The Natural Communities of Georgia

The Natural Communities of Georgia

LESLIE EDWARDS

JONATHAN AMBROSE

L. KATHERINE KIRKMAN

PHOTOGRAPHS BY

HUGH AND CAROL NOURSE

THE UNIVERSITY OF GEORGIA PRESS | ATHENS AND LONDON

© 2013 by the University of Georgia Press
Athens, Georgia 30602
www.ugapress.org
All rights reserved

Designed by April Leidig
Set in Garamond Premier Pro and Seria Sans
    by Graphic Composition, Inc., Bogart, Georgia.
Printed and bound by Four Colour Print Group

The paper in this book meets the guidelines for
permanence and durability of the Committee on
Production Guidelines for Book Longevity of the
Council on Library Resources.

Printed in China

17   16   15   14   13   C   5   4   3   2   1

Library of Congress Cataloging-in-Publication Data
Edwards, Leslie, Ph.D.
    The natural communities of Georgia / Leslie
Edwards, Jonathan Ambrose, and L. Katherine
Kirkman ; photographs by Hugh and Carol Nourse.
        p. cm.
    Includes bibliographical references and index.
    ISBN-13: 978-0-8203-3021-1 (hardcover : alk. paper)
    ISBN-10: 0-8203-3021-3 (hardcover : alk. paper)
    1. Natural history—Georgia. 2. Biotic
communities—Georgia. 3. Ecological regions—
Georgia. 4. Nature conservation—Georgia.
5. Biodiversity conservation—Georgia. 6. Landscape
protection—Georgia. 7. Georgia—Environmental
conditions. 8. Georgia—Description and travel.
I. Ambrose, Jonathan. II. Kirkman, L. Katherine.
III. Nourse, Hugh O. IV. Nourse, Carol, 1933– V. Title.
QH105.G4E38 2013
508.758—dc23
                                        2012008402

British Library Cataloging-in-Publication Data available

Major support for this project was provided by the AGL Resources Foundation. Additional support was provided by the Georgia Department of Natural Resources, Wildlife Resources Division. In-kind support was provided by the Joseph W. Jones Ecological Research Center at Ichauway and Georgia State University.

The
JOSEPH W. JONES
ECOLOGICAL RESEARCH CENTER
•
at Ichauway

This book is dedicated to the memory of Dr. Charles H. (Charlie) Wharton, author of *The Natural Environments of Georgia*. In 2002, Charlie initiated the effort to revise and update his groundbreaking 1978 publication. His enthusiasm, expertise, and vision provided inspiration to the authors and others who contributed to the completion of this work.

Tribute to Charles H. Wharton

DR. CHARLES H. (CHARLIE) WHARTON (Ph.D., University of Florida, 1969) was an outstanding naturalist and conservationist. He was also my teacher, my mentor, and my close friend for more than 30 years. The late Eugene P. Odum, founder of the Institute of Ecology at the University of Georgia, once told me that Charlie was "the most knowledgeable person on Georgia's natural environments." Former Governor and U.S. Senator Zell Miller has proclaimed with pride that the first bill he introduced as a freshman state legislator in 1966 was the Georgia Natural Areas Act, which was drafted by Wharton.

Following the passage of the Georgia Natural Areas Act, Dr. Wharton served as the first chairman of the Georgia Natural Areas Council. Several years later, when Governor Jimmy Carter reorganized state government, the Natural Areas Council was incorporated into the new Department of Natural Resources following a strong recommendation from Wharton. Charlie helped to guide several important land acquisition and conservation planning efforts, beginning with the Carter administration's Georgia Heritage Trust program. The Natural Areas Unit of the Department of Natural Resources became a primary field inventory agency for the Heritage Trust Commission. In 1992, Governor Miller appointed Wharton chairman of the Preservation 2000 advisory council that oversaw the protection of more than 103,000 acres of important natural habitats in Georgia. He also served as a member of the advisory council for the RiverCare 2000 Program, a land conservation program focused on protection of river corridors.

A tireless advocate for land conservation, Wharton supported federal wilderness designation for the Nantahala and Cohutta portions of the national forest system in Georgia, North Carolina, and other states. He was also an outspoken advocate for greater protection of wetlands and streams across the southeastern United States. In 1970 he wrote "The Southern River Swamp: A Multiple-Use Environment." This report highlighted the environmental, educa-tional, and economic values of river swamps as well as the fallacy of "improving" bottomland areas by channelizing streams. His efforts helped to change federal policy toward stream channelization and led to greater awareness of the value of wetland environments. That work was focused on a channelization project to drain 8,800 acres of the Alcovy River swamps. Beginning in 1987 with my move to the Georgia Wildlife Federation, Charlie advised and assisted in a campaign to conserve the Alcovy River corridor, which led to the development of a permanent home for the Federation at the Alcovy Conservation Center. He was also instrumental in efforts to study and protect other rivers, including the Altamaha and Flint.

Wharton's most significant publication, *The Natural Environments of Georgia*, was produced through a contract with the Georgia Department of Natural Resources. Compiling information from other researchers as well as his own observations and notes from class field trips at Georgia State University, Dr. Wharton developed his own unique classification of the state's natural environments based on physical and biological factors. While acknowledging that many of these natural environments were not well researched, he provided the most comprehensive and detailed description of Georgia's natural diversity that had been assembled to date. In the decades since its publication, this publication has informed and inspired researchers, educators, and naturalists, leading to increased awareness of the state's impressive natural diversity and conservation needs.

A strong supporter of environmental education, Wharton recommended the establishment of education centers in every region of the state to help school children gain a better understanding of the natural diversity of the state. Today, the Georgia Department of Natural Resources manages six regional environmental education centers. These facilities, as well as numerous privately operated education centers around the state, help to deliver the education and outreach programs envisioned by Dr. Wharton.

After the establishment of the Georgia Natural Heritage Program in 1986, Dr. Wharton provided many of the field notes, photographs, correspondence, and maps used in the development of *The Natural Environments of Georgia* to the Department of Natural Resources staff. He continued to collaborate with a variety of groups and individuals to facilitate field research and conservation efforts throughout the state. Late in life, he contacted a group of individuals with a proposal to revise and update his 1978 publication. The small group of individuals that began collaborating with Wharton in 2002 became the nucleus of the larger team that contributed to this book. He would have been very proud of the resulting publication.

Charlie Wharton's commitment to conservation and environmental education is evident even in his last wishes. Upon his death in 2003, Wharton's 129-acre property near the headwaters of the Tallulah River was placed under a conservation easement held by the Georgia Wildlife Federation. In 2006, his estate completed the donation of this property to the Georgia Wildlife Federation and the conservation easement was transferred to The Conservation Fund. The land and facilities at this site will be managed as the Wharton Conservation Center and used for environmental education and research purposes. As the chief executive of the Georgia Wildlife Federation I am proud to manage the Wharton Conservation Center in the manner I know he wanted.

I am also proud to join the authors, contributors, and advisors of this effort as they dedicate this book to the memory of Dr. Charles H. Wharton, a towering figure in the field of natural history and conservation in Georgia. We hope that this book serves to inform and inspire Georgians in the same way that his original work did.

Jerry L. McCollum, Certified Wildlife Biologist

Contents

Preface

THE LANDSCAPE OF Georgia is rich and varied. From cool, moist mountain peaks in the Blue Ridge to the sun-drenched shores of our Atlantic coast, this state boasts an amazing diversity of natural habitats. This diversity of habitats supports an equally impressive variety of plant and animal communities. The ecological diversity of Georgia is our natural heritage, a legacy bequeathed to current and future residents of this state.

From prehistoric times to the present, humans have influenced nearly every aspect of the Georgia environment. The landscape of Georgia today is vastly different from that encountered by the first European explorers, and was vastly different at that time from the landscape present centuries and millennia before. Intensive land use has altered vegetation and has led to extirpation of species and the introduction of non-native species. Human impacts also include altered fire regimes, changes in flow of water through streams and underground aquifers, and increased patterns of erosion and sedimentation. As our human population continues to expand and development increases, many natural habitats and native species are increasingly impacted and pushed toward the edge of extinction. Introduced invasive species and disease organisms threaten the integrity of plant and animal communities. The specter of global climate change provides yet another significant challenge to the maintenance of ecological diversity.

Within this altered landscape, however, one can find assemblages of species that have been minimally impacted by modern human activities or have recovered from anthropogenic alterations through natural species interactions and disturbance processes. These interacting species, the physical environment, and the ecological processes governing them exemplify the natural heritage of our state. Identification of natural communities and understanding the factors that determine their distribution and existence are central to developing an appreciation for the region's ecological diversity and the necessary steps for its conservation. This book seeks to both inform and inspire Georgia's citizenry of this rich natural heritage.

Acknowledgments

WE WOULD LIKE to extend a special acknowledgment to three people who have supported this project from its early beginnings with Charles Wharton and who gave generously of their time and resources to this effort.

Jim Renner was one of the original editors and was instrumental in shaping the scope of the book in its early phases. He helped frame the introductions to the physical setting of the state and its ecoregions; edited some chapter drafts; participated in field excursions; wrote supporting material; contributed to sections for the Blue Ridge, Cumberland Plateau / Ridge and Valley, and Piedmont ecoregions; and interpreted the geologic substrate of some natural communities.

Steve Bowling participated extensively in the field reconnaissance work that was critical to writing the Blue Ridge, Cumberland Plateau / Ridge and Valley, and Piedmont ecoregions, and in particular in providing field reconnaissance of the featured places in those ecoregions. He also helped with creation of plant lists. His deep knowledge of the Georgia landscape and the flora of Georgia were invaluable.

Tom Patrick was extremely helpful in locating appropriate state-owned properties for featured places in the Coastal Plain ecoregion. He participated in field excursions throughout the state, and provided valuable expertise regarding rare plant communities and flora.

CONTRIBUTING AUTHORS

Sean Beeching—"Lichens of Granite Outcrops" for the Piedmont ecoregion

Carlos Camp, Piedmont College—text for herpetofaunal communities for the Blue Ridge, Cumberland Plateau / Ridge and Valley, and Piedmont ecoregions

John Costello, Georgia Environmental Protection Division—text for geology in the paleohistory of the state in chapter 2

Philip Freshley, LandTec SE, Inc.—text on soils in chapter 2

Woodrow Hicks, J. W. Jones Ecological Research Center—text on Coastal Plain geology

Jerry McCollum, Georgia Wildlife Federation—"Tribute to Charles H. Wharton"

Kevin McIntyre, J. W. Jones Ecological Research Center—text on Prescribed Fire Council

Mincy Moffett, Georgia Department of Natural Resources—"Calcareous Seepage Fens" for the Cumberland Plateau / Ridge and Valley ecoregion

Michael Wayne Morris, Troy University—"Ultramafic Barrens and Woodlands" for the Piedmont ecoregion

Todd Schneider, Tim Keyes, and Nathan Klaus, Georgia Department of Natural Resources—text for bird communities of the Blue Ridge, Cumberland Plateau / Ridge and Valley, and Piedmont ecoregions, as well as for portions of the Coastal Plain

Ken Terrell, retired, Georgia State University—text for the paleohistory of the state in chapter 2

Brad Winn, Georgia Department of Natural Resources—"Waterbird Conservation Initiative" for the Maritime ecoregion

REVIEWERS

We are grateful to those who reviewed and edited all or parts of the manuscript during the course of its preparation, often providing helpful comments and materials:

Tom Barclay, Albany, Georgia

Ron Carroll, University of Georgia

Eloise Carter, Emory University/Oxford College

Melissa Caspary, Gainesville State College

Linda Chafin, State Botanical Garden of Georgia

Martin Cipollini, Berry College

Lee Echols, North American Land Trust

Walter George, Natural Resources Conservation Service
Lisa Giencke, J. W. Jones Ecological Research Center
Tom Govus, consulting botanist
Mark Hall, Natural Resources Conservation Service
John Jensen, Georgia Department of Natural Resources
Pamela Knox, Assistant State Climatologist
Lisa Kruse, Georgia Department of Natural Resources
Mincy Moffett, Georgia Department of Natural Resources
Michael Wayne Morris, Troy University

Richard Reaves, CH2M Hill
Michael Roden, University of Georgia
Michael Schafale, North Carolina Natural Heritage Program
Todd Schneider, Georgia Department of Natural Resources
John Paul Schmidt, University of Georgia
Robert Sutter, Enduring Conservation Outcomes, LLC
Richard Ware, Georgia Botanical Society
Tom Wentworth, North Carolina State University
Peter White, University of North Carolina
Robert Wyatt, University of Georgia, Emeritus

ADDITIONAL ASSISTANCE

In addition to those listed above, we would like to thank the following people who assisted in the field, provided expertise or materials, or were instrumental in the preparation of the manuscript.

Robert Addington, The Nature Conservancy
Pamela Adkins-Ramey, Georgia Native Plants Certificate intern
Sara Aicher, U.S. Fish and Wildlife Service
Brett Albanese, Georgia Department of Natural Resources
Jim Allison, consulting botanist
Stephen Anderson, Golder Associates Inc.
Thomas Barclay, retired, Albany, Ga.
Lindsay Boring, J. W. Jones Ecological Research Center
Donnie Bradshaw, Virginia Polytechnic Institute and State University
Jean Brock, J. W. Jones Ecological Research Center
Doug Cabe, Natural Resources Conservation Service
Shan Cammack, Georgia Department of Natural Resources
Timothy Chowns, State University of West Georgia
Martin Cipollini, Berry College
Mike Conner, J. W. Jones Ecological Research Center
Mike Christison, Georgia Botanical Society
Scott Coleman, Little St. Simons Island
Liz Cox, J. W. Jones Ecological Research Center
Alan Cressler, United States Geologic Survey
Maureen Donohue, Chattahoochee River National Recreation Area
Matt Elliott, Georgia Department of Natural Resources

Michelle Elmore, The Nature Conservancy
Steve Friedman, Georgia Department of Natural Resources
Beth Grant, Friends of Lost Creek Forest
Mike Harris, Georgia Department of Natural Resources
Malcolm Hodges, The Nature Conservancy
John Holman, Forestry Consultant, Moultrie, Georgia
Gwen Iacona, J. W. Jones Ecological Research Center
Amy Jenkins, Florida Natural Areas Inventory
Ann Johnson, Florida Natural Areas Inventory
Royce Knight, Georgia Native Plant Certificate intern
Lisa Kruse, Georgia Department of Natural Resources
John Lathem, Natural Resources Conservation Service
Steve Lawrence, Natural Resources Conservation Service
Eamonn Leonard, Georgia Department of Natural Resources
Eric Lindberg, Rome/Floyd ECO River Education Center
Hal Massey, Georgia Botanical Society
Jerry McCollum, Georgia Wildlife Federation
Allison McGee, The Nature Conservancy
Leon Neel, consulting forester
Milo Pyne, NatureServe
Scott Ranger, Georgia Botanical Society
Celisha Rosser, Georgia Department of Natural Resources
Brandon Rutledge, J. W. Jones Ecological Research Center
Chris Skelton, Georgia College and State University

Lora Smith, J. W. Jones Ecological Research Center
Frankie Snow, South Georgia College
Phil Spivey, Georgia Department of Natural Resources
James Sullivan, Georgia ForestWatch
Donald Thieme, Valdosta State University
Nate Thomas, The Nature Conservancy

Jacob Thompson, Georgia Department of Natural Resources
Jean Turn, Clay County Library, Ft. Gaines, Georgia
Larry West, USDA Natural Resources Conservation Service
James Whitney, University of Georgia
Keith Wooster, USDA Natural Resources Conservation Services

Finally, a special thanks to several people whose hard work in helping to compile and cross-check the maps, photographs, appendices, index, reference list, and directions to featured places was critical to the completion of this book.

Chris Canalos
Lisa Cox
Susan Curtis
Melanie Kaeser

Linda May
Scott Pokswinski
Brian Vann

We would also like to thank the University of Georgia Press for their support of this project from its inception through its realization, and in particular four people whose hard work, expertise, and enthusiasm made this book possible: Jon Davies, Christa Frangiamore, Kathi Morgan, and Judy Purdy.

The Natural Communities of Georgia

Introduction

A NATURAL COMMUNITY is an assemblage of native plant and animal species, considered together with the physical environment and associated ecological processes, which usually recurs on the landscape. The *Natural Communities of Georgia* describes these assemblages, identifies factors that govern their distribution, and summarizes the management and conservation challenges that must be addressed to protect their biotic diversity and ecologic functions. The term "natural" is somewhat controversial because of the pervasive influence of human activities on the landscape. In this work, a community is considered "natural" when native species predominate and are distributed across the landscape in response to disturbance factors such as fire frequency, flood regimes, wind disturbances, or physical attributes such as landforms, soil nutrients, or moisture (Comer et al. 2003). Few communities have escaped modern anthropogenic impacts, either directly or indirectly, and consequently natural communities do not necessarily resemble those of pre-European settlement; however, those that have been minimally impacted more closely reflect natural species interactions and disturbance processes that once shaped these assemblages. Thus, vegetation that has been planted by humans, such as agricultural fields, pine plantations, pastures, and gardens, is not considered natural. A biological community that has become reestablished through secondary succession or recolonization within a human-impacted landscape, however, is considered natural. In addition, species assemblages that have been shaped or maintained by long histories of human land use practices, in particular, the fires set by indigenous North Americans, are included within the definition of natural (Grossman et al. 1998; Anderson and Bowles 1999).

The classification system in this book is generally based on the classification of ecological systems developed by NatureServe, an international organization that encompasses a network of conservation data centers and natural heritage programs, including that within the Georgia Department of Natural Resources (NatureServe 2009a). The NatureServe classification system has been adopted because it is based on extensive research and fieldwork, and marks a culmination of classification efforts in the region to date. The NatureServe ecological systems are in turn linked to the National Vegetation Classification System (NVCS), which is widely used by public and private organizations throughout the United States for classifying plant communities or associations. In Georgia, for example, plant associations described in the NVCS are used to determine priorities for conservation and restoration of natural habitats (see below). Given the fact that the NatureServe classification system is national in scope, some deviations from this system were required to adequately represent natural communities in Georgia. Correlations between the NatureServe classification system and the natural communities described in this book are presented in Appendix 1.

A plant community generally represents a finer scale of categorization than an ecological system or a natural community. As defined here, a natural community may encompass many plant communities or associations. The plant communities found within a single natural community can vary due to subtle differences in site characteristics, disturbance history, or other factors, including stochastic (random) events affecting succession and community development.

Organization of This Book

The first two chapters of this book introduce concepts relevant to an understanding of the natural communities of Georgia. The following five chapters include detailed descriptions of specific natural communities by ecoregion of the state. Each of these chapters contains an introduction to the ecoregion describing the physiography, geology, soils, hydrology, human impact, and major disturbance regimes of the ecoregion. Descriptions of each of the natural communities follow, and comprise the following sections:

Introduction. Summarizes the key traits of the community.

Physical Setting and Ecology. Describes the physical factors that shape the community, such as hydrology, soils, substrate, nutrient levels, moisture levels, physiography, and disturbance regimes; identifies specific conservation and management needs.

Vegetation. Characterizes vegetation and variation of plant communities along gradients of moisture, nutrients, and fire; includes distinct community variants. Includes a list of characteristic plant species.

Animals. Identifies representative faunal species of the natural community and features an animal of special interest.

Featured Place. Briefly describes a site in Georgia where an example of the natural community can be viewed by the public. The featured places are chosen for their accessibility and are typically on public land. The descriptions of these sites give a broad perspective of the sites as expressions of the natural community.

The concluding chapter of this book summarizes some of the conservation challenges Georgia will face in the future.

ECOREGIONS

The framework for describing Georgia's natural environments is the ecoregion (G. E. Griffith et al. 2001). Ecoregions (shown on p. 3) are broad physical areas with common abiotic and biotic characteristics, such as geology, physiography, soils, climate, hydrology, wildlife, and vegetation (G. E. Griffith and Omernik 2008). The Georgia Department of Natural Resources and other resource agencies recognize six major (Level III) ecoregions in Georgia: the Blue Ridge, Ridge and Valley, Southwestern Appalachians, Piedmont, Southeastern Plains, and Southern Coastal Plain. For this book, the Southwestern Appalachians ecoregion, commonly referred to as the Cumberland Plateau, is combined with the Ridge and Valley because the two ecoregions share geologic characteristics and many overlapping natural communities. Only a small portion of the Southwestern Appalachians, consisting of Lookout, Pigeon, and Sand Mountains, occurs in the state. The Southeastern Plains and the Southern Coastal Plain are also treated as a single unit called

the "Coastal Plain" because of shared natural communities. The Maritime ecoregion, which corresponds to the Sea Islands/Coastal Marsh Level IV ecoregion of G. E. Griffith et al. (2001), is highlighted as the fifth ecoregion in this book. Each ecoregion has a distinctive assemblage of natural communities.

Blue Ridge. The mountainous northern and northeastern portion of the state, underlain by metamorphic rocks. Most of the ecoregion is more than 1,700 feet above sea level. It has the highest elevations and the greatest annual precipitation in the state. Elevation, slope, and aspect are very important influences. Species common in more northern latitudes occur here.

Cumberland Plateau / Ridge and Valley (combined Southwestern Appalachians and Ridge and Valley ecoregions of G. E. Griffith et al. [2001]). The mountainous northwestern portion of the state underlain by sedimentary rocks. Although ridge top elevations are well below the heights of the Blue Ridge and valleys are at elevations similar to that of much of the Piedmont, the region appears mountainous because of the array of steep, narrow ridges jutting from broad, flat valleys. Natural communities are strongly influenced by soil texture and nutrients, as well as by geology, elevation, aspect, and slope.

Piedmont. The hilly upland of northern Georgia underlain by metamorphic and igneous rocks. The ecoregion is geologically related to the Blue Ridge, but topography is different. Elevations are mostly well below 1,700 feet, and the landscape is a succession of hills and valleys.

Coastal Plain (combined Southeastern Plains and Southern Coastal Plain ecoregions of G. E. Griffith et al. [2001]). The largest ecoregion, covering approximately 60% of the state. The substrate is mostly unconsolidated sediments left behind as sea level has fallen and the land surface has risen in the last 65 million years. Elevation is low and relief is modest. The subdued relief means that even slight variations in elevation lead to significant differences in soil saturation and shallow inundation. Fire is an important influence.

Maritime (Sea Islands/Coastal Marsh Level IV ecoregion of G. E. Griffith et al. [2001]). The smallest of the ecoregions; includes coastal bar-

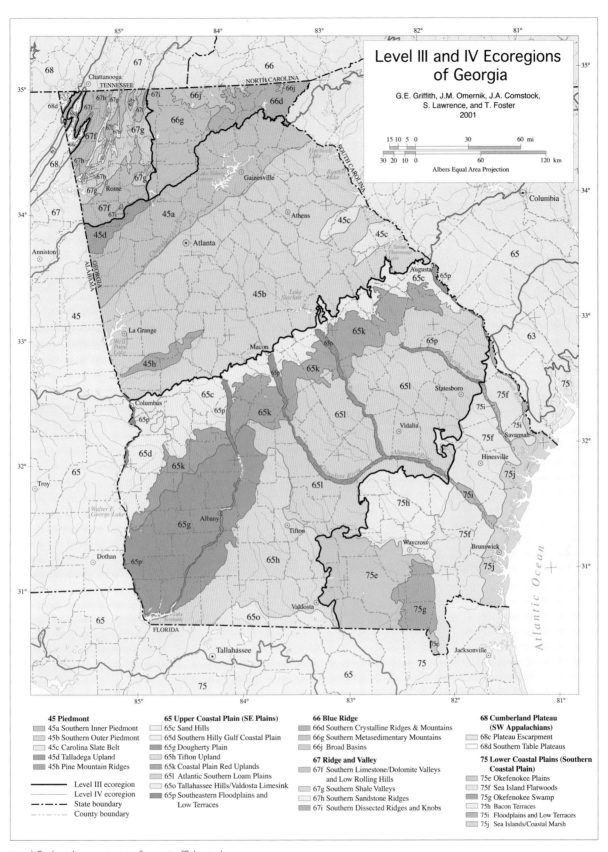

Level III and IV Ecoregions of Georgia

G.E. Griffith, J.M. Omernik, J.A. Comstock,
S. Lawrence, and T. Foster
2001

15 10 5 0   30   60 mi

30 20 10   60   120 km

Albers Equal Area Projection

45 Piedmont
▨ 45a Southern Inner Piedmont
▨ 45b Southern Outer Piedmont
▨ 45c Carolina Slate Belt
▨ 45d Talladega Upland
▨ 45h Pine Mountain Ridges

──── Level III ecoregion
──── Level IV ecoregion
─·─·─ State boundary
─ ─ ─ County boundary

65 Upper Coastal Plain (SE Plains)
▨ 65c Sand Hills
▨ 65d Southern Hilly Gulf Coastal Plain
▨ 65g Dougherty Plain
▨ 65h Tifton Upland
▨ 65k Coastal Plain Red Uplands
▨ 65l Atlantic Southern Loam Plains
▨ 65o Tallahassee Hills/Valdosta Limesink
▨ 65p Southeastern Floodplains and
    Low Terraces

66 Blue Ridge
▨ 66d Southern Crystalline Ridges & Mountains
▨ 66g Southern Metasedimentary Mountains
▨ 66j Broad Basins

67 Ridge and Valley
▨ 67f Southern Limestone/Dolomite Valleys
    and Low Rolling Hills
▨ 67g Southern Shale Valleys
▨ 67h Southern Sandstone Ridges
▨ 67i Southern Dissected Ridges and Knobs

**68 Cumberland Plateau
(SW Appalachians)**
▨ 68c Plateau Escarpment
▨ 68d Southern Table Plateaus

**75 Lower Coastal Plains (Southern
Coastal Plain)**
▨ 75e Okefenokee Plains
▨ 75f Sea Island Flatwoods
▨ 75g Okefenokee Swamp
▨ 75h Bacon Terraces
▨ 75i Floodplains and Low Terraces
▨ 75j Sea Islands/Coastal Marsh

Modified with permission from Griffith et al. 2001

rier islands, nearshore marine and estuarine environments, coastal marshes, and mainland environments within the zone of tidal influence. Natural communities in this ecoregion are strongly influenced by tides, waves, storm events, and salinity gradients.

GENERAL CHARACTERISTICS AND TYPES OF NATURAL COMMUNITIES

The spatial extent and distribution of natural communities on the landscape is generally described using the following terms (Comer et al. 2003). The usage of these terms varies widely among ecologists. The definitions below have been adapted to help provide a uniform treatment for this classification system.

Small patch. A natural community encompassing 1–125 acres. These are usually limited in size by very localized environmental features, such as the extent of an outcrop, seepage area, depressional wetland, or bog.

Large patch. A natural community encompassing 125–5,000 acres. Under natural conditions, these occur over medium to large expanses of the landscape, and are limited by major discontinuities in topographic, geologic, soil, or moisture gradients.

Matrix. A natural community encompassing 5,000–25,000 acres. Matrix environments are those that are dominant on the landscape or in the ecoregion, forming extensive cover across environmental gradients.

Linear. A natural community occurring as a narrow, elongate strip. Linear communities are often found in ecotonal situations, such as transitional zones between rivers and uplands.

Embedded. A natural community completely surrounded by another one.

Interfingered. A natural community that partially extends into another. For example, a riparian stream corridor may extend into a mesic cove forest.

Transitional to; intergraded with. A very gradual transition over space from one community to another. Because natural communities typically intergrade with one another, attempting to distinguish them on the landscape can be difficult because the characteristics of one overlap with the characteristics of another (Whittaker 1956; Wharton 1978; Comer et al. 2003).

Natural communities can generally be distinguished from one another based on the composition and structure of the vegetation, the type of underlying substrate, the predominant soil types, and/or elevation and topographic position (Wharton 1978; Schafale and Weakley 1990; Comer et al. 2003). We use the following definitions:

Forests. Tree-dominated communities with canopy coverage greater than 80%.

Woodlands. Tree-dominated communities where the canopy is 50–80%; these are open stands where the crowns are not usually touching. In addition, stands of markedly stunted trees are treated as woodlands.

Flatwoods. Forests or woodlands that occur on a low, flat, or mildly depressional site, with moist to hydric soils.

Forests

Woodlands

Flatwoods

Prairie

Savanna

Glades and barrens

Savanna. A community dominated by herbaceous vegetation, where mature trees are widely spaced and the canopy is at least 50% open, supporting a dense herbaceous ground cover similar to a prairie.

Prairie. A community dominated by herbaceous vegetation. No mature trees are present, herbaceous ground cover is complete, and exposed gravelly soils or large expanses of rock outcrop are lacking (e.g., soils are deeper than those of barrens).

Barrens. A community where no mature trees are present, ground cover is not complete, and the site has thin, gravelly soils. Barrens are often intermixed with glades on the landscape and referred to as "glades and barrens."

Glade. A community with extensive rock outcrops and patchy vegetation dominated by herbaceous species and shallow, rocky soil.

Chapter 1

GEORGIA'S NATURAL HERITAGE
Conservation Challenges and Management Strategies

ONE OF THE ORIGINAL objectives of *The Natural Environments of Georgia*, authored by Charles H. Wharton in 1978, was to describe the biological diversity occurring in the state and to evoke a sense of stewardship through recognition of the important ecological services these environments provide to society. In his classification, Wharton provided an early framework for inventorying the natural systems of the state and brought to light the prevailing threats to the sustainability of these natural areas. Despite the fact that many of the same threats remain, or have even escalated with rapid population growth in the state, much has changed in Georgia since the late 1970s in regard to publicly owned lands and overall recognition of conservation management of natural resources in the state. While Georgia falls short of many other southeastern states in acreage of public land ownership, significant strides have occurred statewide in land acquisition, multiagency conservation planning, implementation of conservation easements on private properties, and local greenspace initiatives.

Public land ownership in Georgia varies regionally. Approximately 6% of the Cumberland Plateau / Ridge and Valley and the Piedmont ecoregions is in some form of public conservation ownership. Nearly 40% of the total area of the Blue Ridge ecoregion is in state or federal ownership, with a large holding composed of the Chattahoochee National Forest. Publicly owned lands in the Coastal Plain are predominantly properties of the U.S. Department of Defense or the U.S. Fish and Wildlife Service (Okefenokee National Wildlife Refuge). The largest area of the state, represented by middle and southwestern Georgia, has the lowest percentage of lands in

permanent conservation status (approximately 3%). Even so, significant land acquisitions have taken place since 1978, and the majority of these have occurred in the Coastal Plain, especially along the Flint, Ocmulgee, Oconee, and Altamaha River corridors. In addition, certain rare or imperiled community types such as upland longleaf and montane longleaf pine woodlands, sandhills, pitcherplant bogs, blackland prairies, granite outcrops, and Altamaha Grit outcrops have been targeted in these land acquisition projects. From 1978 to 2012, 429,200 acres were added to the lands that the Department of Natural Resources manages (including non-fee lands). Of that total, 350,054 were purchased in fee simple. In addition, more than 250,000 acres of private lands are protected by permanent conservation easements by private land trusts or state agencies (H. Neuhauser, Georgia Land Conservation Center, pers. comm.). Numerous communities throughout the state have taken advantage of private, state, or local funding sources to purchase properties for community greenspace. Many of these county- or city-level projects focus on long-term protection of important conservation areas such as river corridors.

Habitat Loss and Fragmentation

CHALLENGES

The rapidly changing landscape in Georgia due to population growth is one of the most serious stressors of natural communities, impacting their ability to provide critical ecological services. Georgia has experienced extremely rapid population growth

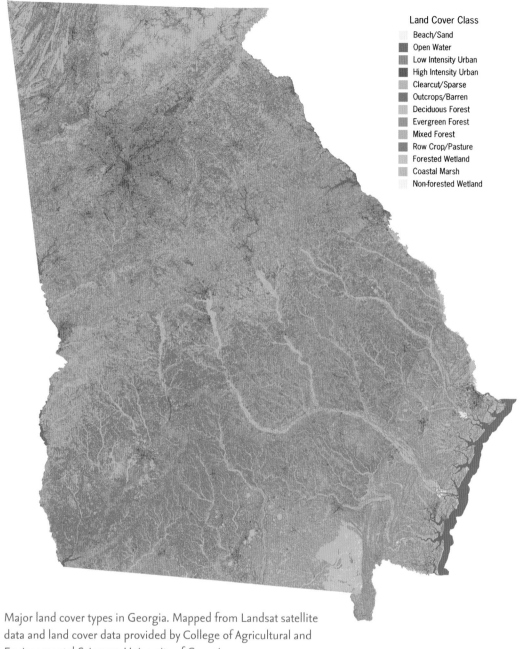

Land Cover Class
Beach/Sand
Open Water
Low Intensity Urban
High Intensity Urban
Clearcut/Sparse
Outcrops/Barren
Deciduous Forest
Evergreen Forest
Mixed Forest
Row Crop/Pasture
Forested Wetland
Coastal Marsh
Non-forested Wetland

Major land cover types in Georgia. Mapped from Landsat satellite data and land cover data provided by College of Agricultural and Environmental Sciences, University of Georgia.

since the 1970s and is ranked the fourth fastest-growing state in the nation. According to the current projection, Georgia's population will increase 46%, from 10.1 to 14.7 million people, by 2030. The highest population density in the state will remain in the Atlanta-metropolitan area, and substantial urban/suburban growth will occur in northern and coastal counties (Georgia Office of Planning and Budget 2010).

Technological developments to benefit agriculture have greatly impacted natural communities in some rural areas. In the 1970s, center pivot irrigation systems became prevalent in the southern part of the state (Rugel et al. 2011). More than 1,000,000 acres of agricultural land are currently irrigated, with half of these occurring within the Dougherty Plain (J. Hooks, University of Georgia, National Environmentally Sustainable Production Agriculture, pers. comm.). Ground-

Landcover by Ecoregion

2008 NARSAL Landcover Class	Blue Ridge	Cumberland Plateau / Ridge and Valley	Piedmont	Coastal Plain	Maritime
Beach/Sand	373	726	15,437	17,974	10,749
Open Water	24,300	11,866	252,455	219,076	77,052
Low-Intensity Urban	100,938	224,750	1,555,684	1,328,834	63,620
High-Intensity Urban	5,607	44,805	364,060	177,392	20,732
Clearcut/Sparse	11,589	35,358	549,607	1,094,620	19,763
Outcrops/Barren	1,495	4,359	13,198	30,243	215
Deciduous Forest	1,148,828	791,955	2,790,697	2,043,532	17,932
Evergreen Forest	261,692	341,243	2,905,295	6,252,858	167,906
Mixed Forest	24,673	61,275	326,253	982,780	9,884
Row Crop / Pasture	81,125	446,594	1,760,542	5,601,321	13,161
Forested Wetland	749	14,532	467,202	4,166,614	115,897
Coastal Marsh	0	0	0	5,995	297,532
Nonforested Wetland	0	242	2,827	98,444	28,753

Source: Natural Resources Spatial Analysis Laboratory, University of Georgia.
Values are acres.

The Okefenokee National Wildlife Refuge is a superb example of publicly owned land in Georgia.

Conservation Land by Ecoregion

Managing Entity	Blue Ridge	Cumberland Plateau / Ridge and Valley	Piedmont	Coastal Plain	Maritime	Total
Georgia DNR fee	25,217	28,859	81,655	193,848	99,160	428,739
Georgia DNR non-fee	240,492	54,826	181,643	171,070	70	648,101
Other state fee	421	190	7,567	21,090	2,330	31,598
Other state non-fee	0	0	4,410	23,760	0	28,170
DOD fee	18,703	2,575	167,863	525,266	8,330	722,737
DOD non-fee	0	102	912	13,612	5,841	20,467
NPS	0	6,393	11,525	1,157	34,420	53,495
NRCS easements	0	0	949	11,232	0	12,181
USFS	399,952	44,441	110,027	0	0	554,420
USFWS fee	0	0	35,078	409,712	29,800	474,590
USFWS non-fee	0	0	633	3,950	171	4,754
Private fee	591	3,692	1,201	56,147	29,590	91,221
Private easements	2,224	12,992	22,005	140,354	9,930	187,505
Local government	928	1,329	9,150	2,626	250	14,283
State and federal	684,785	137,386	602,262	1,374,697	180,122	2,979,252
Total conservation land	688,528	155,399	634,618	1,573,824	219,892	3,272,261
Total ecoregion area	1,696,931	1,987,713	11,003,551	22,045,897	842,315	37,576,407

Source: State Land Conservation GIS (consland11.shp file). Values are acres.

water and surface water pumping can significantly impact aquatic and wetland communities, especially in areas such as the lower Flint River basin.

Mining has been an important industry in Georgia since the early 1800s. Minerals extracted at various times include gold, marble, limestone, coal, bauxite, iron ore, granite, and talc above the Fall Line, and kaolin and sand in the Coastal Plain. In every ecoregion, mining activities have impacted natural communities, and in some cases have profoundly affected local topography, hydrology, and water quality. In recent decades, proposals by corporations to mine phosphates along the coast and titanium on Trail Ridge just east of the Okefenokee have proven very controversial, resulting in a transfer of the proposed mining lands to conservation ownership. Given the fact that many of Georgia's rarest natural communities are edaphically controlled, the impacts of mining

on these communities and their associated rare species can be very significant.

Direct habitat losses occur with conversion of natural communities to residential, industrial, or agricultural uses or through construction of water reservoirs on rivers and streams. In addition, with growing development, formerly large expanses of natural habitat become divided into remnants surrounded by potentially incompatible land uses that negatively impact habitat connectivity and plant and animal dispersal, alter important ecological processes such as nutrient exchanges, and disrupt fire corridors.

MANAGEMENT STRATEGIES

In addition to fee-simple acquisition (purchase of land with all property rights), effective preservation tools include long-term and permanent conservation easements on private lands. These are voluntary

Habitat loss and fragmentation in the form of agricultural fields, buildings, chicken farms, and roads in the Cumberland Plateau / Ridge and Valley ecoregion

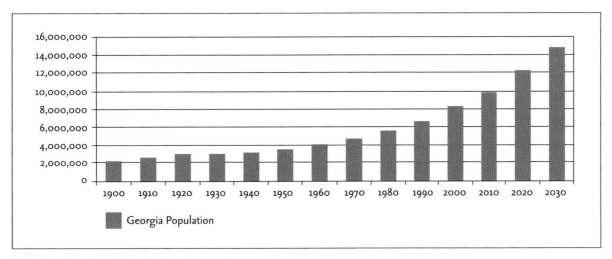

Historic and projected population of Georgia, 1900–2030

Habitat destruction and fragmentation in the urban Atlanta area

agreements that allow landowners to limit the type or amount of development on their properties or to protect sensitive natural habitats. In recent years, protection of land through conservation easements has increased dramatically in Georgia, in part due to federal and state tax incentive programs. State agencies such as the Georgia Department of Natural Resources and the Georgia Forestry Commission have partnered with land trust organizations and private landowners to protect thousands of acres of land through easements. Currently, more than 250,000 acres in Georgia are protected through conservation easements by 52 different organizations (H. Neuhauser, Georgia Land Conservation Center, pers. comm.).

Technical assistance provided by state and federal agencies to private landowners is another important conservation tool that complements land acquisition. In 1995, the Georgia Department of Natural Re-

sources began its Private Lands Program to intensify efforts to promote, encourage, and provide technical assistance for habitat restoration and enhancement on private lands. The Private Lands Program delivers technical assistance to private landowners through U.S. Department of Agriculture (USDA) programs authorized under the Farm Bill as well as a partnership with corporate forest landowners known as the Forestry for Wildlife Partnership. Private Lands Program biologists inform landowners about federal and state programs that provide technical or financial assistance and identify the programs and agencies best suited to meet their habitat management objectives. These biologists also participate in the Sustainable Forestry Initiative (SFI) Implementation Committee for Georgia and assist member organizations (which include forest product companies and timberland investment firms) to meet SFI standards for protection of rare species

The Lula Lake Land Trust of northwest Georgia is one of many entities preserving land, such as this picturesque sandstone cliff, in the state.

and natural communities. Georgia Forestry Commission staff provides training and technical assistance to SFI members to ensure compliance with Best Management Practices for forestry. Continued emphasis in this area will be critical to meeting objectives for conservation of natural habitats throughout the state.

Since 2006, the USDA's Farm Service Agency has overseen a Conservation Reserve Program (CRP) Longleaf Pine Initiative designed to reforest longleaf pine forests on former agricultural lands in nine southern states. As part of this program, 200,000 acres have been planted with longleaf pine. The Wetlands Reserve Program (WRP) is a voluntary program administered by the USDA's Natural Resources Conservation Service offering landowners the opportunity to restore, protect, and enhance wetlands in exchange for retiring eligible land from agriculture. To ensure protection of wetlands that are restored through WRP res-

toration plans, conservation easements are placed on the properties that restrict certain uses; however, landowners retain ownership and recreation rights and control access to the land. The landowners also receive financial and technical assistance for restoring and protecting the wetlands' values and functions. Georgia currently has more than 16,000 acres enrolled as permanent or 30-year conservation easements across 22 counties in the Piedmont and Coastal Plain. Numerous other state and federally funded private landowner incentive programs, such as the Wildlife Habitat Incentives Program (WHIP), the Environmental Quality Incentive Program (EQIP), Partners for Fish and Wildlife (PFW), the Forest Stewardship Program, the Forest Land Enhancement Program (FLEP), and the Bobwhite Quail Initiative (BQI), have been implemented to encourage restoration and maintenance of wildlife habitat and protection of water quality.

Non-native Invasive Species

CHALLENGES

Human activities have resulted in the introduction of most of the non-native species that have become established in natural communities. Although many non-native species do not naturalize and proliferate, those that do can cause considerable or even catastrophic damage to native species. They represent perhaps the second greatest threat to the state's biodiversity, following habitat destruction and fragmentation. Nationwide, nearly half of all threatened or endangered species are imperiled in part because of the impacts of invasive species (Mack et al. 2000).

Some of these invasive species were deliberately introduced into Georgia as crop or horticultural plants, livestock, or pets and later escaped from cultivation or domestication. Others, like kudzu, autumn-olive, Japanese honeysuckle, and bicolor lespedeza, were introduced to control erosion or provide food for wildlife. Still other species were accidentally introduced by importation of food and other materials. A wide-spread invasive plant species, Chinese privet, has colonized floodplain and upland habitats throughout the state, suppressing native vegetation through shading and allelopathic effects. Kudzu is well known in Georgia for its ability to smother entire stands of trees. Nepal grass and Japanese honeysuckle are capable of suppressing the diversity of native herbs in many forested communities, and Chinese wisteria and English ivy can be problematic in local habitats. Cogongrass is a serious threat to the ground cover of many Coastal Plain sites; this aggressive grass, introduced from Africa, outcompetes native grasses and burns intensely.

Feral swine are the most damaging of invasive mammals in Georgia. They were brought to America by European explorers and settlers. Feral swine reproduce abundantly and are voracious, omnivorous feeders. They are particularly destructive in wetland and riparian environments and in rich cove forests, where they wallow in moist areas, uproot and eat native plants, fungi, and amphibians, and denude the forest floor of ground layer vegetation, which contributes to soil erosion and stream sedimentation. On barrier islands,

Kudzu, a non-native invasive species, was introduced in the Southeast for erosion control.

Feral swine reproduce prolifically, are difficult to capture and eradicate, and cause great damage by wallowing and rooting in the soil and feeding on a wide variety of plants and animals.

feral swine are major predators of sea turtle and shorebird nests.

One of the most significant impacts on Georgia's forests was the introduction of chestnut blight (*Cryphonectria parasitica*). This pathogenic fungus, which was most likely imported from Asia, arrived in the state in the early 1900s. It attacked the American chestnut, once one of the most common trees in the Georgia Blue Ridge and upper Piedmont. Because of chestnut blight, the American chestnut has been eliminated as a canopy tree in Georgia. Numerous other pathogens, including Dutch elm disease, laurel wilt, sudden oak death, and dogwood anthracnose, pose serious threats to Georgia's forests. Currently, the eastern hemlock is being decimated at a regional scale by the hemlock wooly adelgid, an insect that was also accidentally introduced from Asia. Other non-native insects harmful to trees include the European gypsy moth, Asiatic gypsy moth, and Asiatic oak weevil. Cave-dwelling bats in the eastern United States are being killed by "white nose syndrome," a disease caused by an introduced fungus (*Geomyces destructans*) that disrupts normal hibernation patterns, causing bats to arouse frequently from torpor and leading to debilitation and death.

With continued introduction of non-native species into the region, newly emerging threats are to be expected. Negative consequences of non-native species to natural environments are often difficult to predict at early stages of introduction, and such future projections may be especially challenging in light of ongoing climate change relative to the ability of introduced species to become invasive (Mooney and Hobbs 2000).

Volunteers work to remove invasive species that have overtaken a bottomland and floodplain natural community.

MANAGEMENT STRATEGIES

Control efforts for invasive species are generally costly and time consuming, and must be maintained for many years to be successful. Invasive plants, for example, must be physically removed or aggressively treated with herbicides. Plants that are wind- or animal-dispersed, or that have seeds that persist in the soil, are particularly difficult to eradicate. Control of feral swine is challenging due to their fecundity and mobility and will require aggressive removal by state and federal agencies to regulate their dispersal. Fungal and insect invasions are difficult to contain because they often spread quickly and pervasively in the absence of natural biological controls. Invasive species management requires careful planning and implementation to provide effective control while minimizing impacts to nontarget species and surrounding natural communities. It also requires focusing limited resources in areas that are likely to produce the most significant benefits (Mack et al. 2000).

The Georgia Invasive Species Task Force, a partnership formalized in 2009 between the Georgia Department of Natural Resources, the Georgia Forestry Commission, the Georgia Department of Agriculture, and the University of Georgia, was established to coordinate the monitoring, reporting, control, and education efforts related to non-native invasive species on a statewide basis. Additional funding is needed for assessment, monitoring, and control of invasive species throughout the state (Georgia Department of Natural Resources 2009a).

Altered Fire Regimes

CHALLENGES

The conservation of many species of plants and animals in the Georgia landscape depends on conservation of fire-dependent habitats. Anthropogenic and lightning-ignited fires were major ecological forces in Georgia for the last several thousand years and it is nearly impossible to separate the impacts of the two sources. The timing, scale, frequency, and intensity of these fires varied from site to site, and this variability, in combination with other local environmental gradients, influenced the diversity of natural communities and species that evolved. The increase in human population and continued urban sprawl prohibit the restoration of historic fire regimes on a broad scale. Thus, fire-dependent communities require prescribed fire management or they will cease to exist.

The Georgia Forestry Commission has performed the primary role in regulating and issuing permits for prescribed fire activities in the state. It is also involved in fighting wild fires and recognizes prescribed fire as the key tool in preventing catastrophic wild fire. This

A prescribed fire in a longleaf pine woodland

agency annually permits prescribed fire on approximately 1,000,000 acres in Georgia. With recent reductions in personnel and budget, its capacity to optimally manage statewide prescribed fire is seriously strained.

During the 20th century, all fire came to be viewed as detrimental to the natural environments of the state. This paradigm was reinforced by early policies of the U.S. Forest Service (USFS) (Earley 2004). Human-set fires were greatly reduced, and both lightning- and human-ignited fires were suppressed. The views of fire promoted during the "Smokey the Bear" era are still held by a significant segment of the public today. Some view prescribed burns in a negative light because of smoke hazards, air pollution, and the fact that a temporarily charred ground layer is not aesthetically pleasing to them. Others perceive negative impacts to wildlife or associate fire only with catastrophic events. Although recognition of the importance of prescribed fire for natural resource conservation and management has grown, there are new constraints on its use in terms of social acceptance and policy.

State policies have been implemented to comply with air quality standards under the Clean Air Act, primarily to clean airsheds impacted by automobile and industrial emissions. These policies may have serious implications for prescribed burning in the future. The Environmental Protection Agency (EPA) sets standards for air quality in the form of the National Ambient Air Quality Standards (NAAQS). In 2007, the EPA revised the NAAQS by lowering permissible levels of fine particulate matter (PM 2.5) from 65 μg to 35 μg per cubic meter. PM 2.5 comes from a variety of sources, including exhaust from internal combustion engines, coal-fired power plants, agriculture, and biomass burning, including prescribed fire. While prescribed fire is a relatively minor source of PM 2.5 compared to the others listed above, it is highly visible and easily targeted for restrictions. Prescribed fire is the only emission source, however, that is managed through a permitting system that ensures that the activity occurs when atmospheric dispersion is optimal.

MANAGEMENT STRATEGIES

Application of prescribed fire to restore and maintain natural habitats on state and private lands is identified as one of the highest-priority conservation actions in the Georgia Department of Natural Resources' State Wildlife Action Plan. One of the challenges of the use of prescribed fire is the identification of natural communities that benefit from prescribed fire, training of land managers in the use of prescribed fire as a tool, and education of the public as to the need for prescribed fire in many Georgia environments. Although some communities such as the longleaf pine communities of the Coastal Plain are clearly dependent on frequent fire, the role of fire in maintaining natural communities in north Georgia is less well established. Because many landscapes have been fire-suppressed for decades, determining the probable fire history of some natural communities requires a holistic examination of indicator species, topography, substrate, soils, and other factors as a guide for establishing habitat restoration objectives. Reintroduction of fire into fire-suppressed sites often requires mechanical or chemical removal of undesirable species to reestablish adequate fuels to carry fires. Buildup of fuels and organic materials in the prolonged absence of fire may also necessitate successive low-intensity fires for fuel reduction as an initial measure before a more regular prescribed fire maintenance regime is implemented.

In 2002, the U.S. Fish and Wildlife Service, the Georgia Department of Natural Resources, the Georgia Forestry Commission, and The Nature Conservancy established the Interagency Burn Team (IBT), a coalition of organizations involved in prescribed burns for biodiversity conservation on public and private lands. The IBT member organizations jointly identify high-priority sites for application of prescribed fire for restoration and maintenance of fire-adapted natural communities. These high-priority sites typically represent exemplary fire-adapted natural communities containing rare species. Members of the IBT collaborate on prescribed burns on these sites, sharing equipment and staff expertise to control management costs. In 2010, the IBT was expanded through the addition of the USFS and the Orianne Society, a private conservation organization.

To expand its capacity for prescribed fire programs to benefit natural communities, the Wildlife Resources Division of the Georgia Department of Natural resources has invested state and federal funds to train its staff, members of partner organizations, and volunteers in prescribed burn methods. It has purchased equipment, protective gear, and supplies, and has established a roving fire team using trained volunteers from the Student Conservation Association,

AmeriCorps, and other organizations. These efforts have resulted in prescribed burns on many thousands of acres of state land annually. These burns are conducted as part of broader habitat restoration projects involving cultivation and planting of native ground cover species, thinning of pine stands, removal of "off-site" hardwoods, and control of invasive exotic species. In addition, the Wildlife Resource Division conducts targeted outreach efforts to increase public awareness of the need for prescribed fires for habitat restoration and management (Georgia Department of Natural Resources 2010).

Other important outreach and advocacy programs are directed by the nonprofit Georgia Prescribed Fire Council (GPFC). This organization includes private landowners, land managers, state and federal agencies, and other nongovernmental conservation organizations. Its mission is to advocate for the use of prescribed fire and to promote public understanding of fire as a management tool. Its basic premise is that the public's willingness to accept prescribed fire and allow its continued use is critical for the future of fire-dependent natural communities. The GPFC has worked closely with the Georgia Forestry Commission and the Georgia Environmental Protection Division (EPD) on revised state smoke management plans to help meet the new U.S. EPA air quality standards. The council also serves as a vehicle for public education, a mechanism for coordination among conservation organization, and an information resource for prescribed fire practitioners and legislators. It has been effective in a campaign for the adoption of resolutions for the use of prescribed fire by the state and nearly all Georgia county governments. For more information on the GPFC, visit its website at http://www.garxfire.com

Altered Hydrology

CHALLENGES

Rapidly increasing economic development and population growth in Georgia has negatively impacted the hydrology of many wetlands and streams, affecting important aquatic and wetland communities and the ecological services that they provide. Hydrologic alterations vary by region, but include construction of hydropower dams, water supply reservoirs, and recreational or agricultural ponds, channelization of streams,

drainage of wetlands by ditches or drainage tiles, and withdrawal of groundwater and surface water.

Numerous large reservoirs have been constructed on major rivers and thousands of small impoundments occur on tributaries throughout Georgia (Merrill et al. 2001; Cowie 2002). Estimates of the number of reservoirs in the state are around 68,000, a much greater number than had been identified by inventories provided by the EPA (Cowie 2002). Numerous new reservoirs are being proposed to meet the growing water demands of the Atlanta metropolitan area. These types of activities often affect a wide variety of species in an area much larger than the footprint of the construction area. For example, construction of dams on major rivers can impact aquatic and wetland systems miles upstream and downstream of the impoundment through alteration of in-stream flows, flood regimes, changes in water quality, and physical isolation of populations of aquatic species. Similarly, stream channelization affects not only the aquatic habitat in the channelized segment, but also downstream areas and adjacent floodplain forests.

Regulated releases of water from impoundments result in downstream flow regimes in which the amplitude and seasonal variation differ from that of free-flowing streams. As a consequence, floodplains do not flood as often or extensively as they would under natural conditions; this diminished flooding reduces the overbank deposition and distribution of nutrient-rich sediments to the floodplain as well as the distribution of nutrients to downstream habitats. The cumulative effects of numerous reservoirs on natural communities and ecological services associated with free-flowing rivers are not well understood, but are of growing concern (Cowie 2002).

In regions such as southwestern Georgia, where there is excessive groundwater withdrawal for irrigation, streamflow depletion can occur due to changes in regional hydrologic gradients (Rugel et al. 2011). In addition to dried stream shoals and segments and reduced nutrient-loading to downstream communities, reduced streamflows affect channel morphology and increase stream temperatures, threatening biota (Pringle and Triska 2000; Bunn and Arthington 2002; Golladay et al. 2004). Wetlands such as seeps or geographically isolated depressional wetlands that are influenced by groundwater may also be impacted by regional groundwater withdrawal.

Lake Winfield Scott, an impoundment in the Blue Ridge ecoregion

Increases in the amount of impervious land surface associated with urbanization can result in significant impacts on water quality and quantity in streams, rivers, and wetlands, particularly in areas where riparian buffer vegetation has been removed. Similarly, disruption of riparian vegetation by cattle and other livestock results in erosion, sedimentation, and increased nutrient inputs of excess nutrients to streams. Nearly 34% of the streams and rivers in Georgia have some form of impaired water quality, with the largest percentage of impacted streams occurring in the Coastal Plain (Georgia Department of Natural Resources 2009). Headwater streams are particularly vulnerable to removal or destruction of riparian buffers, and changes in these upper reaches can threaten the biological integrity of entire river networks through disruptions of food webs (Hutchens and Wallace 2002) and elevated stream temperatures (J. L. Meyer et al. 2003, 2005, 2007). J. L. Meyer et al. (2005) estimated that the regulation that the state legislature passed in 2000 reducing the riparian buffer requirement in

north Georgia trout streams from 100 feet to 50 feet would have significant negative effects on trout populations.

Georgia's total wetland acreage is estimated to be 7.7 million acres, including 378,000 acres of coastal marshlands. Development associated with coastal marshlands has been regulated by the state since 1970 through the Coastal Marshlands Protection Act; however, Georgia relies on federal water quality certification under the Clean Water Act for regulatory protection of freshwater wetlands. Consequently, no protection is provided for geographically isolated wetlands in the state because they no longer receive federal protection. No programs exist for statewide monitoring and assessment of freshwater wetland conditions, so the degree to which wetlands have been degraded by alterations in hydrology or nutrient inputs statewide is not known. A study of Carolina bays in Georgia found that the majority of the smaller bays had hydrologic alterations or other forms of degradation associated with agricultural activities (Vande-

Genachte and Cammack 2002). Similar findings were reported by G. Martin (2010) in sinkhole depressions in southwestern Georgia.

MANAGEMENT STRATEGIES

Mitigation of impacts on streams and rivers due to reservoir construction is required under the Clean Water Act. According to this regulation, any impacts must be compensated with restoration, creation, or preservation of similar habitat; however, monitoring and enforcement of mitigation requirements are often inadequate to ensure compliance (Cowie 2002). Growing pressures for additional water supply impoundments and evidence of increasing impacts from water impoundments and withdrawal suggest that a better understanding of cumulative effects of reservoirs of varying sizes and purposes on system-wide processes is needed. Emphasis on multiple approaches (including water conservation) to meet water demands, as well as avoidance of watersheds with rare species and significant natural communities during reservoir site selection, are important considerations for minimizing environmental impacts. Changes in dam operations that incorporate seasonally variable flows, low flow releases, periodic low flows, and aeration of release waters are potential methods to offset downstream impacts. These approaches have been applied to reservoirs in other states and are being evaluated for implementation in Georgia (Collier, Webb, and Schmidt 2000). Protection of headwater streams from development and protection of isolated wetlands are recognized as critical conservation goals for the state in the State Wildlife Action Plan. The Georgia Department of Natural Resources' Wildlife Resources Division provides guidance on landowner stewardship programs to encourage protection of high-priority habitats, including wetlands and riparian forests.

Prescribed burns must be implemented with great care when near residential areas, as shown here near Pickett's Mill Battlefield Historic Site.

Chapter 2

THE PHYSICAL SETTING

NATURAL COMMUNITIES ARE largely formed from the characteristics of their physical setting: geology, soils, climate, and hydrology. The first part of this chapter describes these characteristics and how they interact to determine the temperature, moisture, and nutrient levels of a site. In addition to the physical setting, various disturbances, such as fire, flooding, windthrow, ice loading, and herbivory, can strongly influence the formation of a natural community; the second part of this chapter describes these disturbances and how natural communities are impacted by them.

Physical setting and disturbance factors are not static. Rather, they are dynamic systems that continually fluctuate and change. The final part of this chapter shows how radically Georgia's flora and fauna have changed through the eons, illustrating that the natural communities of today represent merely a snapshot in time.

PART I.

Characteristics of the Physical Setting

GEOLOGY AND SOILS

Geology. The geology of a region exercises a profound influence on the plant communities that develop. The parent material determines the nutrient levels in the soils, soil texture (which influences both moisture-holding and nutrient-retention capacities), and topography (which influences moisture levels). Georgia consists of a complex array of rock types (see box). The moisture and nutrient levels in turn are primary determinants of vegetation composition. Rocks are of three general types: igneous, sedimentary, and metamorphic. Igneous rocks form when magma (molten rock) slowly cools and solidifies deep in the earth's crust or rapidly

freezes when it is extruded as lava and ash at the earth's surface. Metamorphic rocks form when igneous, sedimentary, or other metamorphic rocks are compressed and heated, usually as a result of continental collision. Sedimentary rocks are formed when igneous, metamorphic, and other sedimentary rocks are eroded and the erosional debris is transported and deposited in the sea, buried over time, and lithified (compressed, cemented, and transformed from loose sediment into hard rock).

Soils. Soils are primarily derived from the bedrock over which they form. Continually interacting with natural environments, soils influence and are influenced by parent material, climate, biota, topography, and time

Dunite, an ultramafic rock, contributes to the formation of a very rare ultramafic barren and woodland natural community in the Blue Ridge ecoregion.

COMMON ROCKS OF GEORGIA

IGNEOUS ROCKS

Granite. A medium- to coarse-grained rock composed of quartz (silica), potassium feldspar (a mineral mostly made up of alumina and silica), and sodium feldspar. Mica and other minerals are present in lesser amounts. Granite is resistant to chemical and physical weathering when it is not split by joints and fractures, so it sometimes forms rock domes, pavements, and residual boulders. Some fertility is imparted by potassium and calcium in the feldspars and various elements in the minor minerals.

Gabbro. A medium- to coarse-grained rock composed of pyroxene (a dark-colored mineral made up of alumina and silica with significant iron, magnesium, and calcium), calcium feldspar, and other minerals. Gabbro often weathers to sticky clay soils. Some fertility is imparted by calcium and elements in the minor minerals.

METAMORPHIC ROCKS

Quartzite. A fine- to coarse-grained rock composed of quartz, usually formed by subjecting sandstone to high pressure and temperature. Quartzite is resistant to chemical weathering, but is usually fractured, so that some quartzites form ridges. Quartzite has no inherent fertility.

Schist. Any metamorphic rock in which the mineral grains align in one direction, but most often a fine- to medium-grained rock composed of mica and quartz. Mica quartz schist is resistant to weathering and forms ledges and ridges. Fertility is low and derived soils are usually acidic.

Gneiss. Any metamorphic rock displaying bands of different mineral composition, but usually a medium- to coarse-grained rock composed of light-colored bands of quartz and feldspar alternating with dark-colored bands of black mica (biotite), hence the term "biotite gneiss." Fertility is modest unless nutrients are derived from an unusual concentration of trace minerals.

Amphibolite. A mafic, medium-grained, black rock composed of hornblende (a member of the amphibole family of aluminosilicate minerals, containing varying proportions of potassium, sodium, calcium, magnesium, and iron) and calcium feldspar. Amphibolite is modestly resistant to chemical and physical weathering, and weathers to form bright orange soil with scattered rock outcrops. Fertility of soils derived from amphibolites is usually good because of the abundant potassium, calcium, and other trace elements in the rock.

Marble. A white or gray fine- to coarse-grained rock composed of calcium carbonate. Marble is a metamorphosed limestone. Like limestone, marble is very easily weathered by rainwater. Calcium is an important plant nutrient and even thin beds of marble can help establish diverse plant communities.

SEDIMENTARY ROCKS

Sandstone. A fine- to coarse-grained rock composed of sand grains and pebbles, usually quartz. Sandstone is resistant to chemical and physical weathering and forms ridges and cliffs. Sandstone has no inherent nutrition, although fertility is sometimes provided by interbedded shale or trace amounts of calcium minerals.

Conglomerate. A variant of sandstone in which the majority of the grains are coarse pebbles or cobbles in a matrix of sandstone.

Shale. A very fine-grained rock composed of clay minerals. Shale forms from muddy sediments, particularly in deltas. The clay minerals are resistant to chemical weathering, but the rock itself breaks into fragments, so that shale forms slopes and low hills and is less likely to form outcrops. Shale has modest amounts of plant nutrients in the clay minerals, and additional nutrition may be imparted by interbedded limestone.

Limestone. A fine-grained hard or soft rock composed of the calcium carbonate skeletal debris of marine organisms, such as corals, mollusks, and plankton. Limestones are also called "carbonate rocks."

Dolomite. A variety of limestone in which magnesium substitutes for some of the calcium.

Chert. A hard, extremely fine-grained rock formed from the silica skeletal debris of marine organisms, such as sponge spicules and diatom husks. Chert resists chemical and physical weathering, so it forms ridges, ledges, and blocky residuum in the more easily eroded limestone. Chert has no inherent fertility.

This soil is very organic: because this site is often saturated with water, plant remains decompose slowly, supporting a bay swamp natural community that can tolerate high amounts of organic material, acidic conditions, and saturated conditions.

Dark, saturated soils promote shallow roots in trees.

(Jenny 1941). As soils weather over time, organic debris, minerals, and chemicals move differentially through the soil column and form distinct layers called "horizons." This process is assisted by the activity of plant roots and soil organisms (bacteria, fungi, nematodes, worms, etc.). The character and arrangement of the soil horizons is called a soil's "profile." Most commonly, soils have three layers: the A horizon, or topsoil; the B horizon, or subsoil; and the C horizon, or parent material. In most soils, the subsoil (B horizon) has a higher clay content than the topsoil (A horizon) or parent material (C horizon). In old, intensively weathered soils, the B horizon is more than 50% clay and the A horizon is more than 50% sand.

A soil's texture, color, structure, pattern of layering in the profile, and landscape position provide clues to the drainage characteristics, seed and root bed limitations, potential fertility, and the types of plants that can survive under those conditions (Freshley 2006). Soil texture is very important to plant growth. Texture is the proportion of sand, silt, and clay-sized particles. A typical loam has about 50% sand, 20% clay, and 30% silt. Loamy soils provide optimal resources for plant growth. Topsoil with a loam or sandy loam texture allows uniform movement of water, good aeration, and unimpeded root growth. The presence of clay in the subsoil helps to retain water, nutrients, and organic material in the lower root zone. At times, however, dominance of clay particles in the soil can block root penetration and perch water or cause it to run off rather than percolating through the soil column. Most soils in Georgia are orange and red due to abundant iron oxides staining the clay particles. White and tan soils are usually indicative of sandy soils, with little iron. Dark brown topsoil indicates staining by organic matter and/or iron oxides. Gray soils usually indicate prolonged saturation. Microbes in waterlogged soils use up available oxygen, stripping it from the reddish iron oxides in a process called "reduction." The reduced iron forms grayish green compounds or is transported away in solution. Soils that have a gray matrix mottled with orange and red typically indicate a fluctuating water table.

Soil scientists classify soils based on their profile characteristics and the extent to which soil development has occurred (U.S. Department of Agriculture 1975). The broadest classification units are soil orders. Most of the soils in Georgia fall into four orders: ultisols (old, weathered soils that are low in nutrients), spodosols (sandy soils with a strongly leached surface layer and a brown hardpan composed of leached iron and aluminum minerals mixed with organic compounds within 6 feet of the surface, found in the southeastern Coastal Plain), inceptisols (young, poorly developed soils, usually on slopes and old stream terraces), and entisols (very young soils with little soil horizon development, usually on floodplains). Two other orders are less common, but important to some natural environments: histosols (dominated by organic material, such as muck and peat) and alfisols (less weathered than ultisols, often with moderate to high base levels).

The narrowest, most homogeneous classification unit applied to soils is the soil series, and it is the unit of mapping for most agricultural soil surveys. Soil series are defined by landscape position and soil profile and are named for their type location (a specific place that represents a norm for the series) and dominant texture (proportion of sand, silt, and clay).

SOIL PH/NUTRIENT GRADIENT

Bedrock geology and the soils that are derived from bedrock determine the availability of many nutrients that are important to plant growth. Very different plant communities develop according to the nutrient levels and pH of a soil. Common terms relating to plant nutrient and pH conditions are defined below.

Acidic/Low pH Soils. Soils with a pH less than 5.

Basic/High pH/Alkaline Soils. Soils with a pH above 7.4.

Circumneutral Soils. Soils with a pH between 6 and 7.4, with 6–7 being most favorable to plant growth.

Rich/Fertile Soils. Soils that are circumneutral or mildly acidic, and possess many base macronutrients, as well as nitrogen, phosphorus, and sulfur.

Sterile Soils. Soils that hold few plant nutrients.

Acidophiles. Plants that are adapted to soils with low pH and few bases.

Calcifuges. Plants that grow poorly on high-calcium soils; they are nearly always acidophiles.

Calciphiles/Calcicoles. Plants that do well with or even require high-calcium conditions.

TOPOGRAPHIC FACTORS

Geology has a strong impact on the topography of an ecoregion, which in turn strongly influences the moisture of a site. Interactions of the topographic characteristics described below create a complex moisture gradient that ranges from mesic (consistently moist) to xeric (very dry), and can also affect nutrient levels.

Aspect. The compass direction a site is facing. Sunlight rarely strikes sites with a north- or northeast-facing aspect, encouraging cooler, moister conditions, in contrast to south and west aspect slopes, which are exposed to more sunlight and hence are warmer and drier due to the resulting high evaporation and transpiration rates.

Gradient. The steepness of a slope. Rainwater runs off steep slopes quickly, dislodging rock and soil particles such that deep soils are unable to form. In contrast, deep soils and moist conditions occur on flatter slopes.

A. The north-facing slope gets very little sun during the day, keeping it cooler. Also, this slope is bowl-shaped, allowing soils to build, and clays and humus, which retain moisture and nutrients, to collect.

B. The southwest-facing slope gets sun nearly all day, especially in the afternoon, when sun angles are still high, making it warmer. In addition, it has a straight shape, which causes water, clays, and humus to travel downhill.

C. Lower slopes, especially those shaded by ridges, are protected from the sun's rays and stay cool.

D. High ridge tops are very exposed to the sun's rays, so unless they are at very high elevations, they tend to be warmer.

Shape. The surface configuration of a slope (concave, convex, or straight). Convex slopes have thin soils that cannot hold much moisture, while concave sites collect more soil and retain more moisture and nutrients.

Position. The relative location on a slope. Except for very broad, flat sites, sites at higher elevation on a slope do not collect moisture, nutrients, and soils, and tend to be more exposed to climatic conditions. In contrast, sites on a lower slope, except for very steep sites, tend to collect soils, nutrients, and moisture.

Exposure. The degree of protection from wind and sun. Exposed sites, particularly at high elevations, are subjected to more sunlight and wind, resulting in drier conditions, while sheltered sites that lie beneath ridges or steep slopes are more protected from these elements and retain more moisture.

In Georgia, topographic factors vary widely across the state, with the most pronounced relief occurring in the Blue Ridge ecoregion and the flattest sites occurring in the southeastern portion of the Coastal Plain ecoregion; the implications of these differences are explored in the introductory sections of each ecoregion chapter.

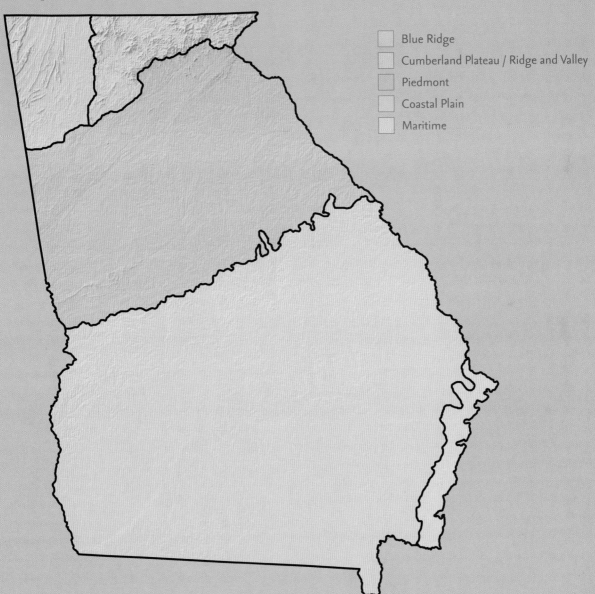

- Blue Ridge
- Cumberland Plateau / Ridge and Valley
- Piedmont
- Coastal Plain
- Maritime

Topography of Georgia. Data from U.S. Geological Survey National Elevation Database.

These sandy soils drain very quickly, creating xeric conditions. The oak saplings in the foreground are clones, sprouting from the root system of a nearby tree. This enables the tree to reproduce even in conditions that are too dry for seeds to germinate.

This open canopy occurs on a very dry site that is supporting a montane longleaf pine community, along with dry-site oaks, which can tolerate the low moisture levels and fairly frequent droughty conditions that thin, fairly sandy soils create.

THE MOISTURE GRADIENT AND PLANT ADAPTATIONS

The moisture gradient is a reflection of the hydrologic, soil texture, physiographic, and microclimatic characteristics of the environment. These categories are defined qualitatively rather than quantitatively, but have significant relevance to the prevailing vegetation of a natural community. While many vegetation characteristics reflect a plant's ability to deal with extreme moisture levels in a particular habitat, most are not visible. Plant morphology (the physical characteristics of the plant's leaves, stems, and growth patterns of the vegetation), however, is often a good indicator of a site's moisture regime, and some common morphological traits are described here.

> **Xeric.** Extremely dry sites. Xeric conditions occur on well-drained sites of very deep sands in the Coastal Plain and on sites throughout the state that possess very thin, rocky, or sandy soils that are exposed to high levels of sunlight. Xeric

sites generally cannot support closed forests with trees that reach full stature. Rather, glades, woodlands, or open forests with stunted trees are characteristic.

> **Subxeric.** Sites that often experience low moisture levels, but not with the frequency or severity of xeric sites. Subxeric sites usually have finer-textured soils or less intense exposure than xeric sites, but edaphic (soil) and topographic traits that foster rapid water loss are present. Vegetation structure ranges from open to closed forest in the absence of frequent fire, with trees of shorter stature than would be reached in moister sites.

Xeric and subxeric sites are dominated by plants that have mechanisms that enable them to conserve moisture. Leaf characteristics that preserve moisture are easily observed. Waxy leaves or needles reflect sunlight, so that the plant does not absorb as much of the sun's rays. Similarly, light-colored hairs on leaves and

This Piedmont oak-pine-hickory forest has grown in dry-mesic (sub-mesic) conditions. Although subject to occasional drought, the soils support tall trees and a closed canopy.

This mesic cove is moist all, or nearly all, of the year. Trees form a closed canopy, and a lush, diverse herb layer carpets the forest floor.

stems reflect sunlight and help the plant retain moisture. Thick leaves or needles reduce the amount of leaf exposed to sunlight. Small plants and leaves reduce the amount of moisture lost through transpiration. Some plants curl their leaves during hot, sunny conditions to reduce exposure to sunlight; others turn their leaves so that the edge of the leaf, rather than the flat surface, is exposed to the sun. Succulent plants, such as cacti, store water in stem or leaf tissue. Plants on subxeric or xeric sites often have either very deep roots that enable them to reach the water table or shallow root systems that permit them to capture rainwater quickly as it infiltrates into the soil.

Dry-mesic/submesic. Sites that receive enough moisture to support a closed forest in the absence of fire. These sites are subject to occasional droughts that preclude the survival of many mesophytic species, such as sugar maple, bitternut hickory, and basswood, beyond the sapling stage.

Mesic. Sites that are moist throughout the year, rarely experiencing droughty, moisture-deficit conditions. Because mesic sites have enough

This hydric site is saturated for much of the year. The pitcherplants shown here can tolerate the high water levels and resulting low-oxygen conditions.

moisture to support closed forests, leaf morphologies that increase sunlight receipt are favored. Leaves are often fairly thin and broad, enabling the plant to absorb as much sunlight as possible. Canopy trees are often characterized by small leaves in the upper canopy, where sunlight is plentiful, and very large leaves on lower limbs that receive far less light. Subcanopy trees may have limbs arranged in a tiered manner that enables the tree to capture sunlight from several angles as the sun changes position during the day.

Hydric. Sites with soils that are saturated or flooded for periods long enough to develop anaerobic conditions and support natural communities dominated by wetland vegetation. These sites are described in detail in the Hydrology section.

CLIMATE

Georgia has a humid, temperate climate, consistent with its geographic location at 31–35 degrees north latitude on the Eastern Seaboard of North America. Climatic conditions differ significantly from north to south, greatly influencing the diversity of natural communities within the state.

Temperature. Elevation tends to increase with latitude, amplifying the differences in average temperatures between the northern and southern parts of the state. Average annual temperatures are in the mid to upper 50s°F in the northern part of the state, low 60s°F in the Piedmont, and upper 60s°F in southeast Georgia (University of Georgia 2012). Average winter temperatures are in the 30s°F in the mountains (ranging from the 20s°F to 50s°F); low 40s°F in much of the Piedmont (ranging from the 30s°F to the 50s°F); upper 40s°F in much of the Coastal Plain (ranging from 30s°F to 60s°F); and low 50s°F near the coast, ranging from the 40s to low 70s°F (G. E. Griffith et al. 2001; University of Georgia 2011). Winter temperature regimes throughout the state include extended periods of mild weather that are punctuated by cold snaps (National Oceanic and Atmospheric Administration 2012). Average summer temperatures are in the low 70s°F in the mountains (ranging from low 60s°F to upper 80s°F); mid to upper 70s°F in much of the Piedmont (ranging from mid 60s°F to 90°F); and upper 70s°F in the Coastal Plain, ranging from low 70s°F to low 90s°F (G. E. Griffith et al. 2001; Univer-

sity of Georgia 2011). The elevations of the mountains cause the Blue Ridge to have the shortest growing season in the state, while the ocean waters and sea breezes reduce temperature extremes along the coast, resulting in the longest growing season there. The average dates of first frost are in October in northern Georgia, November in central Georgia, and December in southern Georgia, and the average dates of last frost are in April in northern Georgia, in March in southern Georgia, and in February along the coast (Hodler and Schretter 1986).

Rainfall. Rainfall in Georgia also varies significantly from north to south. The mountains of north Georgia are the wettest portion of the state, averaging more than 50 inches of precipitation per year in north Georgia, more than 60 inches in northeast Georgia, and exceeding 70 inches in the northeastern corner of the state, with more than 80 inches on some high peaks in the Blue Ridge Mountains (G. E. Griffith et al. 2001; National Oceanic and Atmospheric Administration 2012; University of Georgia 2012). The high precipitation levels in the mountainous areas are due to the orographic effect, in which moist air is pushed up mountain slopes, and cools and condenses as it reaches higher elevations. Most of the Piedmont and Coastal Plain averages 46 to 52 inches of rainfall. During the summer months, a large high-pressure system can settle over the region, leading to periods of drought. Portions of east-central Georgia are the driest on average, being particularly susceptible to receipt of air masses that sink and absorb moisture (Hodler and Schretter 1986; University of Georgia 2012). Periods of drought lasting 2 or more years occur about every 25 years (Stooksbury 2003). Throughout the state, October tends to be the driest month. Frontal activity produces high precipitation totals in late winter or early spring in north Georgia, with the wettest month being March in central and north Georgia. While tropical storms can cause the highest precipitation levels to occur in late summer in southeast Georgia (National Oceanic and Atmospheric Administration 2012), thunderstorms can produce secondary peaks of rainfall totals in July throughout the state (Hodler and Schretter 1986). Relatively little precipitation in Georgia occurs as snow. Portions of the Blue Ridge average 4 to 6 inches of snowfall each year, while other northern areas receive 1 to 2 inches, and the central and southern parts of the state receive negligible amounts (National Oceanic and Atmospheric Administration 2012).

Severe weather occurs most frequently in spring and summer. Tornadoes accompany thunderstorms, with the highest probability of occurrence in April and the lowest in September. Georgia averages approximately 19 tornadoes a year. Tropical depressions, storms, and, rarely, hurricanes affect the state from June through December, with a peak period of activity from August through October (Hodler and Schretter 1986). The shape and position of Georgia's coast (located in a deep curve in the coastline of eastern North America known as the South Atlantic Bight) minimize the likelihood of direct hits by hurricanes, whose paths tend to curve toward the north and east after approaching the coast from the Atlantic Ocean or Caribbean Sea (Southeast Regional Climate Center 2009). Only four hurricanes, none of them major, hit the Georgia coast during the 20th century (Hodler and Schretter 1986). Most tropical storms enter Georgia from the Gulf of Mexico and across the panhandle of Florida.

HYDROLOGY

"Hydrology" is a broad term that refers to the pathways and sources of water on a site—precipitation, surface runoff, groundwater, tides, or flooding—as well as to water depth, flow patterns, and the hydroperiod, which is the seasonal pattern of flooding or inundation. Wetlands are generally considered lands transitional between terrestrial and aquatic systems where the water table is often at or near the surface or the land is covered by shallow water, and which have the following three attributes: (1) at least periodically, the land supports hydrophytes (water-loving plants); (2) the substrate is predominantly undrained hydric (wetland) soil; and (3) the substrate is saturated with

These saturated soils belong to the Iredell soil series and are found in the Piedmont flatwoods natural community. They develop from gabbro bedrock, which weathers to clays that swell when they become saturated with water. The swollen soils prevent water from percolating downward, keeping the surface layers wet, as shown here. The gray color is indicative of the reduced form of iron that occurs when wet soils are low in oxygen.

The Okefenokee Swamp is a wetland that is home to many plants with adaptations to hydric conditions.

water or covered by shallow water at some time during the growing season of each year (Cowardin et al. 1979). This definition emphasizes the role of hydric soils and hydrophytic plants in differentiating wetlands from other environments. Hydric soils are those that are saturated for long enough periods during the growing season that low oxygen conditions occur in their upper horizons (U.S. Soil Conservation Service 1987). Under wet conditions, water fills the soil pores, displacing air. Because oxygen moves slowly through water, plant roots and microbes use it more quickly than it can be replaced. When the soil is saturated and anaerobic conditions occur, iron compounds within the soil change chemically. With repeated wetting and drying, hydric soils display color patterns known as redoximorphic features or mottling. The oxidized form of iron, which occurs when oxygen is present, gives red clay its characteristic color. The reduced form of iron, which occurs in saturated soils, is gray. Continual anaerobic conditions can create a habitat that is stressful or even toxic to plants (Ponnamperuma 1984).

Plant Adaptations to Hydric Sites. When soils are saturated, oxygen levels are low. Thus, many wetland plants develop internal, gas-filled channels in the stems and roots, called "aerenchyma," which allow oxygen movement from the aerial portions of the plant down into the roots (Cronk and Fennessy 2001). Some plant species develop expanded lenticels (called "hypertrophied lenticels") during high-water periods to increase gas exchange in anaerobic conditions. Other species have elongated petioles, which serve to keep their leaves above water when water levels rise. Many plants will have adventitious roots above the low oxygen zone (Mitsch and Gosselink 1993). In addition, plants that are not tolerant of hydric, anaerobic environments typically have decreased water uptake, probably because roots are metabolizing less. Thus, many features of drought-tolerant plants, such as waxy leaves, also occur on wetland plants (Mitsch and Gosselink 1993).

Physiological adaptations to wetland environments include metabolic processes, such as the ability to grow roots in oxygen-deficient situations. Reproduc-

Buttressed trunks are an adaptation to wetland soils.

tive adaptations include prolonged seed viability. Morphological adaptations to the unstable soils, anaerobic conditions, and/or flooded conditions of hydric sites include buttressed tree trunks (trunks with swollen bases), very shallow root systems, and floating leaves, among many others.

Wetland Types. One way of defining wetlands is based on a combination of general vegetation type and physical habitat. These wetland categories include the following (adapted from Mitsch and Gosselink 1993):

Bog. A peat-accumulating wetland that has no significant inflows or outflows and supports acidophilic mosses, especially sphagnum.

Fen. A peat-accumulating wetland that receives some drainage from surrounding mineral soil and usually supports emergent vegetation, such as forbs, grasses, rushes, and sedges. The pH of a fen is circumneutral.

Seepage bog. A wetland that is intermediate between bog and seep. The soil is saturated much of the year by lateral seepage of groundwater from sandy soils of adjacent uplands, with peat accumulation to greater depths than that of a seep but less than that of a bog.

Seep/seepage area/seepage slope. A wetland with either organic or mineral soil that occurs where groundwater discharges to the surface, either due to a break in the topography or to channeling of water by joints in the substrate. Water is not standing, as it is in a bog, but moving, often imperceptibly, downslope.

Marsh. A frequently or continually inundated wetland dominated by emergent vegetation (herbaceous vegetation rooted in water). Marshes can occur in estuarine waters, at the edges of tidal and nontidal rivers, and in naturally impounded areas such as beaver ponds, floodplain pools, and interdune ponds.

Wet prairie. A wetland dominated by herbaceous vegetation, where standing water occurs more frequently than in seepage wetlands, but less frequently than in marshes.

Swamp. A tree-dominated wetland that has standing water or saturated soil all or most of the year. River swamps occur in floodplains and are characterized by flowing waters. Upland depressional swamps occur away from active floodplains and have very little flow.

Bottomland forest. A tree-dominated, seasonally flooded wetland in riparian areas. It is typically interspersed with mesic and hydric habitats, and occurs behind the levees of riverine forests.

Riparian Environments and Watersheds. Georgia has 12 main watersheds, most of which cross ecoregional boundaries. The state is unusual in that nearly all of its rivers originate within the state. The Blue Ridge ecoregion is the headwater for the Savannah, Chatta-

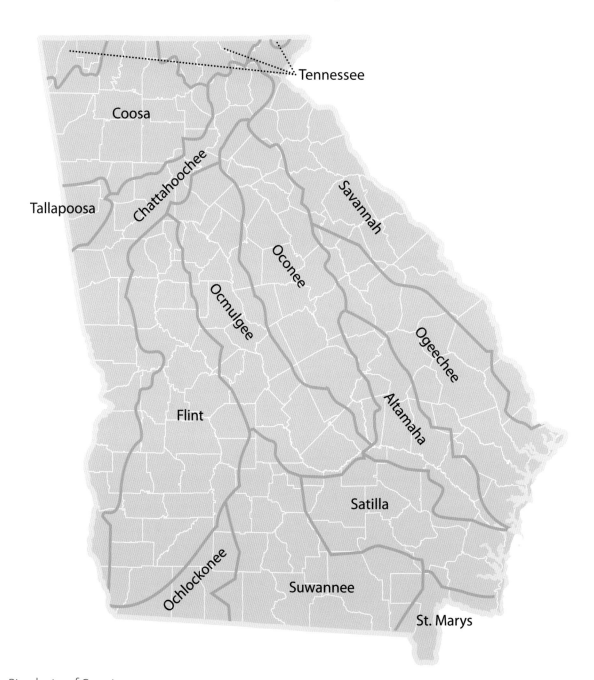

River basins of Georgia

hoochee, and Coosa Rivers and for Georgia's tributaries to the Tennessee River system. As such, it is the divide between the Gulf and Atlantic drainages. The entire Cumberland Plateau / Ridge and Valley ecoregion is drained by the Coosa River system except for the small northwestern-most portion that drains to the Tennessee River. The Savannah, Chattahoochee, and Etowah Rivers flow from the Blue Ridge into the Piedmont, and the Piedmont is the source for numerous tributaries to the Savannah, Chattahoochee, and Coosa River systems. The Piedmont is also the headwater region for the Oconee and Ocmulgee Rivers, the main tributaries of Georgia's largest river, the Altamaha. Other large rivers of the Coastal Plain—the Flint, Ogeechee, and Chattahoochee—also enter the ecoregion from the Piedmont, but several rivers and very large creeks arise within the Coastal Plain, including Ichawaynochaway Creek, the Ochlocknee River, the Satilla River, the Ohoopee River, and Brier Creek. The Okefenokee Swamp is the headwater of both the Suwannee River, which drains to the Gulf of Mexico, and the St. Marys River, which drains to the Atlantic Ocean.

Water flowing in rivers and streams shapes the channel and the adjacent floodplain, forming riparian natural environments. Riparian natural communities occur in all of Georgia's ecoregions, but are more prevalent in the Coastal Plain, where floodplains are larger and well developed. In mountainous regions of north Georgia, substrates are rocky and stream gradients are steep, so these streams are down-cutting through bedrock rather than building floodplains. Average stream discharges are also lower in mountainous terrain because the streams are relatively small; these streams do not increase substantially in size until more tributaries join them at lower elevations, so there is less energy and water for the creation of large floodplains. In contrast, in the Coastal Plain and flatter portions of the Cumberland Plateau / Ridge and Valley, the larger rivers have more energy and water volume for building floodplains. Their lower stream gradient and sandy stream beds allow them to meander and build floodplains through deposition of sediments.

The most important factors influencing vegetation on floodplains are mechanical flood disturbance and soil moisture conditions, which are determined by the flooding regime and water table levels of a site (Sharitz and Mitsch 1993). Because saturation impacts the

amount of oxygen available to a site, Wharton et al. (1982) referred to the soil moisture gradient on floodplains as an "anaerobic gradient." Soil moisture varies on bottomlands according to the microtopography of the bottomland and distance from the stream channel. Depending on topography and distance from the river, sites experience a range of flooding regimes, from nearly continuously flooded to flooding less than once a decade (Mitsch and Gosselink 1993; Christensen 2000). These flood regimes over time carve a complex topography of former levees, small hummocks, swales, and other slight depressions that collect water and clay (Mitsch and Gosselink 1993; Sharitz and Mitsch 1993). Thus, moisture conditions can change over a spatial scale of yards or even inches (Sharitz and Mitsch 1993). (See p. 467 for a diagram of floodplain topography.)

Beaver Ponds and Other Semipermanent Impoundments. Beaver ponds are wetlands that support important plant and animal communities. Indeed, beavers are the only organisms other than humans that create wetlands, and beaver ponds are the only natural ponds in the Piedmont and Blue Ridge ecoregions of Georgia (Godfrey 1997; Batzer, Cooper, and Wissinger 2006).

Beavers construct dams across small to medium-sized streams. The stream and bottomlands behind the dam are flooded, forming a pond. The upland vegetation along the stream dies as the water creates anoxic (very low oxygen) conditions. The site becomes increasingly open as the trees die and as beavers cut down more trees along the pond edge. Thus, the stream and bottomland forest natural communities are converted to sunny, open pond communities dominated by hydrophytic plants in a process that can take up to 30 years (Godfrey 1997). Eventually, the beavers may succumb to predation, disease, or trapping by humans, or may abandon the pond if food resources become scarce. After the beavers are gone and no longer maintaining the dam, it will weaken over time and be breached. The pond drains, and the newly exposed sediments are colonized by new vegetation, eventually succeeding to the stream-side communities that existed prior to the dam's construction (Godfrey 1997; Batzer, Cooper, and Wissinger 2006).

Plants in a beaver pond may be arranged somewhat zonally, from shoreline to deeper waters (God-

A beaver pond. Note the complex topography and differing water levels throughout the habitat, which support a variety of plant communities.

Beaver dam

frey 1997). A classic distribution includes a shoreline flora of buttonbushes, swamp dogwoods, black willows, and tag alders; the pond margin supports emergent vegetation such as cattails, sedges, rushes, and spikerushes; slightly deeper waters support arrowheads and water plantains; and still deeper waters sustain floating vegetation such as water lilies, spatterdocks, water-shields, parrot-feathers, bladderworts, and pondweeds. Such clear zonation, however, is often not evident in beaver ponds. The land that was flooded by the dammed stream waters often has a complex topography with interspersed mounds and depressions, so the plant distribution will reflect the mosaic of water depths. Beaver pond vegetation composition also varies from site to site due to successional dynamics, regional differences in flora, and local precipitation patterns. The vagaries of seed dispersal and germination also affect the plant composition of beaver pond vegetation. Species that may appear in beaver ponds include, in addition to those already mentioned, turtleheads, false-nettles, orange jewelweeds, cardinal flowers, bulrushes, lizard's-tails, mermaid-weeds, American bur-reeds, sensitive ferns, ditch-stonecrops, common elderberries, and Midwestern tickseed-sunflowers.

PART 2.

Disturbance and Succession

A disturbance agent is a force that periodically destroys, damages, or removes vegetation on a site, creating gaps and consequently altering vegetation structure and/or composition. The most common disturbance agents in Georgia are fire, flooding, windthrow, ice-loading, and herbivory. Whether large-scale disturbances or small canopy gaps created by mortality of a single or multiple trees, available sunlight increases, and the water and nutrient resources that were being used by the vegetation prior to removal become available to plants that recolonize the site (Canham and Marks 1985; B. S. Collins et al. 1985; Krebs 2001). The size of the gap is important in determining subsequent species composition because it determines the amount of light, the temperature, and the moisture regime within the gap (Brokaw 1985; B. S. Collins et al. 1985). When gaps caused by the disturbance are medium to large in size (several trees or several acres), the outcome may be a succession of plant communities. Typically, "pioneer" spe-

A downed tree has opened a gap in the forest that will enable new plants to grow, taking advantage of the increased sunlight and nutrients available in the gap.

Pines, and many oaks, require some sun to regenerate. If medium-sized openings do not occur in this forest, eventually the pines (and many oaks) will disappear from the forest, as the older trees die off and new ones cannot become established.

cies that produce light, wind-blown seeds quickly colonize larger gaps. The pioneer species grow rapidly and initially dominate the gap. These species are often short-lived relative to other species, however, and cannot reproduce in the more shaded conditions that develop over time (Grime 2001; Krebs 2001). Eventually, longer-lived, more-shade-tolerant species come to dominate the site until another disturbance occurs.

A process known as "gap phase succession" is common in most forested natural communities in Georgia and is caused by the loss of a single tree or even the large branches of a tree. Saplings of longer-lived species are usually already established in the understory and are "released" by the disturbance—that is, they are able to grow quickly in the greater amounts of sunlight and soil moisture that were made available by the fallen tree or branch (Brokaw 1985; Runkle 1985). Many protected, mesic forests experience these very small gap disturbances and are rarely subjected to medium or large disturbances (Clebsch and Busing 1989; Schafale and Weakley 1990; Bratton 1994).

Often different portions of a natural community experience disturbance at varying times or levels of intensity, such that the community comprises vegetation patches of differing ages and composition (Schafale and Weakley 1990; Comer et al. 2003). These spatial variations in successional stage can cause confusion in identification of a natural community. A stand of pine trees, for example, might be labeled a pine-oak woodland and forest natural community in the Georgia Blue Ridge, but the density of the trees, the surrounding vegetation, and the hardwood seedlings in the understory may indicate that this is actually an early successional phase of the oak-pine-hickory forest natural community.

FIRE

Fire has been a major force in shaping many environments in Georgia, and indeed much of the western hemisphere, for millennia (Pinter, Fiedel, and Keeley 2011). The effects of fire on natural communities in Georgia are complex, and are influenced by weather, climate, topography, soils, vegetation structure and composition, and human activities. Fire that occurs at regular intervals influences both the vegetation structure and composition of a site, and is in turn influenced by them.

Fire's Impact on Vegetation Structure and Composition. Fire regimes greatly influence the vegetation structure of a site. Sites that undergo regular fire are more open because the fire suppresses many fire-intolerant understory plants. Thus, woodlands, savannas, or prairies often predominate on sites experiencing frequent fires. Areas that were previously cleared or partially cleared of canopy trees (through either human or natural disturbance) can be maintained as prairies, woodlands, or savannas if subsequent fires or

Fire is a disturbance agent that structures vegetation by reducing fire-sensitive species.

other disturbance agents occur frequently enough to prevent regeneration of tree species.

Plants adapt to fire through several different strategies: (1) avoidance of fire damage; (2) enduring biomass removal, often by fast regrowth after fire; (3) rapid colonization of a site after a fire; and (4) facilitating fire so that fire-intolerant competitive species are eliminated from the landscape (Barnes et al. 1998). Fire damage is avoided through several morphological adaptations. Thick, insulating bark (as is found in many pines and oaks) protects some trees. Others have buried buds that are protected within the soil. Some species have leaves that sheathe terminal buds or that may have flame-resistant terminal buds. Trees may self-prune branches, preventing the formation of a fire "ladder" that can carry fires to the canopy.

Fast regrowth following biomass removal by fire occurs as a result of the perenniality of plants. Numer-

Longleaf pine is extremely well adapted to fire. Although the needles burned during a recent fire, the growing tip of the tree remains viable.

ous fire-adapted plants have rhizomes, deep tap roots, extensive root systems, or sinker roots that allow for rapid resprouting. Some have adventitious and latent axillary buds that quickly produce new growth after top kill (mortality of the above-ground portion of the tree).

Rapid recolonization often occurs when pioneer species carpet an area with light, wind-borne seeds. In contrast, the seeds of some species are buried in the soil and can persist on fire-prone sites. Some species produce serotinous cones (cones that remain closed and release seeds only after they are exposed to high heat). Many species are stimulated to flower in response to fire, presumably to take advantage of the availability of exposed soil or fire-released nutrients.

Many oak and pine species in Georgia are favored by fire and so will dominate fire-prone sites. Different oaks and pines have varying fire tolerances, depending on the thickness of their bark and their ability to resprout. Shortleaf, pitch, and longleaf pines often have

a competitive advantage over oaks where fire is frequent. In contrast, as fires become less frequent, oaks and other hardwood trees tend to dominate as leaf litter becomes thicker, presumably because their larger seeds can germinate and grow in the presence of the litter (Abrams 2000). Consequently, varied assemblages of species will develop as a result of different fire frequencies.

Fire can also have more subtle effects on vegetation composition by altering nutrient availability and ecosystem processes through changes in soil pH, cation exchange capacity, organic matter oxidation, and soil organism activity in soils. Fuel combustion releases cations, particularly Ca+, Mg+, and K+, which may increase soil pH with ash accretion on the surface (Raison 1979; Certini 2005). Many nutrients become more available for plant uptake at neutral pH values (Bardgett 2005). Over time, ash is gradually removed through leaching or wind. Of particular interest are the fates of two nutrients that are limiting factors for growth in many ecosystems: nitrogen and phosphorus. Much of the total nitrogen is volatilized with combustion of organic material (DeBano et al. 1998), but increases in organic nitrogen, ammonium, and nitrate also usually occur (Boring et al. 1990). The highly soluble form, nitrate, is rapidly leached from soil, whereas ammonium usually binds with clay particles. Available phosphorus, in the form of phosphate, also increases following fire (Certini 2005).

Nutrient cycling and availability are strongly mediated by microbes. Bacteria and mycorrhizal fungi decompose organic material into forms available for plant uptake. Immediately following fire, bacterial and fungal populations decrease. Due to initial increases in pH and nutrients, bacteria recolonize more rapidly than mycorrhizae, although as soils acidify, the mycorrhizae will become abundant (Bardgett 2005). The removal of litter through fire and the resulting exposed dark soil surface increase soil temperature and accelerate the oxidative process.

Interactions of Fire and Vegetation. Fire both impacts and is influenced by vegetation composition and structure. Fire-adapted communities facilitate the distribution and influence of fire, and vice versa.

Some plants are structured such that they carry fire well: fire is able to spread from plant to plant with ease. The southern wiregrass that carpets many longleaf pine forests is an excellent example; not only does the fire spread from grass clump to grass clump, but the narrow southern wiregrass blades dry quickly after rain, igniting more readily than other species. Actually, any dense and dry herbaceous or shrub layer will also spread fire under the right burning conditions. Once a woodland or savanna has become established and maintained by fire, the resulting vegetation promotes low-intensity surface fires that do not harm the fire-tolerant canopy trees. Many perennial species resprout quickly from rootstocks after a fire. Thus, the combination of rapid resprouting and fire-carrying capacity enables them to retain dominance on a site if ignition sources are present.

If fires are suppressed, fire-sensitive woody shrubs and tree saplings eventually dominate the site. Over time they can impact fire frequency, establishing a new threshold through the absence of fine fuels. Once established, fire-sensitive species may alter fuel conditions such that the opportunity for recurrence of fire is reduced. Some evergreen oak leaves, for example, hold

moisture in the litter layer that retards fire movement, while the leaves of many mesophytic species mineralize quickly, so there is not as much duff or litter on the forest floor to spread a fire. When multiple layers of dense vegetation develop over time, the probability of a catastrophic crown fire that can destroy the entire stand increases.

In summary, the importance of fire to vegetation structure and composition is not defined by the effects of a single fire, but by the frequency and continuity of repeated fires: prairies, savannas, woodlands, or forests, dominated by pines, oaks, or both, can arise on a site, depending on the fire regime. A characteristic fire regime can be defined for long periods of time or over large areas based on fire-return interval, disturbance size, and severity of the fire (the amount of biomass consumed). Climate shifts and human intervention can alter these regimes, causing vegetation structure and composition to change accordingly.

The Impact of Weather and Climate on Fire. Fires are more common, spread more quickly, and can be more intense in dry, low-humidity conditions. Fires may also occur more often if opportunities for lightning ignition are more common. The frequency of lightning ignition varies over the state and depends on both the number of thunderstorms an area experiences and the number of strikes that occur without rains that would otherwise put out a fire. The frequency of cloud-to-ground lightning is higher throughout the Coastal Plain than in other parts of the state. Variation in incidence of flashes across the Coastal Plain is attributable to physiographic differences and storm patterns within the ecoregion. In summer months, lightning activity is highest in coastal counties. Other areas of the state with high lightning strike frequencies include the east-central region near the Fall Line and somewhat southwest, and the metropolitan area of Atlanta, due to elevated temperatures caused by impervious surfaces and resulting high incidence of summer thunderstorms (Bentley and Stallins 2005).

During winter months, overall lightning activity declines with decreasing frequency of convection storms, but is greater at this time of year in southwestern Georgia than other parts of the Coastal Plain (Bentley and Stallins 2005). Indeed, based on lightning-caused mortality rates of approximately 1% in a longleaf pine stand in southwest Georgia, the probability of a tree being struck by lightning within its expected

The patchy pattern of plant litter interspersed with bare sand will prevent a fire from spreading far on this sandhill in the Coastal Plain.

lifespan of 300 years is extremely high (R. J. Mitchell, J. W. Jones Center, pers. comm.).

Thus, fire regimes change over time as climate fluctuates. Climate regimes that encompass many dry, droughty periods will encourage more fires. In much of Georgia's developed landscape, however, fire regimes are primarily controlled by prescribed fire management and regulations dictating the climatic conditions necessary to obtain a burning permit.

The Influence of Topography and Soils on Fire. A major way in which topography influences fire is in determining the size of "fire compartments"—areas over which a fire can spread before being halted by a firebreak, which is a landscape feature that discourages fire. Landscape features that serve as firebreaks include bodies of water, steep slopes that foster shaded, cool sites, moist fuels, scarcity of fuels, and roads. Natural fire compartments are smallest in the Blue Ridge and the northernmost Piedmont, where dense incision of streams, steep, shaded slopes, and, on the highest

peaks, frequent precipitation and fog all impede fires. Compartments are somewhat larger in the Cumberland Plateau / Ridge and Valley ecoregion, where wide valleys and broad ridge tops enable fire to spread. The southern Piedmont's gentle topography leads to larger compartments and the largest compartment size in Georgia occurs in the Coastal Plain. Today, firebreaks are more often determined by anthropogenic features.

Exposure is another feature that influences fire frequency, particularly in rugged landscapes. Exposed sites tend to be both dry and particularly vulnerable to lightning strikes due to their prominence in the landscape. Dry ridges that are higher than those surrounding them, particularly west- and south-facing sites that are in storm tracks, will be most susceptible to lightning-ignited fires. In flatter topography, a more even exposure exists over wide swaths of landscape.

Soil texture can also be influential in the spread of fire. Sandy soils drain moisture and dry out quickly, encouraging the spread of fire through dry duff layers. In contrast, humus-rich or loamy soils retain moisture

The plants close to the water along the Jacks River in the Blue Ridge ecoregion experience mechanical damage from floodwaters. Vegetation includes shrubs and herbs that can sway in the floodwaters, as well as trees that resprout from the roots after their trunks are broken by the water's force.

for longer periods, contributing to moist conditions in overlying duff layers. Some very clayey soils form hardpans that create very dry, more fire-prone conditions in the summer, as water over the hardpan quickly evaporates from the surface.

FLOOD DISTURBANCE

Flooding influences vegetation through mechanical damage, deposition of nutrient-rich sediments, and the creation of saturated (anaerobic) soil conditions.

Rivers are in a constant state of flux as they flow across the landscape, continually building up landforms in some areas and eroding them in others. Areas near and within the stream channel, such as point bars, levees, riffles, shallow midstream islands, bars, the edges of large islands, rock outcroppings, and

the channel sides, are the most active sites. These riparian areas have common characteristics that influence vegetation: (1) a continual shifting of sediment as floodwaters deposit and erode sediment; (2) periods of inundation and anaerobic conditions that accompany flooding; (3) mechanical damage caused both by the weight of floodwaters and by the debris carried by the floodwaters; (4) nutrients that are delivered to the sites through flooding; and (5) high levels of sunlight made possible by the open conditions along the river and stream (Malanson 1993; Mitsch and Gosselink 1993; Sharitz and Mitsch 1993).

Riparian areas are most affected by strong floods, where the weight of the water and debris within the water mechanically damage plants, uprooting them and breaking stems. Gaps are continually being formed as

This floodplain has a varied topography, ranging from the levee in the foreground to a swamp behind the levee in the background, which results in a complex mosaic of nutrient and moisture conditions.

trees fall into the stream (Malanson 1993; Sharitz and Mitsch 1993). The increased sunlight caused by the loss of canopy trees enables pioneer species to become established. Trees are snapped by floodwaters; they may resprout after damage. Others are bent low to the ground with a single strong root anchoring them or lean at low angles over the water. Because sediment is often removed from these areas, tree roots are often exposed and sprawl along the ground. Shrubs that can sway and bend with the floodwaters are common and dominate some sites. Tangles of vines sprawling over shrubs, herbs, and saplings are common within the many openings, and herbs often dominate large patches.

Floodwaters also affect floodplains by depositing nutrient-rich alluvium. The distribution of nutrients varies with depositional patterns of river floods. Behind the levees, where nutrient-rich clays have been deposited, lush vegetation may be supported. In active sites, where sands are more prevalent, nutrient levels may be lower (Clark and Benforado 1981; Trimble 1985; Cow-

ell 1992; Sharitz and Mitsch 1993; Ferguson 1997; Edwards et al. 1999; Edwards 2001). While a zonal pattern can exist on floodplains, with more nutrients deposited farther from the river, differences in intensity of flood events and the microtopography of the floodplain often result in a mosaic of nutrient conditions.

WINDTHROW

Trees, particularly on more exposed sites, are often subject to windthrow (toppling by winds, either from the roots or snapping at the trunks) in association with tropical storms, tornadoes, ice storms, and severe thunderstorms. Wind is a significant disturbance agent in Georgia, altering vegetation assemblages by tree blow-downs that create small to large canopy gaps that increase sunlight to the understory and ground layer. Tree fall is more common on steep sites and areas with shallow soil, particularly those on exposed sites in the path of prevailing wind. Where wind disturbance is common, a continual turnover of species may

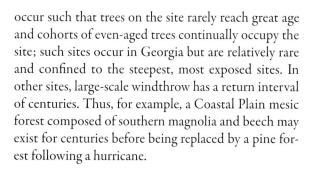

Limbs weighted by ice-glazed needles are subject to breakage.

Herbivory takes many forms. Here a non-native invasive insect, the hemlock woolly adelgid, sucks fluid from the base of eastern hemlock needles, causing the needles to drop off, eventually killing the tree.

occur such that trees on the site rarely reach great age and cohorts of even-aged trees continually occupy the site; such sites occur in Georgia but are relatively rare and confined to the steepest, most exposed sites. In other sites, large-scale windthrow has a return interval of centuries. Thus, for example, a Coastal Plain mesic forest composed of southern magnolia and beech may exist for centuries before being replaced by a pine forest following a hurricane.

ICE-LOADING

Ice-loading occurs when large amounts of ice and snow collect on tree branches, causing them to snap and break off. In some cases, entire trees or even groups of trees are toppled by ice storms. More sunlight is able to reach the lower layers of the forest, enabling small trees that have been suppressed beneath the canopy to be released and grow toward the canopy. Ice-loading is a significant disturbance agent in the Blue Ridge and,

to a lesser degree, in the Cumberland Plateau / Ridge and Valley and Piedmont ecoregions.

HERBIVORY

Herbivory, or animal predation on plants, may greatly influence vegetation structure and composition (Lancaster 1996). Grazing by bison and other native herbivores undoubtedly influenced the herbaceous vegetation of southeastern woodlands and savannas, as did the free-ranging domestic animals that early European settlers set out to graze in forests. More recently, a dramatic increase in white-tailed deer populations due to land use changes and the extirpation of natural predators has resulted in significant impacts on understory vegetation in some forests. Southern pine beetle infestations are capable of causing significant mortality in pine-dominated forests, thinning the stands and hastening a transition to pine-hardwood forests.

The impacts of herbivory are often most noticeable in the case of non-native invasive species. The impacts of feral hogs on southern Appalachian beech gaps have been well documented (Bratton 1975). Grazing and soil disturbance by this omnivorous animal reduce understory herb cover to 10–30% of undisturbed levels and may affect tree growth and nutrient cycling (Singer et al. 1984). Impacts on the herbaceous communities of mesic ravine and bottomland forests have also been noted in Georgia (T. Patrick, Georgia Department of Natural Resources, pers. comm.).

In some cases, the impacts of non-native and native herbivores are linked. A recent study of white-tailed deer herbivory on tree seedlings in areas infested by the hemlock wooly adelgid indicated that deer-browsing significantly decreased the abundance of six native tree species. Results of the study indicated that deer herbivory alters forest response to hemlock woolly adelgid mortality and has the potential to shift the overstory composition of the recovering forest (Eschtruth and Battles 2008).

PART 3.
Paleohistory

Georgia's natural environments are the result of changes occurring over long periods of time, as the biota has responded to changes in continental positions and configuration, topography, local and global climate, immigration and emigration, and competition. The study of the past demonstrates how today's natural environments are a snapshot in time, and how past conditions must be considered to fully understand the natural communities of the present (S. T. Jackson and Hobbs 2009).

PRE-PALEOZOIC, OVER 600 MILLION YEARS AGO (MYA)

A single supercontinent, named Rodinia, existed on earth 2.5 billion years ago. Seven hundred to 650 million years ago, Rodinia split apart into the continents Laurentia (now North America), Gondwana (part of which is now Africa), and smaller fragments. Primitive multicellular and one-celled life forms were in existence.

THE PALEOZOIC ERA, 600–225 MYA

Geology. Between 543 and 360 million years ago, collisions between Laurentia, island arcs, and other land-masses caused two successive orogenies (mountain-building events), in which mountain chains rose in what is now Georgia. Each eroded over the course of millions of years, and the eroded particles were transported to basins and shallow seas. These sediments, along with the reefs and skeletal debris of organisms living in the seas, eventually hardened to form sandstone, shale, limestone, and other sedimentary rocks over time. Many of these rocks are now exposed in the Cumberland Plateau / Ridge and Valley ecoregion.

Between 325 and 260 million years ago, portions of Gondwana began colliding with Laurentia to begin the formation of a supercontinent called Pangaea. This collision caused the rise of the current Appalachian mountain chain, which may have been as high as the Himalayas. In the Blue Ridge and Piedmont ecoregions, the collision caused complex patterns of folding and faulting, and the rocks were metamorphosed (altered and recrystallized by the high temperatures and pressures within the mountains). The sedimentary rocks farther west, in what is now the Cumberland Plateau / Ridge and Valley ecoregion, were not metamorphosed but were uplifted, folded, and slightly faulted. Even farther west in this ecoregion, sedimentary rocks were only slighted warped.

Flora and Fauna. A succession of life forms developed, including hard-shelled invertebrates, fishes, amphibians, reptiles, and primitive plants such as ferns, scale trees, quillworts, horsetails, and conifers. Fossils of marine organisms from this era are found throughout the sedimentary rocks of the Cumberland Plateau / Ridge and Valley ecoregion, while an amphibian trackway in 300-million-year-old rocks is the oldest evidence of terrestrial animals in Georgia (Schneck and Fritz 1985; Tomer 2003).

The largest extinction in earth's history, sometimes called the Great Extinction, took place at the end of the Paleozoic era (Bowring et al. 1998). During "The Great Dying" 96% of all marine animal species and 70% of all terrestrial animal species were extinguished (Benton 2005).

THE MESOZOIC ERA, 225–75 MYA

Geology. Roughly 200 million years ago, Pangaea began to rift apart. Africa split from North America, creating a landscape of fault-block mountains and down-dropped valleys similar to the rift valleys in eastern Africa of today. As the rift valleys widened, they flooded, giving birth to the Atlantic Ocean. Sediments shed from the highlands to the north buried the fault-block mountains and valleys to begin formation of the Coastal Plain. Seventy million years ago, sea levels rose to at least as far as the southern Piedmont of today.

Flora and Fauna. Following the Great Extinction, the Mesozoic era began, ushering in the Age of Dinosaurs. A great variety of life forms must have existed in Georgia during the Triassic and Jurassic periods of the era (225–135 MYA), although the known fossil record for the state starts with the Cretaceous period, which was the final period of the Mesozoic era and lasted from 135 to 70 million years ago. The Georgia coastal zone is thought to have been characterized by large saltwater swamps grading into freshwater swamps, due to the low elevation of the land in relation to the sea (E. B. Robertson 1996). Herbivorous and carnivorous dinosaurs, pterosaurs, fish, and a range of other animals, including a giant crocodilian, *Deinosuchus hatcheri*, existed here (Schwimmer, Padian, and Woodhead 1985; Case and Schwimmer 1988). Fossils from more inland terrestrial environments from this time have not been preserved and so are unavailable for study in Georgia.

Flowering plants most likely first appeared in the Cretaceous. Vegetation was tropical to subtropical in much of Georgia, with ancestors of pawpaw, sassafras, spicebush, magnolia, laurel, and much else (A. Graham 2008). The cooler mountainous areas may have supported ancestors of temperate pines, birches, basswoods, and other hardwoods of today (A. Graham 2008).

Another great terrestrial extinction occurred at the end of the Cretaceous period, as the dinosaurs and other life forms vanished. In North America, plants were particularly devastated, and approximately 57% of plant species became extinct (K. R. Johnson and Hickey 1991). The extinction seems to have been caused by multiple factors, including severe lowering of sea level, dust clouds and acid rain induced by volcanism in India, and meteorite impacts, most prominently the Chicxulub impact on the northern edge of the Yucatan Peninsula.

THE CENOZOIC ERA PRIOR TO THE PLEISTOCENE, 70–2.6 MYA

Geology. The great Cretaceous extinction was followed by the Cenozoic era, the Age of Mammals.

North Georgia remained uplifted and continued eroding, while sediments were being deposited in south Georgia by a gradually receding ocean that was moving south from its previous Cretaceous shoreline in the vicinity of today's Fall Line. As the ocean receded over the succeeding eons, thick layers of sands, silts, clays, and limestone were left behind across the Coastal Plain. The breakup of the supercontinent Pangaea continued (Prothero 2006). North America drifted to the north, moving the southeastern United States to a temperate position from its former tropical location (P. A. Delcourt et al. 1993). Georgia, as well as all of North America, was greatly affected by these processes as the area underwent a gradual cooling through the Cenozoic.

Flora and Fauna. Fossil pollen shows a mixture of tropical and temperate plants (E. B. Robertson 1996). Over time, cooling fostered a warm temperate, mixed deciduous hardwood forest with many similarities to current flora, including alder, birch, hickory, chestnut, beech, holly, sweet gum, black gum, oaks, and elms (Graham 1999).

Sea snakes, barracudas, sharks, and whales swam in the seas over what is now the Coastal Plain. In the absence of dinosaurs, this period became the Age of Mammals (Kurtin 1972): the land animals included horses, rhinos, beavers, red pandas, badgers, and forest-adapted species. The late Cenozoic is famous for the Great American Interchange, which occurred when a land bridge emerged between South America and North America roughly three million years ago (Marshall 1988). The interchange took place in both directions, but more South American groups were displaced by immigrants than groups in North America. Giant ground sloths, armadillos, glyptodonts, porcupines, capybaras, and large, flightless predatory birds are among these arrivals from the south (Marshall 1988).

THE PLEISTOCENE EPOCH, 2.6 MYA–11,700 YEARS AGO

Beginning about 2.6 million years ago, a series of roughly 20 glaciations occurred. Each glaciation lasted roughly 90,000 years, during which time large ice caps would begin building up in the Hudson Bay area and spreading down to the Ohio area, although ranges varied. Interglacials, during which the ice retreated, would follow the ice ages, and most lasted roughly

THE PALEOHISTORY OF GEORGIA

GEOLOGIC ERA	GEOLOGIC EVENTS	SIGNIFICANT LIFE FORMS
Cenozoic: 70 MYA–present	Pleistocene glaciations from 2.6 million to 11,700 years ago; sea levels retreated; development of temperate climate in SE United States.	The Age of Mammals
Mesozoic: 225–70 MYA	Pangaea rifted apart; sea levels rose to the present-day Fall Line or beyond.	The Age of Dinosaurs; first flowering plants
Paleozoic: 600–225 MYA	The supercontinent Pangaea formed, causing the rise of the current Appalachian Mountain chain.	Hard-shelled invertebrates and fishes; movement of life to land, including invertebrates, amphibians, reptiles, and primitive plants
Pre-Paleozoic: over 600 MYA	The supercontinent Rodinia formed, then split apart into Laurentia and Gondwana.	Primitive multicellular and one-celled life forms

Some of the flora extant in Georgia can serve as reminders of the paleohistory of the state. For example, the magnolia family is an ancient one, dating back to the Cretaceous period in the Mesozoic era. The flowers were (and are) pollinated by beetles; bees were not yet present on earth when magnolias appeared. Like some other primitive flowering plants, the flower parts are arranged in a spiral with many stamens and pistils. Here, the stamens are being dropped onto the petal.

10,000 years. During glaciations, sea level was much lower because water evaporated from the oceans and then precipitated as snow to form the glaciers. The shoreline during glaciations was as much as 100 miles farther out from the continental shelf than today. Sea levels rose during interglacials because the glaciers melted, returning water to the oceans.

Each glacial advance caused the location and nature of Georgia's natural communities to change. During each glaciation, plants were forced southward by the cooling climate; some plants colonized the valleys and ravines in the Piedmont and Coastal Plain, where north-facing slopes provided conditions that were warmer than those farther north but cooler and moister than the surroundings. These refugia enabled numerous species to avoid extinction (H. R. Delcourt 2002). Many species moved north again when the ice age ended, with a number of populations remaining in some ravines as southerly disjuncts from their main population centers, as relics of the ice age distributions.

Although estimates vary widely, during the most recent glaciation, northernmost Georgia experienced considerably cooler winters and summers, fostering a boreal mixed hardwood and evergreen forest dominated by pine, spruce, and fir (Barnett et al. 2005; P. A. Delcourt and Delcourt 2008). Southern Georgia was most likely less affected, with temperatures more similar to those in the present, although conditions were drier. While more study is needed, the Coastal Plain probably supported mixed temperate deciduous and evergreen forests. Middle Georgia was a transition zone between north and south (P. A. Delcourt and Delcourt 2008). A stunningly different fauna inhabited Georgia, including jaguars, ground sloths, (possibly) ocelots, American lions, saber-toothed cats, mountain lions, American cheetahs, and many others, with an especially diverse amphibian and reptile fauna (Holman 1967; Ray 1967; Voorhies 1974).

Chapter 3

BLUE RIDGE ECOREGION

Overview

The Blue Ridge ecoregion encompasses the highest mountains in Georgia, with the tallest peaks, the sharpest relief, the most precipitation, and the coolest temperatures of any region in the state. Some mountaintops in the Blue Ridge host species that are typical in habitats 700 miles to the north, but are absent in the Piedmont just 50 miles to the south. Many plant species that were common at lower elevations during the last ice age now survive as remnant (relict) populations only at high elevations, and there are many plant species that are endemic to (found only in) the central and southern Appalachians. Species of salamanders, millipedes, trilliums, and snails also exist in great variety in the southern Appalachians. A large percentage of this ecoregion is protected in the Chattahoochee National Forest as well as in Unicoi, Vogel, Amicalola, and Fort Mountain State Parks.

GEOLOGY, TOPOGRAPHY, AND SOILS

The Blue Ridge ecoregion occupies roughly 1,850 square miles in Georgia, which is less than 5% of the state. European settlers advancing west from the populated seaboard of the mid-Atlantic colonies saw the easternmost escarpment of the Appalachians as a hazy blue ridge looming over the more gently rolling Piedmont. There are 37 peaks above 4,000 feet in elevation, of which 4 are higher than 4,500 feet. The Blue Ridge ecoregion contains all of the mountains in Georgia more than 3,000 feet tall except Mount Yonah in the Piedmont.

The ecoregion is made up of three subregions: the Southern Crystalline Ridges and Mountains, the Southern Metasedimentary Mountains, and the Broad Basins (G. E. Griffith et al. 2001). Each is described below.

The Southern Crystalline Ridges and Mountains. These occur in the easternmost part of the ecoregion. The mountains within this subregion are higher and the relief is sharper than anywhere else in the ecoregion: valleys are often 1,500–2,000 feet below the adjacent summits. The majority of peaks that rise above 4,000 feet in Georgia are found here. The tallest is Brasstown Bald at 4,784 feet (Towns and Union Counties), while peaks on Rabun Bald (Rabun County), Dicks Knob (Rabun County), Hightower Bald (Towns County), Blood Mountain (Lumpkin and Union Counties), Tray Mountain (Towns County), Grassy Ridge (Rabun County), and Little Bald (Towns County) are all 4,400 feet or higher.

The bedrock of this subregion is the most intensely metamorphosed in the ecoregion and is extensively folded and faulted. The most common rock types are gneiss, schist, and quartzite, which weather to fairly acidic, well-drained soils. On steep slopes, these soils are thin and poorly developed. Mafic rocks, such as amphibolite, and ultramafic rocks, such as dunite, occur sporadically, and are intermixed in a large ring around Brasstown Bald. Mafic rock outcroppings form basic soils that foster outcrop, barren, and woodland communities in thin-soiled areas and variants of mid- to low-elevation oak forests or mesic forests in others. A rare ultramafic barren community, with soils that are very high in magnesium and iron, occurs in one dunite outcrop area (see p. 104).

This subregion also includes some lower-elevation areas along the Chattooga River, the lower Tallulah River, the Tugaloo River, and Panther Creek.

The Southern Metasedimentary Mountains. These occur in the western part of the ecoregion. Here the rocks are less strongly metamorphosed than those of the Southern Crystalline Ridges and Mountains and

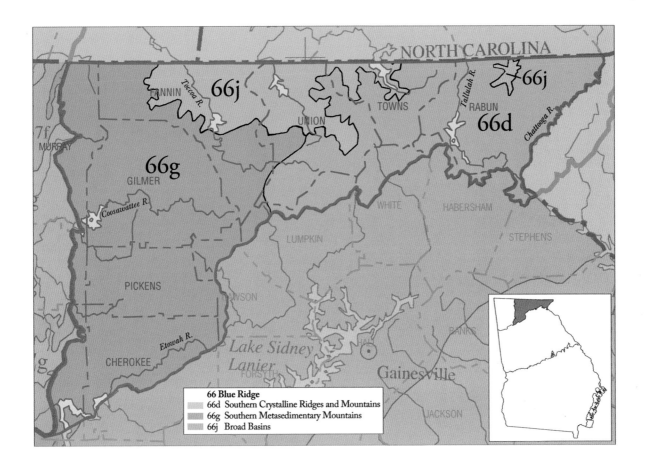

66 Blue Ridge
66d Southern Crystalline Ridges and Mountains
66g Southern Metasedimentary Mountains
66j Broad Basins

consequently retain more similarities to the sedimentary rocks from which they were derived. The characteristic rock types include slate, conglomerate, phyllite, metagraywacke, metasiltstone, metasandstone, quartzite, and marble. Elevations are lower than in the eastern portion of the ecoregion; only a few peaks, such as Rich Mountain (Gilmer County) and Bald Mountain (Murray County) reach above 4,000 feet, so high-elevation communities are much rarer. The ridge tops tend to be broader and flatter than those to the east, and with fewer sharp peaks than they are to the east.

There are several distinct mountain ranges in this subregion. The Cohuttas lie to the northwest and range from 3,000 to 4,000 feet; valleys are 1,000 to 1,500 feet below the mountain crests. The Rich Mountain area is to the east. The Fort Mountain area is in the southwestern portion of the subregion, and rises to 2,840 feet, with stunning views into the Great Valley of the Cumberland Plateau / Ridge and Valley ecoregion. Pine Log (Bartow County), Sharp (Pickens County), and Talona (Gilmer County) Mountains

are the southernmost ridges; they are often deeply dissected by the Coosawattee River and its tributaries. Soils are generally well drained, acidic, brownish, and loamy. The flatter ridge tops allow development of deeper soils, while thinner, more poorly developed soils (inceptisols) occur on steep slopes.

The Broad Basins. These are broad, low-elevation areas (1,600–1,800 feet) that are traversed by larger rivers. The Toccoa River drains the westernmost area, and has been impounded to form Blue Ridge Lake (Fannin County). The central part of the subregion is dominated by Lake Chatuge (Towns County), which was formed by damming the Hiwassee River in Tennessee. This subregion typically contains the best-developed floodplains of the ecoregion. The easternmost portion of the subregion encompasses the southernmost portion of the Little Tennessee River watershed (Rabun County). This subregion is characterized by deeper soils than found elsewhere in the ecoregion: mostly deep, well drained, loamy to clayey ultisols.

This narrow, cascading stream is typical of the Georgia Blue Ridge ecoregion.

RIVER BASINS AND GROUNDWATER

In general, the Blue Ridge receives the most rainfall of any ecoregion in Georgia, but water runs rapidly off the steep slopes and the narrow valleys do not allow development of large floodplains. Elevation along the rocky waterways can drop several hundred feet per mile, creating waterfalls, churning rapids, and deep, narrow, V-shaped valleys. Well-developed floodplains are very rare in the mountains, except for those along low-gradient sections of Youngcane Creek, the Nottely River, Arkaquah Creek, Brasstown Creek, the Hiwassee River, Tiger Creek, and the Little Tennessee River. Similarly, in the Dahlonega Plateau portion of the Blue Ridge, the lower stream gradients of the Coosawattee and Etowah Rivers and their tributaries have permitted the development of fairly well-defined floodplains.

The rivers of the Blue Ridge ecoregion, though close together geographically, take very different paths to the sea. The ridges of Georgia's Blue Ridge form the Tennessee Valley Divide, which separates the drainage basin of the Tennessee River from the Savannah, Coosa, and Chattahoochee River basins. Thus, the northernmost part of Georgia, which is drained by the Tennessee River, is in the Mississippi River basin. Runoff from rainfall in this area eventually flows into the Tennessee, then the Ohio, then the Mississippi River, and finally into the Gulf of Mexico—a distance of more than 1,300 miles.

The Blue Ridge ecoregion contains the headwaters of the Savannah, Chattahoochee, and Coosa Rivers and the Georgia tributaries to the Tennessee River system. As such, it is the continental divide between the Gulf and Atlantic drainages. The principal rivers of the Blue Ridge ecoregion are the Coosawattee, Toccoa, Nottely, Tallulah, and Chattooga, with the Conasauga, Hiwassee, and Little Tennessee also draining large areas. The headwaters of the Etowah and Chattahoochee Rivers drain the southern slopes of the Blue Ridge, but the main reaches of these rivers flow in the Piedmont and beyond.

The Tennessee Valley Authority has impounded the Toccoa, Nottely, and Hiwassee Rivers, and the Georgia Power Company built several dams along the Tallulah River. The U.S. Army Corps of Engineers dammed the Coosawattee River and Etowah River where they flow from the Blue Ridge into the Cumberland Plateau / Valley and Ridge. Collectively, these impoundments resulted in loss of significant acreage of floodplain, bog, seepage, and mesic forest natural communities.

The relatively impermeable bedrock of the Blue Ridge restricts extensive groundwater storage. Limited amounts of water are stored in joints, faults, and bedding planes throughout the ecoregion.

ENVIRONMENTAL FACTORS

The main factors that affect the distribution of the natural communities in the Georgia Blue Ridge include elevation, soil moisture, soil nutrients, hydrology, and fire.

Large changes in elevation play a more important role in the Blue Ridge than in other ecoregions in the state. The air is cooler at high elevations (roughly 3.5°F cooler per 1,000 feet of elevation), so growing seasons are shorter and freezing events are more common. Trees of the higher elevations on the highest ridge tops are exposed to ice glaze and high winds, creating stunted forests. Upper elevations also receive more orographic precipitation: rain, snow, and fog form when moist air is lifted up a mountainside and the moisture then condenses in the cooler temperatures in the higher elevation. Further, soils retain moisture because the cooler temperatures on high peaks mean reduced evapotranspiration. The cool temperatures and wet weather also prevent organic material from decomposing quickly, so thick, acidic soils build up on flat and bowl-shaped areas. Thus, a suite of upper-elevation communities adapted to these conditions—high-elevation rock outcrops, montane oak forests, and northern forests and boulderfields—occurs only in this ecoregion.

Throughout the Blue Ridge, aspect, slope shape, slope position, and exposure interact to create a complex moisture gradient that ranges from mesic to xeric. (see pp. 26–27) A slope that faces north has cool, moist conditions that can extend to lower elevations.

In contrast, slopes that face south receive more sunlight and will often have thinner, less organic soils. Flatter or concave sites that collect more clay and humus are able to retain more moisture and nutrients than convex slopes, where soil particles and rainwater are poorly retained. Ravines and lower slopes below high peaks can experience cold air drainage, which is when cold air from upper slopes moves downslope at night and remains in the ravine, cooling the site and enabling high-elevation plant and animal species to occur at much lower elevations.

Xeric conditions occur on sites with thin, rocky soils, steep slopes, and south-facing aspects because these sites cannot store moisture and receive high sunlight levels. Most glades, barrens, and rock outcrops, as well as many savannas, prairies, and woodlands, occur in xeric conditions. Sites become increasingly moist as topography becomes flatter, aspect moves to the north and east, and soils deepen.

Topography also influences the distribution of soil nutrients in the landscape: concave or flat sites collect more clays and humus, which bind nutrients, while clays and humus run off of convex slopes, leaving sandier particles, which do not bind nutrients. Thus, bottomlands and coves tend to be more fertile than straight and convex sites.

Hydrology—the pathways and sources of water on a site, and the seasonal pattern of flooding—determines the formation of several wetland natural communities in the Blue Ridge. Floodplains and bottomlands occur along rivers and streams where the water table reaches the surface. Spray areas around waterfalls are constantly moist. Seepages occur where there is a break in topography that channels water to the surface, or where rock joints or bedding planes direct water to the surface. Montane bogs and fens form on floodplains or on some flat areas where saturated soil conditions and buildup of organic matter occur.

Fire is an important factor in maintaining oak dominance or pine-oak dominance in some forests and woodlands. It can increase the extent of outcrop and barren communities, and may also play a role in keeping bog and seepage communities more open. Lightning-ignited fires are rare on most southern Appalachian sites (P. A. Delcourt and Delcourt 1997), averaging about 6 per year per 1,000,000 acres (Southern Appalachian Man and the Biosphere 1996c). Most lightning-ignited fires occur on ridge tops and very dry upper slopes that face west to south (P. A. Delcourt and Del-

court 1997). The Blue Ridge, with its deeply incised topography, has smaller fire compartments than other parts of the state, meaning many moist areas, such as mesic coves and stream valleys, are located close to one another, halting the spread of fire. This pattern differs markedly from that of the Coastal Plain or even parts of the Piedmont and Cumberland Plateau / Ridge and Valley ecoregions, where firebreaks are farther apart and lightning-caused fires can travel much farther. Humans have also set fires for centuries or perhaps millennia, increasing the amount of fire the ecoregion has historically experienced (see p. 55).

LAND USE HISTORY AND HUMAN IMPACT

Indigenous Peoples. Humans have played an important role in influencing the species composition of

(LEFT) Trees are coated and glazed with ice more often and more heavily at higher elevations, causing limbs to break off, thereby creating a more open canopy.

(BELOW) Orographic fog is common at high elevations: air cools as it rises, so it cannot hold as much moisture. The resulting fog, rain, or snow keeps the high elevations cooler and moister than lower elevations.

natural communities in the region for 10,000 to 12,000 years. Native Americans cultivated the lower valleys and stream bottoms of larger rivers, clearing and burning to create open areas for agricultural use. The pattern and extent of fires in the landscape varied over the 4,000-year period across the late Archaic, Woodland, and Mississippian periods, indicating that these cultures used fire in different ways, and perhaps for different purposes (Fowler and Konopik 2007). The Cherokee followed the Mississippians, and historical accounts of their land use practices indicate that these Native Americans burned forests for a variety of reasons—to maintain favorable conditions for hunting, to promote forage for game animals, and to maintain agricultural areas. These fires tended to be low-intensity brush fires (Fowler and Konopik 2007). During much of the pre-Columbian period, anthropogenic (human-caused) fires tended to be concentrated in river valleys, where the Native Americans settled and farmed, as well as on upper slopes and ridges, where they hunted and gathered food, including chestnuts (P. A. Delcourt and Delcourt 1997; D. E. Davis 2000; Fowler and Konopik 2007). Native Americans also used fire on the mountain slopes, presumably to drive game and encourage the growth of browse materials for game, though the extent and purposes of this activity in the southern Appalachians are debated. It is likely that mesic forests of lower slopes, coves, and narrow valleys were burned far less frequently and intensely. This selective use of fire in different topographic settings contributed to a complex mosaic of different natural communities in the Georgia Blue Ridge, which ranged from fire-adapted to fire-intolerant.

Agriculture and Grazing. European settlers moved into the Georgia Blue Ridge starting in the early 1800s and transformed the landscape. They settled and farmed mainly in the rich coves and valleys, but community boundaries ran to the top of the mountain ridges and the forested slopes were open to everyone for hunting and food-gathering. Domestic livestock were allowed to range widely on the mountain slopes in some areas. Some homesteads were built on mountaintops, where settlers girdled trees and set fires to maintain high-elevation pastures. The number of small farms, which were family owned and highly diversified, increased dramatically in the southern Appalachians during the 1800s. By 1880, Appalachia had a greater concentration of noncommercial family farms than any other area of the country (Southern Appalachian Man and the Biosphere 1996b).

Agricultural practices continue to negatively affect wetland and stream habitats in some areas of the Georgia Blue Ridge. In cultivated areas that do not have adequate stream buffers, herbicides, fertilizers, and sediments enter the streams from fields, lowering water quality and negatively impacting aquatic fauna. Cattle and other livestock create serious erosion and sedimentation problems when they are not fenced away from streams, by eroding stream banks and contributing to high fecal coliform levels with their waste. Drainage tiles and ditches remaining from previous wetland "improvement" projects that drained water away from wetlands to create arable farmland continue to harm water quality and keep wetlands in a degraded condition.

Industrial Forestry. When the Blue Ridge was first settled by Europeans, small logging and sawmill operations provided lumber and other wood products for local use. Beginning in the 1880s, commercial logging interests began acquiring large tracts of land in the mountains of north Georgia. Some of this land was purchased for as little as one dollar per acre. The timber operations were facilitated by the construction of railroads and sawmills throughout the region. From 1900 to the 1920s, forest cover of the southern Appalachians was significantly reduced by heavy commercial timber harvest. By 1908, a report issued by the U.S. secretary of state estimated that 86% of the timberland in the region had been cleared or was in various stages of regeneration, and that nearly all of this acreage had been burned (Yarnell 1995).

Most of the forests on public lands in the Blue Ridge are maturing second- or third-growth stands, on sites that have been impacted by past logging, grazing, and farming practices. The trees in these stands are often even-aged, rather than multi-aged, as they would be in old growth. Timber harvest of these forests continues in many areas throughout this region. Failure to heed best management practices (BMPs) for forestry can cause increased soil erosion, stream sedimentation, and soil compaction. On the other hand, a properly planned and carefully managed timber harvest operation can be an important tool for restoration and improvement of forest communities.

Today on public lands there is often an increasing emphasis on smaller timber cuts, retention of snags

The trees in this stand appear to be even-aged, indicating that the stand was probably clearcut in the past.

and woody debris in harvest areas, natural regeneration with augmentation from plantings to increase canopy diversity, timber thinnings, and uneven-aged management practices to create greater structural diversity. In the national forest some small, open patches are maintained as wildlife openings to benefit wildlife species such as white-tailed deer and black bear. On private forestry lands in the Blue Ridge, pine plantations and even-aged management for timber production are emphasized.

Overall, forest acreage has declined in the southern Appalachian region by 2% since the mid-1970s. The amount of upland forest previously converted to pine plantations is much lower in the Blue Ridge than in other ecoregions of Georgia. The decline of upland oak and pine-hardwood forests due to fire suppression, selective timber harvest ("high grading"), and other factors, however, have altered forest composition.

Prescribed Fire and Fire Suppression. Differing fire regimes over time have resulted in varying forest composition. European settlers set fires to clear land and improve forage for livestock. The fires set by the earliest settlers were probably low-intensity brush fires similar to those set by Native Americans. Fires became more intense in the late 1800s and 1900s, when used to "clean up" slash in logged-over areas (Fowler and Konopik 2007). In some sites, however, fire frequency may have been reduced by the late 1800s (Fesenmyer and Christensen 2010). The combination of land-clearing (for timber, crops, livestock grazing, and mining), erosional soil loss, and intensive fires resulted in a dramatic increase in forest communities dominated by Virginia, shortleaf, pitch, and Table Mountain pine. Following the establishment of the Chattahoochee National Forest and wildlife management areas, fire suppression programs were implemented throughout the region. Thus, the fire-return interval for most

A forest stand near Warwoman Dell following a fire

sites increased significantly compared to what it had been in the previous few centuries. This regime of active fire suppression lasted for nearly 60 years. During that time, fire-tolerant pine- and oak-dominated stands declined, while less tolerant species such as red maple, tulip-tree, eastern hemlock, black gum, white pine, and black birch increased in abundance. During the same period, successive attacks of southern pine beetle caused substantial declines in many mature pine stands, especially those impacted by drought or other stress factors.

By the 1990s, it was recognized that fire-adapted pine- and oak-dominated stands were declining rapidly, and management plans began to include prescribed fire as a management tool to restore them. Timing and intensity of prescribed fires are important factors in the successful restoration of these communities. For example, periodic low-intensity fires under oak stands appear to increase oak regeneration

while suppressing later successional species such as red maple. It also seems that more frequent and intensive (but not necessarily stand-replacing) fires are needed for maintenance of table mountain and pitch pine woodlands (Brose and Waldrop 2006).

Fire management continues to be a significant issue in this region, particularly at the urban/natural area interface. Concerns about smoke management, air quality, and damage to structures make it difficult to implement prescribed burn plans for restoration and maintenance of fire-adapted communities. Further, while there is general consensus that prescribed fire is necessary to restore and maintain upland pine- and oak-dominated stands, there is considerable debate as to ultimate management objectives. Should we attempt to re-create the vegetation mosaic of the pre-Columbian landscape, the period of early European settlement, or some other previous condition? These are largely value judgments. The goal of maximizing landscape diversity suggests a variety of different fire regimes implemented across various topographic settings. In reality, many of the future decisions involving use of prescribed fire in the Blue Ridge will be dictated by other factors, including public safety concerns, smoke management needs, and air quality standards in the rapidly urbanizing sectors of this region.

Patterns of Land Ownership and Development. By the turn of the 20th century, many settled areas in the southern Appalachians were in poor condition due to overgrazing, uncontrolled burning, unsustainable timber management, and poor cultivation techniques (Ayers and Ashe 1905). In some areas beaver, mink, and otter had been trapped to the point of local extinction, and fish communities had declined with the loss of streamside vegetation and sedimentation of streams. Populations of game animals such as turkey, bear, and deer were critically low due to unregulated hunting.

Widespread concern over the rapid depletion of resources in the southern Appalachians led to the development of the Weeks Act. This federal law, passed in 1911, led to the establishment of 11 national forests in the eastern United States. In 1911, the U.S. Forest Service purchased 31,000 acres from the Gennett family for $7.00 per acre. This was the first acquisition of land for what would in 1936 become the Chattahoochee National Forest (R. Schneider 2002).

A downed chestnut tree on Cowpens Mountain

In the 1930s, the U.S. Forest Service entered into a cooperative agreement with the state of Georgia to establish wildlife management areas and restore populations of game animals and sport fish on national forest lands. Additional acreage was added to the Chattahoochee National Forest in the following decades, eventually resulting in holdings of more than 750,000 acres. In addition, farming decreased significantly after the 1930s. While all regions of Georgia experienced a decrease in the proportion of land in farms from 1935 to 1985, these declines were most pronounced in the Piedmont and north Georgia mountains (E. P. Odum and Turner 1987).

All of these changes transformed the Georgia Blue Ridge from a cut-over, patchy landscape to its current status as the most forested of all the ecoregions in Georgia. It is also one of the most rapidly growing regions, however, as people build vacation and second homes. Commercial areas, roads, and utility lines are built to support these new residents. In addition to direct habitat loss, this development also fragments the landscape, creating migration barriers for wildlife populations, promoting weedy and edge habitat at the expense of forest interior habitat, and providing routes for the incursion of non-native invasive species.

Of all the Georgia ecoregions, the Blue Ridge has the largest percentage of publicly owned conservation land (approximately 39%). This land provides numerous recreational opportunities for the public. In some areas, high levels of recreational use result in significant impacts on natural habitats. Rock-climbing activities can adversely affect cliff vegetation. Overuse of hiking trails can degrade rock outcrops, streams, cove forests, and isolated wetlands, and excessive trampling can destroy plants and severely compact soils. Species restricted to springs, seeps, bogs, caves, and rock shelters are particularly susceptible to impacts from recreational overuse.

Off-road vehicle (ORV) use has also seriously degraded some sites. Heavily used trails erode and cause sedimentation into streams, but the most severe problems occur from illegal off-trail use, which disturbs populations of sensitive species, and causes erosion and churning and compacting of soils. Indiscriminant use of all-terrain vehicles (ATVs) and other vehicles on steep slopes and along stream bottoms has been identified as a major source of disturbance to aquatic and wetland communities (Georgia Department of Natural Resources 2005a).

Non-native Invasive Species. Non-native invasive species have had a significant negative impact on many natural communities of the Georgia Blue Ridge. Non-native invasive plants in the Georgia Blue Ridge include Nepal grass, Japanese honeysuckle, Oriental bittersweet, Chinese privet, silvergrass, multiflora rose, autumn-olive, kudzu, Japanese spiraea, Japanese knotweed, tree of heaven, and princess tree.

Currently, one of the most serious non-native invasive species is the hemlock woolly adelgid, which may eradicate the eastern hemlock throughout this region (see p. 84). This Asian insect infests stands of eastern hemlock and the endemic and rare Carolina hemlock.

The gypsy moth is also a threat, particularly to red oaks in lower-elevation oak forests. Pesticides can be used to control the gypsy moth, but such treatments are not practical on a large scale. It is unclear how much impact the European gypsy moth will have on high-elevation, oak-dominated stands in the near future. Although the moth is attracted to oak hosts, the caterpillars have high mortality rates in the cool, moist conditions prevalent in these often fog-shrouded sites. White oaks are less susceptible to the moth than red oaks.

Non-native fungal diseases have also disrupted forest communities at landscape scales—most famously, the chestnut blight fungus, which eliminated the American chestnut as a canopy tree in Georgia and greatly altered the vegetation and ecology of forests throughout the Blue Ridge (see p. 76). Dogwood anthracnose, which is a non-native fungus, is currently a threat to eastern dogwood trees: it has killed many trees, so there are fewer white blossoms each spring and fewer bright red berries to feed migratory birds in the fall. Dogwoods that are in dense, mesic forest stands appear to be affected most by this disease.

Water Quantity and Quality. Dams and other structures that alter streamflow represent another significant problem for aquatic and wetland habitats in this region. These include large reservoirs such as Rabun Lake, Blue Ridge Lake, Nottely Lake, Chatuge Lake, Lake Burton, and Lake Seed as well as farm ponds, weirs, improperly constructed bridges, and undersized or perched culverts. These structures interfere with normal streamflows, serve as migration barriers for many aquatic species, and contribute to the isolation of populations of aquatic or wetland species and the fragmentation of aquatic and riparian communities.

Increased urbanization is also degrading aquatic habitats through increased runoff and sedimentation, pollution from chemicals that wash off roads and other impermeable surfaces, and loss of supporting floodplain and riparian habitats.

Acidic cove forests are being changed by the hemlock woolly adelgid's deadly effect on hemlocks, which appear in the foreground here.

Natural Communities of the Georgia Blue Ridge

UPLAND FORESTS

Northern Hardwood and Boulderfield Forests. Forests on sheltered, north-facing sites above 3,500 feet in elevation, dominated by yellow birch, American beech, yellow buckeye, striped maple, basswood, and northern red oak. These forests are typically small-patch in Georgia. Boulderfield forests are sites of tightly packed fields of boulders embedded within the northern hardwoods, on high (above 3,200 feet), usually north-facing slopes, most often near the heads of cove forests. The boulders are covered with mosses and vines. Lower-elevation rocky slopes that do not support moss mats and high-elevation species are not considered a part of the boulderfield natural community.

Montane Oak Forests. Oak-dominated forests on sites that are typically more than 3,500 feet in elevation in all locations except for those north- to east-facing sheltered sites that are occupied by cove forests, rocky summits, or northern hardwood and boulderfield forests. Montane oak forests are dominated by northern red oak, scarlet oak, and/or white oak, sometimes mixed in with a few mesophytic species. They are large-patch. The trees are usually stunted, or at least do not reach the heights common in lower elevations.

Cove Forests. Mesic hardwood forests found in sites below 3,500 feet, most often in north-facing coves, but sometimes on moist, protected slopes in other aspects. Tulip-tree, basswood, white ash, American beech, yellow buckeye, northern red oak, and common silverbell are common trees in fertile sites; eastern hemlock, white pine, sourwood, and black birch are common in acidic sites. These forests are large- or small-patch.

Low- to Mid-Elevation Oak Forests. Forests on dry to submesic sites below 3,500 feet in elevation. Oaks, such as rock chestnut oak, white oak, southern red oak, northern red oak, and scarlet oak, may dominate, but in many sites tulip-tree, white pine, red maple, mockernut hickory, pignut hickory, Fraser magnolia, and black gum co-dominate. This matrix forest is the most widespread forest in the Georgia Blue Ridge.

Pine-Oak Woodlands and Forests. Mixed pine and oak woodlands and forest that occur on xeric, convex, rocky, south-facing, thin-soiled slopes and low, narrow ridge tops. These woodlands and forests may also occur on dry to submesic sites subject to fire. Pitch pine, Virginia pine, and/or shortleaf pine make up at least one-quarter of the canopy. Dry-site oaks, such as post oak, blackjack oak, rock chestnut oak, scarlet oak, and southern red oak, are usually mixed in with the pines and may dominate the stand. The trees are often stunted. These woodlands and forests probably once comprised a large-patch system, but now are small-patch.

Montane Longleaf Forests and Woodlands. See page 189 (Cumberland Plateau / Ridge and Valley Ecoregion).

Ultramafic Barrens and Woodlands. A mosaic of barrens and woodlands that occurs over ultramafic rocks. Pitch pine, post oak, and red maple dominate the canopy. Outcrops of very dark ultramafic rocks, which are high in magnesium and iron, are scattered throughout the landscape. These barrens and woodlands are very rare and small-patch.

GLADES, BARRENS, AND ROCK OUTCROPS

High-Elevation Rock Outcrops. Expanses of rock outcrop or cliffs (mafic or nonmafic) above 4,000 feet. These outcrops may have substantial areas covered with Catawba rhododendron, great laurel, and mountain laurel. They occur on Blood Mountain, Brasstown Bald (prior to construction of the visitor center), Rabun Bald, Eagle Mountain, Tray Mountain, Hightower Bald, and most likely some unexplored sites on other peaks above 4,000 feet. They are small-patch.

Low- to Mid-Elevation Mafic Domes, Glades, and Barrens. Outcroppings below 4,000 feet, on mafic rocks, usually in a mosaic of large outcrop domes, glades, and barrens, and savannas or woodlands, although any of those elements may be absent. Mafic indicator plant species include eastern red cedar, white ash, wafer-ash, and coralberry. They are small-patch.

Low- to Mid-Elevation Acidic Cliffs and Outcrops. Nonmafic rock outcrops and cliffs below 4,000 feet. These cliffs and outcrops are often found along river gorges, but can include any outcropping larger than roughly 500 square feet in size in a variety of topographic settings. Herbs, shrubs, and stunted trees grow on ledges and within crevices on the cliffs. They are small-patch.

WETLANDS

Mountain Bogs. Wetland communities that occur on flat, poorly drained locations with deep, peaty soils and scattered hummocks of sphagnum moss. In most bogs, encroaching great laurel rhododendron, tag alder, mountain laurel, and other shrubs shade out the herbaceous layer, but some bogs have portions dominated by forbs and graminoids. They are small-patch.

Seepage Wetlands. Wetland communities that occur on seasonally to semipermanently saturated spots at the heads of streams, on slopes where bedrock is near the surface, on flats beyond the active floodplains of small streams, and on ledges beneath seepage faces of cliffs and rock overhangs. Typically, these are herb-dominated systems with few or no trees rooted in the seep. They are small-patch.

Spray Cliffs. Wetland communities that occur adjacent to waterfalls on cliffs and rocks that are kept constantly moist by the spray. Mosses, liverworts, meadowrues, thyme-leaf bluets, grasses, galax, and saxifrages are common. They are small-patch.

Floodplains, Bottomlands, and Riparian Zones. Forests that occur along rivers and streams with some floodplain development. They support species, such as sycamore, river birch, red maple, sweet gum, green ash, box elder, silver maple, sugarberry, and some oak species, which have some adaptations to the anaerobic conditions induced by flooding. This natural community also includes rocky shoals and boulders that border streams, small levees, point bars, stream banks, and low terraces. These sites are usually linear and small-patch in this ecoregion.

Northern Hardwood and Boulderfield Forests

Northern hardwood forests in Georgia occur on a few sheltered, north-facing sites above roughly 3,500 feet and support yellow birch and other high-elevation species. These large- or small-patch forests are unique and fascinating assemblages of species: many of the canopy trees have northern affinities, while many shrubs and herbs have a southerly distribution. These high-elevation sites support many species that are endemic to the southern and central Appalachians and are notable for their Pleistocene relict species, such as mountain maple, mountain-ash, thyme-leaf bluet, long-stalked holly, rosy twisted-stalk, starflower, and American wood-sorrel. A few high peaks in Georgia harbor northern hardwood stands that are unusual communities for the state and that represent the southernmost examples of this natural community.

Boulderfield forests are variants of northern hardwood forests that occur on fields of tightly packed rocks covered with mosses and vines. Formed during the colder-temperature regimes of the Pleistocene ice ages, they are intriguing geologic relicts of the epoch. Changing climates continue to affect these forests. It is possible that, as temperatures increase, community composition will change in these natural communities, with lower-elevation species replacing those with northern affinities over time.

The transition to the cove forest natural community is gradual and noticeable mainly by a greater abundance of tulip-tree, white ash, cucumber magnolia, and other lower-elevation species, with fewer high-elevation species such as mountain-ash, fire cherry, and yellow birch.

Although they share many species and ecological processes with the forest communities in the eastern hemlock-white pine-northern hardwood region that extends from northern Wisconsin to southeastern Canada and New England, Georgia's northern hardwood forests differ significantly in composition (Delcourt and Delcourt 2000). They support several endemic southern Appalachian shrub and herb species that do not occur in the northern forests and lack some northern species.

PHYSICAL SETTING AND ECOLOGY

In latitudes north of Georgia, northern hardwood forests can be found at any aspect in high elevations. Georgia is more southerly and does not have peaks above 5,000 feet, however, so these forests are limited to high, protected, north-facing slopes. Steep, concave topography shadows the sites and protects them from drying winds and severe temperature changes. Orographic rain and fog are quite common. Soils are acidic, dark, and rich in organic matter because the leaf litter decomposes slowly in the moist, cool conditions. In places, seepages create very moist conditions (Wharton 1978).

Plants are adapted to the relatively short growing season and cool temperatures of the higher elevations. Leaves emerge on trees later in the year than at lower elevations and fall from trees earlier, so the period between flowering and fruit maturation is shorter than that in lower elevations. Late spring frosts often damage plants at high elevations, forcing trees to leaf out a second time. The trees are shorter and the forests more open than those of lower elevations in exposed sites: high winds and ice prune the trees and cause more branches to fall. Ashes, oaks, and beeches tend to lose more small twigs from frost than do birches (Thomas 2000). Some plants, such as sugar maples, accumulate sugars in their cells to lower their freezing point (Thomas 2000). The tree composition changes when small- or medium-sized gaps open due to wind, ice, drought, or other factors (Schafale and Weakley 1990; White et al. 1993). The dominant trees in these forests are usually long-lived, shade-tolerant, late-successional species that became established at different times as gaps opened up and the resulting sunnier conditions "released" the saplings of these trees up into the canopy. Lightning-ignited fires are rare in these moist natural communities and probably would be catastrophic in their impact (Schafale and Weakley 1990).

The northern hardwood plant assemblages of today did not exist during the last glaciation. Instead, boreal forests covered the mountains, and the individual species of northern hardwoods were scattered in varying plant assemblages in refugial areas with special microclimates that enabled species from other regions to survive. Northern hardwood refugia were often ravines in the Coastal Plain and lower Piedmont (H. R. Delcourt 2002), where steep, north-facing slopes created conditions that were cooler than most surrounding sites but not as harsh as in the boreal forest. As the climate warmed, these species migrated north and upslope to the highest areas of Georgia, joining the few relict species that survived the warming trend on the mountain peaks, thereby forming the southern Appalachian northern hardwood communities of today (H. R. Delcourt 2002; but see Loehle 2007 for suggestions as to the possible impact of low carbon dioxide levels on vegetation during the Pleistocene).

VEGETATION

The distinction between cove forests and northern hardwood forests is among the most difficult to make (Wharton 1978; Schafale and Weakley 1990). Here the northern hardwood natural community in Georgia is defined as stands above 3,500 feet that contain yellow birch; may possess a somewhat stunted canopy; and often host high-elevation species, such as minniebush, mountain maple, mountain-ash, rosy twisted-stalk, long-stalked holly, red elderberry, fire cherry, American wood-sorrel, witch's-hobble, and Blue Ridge white heart-leaved aster. These species are not necessarily dominant or common but do testify to cool, moist, high-elevation conditions when present. Coosa Bald (Union County), Hightower Bald (Towns County), Tray Mountain, including the Kelly Ridge Spur (Towns and Habersham Counties), Brasstown Bald (Towns and Union Counties), and Eagle Mountain (Towns County) support northern hardwood stands (usually dominated by boulderfields). With the possible exception of Brasstown Bald, Georgia does not have well-developed northern hardwood sites comparable to those of North Carolina.

In addition to the species already mentioned, northern hardwood forests in Georgia support other mesophytic trees, such as yellow buckeye, basswood, black cherry, and striped maple. These trees dominate because they are shade-tolerant—that is, they are able to grow very slowly under the shade of canopy trees and then shoot up quickly when a gap in the canopy forms above them. Most of these species are also able

Rosy twisted-stalk

Mountain-ash

A clone of American beech trees on Coosa Bald

to reproduce vegetatively, in the form of sprouts at the root crown, or clonally, as with beech, to take advantage of small openings (Chafin and Jones 1989; Coladonato 1991; Sullivan 1994). Although these forests are referred to as "northern hardwoods," yellow buckeye ranges from Georgia only to as far north as Pennsylvania. As seen on Brasstown Bald (Union and Towns Counties) and Coosa Bald (Union County), northern red oak may be common, or the northern hardwoods may intergrade with a white oak-dominated montane oak community on the ridge and with lush cove forests downslope.

The shrub layer includes beaked hazelnut, smooth hydrangea, witch-hazel, mountain holly, Catawba rhododendron, and great laurel. The ground layer may support trout lily, Solomon's seal, mountain black-cohosh, red trillium, mountain angelica, and many others, along with some species common to the cove forest and montane oak forest natural communities.

Beech gaps are a northern hardwood forest subtype that occurs in states north of Georgia but may not exist within this state. Wharton (1978) reported seeing one on Hightower Bald (Towns County), but it has not yet been relocated. Beech gaps are pure stands of American beech, usually found in exposed locations, such as gaps, on high ridges. These stands may originate from a few individuals that reproduce by cloning in response to disturbances such as high winds or ice-loading. They are short, gnarled trees. Small clumps (less than 500 square feet) of American beech on Coosa Bald (Union County), Tray Mountain (Towns and Habersham Counties), and Hightower Bald (Towns County) begin to suggest beech gaps, but these sites are lower in elevation than beech gap forests in North Carolina.

Vasey's trillium. Although typically a plant of the cove forest natural community, Vasey's trillium
is occasionally found above 4,000 feet in Georgia

(LEFT) A boulderfield forest on Coosa Bald

the mosses and boulders. The plant and animal communities of these sites are relicts of the last period of glaciation and represent an important aspect of Georgia's natural heritage.

The thick moss mats that grow on the boulders and the presence of high-elevation species distinguish these forests from mid-elevation rocky cove forests. Lower-elevation rocky slopes that do not support moss mats and high-elevation species are not considered a part of the boulderfield natural community.

The boulders greatly limit rooting space, fostering sparse canopy cover and dense moss mats, vines, and shrubs (Wharton 1978; Chafin and Jones 1989; Schafale and Weakley 1990). Some sites, such as those on Coosa Bald and Tray Mountain, are exposed to wind and ice, so trees with wind-snapped trunks and limbs are common (Chafin and Jones 1989). More sheltered boulderfields, such as those nestled in the coves on the flanks of Hightower and Slaughter Mountains, have fewer broken trees and less open canopies.

Boulderfield communities are different from the cove or hardwood forests around them not only because of the rocks, but also because of the prevalence of birch and the vegetation structure, which is like no other in Georgia. Environmental factors interact to create ideal conditions for yellow and black birch. Birches are pioneer species and, when an opening occurs, can blanket the site with seeds (Chafin and Jones 1989). In boulderfields, windthrow, tree snap, and limb breakage create openings that foster continual birch recruitment (Chafin and Jones 1989). Further, birches can germinate and grow on top of the rocks and logs. They do not have taproots; their roots wrap around the boulders and fallen trees. Basswood has advantages here, as well: its strong, lateral root system firmly anchors the tree where it can find a foothold, and it can resprout after being broken by wind (Chafin and Jones 1989). Basswood, northern red oak, yellow buckeye, and downy or roundleaf serviceberry often rim the boulderfield; American beech is common on Brasstown Bald. Eastern hemlocks are occasionally present because they can germinate on the boulders.

Shrubs and vines are often abundant because they are able to root in the crevices between boulders and on the thick moss mats that cover the boulders. Their low stature makes them less susceptible to windthrow,

BOULDERFIELD FORESTS

Boulderfield forests occur in Georgia on fields of tightly packed, 1- to 10-foot-diameter boulders on slopes above roughly 3,200 feet. Yellow birch and perhaps black birch dominate the stands. Most northern hardwood boulderfields in Georgia occur on north-facing slopes near or at the heads of cove forests just below the highest ridges. The cool temperatures associated with these sites promote thick mosses, rare forbs, and northern ferns. The shredding, bronze bark of gnarled, stunted birch trees contrasts with the moss-cloaked boulders to create a beautiful environment. Seepage areas sometimes flow beneath the rocks. Alpine mammals and salamanders skirt through and they can grow in the greater light levels available from the open canopy. Striped maple, mountain holly, smooth hydrangea, and witch-hazel are common (Chafin 1988); rare, high-elevation species (red elderberry, running strawberry-bush, flowering raspberry, mountain maple, prickly gooseberry, and mountain-ash) also occur.

Composition and diversity differ with the openness of the canopy and the nutrient content of the soils. A small boulderfield along Loggy Branch on Hightower Bald is an excellent example of a low-diversity boulderfield, dominated by running strawberry-bush, prickly gooseberry, pipevine, marginal wood-fern, yellow jewelweed, wood-nettle, Virginia-creeper, yellow birch, and mountain maple. In contrast, the boulderfield above Sosebee Cove is more cove-like, with yellow-wood, Canada waterleaf, and squirrel corn, while boulderfields on Brasstown Bald have more high-elevation species.

Geomorphologists are still debating the formation of southern Appalachian boulderfields. These boulderfields have generally been considered to be the result of freeze-thaw processes in tundra-like conditions (e.g., periglacial processes occurring above the tree line), but estimations of Pleistocene tree-line elevations and climatic regimes in the region differ (Cogbill, White, and Wiser 1997; Loehle 2007), and no studies regarding the origin of Georgia boulderfields have been performed. It is possible that a freeze-thaw regime of exposed rock outcrops during previous glaciations accounts for some of Georgia's boulderfields.

During interglacials, soil partially filled in the voids between boulders, and moss and lichens covered the rocks. As the soil over the rocks deepened, northern hardwood forest interfingered the boulderfields, as can be seen on Tray Mountain (Towns and Habersham Counties), Coosa Bald (Union County), and Brasstown Bald (Towns and Union Counties).

COMPARISONS TO NORTH CAROLINA NORTHERN HARDWOOD STANDS

To best understand the relationship of Georgia's northern hardwood stands to that of more northern regions, it is helpful to contrast them with examples such as those within Craggy Gardens, North Carolina, where northern hardwood stands occur on exposed sites below shrub balds that cloak the mountaintops. In North Carolina, this forest type appears on a wider range of aspects and topographies than in Georgia because the higher elevations and more northerly latitude provide increased orographic moisture and cooler temperatures, so there is a greater amplitude of conditions favorable to these assemblages (White et al. 1993). American beech and yellow birch are much more numerous than they are in any site in Georgia except for Brasstown Bald. Winds are higher at these elevations, growing seasons are shorter, and ice storms are more severe and more frequent than in Georgia, so the trees are more stunted and gnarled. Some high-elevation species, such as mountain-ash, are more common in North Carolina stands. Other high-elevation species common to North Carolina, such as avens, bluebead-lily (last seen in Georgia on Brasstown Bald in the 1940s), and witch's-hobble (last seen in Georgia on Hightower Bald in the 1970s), are not known to occur in Georgia at this time.

CHARACTERISTIC PLANTS OF NORTHERN HARDWOOD AND BOULDERFIELD FORESTS

TREES

Striped maple—Acer pensylvanicum
Sugar maple—Acer saccharum
Mountain maple—Acer spicatum
Yellow buckeye—Aesculus flava
Yellow birch—Betula alleghaniensis
American beech—Fagus grandifolia
Fire cherry—Prunus pensylvanica
Basswood—Tilia americana

SHRUBS AND WOODY VINES

Mountain sweet pepperbush—Clethra acuminata
Beaked hazelnut—Corylus cornuta
Running strawberry-bush—Euonymus obovatus
Witch-hazel—Hamamelis virginiana
Dutchman's-pipe—Isotrema macrophyllum
Prickly gooseberry—Ribes cynosbati
Allegheny blackberry—Rubus allegheniensis

GROUND COVER

Eastern blue monkshood—Aconitum uncinatum
Mountain black-cohosh—Actaea podocarpa
White snakeroot—Ageratina altissima
Common blue cohosh—Caulophyllum thalictroides
Carolina spring-beauty—Claytonia caroliniana
Northern horsebalm—Collinsonia canadensis
Hay-scented fern—Dennstaedtia punctilobula
Fancy fern—Dryopteris intermedia
Dimpled trout lily—Erythronium umbilicatum
Blue Ridge white heart-leaved aster—Eurybia chlorolepis
Common white heart-leaved aster—Eurybia divaricata
Yellow jewelweed—Impatiens pallida
Wood-nettle—Laportea canadensis
Canada mayflower—Maianthemum canadense
Bee-balm—Monarda didyma
Whorled aster—Oclemena acuminata
Giant chickweed—Stellaria pubera
Red trillium—Trillium erectum
Tall white violet—Viola canadensis

ANIMALS

The cool conditions of Georgia's northern hardwood forests have enabled small mammals and amphibians that once inhabited the jack pine-spruce fir forest and alpine tundra of Georgia's mountains during the ice age to survive in isolated populations on the highest mountaintops. Also, some northern breeding birds have the southern extent of their breeding ranges in these high forests. The moist, thick litter supports a rich fauna of amphibians and detritivores (worms, millipedes, snails, and other fauna that feed on decaying vegetation). Small fossorial animals inhabit the boulderfields, being well adapted to traverse the rugged boulder surfaces and rock crevices.

Characteristic mammals include several Pleistocene relict shrews: the masked shrew, long-tailed shrew, smoky shrew, and pygmy shrew (see the Featured Animal). These small insectivores inhabit moist ground under rocks and leaf litter, eating snails, insects and other invertebrates, and some plants. The relict southern red-backed vole, a mouse-like animal that eats plants, also inhabits these forests. Other small mammals include deer mice and northern short-tailed shrews. Southern flying squir-rels feed on the abundant lichens and fungi and den in tree cavities. The noisy red squirrel occasionally can be found here. Larger mammals that inhabit closed forests, such as black bears, also occur in this habitat.

Both mature and early successional northern hardwood forests are important bird habitats. Forest disturbances such as wind and ice storms open up habitat for early successional bird species such as the chestnut-sided warbler and ruffed grouse. Some forest-nesting species, such as the wood thrush and red-eyed vireo, make use of forest openings during postbreeding dispersal, taking advantage of dense cover for the young and foraging on the plentiful insects and fruit found in gaps. Mature stands provide key habitat for the Blackburnian warbler, blue-headed vireo, winter wren, dark-eyed junco, and rose-breasted grosbeak. The black-throated blue warbler, Canada warbler, and veery thrive where the canopy is more open and allows greater development of the shrub layer. The rare and declining cerulean warbler can be found in several cove-like locations that transition to northern hardwoods, where tall super-canopy trees are mixed with gaps to create structural diversity.

This diversity in spring and summer residents stands in marked contrast to the sparse collection of wintering birds. Most of the breeders are obligate insectivores (they eat only insects) that migrate to the neotropics (Central and South America) for winter. Winter species of interest include the yellow-bellied sapsucker, which has bred in the state, the northern saw-whet owl, and the brown creeper. Species of conservation concern include the winter wren and cerulean warbler.

Amphibians, particularly salamanders, can be abundant in boulderfield and northern hardwood forests, and are similar to those described under cove forests on p. 84. Reptiles are uncommon in this natural community because the shady and perpetually cool conditions limit their activity levels.

Pygmy Shrew (*Sorex hoyi*)

The pygmy shrew is the smallest mammal in North America, weighing in at only 0.10 to 0.14 ounce. These shrews are approximately 3 to 4 inches in total length, with the tail accounting for approximately one-third of that length. Like other members of the primitive mammal family Soricidae, the pygmy shrew has a narrow head, pointed nose, inconspicuous ears, and tiny, bead-like eyes without eyelids. Coloration varies from gray-brown in the summer to gray in the winter. The belly is lighter in color than the back and sides (Burt and Grossenheider 1980).

The range of the pygmy shrew extends from the Gaspé Peninsula across Canada to Alaska and south to northeastern Washington, northwestern Montana, Iowa, southern Wisconsin, and Ohio. In the eastern United States, the range includes New England and extends southward along the Appalachian Mountain chain into northern Georgia. Across its range, this species occupies a wide variety of habitats, including evergreen and deciduous forests, swamps, grassy clearings, bogs, and floodplains (Burt and Grossenheider 1980). In Georgia, these diminutive animals are found in cool, moist, high-elevation forests of the Blue Ridge, including northern hardwood and boulderfield forests. These forests typically have thick leaf litter, moist soils, and moss-covered stumps, rocks, and logs that provide suitable microhabitats for the pygmy shrew (Georgia Wildlife Web 2008). While globally secure and often locally abundant within its preferred habitat, the pygmy shrew is considered a species of conservation concern in Georgia due to its restricted range in the state.

The pygmy shrew is a proficient burrower in moist soil and leaf litter, but also uses tunnels made by other animals such as beetles, voles, and moles to find food. The pygmy shrew's diet includes ants, flies, spiders, earthworms, beetles, grubs, and caterpillars. Predators include hawks, owls, snakes, and small carnivores (Georgia Wildlife Web 2008).

The Wagon Train Trail and Summit of Brasstown Bald

The north-facing portion of the summit of Brasstown Bald contains perhaps Georgia's best expression of northern hardwood and boulderfield forests. An excellent vantage point for observation of this gnarled, stunted forest is from Brasstown's summit, facing north and observing the forest from above. Yellow birch is a dominant tree and occurs in higher densities, larger girths, and greater ages than anywhere else in the state. The trees have picturesque peeling bark (especially golden when moistened by fog) and stout trunks, whose tops are pruned by wind and ice. Other high-elevation species include fire cherry (recognizable by the large, dark lenticels in the bark), mountain maple, and mountain-ash. Other northern hardwood

tree species include yellow buckeye, basswood, and black cherry.

Minniebush, a high-elevation shrub often seen on craggy peaks of the Smoky Mountains, grows along the trail, as does the typically high-elevation species Catawba rhododendron, whose vibrant purple flowers bloom in late May to June. Other shrubs include mountain holly, witch-hazel, great laurel, and mountain laurel. Pleistocene relict herbs typical of the few high-elevation sites in Georgia include thyme-leaf bluet, Canada mayflower, and mountain angelica. In early May, the red trillium is striking. Other herbs include Dutchman's britches, American trout lily, Jack-in-the-pulpit, and mountain bunchflower. These species flower here weeks later than in lower elevations.

Often the boulderfields tumble down to the edge of the trail. Thick moss mats cover many rocks. Yellow birch is perched on the boulders with American beech and basswood interspersed among them, along with striped maple, mountain maple, mountain holly, and witch-hazel. Herbaceous species grow in the moss mats. The boulderfields should be viewed from the edge and should not be entered because of the extreme fragility of their ground cover. Even one person may do great damage by trampling the moss mats and causing them to slip off the rocks, reversing decades of vegetative growth.

Location: Brasstown Bald is located south of Hiawasee, north of Helen, and east of Blairsville. From Ga. Hwy. 2 in Blairsville, proceed south on U.S. 19/129/Ga. Hwy. 11 for about 8 miles. Turn left (east) on Ga. 180 and drive 9 miles; turn left (north) on Ga. 180 spur and go 3 miles. Alternatively, from downtown Helen, take Ga. Hwy. 75/17/ Unicoi Turnpike north about 12 miles, turn left (west) onto Ga. 180, and proceed about 6 miles. Turn right (north) onto Ga. 180 spur and proceed 3 miles to Brasstown Bald parking lot. The Wagon Train Trail may be reached by following the path up from the parking lot toward the visitor center; the trailhead is to the right at Google Earth GPS approximate coordinates of N 34.870613/W 083.810205.

Montane Oak Forests

Montane oak forests occur at elevations roughly above 3,500 feet in Georgia, and cover most of the higher ridges and peaks of the Georgia Blue Ridge (Wharton 1978). Oaks, often gnarled and stunted, dominate these stands. Montane oak "orchard forests" underlain by dense carpets of ferns and herbs are among the most beautiful forests in Georgia, while stands of widely spaced, stunted trees barely overtopping evergreen shrubs on high peaks such as Tray Mountain (Towns and Habersham Counties) and Rabun Bald (Rabun County) afford impressive vistas. High-elevation and Pleistocene relict fauna and flora can be found here, and these forests are also important sites for several bird species that do not breed farther south (T. M. Schneider et al. 2010).

Most intact examples of montane oak forest are found in the Chattahoochee National Forest and on a few privately owned lands. Because these forests had less marketable timber and were less accessible than lower-elevation stands, they were sometimes spared from much of the earlier logging that devastated most of the Blue Ridge (Wharton 1978; Riddle 2005). Thus, some old-growth stands remain along some of the higher ridges of Georgia. For example, stands on Double Spring Knob (Towns and Rabun Counties), Springer Mountain (Fannin County), Spaniard Mountain (Towns County), Alex Gap (Rabun County), Wolfstake Knob (Towns County), and Wolf Knob (Rabun County) are dominated or co-dominated by white oaks ranging in age from 210 to 306 years (Riddle 2005). Old-growth northern red oaks are less commonly found in Georgia (Riddle 2005).

Like other high-elevation natural communities of the Georgia Blue Ridge, montane oak forests are susceptible to changes in community composition as a result of global climate change, if temperatures increase and shifts in rainfall patterns cause a greater frequency of periodic droughts.

PHYSICAL SETTING AND ECOLOGY

Soil and moisture vary significantly among high-elevation oak forest sites. Steep, exposed sites are more common on sharper peaks in Georgia's eastern Blue Ridge (the Southern Crystalline Ridges and Mountains subregion), including Tray Mountain (Towns and Habersham Counties), Rabun Bald (Rabun County), Blood Mountain (Lumpkin and Union Counties), Brasstown Bald (Towns and Union Counties), and Black Rock Mountain (Rabun County). The steep slopes have high runoff rates that promote thin soils. Soils can be deeper on the broader ridge tops of Georgia's western Blue Ridge (the Southern Metasedimentary Mountains subregion), including Springer (Fanin County), Bald (Murray County), Cowpens (Murray County), and Grassy (Murray County) Mountains.

These stands are uneven-aged and maintained by gap dynamics, in which younger trees grow in the gaps created by fallen trees or large limbs. Occasional severe events create larger openings. Gale-force winds, lightning strikes, and ice-loading cause more canopy gaps on these high-elevation sites than occur on lower-elevation sites. The trees are shorter than those in more protected sites, most likely because growing seasons are short and high winds and ice-loading prune the trees; as a result, tree growth is concentrated on

thickening the trunk and limbs. The role of fire in the development of montane oak communities is poorly understood. Lightning strikes may be fairly common, but fuel loads are low and high-elevation sites receive much precipitation. Consequently, fires are probably localized, rarely canopy-damaging, and probably most common on drier southerly and lower ridges, where they may open the understory (Schafale and Weakley 1990). Native Americans likely burned some ridges above 4,000 feet, especially broad, flat areas conducive to agriculture and hunting, keeping the forests more open and dry (P. A. Delcourt and Delcourt 1997).

American chestnut trees, often gnarled and stunted like the oaks, once co-dominated or dominated many of these forests. Until the chestnut blight (see p. 76), they made up roughly 20–30% of overall forest cover in the southern Appalachians (D. E. Davis 2000). Old chestnut stumps, salvage debris, twisted, fallen trunks, and numerous root sprouts are still present in most montane oak forests in Georgia (Riddle 2005). These forests are still reorganizing in the aftermath of chestnut dominance and the eventual forest composition

A "chestnut ghost" on Cowpens Mountain

is unclear. In some sites, oaks that were previously established beneath the chestnut canopy now dominate (Stephenson, Ash, and Stauffer 1993). In other sites, pioneer trees, such as black birch, black locust, sassafras, yellow birch, white pine, and tulip-tree, have become established and a more mesophytic community is developing (Wharton 1978).

VEGETATION

A mix of white oak, northern red oak, scarlet oak, and occasionally rock chestnut oak dominates montane oak natural communities, any one of which may control a particular site. Other species suited to dry and/or dry-mesic (submesic) conditions, such as black birch, red maple, and hickories, appear and occasionally co-dominate (Wharton 1978; Riddle 2005). Scarlet oak is very drought-tolerant and dominates on many dry sites, such as portions of Rabun Bald and Tray Mountain. White oaks dominate most of the old-growth forests in Georgia because they can remain suppressed (exist as understory trees below the canopy cover) for up to 90 years, waiting for a canopy gap (U.S. Department of Agriculture Forest Service 2009a). On some flatter sites, such as parts of Bald, Springer, and Cowpens Mountains, tulip-tree and white ash co-dominate with oaks, creating commu-

Great laurel in the shrub layer of an acidic montane oak forest

CHARACTERISTIC PLANTS OF MONTANE OAK FORESTS

TREES

Striped maple—*Acer pensylvanicum*
Red maple—*Acer rubrum*
Downy serviceberry—*Amelanchier arborea*
Pignut hickory—*Carya glabra*
Mockernut hickory—*Carya tomentosa*
White oak—*Quercus alba*
Scarlet oak—*Quercus coccinea*
Rock chestnut oak—*Quercus montana*
Northern red oak—*Quercus rubra*

SHRUBS AND WOODY VINES

Black chokeberry—*Aronia melanocarpa*
American chestnut (sprouts)—*Castanea dentata*
Beaked hazelnut—*Corylus cornuta*
Witch-hazel—*Hamamelis virginiana*

Mountain holly—*Ilex montana*
Mountain laurel—*Kalmia latifolia*
Buffalo-nut—*Pyrularia pubera*
Flame azalea—*Rhododendron calendulaceum*
Catawba rhododendron—*Rhododendron catawbiense*
Great laurel—*Rhododendron maximum*
Smooth highbush blueberry—*Vaccinium corymbosum*
Mountain highbush blueberry—*Vaccinium simulatum*
Deerberry—*Vaccinium stamineum*

GROUND COVER

White snakeroot—*Ageratina altissima*
Tall milkweed—*Asclepias exaltata*
Common hairgrass—*Avenella flexuosa*

Hay-scented fern—*Dennstaedtia punctilobula*
Common white heart-leaved aster—*Eurybia divaricata*
Purple-node Joe-pye-weed—*Eutrochium purpureum*
Mountain Indian-physic—*Gillenia trifoliata*
Wood-nettle—*Laportea canadensis*
Indian cucumber-root—*Medeola virginiana*
Appalachian cow-wheat—*Melampyrum lineare*
Wild bergamot—*Monarda fistulosa*
Whorled aster—*Oclemena acuminata*
Carolina phlox—*Phlox carolina*
New York fern—*Thelypteris noveboracensis*

---

nities that intergrade between cove forest, northern hardwood forest, and montane oak forest natural communities.

Some acidic sites have shrub layers that are strongly dominated by great laurel, mountain laurel, Catawba rhododendron, and/or blackberries and huckleberries, with a scattering of acid-loving ground-layer plants, such as downy rattlesnake-orchid, pipsissewa, galax, and trailing arbutus. These assemblages are fairly common in the Georgia Blue Ridge, with examples on Spaniard (Towns County), Wolfstake (Towns County), and Blood (Lumpkin and Union Counties) Mountains, and on Brasstown Bald along the Arkaquah Trail (Towns and Union Counties).

A rarer assemblage that resembles the shrub balds of more-northern states occurs where oaks and other trees form a woodland, and the trees are so dwarfed they barely reach above the ericaceous shrub understory. This community is well expressed on portions of Rabun Bald (Rabun County), Tray Mountain (Towns and Habersham Counties), Blood Mountain (Lumpkin and Union Counties), Brasstown Bald, and Wildcat Mountain (see the Featured Place).

"Orchard" oak forests have a dense herbaceous layer, often with an open tree canopy and a scattering of blueberries, beaked hazelnut, northern wild raisin, mountain holly, and azaleas. Grasses, sedges, tall forbs, and/or ferns dominate the ground layer (DeLapp 1978; Schafale and Weakley 1990). Orchard oak forests are most common on the wider mountaintops of the Georgia western Blue Ridge (the Southern Metasedimentary Mountains), including Grassy (Murray County), Springer (Fannin County), Buckeye (Murray County), and Bald (Murray County) Mountains. Some also grow on broad areas of the eastern Blue Ridge (the Southern Crystalline Ridges and Mountains subregion), including gentle slopes near the peaks of Rabun Bald (Rabun County) and Blood Mountain (Lumpkin and Union Counties). White oak, or a mix of oak species, often dominates orchard forests, but a pignut hickory-white oak forest occurs on some sites, such as Springer Mountain. In some places, huge expanses of hay-scented and/or New York ferns cover the slopes. Parts of Cowpens (Fannin County), Grassy (Murray County), Tray (Towns and Habersham Counties), and Spaniard (Towns County) Mountains have good examples of these fern carpets.

Wild bergamot

Tall milkweed

Sprouts of an American chestnut tree that succumbed to the blight. The fungus will cause these sprouts to die back before they are old and large enough to produce nuts.

AMERICAN CHESTNUT BLIGHT

At the turn of the 20th century, the American chestnut (*Castanea dentata*) was one of the most important trees in the eastern United States, ranging from Maine to Ohio and south to the panhandle of Florida. They were magnificent trees, growing up to 100 feet in height and 8–10 feet in diameter. They made up roughly 20–30% of all canopy cover in the mountains (D. E. Davis 2000) and more than 50% of cover in some stands in the Georgia Blue Ridge (Jacobs 2007). The tree was able to dominate or co-dominate many stands in the Blue Ridge because it could persist under shaded conditions and then grow at unusually fast rates when a gap opened. It could also grow in a wide range of sites, from moist to dry (Jacobs 2007). Unlike oaks, which do not produce large crops of acorns every year, American chestnuts produced big crops reliably each year, which were a very important source of food for many animals, including white-tailed deer, turkey, black bear, ruffed grouse, and gray squirrel.

This food source dwindled, however, as European settlers harvested huge numbers of American chestnuts for many reasons. The wood was strong and rot-resistant, making it ideal for use in doors, flooring, paneling, fence rails, barns, shingles, railroad ties, telegraph posts, furniture, and musical instruments. Tannins derived from the bark of the tree were used to tan leather.

The American chestnut, though, was ultimately destroyed by blight. First, many chestnuts in the Coastal Plain and Piedmont were killed by black rot (*Phytophthora cinnamomi*) in the 1820s and then again in the 1930s and 1940s. The tree was ultimately devastated, however, by another fungus. In 1904, the American chestnut blight (*Cyphonectria parasitica*) was discovered at the Bronx Zoological Park in New York. This Asian fungus, accidentally introduced with imported nursery stock, quickly spread, leaving in its wake "ghost forests" of dying trees. By 1950, the American chestnut had nearly disappeared from the forests of the eastern United States. Surviving trees produce root sprouts that succumb to the blight after a few years. The fungus, which persists in the soil, is spread by wind, rain, birds, and other animals, and enters the trees through cracks or wounds in the bark. It multiplies quickly and creates cankers that girdle the stem, killing all growth above the canker, usually in one growing season. Now only a few individual trees grow long enough to produce nuts, but these have little chance of developing into mature trees.

Thus, while many chestnut trees had been felled by logging in the Georgia Blue Ridge, the overwhelming loss of the species due to the blight has created a fundamental change in the forests. Oaks, hickories, black locust, maples, American beech, tulip-tree, and other trees became more dominant. Animals that previously fed on chestnuts now rely more heavily on acorns, hickory nuts, and soft mast. Herbivorous insects that

fed on chestnut leaves, flowers, bark, nuts, and stems, and the predators of these insects, were undoubtedly also affected.

Research into methods of breeding resistance to chestnut blight is ongoing, and field biologists continue to search for nut-bearing trees that can be used to augment native germplasm reserves. By conducting successive backcrosses with the blight-resistant Chinese chestnut, groups such as the American Chestnut Foundation hope to produce blight-resistant strains of American chestnut that are morphologically indistinguishable from the original genotype. Another area of research involves an attempt to map the chestnut genome and to identify specific blight-resistant genes. For example, Dr. Scott Merkle at the University of Georgia is using somatic embryogenesis and transgenics to create pure American chestnut seedlings with fungus-resistant genes (University of Georgia Warnell School of Forestry 2011).

ANIMALS

These upper-elevation forests support some animals that are not found in lower elevations. Small Pleistocene relict mammals, including the southern red-backed vole, pygmy shrew, long-tailed shrew, masked shrew, and smoky shrew, occur on the moister stands where soils are deep enough for their runways. Other small mammals found in this habitat include golden mice and eastern woodrats. White-tailed deer can browse and graze throughout these forests, especially where ground layers are dense. Black bears feed on acorns and berries. Open, patchy areas attract many mammals, including bobcats, coyotes, and striped skunks.

The upper-elevation forests attract a unique group of bird species, including the black-throated blue warbler, cerulean warbler, Blackburnian warbler, and Canada warbler. Breeding birds are limited to those that can adapt to the shorter breeding seasons, cooler temperatures, and later insect availability of high-elevation sites (T. M. Schneider et al. 2010). Openings attract a diverse suite of breeding songbirds, including the golden-winged warbler, prairie warbler, chestnut-sided warbler, northern bobwhite, field sparrow, yellow-breasted chat, and indigo bunting. Most of the songbirds are migrants. The golden-winged

warbler was described by early ornithologists as abundant in open oak woodlands in the past, but is known from only five sites in Georgia today. Ruffed grouse, which are often heard drumming, feed on buds and fruit from shrubs such as beaked hazelnut, witch-hazel, mountain laurel, and mountain-ash. Birds that nest in dead trees, such as the red-headed woodpecker and great-crested flycatcher, also appear in relatively open forests. Common ravens are a species of conservation concern in Georgia that occasionally appear in montane oak forests (see the Featured Animal in the high-elevation outcrop natural community on p. 116).

Food supplies for birds and mammals in these natural communities have greatly changed in the past 75 years due to the demise of the American chestnut, which was an extremely important wildlife plant (D.E. Davis 2000). A single tree could produce as much as 10 bushels of nuts that would pile up to 4 inches deep on the forest floor, supplying food for squirrels, wild turkeys, white-tailed deer, bears, raccoons, and grouses (D. E. Davis 2000). Although the faunal communities in this ecosystem did not crash as a result of the chestnut demise (Stephenson, Ash, and Stouffer 1993), the oaks that replaced the chestnuts in the canopy do not equal the chestnuts in mast production, and so ecosystem dynamics no doubt changed dramatically.

Amphibians are not abundant in montane oak forests. The occasional Chattahoochee slimy salamander may be found under coarse woody debris throughout most of the Blue Ridge. The southern Appalachian salamander, another species of the slimy salamander species complex, occurs north and east of Rabun Bald as well as on the mountain itself, where it is greatly outnumbered by the similar southern gray-cheeked salamander. American toads may also occasionally occur here.

Reptiles include the garter snake, which feeds on earthworms, frogs, and salamanders. Ringnecked snakes seek cover under rocks or woody debris. Although rarely larger than a pencil, these little snakes are voracious predators, feeding on a variety of invertebrates as well as small vertebrates, including small salamanders and lizards (K. M. Andrews and Gibbons 2008b). Timber rattlesnakes forage in these forests, which may be well away from their over-wintering dens. Rattlesnakes are ambush predators, and individuals often coil with their heads resting against the top of a fallen log waiting, perhaps for days, for a small mammal to run down the length of the log (Reinert et al. 1984).

FEATURED ANIMAL

Cerulean Warbler (*Dendroica cerulea*)

The cerulean warbler is a strikingly attractive migratory songbird. Males have blue upperparts with two white wing bars and whitish underparts. Females have similar color patterns but are greenish-blue instead of blue. This bird's summer range extends throughout much of the eastern United States and southeastern Canada. Within this range, the main breeding area is in eastern Tennessee, eastern Kentucky, southern and western West Virginia, southeastern Ohio, and southwestern Pennsylvania. Winter habitats include broad-leaved evergreen forests extending from Colombia to Peru and Venezuela (Hamel 2000).

In Georgia, cerulean warblers are found primarily in oak-hickory or cove forests, often near ridge tops where exposure to periodic storms creates forest gaps that serve as favored breeding sites (Klaus 2010a). Cerulean warblers are considered area-sensitive birds because they prefer large tracts of forest. Within those sites, they are typically found in uneven-aged stands containing some very large trees. Cerulean warbler nests are often located in the tallest canopy trees near small forest gaps (Hamel 2000).

Breeding Bird Survey data indicate that this bird has experienced significant declines in the Southeast and throughout its breeding range since the 1960s. While the reasons for this decline are not well understood, important factors may include forest fragmentation and conversion within the breeding range, lack of suitable forest structure (e.g., canopy gaps), and habitat loss along migration routes and on wintering grounds (Klaus 2010a). This bird is protected as Rare in Georgia.

Experimental timber harvest techniques to benefit cerulean warblers are being evaluated in several national forests in the Southeast. In Georgia, protection of large tracts of mature hardwoods forest in the Chattahoochee National Forest as well as experimental openings that attract cerulean warblers may help conserve this species, though efforts to conserve habitat within its wintering grounds are also essential (Klaus 2010a).

Whitley Gap Trail on Wildcat Mountain

The Whitley Gap Trail is a 1-mile spur trail off of the Appalachian Trail (AT) that leads to a particularly picturesque and accessible dwarfed montane oak forest on the north side and ridge crest of Wildcat Mountain. The first 0.5 mile on the AT leading to the trail is a moderate climb to the 3,800-foot elevation ridge top, through mountain laurel, great laurel, and dense herbaceous patches. The dominant trees on the ridge top, including white oak, red oak, scarlet oak, rock chestnut oak, and black birch, are typically stunted and often no more than 25 feet tall, with low, contorted limbs that at times form tunnels over the trail. The trees are barely taller than the dense shrubs, which are also gnarled, creating the effect of a rocky summit or shrub bald. Other tree species include serviceberry, black locust, red maple, mockernut hickory, sourwood, and tulip-tree. Chestnut sprouts (up to 18 feet high) are relatively common, indicating that chestnuts once dominated or co-dominated this site. The southern Appalachian endemic Catawba rhododendron is a dominant shrub. Herbs include New York fern, spi-

derworts, great yellow wood-sorrel, bloodroot, Solomon's seal, eastern flowering spurge, whorled loosestrife, yellow stargrass, Appalachian cow-wheat, black snakeroot, northern horsebalm, summer bluet, lobelia, galax, and veiny hawkweed. Moss and lichens add to the picturesque feel of this site.

A short spur trail leads to Adam's Bald, a very scenic outcrop that is surrounded by and interfingered with shrub-sized white oak, scarlet oak, sassafras, black cherry, and Virginia pine.

Location: From downtown Helen, take Ga. Hwy. 17/ Unicoi Turnpike north approximately 1.3 miles. Turn left (southwest) onto Ga. Hwy. 75 (Alt.); proceed about 2.3 miles. Turn right onto Ga. Hwy. 348/Richard B. Russell Scenic Hwy. and proceed about 7 miles to parking for the trail on the right. The Appalachian Trail crosses Richard Russell Scenic Hwy. at Hog Pen Gap. From the parking area at Hog Pen Gap on Ga. Hwy. 348/Richard B. Russell Scenic Hwy., go south on the Appalachian Trail about 150 yards to find the Whitley Gap Trail. Google Earth GPS approximate coordinates to the parking area: N 34.725922/W 083.839793.

Cove Forests

Cove forests occur in sheltered, concave, flat, or straight sites with north- to east-facing aspects, or on low, protected positions that foster cool, moist conditions. Fertile (circumneutral) coves are dominated by mesophytic tree species such as basswood, bitternut hickory, northern or southern sugar maple, tulip-tree, and yellow buckeye. These forests are beautiful in the spring, with diverse wildflowers, including trilliums, crested iris, showy orchis, yellow lady's-slipper, common blue cohosh, common black-cohosh, dolls'-eyes, yellow mandarin, violets, and ginseng.

Acidic sites typically have a strong evergreen component, with eastern hemlock, white pine, and a dense understory of great laurel and mountain laurel. Although low in diversity, the lush evergreen plant community, which often surrounds streams and waterfalls, provides scenic variety, and helps maintain cool water temperatures. The beauty of the acidic coves is threatened by the hemlock woolly adelgid, a non-native species that is currently devastating the eastern hemlocks.

PHYSICAL SETTING AND ECOLOGY

Mesic sites in the Georgia Blue Ridge are usually found on north- to east-facing slopes and lower protected slopes, although exceptions occur. Till Ridge Cove (Rabun County) faces southeast and Hollifield Ridge on Eagle Mountain (Towns County), a ridge top at 3,600 feet, supports cove hardwoods, most likely because of orographic fog, deep soils, and high soil nutrient levels (Riddle 2005). Coves usually experience gap phase disturbance patterns: small gaps created by the fall of individual trees or branches enable shade-tolerant trees, such as yellow buckeye, sugar maple, and American beech, to reach the canopy, where they can live for centuries and reach enormous dimensions. Windthrow of individual trees is the most common way that gaps are created; lightning and ice glaze also topple trees. Occasionally, ice storms or wind bursts may down several trees, enabling pioneer species such as white pine, tulip-tree, black birch, and black locust to retain a presence and increase diversity in the forest (Clebsch and Busing 1989). Large openings most likely occur only every few centuries (Bratton 1994). Lightning fires occur only in extremely dry years, within a return interval of centuries, and are low-intensity with limited effect (Clebsch and Busing 1989).

The most important factor contributing to fertile (basic or circumneutral) conditions is the presence of nutrient-rich bedrock or colluvium (Pitillo, Hatcher, and Buol 1998). Slope shape and steepness, however, also play a role: concave, gentle slopes collect deeper soils, with greater amounts of clays and humus to hold more nutrients, while on steeper slopes the clays and humus are transported downslope, creating more acidic conditions (Blevins and Schafale 2011). Abundant hemlock needles may contribute to the formation of acidic soils (Whittaker 1956). The hemlocks may also affect soil moisture: some researchers have suggested that the open valley flats of middle elevations and the slopes above valleys at high elevations where some hemlock-dominated forests occur are less mesic than those of fertile coves, perhaps because the superficial root system and hemlock needles reduce water penetration (Whittaker 1956; Schafale and Weakley 1990); this would also be the case where there were fewer clays to hold moisture. It is also possible that in the absence of fire, hemlocks have moved upslope to drier conditions.

VEGETATION

The gap phase dynamics of cove forests encourage dominant trees that are shade-tolerant. Tulip-trees dominate most Georgia Blue Ridge coves now because they colonized after extensive logging in the 19th and 20th centuries. Tulip-trees are long-lived and may dominate for at least two centuries before other more shade-tolerant species, such as yellow buckeye, basswood, American beech, yellow-wood, and sugar maple, take over (Runkle 1985; Clebsch and Busing 1989).

There are two main types of coves: fertile (basic or circumneutral) and acidic. Transitional forests also exist, however, and these may become more common with the demise of the eastern hemlock. Examples of transitional coves include Warwoman Dell (Rabun County) and the Chestnut Lead Trail (Fannin and Gilmer Counties). In some places, such as on Blood Mountain (Lumpkin and Union Counties) and the Bear Hair Trail in Vogel State Park (Union County), some sites are acidic and other sites are more fertile, as steepness and nutrient levels change over small spatial scales.

Fertile cove forests have a rich array of mesophytic tree species, including yellow buckeye, basswood, tulip-tree, white ash, sugar maple, bitternut hickory, black cherry, and yellow-wood. Yellow-wood, an uncommon tree in Georgia, is plentiful in coves on the north side of Brasstown Bald and in Loggy Branch on Hightower Bald (Wharton 1978). Shrubs include beaked hazelnut, American hazelnut, smooth hydrangea, northern hairy spicebush, buffalo-nut, and mountain holly. The ground layer is dense and diverse. There are many celebrated fertile cove forests in Georgia, each with a slightly different composition. The Hambidge Center Trail (Rabun County) features dense populations of Vasey's trillium, dwarf ginseng, crested iris, and showy orchis. Till Ridge Cove (Rabun County), just upslope from the Hambidge Center Trail, has a huge swath of hundreds of great white trillium, as well as bloodroot, common blue cohosh, dolls'-eyes, and many other herbs. Ramp Cove on Kelly Ridge (Towns County) is named for its huge numbers of ramps, while coves in the Alaculsey Valley in the western Cohuttas include fernleaf phacelia, carpets of tall white violet, golden-seal, yellow lady's-slipper, silvery glade fern, and yellow mandarin (Murray County). An unnamed, boulder-strewn cove on the north side of Brasstown Bald has an abundance of green violet and ginseng. Coves on the Gahuti Trail in Fort Mountain State Park (Murray County) have spotted mandarin and many trillium species.

Acidic cove forests grow in submesic to mesic acidic sites on flats near streams; in deep, stream-laced ravines and lower coves; and on steep, sheltered slopes (Wharton 1978; Schafale and Weakley 1990; Porcher and Rayner 2001). Eastern hemlock, white pine, black birch, tulip-tree, Fraser magnolia, and red maple typically dominate, often with dense understories of great laurel and mountain laurel, especially along streams. In the most acidic, densely shaded sites, the ground layer is sparse, with only a few species, including pipsissewa, downy rattlesnake-orchid, Indian cucumber-root, and galax. Painted trillium, which is unusual in Georgia, grows in moist, acidic areas, such as around Lakes Conasauga and Winfield Scott.

An acidic cove forest on the Coleman River near Tate City

Eastern hemlocks can be the longest-lived trees in the Georgia mountains, reaching more than 800 years in age and with diameters of up to 6 feet (Carey 1993; Riddle 2005). Eastern hemlocks are well suited to acidic, deep ravines and shaded colluvial flats. They are shade-tolerant and grow slowly until the canopy opens, and their limbs are layered to catch the maximum amount of insolation throughout the day. Seeds can germinate both on the tipped-up root masses of toppled trees and on moss-covered trunks that have fallen to the forest floor, where the seedlings thrive in the partial sunlight that pierces through the small gaps. They can survive hundreds of years of suppression until a canopy gap opens. They are vulnerable to fire, at least until they are quite large (Carey 1993). The long lifespans and ability to regenerate on root masses, logs, and gaps have enabled them to retain dominance in the past; their destruction by woolly adelgid will utterly change these forests.

OLD GROWTH

Old-growth stands are distinctive because of the beauty and size of the old trees and the uneven-aged trees within them: trees hundreds of years old are neighbors to very young trees. Two old-growth eastern hemlock stands exist around Big Bald Cove in Union County near Brasstown Bald (Riddle 2005). In one, eastern hemlocks are up to 4 feet in diameter and tulip-trees reach 38 inches. Eastern hemlock saplings abound, except where they have been crowded out by great laurel. Red maple, black birch, rock chestnut oak, black gum, and basswood also appear. The other stand has more eastern hemlock biomass than any other known site in Georgia: one eastern hemlock is more than 234 years old, measures 52 inches in diameter, and is 153 feet tall (Riddle 2005). Black birch, Fraser magnolia, basswood, tulip-tree, yellow birch, and common silverbell are also present; unfortunately, the woolly adelgid is devastating the stand. Other notable stands of old trees occur on the Conasauga River Trail (Fannin County) and Holcomb Creek Trail (Rabun County), particularly in the flats between Holcomb Creek and Ammons Falls, where eastern hemlocks reach heights of more than 150 feet and span more than 4 feet in diameter (Carlson 1995).

Some coves, including Ramp Cove (Towns County) and Sosebee Cove (Union County), have large specimens of yellow buckeye, common silverbell, and black cherry, all of which have striking bark patterns that differ markedly from those of younger trees (Duffy 1993; Riddle 2005). Yellow buckeyes in Ramp Cove are more than 4 feet in diameter and may be up to 400 years old; some in Sosebee Cove are more than 175 years old (Duffy 1993). The buckeyes were not logged because of the poor quality of the wood. Grassy Mountain Cove contains some large, old canopy trees, including tulip-trees that are nearly 4 feet in diameter, basswoods up to 34 inches in diameter, yellow buckeyes roughly 3 feet in diameter, black cherries up to 30 inches in diameter, and northern red oaks more than 55 inches in diameter, as well as smaller white ash, bitternut hickory, and cucumber magnolia specimens (Riddle 2005). Similarly, Ramp Gap and Wolf Pen Gap coves in the Rich Mountain wilderness area (Gilmer County) once supported northern red oaks, basswoods, and tulip-trees in a nearly mesic setting prior to logging; now huge common silverbells and yellow buckeyes dominate (Wharton 1978).

Old-growth tree in Sosebee Cove

CHARACTERISTIC PLANTS OF COVE FORESTS

TREES

Southern sugar maple—Acer floridanum

Northern sugar maple—Acer saccharum

Yellow buckeye—Aesculus flava

Black birch—Betula lenta

Bitternut hickory—Carya cordiformis

American beech—Fagus grandifolia

White ash—Fraxinus americana

Common silverbell—Halesia tetraptera

Tulip-tree—Liriodendron tulipifera

Cucumber magnolia—Magnolia acuminata

Fraser magnolia—Magnolia fraseri

White pine—Pinus strobus

Black cherry—Prunus serotina

Basswood—Tilia americana

Eastern hemlock—Tsuga canadensis

SHRUBS AND WOODY VINES

Smooth hydrangea—Hydrangea arborescens

Mountain laurel—Kalmia latifolia

Mountain doghobble—Leucothoe fontanesiana

Northern spicebush—Lindera benzoin

Great laurel—Rhododendron maximum

GROUND COVER

Dolls'-eyes—Actaea pachypoda

Common black-cohosh—Actaea racemosa

Northern maidenhair fern—Adiantum pedatum

White snakeroot—Ageratina altissima

Common blue cohosh—Caulophyllum thalictroides

Northern horsebalm—Collinsonia canadensis

Galax—Galax urceolata

Wood-nettle—Laportea canadensis

Turk's-cap lily—Lilium superbum

Sweet cicily—Osmorhiza spp.

Yellow mandarin—Prosartes lanuginosa

Trilliums—Trillium grandiflorum; T. simile; T. undulatum; T. vaseyi

Mountain bunch-flower—Veratrum parviflorum

HEMLOCK WOOLLY ADELGID

The hemlock woolly adelgid (*Adelges tsugae*) was introduced from Asia into the Pacific Northwest in 1924. In 1951, it was discovered near Richmond, Virginia, and began seriously harming hemlock stands in the eastern United States. It was discovered in Georgia in 2003 and is spreading at an estimated rate of 20–30 miles per year.

The adelgid is an aphid-like insect that sucks fluid from the base of hemlock needles. It may also inject toxins into the tree as it feeds, accelerating needle drop and branch die-back. Although some trees die within four years after infection, some persist in a weakened state for many years. Hemlocks that have been infested by hemlock woolly adelgid typically have grayish-green needles, instead of the normal shiny, dark green ones. Eastern hemlock (*Tsuga canadensis*) and Carolina hemlock (*Tsuga caroliniana*) are more susceptible to hemlock woolly adelgid damage than Asian and western hemlock trees, in part due to native predators that help protect the latter species.

Populations of hemlock woolly adelgid are composed entirely of females that reproduce asexually. In early spring, the over-wintering females lay between 100 and 300 eggs in woolly egg sacs beneath the hemlock leaves. In April or May, larvae known as crawlers emerge from the eggs to search for suitable feeding sites. These crawlers may be transported by wind, birds, or mammals to other nearby hemlocks. Once settled at the base of hemlock needles, the crawlers become immobile nymphs that mature into wingless or winged adult females by early summer.

The winged females die without reproducing, while the wingless females lay another 100 to 300 eggs on the hemlock trees. Crawlers emerge from these eggs to search for suitable feeding sites, then settle and become dormant until October or November, when they resume development. Feeding continues throughout the winter and early spring. Factors that can influence the impact of this pest on hemlock trees include drought, temperature stress, fungal diseases, and infestations of other hemlock pests. Low winter temperatures and heavy thunderstorms can reduce populations of the hemlock woolly adelgid, while mild winters can result in sharp increases in infestations.

Loss of hemlock stands adjacent to streams may cause higher stream temperatures, altering aquatic systems. Current efforts to control the hemlock woolly adelgid in Georgia include drenching the root zone

ANIMALS

Mammals in cove forests include boreal small mammals such as southern red-backed voles, smoky shrews, and masked shrews that can survive in these sites due to cold air draining downslope (Wharton 1978). Hemlock mixed with white pine is the preferred habitat of the red squirrel. Species of Special Concern that may frequent these stands include the starnose mole and hairy-tailed mole, southern red-back vole, and masked shrew. The closed cove forests support numerous other mammals, including white-tailed deer, black bears, raccoons, eastern chipmunks, gray foxes, southern flying squirrels, short-tailed shrews, and several species of forest bats.

Cove forests have an abundance and diversity of nesting songbirds, particularly neotropical migrants. The many flowers and budding leaves attract a wide array of insects, which in turn support a diverse avifauna. Colorful breeding birds include the blue-headed vireo, scarlet tanager, rose-breasted grosbeak, and Blackburnian warbler. The worm-eating warbler may build its ground nest, neatly hidden in clumps of grass on steep slopes with dense understories, while the black-throated blue warbler and hooded warbler nest in the shrub layer. In sites with more open understories, the ovenbird may be present. Small numbers of cerulean warblers nest in tall canopy trees near the edges of forest gaps.

Coal skinks are among the most seldom encountered reptiles in Georgia. They favor damp forests and woodlands in Georgia's Blue Ridge and adjacent upper Piedmont. Georgia's more familiar skinks are conspicuous because they readily sun in the open and climb trees, and their young possess bright-blue tails. Coal skinks, on the other hand, forage within the leaf litter of the forest floor and disappear into burrows at the slightest disturbance. They are most likely to be seen on warm days during winter and early spring when courtship and mating occurs. During this period, males develop tomato-red faces and become aggressive toward other males of their species (Hotchkin, Camp, and Marshall 2001).

The hemlock woolly adelgid. Trees that have been infested by the adelgid can be quickly recognized by the white, cotton-like appearance of this insect's egg sacs.

or injecting hemlocks in high-priority sites with imidacloprid, a soil-active insecticide; direct spraying of foliage with pyrethroids, insecticidal soaps, or horticultural oils; and rearing and release of predatory beetles for biological control. Currently, five laboratories in the Southeast are involved in rearing the predatory beetles as potential biological control of hemlock woolly adelgid populations.

SALAMANDERS

Southern Appalachian coves are perhaps the richest salamander habitats in the world, due to their relatively constant temperatures, abundant leaf litter, cool, moist soils, many downed logs, and damp areas near stony streams (Ford et al. 2002). On rainy nights many salamanders forage in the arthropod-rich leaf litter, and some actually climb vegetation under such conditions to hunt for arboreal insects (Jaeger 1978). In high forests, Blue Ridge southern two-lined salamanders migrate to small seeps to breed during the winter or very early spring and return to the forest when breeding is over. Seepage salamanders, which are tiny salamanders of conservation concern in Georgia, lay eggs under mosses near springs but then reside in the surrounding forest. Ocoee salamanders attach their eggs to the undersides of rocks or in moss, but some then move to coarse woody debris in terrestrial locations within these forests.

Spring salamanders are rarely encountered anywhere but are most common in high-elevation seeps and springs. They may move out onto the forest floor during rainy periods. An example of this diverse salamander community is to be found in Union County's Sosebee Cove (see the Featured Place), which contains all of these species as well as four additional species of dusky salamanders found along the seepages and streams (Camp et al. 2002).

The terrestrial Chattahoochee slimy salamander is particularly abundant in mesic forests throughout Georgia's Blue Ridge. Along the North Carolina line near the headwaters of the Tallulah and Coleman Rivers, the Chattahoochee slimy salamander hybridizes with the red-legged salamander (Highton and Peabody 2000), and many individuals in this area can be found with varying amounts of red on their legs (Wharton 1978). These terrestrial salamanders (woodland-salamander group) secrete a noxious, sticky substance from their tails, and the bright-red patches serve as advertisements of this noxious quality to predatory birds.

Eastern newts occur here and in many other communities as well, as long as there are nearby pools for breeding. The newts first spend a season as larvae in water, then live on land for several years (in this stage they are called red efts), and then return permanently to the pond to breed. In the eft stage the salamanders are bright red, which warns predators of their toxicity and so enables them to wander the forest floor unmolested during the day when humidity is high (D. J. Stevenson and Camp 2008).

Salamanders are particularly sensitive to shade removal by timber harvest; clearcutting practices severely impact amphibian communities (Petranka, Eldridge, and Haley 1993). Consequently, coves supporting old-growth forests sustain the most extensive amphibian assemblages (Ford et al. 2002).

A millipede. The southern Appalachians are known for the diversity of millipedes that exist there. Millipedes eat decaying leaves and other dead plant matter, so they thrive in the organic material that collects in fertile coves.

Woodland Jumping Mouse
(*Napaeozapus insignis*)

Jumping mice (family Zapodidae) can be easily distinguished from other mice of the eastern United States by their long hind legs, large hind feet, and extremely long tails. Two species of jumping mice are native to Georgia: the woodland jumping mouse (*Napaeozapus insignis*) and the meadow jumping mouse (*Zapus hudsonicus*). As their common names suggest, they occupy different habitats, the former found primarily in mesic hardwood forests, stream borders, and mountain bogs, the latter in low-elevation fields and meadows (Burt and Grossenheider 1980; Whitaker 1999).

The range of the woodland jumping mouse extends from Labrador, Quebec, and New Brunswick, west to southeastern Manitoba, Canada, and south in the Appalachian Mountains to eastern Kentucky and northern Georgia (Linzey 1995). In Georgia, this species is restricted primarily to the Blue Ridge ecoregion, where it is found in moist mid- to high-elevation forests.

The woodland jumping mouse is an attractive rodent, with a brownish dorsal surface, yellow-orange sides, and a white belly. The long (5–6 inches) tail is light brown in color with a white tip. The woodland jumping mouse is primarily nocturnal and active only during the warmer months of the year. They may occasionally be seen in the daytime, however, hopping through dense ground layer vegetation. The period from late fall to spring is spent hibernating in a nest in a subterranean burrow. Woodland jumping mice feed heavily on fungi in the genera *Endogone* and *Glomus*. Other foods include seeds, fruits, and insects (Whitaker 1999).

Woodland jumping mice breed from May to August and produce one to two litters averaging four to five young from June to September. Though only occasionally observed, this species is thought to be secure in Georgia. Protection of mature mesic hardwood forests is an important component of the conservation of this species.

Sosebee Cove Trail

Sosebee Cove is the best known cove forest in Georgia, renowned for the diversity and beauty of its herbaceous layer. A 0.5 mile trail loops around part of the cove, and encompasses much of the diversity within this 175-acre site. Tulip-trees now predominate: they became established after selective logging removed the once-dominant old-growth hardwoods. Although a sign states that the cove was logged in 1903, some of the largest trees, including some tulip-trees, are older and some exceed 150 years (Duffy 1993). In particular, yellow buckeyes, which are not valuable timber, were left behind, and a few are now huge; one is more than 185 years old (Duffy 1993). Other species now reaching toward the canopy include black cherry, basswood, white ash, and bitternut hickory. Thus, while not entirely old-growth, Sosebee does demonstrate the diversity of cove forest trees.

Northern spicebush is common in the shrub layer. Spring wildflowers include dimpled trout lily, wood anemone, giant chickweed, Canada columbine, Dutchman's britches, common blue cohosh, squirrel corn, sweet white trillium, large-flowered trillium, showy orchis, common black-cohosh, toothworts, bloodroot, wild geranium, umbrella-leaf, dolls'-eyes, and much more (Nourse and Nourse 2007).

Summer flowering species include wood-nettle, yellow jewelweed, great yellow wood-sorrel, summer bluet, American lopseed, common white heart-leaved aster, foamflower, white snakeroot, and northern horsebalm. Ferns include Goldie's wood-fern, marginal wood-fern, fancy fern, and silvery spleenwort.

Upslope of the road bisecting this high-elevation cove is a large and picturesque boulderfield forest that extends toward the ridge and grades into a mesic cove talus forest in its lowest reaches. Black birches and a few yellow birches grow on the moss-covered boulders, and yellow-woods are present. The flora increasingly resembles that of a northern hardwood forest as elevation increases.

Location: From the square in downtown Blairsville, proceed south on Gainesville Hwy./Ga. Hwy. 11/U.S. Hwy. 19/129 about 10 miles. Turn right (west) on Ga. Hwy. 180 and proceed approximately 3.1 miles to Sosebee Cove parking on the right near the trailhead. Google Earth GPS approximate coordinates to parking area: N 34.763839/W 083.952370.

Low- to Mid-Elevation Oak Forests

Low- to mid-elevation oak forests typically occur below 3,500 feet in Georgia, on dry to submesic sites. These are matrix forests of the Georgia Blue Ridge, covering vast acreages of the ecoregion. These forests can vary widely, from nearly xeric sites dominated by rock chestnut oak and scarlet oak, to nearly mesic sites with northern red oak, tulip-tree, and Fraser magnolia. Oak-dominated forests have decreased in extent over the last century; red maple, tulip-tree, black gum, and white pine dominate many of these stands today, making the community name "oak forest" somewhat problematical. This natural community is the major habitat for most plant and animal species in the ecoregion and reflects most broadly the story of human impact upon the region. Although several old-growth, oak-dominated sites still exist in the Georgia Blue Ridge and are described below, in many places the oaks are apparently unable to regenerate because of the absence of fire.

PHYSICAL SETTING AND ECOLOGY

Soil moisture is an important influence on vegetation composition of low- to mid-elevation oak forests. Vegetation assemblages adapted to drier conditions are found on sites with south- to west-facing aspects, thin soils, steep gradients, exposed slope positions, and convex slope shapes. As conditions range to more northerly aspects, deeper soils, concave or straight sites, and sheltered positions, vegetation composition will intergrade with that of the cove forests.

The natural disturbance regime in these forests is gap phase dynamics, in which disease, insects, drought, windthrow, fire, and lightning cause trees to die and create gaps in the forest canopy (Pickett and White 1985). The size of the gaps varies according to type of disturbance, which in turn is often influenced by topography: dry and exposed sites are more susceptible to larger-scale disturbances, such as fire, powerful thunderstorm downdrafts, and tornadoes (Harmon, Bratton, and White 1983). The gaps are important sources of plant diversity and provide food and habitat because many herbs, vines, and pioneer trees invade them.

The historic role of fire in maintaining oak forests was most likely important but is still subject to debate and ongoing research. The frequency, source, and sites of fires in the region as best understood today are described on p. 57, but the fire suppression policies of the mid- to late 20th century obscured the natural and anthropogengic fire patterns of the past. Reduced oak regeneration in recent years in the southern and central Appalachians, however, appears to be associated with fire exclusion in the last century (Mikan et al. 1994; Abrams 2000). Most oaks are more fire-tolerant than thinner-barked trees such as red maple, white pine, black birch, and black gum in their early years. This advantage to oaks disappears as the other species become more fire-tolerant with age as their bark thickens. Prescribed burns are being conducted on some mountain slopes to maintain oak-dominated forests, but this becomes increasingly difficult where trees other than oaks become more fire-tolerant with age. Careful application of mechanical or chemical treatments in conjunction with fire may be needed to restore oak-dominated stands in some areas.

VEGETATION

Southern Appalachian oak forests are notoriously difficult to classify because they occur along a very gradual gradient of nearly xeric to nearly mesic soils (Whittaker 1956; Wharton 1978). They also vary along a nutrient gradient and according to disturbance history.

Acidic, Dry to Xeric Forests. These forests occur on steep ridgelines and exposed, convex slopes with thin, acidic soils. Rock chestnut oak and scarlet oak dominate with other dry-site tree species and ericaceous shrub layers of mountain laurel and several blueberry and huckleberry species. Roughly 55 such stands in Georgia have been identified as old-growth, ranging up to 260 years of age, and are usually on upper south- to west-facing slopes (Riddle 2005). Presumably, these stands were burned frequently by early settlers and many of them escaped timber harvest because they are on unproductive, inaccessible sites and dominated by less valuable timber species (Riddle 2005). Easily accessed, younger examples of rock chestnut oak-scarlet oak forests are fairly common in Georgia, and can be seen in Fort Mountain State Park (Murray County), Tallulah Gorge State Park (Rabun County), portions of the Bear Hair Trail in Vogel State Park (Union County) (see the Featured Place), and most other

Red maple emerging through the understory on the Bear Hair Trail at Vogel State Park

trails through dry sites. Fire suppression over the past 70 years has increased the amount of black gum, red maple, and white pine on most sites, especially where the evergreen understory is not dense, to the point where oaks can be difficult to find in some stands. There may be few oaks in the mid-story of such forests because they need relatively open-canopy conditions to germinate and survive (Abrams 2000). In some cases, the dense shrub layer that has developed in the absence of fire prohibits tree recruitment into the seedling or sapling layer.

Dry-Mesic (Submesic) Forests. These forests occur in more sheltered, concave, and thicker-soiled sites, where northern red oak, pignut hickory, eastern hemlock, tulip-tree, Fraser magnolia, and white oak become more abundant, creating a mixed hardwood rather than oak-dominated canopy. The shrub and herbaceous layers in these sites are also more diverse. These productive sites were more likely to be logged than drier sites and, consequently, fewer dry-mesic

CHARACTERISTIC PLANTS OF LOW- TO MID-ELEVATION OAK FORESTS

TREES

Pignut hickory—Carya glabra

Mockernut hickory—Carya tomentosa

Flowering dogwood—Cornus florida

Tulip-tree—Liriodendron tulipifera

Fraser magnolia—Magnolia fraseri

Sourwood—Oxydendrum arboreum

White pine—Pinus strobus

White oak—Quercus alba

Scarlet oak—Quercus coccinea

Northern red oak—Quercus rubra

Black locust—Robinia pseudoacacia

SHRUBS AND WOODY VINES

American chestnut (sprouts)—
   Castanea dentata

Black huckleberry—Gaylussacia baccata

Bear huckleberry—Gaylussacia ursina

Mountain laurel—Kalmia latifolia

Buffalo-nut—Pyrularia pubera

Flame azalea—Rhododendron
   calendulaceum

Great rhododendron—Rhododendron
   maximum

Gorge rhododendron—Rhododendron
   minus

Hillside blueberry—Vaccinium pallidum

Deerberry—Vaccinium stamineum

GROUND COVER

Southern harebell—Campanula
   divaricata

Pipsissewa—Chimaphila maculata

Speckled wood-lily—Clintonia
   umbellulata

Pink lady's-slipper—Cypripedium acaule

Hay-scented fern—Dennstaedtia
   punctilobula

Whorled wild yam—Dioscorea
   quaternata

Trailing arbutus—Epigaea repens

Common white heart-leaved aster—
   Eurybia divaricata

Galax—Galax urceolata

Downy rattlesnake-orchid—Goodyera
   pubescens

Quaker ladies—Houstonia caerulea

Naked tick-trefoil—Hylodesmum
   nudiflorum

Eastern Solomon's-plume—
   Maianthemum racemosum

Indian cucumber-root—Medeola
   virginiana

Small Solomon's-seal—Polygonatum
   biflorum

Christmas fern—Polystichum
   acrosticoides

New York fern—Thelypteris
   noveboracensis

Catesby's trillium—Trillium catesbaei

Perfoliate bellwort—Uvularia perfoliata

---

old-growth stands remain in Georgia. Roughly 20 stands were identified in an old-growth inventory, with ages of the stands ranging from 150 to 330 years (Riddle 2005). The younger forests that have developed after logging have large numbers of tulip-trees, white pines, and red maples.

Mafic Forests. These forests occur over amphibolites or some gneisses. White oak and hickories are common, while ericaceous shrubs, such as blueberries and mountain laurel, are less frequent than in other oak forests. American columbo may appear in the herbaceous layer as an indicator plant of mafic conditions. These forests sometimes have a more open canopy, possibly because the soils that form from some mafic rocks are thinner than those that form from the typical acidic rocks (West 2006). Examples of mafic forests occur on the lower reaches of the Arkaquah Trail that leads downslope from Brasstown Bald (Union County) and on the Appalachian Trail leading north from Woody Gap (Union and Lumpkin Counties).

Transitional to Cove Forests. These forests appear as conditions become increasingly moist and fertile and can be difficult to distinguish from cove forests at times (Whittaker 1956; Wharton 1978). They have diverse canopies that include hickories, northern red oak, and white oak, along with a scattering of mesophytic species and a fairly dense and rich herbaceous layer. In Georgia, a few stands that grade to cove forests possess large, old tulip-trees and northern red oaks. One good example occurs on the north face of Betty Mountain (Fannin County), where tulip-trees are 240–255 years old, more than 4 feet in diameter, and up to 138 feet tall; northern red oaks reach more than 3.5 feet in diameter; and cucumber magnolias are nearly 3 feet in diameter and up to 117 feet tall (Riddle 2005). A similar assemblage occurs on the Old Growth (Giants) Trail near Coopers Creek (Union County) and on Mill Creek near Springer Mountain (Fannin County), where huge northern red oaks, white oaks, and giant tulip-trees contrast with smaller trees and saplings in the stand.

ANIMALS

Because these forests are extensive, with many habitat niches and a wide range of food sources, they are the primary habitat for the animals typically associated with the Georgia Blue Ridge. Characteristic mammals include white-tailed deer, bobcats, striped skunks, gray foxes, moles, shrews, mice, voles, southern flying squirrels, coyotes, black bears, and bats, including hoary, evening, eastern pipstrelle, and big brown. Uncommon species include the least weasel and Rafinesque's big-eared bat (see the Featured Animal). Acorns are an important food source in these forests, and oak acorn cycles probably exercise a strong influence on animal populations in the Georgia Blue Ridge. Oaks do not produce the same amount of acorns year after year; they sporadically produce large crops of acorns in some years and far fewer acorns in other years. This variable production helps ensure oak reproduction because low acorn production years cause a reduction in some animal populations so that during high acorn production years some acorns escape predation. Effects are complex, though: one study found that mice populations rose with increasing red oak acorn production, but populations of a shrew were unaffected; the shrew population rose when more red maple seeds were available (Schnurr et al. 2002).

The yellow-billed cuckoo preys on gypsy moths and thrives during outbreaks of this forest pest. Mature examples of oak forests are important woodpecker habitat because of the abundance of acorns and insects. Notable breeding birds include wood thrush, ovenbird, black-and-white warbler, scarlet tanager, eastern wood-pewee, red-eyed vireo, and American redstart. The golden-winged warbler, a species of conservation concern, can be found occasionally in canopy gaps of these forests; efforts are under way to provide habitat for this species on Brawley Mountain, where openings that the warbler requires are being created in the multistoried forest.

Both reptiles and amphibians occur on submesic sites, although amphibians are more common on moister sites. Eastern kingsnakes and fossorial snakes, including the ringnecked snake, plain-bellied snake, northern pine snake, and eastern worm snake are found here. Smooth earth snakes may also occur in the drier forests. Ground skinks are abundant in the leaf litter of the forest floor. Eastern milk snakes and northern pine snakes are very secretive components of the reptile fauna (Wharton 1978). In more mesic forests, the Chattahoochee slimy salamander is abundant, and spotted salamanders may occur if suitable breeding habitat (shallow depressions that pond water during the winter) is present in the forest or nearby.

Rock chestnut oak is a common tree of low- to mid-elevation oak forests in the Georgia Blue Ridge. Its acorns are a food source for many animals. The leaves, shown here, somewhat resemble those of American chestnut.

Rafinesque's Big-Eared Bat
(*Corynorhinus rafinesquii*)

This secretive and enigmatic bat, named for the famous French naturalist Constantine Rafinesque (1783–1840), is notable for the size of its ears, often more than 1 inch in length and equal to one-fourth of the bat's total body length. Rafinesque's big-eared bat is generally brownish-gray in appearance with a whitish belly. Two large, conspicuous glands are present on either side of the snout, and form prominent lumps on the top of the nose (Burt and Grossenheider 1980).

Rafinesque's big-eared bat ranges widely throughout the southeastern United States, but is usually found in low numbers. While it is thought to occur throughout Georgia, most documented occurrences are from the Blue Ridge and Coastal Plain. Typical roosting sites are located in or near mature forests, including bottomland and upland hardwood forests as well as pine flatwoods, and often near water. This bat roosts in hollow trunks and the loose bark of trees, the entrance zones of caves and abandoned mines, wells, buildings, and crevices in rock ledges. It emerges from its roost well after dark to forage in the forest canopy. The flight of Rafinesque's big-eared bat is slower than that of most other bats, and at times it appears to hover in the air. Its diet includes a wide variety of flying insects (Ozier 2008).

Little is known of the overall population size of Rafinesque's big-eared bat in Georgia. Recent surveys in Georgia have demonstrated the importance of hollow trees in river swamps and bottomland hardwood forests in the Coastal Plain as roosting areas, and have shown this bat to be more abundant than previously thought. There is some evidence that this species has been impacted by former use of persistent pesticides, loss of mature forest stands, and removal of hollow trees. Rafinesque's big-eared bat is state-protected as Rare in Georgia (Ozier 2008).

Bear Hair Gap Trail

The Bear Hair Gap Trail, located in Vogel State Park, clearly illustrates the oak forest transition into other forest types as topography and aspect change. In addition, there are several stands of mature oaks along the trail in a region where oak domination is becoming increasingly rare. The approach consists of the acidic variant of a cove forest natural community, dominated by eastern hemlock (now being struck by the hemlock woolly adelgid), along with sourwood, tulip-tree, and sweet gum. The cove forest natural community grades into a northern red oak-dominated stand with white oak, red maple, rock chestnut oak, white pine, mockernut hickory, and horsesugar, then changes back to cove forest conditions near a stream. The Bear Hair Gap Trail itself starts in low, fairly flat topography that supports an oak forest that grades into an acidic cove natural community, with white oak, eastern hemlock, black birch, black gum, sourwood, red maple, northern red oak, rock chestnut oak, Fraser's magnolia, common silverbell, striped maple, and great laurel.

The trail moves back into more concave, north-aspect mesic sites with cove species, such as basswood and yellow buckeye, and a dense, diverse herb layer. As the trail continues through drier conditions, the rich herb layer disappears, and pioneer tree species, such as black birch, black locust, tulip-tree, and red maple, become common. American chestnut sprouts indicate that the tree was once a canopy species here. Steep slopes support rock chestnut oak, scarlet oak, and sourwood, often with a dense mountain laurel understory and a sparse ground layer. The trail continues in this manner, slipping in and out of oak, cove, seep, and rock outcrop natural communities.

Location: From the square in downtown Blairsville, proceed south on Gainesville Hwy/Ga. Hwy. 11/U.S. Hwy. 19/129 about 10.5 miles. Turn right onto Vogel State Park Rd. and continue straight less than 0.5 mile to the visitor center. A map of the Bear Hair Gap Trail is available in the visitor center. Google Earth GPS approximate coordinates to visitor center: N 34.765711/ W 083.924163.

Pine-Oak Woodlands and Forests

Pine-oak woodlands and forests in the Georgia mountains are dominated or co-dominated by pitch pine, Virginia pine, shortleaf pine, Table Mountain pine, and dry-site oaks. These forests typically have an ericaceous shrub layer and are often called "pine-oak heath" communities (Schafale and Weakley 1990; Porcher and Rayner 2001; Spira 2011). During pre-Columbian and early settlement periods, when fires were more frequent, such forests were more common in the southern Appalachians. Most likely, some pine-dominated stands had a fairly dense herbaceous ground layer that added important diversity to southern Appalachian forests (Harrod, Harmon, and White 2000; K. J. Elliott and Vose 2005).

Mature pine-oak woodlands and forests are now rare in the Georgia Blue Ridge. Because of the diversity they contribute to the ecoregion, restoring pine-oak woodlands is the largest single restoration objective of the Land and Resource Management Plan for the Chattahoochee-Oconee National Forests. Woodland restoration will create complexes of open habitat varying from grassland to woodland conditions, often grading into surrounding open forest. This pattern is meant to mimic the historical conditions created and maintained by variations in fire intensities due to slope, aspect, landform, and soil type (Georgia Department of Natural Resources 2005a).

PHYSICAL SETTING AND ECOLOGY

Pine-oak woodlands and forests occur most often on xeric, rocky, exposed, thin-soiled ridge tops and steep west- to south-facing slopes with thin, infertile soils, usually over acidic gneiss or quartzite (Harrod, Harmon, and White 2000). These slopes are prone to erosion that transports nutrient-retaining clays and organic material downslope, leaving sterile, acidic sands

Trailing arbutus. This small, woody sub-shrub is in the heath family and often grows in dry, acidic sites. It flowers in early spring and has a delicate, sweet scent.

behind. The pine needles and oak leaves in the leaf litter further acidify the soil. In addition to the low-nutrient and moisture conditions, these sites are exposed to lightning strikes, ice storms, and high winds, so blow-downs, fire, and ice-loading create a coarse-grained disturbance pattern that can often result in uneven-aged stands (Brose and Waldrop 2006).

Southern pine beetles (*Dendroctinus frontalis*) kill large numbers of pines in the Georgia Blue Ridge. The rice-sized beetles invade pines by boring into the bark and excavating winding paths and egg galleries that eventually girdle the tree (R. N. Smith 1991). Southern pine beetles are a natural part of the pine ecosystem. Over the centuries, they have periodically ravaged pine stands, hastening the takeover of the canopy by oaks or creating fuel loads for catastrophic fires (R. N. Smith 1991). The beetles are particularly problematical after drought, when the defenses of the stressed trees are low (R. N. Smith 1991). The beetle kill does not produce ideal conditions for pine stands to regenerate because the thick duff on the forest floor restricts

pine germination, so typically oaks, white pine, black gum, and red maple that were in the understory grow into the canopy and dominate the stand (R. N. Smith 1991).

Fire is generally needed to maintain pine-oak dominance, except on some very rocky sites, such as the cliff edges on Holly Creek (Murray County), Grassy Mountain (Murray County), and Tallulah Gorge (Rabun County) (Harmon, Bratton, and White 1983). Without fire, pines are replaced over time by dry-site oaks, which in turn can be replaced by red maple, black gum, and white pine. More study is needed on optimal fire regimes for these pine-oak communities. For example, stand-replacing fires were once considered essential to maintain Table Mountain pine-pitch communities, but more recent research suggests that less severe fires, combined with other disturbance, will maintain stands of uneven-aged trees (Brose and Waldrop 2006). Although the exposed, dry ridge sites are more prone to lightning-set fires than other sites in the Blue Ridge, anthropogenic (human-caused) fires set by Native Americans and early European settlers most likely promoted pine-oak natural communities (Harrod, White, and Harmon 1998).

Fire exclusion during the previous century has obscured understanding of the ecology and distribution of the pine-oak woodlands and forests in the Georgia Blue Ridge. Fire exclusion is a critical factor contributing to the decline of rare species such as the red-cockaded woodpecker, turkeybeard, smooth purple coneflower, and pink lady's-slipper. Although management with prescribed fire to perpetuate these forests is a conservation priority, restoration of fire to fire-suppressed sites is difficult (K. J. Elliott and Vose 2005). Older pine trees can be injured because fires can cause damage to fine roots near the soil surface in deep pine litter, and smoldering fires may also damage the trees' cambium layer. Fuel accumulation in the shrubby understory also creates hazards for crown fires and smoke management difficulties with reintroduction of prescribed burning (Waldrop, Mohr, and Brose 2006). At times thinning of the canopy through felling trees and selective use of herbicides (which should be used as sparingly as possible) can help create a patchy distribution of open-canopied stands with a grassy understory (Georgia Department of Natural Resources 2005a).

VEGETATION

The fire-adapted pines that dominate pine-oak stands in the Georgia Blue Ridge are described on pp. 99–100. White pine is also common on fire-excluded sites. Common oaks include blackjack oak, post oak, rock chestnut oak, scarlet oak, black oak, and southern red oak. Oaks can be top-killed by fire as saplings, but they can resprout after fire and become fire-tolerant as their bark thickens. They grow more slowly than pines in open conditions, and some are shade-tolerant enough to establish beneath a pine canopy. Other trees that occur in these stands are red maple and black gum, which are less fire-tolerant but more shade-tolerant than oaks. Like many oaks, they can resprout if top-killed by fire, and the fire tolerance of these species increases as their tree diameter increases (Harrod, White, and Harmon 1998).

Ericaceous shrubs (heaths), such as mountain laurels, azaleas, and blueberries, usually dominate the shrub layer. These shrubs resprout after fire, and so can stay dominant on a site once established. The ground layer is often sparse, with grasses, composites, legumes, and bracken fern. It is possible that during earlier periods of more frequent fire, many of these forests had a dense herbaceous ground cover of graminoids, legumes, and composites (Harrod, Harmon, and White 2000; Govus 2002a).

Common butterfly-weed

PINE-OAK ASSEMBLAGES IN THE GEORGIA BLUE RIDGE

Several different pine-oak plant assemblages occur in the Georgia Blue Ridge. Virginia pine–dominated communities are common in dry-mesic (submesic) sites because Virginia pine seeds into many sites following timber harvest. Most of these are early successional stands that will develop into low-elevation oak natural communities over time. Virginia pine does retain dominance on a few rocky sites, however. On a rocky, remote site on Grassy Mountain in the Cohuttas (Murray County), Virginia pines are more than 85 years old (Riddle 2005). Virginia pines co-dominate with scarlet oaks on a site in Fort Mountain State Park (Murray County) and with rock chestnut oaks on Doogan Mountain in the Cohuttas (Murray County). A Virginia pine woodland with deergrass and big bluestem grows along the Appalachian Trail on the eastern side of Levelland Mountain in Union County (Govus 2007).

There are a few shortleaf pine–dominated stands in the Georgia Blue Ridge. Holly Creek Preserve (Murray County) is a Nature Conservancy–owned property in the far western portion of the Cohuttas that occurs on a thin ridge, where shortleaf and Virginia pines are mixed with invading black gums, white pines, and red maples. The shrub layer varies from dense great laurel thickets under shortleaf pine to sparse blueberry and mountain laurel. Stumps of shortleaf occur throughout this site. Shortleaf pines more than 2 feet in diameter and up to 240 years old grow on a ridge crest at Reed Branch on Rand Mountain in Rabun County (Riddle 2005). Another shortleaf tract exists between Warwoman Creek and Burrell's Ford (Rabun County), where shortleaf pines are up to 300 years old and nearly 3 feet in diameter (Carlson 1995).

Pitch pine–Virginia pine–chestnut oak–scarlet oak forests are scattered throughout the Georgia Blue Ridge (Carlson 1995; Riddle 2005). These mixed pine-hardwood forests often have a dense heath understory beneath the canopy trees. Pitch pines occur in several stands that rock chestnut oak now dominates; they may have dominated when fire was more common. On Snake Knob (Towns County), pitch pines that are more than 100 years old and only 18 inches in diameter co-dominate with scarlet oak (Riddle 2005). At Stillhouse Branch (Rabun County), pitch pines reach more than 155 years old and 2 feet in diameter, and are prominent in the canopy (Riddle 2005). On Almond Bald in Black Rock Mountain State Park (Rabun County), pitch pine is the main canopy tree, thinly scattered over tall, dense thickets of great laurel and mountain laurel (Carlson 1995).

Mixed pine-oak woodlands or savannas with a dense herbaceous layer may have existed on some sites in the Georgia Blue Ridge. For example, the Ten-Time Burn Area, located at about 1,500-feet elevation on a south-facing slope in the Cohuttas of Georgia, is a former loblolly pine plantation that has been converted to an open hardwood-pine stand. The canopy is Virginia pine mixed with shortleaf pine and some residual loblolly pines. Oaks include scarlet oak, rock chestnut oak, and some white oak. Common little bluestem and other fire-fostered species make up the ground layer (Govus 2002a).

A rare assemblage occurs on the upper slopes and cliff tops of the Tallulah Dome quartzite geologic formation (Rabun and Habersham Counties) west of Tallulah Gorge State Park. Virginia pine, shortleaf pine, pitch pine, and Table Mountain pine mix with rock chestnut oak and other dry-site oaks to form an open and stunted forest, with contorted, bonsai-like pines perched on picturesque lookouts. Mountain laurel, trailing arbutus, sparkleberry, and other ericads make up the understory.

At least three stands dominated by a mix of Table Mountain pine, pitch pine, and rock chestnut oak occur in the Georgia Blue Ridge on steep, south-facing slopes south of Rabun Bald (Brose and Waldrop 2006). They have either dense mountain laurel shrub layers or understories dominated by sourwood, red maple, and black gum. The U.S. Forest Service is restoring open understory conditions in these stands through use of prescribed fire (Brose and Waldrop 2006).

PINES OF THE GEORGIA BLUE RIDGE

The most common pines of the Georgia Blue Ridge are Virginia pine, shortleaf pine, pitch pine, and Table Mountain pine. These pines differ in lifespan, drought tolerance, and adaptations to fire. Virginia pines are less resistant to fire than other mountain pines, especially in the sapling stage, although mature individuals can apparently survive fire (Sullivan 1993). They are drought-hardy and can grow at all elevations in the Georgia Blue Ridge (K. K. Carter and Snow 1990; Sullivan 1993). They produce frequent, heavy seed crops; thus, they can quickly invade old fields, roadsides, logged areas, and intensively burned areas in the mountains (Sullivan 1993; Kirkman et al. 2007). They have shallow root systems, making them prone to windthrow, and are short-lived, rarely exceeding 90 to 125 years in age (Sullivan 1993).

Shortleaf pines are more restricted to low-elevation sites than the other mountain pines (Kirkman et al. 2007), generally occurring at elevations below 2,500 feet. They have medium-thick bark and are more fire-tolerant than Virginia pines (Carey 1992a). They are able to sprout prolifically after a canopy fire from dormant buds within the bole and at the base (Carey 1992a). Shortleaf pines are fairly long-lived trees, and some more than 200 years old exist in Georgia (Carlson 1995; Riddle 2005). Shortleaf pine is capable of growing a deep taproot and so is resistant to windthrow if soils are deep enough to enable the taproot to develop (Carey 1992a).

Pitch pine, which occurs at all elevations in the Blue Ridge in Georgia, is one of the most fire-adapted trees in this region. Young trees of this species have thick, fire-resistant bark. Pitch pines can also resprout after a fire, due to a crook at the base of the trunk that bends into the soil, which protects growth buds during a fire so that they can resprout. In addition, a new limb can become the growth leader if fire kills the terminal leader, and the crown can produce new needles if the heat of the fire has killed the foliage (Carey 1992c). A pitch pine can grow slowly from root sprouts, being contorted, ravaged, and flat-topped from frequent fire damage, yet continue to survive in and even dominate a site where fires are frequent. Pitch pine produces both serotinous cones (cones that are normally closed but that open during a fire) and nonserotinous cones.

Virginia pine has many cones, with two short, twisted needles per bundle.

Pitch pine can often be identified by its epicormic needles, which sprout directly out of the tree trunk. The needles are three to a bundle; the cones have very short stalks and prickles.

Pitch pine is also capable of developing deep roots in rock crevices and sends out shallow lateral roots that can capture rainwater before it runs off the steep slopes (Carey 1992c).

Table Mountain pine is a fire-adapted tree that is scattered on a few xeric or dry sites, in such sites as Tallulah Gorge (Rabun and Habersham Counties), Glade Mountain (Rabun County), Smithgall Woods Conservation Area (White County), the upper Piedmont near Curahee Mountain (Stephens County), and Rabun Bald (Rabun County). Like pitch pine, the seedlings can survive surface fires because they have a crook just above or below the root crown to protect their buds, and can produce both serotinous and nonserotinous cones. Table Mountain pines have intermediate bark thickness—their bark is thicker than that of Virginia pine but less thick than that of pitch pine. Table Mountain pines can facilitate cyclical patterns of regeneration: dense stands of the pines create high fuel loads in the crowns that eventually encourage hot fires that open the serotinous cones. The opened cones disperse seeds prolifically onto the recently burned bare mineral soil, starting a new, even-aged cohort (Carey 1992b). Recent studies indicate, however, that multi-aged stands of Table Mountain pine do occur in the southern Appalachians, apparently fostered by windthrow-driven gap dynamics, with the pines reproducing even in the presence of duff on the sites (Brose and Waldrop 2006).

Table Mountain pine is superbly adapted to harsh sites. It has long limbs that can curve down almost to the ground, conserving moisture and protecting the surface roots from sun exposure (although it also makes them vulnerable to breakage from ice-loading).

Table Mountain pine has larger cones with prickles, two needles per bundle, and often develops a large, flat top as it ages.

It often develops a taproot in a rock crevice, with a spreading root system of sinker roots that penetrate to soil in adjacent crevices, providing access to moisture and nutrients as well as promoting wind resistance.

CHARACTERISTIC PLANTS OF PINE-OAK WOODLANDS AND FORESTS

TREES

Shortleaf pine—*Pinus echinata*
Table Mountain pine—*Pinus pungens*
Pitch pine—*Pinus rigida*
White pine—*Pinus strobus*
Virginia pine—*Pinus virginiana*
Scarlet oak—*Quercus coccinea*
Southern red oak—*Quercus falcata*
Blackjack oak—*Quercus marilandica*
Rock chestnut oak—*Quercus montana*
Post oak—*Quercus stellata*
Black oak—*Quercus velutina*

SHRUBS AND WOODY VINES

Common New Jersey tea—*Ceanothus americanus*
Huckleberries—*Gaylussacia spp.*
Mountain laurel—*Kalmia latifolia*

Great laurel—*Rhododendron maximum*
Gorge rhododendron—*Rhododendron minus*
Horsesugar—*Symplocos tinctoria*
Blueberries—*Vaccinium spp.*

GROUND COVER

Honesty weed—*Baptisia tinctoria*
Butterfly pea—*Clitoria mariana*
Woodland coreopsis—*Coreopsis major*
Poverty oat-grass—*Danthonia spicata*
Trailing arbutus—*Epigaea repens*
Eastern flowering spurge—*Euphorbia corollata*
Appalachian sunflower—*Helianthus atrorubens*
Small-headed sunflower—*Helianthus microcephalus*
Quaker ladies—*Houstonia caerulea*

Common stargrass—*Hypoxis hirsuta*
Upland dwarf iris—*Iris verna*
Carolina lily—*Lilium michauxii*
Eastern sensitive-briar—*Mimosa microphylla*
Eastern needlegrass—*Piptochaetium avenaceum*
Silkgrass—*Pityopsis graminifolia*
Bracken fern—*Pteridium aquilinum*
Black-eyed Susan—*Rudbeckia hirta*
Common little bluestem—*Schizachyrium scoparium*
Licorice goldenrod—*Solidago odora*
Yellow indiangrass—*Sorghastrum nutans*
Pencil-flower—*Stylosanthes biflora*
Virginia goat's-rue—*Tephrosia virginiana*

ANIMALS

These dry, nutrient-poor forests have fewer species than richer, moister environments, but can be havens for several rare species suited to the harsh conditions. The pine trees provide important habitat components here; their foliage and bark provide niches for unique insects and their predators. Although pitch pine cones are usually serotinous, some cones open and shed seeds in midwinter, providing a food source for over-wintering birds.

Mammals that inhabit or visit more open areas include red fox, striped skunk, coyote, white-tailed deer, opossum, black bear, and eastern chipmunk. Birds include those that glean caterpillars, beetles, and cicadas from the pine foliage and tree bark, such as the pine warbler, summer tanager, and yellow-throated vireo. Species that also excavate insects from the relatively soft wood of the pines include the brown-headed nuthatch, Carolina chickadee, and tufted titmouse. The northern flicker seems to prefer these dry ridge tops, where its favorite food—ants—can be found in abundance. Pitch pine seeds are eaten by over-wintering pine siskins and red crossbills. Ground-feeding birds, including the dark-eyed junco (on the highest sites) and chipping sparrow, exploit open stands that are rich in grasses, sunflower seeds, and blueberries. Once these ridges may have been home to even more specialized pine-loving birds, such as the red-cockaded woodpecker and Bachman's sparrow, but these species have been extirpated from the Blue Ridge, most likely due to changes in the disturbance regime (T. M. Schneider et al. 2010). The red crossbill, a species of Special Concern, is occasionally found in this natural community.

The dry environment supports reptiles, whose leathery, scaly skin conserves water and whose long bodies dispel heat quickly. Examples include eastern fence lizards, five-lined and broadhead skinks, and green anoles. Snakes include timber rattlesnakes, black racers, smooth earth snakes, eastern milk snakes, rat snakes, northern pine snakes, and copperheads. Amphibians are rare, but American and Fowler's toads may occur here, the American toad being more common at higher elevations (Floyd 2008a).

Red Squirrel (*Tamiasciurus hudsonicus*)

The red squirrel is one of four tree squirrels native to Georgia and the least abundant. This small but vociferous squirrel typically announces its presence by a loud, ratchet-like call from an overhead tree branch. The fur is typically reddish or yellowish on the back and sides and whitish on the belly. In winter, red squirrels sport tufts of hair extending from the tips of their ears; in summer, they usually have a dark brown or black stripe extending laterally along their bodies (Burt and Grossenheider 1980).

The range of the red squirrel extends from Alaska eastward throughout much of Canada, southward in the Rocky Mountain states to Arizona and New Mexico, and in the eastern United States as far south as Georgia and South Carolina (Burt and Grossenheider 1980). In the northern portions of its range, the red squirrel occupies pine or spruce forests as well as mixed hardwood and pine-hardwood forests. In Georgia, this species is found primarily in stands of Virginia pine or eastern hemlock and sometimes in mixed hardwood forests. Charles Wharton (1968) provided the first scientific account of the red squirrel's distribution in Georgia.

Active throughout the year, this squirrel is solitary except during the breeding season. Its diet consists of a wide variety of seeds, nuts, and fungi, as well as insects, small reptiles, mice, and bird eggs. The red squirrel stores harvested pine cones and other foods under logs, at the base of trees, or underground. In so doing, it helps to disperse seeds as well as fungi that are beneficial for tree growth. Red squirrels may shift their home ranges seasonally in the Georgia mountains, moving downslope to forage in lower-elevation sites in the winter months (Wharton 1968). Though globally secure, this species is uncommon in Georgia and may have declined in abundance in recent decades due to habitat loss.

Tallulah Gorge State Park

Tallulah Gorge is a striking gorge carved by the Tallulah River through quartzite cliffs that are up to 600 feet in height. Five waterfalls tumble through the gorge, with spectacular views. This site is also the Featured Place for the low- to mid-elevation acidic cliff and bluff natural community, so they can be studied together.

The North Rim Trail starts at the back of the visitor center and passes through small-patch pine-oak woodlands near the cliff edges (the low- to mid-elevation oak forest natural community grows away from the cliff edges). Trees include Virginia pine, rock chestnut oak, black gum, sand hickory, post oak, Table Mountain pine, scarlet oak, white pine, southern red oak, blackjack oak, red maple, sourwood, and American persimmon. Shrubs and woody vines include mountain laurel, horsesugar, hillside blueberry, deerberry, gorge rhododendron, sparkleberry, greenbriers, and Hercules'-club. The ground layer supports trailing arbutus, Maryland golden-aster, silkgrass, and galax.

The South Rim Trail is reached by descending the stairs and crossing the river. All of Georgia's montane pines are here, including Virginia pine, pitch pine, shortleaf pine, white pine, and Table Mountain pine. A few Carolina hemlocks, rare in Georgia but a signature species of this natural community, are also present directly across from the visitor center. They are within feet of an eastern hemlock, allowing a direct comparison of the two species. Serviceberry, black gum, rock chestnut oak, blackjack oak, and other dry-site species occur with the pines. Stiff-leaved aster, southern harebell, and goldenrods flower in late summer and fall.

A prairie-like area under a powerline on the south rim affords a good opportunity to contemplate the vegetation that would occur here if fire occurred more regularly, including fireweed, aster, ragweed, licorice goldenrod, veiny hawkweed, trailing arbutus, woodland coreoposis, Maryland golden-aster, pussy toes, and silkgrass.

Location: Tallulah Gorge State Park is located on U.S. 441/23 and Ga. Hwy. 15 within the city limits of Tallulah Falls. At approximately 0.25 mile north of Tallulah Falls Dam turn east off of U.S. 441/Ga. Hwy. 15 onto Jane Hurt Yarn Center Dr. Continue just under 1 mile to the interpretive center. Google Earth GPS approximate coordinates to interpretive center: N 34.739820/ W 083.390578.

Ultramafic Barrens and Woodlands

Ultramafic barrens and woodlands are natural communities that develop over ultramafic rocks, which have extremely high levels of magnesium and iron. Ecologists have long been intrigued by the unusual plant communities that develop over these unusual rocks, which they have referred to generically as "serpentine." These sites support a very unusual community of pitch pines, dry-site oaks, and glade-like, grassy openings with some Coastal Plain and prairie species. Ultramafic barrens and woodlands contrast starkly with the southern Appalachian oak forests growing on the more acidic bedrock surrounding them, adding diversity to the ecoregion.

The few southern Appalachian ultramafic woodlands that are known in Georgia are currently protected and managed by the U.S. Forest Service. These rare natural communities support several rare and near-endemic species, increase the overall biodiversity of the Blue Ridge, and serve as outdoor classrooms for students of geology and ecology. Additional surveys of known and suspected ultramafic woodland sites are needed. In addition, inventories of invertebrate communities in these rare habitats will provide a more complete picture of their contribution to regional biodiversity.

PHYSICAL SETTING AND ECOLOGY

Ultramafic rocks have very high levels of magnesium and iron. Outcrops of these rocks are uncommon on the earth's surface, and occur patchily within the Georgia Blue Ridge. The best-known ultramafic body in the Georgia Blue Ridge is the Lake Chatuge sill, which forms a ring around Brasstown Bald (Hartley and Penly 1974). The sill consists of dunite and related mafic and ultramafic rocks subjected to varying degrees of metamorphism and chemical alteration. Dunite and most other unmetamorphosed ultramafic rocks are not resistant to weathering, so that the trace of the Lake Chatuge sill is expressed in valleys and gaps, such as the Young Harris Valley and the basin of

Dunite is an ultramafic rock. Here it is shown from the Davidson Creek Botanical Area, coated with lichens.

Lake Chatuge. Dunite and other amphibolites, however, can be seen at the Davidson Creek Botanical Area at the Popcorn Overlook on U.S. 76 and on the shore of Lake Chatuge near Lower Bell Creek Church. Chloritic soapstone is exposed in Track Rock Gap.

The mineral and chemical composition of ultramafic rocks produces unusual soils (Brooks 1987). The soils are highly variable (Mansberg and Wentworth 1984; Tyndall and Hull 1999), but in general they have (1) a high pH, averaging 6.8, although preliminary tests indicate a pH closer to 6.0 in the Georgia Blue Ridge; (2) a high magnesium to calcium ratio, due to high levels of magnesium; (3) low levels of nutrients such as phosphorus, potassium, and nitrogen; (4) high concentrations of nickel and chromium, which may be harmful to plants; and (5) commonly, low levels of calcium. Soils derived from ultramafic rocks in Georgia are typically sandy, but are olivine and pyroxene sands rather than quartz sands. The high magnesium to calcium ratio, lack of plant nutrients, and, arguably, presence of potentially toxic trace elements create a harsh

environment sometimes called the "serpentine syndrome," which eliminates plants not well adapted to the extreme conditions.

Openings in the canopy occur when windstorms topple trees rooted in the shallow soils. Soil depth also appears to be an important factor regulating plant structure in ultramafic sites, with shallow soils supporting grasslands, slightly deeper soils supporting savannas, and woodlands or forests occurring on the deepest soils (Tyndall and Hull 1999). While the shallow soils maintain an open environment by fostering tree fall and limiting moisture, rooting space, and nutrients, fire also contributes to open conditions. Where soils are dry, the conditions encourage fire, which appears to be an important component for maintaining woodlands or barrens. Fire has been postulated to play a role in maintaining shallow soils in a Pennsylvania site (Arabas 2000). Prescribed fire management has been used regularly in North Carolina's well-known Buck Creek Serpentine Barren. This management tool would be beneficial for habitat enhancement at Track

Trees tip over easily in the shallow soils that develop over many ultramafic rocks.

Rock Gap and Popcorn Overlook, where the understory is becoming dense and is crowding out the herbaceous layer. Careful planning is needed, however, to ensure that construction and maintenance of firebreaks does not impact the integrity of this small but significant site.

Ultramafic bedrock does not always lead to unusual plant communities (Schafale and Weakley 1990). For example, at Track Rock Gap (Union County), best known for the hieroglyphics of animal tracks carved in large soapstone boulders, most of the vegetation is dry oak-pine forest, with the exception of a small area where there is a dense herbaceous layer with white goldenrod, eastern gray goldenrod, rosinweed, small-leaved white snakeroot, and Appalachian sunflower. Topography, land use history, mineral content of the bedrock, soil moisture, soil depth, and introduction of nonmafic material by flooding or downslope movement of colluvium may all play a role in determining vegetation composition over ultramafic substrates.

VEGETATION

Pitch pine is dominant: it is favored by a regime of fire and windthrow because it produces both serotinous cones (generally closed and opened only by fire) and nonserotinous cones (Carey 1992b). This natural community supports more base-loving species than do acidic pine-oak forests. For example, eastern ninebark, nodding onion, nettle-leaf sage, skunk meadowrue, whorled milkweed, and woodland muhly are all found at the Davidson Creek site (see the Featured Place). Post oak is more common than on many sites, not only because of the xeric conditions but also because it selectively accumulates calcium, retaining it at much higher levels than many other oaks (F. L. Johnson and Risser 1974), which may provide a competitive advantage in this limited-calcium environment.

Many adaptations to dry conditions are evident in the plant species associated with this community, many of which are also found in acidic woodlands and forests. Common little bluestem and other grasses, for example, roll their leaves to minimize water loss

Blazing-star

in droughty conditions, while white goldenrod has a dense covering of whitish hairs on its stems and leaves that reflect sunlight and trap humidity. Rattlesnake-master has thick, waxy leaves that retard water loss, while the small leaves of blazing-stars, whorled milkweed, and pitch pines reduce water loss through decreased surface area. Legumes, such as lespedezas and tick-trefoils, convert nitrogen in the atmosphere to forms that are usable by plants, thus supplementing the low amounts available in the soils.

Acid-loving plants, such as mountain laurel, trailing arbutus, blueberries, and teaberry, occur patchily in these woodlands in Georgia, and ericaceous shrubs occur as dense undergrowth in Pennsylvania and North Carolina serpentine barrens (Mansberg and Wentworth 1984). The reasons for this remain unknown and deserve more research. One study has found that pH was higher in savanna-like areas than in areas that supported a pitch pine forest (Kelly and Cumming 2005). It has also been noted that one variety of deerberry (*Vaccinium stamineum*) can grow well in mafic areas, which is unusual for plants in the blueberry genus (Weakley 2010).

CHARACTERISTIC PLANTS OF ULTRAMAFIC BARRENS AND WOODLANDS

TREES

Red maple—Acer rubrum
Mockernut hickory—Carya tomentosa
Black gum—Nyssa sylvatica
Shortleaf pine—Pinus echinata
Pitch pine—Pinus rigida
White pine—Pinus strobus
Virginia pine—Pinus virginiana
Scarlet oak—Quercus coccinea
Southern red oak—Quercus falcata
Post oak—Quercus stellata

SHRUBS AND WOODY VINES

Common New Jersey tea—Ceanothus
 americanus
Eastern ninebark—Physocarpus
 opulifolius
Hillside blueberry—Vaccinium pallidum
Deerberry—Vaccinium stamineum

GROUND COVER

Nodding onion—Allium cernuum
Big bluestem—Andropogon gerardii
Whorled milkweed—Asclepias
 verticillata
Southern harebell—Campanula
 divaricata
Woodland coreopsis—Coreopsis major
Poverty oat-grass—Danthonia spicata
Common rough fleabane—Erigeron
 strigosus
Rattlesnake-master—Eryngium
 yuccifolium
Teaberry—Gaultheria procumbens
Bowman's-root—Gillenia trifoliata
Small-headed sunflower—Helianthus
 microcephalus
Veiny hawkweed—Hieracium venosum
Yellow stargrass—Hypoxis hirsuta

Lespedezas—Lespedeza spp.
Blazing-stars—Liatris spicata; L.
 squarrulosa
Royal fern—Osmunda regalis
Common wild quinine—Parthenium
 integrifolium
Bracken fern—Pteridium aquilinum
Nettle-leaf sage—Salvia urticifolia
Common little bluestem—
 Schizachyrium scoparium
Licorice goldenrod—Solidago odora
Yellow indiangrass—Sorghastrum
 nutans
Skunk meadowrue—Thalictrum
 revolutum

ANIMALS

Animal species and populations vary according to the proportion of oaks and pines on a site and the density and diversity of the ground cover. The open vegetation structure and the mix of pine and oak species in this natural community cause it to support a fauna that is very similar to the pine-oak woodland and forest natural community. These dry, nutrient-poor forests have fewer species than richer, moister environments. Although pitch pine cones are usually serotinous, some cones open and shed seeds in midwinter, providing a food source for over-wintering birds.

Mammals include black bear, red fox, striped skunk, coyote, white-tailed deer, opossum, and eastern chipmunk. Birds include the pine warbler, summer tanager, yellow-throated vireo, brown-headed nuthatch, Carolina chickadee, tufted titmouse, and chipping sparrow. The northern flicker will search for ants on dry, rocky areas. Pitch pine seeds are eaten by over-wintering pine siskins and red crossbills.

The dry environment supports reptiles, including the eastern box turtle, eastern fence lizards, five-lined and broadhead skinks, glass lizards, and green anoles. Snakes include northern pine snakes, timber rattlesnakes, black racers, smooth earth snakes, milk snakes, rat snakes, and copperheads. Amphibians are not common in this natural community because it is too dry, although Fowler's and American toads may appear.

These pine forests provide important habitat for insects; the foliage and bark of the trees provide niches for unique insects and their predators, while the abundant grasses and forbs provide grazing and nectar-gathering opportunities for a variety of bees, moths, butterflies, grasshoppers, flies, and beetles. These insects are in turn prey for many of the birds and reptiles listed above.

Fringed gentian is a rare plant that is associated with ultramafic rock.

Northern Pine Snake (*Pituophis melano-leucus melanoleucus*)

The northern pine snake is, as its name suggests, a denizen of pine-dominated forests. This large, thick-bodied snake is distinctively colored, with a whitish or cream-colored background and black or dark brown blotches. Like other pine snakes, this species is adept at burrowing through leaf litter and loose soil (Tuberville and Mason 2008).

The northern pine snake's primary range extends from north-central South Carolina westward into northern Georgia, eastern and central Tennessee, and central Alabama. Disjunct populations of the northern pine snake occur in central Kentucky and southwestern Tennessee, in New Jersey, and along the Blue Ridge Escarpment in Virginia and West Virginia. Preferred habitats include sandhills, pine barrens, and dry mountain ridges, usually near pine woods (Conant and Collins 1998). Loblolly, pitch, or Virginia pines are usually the dominant trees in their habitat, but they are occasionally found in mixed oak or other plant associations if the soil is loose enough to allow burrowing.

In Georgia, these snakes are found primarily in the Blue Ridge and Piedmont, usually in pine-dominated stands but sometimes in hardwood forests. While they are capable of climbing trees, they spend the vast majority of their time on the ground, often concealed under leaf litter. Because of their secretive behavior they are often overlooked, but may rarely be observed crossing roads or trails. They are considered uncommon in the state, but not imperiled (Tuberville and Mason 2008).

Northern pine snakes have a varied diet that includes mice, moles, chipmunks, squirrels, birds, rabbits, and eggs of various animals. Occasionally, a northern pine snake will enter an animal burrow and consume the inhabitant, then take possession of the burrow (Tuberville and Mason 2008).

Davidson Creek Botanical Area at the Popcorn Overlook

The Davidson Creek ultramafic barren site near U.S. 76 is a landscape of depressions, mounds, and lichen-coated dunite rocks. Biotite gneiss, dunite, and serpentinite rocks have all been identified here (S. Ranger, Atlanta, pers. comm.).

To reach the barrens and woodland area, cross the road on the northern side of the pull-in, and follow the trail. Teaberry (sometimes called wintergreen), a small, ground-hugging shrub that smells like wintergreen and has been used to flavor teas and breath mints, grows along the trail near mountain laurel and Bowman's root. An opening occurs, with diverse grasses and rattlesnake-master, at the top of the hill.

Beyond the opening and along the hill crest (off-trail to the right), the forest opens up, and pitch pine, Virginia pine, red maple, post oak, blackjack oak, sourwood, dogwood, and sassafras occur. Grasses and many forbs, including eastern flowering spurge, blazing-stars, milkweeds, goldenrods, and sunflowers, form a dense to patchy ground cover. The best expression of Appalachian ultramafic woodland occurs on the western side of the hill, where pitch pines (identified by the epicormic needles that grow directly out of the trunks) and stunted blackjack oaks grow above a dense, grassy groundcover. Gray-green boulders laced with lichens are strewn over the landscape. Trenches dug by prospectors are still present: they were mining for asbestos, which occurs in veins through the dunite. Red maples were invading many sites due to the absence of fire, but, as can be seen by the charred trees, prescribed fires are now being implemented. Ground-water surfaces in places and collects around rocks, creating small, moist areas where royal fern grows.

In early spring, trailing arbutus appears, followed by bird's-foot violet, barren strawberry, and Catesby's trillium, which yield to yellow stargrass, veiny hawkweed, mountain laurel, daisy fleabane, Robin's plantain, and woodland coreopsis, followed by whorled milkweed, blazing-stars, nettle-leaf sage, licorice goldenrod, and woodland sunflower (Govus 2001).

Location: From Main St. in Clayton, go west toward Hiawassee on U.S. 76/Ga. Hwy. 2/Lookout Mountain Scenic Hwy. approximately 12 miles. There are picnic tables at the site and an interpretive sign that briefly describes the geology and ecology of the area. The serpentine woodland is located on the south side of U.S. 76, across the highway from the overlook. Google Earth GPS approximate coordinates to the overlook: N 34.874897/W 083.574616.

High-Elevation Rock Outcrops

High-elevation rock outcrops are large vertical or horizontal rock outcrops that occur above 4,000 feet. On clear days, views from Georgia's high-elevation outcrop natural communities are spectacular, with panoramas of 8 to 10 ridges receding into the distance. Some views reach into the Piedmont, with Mount Yonah (White County) a prominent feature.

These outcrops are placed in a separate natural community because of their high-elevation flora. Some summits in Georgia support plants that are Pleistocene relicts. Blood Mountain (Lumpkin and Union Counties), in particular, harbors a high density of rare disjunct and endemic plants that inhabited rock outcrops or other montane habitats during the Pleistocene. Other ridges, such as Rabun Bald (Rabun County), Eagle Mountain (Towns County), Hightower Bald (Towns County), and Brasstown Bald (Towns and Union Counties), have records of high-elevation species. Indeed, because high-elevation outcrop communities are rare and distributed sporadically throughout the southern Appalachians, they harbor a number of rare species, as well as some plant communities that are globally imperiled (Wiser, Peet, and White 1996; Wiser 1998). Heavy and repeated use by rock climbers and hikers can cause damage to the fragile plant communities. Visitors should remain on established trails, realizing that the small, wizened forbs, shrubs, mosses, and lichens represent decades of growth under severe environmental conditions.

Shrub balds are communities of ericaceous (heath) or other high-elevation shrubs that typically occur above 5,000 feet in the southern Appalachians. Georgia does not have any known well-developed shrub balds comparable to the shrubby expanses on the wind-shorn high peaks of the Great Smoky Mountains. Areas similar to shrub bald communities, how-

Orographic fog often keeps high-elevation outcrops cool.

ever, occur on the pinnacle of Tray Mountain (Towns and Habersham Counties), around the rocky summits of Blood Mountain (Lumpkin and Union Counties) and Rabun Bald (Rabun County), and in openings in the montane oak community on Wildcat Mountain at Whitley Gap (White County). These sites are classified and discussed under the montane oak natural community (p. 74).

PHYSICAL SETTING AND ECOLOGY

Hydrology, geology, soil, and aspect interact to create differing conditions on high-elevation rock outcrops. The mineral composition of an outcrop affects the vegetation by influencing nutrient levels and habitat formation (Wiser, Peet, and White 1996). The bedrock type also dictates the tendency to weather into depressions and patterns of jointing in the rock, which in turn influence the accumulation of soils and the subsequent development of plant communities. Cliff-like

summits occur on Rabun Bald (Rabun County) and Hightower Bald (Towns County) and have ledges on which soil collects, while flatter sites, such as sites on Blood Mountain (Lumpkin and Union Counties) and Brasstown Bald (Towns and Union Counties), have depressions that host islands of vegetation.

Soil moisture levels vary from moist and organic to dry mineral soils. Hydrology varies from microsite to microsite, from summit to summit, from season to season, and from year to year. Seepage varies from constant to flowing only after heavy rains, depending on the pattern of rock fractures that store groundwater. Where seepage water is not present, the thin soils and bare rocks dry quickly after rain in areas exposed to sunlight (Schafle and Weakley 1990). In the highest elevations, especially those facing north, pockets of soil remain moist and plant decomposition is slow, creating organic soils. Thus, the cliffs and flat rocks of Georgia's high peaks have communities that differ within the

Mountain cinquefoil occurs on high-elevation outcrops. Although it looks like an herbaceous plant, it is actually a very small, woody evergreen sub-shrub.

space of a few feet. Aspect can also be an important hydrological control: south- and west-facing rocky summits lose considerably more moisture from evaporation and plant transpiration than north- and east-facing ones. The high elevations also experience higher precipitation rates because water vapor condenses in the cooler air and the plants lose less moisture in the cooler temperatures (Wiser, Peet, and White 1996; Wiser 1998). In some locations the fog that shrouds these sites and condenses on the plants may be acidic, and ozone may be hampering growth (Southern Man and the Biosphere 1996a). Further study is also needed to assess the effects of atmospheric pollutants on the vegetation of these high-elevation sites in Georgia.

VEGETATION

High-elevation outcrops tend to be complex mosaics of vegetation. Lichens and mosses colonize bare rock. Low-lying forbs and shrubs become established in cracks and depressions; seeps encourage mountain-dwarf dandelion (Wiser, Peet, and White 1996). Large islands and areas surrounding the outcrop host dense stands of mountain laurel, Catawba rhododendron, serviceberry, stunted oaks, and other small trees and shrubs. On the peak of Rabun Bald (Rabun County), dwarf pussy willow, bristly locust, and beaked hazelnut predominate in shrubby areas. Shrubby St. John's-wort is common on Blood Mountain (Lumpkin and Union Counties) and on outcrops near Brasstown Bald in Towns and Union Counties (Govus 2002b).

Most plants of these sites are perennial, reflecting the short growing season: annual plants generally do not have time to germinate, flower, and set seed in one season (Grime 2001; Wiser 1994). About one-fifth of the species, including some of the rhododendrons, hypericums, club mosses, and mountain laurel, are evergreen (Wiser 1994), which maximizes the opportunities for photosynthesis on warm days throughout the year (Grime 2001). Winter leaves turn red on some plants, such as three-toothed cinquefoil and Michaux's saxifrage: anthocyanins in the red leaves enable them to absorb infrared light from the sun. Most high-elevation outcrop plants flower in the summer, avoiding the danger of an early frost that can occur in upper elevations (Wiser 1994).

The species in these communities are also adapted to cold, harsh conditions that bear similarities to the Pleistocene outcrops and alpine tundra of which a few of the plants are relicts. To survive the extremes of cold, drought, and damaging winds, many high-elevation plants, such as granite dome hypericum, mountain-dwarf dandelion, silverling, Michaux's saxifrage, and three-toothed cinquefoil, grow in low-lying tussocks, bunches, or cushions. Their branches or leaves are tightly packed to retain moisture from rain and fog and reduce breakage from wind or ice. Their low stature enables them to benefit from the warmth that occurs inches off the ground, where the rocks are radiating the sun's heat (Capon 1994; Grime 2001). Many plants, such as mountain-dwarf dandelion, St. John's-wort, mountain laurel, and three-toothed cinquefoil, also have cup-shaped flowers that gather in heat (Capon 1994). Just as they preserve the heat during cold periods, the plants in exposed areas must avoid desiccation on dry rocks during warm summer days: the small, waxy, hairy, or curled leaves on St. John's-worts, saxifrages, alumroots, silverling, rhododendrons, grasses, and sedges reduce water loss. The lichens and mosses are poikilohydric—that is, they shrivel up and go dormant in drought and soak up water like a sponge and photosynthesize during wet periods (Capon 1994).

In contrast to some open areas, the ericaceous shrubby areas tend to be low in diversity, presumably because the herbs are outcompeted by shrubs. The shrubs' dense shade and thick leaf litter also often preclude trees from becoming established (Wiser, Peet, and White 1996).

The role of fire in determining vegetation on rocky summits is not known. Presumably the high elevation and exposed nature of rocky summits make them vulnerable to frequent lightning strikes, but the moist nature of shady high-elevation sites, the expanse of bare rock that acts as a firebreak, and the light fuel loads of the rocky areas prevent extensive or frequent fires (Wiser, Peet, and White 1996).

CHARACTERISTIC PLANTS OF HIGH-ELEVATION ROCK OUTCROPS

TREES

Downy serviceberry—Amelanchier arborea
Black birch—Betula lenta
Virginia pine—Pinus virginiana
White oak—Quercus alba
Scarlet oak—Quercus coccinea
Northern red oak—Quercus rubra

SHRUBS AND WOODY VINES

Black chokeberry—Aronia melanocarpa
Beaked hazelnut—Corylus cornuta
Smooth southern bush-honeysuckle—Diervilla sessilifolia
Witch-hazel—Hamamelis virginiana
Mountain laurel—Kalmia latifolia

Catawba rhododendron—Rhododendron catawbiense
Great rhododendron—Rhododendron maximum
Upland willow—Salix humilis
Smooth highbush blueberry—Vaccinium corymbosum
Deerberry—Vaccinium stamineum

GROUND COVER

Mountain angelica—Angelica triquinata
Southern harebell—Campanula divaricata
Rock harlequin—Capnoides sempervirens
Woodland coreopsis—Coreopsis major
Glade rushfoil—Croton willdenowii

Rock alumroot—Heuchera villosa
Cliff saxifrage—Hydatica petiolaris
Pineweed—Hypericum gentianoides
Shrubby St. John's-wort—Hypericum prolificum
Mountain dwarf-dandelion—Krigia montana
Early saxifrage—Micranthes virginiensis
Whorled aster—Oclemena acuminata
Appalachian rock-pink—Phemeranthus teretifolius
Appalachian milkwort—Polygala curtissii
Common little bluestem—Schizachyrium scoparium
Twisted-hair spikemoss—Selaginella tortipila

ANIMALS

Typical mammals of high-elevation rock outcrops include southern red-backed voles, small, mouse-like mammals that inhabit treeless mountain balds, presumably where some protection is offered by rhododendron and laurel. Bats, such as big brown bat and small-footed myotis, hibernate in rock crevices or caves, returning to the same places year after year. They inhabit nearby oak forests in the summer to feed on small insects and moths. Eastern woodrats gather acorns, hazelnuts, berries, and ferns in the adjoining oak forests. They gather twigs, mosses, and leaves to build nests in deep crevices. Usually, the nests are roughly 20 inches in diameter, but the efforts of several generations of eastern woodrats can result in nests up to 12 feet long, 6 feet wide, and 3 feet high. Many other creatures, including mice, spiders, toads, and lizards, find shelter in woodrat nests. Mice forage on insects in herb tussocks and nest in rock cavities.

High-elevation rock outcrops do not provide much breeding habitat for birds, but the scrubby edges around them do attract some species, such as dark-eyed junco, ruffed grouse, indigo bunting, and chestnut-sided warbler. The common raven, a rare breeding bird in north Georgia, nests on cliff-like summits (see the Featured Animal). The summits are excellent spots to watch for migrating hawks and turkey vultures, as well as barn swallows and northern swallows swirling around the peaks.

The thin soils of the outcrops do not hold enough moisture to supply suitable habitat for amphibians. Reptiles are able to tolerate dry conditions, but their activities are limited seasonally by relatively low temperatures. If deep crevices provide access to underground retreats, timber rattlesnakes may choose near-summit outcrops with southerly or westerly exposures as hibernation dens. The available season for foraging for prey such as small mammals is necessarily short, and thus, high-elevation timber rattlesnakes seldom reach the sizes that their low-country counterparts do. Gravid female rattlesnakes, which typically give birth to 6–10 young in the fall, use exposed rocks on which they bask during the summer to help incubate the developing embryos. Garter snakes are the most common snake species encountered on summit balds. Other reptiles include eastern fence lizards and skinks, all of which use exposed outcrops for basking and for hunting insect prey.

Rock harlequin

Common Raven (*Corvus corax*)

Famed in myth and literature, the common raven is the largest member of the crow family (Corvidae). In addition to being much larger and heavier than the American crow, the raven has a longer, more wedge-shaped tail, a heavier and more curved bill, and a ruff of feathers on its neck. In flight, the raven alternately glides and flaps more like a hawk than a crow and can descend rapidly from great heights to its perch. The call of the raven has been described as a guttural croak (Boarman and Heinrich 1999).

Ravens occur widely across the eastern hemisphere from northern Europe and the British Isles through central Asia to northwestern India, Iran, northwestern Africa, and the Canary Islands. In the western hemisphere the raven is found from northwestern Alaska throughout much of Canada, the western United States and Central America south to Nicaragua, the northern portion of the American Midwest and New England, and the southern Appalachians south to Georgia.

Ravens are found in a wide variety of habitats, including tundra, seacoasts, open riverbanks, rocky cliffs, mountain forests, plains, deserts, and scrubby woodlands (Boarman and Heinrich 1999). In Georgia, these birds are typically found only in remote forested locations at elevations above 3,500 feet, usually in the vicinity of rocky cliffs or ledges in a few locations in Rabun, Towns, Union, and Lumpkin Counties (T. W. Johnson 2010b).

Ravens are intelligent and highly social, with a diverse suite of calls, nonvocal sounds, and physical displays. These birds often perform aerial acrobatic maneuvers, such as tumbles and rolls, which resemble play behavior. These behavioral traits probably account for the raven's prominence in native cultures throughout its range. Ravens are primarily scavengers and opportunistic predators, with a diet that includes carrion, small mammals, berries, nuts, insects, amphibians, reptiles, crayfish, and the eggs and young of other birds (Boarman and Heinrich 1999).

Blood Mountain (Lumpkin and Union Counties)

The summit of Blood Mountain is unparalleled in Georgia in terms of its extent, species composition, and far-ranging views. The site is reached by hiking a picturesque portion of the Appalachian Trail to the peak of Blood Mountain, passing through coves, low- to mid-elevation oak forest, acidic cliff, and outcrop natural communities, pine-oak natural communities, and montane oak (with much white oak) natural communities before finally arriving at the summit.

The summit is approximately an acre in size, with spectacular views in all directions. A mosaic of plant communities grows here. Expanses of bare rock are interlaced with herbaceous vegetation growing in cracks and depressions. Stunted white oaks, northern red oaks, and Virginia pines are scattered throughout larger islands of vegetation, and thickets of rhododendrons and mountain laurels are scattered throughout. Perhaps more than any other site in Georgia, Blood Mountain possesses a portion of what Weakley (2010, p. 887) calls "the remarkable 'pseudo-alpine' flora of high elevation rocky summits." While some of the pseudo-alpine species are missing, Blood Mountain does possess several representative species, including three-toothed cinquefoil, silverling, rock alumroot, and Michaux's saxifrage. Other high-elevation plants on the summit include Catawba rhododendron, mountain-dwarf dandelion, black chokeberry, and mountain angelica. Other notable plants include witch-hazel, smooth southern bush-honeysuckle, black birch, serviceberry, deerberry, and shrubby St. John's-wort. The western side of the summit is a good example of ever-green shrub-type high-elevation oak forest.

Location: Blood Mountain is located on U.S. 19 and 129, roughly 21 miles north of Dahlonega, and just north of the Walasi-Yi Center at Neel's Gap. To reach parking for the Byron Herbert Reece Access Trail from the square in downtown Blairsville, proceed south on Ga. Hwy. 11/U.S. Hwy. 19/129 about 13.5 miles. The parking area is on the west side of the highway. Follow the Byron Herbert Reece Access Trail about 0.8 mile until the Appalachian Trail intersects it. The Blood Mountain summit is roughly 1.5 miles from the intersection. Google Earth GPS approximate coordinates to the parking area: N 34.741993/W 083.922666.

Low- to Mid-Elevation Mafic Domes, Glades, and Barrens

Mafic domes, glades, and barrens are open, rocky habitats that occur on mafic bedrock. Generally, a mosaic of barrens, woodlands, and glades is present over a dome-like substrate. Tree species that are usually indicative of fairly high nutrient conditions are present, particularly red cedar and white ash (R. S. Griffith 1991), and some base-loving species occur in the shrub and herbaceous layers. A unique convergence of species common to upper elevations, southern Appalachian endemics, base-loving species, xeric-adapted species, rare seepage species, and prairie species (Govus 2002b) can form globally imperiled vegetation assemblages. Although many other sites exist, eight examples of this natural community have been partially inventoried in Georgia, comprising roughly 125 acres;

together they host 11 species that are protected in the state and many endemic species (Govus 2002b). Views from the high, remote outcrops are outstanding.

PHYSICAL SETTING AND ECOLOGY

Mafic rocks (rocks rich in magnesium and iron) occur throughout the Blue Ridge and Piedmont. Compared to ultramafic rocks, they typically have less magnesium and iron and more calcium, so this natural community differs notably from the ultramafic barren and outcrop community. The bedrock is amphibolite or biotite gneiss with veins of hornblende. Nutrient levels can vary spatially because nutrient-rich veins of rock are interspersed with more acidic substrates, or because runoff from a mafic site pours onto an acidic one; the result is a mix of acid- and base-loving species growing within close proximity (Small and Wentworth 1998).

Topography ranges from nearly level to cliff-like (Govus 2002b). Soil depth also varies, ranging from bare rock, to shallow depressions or crevices with several inches of soil, to woodland soils that are up to 15 inches or more deep. Mafic rocks can weather to develop heavy, clayey soils that swell when wet, but shrink and crack when dry, making rooting in the soil difficult. The clays may form hardpans that prevent rainwater from percolating into the soil during the wet season. Also, water adsorbs tightly to the clay minerals, so that plants are unable to take up all of the moisture in the soil.

Rock outcrops are xeric environments because very little soil can build up to store moisture. Most mafic domes in Georgia are even drier because they face south to east (Govus 2002b), and water runs off the dome-like topography quickly. There are a few exceptions, however, where orographic fog keeps these sites moister and cooler than outcrops.

The exposed topography subjects these communities to lightning, but it is likely that lightning-ignited fires are spotty and low-intensity due to natural fire-breaks caused by rock outcrop expanses and the relatively sparse fuel load. Eastern red cedar, which is not fire-tolerant, is therefore common.

Trees and shrubs develop on deeper soils; forbs and grasses grow in shallow depressions and rock. As in all outcrop and cliff communities, droughts can cause vegetation to die back and intense storms may cause soil and plants to slough off of the outcrop.

VEGETATION

The mafic rock, combined with moderately high elevations and open, dry settings, creates a unique suite of species. White ash, usually an indicator of elevated calcium conditions when abundant (R. S. Griffith 1991), appears on nearly every site inventoried (Govus 2002b). Rock chestnut oak and eastern red cedar are also important canopy components, and pignut or mockernut hickory often appears. The shrub

Mafic glades and barrens are often a complex mix of vegetation structure.

layer may include blueberries, fringe-tree, and some calcium-loving shrubs such as wafer-ash, coralberry, or ninebark; in higher elevations black chokeberry and roundleaf serviceberry can appear. The herbaceous layer can be diverse, and, like the shrub and tree layers, contains species found on both acidic and more basic soils. Grasses or sedges may dominate, and higher sites may support mountain dwarf-dandelion and Beadle's mountain-mint, which are both southern Appalachian endemics.

Each inventoried site has a somewhat unique composition (Govus 2002b). Cedar Mountain (Union County), at roughly 3,000 feet in elevation with a southern aspect, has a woodland canopy of dwarfed common shagbark hickory. Eagle Mountain (Towns County), where steep outcrops vary from mid- to high (4,240 feet) elevations (with upper elevations qualifying as rocky summits), has abundant moss and huge colonies of lichens, which are probably thriving due to fog interception. Long Mountain (White County), at roughly 2,000 feet, supports an unusual assemblage of Canada columbine, northern red oak, pignut hickory, northern hackberry, American columbo, and common black-cohosh.

Eastern red cedar

EASTERN RED CEDAR

Eastern red cedar is well adapted to mafic domes, barrens, and woodlands because it favors soils that are low in phosphorus and high in calcium, with circumneutral to basic pH. Seedlings of red cedar are exceptionally drought-tolerant and can establish on the bare ground of erosion-prone sites (M. D. Anderson 2003). Because it can quickly develop taproots in crevices and has a shallow, fibrous root system (Converse 1983), red cedar often out-competes hardwoods in this natural community (Small and Wentworth 1998; R. C. Anderson, Fralish, and Baskin 1999). The foliage of red cedar concentrates calcium, and accumulation of needle litter can in turn further increase calcium levels in the soil (M. D. Anderson et al. 2003). The trees are typically stunted and gnarly (red cedar generally needs more than 1 foot of soil to grow more than 30 feet tall). Red cedars can live for 300 to 450 years. A 50-year-old tree can have a diameter of less than 2 inches in thin, dry soils (Converse 1983; M. D. Anderson 2003).

CHARACTERISTIC PLANTS OF LOW- TO MID-ELEVATION MAFIC DOMES, GLADES, AND BARRENS

TREES

Pignut hickory—*Carya glabra*
Hawthorns—*Crataegus spp.*
White ash—*Fraxinus americana*
Eastern red cedar—*Juniperus virginana*
Shortleaf pine—*Pinus echinata*
Virginia pine—*Pinus virginiana*
Rock chestnut oak—*Quercus montana*

SHRUBS AND WOODY VINES

Black chokeberry—*Aronia melanocarpa*
Fringe-tree—*Chionanthus virginicus*
Smooth hydrangea—*Hydrangea arborescens*
Shrubby St. John's-wort—*Hypericum prolificum*
St. Andrew's cross—*Hypericum stragulum*
Wafer-ash—*Ptelea trifoliata*
Smooth sumac—*Rhus glabra*
Coralberry—*Symphoricarpos orbiculatus*
Sparkleberry—*Vaccinium arboreum*
Deerberry—*Vaccinium stamineum*

GROUND COVER

Big bluestem—*Andropogon gerardii*
Common hairsedge—*Bulbostylis capillaris*
Southern harebell—*Campanula divaricata*
Hairy lipfern—*Cheilanthes lanosa*
Hairy coreopsis—*Coreopsis pubescens*
Poverty oat-grass—*Danthonia spicata*
Marginal wood-fern—*Dryopteris marginalis*
Common bottlebrush grass—*Elymus hystrix*
Creeping aster—*Eurybia surculosa*
Sunflowers—*Helianthus spp.*
Rock alumroot—*Heuchera villosa*
Cliff saxifrage—*Hydatica petiolaris*
Pineweed—*Hypericum gentianoides*
Mountain dwarf-dandelion—*Krigia montana*
Appalachian ragwort—*Packera anonyma*
Appalachian rock-pink—*Phemeranthus teretifolius*
Glade knotweed—*Polygonum tenue*
Little bluestem—*Schizachyrium scoparium*
Rock spikemoss—*Selaginella rupestris*
Narrow-leaf white-topped aster—*Sericocarpus linifolius*
Licorice goldenrod—*Solidago odora*
Yellow indiangrass—*Sorghastrum nutans*
Common clasping aster—*Symphyotrichum patens*
Blunt-lobed cliff fern—*Woodsia obtusa*

ANIMALS

The dry, open areas of montane mafic glades and barrens offer little shelter or nesting habitat for most species, but the many herbaceous species provide food for pollinators and animals that eat the seeds. Islands of shrubs and trees provide shelter, nesting sites, and food for browsers and those that eat the fruits of the trees and shrubs. Eastern red cedar is valuable because it offers year-round screening from wind and predators, and its berry-like cones persist through the winter and are consumed by many birds and small mammals.

Typical mammals that may venture onto the outcrops include southern red-backed voles, eastern chipmunks, and eastern woodrats. Crevices and overhangs are less common on mafic domes than on cliffs and many rocky summits, but bats may hibernate in those that do exist. Many birds, including cedar waxwings, purple finches, and ruffed grouse, eat the seeds within red cedar cones. Hummingbirds will nest in red cedars. Seeds from grasses and composites attract juncos and chipping sparrows. The herbs appeal to insects, which in turn attract insectivorous birds, such as phoebes, peewees, bluebirds, and others. Herbs, such as sunflowers and yellow indiangrass, also provide seeds for ground-feeding birds.

Rocky areas are inhospitable areas for amphibians, which require more moisture, but a variety of insects and lizards, such as eastern fence lizards, broadhead skinks, and five-lined skinks can survive in these xeric environments. Characteristic snakes include timber rattlesnakes (see the Featured Animal) and copperheads, whose gravid females use sites with southern or western exposures to help incubate developing embryos during the late summer and fall. As the sun warms the rocks on summer days, the snakes retreat to hideaways under large rocks. Hikers on the Appalachian Trail commonly sit to rest or eat on such rocks, often unaware of copperheads hidden beneath.

Timber Rattlesnake (*Crotalus horridus*)

Sometimes called the "velvet-tail," "canebrake," or "banded" rattler, the timber rattlesnake is found over a large portion of the eastern and Midwestern United States, ranging from New England to northern Florida and as far west as Texas, Oklahoma, Kansas, and Nebraska (Conant and Collins 1998). In Georgia, this species is found throughout most of the state, but may be absent from the Tallahassee Redhills region (W. H. Martin et al. 2008).

Timber rattlesnakes grow to lengths of approximately 33–60 inches, with Coastal Plain individuals typically larger than those from north Georgia. This stout snake has a broad, triangular head and a series of dark chevron-shaped cross bands. In the north Georgia mountains, timber rattlers from higher elevations tend to have a yellowish or olive brown ground color, while individuals at lower elevations tend to be dark brown to blackish. In the Coastal Plain, timber rattlesnakes tend to be tan, gray, or brown, often tinged with pink.

In the Piedmont and Coastal Plain, preferred habitats include upland forests, swamps and floodplains, wet pine flatwoods, and hydric hammocks (Mount 1975). In the mountains, favored habitats include upland hardwood and pine-hardwood forests, especially in areas with rocky slopes and ledges that provide suitable denning sites. Prey items include mice, shrews, chipmunks, squirrels, and weasels, as well as ground-nesting birds and lizards. Heat-sensitive sensory organs located on the sides of the head help timber rattlers locate warm-blooded animals, even in total darkness. When its prey is within range, the snake lunges forward with mouth open, striking and injecting venom through a pair of fangs.

Though this species is currently considered globally secure and abundant in the Coastal Plain, timber rattlesnake populations are reportedly declining in north Georgia. This decline is due primarily to habitat destruction and persecution by humans (W. H. Martin et al. 2008).

Big Cedar Mountain

The eastern slope of Big Cedar Mountain is a diverse, accessible mafic outcrop, with stunning vistas that reach to Mount Yonah and beyond. The uppermost portion has a gentle gradient, but the gradient is steep below and care should be exercised in exploring this site. This picturesque outcrop is a mixture of seepage areas, bare rock, glades, small woodlands, and barrens. The trees are stunted, and some are flagged, with limbs that appear to have been damaged by ice on this exposed site. Eastern red cedar is abundant downslope, but not at the summit of the outcrop. Other species, including pignut hickory, white oak, rock chestnut oak, American persimmon, and Virginia pine, mix with the eastern red cedar to form a classic expression of this mafic dome and barren natural community. Common shrubs and woody vines include fringe-tree, deerberry, wafer-ash, black chokecherry, and poison ivy. Herbaceous species are scattered throughout in cracks and shallow depressions. Forbs include common hairy coreopsis, spreading sunflower, small-headed sunflower, southern harebell, rock alumroot, nodding ladies'-tresses, ragweed, Michaux's saxifrage, Turk's-cap lily, Solomon's-seal, goldenrod, and Appalachian bluet. Grasses include Nuttall's reed grass, slender muhly, mountain oat-grass, slender-stemmed witchgrass, and big bluestem. There is also a seepage area with sphagnum moss (Govus 2002a).

Location: Big Cedar Mountain is located along the Appalachian Trail off of Ga. Hwy. 60, roughly 15 miles northwest of Dahlonega and 2 miles southwest of Suches. From Dahlonega, take Ga. Hwy. 60 north approximately 15 miles. Woody Gap is well marked with parking available on the right. From Woody Gap, walk roughly 1 mile east and then north on the AT to a small outcrop on the southwest side of the mountain. The larger, east-facing outcrop described here is located several hundred feet farther up the trail. Google Earth GPS approximate coordinates to the parking area: N 34.677779/W 083.999824.

Low- to Mid-Elevation Acidic Cliffs and Outcrops

Low- to mid-elevation acidic cliffs and outcrops are steep cliffs or overhanging rock outcrops that occur on low- to mid-slopes of nonmafic rock up to 4,000 feet, often forming gorges or river bluffs. These natural communities have a distinct flora, support rare and endemic species, and form important patches of diversity within the generally forested region of the Georgia Blue Ridge; they also provide habitat for many bryophytes as well as relict plant species (Newell and Peet 1998; Larson, Matthes, and Kelly 2000). Cliffs provide niches for hibernating mammals and reptiles, and their inaccessibility makes them ideal nesting and feeding places for vultures, hawks, and swallows.

PHYSICAL SETTING AND ECOLOGY

Bedrock, aspect, elevation, slope position, slope shape, and hydrology interact to create many microhabitats on cliffs and outcrops (Newell and Peet 1998; Larson, Matthes, and Kelly 2000). In narrow gorges where the sunlight does not penetrate, slope position primarily affects moisture levels and temperature. Upper cliff faces are hotter and drier than lower ones because they receive more sunlight. This gradient can be seen along the Chattooga River (Rabun County) and Tallulah Gorge (Rabun and Habersham Counties), where Virginia pine may cling to upper cliffs, while eastern hemlocks take hold on lower ones (Riddle 2005). In wider valleys, aspect is important: south- to west-facing cliffs are hotter and drier than north-facing ones because they are more exposed to sunlight. This pattern is notable in Tallulah Gorge State Park (Rabun and Habersham Counties; see the Featured Place). Wind is also a factor on exposed sites: it contributes to dry conditions and blows down trees (Newell and Peet 1998). Higher cliff and rock outcrops begin to resemble the high-elevation outcrop natural community, as seen on Wildcat Mountain and proceeding up the flanks of Blood Mountain.

Moisture conditions range from hydric on seep-fed ledges, as described under seepage wetlands (p. 137), to xeric bare rock. Rock crevices store water and protect roots from sunlight, enabling plants such as pines

Ledges, talus, and crevices on cliff walls provide distinct habitats, as seen here at Raven Cliffs.

and mountain laurel to grow. Soils vary from mineral soils that collect as particles erode from above to organic soils that form on some seep-fed ledges. Soil depth also varies: wide ledges can build up deep soils that support trees and shrubs, while vines and perennial herbs grow on smaller ledges with shallow soils.

The variety of microhabitats on a cliff face is closely related to the bedrock composition. Rock that erodes very easily can crumble too quickly to provide many stable habitats, whereas erosion-resistant rock, such as gneisses and the quartzite of Tallulah Gorge (Rabun and Habersham Counties), has many fractures that store water and erode to form crevices and ledges (Larson, Matthes, and Kelly 2000).

The harsh growing conditions caused by low moisture levels, intense sunlight, shallow soils, and wind limit vegetation to those plants with adaptations to drought and low nutrient levels. Many have thick,

waxy, and hairy leaves that retain moisture. Often plants grow very slowly due to the low nutrient and water levels. Lichens and mosses are poikilohydric—they are able to dehydrate completely and go dormant during drought, then spring back and photosynthesize when moistened by rain. Trees with wind-blown seeds, such as pines, may colonize crevices where the roots stay moist. Annuals are typically rare on cliffs (Larson, Matthes, and Kelly 2000). Some perennial plants grow roots that spread over ledges to absorb rainwater before it runs off. Less drought-adapted plants are confined to moister, north- to east-facing sites, low sites receiving little insolation, or sites where they can plant their roots into moist crevices (see the Featured Place for the floodplain and bottomland natural community [p. 150], where a moist cliff community is mentioned).

The patterns of vegetation succession on cliffs and outcrops are not well studied, but plant communities are probably relatively stable once established (Schafale and Weakley 1990). Plant communities may be destroyed by rock slides, sloughing off after heavy storms, or drought. In favorable areas trees, though small and contorted, may be quite old (Larson, Matthes, and Kelly 2000).

VEGETATION

Cliffs support a complex mosaic of communities, where variations in soil moisture, depth, and texture create many different conditions on the same cliff face. Lichens, mosses, and liverworts adorn otherwise bare rock. Contorted trees, such as Virginia pine, pignut hickory, shortleaf pine, sparkleberry, and rock chestnut oak, and shrubs or woody vines, such as deerberry and poison ivy, root in crevices or on deep

Southern harebell

ledges banked with soil. Dry to xeric communities occur on thin-soiled, sunny ledges, with grasses and perennial forbs, including mats of twisted-hair spikemoss, dwarf-dandelion, and oat-grasses (Gaddy 1998), as well as little bluestem, wide-leaved spiderwort, florist's gayfeather, southern harebell, pinweed, Appalachian beardtongue, and pineweed. Mesic to submesic conditions (ranging from evenly moist all year to sites subject to occasional drought) occur in shady spaces on north-facing cliffs or under rock overhangs, which can support wild hydrangea, foamflower, saxifrages, spleenworts, doghobble, climbing hydrangea, witchhazel, mountain laurel, great laurel, wood-ferns, alumroots, and white wood asters.

ANIMALS

Cliffs are difficult habitats for most wildlife because of their inaccessibility and extreme environmental conditions. They tend to be visited by animals for specialized purposes but have few year-round residents. The "urban cliff hypothesis" speculates that many animals now found in urban environments, including some species of rats, mice, birds, and bats, first cohabited with people in prehistoric rock shelters and caves. Rodents comprise most of the small mammals that use cliffs; mice, red squirrels, voles, and eastern chipmunks have all been trapped on cliffs in other areas (Larson, Matthes, and Kelly 2000). Some bats, such as the eastern small-footed myotis, big brown, hoary, and eastern pipistrelle, use crevices and ledge overhangs for hibernation and for summer daytime retreats. Since many cliffs are near rivers, they are ideal launching pads for nocturnal flights over the river in search of flying insects. Overhanging rock shelters and cave-like areas in cliffs (Larson, Matthes, and Kelly 2000) attract many mammals for shelter or hibernation.

CHARACTERISTIC PLANTS OF LOW- TO MID-ELEVATION ACIDIC CLIFFS AND OUTCROPS

TREES

Downy serviceberry—Amelanchier arborea
Shortleaf pine—Pinus echinata
White pine—Pinus strobus
Virginia pine—Pinus virginiana
Rock chestnut oak—Quercus montana

SHRUBS AND WOODY VINES

Red chokeberry—Aronia arbutifolia
Black huckleberry—Gaylussacia baccata
Smooth hydrangea—Hydrangea arborescens
Shrubby St. John's-wort—Hypericum prolificum
St. Andrew's cross—Hypericum stragulum
Virginia-creeper—Parthenocissus quinquefolia
Great laurel—Rhododendron maximum
Gorge rhododendron—Rhododendron minus

Winged sumac—Rhus copallinum
Smooth blackberry—Rubus canadensis
Sparkleberry—Vaccininium arboreum
Deerberry—Vaccinium stamineum
Northern wild raisin—Viburnum cassinoides

GROUND COVER

Ragweed—Ambrosia artemisiifolia
Big bluestem—Andropogon gerardii
Mountain spleenwort—Asplenium montanum
Wavy hairgrass—Avenella flexuosa
Common hairsedge—Bulbostylis capillaris
Southern harebell—Campanula divaricata
Woodland coreopsis—Coreoposis major
Glade rushfoil—Croton willdenowii
Silky oat-grass—Danthonia sericea
Marginal wood-fern—Dryopteris marginalis

Common roundleaf eupatorium—Eupatorium rotundifolium
Creeping aster—Eurybia surculosa
Rock alumroot—Heuchera villosa
Cliff saxifrage—Hydatica petiolaris
Pineweed—Hypericum gentianoides
Mountain dwarf-dandelion—Krigia montana
Blazing-star—Liatris spicata
Appalachian beardtongue—Penstemon canescens
Appalachian milkwort—Polygala curtissii
Appalachian rockcap fern—Polypodium appalachianum
Common little bluestem—Schizachyrium scoparium
Twisted-hair spikemoss—Selaginella tortipila
Goldenrods—Solidago spp.
Wide-leaved spiderwort—Tradescantia subaspera

Cliffs can be excellent places to observe raptors that lift on winds generated by the steep topography. Especially in autumn, the broad-winged hawk, red-tailed hawk, Cooper's hawk, and sharp-shinned hawk can often be seen in migration. The turkey vulture often nests under overhanging ledges and in shallow caves. The dark-eyed junco hops around the grassy edges of cliffs, searching for seeds and insects. Other species that may nest on exposed cliffs include the eastern phoebe, the northern rough-winged swallow, and the barn swallow. The peregrine falcon is a species of Special Concern that formerly bred in the Georgia Blue Ridge. Historically, the peregrine falcon nested on cliffs in Georgia, but the state's breeding population is currently limited to several pairs nesting on tall buildings in the Atlanta metropolitan area.

Dry cliffs are habitat for the reptiles described under mafic outcrops. Streamside salamanders such as Ocoee, seal, and spring salamanders are associated only with cliffs that are permanently wet, with a thin, flowing sheet of water. In eastern Rabun County, the green salamander (*Aneides aeneus*), a species of Special Concern, inhabits moist, shaded cliffs that are not actually wet but have narrow, horizontal crevices that maintain a humid microatmosphere.

FEATURED ANIMAL

Green Salamander (*Aneides aeneus*)

The green salamander is a medium-sized member of the family Plethodontidae. This salamander can be readily identified by its greenish, lichen-like splotches and flattened head and body. The green salamander occurs in hilly or mountainous areas from northeastern Mississippi to southern Pennsylvania (Petranka 1998). In Georgia, this species occurs in scattered populations in the Cumberland Plateau / Ridge and Valley and northeastern portions of the Blue Ridge and upper Piedmont from the eastern half of Rabun County to the Tugaloo River valley just south of Tallulah Gorge. These two disjunct areas of distribution may represent diverging genetic groups within the species (M. J. Elliott 2008a).

Green salamanders are adapted to living in and around cliffs and outcroppings, especially those with abundant cracks and crevices. They prefer moist but not wet or inundated outcrops, and are also found in trees surrounding rock outcrops. During the warm months, green salamanders may be active on cloudy or rainy days, but are more active at night. Their color pattern serves as camouflage, helping them blend in with lichen-covered rocks and tree trunks. Flattened heads and bodies help green salamanders fit between narrow crevices, and expanded toe tips aid in climbing vertical surfaces.

Crevices in cliffs and outcroppings serve as shelter, foraging areas, and brooding sites for this species. Green salamanders breed from spring to fall. The eggs are deposited on the upper surface of the rocky crevice and guarded by the female until hatching occurs. During winter, green salamanders may aggregate deep within the crevices to avoid freezing temperatures.

Green salamander populations in the Blue Ridge have declined since the 1970s; factors in this decline may include climatic changes, habitat loss, disease, and overcollecting (M. J. Elliott 2008a). Populations in the Cumberland Plateau / Ridge and Valley ecoregion are thought to be stable. Due to its limited range and relative scarcity, the green salamander is protected in Georgia.

Tallulah Gorge State Park

The cliff faces of the spectacular Tallulah Gorge are up to 600 feet high. The North and South Rim Trails offer excellent views of the cliffs. These trails are also the Featured Place for the pine-oak woodland and forest natural community, which interfingers with the cliff vegetation. The river runs east-west through the park, and the cliffs face south and west so that the impact on vegetation of north versus south aspect is evident. Vegetation changes also correspond to elevation changes, as seen when going down the steps to the gorge and over the river. Additionally, the cliffs here have many microhabitats, crevices, ledges, talus, rock faces, cliff tops, and seeps.

Starting at the observation points along the North Rim Trail, there are panoramic cliff views. The xeric, south-facing cliffs support Table Mountain pine, Virginia pine, scarlet oak, sourwood, red maple, black gum, and rock chestnut oak. White pine, eastern red cedar, and downy serviceberry also appear on some crevices, ledges, and steep slopes. Shrubs include deerberry, sparkleberry, hillside blueberry, Hercules'-club, American beautyberry, mountain laurel, gorge rhododendron, and winged sumac. Herbs include blazingstars, goldenrods, silkgrass, sedges, asters, woodland coreopsis, wavy hairgrass, and old-field broomsedge.

As one descends down the stairs, conditions change to dry-mesic, and the community transitions to low- to mid-elevation oak forest, with rock chestnut oak, gorge rhododendron, white pine, eastern hemlock, mapleleaf viburnum, and sweet-shrub. Across the river, the north-facing cliff base hosts sweet gum, red maple, white pine, and tulip-tree. Galax, mountain laurel, American beautyberry, common silverbell, smooth hydrangea, smooth southern bush-honeysuckle, and cinnamon fern grow among some talus. As one moves upslope to the North Rim Trail, there are small patches of moist cliff outcrops with mosses, lichens, American holly, great rhododendron, gorge rhododendron, mountain laurel, poison sumac, mountain doghobble, red maple, and climbing hydrangea.

Location: Tallulah Gorge State Park is located on U.S. 441/23 and Ga. Hwy. 15 within the city limits of Tallulah Falls. At approximately 0.25 mile north of Tallulah Falls Dam, turn east off of U.S. 441/Ga. Hwy. 15 onto Jane Hurt Yarn Center Dr. Continue just under 1 mile to the visitor center.

Mountain Bogs

Mountain bogs are wetlands that occur on flat, poorly drained sites with peaty soils. Some have sphagnum moss in mounds more than 1 foot deep. Bogs are distinguished from seeps by having deep, peaty soils, high acidity, and more sphagnum buildup than occurs in seeps; in bogs the sphagnum frequently forms blankets and mounds, which rarely if ever occur in seepage areas. Georgia's mountain bogs support many rare species, including purple pitcherplant, swamp pink, sheep laurel, Cuthbert's turtlehead, and bog turtles (Patrick and Moffett unpubl. data). The flowering plants, along with carpets of red and green sphagnum mosses, make some bogs particularly beautiful. The bogs are

also important chronicles of how vegetation and climate have changed over time because they may hold pollen that has been deposited, layer by layer, in the peat over thousands of years (H. R. Delcourt 2002). Through pollen analyses, for example, it was learned that jack pine–spruce–fir communities once covered the Blue Ridge Mountains in Georgia (H. R. Delcourt 2002).

Mountain bogs are among the most endangered natural communities in the state. Most mountain bogs in Georgia were lost or seriously degraded when they were drained for agriculture or impacted by excess nutrients from adjacent agricultural land (Richardson and Gibbons 1993). Drainage methods included ditch construction, stream channel modification, and installation of drainage tiles or buried hollow logs with

Mountain bogs are typically embedded within forests, and often have a mosaic of vegetation, with pools of water, sphagnum mounds, swaths of herbaceous plants, trees, and shrubby areas.

bored holes. Once in place, the buried logs do not rot because of the acidic, low-oxygen conditions. Bogs near stream floodplains were often the first mountain habitats to be drained and converted to farmland by early settlers because they were flat, with rich soils and a nearby water supply. Other low-lying bogs have been inundated by reservoirs or obliterated by development.

PHYSICAL SETTING AND ECOLOGY

Bogs are traditionally defined as peat-forming, acidic, nutrient-poor wetlands that are ombrotrophic (they

are replenished by precipitation), with thick layers of peat that block groundwater from entering them (Mitsch and Gosselink 1993). In contrast, fens are defined as less acidic habitats that receive fresh groundwater inputs and are often dominated by graminoids (Schafale and Weakley 1990; Mitsch and Gosselink 1993). In general, the acidic bedrock of the Georgia mountains prevents the formation of true fens, but a combination of groundwater seepage, high levels of rainfall, and acidic soils blurs the differences between bogs and fens (Porcher and Rayner 2001). While most southern Appalachian bogs appear to be acidic (Schafale and Weakley 1990), there is a lot of species overlap along the gradient of fen to bog, and some of Georgia's bogs might be considered "poor fens" (Mitsch and Gosselink 1993; Porcher and Rayner 2001). The relationship between pH and vegetation in Georgia mountain bogs, however, has not yet been studied.

Hydrology is the most important environmental influence but because the mountain bogs in Georgia have been degraded through drainage or disruption of natural disturbance regimes, their natural processes are not well understood (Schafale and Weakley 1990). One hydrologic setting occurs in Tom's Swamp (Rabun County), Hedden Bog (Rabun County), Hale Ridge (Rabun County), and Keener Creek (Rabun County), which are all situated at flat valley heads and receive water from both precipitation and seepage from adjacent slopes. Another hydrologic setting for mountain bogs was once more common just above the active floodplains of some mountain rivers in Georgia, such as the Little Tennessee, as evidenced by patches of dark, black soil that can still be seen in what are now agricultural fields (S. Bowling, Atlanta, pers. comm.). These former bogs would have developed on clayey alluvial soils where water ponded in low spots behind old levees and in swales and abandoned stream channels that had filled with organic matter (R. Sutter, Enduring Conservation Outcomes, pers. comm.).

Beaver dams may also catalyze the formation of some bogs or change the hydrology of existing ones, such that bogs form as beaver ponds fill in with organic material and sediment (Schafale and Weakley 1990). In Hedden Bog (Rabun County), which has a more open canopy and larger expanses of forbs than the other bogs, recent beaver activity has killed many trees, resulting in a mosaic of seepy areas, peat mounds, forest, and stream channels. Indeed, evidence of recent and past beaver activity is apparent in many of the large bog complexes in Georgia (M. Moffett, Ga. DNR, pers. comm.).

It has been suggested that when beavers were abundant and mountain wetland systems were less fragmented, orderly stages of succession facilitated by the creation, maturation, and eventual abandonment of beaver ponds/swamps could occur. Following abandonment of a pond by beavers, there would be dam breakage, exposed mineral and organic flats, and an abundance of sphagnum moss on the pond fringes. Herbs and graminoids, including rare bog flora, would then colonize the area. Fires may have occasionally occurred, enabling the bog to survive a few more years before it succeeded to a shrub or tree bog. At some point, the beaver may have returned to reclaim the area and start the process all over again. Thus, there could be enough bog complexes in varying stages of succession at any given time to function as a sort of "meta-dynamic" system (Morehead and Russel 1998).

Restoration of natural hydrologic conditions to mountain bogs is often difficult (Somers et al. 2000). Even partially functioning drainage ditches constructed decades ago can significantly alter bog hydrology, and buried pipes and tiles may be difficult to detect and remove.

In addition to hydrology, sphagnum mosses are major contributors to the acidic, peaty conditions of mountain bogs because their overlapping branches and leaf anatomy allow them to take up 15–23 times their dry weight in water (Mitsch and Gosselink 1993). Only the uppermost layers of sphagnum grow. The lower layers die and partially decompose to peat; hence, the common name "peat moss" (Mitsch and Gosselink 1993). Soils in mountain bogs are peaty because dead sphagnum, herbs, and shrubs can only partly decompose in the wet, cool conditions. Over time, the peat can grow into hummocks or domes or can spread out over adjoining areas like a blanket (Mitsch and Gosselink 1993). Mountain bogs are acidic because the slowly decomposing plant remains release humates (a broad family of organic compounds including tannic acids) and because living sphagnum moss produces organic acids (Mitsch and Gosselink 1993). Nutrients have little opportunity to enter a bog except by occasional floods and windblown dust.

The combination of saturated soils, low nutrients, and acidic conditions limits the types of plants that can become established. Alders adapt by fixing nitrogen from the atmosphere, while the laurels and rhodo- dendrons, with their associated mycorrhizal fungi, obtain nitrogen and phosphorus from the organic peat (J. E. Smith, Molina, and Perry 1995; Grime 2001). These evergreen plants can also photosynthesize all year, an advantage in an area where low-nutrient conditions slow energy production. Pitch pine, which appears on the most xeric, exposed sites of the Appalachians, also survives the low-nutrient conditions and constant wetness of mountain bogs, perhaps partnering with the same or similar mycorrhizae associated with the laurels (J. E. Smith, Molina, and Perry 1995).

Encroachment by shrubs and trees, including red maple, American holly, huckleberry, black gum, great laurel, and mountain laurel, are apparent in most of Georgia's bogs, particularly at Hale Ridge (Rabun County), Tom's Swamp (Rabun County), parts of Cooper Creek (Union County), Commissioner's Rock (Rabun County), and Keener Creek (Rabun County). Historically, multiple disturbance agents (grazing, fire, clearing) may have reduced dominance by shrubs (Schafale and Weakley 1990). Although the historic role of fire in mountain bogs is poorly understood, these woody invaders are now being removed through prescribed burning and hand-cutting. Ongoing efforts to restore mountain bogs are being conducted by the Georgia Plant Conservation Alliance and others.

VEGETATION

Mountain bogs encompass a mosaic of vegetation consisting of open alder thickets, heath tangles, or forests punctuating open expanses of herbaceous plants. Trees such as black gum, red maple, white pine, pitch

Purple pitcherplant

CHARACTERISTIC PLANTS OF MOUNTAIN BOGS

TREES

Red maple—Acer rubrum
Sweet gum—Liquidambar styraciflua
Tulip-tree—Liriodendron tulipifera
Black gum—Nyssa sylvatica
Pitch pine—Pinus rigida
Rock chestnut oak—Quercus montana

SHRUBS AND WOODY VINES

Tag alder—Alnus serrulata
Black chokeberry—Aronia melanocarpa
Mountain sweet-pepperbush—Clethra
    acuminata
Bear huckleberry—Gaylussacia ursina
Winterberry—Ilex verticillata
Carolina bog myrtle—Kalmia carolina
Mountain laurel—Kalmia latifolia
Maleberry—Lyonia ligustrina

Sweet azalea—Rhododendron
    arborescens
Great laurel—Rhododendron maximum
Allegheny blackberry—Rubus
    allegheniensis
Common elderberry—Sambucus
    canadensis
Greenbriers—Smilax spp.
Smooth highbush blueberry—
    Vaccinium corymbosum
Hillside blueberry—Vaccinium pallidum
Northern wild raisin—Viburnum
    cassinoides
Yellowroot—Xanthorhiza simplicissima

GROUND COVER

Fly-poison—Amiathium muscitoxicum
Sedge—Carex crinita
White turtlehead—Chelone glabra

Pink lady's-slipper—Cypripedium acaule
Orange jewelweed—Impatiens capensis
Common rush—Juncus effusus ssp.
    solutus
Cardinal flower—Lobelia cardinalis
Indian cucumber-root—Medeola
    virginiana
Royal fern—Osmunda regalis
Cinnamon fern—Osmundastrum
    cinnamomeum
Small green wood orchid—Platanthera
    clavellata
Roughleaf goldenrod—Solidago patula
Peat mosses—Sphagnum spp.
Swamp aster—Symphyotrichum
    puniceum
New York fern—Thelypteris
    noveboracensis

---

pine, or eastern hemlock are widely dispersed and sometimes stunted. The plant list above reflects the dominant plants of Georgia's mountain bogs, but each bog has its own character and suite of rare species (Patrick and Moffett, unpubl. data). For example, one bog, though drained and strangled by great laurel, supports swamp pink, painted trillium, and pink lady's-slipper. Another, very remote bog that consists mostly of shrubs, has clearings in which purple pitcherplants and swamp pinks are being planted by the Georgia Plant Conservation Alliance. Yet another has a seep-like character in places and supports many rare species including the purple fringeless orchid, purple pitcherplant, and marsh bellflower. Another is a network of wet, mucky, hummocky channels, with open, seepy expanses where jewelweed, hollow-stem Joe-pye-weed, and Cuthbert's turtlehead all bloom at once.

ANIMALS

Prior to European colonization, bogs were probably rich in animal life because the mosaic of open herbaceous areas, peat mounds, shrub thickets, and seasonal pools creates many microhabitats. Much of this habitat diversity has been lost due to shrub invasion, fire suppression, ditching, and draining, thereby decreasing faunal diversity.

Small mammals inhabit the soil and ground layers, particularly where the soil is damp but not completely saturated. Starnose moles burrow in the muck, searching for grubs and earthworms. The "tentacles" of these bizarre-looking animals help them feel their way through their dark domains (L. Brown 1997) and detect food (Burt and Grossenheider 1980); it is possible that the proboscis detects the electrical fields of earthworms and other prey. Meadow voles cut the grass and sedge stalks that have seed heads and cache them in runways. Pine voles construct runway systems in sphagnum bogs, as well. The voles also help, on a small scale, to keep the bog open: when eating the inner bark of small red maples, they sometimes girdle and thereby kill them. Southern bog lemmings burrow in mucky soils and eat sedges and grasses. They leave telltale bright green droppings because they do not digest chlorophyll. Mammals of Special Concern include the southern bog lemming and the starnose mole.

Mountain bogs are important foraging areas for ruffed grouse and (in the winter) American woodcock because the diverse plant communities provide a wide variety of food and the thick vegetation provides protection from predators. Several swallows and the eastern wood-pewee use bogs because the open habitat allows them to catch prey on the wing. The common yellowthroat makes its home among the herbaceous vegetation of these habitats. The willow flycatcher specializes on the woody brush within bogs. Now relatively rare in Georgia, this species may have nested in greater numbers when bog habitats were more common. The black-billed cuckoo, a species of conservation concern, may frequent mountain bogs.

Amphibians are better adapted to fen-like environments than bogs; the humic acids in sphagnum bogs harm the gills of many amphibians. The four-toed salamander, a species of Special Concern, nests in hummocks of sphagnum moss (M. J. Elliott 2008b); spring, red, and mud salamanders may inhabit less acidic bogs, along with northern cricket frogs, pickerel frogs, and green frogs. This environment does not support many reptiles, but it does harbor the rare bog turtle.

FEATURED ANIMAL

Bog Turtle (*Glyptemys muhlenbergii*)

The bog turtle is a small, semiaquatic turtle found in the eastern United States. A bright yellow or orange blotch on each side of the head and neck is a distinctive feature of this otherwise nondescript turtle. The body color is generally blackish or dark brown, with orange-red highlights on some individuals. The carapace (upper shell) is black or dark brown, sometimes with a lighter brown sunburst pattern on each scute (shell plate) (Carr 1952; Conant and Collins 1998).

Bog turtles are found in scattered populations ranging from New York, Massachusetts, New Jersey, and Pennsylvania southward to North Carolina, Tennes-

see, and Georgia. Preferred habitats include open bogs and fens, wet meadows, and slow-moving, mud-bottomed streams in open areas (Ernst, Lovich, and Barbour 1994). In the Blue Ridge of Georgia, bog turtles are known from only about a half-dozen locations. Many of these sites have been maintained in an open condition by periodic disturbance, including fire, beaver activity, and livestock grazing. Although generally very secretive, bog turtles can sometimes be observed basking in the open, especially after emerging from hibernation in the early spring. Their diet includes slugs, worms, insects, seeds, leaves, and carrion (Fahey 2008).

Because mountain bogs represent dynamic successional habitats, bog turtles must seek out new sites when these habitats become overgrown with woody vegetation or otherwise unsuitable (Bury 1979). The small size and widely scattered distribution pattern of intact mountain bogs in Georgia make this a significant challenge. In the past, beaver activity helped to create and maintain suitable habitat for bog turtles, but overharvest of beaver in the Blue Ridge may have significantly reduced habitat availability. In addition, some bog sites have been drained, filled in, or invaded by non-native species. Road construction and other types of development also hinder the bog turtle's ability to disperse to new sites. Conservationists are working to restore bog turtle populations in Georgia through habitat restoration as well as captive propagation and release of turtles (Fahey 2008).

Songbird Trail Bog in the Lake Conasauga Recreation Area

Most bogs in Georgia contain so many rare species prized by collectors that their locations cannot be disclosed because unscrupulous people will poach the plants. On the Songbird Trail in the Lake Conasauga Recreation Area in the Cohutta Mountains, however, small boggy areas can be found along the edge of a wetland that was created by beavers. The mucky, organic soils of bogs are easily seen here, as are the characteristic clumps of sphagnum mosses. These small bogs offer a notable contrast to the drier forest along the trail. For example, one such area, roughly 300 square feet on a flat, low site, supports a dense layer of sphagnum moss. Fern-leaf moss is scattered throughout. Characteristic trees include tulip-tree, black birch, black gum, red maple, and eastern hemlock. Shrubs include mountain laurel, great laurel, and maleberry,

all of which bloom in May. Herbs include a turtlehead, cinnamon fern, cowbane, roughleaf goldenrod, and sedges.

Location: Lake Conasauga is located in the Cohutta Wilderness. Take U.S. 411/Ga. Hwy. 2/61/S 3rd Ave. north from Ga. Hwy. 2/Fort St. in Chatsworth for 4 miles. Turn right (east) at the traffic light in Eton, and proceed east on Forest Service Rd. 18/Old CCC Camp Rd. about 10 miles. Turn left on Forest Service Rd. 68 and drive 11 miles toward Conasauga Lake. Turn left on Forest Service Rd. 49 until you reach the "overflow camping area," where parking is available to access Songbird Trail. (Service Rd. 49 may not be posted. Follow signs for the "Overflow Camping Area" and Song Bird Trailhead.) The bogs are less than 0.5 mile from the camping area along the Songbird Trail. Google Earth GPS approximate coordinates to the campground are N 34.860746/W 084.649756.

Seepage Wetlands

Seepage wetlands occur where groundwater emerges at the surface on a slope, creating frequently saturated conditions and a relatively constant flow of water that usually fosters an herbaceous community. Seeps in the Georgia Blue Ridge vary in character and species composition. Mafic bedrock seepage areas host rare plants in expanses of meadow-like areas. One very rare seepage bog has large swaths of pitcherplants and Coastal Plain species. Streamhead seeps form picturesque grottoes, with trickles of cold, clear water, mossy stones, and an array of lush foliage with tall ferns. Seepage areas often cross through and under boulderfields. The seeps are important areas for amphibians, particularly as breeding sites for numerous salamanders.

PHYSICAL SETTING AND ECOLOGY

Mountain seepage areas can form in multiple ways. Groundwater that moves through rock fractures may reach the surface where the fractures intersect the hillside. Bedrock close to the surface may halt the percolation of rain and channel water to the surface of shallow bedrock. Groundwater also emerges where there is an abrupt change in slope, such as steepening into the side of a ravine or shallowing where a slope meets a flat floodplain. Rock crevices may channel groundwater to the surface. Seepage rates often vary with precipitation and soil depth. Seeps that are supplied by larger volumes of soil and fractured rock have more reliable flows.

The soil texture of seepage wetlands varies. Texture may be sandy or gravelly on steeper slopes where faster water flow winnows out clays and silts, leaving heavier materials behind. But mucky clays and thin layers of organic materials can collect at the base of slopes or on very gentle slopes. At high elevations, the soils may be more organic because the low temperatures and constant saturation create low-oxygen conditions that slow decomposition of plant material, blurring the line between mountain bogs and seeps, so seeps and bogs are sometimes classified as a single natural community (Wharton 1978; Porcher and Rayner 2001). In general, seeps have only minor amounts of peat accumulation and tend to be more herb-dominated than mountain bogs (Schafale and Weakley 1990).

Nutrients within seeps vary with the nature of the bedrock and colluvium through which the water flows, affecting plant composition (Schafale and Weakley 1990). For example, at Track Rock Gap (Union County), high calcium levels supplied by mafic colluvium and bedrock support base-loving species such as Virginia mountain-mint, fringed gentian, and swamp lousewort.

Although openings in the tree canopy or fluctuations in water level may occasionally shift species dominance, seepage wetland communities are probably quite stable (Schafale and Weakley 1990). Groundwater temperature does not vary greatly, and the saturated conditions and (typically) dappled shade limit the species that can colonize the sites. Two seepage sites that are being artificially maintained include an area under a powerline at Track Rock Gap (Union County) and a natural area that has been set aside on a golf course on U.S. 76 near Hiawassee (Towns County).

VEGETATION

Seepage plants include cutleaf coneflower, orange jewelweed, turtlehead, hollow-stem Joe-pye-weed, royal fern, kidney-leaved grass-of-Parnassus, Turk's-cap lily, cliff saxifrage, southern lady fern, New York fern, cinnamon fern, tassel-rue, lady-rue, thyme-leaf bluet, fragile fern, branch-lettuce, eastern blue monkshood, and water hemlock. Many of these herbs have a growth form that anchors them in the wet soils and helps them to persist and dominate seepage areas. For example, cinnamon fern, royal fern, and turtlehead spread by stout stolons or rhizomes, forming dense clumps that other plants cannot penetrate. Such dense herbaceous stands often demarcate seepage areas from the surrounding forest. Trees may appear at the edge of a seep and shade it, but generally the soils are too wet

Kidney-leaved grass-of-Parnassus

to support trees rooted within the seepage area (Schafale and Weakley 1990).

Seepage wetlands may intergrade into cove natural communities, with umbrella-leaf, wood-nettle, and other rich cove species appearing.

High Base (Mafic) Seeps. These occur where seepage water traverses mafic or otherwise base-rich rock to create rich assemblages of species that can include several protected species. Well-developed basic seeps are rare in Georgia. One occurs at the Brasstown Valley Parnassia Seeps (Towns County) and one at Track Rock Gap (Union County). Another has been set aside as a natural area on a golf course on U.S. 76 near Hiawasee (Towns County), and supports southern agrimony, orange jewelweed, Virginia mountain-mint, swamp rose, sycamore, swamp lousewort, cutleaf coneflower, hollow-stem Joe-pye-weed, Carolina wild-petunia, and common wingstem.

Vertical Rock Outcrop Seeps. These occur on ledges beneath seepage areas on cliffs. Deep layers of soil, sometimes peaty in nature due to the presence of sphagnum or the buildup of partially decomposed plant remains, develop on the ledges. These communities closely resemble bogs. Examples occur on Buck Knob (Towns County), Tallulah Gorge (Rabun County), and Grassy Mountain (Murray County), and support common grass pink, roundleaf sundew (a carnivorous plant), royal fern, tag alder, poison sumac, and monkey-face orchid (Gaddy 2000; Govus 2002b).

Montane Seepage Bog. In Georgia, this nearly qualifies as a mountain bog, but has too much surface flow to support the deep, peaty soils associated with true bogs. It is a hybrid between seepage wetlands and bogs. It occurs on saturated, acidic, sandy soil with some organic matter and is dominated by graminoids and forbs, with several carnivorous plants. This community is extremely rare and is described in the box below.

REED BRANCH WET MEADOW MONTANE SEEPAGE BOG

Georgia has one montane seepage bog, Reed Branch Wet Meadow (Union County), which is owned by The Nature Conservancy. This very gently sloping site collects enough water to support sphagnum moss but lacks the deep peat layers associated with bogs. It contains more than 1,400 federally endangered green pitcherplants and a unique assemblage of Coastal Plain, northern bog, and prairie species.

Disjunct Coastal Plain taxa include eastern beard grass, pipewort, slender marsh-pink, Virginia meadowbeauty, threeway sedge, narrowleaf sunflower, and bushy bluestem. Species affiliated with northern bogs include swamp aster, roundleaf sundew, and northern white colic-root. Prairie species (away from the seepiest areas) include yellow indiangrass and common little bluestem.

Green pitcherplants in bloom at the Reed Branch Wet Meadow Preserve

CHARACTERISTIC PLANTS OF SEEPAGE WETLANDS

Eastern blue monkshood—*Aconitum uncinatum*

White turtlehead—*Chelone glabra*

Water hemlock—*Cicuta maculata*

Umbrella-leaf—*Diphylleia cymosa*

Roundleaf sundew—*Drosera rotundifolia*

Hollow-stem Joe-pye-weed—*Eutrochium fistulosum*

Thyme-leaf bluet—*Houstonia serpyllifolia*

Orange jewelweed—*Impatiens capensis*

Yellow jewelweed—*Impatiens pallida*

Turk's-cap lily—*Lilium superbum*

Branch lettuce—*Micranthes micranthidifolia*

Bee-balm—*Monarda didyma*

Royal fern—*Osmunda regalis*

Cinnamon fern—*Osmundastrum cinnamomeum*

Cowbane—*Oxypolis rigidior*

Golden ragwort—*Packera aurea*

Kidney-leaved grass-of-Parnassus—*Parnassia asarifolia*

Cutleaf coneflower—*Rudbeckia laciniata*

Roughleaf goldenrod—*Solidago patula*

Oval ladies'-tresses—*Spiranthes ovalis*

Swamp aster—*Symphyotrichum puniceum*

Lady-rue—*Thalictrum clavatum*

New York fern—*Thelypteris noveboracensis*

Foamflower—*Tiarella cordifolia*

Tassel-rue—*Trautvetteria caroliniensis*

White-hellebore—*Veratrum viride*

Blue marsh violet—*Viola cucullata*

ANIMALS

The tall grasses and forbs that characterize some seeps provide good cover for some mammals, and the insects that graze on the herbs provide food for mammals, as well. Raccoons, opossums, coyotes, red foxes, bobcats, striped skunks, eastern cottontails, and white-tailed deer all frequent moist, brushy areas. Seepage wetlands in the Georgia Blue Ridge are generally too small to support distinct populations of birds, but instead serve bird populations from the surrounding habitats. Large numbers of ruby-throated hummingbirds are attracted to seeps when jewelweeds, bee-balm, and other nectar-producing plants are blooming.

Seeps are important environments for amphibians. Seal salamanders lay their eggs under rocks within shallow areas of current and may wander out into the leaf litter zone of the forest to forage during wet weather. Ocoee salamanders are abundant in mountainous seepages and small streams, and seepage salamanders may be common under leaf litter near seepages that drain cove forests. Spring salamanders are unusually common in high-elevation seeps and springs (Wharton 1978) and may move out onto the forest floor during rainy periods. An example of this diverse salamander community is found in Union County's Sosebee Cove, which contains all of these species as well as four additional species of dusky salamanders (Camp et al. 2002).

The herbs of seepage areas supply habitat for many invertebrates; in particular, seeps support the host plants of many butterflies. Nettles nourish the caterpillars of question mark, green comma, and red admiral butterflies. Sedges host the caterpillars of Appalachian eyed brown, Georgia satyr, and dun skipper butterflies. Violets feed the caterpillars of variegated fritillary, Aphrodite fritillary, Diana fritillary (see the Featured Animal), and great spangled fritillary butterflies. The caterpillars of black swallowtail butterflies consume water hemlock, which is violently toxic to mammals, including people.

Diana Fritillary (*Speyeria diana*)

The Diana fritillary is a member of the family Nymphalidae, or brush-footed butterflies. The wingspan of adults ranges from 3.4 to 4.4 inches. Males are brownish-black with orange wing margins. Females are blue-black with blue and whitish spots (Vaughan and Shepherd 2005b).

This species appears to be confined primarily to two separate areas—the Appalachian region from the Virginias and eastern Kentucky into northern Georgia and Alabama; and the Ozark and Ouachita Mountains of Missouri and Arkansas. In Georgia, it is found primarily in the Blue Ridge, with a few historic occurrences in the Piedmont. Collections have been recorded from Rabun, Union, Towns, Fannin, White, Cherokee, Fulton, and DeKalb Counties (L. C. Harris 1972). The Diana fritillary's preferred habitats include openings in mesic forests and low-elevation wetlands.

Adult males emerge from metamorphosis in June, and are followed shortly after by females. After mating, the female deposits her eggs on the forest floor. The eggs may be attached to dead leaves, twigs, or other material. The caterpillars hatch from eggs in the fall, over-winter in the leaf litter, and emerge the following spring to search for food (L. C. Harris 1972). The primary food plants of the larvae are violets. Adults feed on a variety of nectar sources, including milkweeds, Joe-pye-weed, buttonbush, white horse-mint, coneflowers, and ironweed (Scholtens 2005).

Known threats to this species include forest conversion and insecticides. This species seems to be particularly susceptible to *Bacillus thuringensis*, a bacterium used to control gypsy moths. Historic records indicate that the Diana fritillary underwent a major decline and range contraction, possibly due to intensive silvicultural practices and pesticide use. Some researchers believe that this species is recovering in areas where second-growth forests are becoming mature and gypsy moth-spraying is not widespread (NatureServe 2009c). While large clearcuts are likely detrimental, creation of small openings may be beneficial in promoting the growth of nectar plants.

Track Rock Gap Archeological Preserve

Track Rock Gap is best known as a 52-acre site that preserves petroglyphs that have been carved in large ultramafic rocks. These mysterious and possibly ancient petroglyphs appear to depict mammal and bird tracks, as well as human footprints and various geometric designs. The petroglyphs occur at the end of a short trail that originates in the parking lot at the site.

After viewing the petroglyphs, walk downhill to see the seepage wetlands at the base of the Arkaquah Trail. Because large seepage wetlands, as well as mafic substrates, are uncommon in the Georgia Blue Ridge,

this site supports unusual species and plant assemblages. Three seepage conditions are present. First, some seepage habitat occurs along the roadside ditches on both sides of the road. These ditches support fringed gentian, which has iridescent, fringed blue petals and blooms from late September to early November. A second type of seepage is maintained as a wet meadow by mowing a stream terrace under the powerline that traverses the site. This meadow has densely growing, tall forbs, many of which are 3 to 6 feet in height. Hollow-stem Joe-pye-weed, roughleaf goldenrod, Maryland meadow-beauty, swamp lousewort, downy agrimony, southern agrimony, cowbane, oval ladies'-tresses, eastern swamp milkweed, nodding ladies'-tresses, and many grasses and sedges grow here. A third area is the forested seepages that occur on the stream floodplain at the base of the slope, within a complex mosaic of seepage, cove forest, and bottomland natural communities, with monkey-flower, royal fern, Jack-in-the-pulpit, wild comfrey, lobelias, turtlehead, northern horsebalm, sweet gum, and red maple.

Location: Track Rock Gap is located on Trackrock Rd. off U.S. 76, northwest of Blairsville and 4 miles southwest of Young Harris. From the square in downtown Blairsville, go south about 2.8 miles toward Cleveland, Georgia, on Ga. 11 S/U.S. 129 S/U.S. 19 S/Cleveland St. Turn left at Town Creek School Rd. (CR 234) and go 1 mile. Turn left at Trackrock Gap Rd. and go approximately 3.8 miles. The Track Rock Gap parking lot will be on the left. Google Earth GPS approximate coordinates: N 34.883383 /W 083.877403.

White turtlehead

Spray Cliffs

Spray cliffs are areas on cliff faces that are kept constantly wet by misting and splashing from waterfalls. They usually occur in ravines and gorges and include the cliff over which the waterfall plunges, as well as the surrounding grottoes, plunge pool rocks, and other wet surfaces. This natural community has a unique mix of plants. Often shrouded in eastern hemlocks and rhododendrons, the spray cliffs can be exceptionally diverse in mosses and liverworts of widely differing origins (Zartman and Pittillo 1998). Several forbs, including lady-rue, umbrella-leaf, brook-saxifrage, thyme-leaf bluet, and kidney-leaved grass-of-Parnassus, are endemic to the southern Appalachians and were present here millions of years ago when the southeastern United States had a warmer climate (Schafale and Weakley 1990; Weakley 2010). Other taxa are tropical disjuncts or are closely related to tropical species; still

others are typically more northern in distribution and are presumably Pleistocene relicts (Weakley and Schafale 1990; Zartman and Pittillo 1998).

PHYSICAL SETTING AND ECOLOGY

Topography, elevation, and hydrology interact on spray cliffs to create a protected, humid, cool habitat that is buffered from disturbance and temperature extremes (Weakley and Schafale 1990). Spray cliff temperatures vary on average from 25°F to 73°F during the year, compared with those of adjacent ridge sites (from 3°F to 83°F) (Zartman and Pittillo 1998). The steep ravine slopes admit little sunlight, trap humidity from the waterfall spray, and block drying winds, so the sites stay cool and temperature variation is moderated; cold air drainage can amplify the coolness. The Blue Ridge Escarpment is particularly known for its spray cliff vegetation because moist air from the Atlantic Ocean rises when it encounters the Appalachians and condenses, creating high precipitation rates and relative

Microhabitats on a spray cliff

The lack of soil on the steep, rocky cliffs limits plant colonization to microhabitats such as crevices, seepage areas, cliff ledges, caves behind waterfalls, the stream edge, and rock ledges surrounding plunge pools. Soils that collect on the ledges tend to be organic and acidic because plant remains decompose very slowly in the wet, cool natural environment. Soil depth varies with the size of the pocket or ledge on which accumulation occurs.

The survival of endemic, northern, and tropical species attests to the stability of the spray cliff communities (Schafale and Weakley 1990). Protected grottoes in boulder piles, deep crevices, and recesses behind waterfalls may be undisturbed for long periods, fostering old-vegetation communities with rich bryophyte populations. Closer to the flood zone, floods may disturb vegetation every year, so species turnover is probably greater in these sites (Zartman and Pittillo 1998).

VEGETATION

Trees and shrubs are most often those of the acidic cove community; they grow on the edge of the spray cliff and occasionally within cracks on the cliff. No vegetation community dominates all, or even most, spray cliffs because the waterfalls are isolated from one another and dry natural communities between them hinder the spread of species from one waterfall to the next (Zartman and Pittillo 1998). Spray cliffs also differ markedly from one another due to the wide variation in habitat. Some are nearly barren, others have a complex topography hosting many different vegetation types and species; some are far richer in bryophytes than others (Schafale and Weakley 1990).

Each spray cliff community develops its own character. For example, Martin Creek Falls (Rabun County) is a large waterfall that was visited by William Bartram, who described it as an "unparalleled cascade" of Falling Creek; it was later visited and described by Francis Harper, who found it "wondrously enchanting" (Harper 1998, p. 387). The spray cliffs at this site host foamflower, Jack-in-the-pulpit, branch lettuce, mountain meadowrue, great blue lobelia, Virginia bugleweed, alumroot, and numerous mosses and liverworts. Shrubs include mountain pepperbush, tag alder, great laurel, yellowroot, and witch-hazel. In DeSoto Falls Scenic Area (White County), a waterfall is bordered by multiple spray cliff ledges that provide microhabitats for Christmas fern, alumroot, climbing

humidity within many gorges (Zartman and Pittillo 1998). In some more exposed sites, however, a south- to west-facing aspect or exposed position will increase dryness and temperature variability on spray cliffs.

Spray cliffs are classified as wetlands because constant waterfall spray moistens the rocks and saturates the soils that build on them. The extent and regularity of the spray will depend on the size of the stream. Seepage on cliff walls often adds additional moisture to a site. Flooding, along with waterfall spray, is an important influence on the vegetation because some plants are able to tolerate flooding better than others. Flooding regimes vary from site to site and from season to season, depending on the size of the stream and the precipitation patterns within its watershed. Some streamside sites flood almost annually, some flood only during huge rain events, and some sites may never flood (Zartman and Pittillo 1998). In drought years, the streamflow declines and waterfall spray and flooding are considerably less.

hydrangea, and northern horsebalm. In contrast, Ada Hi Falls in Black Rock State Park (Rabun County) encompasses a small spray cliff with umbrella-leaf, foam-flower, and mountain meadowrue.

The variety in habitat and species among spray cliffs was well captured in a study along the Blue Ridge Escarpment in Rabun County (Zartman and Pittillo 1998). Gold Mine Creek is a nearly vertical spray cliff with a north-facing aspect that supports a rich diversity of mosses and other bryophytes, including a southern Appalachian endemic moss. Lower Sarah Creek harbors a classic heavy shade wet grotto community, with both tropical and northern temperate species. White turtleheads dominate over delicate fern moss, thyme-leaved bluet, mountain meadowrue, a disjunct tropical moss, a rock clubmoss that is a northern temperate species of Special Concern, and a tropically affiliated moss.

ANIMALS

Little study has been made of spray cliff fauna. It is likely that there are some interesting and perhaps rare invertebrate species, but the inaccessibility of these sites makes inventory difficult. Small habitat size and precarious footing limits the vertebrate fauna: animals must be able to crawl over steep, slick rocks or fly from

Jack-in-the-pulpit grows on spray cliffs.

CHARACTERISTIC PLANTS OF SPRAY CLIFFS

TREES

Red maple—*Acer rubrum*
Black birch—*Betula lenta*
Eastern hemlock—*Tsuga canadensis*

SHRUBS AND WOODY VINES

Tag alder—*Alnus serrulata*
Mountain sweet pepper-bush—*Clethra acuminata*
Climbing hydrangea—*Decumaria barbara*
Witch-hazel—*Hamamelis virginiana*
Smooth hydrangea—*Hydrangea arborescens*
Mountain doghobble—*Leucothoe fontanesiana*

Great laurel—*Rhododendron maximum*
Yellowroot—*Xanthorhiza simplicissima*

GROUND COVER

Jack-in-the-pulpit—*Arisaema triphyllum*
Brook-saxifrage—*Boykinia aconitifolia*
White turtlehead—*Chelone glabra*
Umbrella-leaf—*Diphylleia cymosa*
Hollow-stem Joe-pye-weed—*Eutrochium fistulosum*
Galax—*Galax urceolata*
Alumroots—*Heuchera villosa*; *H. parviflora*
Thyme-leaf bluet—*Houstonia serpyllifolia*
Cliff saxifrage—*Hydatica petiolaris*

Orange jewelweed—*Impatiens capensis*
Lobelias—*Lobelia amoena*; *L. siphilitica*
Virginia bugleweed—*Lycopus virginicus*
Cowbane—*Oxypolis rigidior*
Kidney-leaved grass-of-Parnassus—*Parnassus asarifolia*
Meadow spikemoss—*Selaginella apoda*
Roughleaf goldenrod—*Solidago patula*
Lady-rue—*Thalictrum clavatum*
Delicate fern moss—*Thuidium delicatulum*
Tassel-rue—*Trautvetteria caroliniensis*
Sweet white violet—*Viola blanda*

ledge to ledge. Most mammals of this natural community are probably only occasional visitors.

Spray cliffs do not host a wide range of bird species, although the dense shrubs surrounding them can provide habitat for the hooded warbler, worm-eating warbler, Kentucky warbler, and Acadian flycatcher. Other warblers, tanagers, and thrushes that nest in the surrounding forests may be drawn to the reliable water source.

The wet environment is very favorable for amphibians, particularly dusky salamanders. Ocoee and seal salamanders shelter and lay eggs in rock cracks and crevices. Black-bellied salamanders are common in large, wet crevices, and Ocoee salamanders may be abundant on wet cliff faces. Dwarf black-bellied salamanders occur on spray cliffs on both sides of the Blue Ridge divide in Union, Towns, Lumpkin, and Gilmer Counties. The spring salamander occurs occasionally and feeds on small salamanders like Ocoee salamanders and the young of larger species.

FEATURED ANIMAL

Dwarf Black-Bellied Salamander (*Desmognathus folkertsi*)

The dwarf black-bellied salamander is a relative of the common black-bellied salamander (*D. quadramaculatus*). Black-bellied salamanders are the largest and most robust of the dusky salamanders, with body lengths exceeding 7 inches. They are also the most aquatic, seldom straying far from mountain streams and often seeking shelter under rocks within these streams.

Though similar in coloration and overall appearance to the common black-bellied salamander, the dwarf black-bellied salamander is approximately 30%

smaller at every developmental stage. Adults range from 4.5 to nearly 6 inches in total length, with males typically larger than females (Camp et al. 2002). The distribution of the dwarf black-bellied salamander is not well known. Populations have been documented from the Conasauga, Hiwassee, Nottelly, Toccoa, Chattahoochee, and Savannah River drainages in Georgia. This species has also been recently documented from North Carolina (Rothermel et al. 2007). Within this range, dwarf black-bellied salamanders are abundant in small to medium-sized high-gradient streams with rocky streambeds (Camp 2008a).

The dwarf black-bellied salamander shares habitat with the common black-bellied salamander, but appears to be slightly more aquatic. Dwarf black-bellies tend to be found within the stream channel, while their larger relatives are found along the stream bank (Camp et al. 2002). Dwarf black-bellied salamanders are most abundant in shallow areas of streams, where they take cover under rocks during the day. At night they emerge to forage for food, which probably consists of small invertebrates. This species has an aquatic larval stage that lasts two years; sexual maturity is thought to occur at an age of four to five years (Camp 2008a).

Though restricted in its range, this salamander is abundant where it occurs. Potential threats to local populations include over-collection, habitat degradation, and introduced diseases. Natural predators of dwarf black-bellied salamanders likely include snakes, birds, and small mammals (Camp 2008a).

Helton Creek Falls

Helton Creek Falls is a very picturesque yet accessible waterfall near Vogel State Park that is an excellent example of the spray cliff natural community. This beautiful, secluded site is nestled in a deep ravine that is shrouded by trees and shrubs; it also possesses a large spray cliff with numerous microhabitats. Moisture-loving plants are rooted among large boulders, on sandy deposits between the rocks, and on an extensive set of cliff ledges that cascade down the cliff over which the water falls. The site has two separate water-fall areas. The lower (downstream) portion of the falls is about 30 feet high. Here the rocks are scoured and support little vegetation; representative species include bugleweed, ebony spleenwort, and partridge-berry. The second falls, just upstream, is roughly 50 feet high. Here it is possible to traverse different portions of the spray cliff natural community and observe how vegetation composition changes. Mosses and lycopodiums drape many of the ledges, as well as some rocky areas around the pool below the falls. Tag alders line some cliff sides, while a canopy of tulip-tree, red maple, eastern hemlock, black birch, and Fraser magnolia rims the falls. These trees rise above mountain sweet-pepperbush and great laurel. Sands collecting around logs and rocks near the plunge pool support bugleweed and orange jewelweed, lady-rue, a cutgrass, foamflower, greenfruit clearweed, New York fern, southern lady fern, sweet white violet, round-leaf yellow violet, hollow-stem Joe-pye-weed, yellowroot, and a lobelia. Witch-hazel and smooth hydrangea also grow at the base of the falls.

Location: From the square in downtown Blairsville, proceed south on Gainesville Hwy./Ga. Hwy. 11/U.S. Hwy. 19/129 about 12 miles. Turn east on Helton Creek Road. Travel 2.3 miles (the pavement ends after 0.7 mile) to the parking area on the right, just beyond the trailhead sign. Google Earth GPS approximate coordinates to parking: N 34.753328/W 083.894289.

Cliff saxifrage

Floodplains, Bottomlands, and Riparian Zones

Floodplains, bottomlands, and riparian zones occur along rivers and streams where topography and riparian processes have resulted in some floodplain development. At least some species that are adapted to flooding conditions are present. Typical canopy trees are sycamore, river birch, red maple, sweet gum, green ash, sugarberry, box elder, silver maple, and some oak species.

This natural community includes rocky shoals and boulders that border streams, small levees, point bars, stream banks, and low terraces. Animal life is fostered by the ecotonal (transition from river to forest) habitat, along with canebrakes and shrubby areas that can support many bird and mammal species. In contrast to the broad bottomlands of the Coastal Plain, this natural community is small-patch in the Blue Ridge because floodplain features are poorly developed or nonexistent. Floodplain communities were best developed in the Broad Basins subregion, but agriculture and dams have eliminated most if not all of the larger examples.

PHYSICAL SETTING AND ECOLOGY

Throughout the Georgia Blue Ridge, streams have steep gradients and are cutting down through the rock instead of meandering from side to side to create broad floodplains (Christopherson 2009). Floodplains and riparian zones occur in small patches on poorly developed floodplain landforms including sand bars, shoals, boulder outcrops, small levees, and narrow streamside terraces. The streambeds tend to be rocky, with less sand or clay alluvium than those of the Piedmont or Coastal Plain.

On frequently flooded sites, such as point bars, shoals, and stream banks, vegetation must withstand the force of the floodwaters, so plants are often herbaceous or shrubby, with deep roots and flexible stems that can withstand flooding without snapping.

Orange jewelweed often covers large areas of floodplains.

Gradients are steep in many Blue Ridge streams. These streams are still cutting down through bedrock, rather than developing floodplains.

Acidic mesic cove natural communities often border streams.

The trees are often pioneer species and may be multitrunked, which is at times an indicator that they have been broken in the past by floodwaters and are resprouting. Farther from the stream, sites are either mesic or hydric, with mesic areas on higher ground.

VEGETATION

The vegetation is a mix of herbs, shrubs, and trees that are responding to the fine-grained flooding conditions that occur on these sites. Both mesophytic and bottomland species are present. Trees include sycamore, sweet gum, box elder, green ash, red maple, river birch, tulip-tree, American elm, sugarberry, musclewood, silver maple, and, in less disturbed areas, willow oak, cherrybark oak, swamp chestnut oak, silverbell, bitternut hickory, southern sugar maple, American holly, white oak, elms, and common silverbell. Shrubs include tag alder, mountain bushy St. John's-wort, Virginia water-willow, buttonbush, northern spicebush, American hazelnut, and common pawpaw. Woody vines, such as poison ivy, Virginia-creeper, greenbriers, grapes, and cross-vine, are common. Many herbaceous species are present, including river cane, sedges, grasses, orange jewelweed, golden ragwort, cutleaf coneflower, wingstem, sedges, false-nettle, cinnamon fern, knotweeds, spring beauties, Jack-in-the-pulpit, river oats, and American water-willow.

In the Georgia Blue Ridge, acidic cove forest natural communities often border the stream. Thus, eastern hemlock, great laurel, mountain laurel, mountain doghobble, black gum, black birch, Fraser magnolia, and white pine can be tightly interfingered among the floodplain landforms or occupy large stretches of the streambank.

CHARACTERISTIC PLANTS OF FLOODPLAINS, BOTTOMLANDS, AND RIPARIAN ZONES

TREES

Box elder—Acer negundo
River birch—Betula nigra
Sugarberry—Celtis laevigata
Green ash—Fraxinus pennsylvanica
Sweet gum—Liquidambar styraciflua
Tulip-tree—Liriodendron tulipifera
Sycamore—Platanus occidentalis
Willow oak—Quercus phellos
Black willow—Salix nigra

SHRUBS AND WOODY VINES

Tag alder—Alnus serrulata
Cross-vine—Bignonia capreolata
Trumpet-creeper—Campsis radicans
Buttonbush—Cephalanthus occidentalis
Climbing hydrangea—Decumaria
    barbara
Virginia-willow—Itea virginica
Common elderberry—Sambucus
    canadensis
Grapes—Vitis spp.
Yellowroot—Xanthorhiza simplicissima

GROUND COVER

Jack-in-the-pulpit—Arisaema triphyllum
River cane—Arundinaria gigantea
False-nettle—Boehmeria cylindrica
Sedges—Carex spp.
River oats—Chasmanthium latifolium
Hollow-stem Joe-pye-weed—
    Eutrochium fistulosum
Orange jewelweed—Impatiens capensis
American water-willow—Justicia
    americana
Royal fern—Osmunda regalis
Knotweeds—Polygonum spp.
Cutleaf coneflower—Rudbeckia
    laciniata
Common wingstem—Verbesena
    alternifolia

ANIMALS

This is a rich natural community for mammals as a result of the ecotones between bottomland, riverfront, and stream habitats. Minks are carnivorous mammals that den under the roots of trees along the stream in the abandoned lairs of other mammals. They feed on a wide variety of animals, including mammals, birds, eggs, insects, frogs, crayfish, turtles, and fish. River otters also den in river banks, and have a similarly broad range of prey items, but rely heavily on fish as a major portion of their diet in north Georgia. Muskrats den in stream banks, with holes to the surface hidden under plant growth or debris. They are omnivorous, feeding on a variety of aquatic plants as well as small animals; they are occasionally preyed on by mink and river otters (L. Brown 1997; Fergus 2003). Mink, muskrat, and river otter are found primarily along the river's edge, but may use other aquatic habitats in the floodplain, including marshes and ponds. Other mammals found in floodplain communities include raccoon, beaver, gray squirrel, golden mouse, black bear, deer mouse, silver-haired bat, gray fox, bobcat, coyote, short-tailed shrew, eastern mole, and opossum. Big brown bats will forage over rivers in the evening, and roost under loose tree bark during the day. Evening bats hunt above the tree canopy in search of flying insects, foraging along streams in bottomlands and roosting in loose bark or hollow trees during the day (Georgia Wildlife Web 2008).

The yellow-throated warbler will nest in sycamore trees along some of these streams and rivers (Bettinger 2010). Understory trees along wider stream corridors provide nesting sites for the Acadian flycatcher, while root tangles and bank crevices provide nest sites for the Louisiana waterthrush (W. D. Robinson 1995; Whitehead and Taylor 2002). Black-throated green warblers use eastern hemlock trees of the cove forest natural community for nesting and foraging sites during the breeding season and feed in these trees during migration (Morse 1993). Other warblers, including the Blackburnian, Cape May, and yellow-rumped, often feed in the eastern hemlock during migration (Morse 1994; Baltz and Latta 1998; P. D. Hunt and Flaspohler 1998). Areas of river scour provide brushy habitats that are often used by white-eyed vireos and common yellowthroats for nesting and during migration (Hopp, Kirby, and Boone 1995; Guzy and Ritchison 1999; T. M. Schneider et al. 2010).

Small stream floodplains have a diverse salamander fauna, including Blue Ridge two-lined salamanders, spring salamanders, spotted dusky salamanders, and mudpuppies. Characteristic frogs include northern cricket frogs, green frogs, bullfrogs, southern leopard frogs, and pickerel frogs. The secretive and rarely observed wood frog breeds in temporary pools near Blue Ridge streams during the winter months.

Beaver (*Castor canadensis*)

The beaver, a member of the family Castoridae, is North America's largest rodent. Adults range from 25 to 30 inches in body length, with a 9- to 10-inch tail. The fur is rich brown in color and the tail is paddle-shaped, dark, and scaly. Beavers have a pair of very large incisors that are used for felling and manipulating trees as well as for foraging and defense. Their broad, flat tails are used for stability while sitting, feeding, and swimming. In addition, the tail of the beaver serves as a warning device; when intruders are detected, the tail is slapped vigorously on the water, making a loud sound. Males and females are very similar in appearance (Burt and Grossenheider 1980).

Beavers are widely distributed throughout North America and are found statewide in Georgia wherever suitable habitat exists. They are primarily nocturnal. Their presence is most often indicated by the dams and lodges that they construct and their impact on trees and shrubs near the dam (Burt and Grossenheider 1980).

The diet of beavers varies seasonally. During the winter, preferred foods include twigs and bark of sweet gum, ash, willow, poplar, cottonwood, pine, and fruit trees. During the spring and summer, beavers relish aquatic plants and the tender green shoots of woody plants (Georgia Department of Natural Resources 2003).

Beaver dams can significantly alter the characteristics of a stream and floodplain by impounding upstream areas, drowning flood-intolerant trees, and increasing the extent of open-water habitats and shrub- or herb-dominated wetlands (see page 33 for a discussion of beaver ponds). Over time, the beavers may abandon an area and move to another site, allowing the floodplain environment to return to its former state as the dam disintegrates and the stream returns to its former channel. The ponds and wetlands created by beavers serve as important habitats for a wide variety of plants and animals, including numerous species of waterfowl and other migratory birds. Periodic beaver activity is thought to be important for the maintenance of rare wetlands, including bogs and fens.

Beavers are social animals and usually live in family units called "colonies." A single colony may contain a breeding adult pair and both yearling and juvenile offspring. Members of the colony work together to build and repair dams and lodges and to defend their territory from other beavers (Georgia Department of Natural Resources 2003).

In the late 1800s and early 1900s, the beaver population in Georgia was greatly reduced due to high demand for pelts, unregulated trapping, and habitat loss. Trapping regulations combined with restoration efforts initiated in the 1940s resulted in the successful reestablishment of local populations throughout the state. Today the beaver population in Georgia is secure and trapping pressure is low (Georgia Department of Natural Resources 2003). Public pressure to remove "nuisance" beavers from urban and suburban areas is increasing, while beavers have yet to reestablish populations in some remote mountainous areas of the state.

Jacks River Trail

The confluence of the Jacks and Conasauga Rivers exhibits many facets of the floodplain and bottomland natural community. Three different sites are featured here. The first is the Cottonwood Patch campground, which has an excellent example of bottomland forest. A trail leads through bottomland to the Conasauga River. Floodplain trees include river birch, sycamore, red maple, sweet gum, tulip-tree, and musclewood. The dense ground and shrub layers support bottomland plants, including orange jewelweed, yellow jewelweed, wingstem, hollow-stem Joe-pye-weed, trumpet-creeper, poison ivy, cutleaf coneflower, buttonbush, American water-willow, and river cane.

The second site is the trailhead of Jacks River Trail, and it is an excellent example of the floodplain along the river channel, with picturesque boulders and shoals. Vegetation on the bank and tucked between river rocks includes river birch, tag alder, Virginia-creeper, royal fern, muscadine, poison ivy, American water-willow, smooth southern bush-honeysuckle, royal fern, yellowroot, mosses, sedges, witch-hazel, red maple, sweet gum, mountain-mint, witchgrasses, blackberries, mountain doghobble, and hollow-stem Joe-pye-weed. A cove community, with eastern hemlock, white pine, common silverbell, basswood, eastern redbud, musclewood, and tulip-tree, occupies much of the stream bank. Moist cliffs with saxifrages, foamflower, mountain laurel, spiderwort, naked tick-trefoil, great laurel, and mountain doghobble flank the left side of the trail.

The third site is the Snorkeling Hole, located just over the state line in Tennessee. It is known for demonstrating the great aquatic diversity of the Conasauga River, which is best seen when snorkeling. Signs note that roughly 40 native fish, including redeye bass, freshwater drum, green sunfish, shiners, minnows, and the Coosa darter are here; other sources report up to 70 fish species, along with a diversity of mussels. The entire Conasauga watershed has 761 aquatic species.

Location: At approximately 13 miles north of Chatsworth on U.S. Hwy. 411/Ga. 61/2, turn right (east) at Old Hwy. 2 by Cisco Baptist Church. After roughly 1.8 miles, the road will turn to gravel. At approximately 8 miles from U.S. 411/Ga. 61/2 Cottonwood Patch Camp is on the left. After viewing the Conasauga River at the camp, return to the road and proceed north approximately 1 mile to Jacks River Bridge. Across the bridge, the Jacks River trailhead will appear soon on the right. To reach the Snorkeling Hole, turn left onto Ladd Springs Rd. immediately after Jacks River Bridge and proceed about 0.5 mile, crossing the state line into Tennessee, to the Conasauga Trail Head parking lot. Google Earth GPS approximate coordinates to Cottonwood Patch Camp: N 34.980424/W 084.638373.

Cutleaf coneflower

Chapter 4

CUMBERLAND PLATEAU | RIDGE AND VALLEY ECOREGION

Overview

The Cumberland Plateau / Ridge and Valley ecoregion occupies about 15% of the state. Wharton (1978, p. 108) noted that "nowhere in Georgia is the bedrock geology of the land more visible, exciting, or easier to relate to landform than in [this] region." Hillsides and road cuts reveal the tilted beds of bedrock, where very different types of rock are layered over one another. Erosion-resistant sandstone often caps the ridges, which feature dry forests with stunted trees, scenic views into the valleys below, steep cliffs, and towering rock outcroppings. In contrast, valley floors are underlain by more easily eroded limestone that fosters rich forests with extravagant spring wildflower displays, as well as unique calcareous fens, glades, and prairies with many rare species.

Vegetation influences from the west and the north are recognizable here. Calcareous glades share many endemic species with glades of Kentucky and Tennessee, while the Coosa prairies host disjunct Midwestern species. A Coastal Plain influence also occurs because the Coosa River valley forms a migration corridor from the Alabama Coastal Plain. These complex biogeographical relationships, combined with the varied geology of the region, make the Cumberland Plateau / Ridge and Valley ecoregion of Georgia unique to the state, with an unusually high diversity of natural communities, especially given its small areal extent.

The Cumberland Plateau / Ridge and Valley ecoregion viewed from Zahnd Natural Area

GEOLOGY, TOPOGRAPHY, AND SOILS

The Cumberland Plateau / Ridge and Valley ecoregion is about 3,122 square miles in size and is characterized by broad plateaus and a series of southwest- to northeast-trending ridges and narrow, parallel valleys. The southwestern Appalachians (Cumberland Plateau) and the Ridge and Valley ecoregions of G. E. Griffith et al. (2001) are combined here because they are both small in extent, have very similar bedrock and soils, and share many overlapping natural communities.

This ecoregion was formed from ancient coastal margins and inland seas. From roughly 570 million to 300 million years ago, seas advanced into and retreated from the interior of North America several times. Sediments were laid down in successive layers and over millions of years formed the major rock types found today: sandstone (from sand deposited in beaches, estuaries, and river channels), shale (from the muddy ocean bottom), limestone (from coral reefs and other calcareous skeletal debris), chert (where sponges and diatoms left mostly siliceous skeletal debris), and coal (from peat-filled swamps). When Africa and North America collided between 290 and 250 million years ago, these layers were folded and, in some cases, faulted. Since then, erosion has dissected the landscape, forming the valleys and ridges of today.

The ecoregion has six subregions, which are distinguished by differences in their physiography and geology.

Southern Limestone / Dolomite Valleys and Low, Rolling Hills.

This subregion consists of valleys and low, rounded hills. This area, along with portions of the Southern Shale Valleys, is often called the Great Valley. The geology is mostly limestone and cherty dolostone from the Knox and Conasauga Formations (described on p. 157). Limestone is easily dissolved by weakly acidic rainwater, so it erodes rapidly, forming valleys. Dolomite, which has more magnesium and less calcium, is slightly less susceptible to weathering and often forms low hills. Soils vary depending on whether they developed from limestone, dolomite, or chert. Soils that form over limestone are composed mostly of clay that remains after the calcium carbonate dissolves and may be moderately to poorly drained, although some areas have deep, rich soils. Limestone-derived soils are less acidic and more fertile than those formed from other rocks. Because limestone weathers unevenly, the depth to bedrock is variable, ranging from a few inches to more than 100 feet. The chert layers in the Knox formation resist chemical weathering, so as the limestone and dolomite dissolve away, many chert fragments remain. These chert fragments are called "float" and often form ledges or cliffs.

The dolomites and limestones of this subregion contribute greatly to the biodiversity of the state. They foster rare communities and diverse community variants in calcareous glades, barrens, fens, cliffs, and forests.

Southern Shale Valleys.

This low-lying subregion is made up of rolling valleys and rounded hills that are composed mainly of shale, or a shaly limestone, with some clayey sediment. Some shale outcrops are so highly weathered they can be ripped with a plow or even crumbled by hand. The soils tend to be deep and acidic. Exceptions occur, however, such as along stretches of the Coosa River, where carbonates are present near the surface. The valleys of the Coosa River and its tributaries can be as low as 600 feet. Some shale- or limestone-shale-derived soils are silty with abundant shale fragments; others are sticky clays that cause water to pond during the winter and early spring, creating wetlands such as flatwoods and wet prairies.

Southern Sandstone Ridges.

This subregion is made up of north- to northeast-trending linear ridges that alternate with the Southern Shale and Southern Limestone / Dolomite Valleys subregions. Sandstone resists chemical and physical weathering, and so forms ridge caps and cliffs. It consists of quartz sand with trace amounts of clay and iron and yields thin, stony, sandy, nutrient-poor soils. While most ridges are typically capped by sandstone, a few are topped by shale, siltstone, or conglomerate. The Armuchee Ridges make up much of this subregion, and include Johns Mountain, Rocky Face, Taylor Ridge, Horseleg Mountain, Simms Mountain, and Lavender Mountain. Much of this area is located in the Chattahoochee National Forest. The dry, acidic soils of this subregion foster oak-pine-hickory forests, pine-oak woodlands, sandstone glades and barrens, and rare montane longleaf pine woodlands and forests.

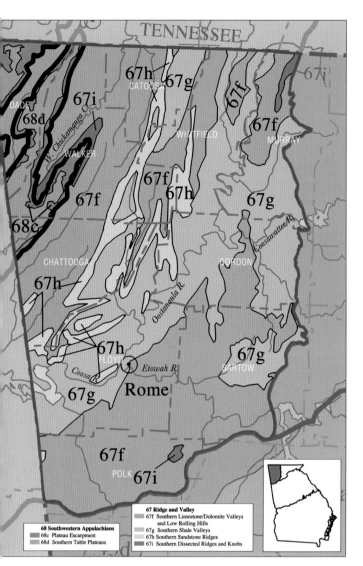

be more than 1,000 feet. A series of bedrock strata is exposed along the high escarpment slopes, including limestone, shale, siltstone, and conglomerate. Soils on slopes are derived from shale and from sandstone and shale colluviums. Talus slopes, often made up of sandstone blocks, occur on some of the lower portions of the escarpment.

Southern Table Plateaus. Often referred to as the Cumberland Plateau, this subregion consists of the broad, flat caps of Sand, Lookout, and Pigeon Mountains (often composed of the Lookout Sandstone/Gizzard Formation) which are predominantly Pennsylvanian-age sandstone, with some shale and conglomerate. The sandstone resists chemical and physical weathering, and so forms ridge caps and cliffs. The sandstone is a little downwarped, so the highest portions of the caprock are along the rim of the mountains and the lower portions are in the middle of the plateau. The Little River follows these lower areas. The highest point of the ecoregion (2,392 feet) is on the western brow of Lookout Mountain.

Sandstone consists of quartz sand with trace amounts of clay and iron that yield thin, stony, acidic, sandy, nutrient-poor soils. These soils foster oak-pine-hickory forests, pine-oak woodlands, sandstone glades and barrens, and dramatic cliff and outcrop communities, as exemplified on Zahnd Natural Area (Walker County) and at Rocktown (Walker County).

Southern Dissected Ridges and Knobs. This subregion is of very limited extent in Georgia, occurring in just a few areas. These ridges and knobs tend to be small and broken, in contrast to the long ridges and plateaus that characterize most of northwest Georgia. Shale is a common bedrock, but many knobs are interbedded with chert, siltstone, sandstone, and limestone. The shale-derived soils may be silty with abundant shale fragments.

Plateau Escarpment. The escarpment subregion is made up of the steep slopes that undergird the long plateau caps of the southern table plateaus. High-gradient streams cut through the slopes. Relief can

MAJOR ROCK FORMATIONS OF THE CUMBERLAND PLATEAU / RIDGE AND VALLEY ECOREGION

Individual rock formations are recognizable throughout the ecoregion, and are often one of the most important factors in the development of natural communities. They range from tens to hundreds or thousands of feet thick and can extend for many miles.

Lookout Sandstone/Gizzard Formation. Sandstone and conglomerate containing interbedded shale, siltstone, and coal. This formation is prevalent on the caps of Sand, Pigeon, and Lookout Mountains in extreme northwest Georgia and on Little Sand and Rock Mountains farther east. Sandy sediments that formed these rocks were deposited during the Pennsylvanian period.

Pennington Formation. Shale containing siltstone and occasionally fine-grained sandstone. The Pennington was deposited during the Mississippian period. This formation is beautifully exposed along Dougherty Gap Road at the southern end of McLemore Cove between Lookout and Pigeon Mountains and along Georgia Highway 48 between Cloudland and Menlo Counties.

Bangor Limestone. Calcareous limestone and dolostone, with a cherty layer near the base, deposited during the Mississippian period. Bangor Limestone is typically buried beneath debris from the overlying formations on the Lookout and Pigeon Mountain slopes. It is cavernous, however, and exploration of several area caves, including Pettijohns Cave in the Crockford–Pigeon Mountain Wildlife Management Area (Walker County), provides opportunities for examining this formation

Fort Payne Chert. Limestone containing abundant chert, deposited during the Mississippian period. The upper part of the formation is siltstone in some locales. Beds of shale, shaly limestone, and siltstone are scattered throughout the formation. This formation occurs on upper and middle hillsides around the edges of Sand, Lookout, and Pigeon Mountains. Limestone that is part of the Fort Payne Chert is exposed in the cliff walls of the Pocket in the Crockford–Pigeon Mountain Wildlife Management Area in Walker County.

Red Mountain Formation. Interbedded sandstone, siltstone, and shale, with some partly silty and sandy limestone, deposited during the Silurian period. This sandstone caps some of the Armuchee Ridges, such as Rocky Face Mountain, Johns Mountain, Taylor Ridge, and Horseleg Mountain.

Chickamauga Limestone. A calcareous limestone that forms the lowermost hillslopes of the Armuchee Ridges and extends northward from Pigeon Moun-

Sandstone, which is resistant to erosion, forms the cliffs seen here. Shale forms the tree-covered slopes and limestone typically occurs on valley floors.

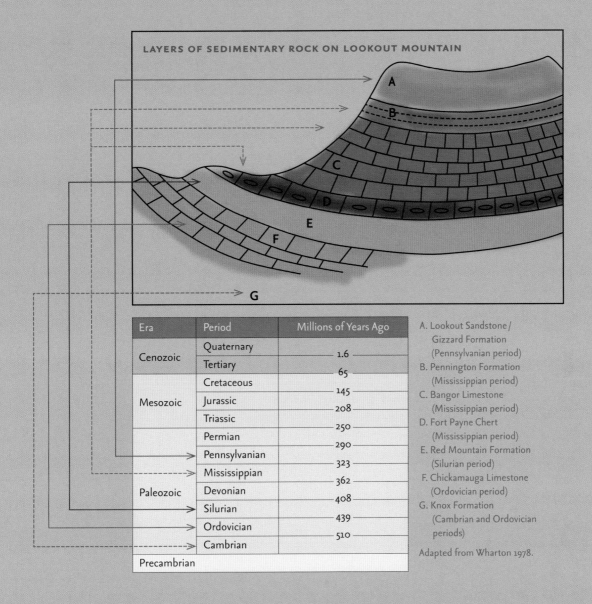

LAYERS OF SEDIMENTARY ROCK ON LOOKOUT MOUNTAIN

Era	Period	Millions of Years Ago
Cenozoic	Quaternary	
		1.6
	Tertiary	
		65
Mesozoic	Cretaceous	
		145
	Jurassic	
		208
	Triassic	
		250
Paleozoic	Permian	
		290
	Pennsylvanian	
		323
	Mississippian	
		362
	Devonian	
		408
	Silurian	
		439
	Ordovician	
		510
	Cambrian	
Precambrian		

A. Lookout Sandstone /
 Gizzard Formation
 (Pennsylvanian period)
B. Pennington Formation
 (Mississippian period)
C. Bangor Limestone
 (Mississippian period)
D. Fort Payne Chert
 (Mississippian period)
E. Red Mountain Formation
 (Silurian period)
F. Chickamauga Limestone
 (Ordovician period)
G. Knox Formation
 (Cambrian and Ordovician
 periods)

Adapted from Wharton 1978.

tain, forming low hills where the sandstone cap has been removed. Chickamauga Limestone was deposited during the Ordovician period.

Knox Formation. Interstratified limestone, dolostone, chert, and shale that have weathered to form the Great Valley between Cartersville and Rome (Butts and Gildersleeve 1948) and forms most valleys between the Armuchee Ridges. This formation was deposited during the Cambrian and Ordovician periods.

Conasauga Shale. Shales and carbonates that form nondescript rolling terrain in the Great Valley and portions of the Armuchee Ridges. The largest outcrop area is southwest of Rome, where Conasauga Shale crops out over more than 100 square miles along the Coosa River. This formation was deposited during the Cambrian period.

Rome Formation. Brightly colored (maroon, orange, and yellow) siltstone, shale, and sandstone, with rare dolostone and limestone. This formation was deposited during the Early Cambrian period. It is typically the oldest rock unit encountered in the Cumberland Plateau / Ridge and Valley. It occurs near Rome and Cartersville.

RIVER BASINS AND GROUNDWATER

The river basins of the Cumberland Plateau / Ridge and Valley ecoregion vary according to the topography and substrate. Stream bottoms on the sandstone caps are rocky and the streams do not meander much in the resistant rock, so floodplains are nonexistent or patchy and narrow. Some stretches form a chute-like environment, with many scour areas. These streams can have very low flows in the summer when the sandstone-capped ridges are dry. The Little River is unusual because unlike most rivers, which flow in valleys, it flows on the top of Lookout Mountain, in the down-warped trough portion in the center of the plateau. Forks of the Little River flow southwestward down this trough before joining together and plunging off the mountain through the spectacular Little River Canyon of Alabama.

In the Plateau Escarpment subregion, streams cascade down steep slopes, forming narrow, rocky channels with little to no floodplain development. Some waterfalls occur where sandstone meets more easily eroded shale; these waterfalls are often dry in summer. Most of these streams join to form the Coosa River watershed, creating what is known as a "trellis" pattern because the escarpment streams flow off the ridges at right angles to the streams that flow in the parallel valleys.

Most of the region is drained by the Coosa River system, which flows to the Gulf of Mexico. Because it is cutting through more easily erodible limestone or dolomite, the Coosa River is unusual for a river flowing in a mountainous region: it has cut a wide floodplain and meanders broadly over the floodplain, resembling a Coastal Plain river in some places, complete with abandoned meanders, backswamps, and levees.

The Conasauga and Coosawattee Rivers are major streams in the Coosa watershed. They join to form the Oostanaula River near Calhoun and then proceed southward toward Rome. The Conasauga River exits the Cohutta Mountains of the Blue Ridge ecoregion, heading northwestward into the Great Valley of Tennessee. Less than 10 miles from the Ocoee River it arcs to the south, turning away from the Tennessee drainage and heading south to become part of the Coosa River system. This odd pattern suggests that the upper reach of the Conasauga was originally a Tennessee (Ocoee) River tributary but was captured by an arm of the Oostanaula River. The spectacular aquatic biodiversity of the Tennessee and Coosa systems was further increased by divergent evolution of fish and mussel species stranded in the Conasauga when it was diverted into an entirely different drainage system.

The Oostanaula River joins the Etowah River in Rome to form the Coosa. The Etowah River flows westward from the Blue Ridge and Piedmont and enters the ecoregion near Cartersville. The Chattooga River flows southwestward from around Summerville to join the Coosa in Alabama in Lake Weiss. The northwestern-most portion of this ecoregion is drained by northeastward-flowing streams, most notably Chickamauga Creek, which are tributaries to the Tennessee River. The Tennessee River eventually flows into the Mississippi and the Gulf of Mexico.

KARST FEATURES OF THE CUMBERLAND PLATEAU / RIDGE AND VALLEY

Karst topography is a distinctive suite of landforms, including caves, sinkholes, springs, and disappearing streams, which develop in limestone because of the way it weathers in humid climates: the limestone dissolves along bedding planes, fractures, and joints, so weathering progresses rapidly in any zone of weakness where water can infiltrate. Below the surface, the fractures, joints, and bedding planes eventually enlarge as they dissolve to form voids and conduits and, eventually, caves. (See diagram on p. 449.) Karst topography is not well developed in the Cumberland Plateau / Ridge and Valley ecoregion because in many places limestone is not near the surface, relief is modest, and thick clay soils mantle most of the pinnacles and voids weathered into the limestone. Nonetheless, notable karst features do occur.

Sinkholes are depressions that form when limestone erodes from beneath the surface until the weight of the surface rock causes a collapse. Sinkholes are particularly common in the Knox Formation, which underlies much of the Southern Limestone / Dolomite Valleys and Low, Rolling Hills subregion, but they also occur in other limestone formations. They do not typically pond water in this ecoregion in Georgia but occur as steep-sided, vegetated depressions.

Impressive caves have formed in the ecoregion. The most extensive ones occur along the flanks of Pigeon, Lookout, and Sand Mountains (the Plateau Escarpment subregion), where the Bangor and Chickamauga Limestones are hundreds of feet thick. Ellison's Cave in Walker County has passages with a total length of almost 12 miles, including the 2 deepest cave drops in the continental United States: 586 feet and 444 feet. Other caves are scattered throughout the ecoregion wherever limestone crops out.

Groundwater occurs in huge quantities within the thick units of limestone and dolomite. Where the extensive network of subsurface, interconnected fissures in the weathered limestone intersect with the surface, they produce springs that discharge thousands and sometimes millions of gallons of pale blue water each day. Large springs are found where limestone occupies a significant thickness of the sedimentary sequence and outcrops on the valley floor. Regal Spring, on the banks of Armuchee Creek, discharges as much as 14 million gallons per day gathered through a network of interconnected fissures in the Knox Group carbonates forming the valley. Blue Hole, located at the eastern base of Pigeon Mountain, is an easily accessible and picturesque spring.

The Blue Hole, a well-known site at the foot of Pigeon Mountain, where a spring emerges from limestone bedrock

ENVIRONMENTAL FACTORS

The main factors that affect the distribution of the natural communities of the Cumberland Plateau / Ridge and Valley ecoregion in Georgia include soil moisture (which results from a complex interaction of slope aspect, relief, shape, exposure, and position), soil nutrients, hydrology, and fire, which is an important influence in shaping some communities.

Both soil moisture and soil nutrients are dependent on geology. Sandstone consists of quartz sand with trace amounts of clay and iron and yields thin, nutrient-poor soils. It resists chemical and physical weathering, so it forms ridge caps and cliffs. Shale is composed of aluminum-rich clay minerals with modest amounts of potassium and trace amounts of calcium carbonate and phosphate minerals. The rock easily crumbles so that shale typically forms scree slopes below sandstone cliffs or makes low hills rising slightly from limestone valley floors. The tight, sticky texture of the clay soils can retard rooting and limit access to water and nutrients. Limestone and dolo-

mite are composed of calcium carbonate and calcium-magnesium carbonate minerals. Limestone is easily dissolved by weakly acidic rainwater, so it rapidly erodes away, forming valleys. Dolomite, which has more magnesium and less calcium, is slightly less susceptible to chemical dissolution and can form low hills in the limestone valleys. The silica in chert is resistant to weathering, so it forms ledges and cliffs.

Because of the distinctive geology (no other portion of the state is made up of layers of sedimentary rock), there is a very different spatial distribution of natural communities in this ecoregion compared to that of all others. Natural communities are organized vertically because the landscape changes from calcium and dolomite in the valleys to shales on many mid-slopes or low ridges and sandstone and occasionally conglomerates on the plateau tops.

Dry, acidic natural communities form over the sandstone ridge tops. Aspect, slope shape, slope position, and exposure interact to create a moisture gradient here and on the mid-slopes below that ranges from

Sandstone on Lookout Mountain

Calcareous cliffs on Pigeon Mountain

submesic to xeric in these upper positions. North-aspect slopes foster cool, moist conditions because they rarely receive direct sunlight. In contrast, south-aspect slopes with greater exposure to sun experience higher temperatures and markedly more evapotranspiration. Flat or concave sites that collect more soil retain more moisture and nutrients. Exposed ridges and peaks—especially on the western sides of ridges—are more vulnerable to high winds, higher temperatures, and greater incidence of lightning strikes than more protected slopes.

More diverse communities occur over dolomite or limestone in the lower landscape positions. The moisture levels of these communities vary according to the amount of clay levels and soil depths. Often valley floors will collect thick, loamy soils that foster diverse mesic forests. Some valley floors or lower slopes, however, have an easily erodible substrate that maintains thinner soils and supports drier calcareous forests, while very thin soils with some exposed rock surface form cliffs, glades, prairies, woodlands, or barrens. The occurrence of limestone may lead to high plant diversity and the occurrence of rare plant species.

Hydrology plays a large role in forming several natural communities in this ecoregion. Several types of wetlands occur. Floodplains and bottomlands vary across the ecoregion, as discussed on p. 158. Depressional wetlands sometimes form where limestone layers beneath overlying substrates collapse and cause a depression that, in some cases, fills with water over time. Flatwoods and wet prairies occur when sticky clay soils pond water during the winter and spring. Seepage areas occur in swales on the sandstone ridge tops, as well as on calcareous substrates.

Fire has influenced the vegetation structure and composition of many natural communities, including acidic oak-pine forests, pine-oak woodlands, dry calcareous forests, prairies, glades, barrens, and seepage areas. As discussed on p. 36, regular fire results in the dominance of fire-tolerant species, as well as a more open vegetation structure, while the absence of fire encourages fire-intolerant species and, in general, a more closed structure. The frequency of fires caused by lightning ignition is not known: it is very difficult to separate human-caused from lightning-caused fire regimes (Pinter, Fiedel, and Keeley 2011). Lightning-ignited fires would have been rare on most southern Appalachian sites (P. A. Delcourt and Delcourt 1997), averaging about six per year per million acres (South-

ern Appalachian Man and the Biosphere 1996c). Most likely, lightning-ignited fires were more common in the Cumberland Plateau / Ridge and Valley ecoregion than in the much more highly dissected Blue Ridge ecoregion, but much less common than in the Coastal Plain ecoregion. Within the ecoregion, topography, aspect, soil moisture, and fire compartment size (the extent to which a fire can spread before encountering a moist or hydric firebreak) all vary, and so it is likely that natural fire patterns differ over the landscape accordingly. Most of the lightning-ignited fires would occur on exposed ridge tops and xeric, upper slopes that face west to south (Southern Appalachian Man and the Biosphere 1996b; P. A. Delcourt and Delcourt 1997). Humans have also greatly influenced fire patterns, however, as discussed in the following section.

LAND USE HISTORY AND HUMAN IMPACT

Indigenous Peoples. The Cumberland Plateau / Ridge and Valley ecoregion was inhabited by nomadic paleo-Indians as early as 13,000 to 14,000 years before the present (Hester 1970). Native Americans used fire over millennia to hunt and drive game; to clear the understory for travel; to prepare land for agriculture; and to reduce leaf litter when searching for chestnuts. Most likely, fires increased with the advent of the woodlands culture 3,000 to 4,000 years ago (Fesenmyer and Christensen 2010). These anthropogenically ignited fires were typically low-intensity brush fires, usually on ridge tops and south-facing slopes. Native Americans also cleared some lands for agriculture in localized areas (P. A. Delcourt and Delcourt 1997; D. E. Davis 2000; Fowler and Koponik 2007). The first inhabitants of the region to develop large permanent settlements were the Mississippian mound builders, who lived in the area from A.D. 900 to the 1600s. This was a complex, agrarian-based society that performed religious rituals associated with unique earthen mounds. They had a much greater impact than earlier inhabitants on the landscape, clearing vast areas of bottomland for cultivation and settlement. After coming into contact with members of Hernando DeSoto's expeditionary forces in 1540, the Mississippian mound builders began to succumb to a variety of European diseases to which they had no immunity. They were followed in the 1700s by the Cherokee, who set fires, hunted wild game, and raised crops in small agricultural plots in the fertile bottomlands along major rivers.

Agriculture and Grazing. The European settlers who followed the Cherokee had a more profound impact on the landscape. They cleared forests for farms and imported thousands of cattle and hogs. In the early 1800s, the major agricultural crop in this region was corn, but after the Civil War cotton became more prevalent. Dalton and Rome soon became prominent centers of the cotton trade (D. E. Davis 2000). As the demand for cotton grew, many of the remaining forests in the Great Valley were cleared and placed into cultivation. Roads were built to haul cotton and other goods to market, and flatboats and steamboats traveled the waters of the Oostanaula, Etowah, and Conasauga Rivers. Cotton production in the Great Valley continued well into the mid-20th century and stimulated the development of the textile industry.

Industrial Forestry. Much of the original forest cover in the region has been cut over, either to provide charcoal for iron smelting or for lumber. Large-scale timber operations funded by northern industrialists removed most of the remaining mature and old-growth stands. The Conasauga Lumber Company, based in Cincinnati, Ohio, owned 70,000 acres in Murray, Fannin, and Gilmer Counties and logged much of what is now known as the Cohutta Wilderness as well as the headwaters of Holly Creek and old-growth stands along the Conasauga River (D. E. Davis 2000). Industrial timber extraction reached its peak in the 1920s.

Many forests were "high-graded" in the past, with selective removal of economically important timber trees. Others have been wholly or partially converted to pine plantations through clearcutting and, in some cases, aerial seeding of pines (often with mixed success), though this type of conversion is much less common today. Much of the industrial pine plantation acreage in this region lies in the Great Valley near Rome.

Conversion of upland hardwood and pine-hardwood forests to pine plantations has also resulted in impacts to wildlife diversity. While not as widespread in this region as in other areas of the state, this change in land use has resulted in decreased habitat for a number of declining bird species: the birds dependent on mature forest are less secure here than in any other physiographic area in the southern Appalachians. The long-term health of populations of declining birds, including Acadian flycatcher, wood thrush, and yellow-throated warbler, will depend on main-tenance and management of these remnant forests as well as targeted restoration efforts. Restoration of more natural species composition in these stands may require timber-thinning as well as selective removal of some species and replanting of underrepresented species.

Prescribed Fire and Fire Suppression. Early settlers often burned the woods to provide new forage for their livestock. The fire-setting proclivities of early European settlers, as well as more intensive, stand-replacing "industrial" fires in the 1800s and early 1900s set by loggers and farmers, are acknowledged as having promoted pine-oak environments (Harmon, Bratton, and White 1993; Schuler and McClain 2003; Fowler and Koponik 2007), although in some instances fire frequencies were lower in the past 250 years than in earlier centuries (Fesenmyer and Christensen 2010). By the mid-20th century, policies of fire suppression were in place.

Although many natural communities in this ecoregion do not require fire, those that do have declined in extent due to fire suppression, creating a significant challenge to the maintenance of habitat diversity in this region. Throughout the region, a lack of fire has resulted in the decline in the extent and quality of habitats such as some seepage areas, sagponds, montane longleaf pine woodlands, oak and pine-oak woodlands and forests, calcareous prairies, canebrakes, and calcareous glades and barrens. Red maple and black gum have increased in abundance, while oaks and pines have decreased because they are less shade-tolerant and cannot regenerate under the closed canopy that occurs without regular fire (Lorimer 1993; Arthur, Paratley, and Blankenship 1998). Urbanization has amplified the problem because concerns about smoke management, air quality, and damage to structures make it difficult to implement prescribed burn plans for many of these important habitats (Sutter et al. 2011). Development of local fire management plans that provide opportunities for prescribed burns to facilitate habitat restoration while maintaining public health and safety will be critical for maintenance of many of the region's significant natural environments.

Patterns of Land Ownership and Development. In 1924, Georgia's state geologist declared that the cutover landscape of this region had lost much of its productive potential, making it a candidate for inclusion in the emerging national forest system in the Southeast. In the 1920s, the U.S. Forest Service began to buy up tracts of land for a newly authorized national forest in north Georgia. In 1930, the Service purchased 23,000 acres from the Conasauga Lumber Company, which became part of the Chattahoochee National Forest in 1937. Today the Armuchee Ranger District contains approximately 65,000 acres in the Cumberland Plateau / Ridge and Valley.

Second-growth hardwood forests on privately owned properties have been fragmented or destroyed more recently by residential developments, roads, utility corridors, and commercial centers as Chattanooga and Atlanta expanded. From 1974 to 2005, urban land cover more than tripled (Georgia Department of Natural Resources 2009b). Increasingly, houses and subdivisions are being constructed in more remote locations, including secluded coves; steep, forested slopes; and along the brows of Lookout Mountain and Sand Mountain (Georgia Department of Natural Resources 2005a). The region is fragmented by carpet manufacturing and other forms of industrial production. Row crop production, livestock grazing, and forestry are still prevalent in rural areas.

In recent years, private conservation groups, including the Open Space Institute, the Lyndhurst Foundation, The Nature Conservancy, the Georgia Land Trust, the Lookout Mountain Conservancy, and the Benwood Foundation, have partnered with the Georgia Department of Natural Resources to identify high-priority lands in this ecoregion and to obtain conservation easements on private lands adjacent to or in close proximity to existing conservation lands. The goal of this effort is to provide greater capacity for landscape-scale conservation and management of natural habitats and species of conservation concern in this region.

For some habitats, unmanaged recreational use represents a serious problem. High levels of use by rock climbers may threaten habitats such as sandstone barrens and limestone ledges, impacting plant communities and rare species through trampling, dislodgement of vegetation, and increased soil erosion. Similarly, cave exploration by careless cavers can degrade cave formations and populations of rare cave fauna. The Georgia Department of Natural Resources and private conservation organizations such as the Southeastern Cave Conservancy have worked to protect sensitive cave habitats from damage by constructing gates.

Cave-dwelling bat populations have begun to decline steeply in the eastern United States and adjacent Canada as a result of mortality from a disease known as white nose syndrome. This disease, caused by a recently identified fungus, is expanding and has now been documented as far south as Tennessee and Alabama. In all likelihood, this disease will soon reach caves in northwest Georgia. Any actions that increase stress or cause arousal in hibernating bats, such as recreational cave use, can exacerbate the effects of the disease (U.S. Fish and Wildlife Service 2010).

Use of off-road vehicles (ORVs) in or near streams, springs, calcareous flatwoods, calcareous prairies, and calcareous glades can damage those natural communities and the rare species within them. Careful monitoring and control of public access to these sensitive sites are significant priorities for land managers in this ecoregion.

Road and utility corridors may serve both beneficial and negative roles. Openings, which are maintained by mowing or herbicide application, may provide refugia for species that rely on open habitats. Road and utility corridor management, however, can pose problems for some nonforested natural communities, including calcareous prairies, acidic meadows, sagponds, glades, barrens, and seeps, particularly through extensive herbicide use. The Georgia Department of Natural Resources is working with managers of road and utility rights-of-way to encourage the implementation of vegetation management schemes that minimize impacts on rare species and sensitive habitats.

Non-native Invasive Species. Non-native invasive species pose significant threats to natural communities in this region. Notable examples of non-native invasive plant species of concern in this region include Nepal grass, Chinese privet, Japanese honeysuckle, oriental bittersweet, princess tree, silvergrass, and autumn-olive (Georgia Department of Natural Resources 2005a).

Water Quality and Quantity. More than 200 years of post-settlement conversion of forest and woodland habitats to agricultural uses have resulted in the loss of nearly all floodplain forests in this region. Drainage ditches and underground tile systems have been constructed to drain most floodplains for agriculture. Of those floodplains that remain, many have been impacted by point-source pollution, stream bank destabilization, and sedimentation from multiple sources (Georgia Department of Natural Resources 2005a). Sediments enter the streams when it rains due to poor storm water controls on construction sites, roads, improper postconstruction stormwater controls on developed areas, and poor agricultural practices. In several watersheds, such as West Chickamauga Creek and the Conasauga River, vegetated stream buffers are often too narrow to provide adequate erosion control, and in some areas livestock have unrestricted access to the streams. The livestock destabilize the stream bank, increasing erosion and degrading habitat for aquatic species. In some areas, local land trusts have partnered with private landowners and the local government to protect stream buffers by purchasing conservation easements. For example, Walker County and the Georgia Land Trust have collaborated to protect stream banks in the Chickamauga Creek watershed, using state and local funds. Similarly, in the Conasauga River basin, the USDA Natural Resources Conservation Service, the Conasauga River Alliance, and The Nature Conservancy are working to implement conservation easements along stream corridors.

Groundwater withdrawals for industrial, municipal, and residential uses, along with quarrying and contamination of groundwater, represent potential impacts to sensitive karst environments such as caves. This region contains the vast majority of Georgia's nearly 600 caves. Most of these caves are found on private land, and only a few have been adequately surveyed for rare cave fauna. Occurrences of several rare species, including gray myotis, Tennessee cavefish, and Tennessee cave salamander, have been documented from these caves. All of these species are particularly sensitive to changes in the quantity or quality of water in underground streams.

Upstream impoundments on the Coosawattee and Etowah Rivers have altered flow regimes such that the connections between river and floodplain habitats have largely been severed. Most of the major river impoundments (e.g., Lake Allatoona, Carter's Lake, Weiss Lake) affecting streams in this area lie outside of Georgia's portion of the Cumberland Plateau / Ridge and Valley, but the impacts of these impoundments extend upstream and downstream of the dams. These impacts include loss of stream habitat, changes in flood and inundation regimes, changes in channel depth, alteration of the sediment regime, creation of migration barriers, isolation of subpopulations, and alteration of temperature and oxygen regimes in the aquatic environment (Georgia Department of Natural Resources 2005a). Development of new water supply reservoirs to serve a burgeoning human population in this region has the potential to negatively impact aquatic communities and species of conservation concern. Careful evaluation of water supply alternatives and protection of streams harboring rare species are important considerations for maintenance of diversity.

Within the ecoregion, some impaired floodplain sites are being restored to more natural conditions. For example, the state-owned Conasauga River Natural Area in Murray County was overrun with Chinese privet and other non-native invasive plants and impacted by ditches and drainage tiles. Long-term management objectives for this site include reestablishment of more natural hydrologic conditions and restoration of native floodplain vegetation. Management programs along the Coosa River near Rome include mechanical and chemical treatments to remove non-native invasives and restoration of more natural hydrologic conditions. Overall, this region has seen a significant increase in streamside forests, more than any other region of the state, but still, nearly 40% of recently assessed streams were judged to be poor or very poor in terms of the Index of Biotic Integrity (Georgia Department of Natural Resources 2009b). Given the high number of imperiled mollusks in this ecoregion, improvements in water quality are a high priority for maintenance of wildlife diversity (Georgia Department of Natural Resources 2005a).

Natural Communities of the Cumberland Plateau / Ridge and Valley

UPLAND FORESTS

Mesic Forests. These occur in protected sites where soils are deep and rich, such as valley floors, ravines, protected coves on slopes, and the bottoms of some large sinkholes. They are often dominated by a diversity of late successional mesophytic species, such as basswood, American beech, yellow buckeye, tulip-tree, and southern sugar maple. Mesic forests are typically small-patch in the ecoregion today.

Dry Calcareous Forests. Deciduous forests that occur over dry to dry-mesic soils and support species associated with high-calcium soils, such as chinquapin oak, Shumard oak, chalk maple, white ash, eastern red cedar, eastern redbud, elms, hickories, coralberry, fragrant sumac, and Carolina buckthorn. Ericads are sparse to absent. Dry calcareous forests are large-patch.

Acidic Oak-Pine-Hickory Forests. Forests that occur on acidic substrates, such as sandstone, chert, and some shales. These forests, which range from xeric to dry-mesic, are usually dominated by oaks, such as rock chestnut oak, white oak, black oak, post oak, blackjack oak, southern red oak, and scarlet oak, with some hickories, black gum, red maple, and pines. These forests are large-patch in much of the ecoregion.

Pine-Oak Woodlands. Forests and woodlands that occur on xeric, rocky, exposed sites. They are usually dominated by Virginia pine and/or shortleaf pine, and dry-site oaks. These communities typically have an ericaceous shrub layer. The trees are often stunted. These forests were most likely large-patch when fire was more frequent; they are small-patch today.

Montane Longleaf Woodlands and Forests. Longleaf pine–dominated woodlands and forests that occur in a few xeric to dry montane sites. Associated (and at times co-dominant) species include dry-site oaks, such as scarlet oak, rock chestnut oak, and post oak, along with scattered shrubs and a fairly dense herbaceous layer. They are small-patch.

ROCK OUTCROPS, PRAIRIES, AND BARRENS

Calcareous Prairies and Barrens (Coosa Prairies). Grasslands that occur in a mosaic of deep-soil prairies and shallow-soil barrens restricted to calcareous substrates in the Coosa River Valley. Composites, including sunflowers, coneflowers, and blazing-stars, dominate along with the dominant grasses of the tallgrass prairie of the American Midwest: big bluestem, switchgrass, yellow indiangrass, and common little bluestem. These prairies are small-patch.

Calcareous Glades, Barrens, and Woodlands (Cedar Glades). Areas of exposed limestone interspersed with barrens, shrubby areas, and small islands supporting woodlands of stunted trees. They are dominated by eastern red cedars and are often called cedar glades. They are small-patch.

Acidic Glades and Barrens. Mosaics of bare rock, glades, barrens, and woodlands that occur on flat to gently sloping expanses of exposed sandstone or conglomerate on the caps of ridges. These are very dry areas supporting drought-tolerant herbaceous species as well as bryophytes with scattered Virginia pine, rock chestnut oak, and other dry-site oaks and pines. They are small-patch.

Calcareous Cliffs. Vertical to near vertical rockfaces that have high levels of calcium and occur on bluffs along rivers and on the sides of some valleys and canyons in the Ridge and Valley, often as small patches embedded within the mesic forest natural community. Vegetation grows on ledges and is rooted within the crevices of the rock.

Acidic Cliffs and Rock Outcrops. Steep to vertical outcroppings that often form bluffs along rivers or streams. Vegetation is sparse and limited to crevices within the rocks and shallow ledges. Moisture levels range from xeric to wet cliffs near waterfalls. They are small-patch.

WETLANDS

Flatwoods. Open to closed forests on gently rolling to flat, calcium-rich terrain. They are considered wetlands because depressional areas within them pond water during the winter and early spring; they are also known as upland depression swamps. Dominant tree species include willow oak, white oak, Shumard oak, cherrybark oak, green ash, white ash, and sugarberry. They are small-patch today in most areas, but large-patch examples may have occurred prior to ditching and draining activities.

Calcareous Seepage Fens. Herb-dominated complexes of seeps, springs, and small streams with soils high in calcium and magnesium that typically occur in valleys. They are small-patch.

Acidic Seepage Wetlands. Open forests in shallow swales or near streamheads on the caps of the Cumberland Plateau and ridges in the Ridge and Valley. They usually form in shallow swales or depressions or near streamheads. Red maple, black gum, sweet gum, tag alder, cinnamon fern, and royal fern are typical species. They are small-patch.

Sagponds and Sinkholes. Depressional wetlands with vegetation that is often distributed in a zonal pattern and ranges from open water to open forest. Typical woody species include red maple, sycamore, willow oak, black gum, sweet gum, green ash, southern wild raisin, tag alder, and buttonbush. They are small-patch.

Floodplains, Bottomlands, and Riparian Zones. Forests and vegetation patches that occur along streams, large creeks, and rivers and are characterized by trees and shrubs that can grow to maturity on soils that are saturated for limited periods, such as cherrybark oak, willow oak, swamp chestnut oak, Shumard oak, overcup oak, sweet gum, red maple, water oak, river birch, sycamore, tulip-tree, green ash, and box elder. This natural community encompasses a wide variety of habitats, including large and small floodplains as well as scour areas along streams. These sites are small-patch today. In the past, some large-patch examples would have occurred in the Coosa watershed.

Mesic Forests

Mesic forests occur in protected sites where soils are deep and rich, such as valley floors, ravines, protected coves on slopes, and the bottoms of some large sinkholes (Hinkle et al. 1993). Tulip-tree is the most common dominant tree in most sites now, but late successional mesophytic trees, such as basswood, American beech, yellow buckeye, and southern sugar maple, will eventually dominate. Northern red oak and white oak are common in some sites (Hinkle et al. 1993). September elm, Ohio buckeye, and blue ash, which are absent in other ecoregions and rare in Georgia, are notable elements of these forests. These natural communities can be lush and beautiful, particularly in the spring, when a rich diversity of spring wildflowers bloom, including celandine-poppy, Virginia bluebells, bent trillium, decumbent trillium, dwarf larkspur, and fern leaf phacelia, which are uncommon in other parts of the state.

Outstanding examples of mesic forests occur along the Shirley Miller Wildflower Trail in Crockford–Pigeon Mountain Wildlife Management Area (Dade County) (see the Featured Place), in Sitton Gulch in Cloudland Canyon State Park (Dade County), near Carter's Lake re-regulation dam (Murray County), and on some low slopes on Black's Bluff Preserve (Floyd County). These forests achieve their richest expression in the Southern Limestone / Dolomite Valleys subregion and to a lesser degree in the southern shale valleys, particularly where a shaly limestone substrate exists.

PHYSICAL SETTING AND ECOLOGY

Substrate and slope position are two key factors in the formation of mesic forests. These two features are often closely related in this ecoregion because the valley floors are often calcareous, which means that the most protected, moist sites within this ecoregion are also often the most nutrient-rich, so exceptionally diverse and lush plant communities are able to develop. In some cases, the soils on the valley floor may be less fertile and support less diverse forests.

Gap phase disturbance patterns occur here: small gaps are created by the fall of individual trees or branches, allowing shade-tolerant trees that have become established in the understory to reach the canopy, where they can live for centuries. Windthrow of individual trees is the most common way that gaps are created. Occasionally, tornadoes or thunderstorm downbursts may fell multiple trees, enabling pioneer species, such as black locust or tulip-tree, to retain a presence and increase diversity in the forest (Clebsch and Busing 1989). Such large openings probably occur only every few centuries on a particular site (Bratton 1994).

Lightning fires most likely occur only in extremely dry years, within a time frame of centuries, and under natural conditions are generally low intensity with limited effect (Clebsch and Busing 1989). Therefore, prescribed fires set near mesic forests should be managed with great care to ensure that the fire does not spread to these fire-intolerant habitats. Fires in this habitat will kill the dominant trees directly or weaken them so that they are vulnerable to insects and diseases.

VEGETATION

Vegetation is diverse, with dense herbaceous layers, sparse to moderate shrub layers, and canopies with tulip-tree and late successional, mesophytic trees. The plant assemblages vary in composition according to the levels of nutrients in the soils and the successional stage of the forest. Where base levels are higher, calciphiles are more predominant and a wide diversity of trees can be present, including basswood, yellow-wood, American beech, black walnut, blue ash and other ashes, southern sugar maple, tulip-tree, Ohio buckeye, bitternut hickory, and Carolina shagbark hickory. Where nutrient levels are lower, white oak may dominate the forest, with American beech, sweet gum, or tulip-tree as co-dominants; these stands sometimes border small streams, as exemplified on the Pocket Trail in the Pocket Recreation Area. Acidic environments may have eastern hemlock as an important component. Typical shrubs include smooth hydrangea, northern spicebush, common pawpaw, oakleaf hydrangea, Appalachian mock-orange, and wafer-ash.

The herbaceous layer can be "exceedingly rich and varied," as the noted ecologist Lucy Braun described (Braun 1950, p. 45), with bent trillium, lance-leaf trillium, southern red trillium, Canada waterleaf, Canada columbine, two-leaved miterwort, decumbent trillium, yellow lady's-slipper, wild hyacinth, celandine-poppy, toothworts, common black-cohosh, common blue cohosh, fernleaf phacelia, spring-beauty,

Twinleaf

dolls'-eyes, Dutchman's britches, yellow-mandarin, and many more.

ANIMALS

Characteristic mammals of this community include the eastern chipmunk, short-tailed shrew, pine vole, gray squirrel, white-tailed deer, golden mouse, gray fox, least shrew, eastern mole, southern flying squirrel, opossum, black bear, and raccoon. Several species of bats can inhabit these forests, including big brown, eastern pipistrelle, evening, hoary, and little brown. In addition, caves in limestone cliffs along the edges of this natural community provide shelter for a variety of cave bats, including rare species such as the gray and Indiana bats. Sites with large trees provide breeding habitat for the black-and-white warbler, and in some cases the worm-eating warbler (Kricher 1995; Hanners and Patton 1998). Other bird species with an affinity for hardwood forests, such as the red-eyed vireo, wood thrush, and tufted titmouse, nest here as

CHARACTERISTIC PLANTS OF MESIC FORESTS

TREES

Southern sugar maple—Acer floridanum

Yellow buckeye—Aesculus flava

Bitternut hickory—Carya cordiformis

Common shagbark hickory—Carya ovata

American beech—Fagus grandifolia

White ash—Fraxinus americana

Common silverbell—Halesia tetraptera

Tulip-tree—Liriodendron tulipifera

Umbrella magnolia—Magnolia tripetala

Basswood—Tilia americana

SHRUBS AND WOODY VINES

Common pawpaw—Asimina triloba

Smooth hydrangea—Hydrangea arborescens

Northern spice bush—Lindera benzoin

GROUND COVER

Dolls'-eyes—Actaea pachypoda

Common black-cohosh—Actaea racemosa

Northern maidenhair fern—Adiantum pedatum

Toothworts—Cardamine spp.

Common blue cohosh—Caulophyllum thalictroides

Silvery glade fern—Diplazium pycnocarpon

Wild geranium—Geranium maculatum

Crested iris—Iris cristata

Virginia bluebells—Mertensia virginica

Fernleaf phacelia—Phacelia bipinnatifida

May-apple—Podophyllum peltatum

Yellow mandarin—Prosartes lanuginosa

Bloodroot—Sanguinaria canadensis

Rue-anemone—Thalictrum thalictroides

Foamflower—Tiarella cordifolia

Trilliums—Trillium spp.

Tall white violet—Viola canadensis

well. In more mature stands where large snags are present, pileated and red-bellied woodpeckers are common (Dobbs 2010; Spivey 2010).

These forests support a rich diversity of salamanders, which forage in the arthropod-rich leaf litter of the forest floor during moist, temperate weather. This salamander fauna can be roughly divided into three components based on the general ecology of the individual species. The dominant group consists of completely terrestrial species that never voluntarily enter standing water, even to lay eggs. The northern slimy salamander, southern red-backed salamander, and southern zigzag salamander take cover under coarse woody debris or in underground burrows during adverse weather, the latter two species retiring to underground retreats for the entire summer. Red efts fit nominally into this group because of their terrestrial habits, but they represent the immature stage of the eastern newt, whose adult stage is an aquatic pond-dweller (D. J. Stevenson and Camp 2008). Largely fossorial (burrowing) marbled and spotted salamanders may occasionally be found in this community.

The second group is strongly associated with the twilight zones of caves or outcrop crevices. These salamanders, such as cave salamanders and Pigeon Mountain salamanders, occasionally forage in the leaf litter zone or more commonly migrate across this zone among scattered patches of preferred habitat. The third group includes species with strong ties to small streams, and they may occur under coarse woody debris away from the streams during periods of humid weather. Red salamanders, southern two-lined salamanders, spring salamanders, long-tailed salamanders, and spotted dusky salamanders fall into this category (Petranka 1998). The terrestrial wood frog may also occur in this habitat, along with Fowler's and American toads.

Common lizards in this community include the ground-dwelling and semi-arboreal broadhead and five-lined skinks, green anole, and eastern fence lizard, as well as the litter-dwelling ground skink. Eastern worm snakes, ringnecked snakes, and the occasional eastern milk snake are fossorial members of the snake fauna. Rat snakes, corn snakes, and common kingsnakes are the abundant constrictors. Common garter snakes search the forest floor for earthworms and amphibians, and black racers feed on lizards and small snakes (K. M. Andrews and Gibbons 2008a; R. N. Reed and Gibbons 2008). Two pit vipers (copperhead and timber rattlesnake) are common in this habitat. The eastern box turtle is the only turtle species present.

Polyphemus Moth
(*Antheraea polyphemus*)

The polyphemus moth is a member of the family Saturniidae (giant silk moths). This large moth has an average wingspan of 6 inches. Besides its size, the most notable feature of this moth is the large, purplish eyespot on each of its two hindwings. These eyespots are the source of its common name, a reference to the cyclops Polyphemus from Greek mythology.

The polyphemus moth is found throughout much of North America, from southern Canada to portions of Mexico. Though found in a variety of habitats, it seems to prefer mesophytic hardwood forests. The larval stage (caterpillar) feeds on the leaves of a variety of trees, including birches, willows, oaks, maples, hickories, basswood, American beech, American chestnut, honey locust, black walnut, sycamore, and American elm (Holland 1968).

There are generally two broods: one that hatches in early spring and one that hatches in late summer. The newly hatched bright yellow caterpillars eat their own eggshells and then begin feeding on their host plants. These voracious larvae can eat approximately 86,000 times their weight in less than 2 months. The full-grown caterpillars, bright green in color and approximately 3.5 inches long, spin tough cocoons of brown silk, usually wrapped around a host plant leaf. These cocoons may remain attached to branches, but usually fall with the leaves in late autumn.

Emerging from their cocoons, the adult moths must pump their wings with fluid (hemolymph) to extend them. The females emit pheromones, which the males can detect through their large, plumose antennae. Males may fly for miles in order to reach a female. After the moths mate, the female spends the majority of the remainder of her life laying eggs, while the male may mate several more times. Adults of this family of moths have only vestigial mouths. Because of this, they do not feed and live as adults for less than one week (Holland 1968; Butterflies and Moths of North America 2009).

from Fort Payne Chert interbedded with limestone, the talus of which forms a rich valley floor. From mid-March to mid-April, this trail has one of the most spectacular wildflower displays in Georgia: nearly all of the species found in the plant lists above occur in this forest. Tulip-trees dominate the canopy, and the rare Ohio buckeye and yellow-wood also occur, along with basswood, American beech, black walnut, and northern red oak.

The Shirley Miller trail begins as an interconnecting series of boardwalks, which were built to prevent trampling of the lush herbaceous cover. The remainder of the walk follows a narrow trail along a stream that leads to the picturesque Pocket Branch waterfall. Throughout late winter and spring a steady progression of wildflowers bloom (Nourse and Nourse 2007). Harbinger-of-spring blooms in late winter. In late March, along the beginning of the boardwalk, large drifts of Virginia bluebells and celandine poppy are in flower. Toothworts, bloodroot, giant chickweed, wild geranium, fernleaf phacelia, foamflower, Dutchman's britches, squirrel corn, rue-anemone, decumbent trillium, two-leaved miterwort, American trout lily, and several other species will also be blooming. As the Virginia bluebells and poppies are in decline in early to mid-April, a spectacular display of bent trillium blooms, along with toadshade trillium and many other forbs. Large swaths of wild hyacinth bloom soon after.

Shirley Miller Wildflower Trail, Crockford–Pigeon Mountain Wildlife Management Area

This trail, on the west side of Pigeon Mountain at the edge of McLemore Cove, winds through a narrow valley with steep cliffs on either side. The cliffs formed

Location: From U.S. Hwy. 27 in Lafayette, drive west, then north on Ga. Hwy. 193 about 8 miles to the intersection with Ga. Hwy. 341/Hog Jowl Rd. (Davis Crossroads). Turn left (south) onto Hog Jowl Rd. While on Hog Jowl Rd. the road will fork at approximately 2.5 miles. Continue left on Hog Jowl for about 0.2 mile and turn left on Pocket Rd. Drive approximately 1.2 miles (the road will turn to gravel) to the parking area. Google Earth GPS approximate coordinates at the parking area: N 34.712538/W 085.379920.

Dry Calcareous Forests

Dry calcareous forests occur over dry or dry-mesic (submesic) soils, and include both calcareous and sub-calcareous conditions. These forests are dominated or co-dominated by many calciphiles, including chinqua-pin oak, Shumard oak, chalk maple, white ash, eastern red cedar, eastern redbud, and many elms and hickories. Few blueberries and rhododendrons are present compared to more acidic forests; instead, distinctive calciphitic species such as coralberry, fragrant sumac, and Carolina buckthorn are abundant. In Georgia, such expanses of calcareous forests are rare because acidic soils tend to predominate throughout the state. Good examples of calciphytic forests are found around the cedar glades in Chickamauga and Chattanooga National Military Park (Walker County) (see the Featured Place), on the lower slopes of the eastern side of Lookout Mountain (Dade and Walker Counties) and Pigeon Mountain (Walker County), and on parts of Lavender Mountain at Berry College (Floyd County).

PHYSICAL SETTING AND ECOLOGY

The calcium-rich substrate and the resulting predominance of calciphytic plants are the main factors that distinguish these forests from acidic oak forests. These forests often occur at low elevations (particularly the Southern Limestone / Dolomite Valleys subregion) because the substrates that support them have eroded over time to form valleys. As can be seen on Pigeon Mountain (Walker County) and Black's Bluff (Floyd County), however, small patches can occur on side-slopes where calcareous substrates have outcropped in the Plateau Escarpment subregion or in portions of the southern shale valleys, where limey shales occur. Slope aspect and gradient are important in determining the dry or dry-mesic (submesic) nature of the soils. Steep slopes and west or south aspects will produce drier soils, while gentle slopes and north- to east-facing aspects foster deeper, moister soils (W. L. Lipps 1966; Wharton 1978). This natural community grades into the mesic forest natural community as conditions become more mesic.

Without fire or some other disturbance, these for-

If fire were more common, some dry calcareous forests would be woodlands or prairies with diverse ground layers.

ests will succeed from oak canopies to domination by red maple, tulip-tree, and, in some cases, late successional species such as southern sugar maple and American beech. Tulip-tree comes in as a pioneer species but is long-lived and remains in the canopy. The presence of oaks and pines may reflect past disturbances that opened the forest enough for these species to become established. Gaps were likely created by windfall, especially on steeper bluffs, or through openings from lightning-ignited fires that spread from upper slopes and killed the thin-barked trees (W. L. Lipps 1966; Wharton 1978; Pyne 1982; Schuler and McClain 2003). Thus, the extent of these forests may have varied in the past, depending on fire and drought regimes.

The potential variation in composition over time adds complexity to the development of fire management plans. This natural community has received less attention than others in the region with respect to fire management needs. The Georgia Department of Natural Resources is currently recommending fire-return intervals of five to seven years for some dry calcareous forests, which would be similar to those recommended for acidic oak-pine-hickory forests (Georgia Department of Natural Resources 2009c). The best opportunities for prescribed fire management of such forests will be on large-acreage public tracts such as Crockford–Pigeon Mountain Wildlife Management Area (Walker County), Zahnd Natural Area (Walker County), Cloudland Canyon State Park (Dade County), Chickamauga and Chattanooga National Military Park (Walker County), Johns Mountain Wildlife Management Area (Floyd and Gordon Counties), and tracts within the Armuchee Ranger District of Chattahoochee-Oconee National Forest (Chattooga, Walker, and Floyd Counties).

While prescribed fire is appropriate for some sites because of the lush and diverse herbaceous layer that

Common Bluecurls

it can foster it can destroy the fire-intolerant trees and shrubs that can be important features of this natural community. Regional management plans that promote the persistence of a variety of calcareous forest, woodland, glade, barren, and prairie natural communities are needed.

VEGETATION

These calcareous and subcalcareous forests are closed canopy stands that are distinguished by calcium-loving species in all strata. Tree species include chinquapin oak, Shumard oak, white oak, chalk maple, eastern red cedar, and sugarberry. Hickories, such as pignut,

mockernut, Carolina, and common shagbark, tend to be more common on these higher-base soils than they would be on more acidic sites. Ashes, including white ash and the rare blue ash; elms, such as slippery elm, winged elm, and the rare September elm; and hawthorns are also more abundant (Schafale and Weakley 1990). Shrubs and woody vines include high-base indicators such as coralberry, wafer-ash, Carolina buckthorn, fragrant sumac, and American rattan. The herb layer tends to be sparse where the forest is closed, and will include many widespread calciphiles, such as Indian pink, nettleleaf noseburn, nettle-leaf sage, and dwarf larkspur.

Plant composition will vary according to the level of bases and moisture in the soil. Where base levels are lower, calciphiles, hickories, elms, and ash will be tend to be less common, and ericads, such as blueberries, mountain laurel, azaleas, and sourwood, will appear, as will more oak and pine species, including southern red oak, post oak, Virginia pine, and shortleaf pine. Where conditions become moister, more mesophytic species may appear, and the community will grade gradually into the mesic forest natural community.

ANIMALS

Mammals of dry calcareous forests include the eastern chipmunk, short-tailed shrew, pine vole, gray squirrel, white-tailed deer, golden mouse, gray fox, striped skunk, eastern spotted skunk, least shrew, southern flying squirrel, opossum, and raccoon. Several bats may be present, including the hoary, little brown, evening, eastern pipistrelle, and big brown. The eastern pipistrelle roosts alone under loose bark and in tree cavities in the summer, but in the winter it hibernates in caves with hundreds of other bats.

Bird species breeding here are similar to those in oak-pine-hickory forests and woodlands. Ovenbirds and whip-poor-wills often nest in these forests, the ovenbird building a small, domed nest out of pine straw and leaves and the whip-poor-will laying its eggs on the ground in a small depression (M. A. Van Horn and Donovan 1994; Cink 2002; Beaton 2010b; Straight 2010b). Sites with a significant amount of mature pine may have pine warblers (Rodewald, Withgott, and Smith 1999; Ferrari 2010).

Few amphibians are present, although terrestrial salamanders, including the northern slimy salamander, may be found under coarse woody debris and in

CHARACTERISTIC PLANTS OF DRY CALCAREOUS FORESTS

TREES

Chalk maple—*Acer leucoderme*

Hickories—*Carya carolinae-septrionalis;
C. glabra; C. ovalis; C. tomentosa*

Eastern redbud—*Cercis canadensis*

White ash—*Fraxinus americana*

Eastern red cedar—*Juniperus virginiana*

White oak—*Quercus alba*

Chinquapin oak—*Quercus
muehlenbergii*

Northern red oak—*Quercus rubra*

Shumard oak—*Quercus shumardii*

Post oak—*Quercus stellata*

Elms—*Ulmus alata; U. americana;
U. rubra*

SHRUBS AND WOODY VINES

American rattan—*Berchemia scandens*

Southern-privet—*Forestiera ligustrina*

Carolina buckthorn—*Frangula
caroliniana*

Wafer-ash—*Ptelea trifoliata*

Fragrant sumac—*Rhus aromatica*

Buckthorn bumelia—*Sideroxylon
lycioides*

Coralberry—*Symphoricarpos orbiculatus*

Southern black haw—*Viburnum
rufidulum*

GROUND COVER

Thimbleweed—*Anemone virginiana*

Common smooth rockcress—
Boechera laevigata

Northern leatherflower—*Clematis
viorna*

Dwarf larkspur—*Delphinium tricorne*

Crested iris—*Iris cristata*

Hoary puccoon—*Lithospermum
canescens*

Eastern Solomon's-plume—
Maianthemum racemosum

Solomon's-seal—*Polygonatum biflorum*

Nettle-leaf sage—*Salvia urticifolia*

Black snakeroot—*Sanicula canadensis*

Indian pink—*Spigelia marilandica*

Nettleleaf noseburn—*Tragia urticifolia*

the more submesic sites. The southern red-backed salamander, and possibly Webster's salamander, may also be found (Semlitsch and West 1986; Camp 1988). Reptiles are common in this environment. Lizards that can occur include southeastern five-lined skinks and eastern fence lizards. Fossorial (burrowing) snakes common to dry forests are the smooth earth and southeastern crowned snakes, both of which feed on invertebrates. Larger snakes include black racers and the semi-arboreal rat snake.

Indian pink

Spotted Skunk (*Spilogale putorius*)

The spotted skunk, also known as the "civet cat," is one of two species of skunks occurring in Georgia, the other being the striped skunk (*Mephitis mephitis*). The range of the spotted skunk extends from south-central Canada to northeastern Mexico. In Georgia, this species is more common in the northern portion of the state and appears to be absent from the southeastern portion of the Coastal Plain (Kinlaw 1995).

Spotted skunks are considerably smaller than striped skunks, measuring between 17 and 23 inches in total length and weighing from 1 to 3 pounds. While quite variable in pattern, they typically have four broken white stripes on the back, a white-tipped tail, and white spots on the sides of the body, top of the head, under the ears, and between the eyes. Spotted skunks are far less common than striped skunks and occur at considerably lower densities (Georgia Department of Natural Resources 2005c). They are found in a wide variety of habitats, but seem to prefer open woods, brushy thickets, and edge habitats in rocky terrain. They den in rock piles, under logs, in abandoned burrows of other animals, and occasionally under buildings. The diet of spotted skunks includes small mammals, insects, birds, eggs, carrion, and some plant material (Burt and Grossenheider 1980; Kinlaw 1995).

Eastern spotted skunks breed mostly in late winter and produce litters of four to six young in late spring to early summer. The young are weaned and able to discharge musk at the age of two months. Skunks are well known for their ability to employ chemical defenses, and spotted skunks are no exception. When confronted, they balance on their front feet and spray musk directly over their heads. While this defense is effective against most would-be predators, they often fall prey to great horned owls. Other known predators include bobcats, coyotes, dogs, housecats, and humans (Kinlaw 1995).

Forests of Chickamauga and Chattanooga National Military Park

Dry calcareous forests surround the glades described in the Featured Place for the calcareous glade, barren, and woodland natural community. Common high-calcium tree species that inhabit the forests include chinquapin oak, eastern redbud, sugarberry, white ash, and eastern red cedar; the presence of many hickories, including shagbark, mockernut, and pignut, and elms, such as winged elm and slippery elm, also indicates high-base conditions. Other tree species include post oak, black oak, southern red oak, red maple, black cherry, flowering dogwood, American persimmon, shortleaf pine, and Virginia pine. Shrubs and woody vines found in these forests include the calciphiles coralberry and fragrant sumac, as well as Virginia-creeper, trumpet-creeper, and grapes. The herbaceous layer is somewhat sparse in these closed forests, but may include high-base indicators such as dwarf larkspur and nettle-leaf sage, as well as rue-anemone, yellow stargrass, foxglove beardtongue, and lyreleaf sage. Typical of these calcareous plant communities, ericads, such as azaleas, mountain laurel, and sourwood, are lacking.

Location: From the intersection of Ga. Hwy. 2/Battlefield Pkwy. and Lafayette Rd. in Fort Oglethorpe, travel south on Lafayette Rd. about 1 mile to the park entrance and visitor center. To reach specific glades and view the surrounding dry calcareous forests, follow the directions on p. 209.

Acidic Oak-Pine-Hickory Forests

Acidic oak-pine-hickory forests develop over acidic bedrock. These forests, which range from dry to dry-mesic (submesic), are usually dominated by oaks, such as rock chestnut oak, white oak, black oak, southern red oak, and scarlet oak, with some hickories, black gum, red maple, and pines. They occur throughout the eco-region but are particularly common on sandstone, shale, chert, and conglomerate substrates in the Southern Shale Valleys, the Southern Sandstone Ridges, the Plateau Escarpment, and the Southern Table Plateaus sub-regions. The Armuchee Ridges support many examples of this community; in them, Marshall Forest Preserve (Floyd County) is an old-growth forest that has been extensively studied and offers an outstanding example

(W. L. Lipps 1966; Wharton 1978). Other good examples occur in Cloudland Canyon State Park (Dade County) (see the Featured Place) and Zahnd Natural Area (Walker County).

Xeric forests that are dominated or co-dominated by pines are covered in the section on the pine-oak woodland natural community. Subcalcareous sites, where there is sufficient calcium to support species such as chalk maple, eastern redbud, eastern red cedar, chinquapin oak, white ash, wafer-ash, coralberry, and fragrant sumac, are classified in the dry calcareous forest natural community.

ECOLOGY AND PHYSICAL SETTING

Bedrock, aspect, fire, slope position, slope shape, and slope gradient are the major factors influencing the vegetation of these forests (W. L. Lipps 1966; Wharton 1978). South- to west-facing aspect, thin soils, steep gradient, exposed slope position, convex slope

Vegetation composition is influenced by aspect and slope configuration. Steep, convex slopes have a high rate of runoff, while those with more gentle gradients tend to retain moisture for longer periods.

shape, and narrow ridge tops all contribute to dry conditions; as these factors are ameliorated, sites become more dry-mesic (W. L. Lipps 1966; Wharton 1978).

Aspect plays an important role in this ecoregion because of the predominant southwest-northeast trend of the ridges. West-facing sites are exposed to storms originating from the west and are particularly vulnerable to ice and wind damage. Research in the Marshall Forest Preserve (Floyd County) indicates that ice storms, with a roughly 30-year periodicity, play a role in creating forest gaps and in limiting the northerly spread of some species, such as longleaf pine (W. L. Lipps 1966; Wharton 1978).

Slope position also plays a particularly important role in this ecoregion because of the abrupt transitions in geologic substrate that occur upslope and downslope, as when shale underlies sandstone and is

in turn underlain by limestone. Differences in erosion rates and patterns of these rocks influence soil development processes. Soil derived from shale erodes to form finer, moister soils than does the sandstone that is often upslope. The most acidic and sandy soils occur on sandstone-capped ridges; these exposed sites are also the most xeric and fire-prone. In the lower-slope positions, sites are better protected from drying sunlight and winds, and the soils usually have more clays, which hold on to nutrients and moisture. Work in the Marshall Forest emphasizes the dual influence of substrate and slope position on vegetation composition in acidic forests (W. L. Lipps 1966).

The natural disturbance regime in many sites is gap phase: disease, insects, drought, windthrow, and lightning cause trees to die and create canopy gaps (Pickett and White 1985; Abrams 2000). The size of the gaps

Bedrock is an important factor in determining vegetation composition. The sandy, acidic soils that are created by the sandstone bedrock shown here encourage development of acidic oak-pine forests.

Indian pipes. These plants lack chlorophyll and obtain nutrients by being parasitic on fungi and so can live on shady forest floors. They are members of the ericad, or heath, family, which typically thrives on acidic soils.

varies with the type of disturbance, which is often dictated by topographic setting. Dry, exposed sites are the most susceptible to larger-scale disturbances, such as fire, powerful thunderstorm downdrafts, and tornadoes (Harmon, Pickett, and White 1983). Fire is likely needed to maintain oak-regeneration in this natural community. One study showed that over a period of 156 years, fire intervals ranged from 4 to 32 years for one stand, and that oaks were not able to enter the canopy after fire was no longer present (Schuler and McClain 2003).

The frequency of fires caused by lightning ignition is not known, but presumably varies with slope position and soil moisture conditions. The impact of landscape position on fire regimes in this ecoregion is described on p. 161. Low-intensity surface fires result in the death of the saplings of thin-barked trees, encourage the persistence of oak and pine species, and maintain more open subcanopy and shrub layers. Very frequent or canopy-destroying fires could result in the transformation of these forests to the pine-oak woodland natural community. Judicious application of prescribed fire is important for maintaining the presence of oaks in these forests, although their proximity to developed areas makes prescribed fire programs difficult to implement.

VEGETATION

Several oak species, including rock chestnut oak, white oak, black oak, and southern red oak, often dominate these sites. Other trees include pignut hickory, mockernut hickory, sand hickory, black gum, sourwood, and red maple. On some ridges, such as several in the Marshall Forest Preserve (Floyd County), shortleaf and Virginia pines remain an important element. The shortleaf pines may reach more than 200 years in age in some instances, even without frequent fire, apparently because ice and wind create enough gaps to maintain pioneer species (W. L. Lipps 1966; Wharton 1978). Further studies of pine seedling recruitment,

CHARACTERISTIC PLANTS OF ACIDIC OAK-PINE-HICKORY FORESTS

TREES

Downy serviceberry—*Amelanchier arborea*

Hickories—*Carya glabra*; *C. ovalis*; *C. pallida*; *C. tomentosa*

Flowering dogwood—*Cornus florida*

Sourwood—*Oxydendrum arboreum*

Shortleaf pine—*Pinus echinata*

Virginia pine—*Pinus virginiana*

White oak—*Quercus alba*

Scarlet oak—*Quercus coccinea*

Southern red oak—*Quercus falcata*

Blackjack oak—*Quercus marilandica*

Rock chestnut oak—*Quercus montana*

Post oak—*Quercus stellata*

Black oak—*Quercus velutina*

SHRUBS AND WOODY VINES

American chestnut (sprouts)—*Castanea dentata*

Fringe-tree—*Chionanthus virginicus*

Hairy southern bush-honeysuckle—*Diervilla rivularis*

Carolina jessamine—*Gelsemium sempervirens*

Mountain laurel—*Kalmia latifolia*

Coral honeysuckle—*Lonicera sempervirens*

Blueberries: *Vaccinium arboreum*; *V. corymbosum*; *V. pallidum*; *V. stamineum*

GROUND COVER

Common hairgrass—*Avenella flexuosa*

Woodland coreopsis—*Coreopsis major*

Common white heart-leaved aster—*Eurybia divaricata*

Hairy sunflower—*Helianthus hirsutus*

Veiny hawkweed—*Hieracium venosum*

Yellow stargrass—*Hypoxis hirsuta*

Upland dwarf iris—*Iris verna*

Orange dwarf-dandelion—*Krigia biflora*

Silkgrass—*Pityopsis graminifolia*

Bracken fern—*Pteridium aquilinum*

Goldenrods—*Solidago* spp.

Common clasping aster—*Symphyotrichum patens*

---

however, are needed. American chestnut sprouts may also appear.

Ericaceous shrubs in this community include mountain laurel, Catawba rhododendron, smooth highbush blueberry, hillside blueberry, deerberry, and sparkleberry. Dewberries, blackberries, fringe-tree, and witch-hazel also occur. Woody vines include hairy southern bush-honeysuckle, greenbriers, grapes, and poison ivy. Herbaceous species vary but often include hairy sunflower, goldenrods, veiny hawkweed, eastern flowering spurge, yellow stargrass, bracken fern, common hairgrass, and poverty oat-grass.

ANIMALS

Characteristic mammals of this community include the eastern chipmunk, short-tailed shrew, pine vole, gray squirrel, white-tailed deer, black bear, golden mouse, gray fox, striped skunk, least shrew, southern flying squirrel, opossum, and raccoon. Several bats may be present, including big brown, eastern pipistrelle, evening, and hoary. The avifauna found here is fairly typical of many hardwood forest types in this region. Both summer and scarlet tanagers nest here, with scarlet tanagers more often found at the higher elevations. Black-throated green warblers also nest here at higher elevations, particularly when some conifers are present

(Morse 1993; T. M. Schneider et al. 2010). Steep slopes with larger trees provide nesting sites for worm-eating warblers (Hanners and Patton 1998; Beaton 2010c). Other species that commonly breed here include the tufted titmouse, red-bellied and pileated woodpeckers, red-eyed vireo, wood thrush, great crested flycatcher, and yellow-billed cuckoo (T. M. Schneider et al. 2010).

The forest floor may be occupied by the northern slimy salamander and likely by one or more of its smaller, winter-active cousins (e.g., southern red-backed salamanders and either southern zigzag or Webster's salamander (Highton 1979). Fossorial (burrowing) snakes of this habitat include ringneck and brown snakes. Southeastern crowned and smooth earth snakes may occur in drier sites. Eastern fence lizards, five-lined skinks, and southeastern five-lined skinks are typical inhabitants. Eastern hognose snakes (see Featured Animal) may cruise the forest floor or dig in leaf litter in search of toads. Pine snakes and mole kingsnakes, both constrictors, may also be locally present. Black racers, rat snakes, copperheads, and timber rattlesnakes are among the common terrestrial snakes.

Open areas of these forests host many butterflies, including the hickory hairstreak, coral hairstreak, and great spangled fritillary.

Eastern Hognose Snake
(*Heterodon platirhinos*)

The eastern hognose snake is one of two members of the genus *Heterodon* in the state, the other being the southern hognose snake (*Heterodon simus*), a much rarer species confined primarily to sandy habitats of the Coastal Plain. The eastern hognose snake is found throughout the state in a variety of upland habitats, including oak-pine forests and woodlands, hardwood forests, pine flatwoods, and sandhills, as well as pine plantations and old fields. It is less frequently found in densely wooded or low-lying habitats. This snake often over-winters in piles of logs, rocks, and other materials, as well as in decaying stumps and root holes (Tuberville and Buhlmann 2008).

The common name of this snake comes from its keeled and conspicuously upturned snout. Other names include "puff adder," "hissing adder," or "spreading adder." These names are derived from one of its defensive behaviors, consisting of flattening the head and neck, hissing loudly, and raising its upper body like a cobra. If this fails to deter the intruder and the snake is further harassed, it may roll over on its back, evert its vent, open its mouth, convulse, and expel various body fluids, then lie still as if dead. If the individual is flipped right-side up, it will usually promptly resume its former position, continuing to "play possum" until the threat subsides (Conant and Collins 1998; Tuberville and Buhlmann 2008).

The eastern hognose snake is an avid burrower, using its pointed, upturned snout to push through leaf litter and soil in search of its favorite food, toads. It has enlarged rear teeth that enable it to puncture toads that have inflated themselves as a defense against predation. Other food items include frogs, salamanders, lizards, small mammals, snails, and arthropods. Major predators include kingsnakes, raptors, and carnivorous mammals (Tuberville and Buhlmann 2008).

Cloudland Canyon State Park West Rim Trail

The West Rim Loop Trail in Cloudland Canyon State Park (Dade County) winds through excellent examples of the Cumberland Plateau / Ridge and Valley acidic oak-pine-hickory forest and woodland communities. Some areas are quite open, with picturesque grassy understories and stunted trees that grade into the xeric pine-oak natural community. Small, glade-like openings are common, and along the rim, rock outcrops atop plunging cliffs offer scenic views of the eastern portion of Lookout Mountain and the many sedimentary layers that comprise the mountain. Trees include white pine, southern red oak, downy service-berry, American holly, Virginia pine, shortleaf pine, rock chestnut oak, blackjack oak, post oak, sassafras, red maple, black gum, pale (sand) hickory, mockernut hickory, and pignut hickory. Catawba rhododendron,

mountain laurel, smooth highbush blueberry, sparkle-berry, mapleleaf viburnum, fringe-tree, dewberries, blackberries, witch-hazel, poison oak, and hillside blueberry are some common shrubs. Occasionally, an American chestnut sprout appears. Woody vines include hairy southern bush-honeysuckle, grapes, greenbriers, and Virginia-creeper. Herbaceous species include wavy hairgrass, trailing arbutus, bracken fern, rock alumroot, common clasping aster, veiny hawk-weed, goldenrods, upland dwarf iris, ebony spleen-wort, eastern needlegrass, and poverty oat-grass.

Small glades are embedded within the forest and also appear on the edges of the sandstone cliffs. The glades support dewberries, blackberries, oat-grasses, wavy hairgrass, cladonia or cladina lichens, haircap mosses, mapleleaf viburnum, sparkleberry, smooth highbush blueberry, hillside blueberry, stunted Virginia pine, red maple, post oak, hairy southern bush-honeysuckle, Catawba rhododendron, mountain laurel, and rock chestnut oak. One 30-foot diameter glade occurs outside of the loop portion of the trail, very close to the path that connects the west rim trail to the camping area, and features St. John's-wort, upland dwarf iris, trailing arbutus, sparkleberry, smooth highbush blueberry, Virginia pine, red maple, and red chokeberry.

Location: Cloudland Canyon State Park is located on Ga. 136, 8 miles east of Trenton and I-59 and 18 miles northwest of LaFayette. From Ga. Hwy. 193 in LaFayette, take U.S. Hwy. 27/Ga. 1/Ga. 136/Lyle Jones Pkwy. north about 3 miles. Proceed left on Ga. 136/Lookout Mountain Scenic Hwy. about 17 miles toward Trenton. Turn right onto Cloudland Canyon Park Rd. Take the first road on the left past the park office. Continue approximately 2.2 miles to a gravel road on the left that leads to the West Rim Access Parking. Maps and directions are also available in the park office. Google Earth GPS approximate coordinates at the parking area: N 34.846013/W 085.490785.

Pine-Oak Woodlands

Cumberland Plateau / Ridge and Valley pine-oak woodlands occur on xeric, rocky, exposed sites and range from nearly closed canopy to woodlands. They are usually dominated by Virginia pine and/or shortleaf pine typically with many dry-site oaks. These habitats usually have an ericaceous shrub layer of laurel, rhododendron, blueberries, and/or huckleberries and are often called "pine-oak-heath" communities; however, some have herbaceous understories (Braun 1950; Schafale and Weakley 1990). The pines are often stunted and gnarled. Dry-site oaks may co-dominate with pines on some sites. On the sandstone caps of some ridges, these forests can be quite picturesque, with slightly stunted trees and glade-like openings that provide expansive views of the scenic, folded ridge and valley landscape. These forests are most common in the Southern Sandstone ridges and Southern Table Plateaus subregions and more occasionally on the Plateau Escarpment.

Extensive logging, when followed by burning, creates conditions ideal for Virginia pine to colonize, creating early successional forests that should succeed to acidic oak-pine forests over time (Hinkle et al. 1993). In the past when fire was more common, pine-dominated forests or woodlands mixed with oaks were more widespread, some with a dense grassy ground layer (Braun 1950).

PHYSICAL SETTING AND ECOLOGY

This natural community now mostly occurs on exposed outcroppings of sandstone and conglomerate (such as Lookout Sandstone/Gizzard Formation), where they grade into the acidic cliff and outcrop natural community, as well as on some shale slopes and as small patches within the acidic oak-pine forest natural community (Braun 1950; W. L. Lipps 1966; Wharton 1978; Georgia Department of Natural Resources 2009c). Pines can dominate or co-dominate where there are harsh edaphic (soil) conditions with mineral-bare soils for seedling establishment, where frequent fires allow the pines to reproduce and persist,

Indeed, pine beetle outbreaks can result in a shift in dominance from Virginia and shortleaf pine to dry-site hardwoods, because hardwoods that are growing under the pines are "released" after the pines are killed: no longer suppressed by the shade of the pines, they are able to grow into the canopy.

VEGETATION

The dominant trees are typically Virginia pine and shortleaf pine, along with dry-site oaks, such as black-jack oak, post oak, black oak, southern red oak, rock chestnut oak, and scarlet oak. Red maple, sand hickory, sourwood, pignut hickory, and black gum may also be present. On very rocky, dry sites, the trees are dwarfed, at times nearly to shrub size (Wharton 1978). As described on p. 99, although Virginia pines are the least fire-tolerant of the mountain pines, they are able to maintain a presence because they are drought hardy and produce frequent, heavy seed crops so they can seed in quickly after fire (K. K. Carter and Snow 1990;

Virginia pines after a fire

Cumberland rose-gentian. This rare plant grows in woodlands over sandstone or shale.

or where rocky sites exposed to wind and ice-loading maintain gaps (W. L. Lipps 1966; Wharton 1978). In addition, on some dry calcareous sites, shrink-swell soils apparently create a hardpan that contributes to dry conditions that support a rare pine-oak woodland that is described below (Govus 2003a).

Typically dry-site oaks, red maple, and black gum will take over in the absence of fire, though pines can persist in some nutrient-poor, exposed sites. In the past, the fires that maintained pine stands were ignited by lightning and humans. Lightning ignition would occur most often on dry ridge sites and burn downslope. Both European settlers and Native Americans also set fires in this region, as discussed on p. 161.

Southern pine beetles are natural agents of disturbance that can cause significant tree mortality in dense pine stands. Pine beetle outbreaks are cyclical and tend to cause greatest damage to pines that are already stressed by drought, disease, or overcrowding.

CHARACTERISTIC PLANTS OF PINE-OAK WOODLANDS

TREES

Pignut hickory—*Carya glabra*
Sand hickory—*Carya pallida*
Sourwood—*Oxydendrum arboreum*
Shortleaf pine—*Pinus echinata*
Virginia pine—*Pinus virginiana*
Scarlet oak—*Quercus coccinea*
Southern red oak—*Quercus falcata*
Blackjack oak—*Quercus marilandica*
Rock chestnut oak—*Quercus montana*
Post oak—*Quercus stellata*
Black oak—*Quercus velutina*

SHRUBS AND WOODY VINES

Hairy southern bush-honeysuckle—
   Diervilla rivularis
Carolina jessamine—*Gelsemium*
   sempervirens
Mountain laurel—*Kalmia latifolia*
Blackberries and dewberries—*Rubus*
   spp.
Greenbriers—*Smilax* spp.
Horsesugar—*Symplocos tinctoria*
Blueberries—*Vaccinium arboreum*;
   V. corymbosum; V. pallidum

GROUND COVER

Broomsedges—*Andropogon* spp.
Woodland coreopsis—*Coreopsis major*
Poverty oat-grass—*Danthonia spicata*
Eastern flowering spurge—*Euphorbia*
   corollata
Veiny hawkweed—*Hieracium venosum*
Yellow stargrass—*Hypoxis hirsuta*
Blazing-stars—*Liatris* spp.
Common wild quinine—*Parthenium*
   integrifolium
Little bluestem—*Schizachyrium*
   scoparium
Goldenrods—*Solidago* spp.
Common clasping aster—
   Symphyotrichum patens
Virginia goat's-rue—*Tephrosia*
   virginiana

Sullivan 1993; Kirkman et al. 2007). Their shallow root systems, which make them prone to windthrow, and their short lifespans of 90 to 125 years of age, however, may limit their presence on some sites (Sullivan 1993).

Shortleaf pines are more fire-tolerant than Virginia pines: their bark is thicker, and they can sprout after a canopy fire from buds within their trunks. In addition, they are fairly long-lived trees; individuals more than 225 years of age were found in the Marshall Forest Preserve in Floyd County (W. L. Lipps 1966; Wharton 1978). Because of their fire tolerance and long lifespan, it is likely that shortleaf pines were more common on fire-prone sites than Virginia pines, but both will often be present.

Small trees, shrubs, and woody vines typically include sparkleberry, deerberry, hillside blueberry, mountain laurel, horsesugar, beaked hazelnut, Catawba rhododendron, downy serviceberry, prickly-ash, American persimmon, Carolina jessamine, greenbriers, poison oak, and grapes. Herbaceous species include several grasses, goldenrods, woodland coreopsis, Virginia goat's-rue, pipsissewa, common clasping aster, yellow stargrass, eastern flowering spurge, veiny hawkweed, and numerous other dry-site species.

Coosa Valley pine-oak woodlands are unusual plant assemblages that grow on some dry, calcareous knolls near the Coosa Valley prairies and barrens (Floyd County). They are dominated by shortleaf pine, with post oak and blackjack oak as co-dominants. These woodlands are now rare because most were converted to loblolly pine plantations. The ground cover includes prairie grass species such as little bluestem, big bluestem, eastern beard grass, and rough dropseed and many herbaceous species with prairie affinities, such as the white prairie-goldenrod, ashy sunflower, common wild quinine, blazing-stars, narrow-leaved smooth aster, prairie grass-leaved aster, Appalachian sunflower, stiff-leaved aster, eastern gray goldenrod, hairy sunflower, Virginia goat's-rue, toothed white-topped aster, and southern rattlesnake-master (Govus 2003a). This combination of prairie species, dry-site trees, and calcareous substrate make these woodlands notable.

ANIMALS

Typical mammals of this community are those that prefer the open, ecotonal habitats that occur where dense herbaceous layers are interspersed with canopy trees that provide additional food and shelter; these include red fox, striped skunk, bobcat, white-tailed deer, opossum, and eastern chipmunk. Most forests and woodlands with mature pine trees have breeding pine warblers (Rodewald, Withgott, and Smith 1999). Mature pine stands with dense patches of shrubs will harbor nesting prairie warblers, as will regenerating clearcuts for the first few years after cutting. Mature pine forest stands often support brown-headed nuthatch and eastern wood-pewee (McCarty 1996). Larger examples of these stands with dense, grassy ground cover may have breeding Bachman's sparrows (Gobris 2010). Black-throated green warblers may breed at higher-elevation sites with more mature pine trees, although these sites often can have a significant hardwood component (Morse 1993).

As in other dry sites of the ecoregion, amphibians are not expected to be important members of the herpetofaunal community. Characteristic reptiles likely include southeastern five-lined skinks, slender glass lizards, and ground skinks. Eastern milk snakes and pine snakes are secretive constrictors that have been found in dry forests dominated by Virginia pine in the nearby Cumberland Plateau region of Alabama (Mount 1975).

FEATURED ANIMAL

Eastern Milk Snake (*Lampropeltis triangulum triangulum*)

The eastern milk snake is a member of the family Colubridae, the taxonomic group that includes most of the snake species native to Georgia. It is a close relative of the scarlet kingsnake, but the ranges of these snakes do not appear to overlap in Georgia. The scarlet kingsnake is found primarily in the Coastal Plain and lower Piedmont, while the eastern milk snake is found in the Blue Ridge and the Cumberland Plateau / Ridge and Valley (Jensen 2008a). The common name of this attractive snake comes from a myth that it is capable of sucking milk from cows (Conant and Collins 1998; Jensen 2008a).

The eastern milk snake is found in a variety of habitats, including pine and hardwood forests, woodlands, upland rock outcrops, river bottoms, and even anthropogenic habitats such as fields and farm buildings (Conant and Collins 1998). In natural habitats, individuals are usually found between or under rocks, beneath logs, or underneath the bark of decaying logs and stumps. There is some evidence that the eastern milk snake uses moist, low-elevation habitats during the summer months and moves to drier, high-elevation sites in the fall. Instead of basking in the sun in exposed areas, this shy and secretive snake warms itself on rocks or other objects heated by solar radiation (Jensen 2008a).

The diet of the eastern milk snake includes small mammals, birds, lizards, snakes, salamanders, fishes, worms, and insects, as well as carrion and the eggs of birds and reptiles. Like other members of the genus *Lampropeltis*, this snake is able to prey on venomous pit vipers without serious ill effects, due in part to the fact that its blood has chemical properties that neutralize the pit vipers' venom. Common predators of eastern milk snakes include raccoons, foxes, owls, hawks, skunks, weasels, and opossums (Jensen 2008a).

Zahnd Natural Area

Zahnd Natural Area extends from the summit of Lookout Mountain to the floor of McLemore Cove nearly 1,000 feet below. The shoulders of the escarpment support very picturesque pine-oak woodlands, with the trees, stunted to shrub size in places, forming woodlands among rock outcroppings and on the edges of the escarpment. Geologically, the summit of Lookout Mountain is made up of coarse Pennsylvanian sandstone and conglomerate. Materials in the conglomerate eroded from the ancestral Appalachians and were deposited by westward-flowing rivers. It is this formation that has been eroded by water and wind into the spectacular outcrops and "hoodoos" in the "Little Rock City" in this area. Iron nodules have precipitated into secondary deposits throughout the sandstone and give it a distinctive banded appearance. In places the conglomerate is interbedded with coal deposits. Below the conglomerate is another sandstone formation of similar age and origin.

The outcrops here consist of very picturesque, rounded rocks sometimes called "turtleback rocks." Virginia pine dominates. Hardwoods include red maple, rock chestnut oak, black gum, mockernut hickory, sand hickory, post oak, sassafras, downy serviceberry, and sourwood, which become increasingly common away from the rim as the environment grades into the acidic oak-pine-hickory environment. Mountain laurel, fringe-tree, hillside blueberry, smooth highbush blueberry, sparkleberry, Carolina jessamine, witch-hazel, winged sumac, Virginia-creeper, spiderworts, goldenrods, and grasses are also present.

Take the time to explore this area thoroughly; it contains excellent examples of dry oak-pine-hickory forests, a small stream bottomland dominated by mountain laurel in some areas and herbaceous plants in others, as well as a sagpond, which is described under the sagpond and sinkhole natural community.

Location: Zahnd Natural Area is located on Lookout Mountain approximately 13 miles north of Ga. Hwy. 48 in Cloudland via Ga. Hwy. 157. Although there are no designated hiking trails, there is a path leading into the woods at the Ga. 157 kiosk 4.4 miles north of Dougherty Gap Rd. The kiosk is located on the left (west) side of the road, and a pulloff area by a kiosk is located on the east side of the highway. To reach the pine-dominated stands near the escarpment edge, after parking, walk across the road and follow a short unmarked foot trail on the east side of the highway that leads to the canyon rim. Google Earth GPS approximate coordinates for the pulloff by the kiosk: N 34.650250/W 085.470400.

Montane Longleaf Woodlands and Forests

Montane longleaf pine woodlands and forests occur on steep, rocky, south- to west-facing slopes in the Cumberland Plateau / Ridge and Valley, Piedmont, and Blue Ridge ecoregions of Georgia. Longleaf pine dominates these stands, but a mix of other pines and dry-site oaks can co-dominate (Hermann, Kush, and Stowe 2008). Some montane longleaf pines in Georgia are very old, with the flat tops and thick limbs indicative of great age: a few trees in the Piedmont and Cumberland Plateau / Ridge and Valley ecoregions are over two centuries old (Klaus 2006; Knight 2006). These sites can also be very picturesque, with rocky slopes, open canopies, grassy ground cover, and old, stunted pines. Montane longleaf stands were more widespread when fire was more frequent, but are now among the rarest natural communities in the state and add important biological and aesthetic diversity to the landscape.

Some ecologists refer to all occurrences of longleaf above the Fall Line as "montane" longleaf; others refer simply to "longleaf" (Moore and Fogo 2008). "Montane" as used here refers only to those stands north of the Fall Line that occur on slopes and ridges. At one time longleaf pines also grew in dense stands on gentle slopes, gravelly high terraces, foothills, and valleys near the Coosa River, extending into Alabama; some stands may have occurred on low-lying areas in the Piedmont as well (Wharton 1978; Moore and Fogo 2008). While no examples of these lowland stands remain in Georgia, they "must have been startlingly similar to Coastal Plain flatwoods," with embedded pitcherplant bogs (Wharton 1978, p. 120). Should any such stands be found and restored they would be classified as a new natural community because they would be very different from montane sites (E. F. Andrews 1917; Wharton 1978).

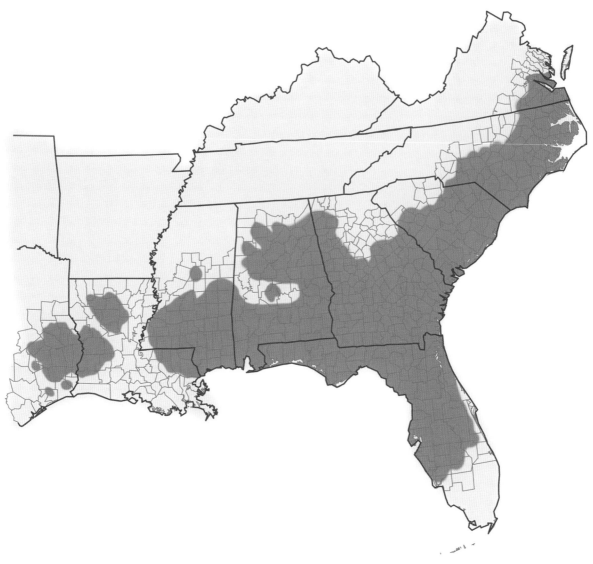

Historic range of longleaf pine. Adapted from Moore and Fogo 2008.

PHYSICAL SETTING AND ECOLOGY

The original distribution of longleaf woodlands above the Fall Line is not known; they may have been fairly widespread. Their current position exclusively on steep sites may be because longleaf pines on the lower slopes and bottoms were removed by settlers and by timber companies that harvested longleaf and re-planted other pine species, such as loblolly. Stands on steep slopes have been reduced by logging and fire ex-clusion.

Montane longleaf pines occur on thin-soiled, well-drained, south- to southwest-facing sites. Well-known stands occur in the Cumberland Plateau / Ridge and Valley on Lavender Mountain and as far north as Tay-lor Ridge, near Trion. A small stand in the Blue Ridge ecoregion occurs on the shores of Lake Allatoona. In the Piedmont, longleaf stands occur over quartz-ite (which erodes to thin, sterile, sandy soils) around Pine Mountain in Talbot, Meriwether, Troup, and Harris Counties, with especially good examples in Sprewell Bluff Natural Area, Camp Thunder near Pine Mountain, Callaway Forest Preserve, and F. D. Roosevelt State Park. Longleaf pines also occur over quartzite and other acidic metamorphic rocks of the Talladega Uplands in Haralson and Paulding Coun-ties and extend along the northern border of the Ridge and Valley in Polk County, as well as on acidic meta-morphic rocks in Fulton County, near Griffin (R. M.

Harper 1905b), and in Sweetwater Creek State Park in Douglas County. They also occur on ultramafic rock in the Georgia Piedmont at Burks Mountain (see p. 319).

Although some longleaf pines occur where steep, fairly inaccessible slopes and dry, rocky, sandy soils enabled a few individuals to regenerate in spite of fire exclusion during the 20th century, longleaf pine usually requires fire to persist: its entire lifecycle is adapted to surviving fire (see p. 368). In the past, most likely a combination of lightning-ignited and anthropogenic (human-caused) fires fostered longleaf stands, though there is much to be learned about the fire regime (Hermann, Kush, and Stowe 2008). Depending on patterns of anthropogenic fire-setting, fire-return intervals may have been longer in some montane sites than they were on typical Coastal Plain longleaf pine sites because the topography is more dissected so that fire compartments—the areal extents in which fires can burn unimpeded by firebreaks such as streams and moist ravines—are smaller. Estimates of historic fire-return intervals vary. One early observer noted that surface fires were prevalent in the region, indicating some areas may have burned twice within a year (F. W. Reed 1905), while analysis of cores from tree stumps in the Piedmont indicated an average fire-return interval of 2.6 years prior to 1840; 1.2 years during early European settlement, 1840–1912; and 11.4 years from 1912 to present (Klaus 2006). A few fire-scarred logs at Berry College revealed fire-return intervals of about 10 to 12 years in the early 1900s.

In Georgia, montane longleaf pine sites are more northerly and are subjected to a different climate regime than those of the Coastal Plain; they experience cooler temperatures and increased incidence of ice storms. Ice storms may be a major control on the distribution of longleaf, with the severity of ice-loading differing according to small variations in slope steepness, aspect, and vegetation structure (W. L. Lipps 1966; Wharton 1978; Lafon et al. 1999; Mou and Warillow 2000; Knight 2006). Windthrow has also been suggested as a possible cause of openings in some stands in addition to fire (Knight 2006).

VEGETATION

The vegetation structure and composition of montane longleaf most likely varies with topography, land use history, and management practices. Where sites are being actively managed with frequent fire and/or her-

Silkgrass

bicides, the canopy may be open; elsewhere they are closed forest. Longleaf pine varies from being an important canopy species (e.g., in portions of Sprewell Bluff Natural Area, FDR State Park, Paulding Forest Wildlife Management Area, and portions of Callaway Forest Preserve) to a scattering of isolated individuals, as in other areas within Paulding Forest (Paulding County), Camp Thunder, and Sweetwater Creek State Park (Douglas County). Other canopy trees include shortleaf pine, loblolly pine, blackjack oak, post oak, scarlet oak, southern red oak, and rock chestnut oak. American chestnut may once have been an important component in some sites: individual trees large enough to flower and bear fruit have been found on the slopes of Pine Mountain (Harris and Meriwether Counties). Blueberries, muscadine grapes, Virginia-creeper, and greenbriers are common in the shrub and woody vine layer (Carter and Londo 2003; Hermann, Kush, and Stowe 2008; Cipollini, unpubl. data).

CHARACTERISTIC PLANTS OF MONTANE LONGLEAF WOODLANDS AND FORESTS

TREES

Shortleaf pine—Pinus echinata
Longleaf pine—Pinus palustris
Scarlet oak—Quercus coccinea
Southern red oak—Quercus falcata
Blackjack oak—Quercus marilandica
Rock chestnut oak—Quercus montana
Post oak—Quercus stellata

SHRUBS AND WOODY VINES

Blackberries—Rubus spp.
Blueberries—Vaccinium arboreum;
    V. pallidum; V. stamineum

GROUND COVER

Broomsedges—Andropogon spp.
Hemp dogbane—Apocynum
    cannabinum

Maryland golden-aster—Chrysopsis
    mariana
Butterfly pea—Clitoria mariana
Woodland coreopsis—Coreopsis major
Oat-grasses—Danthonia spp.
Witchgrasses—Dichanthelium spp.
Common elephant's-foot—
    Elephantopus tomentosus
Dog-fennel—Eupatorium capillifolium;
    E. perfoliatum
Sunflowers—Helianthus spp.
St. John's-worts—Hypericum spp.
Yellow stargrass—Hypoxis hirsuta
Lespedezas—Lespedeza spp.
Blazing-stars—Liatris spp.
Eastern sensitive briar—Mimosa
    microphylla

Appalachian ragwort—Packera
    anonyma
Common wild quinine—Parthenium
    integrifolium
Silkgrass—Pityopsis graminifolia
Bracken fern—Pteridium aquilinum
Little bluestem—Schyzachyrium
    scoparium
Goldenrods—Solidago spp.
Virginia goat's-rue—Tephrosia
    virginiana
Bird's-foot violet—Viola pedata

The herbaceous layers were often dense in the past and are becoming so again with the return of prescribed fires. Common herbaceous species include common little bluestem, fireweed, goldenrods (esp. licorice goldenrod), broomsedges, bracken fern, Bosc's witchgrass, common dog-fennel, smooth trailing lespedeza, horse-nettle, silkgrass, woodland coreopsis, sunflowers, St. John's-worts, yellow stargrass, orange dwarf-dandelion, a blue-eyed grass, boneset, Appalachian ragwort, Maryland golden-aster, hemp dogbane, common elephant's-foot, witchgrasses, and Virginia goat's-rue (Currie et al. 2006; Cipollini 2011).

Some Piedmont longleaf stands, particularly southerly ones, have Coastal Plain elements, such as turkey oak and tread-softly (Carter and Londo 2003). Addi-tional field research may lead to identification of distinctive southern Piedmont longleaf pine forest subtypes. A superb stand of longleaf pine in FDR State Park occurs on the Pine Mountain Trail, starting from the Fox Den Cove trailhead parking lot and proceeding north on the Pine Mountain Trail about half a mile to the intersection of the Pine Mountain Trail and the Pool Trail. Some of the longleaf pines exhibit the thick trunks, heavy limbs, and topped-off growth pattern that the species develops with age. Late fall and winter are excellent times to visit this site because the trees occur in stark relief to the surrounding deciduous dry-site oaks that have dropped their leaves, and trees in the "grass" and "rocket" stages are easily discerned from the trail.

PRESCRIBED FIRE IN MONTANE LONGLEAF

Introducing prescribed fires in montane longleaf stands is a challenging task. Years of fire exclusion have resulted in stands that are overly dense, with many fire-intolerant trees and thick layers of duff (unburned pine needles) and few seed sources. While some advocate clearcutting of mixed stands and planting longleaf pine, the aesthetic and ecological impacts of this approach are problematical. Typically, a slow, careful approach involving a combination of selective removal of hardwoods and prescribed fire is desirable. Reintroduction of fire must be done carefully to avoid damage to desirable species. In general, initial burns must be conducted during cool, moist conditions in order to avoid damaging the vascular tissue of longleaf pines surrounded by deep layers of duff. Under dry conditions, these fires can generate temperatures of 800°F next to the tree trunks. The objective in early years is to reduce the duff layer gradually through a series of "cool" burns, at the same time allowing the resurgence of an herbaceous layer that will serve as fuel for future burns and reducing fire-intolerant species. Other strategies include minimizing the amount of duff smoldering around old trees by raking the litter and duff away; burning when the duff is still moist, within days of 1-inch rains; avoidance of slow-moving back fires; and the extinguishing of smoldering duff around tree bases immediately following the burn (Kush and Varner 2006).

Burning in montane sites presents challenges that do not exist in the flatter lowlands. Erosion rates are higher on the steep terrain, so existing roads and natural firebreaks are used whenever possible. In general, prescribed burns should be set along ridges and allowed to burn downslope under relatively moist conditions. Great care should be taken to avoid detrimental impacts to downslope mesic natural communities: intense fires can seriously harm these beautiful, diverse stands.

In addition, on steep slopes, it is easier for fires to reach the canopy of trees upslope, so care must be taken to ameliorate the intensity of fires. It is possible that fires should be less frequent than on the Coastal Plain because of the danger of soil erosion. Hardwood control could be done on lower slopes with repeated fire due to less danger of soil erosion, but control on

A prescribed fire. The fire will kill back fire-intolerant plants and enables longleaf pines and a diversity of other fire-tolerant plants to grow. If the fire-intolerant plants were not removed, over time they would produce so much shade that many sun-loving plants would disappear.

steeper slopes would involve some combination of mechanical and chemical treatments. Unlike sites on lowlands, the terrain sometimes requires using aerial ignition, which is less precise. Also, wind patterns can be complex on slopes, making smoke and fire management difficult.

In some cases, reduction of the hardwood component of the stand through manual removal of trees and shrubs, as well as chemical treatments, may be appropriate. Herbicides should be applied minimally and with care. This is a short-term approach that will eventually transition to a long-term program of burning that will include growing season burns for effective hardwood control and reestablishment of ground layer diversity.

ANIMALS

Mammals that inhabit or visit woodland areas include red fox, striped skunk, white-tailed deer, opossum, and eastern chipmunk. Montane longleaf pine natural communities are important habitats for a variety of birds. Stands dominated by mature pines usually have numerous brown-headed nuthatches, chipping sparrows, eastern wood-pewees, and pine warblers.

In Berry College longleaf stands, bird abundance and species richness have increased as the stands have become more open. These stands now have greater grass and shrub cover, which encourages more species that forage on small seeds, as well as more ground-nesting birds. The top 10 bird species found in fire-managed stands at Berry College are the Carolina wren, tufted titmouse, golden-crowned kinglet, red-bellied woodpecker, northern cardinal, summer tanager, Carolina chickadee, prairie warbler, indigo bunting, and downy woodpecker (Cipollini, Berry College, pers. comm.).

In the past, some montane longleaf pine sites harbored nesting red-cockaded woodpeckers (McCarty 1996; T. M. Schneider et al. 2010). In areas where trees are widely spaced and the ground cover is dominated by thick grasses, Bachman's sparrow and northern bobwhite can often be found (Dunning 1993). The eastern wood-pewee, great crested flycatcher, and eastern bluebird are also found at the more open sites. Where there are a significant number of hardwood trees within the stand the yellow-billed cuckoo, red-eyed vireo, summer tanager, and yellow-throated vireo often occur (Robinson 1995; T. M. Schneider et al. 2010). Although documentation is somewhat limited, it appears that the red-cockaded woodpecker may have bred in the Ridge and Valley ecoregion histori-

cally (Burleigh 1958), and it is very likely that mature, open stands of longleaf pine were the prime habitat used by this species.

Toads, treefrogs, and terrestrial salamanders may occur in this habitat if deciduous trees comprise a significant portion of the canopy and particularly if adjacent areas are forested by oak-dominated communities. Montane longleaf sites in adjacent states have been found to support Fowler's toad, barking treefrog, squirrel treefrog, eastern narrow-mouthed toad, and eastern spadefoot toad. Webster's salamander occurs along oak-dominated ridges and bluffs having a significant amount of longleaf pine along the Flint River in Upson County (Camp 2008c). Zigzag salamander and southern redback salamander may also occur.

Terrestrial snakes include eastern mole snakes, black racers, eastern hognose snakes, eastern coral snakes, coachwhips, rat snakes, and copperheads. The eastern hognose snake has the most specialized diet of any of these, feeding almost exclusively on toads. Timber and pigmy rattlesnakes may occur locally in undeveloped regions. Fossorial (burrowing) snakes include the largely insectivorous southeastern crowned snakes and scarlet snakes, which feed heavily on the eggs of other reptiles.

The most frequently occurring lizards are the eastern fence lizard and perhaps the five-lined skink, which is fairly common along dry ridges of the Pine Mountain (Harris and Meriwether Counties) area. Six-lined racerunners may occur in and around openings associated with rock outcrops or those created by fallen trees. This species' closest relatives live in western deserts, and racerunners show their desertic tendencies by remaining active in the middle of the day even during the hottest times of the year (Winne 2008).

Pine Warbler (*Dendroica pinus*)

Pine warblers are slightly larger than most wood-warblers, reaching a length of about 5.5 inches. Adult males are olive-green above and have a yellow throat and breast with indistinct black streaking on sides of the breast, a whitish belly, and dark wings with two broad whitish wing-bars. The bill is black and relatively thick for a warbler. Adult females are duller and more variable in color than males (Dunn and Alderfer 2008).

This bird is aptly named, since it nests only in pine trees and spends most of its life in pine-dominated habitats. It is a common breeder in most pine forests of the eastern United States as well as in southeast Canada. In Georgia, the pine warbler breeds frequently in stands of shortleaf, longleaf, loblolly, Virginia, and slash pines. It is one of only a few birds in the Southeast that are considered pine forest specialists (Ferrari 2010).

Pine warblers have a varied diet. The most important foods are insects and spiders, but during late summer, fall, and winter these birds may also consume fruits of bayberry, dogwood, grape, American persimmon, sumac, and Virginia-creeper as well as the seeds of longleaf, pitch, shortleaf, and loblolly pines (NatureServe 2009b). Due to the fact that this bird nests high in the canopy, data on nesting and reproduction are limited. Breeding can begin in early March and may extend to early August. The pine warbler's compact nest is usually constructed among pine needles near the tip of a horizontal branch more than 20 feet off the ground (Ferrari 2010).

Breeding Bird Survey data indicate that populations of the pine warbler have increased in Georgia and the eastern United States since the 1960s. Since almost all of its range is within the United States, loss of wintering habitat is not a significant threat for this bird, which is among the most abundant breeding warblers in Georgia (Ferrari 2010).

ecology. Detailed signs along the trail explain how to identify longleaf pines, management of the stands, and the ecology, fire regime, animals, and plants of the forest. As the signs indicate, these stands are being studied by Berry faculty and students and are being carefully restored and inventoried.

Many of the longleaf pines are magnificent. Some were established more than two centuries ago and have achieved the flat tops and thick limbs that distinguish old longleaf pines. Other tree species include Virginia pine, shortleaf pine, sand hickory, pignut hickory, mockernut hickory, blackjack oak, scarlet oak, rock chestnut oak, southern red oak, post oak, black oak, sassafras, sourwood, and flowering dogwood. Shrubs and woody vines include hillside blueberry, sparkleberry, winged sumac, and muscadine grape. Herbaceous species include woodland (whorled) coreopsis, small-headed sunflower, licorice goldenrod, small-headed sunflower, silkgrass, bracken fern, and several grasses and sedges.

Location: The main entrance to Berry College is located 2 miles north of Ga. Hwy. 20/Turner McCall Blvd. in Rome on U.S. 27. Turn left into Berry College's main entrance. The Longleaf Trail is located on the Mountain Campus portion of Berry College and is displayed in the Berry Campus map as "Old Mill." From the main gate, drive to the roundabout and turn at the first right onto Bertrand Way. Stay on Bertrand Way, driving past the Ford Complex of buildings on the right and past the intersections with Viking Way and Rollins Rd. Bertrand will end at Lavender Mountain Dr. Bear right on Lavender Mountain Dr. and travel approximately 3 miles. Turn right at the five-way crossroads in front of the WinShape Center. Proceed less than 0.25 mile until a small lake (Swan Lake) is visible on your right—bear left at the next road and proceed another 0.25 mile until a pavilion (WinShape Pavilion) is on the left. Turn left and proceed about 0.5 mile until the Old Mill parking area. Look for signs for the Longleaf Pine Trailhead, which is located behind the Old Mill. Google Earth GPS approximate coordinates: N 34.324733/W 085.249266.

Longleaf Trail at Berry College

The Longleaf Trail on Lavender Mountain, within the confines of Berry College, is a short trail that provides an excellent opportunity to experience the montane longleaf natural community and to learn about its

Calcareous Prairies and Barrens (Coosa Prairies)

Calcareous prairies and barrens are a mosaic of deep-soil prairies and shallow-soil barrens. They grow over calcareous bedrock in Floyd County, in the Coosa River watershed in the Southern Limestone / Dolomite Valleys subregion. Composites, including sunflowers, coneflowers, and blazing-stars, dominate, along with some grasses of the American Midwest. This natural community has been documented and inventoried in Georgia by botanists since the early 1990s (Allison 1995; Govus 2003a; R. Ware, Floyd Cty., unpubl. data).

The calcareous prairies and barrens are ecologically significant. They are very diverse, with many rare species, including several endemics and disjuncts (Govus 2003a). Two critically imperiled plant associations are found in this natural community. The plant assemblages have strong affinities with prairies farther west, including those in the Ozarks, Tennessee, and Kentucky and even farther west (R. C. Anderson and Bowles 1999; Baskin, Baskin, and Chester 1999; Heikens 1999).

The prairies and barrens are especially attractive in June, when the prairie coneflower, wavyleaf purple coneflower, Mohr's Barbara's-buttons, and scaly blazing-star are blooming, and again in September–October, when narrowleaf sunflower, whorled sunflower, orange coneflower, many asters, and goldenrods are blooming (Ware 2008c). This natural community has many similarities to the calcareous glade, barren, and woodland (cedar glades) natural community (DeSelm and Murdock 1993; Govus 2003a), but several factors distinguish these communities in Georgia. The dominant and rare plant species differ; soil depth is on average lower in cedar glades; red cedar is much more abundant in the glades; the Coosa prairies lack several cedar glade endemics, such as least glade cress, purple tassels, and Nashville breadroot (Govus 2003a); and the cedar glades lack a number of the rare species found in the calcareous prairies and barrens.

PHYSICAL SETTING AND ECOLOGY

The bedrock is limestone or calcareous shale, particularly the Conasauga Shale. Soil depth ranges from very shallow soils that foster barrens on the upper portions of low ridges and south- or west-facing slopes to thick, shrink-swell soils on flat sites (Govus 2003a). Conditions in the shallow soils are harsh. They may be saturated during wet periods, but are more often xeric and exposed to temperature extremes. The thicker-soiled sites retain much more moisture and so are buffered from the temperature extremes experienced by the dry sites. They have an extreme hydrologic regime because the thick soils are subject to shrink-swell patterns. From winter through early spring, the soils swell and pond water; as the spring and summer progress, the water evaporates and the plants take up and transpire more moisture, so the soils dry out and become cracked, like pavement. What little water is retained in the clayey soils that develop over calcium substrates will adhere strongly to the clay particles and is unavailable to plants.

Except for the most hydric sites and glade-like areas where vegetation is sparse and bare rock acts as a firebreak, anthropogenic (human-caused) fire probably helped maintain some of these sites and extended their range from that of the present. Researchers have chronicled the demise of prairies due to the invasion of woody species when fire was excluded (DeSelm and Murdock 1993; R. C. Anderson and Bowles 1999; Baskin, Baskin, and Chester 1999; Heikens 1999). Fire-return intervals of roughly three to four years maintained savannas in the Ozarks (Heikens 1999). As those intervals increased to 24 years, few openings persisted, with eastern red cedar and blackjack oak being primary invaders. Xeric, thin-soil openings resisted encroachment the longest (Heikens 1999). Prairie maintenance should be similar. Thus, prescribed fire and hand-pruning regimes may need to be implemented in some prairies and barrens to sustain them.

Another important influence on vegetation composition in the prairies is the presence of calcium, which can inhibit plant uptake of other nutrients (Allison 1995). Although calcium is necessary to plants, in abundance it can inhibit the uptake of iron, which is most soluble and available to plants in low pH environments. Ericads, such as blueberries, for example, are dependent on acidic environments where iron is soluble. These plants are not equipped for high-base conditions where iron is bound to other nutrients and not easily available (Cullina 2008). Thus, acid-loving plants are rare in this environment, whereas calciphiles, which have evolved numerous mechanisms to stave off uptake of too much calcium, are favored here (Cullina 2008).

VEGETATION

In both dry and moist communities, grasses and forbs are dominant, with little bluestem, big bluestem, prairie dropseed, yellow indiangrass, side-oats grama, switchgrass, nodding onion, obedient plant, common sneezeweed, and narrow-leaved smooth aster (Allison 1995; Govus 2003a). The plant communities occur along a moisture gradient from moist, deeper-soiled sites to xeric, shallow-soiled ones (DeSelm and Murdock 1993; Govus 2003a), as described below.

Dry Prairies and Barrens. These support interesting disjunct plants, including Great Plains ladies'-tresses, barrens (prairie) milkweed, blue wild indigo, and barrens St. John's-wort. Other dry prairie plants include rosinweed, poverty dropseed, rough blazing-star, hairy wild-petunia, eastern gray goldenrod, obedient plant, common sneezeweed, common eastern coneflower, Virginia marbleseed, prairie grass-leaved aster, nodding onion, glade blue curls, stiff-leaved aster, prairie bluehearts, Canada bluets, lobelia, green milkweed, narrow-leaved smooth aster, side-oats grama, Mexican plum, bird's-foot violet, a rare blazing-star, glade St. John's-wort, shale-barren skullcap, and barrens silky aster (Allison 1995; Govus 2003a; R. Ware, unpubl. data). The diversity of these sites and the many plants unusual to Georgia make these important communities.

Wet Prairies. Wet prairies, which are on moist to hydric sites, are easily identified by the presence of prairie-dock because of its large leaves. Disjunct species include Riddell's goldenrod, whorled loosestrife, Texas plains rush, and Thorn's beaksedge. Narrowly endemic species include whorled sunflower and Mohr's Barbara's-buttons. Other herbs include Virginia mountain-mint, big bishopweed, small-fruited seedbox, swamp thistle, florist's gayfeather, Caribbean miterwort, angle-stem beaksedge, eastern shooting star, and yellow sunnybells (Govus 2003a).

Dry-mesic prairie (Martha's Meadow)

Wet prairie. The large leaves of prairie-dock are often good indicators of a wet prairie.

Dry-Mesic Prairies, Savannas, and Woodlands. These occur on sites that are intermediate between dry and wet sites. A good example of this assemblage is Martha's Meadow at Berry College (see Featured Place). The lush ground cover includes numerous grasses, sedges, several milkweeds, several bedstraws, many legumes, calciphitic herbaceous species such as hoary puccoon, dwarf larkspur, nettleleaf noseburn, nettleleaf sage, indian pink, and much more (R. Ware, unpubl. data).

The canopy composition of these woodlands and savannas differs according to whether they are maintained by fire or mowing. Ironwood, common shagbark hickory, Carolina shagbark hickory, eastern red cedar, eastern redbud, water oak, and black cherry would survive if mowing is the dominant force (in the past grazing would have had a similar impact), keeping a site open but not where fire is frequent. With regular fire, oaks, such as post oak, chinquapin oak, white oak, southern red oak, black oak, and Shumard oak, as well as shortleaf pine and loblolly pine are more abundant.

ANIMALS

Prairies and barrens are very favorable for those mammals that flourish in the ecotone between the prairie and surrounding forest or woodland. Some species forage for food in the prairie, but will find shelter and breed in the forest. Common mammals in prairies are white-tailed deer, eastern cottontail, groundhog, coyote, red fox, white-footed mouse, golden mouse, hispid cotton rat, eastern mole, and striped skunk. Pine voles are influential in maintaining this natural community because they feed on the bases of grass stems and create many runways, thereby aerating the soil, spreading and mixing humus and nutrients, and enabling nongraminoid species to become established in the stirred-up soils (DeSelm and Murdock 1999).

While these remnant prairies are generally too small in size to provide adequate habitat for most nesting grassland birds, they can provide foraging habitat for species such as the eastern bluebird, red-headed woodpecker, and northern flicker that use open areas of grasses and forbs as feeding sites (W. S. Moore 1995; Gowaty and Plissner 1998; K. G. Smith, Withgott, and Rodewald 2000). The red-winged blackbird, American goldfinch, and possibly the blue grosbeak (Ingold 1993; Middleton 1993; Yasukawa and Searcy 1995) nest in some of these prairies, and common

CHARACTERISTIC PLANTS OF CALCAREOUS PRAIRIES AND BARRENS (COOSA PRAIRIES)

Big bluestem—Andropogron gerardii

Milkweeds—Asclepias hirtella; A. viridiflora; A. viridis

Blue wild indigo—Baptisia australis

Prairie bluehearts—Buchnera americana

Prairie purple coneflower—Echinacea simulata

Tall thoroughwort—Eupatorium altissimum

Prairie grass-leaved aster—Eurybia hemispherica

Sunflowers—Helianthus mollis; H. occidentalis; H. verticillatus

Barrens St. John's-wort—Hypericum sphaerocarpum

Blazing-stars—Liatris aspera; L. spicata

Whorled loosestrife—Lysimachia quadrifolia

Mohr's Barbara's-buttons—Marshallia mohrii

Virginia marbleseed—Onosmodium virginianum

Common wild quinine—Parthenium integrifolium

Obedient-plant—Physostegia virginiana

Virginia mountain-mint—Pycnanthemum virginianum

Thorne's beaksedge—Rhynchospora thornei

Common eastern coneflower—Rudbeckia fulgida

Common little bluestem—Schizachyrium scoparium

Yellow sunnybells—Schoenolirion croceum

Rosinweed—Silphium asteriscus

Prairie-dock—Silphium terebinthinaceum

White prairie-goldenrod—Solidago ptarmicoides

Riddell's goldenrod—Solidago riddellii

Southeastern bold goldenrod—Solidago rigida

Great Plains ladies'-tresses—Spiranthes magnicamporum

Prairie dropseed—Sporobolus heterolepis

Narrow-leaved smooth aster—Symphyotrichum laeve

Barrens silky aster—Symphyotrichum pratense

yellowthroats, white-eyed vireos, and indigo buntings may nest in dense shrubs found along the margins (Payne 1992; Hopp, Kirby, and Boone 1995; Guzy and Ritchison 1999). Composites are abundant in these prairies and provide plentiful seeds in late summer and early fall for American goldfinches that nest within or near these sites (Middleton 1993). Field sparrows, and possibly grasshopper sparrows, may use these sites during migration or winter (Carey, Burhans, and Nelson 1994; Vickery 1996).

Being relatively open and dry, the herpetofauna of the dry variants of this natural community is probably similar to that of the calcareous glade and barren natural community. In Alabama, the Coosa Valley has been an important dispersal corridor for Coastal Plain species of amphibians and reptiles (Mount 1975). It is possible that one or more of these species may be discovered in this particular community in Georgia's portion of the Coosa Valley. Potential candidates include oak toads and mole skinks, both of which are inhabitants of open habitats and occur in reasonable proximity to the Georgia line in Alabama. In moister sites, the herpetofauna should be similar to that of the flatwoods in which this environment is typically embedded.

Loggerhead Shrike (*Lanius ludovicianus*)

The loggerhead shrike is a medium-sized bird, gray above and white below, with a distinctive black mask. Its head is large in proportion to its body, hence the name "loggerhead," which also means "blockhead." Other common names for this species include butcherbird, white-rumped shrike, French or Spanish mockingbird, and thornbird (Terres 1980; Yosef 1996). Found only in North America, the loggerhead shrike nests from central Canada through the Great Basin to the southern tips of Baja California, Mexico, and Florida. Loggerhead shrike nesting has been documented throughout Georgia except in and around the Okefenokee Swamp and in the Blue Ridge (Keyes 2010).

The loggerhead shrike inhabits meadows, grasslands, woodlands, abandoned orchards, and other open habitats. Favorite food items include mice and small birds, especially in the winter (Terres 1980). During the summer months, insects, snails, spiders, frogs, snakes, and other animals may also be taken. The loggerhead shrike hunts from exposed perches, swooping down to capture its prey and impaling it on sharp objects such as thorns and barbed-wire fences. Its hooked bill has horny projections that help the shrike grasp and subdue active prey (Yosef 1996).

Despite its wide distribution, the loggerhead shrike has been declining in abundance since the 1960s, and perhaps earlier. The species is now extirpated from most of the Northeast and is nearly extirpated from portions of the upper Midwest. Part of this decline can be attributed to reforestation of open habitats. Much suitable habitat remains unoccupied in these northern states, however, and declines have been recorded in all regions of the country. Use of persistent pesticides, loss of shrubby field edges, loss of wintering habitat, competition with other species, and increased roadside mortality have all been suggested as possible factors in this decline, but further research is needed (Yosef 1996; Keyes 2010).

Berry College

Tiny patches of wet prairie embedded within the flatwoods occur on the campus of Berry College, within the wildlife management area. One small prairie occurs roughly 0.5 mile from the trail around Victory Lake. Prairie-dock, which is an indicator species of moist prairies, occurs here. A common switchgrass of the prairies, *Panicum virgatum*, is also here, as is spider milkweed, a good prairie indicator. Other herbaceous species include sundrops, lobelia, common marsh-pink, black-eyed Susan, common rough

fleabane, wild onion, common hairy coreopsis, narrowleaf vervain, skullcap, Maryland golden-aster, common yellow thistle, and narrow-leaf white-topped aster. The woody species that may invade prairies in the absence of disturbance such as fire or grazing are also illustrated here. Woody invaders on the site include sweet gum, blackjack oak, loblolly pine, American persimmon, willow oak, flowering dogwood, white ash, littlehip hawthorn, sparkleberry, black cherry, American rattan, parsley haw, and red maple (R. Ware 2009d).

Dry-mesic prairie and woodland conditions occur in Martha's Meadow, which is alongside the trail around Victory Lake, beyond the stands described for the flatwoods Featured Place. More than 175 species occur in this very small (less than half-acre) site, which is being maintained as a savanna through mowing. The lush ground cover, as described earlier, supports numerous grasses, sedges, five different milkweeds, several bedstraws, many legumes, calciphitic herbaceous species such as hoary pucoon, dwarf larkspur, nettleleaf noseburn, nettle-leaf sage, indian pink, and much more (R. Ware 2009d). The canopy composition of this woodland differs somewhat from how such woodlands would have appeared if maintained by fire. Fire-intolerant trees, such as eastern red cedar, eastern redbud, water oak, and black cherry, would not have occurred; rather, fire-tolerant oaks, such as post oak, chinquapin oak, white oak, southern red oak, and black oak, would have dominated, perhaps with Shumard oak and some shortleaf pine.

Location: Follow the directions to Berry College found on p. 196. After turning right onto Lavender Mountain Rd., continue less than 0.25 mile and through the avenue of oaks, then turn right onto the gravel road. Park in the small parking lot on the right. Continue walking down the dirt road (Road of Remembrance or Old Stretch Rd.) to the north, around what was previously Victory Lake before the water drained into underground caverns. Go through the metal gate and go approx. 0.75 mile (about 100 yards past metal gate) to a small opening on the left, which is the prairie. Google Earth GPS approximate coordinates for parking area: N 34.298878/W 085.197983.

Calcareous Glades, Barrens, and Woodlands (Cedar Glades)

Calcareous glades, barrens, and woodlands are mosaics of exposed limestone, barrens, shrubby areas, and small woodlands. These sites have long been called cedar glades because of the many eastern red cedars that are present (R. M. Harper 1906; Wharton 1978). The glades are picturesque and distinctive, especially in a moist spring, when a host of spring wildflowers, including nettle-leaf sage, common cinquefoil, Nashville breadroot, purple tassels, spider milkweed, blue wild indigo, and hoary pucoon are all blooming.

Expanses of exposed limestone are rare in Georgia, and so the vegetation of this environment hosts a number of rare, endemic species, including least glade cress, purple tassels, Nashville breadroot, glade St. John's-wort, and Eggleston's violet (Baskin and Baskin 1999; Govus 2003a). These glades and barrens thus contribute important biological diversity to the ecoregion (Braun 1950). Fortunately, superb examples of cedar glades are preserved in Chickamauga and Chattanooga National Military Park (Walker County) (see the Featured Place), where it is possible to visit numerous sites, each with a unique suite of species and topographic features.

This natural community intergrades with the calcareous prairie and barren (Coosa prairies) natural community (DeSelm and Murdock 1993). The differences between the two are described on p. 197.

PHYSICAL SETTING AND ECOLOGY

Calcareous glades, barrens, and woodlands occur in the Southern Limestone / Dolomite Valleys and Low, Rolling Hills subregion, on low, flat, or sloping, north- to south-trending limestones, often in the Chickamauga Limestone, which is a calcareous limestone formation that occurs in the lowermost hillslopes of the Armuchee Ridges and extends northward from

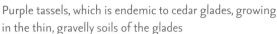
Purple tassels, which is endemic to cedar glades, growing in the thin, gravelly soils of the glades

Glade larkspur

Pigeon Mountain. In addition to the Chickamauga glades, this natural community is found on low ridges on the eastern slope of Pigeon Mountain (Walker County), within openings in the dry calcareous forest natural community. One well-developed glade occurs near Rome on the Knox Formation.

The bare rock and shallow soils create extremes of moisture and temperatures that restrict the plant species to those with adaptations to heat and drought similar to those on granite outcrops (p. 304). Temperatures are very hot in open areas in the summer and quite cold in winter because the shallow soils cannot hold enough moisture to buffer temperature fluctuations. Soils are often saturated in the winter, when transpiration rates are low, but can be very dry in late spring and summer, sometimes below the

permanent wilting point (Braun 1950; Baskin and Baskin 1999). Precipitation differences from year to year cause the glades and barrens to have radically different appearances in different years. When precipitation rates are high, many plants germinate and bloom, whereas in dry, hot years the sites appear depauperate (Nourse and Nourse 2007). The sites also change greatly in appearance with the season; for example, in spring, open glades are "carpeted with flowers, many of them short-lived annuals," but when the annuals die, the xerophytes, such as eastern pricklypear, agave, and croton, become more conspicuous (Braun 1950, p. 131).

Erosion, drought, fire, grazing, frost-heave, shrink-swell soils, and grazing can all contribute to keeping these landscapes open. Erosion maintains some open areas: mildly acidic rainwater runs over the rock and dissolves the limestone, creating depressions, widening crevices, and causing the formation of gravel and flat limestone fragments called "flags" (Quarterman, Burbanck, and Shure 1993; Baskin and Baskin 1999; Christopherson 2009). Long droughts cause the mortality of trees and shrubs. Frost-heaving uproots and so kills seedlings as follows: soil water first freezes, causing the soil particles to rise, and then melts, causing the soil particles to collapse (Quarterman, Burbank, and Shure 1993; Christopherson 2009). The shrink-swell soils that form over calcium bedrock can prevent plants from becoming established because in the summer the soil dries out and forms huge cracks, displacing the plants' roots and drying them out. Browsing and grazing also increase openness (DeSelm and Murdock 1993; Quarterman, Burbank, and Shure 1993; R. C. Anderson and Bowles 1999).

Without fire, trees and shrubs encroach in many parts of the glades and barrens, reducing diversity (Baskin and Baskin 1978; Heikens 1999; NatureServe Ecology South 2008). A fire-return interval of 13–25 years, with local areas experiencing return intervals as low as 7 years, has been suggested as a likely regime (Frost 1998; NatureServe Ecology South 2008). Glades were probably more expansive in the past, encompassing surrounding areas that are now dry calcareous forest.

Fire has largely been excluded from the Chickamauga and Chattanooga National Military Park (Walker and Catoosa Counties) since its creation more than a century ago (NatureServe Ecology South 2008; Sutter et al. 2011). This has led to severe fire-suppressed conditions for all of the forests/woodlands surrounding the glades. The current structure of these forests includes an extremely dense understory of eastern red cedar and other deciduous woody plants that would not occur within forests under a natural fire regime, including Chinese privet, a non-native invasive shrub (Sutter et al. 2011).

As in many other natural communities of this ecoregion, calcium is an important factor in shaping vegetation composition. As described for other calcareous communities in this ecoregion, although calcium is necessary to plants, in abundance it can inhibit the uptake of iron, which is most soluble and available to plants in low pH environments. Ericads, for example, are dependent on acidic environments where iron is soluble. They are not equipped for high-base conditions where iron is bound to other nutrients and less available (Cullina 2008). Thus, ericads are rare in this natural community. Calciphiles, which have evolved numerous mechanisms to stave off uptake of too much calcium or to enable physiological tolerance, are favored here.

Soils build up in crevices between rocks and in shallow depressions created by solution weathering (Baskin and Baskin 1999). The depth of soils is an important physical factor in shaping vegetation on a particular microsite because it influences moisture levels (Quarterman, Burbank, and Shure 1993). Deeper soils retain more water for longer periods of time and are therefore able to support larger plants and more diversity.

Great Plains ladies'-tresses. This rare plant is found over calcareous barrens, in thin, dry soils.

Nashville breadroot growing in a gravel glade

VEGETATION

Differences in soil depth serve to distinguish four different vegetation communities on the cedar glades, each of which intergrades into the next: gravel glades, grassy glades, shrub thickets, and glade woodlands (Quarterman, Burbank, and Shure 1993). Plants also grow in deep cracks in the limestone that fill with soil (Baskin and Baskin 1999). It is possible that plant succession progresses over long periods of time from one community to the next as crevices and depressions grow and soils deepen (Sutter et al. 2011). As in other rock outcrop communities, however, successional processes are disrupted and reversed by drought or the sloughing of vegetation from intense rainfall during high-precipitation events (Schafale and Weakley 1990).

Gravel Glades. These occur in the most xeric conditions (except for bare rock) with less than 0.25 inch of gravel-covered soil. Algae and foliose lichens dominate, along with least glade cress. Lime-barren sandwort can dominate in the spring along with other sum-

mer annuals and mosses (Baskin and Baskin 1999). Deeper parts of the gravel glades will support other herbs, such as poverty dropseed, fleabanes, purple tassels, and witchgrasses (Quarterman, Burbank, and Shure 1993).

Grassy Glades. These are areas where the soil is deeper, though not deep enough to support mature shrubs and small trees. In addition to the species that occur in the deeper parts of the gravel glades, other plants, particularly more perennials, will grow here, including scurf-pea, eastern prickly-pear cactus, and rattlesnake-master. Barrens often develop where the soil is consistently deep enough for perennial grasses, such as little bluestem, to dominate (Quarterman, Burbank, and Shure 1993).

Shrub Thickets. These occur in small islands within the rock outcrops and often support southern-privet, fragrant sumac, Carolina buckthorn, and coralberry, along with seedlings of eastern red cedar, white ash, dwarf hackberry, American rattan, and winged elm

CHARACTERISTIC PLANTS OF CALCAREOUS GLADES, BARRENS, AND WOODLANDS (CEDAR GLADES)

TREES

Hackberries—Celtis occidentalis; C. tenuifolia

White ash—Fraxinus americana

Eastern red cedar—Juniperus virginana

Pines—Pinus echinata; P. virginiana

Chinquapin oak—Quercus muehlenbergii

Post oak—Quercus stellata

Winged elm—Ulmus alata

SHRUBS AND WOODY VINES

Southern-privet—Forestiera ligustrina

Carolina buckthorn—Frangula caroliniana

Fragrant sumac—Rhus aromatica

Coralberry—Symphoricarpos orbiculatus

GROUND COVER

Thimbleweed—Anemone virginiana

Tall coreopsis—Coreopsis tripteris

Purple tassels—Dalea gattingeri

Daisy fleabane—Erigeron strigosus

Glade St. John's-wort—Hypericum dolabriforme

Least glade cress—Leavenworthia exigua

Hoary puccoon—Lithospermum canescens

Rattlesnake-master—Manfreda virginica

Lime-barren sandwort—Minuartia patula

Sundrops—Oenothera fruticosa

Eastern prickly-pear—Opuntia humifusa

Ragworts—Packera anonyma; P. paupercula

Nashville breadroot—Pediomelum subacaule

Hairy phlox—Phlox amoena

Nettle-leaf sage—Salvia urticifolia

Lime stonecrop—Sedum pulchellum

Goldenrods—Solidago spp.

Eggleston's violet—Viola egglestonii

(Quarterman, Burbank, and Shure 1993; NatureServe Ecology South 2008).

Glade Woodlands. These grow in small islands in the glades and often support white ash, dwarf hackberry, eastern red cedar, chinquapin oak, winged elm, Virginia pine, shortleaf pine, post oak, or eastern redbud (Quarterman, Burbank, and Shure 1993; NatureServe Ecology South 2008).

ANIMALS

Small mammals associated with cedar glades have not been inventoried extensively in Georgia. Based on similar habitats in Tennessee, the white-footed mouse may occur in wooded areas and the golden mouse could occur in vine-dominated edge environments. Eastern harvest mice and hispid cotton rats may frequent moist, grassy glades. Other mammals associated with the surrounding forests, such as the eastern chipmunk, might also frequent or traverse the glades (Quarterman, Burbank, and Shure 1993).

Many bird species will use cedar glades depending on the composition and structure of the vegetation. Eastern towhees, brown thrashers, and gray catbirds will nest in shrub thickets (Cimprich and Moore 1995; Greenlaw 1996; Cavitt and Haas 2000) as will white-eyed vireos, indigo buntings, and common yellowthroats (Payne 1992; Hopp, Kirby, and Boone 1995; Guzy and Ritchison 1999; T. M. Schneider et al. 2010). Areas of very sparse vegetation may provide nesting sites for common nighthawks, which place their eggs directly on the ground (Poulin, Grindal, and Brigham 1996). Wintering sparrows will feed on grass and forb seeds. The cedar waxwing feeds heavily on the arils ("berries") of the eastern red cedar from late fall through early spring (Witmer 1996; Witmer, Mountjoy, and Elliot 1997). The larger openings provide feeding sites for northern flickers, eastern phoebes, and eastern wood-pewees (Weeks 1994; W. S. Moore 1995; McCarty 1996).

Several reptile species that typically avoid closed-canopy environments occur in dry, open areas. These include six-lined racerunners, whose closest relatives inhabit prairie and desert environments of the western United States (Reeder, Cole, and Dessauer 2002). These lizards share the heat-loving tendencies of their western relatives and are among the last species to become active in the spring. Moreover, individuals remain active in the middle of the day (Winne 2008), even at ambient temperatures in excess of 95°F. Slender glass lizards are also species of dry, grassy habitats or open woodlands. Five-lined skinks and eastern fence lizards occur if trees are present. Coachwhips and black racers, both of which feed on lizards, are common in open areas, as well (Plummer and Congdon 1994). Rodent-eating snakes such as corn snakes and rat snakes may hunt in these areas, as well. Copperheads and timber rattlesnakes may be found in areas where fallen timber or rocky outcrops provide cover.

Invertebrates are numerous: they graze on the vegetation, pollinate flowering plants, and provide food sources for larger fauna. A study of glades in Tennessee found more than 400 species of invertebrates in the open areas. Ants comprised more than half of all species (Quarterman, Burbank, and Shure 1993, citing Meyer 1937).

FEATURED ANIMAL

Falcate Orangetip (*Anthocharis midea*)

The falcate orangetip is a North American butterfly in the family Pieridae, which includes the whites and sulphurs. These butterflies are found mainly in the eastern United States, from southern New England southwest to south Texas and north to eastern Oklahoma and Kansas. Local populations and stray individuals have been documented from the Florida panhandle, eastern Nebraska, and southern Wisconsin. Falcate orangetips live in open, wet woodlands along waterways, in open swamps, and less often in dry woods and ridge tops (Butterflies and Moths of North America 2009).

This predominantly white butterfly is of moderate size, with a wingspan of 1.375 to 1.75 inches. Each of the male's forewings has a black spot and orange hooked tip; females also have the hooked tip and black spot but lack the orange coloration. The underside of the hindwing has finely patterned green marbling (L. C. Harris 1972).

Adult males patrol on hilltops and flats in March and April, looking for females. After breeding, the females lay their yellow-green eggs singly on host plant flowers. The olive-green larvae feed mainly at night and prefer to eat flowers, flower buds, and seedpods rather than leaves. They are also cannibalistic, feeding on smaller individuals of their own species. After growing to a length of slightly more than 1 inch, the larvae form chrysalises in mid-June and may pupate for two or more years. The chrysalis has a spike-like projection that makes it look like a thorn, which may provide some protection against predation.

The favorite foods of the falcate orangetip caterpillar are plants in the mustard family (Brassicaceae), including rock cresses, glade cresses, winter-cresses, and bittercresses. Adults feed on the nectar of mustards, violets, and other species (L. C. Harris 1972).

Chickamauga and Chattanooga National Military Park

The Chickamauga and Chattanooga National Military Park contains examples of superb calcareous glades and barrens embedded within the calcareous dry forest natural community (and is the Featured Place for that natural community). Three glades are described here.

In Glade 1 mosses and lichens cover much of the ground. Trees include eastern red cedar, post oak, and white ash. Carolina buckthorn is a common shrub. Herbs that bloom in May include nettle-leaf sage, lyreleaf sage, southern ragwort, Nashville breadroot, purple tassels, and Quaker ladies. Glade St. John's-wort is also present.

Glade 2 is picturesque, with moss growing in large mats near a stream at the back of the glade. Trees include loblolly pine and Virginia pine. Plants in bloom during May include hairy phlox, spider milkweed, common cinquefoil, blue wild indigo, lyreleaf sage, southern ragwort, and hoary puccoon. Eastern prickly-pear, thimbleweed, blazing-star, rattlesnake-master, coneflower, and a mountain-mint are also present.

Glade 3 is a marvelous glade. The section nearest the path is nearly prairie-like, with grasses and many cedars. Farther away, the glade slopes more than any other in the park. Trees and shrubs include the calciphiles chinquapin oak, eastern redbud, eastern red cedar, fragrant sumac, and coralberry. Herbs include Nashville breadroot, coneflower, tall coreopsis, pussytoes, nettle-leaf sage, hoary puccoon, hairy phlox, and purple tassels. Lime stonecrop is blooming on a limestone ledge along the path leading to the glade. See Nourse and Nourse (2007) for more information on the glades.

Location: From the intersection of Ga. Hwy. 2/Battlefield Pkwy. and LaFayette Rd. in Fort Oglethorpe, travel south on LaFayette Rd. about 1 mile to the park entrance and visitor center. To reach Glade 1, go north from the visitor center to the intersection of LaFayette Rd. and Reed's Bridge Rd. Turn right (east) on Reed's Bridge Rd. and go 0.3 mile to a parking lot on the right side of the road. There is green-blazed trail here, which crosses the glade for about 100 yards. Google Earth GPS approximate coordinates: N 34.940470/ W 085.251982.

To reach Glade 2, drive an additional 0.6 mile east on Reed's Bridge Rd. to the next parking pull-off on the right. A blue-blazed trail is here; follow it about 200 yards where it intersects with the yellow trail.

To reach Glade 3, continue east on Reed's Bridge Rd. for 0.9 mile to Jay's Mill Rd. Follow Jay's Mill to the intersection with Alexander Bridge Rd. Turn left on Alexander Bridge Rd. and then right on Viniard-Alexander Rd. Drive to the second trailhead on the right; parking is on the left of the trailhead.

Acidic Glades and Barrens

Acidic glades and barrens are small-patch natural communities that are mosaics of rock, glades, barrens, and woodlands on flat to gently sloping expanses of exposed sandstone or conglomerate. Plants grow in the joints within rocks and in shallow depressions where soils accumulate. These are typically very dry communities with drought-tolerant herbs and bryophytes, along with Virginia pine, rock chestnut oak, and other dry-site oaks and pines.

These glades are often picturesque because of the bizarre, beautiful rock formations within some of them. The glades often occur on the Pennsylvanian Sandstones of the Southern Table Plateaus subregion, in Cloudland Canyon State Park (Dade County), in the Lula Lake Preserve (Walker County), on Pigeon Mountain (Walker County), and in Zahnd Natural Area (Walker County). They are also embedded within and grade into the acidic oak-pine forest or pine-oak woodland natural communities.

PHYSICAL SETTING AND ECOLOGY

These glades and barrens are often situated near the edges of the dramatic escarpments of the Cumberland Plateau, which provide striking views. The sandstones and conglomerates that underlie this natural community weather to acidic soils. As the cement that holds the sand and conglomerate particles together dissolves and is transported away, sandy particles often gather in crevices and depressions to form shallow, sandy soils (Quarterman, Burbanck, and Shure 1993; Christopherson 2009). These sites may be saturated for short times after rainfall. Temperatures on the bare rock are extremely high on exposed areas in the summer, creating very harsh conditions so plants in this community have the same adaptations to heat and drought as described for Piedmont granitic outcrops on p. 304. Glades that are embedded within forests are less ex-

In some areas, the bedrock permits only very scattered vegetation, and the acidic glade and barren natural community grades into the acidic cliff and rock outcrop natural community.

posed. Except where soils have accumulated in shallow depressions or flats, plants are restricted to crevices between rocks, creating a patchy, linear pattern of plant growth that is sparser than that on more erodible bedrock or in shallow depressions.

VEGETATION

The harsh conditions conferred by shallow, low-nutrient soils and temperature extremes do not encourage plant diversity. Dry-site trees, often gnarled and stunted to shrub size, occur around the edges of the glades and are rooted in some deep crevices (Wharton 1978). Virginia pine is common: it produces abundant seeds and is very drought tolerant, so it can easily seed into the glades. Other trees include shortleaf pine, rock chestnut oak, downy serviceberry black gum, red maple, black birch, and sand hickory. Shrubs include mountain laurel, fringe-tree (which often grows on the top of large rock outcrops), sparkleberry, Catawba rhododendron, and winged sumac. Dewberries and blackberries are common, and vines, including Carolina jessamine, muscadine, and sum-

Mountain laurel

CHARACTERISTIC PLANTS OF ACIDIC GLADES AND BARRENS

TREES

Downy serviceberry—Amelanchier
  arborea
Black (sweet) birch—Betula lenta
Hickories—Carya glabra; C. pallida;
  C. tomentosa
Sourwood—Oxydendrum arboreum
Shortleaf pine—Pinus echinata
Virginia pine—Pinus virginiana
Rock chestnut oak—Quercus montana
Post oak—Quercus stellata

SHRUBS AND WOODY VINES

Fringe-tree—Chionanthus virginicus
Hairy southern bush-honeysuckle—
  Diervilla rivularis
Carolina jessamine—Gelsemium
  sempervirens

Mountain laurel—Kalmia latifolia
Catawba rhododendron—
  Rhododendron catawbiense
Winged sumac—Rhus copallinum
Dewberries and blackberries—Rubus
  spp.
Blueberries—Vaccinium arboreum; V.
  corymbosum; V. pallidum
Grapes—Vitis aestivalis; V. rotundifolia

GROUND COVER

Old-field broomsedge—Andropogon
  virginicus
Wavy hairgrass—Avenella flexuosa
Reindeer lichens—Cladonia spp.,
  Cladina spp.
Glade rushfoil—Croton willdenowii
Oat-grasses—Danthonia spp.

Marginal wood-fern—Dryopteris
  marginalis
Common white heart-leaved aster—
  Eurybia divaricata
St. John's-wort—Hypericum stragulum
Rock-pinks—Phermeranthus mengesi;
  P. teretifolius
Silkgrass—Pityopsis graminifolia
Common little bluestem—
  Schizachyrium scoparium
Rock spikemoss—Selaginella rupestris
Spiderworts—Tradescantia spp.
Common blue curls—Trichomesta
  dichotomum

mer grape, may sprawl across the glades. Herbaceous species include the marginal wood-fern, Appalachian rock-pink, large-flowered rock-pink, spiderworts, oat-grasses, old-field broomsedge, little bluestem, hairy southern bush-honeysuckle, silkgrass, goldenrods, and asters.

Rocktown (Walker County) on Pigeon Mountain and a privately owned site on Lookout Mountain (Walker County) that is on private property support a rare plant community. In the midst of the towering, sculpted rock formations of Rocktown, extensive, shallow sandstone depressions support elf-orpine, fruticose lichens, haircap moss, black birch, Virginia pine, sourwood, and blueberries.

ANIMALS

Small mammals, such as the white-footed mouse, the eastern harvest mouse, hispid cotton rat, and eastern chipmunk, frequent acidic glades and barrens, as well as a few larger mammals such as eastern cottontail, eastern woodrat, and red fox; other mammals such as the bobcat, gray fox, and coyote from surrounding forests may traverse the glades in search of food. The open areas surrounding larger rock outcrops can provide foraging sites for the insectivorous common nighthawk, chuck-will's-widow, and whip-poor-will (Poulin, Grindal, and Brigham 1996; Straight and Cooper 2000; Cink 2002). Great crested flycatchers and eastern wood-pewees may also use these areas to feed by sallying out into the opening from the forest edge to catch moths and other insects (McCarty 1996; Lanyon 1997). Outcrops and adjacent areas with very sparse vegetation may occasionally serve as nest sites for the common nighthawk, which lays its eggs directly on the ground. Indigo buntings and common yellowthroats nest in dense patches of shrubs along the edges of the outcrops (Payne 1992; Guzy and Ritchison 1999). Chipping sparrows often nest at sites with scattered mature pines (Middleton 1998; T. M. Schneider et al. 2010). Black vultures also use these sites as roosting areas.

Six-lined racerunners are likely to be common because they prefer hot, dry, open areas. Eastern fence lizards and five-lined skinks use these areas, if there is easily accessible cover in the form of standing or fallen timber or cliff crevices nearby. A variety of forest snakes, including black racers and timber rattlesnakes, may exploit these areas for basking during periods of relatively cool weather.

Mole Kingsnake (*Lampropeltis calligaster*)

The mole kingsnake is a secretive member of the family Colubridae and a close relative of the common kingsnake, scarlet kingsnake, and eastern milk snake. Also known as the mole snake or brown kingsnake, this snake is moderate in size—usually less than 3 feet in length. The background color is light brown to reddish, with a series of reddish brown blotches. Older adults may be solid brown or greenish gray. This snake is often confused with the similarly colored and more commonly encountered corn snake (Krysko and Means 2008).

The mole kingsnake is distributed widely across the eastern United States, from Maryland to Mississippi and eastern Louisiana, with disjunct populations in the panhandle of Florida (Conant and Collins 1998). In Georgia, its range is largely restricted to the Piedmont, Blue Ridge, and Cumberland Plateau / Ridge and Valley ecoregions, where it is a resident of upland forests and woodlands. It also inhabits fallow fields and pastures. This is a strongly fossorial species, apparently spending most of its life underground. It is rarely encountered by humans except when it surfaces to prowl at night or after thunderstorms, or when it is uncovered by plowing or digging in the soil (Krysko and Means 2008).

Like other members of the genus *Lampropeltis*, the mole kingsnake is a constrictor and feeds on a variety of vertebrate prey, including mice, lizards, and small snakes. Mating takes place in the spring, and females lay an average of 10–12 eggs underground during the summer. Known predators of mole kingsnakes include common kingsnakes, black racers, and a variety of large birds and mammals (Krysko and Means 2008).

Rocktown

The Rocktown Trail on Pigeon Mountain winds through an acidic oak-pine forest natural community before it enters an area of dramatic, picturesque rock formations unmatched by any other publicly accessible place in the ecoregion. These formations are perched on the edge of the Plateau Escarpment. Within this area, acidic oak-pine forest, pine-oak woodland (dominated by Virginia pine), acidic glade and barren, and acidic cliff and outcrop natural communities intertwine and intergrade nearly imperceptibly with one another. A picturesque glade occurs shortly after entering the Rocktown area. It is located on top of a large, somewhat steeply rounded outcropping that has weathered into interesting knobs and hummocks. Dominant trees include Virginia pine, rock chestnut oak, red maple, scarlet oak, and sourwood. An occasional eastern red cedar appears. Shrubs and woody

vines include fringe-tree, sparkleberry, and American beautyberry. Reindeer lichens and haircap mosses fringe the rocks. Herbs include bracken fern, glade rushfoil, and a goldenrod. Woody vines include muscadine and greenbriers.

The best way to explore the many natural communities of this site is to wander at will, exploring the dramatic outcroppings. Other glade-like openings support the above species as well as blackberries, dewberries, Virginia-creeper, black birch, sand hickory, poison ivy, sassafras, mountain laurel, and spiderworts. A small rockhouse (see the acidic cliff and rock outcrop natural community) occurs in one area.

Location: From U.S. 27/Ga. Hwy. 1/Main St. in LaFayette, proceed west 2.8 miles on Ga. 193/W. Main St. to Chamberlain Rd., turn left, and proceed 3.4 miles. Turn right at the sign for Crockford–Pigeon Mountain Wildlife Management Area onto Rocky Lane. Pass the Department of Natural Resources check station and continue straight on the gravel road of Rocky Lane. The road can be rough, so drive with care. At about 3.4 miles from the check station, Rocky Lane will turn sharply right while another road will continue straight. Proceed right on Rocky Lane to Rocktown. From the sharp right turn continue approximately 1.3 miles and turn left on Rocktown Rd. Proceed about 0.7 mile to the parking area and the trailhead. Google Earth GPS approximate coordinates at Rocktown parking: N 34.658661/W 085.390071.

Advisory: The road that runs up the Plateau Escarpment to reach Rocktown can be difficult to drive due to rough conditions. Zahnd Natural Area described in the text (p. 188) is an alternative site, as is the West Rim Trail glade described on p. 183.

Calcareous Cliffs

Calcareous cliffs are vertical or near-vertical rockfaces that have high levels of calcium. They occur on bluffs along rivers and on the sides of some valleys and canyons, usually as small patches embedded within the mesic forest natural community. These cliffs are generally dry with some seepage areas. This natural community can be quite picturesque, particularly in the spring when calcium-loving wildflowers such as Canada columbine and fernleaf phacelia are blooming on the rocks. Caves often occur at the base of these cliffs, and a number of rare species occur in the caves.

The Southern Limestone / Dolomite Valleys subregion supports many examples of this community. Calcareous cliffs and bluffs occur along larger rivers, such as Whitmore's Bluff along the Oostanala River (Floyd County) and Black's Bluff along the Coosa River (Floyd County), as well as along smaller streams, such as on the Shirley Miller Trail in the Crockford–Pigeon Mountain Wildlife Management Area (see Featured Place) and in Sitton Gulch in Cloudland Canyon State Park (Dade County). It is likely that unexplored calcareous cliffs exist in this ecoregion.

PHYSICAL SETTING AND ECOLOGY

Cliff faces vary in their moisture levels, microhabitat formation, and soil pH (Schafale and Weakley 1990; Larson, Matthes, and Kelly 2000). This may be particularly true for limestone and other calcareous substrates in the eastern United States because they erode easily in the moist climate to form many different habitats, ranging from crevices to fairly deep depressions and ledges on which soils build. Moisture levels vary greatly within small distances on the cliffs, ranging from very xeric niches to permanent seepage areas. They also vary with aspect: southwest-facing cliffs are drier, and north-facing cliffs, particularly those embedded within forests, are more mesic.

CHARACTERISTIC PLANTS OF CALCAREOUS CLIFFS

TREES

Eastern redbud—*Cercis canadensis*

White ash—*Fraxinus americana*

Eastern red cedar—*Juniperus virginiana*

Ironwood—*Ostrya virginiana*

Elms—*Ulmus alata; U. rubra*

SHRUBS AND WOODY VINES

Smooth hydrangea—*Hydrangea arborescens*

Appalachian mock-orange—*Philadelphus inordorus*

Buckthorn bumelia—*Sideroxylon lycioides*

GROUND COVER

Northern maidenhair fern—*Adiantum pedatum*

Sharp-lobed hepatica—*Anemone acutiloba*

Canada columbine—*Aquilegia canadensis*

Lyreleaf rockcress—*Arabidopsis lyrata*

Spreading rockcress—*Arabis patens*

Spleenworts—*Asplenium platyneuron; A. ruta-muraria; A. trichomanes*

Walking fern—*Asplenium rhizophyllum*

Rockcresses—*Boechera canadensis; B. laevigata*

Cutleaf toothwort—*Cardamine concantenata*

Cumberland spurge—*Euphorbia mercurialina*

Crested iris—*Iris cristata*

Early saxifrage—*Micranthes virginiensis*

Roundleaf ragwort—*Packera obovata*

Purple cliff-brake—*Pellaea atropurpurea*

Fernleaf phacelia—*Phacelia bipinnatifida*

Eastern blue phlox—*Phlox divaricata*

Resurrection fern—*Pleopeltis polypodioides*

Bloodroot—*Sanguinaria canadensis*

Mountain stonecrop—*Sedum ternatum*

Blue-eyed grass—*Sisyrinchium spp.*

Rue-anemone—*Thalictrum thalictroides*

Long-spurred violet—*Viola rostrata*

Some researchers have found that the calcareous rock type has little influence on plant composition, presumably because the organic matter that builds up in soils is acidic, mitigating calcareous substrate influences or because soils are leached of calcium; others have found that a high pH substrate does influence plant composition. Still others have found that pH can vary greatly over a cliff face and so has varying influences on plant distribution (Larson, Matthes, and Kelly 2000). Typically, calcareous cliffs in Georgia appear to support both calciphiles and the species of acidic cliffs, with plant composition changing in response to soil moisture levels and pH fluctuations.

VEGETATION

Trees occur on the tops of the cliffs as well as within crevices and ledges on the cliffs. Often they are calciphiles, such as white ash, eastern redbud, or eastern red cedar. Calciphitic shrubs, such as Appalachian mock-orange or buckthorn bumelia, also appear on eroded portions of the cliff, as do smooth hydrangea and Virginia-creeper. Where soils have built up on ledges or on the talus below the cliff, herbs will grow. Canada columbine, eastern shooting star, sharp-lobed hebatica, early saxifrage, mountain stonecrop, and rue-anemone are present. These sites can provide good

Eastern shooting star

habitat for many ferns, such as resurrection fern and several spleenworts. Calciphiles on the cliffs include fernleaf phacelia, Cumberland spurge, and Canada columbine, along with species of acidic cliffs, such as resurrection fern. There are fewer ericads on the limestone cliffs than on acidic cliffs; mountain laurel and sparkleberry, for example, are uncommon.

ANIMALS

Although cliffs can limit wildlife because of their inaccessibility, they can also provide a wide array of habitat niches. Bats are the most common mammals utilizing cliffs. Bats such as eastern pipistrelle and big brown use crevices and ledge overhangs for hibernation and for summer daytime retreats. Since many cliffs are near rivers, they are ideal launching areas for moving over the river at night to catch insects rising over the water. In addition, caves within bluffs are important habitats. The eastern pipistrelle roosts alone in the summer, but gathers in large numbers in hibernacula in the winter, so caves are critically important habitat for this species. The Indiana bat and gray bat, species of conservation concern, use limestone caves for hibernation, as well. Other small mammals include white-footed mice, red squirrels, raccoons, voles, and eastern chipmunks (Larson, Matthes, and Kelly 2000). The caves at the base of many limestone cliffs can provide shelter for many other mammals as well.

Crevices and small caves on these cliff faces can provide nesting sites for black and turkey vultures, which lay their eggs directly on the ground (Kirk and Mossman 1998; Buckley 1999; T. M. Schneider et al. 2010).

Ledges protected by an overhang are often sites for the mud and moss nests constructed by the eastern phoebe (Weeks 1994).

Limestone cliffs and outcroppings support a variety of salamanders, which take refuge in moist crevices. On humid, particularly rainy, nights, salamanders leave these crevices to forage for insects. Surveys of limestone outcroppings of Pigeon Mountain have shown that the crevice-dwelling salamander community includes northern slimy, Pigeon Mountain, cave, and southern zigzag salamanders (Jensen, Camp, and Marshall 2002). All of these salamander species may shelter in the twilight zones of caves to escape harsh surface conditions (Camp and Jensen 2007). When surface conditions are sufficiently moist, individual salamanders migrate from caves to outcrop or forest floor refuges (e.g., beneath downed woody debris), which they then use as jumping-off points for feeding forays into the surrounding forest. Although not normally associated with caves, green salamanders also use limestone outcrops, particularly as over-wintering sites (M. J. Elliott 2008a). Ocoee salamanders occur on wet cliffs of the Cumberland Plateau in northeastern Alabama (Mount 1975) and south-central Tennessee; it is possible that this species also occurs in these habitats in Georgia. Various climbing species of lizard such as green anoles, fence lizards, and five-lined skinks commonly take refuge in outcrop crevices. If splits in the rock open into sufficiently deep refugia, snakes such as timber rattlesnakes, copperheads, and rat snakes may use them as over-wintering dens.

Pigeon Mountain Salamander
(*Plethodon petraeus*)

The Pigeon Mountain salamander is a large wood-land salamander in the family Plethodontidae. Adults range in size from 4.5 to 7 inches in total length. The upper body of adults is black with whitish and brassy spots and a reddish-brown or olive-colored stripe that extends along the dorsal surface from head to tail (Conant and Collins 1998). The Pigeon Mountain salamander is unique among woodland salamanders in that it has expanded toe tips that help it to climb verti-cal surfaces. Its body is slightly flatter and thinner than that of other related woodland salamanders.

This Georgia endemic is known only from the east-ern side of Pigeon Mountain in Walker and Chat-tooga Counties, where it is found in discrete, patchy subpopulations. Deep topographical incisions along the mountain slopes known locally as "gulfs" pro-duce deep coves that support mesic forests. Pigeon

Mountain salamanders reach their greatest abundance within these forests, where they are often associated with cliffs and outcrops. These secretive salamanders typically take refuge in small rock crevices or occasion-ally under logs on the forest floor. They emerge on humid or rainy nights to forage on insects. During the hot summer months, Pigeon Mountain salamanders tend to be found in and around the entrances of caves, where they benefit from cool temperatures and high humidity (Camp and Jensen 2008).

Like other salamanders of the genus *Plethodon*, this species is completely terrestrial, remaining in humid terrestrial microhabitats. Although the eggs and hatchlings of Pigeon Mountain salamanders have not been observed, it is presumed that eggs are depos-ited in clusters in humid underground sites such as caves, and that the hatchlings quickly metamorphose into miniature versions of adults without undergoing an aquatic larval stage. Because of its very restricted range, the Pigeon Mountain salamander is protected by state law in Georgia (Camp and Jensen 2008).

Crockford–Pigeon Mountain Wildlife Management Area

Two parallel trails provide access to picturesque calcareous cliffs that line the small canyon that encompasses the Shirley Miller Wildflower Trail on the west side of Pigeon Mountain. One is the Shirley Miller Wildflower Trail, the Featured Place for the mesic forests. This trail is fairly far from the cliffs through much of the way, but ends in a steep cliff down which an ephemeral waterfall flows. In the spring, fernleaf phacelias bloom abundantly on the rocks. The better trail for cliff viewing is to walk the former (narrow) roadbed that is on the other side of the stream from the Shirley Miller Trail. This road hugs the cliffs for approximately 0.5 to 0.75 mile, allowing close inspection. The cliffs are sparsely vegetated, although substrate has eroded to provide niches for a number of cliff plants. The most notable plant is the Canada columbine, which blooms in late March. Other species include resurrection fern, lady-rue, mountain stonecrop, crested iris, wild geranium, and Cumberland spurge.

Location: From U.S. Hwy. 27 in LaFayette, drive west then north on Ga. Hwy. 193 about 8 miles to intersection with Ga. Hwy. 341/Hog Jowl Rd. (Davis Crossroads). Turn left (south) onto Hog Jowl Rd. The road will fork at approximately 2.5 miles; continue left on Hog Jowl Rd. for about 0.2 mile and turn left on Pocket Rd. Drive approximately 1.2 miles (the road will turn to gravel) to the parking area. Google Earth GPS approximate coordinates at the parking area: N 34.712538/W 085.379920.

Acidic Cliffs and Rock Outcrops

Acidic cliffs and rock outcrops are steep to vertical outcroppings of acidic rock, usually sandstone. Lichens and mosses are scattered over the rock faces, and vegetation is typically sparse and limited to crevices and shallow ledges. Moisture levels range from xeric to wet near waterfalls. This natural community is most dramatic along the upper rim of the Plateau Escarpment subregion, where sculpted cliffs plunge down from the plateau. Some cliff faces also occur in the Armuchee Ridges in the Southern Sandstone Ridges subregion. Exposed expanses of rocks are uncommon, so the acidic cliffs support some rare plant assemblages.

This natural community also includes shallow caves, called "rockhouses." The rockhouses, which are especially well developed in adjacent Tennessee, are particularly picturesque when they occur at the base of a waterfall and the opening is rimmed by lush vegetation. Some large outcrops are also included in this community, with pedestal rocks and narrow alleyways between huge outcroppings. Rocktown (Walker County), a site on Pigeon Mountain, is an especially striking example. (See the Featured Place for the acidic glade and barren natural community.)

PHYSICAL SETTING AND ECOLOGY

The acidic, low-nutrient nature of the bedrock (often the Lookout Sandstone/Gizzard Formation or Red Mountain Formation, described on p. 156) plays a strong role in the vegetation that grows here; few to no calciphiles occur in the plant communities, but ericads are common. In addition, variation in erosion patterns of the bedrock controls the types of microhabitats that develop. Some sandstone outcroppings have few joints and bedding planes: the sandstone breaks off in vertical blocks, creating sheer cliffs with few microhabitats. These cliffs are nearly barren of vegetation. In other

A cave at the base of a cliff at the Lula Lake Preserve

A wet sandstone cliff at Keown Falls

cases, such as in some areas in Cloudland Canyon State Park (Dade County) (see the Featured Place), the substrate has many vertical bedding planes that form soil-collecting crevices and ledges. In Zahnd Natural Area (Walker County), where conglomerate is a common substrate, a striking, rounded effect occurs as the rocks erode, so they are sometimes called "turtleback" rocks. These round outcroppings do not support much vegetation, although some support glades and barrens. Moisture sources are also important. Parts of a few cliff faces are moist nearly year round, due to spray from a nearby waterfall. Because streams on sandstone are exposed to high evaporation rates and there is little moisture storage in the thin soils of the caps of the ridges, however, usually streamflow decreases dramatically in the summer; some streams dry up completely. Given this great variation in moisture, vegetation can range from fairly dense around some waterfalls, such as Keown Falls (Walker County), the Waterfall Trail

in Cloudland Canyon State Park (Dade County), and a waterfall downslope from Rocktown (Walker County), to nearly barren, such as the waterfall at the Lula Lake Preserve (Walker County).

Exposure and aspect also regulate plant establishment. Where a site is very exposed, especially an upper slope that faces south to west, conditions are harsh and plant life, already limited by the lack of nutrients and places to anchor their roots, is very sparse. Turbulence from winds can cause harsh conditions (Larson, Matthes, and Kelly 2000). Cliffs on north- to east-facing slopes, lower slopes, or vertical outcrops embedded within forests or woodlands are considerably shadier and more mesic.

VEGETATION

Trees that grow on cliff shoulders, in between vertical rock outcroppings, and in some crevices include black birch, Virginia pine, rock chestnut oak, mockernut

Vegetation grows in microhabitats on sandstone cliffs along the Cloudland Canyon Waterfall Trail.

wort and marginal wood-fern often appear in crevices; other herbaceous species on the cliffs or outcrops include smooth southern bush-honeysuckle, bluets, spiderworts, rock alumroot, and Carolina lily. Seepage areas on cliffs can support sphagnum moss, lycopodiums, saxifrages, royal fern, Jack-in-the-pulpit, and New York fern.

Because the cliff environment is an uncommon one, rare assemblages of plants have been described from neighboring states for moist cliff habitats, and more fieldwork searching for these assemblages in Georgia is warranted. A special assemblage that occurs in Georgia on dry cliffs with seepage areas includes species such as cave alumroot, roundleaf fire-pink, mountain spleenwort, Bradley's spleenwort, partridge-berry, mountain laurel, and climbing hydrangea.

ANIMALS

Although cliffs are fairly inaccessible, some mammals are able to utilize them. For example, bats hibernate in caves and also find protection within crevices and under ledges. Small mammals such as white-footed mice, raccoons, pine voles, and eastern chipmunks can sometimes find a foothold on portions of a cliff and forage in those areas (Larson, Matthes, and Kelly 2000).

Cliff faces can provide nesting sites for black and turkey vultures, which lay their eggs on ledges (Kirk and Mossman 1998; Buckley 1999; T. M. Schneider et al. 2010). Eastern phoebes build nests using mud and moss (Weeks 1994). Raptors rise up on winds generated by the steep topography and bare rock. Cliff areas are good places to observe migrating broad-winged hawk, red-tailed hawk, Cooper's hawk, and sharp-shinned hawk. Species that may nest on exposed cliffs include the northern rough-winged swallow and barn swallow.

In moist crevices, climbing salamanders such as the green salamander and Pigeon Mountain salamander may be present during periods of sufficient rainfall. For example, vertical sandstone cliffs on Pigeon Mountain support large populations of Pigeon Mountain salamanders (Jensen, Camp, and Marshall, 2002). This species is also common in crevices of the sandstone rimrock (Camp and Jensen 2008).

hickory, and other species from the adjoining acidic oak-pine-hickory forests or pine-oak woodlands. Shrubs include fringe-tree, mountain laurel, sparkleberry, winged sumac, and dewberries. A number of woody vines sprawl over the rocks, including Carolina jessamine, greenbriers, Virginia-creeper, and muscadine. Climbing hydrangea is common on wet cliffs, dominating, for example, the wall behind the waterfall at Keown Falls Trail (Walker County). Mountain spleen-

CHARACTERISTIC PLANTS OF ACIDIC CLIFFS AND ROCK OUTCROPS

TREES

Red maple—Acer rubrum

Black birch—Betula lenta

Virginia pine—Pinus virginiana

Rock chestnut oak—Quercus montana

SHRUBS AND WOODY VINES

Fringe-tree—Chionanthus virginicus

Mountain sweet-pepperbush—Clethra acuminata

Climbing hydrangea—Decumaria barbara

Hairy southern bush-honeysuckle—Diervilla rivularis

Carolina jessamine—Gelsemium sempervirens

Witch-hazel—Hamamelis virginiana

Smooth hydrangea—Hydrangea arborescens

Ashy hydrangea—Hydrangea cinerea

Mountain laurel—Kalmia latifolia

Catawba rhododendron—Rhododendron catawbiense

Gorge rhododendron—Rhododendron minus

Winged sumac—Rhus copallinum

Blackberries and dewberries—Rubus spp.

GROUND COVER

Spleenworts—Asplenium spp.

Wavy hairgrass—Avenella flexuosa

Southern harebell—Campanula divaricata

Sedges—Carex spp.

Marginal wood-fern—Dryopteris marginalis

Alumroots—Heuchera parviflora; H. villosa

Quaker ladies—Houstonia caerulea

Upland dwarf iris—Iris verna

Carolina lily—Lilium michauxii

Partridge-berry—Mitchella repens

Appalachian rockcap fern—Polypodium appalachianum

Roundleaf fire-pink—Silene rotundifolia

Lady-rue—Thalictrum clavatum

Spiderworts—Tradescantia spp.

Sweet white violet—Viola blanda

Spiderworts can be common on acidic cliffs.

Eastern Woodrat (*Neotoma floridana*)

Eastern woodrats are medium-sized rodents in the family Muridae. They have grayish-brown fur on the back and lighter fur on the sides, with a white throat, belly, and feet. They can be distinguished from non-native rats (Norway and black rats) by their hairy tail, larger ears, and white feet. Adults range from 14 to 17 inches in length (Burt and Grossenheider 1980).

The range of the eastern woodrat extends from Connecticut west to eastern Colorado and western South Dakota, south to Texas, and east to Florida. The eastern portion of its range extends along the Atlantic Coastal Plain from Florida to North Carolina. The eastern woodrat has been documented from all regions of Georgia except for the eastern portion of the Piedmont (Georgia Wildlife Web 2008).

Eastern woodrats are found in a variety of natural and manmade habitats, including cliffs, rockhouses, swamps, and occasionally human residences. Where they occur near human communities, these rodents are generally known as "pack rats," due to their habit of incorporating various manmade objects into their nests (Burt and Grossenheider 1980). In the northwestern portion of Georgia, eastern woodrats appear to be restricted to remote rocky cliffs and rockhouses, where they construct loose nests of twigs. These nests typically have several compartments and may be used by multiple generations (Georgia Wildlife Web 2008).

In the Southeast, eastern woodrats produce two to three broods per year, with one to six young per litter. The young are weaned by the age of three to four weeks. The diet of eastern woodrats consists of a variety of seeds, nuts, fruits, and other plant material. Predators include snakes, skunks, coyotes, foxes, hawks, and owls (Georgia Wildlife Web 2008). Though globally secure, eastern woodrat populations are declining in some areas due to loss of habitat, predation from feral cats, and persecution from humans.

The Waterfalls Trail at Cloudland
Canyon State Park

berry, wavy hairgrasss, common white heart-leaved aster, and witch-hazel. Down the trail a tall outcrop with fewer bedding planes supports very little vegetation, but the incipient rockhouse (overhang) beneath it is of interest.

As the trail descends, cliff sites become more protected, with more seepage. Poison ivy is common on cliffs; rock alumroot, ashy hydrangea, and Jack-in-the-pulpit appear in addition to the species already listed. The trail forks, and the first falls is to the left. This waterfall is in a very picturesque setting; moist cliffs support poison ivy, northern horsebalm, black birch, yellowroot, black birch, many mosses and liverworts, a rattlesnake-root, and lady-rue.

Returning to the fork, the trail to the second waterfall also features many dramatic and beautiful cliff faces. In some areas, overhangs keep species beneath them protected from the force of direct precipitation, and here the cave alumroot, which has very delicate leaves, is present. A rest stop with benches occurs in the midst of a Cumberland Plateau / Ridge and Valley mesic forest environment with some species typical of moist forests, including dolls'-eyes, sharp-lobed hepatica, yellow mandarin, basswood, eastern hemlock, umbrella magnolia, and much else. Poison ivy covers much of the cliff face near the falls; some royal fern occurs at the top of the falls.

The Waterfalls Trail at Cloudland Canyon State Park (Dade County) offers many opportunities to view cliff environments, ranging from dry to wet. Almost immediately upon starting the trail, a large, dry rock outcrop can be seen, which supports mountain spleenwort, partridge-berry, hairy southern bush-honeysuckle, mountain laurel, Catawba rhododendron, red maple, and trailing arbutus. Soon thereafter, a large—more than 40 feet tall—dry-mesic outcrop with many bedding planes appears. It supports many species and microniches, with most of the species already listed, as well as Virginia-creeper, hay-scented fern, marginal wood-fern, mapleleaf viburnum, woodland coreopsis, Virginia pine, Christmas fern, smooth highbush blue-

Location: Cloudland Canyon State Park is located on Ga. 136, 8 miles east of Trenton and I-59, and 18 miles northwest of LaFayette. From Ga. Hwy. 193 in Lafayette, take U.S. Hwy. 27/Ga. 1/Ga. 136/Lyle Jones Pkwy. north about 3 miles. Proceed left on Ga. 136/Lookout Mountain Scenic Hwy. about 17 miles toward Trenton. Turn right onto Cloudland Canyon Park Rd. After entering the park, continue straight past the office. The Waterfalls Trail begins across the road from the playground and picnic area. The trail sign is along the railed canyon rim to the left of the parking lot. Maps and directions are also available in the park office. Google Earth GPS approximate coordinates to the trailhead: N 34.613539/W 085.088127.

Flatwoods

Flatwoods are forested wetlands that usually occur within a few miles of the Conasauga, Coosawattee, Oostanaula, and Coosa Rivers on gently rolling to flat, calcium-rich, undulating terrain of streams, small hummocks, and depressions in the southern limestone/dolomite valley subregion (Govus 2003a). These sites are classified as wetlands because the depressional areas within them typically pond water during the winter and early spring; they are also known as upland depression swamps. Mesic to hydric oaks usually dominate, including willow oak, Shumard oak, and cherrybark oak, often with much sugarberry, white ash, green ash, red maple, and, rarely, nutmeg hickory. Many calcium-loving species occur in the shrub and ground layers. In some of the wetter sites, buttressed trees can impart a swamp-like

Coastal Plain feel. Mesic microsites are mixed in throughout.

The calcareous, hydric soils support many rare plants, including narrowly endemic species, species with prairie affiliations, and species that are disjunct from more northern and Midwestern regions (Govus 2003a). Efforts are under way to document and describe additional occurrences in the region.

PHYSICAL SETTING AND ECOLOGY

Flatwoods often occur next to the calcareous prairie and barren (Coosa prairies) natural community over the Conasauga Shale Formation, described on p. 157 (Govus 2003a). Small wet prairies may be embedded within them. High calcium levels in the soils foster the development of vertisols, which are soils with high levels of shrink-swell clays. The clays swell during the winter and early spring, when precipitation rates are high and evaporation rates from the ground and

Fremont's clematis

VEGETATION

The variation in microtopography and wide range of moisture conditions can foster a diverse mixture of mesic species, along with plants that are restricted to more hydric conditions. The canopy may be somewhat open or entirely closed (Govus 2003a). Trees include a range of mesic-hydric oak species, such as willow oak, swamp chestnut oak, Shumard oak, water oak, overcup oak, and cherrybark oak. Other important canopy species include sugarberry, white oak, American elm, loblolly pine, slippery elm, white ash, green ash, Carolina shagbark hickory, pignut hickory, common shagbark hickory, southern sugar maple, red maple, tuliptree, ironwood, musclewood, and sweet gum (R. Ware unpubl. data; Govus 2003a).

In some places, an open canopy encourages dense, diverse shrubs or herbaceous species. Shrubs and small trees often include silky dogwood, southern swamp dogwood, fringe-tree, southern wild raisin, littlehip hawthorn, parsley haw, and buckthorn bumelia (R.

Purple milkweed

transpiration levels from plants are low. This swelling creates a hardpan effect that ponds water in low depressional areas, interspersed with hummocks that are more mesic. In the summer these soils dry out and shrink, developing large cracks. The clays bond the remaining water so tightly that the plants cannot take it up.

As described for other calcareous communities the calcium-rich substrate favors plants adapted to high levels of calcium. Although calcium is necessary to plants, in abundance it can inhibit the uptake of iron (Cullina 2008). Ericads are dependent on acidic environments where iron is soluble and are not equipped for high-base conditions where iron is bound to other nutrients and not easily available (Cullina 2008). Thus, ericads, including azaleas, mountain laurel, great laurel, and sourwood, are relatively rare in this environment, whereas calciphiles, which possess mechanisms that reduce the uptake of too much calcium or that allow them to physiologically withstand it, are favored here.

CHARACTERISTIC PLANTS OF FLATWOODS

TREES

Southern sugar maple—Acer floridanum

Musclewood—Carpinus caroliniana

Carolina hickory—Carya carolinae-septentrionalis

Common shagbark hickory—Carya ovata

Sugarberry—Celtis laevigata

Eastern redbud—Cercis canadensis

Green ash—Fraxinus pennsylvanica

Sweet gum—Liquidambar styraciflua

Overcup oak—Quercus lyrata

Swamp chestnut oak—Quercus michauxii

Water oak—Quercus nigra

Cherrybark oak—Quercus pagoda

Willow oak—Quercus phellos

Shumard oak—Quercus shumardii

Elms—Ulmus americana; U. rubra

SHRUBS AND WOODY VINES

American rattan—Berchemia scandens

Cross-vine—Bigononia capreolata

Silky dogwood—Cornus amomum

Southern swamp dogwood—Cornus stricta

Possum-haw—Ilex decidua

Buckthorn bumelia—Sideroxylon lycioides

GROUND COVER

Nodding onion—Allium cernuum

Bulbous bittercress—Cardamine bulbosa

Spring-beauty—Claytonia virginica

Hammock spiderlily—Hymenocallis occidentalis

Orange jewelweed—Impatiens capensis

False garlic—Nothoscordum bivalve

May-apple—Podophyllum peltatum

Lizard's-tail—Saururus cernuus

Blue-eyed grass—Sisyrinchium spp.

Indian pink—Spigelia marilandica

Skunk meadowrue—Thalictrum revolutum

Ware unpubl. data; Govus 2003a). Woody vines include poison ivy, greenbriers, cross-vine, and American rattan, which is an indicator of calcareous conditions.

The ground layer is very diverse and includes Appalachian ragwort, spring-beauty, bulbous bittercress, false garlic, partridge-berry, lizard's-tail, southern water-plantain, green dragon, indian pink, nodding onion, may-apple, hammock spiderlily, orange jewelweed, boneset, and skunk meadowrue. There are also rare narrow endemics, such as barbed rattlesnake-root, Alabama leatherflower, trailing meadowrue, and Cumberland oak-leach. Openings within these associations can sometimes include other narrowly distributed species such as Mohr's Barbara's-buttons and Alabama warbonnet. Some herbaceous species found in these flatwoods are disjunct northern or Midwestern species, often with prairie affiliations, including purple milkweed, balsam ragwort, Fremont's clematis, and Michigan lily. Other rare species that are found in flatwoods sites include big bishopweed and least trillium (Ware 1999; Govus 2003a).

ANIMALS

Typical mammals of flatwoods include the short-tailed shrew, gray squirrel, white-tailed deer, golden mouse, gray fox, least shrew, eastern mole, white-footed mouse, southern flying squirrel, opossum, and raccoon. Bats may include the hoary, evening, little brown, east-

ern pipistrelle, and big brown. In the winter, wood ducks and hooded mergansers can be found roosting in flooded sections of these forests (Bellrose and Holm 1994; Dugger, Dugger, and Fredrickson 1994; Hepp and Bellrose 1995). The Acadian flycatcher and Louisiana waterthrush often breed in these forests if the right habitat structure is present, the forest corridor is of sufficient size, and, in the case of the waterthrush, the stream contains suitable gravel bars and riffles where it can forage (W. D. Robinson 1995; Mattsson and Cooper 2007). More open stands with larger snags often have nesting northern flickers and other woodpeckers (W. S. Moore 1995). Yellow-billed cuckoos nest here if ample vine tangles or similar thickets of vegetation are present (Hughes 1999). Many other bird species typical of hardwood forests also nest here, including Carolina wrens, Carolina chickadees, red-eyed vireos, wood thrushes, red-shouldered hawks, and northern cardinals (T. M. Schneider et al. 2010).

Temporary pools provide important breeding habitat for a diverse array of frogs and salamanders. Late winter or early spring breeders include upland chorus frogs and mountain chorus frogs. Spring peepers tend to use heavily vegetated, semipermanent ponds, where breeding males often gather in large choruses. Summer-breeding frogs include the fossorial (burrowing) eastern narrow-mouthed toad and the arboreal Cope's gray treefrog, individuals of which move to ponds in response to summer thunderstorms. Northern and/or southern cricket frogs occur as well. Fossorial (burrowing) marbled salamanders lay their eggs in dry basins during the fall, and attendant females guard the eggs until flooding evokes hatching (Scott 2005). Spotted and mole salamanders move to flooded ponds during winter or early spring and attach eggs to submerged vegetation. Three-lined salamanders often breed in ephemeral ponds, and individuals commonly hide under coarse woody debris at or near the water's edge. Eastern newts are aquatic as adults and are abundant in ponds having lengthy hydroperiods.

FEATURED ANIMAL

Conasauga Blue Burrower
(*Cambarus cymatilis*)

The Conasauga blue burrower is a rare crayfish known from the Conasauga and Hiwassee River basins in the Ridge and Valley province of northwestern Georgia and southeastern Tennessee. In Georgia, this species has been collected from only about five locations, mostly in the vicinity of Chatsworth in Murray County. It is found near streams or in low-lying areas with a high water table. This strikingly colored crayfish is deep blue with orange-tipped claws, and reaches a total body length of about 3 inches. Like other crayfishes, it is an opportunistic feeder, eating a variety of plant and animal materials, living and dead; at night it may actively prey on invertebrates that wander close to its burrow entrance (Skelton 2008).

In contrast to stream-dwelling crayfishes, burrowing crayfishes live in a complex system of tunnels that may be relatively far from flowing water. Burrowing crayfishes typically remain in their burrows most of the year, but males leave the burrows to search for females during the breeding season. During the dry part of the summer, the crayfish may plug the burrow openings to help conserve moisture (Skelton 2008).

Reproduction probably occurs during the spring and fall, but males in reproductive condition may be found throughout the year. Although it is difficult to study burrowing crayfishes, some researchers believe they may live as long as 10 years.

The small size of this species' range makes it particularly vulnerable. About one-half of the known populations of this species occurs within the Chatsworth city limits. One location is in a residential neighborhood, and another was along a street that has now been paved over. Only one population of this rare crayfish is known on state property, at Conasauga River Natural Area (Skelton 2008).

The Berry Flatwoods

The campus of Berry College (Floyd County) has a wide expanse of flatwoods that can be easily explored on the trail around Victory Lake, which, having been drained, is now more a marshland than a lake. Immediately along the lake trail, flatwoods can be seen on the right side of the path. Typically during the winter and early spring, and later if the precipitation levels are high, many areas will be shallowly ponded, providing the viewer a good perspective as to the hydrology of the site.

For the next half mile, a good example of the extent and variety of plant composition and structure relative to the microtopography is evident. In some sites the shrub layer is dense, with southern wild rai-

sin, hawthorns, coralberry, and stiff-leaved dogwood; in others the forest understory is open. Typical flatwoods trees, such as red maple, water oak, sweet gum, green ash, pignut hickory, winged elm, American elm, cherrybark oak, willow oak, eastern redbud, and chalk maple, all appear. Woody vines include American rattan, poison ivy, and cross-vine. Herbs include mayapple, hammock spider lily, and river oats.

Where the trail makes a major bend to circle the lake, there is an extensive and picturesque swampy area dominated by bald-cypress and pond-cypress, with knees and fluted, buttressed trunks. These trees are not native to the area; they are primarily coastal plain species. Cypresses were planted long ago on the campus and have naturalized here. Bigleaf snowbell occurs in a small patch here. This tree is very unusual in this part of the state and this may be its only site in Georgia's Cumberland Plateau / Ridge and Valley (R. Ware, Floyd Cty., pers. comm.).

Beyond the cypresses is an impressive flatwoods site, which supports a striking variety of large trees. The topography is classic flatwoods, with many hummocks supporting buttressed trees with roots coated in moss, depressional areas filled with water (after a moist winter), and superb examples of swamp chestnut oak, cherrybark oak, overcup oak, Shumard oak, willow oak, and water oak. There is also winged elm, Carolina hickory, green ash, hawthorns, and ironwood. The herbaceous layer, unfortunately, has been heavily invaded by Nepal grass, but visitors who arrive in early spring, while the Nepal grass is still very short, will see spring-beauty, bulbous bittercress, and lizard's-tail beneath the trees.

Location: Follow the directions to Berry College found on p. 196. The flatwoods described here are found on the west side of Victory Lake. After turning right onto Lavender Mountain Rd., continue less than 0.25 mile and through the avenue of oaks, then turn right onto the gravel road. Park in the parking lot on right. Walk on the dirt road (Road of Remembrance or Old Stretch Road) to the north and then west, around Victory Lake (now dry). The flatwoods will appear on the right side of the trail, on the east and north sides of the lake. Google Earth GPS approximate coordinates for parking area: N 34.298878/W 085.197983.

Calcareous Seepage Fens

Calcareous seepage fens exist as complexes of seeps, springs, and small streams whose hydrology is variable, but reliably moist, at least the majority of the year. Soils are typically circumneutral, organic sandy loams, intermixed with or overlying gravel or chert, and contain elevated levels of calcium and magnesium. Soil and hydrologic conditions promote a graminoid and forb-dominated community, although succession will occur without periodic disturbance. The marquee rare plant species of these systems is the federally Endangered Tennessee yellow-eyed grass. There are also several plant associations affiliated with this system

that are ranked as critically imperiled or imperiled by NatureServe.

Intact and nondegraded southern Ridge and Valley fens are among the rarest wetland habitats in Georgia (J. M. Moffett 2008). Probably never very abundant across the landscape, fens have suffered from a history of either direct conversion to or collateral damage from grazing, agriculture, and silviculture (Kral 1983, 1990). Fens that were spared these immediate anthropogenic impacts tend to exist as small "isolated" islands (the most extreme example of this is a fen community inside a cloverleaf interchange of I-75 near Cartersville). Fragmentation of the landscape from human use and development, as well as the alteration of natural disturbance regimes (beaver extirpation, hydrologic alteration, fire suppression, etc.) have greatly reduced, if not eliminated, opportunities for colonization/movement of fen communities across the landscape and has left these fens highly vulnerable to encroachment and invasion from woody competition and non-native species (J. M. Moffett 2008).

PHYSICAL SETTING AND ECOLOGY

Calcareous seepage fens reflect the influence of unique physiographic, geologic, and edaphic features. They are found primarily in the valley areas of the ecoregion, in the Southern Shale Valleys and the Southern Limestone / Dolomitic Valleys and Low, Rolling Hills subregions.

Seepage fens are a mixture of seeps, springs, spring-runs, and their associated communities. In Georgia, where these seepage fens are associated with streams, the streams are always of the first order (small streams with no tributaries), although in Alabama there are examples of this system known to be associated with second- and third-order streams. The structural geology of the valley, with thrust faults and various layered strata, provides an ample distribution system for groundwater. Seeps and springs are frequently found at contacts between various strata as water filters vertically through porous strata until reaching a nonporous layer and then traveling horizontally to emerge as a spring (Kral 1983, 1990).

Hydrologic regimes vary by site along an ephemeral-intermittent-perennial flow gradient. Fens that developed around ephemeral (e.g., unreliable) isolated seeps, whose flow is mostly dependent on local recharge by precipitation, may experience either low-flow conditions from the late summer through mid-fall, or even complete "seep-failure" during extended periods of drought, such as that in 2007–2008. At the other extreme are sites supported by the nearby presence of a high-volume perennial spring or stream that are wet year-round and experience substrate drying only along the ecotonal margins of the fen. Slopes are

An open calcareous seepage fen

relatively gentle (mostly in the 1–3% range) and do not appear to substantially affect the moisture retention, overall structure, or floral composition among the various fens (J. M. Moffett 2008).

Soils of seepage fens tend to be highly restricted in their distribution. They are typically circumneutral (mean pH 6.6), sandy loams with 5–10% organic matter and containing a gravelly limestone/dolostone/chert component (J. M. Moffett 2008). In many places, the limestone/dolostone once present on the valley floors has dissolved, leaving behind only a "soil-dressing" of cherty residuum (C. B. Hunt 1967; Roberts 1996). Since most fens are small in size (< 600 square yards) and distributed both irregularly and infrequently across the landscape, there is not a designated soil series description attributed to them (J. M. Moffett 2008). Special investigations by the Natural Resources Conservation Service at some of these sites have indicated that these soils are, in fact, unmapped and unnamed entosolic inclusions in a matrix of otherwise dominant hydric soil series (K. Johnson 2000).

Chemical analysis of fen soils shows them to be similar in most respects to soils of the dominant southeastern soil order, ultisols, with the exception of elevated levels of calcium, magnesium, and pH (J. M. Moffett 2008). While this is consistent with the sedimentary nature and origins of the Ridge and Valley, it bears mentioning that the calcium-to-magnesium ratio (1:7) is lower (i.e., relatively more Mg) than that found in habitats considered more purely calcareous. Using Chilingar's (1957) classification scheme of calcareous rocks, geologic parent materials with a calcium-to-magnesium ratio in the 3.5–16 range would be considered highly dolomitic limestones. Variation among sites within circumneutral pH (range 6.1–7.4) reflects, in part, the influence of beaver-flooding and cattle-grazing. These activities can have either an acidifying or an alkalinizing effect on the fen depending on site specificities, and are mediated through increases in nutrient loads, organic matter accumulation, and periods of inundation. Fens with a history or presence of beaver and cattle tend to have "weedier/nutrient-loving species" among their flora, including common cattail, cut-grass, water-primroses, bulrush, and pickerelweed, as well as more non-native invasive species, such as marsh dayflower, Nepal grass, and small carpgrass (Cronk and Fennessy 2001; J. M. Moffett 2008).

Available sunlight and shading due to aspect and canopy extent (both shrub and tree) are variable. There is no discernible pattern regarding fen aspect (e.g., south-facing slope, etc.). Canopy closure (i.e., woody competition) does reduce overall species richness and the reproductive output of certain high-priority conservation species, such as Tennessee yellow-eyed grass (J. M. Moffett 2008). Historically, seepage fens of the southern Ridge and Valley were probably uncommon across the landscape and rather short-lived. Disturbances that maintained fens in an open state likely included beaver activity, ungulate herbivory, and occasional fire. Scouring from flash floods was less likely, given the gentle topography and the fen's primary association with groundwater sources. Fens that may have once existed in Georgia along second- and third-order streams, however, would have experienced flooding disturbances (similar to those in Alabama). Over the long term, fen plant communities probably existed as "fugitive" communities exhibiting metapopulation dynamics (migration and reproduction among individual communities over a larger landscape) and moving across the landscape opportunistically (Hanski and Zhang 1993; J. M. Moffett 2008). The existence of only a few isolated fens means that the ecological/biological value of each surviving fen is greatly increased and, therefore, must be maintained in an early successional state using a variety of approaches (Boyd and Moffett 2003). Since most known fens are located in areas where the use of prescribed fire is impractical, competition from woody trees and shrubs must be controlled using mechanical/manual methods.

One focus of future management activities will be the restoration of degraded seep/spring/fen complexes and the safeguarding of rare fen flora. Instrumental in this effort will be the Georgia Plant Conservation Alliance, a consortium of public and private conservation organizations including the State Botanical Garden of Georgia, the Georgia Department of Natural Resources, the Atlanta Botanical Garden, and the U.S. Forest Service. Fens to be restored and/or developed as rare plant safeguarding sites include Bluebird Springs (Crockford–Pigeon Mountain Wildlife Management Area—GADNR), Interstate Hypericum Springs (GADOT), Mosteller Springs/Mill (private), and a site yet to be determined in the Armuchee Ridges (Conasauga Ranger District—USFS).

VEGETATION

Fens are dominated by herbaceous vegetation. They exist in various shapes, sizes, and configurations nec-

An open calcareous seepage fen dominated by graminoids and forbs. Comparison of this fen with the others depicted here shows the wide variety of vegetation and hydrology in this natural community.

Downy lobelia

essary to accommodate the unique topography and hydrology of a given site. Nevertheless, an "idealized" conceptual fen can be viewed as a series of concentric rings encircling a water source. The innermost ring is a relatively small, wet forb/graminoid glade or meadow. This is bordered by a shrub ring composed primarily of mountain bushy St. John's-wort, which is further enclosed within a ring of the local forest matrix. Over time, shrubs and trees will invade the fen and promote succession. Some fens, however, appear able to resist invasion and succession, due perhaps to unstable soil conditions or unfavorable hydrologic fluctuations.

The relationship between mountain bushy St. John's-wort and the federally Endangered Tennessee yellow-eyed grass is an interesting one. The St. John's-

wort is known to invade the interior of fens and completely shade populations of Tennessee yellow-eyed grass, rendering them almost entirely vegetative (non-flowering). Unfortunately, in the open, unshaded areas, the Tennessee yellow-eyed grass is a poor long-term competitor, and population declines due to thick/aggressive growth of graminoids and forbs. It has been observed that while the Tennessee yellow-eyed grass persists only vegetatively under the St. John's-wort canopy, it persists nonetheless, while most other fen graminoids and forbs do not. J. M. Moffett (2008) suggested that the St. John's-wort may function somewhat analogously to a nurse plant for the Tennessee yellow-eyed grass by providing refuge from herbaceous competition until such time that a disturbance event releases it.

CHARACTERISTIC PLANTS OF CALCAREOUS SEEPAGE FENS

Shallow sedge—Carex lurida

False nutsedge—Cyperus strigosus

Hairy umbrella-sedge—Fuirena squarrosa

Common sneezeweed—Helenium autumnale

Mountain bushy St. John's-wort—Hypericum densiflorum

Orange jewelweed—Impatiens capensis

Smallhead rush—Juncus brachycephalus

Leathery rush—Juncus coriaceus

Cardinal flower—Lobelia cardinalis

Downy lobelia—Lobelia puberula

Small-fruited seedbox—Ludwigia microcarpa

Virginia bugleweed—Lycopus virginicus

Whorled loosestrife—Lysimachia quadrifolia

Axil-flower—Mecardonia acuminata

Winged monkey-flower—Mimulus alatus

Lax hornpod—Mitreola petiolata

Sensitive fern—Onoclea sensibilis

Cowbane—Oxypolis rigidior

Brownish beaksedge—Rhynchospora capitellata

Narrowleaf whitetop sedge—Rhynchospora colorata

Thorne's beaksedge—Rhynchospora thornei

Cutleaf coneflower—Rudbeckia laciniata

Black bulrush—Scirpus atrovirens

Woolgrass bulrush—Scirpus cyperinus

Roughleaf goldenrod—Solidago patula

Marsh fern—Thelypteris palustris

Tennessee yellow-eyed grass—Xyris tennesseensis

ANIMALS

Many animals benefit from the ecotone between the fen and surrounding forest. They forage for insects, reptiles, or seeds in the fen but find shelter and breed in the forest. Others are more full-time inhabitants of the fen. Common mammals are white-tailed deer, eastern cottontail, hispid cotton rat, eastern harvest mouse, groundhog, coyote, red fox, eastern mole, and striped skunk.

Birds that may forage in the fens include the eastern bluebird, red-headed woodpecker, and northern flicker (W. S. Moore 1995; Gowaty and Plissner 1998; K. G. Smith, Withgott, and Rodewald 2000). As in the calcareous prairie and barren natural community the red-winged blackbird, American goldfinch, and possibly the blue grosbeak (Ingold 1993; Middleton 1993; Yasukawa and Searcy 1995) may nest in some grassy areas, and common yellowthroats, white-eyed vireos, and indigo buntings may nest in dense shrubs found along the margins (Payne 1992; Hopp, Kirby, and Boone 1995; Guzy and Ritchison 1999). Field sparrows, and possibly grasshopper sparrows, may utilize the seed sources within the fens when they migrate during the winter (M. D. Carey, Burhans, and Nelson 1994; Vickery 1996).

During times when the sites are moist, the herpetofauna includes the upland chorus frog, mountain chorus frog, spring peeper, eastern narrow-mouthed toad, Cope's gray treefrog, northern and/or southern cricket frogs, marbled salamander, spotted salamander, mole salamander, four-toed salamander, and three-lined salamander. Eastern newts are aquatic as adults and are abundant in ponds having lengthy hydroperiods.

Cherokee Clubtail (*Gomphus consanguis*)

Cherokee clubtails are typically about 2 inches in length. Males and females have differing patterns of coloration. The adult male is dark and slender with blue-green eyes, narrow wings, and a mostly black abdomen. Adult females have a thicker abdomen with greenish and yellow stripes. Immature individuals of both sexes are similar to adults.

The Cherokee clubtail is restricted to the southern Appalachian region of Virginia, North Carolina, Tennessee, Georgia, and Alabama. In Georgia, it is known from six counties (Catoosa, Chattooga, Floyd, Gordon, Walker, and Whitfield) in the Ridge and Valley region, in both the Coosa and Tennessee River drainages (Beaton 2008b).

Larvae are usually found in small streams with silty pool bottoms. Many of these streams are spring-fed. Adults use the same habitats during the breeding season but can also be found in nearby fields, marshes,

and other open habitats. Adults eat almost any flying insect prey they can catch, while larvae eat a variety of aquatic invertebrates.

Adults typically take flight from the end of May to the end of June. Emerging adults crawl out of the water onto nearby vegetation, then disperse into nearby fields and other open habitats. After maturing for a week or two, they return to the breeding site and establish their territories. Males perch low above the water and make periodic short patrols. Females approach the water only when ready to mate, at which time they are quickly captured by males. After mating, the female returns to the stream and deposits her eggs by tapping the end of her abdomen on the surface of the water (Beaton 2008b).

The Cherokee clubtail is protected in Georgia due to its restricted range. Specific threats include impoundments, loss of riparian habitats, stream sedimentation, and input of excess nutrients or toxins associated with poor land management practices.

Mosteller Springs/Mill

Mosteller Springs is a wonderful example of a nearly intact seepage fen. It consists of a primary spring (averaging 1–1.5 million gallons/day output), a spring-run, known locally as "Mostella Branch," and a number of small seeps that feed the spring-run. The spring-head and other portions of the spring-run were initially impounded by the Mosteller family in order to supply waterpower for various commercial operations, including both a grist and a sawmill (ca. 1830). For nearly a century, the mill was a local hub for commercial, social, and religious activities. The primary spring remains impounded to this day, although other water impoundments and/or diversions have since been removed or are no longer functional. What remains is a 0.25 mile stretch of high-quality springhead and spring-run replete with considerable watercress and numerous aquatic snails.

The fen plant community is primarily herbaceous and graminoid in nature. The marquee species is the federally Endangered Tennessee yellow-eyed grass found in cherty/cobbly areas in relatively shallow soils near the spring-run. Alongside it can be found its faithful associates: hairy umbrella-sedge, common sneezeweed, small-fruited seedbox, axil-flower, lax hornpod, and narrowleaf whitetop sedge. The rare Thornes's beaksedge is seen sparingly in the less congested areas. Taller herbs, such as cardinal flower, winged monkey-flower, woolgrass bulrush, and cowbane, exist in areas of deeper/muckier substrate, usually on the edge of the Tennessee yellow-eyed grass patches. Nearly absent from this site is the signature shrub for this habitat, the mountain bushy St. John's-wort. Its paucity may be due to a history of cattle grazing and other land use activities. Restoration and stewardship efforts for this site by the Georgia Plant Conservation Alliance will include augmentation of this species.

Location: From I-75 in Adairsville, exit at #306 and proceed east on Ga. Hwy. 140 approximately 4 miles. The spring/fen complex is south of Ga. Hwy. 140. Access is by permission only from the Thomas Carlton family. Call prior to arrival for permission and parking instructions: (770) 773-3286.

Acidic Seepage Wetlands

Acidic seepage wetlands form in shallow swales, in depressions, and near streamheads, usually on the sandstone caps of ridges and plateaus. Usually, they are open forests with large swaths of cinnamon and royal fern that are a lush contrast to the vegetation of the drier sites that surround the seep. Red maple, black gum, sweet gum, tag alder, cinnamon fern, and royal fern are typical species. Occasionally, mountain laurel, Catawba rhododendron, and/or great laurel are components. In a few instances, the seeps are more open, with a denser herbaceous layer of grasses and sedges. These sunny seeps were more widespread when fire was more common and were important habitat for the now rare and beautiful monkey-face orchid (Chafin 2007).

Acidic seepage wetlands usually occur on the caps of the Cumberland Plateau / Ridge and Valley in the Southern Table Plateaus subregion and occasion-ally within the Armuchee area, within the Southern Sandstone Ridges subregion. Some acidic seepage forests also occur on acidic shale slopes throughout the ecoregion. These are presumed to be very similar in species composition to Piedmont seepage forests, although further inventorying is needed.

PHYSICAL SETTING AND ECOLOGY

These seepage wetlands are often small patches embedded within the acidic oak-pine-hickory forest natural community. Although they are usually over sandstone, they can also form over conglomerate or acidic shale. Water percolates through the substrate and emerges at the surface to form the seeps either because joints channel the water to the surface or because of an underlying hardpan formed by an impermeable substrate near the surface. Sandstones, conglomerates, and some shales foster low-nutrient, acidic soils. The low nutrient levels, along with the shade cast by surrounding trees and the saturated soils, limit plant diversity.

Seeps occur when water is channeled to the surface, sometimes by rock fractures, as shown here.

The rare and beautiful monkey-face orchid grows in acidic seepage areas when there is enough light.

Soapwort gentian

In the past, fire was more common on the caps of the plateaus and ridges of this ecoregion. These fires typically spread from upland sites into the acidic seeps and helped maintain these wetlands, providing conditions for greater species diversity. Many seepage areas would benefit from periodic prescribed fires today. Seepage areas are often surrounded by residential or commercial developments or by pine plantations, however, making implementation of prescribed fire programs difficult.

VEGETATION

Trees, particularly red maple, black gum, and sweet gum, are rooted wherever conditions are dry enough. Shrubs dominate in some areas, and the acidic conditions encourage ericads such as southern highbush blueberry, mountain laurel, or Catawba rhododendron. Other shrubs include silky dogwood and tag alder. Some areas, especially in shadier seeps, have a

CHARACTERISTIC PLANTS OF ACIDIC SEEPAGE WETLANDS

TREES

Red maple—*Acer rubrum*
American holly—*Ilex opaca*
Sweet gum—*Liquidambar styraciflua*
Tulip-tree—*Liriodendron tulipifera*
Black gum—*Nyssa sylvatica*

SHRUBS AND WOODY VINES

Tag alder—*Alnus serrulata*
Black chokeberry—*Aronia melanocarpa*
Cross-vine—*Bignonia capreolata*
Silky dogwood—*Cornus amomum*
Climbing hydrangea—*Decumaria barbara*

Winterberry—*Ilex verticillata*
Swamp dewberry—*Rubus hispidus*
Smooth highbush blueberry—*Vaccinium corymbosum*
Southern wild raisin—*Viburnum nudum*

GROUND COVER

Jack-in the-pulpit—*Arisaema triphyllum*
Southern lady fern—*Athyrium asplenioides*
Sedges—*Carex* spp.
Soapwort gentian—*Gentiana saponaria*
Rushes—*Juncus* spp.
Cardinal flower—*Lobelia cardinalis*

Indian cucumber-root—*Medeola virginiana*
Royal fern—*Osmunda regalis*
Cinnamon fern—*Osmundastrum cinnamomeum*
Cowbane—*Oxypolis rigidior*
Helmet skullcap—*Scutellaria integrifolia*
Peat mosses—*Sphagnum* spp.
New York fern—*Thelypteris noveboracensis*
Primrose-leaf violet—*Viola primulifolia*
Netted chain fern—*Woodwardia areolata*

---

dense growth of ferns, including cinnamon fern, royal fern, and New York fern, along with some sedges and primrose-leaf violet. Sphagnum moss is often present. Sunnier seeps are more diverse and can include monkey-face orchid, helmet skullcap, soapwort gentian, and Piedmont azalea (S. Bowling, Atlanta, pers. comm.; Chafin 2007).

ANIMALS

No mammals appear to be restricted to these habitats, but many from adjoining forests, such as raccoons, opossums, gray foxes, bobcats, coyotes, and white-tailed deer visit these sites for water and, in the case of the raccoons, red foxes, and opossums, to prey on herpetofauna here. The bird species composition at these sites is heavily influenced by vegetation structure. Areas of mature forest will often have breeding red-eyed vireos, wood thrushes, red-shouldered hawks, red-bellied woodpeckers, Carolina chickadees, tufted titmice, and many other songbirds. Open sites with shrubs and herbs often have nesting gray catbirds, white-eyed vireos, and common yellowthroats (Cimprich and Moore 1995; Hopp, Kirby, and Boone 1995; Guzy and Ritchison 1999; T. M. Schneider et al. 2010). Wintering species in this community can include American robins at more forested sites and swamp and song sparrows in brushy habitats (Burleigh 1958).

The most abundant salamanders in this habitat are spotted dusky salamanders, provided there is sufficient cover in the form of coarse, woody debris. The brightly colored red salamander and the salamander-eating spring salamander occur as well. Southern two-lined salamanders nest in these sites, attaching eggs to the undersides of rocks, sticks, or leaves in shallow areas so that the steady water flow continuously bathes the eggs in oxygenated water (S. N. Smith 2008). The long-tailed salamander, which appears to be the ecological equivalent of the Piedmont's three-lined salamander, is an important community member, emerging at night to forage on insects (Godwin 2008b). Northern cricket frogs, tiny insectivorous frogs no bigger than a person's thumbnail, are abundant in this habitat. Upland chorus frogs and, in smaller numbers, spring peepers may breed in these areas. Pickerel frogs, which are toxic to many potential predators, join leopard and green frogs as the most abundant larger frogs. A major predator of seepage amphibians is the northern watersnake (Dorcas 2008), individuals of which occasionally cruise these areas hunting for frogs and salamanders alike. Although not particularly aquatic in habits, common garter snakes may occasionally visit these sites for the same purpose.

Common Yellowthroat
(*Geothlypis trichas*)

This small songbird in the family Parulidae has a plain olive-green back, wings, and tail with a yellow throat and upper chest. Adult males have a distinctive black mask. Females are similar to males, but have an olive-colored face, olive and paler underparts, and occasionally a faint black mask. The common yellowthroat is found throughout much of North and Central America, excluding portions of the American Southwest. It breeds from central Canada through the northwestern and southeastern United States and winters in Central America and the Caribbean. In Georgia, this bird is a summer resident in the northern portion of the state and a year-round resident in the southern portion (Beaton 2010a).

Found in a variety of habitats, the common yellowthroat breeds in sites with dense patches of low vegetation, including marshes, stream banks, and shrubby thickets. It is less commonly found in dry, scrubby vegetation. It feeds on insects, which are usually captured in dense vegetation but sometimes caught in midair.

The breeding season begins by mid-April in Georgia. The female lays from three to six eggs in a cup-shaped nest constructed on the ground or in low vegetation, and both adults care for the young. Fledging occurs in as little as 8 days after hatching, but the adults care for the young for an additional 22–26 days. Often two broods are raised in one season, the adult male taking over care of the first brood while the female incubates a second clutch of eggs (Hofslund 1959).

The common yellowthroat's early migration northward in the spring and late migration southward in the winter make it more susceptible to extreme weather events than other migratory species. In addition, its habit of flying at lower altitudes than other birds during migration makes it more prone to collisions with radio towers (H. M. Stevenson and Anderson 1994). Despite these sources of mortality and a loss of habitat in some regions, this species is still common.

Keown Falls Trail

A gentle, stream-cut swale on John's Mountain Trail above Keown Falls supports a striking seepage area. The best way to reach this seepage area is not by following the John's Mountain Trail from the parking lot, but rather using the Keown Falls Trail, which passes through several natural communities. The trail starts in a mesic forest that grades to a dry calcareous forest, with oaks, hickories, American beech, sourwood, and tulip-tree, and becomes more mesic streamside on the northern (right) part of the loop. The trail begins climbing the slope and loses its calcareous nature as it passes through a dry oak-pine-hickory natural community that contains a small, embedded stand of pines with an ericaceous understory. Keown Falls itself is an excellent example of an acidic cliff natural community (and may be dry in summer). It is picturesque, with sheets of vegetation hanging from moist crevices.

The seep itself is above the falls. It is easy to detect because lush, dense clumps of ferns contrast lushly with the dry oak-pine forest in which it is embedded. Vegetation diversity is low in the seep. Trees here include sweet gum, tulip-tree, red maple, and black gum. The vegetation is distributed in a patchy manner, with smooth highbush blueberry dominating in some sites, while others have a dense herbaceous cover with Jack-in-the-pulpit, cinnamon fern, New York fern, royal fern, lady fern, netted chain fern, and sphagnum moss.

Location: Keown Falls is approximately 15 miles west of Resaca and less than 13 miles east of LaFayette. From U.S. Hwy. 27 in LaFayette, proceed east on Ga. Hwy. 136 for about 12.5 miles. Turn right (south) on Pocket Rd. and continue nearly 5 miles to Forest Service Rd. 702 and the Keown Falls sign on the right. Turn right and proceed 0.6 mile to picnic area and parking. Google Earth GPS approximate coordinates to parking: N 34.613539/W 085.088127. Hike up the trail to Keown Falls from the parking lot. It goes through a wooden shelter. When you reach the observation deck after 0.7 mile, hike north on the John's Mountain Trail about 100 yards (no more than 0.25 mile). The seep will be on your left, and can be found by the mass of ferns.

Sagponds and Sinkholes

Sagponds and sinkholes are depressional wetlands that vary from a few feet in diameter to up to a square mile in size (Greear 1967; Wharton 1978). Sagponds, which often hold water for all or much of the year, are emphasized here because most sinkholes hold water only temporarily if at all in this ecoregion in Georgia. Vegetation is sometimes distributed in a zonal pattern within sagponds, with conditions ranging from open water to open forest. Typical trees and shrubs include red maple, sycamore, willow oak, black gum, sweet gum, green ash, southern wild raisin, tag alder, and buttonbush (Greear 1967; Wharton 1978). Sagponds can be quite picturesque, with buttressed trees somewhat reminiscent of Coastal Plain swamps.

Sagponds are not common on the landscape, and at least one plant assemblage within them is considered globally imperiled by NatureServe. Nowhere is the relationship between the Coastal Plain and the Cumberland Plateau / Ridge and Valley ecoregions clearer than in this natural community. Coastal Plain species most likely migrated northward from Alabama through the Coosa River valley, becoming established in depressional wetlands that have habitat similarities with Coastal Plain environments. At least 24 species of vascular plants in the sagponds are disjunct from the Coastal Plain, along with nearly 50 others typically associated or having affinities with the Coastal Plain flora (Greear 1967; Wharton 1978).

On Cassville Mountain in Bartow County near Adairsville there is a remarkable string of sagponds, currently in private ownership. More than 50 ponds are connected by complex seepage and subsurface hydrology (Greear 1967; Wharton 1978). Other examples occur on Lookout Mountain (Dade County), on Pigeon Mountain (Walker County) (Wharton 1978), and within Zahnd Natural Area (Walker County) (see the Featured Place).

Sagponds and sinkholes are distinguished here by the surficial substrate (Greear 1967). The term "sagponds" as used here is a colloquial description first used by Greear (1967) to describe depressional wetlands that are formed when a dolomite or limestone substrate collapses beneath thick layers of overlying bedrock of a differing substrate (such as chert or sandstone), causing a swale or depression in the overlying rock. This differs from a "sagpond," which is defined by geologists as a small body of water occupying an enclosed depression or sag formed where active or recent fault movement has impounded drainage (J. Costello, Ga. DNR, pers. comm.). When standing on the caps of the ridges and plateaus of the ecoregion, it is difficult to discern whether a depression is due to a natural swale in the sandstone or to a collapse far beneath the surface; hence we use the term "sagpond" for both types of depressional wetland. Sinkholes, in contrast, are usually steeper-sided depressions that occur directly within dolomite or limestone. Very few are known to pond water in Georgia's Cumberland Plateau / Ridge and Valley ecoregion.

It is probable that when the sagpond first forms, water does not pond within the depression. Over time, however, thick layers of sediment and organic mat-
ter build up and as they reach up to 4 feet in depth, less and less water is able to drain out, increasing the amount of time water remains in the sagpond (Greear 1967). Although nutrient levels within soils may play a small role, the most important factor in determining vegetation composition in sagponds appears to be hydroperiod—how long a pond stays filled with water during the course of a year (Greear 1967; Wharton 1978). Sagponds, given their typically gentle gradient, often exhibit irregular, somewhat concentric zones of vegetation determined by hydroperiod and topography.

VEGETATION

The sagponds studied by Greear near Adairsville typically support zonal vegetation patterns, ranging from open water in the center to a forested edge as illustrated in the diagram below (Greear 1967; Wharton 1978). Patterns and species differ somewhat from pond to pond, depending partially on the maximum depth of water and extent of water level fluctuation within the ponds (Greear 1967; Wharton 1978). Willow oak is very common around the margin of many ponds; red maple, shining fetterbush, and black chokeberry are also present around ponds that are full during the growing season. Black gum occurs in ponds that have

Royal fern occurs in sagponds as well as in many other wetland types across the state.

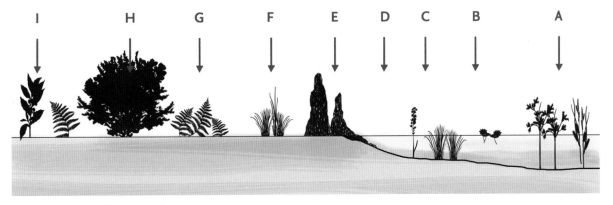

| I | H | G | F | E | D | C | B | A |

Vegetation zones of a sag pond

Each sagpond has a unique zonation pattern that moves from hydric to mesic. For example, vegetation in Quicksand Pond in Bartow County is distributed roughly as follows:

A. Deepwater emergent shrub zone (buttonbush)
B. Open water zone
C. Shallow water emergent shrub zone (buttonbush)
D. Open water zone
E. Aquatic hardwood zone (swamp black gum)
F. Grass-sedge zone
G. Fern zone (Virginia chain fern dominant with royal fern)
H. Marginal heath zone (fetterbush dominant, with red maple and bamboo-vine)
I. Outer ecotone with Piedmont azalea, bracken fern, and haircap moss

Adapted from Wharton 1978, p. 99. Wharton in turn adapted information from Greear 1967.

water through spring and early summer, where the water is at least roughly 1 foot deep. Greear found 24 plants previously known only or primarily from the Coastal Plain. Many were graminoids, including a joint grass, several panic grasses, sedges, and a bulrush. Others include a blue-eyed grass, a violet, shining fetterbush, a marsh-pink, nine lobelias, a goldenrod, a bugleweed, a hawthorn, and gallberry (Wharton 1978, citing Greear 1967).

The sagponds on ridge tops are not as diverse. An excellent publicly accessible example of a sagpond, which is quite large and bears some similarities to the sagponds of the Cassville area, occurs near the Rocktown Trail. The pond is long and oval, measuring roughly 200 by 75 feet. A ditch indicates that the hydrology of this pond has been altered in the past. Stains on tree trunks indicate that water often ponds to around 18 inches or higher. Frogs inhabit the area—a reminder that botanists used to locate sagponds in this area by scouting out the plateau tops in the evening and listening for frogs (S. Bowling, At-

lanta, pers. comm.). There is a somewhat zonal, concentric vegetation pattern, with few species inhabiting areas that are often saturated and trees rimming the edge of the hydric area. Characteristic sagpond plants occur, including distinctive clumps of rushes that dot the pond floor, black gum, saplings of American beech, sourwood, red maple, and tulip-tree. An island of buttonbush is reminiscent of the Cassville sagponds; highbush blueberry is another common shrub. Netted chain fern occurs in some moist areas. Mosses coat the bases of many trees, and sphagnum mosses inhabit hydric areas.

Most sinkholes in the ecoregion do not hold water and support mesic or submesic calcareous plant communities. There is an example of a small limesink that does hold water along the Pocket Trail in the Pocket Recreational Area. This depression is surrounded by red maple, sourwood, and white oak, with stains on the tree trunks indicating the variable water levels. A sparse scattering of royal fern, greenbriers, blueberries, azalea, galax, and thick patches of mosses occur along the rim.

CHARACTERISTIC PLANTS OF SAGPONDS AND SINKHOLES

TREES

Red maple—Acer rubrum

Green ash—Fraxinus pennsylvanicum

American holly—Ilex opaca

Sweet gum—Liquidambar styraciflua

Swamp tupelo—Nyssa biflora

Black gum—Nyssa sylvatica

White oak—Quercus alba

Southern red oak—Quercus falcata

Laurel oak—Quercus laurifolia

Willow oak—Quercus phellos

SHRUBS AND WOODY VINES

Tag alder—Alnus serrulata

Chokeberries—Aronia arbutifolia; A. melanocarpa

Buttonbush—Cephalanthus occidentalis

St. Andrew's cross—Hypericum hypericoides

Possum-haw—Ilex decidua

Gallberry—Ilex glabra

Mountain laurel—Kalmia latifolia

Fetterbush—Lyonia lucida

Greenbriers—Smilax spp.

GROUND COVER

Old-field broomsedge—Andropogon virginicus

Witchgrasses—Dichanthelium spp.

Threeway sedge—Dulichium arundinaceum

Royal fern—Osmunda regalis

Cinnamon fern—Osmundastrum cinnamomeum

Panic grasses—Panicum spp.

Haircap moss—Polytrichum commune

Spotted pondweed—Potomageton pulcher

Bracken fern—Pteridium aquilinum

Beaksedges—Rhynchospora spp.

Peat mosses—Sphagnum spp.

Longspur creeping bladderwort—Utricularia biflora

Virginia chain fern—Woodwardia virginica

ANIMALS

Because these ponds are filled with water most of the year, it is unlikely that many mammals use this as a primary habitat. Mammals of the surrounding forest (either dry calcareous or oak-pine-hickory natural communities), however, might use the sagponds as a source of water, and opossums and raccoons might hunt for amphibians and crayfish in the area. Beaver and muskrats may inhabit the larger sagponds.

Large, open sagponds can provide roost sites for ducks such as the mallard, ring-necked duck, and lesser scaup during migration and winter. More forested ponds may provide roosting sites for the wood duck and hooded merganser, and in some cases, nesting or brood-rearing habitat for the wood duck (Dugger, Dugger, and Fredrickson 1994; Hepp and Bellrose 1995). Forested sites may also provide nesting habitat for green herons, which build stick nests in small trees or shrubs over or adjacent to water (K. L. Davis and Kushlan 1994; Melvin 2010b). Brushy areas within ponds or along their borders often have nesting common yellowthroats (Guzy and Ritchison 1999) and can provide wintering habitat for swamp sparrows (Burleigh 1958; Mowbray 1997).

Fishless pools are used as breeding habitat by many amphibians. Some species such as marbled salamanders, spotted salamanders, Cope's gray treefrogs, spring peepers, and upland chorus frogs breed in temporary and semipermanent ponds throughout most of Georgia. In addition, some ponds are used by amphibians normally thought of as lowland species. For example, barking treefrogs and southern cricket frogs have both been found in Georgia's Cumberland Plateau region (Herrington 2008; Jensen 2008c). In fact, southern cricket frogs have been found living side-by-side with northern cricket frogs in a seasonal wetland atop Lookout Mountain. The mole salamander, a species much more commonly found in the Coastal Plain, has been documented from sagponds on the Cumberland Plateau (see Featured Animal). Relatively permanent ponds may support paedomorphic forms of this species, in which juvenile characteristics are retained in adults. Upland and mountain chorus frogs breed in the winter in shallow ponds having short hydroperiods, spending the remainder of the year as terrestrial members of surrounding forest communities. A number of herpetofaunal species are year-round residents of the more permanent ponds. These species are similar to those found in such ponds in other parts of the state and include eastern newts, green frogs, bullfrogs, southern leopard frogs, northern watersnakes, and common snapping turtles.

Mole Salamander
(*Ambystoma talpoideum*)

The mole salamander is a relatively small member of the family Ambystomatidae, of which there are five species in Georgia (including two newly differentiated species of flatwoods salamander). Adults are 3 to 4.8 inches in length, with a short, stocky body, relatively short and thick tail, and disproportionately large head and feet (Conant and Collins 1998). The back and sides range from gray to brown with flecks of lighter gray. The belly is typically bluish gray with light-colored flecks. Many mole salamanders are paedomorphic, meaning that they fail to metamorphose completely and retain certain larval morphological features as adults (Floyd 2008b).

Until recently, this secretive and relatively inconspicuous salamander was thought to be confined mainly to the Coastal Plain, with isolated popula-tions in other regions of the state (Conant and Collins 1998; Floyd 2008b). In recent years, additional popu-lations have been found in the Piedmont, Blue Ridge, and Cumberland Plateau / Ridge and Valley, leading to a picture of much wider distribution in the state. In the Cumberland Plateau / Ridge and Valley, adults are typically found in upland hardwood and mixed forests that contain sagponds and other isolated wetlands.

Mole salamanders can breed successfully in a variety of ponds, particularly those that are free of predatory fish. The period of breeding ranges from fall to early spring, depending on temperature, rain-fall, and geographic location. Females lay up to several hundred eggs in clusters of varying sizes, often attach-ing these on submerged twigs. After hatching, larvae typically inhabit the ponds for three to four months, then complete their metamorphosis to adults and move out into the surrounding woods. Mole salaman-ders usually reach sexual maturity at two years (Floyd 2008b).

Zahnd Natural Area Sagpond

This is a small sagpond less than 75 feet long. The gentle slope suggests that this small wetland is natural, although it is surrounded by topography that has been altered through human impact, including a nearby borrow pit, an old road, and a ditch paralleling the current road. The site is shady, on an acidic substrate and far away from Coastal Plain migration corridors, but is nonetheless quite picturesque. Mosses coat the tree roots near the water, and sphagnum moss (peat moss) forms patches of green along the pond's rim. The sagpond is particularly picturesque in early spring, when water levels are high, and it provides diversity to the landscape. The pond is rimmed by red maple, sweet gum, black gum, and white oak. Other trees along the rim include sourwood and American holly. A few of the red maples are quite large and hang over the water within the depression. Greenbriers, mountain laurel, a chokeberry, sedges, a blueberry, and cinnamon fern occur beneath the trees. This sagpond can be explored while also observing the Featured Places for the acidic pine-oak-hickory forest and acidic cliff and rock outcrop natural communities.

Location: See p. 188 for directions to Zahnd Natural Area. The sagpond is located very near Hwy. 157, on the west side of the highway, several hundred feet south of the kiosk. A series of ditches precedes the pond. Google Earth approximate coordinates for the sagpond are N 34.654/W 085.471.

Floodplains, Bottomlands, and Riparian Zones

Floodplains, bottomlands, and riparian zones occur along streams, large creeks, and rivers. This natural community is at least occasionally flooded and is characterized by trees and shrubs that can grow to maturity on soils that are saturated for limited periods of time, including cherrybark oak, swamp chestnut oak, Shumard oak, overcup oak, sweet gum, red maple, water oak, tulip-tree, river birch, sycamore, green ash, and box elder (Wharton 1978; Schafale and Weakley 1990; Sharitz and Mitsch 1993). As with floodplain and bottomland habitats throughout the state, the structural and vegetation compositional diversity of these communities and their proximity to water support a diverse array of animal species.

The floodplains of this ecoregion have long been used for farming and settlement. Well-developed expressions of bottomland forests are very rare (DeSelm and Murdock 1993). Mesic areas along small streams that are dominated by upland species such as basswood, tulip-tree, shagbark hickory, northern red oak, and white oak are covered in the mesic forest natural community.

PHYSICAL SETTING AND ECOLOGY

This natural community encompasses a broad range of habitats, from sandy point bars that are constantly changed by floodwater to hydric-mesic bottomlands that rarely flood. Many different plant assemblages are included here, each adapted to differing flood regimes and soil characteristics. In addition, the geology and topography throughout this ecoregion have caused corresponding differences in floodplain, bottomland, and riparian zone characteristics among the streams here. In spite of these differing dynamics, which are described below, the presence of overlapping, hydric species among all of these settings explains their inclusion in this single natural community.

The broad floodplains of the meandering Coosa, Oostanala, and Etowah Rivers resemble those of the Coastal Plain. The Coosa, Oostanala, and Conasauga all cut through the limestone and dolomite of the Great Valley and have well-developed, meandering patterns. The topography of the floodplains of these rivers ranges from steep bluff with little to no floodplain development to a complex mosaic of levees, meander cutoffs, and terraces. For example, the floodplain of the Oostanala by Whitmore's Bluff is narrow, perhaps 30 feet in width, with a dissected levee bordered in places by swales. In contrast, the floodplain of

The Coosa River. Along some stretches this large river has carved a broad, complex floodplain with levees, backswamps, and oxbow lakes, giving it an appearance similar to some floodplains in the Coastal Plain.

the Conasauga near Tilton, Georgia, is much broader, with levees, high terraces, and a slough area. Similarly, the Coosa River near Foster's Bend has an extensive floodplain, with well-developed meanders and ox-bows (Wharton 1978). All of these rivers have a complex, fine-grained mosaic of vegetation influenced by the topography carved by floods. Higher areas support mesic species or a mix of mesic and mesic-hydric species, while depressional areas support mesic-hydric and hydric species. Where steep bluffs descend to the water along the Coosa, Conasauga, and Oostanala, little to no floodplain is present.

The steeply graded streams that plunge down the Plateau Escarpment often have no floodplain at all. On the valley floor, most of the small streams are bordered by low terraces that support mesophytic rather than riparian species. Some small streams do, however, develop small floodplains that support hydric species. A good example of this occurs in New Echota, along Tarvin Springs Branch and New Town Creek, where

flooding of up to 8 feet can occur once a month in late winter and early spring, with floodwaters taking a week to recede. The prolonged inundation encourages wetland plants such as cardinal flower, tag alder, green ash, and swamp chestnut oak, mixed with more mesophytic species (Gomez 2003). In contrast to larger floodplains that experience high discharges, pioneer tree species are not widespread in these smaller floodplains because mechanical damage is not severe enough to create large openings. As in the Piedmont, some of these small streams are incising through alluvium that was deposited when uplands underwent severe erosion due to improvident farming practices in the late 19th- and early to mid-20th centuries (see p. 265). Damage was not as extensive in the Cumberland Plateau / Ridge and Valley ecoregion as it was in the Piedmont, however.

On some sandstone ridge caps, a rare community, known as a scour zone, exists. Scour zones occur in the riparian zones of high-gradient streams along a few

A low terrace near a small stream in Sloppy Floyd State Park is transitional between the bottomland and mesic forest communities.

small streams where bare, erosion-resistant sandstone rock is exposed, creating nearly chute-like conditions in some short stretches. The scour zone is prone to severe drought periods that may stress or kill some vegetation, and pioneer species are favored because of the continual openings created by floods (Malanson 1993). Floods literally scour the sides of the stream. Trees cannot become established because of the force of "flashy," high-velocity water traveling down the stream channels. Virginia spiraea, federally listed as Threatened, is an indicator species, known to occur at two locations in Cloudland Canyon State Park (Dade County), as well as in Lula Lake Preserve (Walker County). The best-known, most easily accessible example of a scour zone occurs along Rock Creek at the Lula Lake Preserve. Conditions along the Rock Creek scour zone range from densely vegetated areas that are dominated by grasses and forbs or by woody shrubs and resprouts battered by floods to exposed cobbles connected by gravel and sand.

VEGETATION

Vegetation in floodplains, bottomlands, and riparian zones is a mosaic of forests, woodlands, shrublands, and herbaceous communities. In general, hydric areas,

In northwest Georgia, stream channels that consist of sandstone scoured by floodwaters are unusual and small in scale. These habitats are more extensive in other states.

CHARACTERISTIC PLANTS OF FLOODPLAINS, BOTTOMLANDS, AND RIPARIAN ZONES

TREES

Box elder—*Acer negundo*
Red maple—*Acer rubrum*
River birch—*Betula nigra*
Musclewood—*Carpinus caroliniana*
Sugarberry—*Celtis laevigata*
Green ash—*Fraxinus pennsylvanica*
Sweet gum—*Liquidambar styraciflua*
Tulip-tree—*Liriodendron tulipifera*
Sycamore—*Platanus occidentalis*
Overcup oak—*Quercus lyrata*
Swamp chestnut oak—*Quercus michauxii*
Cherrybark oak—*Quercus pagoda*
Willow oak—*Quercus phellos*
Shumard oak—*Quercus shumardii*

SHRUBS AND WOODY VINES

Tag alder—*Alnus serrulata*
Cross-vine—*Bignonia capreolata*
Buttonbush—*Cephalanthus occidentalis*
Silky dogwood—*Cornus amomum*
Witch-hazel—*Hamamelis virginiana*
Possum-haw—*Ilex decidua*
Virginia-willow—*Itea virginica*
Southern wild raisin—*Viburnum nudum*
Yellowroot—*Xanthorhiza simplicissima*

GROUND COVER

River cane—*Arundinaria gigantea*
River oats—*Chasmanthium latifolium*
Hollow-stem Joe-pye-weed—*Eutrochium fistulosum*
Orange jewelweed—*Impatiens capensis*
Cardinal flower—*Lobelia cardinalis*
Sensitive fern—*Onoclea sensibilis*
Butterweed—*Packera glabella*
Lizard's-tail—*Saururus cernuus*
Common wingstem—*Verbesina alternifolia*
Netted chain fern—*Woodwardia areolata*

Great blue lobelia

sloughs, swales, small-stream floodplains, and backwater areas where the soils are saturated for long periods, with little mechanical damage caused by strong floods, will support hydric-mesic oak species, including swamp chestnut oak, overcup oak, cherrybark oak, water oak, willow oak, and Shumard oak. Other trees that often grow in these bottomland habitats include swamp tupelo, green ash, sweet gum, red maple, red mulberry, American elm, and sugarberry. Shrubs, vines, and herbs include tag alder, trumpet-creeper, lizard's-tail, cardinal flower, green dragon, creeping Jenny, dotted smartweed, Virginia bugleweed, butterweed, netted chain fern, hammock spiderlily, turtlehead, cinnamon fern, royal fern, common New Jersey tea, southern wild raisin, bluebell, spring-beauty, lanceleaf trillium, river cane, cross vine, and poison ivy.

In areas where floods create many openings in the vegetation, pioneer species, including silver maple, sweet gum, black willow, box elder, river birch, sycamore, and red maple, are able to grow. Shrubs and herbs include Virginia-willow, Virginia spiraea, buttonbush, winged sumac, possum-haw, witch-hazel, yellowroot, tag alder, hollow-stemmed Joe-pye-weed, witchgrasses, common cinquefoil, river oats, and river cane.

Mesic areas, where flooding is not common and soils are not saturated for long periods, support basswood, black walnut, hickories, tulip-tree, American beech, white oak, and southern sugar maple, with shrubs and herbaceous species that include common pawpaw, red buckeye, and may-apple. Some mesic areas near streams on acidic substrates, as seen in Zahnd Natural Area (Walker County), Cloudland Canyon State Park (Dade County), and Lula Lake Preserve (Walker County), support a mesic acidic community with many ericads, such as mountain laurel, trailing arbutus, Catawba rhododendron, and sourwood. Eastern hemlock, black gum, partridge-berry, American holly, American beech, black birch, tuliptree, yellowroot, beaked hazelnut, New York fern, Indian cucumber-root, and witch-hazel may also appear. Sometimes these mesic habitats are woven within the bottomland habitat so closely they cannot be separated. As stated earlier, however, if no hydric species appear, the site should be classified as mesic forest.

ANIMALS

This is a rich habitat for mammals because there are many sources of shelter and food. They benefit from the diversity of vegetation provided by the bottomland, floodplain, and riparian zone habitats, as well as the ecotones between this natural community and the forested natural communities near it. The big brown bat will fly in a straight direction over rivers, searching for beetles. The evening bat, which is smaller than the big brown, will forage along streams in bottomlands, roosting during the day under loose bark and in hollow trees. Minks are carnivorous animals that den under the roots of trees along the stream, in the abandoned dens of other mammals. They roam widely along floodplains looking for their prey, which includes mammals, birds, eggs, frogs, crayfish, and fish. River otters also den in river banks and feed on many of the same prey species. Muskrats are aquatic rodents that den in stream banks; their dens have passages to the surface that are hidden under plant growth or debris. They are omnivorous, feeding on a variety of aquatic plants, as well as crayfish, fish, frogs, and insects (L. Brown 1997; Fergus 2003). These mammals primarily inhabit the river's edge, but may use other aquatic habitats in the floodplain. Other mammals include raccoon, beaver, gray squirrel, golden mouse, hispid cotton rat, silver-haired bat, rice rat, swamp rabbit, gray fox, bobcat, coyote, short-tailed shrew, eastern mole, and opossum.

Bird life is varied. Wood ducks nest in larger cavities in trees along these streams and rivers and in the floodplain forest. Preferred nest cavities are over or near slow-moving or stagnant water (Bellrose and Holm 1994; Hepp and Bellrose 1995). The yellow-throated warbler will nest in sycamore trees along some of these streams and rivers (T. M. Schneider et al. 2010). Understory trees along wider stream corridors provide nesting sites for the Acadian flycatcher, while root tangles and bank crevices provide nest sites for the Louisiana waterthrush (W. D. Robinson 1995; Whitehead and Taylor 2002). Other warblers, including the Blackburnian, Cape May, and yellow-rumped, often feed in eastern hemlock during migration (Morse 1994; Baltz and Latta 1998; P. D. Hunt and Flaspohler 1998). River scour areas provide brushy habitats that can be used by white-eyed vireos and common yellowthroats for nesting and during migration (Hopp, Kirby, and Boone 1995; Guzy and Ritchison 1999; T. M. Schneider et al. 2010).

Large river floodplains support a number of amphibian and reptile species. Completely aquatic, mudpuppies are large salamanders that may use undercuts and bank holes as refuges (Mount 1975). Floodplain swamps along the Coosa River have resident cottonmouths, a species normally associated with the Coastal Plain or lower Piedmont (Wharton 1978). The Coosa River valley is an important dispersal corridor for several amphibian and reptile species that are normally associated with the Coastal Plain in Alabama (see the Featured Animal), including tiger salamanders, oak toads, squirrel treefrogs, eastern glass lizards, and chicken turtles, and that may have as yet undiscovered populations in Georgia.

Riverine turtle species such as loggerhead musk turtles and river cooters use floodplains as nesting sites. Several turtle species, including the common map turtle, the Alabama map turtle, and possibly the Ouachita map turtle, enter Georgia only along rivers and creeks of the Ridge and Valley (Jensen et al. 2008). Painted turtles, river cooters, spiny softshell turtles, and possibly Ouachita map turtles use sand bars for nesting.

Small stream floodplains have a diverse salamander fauna, particularly those of spring-fed streams, which tend to experience less extreme variation in temperature and water flow. Some of the more colorful salamander species, including the southern two-lined and red salamanders, reach their most intense hues in Cumberland Plateau / Ridge and Valley streams. Long-tailed salamanders may be particularly abundant in streams that originate in caves, inside of which individuals live alongside cave salamanders (Camp and Jensen 2007). The most abundant salamander is the spotted dusky salamander. All of these species take cover during the day and forage for insects at night. Northern cricket frogs, green frogs, bullfrogs, south-ern leopard frogs, and pickerel frogs are the most abundant frog species. Pickerel frogs are particularly common along spring-fed streams, and they frequently seek refuge from harsh surface conditions in nearby caves (Godwin 2008a).

FEATURED ANIMAL

Alabama Map Turtle (*Graptemys pulchra*)

The Alabama map turtle is one of several map turtles whose range extends into Georgia via the major rivers of the Ridge and Valley. This member of the family Emydidae exhibits the sexual dimorphism typical of map turtles. While adult males typically have a cara-pace length of less than 5 inches, females may achieve a carapace length of more than 11 inches. Young turtles are strikingly marked with leg stripes, greenish blotches on the head, and a conspicuous keel of spines or knobs on the carapace, but these markings, color patterns, and knobs are less conspicuous on older adults (Moulis 2008).

The range of the Alabama map turtle extends from northwestern Georgia across Alabama and the western panhandle of Florida to Mississippi and eastern Lou-isiana in streams that drain to the Gulf of Mexico (Conant and Collins 1998). In Georgia, it has been found only in the Conasauga and Oostanaula Rivers. This turtle appears to be restricted to streams of mod-erate to large size that support an abundance of mus-sels, which are the adult females' nearly exclusive source of food. The heads of the females are greatly en-larged relative to those of the insectivorous males. The large head and associated jaw musculature give the fe-males the crushing power necessary to successfully feed on mussels. Both males and females frequently bask on snags and tree trunks, quickly diving into the water when disturbed.

The breeding season for Alabama map turtles is from late March through November, during which time they can produce several clutches. Females lay their eggs on sandy banks and sand bars, digging flask-shaped nests with their hind legs. The hatchling map turtles crawl out of their nests and scramble downhill to the water's edge. Because of its restricted range in Georgia, the Alabama map turtle is protected as Rare.

Lock and Dam Park

Publicly accessible trails along major rivers that still possess any natural forest are extremely rare in northwest Georgia. Lock and Dam Park, along the Coosa River in Rome, although altered by human activities appears somewhat close to an unaltered state. A nature trail parallels the river. This trail moves at times through a narrow buffer of trees, but at other times winds through a better-developed floodplain habitat, with cutbanks, levees, and bottomland forest, providing opportunities to see floodplain, bottomland, and riparian zone species along the mesic to hydric spectrum. Pioneer species that grow along the river include river birch, sweet gum, box elder, and sycamore. Bottomland species along the trail include green ash, sugarberry, elms, swamp chestnut oak, cherrybark oak, Shumard oak, ironwood, downy serviceberry, and common silverbell. Some fairly well developed canebrakes occur, and river oats appear on the banks in some areas. Mesic species include bitternut hickory, northern red oak, basswood, tulip-tree, and white oak. The Coosa River Preserve appears at the end of the trail. The trail through the preserve moves through a notable mesic calcareous area with many calcium-loving plants, with the riparian area below it.

The dam is not a major impediment to river flow and does not impede the movement of fish from either side. Rather, it serves as a set of shoals, making boat passage difficult most of the time, but also serving as good habitat for the many native fish that occur in the river. Lake sturgeon were eliminated decades ago by commercial fishing, pollution, and dams. Restocking efforts were started nearly a decade ago, and hopefully over time, the fish will become mature enough to reproduce.

Location: From the major corridor intersection of Ga. Hwy. 20/53/1/U.S. Hwy. 27 and 411 just south of Rome, proceed south on U.S. Hwy. 27/U.S. 411/ Ga. 53/Ga. 1, 3.4 miles to Walker Mountain Rd. on the right. Turn right and proceed west on Walker Mountain Rd. (without a stop, Walker Mountain Rd. changes to Blacks Bluff Rd. at 1.6 miles). Remain straight on Blacks Bluff Rd. approximately 3.4 miles and turn right onto Lock and Dam Park Rd. Proceed straight just under 0.5 mile to parking and park office. Google Earth GPS approximate coordinates to park office: N 34.199367/W 085.257427.

Chapter 5

PIEDMONT ECOREGION

Overview

The term "piedmont" means foothills: the Piedmont ecoregion lies at the foot of the Appalachian Mountains, with a topography that ranges from rugged to gently rolling. In contrast to the sedimentary rocks of the Cumberland Plateau / Ridge and Valley ecoregion and the unconsolidated sediments of the Coastal Plain, the Piedmont (like the Blue Ridge ecoregion) is made up of a mosaic of metamorphic rocks, varying from mafic rocks that foster high-nutrient soils to acidic rocks that render more sterile soils. The variation in topography and soils leads to a mix of natural communities, including fire-influenced woodlands on acidic south-facing ridges, mesic forests on deep, fertile soils, and rock outcrops with panoramic views. Prior to European settlement, Native Americans fostered a landscape that was a complex blend of old-growth forests, prairies, rock outcrops, and woodlands. Much diversity was lost as settlers cleared the forests for agriculture and later populated the Piedmont in huge numbers, destroying and fragmenting habitats. But many reminders of the past remain, which help guide efforts to restore the natural communities of the ecoregion.

The Piedmont ecoregion viewed from Currahee Mountain

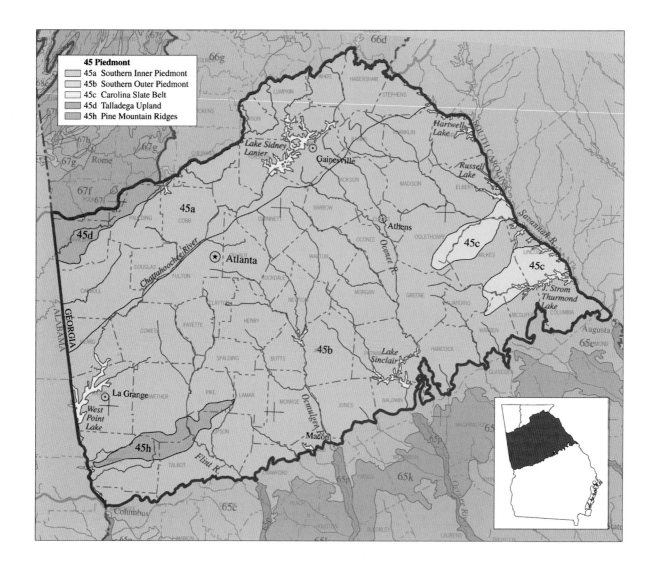

GEOLOGY, TOPOGRAPHY, AND SOILS

The Piedmont ecoregion occupies 17,253 square miles in Georgia, or about 29% of the entire state. The topography varies from dramatic to gently rolling hills. Geologically, the Piedmont is similar to the Blue Ridge in that it is an agglomeration of pieces of the ancient North American continent, island arcs, oceanic crust, and scraps of old continents (terranes) that were repeatedly metamorphosed, folded, faulted, and welded together during collisions between North America, Africa, and smaller pieces of the earth's crust. The most common Piedmont rocks are granitic gneiss and mica schist, with lesser amounts of amphibolite, quartzite, granite, diabase, slate, and various mafic and ultramafic rocks. The ecoregion is divided into five subregions that are distinguished by differences in their topography, geology, and soils, which in turn influence the natural communities that occur in them (G. E. Griffith et al. 2001).

Southern Inner Piedmont. This large subregion makes up nearly one-third of the Piedmont ecoregion. The Dahlonega Plateau is a large upland region in the northeastern portion of this subregion. The ridges in the southern inner Piedmont tend to be higher and steeper than those in the rest of the ecoregion, and north-facing slopes may support many montane plant species. Rock types tend to be mostly gneisses and schists with much silica and aluminum, which yield acidic, nutrient-poor soils. Soils that formed on convex and/or steep slopes are less stable, thinner, and more severely eroded than those of other sites. They often have thin, sandy topsoil layers, and sandy to loamy subsoils, with rock layers at a depth of 3 to 6 feet. Potentially, several natural communities can develop on these dry, thin, sterile soils, particularly if fire occurs regularly, including montane longleaf woodlands, prairies and savannas, glades and barrens, and xeric pine-oak woodlands and forests. Where the soils are a little thicker, oak-pine-hickory forests dominate, except on some concave, north-facing slopes or protected stream terraces, where the moister soil conditions enable Piedmont mesic forests to develop.

Amphibolite, a mafic rock that fosters more circumneutral soils, occurs in thick beds outcropping over hundreds of acres of the Southern Inner Piedmont, including Soapstone Mountain (Banks County), Currahee Mountain (Stephens County), and Pumpkinvine Creek (Paulding County). Glades and barrens, oak-pine-hickory forests, prairies and savannas, pine-oak woodlands and forests, and mesic forests can all develop on these circumneutral soils, depending on soil moisture and depth, as well as fire regime, and all have greater species diversity than their counterparts on the acidic soils of the schists and gneisses.

Another well-known geologic feature of this subregion is the Brevard Fault, a southwest- to northeast-running fault line through which the Chattahoochee River flows. North-facing slopes along the Brevard Fault, especially where marble occurs, can support lush mesic forests.

Southern Outer Piedmont. This subregion makes up almost two-thirds of the Georgia Piedmont ecoregion. The topography is typically lower in elevation and less rugged than that of the inner Piedmont. Exposed layers of granitic rock extend through the center of this subregion, supporting granite outcrops, one of Georgia's most renowned natural communities. As in the Southern Inner Piedmont, schist and gneiss that produce acidic soils are most common and result in the development of the same natural communities as they do in the Southern Inner Piedmont, although typically with fewer montane elements and occasionally with more Coastal Plain species. A highly unusual outcropping of ultramafic rock in the southeastern portion of this subregion forms soils that are very high in magnesium and iron, fostering rare ultramafic barrens. Gabbro, a mafic igneous rock in Jasper County, occupies an area large enough to allow development of unusual xeric pine-oak woodlands that have many

calcium-loving plants. The gabbro also fosters a rare Piedmont flatwoods community.

Carolina Slate Belt. Only a small portion of this subregion extends into Georgia. Metavolcanic and metasedimentary rocks that form silty and silty-clay soils predominate here. Shrink-swell soils that foster unusual natural communities often develop from these rocks. Where base levels are high, the likelihood of rare upland depression swamps and mafic woodland natural communities is strong, but more exploration is needed to confirm the existence of such communities in this region.

Talladega Uplands. This small subregion in the northwestern portion of the ecoregion has some of the highest elevations and steepest slopes in the Piedmont. The ridges here are made up of erosion-resistant quartzite, sandstone, and metaconglomerate rocks that tend to develop sandy, dry, acidic soils. This area is best known for the rare montane longleaf forests and woodlands that can be found on steep, sandy, south-facing slopes.

Pine Mountain Ridges. This subregion is made up of steep ridges (particularly Pine and Oak Mountains) of erosion-resistant quartzite that rise up 300 to 400 feet. The Flint River has carved some stunning gorges through these ridges, best viewed at Sprewell Bluff (Upson County). The sharp relief, combined with proximity to the Coastal Plain, enables an interesting mix of montane and Coastal Plain species to coexist, especially in the seepages and mesic forests. These montane species are often relicts of the Pleistocene, meaning that they were more common in the Piedmont during the last ice age and are now able to survive in some of the cool ravines of the Pine Mountain ridges. The sandy, dry soils that develop from the quartzite also support montane longleaf pine stands, as well as acidic prairies, savannas, and glades and barrens on the dry ridge tops and steep, dry slopes.

RIVER BASINS AND GROUNDWATER

Except for the uppermost reaches of the Etowah, Chattahoochee, and Savannah, the headwaters of Piedmont rivers are all within the ecoregion, so rivers are not particularly large. The Chattahoochee, Flint, Ocmulgee, and Oconee have drainage areas and flows of roughly similar magnitude. The Savannah has a drain-

Shoals spider lilies

age area at least twice that of the others, but its channel in the Piedmont is mostly obliterated by reservoirs. The largest floodplains are on the Oconee River in Greene County, the Flint River–Line Creek–White Oak Creek system between Griffin and Newnan, and the Chattahoochee River below Suwannee and again below Atlanta. The stream valleys are either V-shaped with narrow floors, or, commonly, U-shaped, where alluvium from severe soil erosion collected on valley floors in the previous century (p. 264).

The breadth of floodplains across the Piedmont varies in response to differing geologic controls as well as to topography. Floodplains of even the largest rivers in the ecoregion are rarely more than a few hundred feet wide because the rivers cannot meander widely in the bedrock substrate. In some places, rivers and streams are channeled by faults and joints. The Chattahoochee River, for example, is constrained by the

Brevard Fault as it flows toward Alabama before moving southward. Around Pine Mountain (Harris, Meriwether, and Upson Counties), movement of the Flint River is limited by the quartzite substrate, creating the Flint River Gorge. Sweetwater Creek has what is called a "rectangular" drainage basin shape (Christopherson 2009): it is channeled by the joints in the bedrock of its basin. In all of these places and others like them, the floodplain is narrow and made up of talus (rock fragments that have eroded from the bluffs above) as well as by the alluvium of flood deposits.

Other floodplains in the ecoregion are more alluvial, that is, the stream has been able to move back and forth across the landscape more freely and has deposited alluvium over a broader area. Although no floodplains in the Piedmont approach the well-developed floodplains of the Coastal Plain, broad point bars, levees, and backswamps can be found along stretches of the Ocmulgee, Oconee, Flint, Broad, and South Rivers. A good example of a river swamp—a landform common on the Coastal Plain but less common on the Piedmont—occurs on the Alcovy River.

In general, the more rugged topography of the Southern Inner Piedmont precludes extensive floodplain development and alluvial deposits are coarser, while the outer lower Piedmont has broader interfluves and somewhat broader floodplains with finer alluvial sediments. Hence the Amicalola River, the Chestatee River, and parts of the upper Broad River all somewhat resemble mountain rivers or streams, with narrow, cobbled floodplains and numerous shoals, while the lower Piedmont reaches of the Ocmulgee, Savannah, Flint, and Oconee Rivers—while they certainly support rocky shoals in some stretches—tend to have broader floodplains with deep alluvial deposits of sand, silt, and clay.

The gneisses and schists of the Piedmont are virtually impermeable when unweathered, so there are no predictably productive, regionally extensive aquifers such as those in the Coastal Plain ecoregion. Groundwater moves through fractures and other discontinuities in the bedrock, forming countless small springs and seeps and replenishing streams where it discharges in valley bottoms. Large springs are rare in the Piedmont. Three springs at the base of Pine Mountain are exceptions: Warm Springs, with a discharge of 1,890 gallons per minute; nearby Cold Spring, with a discharge of 2,200 gallons per minute; and Blue Spring, with a discharge of 750 gallons per minute (McCallie 1908).

ENVIRONMENTAL FACTORS

Due to the fairly gentle topography and the primarily acidic substrates of the Piedmont, much of the ecoregion is clothed in dry or submesic oak-pine forests. Many natural communities, however, are distinguished by differences in soil moisture (which results from a complex interaction of slope aspect, shape, exposure, and position), soil nutrients (largely dependent on the underlying geology), hydrology, and fire.

Moisture conditions range along a gradient from xeric (extremely dry) to hydric (saturated). Xeric conditions occur on sites with thin, rocky soils, south-facing aspects, and, often, steep slopes because these sites can experience high runoff and the thin soils cannot store moisture. Most glades and barrens, gran-

Amphibolite

ite outcrops, savannas, prairies, and woodlands occur in xeric or dry conditions. Sites become increasingly submesic (occasionally droughty) to mesic (evenly moist) as topography becomes flatter, aspect becomes more northerly and easterly, and soils deepen, holding more moisture. Oak-pine-hickory forests occur on submesic sites, and mesic forests on the most mesic ones.

The spatially diverse geology of the Piedmont results in a mosaic of soil nutrient conditions throughout the ecoregion, as noted under the descriptions of the subregions above. Mafic rock, which is higher in calcium and other plant nutrients than most Piedmont bedrock, will create more diverse plant assemblages: mafic rock outcrops, woodlands, prairies, and forests all contain more calcium-loving species and a higher diversity of plants than more acidic counterparts. Large expanses of ultramafic rock are very limited in the Georgia Piedmont and can foster the highly unusual ultramafic barren and woodland community.

Hydrology is also an important determinant of natural communities in the Piedmont. Wetlands in the Piedmont include flatwoods, which occur where sticky clays over mafic rocks pond water in the winter and spring, while seepages occur where water is channeled to the surface at topographic breaks or through joints in the bedrock. As discussed under River Basins and Groundwater above, the development of floodplains and bottomlands varies across the Piedmont, depending on the topography and substrate.

Fire is critical to the formation of several natural communities within the Georgia Piedmont, including prairies and savannas, montane longleaf woodlands, most xeric pine-oak woodlands, and ultramafic bar-

Calcium-rich clays swell during the rainy months, creating a hardpan that prevents water from percolating through the soil.

rens and woodlands. In addition, fire can maintain oak domination in oak-pine forests. The impacts of fire on vegetation composition and structure—the ways in which it encourages either woodlands or forests dominated by pine and oak or creates very open natural communities such as prairies and savannas—are described in detail on p. 38, as well as in the descriptions of each of those natural communities.

Fire was once more common on the Georgia Piedmont, and fire-dependent communities were more widespread in the past. The tree species recorded on land-lot surveys performed prior to European settlement indicate a dominance of tree species that were tolerant of fire or required fire to become established (Cowell 1995, 1998; Tuttle and Kramer 2005). The evidence of this fire-tolerant vegetation suggests that a 10- to 50-year fire-return interval time for surface fires, with occasional canopy fires, would have been likely

in the pre-settlement Piedmont in some sites (Cowell 1995).

As was the case throughout the state, there were two main sources of fire: lightning and people. The roles of each in influencing past vegetation patterns on the Georgia Piedmont are unclear (Cowell 1995). Anthropogenic influences are described on pp. 263 and 266, and they most likely played an important role: one study in the Chattooga River basin of the upper Piedmont and lower Blue Ridge found that current lightning ignitions burn up to 2 square miles a year, which the authors concluded could not have resulted in a fire regime that would explain the abundance of oaks and pines that appear on pre-settlement land surveys (Bratton and Meier 1998). Lightning-ignited fires certainly occur in the Piedmont, especially on exposed, dry sites, although their frequency has not been well documented. The timing of the ignitions is weather-dependent: very dry years promote more lightning fires than moister ones, creating an irregular fire regime that would change vegetation composition and structure on a particular site over time. Lightning-ignited fire would not play as great a role in the Piedmont as in the Coastal Plain because fire compartments—areas in which fires burn before meeting a firebreak in the form of streams, rivers, or mesic sites—are smaller in the Piedmont than they are in the Coastal Plain; thus, the fires could not spread as far. Perhaps increased size of fire compartments caused lightning-ignited fires to be more influential on the more southerly, flatter portions of the Piedmont. In rugged areas, sites most likely to experience lightning strikes include dry ridges and upper slopes, while the more mesic, rolling uplands (interfluves) between river corridors would experience lightning-ignited fires less often.

LAND USE HISTORY AND HUMAN IMPACT

Indigenous Peoples. Native Americans certainly influenced the formation of natural communities in the Georgia Piedmont. They played a large role in propagating fire, as reported by travelers and early settlers. They burned for many reasons: to drive game, to rid the landscape of troublesome insects, to promote ground cover that would attract game, and to increase ease of travel. It is likely that buffer zones between tribes were not burned (Silver 1990). It is also possible that the arrival of European traders and the development of a huge new market for animal skins radically changed Native American hunting and increased the fire-setting practices associated with hunting. Thus, there was most likely not a single burning regime that was implemented regularly or evenly over the land-scape through time. Rather, fires were set at different times, with different intensities, for different purposes in different places, creating a mosaic of prairies, woodlands, forests, and savannas that shifted over time.

Native Americans also influenced Piedmont bottomlands through slash and burn agriculture: the bottomlands were cleared for growing crops, most likely burned annually, and abandoned when soil nutrients were depleted. It appears that in most cases erosion was slight because only flat areas were cultivated (Trimble 1974). Many sites were cleared for settlement, as well, although in general these were located away from flood-prone areas (Silver 1990; R. H. Brown 2002). In many Piedmont watersheds, settlement was probably intense during the Mississippian period, as is documented for some Cumberland Plateau / Ridge and Valley sites (D. E. Davis 2000).

Agriculture and Grazing. European settlers had a far more drastic impact on this ecoregion than earlier inhabitants. Settlement of the southern Piedmont by Europeans began in earnest in the 1700s in Virginia (Trimble 1974). By 1770, the wave of immigration had reached eastern Georgia. By 1810, shortly after the Creek Nation had ceded their lands between the Oconee and Ocmulgee Rivers, the central portion of the region was settled, and by 1840, following the removal of both the Creeks and Cherokee, the wave of immigration had spanned the entire Georgia Piedmont (Trimble 1974). The settlers cleared the forests and planted crops: the favorable terrain, fertile soils, and abundant water resources of the region provided an attractive combination for the development of farms and farming communities.

SOIL EROSION IN THE PIEDMONT

The land management practices of white settlers produced drastic changes to the Georgia Piedmont. While the Native Americans most likely limited their agricultural activities to bottomlands, the settlers cleared land throughout the Piedmont and planted cotton, corn, tobacco, and other crops. A "slash and burn" approach to farming was implemented on a grand scale. Trees were cut and either used for building or burned to clear it for agriculture (Silver 1990; R. H. Brown 2002). The land was then farmed until soils were depleted of nutrients and often severely eroded, and the settlers moved on to the next site (Trimble 1985; R. E. Brown 2002). Much of the agriculture concentrated on cotton, which was a cash crop that was exported from Georgia to foreign markets. The invention of the cotton gin, the use of slave labor, and the development of railroads enabled intensive farming on a large scale. Because land was abundant and cheap, no efforts were made to conserve the soil; during winter, fall, and early spring, land lay fallow and exposed to driving rains, leading to staggering erosion rates (Trimble 1985; Magilligan and Stamp 1997; R. H. Brown 2002).

The impact on the landscape was devastating. The Piedmont was nearly denuded of forest and raked with gullies. The gullies, mostly now stabilized by vegetation, are still visible. The Piedmont landscape lost an average of 7.5 inches of topsoil, with some sites losing all topsoil and even parts of the lower soil horizons (Trimble 1985). The eroded soils were washed into streams, choking the channels (Barrows et al. 1917; Trimble 1974; Ferguson 1997; Edwards et al. 1999; R. H. Brown 2002). Over time, these sediments grew deep enough in some streams to bury milldams and raise streambeds 12 feet or more and formed broad bottomlands that covered the lower parts of hillslopes (Trimble 1974; Ferguson 1997).

This agricultural era lasted roughly 150 years on the Piedmont, until the 1920s, when cotton production plummeted due to worn-out soils, market forces that moved production west, and the arrival of the boll weevil. After 1930, many former agricultural fields were allowed to revegetate (Trimble 1974; Magilligan and Stamp 1997; R. H. Brown 2002). In addition, soil

(ABOVE) In the 1800s, much of the Piedmont landscape was cleared, and would have appeared as shown here, with agricultural fields planted on the cleared land.

(RIGHT) Erosion gullies are present throughout the Piedmont—reminders of the severe erosion of the past.

conservation practices were implemented, including contour plowing, maintenance of winter cover crops, the revegetation of steep slopes, and the regrowth of vegetated stream buffers (forested areas along the stream channel). With reduced soil erosion, sediment delivery to streams greatly declined, and streams began to cut down through their sediment-laden channels. Most Piedmont streams are now abutted by steep terraces, some of which are greatly elevated above the water table and no longer flood regularly, fostering mesic forest communities where river swamps and bottomland forests once existed.

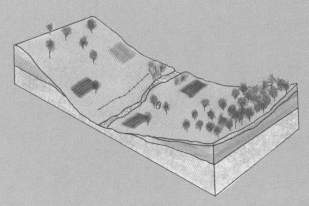

A. At the time of European settlement

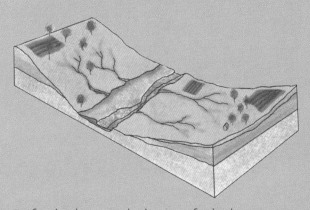

B. After the clearing and cultivation of uplands

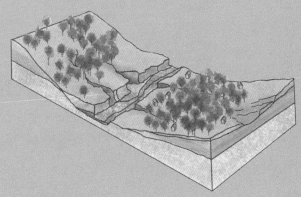

C. After the checking of erosion and the consequent down-cutting of the stream

Changes in the Piedmont landscape along medium-sized streams, 1700–1970

A. The landscape in the early days of European settlement. Bottomlands have been cleared for agriculture and homesteads. Some prairie-like areas exist in abandoned fields. Some canebrakes remain along the floodplain. The streams are not incised, and many probably have gravelly streambeds. Upper and mid-slopes are forested in many areas, with some interspersed open forests and woodlands (and perhaps prairies) where fire has occurred.

B. After comprehensive land-clearing and the creation of agricultural fields with no erosion prevention practices, severe gullying has occurred and the soils have washed into the streams, raising and widening the floodplain. The canebrakes have disappeared.

C. As agricultural fields are abandoned, the land becomes reforested (with gullies still visible) and urbanization intensifies. Former agricultural fields are in differing stages of succession, ranging from prairies to woodlands to forests. Sediments are no longer entering the stream in huge amounts, more water enters the stream because of increased impervious surfaces, and the stream cuts down and widens. The down-cutting causes steep stream banks, with wide terraces on either side of the stream banks.

Modified from Trimble 1974.

Industrial Forestry. Following the decline of agriculture in the Piedmont, many fallow fields were planted in pines, typically loblolly pine. In the 20th century, timber corporations purchased or leased many properties in the Piedmont and implemented large-scale silvicultural operations. These industrial forestry operations created a significant shift in land use and land cover over a few decades. Most conversions occurred on lands formerly cleared for agricultural use, but some sites with second- or third-growth forests resulting from natural regeneration were also converted to pine plantations. Federal programs such as the Conservation Reserve Program provided financial incentives to private landowners to revegetate fallow lands with highly erodible soils, further promoting the conversion of upland sites to pine plantations. In recent years, many of these pine plantations have been converted to other uses as industrial and residential development has increased throughout the region.

Although not as prevalent as it has been in decades past, conversion of upland forests to pine plantations remains a significant factor affecting native biodiversity in some areas. In particular, the Pine Mountain region (Harris, Upson, and Meriwether Counties) has experienced a decline in longleaf pine-hardwood forest as a result of conversion to loblolly pine plantations. Efforts are under way to protect the most significant natural stands in this area from further impacts and to restore native species diversity in other upland sites. Other areas of the Piedmont that contain significant stands of longleaf pine-hardwood forest include the Dugdown-Hightower Mountain area (Haralson and Polk Counties) and Paulding Forest and Sheffield Wildlife Management Areas (Paulding County). Protection and maintenance of all remaining stands of this globally imperiled community type through fee simple acquisition and conservation easements should be a high priority in this region.

Prescribed Fire and Fire Suppression. As noted above, Native Americans and early settlers often set fires that fostered woodlands, savannas, and prairies. Expansion of farms and cotton plantations in the 1800s led to a nearly complete conversion of the native vegetation in much of the Piedmont and a reduction in the influence of fire across much of the landscape. Some exceptions were rocky upland slopes and ridges that were deemed unsuitable for cultivation and were used as woodlots; many of these areas experienced fire, some ignited by lighting and others set by humans to improve habitat for game or to use for open woods livestock grazing. Even after the development of many towns and cities in this region in the late 1800s and early 1900s, more inaccessible and sparsely settled areas such as Pine Mountain probably continued to burn regularly and extensively due to the lack of development. By the early to mid-1900s, however, rural fire suppression campaigns as well as active programs to prevent and fight fires near towns and cities had greatly reduced the percentage of the region that experienced fire on a regular basis.

Fire exclusion continues to be a significant problem for some natural communities in the Piedmont today. Many fire-dependent habitats are now surrounded by highways, subdivisions, or retail centers. Concerns about smoke management, air quality impacts, and damage to structures make it difficult to implement prescribed burn plans for these habitats. Throughout the region, fire suppression has resulted in the decline in the extent and quality of habitats such as oak-pine-hickory forests, oak woodlands and savannas, montane longleaf pine-hardwood forests, serpentine woodlands, and canebrakes. Efforts are under way to restore these fire-dependent communities. In 2008, a team of public agencies and private research and conservation organizations developed a smoke management plan for Georgia that will allow prescribed burning for habitat restoration and maintenance while providing adequate safeguards for public health and safety. Due to its high degree of development and dense human population, the Piedmont will continue to be the most challenging region of Georgia for implementation of prescribed burn programs.

Patterns of Land Ownership and Development. One of the primary factors impacting habitats and species in the Piedmont today is the rapid pace of residential and commercial development and rate of suburban sprawl. Fragmentation degrades natural communities in many ways, including reducing the reproductive capacity of many species, increasing predation of species that typically inhabit interior portions of a forest, enabling the invasion of non-native species, inhibiting the dispersal of native species, and reducing available habitat for wide-ranging species. More than in any other ecoregion in Georgia, development pressures have resulted in the loss or fragmentation of a number of natural communities in the Piedmont, including floodplains and bot-

Prescribed burns are now used in some natural communities to maintain communities that require more frequent fire.

tomlands, oak-pine-hickory forests, granite outcrops, and mesic forests. Much of this impact is driven by the development of industrial and commercial sites along major transportation corridors throughout the region, as well as the huge expansion of the Atlanta metropolitan area.

Because of their prevalence in this region, roads and utility corridors represent important considerations for natural community management, with both harmful and beneficial consequences. Indiscriminant use of herbicides or excessive ground disturbance along existing roads and in utility corridors may impact adjacent terrestrial and aquatic habitats. In addition, newly constructed roads and utility corridors fragment remnant patches of natural communities and can serve as corridors for introductions of non-native invasive species. Utility corridors can also be converted to diverse prairie communities with rare species, however. Thus, vegetation management programs for road and utility corridors should be planned and implemented in a way that minimizes impacts on rare plant populations

and sensitive communities and helps maintain the biological diversity of this region.

Unmanaged Recreational Use. Unmanaged recreational use represents a serious problem for some natural communities. In the Piedmont, river shoals have traditionally been sites of concentrated recreational use (e.g., fishing, picnicking). Today, many of these shoal areas are being heavily damaged by ATV (all-terrain vehicle) and ORV (off-road vehicle) traffic as well as by littering. Similarly, the use of motorized vehicles, bicycles, or horses on granite outcrops as well as excessive foot traffic by outcrop visitors can result in significant impacts to outcrop plant communities and their rare plant associates. For this reason, conservation sites such as Panola Mountain State Park provide access to these sensitive outcrop habitats through guided walks and a boardwalk trail.

Non-Native Invasive Species. One of the obvious and inevitable results of widespread disturbance and

Chinese wisteria smothering native trees

habitat fragmentation is the prevalence of non-native invasive species. Some of the most problematical plants in the Georgia Piedmont are Chinese privet, kudzu, autumn-olive, bicolor lespedeza, Chinese wisteria, Nepal grass, and Japanese honeysuckle. Urban areas are particularly hard hit and are often covered with these non-natives, along with English ivy, winged euonymus, and, increasingly, sacred-bamboo, leatherleaf mahonia, and Bradford pear. In addition to directly competing with native species for resources, these non-native plants can alter the hydrology and fire regime of a natural community. Efforts are under way to restore habitats on many public lands through control of non-native invasive species. Mechanisms of control include mechanical removal of individual plants, careful application of herbicides, and, in some cases, prescribed fire programs. Recent studies have indicated that the choice of invasive species control method may influence community composition, although much work needs to be done in monitoring the return of native species after the removal of the non-natives (Biggerstaff and Beck 2007; Hanula, Horn, and Taylor 2009).

Non-native terrestrial animals in the Piedmont include species such as feral swine that are not native to this continent as well as species that have invaded from other regions of North America, including coyotes and armadillos. As described earlier, feral swine degrade natural communities through their impacts on soils, ground layer vegetation, and water quality. As omnivores, they also prey on a variety of native ani-

mals. Coyotes and armadillos are relatively recent invaders of the Piedmont ecoregion and continue to increase their numbers, becoming significant nuisances in many areas. Their long-term impacts on Piedmont natural communities are unknown, however. Preliminary research indicates that in some areas, coyotes may reduce white-tailed deer populations by culling young and weak individuals (Kilgo et al. 2010), potentially creating more favorable conditions for recovery of vegetation in stands that are currently overbrowsed. Through their burrowing and foraging activities, armadillos may degrade sensitive habitats and reduce populations of ground-nesting birds and other fauna, though these impacts have not been quantified in this ecoregion.

Water Quality and Quantity. The Piedmont is the primary region of water supply reservoirs in Georgia: half of all Georgians drink water from the Chattahoochee River. Construction of dams and other structures that change streamflow represents a significant problem for aquatic species in this region, including rare species such as the Cherokee darter, Etowah darter, and amber darter. Impacts to aquatic fauna from impoundments include direct loss of lotic habitat, barriers to dispersal, alteration of in-stream flows, and impaired water quality (altered temperature and dissolved oxygen regimes). Reductions in streamflow variability by upstream dams cause isolation and dewatering of floodplains in many areas of this ecoregion. Careful planning of future reservoirs coupled with a significant investment in water conservation will be essential for conservation of this region's aquatic biota. Restoration of more natural hydrologic conditions by removal or alteration of dams and other impediments to improve in-stream flows is being considered in some areas. A notable example is the removal of the Eagle and Phenix Dam and City Mills Dam at Columbus, Georgia, and Phenix City, Alabama, an effort that is supported by conservationists, kayakers, and local businesses alike. This restoration project has the potential to benefit several aquatic species native to riverine habitats, including shoal bass, the state Rare bluestripe shiner, the state Threatened alligator snapping turtle and Barbour's map turtle, several species of imperiled freshwater mussels, and the state Threatened shoals spiderlily (Paine et al. 2009).

In addition to the impoundments, the reduction of vegetated stream buffers and loss of permeable water-

This stream is cutting down through its banks because of increased surface runoff of water associated with urbanization. The down-cutting erodes the sides of the channel, causing more sediment to enter the stream.

shed surfaces are major problems in this ecoregion. These problems are related to intensive patterns of development and the resulting high density of roads, utility corridors, lawns, and parking areas near streams. In many areas, the amount of impermeable surface in the local watershed provides very little capacity for amelioration of non-point-source pollution, leads to flash flooding and stream bank scouring, and greatly diminishes groundwater recharge capacity. The lack of permanently vegetated stream buffers contributes to erosion of stream banks allowing large amounts of sediment to enter the streams. Outdated water supply systems, rampant development, and lack of water conservation planning exacerbate problems related to water quantity and, along with poor erosion and sedimentation controls, inadequate sewer systems, runoff from lawns and parking lots, and seepage from septic systems, impact water quality in this rapidly developing region of the state (Kundell and Myszewski 2007).

Restoration of vegetated stream buffers or stream channel morphology has been undertaken through wetland and stream mitigation projects. Continued improvements in stream hydrology, maintenance of vegetated stream buffers, and improvements in erosion and sedimentation control are essential to the protection of aquatic diversity in this ecoregion (Georgia Department of Natural Resources 2005a). In some areas, it is possible that more intensive measures will be needed to stabilize stream banks and remove excessive stream sediments that persist from previous decades of poor land management, but such efforts are difficult and should be undertaken only after extensive planning and assessment of possible negative environmental impacts.

The combined legacy of agriculture and urbanization has drastically changed streams throughout the Georgia Piedmont. The floodplains and channels that now exist are not "natural" but are responses to huge anthropogenic impacts over the last two centuries. Land managers must determine whether, when, and how to intervene to restore such streams. There is no single easy answer. Across the nation, stream restoration efforts have included destruction of dams, removal of excess sediments from floodplains, and reconfiguration of stream channels to address severe bank erosion or channelization impacts. All of these

(ABOVE) Habitat loss and fragmentation are severe in urban areas. Here, goats are eating kudzu that grew in fragmented areas of this urban site.

(RIGHT) Volunteers removing invasive species in the Morningside Nature Preserve in Atlanta

efforts are costly and challenging and have their own negative impacts. For example, if substantial amounts of sediment have been deposited behind dams and on adjacent floodplains, removal of the dam will obviously improve in-stream flows but may choke downstream areas with newly deposited sediments. In addition, the newly downcutting stream channel will be hydrologically disconnected from the adjacent floodplain. Reconfiguring the stream channel and floodplain to improve hydrologic conditions often entails removal of much of the existing vegetation. Depending on the degree of impact and the importance of the aquatic system, extreme measures may need to be employed. Reduction of excessive sediments and stabilization of stream banks are particularly difficult challenges. Excessive sedimentation obliterates spawning beds of fishes, suffocates sensitive mollusks and aquatic plants, reduces overall aquatic diversity, and contributes to flooding problems. In some cases, sand dredges and pumps have been used to reduce in-stream sediment loads. Stream bank stabilization projects often entail planting native riparian zone plants and/or using deadfalls or other materials to reduce bank erosion. These efforts may prove effective if other com-

ponents of watershed improvement are employed, including minimizing the amount of impervious surface in the watershed and maintaining ample vegetated stream buffers.

Another important management challenge is control of non-native invasive species in floodplains. River floodplains are typically used as corridors for sewer lines and other utilities. These utility corridors and their access roads can serve as routes of invasion for non-native species. Many Piedmont floodplains are infested with invasive plants such as Chinese privet, Nepal grass, Japanese honeysuckle, mimosa, and autumn-olive. Chinese privet and Nepal grass in particular can cover large expanses. Removal of these non-native plants often requires a combination of mechanical harvest and use of herbicides. These treatments are generally expensive and may result in a temporary worsening of erosion and sedimentation problems in the treated areas. Further, without a consistent, long-term commitment to invasive species control, the resulting improvements will be short-lived. For these reasons, control of invasive species should be undertaken only after careful consideration of long-term goals and the necessary resources to meet these goals.

Natural Communities of the Georgia Piedmont

UPLAND FORESTS AND WOODLANDS

Mesic Forests. Deciduous hardwood forests that occur on mesic sites, such as lower slopes, steep, north-facing slopes, ravines, well-drained small stream bottoms, and some high stream terraces. American beech is typically an indicator species; basswood, northern red oak, and tulip-tree are other common species. These forests are small-patch to large-patch.

Oak-Pine-Hickory Forests. Forests that occur on xeric to submesic sites. White oak, southern red oak, pignut hickory, mockernut hickory, shortleaf pine, and loblolly pine are especially common.

Pine-Oak Woodlands and Forests. Woodlands and forests that occur on xeric to dry sites (rarely submesic), typically on sharp ridges or on slopes with stony, thin soils. Typical species include a mix of dry-site oaks and pines, including blackjack oak, post oak, scarlet oak, rock chestnut oak, black oak, shortleaf pine, and loblolly pine. They are small-patch now, but were most likely larger-patch at times in the past, when fire was more frequent.

Montane Longleaf Pine Woodlands and Forests. Woodlands and forests that are dominated by longleaf pine and xeric (dry-site) oaks. They occur infrequently on steep, rocky slopes scattered throughout the lower, central, and western Piedmont. They are small-patch. This natural community is described in the Cumberland Plateau / Ridge and Valley ecoregion, where it also occurs.

PRAIRIES, GLADES, BARRENS, AND ROCK OUTCROPS

Prairies and Savannas. Savannas are areas where the herbaceous vegetation dominates and trees beyond the sapling stage are very infrequent and widely spaced (less than 50% closed). Prairies occur where no trees beyond the sapling stage are present. This natural community typically requires anthropogenic fire to maintain the savanna or prairie structure. Soils are deeper than those of the glade, barren, and wood-land natural community. They are small-patch now; they may have been large-patch at times in the past, when fire was more frequent.

Glades, Barrens, and Woodlands. A mosaic of herbaceous or shrub-dominated vegetation with occasional stunted trees that occur on rocky, shallow soils that are interspersed with large expanses of rock outcroppings. These are differentiated from the granite outcrop environment by occurring on substrates that tend to have more joints and so support more vegetation and fewer depressional soil islands; they are also of lesser extent. They are small-patch.

Granite Outcrops. Large expanses of smooth, bare rock, of granite or a granitic gneiss, interspersed with islands of vegetation. Some of these communities occur on dome-like outcrops that have a relief of up to a few hundred feet, while other communities develop on expanses of rock (flatrocks) that have little topographic prominence. They are small-patch.

Ultramafic Barrens and Woodlands. A mosaic of barrens and woodlands that occur on large outcroppings of ultramafic rock. The only known example in the Georgia Piedmont is the Burks Mountain Complex. They are small-patch.

Cliffs, Bluffs, and Outcrops. Fairly vertical cliffs or large outcrops that often form river bluffs that support sparse vegetation that is limited to small microsites within the cliff or bluff. They are small-patch.

WETLANDS

Flatwoods. Shallow, depressional wetlands that form over mafic and possibly slate bedrock in the Piedmont. The soils are shrink-swell, leading to wet conditions in the winter and very dry conditions in summer. Vegetation is a mix of mesic and hydric plants (often calciphiles), including willow oak, Shumard oak, swamp chestnut oak, many hickories, and white ash. They are small-patch.

Seepage Wetlands. Wetlands that may be forested or shrub and herb dominated that occur on stream banks, in a narrow zone along the base of steep slopes that abut stream terraces, and above and around stream-heads. These sites are saturated for at least part of the year. Typically, water is moving imperceptibly toward a stream. This natural community is usually indicated by a canopy of red maple, green ash, sweet gum, and/or tulip-tree and hydric to mesic-hydric species such as southern wild raisin, cinnamon fern, royal fern, orange jewelweed, cutleaf coneflower, and lizard's-tail. They are usually small-patch.

Floodplains, Bottomlands, and Riparian Zones. Forests and areas of patchy vegetation that occur in low-lying areas along creeks and rivers. They are at least occasionally flooded and are characterized by trees that can grow to maturity on soils that are saturated for limited periods of time. Indicator species include river birch, sycamore, cherrybark oak, swamp chestnut oak, and overcup oak. Green ash, red maple, sweet gum, and box elder are common. They range from large-patch to small-patch.

Mesic Forests

Mesic forests occur on evenly moist sites, such as protected, concave-shaped, north- to east-facing slopes, toe slopes near floodplains, and on some stream terraces that no longer experience flooding because the stream has cut down deeply into its former floodplain (see page 265). Mesophytic trees dominate the canopy; American beech is typically an indicator species. Basswood, northern red oak, bitternut hickory, southern shagbark hickory, southern sugar maple, and tulip-tree are other common species. In the northern Piedmont, some mesic forests are similar to mountain cove forests, with a rich, diverse flora that includes some northern species, while in the southern Piedmont, mesic forests can contain a complex mix of Coastal Plain, more northern, and Piedmont species. Rich mesic sites can be particularly beautiful in spring, when carpets of wildflowers are blooming.

Mesic forests occur throughout the Piedmont. Although steep topography exempted some mesic forests from clearcutting and severe erosion, many more stands have been degraded, with their rich top soils

A mesic forest in Mulberry Creek Park

and seed banks severely reduced. Sites supporting rich and diverse flora, with old-growth mesophytic trees and a dense herbaceous layer, are now much rarer than in the past. The most important management approach is to protect them from development or invasion by non-native species.

PHYSICAL SETTING AND ECOLOGY

The soils of these sites range from somewhat acidic to basic. The most fertile sites occur over or near mafic or, more rarely, marble bedrock, but because mesic forests occur on low or concave-shaped slopes, some nutrients are able to collect on most sites. These forests usually experience small gaps due to the death of individual trees from disease, insects, or wind. The saplings of shade-tolerant trees that were growing beneath the canopy trees then grow up into the canopy. These shade-tolerant trees are long-lived, and disturbance that causes tree mortality in a particular area is rare, so over time these forests become a mosaic of multi-aged, shade-tolerant trees.

Fires would naturally be rare and low-intensity in these habitats because of their moist conditions and because they often occur near streams that serve as firebreaks. Care should be taken to ensure that these sites are protected from impacts when prescribed fires are being undertaken in nearby dry sites. Many species of mesic forests have thin barks and are fire-intolerant; they are often killed by fire—sometimes immediately and even several years later as the injured trees succumb to disease, insects, or drought. Destroyed forests take decades or centuries to replace because of the long successional processes required to enable mesophytic trees to reach the canopy.

As with all mesic deciduous forests throughout the state, characteristic plants often have rather large, thin leaves that lose moisture easily but can capture a maximum amount of sunlight in the shaded conditions. These forests also often have many beautiful spring wildflowers, which flower before the trees leaf out so that they can capture the spring sun. The moist, rich soils in many of these forests encourage a greater diversity and density of spring wildflowers than in any other Piedmont natural community. Browsing by dense populations of white-tailed deer as well as rooting and wallowing by feral hogs can significantly reduce the diversity of ground layer vegetation; feral hogs also compact and dislodge the friable, fragile soils of this habitat.

Mesic forests require little active management except when non-native invasive species, particularly Chinese privet, Japanese honeysuckle, Chinese wisteria, English ivy, and autumn-olive, invade and transform the diverse and beautiful ground layer to a monotonous one. Soils in mesic forests are often friable and easily compacted, so recreational use, including off-road vehicles, bicycles, and hiking, should be carefully planned to avoid off-trail use and to prevent erosion. Sites located along steep slopes are particularly vulnerable to soil compaction and erosion.

VEGETATION

The plants that grow in these forests are mesophytes: they are adapted to the moist, cooler conditions and deeper soils that buffer against severe drought. Trees include American beech, northern red oak, basswood, flowering dogwood, ironwood, and tulip-tree. As sites grow more fertile, southern sugar maple, black walnut, Shumard oak, eastern redbud, sugarberry, slippery elm, white ash, red mulberry, Carolina shagbark

Sweet Betsy

hickory, bigleaf magnolia, common silverbell, umbrella magnolia, chalk maple, cucumber magnolia, and alternate-leaf dogwood are more abundant.

Shrubs may include buffalo-nut, Piedmont azalea, sweet-shrub, mapleleaf viburnum, strawberry-bush, and smooth hydrangea. More fertile sites often have more northern spicebush, leatherwood, wafer-ash, American hazelnut, common pawpaw, painted buckeye, red buckeye, and a hybrid of the two buckeyes. "Heath bluffs," with dense understories of mountain laurel, occur in some sites.

The herbaceous layer can include Christmas fern, naked tick-trefoil, may-apple, foamflower, dimpled trout lily, sweet Betsy, dissected toothwort, violets, devil's-bit, beechdrops, giant chickweed, wild geranium, and many ferns. The herbaceous layer in particularly fertile sites can be spectacular, featuring bland sweet cicely, anise-root, sharp-lobed hepatica, southern nodding trillium, bloodroot, common black-cohosh, showy orchis, and yellow lady's-slipper. Sometimes these sites harbor more northern elements, such as ginseng, dolls'-eyes, northern maidenhair fern, American lovage, common blue cohosh, horsebalms, wood-nettle, Vasey's trillium, and Appalachian bunchflower (Braun 1950; Wharton 1978; Govus 2003b; Kruse 2003). Spectacularly diverse sites still remain in the Piedmont: areas in the Oconee National Forest (Jones and Jasper Counties), Pumpkin Vine Creek (Paulding County), and ravines within the Brevard Fault region, for example, have ground covers that are reminiscent of mountain coves.

A unique mix of Coastal Plain and more northern species occurs in some mesic forests of the lower Piedmont near Pine Mountain, in areas such as Pobiddy Creek near Big Lazer Creek Wildlife Management Area (Talbot County); Dripping Rocks at Camp Thunder (Upson County), Cason Callaway Memorial Forest (Harris County), and trails in Franklin Delano Roosevelt State Park (Harris County) (Jones 1974; Radford and Martin 1975; Wharton 1978); along the Fall Line; and on bluffs along the Savannah River. Plants with Coastal Plain affinities that may be found in some of these forests include needle palm, devilwood, wax-myrtle, American wisteria, groundsel tree, dwarf palmetto, American snowbell, Spanish-moss, croomia, fringed campion, and bottlebrush buckeye. (Needle palm, croomia, fringed campion, and bottlebrush buckeye occur in the western portion of the Georgia Piedmont, but are not known from the eastern portion in Georgia, with Macon more or less

Fringed campion (TOP)

Croomia (BOTTOM) is a rare, primarily Coastal Plain plant that appears in a very few southern Piedmont mesic forests in Georgia.

serving as an east-west demarcation that would generally follow the Atlantic Coastal Plain/Gulf Coastal Plain division farther south. Dwarf palmetto occurs to the east.) Swamp bay, ti-ti, bamboo-vine, and southern wild raisin are other Coastal Plain elements in the nearly hydric portions of some of these sites.

ANIMALS

Characteristic mammals of Piedmont mesic forests include the eastern chipmunk, short-tailed shrew, pine vole, gray squirrel, white-tailed deer, white-footed mouse, golden mouse, least shrew, flying squirrel, opossum, striped skunk, and raccoon. Several bats can inhabit these forests, including the big brown, Mexican free-tailed, eastern pipistrelle, evening, little brown, and hoary. The bird life found in these forests varies with the habitat structure of individual sites. Wood thrush, red-eyed vireo, black-and-white war-

CHARACTERISTIC PLANTS OF MESIC FORESTS

TREES

Southern sugar maple—*Acer floridanum*

Musclewood—*Carpinus caroliniana*

American beech—*Fagus grandifolia*

Common silverbell—*Halesia tetraptera*

Tulip-tree—*Liriodendron tulipifera*

Bigleaf magnolia—*Magnolia macrophylla*

Umbrella magnolia—*Magnolia tripetala*

Ironwood—*Ostrya virginana*

Northern red oak—*Quercus rubra*

Basswood—*Tilia americana*

SHRUBS AND WOODY VINES

Buckeyes—*Aesculus pavia; A. sylvatica;* and their hybrids

Common pawpaw—*Asimina triloba*

Strawberry-bush—*Euonymus americana*

Smooth hydrangea—*Hydrangea arborescens*

Mountain laurel—*Kalmia latifolia*

Northern spicebush—*Lindera benzoin*

Piedmont azalea—*Rhododendron canescens*

GROUND COVER

Common black-cohosh—*Actaea racemosa*

Round-lobed hepatica—*Anemone americana*

Jack-in-the-pulpit—*Arisaema triphyllum*

Rattlesnake fern—*Botrypus virginianus*

Toothworts—*Cardamine* spp.

Devil's-bit—*Chamaelirium luteum*

Dimpled trout lily—*Erythronium umbilicatum*

Wild geranium—*Geranium maculatum*

Broad beech fern—*Phegopteris hexagonoptera*

May-apple—*Podophyllum peltatum*

Bloodroot—*Sanguinaria canadensis*

Foamflower—*Tiarella wherryi*

Sweet Betsy—*Trillium cuneatum*

---

bler, whip-poor-will, and many other species nest here (T. M. Schneider et al. 2010). During migration many species that breed much farther north, such as black-poll and Cape May warblers, use these forests as stop-over sites. Armadillos and coyotes have recently invaded these environments.

Mesic forests support a significant amphibian fauna. Terrestrial salamanders take cover under coarse woody debris or in subterranean burrows but forage in the arthropod-rich leaf litter zone of the forest floor during wet weather. The most common are members of the slimy salamander species complex and the diminutive southern red-backed salamander, the latter species being restricted to the western half of the state (Camp 1986). Many southern two-lined salamanders (and Blue Ridge two-lined salamanders along the Dahlonega Plateau) are found in these habitats, breeding in nearby streams during the late winter and early spring (L. L. Smith 2008).

Reptiles include several skink species such as the ground skink, a leaf litter inhabitant. The five-lined skink scampers about the forest floor and on the lower trunks of trees, being particularly fond of the tangled cover provided by fallen trees. The semi-arboreal green anole searches for its prey on the forest floor and among shrubs and low-hanging limbs. Anoles are capable of changing color and can shift from dark brown to bright green or vice versa in response to temperature or other environmental cues (Graeter 2008). Common garter snakes, named for the similarity of their striped patterns to 19th-century men's garters, feed on earthworms, frogs, and toads. The tiny worm and ringnecked snakes, although largely fossorial (burrowing), are often encountered in leaf litter or under cover such as flat rocks or coarse woody debris (J. D. Wilson and Dorcas 2004).

Eastern Box Turtle (*Terrapene carolina*)

A member of the family Emydidae (common water turtles), the eastern box turtle has several unique adaptations for a terrestrial existence. Unlike its more aquatic relatives, such as sliders and cooters, the eastern box turtle has a high, dome-shaped carapace and stout legs and feet that are adapted for traveling on dry ground. The plastron is hinged, allowing the turtle to withdraw its body completely within its shell. This provides protection against predators and may also help the eastern box turtle avoid desiccation during dry periods and hibernation. This turtle is highly variable in color, but usually has yellow or orange blotches on a dark background on the carapace and skin (Cash and Gibbons 2008).

Eastern box turtles can be found in a variety of upland and lowland forests as well as fields and pastures. They seem to prefer a combination of forested and open areas and may take refuge in wet areas during droughts or hot weather. Their diet consists of a wide variety of plant material as well as fungi, earthworms, arthropods, snails, slugs, salamanders, and even carrion. The turtles consume fruits such as blackberries, muscadines, may-apples, and wild strawberries and help to disperse seeds of these plants through their feces (Conant and Collins 1998).

Predators of eastern box turtles include raccoons, foxes, bobcats, skunks, dogs, cats, and feral hogs. Snakes, owls, hawks, crows, and fire ants may prey on young turtles. Another important source of mortality is the automobile, especially during the spring and summer months. The eastern box turtle has declined throughout its range in recent decades due to habitat fragmentation, increased vehicle traffic, predation, and collections for the illegal pet trade (Cash and Gibbons 2008).

gneisses and schists in the area support a less diverse flora (Wharton 1994; Govus 2003b). In Chicopee Woods, the nutrient-rich areas often occur on lower slopes, where the eroded materials from base-rich rocks on upper slopes have collected (Wharton 1994).

The Ed Dodd Trail is a short (0.75 mile) trail by the visitor center that moves through a variety of natural communities. It starts on a dry ridge in an oak-pine-hickory forest community but descends into a lush mesic forest natural community toward the bottom of the slope. Species in the mesic area include northern red oak, American beech, tulip-tree, white oak, flowering dogwood, downy serviceberry, Piedmont azalea, mapleleaf viburnum, black haw, buffalo-nut, smooth hydrangea, mountain laurel, mountain dog-hobble, indian cucumber-root, and galax. Richer sites support basswood, white ash, slippery elm, redbud, red buckeye, painted buckeye (and hybrids of the two), chalk maple, and red mulberry (Wharton 1994; Govus 2003b).

The herb layer is diverse. Species (not all of which are on the Ed Dodd Trail, but are scattered throughout the mesic sites of Chicopee) include common black-cohosh, may-apple, bloodroot, toothworts, dimpled trout lily, fly-poison, American lovage, goat's-beard, New York fern, wild geranium, round-lobed hepatica, wild comfrey, silvery glade fern, American lopseed, broad beech fern, northern maidenhair fern, rattlesnake fern, sweet Betsy, horsebalm, Jack-in-the-pulpit, creeping phlox, blue-stars, wild geranium, foamflower, and southern nodding trillium (Wharton 1994; Govus 2003b).

Chicopee Woods of the Elachee Nature Preserve

Chicopee Woods is located in the area of the Brevard Fault, and the diversity of plant species of the Brevard Fault region are well expressed here. Soil pH ranges from somewhat acidic to circumneutral. The higher pH soils, which are derived from nutrient-rich bedrock, such as metagraywacke, marble, and horneblende gneiss, foster a wide diversity of species. Other

Location: From I-985 near Gainesville, take Exit 17. Go north on Atlanta Hwy. (Ga. Hwy. 13) past Chicopee Woods Golf Course on the right. Turn at the next right at Chicopee Baptist Church and make a quick right onto Elachee Dr. Follow Elachee Dr. for 1 mile through the golf course, across the bridge over I-985, and bear left around the curve leading to the museum center parking lot. Google Earth GPS approximate coordinates to the park office: N 34.246034/ W 082.832234.

Oak-Pine-Hickory Forests

Oak-pine-hickory forests are dry to dry-mesic (sub-mesic) forests with a mix of oaks, pines, and hickories, including white oak, black oak, southern red oak, pignut hickory, mockernut hickory, shortleaf pine, and loblolly pine. These forests are important because they are the matrix forests of the ecoregion: this is the most common natural community of the Georgia Piedmont though its distribution is most likely diminished today compared to pre-settlement times due to significant land use changes. Because these forests are so widespread, they provide habitat for most of the native fauna of the Piedmont. Greater public recognition of this natural community is critical for conservation of biological diversity in the Georgia Piedmont. Because the ecoregion is increasingly urbanized, these forests, which are still growing back after centuries of agriculture, are now threatened by fragmentation and habitat

destruction. To enable the many plants and animals that rely on these forests to survive, careful planning of interconnected conservation lands is needed. Old-growth examples of this community are now very rare. They would have been more common when Native Americans dominated the landscape, particularly in areas that served as buffers between tribes (Silver 1990). Notable sites with old oaks include the William H. Reynolds Memorial Nature Reserve (Clayton County), the Big Trees Nature Preserve in Atlanta, and Fernbank Forest (Dekalb County).

PHYSICAL SETTING AND ECOLOGY

Soil moisture, fire, and soil nutrients all influence the vegetation of oak-pine-hickory forests. Soil moisture ranges from xeric to nearly mesic. Very dry sites occur on steep slopes where the terrain is rugged, such as that of Pine Mountain (Harris County), the Talladega Uplands (Haralson County), parts of the Chattahoochee National Recreation Area (Fulton County), Hard

Labor Creek State Park (Morgan County), Cornish Mountain (Newton County), the Chicopee Woods surrounding the Elachee Nature Center (Hall County), and Sweetwater Creek State Park (Douglas County) (see the Featured Place). More gently rolling land tends to have moister soils because there is less runoff and soils are deeper. Such terrain occurs in many areas, including Indian Springs State Park (Butts County), Ocmulgee Mounds National Monument (Bibb County), and Fort Yargo State Park (Bartow County). The nearly mesic sites intergrade with the mesic forest natural community.

Geology affects the composition of these forests by influencing the nutrient levels in the soils that develop from bedrock. Typically, in the Georgia Piedmont, most soils are acidic and fairly infertile. Where mafic bedrock occurs, however, the forests will be more diverse, with more elms, ashes, hickories, and chalk maple and fewer blueberries, sourwoods, and azaleas. Examples of forests in mafic areas include Curahee Mountain (Stephens County), Soapstone Mountain (Banks County), Soapstone Ridge (DeKalb County), Kennesaw Mountain (Cobb County), Panola Mountain (Henry County), Little Mulberry Park (Gwinnett County), the Oconee National Forest together with the Piedmont National Wildlife Refuge (Jasper, Jones, and Putnam Counties), and the Jarrell Plantation (Monroe County).

The land use history of a site is also important in determining vegetation composition. Many soils retain less moisture and are less fertile than their topography or substrate would typically determine due to severe

Amphibolite bedrock will increase the abundance of base-loving plants and discourage acid-loving ones.

past soil erosion resulting from intensive farming practices that removed most or all of the A horizon and exposed a low-nutrient, clayey B horizon (Trimble 1985; Skeen, Doer, and Van Lear 1993).

During pre- and early post-settlement periods, fire was more of an influence on the composition and structure of these forests. Where fire was more common these forests were more open and contained more fire-adapted oaks and pines (Cowell 1995; Tuttle and Kramer 2005). In some stands, oaks and pines are becoming less common than they were then because disturbance is small-scale: small gaps in the canopy open up after the deaths of individual trees, and consequently shade-tolerant, fire-intolerant trees, instead of oaks and pines, are growing up into the canopy. In some cases, prescribed fires can be used to encourage regeneration of oaks and pines on dry sites where fire would have once been more prevalent.

Non-native invasive plants are a serious threat to the oak-pine-hickory forests of the Georgia Piedmont. In urban areas in particular, huge areas are covered in non-natives, especially English ivy, kudzu, Chinese wisteria, common periwinkle, and Chinese privet. Other problematical species include tree-of-heaven, mimosa, princess tree, chinaberry, thorny-olive, autumn-olive, Japanese honeysuckle, multiflora rose, oriental bittersweet, and Nepal grass. These species are difficult to remove on a permanent basis, and persistent efforts will be needed to reduce their populations.

VEGETATION

Dominant trees include varying mixtures of white oak, rock chestnut oak, black oak, post oak, blackjack oak, southern red oak, pignut hickory, mockernut hickory, sand hickory, shortleaf pine, loblolly pine, and, in the northern Piedmont, Virginia pine and white pine. Other trees include winged elm, red maple, black gum, sourwood, and flowering dogwood. Prescribed fires will foster a higher proportion of fire-tolerant oaks and pines. In addition, loblolly and shortleaf pine remain an important component in many forests because these stands are still early successional forests following agricultural use; over time, hardwoods will dominate, except where severe weather events or fire significantly open the canopy. Shrubs and vines include deerberry, mountain laurel, sweet-shrub, hillside blueberry, muscadine, poison ivy, mapleleaf viburnum, greenbriers, Virginia-creeper, strawberry-bush, sparkleberry, gorge rhododendron, and Piedmont azalea. Some acidic, dry-

CHARACTERISTIC PLANTS OF OAK-PINE-HICKORY FORESTS

TREES

Hickories—Carya glabra; C. ovalis;
    C. ovata; C. pallida; C. tomentosa
Flowering dogwood—Cornus florida
Sourwood—Oxydendrum arboretum
Shortleaf pine—Pinus echinata
Loblolly pine—Pinus taeda
White oak—Quercus alba
Scarlet oak—Quercus coccinea
Southern red oak—Quercus falcata
Rock chestnut oak—Quercus montana
Black oak—Quercus velutina

SHRUBS AND WOODY VINES

Small-fruited pawpaw—Asimina
    parviflora
Strawberry-bush—Euonymus
    americanus
Mountain laurel—Kalmia latifolia
Oconee azalea—Rhododendron
    flammeum
Greenbriers—Smilax spp.
Blueberries—Vaccinium arboreum;
    V. pallidum; V. stamineum
Muscadine—Vitis rotundifolia

GROUND COVER

Pipsissewa—Chimaphila maculata
Butterfly pea—Clitoria mariana
Common wild yam—Dioscorea villosa
Elephant's-foot—Elephantopus
    tomentosus
Eastern flowering spurge—Euphorbia
    corollata
Downy rattlesnake-orchid—Goodyera
    pubescens
Little brown jugs—Hexastylis arifolia
Veiny hawkweed—Hieracium venosum
Common stargrass—Hypoxis hirsuta
Licorice goldenrod—Solidago odora

Pink lady's-slippers

mesic sites are densely covered in mountain laurel and are called "heath bluffs."

While oaks, hickories, and pines appear in nearly all forests, stand composition varies according to the soil moisture levels. Xeric and dry sites have more post oak, blackjack oak, rock chestnut oak, scarlet oak, southern red oak, and black oak. Greater species diversity, with more white oaks and denser vegetation cover, will occur as sites become dry-mesic (submesic). Tulip-tree and northern red oak become more common as moist sites grade into mesic forests.

Nutrient levels also influence plant composition. Oak-pine-hickory forests over- or downhill from mafic substrate are often dominated by white oak and typically have higher occurrences of hickories, elms, white ash, hawthorns, eastern red cedar, wafer-ash, eastern redbud, chalk maple, and viburnums than do more acidic forests (Schafale and Weakley 1990). Typically, they have far fewer ericaceous species, such as blueberries, rhododendrons, azaleas, and sourwoods.

The herb layer is usually sparse because of the closed canopy and may include bracken fern, Virginia goat's-rue, bur-marigolds, eastern flowering spurge, upland dwarf iris, eastern needlegrass, veiny hawkweed, downy rattlesnake-orchid, little brown jugs, Catesby's trillium, pipsissewa, poverty oat-grass, and bluestems, among many other species (Wharton 1978; Schafale and

Weakley 1990; Skeen, Doer, and Van Lear 1993; Govus 2003b). The early successional stands admit more sunlight and therefore have a denser herbaceous layer characterized by many of the herbs listed in the pine-oak woodland natural community.

ANIMALS

The importance of oak-pine-hickory forests to the mammals of the Piedmont is hard to overstate because, being the matrix forest, they are the stands that most mammals rely on for shelter and food. Characteristic species include white-tailed deer, gray fox, bobcat, eastern chipmunk, southern flying squirrel, gray squirrel, raccoon, opossum, and striped skunk. While black bear populations are not established in the Piedmont, dispersing young males often travel along major river corridors in this ecoregion. Several bats can occur in this habitat, including the big brown, eastern pipistrelle, evening bat, hoary, and little brown. As urban areas continue to grow in the Piedmont, thereby shrinking habitat, more and more residents of these areas are encountering these mammals in their backyards and parks. Recent mammalian invaders of these forests include feral swine, coyotes, and armadillos.

Bird life is varied, depending largely on community structure and forest patch size. Breeding summer tanagers are common in mature forests with a significant pine component. Nesting worm-eating warblers can be found in the northern Piedmont on sites with mature hardwood forest on steep slopes that have a dense understory of shrubs and small trees. Early successional forests that occur the first few years after clearcutting have their own unique suite of species. Prairie warblers, blue grosbeaks, indigo buntings, field sparrows, yellow-breasted chats, and many others nest in abundance in these habitats (T. M. Schneider et al. 2010). The specific species composition in these early successional forests depends on many factors, including size and species composition of the trees and shrubs, amount of grass and herbaceous cover, vegetation height, and other environmental conditions. Sites that are planted in widely spaced pines after cutting can harbor nesting Bachman's sparrows and northern bobwhites if enough grass is present in the ground layer (Dunning 1993; Brennan 1999; Gobris 2010; Thackston 2010).

Many amphibians and reptiles occur in these forests. Slimy salamanders, as well as southern two-lined salamanders outside of the winter–spring breeding season, occur in mature deciduous forests, taking cover under coarse woody debris or in underground burrows or root tunnels. The southern red-backed (see the Featured Animal) and Webster's salamanders inhabit the western Piedmont. They are both fiercely territorial, defending moist cover sites (Camp 1999), and the two are rarely found together. Cope's gray treefrog, which lives most of its life high above the ground, signals its presence with short, chirp-like trills emitted during warm, rainy weather. During summer rainstorms, many males descend to temporary ponds and establish breeding choruses, which sound like clusters of ringing cell phones (Greer 2008). Fowler's toads, like toads in general, are more tolerant of dry conditions and are consequently more common than other frogs. Because amphibians are not generally resistant to desiccation, they are rarely encountered in pine-dominated successional stages.

Small, fossorial snakes are important components of this community. They often forage for small invertebrates in the thick leaf litter (J. D. Wilson and Dorcas 2004). Worm and ringnecked snakes are abundant in relatively mesic forests. Brown and plain-bellied snakes may also be common. There is also a diverse fauna of larger terrestrial snakes, including black racers, eastern hognose snakes, eastern kingsnakes, rat snakes, and corn snakes. Rat and corn snakes feed chiefly on endothermic (warm-blooded) animals. The small head of the corn snake restricts its diet to small prey such as mice, while the relatively large head and body of the semi-arboreal rat snake allows it to feed on a variety of additional prey items, including rats, eastern chipmunks, and birds as large as blue jays. Black racers and eastern kingsnakes feed on a variety of vertebrates. The black racer overpowers its prey and swallows it while still alive (K. M. Andrews and Gibbons 2008a). Kingsnakes, being constrictors, can subdue larger, more powerful prey items. The copperhead, fairly common in most Piedmont forests, feeds more heavily on mice. During summer, most copperheads hunt at night and rely on heat receptors located deep inside facial pits to detect endothermic prey (Fitch 1960). Five-lined and broadhead skinks are common. The southeastern five-lined skink can also be relatively common in drier forests such as those along the spine of Pine Mountain (Harris and Meriwether Counties). The ground skink is abundant in the leaf litter. Pine-dominated, early successional communities have fewer reptiles compared to the mature forest, the most common species being eastern fence lizards, southeastern five-lined skinks, black racers, and rat snakes.

Southern Red-backed Salamander (*Plethodon serratus*)

The southern red-backed salamander is a small, slender terrestrial salamander that occurs in hardwood-dominated forests of the western half of Georgia's Piedmont and Blue Ridge and throughout the Cumberland Plateau / Ridge and Valley (Camp 1986). This range extends into portions of neighboring Alabama, Tennessee, and North Carolina. Disjunct populations of the southern red-backed salamander also occur in west-central Arkansas and Oklahoma, central and southeastern Missouri, and central Louisiana (Conant and Collins 1998). Preferred habitats range from mesic hardwood forests along slopes to dry oak-dominated stands on ridge tops. This species is common along the Pine Mountain range of Georgia's western Piedmont, where it is found in dry oak-pine-hickory forests (Camp 2008b).

Southern red-backed salamanders are strongly seasonal, having a surface-active season that lasts from November until April. Warmer months are spent in underground retreats such as old root tunnels (Camp 1988). While on the surface, individuals forage in the leaf litter zone and feed on small arthropods, including ants, termites, mites, and springtails. Coarse woody debris provides cover from predators and prevents desiccation between rainy periods. These refuges are defended as territories against intruding salamanders. During extended dry periods, southern red-backed salamanders may be found in wet leaf packs in gullies or streambeds, or in moist areas near seeps or springs (Conant and Collins 1998; Camp 2008b).

Mating takes place during the winter-active season and involves internal fertilization. The female lays an average of five eggs during late summer in a humid but otherwise dry underground cavity. The entire clutch is suspended as a globe from the roof of the cavity, and the female coils around it and attends it until hatching occurs (Camp 1988). After hatching, the larval salamanders quickly metamorphose into adults without passing through an aquatic stage (Camp 2008b).

Catesby's trillium

forests. Dry-mesic (submesic) stands cover more than 4,100 acres on acidic, low-nutrient sites, such as the slopes immediately surrounding the Elachee Nature Center building complex (Govus 2003b). White oak and rock chestnut oak dominate these stands, along with southern red oak, black oak, pignut hickory, mockernut hickory, black gum, red maple, flowering dogwood, sourwood, and American persimmon. The shrub layer is fairly sparse and includes sweetshrub, deerberry, mapleleaf viburnum, strawberrybush, and hillside blueberry. Herbs include wild ginger, rattlesnake-orchid, pipsissewa, naked tick-trefoil, Solomon's-plume, halberd-leaf violet, cranefly orchid, and veiny hawkweed.

As the trail approaches ridges or knobs, or high slopes with south or west aspects, increasingly xeric soil conditions support more species adapted to droughty conditions. In particular, along the higher portions of the West Lake Trail, the start of the Ed Dodd Trail, and some of the other high ridges in the southern portion of the preserve, scarlet oak, southern red oak, and post oak become more dominant. Sweetshrub and mapleleaf viburnum become less common, while sparkleberry and other blueberries are somewhat more abundant. Gorge rhododendron also appears in the eastern part of the preserve. Bracken fern, goat's-rue, eastern flowering spurge, and eastern needlegrass are also associated with drier soil conditions (Govus 2003b).

Chicopee Woods

The Chicopee Woods that surround the Elachee Nature Center well exemplify how topography and aspect influence the plant composition of oak-pine-hickory forests, and how those forests grade into mesic

Location: From I-985 near Gainesville, Georgia, take Exit 17. Go north on Atlanta Hwy. (Ga. Hwy. 13) past Chicopee Woods Golf Course on the right. Turn at the next right at Chicopee Baptist Church and make a quick right onto Elachee Dr. Follow Elachee Dr. for 1 mile through the golf course, across the bridge over I-985, and bear left around the curve leading to the museum center parking lot. Google Earth GPS approximate coordinates to the park office: N 34.246034/ W 082.832234.

Pine-Oak Woodlands and Forests

Pine-oak woodlands and forests are typically dominated by a mix of dry-site oaks and pines; occasionally oaks or pines alone will dominate a site. Blackjack oak, post oak, rock chestnut oak, scarlet oak, black oak, shortleaf pine, and loblolly pine are common species. This natural community usually occurs on xeric or dry sites, but occasionally fire will foster this community on a dry-mesic (submesic) site. On xeric sites, trees may be slightly stunted, with sparse herbaceous and shrub layers. These forests are similar to oak-pine-hickory forests but differ in vegetation composition and structure, usually because fire is more prevalent and soils are drier.

This natural community appears throughout the ecoregion, particularly on the quartzite ridges of the Talladega Uplands and Pine Mountain Ridges subregions. Areas with shrink-swell soils, such as the mafic areas within the Oconee National Forest in the Southern Outer Piedmont subregion and metavolcanic areas of the Carolina Slate Belt subregion also support pine-oak woodlands. Good examples of such sites occur in the Pine Mountain area (Harris and Troup Counties).

Fire exclusion has caused well-developed woodlands in the Georgia Piedmont to become rare, but some woodlands are being restored at Currahee Mountain in the Chattahoochee National Forest (Stephens County), Dawson Forest Wildlife Management Area (Forsyth County), Oconee National Forest (Jasper County), and other areas.

PHYSICAL SETTING AND ECOLOGY

Three factors primarily influence vegetation structure and composition: fire, soil nutrient levels, and soil moisture levels. Woodlands were more common in the Georgia Piedmont prior to fire exclusion and the widespread conversion of the landscape to agriculture. (See p. 262 for a discussion of fire regimes during Native American and European colonization eras.) Frequent fire promotes pine and oak dominance and fosters open woodlands with dense herbaceous covers; lack of fire promotes a closed canopy and more fire-intolerant species.

This forest near Toccoa Creek is being managed with prescribed burns to open the canopy, encouraging a dense and diverse ground layer.

A management priority in Georgia is to transform some dense forests to woodlands using prescribed fire. The difficult restoration challenge is to enable canopy pines and fire-adapted oaks to survive while suppressing fire-intolerant woody plants and stimulating the growth of grasses and other fire-tolerant ground-layer plants. Often, the stand must first be opened up through judicious thinning to minimize the possibility of catastrophic crown fires. Initial burns are usually conducted under moderate weather conditions to reduce duff and kill fire-intolerant understory species while protecting the overall integrity of the stand. Under ideal conditions, fires can be set using existing roads and natural firebreaks to avoid unnecessary soil disturbance; in other situations, new firebreaks must be established to protect sensitive areas. The long-term goal is to establish a diverse suite of woodland stands that can be maintained primarily through periodic fires that burn over relatively large areas without excessive firebreak construction and maintenance.

Soil nutrient levels also influence the vegetation composition. Base-loving species are more common over mafic bedrock. Where fire is excluded, base-loving species will occur in the canopy as well as the ground layer. Where fire is more frequent on these sites, fire-tolerant oaks and pines will dominate the canopy, but base-loving species in the ground cover will distinguish these sites from more acidic ones.

Soil moisture is also influential in determining the structure and composition of this community. Xeric conditions occur on shallow soils over bedrock or hard lower soil horizons, as well as soils that develop hardpans and/or have shrink-swell tendencies. The dry conditions promote more fires, which foster greater openness and, in turn, drier conditions. Where conditions are less xeric, more fires are required to maintain an open environment because understory species will grow more quickly in moister conditions. These moister sites, when maintained as woodlands through prescribed fire, may have a denser ground cover than drier terrain.

Soils that have developed from mafic bedrock underlie a woodland on Currahee Mountain.

Common elephant's-foot often grows in woodlands.

VEGETATION

Dry-site oaks, such as blackjack oak, post oak, rock chestnut oak, scarlet oak, black oak, and southern red oak, characterize these sites, along with shortleaf pine and loblolly pine. Post oak and shortleaf pine are often the dominant species where fire is frequent (Cowell 1995; Tuttle and Kramer 2005). Blackjack oak can co-dominate, particularly on clayey soils. Shrub species vary by nutrient conditions. Oaks are often the main dominants after fire because some species have thick bark that can withstand fire or they are able to resprout after fire. Pine may dominate following fires that occur after large blow-downs caused by tornadoes, severe thunderstorms, and hurricanes (Skeen, Doerr, and Van Lear, 1993).

Understory trees include sourwood and flowering dogwood. Shrubs and vines often include blueberries, dewberries, huckleberries, blackberries, Carolina jessamine, sumacs, muscadine, and greenbriers. The ground layer can vary widely and include many species of dry and sunny places, such as hemp dogbane, common wild quinine, various asters, goldenrods, sunflowers, and other composites; legumes, such as pencil-flower, lespedezas, Virginia goat's-rue, and spurred butterfly pea; and graminoids, such as eastern needlegrass, bluestems, and oat-grasses, along with much else (Wharton 1978; Schafale and Weakley 1990; Cowell 1992; Skeen, Doer, and Van Lear 1993; Govus 2003b).

Mafic woodland communities are a subtype of pine-oak woodlands that are rare in Georgia but can develop over mafic rock-derived soils on high knolls where the xeric conditions and high base levels combine to create unusual conditions. One example is the open stunted forest that occurs in the Oconee National Forest over a very hard C horizon of clay or saprolite (partially weathered rock) about 1 foot below the surface. Such woodlands have the potential to occur in the Carolina Slate Belt subregion, as well. Where fire has not occurred in recent times, thin-barked woody species co-dominate with fire-tolerant species; a more pronounced shrub layer also develops. These woodlands are dominated by somewhat stunted post oaks and black oaks, with Carolina shagbark hickory, pignut hickory, white ash, white oak, eastern red cedar, redbud, and shortleaf pine. Carolina shagbark hickory, white ash, white oak, eastern red cedar, and redbud would be much less common if fire were more frequent.

Where prescribed fire is applied over mafic sites, some rare and beautiful stands result. On some slopes of Currahee Mountain (Stephens County) and other mafic sites near Toccoa in Stephens County, canopy trees include shortleaf pine, blackjack oak, post oak, sand hickory, white oak, pignut hickory, and Virginia pine. Increased fire frequency should result in the reduction of hickories over time. Many high-base indicator species occur in the dense, diverse herb layer, including Carolina thistle, white prairie-goldenrod, curlyheads, nettleleaf noseburn, and nettle-leaf sage; other common herbs include common wild quinine and few-flowered nutrush among much else. The federally Endangered smooth purple coneflower is a stunning element in some sites.

PIEDMONT SANDHILLS

The Molena sands along the Flint River in Pike and Clayton Counties apparently were blown by Pleistocene winds over the bedrock to create unique Piedmont sandhill conditions (J. Costello, Ga. DNR, pers. comm.). These areas support unusual plant assemblages. Sand laurel oak, which is a Coastal Plain species that is found on well-drained sands but near a shallow water table, is a common dominant. Other canopy trees include post oak, loblolly pine, black oak, southern red oak, and sassafras. Where the sites grade down closer to the water table, willow oak can dominate, and sweet bay appears with river cane and silky dogwood. Where the forest is more closed, herbs are sparse. Sites that are kept open support loblolly pine, numerous grasses, eastern prickly-pear, sparkleberry, and other dry-site species. These stands require a more thorough inventory.

(RIGHT) Piedmont sandhills

CHARACTERISTIC PLANTS OF PINE-OAK WOODLANDS AND FORESTS

TREES

Sand hickory—Carya pallida
Sourwood—Oxydendrum arboreum
Shortleaf pine—Pinus echinata
Loblolly pine—Pinus taeda
Scarlet oak—Quercus coccinea
Southern red oak—Quercus falcata
Blackjack oak—Quercus marilandica
Rock chestnut oak—Quercus montana
Post oak—Quercus stellata
Black oak—Quercus velutina

SHRUBS AND WOODY VINES

Sumacs—Rhus spp.
Sparkleberry—Vaccinium arboreum

Hillside blueberry—Vaccinium pallidum
Deerberry—Vaccinium stamineum

GROUND COVER

Old-field broomsedge—Andropogon
    virginicus
Maryland golden-aster—Chrysopsis
    graminifolia
Oat-grasses—Danthonia spp.
Sunflowers—Helianthus spp.
Veiny hawkweed—Hieracium venosum
Lespedezas—Lespedeza spp.
Common wild quinine—Parthenium
    integrifolium

Eastern needlegrass—Piptochaetium
    avenaceum
Silkgrass—Pityopsis graminifolia
Little bluestem—Schizachyrium
    scoparium
Licorice goldenrod—Solidago odora
Yellow indiangrass—Sorghastrum
    nutans
Pencil-flower—Stylosanthes biflora
Asters—Symphyotrichum spp.
Virginia goat's-rue—Tephrosia
    virginiana
Bird's-foot violet—Viola pedata

ANIMALS

Typical mammals of these forests and woodlands include white-tailed deer, red foxes, gray foxes, bobcats, pine voles, short-tailed shrews, eastern chipmunks, gray squirrels, raccoons, opossums, striped skunks, and oldfield mice. Many birds occur in Piedmont woodlands, including eastern wood-pewee, red-headed woodpecker, northern flicker, eastern bluebird, and many other species. Suitability of a site for a particular bird species depends on habitat structure, including size and density of trees, number of standing dead trees (snags), species composition and density, and height of the herbaceous ground cover. If patches of shrubs are present, species such as the indigo bunting and white-eyed vireo may use the site (T. M. Schneider et al. 2010). Breeding summer tanagers are common in mature forest with a significant pine component. Sites that are planted in widely spaced pines after cutting can harbor nesting Bachman's sparrows and northern bobwhites if enough grass is present in the ground layer (Dunning 1993; Brennan 1999; T. M. Schneider et al. 2010). Red-cockaded woodpeckers are found in a few shortleaf pine stands such as the Piedmont National Wildlife Refuge (see the Featured Place).

Amphibians are rare in this relatively dry environment. Pine-dominated, successional communities are poor in reptile species relative to the mature forest, the most common reptiles being eastern fence lizards, southeastern five-lined skinks, black racers, and rat snakes. Black racers are generalists, preying on a variety of vertebrates (K. M. Andrews and Gibbons 2008a). Scarlet, southeastern crowned, and smooth earth snakes tend to favor drier forests, as on the ridges and bluffs of the Pine Mountain region in Harris County and surrounding areas.

Gray Fox (*Urocyon cinereoargenteus*)

The gray fox is found throughout the eastern United States, westward to northwestern Oregon, central Nevada, and northern Colorado, and southward to Central America. Found in every region of Georgia, this fox uses a wide variety of habitats, but is more common in forests and woodlands. It is slightly smaller than the red fox, which is typically found in more open habitats such as fields and forest edges. The gray fox is unique among canids in its ability to climb trees (Georgia Wildlife Web 2008).

This fox is grayish on top and reddish-brown below, with whitish fur on the throat, chest, and around the eyes. A black stripe extends from the base of the tail and ends in a black tip. Another black stripe crosses the face from nose to eyes and then to the sides of the head. The gray fox has a distinctive bark and will also squeal or growl. Gray foxes are primarily nocturnal but may also be observed shortly after dawn and before dusk (Georgia Department of Natural Resources 2004).

Gray foxes are monogamous, and both sexes care for the young. Dens are usually made in rocky outcrops, at the base of cliffs, or under large boulders, typically surrounded by dense vegetation. Breeding takes place from January to April, and the young are born about 53 days later. Pups stay with the parents until about three months of age, when they become independent (Georgia Department of Natural Resources 2004).

The diet of the gray fox includes rabbits, rats, mice, squirrels, birds, and insects, as well as a wide variety of fruits, nuts, and berries. Known predators include large raptors, coyotes, and bobcats. Abundant in Georgia, the gray fox is hunted as a game animal and trapped for its fur (Georgia Department of Natural Resources 2004).

Red-Cockaded Woodpecker Trail in the National Piedmont Wildlife Refuge

The Red-Cockaded Woodpecker Trail contains some of the most extensive woodlands in the Georgia Piedmont. After decades of use for agriculture and loblolly pine plantations, this site is now being managed toward more natural conditions and also emphasizes restoration of red-cockaded woodpecker populations and habitat. The birds can sometimes be seen flitting through the trees along part of the trail, especially in the early morning during the breeding season.

The trail winds through dry, open forests and woodlands, as well as closed forests in moister soils. Some of the driest, most open sites occur along the gravel road that traverses the uppermost portion of the slope. Loblolly pines with fire-scarred trunks dominate. Shortleaf pine is common in some areas and grows among the loblolly pine. Fire-intolerant trees, such as tulip-tree, white oak, southern red oak, black gum, mockernut hickory, and red hickory, reach the canopy in a few areas, indicating a less intensive fire regime.

In the open forests and woodlands, the ground and shrub layers are dense with 3- to 4-foot-high resprouting trees and shrubs, including tulip-tree, sweet gum, black cherry, post oak, pignut hickory, dogwood, winged elm, black gum, American beautyberry, sparkleberry, deerberry, and winged sumac. A few areas have expanses of herbaceous species, including bluestems, oat-grasses, needlegrass, yellow indiangrass, butterfly pea, common elephant's-foot, licorice goldenrod and other goldenrods, thoroughworts, heal-all, hemp dogbane, and lespedezas. As the trail winds through mesic and unburned areas, it provides an excellent illustration of how fire and soil moisture influence vegetation composition and structure, with dry-site oaks, pines, and an open structure dominating in drier areas where fire has occurred, and closed forest with more mesic species in moister sites that have not experienced fire.

Location: From I-75 at Forsyth, 30 miles north of Macon, take exit 186 (Juliette Rd./Tifton College Dr.) east toward Juliette. From the Ocmulgee River in Juliette, proceed easterly on Round Oak–Juliette Rd. for approximately 8 miles. Turn left on the access road for Allison's Lake and the Piedmont National Wildlife Refuge visitor center. The trailhead kiosk is on the right at 1.3 miles from Round Oak–Juliette Rd. at Google Earth GPS approximate coordinates of: N 33.114788/W 083.685084.

Prairies and Savannas

Prairies are dominated by herbaceous species, with no trees beyond the sapling stage present. Soils are deeper than those of barrens. Savannas are dominated by herbaceous vegetation with widely spaced trees that comprise no more than 50% cover. Well-developed prairies occur in the Georgia Piedmont and are maintained by burning and mowing, as in Pickett's Mill State Historic Site (Paulding County) (see the Featured Place), Panola Mountain State Park (Henry County), Sweetwater Creek State Park (Douglas County), the Georgia Botanical Garden (Clark County), a powerline near Currahee Mountain (Stephens County), and several other powerline sites.

Prairies and savannas were probably more common over the Georgia Piedmont during pre-settlement and early settlement times, when anthropogenic (human-caused) burning was more widespread (Cowell 1995; Juras 1997). These environments can be strikingly beautiful during late spring and summer. Flowering forbs, with grassland species such as sunflowers, asters, black-eyed Susans, thoroughworts, goldenrods, and blazing-stars, which are reminiscent of the woodlands and prairies of the Midwest, bloom in profusion. Some sites, particularly over nutrient-rich substrates, also support rare species such as smooth coneflower, curlyheads, and Georgia aster, and provide a diversity of habitats and food sources for many insects, birds, and mammals.

Former agricultural fields are often called "old fields" by ecologists. Abandoned old fields undergo predictable successional stages from fields to forests over time, with dominant vegetation gradually changing from herbs to shrubs and trees. Some are being restored as a prairie and savanna natural community.

PHYSICAL SETTING AND ECOLOGY

The factors that influence the formation and species composition of woodlands and savannas in the Georgia Piedmont are fire, soil nutrients, and soil texture. On the Georgia Piedmont, vegetation structure varies with fire frequency and with the trees that are present or seed into the site. Where fires are frequent, and few to no trees were established prior to the frequent fire regime, a prairie or savanna will be maintained (unless longleaf pine is present on the site). Once an area is dominated by woodland, savanna, or prairie vegetation, grasses will facilitate the spread of fire that in turn encourages greater grass abundance.

In prior decades, when lightning- and human-set fires were more common in the Georgia Piedmont,

a dynamic and complex mosaic of natural communities would have occurred. Some research suggests that prairies occurred on dry uplands in flat to rolling topography that were located farthest from firebreaks (Cowell 1995). Others suggest that prairies may have been more limited to fallow agricultural fields along river bottomlands, which would have had a brief existence and a prairie-like character before being returned to agriculture. These fields would have had few rare species and would not be considered "true prairies" by all researchers (Schafale 2011).

The restoration of Piedmont prairies and savannas is an arduous and long-term endeavor. Naturally dry sites, such as those over shrink-swell soils, are probably easiest to maintain as prairie, and, because these soils have much calcium, often host more rare plants; some researchers consider these the "true prairies" of the Piedmont (Schafale 2011). In some instances, powerlines that have been continually mowed over time support an abundance of native species. Former agricultural fields ("old fields") are more difficult to transform into native prairie habitat because of the many non-native species that these fields typically possess. Methods used to combat these non-native invasive species include selective use of herbicides as well as mechanical removal and application of prescribed fire. Often within a few years, the non-natives are far less prevalent and restoration of native species can be started, often through the introduction of seeds harvested from appropriate species close to the restoration area, especially little bluestem, old-field broomsedge, and yellow indiangrass. The grass seeds are broadcast over the site, and other natives will seed in over time, transported by winds and birds. Prescribed fires are set every year or two to maintain the prairie structure and to prevent trees and shrubs from taking over the site. Because this is labor- and time-intensive, and staff is typically limited in these efforts, it is often wise to work on small plots at first and extend the scope of the restoration effort over time.

VEGETATION

Warm season grasses typically dominate the ground cover, especially yellow indiangrass, bluestems, and eastern needlegrass. Grasses have vertical, long, narrow blades that minimize moisture loss, making them well adapted to exposed environments. Legumes, such as Virginia goat's-rue, lespedezas, butterfly peas, and pencil-flower, are also common, along with many

CHARACTERISTIC PLANTS OF PRAIRIES AND SAVANNAS

Bluestems—Andropogon spp.

Spurred butterfly pea—Centrosema
   virginianum

Maryland golden-aster—Chrysopsis
   mariana

Butterfly pea—Clitoria mariana

Woodland coreopsis—Coreopsis major

Oat-grasses—Danthonia spp.

Lovegrasses—Eragrostis spp.

Thoroughworts—Eupatorium spp.

Eastern beard grass—Gymnopogon
   ambiguus

Sunflowers—Helianthus spp.

Veiny hawkweed—Hieracium venosum

Lespedezas—Lespedeza spp.

Blazing-stars—Liatris spp.

Eastern sensitive-briar—Mimosa
   microphylla

Common wild quinine—Parthenium
   integrifolium

Maypop—Passiflora incarnata

Eastern needlegrass—Piptochaetium
   avenaceum

Silkgrass—Pityopsis graminifolia

Fragrant rabbit tobacco—
   Pseudognaphalium obtusifolium

Bracken fern—Pteridium aquilinum

Mountain-mints—Pycnanthemum spp.

Black-eyed Susan—Rudbeckia hirta

Little bluestem—Schizachyrium
   scoparium

Rosinweed—Silphium compositum

Goldenrods—Solidago spp.

Yellow indiangrass—Sorghastrum
   nutans

Pencil-flower—Stylosanthes biflora

Virginia goat's-rue—Tephrosia
   virginiana

Bird's-foot violet—Viola pedata

Georgia aster is a rare plant that flourishes in some Piedmont prairies.

composites, such as sunflowers, black-eyed Susans, asters, elephant's-foot, goldenrods, thoroughworts, rosinweed, and Carolina thistle. Other common herbs include bergamot, eastern flowering spurge, greasy grass, common wild quinine, and few-flowered nutrush among much else.

Mafic hardpan savannas and prairies support calciphitic species such as Carolina thistle, white prairie-goldenrod, curlyheads, nettleleaf noseburn, and nettleleaf sage. The federally Endangered smooth purple coneflower is a stunning element of this rare community subtype.

ANIMALS

In pre-settlement and early settlement times, the Piedmont was a complex landscape of savannas, prairies, woodlands, and forests and would have been characterized by numerous ecotones supporting high animal diversity. Today, this natural community is favorable habitat for white-tailed deer, which prefer early successional and edge habitats because they are high in forage. Small mammals can graze on herbs, consume seeds and small insects, and are important seed dispersers in woodlands (DeSelm and Murdock 1993). Small mammals such as eastern harvest mouse (see the Featured Animal), deer mouse, meadow vole, southeastern shrew, least shrew, and eastern mole are grassland denizens (DeSelm and Murdock 1993).

Due to the dry nature of these areas, amphibians are not important faunal elements. Reptiles associated with dry, relatively open environments include the six-lined racerunner, eastern fence lizard, and southeastern five-lined skink. The slender glass lizard, a legless species that feeds on insects and small vertebrates, is also a likely member of the reptile fauna. Terrestrial snakes probably include black racers and coachwhips, both of which are common in relatively open or ecotonal situations. These two species are active, diurnal hunters, feeding on lizards, snakes, and other small vertebrates (K. M. Andrews and Gibbons 2008; Tuberville and Gibbons 2008).

FEATURED ANIMAL

Eastern Harvest Mouse
(*Reithrodontomys humulis*)

A member of the family Muridae, the eastern harvest mouse is about 4 to 5.5 inches long, is rich brown to brownish gray in color with a grayish white belly, and has large ears and dark eyes. The tail is grayish above and white below. Like other members of its genus, the eastern harvest mouse has a vertical groove running down the front of each upper incisor; this characteristic is the basis for the name *Reithrodontomys*, or "grooved-tooth mouse" (Stallings 1997).

This species is distributed widely across the southeastern United States from Virginia west to southern Arkansas, south to eastern Texas, and east throughout northern Florida. The eastern harvest mouse can be found statewide in Georgia in suitable habitats. Preferred habitats include woodlands, prairies, savannas, wet meadows, fallow fields, brushy thickets, and pastures (Georgia Wildlife Web 2008).

The eastern harvest mouse is mostly nocturnal but may be active during the day in periods of cold weather. Its diet consists mainly of seeds but may also include insects, fruits, and grasses. An agile climber, this mouse often forages above ground in dense vegetation. Its small size and weight allow it to climb individual stems of grass to harvest seeds. Unlike other small rodents, the eastern harvest mouse does not construct its own pathways through dense vegetation. Instead, it uses the burrows and runways of other species such as the hispid cotton rat (Georgia Wildlife Web 2008).

Eastern harvest mice may breed year-round, but breeding usually peaks in spring and fall. Adults construct a small, spherical nest out of grasses or other plant materials at or just above ground level in dense vegetation. The young (usually two to four) are born after a gestation period of three weeks. They are weaned within a month and reach sexual maturity at three to four months (Stallings 1997). Likely predators of eastern harvest mice include owls, hawks, snakes, foxes, and weasels.

Pickett's Mill Battlefield Historic Site

Pickett's Mill Battlefield Historic Site contains some excellent examples of restored prairie habitat. The fields were once old corn fields and for a long period were maintained by the park through mowing to retain the vegetation structure that would have existed during the Civil War. Now prescribed fire is also a part of the management regime. It is possible to explore different prairies from field to field by walking along established trails in the park and noting the diversity of each prairie. These sites support many native herbaceous species and are particularly beautiful in the fall, between September and mid-November, when the composites are in flower. The diversity of grasses and flowering forbs is impressive. Herbs include little bluestem, old-field broomsedge, Maryland golden-aster, long-stalked aster, common clasping aster, eastern sensitive-briar, hyssopleaf eupatorium, Georgia aster, blazing-stars, goldenrods, hairy sunflower, mountain-mints, greasy grass, fragrant rabbit tobacco, eastern flowering spurge, downy lobelia, eastern silvery aster, eastern beard grass, black-eyed Susan, beaked panic grass, bent-awn plume grass, and purple lovegrass.

Location: Take I-20 exit 44. Turn onto Thornton Rd./U.S. 278 West. Follow U.S. 278 West for 10 miles. Make a right onto Ga. Hwy 92. Travel north on Hwy. 92 for approximately 6 miles. Look for brown Pickett's Mill signs. Turn left onto Due West Rd. Continue 2 miles. Turn right onto Mt. Tabor Church Rd. The site is 0.5 mile on the right. Google Earth GPS approximate coordinates for the parking lot at the Visitor Center: N 33.625133/W 084.175017.

Glades, Barrens, and Woodlands

Piedmont glades, barrens, and woodlands occur on rocky, shallow soils that are interspersed with large expanses of rock outcroppings. The vegetation is usually a mosaic of herbaceous areas, shrubs, and widely spaced, stunted trees, although any of these vegetation components may predominate in a particular site. Because Piedmont natural communities are typically forested, these open areas are unusual and add diversity to the landscape. The natural community supports several rare species and plant assemblages over mafic rocks such as amphibolite. Interesting disjunct species may be present, partly because the openness and dryness of the environment create conditions similar to those of the western prairies and the Coastal Plain. Views from the outcrops are often striking panoramas of rolling hills.

This natural community is very similar to the granite outcrop natural community but does not contain the expanses of bare rock found in that natural community. In contrast to the huge acreages encompassed by Stone Mountain (Dekalb County), Heggie's Rock (Columbia County), Arabia Mountain (Dekalb County), and other notable granite outcrops, glades and barrens are generally less than an acre in extent. This natural community has some similarities to ultramafic barrens and woodlands, as well. The unusual soils, unique vegetation composition, and extreme rarity of the ultramafic sites, however, warrant their treatment as a separate natural community (Schafale and Weakley 1990).

PHYSICAL SETTING AND ECOLOGY

A mosaic of rock outcroppings, scattered trees and shrubs, and patches of herbaceous vegetation is typically present: the shrubs and trees inhabit deeper soil pockets among the rocks and around the edges of the glades and barrens. Conditions vary from harsh in the sunniest, rockiest areas, where sites approach the nearly desert-like conditions of exposed cliffs and rock outcrops, to dry-mesic (submesic) conditions within some tree-shaded sites.

This natural community typically occurs on mid- to upper slopes of ridges over a range of rock types, from base-rich mafic rocks to acidic substrates. The open structure is primarily due to the edaphic (soil) conditions: the thin, drought-prone soils and expanses of rock outcrop prevent establishment of dense tree and shrub cover. Fire also may play a role in keeping some sites open and is likely critical to maintaining glade conditions where soils are deeper. The natural fire frequency of these sites is not known and may well differ from site to site: glades and barrens in exposed sites are most likely subjected to fairly frequent lightning strikes, but the patchy vegetation cover may limit the intensity and extent of fires. Windstorms may also play a role in maintaining open conditions.

VEGETATION

Most of the species present in the glade, barren, and woodland natural community are adapted to xeric and dry conditions. Grasses, for example, may go dormant during dry periods or roll their leaves to prevent moisture loss; leaves on many plants may be thick or waxy or possess hairs that slow moisture loss by trapping air near the leaf's surface. Rocks may be coated in crustose lichens, and reindeer mosses and rock moss are often present.

A notable difference in species composition occurs between acidic and mafic conditions as described below, with mafic rocks supporting base-loving species as well as many of those typical of acidic outcrops.

Acidic Glades, Barrens, and Woodlands. These occur on acidic substrates, such as quartzite and many schists and gneisses. Examples are not common in the Georgia Piedmont. Several examples occur on quartzite in the southern part of the Piedmont in the Sprewell Bluff Natural Area near Sprewell Bluff State Park (Upson and Talbot Counties), and others most likely occur on other acidic outcroppings, such as a site on Currahee Mountain (Stephens County). Tree species include post oak, blackjack oak, rock chestnut oak, mockernut hickory, winged elm, pignut hickory, sand hickory, Virginia pine, and shortleaf pine (Cruse 1997). Shrubs include fringe-tree, one-flower hawthorn and other hawthorns, St. John's-worts, smooth sumac, winged sumac, curlyleaf yucca, gorge rhododendron, and blueberries, such as sparkleberry and hillside blueberry. Woody vines include greenbriers, yellow honeysuckle, trumpet-creeper, and Virginia-creeper. Com-

Carolina phlox

mon forbs include goldenrods, trailing phlox, sunflowers, yellow passionflower, silkgrass, early saxifrage, Appalachian ragwort, Appalachian rock-pink, woodland coreopsis, fire pink, common wild quinine, eastern prickly-pear, eastern flowering spurge, hyssopleaf eupatorium, sessile-leaf eupatorium, hairy angelica, butterfly pea, pineweed, rattlesnake-master, and wide-leaved spiderwort. Grasses are common and include little bluestem, big bluestem, silky oat-grass, eastern needlegrass, few-flowered nutrush, yellow indian-grass, melic grass, and witchgrasses. Ferns can include bracken fern, ebony spleenwort, woolly lipfern, and hairy lipfern.

Mafic Glades, Barrens, and Woodlands. These occur on base-rich bedrock, such as amphibolites and hornblende gneiss. On some sites, the rock erodes to a distinctive "pea gravel" that covers flat rock outcrops (Schafale and Weakley 1990). In addition to the species listed in the acidic glades variant, plants that in-

A mafic barrens and woodlands on Soapstone Mountain

dicate high-base conditions or circumneutral soils are present. As is true of other base-rich environments, canopy trees will usually include a greater abundance of hickories and elms, including pignut hickory, mockernut hickory, sand hickory, winged elm, slippery elm, and American elm, than acidic environments (Schafale and Weakley 1990). Shrubs and small trees that are often indicators of circumneutral soils include chalk maple, wafer-ash, dwarf hackberry, eastern red cedar, southern black haw, aromatic sumac, coralberry, and eastern redbud. Collectively, these sites can support a number of rare species, including short-spurred corydalis, curlyheads, eastern prairie anemone, thimbleweed, smooth purple coneflower, Georgia rockcress, Missouri rockcress, and Georgia aster.

Examples of mafic glades, barrens, and woodlands occur in several areas. Cedar Mountain (Douglas County on private property undergoing development) has an abundance of the distinctive pea gravel substrate and a unique array of granite outcrop species mixed with typical mafic glade species. Soap-

stone Mountain (Banks County) possesses a striking and diverse example that represents a globally threatened plant assemblage. Kennesaw Mountain (Cobb County) (see the Featured Place) and Goat Rock Dam, which is located on a bluff overlooking the Chattahoochee River in the southwest Piedmont (Harris County), are also important examples that support rare species.

ANIMALS

Common mammals that likely inhabit this natural community include gray fox, red fox, eastern chipmunk, white-footed mouse, old-field mouse, hoary bat, cotton mouse, big brown bat, red bat, silver-haired bat, evening bat, hispid cotton rat, eastern cottontail, opossum, southeastern shrew, least shrew, short-tailed shrew, eastern mole, and gray squirrel.

Glades are generally small enough in extent that they cannot support distinct bird communities. When surrounded by open pines with a grassy ground layer or other grassland habitat, however, many grassland

CHARACTERISTIC PLANTS OF GLADES, BARRENS, AND WOODLANDS

TREES

Dwarf hackberry—*Celtis tenuifolia*
Eastern red cedar—*Juniperus virginiana*
Shortleaf pine—*Pinus echinata*
Blackjack oak—*Quercus marilandica*
Rock chestnut oak—*Quercus montana*
Post oak—*Quercus stellata*

SHRUBS

Fringe-tree—*Chionanthus virginicus*
Wafer-ash—*Ptelea trifoliata*
Sumacs—*Rhus spp.*
Sparkleberry—*Vaccinium arboreum*
Hillside blueberry—*Vaccinium pallidum*
Curlyleaf yucca—*Yucca filamentosa*

GROUND COVER

Bluestems—*Andropogon spp.*
Rockcresses—*Boechera spp.*
Common hairsedge—*Bulbostylis capillaris*
Lipferns—*Cheilanthes spp.*
Reindeer mosses—*Cladonia spp., Cladina spp.*
Oat-grasses—*Danthonia spp.*
Eastern flowering spurge—*Euphorbia corollata*
Grimmia mosses—*Grimmia spp.*
Pineweed—*Hypericum gentianoides*
Rattlesnake-master—*Manfreda virginica*

Eastern prickly-pear—*Opuntia compressa*
Appalachian ragwort—*Packera anonyma*
Appalachian rock-pink—*Phemeranthus teretifolius*
Eastern needlegrass—*Piptochaetium avenaceum*
Silkgrass—*Pityopsis graminifolia*
Nettle-leaf sage—*Salvia urticifolia*
Little bluestem—*Schizachrium-scoparium*
Fire pink—*Silene virginiana*
Goldenrods—*Solidago spp.*
Spiderworts—*Tradescantia spp.*
Nettleleaf noseburn—*Tragia urticifolia*

birds can be present. In these situations several species of declining grassland birds, including Bachman's sparrow and northern bobwhite, can be found (T. M. Schneider et al. 2010). Patches of bare ground and rock may attract mourning doves and, near the Fall Line, common ground-doves (Mirarchi and Baskett 1994; Bowman 2002; M. F. Hodges 2010). Open conditions may also attract northern flickers, which prefer open habitats where they primarily forage on the ground for ants. This species nests in large, isolated snags in somewhat open habitat (W. S. Moore 1995).

Unless the underground rock creates a wet seepage by impeding normal water percolation, amphibians are largely nonexistent in this natural community. The exception is the occasional Fowler's toad, which may wander into this zone from neighboring hardwood forests, particularly during wet weather. The reptile fauna is strongly dominated by lizards. Eastern fence lizards and skinks such as the southeastern five-lined skink are particularly abundant, feeding on insects and escaping predators by taking cover under rubble or by rapidly climbing trees. Large, relatively mobile snakes such as black racers and rat snakes may be occasionally encountered in this community.

Fire pink

Bachman's Sparrow *(Aimophila aestivalis)*

Bachman's sparrow is a rather nondescript resident of mature pine woods and open habitats of the Southeast. In appearance it is similar to other field sparrows—about 6 inches in length, with a long, rounded tail, alternating reddish-brown and gray stripes running down its back, and a broad, reddish-brown stripe above the eye. The cheek, upper breast, and throat are gray or buff-colored, while the lower breast and abdomen are generally whitish. The wing and tail feathers are reddish-brown, and the beak is dark gray to gray-brown. Males and females have essentially the same coloration (Dunning 1993).

Its cryptic coloration provides protection for this bird, which lives among the thick grasses and forbs of open forests and woodlands. In the Coastal Plain, Bachman's sparrow is often found in association with the red-cockaded woodpecker in longleaf pine–wiregrass communities. In the Piedmont, it is found in open pine stands, old-field habitats (abandoned pastures or croplands), edges of cultivated fields, and regenerating forests. Its foods include a variety of beetles, grasshoppers, bugs, millipedes, snails, spiders, crickets, seeds of grasses, sedges, and some forbs. The song of Bachman's sparrow is very distinctive, consisting of a complex series of trills and whistles; it has been described as "sweet" and "ethereal" (Terres 1980, p. 338).

Formerly found throughout the Southeast in suitable habitat, Bachman's sparrow has become increasingly rare as open pine stands have been converted to dense pine plantations with little or no ground cover and as grassy fields have been converted to intensively grazed pastures, row crops, or lawns. The national Breeding Bird Survey has documented a steady decline in numbers of this bird over the past 30 years. Bachman's sparrow was added to the state protected species list in Georgia as Rare in 1992. Maintenance of open, periodically burned pine stands and other grassy habitats is essential for conservation of this bird (T. Schneider and Keyes 2010).

Kennesaw Mountain

An unusual combination of plants occurs on Kennesaw Mountain because of its geologic diversity and the proximity of the Cumberland Plateau / Ridge and Valley and Blue Ridge ecoregions: endemic, disjunct, and prairie species are scattered across the mountain. Several glade, outcrop, and woodland areas occur along the trail that leads to the top of the mountain from the visitor center. Along with rock chestnut oak, the glades and woodlands possess many base-loving trees and shrubs, including eastern red cedar, wafer-ash, and sugarberry. Prickly-ash, a mafic site indicator plant that is more common in Ontario, occurs along the trail. Apparently, the plants are only producing male flowers, so sexual reproduction of this species cannot occur here (L. S. Ranger 2007).

Stone Mountain mint is also present. It is unusual in Georgia, and is endemic to the Southeast, with a limited distribution in Tennessee, Alabama, and North Carolina. Missouri rockcress, a mafic indicator plant that is common in the Ouachitas and disjunct in Georgia, is also present. Elsewhere on Kennesaw and Little Kennesaw Mountains, outcrops support eastern prickly-pear, smooth spiderwort, hairy lipfern, yellow honeysuckle, and short-spurred corydalis, which is a mafic rock indicator plant (L. S. Ranger 2007).

A rare mafic shrub glade community—the only one known—occurs on the southwestern side of the peak of Kennesaw Mountain. Shrubs include hairy mock-orange (which is a mafic indicator species and endemic to the southern Appalachians), wafer-ash, fringe-tree, and one-flower hawthorn. Other species in the glade include little bluestem, big bluestem, common hairsedge, poverty oat-grass, wide-leaved spiderwort, sessile-leaf eupatorium, hemp dogbane, common smooth rockcress, curlyleaf yucca, ebony spleenwort, Appalachian rock-pink, pineweed, fire pink, and eastern flowering spurge. Scattered, stunted trees include pignut hickory, winged elm, and blackjack oak (L. S. Ranger 2007; NatureServe 2009a).

Location: From I-75 in Cobb County, take exit 269 (Barrett Pkwy.) and proceed west 2 miles to Old U.S. 41. Turn left. Continue on Old U.S. 41S and proceed right onto Stilesboro Rd. The visitor center will be immediately on the left. Google Earth GPS approximate coordinates: N 33.983234/W 084.578362.

Granite Outcrops

Granite outcrops are large expanses of granitoid rock, usually a granitic gneiss, interspersed with islands of vegetation. Some of these outcrops form domes with topographic relief of a few hundred feet, while others are "flatrocks" with very gentle gradients. These outcrops are considered among the crown jewels of Georgia natural communities because they feature a suite of endemic or nearly endemic species (Shure 1999; Murdy and Carter 2000; Wyatt and Allison 2000). Georgia has more of these outcrops than any other state and is the center of endemism for granite outcrop species, possessing the greatest concentration of these globally rare species (Murdy 1968; Quarterman, Burbanck, and Shure 1993; Shure 1999). The high number of endemic species suggest that these outcrops probably support a very old biota, with species evolving on these isolated outcrops over long periods of time (Wharton 1978; Quarterman, Burbanck, and Shure 1993; Shure 1999). The outcrops can be spectacular, with colorful and richly textured rock gardens nestled against a backdrop of panoramic vistas.

This important, fragile natural community is unappreciated by many landowners. Traditionally, granite outcrops have been used as dumping grounds, loading decks for timber harvest, ORV (off-road vehicle) trails, parking lots, camping and picnicking areas, and other inappropriate uses (Murdy and Carter 2000). Removal of vegetation in and around the outcrops and excessive vehicular or foot traffic can destroy the vernal pools and the extremely rare plants and animals within them. Many outcrops have been destroyed by mining, and the impacts of former mining activities are evident on most outcrops.

Granite outcrops are scattered throughout the Piedmont. Several outstanding granite outcrops have been protected by state, local, and private entities, including Arabia Mountain (Dekalb County), Stone Mountain

(Dekalb County), Panola Mountain (Henry County), Heggie's Rock (Columbia County), Rock and Shoals Outcrop (Clarke County), and Camp Meeting Rock (Heard County).

PHYSICAL SETTING AND ECOLOGY

Ecologists conventionally refer to this natural community as "granite outcrop" (Quarterman, Burbanck, and Shure 1993). In actuality, the mineral composition of the rocks varies within the granitoid family: for example, Arabia Mountain is composed of Lithonia gneiss; Stone Mountain of Stone Mountain granite; Panola Mountain of Panola granite; Heggies Rock of Appling granite; and Rock and Shoals of Athens gneiss. Thus, although three of the largest domes—Stone, Panola, and Arabia Mountains—are within 20 miles of each other, they are made up of different rocks.

The granitoid rocks chemically weather in a process known as hydrolysis, in which the feldspar minerals are eroded away by rainwater, which is mildly acidic (Christopherson 2009). In flatter areas, this process sometimes carves out small depressions that enlarge over time. It is these depressions that support much of the flora of the outcrop.

As is the case for all outcrop natural communities, conditions on the large areas of exposed rock are harsh. Temperatures on the bare rock on a summer's day can reach 122–131°F (Shure 1999). In summer, evaporation rates are very high, rainfall runoff is rapid, and the thin soils dry quickly. In winter and early spring, soils may remain saturated for long periods due to seepage from joints and because the rocky substrate prevents water from percolating out of the soil.

The hot, dry conditions foster plant life that is strikingly different from that of the forests that predominate on the Piedmont. Indeed, these outcrops have been called "micro-environmental deserts" (Quarterman, Burbanck, and Shure 1993; Shure 1999), with many plant species or genera that are common in the southwestern United States, such as curlyleaf yucca, eastern prickly-pear, Appalachian rock-pink, and flatrock portulaca (Wyatt and Allison 2000). Some of the plants are perennials that grow very slowly, such as common haircap moss, rock spikemoss, and woolly ragwort. Others have a winter annual life history: seeds germinate after early autumnal rains and produce rosettes of frost-resistant leaves. In the spring, temperatures rise, and the plants grow stalks, then flower. The seeds mature by mid- to late spring, when the shallow soils have dried out, so the plants survive the extremely hot, dry summer months as drought-resistant seeds. Examples of winter annuals on Georgia outcrops include Confederate daisy, pineweed, Appalachian sandwort, elf-orpine, Puck's orpine, and snorkelwort (Shure 1999; Murdy and Carter 2000). Many outcrop plants, including hairy lipfern, glade rushfoil, and hairy spiderwort, are covered with whitish hairs that reflect sunlight and reduce evaporative water loss (Allison and Wyatt 2000; Murdy and Carter 2000).

Other interesting adaptations to dry, hot conditions are numerous on the outcrops. Plants often have finely dissected, very small, or linear leaves, which also reduce the surface area susceptible to moisture loss. Others, such as elf-orpine, Appalachian rock-pink, eastern prickly-pear, and curlyleaf yucca, are succulent and store water in swollen stems and leaves. Another adaptation for water conservation is small size; one species, known as little people, is thought to be the smallest terrestrial flowering plant on earth (Weakley 2010, citing Morgan and Soltis 1993). Yellow sunnybells (common in moist areas) have a deeply buried bulb that remains dormant through the summer drought. Mosses and lichens are poikilohydric, that is, they dry out and darken with drought but immediately turn green and photosynthesize in response to moisture. The rock moss illustrates this adaptation dramatically: it is black when dry but turns green when wet (Quarterman, Burbanck, and Shure 1993; Shure 1999; Wyatt and Allison 2000).

Although individual trees are exposed to lightning, widespread fire is probably rare on the outcrops because fuel is sparse and the large expanses of bare rock act as firebreaks.

VEGETATION

Granite outcrops support several different plant communities, including successional assemblages that develop within soil-filled depressions (soil islands), as described above; outcrop margins; plants on exposed rock; and vegetation within temporary pools (Shure 1999). Seepage areas on granite outcrops are covered in the seepage wetland natural community.

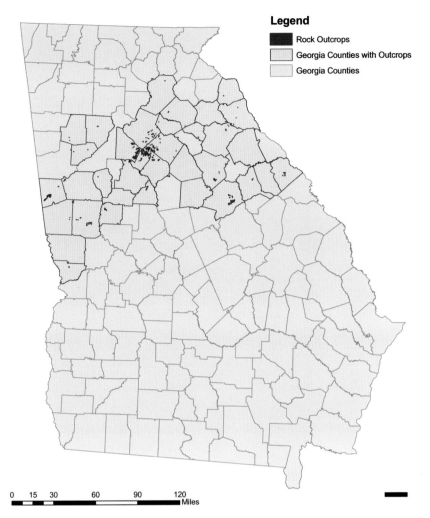

Legend
■ Rock Outcrops
▨ Georgia Counties with Outcrops
▫ Georgia Counties

0   15   30   60   90   120
                                      Miles

*Granite rock outcrop polygons suppied by the Natural Resources Spatial Analysis Labratory (NARSAL 2006).

Granite outcrop distribution in Georgia. Map by Melissa Caspary.

Successional Soil Communities. The soil-filled depressions of granite outcrops have long been studied as a classic example of primary succession, which is the process whereby the bare rock transitions to a habitat that supports a plant community. Four successional stages have been identified on granite rock outcrops (Burbanck and Platt 1964; Burbanck and Phillips 1983; Quarterman, Burbanck, and Shure 1993; Shure 1999). Some caveats must be noted in regard to these successional stages. First, vegetation assemblages often intergrade between the stages described below so that not all examples are clear cut. Also, plant distribution among the outcrops is uneven, so a species may

be abundant on one outcrop and not present on another (Wyatt and Allison 2000). Further, there have been few studies of this process: a 22-year study (Burbank and Phillips 1983) provides the best idea so far of how succession operates in these natural communities, but no longer-scale work has been performed. Certainly, the rate of change can be very slow: transition from bare rock to an oak-pine-hickory forest may take more than 1,000 years (Burbanck and Platt 1964; Quarterman, Burbanck, and Shure 1993; Shure 1999). In addition, while development may occur through a steady progression of successional stages, the progression may be disrupted by drought or flooding that re-

Haircap moss

verts the vegetation to an earlier phase. Finally, not all areas will eventually support trees because some topographic conditions will preclude the development of depressions that are large enough to contain an adequate depth of soils.

The first stage of succession, the elf-orpine community, occurs when soils in a depression are roughly 1 to 3.5 inches deep and elf-orpine is the dominant species. The soils are coarse to medium sands that are acidic and infertile. They experience extreme conditions that limit the plant species that can grow here. Acute fluctuations in moisture level occur because the shallow soils dry out very quickly in spring, summer, and fall but can be saturated after rains. Temperatures also fluctuate greatly because the rock absorbs heat quickly, yet releases heat rapidly when ambient conditions cool.

Vegetation on a granite outcrop

Dish Gardens on Arabia Mountain

A. Exposed rock community
B. Elf-orpine community
C. Lichen-annual herb community
D. Annual-perennial herb-haircap moss community

ELF-ORPINE

This bright red, succulent plant forms striking swaths of color that are a classic feature of Piedmont rock outcrops. Elf-orpine is well adapted to withstand the extreme moisture conditions of shallow granite substrates. An annual, it germinates in the fall, during which time it is able to withstand droughts, and spends the winter as a small rosette. It flowers and completes its lifecycle in the spring, prior to the hot, dry conditions of summer (Shure 1999). Ants are the key pollinators (Wyatt 1981). The seeds remain in capsules at the top of erect dead plants, so they are slightly less exposed to the hot temperatures at the surface of the granite (Shure 1999; Murdy and Carter 2000). Other annuals, such as Confederate daisy, Appalachian sandwort, and pineweed, may germinate during moist years, but they usually will not live to set seed because of the harsh conditions. Elf-orpine communities can be relatively stable for a long time (Burbanck and Phillips 1983).

Elf-orpine

Rock moss. This moss, which can be black when dry, turns green when water is poured over it.

The second recognized successional stage, which may not be reached for decades or centuries, is the lichen-annual herb community. This community occurs on soils that are roughly 3 to 7 inches deep and can support some annual species, including elf-orpine, Appalachian sandwort, southern bentgrass, granite flatsedge, flatrock draba, poorjoe, little people, Small's portulaca, Appalachian rock-pink, glade rushfoil, pineweed, eastern prickly-pear, and Confederate daisy (Shure 1999; Murdy and Carter 2000). The sandy soils contain more organic matter and are deeper than those of the elf-orpine community, and thus retain more moisture. The presence of *Cladonia* lichens is important to the successional process because they trap debris, which builds up the soils and also provides a protected niche for other species to germinate. More annual species are able to survive, and diversity increases. With the establishment of more annual species, vegetation density and plant litter increase, and the site is less prone to the temperature extremes of the elf-orpine community. Plants do not totally cover the site, however, and conditions are still harsh, with sus-

ceptibility to drought and flooding that can destroy the community (Shure 1999).

The third recognized stage, the annual-perennial herb haircap moss community, occurs when soils are 5 to 16 inches deep and at least 2 perennial plants are present. Common perennials include woolly ragwort, Appalachian rock-pink, eastern prickly-pear, blazing-stars, old-field broomsedge, little bluestem, smooth spiderwort, hairy spiderwort, and large-flowered coreopsis (Quarterman, Burbanck, and Shure 1993; Shure 1999; Murdy and Carter 2000). This stage is marked by the presence of haircap moss, which, by trapping soil particles, is a major soil builder of these communities; rock moss may also help build soils (Quarterman, Burbanck, and Shure 1993, Murdy and Carter 2000). The deeper soils hold more water than the lichen-annual herb sites, enabling additional plant species to become established. As soils build, vegetative cover increases, and more organic matter is added to the soil as vegetation decomposes. In a positive feedback cycle, the depression grows deeper as the water held in the soil and the acidic organic material contributed by the vegetation cause increased weathering of the rock; as the depression deepens, soil depth and plant species diversity increase. Drought, or sloughing of the vegetation after violent rains, can cause a reversal of this stage to an earlier one.

The fourth recognized stage, the herb-shrub-tree community, develops on larger, deeper, and more organically rich soil islands compared to those of shallow depressions of earlier stages. Many of the herbs of the annual-perennial community appear, but with the addition of shrubs, woody vines, and trees or tree seedlings. The deepest soil islands support loblolly pine or Virginia pine, and vegetation includes pignut hickory, mockernut hickory, serviceberry, Georgia oak, post oak, dwarf hackberry, blackjack oak, rock chestnut oak, greenbriers, sparkleberry, curlyleaf yucca, eastern red cedar, fringe-tree, cross-vine, and eastern winged sumac.

Marginal Communities. Marginal communities occur at the edge of the rock outcrop, next to the adjacent forest (Shure 1999). Although the soil may be the same depth as that of some of the deeper depressional islands, these areas are moister because water is received from upslope runoff and shade is provided by the adjacent forest or woodland. Plant assemblages here can be very diverse because they contain both outcrop and woodland or forest species. The increased moisture enables the presence of species common to woodlands, including Virginia pine, loblolly pine, fringe-tree, post oak, deerberry, winged elm, pignut hickory, mockernut hickory, various oaks, eastern winged sumac, muscadine grape, grasses, greenbriers, eastern red cedar, and many forbs (Quarterman, Burbanck, and Shure 1993; Shure 1999).

Exposed Rock Communities. Exposed rock communities host mosses and lichens. Although the rock may appear barren, it is typically coated by microscopic lichens that darken the rock (Murdy and Carter 2000). Many of the lichens are crustose (see box). Rock moss is an important pioneer on bare rock and may in some instances form mats, which can in turn lead to a successional progression to annual and perennial herbs similar to the soil island successional process. Such processes vary in their rate and extent, however (Shure 1999).

Vernal (Temporary) Pools. Vernal (temporary) pools occur on some large, domed outcrops, in shallow, flat-

The rare, endemic Confederate daisy blooming near a vernal pool

bottomed depressions that have a rim that prevents them from draining after a rain. The depressions temporarily fill with water during the winter and early spring months, then totally dry out during late spring, summer, and fall. Some foster a globally imperiled community that supports endemics that are adapted to these unique sites: black-spored quillwort and mat-forming quillwort, snorklewort, and the near-endemic elf-orpine.

Snorklewort has an interesting growth form and reproductive habit. It is a winter annual with both submerged and floating leaves, and it bears flowers both on elongated floating stems and at the plant base where they are submerged. The submerged flowers are cleistogamous, which means that the flower does not open but instead self-pollinates. If the pools dry up, and the flowers are no longer submerged, they will open (Murdy and Carter 2000; Nourse and Nourse 2007).

LICHENS OF GRANITE OUTCROPS

Lichens survive where few other living things can. Endolithic lichens (those that live between the mineral grains in rock) of the genera *Polysporina* and *Sacogyne* have developed the strategy of placing the lichen machinery, the photosynthesizing algae and its attendant hyphae, inside the rock. The spore-bearing structures (the apothecia and pycnidia) break through to the surface, but the rest of the lichen inhabits a ready-made greenhouse among quartz crystals, which is no cooler than the surface but quite a bit wetter.

Lichens in the genus *Xanthoparmelias*, often called Xanthos, are the most obvious lichens on the outcrop. They are large, leafy lichens, somewhat yellow-greenish as the *xantho-* of their name suggests. They can be seen on Stone and Arabia Mountains in areas that have been protected from foot traffic. The Xanthos seem to be in direct competition with rock moss, which evidently has the same habitat requirements. The moss and the lichens are probably engaged in a centuries-long battle for the same patches of rock.

What appears to be bare rock can often in fact be a number of lichen crusts that can tolerate full sun. One of the most common of these is *Rinodina tephraspis*, which, like the Xanthos, will also grow on stone walls and gravestones. Two members of the genus *Acarospora* are found in the same situation. Other crusts commonly encountered out in the open are two species of *Diploschistes*, whose name means two-layered, a reference to its double-ringed apothecia. Two species of the genus *Buellia* are also common on sunny rocks, as is *Lecanora oreinoides*; all three are black spot lichens. On occasion, one also sees lichens of the genus *Verrucaria*, tiny organisms growing with cyano-lichens, *Peltula* and the Lichinaceae. A lichen that is usually described as aquatic, or at least amphibious, is *Dermatocarpon luridum*. Its leaves are lurid green when wet, and it is often found with the cyano-lichens.

Four species of *Cladonias* often occur on the sand and gravel that accumulates in solution pits, at the foot of exposed slopes, and in the low areas adjacent to the rocks. *C. caroliniana*, with the coarsest branches of the four, is endemic to rock outcrops. *C. subtenuis* and *rangiferina* (reindeer mosses) can also be seen on open road cuts all over the state. The red-berried *C. leporina* also inhabits the sands of south Georgia.

There is evidence that acid rain and deposition of airborne pollutants have resulted in the disappearance of the foliose lichen *Xanthoparmelia* from xeric, south-facing slopes on Stone Mountain and Arabia Mountain. In some places this species has been replaced by a crustose lichen, but in most areas all of the lichens have disappeared.

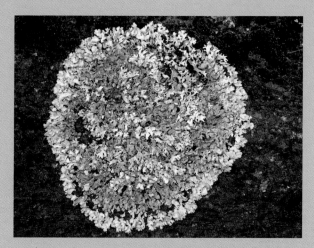

Xanthoparmelia conspersa

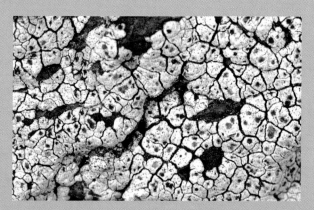

Lecanora oreinoides

Cladonia rangiferina

CHARACTERISTIC PLANTS OF GRANITE OUTCROPS

TREES

Downy serviceberry—*Amelanchier arborea*
Eastern red cedar—*Juniperus virginiana*
Loblolly pine—*Pinus taeda*
Georgia oak—*Quercus georgiana*

SHRUBS AND WOODY VINES

Fringe-tree—*Chionanthus virginicus*
Eastern winged sumac—*Rhus copallina*
Greenbriers—*Smilax spp.*
Sparkleberry—*Vaccinium arboreum*
Curlyleaf yucca—*Yucca filamentosa*

GROUND COVER

Old-field broomsedge—*Andropogon virginicus*
Reindeer lichens—*Cladonia spp., Cladina spp.*
Large-flowered coreopsis—*Coreopsis grandiflora*
Glade rushfoil—*Croton wildenowii*
Granite flatsedge—*Cyperus granitophilus*
Elf-orpine—*Diamorpha cymosa*
Poorjoe—*Diodia teres*
Rock moss—*Grimmia laevigata*
Confederate daisy—*Helianthus porteri*
Pineweed—*Hypericum gentianoides*

Blazing-star—*Liatris microchephala*
Sandwort—*Minuartia uniflora*
Prickly-pear—*Opuntia spp.*
Woolly ragwort—*Packera tomentosa*
Flatrock phacelia—*Phacelia maculata*
Appalachian rock-pink—*Phermeranthus teretifolius*
Haircap moss—*Polytrichum commune*
Small's portulaca—*Portulaca smallii*
Little bluestem—*Schizachyrium scoparium*
Yellow sunnybell—*Schoenolirion croceum*
Spiderworts—*Tradescantia spp.*

ANIMALS

Characteristic mammals of larger forested soil islands include pine voles, southeastern shrews, eastern harvest mice, and an occasional eastern cottontail or gray squirrel. White-tailed deer, gray fox, and raccoon have also been observed on granite outcrops (Quarterman, Burbanck, and Shure 1993). Several species of birds make use of the varying microhabitat conditions on granite outcrops. The mourning dove, a habitat generalist, often feeds on bare ground or among the sparse vegetation on rock outcrops (Mirarchi and Baskett 1994), and northern bobwhite and Bachman's sparrow may frequent grassy ecotonal areas. Turkey vultures sometimes soar above the outcrops on thermals generated by the exposed rock and roost in isolated trees within or adjacent to the outcrop complex. Many birds from the surrounding landscape use the shallow pools and puddles found in the rock for bathing. Species such as the indigo bunting, yellow-billed cuckoo, and blue grosbeak nest in scrubby patches of vegetation (T. M. Schneider et al. 2010). Occasionally, vegetation on these outcrops burns as a result of lightning strikes, prescribed fire, or arson. These fires, or mortality of trees due to drought, provide snags for cavity nesters such as the eastern bluebird and Carolina chickadee, as well as a flush of soft mast that draws summer tanagers, gray catbirds, and other species in abundance.

Reptiles are more common than amphibians on these very dry sites. Six-lined racerunners are characteristic of xeric, open areas and are commonly associated with exposed outcrops. Eastern fence lizards, six-lined racerunners, and southeastern five-lined skinks may range out onto the rock from the surrounding forest or forested islands to bask or forage for insects. Black racers and coachwhips, in turn, are diurnal, active hunters and may cruise along outcrop edges in search of potential lizard prey. Copperheads are more nocturnal and lie in wait to ambush small mammal prey. Timber rattlesnakes are also ambush predators and may use rock outcrops for hunting or basking in areas of the Piedmont where populations persist. Frogs from nearby deciduous forests may use flooded depressions as breeding sites, with upland chorus frogs breeding in shallow pools during winter and Cope's gray treefrogs doing so in the summer.

Several arthropods are endemic to granite outcrops (Quarterman, Burbanck, and Shure 1993). Some forage at night to avoid the harsh daytime conditions, and some have cryptic coloration that makes them nearly imperceptible against lichens and granite, as a protection against predators. The endemic lichen or rock grasshopper is also cryptically colored and inhabits exposed rock, crevices, rubble heaps, and elf-orpine communities, feeding on lichens and mosses (see Featured Animal). The lichen spider is also endemic and cryptically colored to match the lichen-colored rock surface. The spiders live under rocks and in crevices by day and feed at night on arthropods. An endemic species of Caeculid mite comes out at night to eat fungi in moist areas. An endemic orange and greenish-black beetle forages during the day on arthropods, detritus, mites, and elf-orpine seeds and pollen (Quarterman, Burbanck, and Shure 1993). One species of walking stick occurs mainly on granite outcrops, hiding in dead pines during the day and browsing on herbs nocturnally. The diversity of insects, such as leafhoppers, treehoppers, grasshoppers, and crickets, increases with each successional stage of the depression communities and varies by season. Insect diversity and abundance are highest when the Confederate daisy is in flower (Quarterman, Burbanck, and Shure 1993).

The sunflower moth is a noctuid moth that is widely distributed in the Midwest but not well known from the Southeast. The larva (caterpillar) of this species avoids predation by cryptic coloration and behavior that allows it to hide among the flower heads of the Confederate daisy. The lifecycle of this moth is closely matched to that of its fall-flowering host plant. Adults lay their eggs in late August to early September; as they grow, caterpillars feed on the pollen, then the flowers, and finally the developing seeds of the Confederate daisy. They pupate by mid-October. The caterpillar responds to threats by curling around the flower head and blending in (E. Carter, Oxford College of Emory University, pers. comm.).

FEATURED ANIMAL

Lichen or Rock Grasshopper (*Trimerotropis saxatilis*)

This grasshopper is a member of the Acrididae family of short-horned grasshoppers. Most of the 40-plus species in the genus *Trimerotropis* are found in the western United States, while only a few are found in the Southeast. This distribution indicates a tendency for adaptation to dry habitats within this group of grasshoppers.

The lichen grasshopper exists in relatively small and isolated populations across several states in the Southeast and Midwest, including Arkansas, Georgia, Illinois, Kansas, Kentucky, Missouri, North Carolina, Oklahoma, and Tennessee. The preferred habitat of this species includes rocky outcrops and glades in a variety of topographic settings.

The coloration of this slow-moving grasshopper is variable, with a background color ranging from pink, brown, green, or light gray, with dark brown or black splotches, making it well-camouflaged for life on lichen-covered outcrops. Its cryptic coloration helps it hide from predators such as birds while it is on the outcrop surface.

Studies of this species within the heart of its range indicate that populations are relatively small (< 280 adults per year) and fluctuate from year to year (Gerber and Templeton 1996). Gene flow between populations is very low, and closed canopy forest appears to serve as an effective barrier to dispersal. The lichen grasshopper is currently ranked as a globally vulnerable species due to its relatively small and demographically isolated populations. Presumed threats to this species include habitat destruction or degradation and overuse of chemical insecticides.

Davidson–Arabia Mountain Nature Preserve

The Bradley Peak Trail on Arabia Mountain moves through superb examples of the granite outcrop natural community: the views from the top of the mountain are far-ranging, and the successional plant communities are very well developed. Take care when walking on the outcrop: never walk on the gravelly areas because trampling can crush the elf-orpine seeds, which prevents them from germinating. The trail winds through many classic granitic outcrop vegetation communities, and nearly all of the plants and plant communities described on pp. 306–309 are here. These range from bare rock, to very shallow soils that support the elf-orpine community, to herb-shrub-tree communities in the deepest depressions.

The trail is striking throughout the year. In March, the snorkelwort blooms in some pools. Only outcrops with some flat areas can support the temporary pools that host the snorkelwort; nearby Panola Mountain does not have this plant and its related community. The annual-perennial haircap moss communities are beautiful in mid-April, when masses of the bright red elf-orpine contrast with the swaths of white blossoms of the sandwort and the yellow flowers of the woolly ragwort. Note the zonal pattern of vegetation in some depressions, where plant composition varies with soil depth. As spring and summer continue, large-flowered coreopsis, meadow-beauties, sundrops, and much else will bloom. The mountain gets very hot and dry in the summer. Species such as curlyleaf yucca and eastern prickly-pear remind the visitor that this is indeed a "desert microhabitat." Fall brings the blooms of blazing-stars and Confederate daisies, which vary in abundance from year to year, while black gum leaves turn red and the eastern prickly pear and crossvine are in fruit.

Location: From I-20, take Lithonia exit 74 (Evans Mill Rd.) south. After one block, Evans Mill Rd. turns right at the traffic light. Continue straight through to the intersection onto Woodrow Dr. and drive about 1 mile to Klondike Rd. Turn right on Klondike Rd. The Nature Center is on the right at 3787 Klondike Rd. Google Earth GPS approximate coordinates to parking: N 33.672384/W 084.116139. The south parking lot and trailhead for Bradley Peak Trail are about 1 mile farther south from the Nature Center, on the east side of the road.

Ultramafic Barrens and Woodlands

Ultramafic barrens and woodlands are extremely rare communities in the Piedmont ecoregion. Although small outcroppings of ultramafic rock appear at the surface in the Piedmont, the Burks Mountain Complex, sandwiched between Georgia Highway 104 and the Savannah River near Pollards Corner in Columbia County, is a superb example of a large expanse of ultramafic rocks with an intact, classic expression of the grassy barrens and xeric oak-pine woodlands that are closely associated with soapstone- and serpentine-like rock. This discussion is, therefore, centered around Burks Mountain. Burks Mountain also supports longleaf pine, as discussed on p. 319.

The importance of this site to Georgia's natural heritage can scarcely be overstated. Because of its location in the lower Piedmont in close proximity to the Fall Line, the Savannah River, and the Atlantic Coastal Plain, Burks Mountain supports both Coastal Plain and Piedmont species. The ecological richness associated with this location is further enhanced by the ultramafic substrate, which contributes to the presence of rare species. Due to its very limited occurrence in the state, this natural community is of high conservation concern, but no permanently protected examples of this natural community occur in Georgia. Burks Mountain is the only known station within the state for species like yellow nailwort and Dixie Mountain breadroot. Therefore, long-term protection of this area is strongly encouraged.

PHYSICAL SETTING AND ECOLOGY

The most important factor in the development of this natural community is the ultramafic rock, visible around Burks Mountain as grayish-green or reddish-brown outcrops. These rock formations appear in mounds or as flatrock and may contain many shallow depression pits. Occasionally, loose gravel is present on the surfaces of the outcrops. Soils here have an acidic to circumneutral pH (up to 6.2), abundant rock fragments in an otherwise shallow (approximately 1 foot) sandy loam, extremely high magnesium levels, very high magnesium to calcium ratios, and elevated levels of toxic metals such as chromium and nickel (Allison, Morris, and Egan 2006). The bedrock at this

Tall ironweed

site has been described as weathered soapstone, which is largely talc. Cocker (1991a, 1991b) classifies the bedrock as an altered serpentinite. Both soapstone and serpentinite are magnesium-rich metamorphic rocks that are formed through recrystallization in the presence of water. Plants occurring here must be adapted to shallow soils, low nutrient (such as nitrogen) levels in the substrate, potentially high toxic metal soil content, and excessively well-drained conditions during at least part of the year. Invasive species are nearly absent on this substrate, evidence that the soils and growing conditions are stressful to many of these plants.

Peaks of the Burks Mountain Complex, particularly at Ferry Road Knob, another monadnock just to the east of Burks Mountain proper, are capped by silica-rich rocks that support oak-pine-hickory forests, with ericaceous trees and shrubs such as sourwood, sparkleberry, deerberry, and mayberry, as well as Piedmont azalea. These erosion-resistant rocks are likely responsible for the persistence of the monadnocks in this complex; once these caps have eroded away, the less resistant soapstone and altered serpentinite downslope will erode quickly.

The presence of longleaf pine in the adjacent woodlands suggests that periodic natural fires have assisted in maintaining the open, grassy barrens and wood-lands at this site (see box). At present, longleaf occurs with shortleaf and loblolly pines, as well as a number of hardwood tree species such as post and blackjack oaks and several hickories. In the past, if fire was more frequent, a more open vegetation structure and greater dominance by longleaf pine may have occurred. Thus, mowing and bush-hogging in the powerline rights-of-way that cross Burks Mountain have benefited many of the plants inhabiting the open soapstone and serpentinite barrens. In fact, many of these plants have migrated to the artificial openings. Periodic prescribed burns would likely benefit these same species and help prevent the glade-like openings from encroachment by understory shrubs and vines.

VEGETATION

Open, grassy barrens with many species of herbs and a few shrubs are present where there is very thin soil over the outcropping ultramafic rock. These barrens support little bluestem, silky oat-grass, three-awn grasses, other grasses, composites such as daisy fleabane, blazing-star, goldenrods, and asters; various legumes like tick-trefoils, butterfly peas, pencil-flower, lespedezas, and wild indigoes; Georgia calamint, false garlic, and Cuthbert's onion (Morris et al. 2008). Occasionally, these plants are pioneers in very small soil pockets on the

Dixie Mountain breadroot

Blazing-star

outcrops. Other pioneers include an estimated 100 lichen species, including species not yet discovered and described in the scientific literature (S. Beeching, Atlanta, pers. comm.).

Xeric pine-oak woodlands or open forests develop where the soil is deeper around the outcrops. Canopy trees include shortleaf, loblolly, and longleaf pines, and both blackjack and post oak. Understory trees and shrubs may be dense or sparsely distributed, and include flowering dogwood, American persimmon, sweet gum, black cherry, winged elm, wax-myrtle, winged sumac, fragrant sumac, blackberries, Carolina rose, and American beautyberry (Morris et al. 2008).

Because of its location in the lower Piedmont in close proximity to the Fall Line, the Savannah River, and the Atlantic Coastal Plain, the Burks Mountain Complex contains a fascinating and unique mix of plants. In the xeric sites, there is a mixture of species typically found in upland pine-oak forests of the Piedmont such as many composites and legumes, taxa

characteristic of sandhill habitats in the Coastal Plain including a dropseed and an ironweed, and even prairie indicator species like side-oats grama, big bluestem, and green milkweed. A circumneutral soil pH and a history of fire in the open grassy barrens have likely contributed to the presence of prairie species.

Also influencing the plant diversity are elements from nearby granite outcrops characteristic of the Piedmont and from not-too-distant Altamaha Grit outcrops of the upper Coastal Plain. The latter include the near Georgia endemic pineland Barbara's-buttons and the former includes Appalachian rock-pink. Some of the most unusual taxa at Burks Mountain and environs are those closely associated with basic rocks in other regions of the eastern United States such as yellow nailwort (also called yellow whitlow-wort) and curlyheads. Burks Mountain is the only station in Georgia for the former and is the southernmost station known for the latter. Other unique plants occurring here prefer rocky habitats along the Fall Line

CHARACTERISTIC PLANTS OF ULTRAMAFIC BARRENS AND WOODLANDS

TREES

Shortleaf pine—*Pinus echinata*
Longleaf pine—*Pinus palustris*
Loblolly pine—*Pinus taeda*
Blackjack oak—*Quercus marilandica*
Post oak—*Quercus stellata*

SHRUBS AND WOODY VINES

Georgia calamint—*Clinopodium georgianum*
Carolina jessamine—*Gelsemium sempervirens*
Fragrant sumac—*Rhus aromatica*
Winged sumac—*Rhus copallina*
Sand blackberry—*Rubus cuneifolius*

GROUND COVER

Cuthbert's onion—*Allium cuthbertii*
Big bluestem—*Andropogon gerardii*
Thick-pod white wild indigo—*Baptisia alba*
Creamy wild indigo—*Baptisia bracteata*
Common rough fleabane—*Erigeron strigosus*
Pineweed—*Hypericum gentianoides*
Velvety lespedeza—*Lespedeza stuevei*
Blazing-star—*Liatris virgata*
Pineland Barbara's-buttons—*Marshallia ramosa*
False garlic—*Nothoscordum bivalve*
Dixie Mountain breadroot—*Pediomelum piedmontanum*

Appalachian rock-pink—*Phemeranthus teretifolius*
Silkgrass—*Pityopsis aspera* var. *adenolepis*
Glade knotweed—*Polygonum tenue*
Bracken fern—*Pteridium aquilinum*
Common little bluestem—*Schizachyrium scoparium*
Yellow indiangrass—*Sorghastrum nutans*
Rough dropseed—*Sporobolus clandestinus*
Sandhills dropseed—*Sporobolus junceus*
Ironweed—*Vernonia acaulis*

and in the Piedmont of the Carolinas, their ranges barely crossing the Savannah River into Georgia; these include the very rare and recently described Dixie Mountain breadroot, stemless ironweed, and a blazing-star species (Piedmont gayfeather).

Regardless of origin, the majority of these plants are drought-tolerant herbs and a few shrubs and scattered trees, especially where the ultramafic rock is close to the surface. Among the adaptations to conserve water that many of these plants possess are highly reduced or narrow leaves (e.g., pineweed), waxy leaf surfaces (e.g., wax-myrtle and winged sumac), grayish or whitish hairs covering above-ground plant parts (as in many golden-asters, to trap escaping moisture and/or to minimize leaf surface temperature when exposed to bright sunshine), and thick bulb- or corm-like underground storage organs for harsh periods when the plants should remain dormant (e.g., blazing-stars). Other adaptations include leaves that can shift their position with respect to the sun, as in a number of legume species, and leaves that can roll longitudinally during drought periods due to the presence of bubble-like bulliform cells that either take up or lose water in the epidermal tissues (in many grasses).

To help curb herbivory, some mint species, including Georgia calamint, which is abundant at this site,

have concentrated pungent or highly aromatic oils and other chemical compounds. In addition, the oils may function in facilitating the spread of fire. This is not unlike many plants found in Mediterranean climates and in the chaparral. Wax-myrtle and legumes such as species of wild indigo and lespedezas have mutualistic associations with nitrogen-fixing bacteria and, in effect, "fertilize" the soil around them.

ANIMALS

Open areas and their ecotones with adjacent open woodlands at Burks Mountain and environs help support a wide array of insects; reptiles, such as eastern fence lizards, green anoles, and eastern box turtles; and a number of game species, such as northern bobwhite, wild turkey, mourning dove, and white-tailed deer.

Birds are diverse in the area. The ruby-throated hummingbird has been observed taking nectar from coral honeysuckle. Other birds seen at Burks Mountain include brown-headed nuthatches, Carolina chickadees, tufted titmice, blue jays, cardinals, eastern bluebirds, and various woodpeckers in the xeric forests and barrens, and turkey vultures and red-tailed hawks soaring overhead.

Among the butterfly species occurring here are a number that feed on legumes as caterpillars: cloudless sulphur, sleepy sulphur, long-tailed skipper, and eastern tailed-blue. The latter two taxa, along with the common buckeye and the pipevine swallowtail, have been observed visiting the flowers of the recently described Dixie Mountain breadroot (Allison, Morris, and Egan 2006). Common buckeye butterfly caterpillars eat false foxgloves. Caterpillars of pipevine swallowtails feed on Virginia snakeroot in the adjacent woodlands; the resulting concentration of distasteful alkaloid compounds in their bodies affords them protection from predators. Red-spotted purples, spicebush swallowtails, and dark forms of female eastern tiger swallowtails resemble the distasteful pipevine swallowtails and benefit from this mimicry through reduced predation pressure. A blazing-star species here serves as a nectar food plant for the long-tailed skipper and gulf fritillaries; caterpillars of the latter use passionflower as a larval food plant. The cloudless sulphur has been observed here visiting flowers of Georgia calamint for nectar. The eastern tiger swallowtail, also present at the Burks Mountain Complex, has larvae that eat black cherry and tulip-tree leaves. One butterfly species that utilizes some of the grasses in the area during its larval stage is the wood nymph; the adults of this species frequently perch on the trunks and leaves of scrub oaks in the xeric woodlands.

FEATURED ANIMAL

Pipevine Swallowtail (*Battus philenor*)

A common and showy member of the swallowtail family (Papilionidae), the pipevine swallowtail is widely distributed across the southern half of the United States and ranges south to southern Mexico. Adults have occasionally been found as far north as southern Manitoba, Canada. Pipevine swallowtails are found in a wide variety of habitats in Georgia, including glades, open woodlands, and woodland edges (L. C. Harris 1972).

This butterfly has a wing span of 2.75 inches to 5 inches. Its forewings are black above and gray below. Males and females differ in the size and arrangement of spots on the hindwing, but both have metallic blue coloration, a single row of seven orange spots, and small cream-colored dots at the edge of the wing.

As larvae (caterpillars), pipevine swallowtails feed only on plants in the genus *Aristolochia* (commonly known as pipevines). As adult butterflies, however, they feed on nectar from a wide assortment of plants. Pipevine swallowtails can learn to associate certain flower colors with nectar supplies and may be as intelligent as honeybees in this respect (Milius 1998).

In the eastern United States and in California, adults fly primarily in late spring and summer, but the butterfly is more commonly seen in late summer and fall in the South and Southwest. Where temperatures are milder, adults may fly continuously. In lowland tropical Mexico they may be found in any month (Ramos 2001).

MONTANE LONGLEAF PINE FORESTS ON BURKS MOUNTAIN

The Burks Mountain ultramafic woodlands support montane longleaf pine. As noted in the description of the montane longleaf pine woodland and forest natural community on p. 189, the montane longleaf pine forest natural community differs from most natural Coastal Plain longleaf pine communities in that longleaf pine does not usually form continuous, unbroken stands. Instead, other southern yellow pines, such as shortleaf and loblolly pine, often co-occur with longleaf. In addition, several species of scrub oaks, upland hickories, and other hardwoods may comprise a significant portion of the semi-open to mostly closed canopy in this natural community. The character of the Burks Mountain ultramafic woodlands certainly matches this in terms of the semi-open canopy and admixture with other pine and hardwood tree species. Another way in which the Burks Mountain ultramafic woodlands are similar to other montane longleaf pine woodlands is that this habitat type is primarily present on south-facing ridges on dry, rocky substrates. Frequent fire is needed to maintain montane longleaf pine forests, although the semi-open nature of the forest at Burks Mountain is also due to the unusual altered serpentinite bedrock on which few tree species can grow, except in areas where soil pockets are deep enough to support the long taproots of pines and hardwoods.

In montane longleaf, fires tend to occur with less frequency than they do in most Coastal Plain longleaf pine forest types; this appears to be the case at Burks Mountain, as well. The community at Burks Mountain is not as open and park-like as well-maintained longleaf pine forests are in some parts of the Coastal Plain of Georgia, where natural and controlled burns may occur at intervals of one to five years. Leaf litter accumulation on the forest floor is generally greater in montane longleaf, including Burks Mountain, than in many longleaf pine forests in the Coastal Plain. Regeneration of montane longleaf can be more problematic as a result.

While there are many similarities between plant species present at Burks Mountain and in montane longleaf woodlands occurring elsewhere, there are also some marked differences. For example, Georgia-plume and pineland Barbara's buttons, both frequently associated with the Altamaha Grit outcrop system of the Atlantic Coastal Plain, are found at the Burks Mountain Complex. Other species more indicative of sandhill habitats in the Coastal Plain are present at Burks Mountain, probably owing to the geographic location near the Savannah River and close proximity to the Fall Line, including tall ironweed and pineywoods dropseed.

Longleaf pine on Burks Mountain

Cliffs, Bluffs, and Outcrops

Cliffs, bluffs, and outcrops are vertical to nearly vertical cliffs that often form along Piedmont rivers. Very large rock outcroppings with steep vertical faces are also included here. Vegetation is sparse and limited to small microsites on sheer cliffs, but often river bluffs have eroded to supply many holds for trees and shrubs and thus intergrade into the Piedmont oak-pine-hickory forest natural community. The glade, barren, and woodland natural community is often embedded on low-gradient outcroppings on bluffs. Cliffs and bluffs provide vegetation diversity and niches for mammals and reptiles. They are ideal nesting and feeding places for turkey vultures, hawks, and swallows.

Cliffs and bluffs are interspersed throughout the Georgia Piedmont. Most striking is Mount Yonah, made up of granitic gneiss. Pine Mountain (Harris and Meriwether Counties) has stunning quartzite cliffs and bluffs, which can be viewed at Sprewell Bluff and along the trail to Dripping Rock at the Camp Thunder Boy Scout Camp (see Featured Place). The Chattahoochee River bluffs are made up of mica schist and are a dramatic feature in several areas of the Chattahoochee River National Recreational Area, most notably around the Palisades (Fulton and Cobb Counties). Increasing development near the cliff edges of the Chattahoochee River has degraded habitats and aesthetics of some sites. A cliff at the end of the road leading to the top of Currahee Mountain (Stephens County) is also notable and grades into the glade and barren natural community. A few striking bluffs loom above the stream at Sweetwater Creek State Park, with good views to the rapids below. Small cliffs and bluffs are also present on many of the so-called mountains scattered throughout the Piedmont. For example, Big Mountain in Oglethorpe County rises 100 feet or so from the surrounding landscape on erosion-resistant siliceous rock that is exposed in cliffs and ledges at its peak.

PHYSICAL SETTING AND ECOLOGY

Slope position affects moisture and temperature levels: upper cliff faces are hotter and drier than lower ones because they are more exposed to sunlight and wind. Valley width is also important. In wider valleys, aspect is influential (Larson, Matthes, and Kelly 2000); south- to west-facing cliffs rimming wide valleys are hotter and drier than north-facing ones because they are more exposed to sunlight and experience higher evapotranspiration rates. Wide valleys also increase the exposure of a cliff wall to sunlight and drying winds, as seen around Pine Mountain (Harris and Meriwether Counties), where sites along narrow ravines that are rarely exposed to the sun have a very different flora than those facing wide river channels.

Moisture levels are generally fairly low on most Piedmont cliffs because moisture sources are confined to water stored in joints, bedding planes, fractures, and the shallow soils that develop on ledges. In a few places, however, seeps provide a hydric environment for at least a portion of the year; seepages are especially common at the base of the quartzite cliffs in the Pine Mountain area. Further, some ledges or crevices are able to collect more soil, which will store more water. On bare rock and shallow soils of cliffs, moisture levels will fluctuate greatly because there is no moisture-holding soil or shade from trees to mediate ambient conditions.

Nutrient levels also play a role in plant composition. Although most cliffs and bluffs are acidic in the Georgia Piedmont, cliffs with higher nutrient levels, such as at Panther Creek, will support calciphitic plants, such as eastern columbine.

In general, the harsh growing conditions on cliffs limit vegetation to those plants with adaptations to drought and low nutrients. Many of the plants on cliffs grow very slowly due to low nutrient and water levels. Lichens and mosses are poikilohydric—they are able to dehydrate completely and go dormant during drought, then spring back and photosynthesize when moistened by rain. Trees with wind-blown seeds, such as pines, may colonize crevices where the roots stay moist. Annuals are typically rare on cliffs (Larson, Matthes, and Kelly 2000). Some grasses and sedges become dormant during dry summer conditions. Some perennial plants grow roots that spread over ledges to absorb rainwater before it runs off. These plants are drought adapted, with small, rolled, hairy, or waxy leaves that help retain moisture, or with light-colored surfaces that

Wide river valleys allow more sunlight to strike the cliff face.

reflect sunlight rather than absorb it. Less drought-adapted plants are confined to moister, north- to east-facing sites, low sites receiving little insolation, or to sites where vegetation can root into moist crevices.

VEGETATION

Bryophytes and lichens often cover portions of the exposed rock; vascular plants occur where soil gathers on ledges and crevices. Some of these microsites may be deep enough to support shrubs or even trees; others support only herbs. The woody plants are usually species from surrounding forests, and most are xerophytic. Common trees on bluffs include rock chestnut oak, sand hickory, winged elm, red maple, eastern red cedar, southern red oak, shortleaf pine, Virginia pine, and sourwood. Shrubs include sparkleberry, wafer-ash, century plant, yellowroot, blueberries, gorge rhododendron, and mountain laurel. Typical ground-layer plants

CHARACTERISTIC PLANTS OF CLIFFS, BLUFFS, AND OUTCROPS

TREES

Eastern red cedar—Juniperus virginiana
Shortleaf pine—Pinus echinata
Virginia pine—Pinus virginiana
Southern red oak—Quercus falcata
Blackjack oak—Quercus marilandica
Rock chestnut oak—Quercus montana
Post oak—Quercus stellata
Winged elm—Ulmus alata

SHRUBS AND WOODY VINES

Downy serviceberry—Amelanchier
  arborea
Fringe-tree—Chionanthus virginicus
Mountain laurel—Kalmia latifolia

Gorge rhododendron—Rhododendron
  minus
Sparkleberry—Vaccinium arboreum

GROUND COVER

Old-field broomsedge—Andropogon
  virginicus
Ebony spleenwort—Asplenium
  platyneuron
Hairy lipfern—Cheilanthes lanosa
Oat-grasses—Danthonia sericea;
  D. spicata
Marginal wood-fern—Dryopteris
  marginalis
Alumroots—Heuchera spp.

Veiny hawkweed—Hieracium venosum
Carolina lily—Lilium michauxii
Appalachian rock-pink—Phemeranthus
  teretifolius
Common rockcap fern—Polypodium
  virginianum
Early saxifrage—Saxifraga virginiana
Little bluestem—Schizachyrium
  scoparium
Rock spikemoss—Selaginella rupestris
Spiderworts—Tradescantia spp.
Bird's-foot violet—Viola pedata
Blunt-lobed cliff fern—Woodsia obtusa

---

include poverty oat-grass, silky oat-grass, bluestems, smooth spiderwort, Appalachian rock-pink, veiny hawkweed, bird's-foot violet, Carolina lily, and stiffleaf coreopsis, along with rock outcrop specialists such as common rockcap fern, liverworts, early saxifrage, alumroots, common spikemoss, lipferns, mosses, liverworts, and several grasses (Wharton 1978; Schafale and Weakley 1990).

ANIMALS

Cliffs provide a constraint to most vertebrate animals due to their inaccessibility and extreme environmental conditions. Thus, they tend to be visited by animals for specialized purposes but have few year-round residents. Overhanging rock shelters and cave-like areas in cliffs attract many mammals for shelter or hibernation. Mammals may include white-footed mice, raccoons, pine voles, and eastern chipmunks (Larson, Matthes, and Kelly 2000). Some bats use deep crevices and ledge overhangs for hibernation and for summer daytime retreats. Since many cliffs are near rivers, they are used as launching pads for bats' nocturnal flights over the river in search of flying insects. Caves in cliff faces are utilized for roosting and hibernation by some bats, including big brown, Mexican free-tailed, eastern pipistrelle, and hoary (Larson, Matthes, and Kelly 2000).

Bird communities found here generally reflect those of the surrounding landscape, but exposed rock faces

Bird's-foot violet

provide unique nesting sites used by several species. Black and turkey vultures often nest on ledges near cliff tops, while Carolina wrens will frequently nest in smaller crevices or among exposed tree roots. Northern rough-winged swallows and cliff swallows may use these sites as well. Rock ledges with overhangs provide sites for the eastern phoebe's distinctive nest, which is cup-shaped and made of a mixture of mud, moss, and leaves (T. M. Schneider et al. 2010). Often these cliffs serve as communal roost sites for vultures during the fall and winter because they get abundant early light and afford an easy takeoff in the morning before thermals form (Kirk and Mossman 1998). Bluffs provide convenient loafing and hunting perches for red-tailed hawks and bald eagles when near larger rivers.

Eastern fence lizards and various skinks, as well as green anoles in more mesic forests, occasionally climb across vertical outcrops and use the crevices as cover sites. An exceptionally mesic forest at the foot of the Blue Ridge escarpment in Stephens County contains exposed outcrops of partially metamorphosed limestone. These provide habitat for the scansorial (tree-climbing) green salamander, which uses outcrop crevices as retreats when not foraging in trees (M. J. Elliott 2008a).

FEATURED ANIMAL

Turkey Vulture (*Cathartes aura*)

The turkey vulture, also known as the "turkey buzzard," is a member of the family Cathartidae, which in Georgia includes only two species, the turkey vulture and the black vulture. While similar in terms of life history, the two are easily distinguished by head coloration. The turkey vulture's nearly bald head is reddish in color and it has a whitish bill, while the black vulture's head and bill are dark gray to black (Kirk and Mossman 1998).

The turkey vulture is the most widely distributed vulture in the Western Hemisphere, breeding from southern Canada to the southernmost portions of South America. North American populations of the turkey vulture have increased in recent decades, and the breeding range has expanded northward. This large raptor is a common year-round resident throughout Georgia, often roosting communally in large numbers in forested areas (Schmalz 2010).

The turkey vulture has several adaptations for life as a roving carrion feeder. Its large wingspan (up to 70 inches) allows it to take advantage of thermal wind currents to stay aloft for long periods of time. A very keen sense of smell helps it locate carrion even under dense vegetation. It tends to forage solitarily, but several individuals may congregate at a carcass to feed. Turkey vultures may be displaced by more aggressive black vultures, which often follow turkey vultures to a food source.

Turkey vultures nest in cavities beneath boulders, on cliff ledges, in hollow trees, logs, and stumps, and in caves and abandoned buildings. No nest is constructed; instead, one to three eggs are laid directly on the surface of the ground (Kirk and Mossman 1998).

Despite being persecuted as a winged "varmint," poisoned by ingested lead shot, and occasionally hit by automobiles, the turkey vulture's numbers have increased in recent decades. This may be due to an increase in road-killed animals along highways (Schmalz 2010).

Camp Thunder

The riverside trail in Camp Thunder is sandwiched between the rocky, scenic Flint River and the bluffs that rise above it and offers views of both xeric and hydric cliff conditions. Seeps, formed as water percolates through the cliffs and emerges at the cliff bases, support cinnamon fern, along with the Coastal Plain species ti-ti, tag alder, red bay, mayberry, and coastal fetterbush.

Roughly 0.75 mile along the trail, prominent cliffs appear on the left (these will be noted earlier by keen observers), with steps leading to the cliff base. The cliffs face west, and the soils are mostly dry to xeric. Longleaf pines are scattered along the tops of the cliffs. Other trees include blackjack oak, loblolly pine, pig-

nut hickory, sweet gum, red maple, and rock chestnut oak. Shrubs on the cliffs and along the base include mountain laurel, mayberry, oakleaf hydrangea, horsesugar, sparkleberry, and gorge rhododendron. Herbs include American bellflower, goldenrods, veiny hawkweed, bird's-foot violet, Bradley's spleenwort, and stiff-leaved aster.

Roughly 0.25 mile farther down the trail, turn left where there is a tributary entering the river and follow the trail markers to Dripping Rock to view a moist cliff plant assemblage. The trail moves through mesic forest as well as floodplain and bottomland, with an outstanding mix of Piedmont, Coastal Plain, and montane species, including ti-ti, mountain laurel, northern red oak, rock chestnut oak, sweet bay, kidney-leaved grass-of-Parnassus, southern wild raisin, royal fern, horsesugar, oakleaf hydrangea, and common silverbell.

Roughly 0.5 mile down the trail, the Dripping Rock cliffs appear deep within a ravine that protects them from the western sun. Mosses, liverworts, and meadow spikemoss form a dense curtain of vegetation. Other plants include mountain laurel, primrose-leaf violet, southern lady fern, red bay seedlings, climbing hydrangea, azalea, yellowroot, and dewberries.

Location: From U.S. Hwy. 19 in Thomaston, take Ga. Hwy. 74 west for about 13 miles. Look for the sign to Camp Thunder on the left. Turn left onto Thundering Springs Rd. (stay right immediately after turning off of Ga. Hwy. 74) and proceed 0.6 mile to Dripping Rock Rd. on the right. Turn right on Dripping Rock Rd. and drive roughly 2.5 miles to the parking area. Walk to the west for a short distance to reach the trail along the Flint River. Google Earth GPS approximate coordinates: N 32.632367/W 084.53125.

Flatwoods

Flatwoods are shallow depressional wetlands that form over mafic bedrock. This natural community is known by several names, including "Monticello Glades," for the town near which they were first described in Georgia; "Iredell Flatwoods," for the type of soil on which they are frequently found; "upland depression swamps," for their topography; and "gabbro glades," for the type of bedrock that can foster their development. In the Georgia Piedmont, flatwoods are known primarily from the Oconee National Forest in the lower Piedmont (see the Featured Place). It is possible, however, that a portion of the Slate Belt subregion also supports this natural community. Flatwoods

Gabbro in the Monticello Glades

are significant from a conservation perspective because high-base mesic-hydric sites are rare in the Georgia Piedmont and support unusual plant assemblages.

These sites are very scenic in mid-April, when water ponds over shrink-swell soils and swaths of Atamasco-lilies are blooming concurrently with eastern redbud, flowering dogwood, and hawthorns. Broad drifts of saw palmetto, a Coastal Plain species, add a distinctive character to this Piedmont natural community. Populations of Oglethorpe oak, which is a state-protected species, are present in some sites.

PHYSICAL SETTING AND ECOLOGY

Flatwoods occur on flat to gently sloping areas over gabbro mafic rocks. The gabbro fosters the Iredell and Enon soil series, which have shrink-swell tendencies. In winter and spring, when precipitation rates are high, the soils swell, evapotranspiration decreases, and water ponds above the impermeable surface for extended periods of time. A soil core taken in April revealed that 8 inches below the surface the substrate was stiff clay and impermeable. In summer and fall, as the water table drops, the Iredell soil shrinks and becomes almost pavement-like, with limited moisture availability, even though the water table may be only 1 or 2 feet below the soil surface. These extremes of water availability, along with the high nutrient levels in the gabbro-derived soils, contribute to the interesting vegetation assemblage here, where plants in some areas must be able to tolerate both saturation and extreme dryness, while others colonize sites that are more mesic in nature (J. Ambrose 1990).

The role of fire needs to be further studied for this natural community. Some upland depression swamps on the Oconee National Forest have been subjected to prescribed burns in recent years. These sites would burn in summer or fall under natural conditions of lightning ignition. Fires occurring late in the growing season would reduce the hardwood component of the canopy and subcanopy, allowing pines and herbaceous plants to become more prevalent. In South Carolina, a Piedmont flatwoods site known as Camassia Flats is being maintained by prescribed fire, as it probably was in pre-settlement times. It is possible that a seasonally

Coral beads

The vegetation composition is a rare, complex mix of mesic and hydric plants. Dominant trees are typically willow oak, Shumard oak, swamp chestnut oak, and white ash. Other species common to the flatwoods, whose presence increases in high-base soils, include eastern redbud, ironwood, elms (American, slippery, and winged), hickories, eastern red cedar, chalk maple, southern sugar maple, sugarberry, hawthorns, red mulberry, buckthorn bumelia, and dwarf palmetto. Vines, including muscadine, American rattan, trumpetcreeper, coral beads, cross-vine, greenbriers, Carolina spinypod, yellow passionflower, and coral honeysuckle, are abundant and diverse. Herbs can be diverse as well, including a wide range of both hydric and mesic species, including spring-beauty, Christmas fern, early meadowrue, and false garlic.

variable fire regime applied across a suite of sites may be beneficial in promoting overall diversity among these habitats, but, given the number of mesophytic species also present, this issue should be studied with care.

OGLETHORPE OAK

The Oglethorpe oak is a dominant tree in some portions of the Monticello Glades site in Oconee National Forest but absent in nearby sites with similar soils and hydrology. While characteristic of the flatwoods, this rare tree is found in a variety of other habitats with poorly drained soils that become parched in summer, as well as on slopes adjacent to these wetlands. Oglethorpe oak was described as a species by the late Wilbur Duncan, a botany professor at the University of Georgia. Duncan named the tree in honor of General Oglethorpe, the colonial governor of Georgia. A member of the white oak group, this tree is vulnerable to the chestnut blight in some settings, including the Monticello Glades site.

(ABOVE) The leaves of Oglethorpe oak

(LEFT) The bark of Oglethorpe oak

327

CHARACTERISTIC PLANTS OF FLATWOODS

TREES

Carolina shagbark hickory—*Carya carolinae-septentrionalis*
Red hickory—*Carya ovalis*
Eastern redbud—*Cercis canadensis*
Flowering dogwood—*Cornus florida*
White ash—*Fraxinus americana*
Green ash—*Fraxinus pennsylvanica*
Eastern red cedar—*Juniperus virginiana*
Swamp chestnut oak—*Quercus michauxii*
Cherrybark oak—*Quercus pagoda*
Willow oak—*Quercus phellos*
Shumard oak—*Quercus shumardii*

SHRUBS AND WOODY VINES

River cane—*Arundinaria gigantea*
American rattan—*Berchemia scandens*
Cross-vine—*Bignonia capreolata*
Trumpet-creeper—*Campsis radicans*
Fringe-tree—*Chionanthus virginicus*
Coral beads—*Cocculus carolinus*
Southern swamp dogwood—*Cornus stricta*
Hawthorns—*Crataegus* spp.
Possum-haw—*Ilex decidua*
Dwarf palmetto—*Sabal minor*
Buckthorn bumelia—*Sideroxylon lycioides*

GROUND COVER

Sedges—*Carex* spp.
Spring-beauty—*Claytonia virginiana*
Witchgrasses—*Dichanthelium* spp.
False garlic—*Nothoscordum bivalve*
Christmas fern—*Polystichum acrostichoides*
Skullcaps—*Scutellaria* spp.
Early meadowrue—*Thalictrum dioicum*
Atamasco-lily—*Zephyranthes atamasca*

ANIMALS

Typical mammals of this community include the short-tailed shrew, pine vole, gray squirrel, white-tailed deer, golden mouse, least shrew, eastern mole, southern flying squirrel, opossum, raccoon, coyote, gray fox, bobcat, eastern chipmunk, striped skunk, and several bats, including the hoary, little brown, evening, eastern pipistrelle, and big brown. Birds include green herons, which often nest at these sites in thickets surrounding ponds or other standing water. When cavity trees are available the wood duck will also nest here. Common yellowthroats, white-eyed vireos, and hooded warblers may nest in areas with a dense shrub layer, while prothonotary warblers use areas with extensive standing water with snags. The American woodcock will use these flatwoods for nesting, as stopover habitat during migration, and in winter. This species prefers to feed in moist soils along pond edges and similar areas (Keppie and Whiting 1994; Dobbs 2010).

Temporary pools provide important breeding habitat for a diverse array of frogs and salamanders. Late winter or early spring breeders include upland chorus frogs, which breed in shallow, temporary pools throughout the Georgia Piedmont (Moriarty Lemmon 2008). Spring peepers tend to use heavily vegetated, semipermanent ponds, where breeding males often gather in large choruses. Summer-breeding frogs include the fossorial eastern narrow-mouthed toad and the arboreal Cope's gray treefrog, individuals of which move to ponds in response to summer thunderstorms. Northern cricket frogs, squirrel treefrogs, and green treefrogs (see Featured Animal) may also breed in these wetlands. Marbled salamanders lay their eggs in dry basins during the fall, and attendant females often guard the eggs until flooding induces hatching (Scott 2005). Spotted and mole salamanders move to flooded ponds during winter or early spring and attach eggs to submerged vegetation. The four-toed salamander, a species commonly associated with ponds having considerable amounts of sphagnum, often lays eggs in communal nests, which are then guarded by one or two females (M. J. Elliott 2008b). Three-lined salamanders often breed in ephemeral ponds, and individuals commonly hide under coarse woody debris at or near the water's edge. Eastern newts are aquatic as adults and are abundant in ponds having lengthy hydroperiods.

Green Treefrog (*Hyla cinerea*)

This attractive frog has smooth, moist skin, a bright yellowish-green back often with a sprinkling of small yellow spots, and a whitish throat and belly. A light-colored "racing stripe" extends laterally along each side of the body. This stripe may be indistinct or absent in some individuals. The bright green color may shift to pale green, yellowish, olive, or slate gray, depending on temperature, stress, or other factors. Toes on the front and hind feet have expanded terminal disks that allow the frog to adhere to smooth or slippery surfaces (Rothermel 2008).

Green treefrogs, once restricted primarily to the Coastal Plain region in Georgia, have been expanding their range northward in recent decades and can now be found throughout much of the Piedmont. They inhabit a variety of wetland and mesic environments, including bottomland hardwood forests, river swamps, Carolina bays, cypress ponds, beaver swamps, and mesic hardwood forests adjacent to ponds (Rothermel 2008).

The green treefrog has a distinctive call that has been described by some as resembling a duck's quack and by others as a nasal bark or bell-like sound (Conant and Collins 1998). During the breeding season male frogs generally begin calling for mates just before dusk on warm, humid evenings, and these choruses may last for several hours. They may also begin calling well before dusk, especially just before and during summer thunderstorms. For this reason the green treefrog is known by some as the "rain frog" (Conant and Collins 1998).

Food sources include moth and beetle larvae, crickets, bugs, flies, and beetles. Predators of green treefrogs include fish and aquatic insects (for tadpoles), watersnakes, raptors, crows, and other birds.

Atamasco lily

The Monticello Glades of the Oconee National Forest

The Monticello Glades are a superb expression of Piedmont flatwoods. They occur on Iredell soils, which form over gabbro bedrock. The clays in the soils swell when they are wet, forming an impermeable layer that ponds water in winter and late spring. In the summer, as plants transpire greater amounts of water, the soils are much drier and shrink. Plant diversity is high, including Coastal Plain and Piedmont plants, hydric- and mesic-adapted plants, plants that prefer circumneutral soils, and many generalists. In April, the water is still ponded and swaths of Atamasco-lilies, eastern redbud, flowering dogwood, and hawthorns are in bloom. Drifts of saw palmetto, along with pars-

ley haw and buckthorn bumelia, provide a Coastal Plain feel to this scenic landscape.

Monticello Glades covers several acres, with hydric areas that are interwoven with mesic sites, so that a nearly imperceptible gradient of hydric to mesic species occurs. Trees include willow oak, red maple, white oak, pignut hickory, mockernut hickory, Carolina shagbark hickory, red hickory, sweet gum, post oak, American beech, shortleaf pine, flowering dogwood, southern sugar maple, eastern redbud, ironwood, American elm, slippery elm, winged elm, Shumard oak, green ash, white ash, eastern red cedar, chalk maple, red mulberry, and southern hackberry. The state-protected Oglethorpe oak also grows here. Shrubs and woody vines include mayberry, fringetree, coral honeysuckle, muscadine, Virginia-creeper, American rattan, greenbriers, and poison ivy. The diverse ground cover includes violet wood-sorrel, blue-stars, southern twayblade, spring-beauty, false garlic, Christmas fern, melic grass, river oats, adder's-tongue fern, and hairy buttercup. Resurrection fern grows on some trees. Numerous other species occur as the natural community grades into floodplain and bottomland and mesic forest natural communities.

Location: From Ga. Hwy. 83 in Monticello, take Ga. 11/Hillsboro St./Macon Rd. south about 4.3 miles. Turn right (west) at Feldspar Rd. and proceed about 0.4 mile. Park on the right-hand side of the road, opposite the feldspar trailings pond. From there, walk north-northeast, crossing the railroad tracks, about 0.35 mile, to the flatwoods. Google Earth GPS approximate coordinates for the "heart" of the glades (some of the wettest flats): N 33.254714/W 083.681722. There is no designated trail.

Seepage Wetlands

Seepage wetlands are saturated for at least part of the year, and typically water is moving imperceptibly toward a stream or draw. These form in many ways. At the edges of stream banks, groundwater enters the stream in slow trickles. At the base of slopes, groundwater is transported to the soil's surface with the abrupt change in gradient. Striking examples of gradient-change seep areas occur in the Pine Mountain area (Harris, Meriwether, and Upson Counties), where water percolates through quartzite and emerges at the base of cliffs or steep slopes, often onto colluvial flats (see the Featured Place for cliffs, bluffs, and outcrops). Seeps also occur in more gently sloping areas where shallow soils overlie bedrock: on rock outcrops in the Piedmont, for example, seeps occur where soils adjoin bare rock. Seepage plants include green ash, red maple, tulip-tree, southern wild raisin, cinnamon fern,

royal fern, orange jewelweed, cutleaf coneflower, and lizard's-tail. Seeps are often shaded by adjoining forest, but in a few cases they are open and herb-dominated.

Usually, Piedmont seeps occur as a small patch community encompassing no more than a few hundred square feet and often far less. Occasionally, however, they may be up to an acre in size. Seep communities are rarer than they once were for many reasons: many have been obliterated by development; others have been trampled and overgrazed by livestock, damaged by off-road vehicles, flooded by impoundments, or ditched and drained for agriculture.

PHYSICAL SETTING AND ECOLOGY

As described above, seepage areas occur where there are breaks in a slope or joints within rocks that channel water to the surface, resulting in a slow flow of water downhill. The soils of seepage wetlands vary in texture: they can be sandy or gravelly on steeper slopes where faster seepage flow winnows out clays and silts,

Water is seeping from the soil onto the bare rock.

leaving heavier soil particles, such as sands, behind. Often clays can collect at the base of slopes, on gentle slopes, or on terraces (former floodplains).

Nutrient levels vary with the nature of the bedrock and colluvium through which the seepage water flows. Most sites in the Piedmont are fairly acidic; seeps moving through calcium-rich areas will support more calciphitic plants and have greater species diversity.

Usually, trees provide at least partial shade to seepage areas, although prolonged high moisture levels may constrain tree establishment in some sites. Openings in the tree canopy or fluctuations in water level may occasionally shift species dominance, but these communities are probably fairly stable (Schafale and Weakley 1990). Fires are rare in these hydric areas.

VEGETATION

Wetland tree species such as red maple, water oak, tuliptree, and sweet gum often dominate. Shrubs include tag alder, southern wild raisin, poison sumac, horsesugar, Virginia-willow, yellowroot, silky dogwood, and but-

tonbush; herbs include monkey-face orchid, lizard's-tail, orange jewelweed, cowbane, cinnamon fern, royal fern, false-nettle, cutleaf coneflower, soapwort gentian, kidney-leaved grass-of-Parnassus, white turtlehead, arrowhead, cardinal flower, netted chain fern, New York fern, tassel-rue, common groundnut, sedges, river cane, and bulrushes. The composition can vary greatly from site to site. For example, a dense cover of ferns is present in one Currahee Mountain seepage area (Stephens County), while a broad, marsh-like habitat occurs on Burks Mountain (Columbia County). Seepage areas on streamside slopes on Pine Mountain (Harris and Meriwether Counties) support several species typically associated with the Coastal Plain, such as ti-ti, gall-berry, and sweet bay (described in the Featured Place for the cliff, bluff, and outcrop natural community on page 324). These are mixed in with more northern species, such as mountain laurel and galax, as well as typical Piedmont seepage species. When fire was more common, some seepage areas on floodplains may have hosted canebrakes.

Orange jewelweed

Cardinal flower

The nutrients within the substrate through which the seep flows also affect the composition of vegetation. On Burks Mountain (Columbia County), both the southerly location and the circumneutral soils contribute to unusual assemblages that include dwarf palmetto, which is primarily a Coastal Plain species, as well as green fringed orchid, which is typically found farther north over circumneutral soils. On Soapstone Mountain (Banks County), in the northernmost Piedmont, high base levels in a seepage wetland area support Virginia mountain-mint and eastern ninebark along with typical seepage plants (Cruse 1997). It is likely that seeps occurring over marble or other base-rich substrate in the Brevard Fault have some calciphiles, but more exploration is needed.

Seeps on granite outcrops may support Piedmont quillwort, monkey-flowers, arrowhead, cardinal flower, orange jewelweed, and common marsh-pink, as well as a few unusual wetland species, including several plants that are more common to the Coastal Plain, such as the peat moss *Sphagnum cyclophyllum*, flatrock pimpernel, and bladderworts (Wyatt and Allison 2000). Other interesting species found on the granite outcrop seeps include false-pimpernel, horned bladderwort, and yellow-eyed grass (Wyatt and Allison 2000; Nourse and Nourse 2007).

CHARACTERISTIC PLANTS OF SEEPAGE WETLANDS

TREES

Red maple—*Acer rubrum*
Sweet gum—*Liquidambar styraciflua*
Tulip-tree—*Liriodendron tulipifera*

SHRUBS AND WOODY VINES

Tag alder—*Alnus serrulata*
Silky dogwood—*Cornus amomum*
Possum-haw—*Ilex decidua*
Winterberry—*Ilex verticillata*
Virginia-willow—*Itea virginica*
Common elderberry—*Sambucus canadensis*
American snowbell—*Styrax americanus*
Southern wild raisin—*Viburnum nudum*

GROUND COVER

Common groundnut—*Apios americana*
Sedges—*Carex* spp.
Soapwort gentian—*Gentiana saponaria*
Orange jewelweed—*Impatiens capensis*
Cardinal flower—*Lobelia cardinalis*
Bugleweeds—*Lycopus* spp.
Monkey-flowers—*Mimulus* spp.
Royal fern—*Osmunda regalis*
Cinnamon fern—*Osmundastrum cinnamomeum*
Cowbane—*Oxypolis rigidior*
Kidney-leaved grass-of-Parnassas—*Parnassia asarifolia*
Small green wood orchid—*Platanthera clavellata*
Cutleaf coneflower—*Rudbeckia laciniata*
Arrowheads—*Sagittaria* spp.
Lizard's-tail—*Saururus cernuus*
Tassel-rue—*Trautvetteria caroliniensis*
Netted chain fern—*Woodwardia areolata*
Atamasco-lily—*Zephyranthes atamasca*

ANIMALS

These sites are not large enough to support a unique mammalian fauna; mammals from surrounding mesic forest or nearby bottomlands pass through and likely utilize shallow pools in this environment as water resources. Characteristic birds include the ruby-throated hummingbird, which often feeds on the nectar of orange jewelweed found in these seepage wetlands and nests in adjacent forest (see the Featured Animal). Patches of shrubs provide nest sites for the common yellowthroat and gray catbird (T. M. Schneider et al. 2010). In winter, the swamp sparrow will take up residence in these wetlands, using brushy and grassy areas (Mowbray 1997). Red-eyed vireo may occur in forested seepage areas.

These areas are excellent amphibian habitats. The spotted dusky salamander tends to be abundant in seepage areas, provided cover is available in the form of coarse woody debris or rocks. Individuals leave such sites at night to forage on insects. This species is replaced by the ecologically similar Ocoee salamander along the Dahlonega Plateau and in the adjacent Brevard Fault zone (Floyd and Camp 2008). The seal salamander, a related but larger species, occurs in seepages along the Dahlonega Plateau and in the western Piedmont. The seepage salamander is one of Georgia's smallest salamanders and occurs locally in the leaf litter zones of deciduous forests near seepages in the topographically diverse Brevard Fault zone and possibly in the western Piedmont (Harrison 2005). The three-lined salamander is a typical resident, and southern two-lined salamanders often breed in such sites, the females attaching eggs to the undersurfaces of rocks, sticks, or vegetative debris. Along the Dahlonega Plateau and in the Brevard Fault zone, there is a narrow zone of sympatry between the southern two-lined and the Blue Ridge two-lined salamander, the former reproducing in small montane seepages and the latter occurring in seepages of more lowland character (Camp et al. 2000). The red salamander is fairly common, and the spring salamander, which preys on other salamanders, occurs occasionally. Boggy sites form ideal habitat for four-toed salamanders, which commonly lay eggs as part of communal nests in or under rotting logs at the water's edge. Upland chorus frogs and a few spring peepers may breed in shallow, vegetated seepages. Pickerel frogs, southern leopard frogs, and northern cricket frogs are all common residents in sites with small pools. Among reptiles, northern watersnakes, common garter snakes, and eastern ribbon snakes often forage in these areas in search of amphibian prey.

Ruby-Throated Hummingbird (*Archilochus colubris*)

The ruby-throated hummingbird is seen throughout Georgia in the spring, summer, and early fall, often frequenting gardens and hummingbird feeders. It is the only hummingbird known to breed in the eastern United States (Beaton, Sykes, and Parrish 2003). This tiny (3.75 inches long) bird is brilliant metallic green on its back. Males have black chins and deep red throats, while females have whitish throats. Hummingbirds are known for their aerial acrobatics; they can fly very straight and fast but can also stop abruptly and move up, down, or backward with great precision. They feed on nectar as well as insects collected from spider webs, captured in the air, or extracted from flowers (Burleigh 1958; T. W. Johnson 2010a).

Forested seeps are excellent habitats for these birds because trees bordering the seeps provide shelter and nesting opportunities while flowering plants and insects in these wetlands serve as sources of food. Hum-mingbirds visit sunny seeps to feed on flower nectar, creating an audible buzz while darting from flower to flower. They embark on roughly 14–18 foraging trips per hour, each bout lasting less than a minute. Between foraging events, they perch quietly for about four minutes, while their crop half empties (Ehrlich, Dubkin, and Wheye 1988).

In Georgia, the breeding season begins in late March or early April with the arrival of males from wintering grounds in Central America, south Mexico, and southern Florida. Females arrive 1 or 2 weeks later and begin constructing tiny nests 6 to 45 feet above the ground on horizontal tree branches. The nest is made of plant materials reinforced with spider webs and is covered in lichens (Robinson, Sargent, and Sargent 1996). Two broods of one to two young are normally produced each year in Georgia. The ruby-throated hummingbird is globally secure and may have increased in abundance in recent decades due to the popularity of hummingbird feeders (T. W. Johnson 2010a).

Dawson Forest Wildlife Management Area

Numerous seepage plant assemblages occur in the Dawson Forest Wildlife Management Area, affording an excellent opportunity to see how seeps vary over the landscape. An easily accessible trail for viewing seeps starts at the bottom of the parking area. Several hundred yards from the trailhead, a seepage area occurs near the bridge foundation, with false-nettle, yellowroot, river cane, and orange jewelweed. Past the bridge, seepages near the river host cinnamon fern, cutleaf coneflower, common groundnut, downy lobelia, and New York fern. Proceeding along the trail, a well-drained riparian area appears on the right (soil cores to 3 feet reveal a sandy soil), which supports river birch, witch-hazel, white pine, sweet gum, and heaths, while on the left, mesic and seepage areas are interspersed. Areas of cinnamon fern are underlain by gleyed soils at 2 feet. A spring seep at the base of the slope roughly 50 feet from the trail hosts sphagnum moss, winterberry, cinnamon fern, and white turtlehead. An overlook on the trail occurs near additional seepy areas that support winterberry, common groundnut, bamboo-vine, tag alder, and mountain doghobble. Proceeding along the trail, a right-hand fork leads to a rocky, scenic stretch of shoals in the Amicolola River. Seepage areas by the river and among the rocks support tag alder, hollow-stem Joe-pye-weed, maleberry, black gum, and orange jewelweed.

Returning to the trail fork, the main trail enters an upland forest, with several seepage areas occurring along this trail, featuring royal fern, bugleweed, southern lady fern, river cane, climbing hydrangea, cross-vine, white turtlehead, soapwort gentian, Jack-in-the-pulpit, foamflower, small green wood orchid, netted chain fern, orange jewelweed, southern wild raisin, winterberry, New York fern, and, at the last stream before the trail begins an inexorable upward climb, kidney-leaved grass-of-Parnassas.

Location: From the intersection of Ga. Hwy. 9 and Shoal Creek Rd. in downtown Dawsonville, proceed west on Ga. Hwy. 53/Main St./Jasper St. for about 6 miles. The parking area is on the right side of the road. Proceed down the stairs from the parking area, to the start of the trailhead, which begins along the Amicalola River. Google Earth GPS approximate coordinates: N 34.426300/W 084.212140.

Floodplains, Bottomlands, and Riparian Zones

Piedmont floodplain forests are found in low-lying areas along large creeks and rivers. They are at least occasionally flooded, and are characterized by trees that can grow to maturity on soils that are saturated for limited periods of time, including cherrybark oak, swamp chestnut oak, Shumard oak, overcup oak, sweet gum, red maple, water oak, tulip-tree, green ash, and box elder (Wharton 1978; Schafale and Weakley 1990; Sharitz and Mitsch 1993).

Although somewhat limited in extent on the Piedmont compared with the Coastal Plain, floodplain forests can be lush and diverse natural communities, with rich, moist soils and many layers of vegetation. The structural and compositional diversity, as well as the proximity to water, provide habitat and food for many bird and mammal species; they are arguably one of the most diverse environments of the Piedmont (M. A. Godfrey 1997). Because of the moist soils, which protect against fire and drought, it is likely that

in natural conditions the bottomlands would support many large, old-growth trees, with pioneer trees appearing in gaps and along the most geomorphically active areas of the river channel (Malanson 1993; Sharitz and Mitsch 1993; Christensen 2000).

The rich, moist soils and flat, valley bottom locations make bottomlands ideal for human habitation and development. Few to none of the streams in the Georgia Piedmont are in pristine shape; rather, they are responding to severe human impacts that have occurred, particularly in the times since European settlement. Indeed, the changes in Piedmont streams over the past two centuries are among the most far-reaching examples of human impact on the state's natural communities. Both Native Americans and European settlers altered floodplains, although the latter had a far greater impact (see p. 264).

PHYSICAL SETTING AND ECOLOGY

Depending on the numerous factors described on p. 260, some stretches of rivers and large creeks have large, well-developed sandy point bars and floodplains, while others have rocky shoals and borders. Ex-

Some of the larger Piedmont rivers have stretches with well-developed floodplain topography, such as the large point bar shown here.

amples of the latter can be seen on the Flint, Chattahoochee, Apalachee, Ocmulgee, Savannah, and Broad Rivers. Levees are well developed along some river stretches, such as along portions of the Oconee near Athens, the Ocmulgee near Scull Shoals Historic Site, and the Chattahoochee River near the Chattahoochee Nature Center. Some streams are downcutting rapidly, with essentially no developed floodplain, while others are still aggrading in some stretches. Some terraces—flat areas characterized by fairly steep sides that form as a stream downcuts (see diagram on p. 265)—are too high to be affected by frequent floods and are classified as Piedmont mesic forest natural communities. Many others still support hydric or mesic-hydric species and are included here.

The two main controls on vegetation composition and structure are the mechanical damage imposed by flooding and the moisture regime of a site. These factors lead to a somewhat zonal vegetation pattern, from the geomorphically active stream channel to the infre-

quently flooded areas farthest from the stream, as described on the following pages.

The land use history of these sites is another important factor. As noted, many bottomland sites were cleared and farmed by Native Americans, followed by intensive cultivation by European settlers for centuries. Domestic pigs and cattle, as well as deer, have long browsed and grazed on these sites. Seedbanks have been plowed up; most bottomlands are broader and higher than they once were because sediments eroded from upland sites buried the bottoms of the hillslopes bordering some streams, as described on page 264. Now, as streams downcut rapidly, the terraces on either side are becoming mesic rather than hydric.

In many cases, Chinese privet has taken over these bottomland sites, greatly reducing the diversity of native species. All of these changes create challenges to restoration efforts. Such physically altered sites cannot be returned to pre-settlement conditions, and revegetation may be limited by depauperate seedbanks and

River cane growing on an inactive bottomland

scarce propagule sources. Knowledge about floodplain and bottomland restoration (particularly where Chinese privet occurs) will continue to evolve (Hanula, Horn, and Taylor 2009).

VEGETATION

There are three main vegetation assemblage types within this natural community, often occurring on a fine scale in close and overlapping proximity to one another: (1) geomorphically active areas along the channel; (2) less geomorphically active areas on bottomland sites; and (3) small, narrow bottomlands that occur along small streams.

Geomorphically Active Areas (Riparian Zones). Vegetation composition on very active, frequently flooded sites (such as the point bar shown in the photo on p. 338) is limited to those pioneer species that can withstand mechanical damage, are favored by high levels of sunlight, can grow rapidly between distur-

bance events, and are able to withstand the anaerobic conditions that accompany periods of floodwater inundation. Trees that grow in these conditions include river birch, sycamore, some hawthorns, black willow, water hickory, sweet gum, cottonwood, water oak, box elder, green ash, and black willow. Shade-tolerant species that can also appear include sugarberry, American elm, and red maple. Black willow can survive on very actively reworked areas. It can withstand breakage, and, indeed, broken stems are capable of being transported downstream and rooting in sediments there. Cottonwood also occurs on these highly disturbed areas. Both are pioneer species with light, wind-dispersed seeds, the ability to resprout rapidly between flood events, and tolerance to flooded conditions (Sharitz and Mitsch 1993).

The canopy along streambanks is more open and the shrub layer is denser than that of the forests behind them because of the mechanical forces imposed by the flooding. Trees are frequently snapped by floodwaters and resprout after damage, so many are multi-trunked. Others are bent low to the ground with a single strong root anchoring them or lean precipitously at low angles over the water. Tree roots are frequently exposed and sprawl along the ground.

Shrubs that can sway and bend with the floodwaters are common and dominate some sites. They include buttonbush, swamp dogwood, Virginia-willow, swamp rose, and common elderberry. Tangles of vines sprawling over shrubs, herbs, and saplings are common within the many openings caused by the trees that have fallen during floods. Characteristic vines include trumpet-creeper, cross-vine, climbing hydrangea, grapes, Virginia-creeper, and poison ivy (Wharton 1978). Herbs often cover large patches and anchor the soils. Common taxa include sedges, rushes, witchgrasses, wingstems, knotweeds, and orange jewelweeds (Wharton 1978; Schafale and Weakley 1990). In somewhat protected areas, such as areas between rocks or on some low banks, ferns such as royal fern and lady fern appear.

Less Geomorphically Active Bottomland Areas (Floodplains and Bottomlands). Away from the most active areas, the tree canopy becomes more closed, and species that are less able to withstand mechanical damage become more prominent. In areas that have been out of cultivation for a long time, hydric and hydric-mesic oak species, such as cherrybark oak, swamp chestnut oak, overcup oak, Shumard oak, willow oak, and water oak occur. Other species that occur with the oaks include green ash, slippery elm, winged elm, black walnut, honey locust, bitternut hickory, sweet bay, and tulip-tree. Bottomlands with well-developed oak canopies are fairly rare in the Georgia Piedmont, although they can be found scattered along the Oconee, Alcovy, Ocumulgee, and Flint Rivers. Far more common are early successional forests, with cohorts of younger trees that have sprung up following agriculture or clearcutting, including sweet gum, southern hackberry, loblolly pine, tulip-tree, green ash, box elder, and red maple; the Oconee River at the State Botanical Garden supports a good example of this (Wharton 1998). Mesic sites may include white oak, American beech, basswood, and southern sugar maple. Often these species will interfinger on a fine scale within the bottomland, making the transition from hydric to mesic sites nearly imperceptible. A very few bottomlands in the Georgia Piedmont support southern catalpa (seen

A narrow stream bordered by a natural community that is transitional between the mesic forest and floodplain, bottomland, and riparian zone natural communities

on streambanks as well), water tupelo, and/or sweet bay (Wharton 1978). Notable Piedmont examples of water tupelo stands can be found in the Alcovy and Flint River systems.

The subcanopy of many bottomland sites will include common silverbell, musclewood, ironwood, sugarberry, common pawpaw, red mulberry, silky dogwood, and alternate-leaf dogwood. Shrubs may include patches of river cane, yellowroot, spicebush, American beautyberry, American hazelnut, Piedmont azalea, and southern black haw. Woody vines are an important component and include poison ivy, poison oak, Virginia-creeper, climbing hydrangea, cross-vine, trumpet-vine, climbing dogbane, grapes, and greenbriers.

The herbaceous layer can be diverse in areas and nearly barren in others and will vary from mesic species to hydric ones depending on the microsite. Ground

CHARACTERISTIC PLANTS OF FLOODPLAINS, BOTTOMLANDS, AND RIPARIAN ZONES

TREES

Box elder—Acer negundo
Red maple—Acer rubrum
River birch—Betula nigra
Musclewood—Carpinus caroliniana
Southern hackberry—Celtis laevigata
Green ash—Fraxinus pennsylvanica
Sweet gum—Liquidambar styraciflua
Tulip-tree—Liriodendron tulipifera
Sycamore—Platanus occidentalis
Swamp chestnut oak—Quercus
    michauxii
Water oak—Quercus nigra
Cherrybark oak—Quercus pagoda
Black willow—Salix nigra

SHRUBS AND WOODY VINES

Tag alder—Alnus serrulata
Cross-vine—Bignonia capreolata
Buttonbush—Cephalanthus occidentalis
Climbing hydrangea—Decumaria
    barbara
Virginia-willow—Itea virginica
Spicebush—Lindera benzoin
Swamp azalea—Rhododendron viscosum
Yellowroot—Xanthorhiza simplicissima

GROUND COVER

River cane—Arundinaria gigantea
False-nettle—Boehmeria cylindrica
Sedges—Carex spp.
River oats—Chasmanthium latifolium
Orange jewelweed—Impatiens capensis
Rushes—Juncus spp.
Cardinal flower—Lobelia cardinalis
Sensitive fern—Onoclea sensibilis
Royal fern—Osmunda regalis
Cinnamon fern—Osmundastrum
    cinnamomeum
Green arrow-arum—Peltandra virginica
Cutleaf coneflower—Rudbeckia
    laciniata
Broadleaf arrowhead—Sagittaria
    latifolia
Lizard's-tail—Saururus cernuus
Netted chain fern—Woodwardia
    areolata
Atamasco-lily—Zephyranthes atamasca

cover includes cutleaf coneflower, orange jewelweed, broadleaf arrowhead, river cane, river oats, cinnamon fern, cardinal flower, green arrow-arum, royal fern, Atamasco-lily, lizard's-tail, false-nettle, wingstems, climbing hempweed, netted chain fern, and many sedges, rushes, and grasses. Where the terrain becomes more mesic, herbs typical of mesic forests will be common.

Narrow Small Stream Bottomlands. These areas occur on narrow floodplains with a steep gradient, typically along first-order streams (small streams with no tributaries) but occasionally are found on larger streams. These sites are only briefly and rarely flooded and are transitional between the floodplain and bottomland and mesic forest natural communities. The canopy can include a mixture of sweet gum, tulip-tree, red maple, green ash, and black gum. Other species that may be present are white oak, northern red oak, sycamore, and American beech. The understory can include sourwood, ironwood, musclewood, American holly, black cherry, and flowering dogwood. The shrub layer can include witch-hazel, strawberry-bush, southern wild raisin, Piedmont azalea, and mountain doghobble. The herbaceous layer is typically well developed. New York fern, south-

ern lady fern, Christmas fern, Jack-in-the-pulpit, and Solomon's-plume are some of the common species that can be found in these briefly flooded environments (Govus 2003b).

Many small streams have broad terraces caused by the erosion of the uplands and subsequent deposition in the stream valley. These terraces will have the same vegetation as the less geomorphically active bottomland sites described above.

ANIMALS

This natural community is rich in wildlife. Bats include the big brown, eastern pipistrelle, evening, hoary, and little brown, which will roost under the loose bark of trees in the bottomlands and floodplains. Minks den under the roots of trees near streams. They feed on fish, crawfish, insects, frogs, snails, young turtles, birds, eggs, snakes, and a variety of mammals. River otters also den in the river bank and eat many of the same animals, with a strong preference for fish. They utilize stream banks as chutes to slide down riverbanks head first into the water (L. Brown 1997; Fergus 2003). Muskrats den in burrows excavated in stream banks. They are omnivorous, feeding on a wide variety of aquatic plants as well as crayfish, fish, frogs, and insects, and are preyed on by mink and river otter

(L. Brown 1997; Fergus 2003). Other native mammals of floodplains include raccoon, beaver, gray squirrel, golden mouse, deer mouse, meadow vole, rice rat, hispid cotton rat, swamp rabbit, gray fox, bobcat, short-tailed shrew, eastern mole, and opossum. Though no self-sustaining populations of black bear are known in this region, individuals from the Blue Ridge often use Piedmont river floodplains as dispersal corridors.

This natural community also supports a diverse community of birds because of the food sources and habitats associated with the aquatic-upland ecotones here (Edwards 2010). The dense vine tangles that occur in these forests are preferred nesting sites for the American redstart. When beard moss or Spanish-moss are plentiful, the northern parula often nests in these forests. Dense patches of shrubs provide nesting and foraging sites for the white-eyed vireo and common yellowthroat, and both of these species can be common here (T. M. Schneider et al. 2010). The yellow-billed cuckoo and hooded warbler often nest in canopy gaps with dense shrubs, often along a creek or river (Evans, Ogden, and Stutchbury 1994; Hughes 1999).

Several species are only found along rivers and streams and in associated forests. Clean, shallow streams provide foraging habitat for the Louisiana waterthrush, which feeds on aquatic invertebrates found in stream riffles and pools. This species nests in crevices in the stream bank. Another common riparian species, the Acadian flycatcher, constructs a flimsy nest in bottomland forest, often directly over a stream. Where floodplains widen, dense understory thickets of cane or privet provide feeding and nesting habitat for Swainson's and Kentucky warblers. More interior areas of these forests often have nesting northern parulas, great-crested flycatchers, and eastern wood-pewees. Areas that have snags, tree cavities, and standing water often provide nesting habitat for the prothonotary warbler (Jensen 2010). During migration, many species move through Georgia using these forested stream corridors as avian highways. Migrants such as the Canada warbler, the chestnut-sided warbler, and occasionally the yellow-bellied flycatcher are just a few of these species.

Many reptiles and amphibians also occur in bottomlands and floodplains. The combination of mesic conditions, friable soil, and abundant coarse woody debris offered by many floodplains provides ideal habitat for both fossorial and terrestrial salamanders.

Southern two-lined and three-lined salamanders are abundant. Red salamanders, marbled salamanders, spotted salamanders, and four-toed salamanders are frequent residents, although they may be infrequently encountered due to their fossorial (burrowing) nature. Mud salamanders and mole salamanders occur spottily across the Piedmont, both species being more abundant in the Coastal Plain (Wharton 1978). Spotted dusky salamanders often find cover along the edges of pools or seepages. The terrestrial eft stage of the eastern newt may be seen wandering along the forest floor, while adults live in floodplain pools, especially those that are semipermanent (Stevenson and Camp 2008). Several fossorial frogs, including Fowler's toad, eastern narrow-mouthed toad, and eastern spadefoot, dig in the sandy substrates and breed in floodplain pools. Narrow-mouthed toads and spadefoots tend to breed in simultaneous pulses evoked by heavy rain and have been dubbed "explosive breeders." Cope's gray tree-frogs breed in storm-created pools during summer (Greer 2008). The secretive terrestrial wood frog breeds in the Flint River floodplain in Upson County; it is likely present in other Piedmont floodplains, particularly in the western half of the state. Bird-voiced treefrogs occur locally in floodplains that have fairly permanent pools such as along the Alcovy River in Newton County (Wharton 1978). Upland chorus frogs and spring peepers breed in small, shallow pools and larger, semipermanent pools, respectively. Northern cricket frogs and southern leopard frogs are common and may be seen wandering across the floodplain, while green frogs and bullfrogs remain along the river's edge or around semipermanent pools.

Northern watersnake, redbelly watersnake, brown watersnake, and queen snake are abundant along Piedmont rivers and can be seen lying on banks, on downed trees, or in overhanging vegetation along the river's edge (Gibbons and Dorcas 2004). Aquatic turtles that occasionally wander into the floodplains include both bottom-dwelling (e.g., snapping turtles, eastern mud turtles, and common musk turtles) and basking (e.g., painted turtles and pond sliders) species (Wharton 1978). Some riverine turtles, such as river cooters, spiny softshells, loggerhead musk turtles, and, on the Flint and Chattahoochee Rivers, Barbour's map turtles, rarely leave the rivers except to nest, which they do on higher terraces or sand bars. As it is in other mesic forests, the eastern box turtle is a common terrestrial resident.

Broad River Burrowing Crayfish (*Distocambarus devexus*) and Piedmont Blue Burrower (*Cambarus harti*)

The Broad River burrowing crayfish was described as a species in 1981 (Hobbs 1981). This crayfish constructs and lives in simple or complex burrows in wet areas near streams. Though designated a primary burrower (as distinguished from a stream-dwelling crayfish), this crayfish species has also been collected from temporary pools within floodplains. Very little is known about the behavior of this secretive crayfish.

As its common name suggests, this species is apparently restricted to the Broad River watershed of Georgia. It has been documented from five locations spanning three counties: Wilkes, Washington, and Elbert (Skelton et al. 2000). Because this species is usually confined to underground burrows, it is difficult to assess population levels within its range. It appears to be genuinely rare and is listed as critically imperiled. Threats to this species include land disturbance within its habitat, stream impoundments, and over-collection for the pet trade. This species is protected by state law in Georgia.

The Piedmont blue burrower, also described taxonomically in 1981, reaches a maximum size of about 3 inches. As its name suggests, its body coloration is a striking shade of deep blue. It lives in complex burrows adjacent to streams or in low areas where the water table is near the surface of the ground. The Piedmont blue burrower is known definitively from two localities in Meriwether County, Georgia. Skelton et al. (2000) found bluish crayfish specimens that may represent this species at six additional locations in Meriwether County, but none were males and thus the identifications are considered tentative (positive identification of crayfishes depends on examination of adult males). Because of its secretive nature, population levels within its restricted range are difficult to estimate, but this species is currently listed critically imperiled. Threats include destruction or degradation of habitat and over-collection for the pet trade. Like the Broad River burrowing crayfish, this species is protected in Georgia by state law.

Alcovy Conservation Center

The Alcovy Conservation Center is owned and managed by the Georgia Wildlife Federation. It offers an unparalleled example of a complex river bottomland natural community. Both Wharton (1978) and Radford and Martin (1975) acclaimed the Alcovy River swamps as among the most significant natural communities of the Piedmont region of the eastern United States, most particularly because of the rarity of mature water tupelo stands in this ecoregion. The trails through the floodplain have signposts identifying many bottomland species, including overcup oak, swamp chestnut oak, musclewood, cherrybark oak, willow oak, red maple, red mulberry, tulip-tree, green ash, sweet gum, and water tupelo.

This is a classic example of the complex mosaic of landforms that well-developed floodplains possess, with many swales, small creek channels, terraces, a levee, and a large bottomland swamp area. The swamp area is dominated by water tupelo with buttresses and knees and is particularly picturesque when water levels are high, mirroring the trees and sky. Other plants in the swamp include red maple, swamp chestnut oak, overcup oak, and willow oak. Throughout the low-lying bottomland, hydric to moist sites support

Virginia-willow, green arrow-arum, orange jewelweed, winterberry, bugleweeds, sweet gum, swamp tupelo, sensitive fern, spicebush, lizard's-tail, cutleaf coneflower, Atamasco-lily, river oats, hawthorns, marsh St. John's-wort, climbing hydrangea, and American elm. Green ash and river birch often overhang stream areas (Radford and Martin 1975; Wharton 1978).

Higher, well-drained areas interspersed within the floodplain often support American beech, musclewood, trumpet-creeper, southern sugar maple, sweet gum, bitternut hickory, loblolly pine, water oak, green ash, common pawpaw, and mayberry (Radford and Martin 1975; Wharton 1978). Dense stands of river cane cover some higher mounds. River cane also dominates the levee adjacent to the river, with an overstory of swamp chestnut oak, river birch, swamp tupelo, and southern sugar maple.

Location: From Atlanta take Exit 93 off I-20 to Hazelbrand Rd. Turn north off the exit ramp. Cross back over the interstate, and turn right onto Hazelbrand Rd. near the Home Depot. Travel approximately 1.5 miles. Cross over the Cornish Creek Bridge, and turn right into the driveway. Google Earth GPS approximate coordinates for the parking lot: N 33.62781/ W 083.798161.

Piedmont azalea

Chapter 6

COASTAL PLAIN ECOREGION

Overview

The Coastal Plain is Georgia's largest ecoregion, comprising more than half the area of the state. It lies south of the Fall Line. Roughly parallel bands of sediments occurring from the Fall Line to the eastern sea coast range in age from oldest (upper Cretaceous, 150 million years ago) to most recent at the present-day coastline. Since the Cretaceous period, the Atlantic Ocean and the Gulf of Mexico have advanced and retreated to expose overlapping and intermixed layers of sands and clays. The resulting terrain consists of relatively flat, broad plains situated between rivers, numerous wetlands and swamps, and areas of rolling hills. This vast landscape once promoted the spread of lightning-ignited and anthropogenic fires, fostering exceptionally diverse plant communities adapted to frequent fire. A radical increase in the extent and intensity of anthropogenic disturbance has occurred since European settlement, and most land is now devoted to tree farms and agriculture. Less than 2% of the formerly dominant longleaf pine forests remain, and many wetlands have been degraded by draining and filling. Nonetheless, some outstanding tracts of land remain that attest to the natural heritage of southern Georgia, and these remnant natural communities can provide inspiration and guidance for restoration and rehabilitation of altered ecosystems.

The longleaf pine forest—once the dominant upland vegetation type of the Coastal Plain

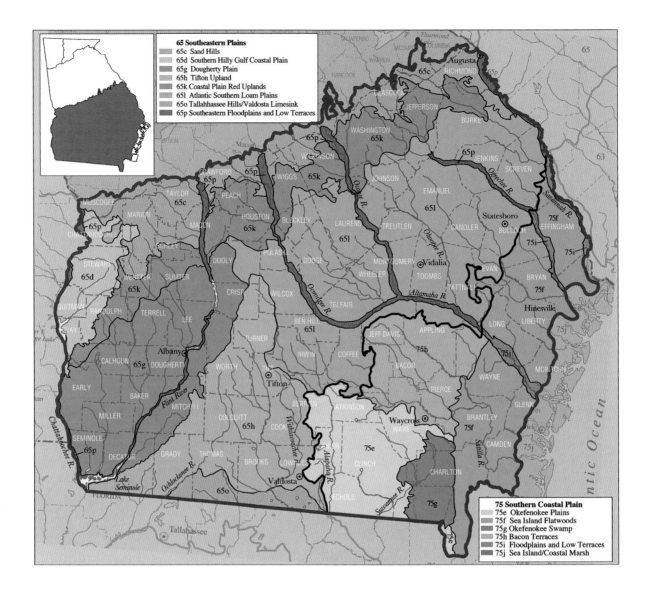

65 Southeastern Plains
- 65c Sand Hills
- 65d Southern Hilly Gulf Coastal Plain
- 65g Dougherty Plain
- 65h Tifton Upland
- 65k Coastal Plain Red Uplands
- 65l Atlantic Southern Loam Plains
- 65o Tallahassee Hills/Valdosta Limesink
- 65p Southeastern Floodplains and Low Terraces

75 Southern Coastal Plain
- 75e Okefenokee Plains
- 75f Sea Island Flatwoods
- 75g Okefenokee Swamp
- 75h Bacon Terraces
- 75i Floodplains and Low Terraces
- 75j Sea Island/Coastal Marsh

GEOLOGY, TOPOGRAPHY, AND SOILS

The Coastal Plain ecoregion occupies about 35,650 square miles in Georgia. Its boundary with the Piedmont ecoregion, the Fall Line, is a band about 20 miles wide stretching across the state from Columbus, through Macon and Milledgeville, to Augusta. This zone is named for the rapid fall of Piedmont rivers where they have cut downward through hard bedrock (weather-resistant crystalline clay and granite) to meet lower reaches in the loose sands of the Coastal Plain. The steep change in elevational gradient gives rise to rapids and waterfalls as streams cross this transition.

In Georgia, the Atlantic Coastal Plain transitions to the Gulf Coastal Plain with subtle differences in sedi-ment composition and topography. Some classification systems divide the region into an Atlantic Coastal Plain and a Gulf Coastal Plain based roughly on drainage areas of the Atlantic Ocean or Gulf of Mexico (The Nature Conservancy 1999). Others divide the region into an upper and lower Coastal Plain (G. E. Griffith et al. 2001; Environmental Protection Agency 2007). In this case, the lower Coastal Plain (or Southern Coastal Plain) refers to the lower elevation and nearly flat landscape composed of a series of terraces that reflect relatively recent sea-level positions. In contrast, the upper Coastal Plain (or Southeastern Plains) refers to the more highly dissected, rolling landscape of higher elevations. Because numerous plant communities overlap throughout the region, we consider the entire portion of the state that lies south of the Fall Line as one ecoregion. The tidally influenced portion of the Atlantic Coastal Plain is treated as the Maritime ecoregion in chapter 7.

In general, the most recently deposited soils of the flat and younger lower Coastal Plain are coarser and less weathered than those of the upper Coastal Plain. Still, many soil orders may be found within a distance of several hundred yards extending from uplands to rivers due to variation in topography and hydrology (Hubbard et al. 1985). Particularly in the Coastal Plain with its relatively low elevational gradient, the position and duration of the water table is an important property that influences soil development and nutrient availability, and in turn, vegetation development. Differences in histories of sea-level changes are reflected in topography and substrate that are well characterized as subregions of the Coastal Plain by Omernik (1987) and G. E. Griffith et al. (2001).

Fall Line Sandhills. The Fall Line Sandhills and adjacent Coastal Plain Red Uplands occupy the northernmost part of the Coastal Plain where Cretaceous sands overlap the crystalline rocks of the Piedmont. Along the lower edge of the Piedmont ecoregion, sediments weathered from the uplands were deposited near the shore and formed the Fall Line Sandhills, a narrow, hilly band of deep sands. This belt of red, yellow, and white sandy hills is about 50 miles wide south of Columbus and narrows to only 10 or 15 miles wide near Augusta. Elevations of the sandhills are similar to those in the Piedmont, with maximum hilltops up to 700 feet in western Georgia but only 400 to 500 feet in eastern Georgia. Stream valleys lie 50 to 250 feet below the adjacent ridge tops. As a result of the abrupt change at the Fall Line to a shallower elevational gradient and the presence of easily eroded sands, Piedmont rivers form large, swampy floodplains as they enter the Coastal Plain. Magnolia Swamp on the Flint River (Crawford and Taylor Counties), Bond Swamp on the Ocmulgee River (Bibbs and Twiggs Counties), and the Oconee River Swamp at Beaverdam Wildlife Management Area (Wilkinson County) are each 3 miles across, many times larger than any floodplains in the Piedmont.

Coastal Plain Red Uplands. These uplands forge a transitional area between the Fall Line Sandhills and subregions of lower relief. A dissected flat-topped plateau embedded within the Red Uplands occurs between the Flint and Ocmulgee Rivers in Peach, Houston, and Macon Counties and is sometimes called the Fort Valley Plateau (Clark and Zisa 1976). In this region, soils are derived from reddish Eocene sand and clay formations. Because the sea retreated and exposed these sediments millions of years ago, the soils are generally more highly weathered than those in the lower Coastal Plain. These ultisols are mostly well drained with a brown or reddish brown loamy or sandy surface layer and red clay-rich subsoils. Here a greater abundance of clay than that in surrounding areas has prevented erosion, although valley walls are still quite steep (50–150 feet deep). Calcareous soils with thin beds of limestone and dolomite are occasionally present, which foster a patchwork of natural prairie similar to that of the Black Belt of Alabama and Mississippi.

Southern Hilly Gulf Coastal Plain. The landscape of the Southern Hilly Gulf Coastal Plain of the western part of the state is characterized by irregular plains and gently rolling hills and soils developed over sand, clay, and marl formations. Throughout this region differential erosion has occurred, exposing various sediment formations at the surface with soils ranging from those dominated by acidic sands to those with more clay, silt, and/or calcium (Magilligan and Stamp 1997). These older soils are generally more highly weathered than those of the lower Coastal Plain.

Dougherty Plain. In the southwestern part of the state, the Dougherty Plain is a nearly level subregion, encompassing most of the Flint River drainage from Cordele, Georgia (Crisp County), to Lake Seminole at the Florida border. This subregion is sharply delineated toward the east by the base of the Pelham Escarpment, a slope of a 100-foot rise to the Tifton Uplands. From the Flint River, the Dougherty Plain slopes gently to the southwest, with elevations ranging from almost 300 feet in the northeast to less than 100 feet at Lake Seminole. The northwestern boundary is a gradual transition to the Fall Line Sandhills. The Dougherty Plain, with limestone near the soil surface, is characterized by karst topography, where numerous sinkholes and springs have developed across the nearly flat sandy plain. Upland soils are usually loams or sandy loam ultisols. The depth to an accumulated clayey layer varies widely and is a major factor in soil drainage. Rainfall infiltrates rapidly into the unconsolidated deposits, so small streams are uncommon; however, the region is notable for several large, southward-flowing tributaries of the Flint River, including Ichawaynochaway, Muckalee, Chickasawhatchee, and Kinchafoonee Creeks.

Tifton Uplands. The Tifton Uplands is a wedge-shaped district extending from the Florida state line to its northern apex at the juncture of Dooly, Crisp, and Wilcox Counties. Its western boundary is the base of the Pelham Escarpment on the Dougherty Plain. The eastern boundary follows the drainage divide between the Alapaha and Suwannee Rivers (Clark and Zisa 1976). The Tifton Uplands is underlain by sands and clays, and the topography consists of low, rolling hills that are extensively dissected by many small streams. Relief can be as great as 50 to 100 feet in the major stream valleys. Upland soils of the Tifton Uplands are well drained, brownish, and loamy ultisols, often with iron-rich or plinthic layers. Plinthite is found in weathered soils subjected to repeated wetting and drying due to a fluctuating water table. The wetting and drying sequesters iron oxides and hydroxides, eventually forming brick-red and orange iron concretions, nodules, and ironstone hardpans. Exposure of indurated (hardened) sandstone, referred to as Altamaha Grit, occurs as outcroppings in this region and extends into the Atlantic Southern Loam Plains. The clay subsoils are often sticky when wet.

Tallahassee Hills and Southern Limesink Region. An adjacent subdivision, the Tallahassee Hills, is distinguished from the Tifton Uplands by the presence of more rolling topography and deep ravines. The area around Moultrie and Thomasville is extensively dissected by tributaries of the Ochlockonee and Little Rivers. Despite similar geology, the lower drainage areas of the Withlacoochee and Alapaha Rivers are flatter and underlying limestone is closer to the surface. As a result, numerous large, round sinkhole depressions form lakes and ponds (Hubbell, Laessle, and Dickinson 1956). This area is referred to as the Southern Limesink Region (Veatch and Stephenson 1911). Grand Bay, including Banks Lake northeast of Valdosta, is the largest natural lake in Georgia, with an area of about 13,000 acres (The Nature Conservancy 2009). Both the Tallahassee Hills and the Southern Limesink Region have a rolling, hilly topography with ultisols characterized by reddish, weathered, clayey sands and sandy clays. Sandy and clayey flats occur between the blackwater streams and swamps and limesink ponds.

Atlantic Southern Loam Plains. This area, also called the Vidalia Uplands, is the largest ecoregional subdivision of the Coastal Plain, encompassing the entire area between the Ocmulgee River and the coastal terraces, except for the portion included in the Fall Line Sandhills. The boundary separating the southern edge of the Southern Loam Plains from the Bacon Terraces is the Altamaha drainage divide, a ridge that parallels the river only a few miles south of its course. The Southern Loam Plains is similar to the northern portion of the Tifton Uplands, having comparable geology and topography. The regional slope is to the southeast, with elevations ranging from 150 to 500 feet. The terrain is dissected by a well-developed dendritic drainage network with low, rounded hills and broad slopes between the streams. Some of the river banks are quite steep, for example, along the Savannah River in Burke County, the Ogeechee River south of Millen (Jenkins County), the Ohoopee River northeast of Vidalia (Toombs County), the Oconee River near Soperton (Treutlen County), and the Altamaha River in Jeff Davis County. Oval-shaped Carolina bays are found on this landscape between Waynesboro and the Ogeechee River (Burke County) and in eastern and southern Screven County. The soils of this subregion are primarily ultisols and are more finely textured (loamy) than the coarse, sandy soils of the adjacent Sea Islands and Flatwoods. The aeolian (wind-deposited) sand dunes positioned along the east side of the Ohoopee and Canoochee Rivers and other large streams are conspicuous environments that are easily identified on aerial photographs.

Floodplains and Low Terraces. The Floodplains and Low Terraces comprise a riverine region of large, sluggish rivers and backwaters with ponds, swamps, and oxbow lakes. This subregion includes the major river systems, such as the Chattahoochee, Flint, Ocmulgee, Oconee, Ogeechee, and Savannah, that originate in or cross the Piedmont. Floodplains are generally proportional to the size of the stream, except where they are deeply incised into limestone bedrock. Floodplain soils are often relatively recent in origin due to erosion and deposition and are classified as inceptisols because they lack a subsurface clay layer accumulated from horizons above.

Bacon Terraces. This subregion is a series of subtle, step-like terraces, representing the highest recognizable remnants of the ancient sea bottoms that form the coastal terraces parallel to the modern-day coastline (Clark and Zisa 1976). The subregion is essentially the drainage basin of the Satilla River, excluding the headwaters that lie in the Southern Loam Plains. It is sparsely dissected by few small streams, but is drained by several long, straight, parallel creeks. Wet flatwoods and bay swamps occupy portions of the flats between streams. An exceptionally large swamp complex extending over 100 square miles is east of Baxley in the headwaters of Little Satilla Creek.

Okefenokee Swamp and Okefenokee Plains. The Okefenokee Swamp and adjacent Plains are bounded by the Alapaha-Suwannee drainage divide on the west, Trail Ridge on the east, and the Satilla River on the north (Clark and Zisa 1976). This flat coastal terrace encompasses nearly the entire Suwannee River drainage basin, except for the small portion in the southeast drained by the St. Marys River. The Okefenokee Swamp is a 660-square-mile peat-filled swamp. Forested wetlands cover large portions of the sandy flats throughout the rest of the Okefenokee Plains. The land has very little relief or stream dissection and slopes gently from west to east. Soils are generally poorly drained.

Sea Island Flatwoods. The Sea Island Flatwoods encompass the entire lower coastal region of Georgia lying east of Statesboro (Bulloch County) and Jesup (Wayne County) and west of the Sea Islands/Coastal Marsh region. This area lies east of the Orangeburg Escarpment and consists of alternating bands of sandy ridges and sandy and clayey wet flatwoods. These features are the remnants of coastal islands and back barrier marshes that formed during fluctuating sea-level stands of the past two million years (Hoyt and Hails 1967). During the Pleistocene epoch, the seas advanced and retreated several times over the area, possibly in response to colder glacial and warmer interglacial episodes (Thieme 2006). These are young soils

with little differentiation in soil horizons to depths of 40 inches or more and are classified as entisols. The entisols vary greatly according to landform. The former barrier dunes and shorelines are dominated by coarse sands of the Pleistocene-Pliocene, which are deep, nutrient-poor sands that may be excessively drained in uplands. Wet entisols occur on landscapes that are nearly level and are often associated with salt marshes that have a high sulfur content. Formerly embayed areas are dominated by finer-textured loamy and clayey entisols. A prominent topographic feature is Trail Ridge, a 130-mile-long narrow sand ridge extending from Starke, Florida, nearly to the Altamaha River, which forms the abrupt eastern edge of the Okefenokee Swamp.

RIVER BASINS AND GROUNDWATER

River drainage patterns in Georgia are conspicuously altered as they cross the Fall Line into the Coastal Plain. Unconstrained by resistant bedrock, rivers meander in the unconsolidated sediments and form broad floodplains. The principal rivers of the Coastal Plain, originating in the Piedmont or Blue Ridge, are the Savannah, the Ogeechee, the Oconee, the Ocmulgee, the Flint, and the Chattahoochee. The Savannah and Ogeechee Rivers flow to the Atlantic Ocean. The Oconee and the Ocmulgee Rivers join to form the Altamaha River, which also empties into the Atlantic Ocean. The Flint and Chattahoochee Rivers converge at the Florida line, forming the Appalachicola River, which flows into the Gulf of Mexico.

The origins of the headwaters of rivers and streams that occur in the Coastal Plain are often used to distinguish river systems because the source can have a significant role in the water chemistry, stream velocity, and the amount of suspended and dissolved matter that is transported (J. L. Meyer 1990). Those originating and having a significant portion of their watershed area in the Piedmont are called "brownwater" or "alluvial" streams because they are laden with sediment derived from severe stream erosion in the Piedmont (see p. 264). Those originating in the Coastal Plain are called "blackwater" or "nonalluvial" because they are typically clear and stained the color of tea due to tannins leached from the streamside vegetation. Despite the seemingly straightforward definition, the designation can be confusing because stream channel morphology, water chemistry, and sediment transport functions can vary greatly within this region due to variations in geology, topography, and soils.

Low-gradient streams (those having little change in elevation per unit river length) that originate in the Coastal Plain have generally escaped impoundment for hydroelectric projects or use for sewage assimilation. Because of their beauty, several Coastal Plain rivers in Georgia have been listed in the Nationwide Rivers Inventory as significant free-flowing streams potentially deserving wild and scenic river designation. These include the Alapaha River, Canoochee River, Ebenezer Creek, Ichawaynochaway Creek, Kinchafoonee Creek, Little Ohoopee River, Muckalee Creek, Ochlockonee River, Ohoopee River, Satilla River, Spring Creek, and Withlacoochee River.

The sediment-laden Savannah River carries a large volume of water in the state. From its headwaters in the Blue Ridge Mountains of North Carolina, it traverses more than 300 miles to the eastern coast, forming most of the boundary between Georgia and South Carolina, with a basin of 10,577 square miles. It is impounded by three large lakes, Hartwell, Richard B. Russell, and Clark Hill (also known as Lake Thurmond). These impoundments have significantly modified the flooding regimes of this river, creating "pulsing" of daily flows and reducing the frequency and amplitude of flood events. As it crosses the Coastal Plain, the river becomes increasingly stained from the dissolved organic compounds of adjacent floodplains (Smock et al. 2005).

The Altamaha River, formed by the confluence of the Oconee and Ocmulgee Rivers, is known as "Georgia's Little Amazon." Its entire drainage basin lies within Georgia and represents nearly one-quarter of the state's area (14,200 square miles). The Altamaha is usually muddy with sediments transported by the Ocmulgee and Oconee Rivers, which originate in the Piedmont and foothills of the Blue Ridge, respectively. The major tributary of the Altamaha downstream of its confluence with the Oconee and Ocmulgee is the Ohoopee River; its clear, tea-colored water contrasts sharply with that of the Altamaha. Currently, there are no dams on the Altamaha River proper; however, numerous drinking-water supply reservoirs occur within the upper watershed and others have been proposed to meet rapidly increasing urban demands. As with the Savannah River, these upstream dams reduce the frequency and amplitude of floods, thereby disrupting the ecological connections between the river and its floodplain.

The Flint River is also contained entirely within the state, originating near Atlanta (at Hartsfield-Jackson International Airport) in the Piedmont ecoregion, and draining approximately 8,500 square miles. It has a long, narrow basin that flows southerly in a wide eastward arc to the Florida state line. It is one of 42 rivers in the mainland United States that has a free-flowing stretch greater than 125 miles long (Couch, Hopkins, and Hardy 1996). Both the Altamaha and the Flint Rivers have been declared as among the most threatened rivers in the United States by the American Rivers Association, based on their ecological significance and threats of water impoundments (American Rivers 2002, 2009). As the Flint River flows from the Piedmont into the upper Coastal Plain and encounters gentler, sandy terrain, it becomes broader and more sinuous. Farther downstream, it enters the Dougherty Plain, and the character of the river changes dramatically again because of the influence of the near-surface limestone. Below Montezuma, the muddy water is diluted by significant inputs from spring-fed water sources. Here it is hydraulically connected to the Floridan aquifer system, where it receives substantial amounts of ground water discharge (Torak et al. 1991). Its channel becomes less sinuous and is deeply incised through erosion and down-cutting into the limestone bedrock, resulting in steep bluffs along some sections. The Flint and the Chattahoochee Rivers join at the Florida boundary to form the Appalachicola River, which flows southward to the Gulf of Mexico. The Chattahoochee River is also deeply entrenched as it flows along the Georgia and Alabama boundary, and, consequently, few swamps have developed along this stretch of the river north of the Florida line. Several of the tributaries to the Chattahoochee form deep, narrow gorges near their confluence with the river, indicating a recent down-cutting of the river from that of more ancient base levels (LaForge et al. 1925). The Appalachicola/Chattahoochee/Flint River basin has been at the heart of a tristate (Georgia, Alabama, and Florida) water dispute for decades.

The Ogeechee River originates in the lower Piedmont ecoregion, just a few miles from the Coastal Plain, and is totally free-flowing as it meanders to the Atlantic. Like many Coastal Plain rivers, it is characterized by tea-colored water, sluggish flow, and low

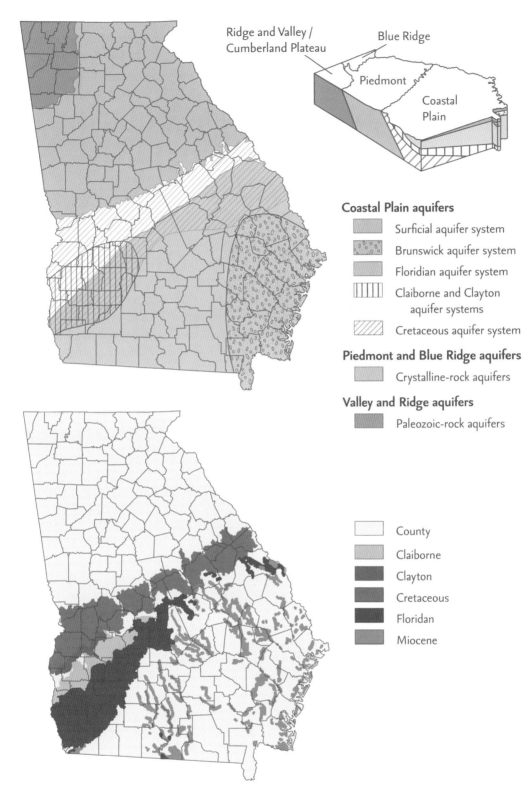

Aquifers of Georgia (TOP) and aquifer recharge areas of the Georgia Coastal Plain (BOTTOM).
Georgia Wildlife Federation, The Flint River. Georgia Wildlife Natural Georgia Series, Issue 7.
Georgia Wildlife Federation, 2002.

swamplands within its floodplain. Because it is not impounded, it exhibits a seasonal pattern of flow; in summer flows are extremely low, but in winter it frequently overflows its banks and substantial flooding can continue for weeks or months (Smock, Wright, and Benke 2005). Just upstream of the confluence with the Canoochee River, and approximately 30 miles from its mouth, the Ogeechee River becomes tidally influenced. Other sluggish, clear, tea-stained Coastal Plain rivers include the Satilla, the Suwannee, and the St. Marys. The Satilla River originates within the Bacon Terraces district of the lower Coastal Plain and flows generally southeastward to the Atlantic Ocean. The headwaters of the Suwanee River are tributary streams that feed into the Okefenokee Swamp; exiting the Okefenokee, the Suwanee flows southwestward through Florida to the Gulf of Mexico. Other streams within the larger Suwannee basin include the Alapaha and Withlacoochee Rivers, which originate in the Tifton Uplands and flow generally southward, joining the Suwannee River in Florida. Originating in the Okefenokee Swamp basin, the St. Marys River exits the swamp on its southeastern side, flowing in a circuitous route through a gap in the Trail Ridge, then eastward to the Atlantic Ocean.

Groundwater conditions in the Coastal Plain differ from those in the other ecoregions because of the unique geomorphology of the region. The unconsolidated porous and permeable sands and limestone layers are saturated with water. These below-ground water-bearing geological formations are called "aquifers." The principal aquifers of the Coastal Plain are, from shallowest to deepest, surficial aquifer, the upper and lower Brunswick aquifers, the upper and lower Floridan aquifers, the Claiborne aquifer, the Clayton aquifer, and the Cretaceous aquifer system (Peck et al. 1990). The surficial aquifer consists of rainfall that has infiltrated into the soil and sediments. The low relief and elevation allow the surficial aquifer, or water table, to be near the surface throughout much of the Coastal Plain; thus, this aquifer most strongly influences natural communities. This water flows laterally until it discharges into streams or the ocean. The water level of the surficial aquifer generally rises rapidly during wet periods and declines slowly during dry periods (Cressler 1998). It usually fluctuates seasonally, reflecting precipitation and evapotranspiration patterns in the Coastal Plain. It is generally highest during winter

when most plants are dormant and lowest in late summer when plants are most actively withdrawing water from the soil and transpiring it into the air. The surficial aquifer is sometimes augmented by upward discharge from deeper aquifers and overbank flooding from streams and rivers.

The thickness of the surficial aquifer increases toward the coast. Thus, areas of low relief in the lower Coastal Plain, such as pine flatwoods, are strongly influenced by the surficial aquifer. Locally, thin clay beds create confined or semiconfined conditions within the surficial aquifer, resulting in a saturated zone elevated above the water table. The surficial aquifer emerges laterally along lower portions of slopes, forming seeps where wetlands such as bogs develop. In the Fall Line Sandhills of the upper Coastal Plain, there is enough discharge to form springs and small streams that undermine the sands and carve out steephead amphitheaters and gullies. The spring water issuing from the sandhills is clear; however, if discharge is modest, the water quickly turns tea-colored as it seeps and flows through accumulated organic matter. Big Sandy Creek (Wilkinson County) and Reedy Creek (Jefferson County) are good examples of clear-water streams flowing over white or tan sand among flats and hummocks of a black, mucky floodplain.

Below the surficial aquifer is a series of aquifers, and each aquifer is generally confined within a specific geologic unit. There are two types of aquifers: (1) confined aquifers, in which the water supply is sandwiched between two impermeable layers of soil or rock, such that water cannot pass through; and (2) unconfined aquifers, in which the water supply has an impermeable layer below it but not above it. A confined aquifer that is under pressure is called an "artesian aquifer"; the pressure can often push water to the surface as a spring. Groundwater moves through numerous interconnected sinks, caves, fissures, and other conduits of the underlying limestone and may emerge in uplands or rivers as springs. Between Albany and Bainbridge more than 20 large springs connect the Flint River with the Floridan aquifer, discharging millions of gallons per day. Groundwater is often readily available in large quantities for human use, and wells are installed throughout the Coastal Plain for human consumption, industrial use, and irrigation. These Coastal Plain aquifers are recharged by infiltration of precipitation where the limestone of the aquifer is near the soil sur-

Spring located on Spring Creek in the Dougherty Plain

face. From the Fall Line a stepped sequence of recharge areas occur southeastward, with the oldest limestone formations to the north and younger formations successively to the south and east. The lower Flint River basin is a major recharge area for the upper Floridan aquifer. Many streams in the Flint River watershed, as well as the Chickasawhatchee Swamp, are hydraulically connected with the aquifer through numerous karst sinks, sinkhole ponds, exposed limestone on the surface, and streambeds incised into the limestone bedrock. During extended droughts the flow even reverses in some springs, with water flowing from the river into the spring (Hicks 1995). Recharge of the upper Floridan aquifer also occurs within the streambed of the Withlacoochee River in Lowndes County, where numerous sinkholes have developed (Davis and Hicks 2001). Evidence of this can be seen during dry summer months when portions of this river disappear below ground.

ENVIRONMENTAL FACTORS

The three most important environmental factors shaping vegetation in the Georgia Coastal Plain are hydrology (the moisture regime), soil texture, and fire. Often, these factors are interrelated: soil texture (which helps determine soil moisture) and hydrology greatly influence the spread of fire. The topography, coupled with unconsolidated sediments, creates conditions favorable not only for the spread of fire but also for the formation of wetlands.

The moisture regime (the movement or retention of water in the soil) determines the excess or deficiency of water to plants. Because plants are adapted to varying degrees of soil moisture, water availability is a major influence on the development of plant communities. In the Coastal Plain, soil moisture is primarily regulated by three factors: the position of the water table, the presence of clayey soil horizons that impede or slow the rate of infiltration of water through the soil, and the moisture-retention properties of individual soil horizons (Brown, Stone, and Carlisle 1990). The position of the water table may be a determining factor in the depth of well-aerated soils. For example, in bottomlands, swamps, and marshes, when the water table drops well below the soil surface during dry periods, the soils may actually be well drained and aerated. In contrast, when the water table is near the surface for extended periods, plants must be able to tolerate the low oxygen (anaerobic conditions) of saturated soils. The water table can rise and fall during the course of a year, so both the depth of inundation or soil saturation and the hydroperiod (timing and duration of inundation) determine the composition of vegetation. Similarly, "perched" water tables occur when a subsurface layer within the soil restricts downward percolation. These subsurface layers can be extremely dense clay layers or hardpans such as those often associated with spodosols. When associated with a depression, such layers can result in geographically isolated wetlands.

Soil texture is also an important moisture-retention factor. During precipitation events, water moves quickly through coarse particles such as sands that have large openings between the particles but moves slowly through finer-textured soils that have more silt, clay, or small sand particles. In addition to controlling water movement in soil, texture influences nutrient availability. Nutrients can bond to clays and to a lesser degree to silts but not to sands, so very sandy soils have few nutrients. Soil texture is also a major factor in soil erosion. Poorly consolidated sands erode quickly, whereas soils rich in clay are more erosion-resistant. This is well illustrated in Providence Canyon State Park, where erosion gullies 150 feet deep formed within a matter of decades in the sandy, poorly consolidated Providence Formation (Magilligan and Stamp 1997).

The frequency and intensity of fire has a dramatic effect on species composition and the diversity of communities, particularly as species sort out across an environmental gradient based on fire tolerance and moisture requirements. Fire is a chronic disturbance that suppresses fire-intolerant species, particularly hardwoods, and fosters fire-tolerant species such as longleaf pine and many perennial grasses and forbs. Where fire is excluded, vegetation is eventually dominated by hardwoods, regardless of water availability.

Historically, the return interval between fires for a given site was based on ignition source and the probability of fire spreading across the landscape as determined by the hydrology, soils, and topographic positions in the landscape. Natural elements of fire suppression included bodies of water, steep slopes, moist fuels, or scarcity of fuels. Many communities embedded within the upland longleaf pine forests, such as depressional wetlands, seepages, or transitional zones into riparian bottomlands, were dependent on fires that originated in the uplands. In the past, ignition sources were lightning, Native Americans, and European settlers. The frequency of cloud-to-ground lightning is higher throughout the Georgia Coastal Plain than in other parts of the state. Variation in incidence of flashes across the Coastal Plain is attributable to physiographic differences and storm patterns within the region. In summer months, lightning activity is highest in coastal counties with frequencies of more than five flashes per square mile per year. Other areas of frequent cloud-to-ground lightning are near the Fall Line and the metropolitan area of Atlanta. During winter months, overall lightning activity declines with decreasing frequency of convection storms; however, it is greater at this time of year in southwestern Georgia than in other parts of the Coastal Plain (Bentley and Stallins 2005). In longleaf pine stands, lightning strikes have been observed to be the primary factor in mortality of large trees (Outcalt 2008). Both Native Americans and European settlers frequently set fires, though the degree of the anthropogenic role in shaping Coastal Plain vegetation is debated (Pyne 1982; Kreech 1999; Earley 2004).

LAND USE HISTORY AND HUMAN IMPACT

Indigenous Peoples. Humans have inhabited the Coastal Plain of Georgia for roughly 12,000 to 14,000 years, beginning with the paleo-Indian hunters of large mammals (Hudson 1976). The archaic hunter-gatherers were most common along the coast by 8,000 to 10,000 years ago and gradually began to occupy major river and creek drainages throughout the state in semipermanent villages about 5,000 years ago (Hudson 1976). Further increases in indigenous populations occurred with the development of agriculture. Cultivated lands were generally restricted to rich bottomlands along river corridors (Hudson 1976; Silver 1990). Many areas of the Coastal Plain of Georgia were densely populated by indigenous peoples at

Many natural communities in the Coastal Plain are shaped by frequent fire.

the time they were encountered by the first Spanish explorers (Hudson 1976; Silver 1990). By the time of European settlement in Georgia in the 1700s, populations of native peoples had actually been in decline for nearly a century as a result of disease and war (Silver 1990; Earley 2004).

The impact of Native Americans in shaping the forests of the Coastal Plain has been increasingly recognized (Pyne 1982; S. Ware, Frost, and Doerr 1993; Kreech 1999; Earley 2004). Although native settlements were primarily associated with fertile bottomland sites and river systems, the longleaf pine uplands were extensively used for hunting. Indigenous peoples purposely burned areas to perpetuate desired plant and animal species (Pyne 1982; Silver 1990). Some early historical accounts suggest that extensive burning and clearing forest undergrowth by natives occurred on an annual basis (Earley 2004). The high frequency of fire for many centuries for cultural land management practices, coupled with frequent lightning-ignited fires, potentially provided open grazing land supporting large herds of buffalo that have been suggested to have existed during the period of 1500 to 1700 in parts of the Southeast (Rostland 1960).

Agriculture and Grazing. With British settlement of coastal areas and barrier islands in the 1730s and lift-

Lightning strikes frequently occur in the Coastal Plain and are a potential source of ignition of fire. Most ignitions today occur as a result of management with prescribed fire.

ing of the prohibition on slavery in the 1750s, extensive acreages were cultivated for rice, indigo, and sugarcane (Stewart 1996). Rice culture in Georgia was concentrated primarily along the tidally influenced portions of the Savannah, Ogeechee, and Altamaha Rivers. In the late 1700s, many European settlers maintained open range herds of livestock and burned the surrounding landscape frequently to encourage forage, similar to practices of Native Americans (Pyne 1982; Silver 1990). The interior Coastal Plain remained largely undeveloped until after the Civil War (Wetherington 1994). Soon thereafter, the most fertile soils of the upper Coastal Plain were cleared and planted in cotton. Late in the 1800s, the interior of the Coastal Plain experienced massive population growth and land-clearing spurred by railroad construction throughout the region (Wetherington 1994). Following the economic depression of the 1930s, the amount of cultivated land throughout the state declined (E. P. Odum and Turner 1987). In the Coastal Plain, this decline was greatest in the eastern parts of Georgia, including Laurens, Emanuel, and Screven Counties, although it was also very severe in other counties, such as Stewart County (Magilligan and Stamp 1997; R. H. Brown 2002).

After World War II, a combination of mechanization, fertilizers, pesticides, and improved crop varieties led to a decrease in demand for manual labor and thus instigated mass movement of populations to urban areas in search of employment. Farms became fewer and larger. Much of the land taken out of production was put into pasture or forest plantations. Acreage in cropland again increased in the Coastal Plain with the introduction of center pivot irrigation systems to the region in the 1970s. By 2001, more than 17,000 systems were in operation, irrigating 1,500,000 acres (Harrison and Tyson 2001). These irrigation systems use water from surface streams or groundwater of the Floridan aquifer.

Given the high proportion of land cover represented by wetlands in the Coastal Plain relative to ecoregions north of the Fall Line, alterations to seasonally inundated or saturated environments by drainage efforts for agriculture have been far greater in this ecoregion. Despite this fact, quantification of the acreage of drained wetlands is difficult and estimates are inconsistent (Shepard et al. 1998; R. H. Brown 2002). Conversion of wetlands began early in the settlement of the state with the cultivation of rice, where water

control structures were needed to regulate flooding. Extensive acreage of productive farmland was attained by clearing and ditching bottomlands along major rivers during periods of early settlement. In the 1800s, new farm equipment, such as plows, rakes, and cultivators, increased the capability of cultivating soils previously considered infeasible. An early plan to drain the entire Okefenokee Swamp for access to timber and to convert the land to agriculture was proposed but finally deemed unachievable (Dahl and Johnson 1991). To encourage farmers to convert wetlands to agricultural land, federal programs provided financial incentives for drainage of low-lying lands as a means to control mosquito-borne diseases and promote more agricultural land use (U.S. Department of Agriculture 1956; Dahl and Johnson 1991). Through the 1970s, channelization of natural streams and construction of artificial canals for wetland drainage were also promoted with federal financing for conversion to agricultural production (Heimlich et al. 1998). Many isolated wetlands of the Dougherty Plain and seepage slope bogs of the Tifton Uplands have been converted to farm ponds.

Free-range livestock grazing was prevalent in the Coastal Plain until the late 1800s and early 1900s, when fence laws were enforced (Wetherington 1994). The impacts of this historical practice on the native ground cover are difficult to assess because the practice was so widespread. The long-held tradition of burning the forest for forage, however, helped to perpetuate fire-maintained ecosystems (Silver 1990; Frost 2006). Although contained by fencing, much of the cattle grazing in the region continued in open forestlands until the 1950s, when pasture improvement and development became a widespread practice, particularly in the upper Coastal Plain. This included application of lime and fertilizer as well as seeding of pasture grasses, such as coastal Bermuda grass, bahia grass, and dallis grass.

Industrial Forestry. Up to the time of the Civil War, longleaf pine stands along rivers and streams were harvested and transported by water to downstream mills. Later, with the technological advances of the steam engine and railroad, the more inaccessible forests became targeted for their prized heartwood timber. The logging boom in the late 1800s came at the expense of vast acreages of virgin pine forests. At about the same time, the naval stores industry was developing in Georgia.

Center pivot irrigation systems use water for agricultural crops from streams or from groundwater of the Floridan aquifer.

Naval stores is a collective name for products rendered from the oleoresin of pine trees such as tar, pitch, spirits of turpentine, and rosin. The name was derived from the practice of applying pitch and tar to wooden ships as a preservative. As the pine forests diminished in Virginia and the Carolinas, the practice became widespread in Georgia in the late 1800s. At its peak in 1910, nearly 8 million acres of southeastern pine forests were in production, rendering 600,000 metric tons of rosin and turpentine (A. W. Hodges 2006). By the early 1900s, expansive areas were nearly stripped clean of longleaf pine trees by these two economic drivers. To replace the forests, large acreages were replanted with loblolly and slash pine and fire was excluded to protect these less fire-tolerant species (Wakeley 1935; R. H. Brown 2002; Frost 2006). Huge acreages were also converted to cropland (Walker 1991; Wetherington 1994).

Today, much of the marginally productive crop land in the Coastal Plain has been converted to commercial production of slash or loblolly pine pulpwood using intensive silvicultural management. The commonly used techniques include site preparation to clear debris and vegetation prior to planting, application of herbicide treatments to control competing woody and herbaceous plants during seedling establishment, and fertilization for maximum growth. In poorly drained flatwoods sites, raised planting beds are constructed as mounded rows that allow the roots of newly planted seedlings to remain above seasonal water-level fluctuations. For pulpwood, sites are harvested at about age 12–15 years. For chip and sawlog production, sites are clearcut in about 25 years. Prescribed fire is generally not employed as a management technique in young plantations because slash pine and loblolly pine are not fire-tolerant at the sapling stage. Structural and

Vast acreages of virgin longleaf pine forests once dominated the Coastal Plain.

ated forest depends on the degree of advanced regeneration (saplings or sprouts present at the time of cut) and the degree of alteration to the hydrologic regime with removal of the canopy and decrease in transpiration (Lockaby et al. 1994). In many bottomland sites, the practice of high-grading stands (removing only the most valuable trees) has altered the species composition of regenerating stands because it favors opportunistic species, or understory species, that are more shade-tolerant beneath the residual canopy species (Kellison et al. 1998).

Prescribed Fire and Fire Suppression. In the early 20th century, the fact that longleaf pine forests were not regenerating following massive timber removal was blamed on the woods-burning practices of the local residents, as well as hogs rooting up the seedlings. To oppose this practice, a full-blown fire suppression policy was implemented by the U.S. Forest Service by the 1920s in an attempt to promote forest regeneration. A regional group formed by the Southern Forestry Congress, the American Forestry Association, and state foresters, known as the "Dixie Crusaders," assumed the role of educating the rural population about the destructiveness of fire to timber production. These anti-fire sentiments persisted for many decades and further contributed to the region-wide succession of cut-over longleaf pine stands to mixed pine-oak forests (Walker 1991; R. H. Brown 2002; Earley 2004). Several early champions of fire in southern forests, including H. L. Stoddard, H. H. Chapman, R. M. Harper, and S. W. Greene, countered these fire-suppression policies. Eventually, a new attitude emerged among foresters in the South with the increased recognition that prescribed fire could reduce fuel hazards, encourage pine regeneration, and improve forage and game conditions. Even after official policies embraced prescribed fire, public education was set back enormously by "Smokey the Bear" and other fire-prevention campaigns.

Patterns of Land Ownership and Development. The Coastal Plain ecoregion covers approximately 22,045,897 acres in Georgia. Approximately 14% of the ecoregion is in some form of permanent or long-term conservation ownership. The Georgia Department of Natural Resources manages approximately 200,000 acres owned in fee simple by the state of Georgia and an additional 170,00 acres in leases or management agreements. Federal land ownership in-

species diversity in pine plantations is greatly reduced relative to natural pine stands.

Nearly all bottomland forests in Georgia have been cut over several times since European settlement. The first major period of clearing of bottomland hardwood forests came in the early 1900s, as railroad and tram lines made commercial harvest of these vast forests possible and profitable. Current silvicultural activities often consist of clearcutting canopy hardwood trees and allowing regeneration from stump sprouts (Walbridge and Lockaby 1994; Lockaby, Stanturf, and Messina 1997). The composition of the regener-

Planted pine stands for commercial production of timber products now replace much of the natural forest stands of the Coastal Plain.

cludes approximately 413,662 acres managed by the U.S. Fish and Wildlife Service, 538,878 acres managed by the Department of Defense, 1,157 acres managed by the National Park Service, and 11,232 acres managed by the Natural Resources Conservation Service. Almost half of the federal land is found in two properties—Okefenokee National Wildlife Refuge and Fort Stewart Military Reservation.

Approximately 60% of the land of the Coastal Plain is forested, and most of this forest land is owned by nonindustrial private landowners. Of the total commercial timberlands, approximately 20% is owned by industrial timber companies. Until recently, many of the largest tracts of forested land in the Coastal Plain of Georgia have been held by industrial timber companies. Large-scale divestiture of properties by timber companies has occurred in recent years in response to changing economies of forestry products, tax structures, and increasing recreational and land development opportunities with spiraling trends in urbanization (Clutter et al. 2005). Between 1996 and 2004,

more than 2,000,000 acres of commercial timberland were sold in Georgia. Most of these properties have been acquired by timber investment and management organizations (TIMOs), which are organizations that manage the property and timber assets for an institution. While much of the land held by TIMOs will continue to be managed for timber products, at least for the short term, thousands of acres of timberland in the Coastal Plain will be sold for residential development. Given increasing development pressures and elevated property values along the Atlantic coast and Florida boundary, significant conversion of timberland to other land uses is predicted for these regions (Wear and Newman 2004; Clutter et al. 2005).

From a conservation perspective, this recent divestiture of lands by larger timber companies has provided unprecedented opportunities for public land acquisition of several large tracts of forest land of ecological significance, particularly along the Altamaha River corridor. Other notable acquisitions in the Coastal Plain include Chickasawhatchee Wildlife Management Area and Silver Lake Wildlife Management Area in southwestern Georgia. Increased funding for public acquisition of properties and purchase of conservation easements is critical in the next few years as such properties become available for sale.

Current land use in the Coastal Plain has promoted a highly fragmented landscape that has major impacts on the sustainability of remnant natural communities. Reconnecting habitats is becoming an important conservation priority for many species, particularly faunal species that have a large home range, such as indigo snakes (Moler 1985, 1992; Means 2006), Sherman's fox squirrels (L. M. Conner 2001), or gopher tortoises (Eubanks et al. 2003). For many amphibian species, disruption of migration corridors between upland habitat used for refuge and temporarily ponded wetlands used for reproduction is detrimental (Semlitsch 2000; Semlitsch and Bodie 2003).

Fragmentation also significantly affects adjacent forested uplands in terms of lowered conductivity of fire. As a consequence, management of fire-maintained ecosystems of the Coastal Plain requires the application of prescribed burning to meet the objectives of fuel reduction or hardwood control. Difficulties in managing natural communities with fire are increasing, particularly in urban-forest interfaces, where smoke management issues, air quality regulations, as well as the lack of practitioners trained in the use of prescribed fire threaten to limit this option region-wide. Consequently, the feasibility of using prescribed fire in the future is an emerging and critical policy concern.

Non-native Invasive Species. Feral hogs occur throughout Georgia and are on most public conservation lands, where they are considered an invasive nuisance species requiring active control. Feral hogs include free-ranging Eurasian breeds (called Russian boars) and domestic pigs, as well as hybrids. Hogs were introduced into the region by European explorers and settlers as early as the 1500s (Bakeless 1961); populations had exploded by the 1700s throughout coastal regions of the Southeast (Frost 2006). Feral hogs played a large role in the decline of longleaf pine forests in the early 1900s because they consumed the roots of regenerating pine seedlings following a period of widespread timber removal (Mattoon 1922; Wakeley 1954). Hogs are also extremely destructive to vegetation in bottomland forests, swamps, and other wetlands, where they root around for food and

Most remnant tracts of natural longleaf pine communities occur within a landscape that has become highly fragmented by urban or agricultural land uses.

severely disturb the soil and ground cover over large areas. They are omnivorous, consuming plant roots, acorns, insects, amphibians, and crops. Consequently, they compete for mast foods of wildlife game species such as deer, quail, and turkey. In these wetland habitats, they also consume large numbers of frogs and salamanders, ground-nesting birds, and young turtles (Jolley 2007).

Several invasive plant species, including Japanese climbing fern, Japanese honeysuckle, Chinese privet, spring silverberry, cogongrass, bicolor lespedeza, sericea lespedeza, mimosa, chinaberry, and Chinese wisteria, are serious threats to natural communities of the Coastal Plain. Many of these non-native species were deliberately introduced as ornamentals, for erosion control, or for wildlife benefit. Some have a long history of introduction into the Southeast. For example, the Chinese tallow-tree was cultivated in China for seed oil. Introduction of this tree into the Southeast as an ornamental and resource for soap is attributed to Benjamin Franklin (Bell 1966). Since the late 1700s, Chinese tallow-tree has invaded abandoned fields, bottomlands, and tidal swamps throughout much of the Coastal Plain.

Other species are of more contemporary introduction, but have rapidly become serious pests. An invasive species of increasing concern in the Coastal Plain of Georgia is cogongrass. This grass was introduced into Florida in the 1930s and 1940s as forage for cattle. Soon after, it was recognized that it had little value as forage, but its aggressive rhizomes and tolerance to fire facilitated its invasive habit. Cogongrass has been inadvertently transported in soil during roadway construction and proves difficult to eliminate, once established (Miller 2003). It is now found throughout Florida and is rapidly encroaching into southern counties of Georgia. This federally listed noxious weed forms dense patches and can quickly dominate a site, displacing native vegetation. It not only competes with native species, but changes the properties of the litter and upper soil layers (Lippincott 1997). The highly flammable leaves increase fuel loads, and resultant fires tend to be hotter than those dominated by wiregrass and other native species. Fire induces flowering and seed production of cogongrass, as well as reduces competition from other plants (Bryson and Carter 1993); thus, establishment in longleaf pine stands is of concern. Aggressive public education campaigns are under way to alert natural resource professionals and landowners to this potentially devastating invader in the Coastal Plain; Georgia state agencies take immediate action to control this species whenever it is first sighted.

Another serious pest in the Coastal Plain is Japanese climbing fern, introduced from Asia as an ornamental. This viny fern invades readily along roadsides and in pine plantations and other disturbed sites but also poses a threat to natural communities such as longleaf pine stands, mesic slope forests, and bottom-

Cogongrass is an introduced noxious weed that is a serious threat to natural fire-maintained communities in the Coastal Plain because of its tolerance to fire and aggressive establishment.

land hardwood forests. It forms dense mats engulfing the ground and shrubs and can grow into tree canopies, blocking sunlight for the vegetation beneath. The foliage dies back in the winter, leaving a ladder of fuel that can result in catastrophic canopy fires. The spores are easily dispersed by wind.

Water Quantity and Quality. Withdrawals from groundwater and streams for irrigation during periods of peak water demand for crops and municipal use in populated areas have dramatic effects on aquifer water levels and river flow (Rugel et al. 2011). For example, water levels in the Clayton aquifer have declined as much as 140 to 150 feet in the Albany area since the 1940s, although the rate of decline has stabilized with limitations on current use (W. Hicks, J. W. Jones Center, pers. comm.). Reduced streamflow in the lower Flint River basin has been attributed to extensive groundwater withdrawals from the Floridan aquifer for center pivot irrigation (Rugel et al. 2011). The long-term effect of agricultural withdrawal on the upper Floridan aquifer in the Flint River basin is not clear; however, seasonal increases in duration as well as the magnitude of groundwater level declines have been documented (Torak and Painter 2006). Radium Springs, near Albany, is the largest spring in Georgia, and can discharge as much as 70 million gallons

Agricultural runoff, unfenced pastures along river banks, and irrigation are significant threats to the rivers and floodplain forests of the Coastal Plain.

per day. Even so, Radium Springs ceased to flow for the first time during the summer of 1981; now, it frequently ceases to flow during the summer months as a result of heavy irrigation pumping from the upper Floridan aquifer, coupled with recurring drought. Reduced flow from artesian wells in the Savannah area from pumping of groundwater from the upper Floridan aquifer was noted as early as 1905 (McCallie 1908). Today, water withdrawal around Savannah is inducing salt water to infiltrate into the aquifer in coastal South Carolina (Krause and Randolph 1989; Clarke, Hacke, and Peck 1990). Similarly, water withdrawal in Brunswick is causing saline groundwater to migrate upward, contaminating the upper Floridan aquifer in Georgia (Jones 2001; Falls et al. 2005).

Agricultural impacts also include increased levels of nitrate in the ground and surface waters of the Coastal Plain through non-point-source runoff due to fertilizer inputs (Beck et al. 1985) and cattle grazing along

stream banks (Armour, Duff, and Elmore 1991). Agricultural runoff, unfenced pastures along river banks, and irrigation are significant threats to the rivers and floodplain forests of the Coastal Plain. Damage to vegetation through trampling by cattle along the edge of rivers causes erosion of the stream bank and substantial siltation. Residential and recreational development pressures along these streams and rivers in the Coastal Plain are sharply increasing, with negative impacts on water quality, aesthetics, habitat, and water storage. Ongoing efforts to protect riparian vegetation to maintain such ecological functions include federal and state incentive programs for private landowners for fencing to exclude cattle access, promotion of tax incentives for donated conservation easements, and land acquisition through public greenspace programs. A better understanding of the flow regimes necessary for sustaining aquatic ecosystems of regional rivers and creeks is critically needed.

Natural Communities of the Georgia Coastal Plain

UPLAND FORESTS

Sandhills and River Dunes. Woodlands with xerophytic vegetation of stunted turkey oak and scattered longleaf pine with sparse ground cover or thick mats of lichens; occurring on ultra-xeric sandhill sites.

Dry Upland Longleaf Pine Woodlands. Woodlands or forests of longleaf pine, turkey oak, bluejack oak, and sand post oak; occurring on nearly level to undulating terrain with a continuous species-rich ground cover dominated by wiregrass; includes sites with increased amount of clays that support blackjack oak.

Mesic Upland Longleaf Pine Woodlands. Widely spaced longleaf pine woodlands or forests with dense wiregrass and species-rich herbaceous ground cover; occurring on upland, well-drained to wet-mesic fine-textured soils; includes a fire-maintained ecotonal zone between dry uplands and hydric conditions of seepages or depressional wetlands.

Dry Evergreen Oak Woodlands. Woodlands or forests dominated by broadleaf evergreen species, primarily laurel oak, live oak, and sand live oak; usually occurring as marginal strands on well-drained mid-slope positions between xeric sandhill woodlands and seepage swamps where fire has been excluded or is infrequent, on excessively drained sandy domes of old marine bars within pine flatwoods, and occasionally on deep sandy soils of river banks; includes rare occurrences of scrub oaks, myrtle oak, and Chapman's oak.

Dry Deciduous Hardwood Forests. Deciduous or mixed-deciduous hardwood forests, including southern red oak, post oak, white oak, water oak, laurel oak, live oak, pignut hickory, mockernut hickory, and sand hickory; occurring on sandy or loamy soils of river bluffs, upper ridges of slope forests, or on the mid- to lower slopes of sandhills between xeric ridge vegetation and seepage swamps, or embedded within longleaf pine sites where streams and other firebreaks shield them from fire.

Mesic Slope Forests. Closed-canopy, diverse mixed evergreen-deciduous forests, often with American beech and southern magnolia; occurring on well-drained but mesic acidic and calcareous soils of steep slopes or bluffs, often associated with ravines and terraces along streams or seeps, as well as along upper walls of deep sinkholes.

ROCK OUTCROPS, PRAIRIES, AND BARRENS

Acidic Glades, Barrens, and Rocky Woodlands. Open woodlands or barrens of pines and hardwoods interspersed with small to extensive outcroppings of indurated sandstone (often called Altamaha Grit) and ironstone in the upper Coastal Plain.

Blackland Prairies and Woodlands. Rare, small, open grasslands within a forested matrix of pines or mesic slope forests; occurring in a few locations on alkaline clay soils underlain by calcareous parent material in the Fall Line Red Hills of Houston, Peach, Twiggs, and Bleckley Counties within the Ocmulgee River drainage.

WETLANDS AND LOWLANDS

Pine Flatwoods. Open forests dominated by longleaf pine, slash pine, and pond pine, often occupying extensive areas of low relief in the lower Coastal Plain; occurring on deep, sandy marine deposits of coastal terraces, often where soils with a spodic horizon have formed in response to fluctuating water levels.

Seepage Slope Herb Bogs. Open patches of herbaceous wetland plants (often with pitcherplants) with few scattered pines; occupying low swales and lower slopes in frequently burned pine uplands, particularly in the Tifton Uplands, Tallahassee Hills, Southern Loam Plains, and Fall Line regions where the soil is saturated much of the year by lateral seepage of groundwater from sandy soils of adjacent uplands.

Seepage Slope Swamps and Shrub Bogs. Open forests or dense shrubby vegetation dominated by evergreen species, including loblolly bay, sweet bay, and red bay with numerous other shrubby species; occupying seepage areas with seasonally to semipermanently saturated soils and peat accumulation; includes canebrakes and Atlantic white cedar swamps.

Depression Marshes and Cypress Savannas. Meadowlike wetlands or open cypress stands dominated by grasses and sedges; occurring in seasonally flooded depressions with gently sloping sides and relatively flat bottoms, such as Carolina bays and limesinks.

Cypress-Gum Ponds. Forested wetlands dominated by pond-cypress and swamp tupelo in seasonally flooded depressions, such as Carolina bays and limesinks.

Depression Oak Forests. Forested islands of live oak and laurel oak with little to no ground cover; occurring in shallow basins that are infrequently inundated and have been excluded from fire.

Cypress-Tupelo River Swamps. Bald-cypress and water tupelo river swamps; occurring in backswamps, secondary channels, sloughs, and swales of river and larger stream floodplains.

Bottomland Hardwoods. Diverse forest assemblages of deciduous hardwood species adapted to periods of inundation including water oak, willow oak, laurel oak, Shumard oak, swamp chestnut oak, red maple, sweet gum, green ash, overcup oak, and water hickory and evergreen species such as southern magnolia and live oak; occurring on relict natural levees, terraces, point bar ridges, and other relatively high parts of floodplain flats along blackwater and alluvial streams; includes bottomland canebrakes.

Riverbanks and Levees. Hardwood-dominated forests bordering the river channel on active levees and banks of medium to large blackwater and alluvial streams and rivers; includes pioneer species establishing on recent alluvial deposits (willows, cottonwood, and ti-ti) as well as species established on more stable soils (river birch, water-elm, catalpa, and sycamore); does not include evergreen-dominated forests of live oak, laurel oak, and sand live oak (see dry evergreen oak woodlands).

Small Stream Floodplain Forests. Dense forests of broadleaved evergreen and deciduous trees, shrubs, and vines (mix of species typically more restricted to distinct levees or backswamps or bottomlands in larger river systems); occurring on narrow floodplains of headwater drainages and low-gradient small creeks and streams of acidic, tannic water.

Okefenokee Swamp. A mosaic of communities including pine uplands, forested wetlands of bay, cypress, and black gum, shrubby wetlands, and extensive prairies of emergent aquatic vegetation located in a vast peat-filled basin in the southeastern part of the state.

An Overview of Upland Longleaf Pine Woodlands

An extensive mosaic of longleaf pine-dominated woodland and savanna habitats (consisting of sandhills, upland pine forests, seepage slopes, and flatwoods) once dominated the southeastern Coastal Plain from Virginia south to Florida and west to Mississippi, covering more than 90 million acres (S. Ware, Frost, and Doerr 1993). These communities, which range from extremely xeric sites on sandhills and river dunes to wet-mesic sites, were strongly shaped by a long history of natural fire disturbance and today must be maintained with frequent prescribed fire. Thus, the longleaf pine forest is often referred to as the "fire forest." The wide range in soil, topography, and hydrologic conditions, as well as variable fire regimes, contribute to the development of habitat that harbors the most species-rich plant communities in North America. This once dominant and biologically diverse ecosystem is now considered one of the most globally imperiled (Noss, Laroe, and Scott 1985; S. Ware, Frost, and Doerr 1993; America's Longleaf 2009).

Prior to widespread deforestation following European settlement, fires ignited in this forest by lightning or by Native Americans moved extensively across the landscape due to the continuous vegetation and presence of flammable fuels. The herbaceous ground cover and pine needles provided the fuel to feed the fire until interrupted by creeks and rivers. The upland longleaf pine forest requires fire to reduce encroachment by fire-intolerant hardwoods. Today, given the fragmentation of the Coastal Plain landscape, the small remaining parcels of this forest type, and overall regional fire suppression, the fire-dependent longleaf pine forests now rely on prescribed fire management to persist.

Since the early 1800s, nearly 98% of the longleaf pine forests have been eliminated due to agricultural conversion, industrial pine plantations, urban development, and fire suppression (Noss, Laroe, and Scott 1985; S. Ware, Frost, and Doerr 1993). Today, the relict stands are confined primarily to sites that were either too wet or too dry for agricultural cultivation (seepage slopes and sandhills). Thus, examples of the once wide-ranging subxeric to mesic upland sites with undisturbed native ground cover are extremely rare because they have been almost entirely converted to agriculture (R. M. Harper 1906; S. Ware, Frost, and Doerr 1993). An exception is in southwestern Georgia, where some of the most extensive remnants of the upland longleaf pine forests have persisted on private lands. These relict tracts occur primarily as a result of landowner objectives of maintaining game bird habitat, particularly for the northern bobwhite (Outcalt 1994). The historical and continued use of frequent prescribed fire to promote open forest conditions for this game species has perpetuated sizable tracts of longleaf pine, principally in the Dougherty Plain, the Tifton Uplands, and the Tallahassee Hills. Among the vestiges of longleaf pine stands that remain in the Coastal Plain, these stands are particularly significant because they occur on relatively fertile soils.

Vegetation development in longleaf pine forests is controlled by a complex interaction of fire frequency, soil characteristics, topographic position, and past land uses. Broad patterns of vegetation composition across the state are associated with soils and physiography and coincide particularly well with the ecoregions defined by Omernik (1987) and G. E. Griffith et al. (2001) that have been adopted by the U.S. Environmental Protection Agency and other government agencies. Similar ecoregional-level vegetation distinctions have been observed throughout the range of the longleaf pine ecosystem (Peet 2006). Local compositional variation and patterns of species richness in the longleaf pine upland forests, driven by gradients in soil moisture and texture, may also occur across relatively small landscape scales (Kirkman et al. 2001; Peet 2006). This complexity has challenged the development of a cohesive and operative classification system for the longleaf pine ecosystem. Here we separate upland longleaf pine communities into xeric sandhill

and river dune longleaf pine woodlands, dry upland longleaf pine forests, mesic upland longleaf pine forests, and rocky upland longleaf pine woodlands and glades, and discuss physiographic variations within these groups.

Prescribed Fire Management and the Longleaf Pine Ecosystem. Frequent fire is essential to the perpetual regeneration of the longleaf pine forest and to the maintenance of the characteristically high biological diversity and of rare species. Considerable debate has occurred relative to the natural fire frequency under which this fire-dependent ecosystem evolved and how such estimates should be incorporated into management prescriptions (Komarek 1974; Glitzenstein, Streng, and Wade 2003; Frost 2006; Glitzenstein et al. 2008, 2011). Furthermore, pre-Columbian lightning-ignited fire is thought to have occurred primarily in the summer months between the end of May and August (W. J. Platt, Evans, and Davis 1988; Robbins and Myers 1992). Based on the rationale that this regularity in season probably exerted significant evolutionary influence on plant reproduction, the use of growing season prescribed fire has been advocated as essential timing for management of the ecosystem (W. J. Platt, Evans, and Davis 1988; Brewer and Platt 1994). Supporting this argument is the abundant flowering response of wiregrass when it is burned in late spring and summer and the near absence of flowering when burning occurs at other times of the year (Parrott 1967; Seamon et al. 1989). Despite this strong response of wiregrass to late season fires, other studies imply that most plant species are not dependent on a particular season of fire for successful reproduction (Kirkman et al. 1998; Hiers, Wyatt, and Mitchell 2000), and, furthermore, that season of fire is not a controlling factor in the long-term maintenance of species richness (Glitzenstein et al. 2008).

Traditional land management for wildlife has included setting fire from February to late April following the passage of cold fronts through the region because of low humidity and increased vertical smoke dispersion and avoidance of impacts to ground-nesting birds (Stoddard 1935; Lemon 1949; Wade and Lunsford 1989). The philosophic trend to emphasize growing season fire (May–June) that emerged under the assumption that fires occurring during the natural fire season were the most ecologically favorable for perpetuating fire-dependent species (W. J. Platt, Evans,

Prescribed fire is essential to the perpetual regeneration of the longleaf pine forest and for the maintenance of high biological diversity.

less frequent fire. Because the timing and fuel conditions under which fire is applied do have an effect on hardwood response, fuel reduction, smoke dissipation, wiregrass reproduction, longleaf pine regeneration, and response of wildlife, fire prescriptions should be based on clearly stated goals and objectives for a given burn unit. Thus, a fire regime that incorporates frequent fire with varied season of burning depending on objectives of the site is strongly advocated (Hiers, Wyatt, and Mitchell 2000).

Reintroduction of fire into extremely fire-suppressed sites can be problematic and may lead to excessive tree mortality. In the absence of frequent fire, substantial accumulations of surficial organic materials (leaf litter, sloughed bark) occur, particularly around the bases of large pines (Varner et al. 2005). These duff piles may accumulate to depths of 1 to 2 feet and provide sites where longleaf pine roots develop. Consequently, when fire is reintroduced, flaming and smoldering duff can cause direct damage to the canopy, stems, and roots that leads to death. Tree mortality may also be associated with indirect effects due to increased physiological stress associated with damaged roots (Varner et al. 2005). Thus, it may be necessary to reduce duff by raking or to introduce multiple low-intensity fires over many years to gradually reduce the organic material before more aggressive burning for hardwood reduction is feasible. This restoration approach is being practiced in a fire-suppressed, old-growth longleaf pine stand at Moody Forest (Appling County) through cooperative management by the Nature Conservancy and the Georgia Department of Natural Resources.

Biology of the Longleaf Pine. The long needles and very large cones make longleaf pine one of the most distinctive pines in the state. It has greater longevity than other southern pines, surviving for more than 300 years (occasionally up to 500 years). Because it evolved in an environment of frequent fire, this species has developed many adaptations for survival and growth (Myers 1990). For example, the strategy of longleaf pine for regeneration in a fire-prone habitat is the seedling grass stage. The year after germination, young seedlings enter into a stage in which they resemble a clump of grass and are very well protected to survive frequent fire because the long tuft of needles protects the bud from the heat of low-intensity fire. Seedlings may persist in the grass stage without stem growth for 3 to 25

and Davis 1988; Robbins and Myers 1992) has led to a "season of fire" controversy among conservation management practitioners.

Alternatively, fire frequency has been demonstrated to be one of the most important drivers of community structure (Wells and Shunk 1931; Lemon 1949; Glitzenstein, Streng, and Wade 2003; Kirkman et al. 2004b; Glitzenstein et al. 2008, 2011) and, arguably, is one of the most critical aspects of a long-range fire management plan (Jack, Neel, and Mitchell 2006; McIntyre et al. 2008). In this context, fire management is thought of as a recurring process or regime rather than a discrete event, with the community responding to repeated fire through time. For most sites, a fire-return interval of no longer than two to three years should be a management goal for preventing hardwood invasion. A practical consideration of restricting prescribed fire to either the dormant or growing season is that this constraint will limit the number of days available to burn, and ultimately leads to

Longleaf pine in the grass stage

Longleaf pine seedlings that have regenerated in a canopy opening

Longleaf pine in the rocket stage

years, during which time they store sufficient carbon in the taproot to support rapid height growth. Once seedlings emerge from this stage, they rapidly bolt, attaining height growth of 4 to 5 feet in a single growing season, called the "rocket stage" (Wahlenberg 1946). Longleaf pine seedlings may be vulnerable to fire when height growth is initiated if the bud is exposed to flames. Once they reach a sapling stage of about 3 feet in height, these pines are again very resistant to damage from fire (Boyer 1987). The ability of longleaf pine

to withstand fire at an early stage of development contrasts dramatically with slash and loblolly pine seedlings and saplings, which need nearly 15 years of fire exclusion for successful establishment (Myers 1990).

Longleaf pines produce abundant cones every five to seven years (called "mast years"). If the large cone crop coincides with prescribed fire a few months prior to cone fall, the reduced ground cover provides suitable exposed soil conditions for seedling establishment. Relative to those of other pines, the seeds are large and have a persistent wing that makes it difficult for them to reach bare soil when dense vegetation is present. Seeds also germinate the same year that they are released. In natural stands of longleaf pine, successful seedling establishment occurs in small canopy openings where adult trees have died (usually from lightning strike). Because of the longevity of the trees and regeneration within gaps, natural stands of longleaf pine are multi-aged.

Young pines are more likely to grow faster in open gaps than near an adult pine because there is more sunlight and less competition for nutrients (McGuire et al. 2001). Also, the pine needles that accumulate around mature trees fuel more intense fire that often eliminates the smaller and younger trees nearby. Thus, fire and competition encourage regeneration in gaps away from adult trees (W. J. Platt, Evans, and Rathbun 1988; Palik and Pederson 1996). Unlike other pines, longleaf pine can be suppressed in the mid-story for years to even decades by the canopy of other pines and then grow quickly into the canopy when a gap is formed. The tree can attain a height of 80 to 100 feet and a bole diameter up to 3 feet. Trees greater than 100 years of age become more flat-topped in stature, as growth occurs more in lateral branches rather than vertically at the top of the crown.

The extremely flammable long, heavy needles of longleaf pine facilitate the spread of fire (Fonda 2001), particularly when fallen needles are held off the ground by clumps of wiregrass. When suspended, longleaf pine needles remain dry and decompose much less rapidly than those on bare soil (Hendricks and Boring 1999; Boring et al. 2004). Consequently, the combination of the highly flammable wiregrass and the accumulated needles increases the potential to carry a fire.

Bark of mature longleaf pine trees is thick and layered, insulating the bole from fire. The flat plates of bark also dissipate heat by sloughing off during fire. The fire tolerance of this species is maintained with frequent, low-intensity fire. Following prolonged fire exclusion and buildup of fuels and organic duff, pine roots develop close to the surface, and then, even mature trees can be vulnerable to reintroduction of fire (Varner et al. 2005). Contributing to this tree's exceptional longevity is the extremely resinous sapwood, which protects it from insect pests and pathogens (J. D. Hodges et al. 1979).

The Biology of Southern Wiregrass. Southern wiregrass is a dominant ground cover species and is often considered to be a key component of the fire-dependent longleaf pine ecosystem due to its function as a high-quality fuel source (W. J. Platt, Evans, and Davis 1988; Clewell 1989; Hardin and White 1989). Wiregrass is also known as pineland three-awn, named for the three spike-like appendages associated with the mature spikelet. Depending on the taxonomic authority, wiregrass is either recognized as a single species, *Aristida stricta*, or is separated into two species, with the more southern taxon called *A. beyrichiana*. Arguments for two species are based on a distributional break in South Carolina and a difference in leaf and sheath pubescence in northern and southern populations (Peet 1993). Others contend that these differences do not warrant distinction at the species level (Kesler, Anderson, and Hermann 2003; Wunderlin and Hansen 2003).

Wiregrass (in the broad sense) once occurred in abundance from southeastern North Carolina, south to

Southern wiregrass is a dominant grass that serves as an important fuel.

southern Florida, and westward to southern Alabama and coastal Mississippi, but little of this native ground cover remains today. Although the historic range is not entirely concurrent with that of longleaf pine, it occurs across a significant portion of it. Recognition of the importance of this ground cover species in the long-term maintenance of the longleaf pine ecosystem has stimulated a growing interest in restoration and the development of commercially available seed sources of wiregrass and other functionally important species.

Wiregrass is a nonrhizomatous bunch grass with numerous narrow, long leaf blades that are enrolled, giving it a wiry characteristic. Clumps of wiregrass form a dominant matrix in the ground cover. The vertical arrangement of highly sclerenchymous tillers (composed of plant tissue with thickened, dry cells) supports accumulated pine needle litter, providing a spatially continuous fuel that increases the overall pyrogenicity of the ground cover (Landers 1991; Boring et al. 2004). Thus, abundant wiregrass in the ground cover greatly enhances opportunities for fire management because it carries a sustained, evenly burning fire under a wider range of humidity conditions than other fuel types.

Some of the natural history characteristics of wiregrass produce difficulties in restoration and regeneration of the species on sites where it has been eliminated. One factor is that initiation of flowering and viable seed production is dependent on a late season fire (May–July), as opposed to earlier burn dates. Additionally, wiregrass does not recover readily from intense soil perturbations (Clewell 1989; Outcalt and Lewis 1990; Outcalt 1992). Not only is wiregrass vulnerable to root disturbance, it has an extremely slow rate of reestablishment as the dominant species in sites once removed (Clewell 1989; Outcalt 1992). Thus, its presence has been used as an indicator of soils that have not been subjected to agricultural cultivation. The loss of wiregrass across vast areas due to disturbance and the paucity of viable seed production caused by the prevalent land management practices of winter-burning or absence of fire are factors contributing to a lack of reinvasion of wiregrass in cultivated or disturbed sites. Even when viable seed is produced, the rate of expansion due to seed dispersal is very low (Mulligan, Kirkman, and Mitchell 2002). The percentage of viable seeds produced varies from year to year, and the germination and establishment from seeds is dependent on adequate precipitation in spring.

Once established, wiregrass is extremely persistent and is thought to be a long-lived species (Clewell 1989). It is very drought tolerant and occurs across a broad ecological gradient from periodically saturated soils to xeric sandhills. Although frequent fire is required for wiregrass to retain dominance over fire-intolerant hardwoods, wiregrass can persist in low-light situations under dense canopy cover for many years (Mulligan, Kirkman, and Mitchell 2002). Following reintroduction of fire, suppressed wiregrass plants can respond vigorously.

Ground cover vegetation that has not been subjected to intense below-ground disturbances (mechanical or chemical) or a history of intense grazing has appreciably higher species richness than that of disturbed sites, even after decades of "recovery" (Hedman, Grace, and King 2000; Kirkman et al. 2004a). Thus, the presence of wiregrass as a dominant ground cover component suggests an "old-growth" characteristic of vegetation regardless of the age of the canopy trees.

Ecological Forestry. Managing longleaf pine stands to extract timber with a goal of sustaining an uneven-aged forest with diverse ground cover requires management strategies to promote fuels necessary for frequent prescribed fire. One approach that has been applied to several large private properties of southwestern Georgia and northern Florida is the Stoddard-Neel silvicultural method, a single-tree selection system (Jack, Neel, and Mitchell 2006; Kirkman and Mitchell 2006; Neel, Sutter, and Way 2010). Tree selection for harvest depends on the site conditions and spatial distribution of trees within the stand. Cutting is designed to release grass-stage seedlings or enhance forest openings to encourage new regeneration, but opening size and total area are restricted to maintain the canopy cover needed to produce litter and to control hardwood encroachment (Jack, Neel, and Mitchell 2006). In addition to overstory retention for continual production of fuels, avoidance of soil disturbances that disrupt ground cover root systems is considered an essential management priority for ecological forestry practices. The impacts of grazing by cattle on the native ground cover have been little studied, although loss of legumes with even moderate grazing is likely (Stoddard and Komarek 1941; C. Frost, Walker, and Peet 1986).

A canopy reduction approach with variable overstory retention has also been advocated as a restoration alternative to clearcuts in the conversion of single-age slash or longleaf pine plantations to multi-age longleaf pine forests (Kirkman et al. 2007). Reintroduction of native ground cover species may be necessary where land use disturbances have eliminated the vegetation. Numerous restoration efforts are under way on state and federal lands in the Georgia Coastal Plain and a growing interest is emerging on private lands. Management activities range from habitat rehabilitation with hardwood removal and reintroduction of fire in fire-excluded longleaf pine sites to planting longleaf pine seedlings and establishing wiregrass as a fine fuel in extremely disturbed sites. Hardwood reduction may be necessary in sites that have been excluded from fire for long periods, particularly where off-site species have encroached in the absence of fire (Kane, Varner, and Hiers 2008). Federal and state landowner incentive programs have promoted longleaf pine establishment and use of prescribed fire to remove marginally productive agricultural lands from production and to encourage wildlife habitat. The long-term success of such large-scale restoration efforts will require development of commercial sources of regional plant materials for reintroduction.

Sandhills and River Dunes

Sandhills and river dunes are ultra-xeric woodland communities restricted to deep sands of ridges and knolls of the Coastal Plain. They occur throughout the Coastal Plain but are particularly prominent in two main locations in Georgia: along the Fall Line and on northeastern banks of major rivers. These infertile woodlands are often quite picturesque, featuring stunted trees and areas of bare sand and thick lichen cover. The structure of the plant community is highly variable, depending on fire frequency, fertility, and previous timber removal. An open canopy of scattered longleaf pine with a subcanopy of turkey oak is present, although fire-suppressed or cut-over sandhills may be strongly dominated by turkey oak. The ground cover is extremely sparse on these dry, sterile sites, yet this habitat harbors more than 30 plant species of concern. Several fossorial animal species (those

adapted for digging and living underground) or species uniquely associated with gopher tortoise or pocket gopher burrows are among faunal species of concern. Several public lands offer notable examples of this scenic community with characteristic elfin trees and lichen-encrusted sands: examples include George L. Smith State Park (Emanuel County), Little Ocmulgee State Park (Telfair County), Ohoopee Dunes Natural Area (Emanuel County) (see the Featured Place), and the Savannah-Ogeechee Canal Museum and Nature Center (Chatham County).

PHYSICAL SETTING AND ECOLOGY

Sandhill woodlands occur throughout the Coastal Plain on isolated upland ridges and knolls with deep (10–20 feet), coarse, sandy soils. These excessively drained soils result in very xeric and infertile conditions due to rapid leaching of moisture and nutrients from the sandy soil. The xeric sandhill longleaf pine woodlands often transition downslope into dry longleaf pine communities where soils have a higher proportion of clay and silt (Bozeman 1971). A good example of this transition can be seen at Ohoopee Dunes Natural Area.

The two most commonly recognized deep sandy communities are the Fall Line sandhills and river-associated dunes. Fall Line sandhills occur on conspicuous sand ridges ranging from 300 to 700 feet above mean sea level in the upper Coastal Plain (R. M. Harper 1906; Wharton 1978). In Georgia, these sandhills form a narrow, discontinuous belt of deep sands across the state from Richmond County (Augusta) to Chattahoochee County (Columbus) and are continuous with Fall Line hills that extend into the Carolinas. Fall Line sandhills are composed primarily of Cretaceous-age and some Eocene-age marine sands and clays deposited over the crystalline and metamorphic rocks of the Piedmont (see overview of Coastal Plain). Across the state, this band of rolling to hilly deep sands of the Fall Line transitions into a parallel band of less hilly terrain with finer-textured soils. Examples of sandhills of Miocene origin occur in Wilcox, Pulaski, Taylor, and Talbot Counties. An accessible example is Fall Line Sandhills Natural Area in Taylor County.

River dunes are extremely deep sand ridges that occur parallel to and east or northeast of major streams in the Coastal Plain of Georgia, such as the Altamaha River (McIntosh and Long Counties), the Ohoopee River (Tattnall County), the Flint River (Dougherty County), and the Canoochee River (Bulloch and Candler Counties) (R. M. Harper 1905b; Thorne 1949b; Ivester and Leigh 2003). The river dunes were formed between 15,000 and 30,000 years ago, when westerly winds transported sands from exposed river bars onto the east and northeast banks of major streams, forming high ridges. Later, the dunes were reshaped by wind and rain erosion and altered by flood events (Cooke 1945; MacNeil 1950; Bozeman 1971; Ivester and Leigh 2003). Soil development, such as increased clay in the B horizon or spodic horizons, has occurred over thousands of years. Today, these dunes are inactive because vegetation has secured their surface, reducing wind action (Ivester and Leigh 2003).

Dunes along the Ohoopee and Canoochee Rivers lie parallel to these rivers for distances exceeding 60 miles. The Ohoopee Dunes have been dissected by streams and eroded such that distinct bands associated with depositional periods are somewhat obscured. In contrast, dune fields along the Canoochee are more reflective of distinct phases of aeolian sedimentation (Ivester and Leigh 2003). An isolated field of dunes occurs along the Flint River in Dougherty County and is the westernmost river dune in Georgia. Another extensive dune system lies near the southeastern edge of the dune cluster along the Altamaha River, about 25 miles downstream from its confluence with the Ohoopee River. Here several bands of dunes extend to nearly 2.5 miles from the modern river channel (Ivester and Leigh 2003).

Fire plays a key role in the successional dynamics and structure of this community, although prolonged region-wide fire exclusion has degraded the condition of many sites (Pessin 1933; Faust 1976). The natural fire return interval probably varied from 5 to 10 years, depending on the fertility of the site and accumulation of fuels. Vegetation change in the absence of fire occurs more slowly on the most xeric sites (Bozeman 1971; S. Ware, Frost, and Doerr 1993). Due to the slower rate of hardwood encroachment, the maintenance of vegetation of xeric systems does not require fire as frequently as that of more fertile conditions.

Expanses of bare sand and patchy vegetation create natural firebreaks. Leaf litter accumulates directly beneath clusters of oaks or pines, forming islands of vegetation and organic debris in the sandy matrix. Over time, as these islands expand and grasses and forbs become established, they become large enough and contain enough fuel to foster fire. Initial establishment of young oak seedlings is dependent on a fire-free period or patchiness within a burned area that provides a fire-free microsite for establishment. Once established, some oaks, such as turkey oak, are extremely fire-tolerant (Heyward 1939; Rebertus, Williamson, and Moser 1989; Cavender-Bares, Kitajima, and Bazzaz 2004). Frequent fire reduces the density of oaks and, conversely, periods of fire suppression may result in thick stands of oaks. Removal of pine canopy eliminates pine needles as a source of fuel, further contributing to fire exclusion. Due to their topographic position and proximity to a water body or swamp, river dune habitats may have a lower natural fire-return interval than other sandhill sites (Goebel et al. 2001).

The deep, sandy soils and barrenness of sandhill communities often invite recreational activities, such as off-road vehicle use, that are detrimental to the habitat for fossorial species, as well as rare plant species. Conservation management often requires reintroduction of fire regimes. On sites where longleaf pine has been harvested and seed sources are insufficient for regeneration, restoration may require planting pines and grasses to establish fuels necessary for prescribed fire. Because of the excessively drained soils, successful establishment of planted pine seedlings is highly dependent on adequate rainfall during the season of planting. Mechanical or chemical reduction of hardwoods is often used as a restoration tool to accelerate structural changes (Provencher et al. 2001).

VEGETATION

On very coarse sands, the most xeric sites are dominated by a scattered overstory of longleaf pine and an understory dominated by turkey oak. Turkey oak, one of the most drought-tolerant oak species (Donovan, West, and McLeod 2000), is a clonal tree that grows very slowly on dry soils; thus, the understory trees usually occur as stunted patches with an open canopy, even when quite old (Berg and Hamrick 1994). Large areas of bare sand may be present with dense patches of lichens. Past land use that included the harvest of the longleaf pine canopy often results in nearly complete oak dominance even after many decades because the extremely sterile conditions of the site discourage reestablishment of the pines. This condition becomes further reinforced when historically the source of pine seeds was totally removed (Myers 1990). Turkey oaks, through clonal reproduction, can persist on the open sites indefinitely.

Sand post oak, sassafras, and American persimmon may occur in addition to turkey oak. Sand live oak occurs as scattered individuals or dome-like clumps. Several shrubs and herbaceous ground cover species are uniquely associated with sandhill vegetation. For example, in the Fall Line ultra-xeric sandhills of Fort Benning and the river dunes of Ohoopee Dunes Natural Area, Little Ocmulgee State Park, and Big Hammock Natural Area, the rare woody goldenrod is often a prominent dwarf-shrub. The sandhill golden-aster is endemic to Fall Line sandhills and occurs primarily in Taylor County and surrounding areas, including Fall Line Sandhills Natural Area. Sandhill rosemary, a Threatened species in Georgia, is found primarily in xeric river dune habitats. This evergreen shrub has needle-like and aromatic leaves that resemble rosemary. Although this species is killed by fire, it will vigorously reseed. The herbaceous ground cover

Woody goldenrod

of extremely dry sandhill sites may range from nearly barren to sparse ground cover of xerophytic species including tread-softly, arrowfeather, southern wiregrass, milkpea, savanna hairsedge, sandhill wild-buckwheat, gopher-apple, and wire-plant. Many of these species have morphological or physiological traits that protect them from excessive sunlight and prevent water loss, such as small, curled evergreen leaves, waxy or hairy leaves or stems, and reduced leaf size (R. M. Harper 1906; Abrahamson et al. 1984).

The distribution of oak species is due to their individual tolerances to dry soil conditions and to variation in fire regimes caused by the amount and patchiness of fuels across the moisture gradient (Monk 1968; Jacqmain, Jones, and Mitchell 1999). For example, where slightly finer soil textures enable more moisture and nutrients to be retained in the sandy soils, sand post oak and bluejack oak share dominance with turkey oak (Jacqmain, Jones, and Mitchell 1999). Of

CHARACTERISTIC PLANTS OF SANDHILLS AND RIVER DUNES

TREES

Longleaf pine—Pinus palustris
Bluejack oak—Quercus incana
Turkey oak—Quercus laevis
Sand post oak—Quercus margarettae

SHRUBS AND WOODY VINES

Dwarf huckleberry—Gaylussacia
  dumosa
Poison oak—Toxicodendron pubescens
Sparkleberry—Vaccinium arboreum
Mayberry—Vaccinium elliottii

GROUND COVER

Sandhills bluestar—Amsonia ciliata
Southern wiregrass—Aristida
  beyrichiana
Arrowfeather—Aristida purpurascens
Savanna hairsedge—Bulbostylis
  ciliatifolia
Tread-softly—Cnidoscolus stimulosus
Sandhill wild-buckwheat—Eriogonum
  tomentosum
Milkpeas—Galactia spp.
Gopher-apple—Licania michauxii

Pink sandhill lupine—Lupinus villosus
Rugel's nailwort—Paronychia rugellii
Silkgrass—Pityopsis graminifolia
Sandhill jointweed—Polygonella
  polygama
Wire-plant—Stipulicida setacea
Southern sandgrass—Triplasis
  americana

these species, bluejack oak occurs across the greatest range of soil moisture conditions (Cavender-Bares, Kitajima, and Bazzaz 2004). All three of these oak species have traits that are related to fire tolerance and postfire recovery, such as thick bark and the ability to resprout from rhizomes (Cavender-Bares, Kitajima, and Bazzaz 2004). Turkey oaks have a highly efficient water-use metabolism relative to that of other species of oaks (Donovan, West, and McLeod 2000). The unusual vertical leaf orientation of turkey oak has been suggested as a drought-avoidance mechanism, although the increased survival value has not been demonstrated (Pallardy and Kozlowski 2008).

Spatial patchiness and variability in historical fire frequency, season, and intensity permit oaks to reach and maintain tree size in varying densities in sandhill sites (Greenberg and Simons 1999). In moister sites, the shrub stratum may transition into sparkleberry, mayberry, deerberry, dwarf huckleberry, yellow hawthorn, and poison oak. The slightly higher fertility and greater moisture retention of these soils are reflected in a more continuous ground cover with higher species richness than ultra-xeric sites. Common species include wiregrass, seymeria, southern oak-leach, bracken fern, common little bluestem, and several species of legumes. Increased abundance of ground cover provides fine fuels necessary to carry fire; thus, more productive sites are able to burn more frequently, provided that fire ignition occurs. The frequency of fire strongly controls the establishment and abundance of oaks.

ANIMALS

The gopher tortoise is a land tortoise that is often associated with xeric longleaf pine communities. In Georgia, this species is classified as Threatened. Gopher tortoises excavate deep burrows that are also a critical resource for many species that are found in sandhill habitats. More than 250 species of vertebrate and invertebrate animals have been documented making use of active or abandoned tortoise burrows (see p. 384). Mole skinks are small, slender lizards with a distinctive long, red tail. They are adept at burrowing, preferring loose sandy soil, such as sandhill habitats and pocket gopher burrows. These secretive lizards wriggle, or "swim," through sand or loose soil, often disappearing in a flash as soon as they are discovered. They prey on tiny insects, spiders, and other invertebrates. Their range is coincident with that of the southeastern pocket gopher (Means 2006).

Snakes that are particularly associated with longleaf pine–turkey oak or barren sandhill communities include the eastern indigo snake, the eastern diamondback rattlesnake, the Florida pine snake, and the southern hognose snake. The federally and state Threatened eastern indigo snake is typically associated with xeric sandhill habitat that is interspersed with wetlands such as swamps, streams, and canals. They occur primarily in the lower Coastal Plain and in the Tifton Uplands (Diemer and Speake 1983; Stevenson, Moulis, and Hyslop 2008). This thick-bodied, shiny, bluish black snake is the largest nonvenomous native snake in North America, reaching a length of as many as 8 feet. The indigo snake often seeks refuge in gopher tortoise and armadillo burrows and in longleaf pine stump holes for nesting and retreat. It is known for its ability to eat venomous snakes, such as rattlesnakes, and it feeds on other nonvenomous snakes, frogs, and rodents (Ernst and Ernst 2003; Means 2006). Habitat loss from development and agriculture, habitat degradation due to lack of fire and human activities, and collection for the pet trade have led to significant reductions in populations of eastern indigo snakes.

Florida pine snakes are frequently found in barren sandhill communities or longleaf pine–turkey oak sites. They spend much of their time underground, particularly in association with gopher tortoise or pocket gopher burrows (Franz 1992, 2005; Means 2006). These large, grayish-brown snakes are excellent burrowers, and they dig both hibernacula and summer dens in the sandy soil. Their diet consists of ground-dwelling birds and their eggs, southeastern pocket gophers, and other small mammals (Ernst and Ernst 2003; Means 2006). In Georgia, pine snakes are listed as Threatened.

The southern hognose snake is considered to be one of the most xeric-adapted species in the eastern United States. It is an extremely fossorial species, with an upturned snout adapted to dig up its prey (mostly toads) in burrows and in the stump and root holes of rotting pines (Means 2006). In Georgia, it is listed as Threatened. It appears to have declined substantially throughout its range. Although not restricted to sandhill sites, the eastern diamondback rattlesnake is another species that often occurs in association with gopher tortoise burrows. These large, venomous snakes with brown, tan, or yellowish diamond-shaped patterns are restricted to the Coastal Plain of the Southeast, from southern North Carolina to eastern Louisiana, occurring primarily in Florida and southern Georgia. The eastern diamondback rattlesnake receives no federal protection despite the fact that it has declined over much of its range due to habitat destruction, deliberate killing, and highway mortality.

Gopher frogs are found in sandhills as well as other longleaf pine sites in association with depres-sional wetlands. This frog is very secretive and hides in upland burrows, including gopher tortoise burrows, longleaf pine stump holes, and crayfish burrows. These sites provide refuges with relatively stable temperature and humidity. This species requires access to temporary ponds for reproduction. This frog is a Protected species in Georgia and is a candidate for federal listing (see p. 454).

Numerous scarab beetles are endemic to xeric longleaf pine uplands and feed on the dung of vertebrate inhabitants. Three scarab beetle species occur only in pocket gopher burrows, and two are obligate associates of the gopher tortoise (Skelley and Gordon 2001). Other species of scarab beetles dig their own burrows, leaving conspicuous mounds of sand at the entrance to tunnels that may be up to 8 feet deep (Olson, Hubbell, and Howden 1954). A newly described species of beetle, *Polyphylla donalsoni*, is known only from the dunes associated with the Ohoopee River (Skelley 2003). Likewise, several rare species of grasshopper have been found within these dune systems (Hill 2009). Eastern harvester ants are conspicuous residents of xeric longleaf pine communities because of their distinctive mounds. The flattened mound is often covered with small pebbles or charcoal from burned areas (Gordon 1984). This large ant species is most active in rather low relative humidity (below 55%) and in high temperatures (> 85°F), gathering seed for storage in the mound.

Sites that are open with significant grassy ground cover often harbor Bachman's sparrows and blue grosbeaks. If adequate snags are present, cavity nesters such as the great crested flycatcher, American kestrel, and eastern bluebird will nest here. A large percentage of the viable populations of the federally Endangered red-cockaded woodpecker remaining in Georgia occur on Fort Benning and Fort Stewart in sandhills and river dunes that have 80- to 120(+)-year-old longleaf pine stands. Although this bird was once abundant throughout the longleaf pine forests of the southeastern Coastal Plain, loss of habitat and removal of old pine trees that are critical for nest cavity construction have greatly reduced populations of this woodpecker. (See p. 392.)

Southeastern Pocket Gopher
(*Geomys pinetis*)

The southeastern pocket gopher, also known locally as "sandy-mounder" or "salamander," is a medium-sized rodent associated with sandy upland communities of the Coastal Plain. Pocket gophers are medium to dark brown on the upper parts of the body and grayish beneath. They are about 10 to 12 inches long and have stout front legs with large claws for digging. They have a hairless tail and small eyes and ears. Pocket gophers are related to moles, but can be distinguished by their larger body size and large incisor teeth.

This fossorial mammal requires deep, well-drained sandy soils to dig extensive tunnel systems and is rarely seen above ground. The presence of the pocket gopher is easily detected by its tunnels; it pushes excess soil to the surface, creating conspicuous mounds of sand. It occurs most abundantly in longleaf pine–turkey oak sandhills in Georgia, Florida, and Alabama, but it is also found in other upland Coastal Plain habitats with well-drained sandy or gravelly soil. Within its tunnel system, the pocket gopher feeds on fleshy rhizomes, roots, bulbs, and tubers. Food is temporarily stored in cheek pouches and then emptied into food storage chambers in the burrow. Pocket gophers also build nests deep within the burrow and breed throughout the year. They are the major prey of pine snakes that frequent the burrows (Franz 2005). The pocket gopher has greatly declined throughout most of its range (Means 2006) and is protected in Georgia.

Ohoopee Dunes Natural Area

Ohoopee Dunes Natural Area consists of five tracts in Emanuel County, near Swainsboro in east-central Georgia. Three parcels are owned by the Georgia Department of Natural Resources, one by the Nature Conservancy, and one by the U.S. Fish and Wildlife Service. These protected tracts are part of the dune system that stretches more than 35 miles along the Ohoopee River and covers around 40,000 acres. The Hall's Bridge Tract features a scenic loop trail (approximately 1.5 miles) that traverses the characteristic elfin forest of stunted turkey oak, sand live oak, and occasional longleaf pine. Shrubs of particular interest along this trail are the rare sandhill rosemary, woody goldenrod, and scarlet wild basil. Scattered among the bare white sands and lichens are Carolina sandwort, gopher-apple, goat's-rue, prickly-pear, sandhills bluestar, southern oak-leach, and blazing-star. Across

a moisture gradient ranging from ultra-xeric sandhill to wetlands, several other examples of vegetation associated with sandhill vegetation can be observed, including dry upland longleaf pine forests, seepage swamps, floodplain bottomlands, and floodplain swamps. A species endemic to this site is the Ohoopee Dunes moth. The larvae of this species use the woody goldenrod as a food source (Covell 1984).

Location: To reach the Hall's Bridge tract, go north from Norristown on U.S. Hwy. 221/Ga. 171 for 0.7 mile to Hall's Bridge Rd./CR 160. Turn right on Hall's Bridge Rd. and proceed for 1.6 miles to the entrance and kiosk on the left, just past the end of Hall's Bridge. The tract is located both to the north and south of the road and is bordered by the Little Ohoopee River to the west. Google Earth GPS approximate coordinates at the parking area: N 32.528414/ W 082.456650.

Dry Upland Longleaf Pine Woodlands

Dry upland longleaf pine woodlands occur on sandy soils on nearly level to undulating terrain throughout the state (Wells and Shunk 1931; Peet 2006). This droughty community is characterized by the presence of longleaf pine in the canopy and oak mid-story species such as turkey oak, bluejack oak, sand post oak, and southern red oak. It contrasts with that of sandhill and river dune woodlands with a more continuous, species-rich ground cover dominated by wiregrass. Also, due to greater fertility and soil moisture, trees are not as stunted as those of sandhill and river dune vegetation.

As is the case for all longleaf pine communities, the dry upland longleaf pine woodlands are globally imperiled as a result of habitat degradation from fire exclusion and extensive land use conversion. Numerous examples of habitat restoration of this once widespread community are under way on several Georgia state parks, wildlife management areas (WMAs), and natural areas. Rare animal species that are associated with these sites are similar to those on sandhills or more mesic upland longleaf forests.

PHYSICAL SETTING AND ECOLOGY

Although now regionally rare, remnant dry upland longleaf pine woodlands are scattered throughout the Coastal Plain. These woodlands may develop on the lower slopes of sandy summits and ridges that support the ultra-xeric sandhill or river dune community. They also develop in shallow depressions within excessively drained sites where soil horizons have accumulated slightly more silt or clay at subsurface depths of about 3 to 6 feet.

In areas of highly dissected topography, such as the Coastal Plain Red Hills and associated Fall Line Sandhills region, the transition from ultra-xeric woodland (the sandhill and river dune longleaf pine woodland community) to these subxeric forests can be particularly dramatic. Dry upland longleaf pine woodlands also occur on the deep marine sands of the lower Coastal Plain on more level terrain that transitions to the longleaf pine flatwoods community. On the upper Coastal Plain, dry upland longleaf pine woodlands develop on small knolls that form as caps of deep sand over loamy or clayey soils, such as in the Atlantic Southern Loam Plains (Vidalia Uplands), Tallahassee Hills, and the Tifton Uplands (Peet 2006). Dry upland longleaf pine woodlands or forests often transition into wet longleaf pine or slash pine seepage slopes, where groundwater emerges along the gentle slope, eventually developing into a seepage slope herb or shrub bog. Such juxtaposition of communities can be observed along upland trails in Reed Bingham State Park (Cook County) (see the Featured Place) and along Big Creek Nature Trail in Laura S. Walker State Park (Ware County). Dry upland longleaf pine woodlands in the Dougherty Plain often extend to the edge of the river bank rather than grade into a floodplain or seepage slope as in most other subregions of the Coastal Plain because streams and rivers of this landform are often deeply incised into the limestone substrate; hence, they lack a well-developed floodplain that would restrict frequent fire (Goebel et al. 2001). Such deep, sandy sites occur along large tracts of frequently burned longleaf pine uplands adjacent to the Flint River and Ichawaynochaway Creek in Dougherty, Mitchell, and Baker Counties.

As is the case for all longleaf pine communities, fire is a dominant factor structuring the dry upland longleaf pine woodland composition, as it interacts with landform, soil texture, and hydrologic regime. A prescribed fire-return interval of two to three years is needed to maintain this longleaf pine community. Otherwise, hardwoods will encroach and grow large enough to withstand fire. The presence of dense hardwoods and resultant leaf litter then shade out the herbaceous ground cover and prevent longleaf pine regeneration. Efforts to restore dry upland longleaf pine woodlands are under way in several state parks, in Georgia WMAs, on the Nature Conservancy properties, and on U.S. military bases on sites that have been fire-suppressed, or where the longleaf pine has been harvested and converted to plantations of other pine species. Relative to ultra-xeric sand ridge conditions, a greater frequency of prescribed fire management is necessary to control hardwood encroachment on subxeric upland longleaf pine sites because of in-

creased growth rates associated with these more fertile sites.

VEGETATION

Dry upland longleaf pine woodlands, when frequently burned and minimally disturbed, have widely spaced pine trees with few understory shrubs and a continuous ground cover typically dominated by southern wiregrass. Longleaf pine strongly dominates the canopy, and scrub oaks are primarily maintained in the ground cover or understory strata as sprouts that are killed back to the roots when burned frequently. With longer fire-return intervals, oaks such as turkey oak, bluejack oak, sand laurel oak, sand post oak, and southern red oak occur as mid-story or canopy trees. Other common woody understory species include American persimmon, sassafras, winged sumac, blackberry, sparkleberry, and poison oak.

Although wiregrass appears to strongly dominate, the ground cover typically supports a diverse array of species, including numerous perennial grasses, com-

Gopher-apple

posites, and legumes, that depend on a fire-maintained habitat. The ground cover of these sites is less species-rich than that of more mesic locations, which are associated with increased silt content (Kirkman et al. 2004b; Peet 2006). Soil moisture is likely a limiting resource for seedling establishment, and fewer species are adapted to the more drought-prone end of the gradient, although numerous species span the entire gradient from sandy to loamy soils (Kirkman et al. 2001; Iacona, Kirkman, and Bruna 2010).

Common legumes of well-drained sites include spurred butterfly pea, butterfly pea, dollarweed, erect milkpea, rabbitbells, lupine scurfpea, goat's-rue, pencil-flower, Florida sensitive-briar, and numerous species of lespedeza and tick-trefoils (Thorne 1949b; Drew, Kirkman, and Gholson 1998). (See p. 382.) In addition to southern wiregrass, other common grasses are also considered to be functionally important species because of their role in providing fine fuel necessary to carry fire. Some of these include species of bluestem, several species of broomsedge, lopsided indiangrass, yellow indiangrass, witchgrasses, rough dropseed, hairgrass, arrowfeather, and sandhills dropseed. Composites can be a striking component of these forests, particularly when blooming in the fall. Common species include silkgrass, several species of blazing-stars, licorice goldenrod, Maryland golden-aster, and numerous species of thoroughworts and American asters. Other herbaceous species that are frequently associated with dry upland longleaf pine woodlands include bracken fern, gopher-apple, silver croton, southern oak-leach, and pitted stripeseed (Thorne 1949b; Drew, Kirkman, and Gholson 1998).

A blackjack-mixed oak variant occurs where a clayey horizon, sandstone, or ironstone is present beneath the surface. Sites with increased clay within roughly 3 feet of the soil surface are particularly prevalent in the Fall Line hills (Bozeman 1971). In these longleaf pine-dominated sites, blackjack oak is more common in the mid-story than other scrub oaks such as turkey oak and bluejack oak. Shortleaf pine is also frequently present in sites that were previously cultivated (R. M. Harper 1943; Thorne 1949b; Monk 1968; Weaver 1969; Peet 2006). Blackjack-mixed oak–dominated woodlands embedded in some dry longleaf pine woodlands in the Tifton Uplands and Atlantic Southern Loam Plains are associated with scattered indurated sandstone outcrops (Altamaha Grit; see also acidic glades, barrens, and rocky woodlands). Here a scattered canopy of longleaf pine and an understory of stunted blackjack and sand post oak are present. Another example of this variant of longleaf pine woodland occurs in an old-growth stand at Moody Forest Natural Area (Appling County), jointly owned and managed by the Nature Conservancy and the Georgia Department of Natural Resources. This woodland type can be viewed along the Upland Loop Trail. At this site, southern red oak is also abundant and probably reflects fire suppression.

Rugel's nailwort (sand squares)

THE ECOLOGICAL IMPORTANCE OF LEGUMES

Legume species are an important component of the longleaf pine ecosystem because of their abundance and their roles in nitrogen fixation and as a food source for wildlife. Most native legumes are perennial species that are well adapted to resprouting following fire. Although legumes do not require fire to flower, several species experience a burst of flowering following fire. The majority of legume species require a bee pollinator for successful pollination. Seeds of many species have a hard seed coat that is impermeable to water and enables them to remain viable in the soil for many years, until conditions become favorable for germination.

Native legumes are often an important component of the vascular flora of longleaf pine communities, particularly on more fine-textured (loamy) soil. In some localities, stem density estimates exceed 280,000 stems per acre (Hainds et al. 1999). Particularly common species are butterfly pea, Pursh's rattlebox, rabbitbells, white tassels, summer farewell, dollarweed, snoutbean, pencil-flower, goat's-rue, leather-root, and numerous species of tick-trefoil, milkpea, and lespedeza.

Many species of legumes are nitrogen fixers, meaning they have the ability to convert atmospheric nitrogen into forms usable by plants. Legumes have a mutualistic relationship with special types of soil bacteria, called "rhizobia," which penetrate legume roots and create small growths, called "nodules." The legume provides the rhizobia with energy and nutrients, and in return, the rhizobia transform atmospheric nitrogen into usable nitrogen compounds that are eventually returned to the soil. This process is particularly important in the fire-dependent longleaf pine ecosystem, where frequent burning leads to the loss of significant amounts of organic nitrogen from the soil (Boring et al. 2004).

The high nutrient and protein contents of leguminous species render them preferred forage for many herbivores, including white-tailed deer, gopher tortoises, rabbits, and pocket gophers. Legumes are also abundant producers of seeds, which are an important component of the diets of northern bobwhite, wild turkey, seed-eating songbirds, and small mammals. Several species have bushy growth forms that provide cover for ground-nesting birds.

Butterfly pea

Virginia goat's-rue

CHARACTERISTIC PLANTS OF DRY UPLAND LONGLEAF PINE WOODLANDS

TREES

Longleaf pine—Pinus palustris
Sand live oak—Quercus geminata
Sand laurel oak—Quercus hemisphaerica
Bluejack oak—Quercus incana
Turkey oak—Quercus laevis
Sand post oak—Quercus margarettae

SHRUBS AND WOODY VINES

Sand blackberry—Rubus cuneifolius
Dune greenbrier—Smilax auriculata
Poison oak—Toxicodendron pubescens

GROUND COVER

Sandhills bluestar—Amsonia ciliata
Southern wiregrass—Aristida beyrichiana
Arrowfeather—Aristida purpurascens
Slimleaf pawpaw—Asimina angustifolia
Maryland golden-aster—Chrysopsis mariana
Butterfly pea—Clitoria mariana
Rabbitbells—Crotalaria rotundifolia
Silver croton—Croton argyranthemus
Florida tick-trefoil—Desmodium floridanum
Pineland tick-trefoil—Desmodium strictum
Erect milkpea—Galactia erecta
Gopher-apple—Licania michauxii
Florida sensitive-briar—Mimosa quadrivalvis
Silkgrass—Pityopsis graminifolia
Bracken fern—Pteridium aquilinum
Dollarweed—Rhynchosia reniformis
Common little bluestem—Schizachyrium scoparium
Slender bluestem—Schizachyrium tenerum
Indiangrass—Sorghastrum nutans; S. secundum
Rough dropseed—Sporobolus clandestinus
Sandhills dropseed—Sporobolus junceus
Virginia goat's-rue—Tephrosia virginiana
Southern sandgrass—Triplasis americana

ANIMALS

Animal species associated with dry upland longleaf pine woodlands are similar to those described for xeric sandhills and river dunes. Some species, such as gopher tortoises and pocket gophers, are most strongly associated with deep sands. Population densities may tend to decline with increases in fine-textured soil, particularly where the transition along a natural gradient is very abrupt or where the subxeric habitat is truncated by land use alterations. Alternatively, where extensive areas of dry upland longleaf pine woodlands are present, such as in the Dougherty Plain, populations of fossorial species may be extremely high (Eubanks et al. 2002).

Conservative estimates of the number of arthropod species associated with dry upland longleaf pine sites range from 4,000 to 5,000, and about 10% of these species might be considered endemic (Folkerts, Deyrup, and Sisson 1993). At least 50 species of spiders are common in the longleaf pine ecosystem (Hölldobler 1971). Commonly encountered in dry upland longleaf pine habitats is the intriguing trapdoor spider that constructs small burrows with a camouflaged trapdoor made of soil particles, vegetation, and web silk. The trapdoor is hinged on one side with silk. These nocturnal spiders prey on other arthropods or small vertebrates that venture too close to the half-open trapdoor. When the spider detects the prey by vibrations, it leaps out of its burrow and captures the prey, holding on to the trap door with one leg. The large and conspicuous golden orb weaver is often encountered in sandhill and dry longleaf pine sites. This species makes a strong golden web that can stretch more than 6 feet across. Another group of insects with adaptations to the sandy environment are the antlions. The larvae, also called "doodlebugs," construct funnel-shaped pitfall traps in the sand to snare ants as prey (Folkerts, Deyrup, and Sisson 1993).

At least 400 species of butterflies and moths are estimated to be associated with sandhill and dry upland longleaf pine communities. Most commonly sighted are the common buckeye, which use species of the plant family Scrophulariaceae, particularly species of southern oak-leach, as larval host plants. Larvae of the zebra swallowtail butterfly feed on species of pawpaw. Another Lepidopteran species that may be present in this community is the yucca moth, the only insect that is able to pollinate yucca flowers (Folkerts, Deyrup, and Sisson 1993).

Several hundred species of ants are estimated to occur in subxeric longleaf pine sites (Folkerts, Deyrup, and Sisson 1993), the most conspicuous being the eastern harvester ant. Ant species are extremely diverse in their habitat specializations, ranging from strictly subterranean to completely arboreal; some nest in the soil and forage above ground (Folkerts, Deyrup, and Sisson 1993). The seeds of some plant species, such as pitted stripeseed, tread-softly, species of milkworts, and violets, are dispersed by ants (Stamp and Lucas 1990). The red imported fire ant, introduced to the Southeast in the 1950s, has become one of the most dominant ant species, even in relatively undisturbed longleaf pine ecosystems; however, there is little evidence that the introduction of this species results in a decline in native ant species (King, Tschinkel, and Ross 2009; Stuble 2009). Negative impacts of red imported fire ants are particularly associated with mortality of young mammals, reptiles, and ground-nesting birds (Allen, Epperson, and Garmestani 2004).

GOPHER TORTOISE (*GOPHERUS POLYPHEMUS*)

The gopher tortoise is the official state reptile of Georgia. It is widely distributed in the Coastal Plain except for the Okefenokee Swamp and the barrier islands. It is a long-lived species, with a lifespan up to 60 years.

The gopher tortoise excavates deep burrows up to 33 feet long in sandy soils that provide winter hibernacula, shelter from fire and summer heat, and refuge from predation. The unbranched burrows also provide habitat for hundreds of invertebrate and vertebrate species (Folkerts, Deyrup, and Sisson 1993). For this reason, the gopher tortoise has been termed the "keystone species" of the longleaf pine community, meaning its existence is critical to the survival of many other species. Other rare species that are closely associated with the gopher tortoise burrows include eastern indigo snakes and southern pine snakes (Witz, Wilson, and Palmer 1991).

Gopher tortoises graze on grasses and forbs in open stands of the longleaf pine ecosystem. Based on home ranges, an area of 100 acres of open, fire-maintained forest is necessary to support a minimum viable population size of 50 individuals (U.S. Fish and Wildlife Service 1990). The widespread loss and alteration of the longleaf pine-wiregrass ecosystem has eliminated many tortoise populations and isolated most others. The naturally low fecundity is only worsened by isolation, unnaturally high populations of raccoons and other predators, suboptimal habitat conditions, and other factors (Lohoefener and Lohmeier 1981). Tortoises forced into roadside habitats due to a lack of suitable surrounding land are more vulnerable to vehicle impacts and collection by humans. In the past, tortoise populations in many areas were decimated by human exploitation for food, a practice that is now illegal but likely continues in some areas. The introduction of gasoline into the burrows of gopher tortoises or destruction of the burrows to extract rattlesnakes is also illegal.

Restoration of habitat is a critical need for this species. Recent management efforts to restore and enhance appropriate habitat are ongoing at Fort Stewart, Fort Gordon, and Fort Benning, as well as on several state properties, such as Seminole State Park, General Coffee State Park, and Reed Bingham State Park. A multi-agency program was initiated in 2008 to restore gopher tortoise populations in Alabama, Georgia, Florida, and South Carolina.

Gopher tortoise

Sherman's Fox Squirrel
(*Sciurus niger shermani*)

Sherman's fox squirrel is the largest of eight subspecies of fox squirrel in the Southeast. It weighs up to 2 pounds and is approximately 30 inches in length.

Sherman's fox squirrels are quite variable in coloration, being silver, gray, black, or rusty gold. Often they have black masks and distinct white markings on the nose, ears, and feet that are particularly striking. The tail is long and bushy and tipped with tawny hairs. In Georgia, the preferred habitat of the Sherman's fox squirrel is mature, open upland longleaf pine forests. Its large size enables the fox squirrel to tear apart large longleaf pine cones to eat the pine seeds, but acorns, fungi, and fruit are also important components of its diet.

Sherman's fox squirrel requires large tracts of mature open pine-oak stands for its home range; a single male fox squirrel requires about 100 acres (L. M. Conner and Godbois 2003; Perkins and Conner 2004). In open pine stands, some large hardwood trees are desirable as a food source and for nesting sites (Perkins, Conner, and Howze 2008). A decrease in Sherman's fox squirrels has been attributed to loss of longleaf pine forests. This subspecies does not occur in the same habitat as that of gray squirrels, so competition between the two species is not considered to be a factor (Perkins and Conner 2004). Management practices to improve habitat for fox squirrels generally target forest structure and tree species composition, particularly reduction of dense understory vegetation and retention of some mature mast-producing hardwoods (Perkins, Conner, and Howze 2008).

Although hunting mortality is not considered to be a major factor controlling squirrel populations (L. M. Conner 2001), intensively hunted populations may be particularly vulnerable to overharvest depending on their level of isolation and potential for recolonization from nearby refuges (Nixon et al. 1974; Herkert, Nixon, and Hansen 1992).

Reed Bingham State Park

Along several trails in Reed Bingham State Park (Cook and Colquitt Counties), examples of dry upland longleaf pine woodlands can be visited, including an area designated as a gopher tortoise management area. A 1-mile loop, the Gopher Tortoise Bike Loop Trail, features a remnant longleaf pine forest that has dense wiregrass ground cover. This trail is near the border of the park boundary and is downslope from an upland ridge just east of the park. Evidence of prior fire suppression is apparent with the presence of live oak, water oak, bluejack oak, and sand live oak. With aggressive prescribed fire management, the hardwood component is being reduced with each successive burning. Numerous species typical of the fire-maintained community are present, including fall-blooming composites such as blazing-star, long-stalked aster, eastern silvery aster, and silkgrass, and grasses such as Tracy's bluestem, yellow indiangrass, arrow-feather, and common little bluestem. Other typical species include rattlesnake-master, gopher-apple, slim-leaf pawpaw, narrow-leaved lespedeza, and Florida sensitive-briar. About 0.5 mile along the trail, wetter conditions associated with seepage from the adjacent slope are present. Here, indicators of wet soils include little gallberry, ti-ti, Florida dropseed, and saw palmetto. Another trail, the Upland Trail, ascends from the floodplain of the Little River Swamp to the open, upland subxeric forest. Species such as gopher-apple and turkey oak are indicative of dry conditions.

Location: From Hwy. 319 in Moultrie, take Hwy. 37 east approximately 14 miles. Turn north on Evergreen Church Rd. and then east on Reed Bingham Rd. to the park entrance. Parking is available at the Gopher Tortoise Loop and trailhead at the Upland Loop Trail. Google Earth GPS approximate coordinates at park entrance: N 31.161449/W 083.540329.

Mesic Upland Longleaf Pine Woodlands

Mesic upland longleaf pine woodlands occur on upland, well-drained, fine-textured soils of the Coastal Plain. These woodlands have widely spaced longleaf pines, a minor mid-story, and a dense ground cover dominated by wiregrass. The exceptionally diverse ground cover of frequently burned sites renders their recognition as the most species-rich vegetation in North America, surpassing even that of the southern Appalachian coves.

Although mesic longleaf pine woodlands were once the dominant vegetation matrix across vast acreages of the Coastal Plain (Peet 2006), these communities are very rare today because the more fertile loamy soils have largely been converted to agriculture. In Georgia, the remnant stands that escaped the plow and have been frequently burned are mostly on privately owned properties in the southwestern part of the state. Two

particularly noteworthy old-growth sites are tracts in Thomas County. Several privately owned stands of high-quality second-growth longleaf pine with native ground cover occur in Thomas, Worth, Baker, and Dougherty Counties. Extensive second-growth stands of mesic longleaf pine and native ground cover are managed by the J. W. Jones Ecological Research Center at Ichauway (Baker County). Outstanding examples of mesic longleaf pine forests with public access occur at Silver Lake Wildlife Management Area (Decatur County) (see the Featured Place).

PHYSICAL SETTING AND ECOLOGY

The soils of these upland longleaf pine woodlands, loamy sands over clay subsoils, dominate the landscape of major physiographic landforms of the upper Coastal Plain. The soil usually exhibits a soil horizon with a significant accumulation of clay (argillic horizon) within 3 feet of the soil surface, in contrast to subxeric or xeric sites in which a layer of accumulation of clay is much deeper (Goebel et al. 2001). The presence of fine-textured silt and clay in these loamy soils offers greater moisture and nutrient retention properties than that of the sandier substrates of subxeric conditions. Soils with increased surficial clay are characterized by the presence of plinthite (pebble-like iron residues associated with repeated wetting and drying of soil). Thus, soil texture is a strong influence on the species assemblages in this community.

Additionally, other factors, such as terrain of the physiographic landform, geologic strata, and fire regime, are strong drivers of vegetation composition, particularly as they control the development of vegetation in embedded wetlands and the transition zones from uplands to wetlands. In this physiographic region, a gradient of increasing mesic conditions is associated with upland-wetland ecotones of limesink depressional wetlands. For longleaf forests managed with frequent fire, where burning extends from the upland into the isolated wetland, the longleaf pine forest with an herbaceous ground cover is continuous to the edge of the depressional wetland (Kirkman, Drew, and Edwards 1998). Factors associated with the geomorphology of the Dougherty Plain, including relatively low topographic relief, the presence of permeable sandy soils, and the absence of shallow groundwater, restrict the development of seepages supporting acidic bogs and the associated flora that is characteristic of adjacent subregions.

In contrast to the Dougherty Plain, topography of the Tifton Uplands, Tallahassee Hills, and the Vidalia Uplands is rolling, sculpted by surface drainage. This terrain provides the slope and soil conditions where groundwater emerges at the base of a slope, forming seepage slope swamp and shrub bogs, seepage slope herb bogs, or small stream floodplain forests (R. M. Harper 1906). Thus, mesic upland longleaf pine sites occur across a wide soil moisture gradient associated with a gradual transition into more permanently saturated conditions, such as that at Doerun Pitcherplant Bog Natural Area (Colquitt County). In the Southern Hilly Gulf Coastal Plain (Chattahoochee County), rolling hills with loamy soils, dissected by rivers and creeks, are characteristic. This physiographic subregion may support upland longleaf pine forests that rapidly transitions into steep mesic hardwood ravines.

As true for all longleaf pine communities, fire is a dominant factor structuring the mesic upland longleaf pine woodland composition, as it interacts with landform, soil texture, and hydrologic regime. Hardwood encroachment occurs more rapidly on the more fertile silty soils than on sandy sites. Maintenance of open longleaf pine forests on silty or loamy upland sites requires fires with return intervals of two to three years (Neel, Sutter, and Way 2010).

VEGETATION

Loamy upland soils support an open-canopied forest dominated by longleaf pine, with few mid-story trees and shrubs and a continuous and species-rich ground cover dominated by wiregrass. This community lacks the species restricted to the wettest and driest conditions of the longleaf pine communities, but contains many species common across the wet-mesic to dry-mesic gradient in fire-maintained sites. As in subxeric sites, grasses, perennial legumes, and composites are numerous in the ground cover of these upland forests; however, the number of species within a small area, or species-packing, is higher in the more mesic conditions. Relative to subxeric sites, wiregrass is more ro-

Pine lily

bust, forming a densely carpeted ground layer, with numerous species established among the clumps of wiregrass. The diverse assemblage of legume species is particularly important to ecosystem function in their role of replenishing organic nitrogen to the soil that is lost through volatilization during fire (Hendricks and Boring 1999; Boring et al. 2004). Oak species occur primarily in shrub layers and occasionally in the midstory and include southern red oak, live oak, water oak, and bluejack oak.

Based on its low recolonization potential, the presence of wiregrass has been widely recognized as an indicator of the absence of prior soil disturbance. Based on their vulnerability to disturbance and slow rate of recovery, several other species have been identified as indicator species of relatively undisturbed reference conditions for longleaf pine woodlands. These species, although not exclusive to mesic longleaf pine communities, include blue twinflower, bracken fern, Carolina wild-petunia, Virginia goat's-rue, Walter's violet, perennial sand bean, dwarf huckleberry, Florida sensitive-briar, and needle witchgrass (Hedman, Grace, and King 2000; Dale, Beyeler, and Jackson 2002; Kirkman et al. 2004a).

The absence of wiregrass in the remnant stands of mesic longleaf pine woodlands at Fort Benning in Muscogee and Chattahoochee Counties is intriguing. The lack of wiregrass may reflect historical land use disturbances or may represent the northwestern range limits of the species in Georgia (Mulligan and Hermann 2004). Almost no upland longleaf pine forest sites that occur on the Red Uplands that are transitional to the Fall Line Sandhills region have escaped a prior history of cultivation because of their soil fertility. Thus, the degree to which current species assemblages are a response to soil fertility, land use history, fire suppression, or a combination of factors is unclear. For example, in the Southern Hilly Gulf Coastal Plain region of Fort Benning (Chattahoochee County), extensive woodlands of open longleaf pine occur on loamy soils of old-field sites, where frequent fires have been associated with military missions as well as current land management practices. Here species of bluestem dominate the ground cover and wiregrass is absent. Curiously, wiregrass is also absent from infertile longleaf pine sandhill sites that presumably were never cultivated.

The highest species richness occurs on mesic sites having a history of frequent fire and absence of soil disturbance. Exceptionally high numbers of species have been reported in the Dougherty Plain with upper ranges exceeding 50 species per 10 square feet (Drew, Kirkman, and Gholson 1998; Kirkman, Drew, and Edwards 1998; Kirkman et al. 2004b). Other similarly species-rich sites have been reported in the Tallahassee Hills (S. Hermann, Auburn University, pers. comm.). Herbaceous species indicative of wet-mesic conditions include narrowleaf sunflower, wand goldenrod, smooth meadow-beauty, golden colic-root, candyroot, toothache grass, pine lily, fringed orchids, large spreading pogonia, and rose pogonia. Several herbaceous species are notably more common on the clayey or loamy surficial soils. For example, species such as western Sampson's snakeroot, bog honeycomb-head, and Walter's aster are commonly encountered in the Tifton Uplands and Tallahassee Hills but not on the Dougherty Plain (S. Hermann, Auburn University, pers. comm.; Kirkman, unpubl. data; Patrick, unpubl. data). The federally Endangered species chaffseed occurs in frequently burned mesic sites, but the exact topographic context may vary by subregion. For example, in several localities in the Dougherty Plain, habitat for this species is consistently associated with mesic zones adjacent to isolated depressional wetlands, whereas in the Tifton Uplands and on the Atlantic Southern Loam Plains, the species occurs more generally across upland sites.

Other less fire-tolerant pine species may co-dominate with longleaf pine, either because of fire suppression or periodic moist soil conditions, coupled with less frequent fire. For example, slash pine and loblolly pine do not have the same fire-tolerant characteristics in the seedling stage as those of longleaf pine, thus these species require the absence of fire for 10 to 15 years for successful establishment. Shortleaf pine becomes more common in the absence of fire on soils with increased clay, particularly in the Fall Line hills (R. M. Harper 1943; Dilustro et al. 2002; Dilustro, Collins, and Duncan 2006; B. Collins et al. 2006), as well as in parts of the Tallahassee Hills. In the absence of frequent fire in these sites, blackjack oak becomes abundant. In the Tifton Uplands and on the Dougherty Plain, loblolly pines or shortleaf pines most often will succeed into sites previously dominated by longleaf pine stands. In the absence of fire, oaks and hickories, including mockernut hickory, sand hickory, red hickory, live oak, sand post oak, water oak, laurel oak, and southern red oak, become prevalent.

CHARACTERISTIC PLANTS OF MESIC UPLAND LONGLEAF PINE WOODLANDS

TREES

Longleaf pine—Pinus palustris
Southern red oak—Quercus falcata
Sand laurel oak—Quercus hemisphaerica

SHRUBS AND WOODY VINES

Dwarf huckleberry—Gaylussacia dumosa
Sassafras—Sassafras albidum
Poison oak—Toxicodendron pubescens
Southern evergreen blueberry—Vaccinium myrsinites

GROUND COVER

Big bluestem—Andropogon gerardii
Old-field broomsedge—Andropogon virginicus
Southern wiregrass—Aristida beyrichiana
Arrowfeather—Aristida purpurascens
Needle witchgrass—Dichanthelium aciculare
Blue twinflower—Dyschoriste oblongifolia
Narrow-leaved lespedeza—Lespedeza angustifolia
Hairy lespedeza—Lespedeza hirta
Common elegant blazing-star—Liatris elegans
Florida sensitive-briar—Mimosa quadrivalvis
Hairgrass—Muhlenbergia capillaris
Silkgrass—Pityopsis graminifolia
Bracken fern—Pteridium aquilinum
Dollarweed—Rhynchosia reniformis
Black-eyed Susan—Rudbeckia hirta
Common little bluestem—Schizachyrium scoparium
Licorice goldenrod—Solidago odora
Yellow indiangrass—Sorghastrum nutans
Lopsided indiangrass—Sorghastrum secundum
Sandhills dropseed—Sporobolus junceus
American aster—Symphyotrichum adnatum
Virginia goat's-rue—Tephrosia virginiana
Tall ironweed—Vernonia angustifolia

ANIMALS

Characteristic birds of longleaf pine forests include northern bobwhite, Bachman's sparrow, red-cockaded woodpecker, and brown-headed nuthatch. Although they are not restricted to this community, these species are year-round residents and breed in longleaf pine forests (Engstrom 1993). The northern bobwhite was once dependent on the open habitat of the longleaf pine ecosystem, although it now persists in pastures, fencerows, and other agricultural landscapes (Kellogg et al. 1972; S. Ware, Frost, and Doerr 1993). This species nests in the dense ground cover of fire-maintained longleaf pine forests. Availability of insects for food and cover to hide from predators are important habitat needs of the northern bobwhite that are provided by herbaceous ground cover in open pine forests (Stoddard 1931). The Bachman's sparrow was once called the "pine-woods sparrow" because of its preference for open pine woods habitat of the Southeast, particularly longleaf pine communities. This species has been steadily declining throughout its range, and in Georgia it is considered rare and local (Gobris 1999). Bachman's sparrow is a ground-nesting species that feeds primarily on seeds and insects (Dunning 1993). The red-cockaded woodpecker is a federally Endangered species and is considered Imperiled in Georgia (Ozier 1999a). This bird depends on living pine trees (usually greater than 90 years old) that are infected with heartrot for nesting cavities. Thus, its decline is attributable to loss of habitat with older pine trees (J. A. Jackson 1994). It is the only woodpecker in North America that nests exclusively in live trees. Foraging habitat for this species is open pineland (see the Featured Animal). The brown-headed nuthatch is a resident in pine forests from eastern Texas and extreme southeastern Oklahoma through the southern coastal states north to Delaware. It is particularly associated with open, periodically burned, mature forests and most often nests in snags or dead branches of live trees. It is one of only a few bird species that has been documented using a tool (flakes of bark) to pry off other pieces of bark to expose insects. The brown-headed nuthatch is decreasing throughout its range because of habitat degradation (Withgott and Smith 1998).

Reptiles and amphibians represent a diverse group of vertebrate specialists in the upland longleaf pine forests (Means 2006). The only specialist turtle in the longleaf pine forests is the gopher tortoise; its importance is discussed in the sandhills section. In addition to the indigo snake, eastern diamondback rattlesnake, pine snake, and hognose snake described in the sandhills section, other longleaf pine specialist snakes in Georgia include the scarlet snake and eastern coral snake. Both species are fossorial and rarely seen, using gopher tortoise burrows and stump holes as refuge. The scarlet snake is nocturnal and feeds primarily on eggs of other reptiles. The venomous eastern coral snake is active both day and night, and its diet consists primarily of other small snakes and slender lizards (Means 2006).

Numerous invertebrate species that are specialists in this ecosystem are associated with gopher tortoise burrows or pocket gopher burrows. See sandhills and river dunes descriptions.

Two mammals are longleaf pine specialists in Georgia: Sherman's fox squirrel and the pocket gopher. Sherman's fox squirrel, commonly called the "raccoon squirrel," is larger than the gray squirrel, weighing up to 2 pounds. This variably colored tree squirrel forages extensively on the ground for longleaf pine seeds, acorns, fungi, and fruit (Weigl et al. 1989). Fox squirrels avoid closed-canopy hardwoods, the preferred habitat of the gray squirrel. Pocket gophers are fossorial mammals in this community and are discussed in the sandhills and river dunes section. Several species of small mammals are common including the hispid cotton rat, the cotton mouse, the eastern harvest mouse, the least shrew, the short-tailed shrew, and the flying squirrel.

Larger mammals frequently encountered in longleaf pine communities, although they are habitat generalists, include white-tailed deer, coyotes, bobcats, and raccoons. The nine-banded armadillo was introduced into the United States in Texas in the early 1900s. This invasive species now extends throughout the Southeast. In Georgia, armadillos occur primarily in the Coastal Plain but have recently invaded the Piedmont. The shell (carapace) of this unusual mammal is made up of scutes, or bony plates, attached to a tough epidermal skin layer. Armadillos dig burrows or occupy those of tortoises or other fossorial species. Armadillos consume a wide range of invertebrates, including insects, ants, millipedes, centipedes, snails, leeches, and earthworms. They are also predators of salamanders, toads, frogs, lizards, skinks, small snakes, and gopher tortoise eggs (Gammons, Mengak, and Conner 2009).

Blazing-star

Red-Cockaded Woodpecker
(*Picoides borealis*)

The red-cockaded woodpecker is the only woodpecker that makes its nest in living pine trees and was once a common bird of longleaf pine woodlands. Populations of this enigmatic bird declined precipitously with the loss and degradation of longleaf pine forests, and it has been federally listed as Endangered since 1970 (Engstrom and Sanders 1997). Today, most remaining red-cockaded woodpeckers exist on public lands such as national forests, national wildlife refuges, and military bases where large tracts of woodland habitat have been maintained in suitable condition. Approximately 14% of the total population in the Southeast is in Georgia.

The excavation of the cavity in old trees can take several years (Hooper, Lennartz, and Muse 1991). Old trees are preferred because these trees have more heartwood than sapwood. Heartwood is more often infected with redheart fungus, which softens the tissue and facilitates cavity excavation. In addition, the

low resin flow of heartwood is less problematic to the bird within the cavity. The woodpeckers make use of the resin flow on the exterior of the tree as a defense against nest predators by pecking resin wells around the external opening of the cavity that results in a distinctive white flow of resin down the bole.

The red-cockaded woodpecker has an uncommon social system known as cooperative breeding. The birds live as family groups of two to five individuals, and the breeding pair is often accompanied by male offspring from a previous year, known as "helpers." The young males remain in the cluster and help rear the nestlings. The red-cockaded woodpecker forages in open forests of longleaf pine, where its main food is arboreal ants and other arthropods (R. N. Conner et al. 1994; Hess and James 1998).

One successful conservation strategy includes translocation of highly isolated red-cockaded woodpeckers to recipient sites that will be managed for conservation purposes. In such cases, artificial cavities for nesting are used to enhance the establishment success of the translocated birds.

CHAFFSEED
(*SCHWALBEA AMERICANA*)

Chaffseed is a federally Endangered herbaceous species in the family Orobanchaceae and grows in association with fire-maintained longleaf pine–wiregrass communities of the southeastern Coastal Plain. Chaffseed is a fire-adapted species that flowers almost exclusively after a fire, regardless of season of burn. Identification of chaffseed in unburned areas is difficult because plants will remain in a nonflowering vegetative state with small sprouts that are often hidden under thick vegetation. This species may also persist in a below-ground dormant state through periods of short-term fire exclusion (Norden and Kirkman 2004). Historically, chaffseed ranged from New York to Texas but has been reduced to a fraction of its original range due to fire exclusion and habitat destruction. In Georgia, this species occurs primarily on private land in only four counties. It is associated with frequently burned sites, often in moist, ecotonal zones between upland pine forests and seasonally inundated isolated wetlands. This rare plant is hemi-parasitic, which means that in addition to being photosynthetic, it obtains nutrients (primarily nitrogen) from a host plant via modified roots, called "haustoria." Numerous species are potential hosts for this species, including silkgrass, gallberry, colic-root, witchgrasses, and southern wiregrass (Helton, Kirkman, and Musselman 2000). Chaffseed is bee-pollinated, although cross pollination is not necessary for viable seed production. The leaves are a food source for the common buckeye butterfly caterpillar.

Chaffseed

Silver Lake Wildlife Management Area

Silver Lake Wildlife Management Area is a 9,200-acre tract managed by the Georgia Department of Natural Resources, adjacent to Lake Seminole in southwestern Georgia (Decatur County). Several localities on this property exhibit excellent examples of frequently burned longleaf pine and wiregrass. Soils are loamy sands over clay on gently rolling terrain. An easily accessible site with numerous red-cockaded woodpecker cavity trees is located in the vicinity of Star Pond. The canopy at this locality is dominated by longleaf pine and occasional slash pine. The dense ground cover is very species-rich, and wildflowers are particularly showy in early June and in late October. Although it is dominated by a nearly continuous ground cover of wiregrass, an extraordinary number of other species are interspersed between clumps of wiregrass. Here numerous perennial grasses such as big bluestem, common little bluestem, broomsedge, and indiangrass are intermixed with legumes such as tick-trefoil, lespedeza, snoutbean, goat's-rue, Florida sensitive-briar, and composites including species of American aster, goldenrod, blazing-star, and thoroughwort. An interesting feature of this site is that the regional groundwater table has been elevated due to the impoundment of Lake Seminole. Consequently, numerous depressional wetlands that were formerly seasonally ponded are now permanently wet. The open upland forest and pond-shores at this site provide excellent opportunities for bird-watching.

Location: Take Ga. Hwy. 253 south from Bainbridge about 9.3 miles to CR 310/Yates Spring Rd. Turn left on Yates Spring Rd. and continue approximately 2.6 miles to WMA check station sign. Turn right onto Silver Lake Rd. and continue to check station. Follow signs to Star Pond and Silver Lake South. Park at Star Pond. Google Earth GPS approximate coordinates at the parking area: N 30.800520/W 084.769049.

Dry Evergreen Oak Woodlands

Dry evergreen oak woodlands are dominated by broadleaf evergreen or semi-evergreen species, primarily laurel oak, live oak, and sand live oak. They develop on dry, sandy, infertile soils that have been excluded from fire or where fire is infrequent. Usually, these forests occur as a marginal band on well-drained mid-slope positions between sandhill woodlands and seepage swamps. They also occur on excessively drained sandy domes of old marine bars within pine flatwoods and occasionally on deep, sandy soils of river banks. These communities are sometimes called xeric hammocks or evergreen broadleaf hammocks, and they often bear a striking similarity to maritime forests. The term "hammock" has been used interchangeably with several community types and applied across a wide range of soil conditions. In many instances, "hammock" refers to any mixed evergreen-deciduous vegetation that occurs as a narrow band or island, as opposed to more extensive pine-dominated communities (R. M. Harper 1905a; W. J. Platt and Schwartz 1990).

Despite the low fertility and water-holding capacity of the soils, most of these sites in Georgia have been converted to slash or loblolly pine plantations and only a few state-protected sites occur. One exemplary site, Big Hammock Natural Area (Tattnall County), features one of the largest populations of myrtle oak in Georgia as well as habitat for the state-protected Georgia-plume.

PHYSICAL SETTING AND ECOLOGY

Dry evergreen oak woodlands typically develop on sandy, dry, nutrient-poor soils where they have experienced periods of exclusion from frequent fire. This vegetation may occur as a transitional band along a sandhill ridge where fire occurs infrequently on edges of sandy slopes and lips of ravines into seepage areas (Bozeman 1971; Myers 1990). These forests also occur on sandy ridges or knolls in pine flatwoods or occasionally along deep, sandy river banks or dunes (R. M. Harper 1905b; Thorne 1949b). Soils along the sand ridge slopes may vary with underlying layers of mottled clay and sand. Studies by Monk (1968) and Bozeman (1971) indicated an increase in available nutrients across a transitional gradient between sandhills and evergreen forests. Both investigators concluded that a successional sequence existed between sandhill vegetation and xerophytic evergreen forests with the release from fire. Even so, the historical fire-return interval is unclear. Some evidence suggests that establishment of evergreen oak species is dependent on fire exclusion for at least 10 to 15 years (Guerin 1993). Once established, these oak species may persist through resprouting even after fire is reintroduced into the community. The thick bark of sand live oak and live oak provides some resistance to fire, particularly after the trees exceed 6 to 10 feet in height. In the long absence of fire, laurel oak and live oak form a canopy that shades the ground and reduces herbaceous growth. Furthermore, the evergreen oak litter does not readily carry fire except under the most catastrophic conditions. The resulting shaded habitat and absence of fire allow more mesic, fire-intolerant species to establish (Bozeman 1971; Daubenmire 1990).

The use of fire is an important consideration in the long-term management of a range of conditions of evergreen broadleaf forests, woodlands, and scrub. Because of widespread removal of longleaf pine on many sandhill sites, the absence of needles has resulted in a decrease in fire frequency, even under prescribed fire management. Therefore, restoration of adjacent upland sites by planting longleaf pine may be necessary to promote the fuels essential for fire management.

On publicly owned properties, unauthorized use of off-road vehicles, littering, and garbage-dumping can be problematic to ground cover vegetation. Many privately owned sites have been converted to off-site pine plantations (i.e., fast-growing species such as slash and loblolly pine). Most remnant tracts are highly fire-suppressed, and they are increasingly targeted for residential development.

VEGETATION

Vegetation is dominated by several evergreen species, including sand laurel oak, live oak, sand live oak, devilwood, sparkleberry, and red bay. Canopy cover ranges from park-like woodlands to open forest or even closed canopy depending on fire history. In addition to different dominant species, the evergreen forest differs from the adjacent turkey oak–longleaf pine vegetation in having a greater diversity of woody species, a higher density of stems, and greater total basal area. An emergent longleaf pine canopy may be pres-

Georgia-plume

ent in younger stands, but pine is unlikely to reproduce within a shaded or fire-excluded environment (Daubenmire 1990).

Common understory plants include saw palmetto, myrtle oak, staggerbush, crookedwood, shining fetterbush, sparkleberry, deerberry, black cherry, American beautyberry, American persimmon, and devilwood. The thick stands or domes of Chapman oak and myrtle oak are considered to be similar to vegetation in Florida called "scrub" (Laessle 1958; Laessle and Monk 1961; Bozeman 1971). Monk (1966) suggested that evergreen species are favored in nutrient-poor

CHARACTERISTIC PLANTS OF DRY EVERGREEN OAK WOODLANDS

TREES

Sand live oak—*Quercus geminata*

Sand laurel oak—*Quercus hemisphaerica*

Water oak—*Quercus nigra*

Live oak—*Quercus virginiana*

SHRUBS AND WOODY VINES

Red buckeye—*Aesculus pavia*

Small-fruited pawpaw—*Asimina parviflora*

Georgia-plume—*Elliottia racemosa*

Crookedwood—*Lyonia ferruginea*

Devilwood—*Osmanthus americanus*

Red bay—*Persea borbonia*

Chapman oak—*Quercus chapmanii*

Myrtle oak—*Quercus myrtifolia*

Saw palmetto—*Serenoa repens*

Dune greenbrier—*Smilax auriculata*

Horsesugar—*Symplocos tinctoria*

Sparkleberry—*Vaccinium arboreum*

Smooth highbush blueberry— *Vaccinium elliottii*

Muscadine—*Vitis rotundifolia*

GROUND COVER

Sandhill beaksedge—*Rhynchospora megalocarpa*

Sandhill skullcap—*Scutellaria arenicola*

Licorice goldenrod—*Solidago odora*

---

sites based on their efficient metabolic use of nitrogen, as well as their gradual turnover of leaf material. Leaf retention circumvents a seasonal pulse of decomposition that would otherwise result in rapid leaching of nutrients from sandy soils.

The herb layer is generally very sparse or absent but may contain scattered wiregrass, sandhill beaksedge, or witchgrasses. Common vines include muscadine and dune greenbrier. Associated with slightly increased soil moisture and prolonged fire exclusion, other species that are often present are spruce pine, small-fruited pawpaw, southern magnolia, pignut hickory, sweet gum, ironwood, and water oak. When subxeric evergreen vegetation develops within a pine flatwoods community, the understory is often strongly dominated by saw palmetto.

In Georgia, several sites of this xerophytic evergreen vegetation are notable because they are the habitat of the beautiful state-Threatened Georgia-plume. The small tree was first discovered in Georgia by William Bartram in 1773 and was also documented in 1875 by Stephen Elliott. Then, this species was not seen again until it was rediscovered in 1901 (Patrick, Allison, and Krakow 1995). Although fewer than 40 extant populations of Georgia-plume occur in Georgia, several sites are protected on public and private properties, including the Georgia Department of Natural Resource's Big Hammock Natural Area (Tattnall County), the Nature Conservancy's Charles Harrold and D. G. Daniels Preserves (Candler County), and six populations on Fort Stewart and Hunter Army Airfield (Liberty and Tatnall Counties).

Georgia-plume is a small, deciduous, clonal tree or shrub with extremely showy white flower clusters that bloom in June–July. Localized populations occur on sandy ridges across a wide range of soil conditions. The role of fire in the life history of this species is not well understood, although low-intensity fire is considered necessary to reduce competing vegetation. Several populations on Fort Stewart are currently being monitored for response to fire management practices. Growth of extant populations has been hindered by lack of sexual recruitment (Godt and Hamrick 1999). Vegetative propagation for reintroduction purposes, including development of tissue culture techniques for regeneration, is currently in progress (Woo and Wetzstein 2008).

Leechbrush is also a noteworthy species, found in the subxeric evergreen zone between the sandhill community and swamp of the Little Ohoopee River.

ANIMALS

Many of the same species associated with xeric sandhills or dry upland longleaf pine woodlands, such as gopher tortoises and pocket gophers, are present, except where closed-canopy conditions exist. Snakes that may be encountered are scarlet, black racer, eastern diamondback rattlesnake, eastern indigo, corn, rat, and eastern hognose. Also associated with dry upland habitats are coachwhip snakes. This species is strictly diurnal and is resistant to desiccation; it can remain active even at very high temperatures (Tuberville and Gibbons 2008). Another diurnal species, the eastern coral snake (see the Featured Animal), is fossorial and secretive and shelters in gopher tortoise burrows. Lizards that might be encountered in this xeric habitat include broadhead skink, slender glass lizard, eastern fence lizard, and ground skink.

The shade, cover, and source of mast contrasts with that of adjacent open forests dominated by longleaf pine or turkey oak. This habitat probably provides refuge for small mammals. An abundance of fall-fruiting species in these habitats correlates with fall migration and over-wintering of migratory birds, including swamp sparrow, white-throated sparrow, chipping sparrow, house wren, and common yellowthroat (Skeate 1987). The more common breeding species include summer tanager, prairie warbler, yellow-breasted chat, and blue grosbeak.

FEATURED ANIMAL

Eastern Coral Snake (*Micrurus fulvius*)

The eastern coral snake is one of two species of coral snakes in the United States. It is found in the Atlantic Coastal Plain from North Carolina south to Florida, and west along the Gulf Coast to eastern Louisiana (Conant and Collins 1998).

This is a slender snake, rarely exceeding 39 inches in length, with smooth, glossy scales and alternating bands of black, yellow, and red. This snake is sometimes confused with similarly patterned nonvenomous snakes, including the scarlet snake and scarlet kingsnake, but the coral snake is the only one that has a black snout and a pattern of red bands adjacent to yellow bands (hence the warning rhyme, "Red touch yellow, can harm a fellow"). In contrast with venomous snakes such as rattlesnakes, copperheads, and cottonmouths, the coral snake has a small head, small eyes, and short, relatively inconspicuous fangs. It must grasp its prey and chew in order to inject its venom (Conant and Collins 1998; Stevenson and Moulis 2008). It feeds exclusively on other small snakes and glass lizards.

Coral snakes are usually secretive and fossorial, hiding under leaves or debris, in decomposing logs and stumps, and in similar areas. They are infrequently seen traveling on the surface of the ground in search of prey. Males are particularly active during spring, when they are searching for mates. This snake is found in a variety of habitats, from sandhill scrub and open pine woodlands to hardwood-dominated hammocks and upland borders of ponds and lakes. It apparently avoids extensive wetlands and areas with saturated soils. The eastern coral snake is thought to occur throughout much of the Coastal Plain of Georgia, but records are lacking for many counties in the middle and upper portions of this physiographic province (Stevenson and Moulis 2008).

Big Hammock Natural Area

Big Hammock Natural Area is an 801-acre, state-owned tract in Tattnall County that adjoins the 5,566-acre tract of Big Hammock Wildlife Management Area. A large portion of this site is a Pleistocene sand ridge that rises above the northeast side of the Altamaha River floodplain. This site is one of the most undisturbed broadleaf evergreen forests along the Altamaha River and contains the largest population of Georgia-plume in the state, as well as one of the largest stands of the shrubby myrtle oak (a species more typical of scrub vegetation in Florida).

The transitional position of the evergreen forest relative to the driest upland sites and wetter seepage areas and alluvial swamp can be easily observed along the 1.3-mile nature trail. The most xeric portions of the sand ridge of the natural area are dominated by turkey oak and longleaf pine. The xerophytic evergreen forest is characteristically dominated by live oak, laurel oak, sand live oak, devilwood, and sparkleberry. Other frequently occurring species are saw palmetto, pignut hickory, and Georgia-plume. In places, powder puff lichen forms a dense ground cover.

Most of the longleaf pine timber was harvested on the sandhill prior to acquisition by the state, which likely contributed to fire exclusion, coupled with the natural firebreaks of the adjacent cypress-tupelo strands. Approximately 50 acres in the center of the evergreen forest were cleared for agriculture but have been abandoned for nearly 100 years. This disturbed site has undergone succession back to a park-like stand of evergreen broadleaf hardwoods.

Location: From the intersection of Ga. Hwys. 23 and 144 (northwest of Glennville), proceed approximately 6 miles and turn left onto Ga. Hwy. 169/144. Proceed west for 6 miles to CR 441 (Mack Phillips Rd.). Turn left and continue 2 miles to a parking area on the right, a short distance past a National Natural Landmark site monument. Google Earth GPS approximate coordinates at the parking area: N 31.86608/W 082.05169.

Dry Deciduous Hardwood Forests

Dry deciduous hardwood forests typically develop on sandy or loamy soils of river bluffs, upper ridges of slope forests, or the mid- to lower slopes of sandhills between xeric ridge vegetation and seepage swamps, or they are embedded within longleaf pine sites where streams and other firebreaks shield them from fire. They also occupy a broader range of uplands where fire has been excluded and thus are more widespread in the Coastal Plain than in the past, when fire was more common and would have fostered longleaf pine communities (S. Ware, Forst, and Doerr 1993). The canopy dominants are deciduous oaks and hickories. Often, several evergreen species such as live oak, sparkleberry, and loblolly or longleaf pine are also present. Forest composition is variable and is dependent on soils and fire history. The vegetation of this community is dis-tinguished from that of the dry evergreen oak woodland community by dominance of deciduous hardwoods as opposed to evergreen hardwoods and scrub.

PHYSICAL SETTING AND ECOLOGY

These forests occur on dry to mesic soils, typically on mid-slopes of sandhills, river edges, or sandy ridges of more mesic hardwood communities. Soils range from coarse sands to sandy loams or clays. Commonly, soils along a sand ridge slope vary considerably with under-lying layers of mottled clay and sand. The presence of clay influences the species present because of increased nutrients and water retention characteristics. Species composition also varies with acidic or calcareous sub-strates. This community occurs within a historically fire-influenced and pine-dominated matrix. In the past, these woodlands were limited to sites that were excluded by fire due to landscape position (adjacent to rivers), topography (steep slopes), or relatively inflam-mable vegetation (hardwood leaf litter). With current

CHARACTERISTIC PLANTS OF DRY DECIDUOUS HARDWOOD FORESTS

TREES

Pignut hickory—Carya glabra
Sand hickory—Carya pallida
Mockernut hickory—Carya tomentosa
White oak—Quercus alba
Southern red oak—Quercus falcata
Sand live oak—Quercus geminata
Sand laurel—Quercus hemisphaerica
Bluejack oak—Quercus incana
Water oak—Quercus nigra
Post oak—Quercus stellata
Live oak—Quercus virginiana
Winged elm—Ulmus alata

SHRUBS AND WOODY VINES

Small-fruited pawpaw—Asimina
    parviflora
Dangleberry—Gaylussacia frondosa
Carolina jessamine—Gelsemium
    sempervirens
Witch-hazel—Hamamelis virginiana
Red bay—Persea borbonia
Carolina laurel cherry—Prunus
    caroliniana
Saw palmetto—Serenoa repens
Eastern gum bumelia—Sideroxylon
    lanuginosum
Sarsaparilla-vine—Smilax pumila
Horsesugar—Symplocos tinctoria

Sparkleberry—Vaccinium arboreum
Deerberry—Vaccinium stamineum

GROUND COVER

Ebony spleenwort—Asplenium
    platyneuron
Slender spikegrass—Chasmanthium
    laxum
Autumn coralroot—Corallorhiza
    odontorhiza
Partridge-berry—Mitchella repens
Woods-grass—Oplismenus hirtellus

widespread fire exclusion, subxeric upland communities are increasingly dominated by fire-intolerant deciduous hardwood species.

VEGETATION

Dry deciduous hardwood forests are quite variable in composition and degree of dominance by deciduous or evergreen species. The overstory is composed of deciduous oaks and hickories such as southern red oak, white oak, water oak, post oak, pignut hickory, mockernut hickory, and sand hickory. Evergreen and semi-evergreen species often include laurel oak, live oak, devilwood, sand live oak, and sparkleberry. Frequent understory species include dangleberry, deerberry, witch-hazel, small-fruited pawpaw, yucca, dwarf palmetto, saw palmetto, horsesugar, and red bay. An occasional longleaf pine or loblolly pine may be present. The ground cover is usually composed of shade-tolerant species such as partridge-berry, Virginia-creeper, violets, several species of sedges, sarsaparilla-vine, ebony spleenwort, and spanglegrass.

In the Red Uplands subregion, such as sites on Fort Benning (Muscogee and Chattahoochee Counties), white oak, post oak, shortleaf pine, and pignut hickory are prevalent. With increased presence of clay, blackjack oak becomes more common (R. M. Harper 1943; Thorne 1949b). Other common species include flowering dogwood, sweet gum, ironwood,

and American holly (S. Ware, Frost, and Doerr 1993). In soils with elevated calcium, such as along the riverbanks of the Flint River (Mitchell, Dougherty, and Baker Counties), "calciphiles," those species of plants that thrive in basic to circumneutral soil conditions, such as southern sugar maple, Sebastian-bush, wafer-ash, eastern redbud, and eastern red cedar, become more common (Thorne 1949b; Drew, Kirkman, and Gholson 1998).

Carolina jessamine

Greater dominance of pine may occur in ecotonal areas adjacent to upland longleaf pine plant communities and with greater exposure to more frequent fire, resulting in a pine-oak-hickory forest variant. The pine species present depend on soils and land use history. On previously cultivated, clayey sites shortleaf pine will become established where upland longleaf pine forests once occurred (Thorne 1949b). In sandier conditions, longleaf pine may be present if it occurs in adjacent uplands. More fire-tolerant species such as bluejack oak or turkey oak may be present (Hubbell, Laessle, and Dickinson 1956). In such cases with occasional fire, a dense ground cover layer may exist, including common little bluestem, slender bluestem, yellow indiangrass, silver plume grass, and species of legumes such as tick-trefoils and goat's-rues.

Floral diversity is impacted through competition with invasive non-native species such as Chinese privet, Japanese climbing fern, and sacred-bamboo. In sites with clayey soils, kudzu may be problematic. In stands where pines co-dominate, occasional prescribed fires (every 3 to 10 years) would be necessary to maintain the open forest and ground cover.

ANIMALS

As with mesic bluff and slope forests, the bird species composition in dry deciduous forests or mixed pine-hardwood forests is heavily influenced by the forest structure. Shrubs and vines such as hawthorns, flowering dogwood, viburnums, and Virginia-creeper produce fruits that are attractive to migratory birds. During migration and breeding season, birds at these sites include Kentucky warbler, northern parula, yellow-throated vireo, summer tanager, eastern towhee, cardinal, red-eyed vireo, Carolina wren, red-bellied woodpecker, tufted titmouse, and many others. Year-round residents include Cooper's hawk and blue-gray gnatcatcher. Acorns are consumed by wild turkeys as well as by numerous mammal species.

Common reptiles associated with deciduous hardwood or mixed pine-hardwood stands are the rat snake, corn snake, copperhead, scarlet kingsnake, and scarlet snake. The eastern hognose snake, which is widely distributed in the Coastal Plain, primarily occurs in dry upland habitats with sandy soils. Box turtles, green anoles, broadhead skinks, and ground skinks are also common inhabitants of the forest floor.

Southern flying squirrels are frequently found in hardwood and mixed hardwood-pine forests. They nest in dead snags with abandoned woodpecker holes or natural cavities. Where Spanish-moss drapes tree limbs, bats such as the northern yellow, Seminole (see the Featured Animal), and eastern pipistrelle often roost within the clumps. These species of bats are active all year.

Dry upland deciduous forest

Seminole Bat (*Lasiurus seminolus*)

The Seminole bat is a medium-sized bat in the family Vespertilionidae (vesper or evening bats), with a wingspan of 11 to 13 inches. Its fur is rich mahogany brown in color and tipped with white. The ears are relatively short, giving the Seminole bat a compact appearance, and the tail membrane is covered with fur on its upper surface (Burt and Grossenheider 1980).

The Seminole bat is distributed widely throughout the southeastern United States, from Virginia to eastern Texas and Oklahoma. Individuals have been observed as far north as New York and Pennsylvania and as far south as Bermuda and Veracruz, Mexico (Harvey, Altenbach, and Best 1999). It is considered common throughout most of its range and occupies a variety of habitats, from dry upland mixed deciduous forests to lowland hardwood-pine forests and river swamps.

The range of this bat generally coincides with the distribution of Spanish-moss in which it often roosts.

The Seminole bat usually chooses a clump of Spanish-moss on the southwest-facing side of a tree at a height that will allow the emerging bat to drop out of the roost and take wing before touching the ground. Trees near the edge of a stand are often preferred. Other roosting sites include the undersurfaces of loose bark and the interior of caves (Harvey, Altenbach, and Best 1999).

This species uses a variety of winter roosts, including the canopy of hardwood trees, hanging vines, pine needle clusters suspended in understory vegetation, and even leaf litter on the forest floor. In contrast, summer roosts are almost exclusively in live canopy pines. Because winter roosts are often located close to the ground, prescribed burns conducted during the winter months have greater potential to impact roosting bats (Hein, Castleberry, and Miller 2005, 2008). The Seminole bat usually emerges from its roost early in the evening and feeds at or just above the tree canopy. It is active throughout the year, taking flight during relatively warm nights in the middle of winter.

Providence Canyon Outdoor Recreation Area

A 3-mile loop trail that starts behind the visitor center winds through an excellent example of mature dry deciduous hardwood forest. The trail begins on a broad, south-facing slope dominated by southern red oak, blackjack oak, white oak, post oak, water oak, rock chestnut oak, northern red oak, black oak, various oak hybrids, sand hickory, mockernut hickory, pignut hickory, black gum, sweet gum, winged elm, tulip-tree, shortleaf pine, and loblolly pine. The shrub layer includes sparkleberry, muscadine, devilwood, American beautyberry, mapleleaf viburnum, hawthorns, southern black haw, wax-myrtle, and American holly. At the bottom of the slope, the trail runs into Turner Creek, a braided stream that is choked with alluvium eroded from the gullies upstream. The trail crosses the creek and continues up the north-facing slope. The lower portion of the slope supports a very unusual rock chestnut oak-gorge rhododendron assemblage that is strongly reminiscent of the Piedmont and Blue Ridge, save for the Spanish-moss hanging from the tree limbs and the presence of the rare plumleaf azalea. Proceeding upslope along the trail, conditions become drier, and the open canopy is dominated by stunted blackjack oak, sand post oak, and post oak, providing a marked contrast to the northern red oak and rock chestnut oak on other portions of the trail. As it loops back toward the visitor center, the latter half of the trail affords striking views of the erosion gullies that are carved into fanciful shapes with strata ranging in color from lavender to orange.

Location: The Recreation Area is located 7 miles west of Lumpkin on Ga. Hwy. 39C. Note: the visitor center is now closed, but it is still possible to access the trail behind it. Google Earth GPS approximate coordinates at the recreation area entrance: N 32.067505/W 084.903674.

Mesic Slope Forests

Mesic slope forests are mixed evergreen-deciduous forests that occur on well-drained but mesic soils of steep slopes or bluffs, often associated with ravines and terraces along streams or seeps, as well as along upper walls of deep sinkholes. These forests are remarkably diverse, typically including American beech, southern magnolia, basswood, American holly, and spruce pine as well as numerous species of oaks and hickories. The mid-story is also an extremely diverse mix of evergreen and deciduous species. In Georgia and northern Florida, mixed evergreen-deciduous forests contain the largest number of species of trees and shrubs per unit area in North America (W. J. Platt and Schwartz 1990). These communities contrast dramatically with the surrounding upland landscapes, particularly if the upland is maintained with frequent prescribed fire. The slope habitats are protected from fire by their

steep terrain and by the accumulation of a thick, moist litter layer.

Several associated species of plants are disjunct from the southern Appalachians, or are at least more commonly allied with mountain flora (Thorne 1949a). Some ravine forests may represent relicts of more northerly mixed mesophytic vegetation that persisted during glaciations. The ravines served as refugia for these species, which migrated north during interglacials (Batista and Platt 1997; Delcourt 2002). At least 25 Special Concern plant species are associated with this habitat (Chafin 2007).

PHYSICAL SETTING AND ECOLOGY

This community occurs on a wide range of topographic and soil conditions. Diverse hardwood forests occur on steep north or northeast-facing river bluffs, particularly along the Savannah River and the lower Chattahoochee and Flint Rivers. They also develop on lower bluffs associated with seepages, such as

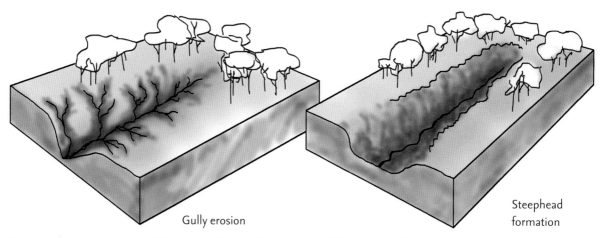

Gully erosion

Steephead
formation

Gully erosion versus steephead formation. The sketch depicts the difference in surface erosion from water cutting downward versus a spring-fed stream cutting from below away from the mouth of the stream.

those along the Alapaha River (Echols County), the Satilla River (Camden County), and the Ogeechee River (Bulloch and Wilcox Counties). Additionally, dry steep-walled limestone sinkholes may also provide conditions for mesic hardwood forests.

In the lower Pelham Escarpment in Decatur County and adjacent Florida, very steep ravines, called "steepheads," which form by erosion of springs, have particularly well-developed hardwood forests. Such unique ravines form along the west-facing escarpment of the Tifton Uplands and east of Lake Seminole overlooking the Dougherty Plain. Streams that flow into the Flint River (now Lake Seminole) have their spring-fed origins in amphitheaters, or steepheads, at the edges of the upland terrace. These springs and runs have chiseled channels into the substrate away from the mouth of the stream. Over time, this continuous headward undercutting (as opposed to downward erosion from the top of the slope) has resulted in narrow, steep-sided ravines that may be 50 to 100 feet deep. The resulting highly dissected landscape of deep ravines and streams contrasts drastically with the adjacent sandhill or clayhill uplands. Distinct distribution of species occurs relative to slope position, with hydric species on lower slopes, mesic species on mid-slopes, and xeric species on upper slopes. The cool, humid, sheltered environment provides habitat for numerous salamanders and frogs (Means 2000). A small ravine that is now only a remnant example of a former steephead system that existed prior to the construction of

the Jim Woodruff Dam can be accessed in Decatur County near the U.S. Army Corps of Engineers office at the southern end of Lake Seminole. Exemplary mesic slope forests in steepheads are best observed just south into Florida (at Appalachicola Bluffs and Ravines Preserve and Torreya State Park).

Soils range from silty clays to silty clay loams, and soil pH ranges from acidic to basic, depending on the influence of calcareous substrates. Calcareous sites, resulting from outcrops of limestone or marl, occur along the slopes and bluffs of the Savannah, Flint, Chattahoochee, and Ocmulgee Rivers and their tributaries. The species composition of these forests is dynamic, with environmental conditions continually changing spatially and temporally. A complex and variable disturbance regime promotes the establishment of a diverse suite of species with varying regeneration strategies, from short-lived pioneer species to long-lived, shade-tolerant late-succession taxa (Batista and Platt 1997). Small gaps caused by mortality of individual trees through windthrow, insect infestation, or senescence enable the saplings of shade-tolerant species to grow into the canopy. Medium to large gaps are caused by hurricanes (W. J. Platt and Schwartz 1990; Batista and Platt 1997; Batista, Platt, and Macchiavelli 1998). The degree and patterns of hurricane damage are variable and create a patchwork of vegetation age and structure by enabling the establishment of pioneer species in areas of large blow-down adjacent to less-disturbed stands.

Underwood's trillium

Impoundment of rivers, streams, and tributaries associated with the ravines are a threat to these communities. On public and private lands, invasive species, such as Japanese climbing fern, Japanese honeysuckle, and Chinese privet, can become extremely dominant. These species often become established following a canopy disturbance. Once established, they are extremely persistent and difficult to control.

Aside from actual site conversion, feral hogs present one of the biggest threats to floristic diversity in these forests (Engeman et al. 2007). Feral hogs can be especially difficult to control in sensitive mesic slope communities because they often travel extensively along floodplain corridors and venture upslope to forage in the adjacent mesic forests. This problem is particularly acute at Montezuma Bluffs Natural Area and Big Grocery Creek in the Oaky Woods Wildlife Management Area. Other potential threats to ravine plant and animal species include water pollution, groundwater use, erosion from upland disturbances, human trampling, and trash dumping (Enge 2005).

VEGETATION

Often, Coastal Plain mesic slope forests are referred to as "hammocks" (R. M. Harper 1905a; W. J. Platt and Schwarz 1990; Goebel et al. 2001) or "southern mixed hardwoods" (S. Ware, Frost, and Doerr 1993). Mature forest stands of mixed hardwoods are best developed along mid- to lower slopes. They are exemplified by a closed canopy of American beech, southern magnolia, white oak, sweet gum, swamp chestnut oak, basswood, Shumard oak, pignut hickory, and spruce pine. Species composition, diversity, and proportion of evergreen and deciduous trees in this community vary throughout the Coastal Plain (Thorne 1949a, 1949b; Batista and Platt 1997). For example, American beech and southern magnolia are often strong canopy dominants, as exemplified in the ravines at Montezuma Bluffs Natural Area (Macon County) (see the Featured Place), Kolomoki Mounds Historic Site (Early County), and Lost Creek Natural Area (Thomas County). Magnolia Bluff, a steep, west-facing bluff along the Satilla River (Camden County), has an interesting mix of American beech, southern magnolia, floodplain species, and cabbage palm. Excellent examples of abrupt transitions from floodplain to mesic slope forests dominated by southern magnolia can be observed along the Bird Trail at Reed Bingham State Park (Cook County) and in Lost Creek Natural Area. In some diverse slope forests, beech and magnolia are less dominant components than that of the Upatoi Bluffs at Fort Benning (Stewart County) or the bluff forests along Cohelee, Town, and Cemochechobee Creeks (Clay County), or the Flint River as it traverses the Dougherty Plain. A globally significant mesic slope forest occurs on steep slopes and bottoms of Grocery Creek and Crooked Creek, tributaries of the Ocmulgee River in Twiggs, Bleckley, and Pulaski Counties. These forests are associated with the calcareous outcrops of the blackland prairies of Oaky Woods Wildlife Management Area and harbor numerous rare species.

Structurally, the forest is usually multitiered with an understory of evergreen or tardily deciduous species such as American holly, southern wax-myrtle, horsesugar, dwarf palmetto, and devilwood, and deciduous species such as ironwood, flowering dogwood, and common two-wing silverbell. The abundant evergreen trees and shrubs are distinctively different from those in Piedmont slope forests and probably reflect the longer growing season of the Coastal Plain. Often species of native azalea, such as Florida flame azalea, Piedmont azalea, Oconee azalea, and plumleaf azalea, are present. In some forests, needle palm is an obvious understory component, as seen at Montezuma Bluffs Natural Area (see Featured Place). Characteristic species of vines and herbaceous species are sarsaparilla-vine, cross-vine, climbing hydrangea, eastern poison ivy, common greenbrier, summer grape, green dragon, and Christmas fern. Spanish-moss is a frequent epiphyte. Some stands, such as Montezuma Bluffs Natural Area or Wolf Creek Ravine (Grady County), or portions of Providence Canyon, and the Upatoi Bluffs have exceptionally showy spring ephemerals including several species of trillium, orchids, bloodroot, eastern blue phlox, cutleaf toothwort, and American trout lily carpeting the ground layer. The protected environment of some bluff forests, such as Shell Bluff and Griffin's Landing (Burke County), harbor species that are more frequently found in the Blue Ridge or Piedmont ecoregions, including northern red oak, black oak, common pawpaw, common shagbark hickory, and basswood. Other species with more northern affinities include little brown jug, may-apple, thimbleweed, spring-beauty, dolls'-eyes, and mountain laurel. Often, trees are dramatically draped with Spanish-moss or resurrection fern.

With decreasing moisture on sandier upper slopes, sand laurel oak, southern red oak, post oak, loblolly pine, and eastern red cedar become more common, and the forest transitions to dry upland deciduous hardwoods or, where frequent fire occurs, to longleaf pine–dominated forests. The transition to upland longleaf pine–dominated sandhills can be quite rapid. Lower slopes, particularly those in transition to adjacent bottomlands, feature musclewood, laurel oak, and water oak (Kwit et al. 1998). Particularly illustrative examples of such transitional zones can be seen at Griffin's Landing and Shell Bluff along the Savannah River. These east-facing bluffs are bordered upslope by xeric sandhills and downslope by cypress-tupelo river swamp and/or bottomland hardwood forests.

Calciphilic species are often present where exposed limestone is present. For example, Shumard oak, chinquapin oak, basswood, Carolina buckthorn, chalk maple, needle palm, oakleaf hydrangea, bottlebrush buckeye, and red buckeye prefer soils of higher pH with higher availability of base cations such as calcium, magnesium, and potassium (Porcher and Rayner 2001; Cavender-Bares, Kitajima, and Bazzaz 2004). Other species often associated with calcareous environments are Chattahoochee trillium, leatherwood, indian pink, Flyr's false-boneset, and threeflower hawthorn. High species richness is frequently encountered on soils that are high in calcium and phosphate (Monk 1965, 1967; W. J. Platt and Schwartz 1990).

The steepness of the terrain is often associated with unique features of the underlying geologic strata, as evidenced within the deep gorges of tributaries to the Chattahoochee River near Fort Gaines in Clay and Early Counties (R. M. Harper 1943). Here the exposed, fossil-rich marl cliffs support prominent sprays of southern maidenhair fern. Habitat for this fern also occurs in the beech-magnolia forests associated with dry sinkholes that connect to underground cavern systems in the Dougherty Plain and Pelham Escarpment.

Although the area of steephead ravines is minimal in Georgia and Florida, their botanical uniqueness has been recognized since the 1800s (Gray 1875), particularly in harboring the federally Endangered Florida torreya and the Florida yew (in Florida). The spring-

CHARACTERISTIC PLANTS OF MESIC SLOPE FORESTS

TREES

Bitternut hickory—*Carya cordiformis*
Pignut hickory—*Carya glabra*
Red hickory—*Carya ovalis*
Mockernut hickory—*Carya tomentosa*
Eastern redbud—*Cercis canadensis*
American beech—*Fagus grandifolia*
Tulip-tree—*Liriodendron tulipifera*
Southern magnolia—*Magnolia grandiflora*
Spruce pine—*Pinus glabra*
Loblolly pine—*Pinus taeda*
White oak—*Quercus alba*
Laurel oak—*Quercus laurifolia*
Swamp chestnut oak—*Quercus michauxii*
Chinquapin oak—*Quercus muehlenbergii*
Water oak—*Quercus nigra*
Shumard oak—*Quercus shumardii*
Basswood—*Tilia americana*

SHRUBS AND WOODY VINES

Southern sugar maple—*Acer floridanum*
Red buckeye—*Aesculus pavia*
Common two-wing silverbell—*Halesia diptera*
American holly—*Ilex opaca*
Devilwood—*Osmanthus americanus*
Needle palm—*Rhapidophyllum hystrix*
Piedmont azalea—*Rhododendron canescens*
Dwarf palmetto—*Sabal minor*
Sarsaparilla-vine—*Smilax pumila*

GROUND COVER

Green dragon—*Arisaema dracontium*
Longleaf spikegrass—*Chasmanthium sessiliflorum*
Virginia snakeroot—*Endodeca serpentaria*
Eastern blue phlox—*Phlox divaricata*
Mottled trillium—*Trillium maculatum*
Relict trillium—*Trillium reliquum*
Underwood's trillium—*Trillium underwoodii*
Common Atamasco-lily—*Zephyranthes atamasca*

Florida torreya

fed streams and cool microclimates of these deeply dissected ravine systems support numerous species more reminiscent of the southern Appalachians as well. Florida torreya is endemic to three counties in Florida and extends 1 mile north into Decatur County, Georgia. This evergreen species is extremely threatened by a fungal blight that has decimated the population. Historically, the strong, durable wood of the Florida torreya was harvested for fence posts, and this species was favored locally as a Christmas tree. Efforts to protect the Florida torreya from extinction include that of the Georgia Plant Conservation Alliance. Through partnerships with other organizations, this institution has planted collections of clones of the wild trees for safeguarding. Trees are planted in areas farther north outside of the plant's current range but within its former range of occurrence. Florida torreya trees planted in the Piedmont are less susceptible to the fungal blight, and some even appear to be free of it.

ANIMALS

Along most forested slopes, there is an opposing moisture and fire gradient, such that vegetation is influenced by frequent fire on upper slopes as it grades into pine forests and governed by excessive moisture as lower slopes transition into wetlands (Clewell 1986; W. J. Platt and Schwartz 1990; Enge 2005). On very steep slopes, the extended moisture gradient provides suitable habitat for a wide diversity of herpetofauna (Enge 1998, 2005). Particularly on north-facing slopes, the presence of evergreen species serves to moderate the temperature extremes in winter and summer, thus providing rather stable microclimates for amphibians. Similar to distribution patterns of vegetation, amphibians with strong northern affinities may be present, including the dusky salamander, four-toed salamander, and red salamander (Means 2000). Within the steep mesic slopes of steepheads, numerous species of invertebrates, particularly caddisflies, have been documented that are more commonly encountered in the southern Appalachians. These species are indicators of high water quality conditions and cooler climates (Hubble, Laessle, and Dickinson 1956; Entrekin et al. 1999). Although not restricted to mesic slope forests of the Coastal Plain, Rafinesque's big-eared bat roosts in caves, hollow trees, and crevices in rock ledges of these forests.

Birds include summer tanager, wood thrush, cardinal, red-eyed vireo, Carolina wren, and many others. The bird species composition of a site depends on the forest structure, particularly the density and height of the shrub layer and subcanopy trees, canopy closure, and similar factors.

FEATURED ANIMAL

Apalachicola Dusky Salamander (*Desmognathus apalachicolae*)

The Apalachicola dusky salamander, a member of the family Plethodontidae, is a small salamander with five to seven pairs of tan or reddish blotches on the back. The blotches coalesce on the lower back to form a slight stripe bordered by a scalloped pattern of darker pigments. Color is variable among individuals and also varies according to temperature and background materials. Older adult males may be uniformly black or brown (Means 2008a).

This secretive salamander is mostly confined to the Coastal Plain, where it is found in deep, shaded ravines, primarily along seepage tributaries to the Chattahoochee River, the Flint River, and the Ochlockonee River. Although once considered a southern extension of the northern dusky salamander, it is now recognized as a separate species. Two other species of salamander, the red salamander and the southern two-lined salamander, are frequently found in the same habitats. Apalachicola dusky salamanders spend the daytime under logs, rocks, and leaf litter, usually in the vicinity of seeps or headwater streams. They often dive in the water to escape when uncovered. At night, they leave their hiding places to forage for food items, which are thought to consist mainly of small invertebrates. They may remain active much of the winter because of the relatively warm temperatures associated with seepages.

Reproduction occurs from May until November (Means 2008a). Females lay their eggs in a small chamber under moist leaf litter and watch over the eggs until they hatch. Larval salamanders live in the shallow headwater streams until they metamorphose into adults (Means 2008a).

Montezuma Bluffs Natural Area

Montezuma Bluffs Natural Area (Macon County), located along dissected terraces above the Flint River, features a mature mesic slope forest with exceptional displays of spring wildflowers. This 500-acre natural area is managed by the Georgia Department of Natural Resources. A hiking trail winds downslope and through the open forest composed of American beech, southern magnolia, and many of the typical mesic forest associates such as red buckeye, southern sugar maple, swamp chestnut oak, Shumard oak, white oak, spruce pine, and red hickory. Needle palm is also a conspicuous component of the forest. Along this trail are dense colonies of cutleaf toothwort, eastern blue phlox, bloodroot, wild ginger, Atamasco-lily, and several species of trillium.

Location: From the intersection of W. Railroad St. and Ga. Hwy. 49 in Montezuma, proceed approximately 2.2 miles north on Ga. 49, and turn left (west) on Crooks Landing Rd. In less than 1 mile, the road will begin to descend sharply; a large gravel parking area is located on the north side of the road. Google Earth GPS approximate coordinates at the parking area: N 32.337004/W 084.028630.

Acidic Glades, Barrens, and Rocky Woodlands

Acidic glades, barrens, and rocky woodlands are open mosaics of plant communities that usually occur on outcroppings of sandstone (often called Altamaha Grit) and ironstone in the upper Coastal Plain. A rare outcrop, composed of flint kaolin, a hard, flinty conglomerate of metamorphosed sediments, occurs in Fall Line counties. Rocky outcrops occur as boulders or flat rocks on hillsides, on gently rolling terrain, or along river banks. Vegetation on these rocky substrates exists as a mosaic of grasslands embedded within sparse longleaf pine woodlands, depending on the degree of bare rock and amount of fine-textured soil. Common species include blackjack oak, turkey oak, southern red oak, sparkleberry, and numerous grasses and forbs. The sandstone glade communities support several rare species, and several interesting biogeographic relation-ships unite these glades with other rock outcrop plant communities throughout the state.

Acidic glades, barrens, and rocky woodlands are distinctive in the Coastal Plain because there are very few areas where rocks outcrop on the surface among the unconsolidated sands and clays that typically characterize this ecoregion. The Altamaha Grit outcrops, such as those at Broxton Rocks Preserve (Coffee County), can be particularly picturesque, featuring large outcrops more than 30 feet in height and even streams with waterfalls. The damp, shaded crevices between the rocks enable species from the southern Appalachians as well as the tropics to occur here.

PHYSICAL SETTING AND ECOLOGY

In general, the sandstone and ironstone outcroppings occur in different regions of Georgia, usually embedded within the dry upland longleaf pine woodland community. The sandstone outcroppings occur in the Tifton Uplands and Atlantic Southern Loam Plains

Ironstone outcrops in longleaf pine woodlands

(Vidalia Uplands) subregions, while the ironstone outcrops occur primarily on the uplands of the Southern Hilly Gulf Coastal Plain and Red Hills regions.

The Altamaha Grit sandstone outcrops were described around the turn of the 20th century by Roland Harper (R. M. Harper 1906). The outcrops are an above-ground exposure of a geologic formation composed primarily of a cemented conglomerate of sandstone, clay, sand, quartz, and iron oxide pebbles (Huddlestun 1988). This indurated sandstone bedrock is limited to Georgia but covers an extensive region within the upper Coastal Plain. Sporadic outcrops of indurated sandstone commonly occur as flat rocks and boulders on hillsides, on gently rolling terrain, or along river banks. Although large expanses of flat rocks are somewhat rare, a notable example is located on the Broxton Rocks Preserve, owned by the Nature Conservancy (within the Broxton Rocks Conservation Area; see the Featured Place).

Historically, Harper referred to the Tifton Uplands and the Southern Loamy Plains (Vidalia Up-

lands) subregions as the "Altamaha Grit Region" because of the prevalence of sandstone outcroppings. He assumed that this area reflected one geologic origin. More recently, the Altamaha Grit has been determined to be of formations ranging in age from Oligocene to Pleistocene (Huddlestun 1988). Therefore, the term "Altamaha Grit" no longer has the meaning Harper originally ascribed to it but remains the term in use among ecologists to describe the 15,000 square miles of sandstone that underlie the region and the outcroppings of that sandstone. The term picked up widespread usage with the protection of the very picturesque Broxton Rocks area (see the Featured Place).

The sandstone bedrock gives rise to sandy loam soils containing large amounts of plinthite (hard, small, round concretions containing iron). Plinthite forms on exposure to repeated wetting and drying, especially if it is also exposed to heat from the sun. Plate-like masses of ironstone occur in many parts of the Coastal Plain, particularly the uplands in the Southern Hilly Gulf Coastal Plain and Red Hills regions. Here erosion-resistant hills that are capped by ironstone protrude on the rolling landscape (Peet 2006). They are formed by wetting and drying processes similar to those that form the plinthite of the Tifton Uplands and Atlantic Southern Loam Plains. In this case, the iron segregates out of unconsolidated substrates into a subsurface crust that breaks into irregular inch-thick slabs and plates. In southwestern Georgia, ironstone outcrops occur on the undulating hills of highly weathered soils. Few examples of such areas that still support longleaf pine remain; exceptions are the rocky woodlands located on the southwestern part of Fort Benning in Chattahoochee County. Similarly, sites with exposed ironstone occur in areas transitional to the Fall Line Sandhills, and are particularly abundant in Marion, Sumter, Schley, Macon, Houston, Pulaski, Burke, Richmond, Columbia, and McDuffie Counties, but most of these sites no longer support longleaf pine. One small, but accessible example occurs at McDuffie Public Fishing Area south of Dearing, Georgia, called Iron Hill (McDuffie County).

"Flint kaolin" occurs with other kaolin deposits just south of Georgia's Fall Line and most notably in Columbia County; its high opaline-silica content makes it too hard for commercial use and also prone to form erosion-resistant outcrops that support vegetation similar to that of Piedmont granite outcrops and Altamaha Grit.

Soil depth varies with topography, collecting in crevices and shallow depressions in the rock, ranging from bare rock to several inches of soil in depressions and up to 15 inches or more in woodlands. The sandy loam soil is well drained. Similar to other outcrop environments that occur throughout the state, growing conditions are harsh, particularly in the open glades and barrens. Here high temperatures and drought conditions are characteristic.

Fire is important in maintaining the longleaf pine and ground cover component of rocky woodlands that fringe these sites and some islands of vegetation within the outcrop site. The role of fire is probably less important in the glade communities, where it would be halted by expanses of rock and the absence of fuel.

VEGETATION

Vegetation in these rocky communities forms a mosaic of plant species, depending on substrate, soil texture, soil depth, moisture, degree of outcropping, and fire-return intervals. In some cases, vegetation associated with outcrops is somewhat reminiscent of granite outcrops of the Piedmont, with species having adapted to droughty conditions. Rocky woodlands grade into a dry upland longleaf pine matrix with increased soil depth (Peet 2006).

The Altamaha Grit flatrock outcrops of sandstone may be bare to patchily vegetated, where accumulations of soil occur in depressions or cracks in the rocks. Distinctive rockland species include rock-pinks, Cuthbert's onion, Georgia beargrass, grit purslane, Georgia beardtongue, little people, early saxifrage, larkspur, and woolly ragwort. Scattered trees and shrubs, including longleaf pine, blackjack oak, and sparkleberry, can be rooted in deeper soils or crevices (Peet 2006). Both extensive flat outcrops and large bouldery outcrops occur at the Broxton Rocks Preserve (Coffee County) owned by the Nature Conservancy (see the Featured Place). Other examples of this community occur on Flat Tub Landing Wildlife Management

Georgia beardtongue

CHARACTERISTIC PLANTS OF ACIDIC GLADES, BARRENS, AND ROCKY WOODLANDS

TREES

Shortleaf pine—Pinus echinata
Longleaf pine—Pinus palustris
Southern red oak—Quercus falcata
Turkey oak—Quercus laevis
Sand post oak—Quercus margarettae
Blackjack oak—Quercus marilandica

SHRUBS AND WOODY VINES

Dwarf huckleberry—Gaylussacia dumosa
Mountain laurel—Kalmia latifolia
Sassafras—Sassafras albidum

Horsesugar—Symplocos tinctoria
Sparkleberry—Vaccinium arboreum

GROUND COVER

Elliott's bluestem—Andropogon elliottii
Splitbeard bluestem—Andropogon ternarius
Old-field broomsedge—Andropogon virginicus
Southern wiregrass—Aristida beyrichiana
Georgia beargrass—Nolina georgiana
Switchgrass—Panicum virgatum

Silkgrass—Pityopsis graminifolia
Bracken fern—Pteridium aquilinum
Little bluestem—Schizachyrium scoparium
Slender bluestem—Schizachyrium tenerum
Yellow sunnybell—Schoenolirion croceum
Virginia goat's-rue—Tephrosia virginiana
Curlyleaf yucca—Yucca filamentosa

Area in Coffee and Jeff Davis Counties. Rocky woodlands form a surrounding matrix, composed of sparse longleaf pine canopy with ground cover dominated by grasses, including splitbeard bluestem, little bluestem, and southern wiregrass. Oaks, including sand post oak and blackjack oak, are present in areas that burn infrequently (see dry upland longleaf pine woodlands). This complex of rocky woodlands and glades is considered critically imperiled because of its rarity in the region.

Similarly, in regions of the upper Coastal Plain on sites with sporadic outcrops of ironstone, widely spaced stands of longleaf pine are characterized by patchy ground cover that develops among bare soil and exposed rock. For example, at Fort Benning and other sites in Chattahoochee County, steep, strikingly rocky hillsides with eroded loamy soils are dominated by longleaf pine with a sparse ground cover of common little bluestem, big bluestem, splitbeard bluestem, Elliott's bluestem, switchgrass, silkgrass, curlyleaf yucca, bracken fern, and numerous species of legumes, when frequently burned. Other scattered trees include turkey oak, southern red oak, and blackjack oak. Conspicuous exposures of ironstone rubble occur in erosion gullies that form on steep hillslopes. Here mountain laurel, sparkleberry, and horsesugar are notably associated with crevices among the rocks in the lower gullies, where moisture accumulates from surficial drainage (Peet 2006). Restricted access to sandstone outcrops for recreational vehicle use is needed to limit potential damage to plant communities and destabilization of substrates. Excessive soil erosion is a concern in the rolling terrain and sandy loam soils associated with ironstone woodlands and glades.

ANIMALS

The acidic glade, barren, and rocky woodland community is usually interspersed within a matrix of longleaf pine woodlands or mixed pine-hardwoods and provides habitat to a similar suite of species associated with other longleaf pine communities. For example, two noteworthy longleaf pine bird associates that nest at the Broxton Rocks Preserve are Bachman's sparrow and the red-cockaded woodpecker. The southeastern American kestrel (J. W. Parrish 2010a), as well as ground-doves, are associated with open pine forests of the Coastal Plain managed with frequent fire (M. F. Hodges 2010). Common nighthawks, which frequently nest directly on rock outcrops or on the ground of open woodlands, are also found in this habitat (Straight 2010a).

Although eastern woodrats inhabit a wide variety of communities, they frequently nest among rocky fissures and boulders. These nocturnal rodents, often called "pack rats," line their nests with sticks, leaves, bones, pebbles, or other miscellaneous items available in the environment.

Yucca Giant-Skipper (*Megathymus yuccae*)

The yucca giant-skipper is a relatively large and robust butterfly, with a wingspan of approximately 2 to 3 inches. The sexes are similar, but females are generally larger than males. Yucca giant-skippers are fast and powerful fliers, producing an audible "whizzing" sound as they dart from place to place (Daniels 2008). They typically fly in the late afternoon and early evening, remaining hidden in vegetation during the early part of the day (L. C. Harris 1972).

This butterfly is found in a variety of natural and anthropogenic habitats, including rock outcrops, coastal dunes, pine savannas, sandhills, desert canyons, pine flatwoods, grasslands, old fields, and utility corridors. It is widely but patchily distributed across the southern half of the United States from North Carolina to California and south into Mexico. The yucca giant-skipper has been documented throughout the northern two-thirds of Florida. In Georgia, it has been collected primarily in the Coastal Plain and Piedmont (L. C. Harris 1972; Beohm 2010). Despite its broad geographic range, the yucca giant-skipper is local and uncommon; large numbers of adults are seldom observed (Daniels 2008).

The yucca giant-skipper produces one brood each year from February to May, depending on location. Males typically perch conspicuously in the open on yucca leaves and stalks, dead stumps and twigs, or fallen leaves on the ground. After breeding, the females glue their eggs to the leaves of the host plants. Following hatching in about 10 days, the young caterpillars feed near the leaf tips and may web them together with silk. Older caterpillars bore into the plant crown and feed within the large, fleshy root, constructing a tunnel capped at its opening by a silken chimney or tent. The fully grown caterpillars over-winter inside the yucca plant and pupate in late winter or early spring (L. C. Harris 1972). The emerging adults do not feed, relying instead on ample reserves of body fat developed during the larval (caterpillar) stage.

Broxton Rocks Preserve and Flat Tub Landing Wildlife Management Area

Broxton Rocks Preserve is owned and managed by the Nature Conservancy, and the adjoining Flat Tub Landing Wildlife Management Area is owned by the state and managed by the Georgia Department of Natural Resources. Together, this conservation area is a 13,500-acre tract in northern Coffee County and Jeff Davis County near Douglas, Georgia. This rugged sandstone outcrop and longleaf pine forest represents the largest single extrusion of the Altamaha Grit. The boulders, crevices, and flat outcrops amid the long-leaf pine forest provide unique habitats for several rare plants such as the grit purslane, the silky dwarf morning-glory, and the state Threatened Georgia-plume. Two rare ferns—the dwarf filmy fern, which normally occurs in the southern Appalachians, and the rare shoestring fern, which is usually found in the tropics—are also present. The green-fly orchid normally grows on trees but here occurs on the rock walls. Other species of interest are early saxifrage, prairie larkspur, spring-beauty, rock-pinks, sandwort, pine-land Barbara's-buttons, yellow sunny bell, sand spike-moss, and several species of quillwort. Rocky Creek, an ephemeral tributary of the Ocmulgee River, dissects part of the outcrop. During wet periods, water gushes over the rock ledges, forming a scenic waterfall; at other times it is only a trickle.

The federally Threatened indigo snake and state Threatened gopher tortoise also inhabit the area. The Nature Conservancy and the Georgia Department of Natural Resources are restoring the original longleaf pine–wiregrass community through prescribed fire and planting longleaf pine and southern wiregrass.

Location: Access to Broxton Rocks Preserve is best arranged by contacting the Nature Conservancy Office in Atlanta, or the city of Douglas, Georgia, via email: tourism@cityofdouglas.com. To Flat Tub Landing Wildlife Management Area: From downtown, Douglass, take Ga. Hwy. 441 north for approximately 20 miles. Turn right (east) onto Ga. Hwy. 107 and proceed for 8 miles to Flat Tub Wildlife Management Area. Look for the sign on the left. Google Earth GPS approximate coordinates: N 31.761962/W 082.831737.

Blackland Prairies and Woodlands

Blackland prairies are rare herbaceous communities in Georgia, occurring in a few locations in the Coastal Plain Red Uplands of Houston, Peach, Twiggs, and Bleckley Counties. They occur as small, open grasslands within a forested matrix of pines or mesic slope forests. Blackland prairies are part of a complex of blackland prairies and woodlands limited to a few localities on rolling hills within the Ocmulgee River drainage. They occur on alkaline, clay-rich soils derived from marl, chalk, or limestone. Shrink-swell soils have limited the growth of trees and shrubs but have supported the formation of an interesting and rare plant community dominated by grasses and showy wildflowers. Many of these species are also associated with the fire-maintained ground cover of longleaf pine uplands. Several species are more commonly associated with western prairies or limestone glades and are considered rare in Georgia.

Blackland prairies and the associated mesic slope forests are of significant conservation interest because of their uncommonness in Georgia and the presence of numerous rare plant species. Only a few high-quality examples of blackland prairie remain in Georgia, and thus protection of these sites and the surrounding complex of mesic chalk forests and bottomlands is a high priority. Nine remnant prairies have been documented on the Ocmulgee and Oaky Woods Wildlife Management Areas, recently acquired by the state.

PHYSICAL SETTING AND ECOLOGY

The dominant factors controlling vegetation of the blackland prairies are the combination of shallow, alkaline clay soils, the steep, rolling topography and associated erosion, and fire. The distinctive chalky,

The marly soils of blackland prairies have shrink-swell properties that result in cracking or heaving as moisture content varies.

clay-rich soils conspicuously change in volume with changes in moisture content. During dry periods, the soil volume shrinks, and deep, wide cracks form; when wet, the soil volume expands and the soil takes on a very sticky consistency. The shrink-swell properties of the soils make them marginally suitable for agricultural production. Even though such soils can create serious engineering problems for construction (Rosser and Moore 1982), these remnant grassland communities are under considerable development pressure in this area of the state (Foskett 2006).

Characteristically, the soils are somewhat poorly drained to moderately well-drained silty clays. The shrink-swell properties result from weathering of aluminosilicate minerals (Woods 1967). In some areas, as can be readily observed at the former Oaky Woods Wildlife Management Area (Houston and Pulaski Counties), the upper soil horizons have eroded, reveal-

ing the distinctive light gray, marly subsurface (Echols 2007).

Many sites of the more fertile soil types were converted to pasture or industrial longleaf pine plantations decades ago. Although the shallow soils over limestone may retard encroachment of hardwoods, fire has played a role in maintaining the openness of the sites. In the prolonged absence of fire, hardwoods eventually dominate the sites (Lawless 2005). While localized, the presence of the unique soil type suggests that the open prairie vegetation was likely more extensive prior to settlement (Echols 2007).

The use of frequent prescribed fire is essential to the long-term maintenance of this community. The history of fire suppression, encroachment by hardwoods, and conversion to planted pine may require mechanical removal of undesirable species to reintroduce prescribed fire. This community is also threatened by

Prairie coneflower

Starry rosinweed

severe erosion associated with roads on steep slopes. Soil compaction and deep ruts are caused by uncontrolled off-road vehicular traffic. The prairie vegetation is vulnerable to soil disturbances by feral hogs, particularly in the wettest soils.

VEGETATION

The vegetation on the blackland prairies of Georgia is quite similar to that found in central Alabama and Mississippi and may be an extension of the same community (Rostland 1957; Peacock and Schauwecker 2003). The prairie vegetation is dominated by perennial grasses and forbs, and the ground cover may range from sparse to nearly complete. Dominant grasses include indiangrass, big bluestem, old-field broomsedge, arrowfeather, hairgrass, rough dropseed,

and poverty dropseed. A conspicuous increase in grass cover following reintroduction of prescribed fire was noted by Echols (2007), suggesting that dominance by grasses would continue with regular fire management. While dominants may vary across the prairie opening or among prairie sites, the relationship to previous land use or soil characteristics is unclear (Echols 2007).

Some common species present that are associated with western limestone prairies include side-oats grama, whitlow-grass, Ozark bedstraw, Drummond's skullcap, prairie coneflower, and diamond-flower. Forbs that occur sporadically throughout include cedar glade, daisy fleabane, butterfly-weed, green milkweed, whorled milkweed, New England aster, Dakota vervain, common eastern coneflower, azure sage, and starry rosinweed.

CHARACTERISTIC PLANTS OF BLACKLAND PRAIRIES AND WOODLANDS

TREES

Dwarf hackberry—Celtis tenuifolia
Eastern redbud—Cercis canadensis
Eastern red cedar—Juniperus virginiana
Chinquapin oak—Quercus muehlenbergii
Bastard oak—Quercus sinuata
Winged elm—Ulmus alata

SHRUBS AND WOODY VINES

American rattan—Berchemia scandens
Eastern roughleaf dogwood—Cornus asperifolia
Cockspur hawthorn—Crataegus crus-galli
Littlehip hawthorn—Crataegus spathulata
Three-flower hawthorn—Crataegus triflora
Carolina buckthorn—Frangula caroliniana

Eastern gum bumelia—Sideroxylon lanuginosum
Dune greenbrier—Smilax auriculata
Southern black haw—Viburnum rufidulum

GROUND COVER

Big bluestem—Andropogon gerardii
Arrowfeather—Aristida purpurascens
Common butterfly-weed—Asclepias tuberosa
Whorled milkweed—Asclepias verticillata
Green milkweed—Asclepias viridiflora
Cherokee sedge—Carex cherokeensis
Beaked panic grass—Coleataenia anceps
Prairie larkspur—Delphinium carolinianum
Cedar glade daisy fleabane—Erigeron strigosus

Dakota vervain—Glandularia bipinnatifida
Diamond-flower—Houstonia nigracans
Hairgrass—Muhlenbergia capillaris
Boykin's milkwort—Polygala boykinii
Prairie coneflower—Ratibida pinnata
Common eastern coneflower—Rudbeckia fulgida
Azure sage—Salvia azurea
Starry rosinweed—Silphium asteriscus
Eastern gray goldenrod—Solidago nemoralis
Yellow indiangrass—Sorghastrum nutans
Rough dropseed—Sporobolus clandestinus
Poverty dropseed—Sporobolus vaginiflorus
New England aster—Symphyotrichum novae-angliae

With fire suppression and/or deeper soils, woody species, including dwarf hackberry, eastern redbud, eastern roughleaf dogwood, cockspur hawthorn, littlehip hawthorn, three-flower hawthorn, American persimmon, Carolina buckthorn, white ash, eastern red cedar, chinquapin oak, bastard oak, eastern gum bumelia, winged elm, and southern black haw, are more abundant. Common vines include American rattan and dune greenbrier.

ANIMALS

Little information regarding fauna of the blackland prairies in Georgia is available, given the rarity of this community in the state. In Alabama, where blackland prairie habitats are more common, no locally endemic vertebrates are reported (Schotz and Barbour 2009). The openness of the prairie and woodland communities has been noted as ideal habitat for the long-tailed weasel, as well as numerous grassland bird species. Of particular conservation interest are American kestrels, grasshopper sparrows, and northern harriers. Numerous beetle and moth species are restricted to blackland prairies in Alabama and Mississippi (DeSelm and Murdock 1993; R. L. Brown 2003), and these habitat specialists may also be found in similar sites in Georgia.

Black Bear (*Ursus americanus*)

Black bears are found in three distinct regions in Georgia: the north Georgia mountains, along the Ocmulgee River drainage system in the central part of the state, and in the Okefenokee Swamp. Bears typically live in swamps and forested areas, especially mature mixed pine stands that offer a plentiful supply of natural foods and forests and thickets for escape. Standing, hollow trees are common den sites for Georgia bears, particularly in the Coastal Plain. Brush piles, rock crevices, caves, or other places that offer protection may also be used (Georgia Wildlife Web 2008).

Black bears have poor eyesight but an excellent sense of smell. They are good tree climbers, can swim well, and are able to run at speeds of up to 30 miles per hour. The typical lifespan of a bear is about 8 to 15 years. Adult bears are generally up to 6 feet in length and about 3 feet high at the shoulder. Female adult bears can weigh up to 300 pounds and attain breeding status at about 3 to 5 years of age. Adult males can weigh more than 500 pounds and may breed as early as 1.5 years of age (Georgia Wildlife Web 2008).

Bears are omnivorous, feeding on berries, fruits, acorns, grasses, and animal matter, including insects or mammals. Bears can become attracted to human food when their natural diet sources are scarce. A diet of garbage and other unnatural foods can result in malnutrition and a shortened lifespan. Black bears were common in the state at the time of European settlement; however, subsequent habitat loss and unrestricted hunting contributed to significant population declines. More recently, the black bear population in Georgia has rebounded to a total of at least 5,100 individuals due to strict enforcement of hunting regulations, sound wildlife management practices, and protection of habitat.

Oaky Woods Wildlife Management Area

A complex of remnant blackland prairies and mesic slope forests occur in the 19,200-acre Oaky Woods Wildlife Management Area in southeast Houston County near Kathleen, Georgia. This property is partly owned and partly leased by the Georgia Department of Natural Resources. This tract is considered to be extremely important wildlife habitat in addition to harboring plant communities unique to Georgia (see also mesic slope forests).

Dakota Prairie is located in the northwestern portion of the Oaky Woods Wildlife Management Area. Roads accessing this site exhibit the eroded calcareous soil and hilly topography. The 9-acre prairie site is surrounded by planted pine. The herbaceous vegetation is sparse to continuous and is dominated by species such as diamond-flower, prairie coneflower, and poverty grass. This prairie is spectacularly showy in July, when prairie coneflowers are in full bloom. Later in

the season, various asters and grasses are highly visible, including hairgrass, eastern gray goldenrod, and New England aster. Encroachment by woody calciphiles such as southern red cedar, eastern red bud, and chinquapin oak is evident.

Big Prairie is located within the central portion of Oaky Woods Wildlife Management Area. This site exhibits deeper soils than Dakota Prairie and exhibits a stronger dominance of perennial prairie grasses such as big bluestem and yellow indiangrass. The rare Georgia aster can be seen blooming along the prairie edges during the fall.

Location: From the intersection of Ga. Hwy. 127 and Ga. 247 in Kathleen, go south on Ga. 247 about 0.7 mile. Turn left (east) onto Oaky Woods Rd. Proceed about 1.5 miles to the main gate. Google Earth GPS approximate coordinates at the entrance: N 32.486095/ W 083.58182.

Pine Flatwoods

Pine flatwoods occur primarily in areas of low relief in the outer Coastal Plain, on deep, sandy, acidic soils. The water table is close to the surface and results in periodic saturation, particularly in the winter. During droughts, the soil conditions are extremely dry. Pine flatwoods that are maintained by prescribed fire are typically dominated by longleaf pine, slash pine, or pond pine, depending on drainage and fire frequency. Saw palmetto, low-statured shrubs, grasses, and forbs compose the understory and ground cover. In the absence of fire, shrubs become more dominant, often forming nearly impenetrable thickets. Once occupying vast stretches of the lower Coastal Plain, pine flatwoods in Georgia have largely been converted to slash or loblolly pine plantations for industrial forestry.

The term "flatwoods" has been widely applied to many pine-dominated sites in the southeastern Coastal Plain (Christensen 2000). Here we follow Abraham-son and Hartnett (1990) and Peet (2006) in restricting the application to pine stands associated with poorly drained acidic soils of the lower Coastal Plain.

PHYSICAL SETTING AND ECOLOGY

Pine flatwoods are distributed throughout the lower Coastal Plain on sandy marine deposits associated with former shorelines and marsh deposits during the Pleistocene epoch. A transition from the Tifton Up-lands to the lower Coastal Plain can be observed along U.S. Highway 341 in Jeff Davis County, just south of Hazelhurst (Wharton 1978). The flat topography results in periodic soil saturation, depending on rainfall.

Flatwoods soils are poorly drained acidic sands with low nutrient availability, low clay content, low organic matter content, and low cation exchange capacity (Abrahamson and Hartnett 1990). Many flatwoods soils are spodosols and can be recognized by a distinctive color change in subsurface horizons. The characteristic spodic horizon is formed when organic materials from plant roots are translocated downward by water percolation and accumulate at the lower depths of root penetration. Typically, spodosols have an upper subsurface horizon of light-colored sands from which clay and silt have been removed. The spodic horizon will appear as a darker brownish-black beneath the light-colored upper horizon. Below the spodic horizon, the light-colored parent materials will again be present. Spodosols are usually strongly acidic. In some cases, iron, aluminum, and organic compounds of the spodic horizon cement the sand grains together, forming a rock-hard layer that can create a perched water table (Buol 1973). Although flatwoods soils with spodic horizons are common, considerable variation occurs among soils within large areas of flatwoods. Also frequently present are wet ultisols and alfisols (Edmisten 1963; Abrahamson and Hartnett 1990; Stout and Marion 1993; Harms, Aust, and Burger 1998).

The hydrology of flatwoods is strongly influenced by local precipitation and groundwater level, elevation, and the presence of water-restrictive soil horizons. Flatwoods hydrology ranges from standing water for several months per year, to only brief inundation during extreme high-water periods, to merely subsurface saturation. Generally, they are well drained or even droughty during the summer but saturated during winter or periods of greater rainfall. Often flatwoods sites have numerous wet depressions, wetland cypress ponds, oak domes, small floodplain swamps, or scrubby intermediate zones embedded within.

As in all Coastal Plain pine communities, the relationship among fire, soils, and hydroperiod shapes vegetation and modifies successional trajectories. Fire is an important factor in reducing competition from hardwoods and increasing the abundance of grasses and forbs. Today, few stands of flatwoods resemble natural or pre-settlement conditions. Historically, longleaf, slash, and pond pine were dominant trees, and these species were distributed across a hydrologic and fire gradient. With the removal of much of the virgin longleaf pine in the early 1900s and reduced frequency of fire, slash pine expanded its range from predominantly wet sites and mixed stands of longleaf and slash pine to become prevalent throughout the area (Gunter 1921; Edmisten 1963). In the last 50 years, much of the natural pine-dominated flatwoods sites have been converted to industrial slash or loblolly pine plantations managed intensively for fiber production. Intensive site manipulation is commonly associated with silvicultural practices for even-aged slash

pine pulpwood production. Conversion of a site from original flatwoods vegetation to a pine plantation occurs through harvesting the canopy, clearing the remaining vegetation, piling and burning the slash, and sometimes construction of drainage ditches. Bedding in flatwoods is a common practice of mounding soil in rows for planting sites to keep the roots of planted seedlings above the water table during early establishment (Harms, Aust, and Burger 1998).

Catastrophic wildfire hazard is a result of fire exclusion and the buildup of flammable fuels in pine flatwoods. The absence of fire for one to two decades significantly increases the risk of wildfire during drought (Edmisten 1963). For example, wildfires in the Okefenokee Swamp escaped into privately owned slash pine plantations and burned thousands of acres of timber, threatened homes, closed roads, and created smoke that drifted over much of Georgia and northern Florida during a drought in 2007. Many of these destroyed stands had not been managed with prescribed fire for fuel reduction. Increased public recognition of the importance of prescribed fire in fire-prone communities is a serious educational need.

VEGETATION

Species that reside in flatwoods are adapted to extremes in soil moisture from periodically saturated to droughty conditions. Although most of the flatwoods in Georgia are now dominated by planted slash pine, natural stands may be dominated by longleaf or slash pine or a combination of the two. At River Creek Wildlife Management Area (Thomas County), a continuum of flatwoods conditions can be observed. Longleaf pine is usually associated with better drained and more frequently burned sites, slash pine with less well-drained sites, and pond pine with the wettest sites (Edmisten 1963; Snedaker and Lugo 1972; Abrahamson and Hartnett 1990).

Both slash and pond pine trees have root systems that are well adapted to wet soil conditions. Slash pine roots are composed of aerenchymous (air-filled) tissues that provide a mechanism for the tree to extend its roots into anaerobic, waterlogged soils. Consequently, slash pine can withstand inundation for several months or even a few years (Topa and McLeod 1986; Fisher and Stone 1990; Tiner 1999). Slash pine and pond pine do not have the fire-resistant grass stage as found in longleaf pine and thus must have a fire-free period for seedling establishment. In spite of its sen-

Deer's tongue

sitivity to fire at an early age, pond pine depends on periodic fire to maintain stand dominance because it produces serotinous cones, requiring the heat of fire to open (Burns and Honkala 1990; Stout and Marion 1993). Pond pine is also able to resprout from buds located along the main stem (epicormic buds) to produce new branches if its branches are killed by fire (Wade and Ward 1973).

Saw palmetto is the most obvious understory plant of the flatwoods, with fan-shaped leaves and large, horizontal stems. This species reaches heights of 3 to 7 feet and can form nearly complete cover. Dead leaves remain on this evergreen plant, providing extremely flammable fuels. It resprouts vigorously following fire. Other shrubby species, such as staggerbushes and little gallberry, are common understory constituents if burning has been suppressed. Frequently burned sites, particularly those with drier soils, favor grasses and forbs (Edmisten 1963). Ground cover in these sites includes southern wiregrass, toothache grass, Florida dropseed, numerous species of chaffheads, yellow-eyed grass, blazing-stars, thoroughworts, flat-topped goldenrod, and dwarf live oak. Species of adjacent communities invade flatwoods when fire is suppressed.

Pond pine flatwoods

CHARACTERISTIC PLANTS OF PINE FLATWOODS

TREES

Slash pine—*Pinus elliottii*
Longleaf pine—*Pinus palustris*
Pond pine—*Pinus serotina*

SHRUBS AND WOODY VINES

Huckleberry—*Gaylusaccia frondosa*
Dahoon—*Ilex cassine*
Little gallberry—*Ilex glabra*
Hairy wicky—*Kalmia hirsuta*
Crookedwood—*Lyonia ferruginea*
Staggerbush—*Lyonia fruticosa*
Wax-myrtle—*Morella cerifera*
Dwarf live oak—*Quercus minima*
Saw palmetto—*Serenoa repens*

Dune greenbrier—*Smilax auriculata*
Bamboo-vine—*Smilax laurifolia*

GROUND COVER

Old-field broomsedge—*Andropogon virginicus*
Southern wiregrass—*Aristida beyrichiana*
Toothache grass—*Ctenium aromaticum*
Flat-top goldenrod—*Euthamia caroliniana*
Coppery St. John's-wort—*Hypericum denticulatum*
Common elegant blazing-star—*Liatris elegans*

Switchgrass—*Panicum virgatum*
Silkgrass—*Pityopsis graminifolia*
Blackroot—*Pterocaulon pycnostachyum*
Smooth meadow-beauty—*Rhexia alifanus*
Pale meadow-beauty—*Rhexia mariana*
Little bluestem—*Schizachyrium scoparium*
Florida dropseed—*Sporobolus floridanus*
American asters—*Symphyotrichum adnatum; S. walteri*
Deer's-tongue—*Trilisa odoratissima*
Drummond's yellow-eyed grass—*Xyris drummondii*

The highly flammable properties of southern wiregrass and saw palmetto contribute to the spread of fire (Laessle 1942; Mutch 1970). In the absence of fire, fire-sensitive swamp hardwoods, such as laurel oak, water oak, sweet gum, and wax-myrtle, or bay species, such as sweet bay, red bay, and loblolly bay, may replace pines as canopy dominants (Edmisten 1963; Monk 1968). The rate of invasion of hardwoods into flatwoods depends on soil pH, proximity to hardwood swamps or bay swamps, retention of pines in the canopy, and modifications of hydrology (Edmisten 1963; Monk 1968; Abrahamson and Hartnett 1990).

ANIMALS

Longleaf pine flatwoods are inhabited by numerous vertebrates depending on the type of embedded uplands or wetlands within the site. Two commonly occurring amphibians in drier pine flatwoods are the pine woods treefrog and the oak toad, although neither species is restricted to this habitat; they also occur in longleaf pine sandhills. During the nonbreeding season, these species reside under bark or rotting logs. The pine woods treefrog climbs into pine trees and breeds in temporary aquatic habitats such as cypress-gum ponds. In wetter pine flatwoods, the little grass frog is present, and its breeding and nonbreeding habitats do not necessarily differ (W. B. Cash 2008).

The pine woods snake has a localized distribution in Georgia, restricted primarily to pine flatwoods in the southeastern part of the state (see the Featured Animal). In the Coastal Plain, pygmy rattlesnakes are frequently associated with saw palmetto thickets (Glaudas 2008). Other commonly encountered snakes in pine flatwoods are eastern diamondback rattlesnake and black racer.

Mature pine flatwoods that are frequently burned may harbor the red-cockaded woodpecker, Bachman's sparrow, and pine warbler. No mammals are exclusive to flatwoods; white-tailed deer are common. Although not commonly found in the lower Coastal Plain of Georgia, black bears occur in the Okefenokee Swamp and adjacent sites in Florida. Small mammals include raccoon, cotton mouse, hispid cotton rat, and gray fox. The two most common introduced vertebrates of flatwoods are the nine-banded armadillo and feral hog (Abrahamson and Hartnett 1990).

The palmetto tortoise beetle is a beautiful metallic blue beetle that is commonly found feeding on saw palmetto. This distinctive, small, round-bodied beetle has alternating longitudinal rows of pits and ridges on its back. The distal parts of the legs (tarsi) are greatly enlarged with numerous adhesive bristles for grasping the leafy substrate and preventing other predatory insects from dislodging it (Beshear 1969).

Pine Woods Snake (*Rhadinea flavilata*)

The pine woods snake, also known as the yellow-lipped snake, is a member of the family Colubridae. This snake is rather small and slender; adults are approximately 10 to 13 inches long, and females are larger than males. Coloration is golden brown to reddish brown on the back and paler on the sides. The belly is white, pale yellow, or yellowish green. The head of the pine woods snake is darker in color than the rest of the body, with a dark line that extends from the snout to the back edge of the jaw. The upper lip is white to pale yellow in color (Lamb and Gibbons 2008).

The pine woods snake is found in damp woodlands, especially pine flatwoods but also occasionally in hardwood hammocks and within forest habitats on coastal islands (Conant and Collins 1998). Pine woods snakes seem to prefer moist areas with an abundance of fallen logs and rotting stumps. They are typically found under loose bark or within decaying stumps or boles of pine trees, more rarely in loose soil or leaf litter; around homesites they may occasionally be found under boards or in woodpiles. Though harmless to humans, this rear-fanged snake produces mildly toxic venom that helps it subdue larger prey.

In Georgia, this species of conservation concern is known from only a handful of counties in the southeastern portion of the lower Coastal Plain. In neighboring South Carolina its range is a larger portion of the lower Coastal Plain, with an apparently disjunct population in the upper Coastal Plain near the Savannah River. It is possible that this secretive and rarely observed species is more widely distributed in Georgia than currently known (Lamb and Gibbons 2008).

Okefenokee National Wildlife Refuge

The Okefenokee National Wildlife Refuge contains an excellent and easily accessible example of longleaf pine flatwoods adjacent to the U.S. Fish and Wildlife Service headquarters office located near the east entrance of the refuge. This upland site features a relatively uniform stand of second-growth longleaf pine (about 60 to 80 years old) because most of the older trees were removed in timber harvest operations in the 1920s and 1950s. Although not yet old-growth, this stand is mature enough to harbor numerous red-cockaded woodpeckers. Cavity trees are easily identified because they are marked with a band of white paint. The ground cover is strongly dominated by saw palmetto, but southern wiregrass and numerous ground cover species are scattered throughout. A mixture of woody evergreen species includes gallberry, southern wax-myrtle, shining fetterbush, and sparkleberry; dwarf live oak is also present, with the density and height depending on fire. Aggressive fire management in recent decades has promoted the herbaceous ground cover, reduced woody vegetation, and encouraged regeneration of longleaf pine. Along Swamp Island Drive a transition from longleaf pine to slash pine and pond pine flatwoods can be viewed across the gradient from the upland to a drain. A stark contrast exists along the refuge boundary of this drive between the frequently burned natural longleaf pine flatwoods of the refuge and the adjacent privately owned slash pine plantation that is typical of land conversion of flatwoods sites throughout the Coastal Plain.

Location: From Main Street in Folkston, take Okefenokee Dr. (Ga. Hwy. 121/23) south for 7 miles to the east entrance of the wildlife refuge at the Suwannee Canal Recreation Area. Just past the entrance gate, the office headquarters is located on the right. Swamp Island Dr. is a short loop drive located off Entrance Dr. Google Earth GPS approximate coordinates at headquarters area: N 30.739392/W 082.116934.

Seepage Slope Herb Bogs

Seepage slope herb bogs are some of the showiest natural gardens of the Georgia Coastal Plain. They are open wetlands found in low swales and lower slopes in frequently burned pine uplands, particularly in the Tifton Uplands, Tallahassee Hills, and Fall Line regions. They occur as openings in the pine forest or with scattered pines where the acidic soil is saturated much of the year by lateral seepage of groundwater from sandy soils of adjacent uplands. Seepage slope herb bogs are kept open by frequent fire that prevents shrub and tree invasion and fosters the diverse herbaceous community. These communities are often known as pitcherplant bogs because of the presence of the distinctive pitcherplant species and other insectivorous plant species that occur in the wetlands. Vast expanses of pitcherplants may occur in frequently burned sites and are particularly showy when flowering in April. In Georgia, more than 40 species of Special Concern occur in pitcherplant bogs and hillside seeps. Many of these wetland sites have been degraded by fire exclusion or destroyed by impoundment and conversion to farm ponds.

PHYSICAL SETTING AND ECOLOGY

The poorly drained soils of seepage bogs are usually acidic and nutrient-poor, occupying low sites within rolling sandy uplands. The soils are usually sands with a surface layer of organic material or peat and are often underlain by a clay hardpan (Plummer 1963; Folkerts 1991). Discharge of water occurs where the downslope percolation of water is restricted by a layer of impermeable clay (Folkerts 1991). The contour of a bog at the base of a slope may be concave to flat and the bog typically drains into a small stream. These wetlands are seasonally to semipermanently saturated but are seldom

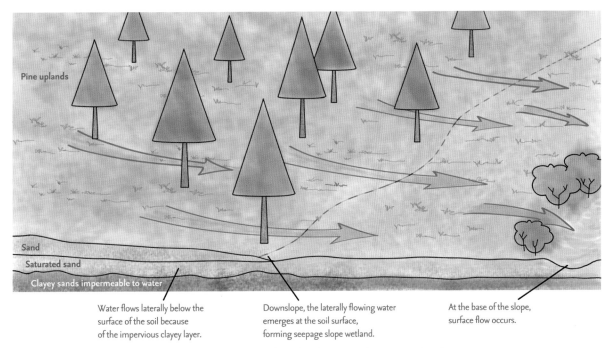

Seepage slope hydrology. Adapted from the book *Priceless Florida*, copyright © 2004 by Ellie Whitney, D. Bruce Means, and Anne Rudloe. Used by permission of Pineapple Press, Inc.

Labels within the figure:

Pine uplands

Sand

Saturated sand

Clayey sands impermeable to water

Water flows laterally below the surface of the soil because of the impervious clayey layer.

Downslope, the laterally flowing water emerges at the soil surface, forming seepage slope wetland.

At the base of the slope, surface flow occurs.

flooded. They are maintained by frequent fire, with an approximate fire-return interval of every two to three years. Fire retards shrub and tree invasion and encourages dominance of grasses and herbs. Periodic dry-down and fire prevent deep layers of peat from accumulating. Both fire and seepage hydrology are significant factors in the development of a diverse community of grasses, sedges, composites, orchids, and pitcherplants. In the absence of fire, this wetland succeeds to a seepage shrub bog (McDaniel 1971). Many of the pitcherplant bogs that once occurred in the Coastal Plain ecoregion have been lost due to fire exclusion, impoundment for small farm ponds, or conversion to pasture (Plummer 1963; Folkerts 1982). Some seepage bogs have been maintained in Georgia in the absence of fire, where openings are perpetuated within powerline transmission corridors as they extend across hillside seeps. For example, the seepage bogs at Blackjack Crossing (Talbot County) owned by the Nature Conservancy and at Gordonia-Alatamaha State Park (Tattnall County) occur at the base of a series of steep slopes within the powerline corridor. The juxtaposition of dense, nearly impenetrable woody vegetation adjacent to the herbaceous bog within the corridor illustrates the seepage slope swamp and shrub bog community development in the absence of fire. In this case, the mechanical re-

Seepage herb bog located in powerline right-of-way

duction of woody vegetation associated with powerline corridor maintenance helps to facilitate the herbaceous bog communities. Several relict bogs that have been perpetuated by powerline corridors are being protected and monitored through cooperative agreements between the Georgia Department of Natural Resources, private landowners, and utility companies.

VEGETATION

The herb bog often appears within a gap or thinner canopy of longleaf pine, slash pine, or pond pine than that of the surrounding upland longleaf pine savanna. The ground cover in frequently burned sites is extraordinarily diverse and harbors numerous species of concern in Georgia. The moisture conditions change gradually across a broad expanse, creating a mosaic of growing conditions. Grass and sedge dominants include species of three-awn grasses, broomsedge, toothache grass, dropseed, beakrushes, and nutrushes. Showy orchids often include large spreading pogonia, common grass-pink, rose pogonia, yellow fringed orchid, small white fringed orchid, and several species of ladies'-tresses. Other commonly encountered species are hatpins, bog buttons, yellow-eyed grasses, meadow-beauties, colic-roots, and milkworts. Carnivorous plants are a notable feature of seepage slope herb bogs and are an adaptation to the nitrogen-limited environment (see carnivorous plants). The most conspicuous are the pitcherplants, such as trumpet pitcherplants, parrot pitcherplants, and hooded pitcherplants. The most common shrubs are gallberry, southern wax-myrtle, sweet bay, and shining fetterbush. In the absence of fire, these species can dominate the site. Pond pine and slash pine may also be scattered throughout.

Yellow fringed orchid

Pitcherplant bog

CARNIVOROUS PLANTS

Four common plant genera have leaf modifications for trapping and digesting insects as a source of nutrients. These include pitcherplants, bladderworts, sundews, and butterworts. Because of their intriguing food habits and morphology, all of these species are vulnerable to over-collecting by carnivorous plant enthusiasts (Folkerts 1982).

Pitcherplants have funnel-shaped or tube-shaped leaves that are open at the top and are completely or partially covered by a specialized flap, or hood. Leaves of some species are tall and resemble pitchers, partially filled with water. These modified leaves serve as a pit-fall trap to passively ensnare insects and digest them as an additional source of nutrients for the plant. The leaves are musky-scented from nectar secreted near the orifice to attract insects. Downward-directed hairs occur on the inside of the "pitcher" and prevent the insect from escaping. Once the insect falls to the base of the leaf, digestive enzymes decompose the prey. There is a progression throughout the season toward carnivorous or detritivorous insects as the odor of trapped and decaying insects brings even more victims. By gently tearing open the pitcher, numerous insects can be viewed in various stages of decomposition in the base of the leaf. In addition to devouring insects, pitcherplant leaves also serve as habitat for some insects, including several species of mosquito, moths, blowflies, and an aphid whose larvae complete their lifecycle within the pitcher without being digested (Folkerts 1982; Rymal and Folkerts 1982). Also, treefrogs often hide inside trumpet pitcherplants to forage for insects and spiders attracted to the leaves of the plant.

As well as highly modified leaves, pitcherplants also have unusual flowers. The flower droops on the end of a slender stalk and has pendulous petals. The style is an upside-down, umbrella-shaped structure in which the points of the umbrella are the pollen receptor sites. Because the flower droops, the style is positioned as the lowest structure, and the ovary and stamens that

Trumpet pitcherplant

Parrot pitcherplant

433

actually develop below the style are positioned above it. Nectar on the style attracts bumblebees, blowflies, and other insects. As these insects crawl around the cup of the umbrella, pollen shed from the stamen becomes attached to them and they serve as pollinators as they move from plant to plant. The primary pollinators are bumblebees (Schnell 2002).

Seven species of pitcherplants are known from the Georgia Coastal Plain. Trumpet pitcherplant is one of the largest of the pitcherplant species, reaching heights of nearly 3 feet. The hollow, trumpet-shaped leaves are greenish yellow, broadest at the mouth with a reddish throat and gradually narrower to the base. The lids are suberect. The sepals are green, and the petals are bright yellow. It also produces flattened, sword-shaped leaf blades, called "phyllodes," which remain green during the winter (Schnell 2002). The hooded pitcherplant can be recognized by its leaf, which is recurved on the apex, forming a hood that nearly closes the orifice and

aids in trapping insects. The leaf is a green to reddish purple with translucent spots on the back of the hood that actually transmit light inside the pitcher as an additional mechanism to lure insects toward the interior leaf surface window rather than escaping out of the leaf. The flowers of this species are yellow. This species of pitcherplant has the widest range of habitat requirements, and is often seen on moist road rights-of-way when herbicide application is not part of roadside maintenance.

The parrot pitcherplant is Threatened in Georgia. It is recognized by its tube-like leaves with a prominent wing along the upper half. The leaf hood is a rounded chamber with a beak-like appearance, resembling a bird's head. The leaves have translucent windows near the apex and hood. The leaves range from reddish purple to green, and the mature leaves are often partially reclining. The stigma of this species is whitish, but the petals are deep red.

The whitetop pitcherplant is recognized by its large, deep crimson flowers and the striking white and red-veined top of the gradually flaring pitcher and

Hooded pitcherplant

Whitetop pitcherplant

overarching lid. This species is Endangered in Georgia and is a candidate for federal listing. In Georgia, it is restricted to five counties in the southwestern part of the state and occurs along red maple–black gum swamps. Because the leaves are so showy, they are often used by florists.

Green pitcherplant is federally Endangered and is very rare in Georgia. Formerly known from a few sites in the Coastal Plain of Georgia, it is now known only from the Blue Ridge Mountains. It has tall, trumpet-shaped greenish yellow leaves that resemble those of the trumpet pitcherplant, but the pitchers are greenish throughout, lacking the reddish throats of trumpet pitcherplant. Green pitcherplant also differs in that the phyllodes arch away from the plant in a distinctive sickle shape.

Purple pitcherplant is also called "northern pitcherplant" because its range extends throughout Canada and into Newfoundland. The leaves of this species range from green to reddish with red veins. The pitcher is distinctively wide and short, and has a crescent wing facing toward the center of the plant and an expanded, curly lid. The sepals and roundish petals are red. This species occurs in the Blue Ridge Mountains.

Sweet pitcherplant is listed as Endangered in Georgia. It is restricted primarily to the upper Coastal Plain and the Fall Line Sandhills. The mature leaves are erect, broadest at the mouth, and gradually tapered below. They are green with some red or purplish veins. The hoods are sharply pointed with entire margins. Hybrids of hooded pitcherplant and trumpet pitcherplant can be seen at Doerun Pitcherplant Bog Natural Area.

The leaves of butterworts employ a different method of trapping their prey. Their wide leaves bear short hairs that secrete a sticky, mucilaginous substance that functions as an adhesive, snaring small insects such as gnats or midges. The leaves also have small, round hairs with digestive enzymes. When an insect becomes trapped, the leaf edges enroll and the insect is digested. Once the insect is digested, the leaf edges unroll and the leaf becomes nearly flat. The nodding flowers are asymmetrical in shape with fused petals and a spur. In the Coastal Plain of Georgia, four species of butterwort occur (Jones and Coile 1988).

The sundews have small, linear leaves with sticky leaf hairs that glisten in the sunlight. These mucinous droplets serve as an adhesive to trap insects. Once the insect is trapped, digestive enzymes are produced and secreted by the glandular hairs. The flowers of sundews occur on a slender stalk and are white to pinkish, depending on the species. One species of sundew, called "Tracy's sundew," is particularly rare in Georgia.

Bladderworts have still another trapping mechanism that functions in an aquatic environment. Several species of floating bladderworts have modified leaves that serve as basket-like snap traps below the surface of the water, where they snare microscopic organisms. These small suction traps open and close extremely rapidly, and the cavity structure is lined with digestive glands (Schnell 2002). Some terrestrial species of bladderworts occur in moist soils of bogs or ditch banks. More than a dozen species of bladderworts occur in Georgia (Jones and Coile 1988).

Dwarf sundew

Swollen bladderwort

Yellow butterwort

CHARACTERISTIC PLANTS OF SEEPAGE SLOPE HERB BOGS

TREES

Slash pine—Pinus elliottii
Longleaf pine—Pinus palustris
Pond pine—Pinus serotina

SHRUBS AND WOODY VINES

Evergreen bayberry—Morella caroliniensis
Wax-myrtle—Morella cerifera
Odorless bayberry—Morella inodora

GROUND COVER

Old-field broomsedge—Andropogon virginicus
Rayless-goldenrod—Bigelowia nudata
Sunbonnets—Chaptalia tomentosa
Combs panic grass—Coleataenia longifolium

Toothache grass—Ctenium aromaticum
Witchgrasses—Dichanthelium spp.
Dwarf sundew—Drosera brevifolia
Narrowleaf sunflower—Helianthus angustifolius
Savanna hibiscus—Hibiscus aculeatus
Coppery St. John's-wort—Hypericum denticulatum
Redroot—Lachnanthes caroliniana
Common bogbuttons—Lachnocaulon anceps
Hairgrass—Muhlenbergia capillaris
Blue butterwort—Pinguicula caerulea
Crested fringed orchid—Platanthera cristata
Snowy orchid—Platanthera nivea
Orange milkwort—Polygala lutea
Candyroot—Polygala nana

Smooth meadow-beauty—Rhexia alifanus
Pale meadow-beauty—Rhexia mariana
Beakrushes, beaksedges—Rhynchospora spp.
Trumpet pitcherplant—Sarracenia flava
Hooded pitcherplant—Sarracenia minor
Parrot pitcherplant—Sarracenia psittacina
Netted nutrush—Scleria reticularis
Ladies'-tresses—Spiranthes praecox
Wireleaf dropseed—Sporobolus teretifolius
Yellow hatpins—Syngonanthus flavidulus

ANIMALS

No birds are specialists of seepage slope herb bogs; however, some of the over-wintering grassland specialists, such as Henslow's sparrows, are likely to be present. Year-round longleaf pine associates that occur in seepage bogs are the brown-headed nuthatch, northern bobwhite, and red-cockaded woodpecker.

The green treefrog and squirrel treefrog are common inhabitants within pitchers of pitcherplants, where they can take advantage of the ready source of insects. Another treefrog species, the pine barrens treefrog, has not been verified in Georgia. Based on its range in the surrounding states of Alabama, Florida, and South Carolina, there is a possibility of its occurrence in highly acidic seepage sites (Jensen et al. 2008a). The mimic glass lizard is extremely rare in Georgia and may be extirpated from the state. Its habitat includes herbaceous seepage bogs and pine flatwoods that are always closely associated with upland longleaf pine–wiregrass habitats (Jensen 2008b).

Some insects are able to live within the leaf pitchers of pitcherplants without being ensnared and di-gested. Several flies are obligate associates of pitcherplants; the larvae develop within the pitcher, ingesting trapped prey. Several wasp species may nest in pitchers, although they are not obligate associates. One species, known as a grass-carrying species, builds a nest in the bottom of the pitcher with a wad of coiled grass. Eggs are deposited on the grass plug, and another wad of grass is placed over the brood chamber. Often, a tuft of grass can be observed protruding from the pitcher orifice. After the larvae hatch, they prey on paralyzed insects that become trapped. Several moth species feed on pitcherplant tissue and complete their entire life-cycles within the pitcher. Eggs of these moths are laid on the inside wall of a pitcherplant in early spring following pupation. Prior to pupation, the larva cuts a tiny drainage hole in the wall of the pitcher, where it will attach. As newly hatched larvae feed, they girdle the upper pitcher, causing it to wilt and flop, closing the orifice. Adults fly to new pitchers in search of mates, and copulation occurs within the pitcher (Rymal and Folkerts 1982).

Say's Spiketail (*Cordulegaster sayi*)

Say's spiketail is a rare, strikingly colored dragonfly. Adults are typically 2.4 to 2.7 inches in total length, making this the smallest spiketail in its range. Males and females have similar coloration (Dunkle 2000; Beaton 2007). Say's spiketail is found primarily in the eastern Coastal Plain of Georgia and Florida. It is currently known from only about 25 sites, most of these in Georgia. Many of these habitats are very small and support fewer than 30 adult Say's spiketails (Beaton 2008a). Recent surveys suggest that extirpations have occurred at some of these sites due to drought or habitat alteration.

Say's spiketails typically take flight from the middle of March to late April. Upon emergence from the larval stage, adults crawl away from the seep and move into nearby open habitats. After maturing for a week or two, they return to the seep to establish territories. Say's spiketail can be difficult to see in its breeding habitat and is more often observed feeding

in nearby scrub oak sandhills, brushy fields, or grasslands. When feeding, Say's spiketail often perches on plant stems near the ground and may defend its feeding perch (Dunkle 2000). It also patrols the tree canopy looking for its prey. Food items include a wide variety of insects, especially bees and wasps (Beaton 2008a).

Prior to breeding, males patrol the seepage areas, alternately hovering and perching in anticipation of approaching females. After mating, females deposit their eggs by hovering over the seep and thrusting the tip of their abdomens vertically into the mucky substrate. Recent studies indicate that this species may persist in a larval form for three years, feeding on various aquatic macroinvertebrates (Beaton 2008a).

Say's spiketail is state-listed as Threatened. Threats to this species include prolonged drought and habitat destruction or degradation from commercial or residential development. Protection of seepage zones and adjacent foraging habitats is necessary for the conservation of this species.

Doerun Pitcherplant Bog Natural Area

Doerun Pitcherplant Bog Natural Area is a relict long-leaf pine–wiregrass ecosystem situated in the Tifton Uplands (Colquitt County), bordering the Ochlocko-nee River. In addition to featuring one of the few large pitcherplant bogs remaining in the Coastal Plain of Georgia, the 651-acre site contains forested up-lands, swales, flats, depressions, intermittent stream drainages, river floodplains, planted pine stands, and cleared agricultural lands. The pitcherplant bog occu-pies about 100 acres in the seasonally saturated slope, flat, and branch head wetlands, and in transition zones to riverine wetlands. Numerous carnivorous plants, including three pitcherplants (trumpet pitcherplant, hooded pitcherplant, and parrot pitcherplant), sun-dews, and butterworts are present. Dominant grasses include dropseed grasses; other species include snowy orchids, bogbuttons, pipeworts, yellow-eyed grasses, and meadow-beauties. In addition to the three pitcher-plant species, the bog honeycomb-head is also state-protected and chaffseed is federally protected. Other species of conservation concern include odorless bay-berry, savanna cowbane, wireleaf dropseed, pinebar-ren sedge, Tracy's sundew, snowy orchid, pondspice, and sandhill angelica. The extremely rare autumn beakrush was apparently known from the area early in the 20th century.

Location: From Moultrie, at the intersection of U.S. 319 and the Moultrie Bypass, go north on Ga. Hwy. 133 about 10 miles. Turn right into the natural area on the gravel drive. Trailhead is at parking lot kiosk. Google Earth GPS approximate coordinates at the entrance area: N 31.286281/W 083.887969.

Seepage Slope Swamps and Shrub Bogs

Seepage slope swamps and shrub bogs occur in small patches or as long, connected dendritic networks on slopes in dissected terrain where a clay lens or other impermeable layer forces groundwater to seep out at the base of the slope and flow across it. These wetlands usually occur in headwater streams or ravines; however, they may also occur along the edges of floodplains, where there is significant groundwater seepage from adjacent sandy slopes. The soil is perennially wet, which permits peat accumulation to occur. These communities are characterized by the presence of evergreen shrubs or trees, particularly those known colloquially as "bays": sweet bay, loblolly bay, and swamp bay. Often these communities have a dense, nearly impenetrable shrub layer, and occasionally thickets of river cane, called "canebrakes," develop in these habitats. Atlantic white cedar dominates seepage swamps near the Fall Line, which represents a rare vegetation assemblage in Georgia. Seepage swamps are often called "still water swamps," "groundwater swamps," or "non-

flowing water swamps." They may also be referred to as bayheads, baygalls, or pocosins, although these names are more locally used in Florida or the Carolinas.

PHYSICAL SETTING AND ECOLOGY

In Georgia, seepage slope swamps and shrub bogs are prevalent along the Coastal Plain Fall Line Sandhills associated with Miocene clay ridges and in the Tifton Uplands. They develop in low swales and depressions, lower slopes, and poorly drained flats, and are often associated with the heads of blackwater creeks. In some cases, a creek-side bay swamp develops, such as that along Whitewater Creek and Cedar Creek (Taylor County) and along Seventeen Mile Creek (Coffee County). These communities are infrequently inundated with standing water, or, if briefly inundated, the water does not remove the thick peat substrate.

Seasonally to semipermanently saturated soils are characteristic of these seepage swamps and shrub bogs, and the resulting peat accumulation strongly influences community development. Peat is the partially decomposed remains of plants. It builds up in situations with continuous poor drainage where decomposition is slow due to low-oxygen conditions. The soils are variable but usually wet, acidic, and peaty, mixed with sands, and frequently underlain by a clay hardpan. These sites receive water directly from lateral seepage from adjacent areas, as well as precipitation; however, the relative contribution of water source varies from site to site. In general, the height of the vegetation increases with decreasing thickness of peat deposits. Sites with extremely deep peats are often dominated by dwarfed trees.

Although this community occurs in landscapes that once had frequent fire under natural conditions, the frequently saturated soils sometimes limited fire spread, creating a less frequent fire-return interval. During periods of prolonged drought, these habitats may burn. Frequently burned sites tend to have a dense layer of low-growing shrubs, while infrequently burned sites have a greater abundance of deciduous hardwood trees. Shrub bogs are less frequently burned than herb bogs and are successionally related in some topographic situations.

Seepage slope swamps and shrub bogs are vulnerable to changes in local streamflow and groundwater flow as well as to sedimentation from upslope disturbances. They are also impacted by fire suppression in the adjacent uplands, which prevents even infrequent fires from occurring in the lower slopes. Throughout the Coastal Plain, much of the longleaf pine in upland sites adjacent to seepages has been removed. These former longleaf pine sites are now in agriculture or urban use, silvicultural pine plantations, or dominated by xeric hardwoods and are no longer managed with prescribed fire. Thus, the downslope seepage bogs and swamps are increasingly exposed to less frequent fire.

VEGETATION

In addition to dominance by sweet bay, loblolly bay, and swamp bay, the vegetation of shrub bogs and seepage swamps usually includes canopy trees such as red maple, swamp tupelo, loblolly pine, pond pine, laurel oak, and water oak. The vine/shrub layer is a dense

Sweet bay

mixture of swamp bay, buckwheat-tree, shining fetterbush, maleberry, coastal doghobble, southern wild raisin, big gallberry, dahoon, ti-ti, wax-myrtle, swamp azalea, poison sumac, coastal sweet-pepperbush, bamboo-vine, and coral greenbrier. These trees, shrubs, and vines can form almost impenetrable thickets. The herbaceous ground layer vegetation is sparse, consisting mainly of ferns such as Virginia chain fern, cinnamon fern, and sensitive fern, as well as sphagnum moss. The wetland community is often bordered upslope by a longleaf pine–scrub oak woodland and downslope by a bottomland forest adjacent to a creek. Typically, the creek bank is dominated by Ogeechee lime and bald-cypress. Adjacent to the creek is a bottomland dominated by water oak, swamp tupelo, sweet gum, and red maple. At the base of the slope is a swamp dominated by loblolly bay and sweet bay with trunks up to 15 inches in diameter. The trees form a closed evergreen canopy, with open forest structure beneath. In some areas, pond pine and loblolly emerge through the canopy and red bay is often very common. Upslope from the seepage swamp, a seepage shrub bog is frequently present, dominated by buckwheat-tree, southern black haw, large gallbery, and crookedwood. A wide range of seepage swamp and shrub bog conditions occurs on private properties along several creeks in Coffee County. Other examples include a shrub bog at Reed Bingham State Park (Cook County), a bog along I-16, 2.8 miles northwest of Ogeechee River (Bryan County), and a shrub bog in the Townsend Wildlife Management Area (McIntosh County) (see the Featured Place).

Atlantic White Cedar Swamps. Atlantic white cedar swamps are uncommon in Georgia and are restricted to the eastern and western ends of the Fall Line Sandhills region. Atlantic white cedar, which is state-listed as a Rare species, is the canopy-dominant tree, occurring in narrow riparian bands intermixed with sweet bay and pond pine. The evergreen understory of shrubs and vines of this wetland community is extremely dense. At least 12 other Georgia rare plant species occur in this community. While extremely rare and localized in Georgia, white cedar swamps are much more extensive in other regions of the Southeast (North Carolina, Virginia, and Florida) (Christensen 2000). Examples of this regionally rare forested wetland occur along the Sandy Run Creek drainage at Fort Gordon in Richmond County and along

Seepage swamp

several small to medium-sized clear streams in Taylor, Talbot, Schley, Peach, and Marion Counties on privately owned properties. With the exception of military reservations, no sites in Georgia are under public protection.

White cedar swamps occur on sites in which soils are continually moist and where neither flooding nor fire is frequent. Typically, they are associated with deep peats over sandy soil (Christensen 2000). This species may once have been more widespread in Georgia; however, factors currently restricting its distribution are not known (Laderman 1989).

The vegetation dynamics of white cedar swamps are also not well understood, but infrequent fires (25–100+ years) are likely necessary for long-term persistence (Buell and Cain 1943; Christensen 2000). White cedar is neither shade- nor fire-tolerant. It is a rapid colonizer and after fire may regenerate from seed residing in layers of peat (Penfound 1952). Often, stands are of uniform age (Christensen 2000). With prolonged

Atlantic white cedar

fire exclusion in these sites, hardwood or bay species may become dominant; with frequent fire the community may develop into a streamhead shrub bog (Ewell 1990).

Canebrakes. Canebrakes are dense thickets of small cane (also called switch cane) and are considered here as a variant of shrub bog because of the structure and woodiness of the culms. These communities were once much more pronounced, occurring as large patches in seepage slopes and river bottoms throughout the Southeast (S. G. Platt and Brantley 1997; S. G. Platt, Brantley, and Rainwater 2001) (see bottomland hardwoods). Due to fire suppression and agriculture, only remnant patches remain, and these often intergrade with longleaf pine savannas, pond pine savannas, evergreen shrub bogs, or bottomland forests. Canebrakes provide important habitat for Swainson's warbler and the possibly extinct Bachman's warbler. Malone Canebrake, located at Fort Benning (Chattahoochee County), is an excellent example of a critically imperiled seepage shrub bog strongly dominated by small cane. It occurs in small patches with saturated soil within the highly dissected landscape of the Fall Line Sandhills. High-frequency fires have been associated with this site due to daily military live fire training exercises.

Canebrake

CHARACTERISTIC PLANTS OF SEEPAGE SLOPE SWAMPS AND SHRUB BOGS

TREES

Red maple—Acer rubrum
Loblolly bay—Gordonia lasianthus
Sweet bay—Magnolia virginiana
Swamp tupelo—Nyssa biflora
Swamp bay—Persea palustris
Slash pine—Pinus serotina
Laurel oak—Quercus laurifolia
Water oak—Quercus nigra

SHRUBS AND WOODY VINES

Small cane—Arundinaria tecta
Coastal sweet-pepperbush—Clethra
    alnifolia
Ti-ti—Cyrilla racemiflora
Dahoon—Ilex cassine
Big gallberry—Ilex coriacea
Coastal doghobble—Leucothoe axillaris
Maleberry—Lyonia ligustrina
Shining fetterbush—Lyonia lucida
Swamp bay—Persea palustris

Swamp azalea—Rhododendron viscosum
Bamboo-vine—Smilax laurifolia
Coral greenbrier—Smilax walteri
Poison sumac—Toxicodendron vernix
Southern wild raisin—Viburnum nudum

GROUND COVER

Sensitive fern—Onoclea sensibilis
Cinnamon fern—Osmundastrum
    cinnamomea
Virginia chain fern—Woodwardia
    virginica

ANIMALS

Although present throughout the Georgia Coastal Plain, the dwarf salamander is most commonly found in acidic wetlands, migrating to and from breeding sites from July to October. Other salamanders common to the leafy organic matter or sphagnum of seepage swamps are the Gulf Coast mud salamander and the southern dusky salamander (Means 2008b). The two-toed amphiuma and greater siren are among the largest salamanders in North America (Sorenson 2008; Sorenson and Moler 2008). They are found in a variety of wetland habitats but are most commonly associated with thick vegetation and mucky organic soils. These salamanders can tolerate dry periods by burrowing in muck and remaining in a dormant state (Sorenson 2008; Sorenson and Moler 2008). Mud snakes are aquatic snakes that occur primarily in the Coastal Plain in acidic swamps and wetlands. They are dietary specialists, eating only salamanders, especially amphiumas and sirens. Spotted turtles, restricted to the Coastal Plain, occur in seepage swamps and shrub bogs, as well as other wetland habitats (see the Featured Animal).

Birds associated with this community are not specialists; likely inhabitants include pileated woodpeckers, downy woodpeckers, Acadian flycatchers, yellow-throated vireos, red-eyed vireos, prothonotary warblers, worm-eating warblers, and Kentucky warblers (Sharitz and Gresham 1998).

The palamedes swallowtail is also known as the laurel swallowtail because it is particularly common in Coastal Plain swamps and adjacent pine forests where its host plants, red bay, swamp bay, and sassafras, are abundant. Hessels' hairstreak is a small, rare butterfly associated with seepage swamps that harbor white cedar, its host plant (Vaughan and Shepherd 2005a).

Spotted Turtle (*Clemmys guttata*)

The spotted turtle is one of Georgia's smallest and most attractive reptiles. This species has a maximum body length of about 5 inches and a smooth, dark carapace with yellow or cream-colored spots. It is distributed from southern Maine to central Florida along the Atlantic Coastal Plain and portions of the Piedmont. In addition, it is found in states surrounding the Great Lakes and across the upper Midwest as far west as northeastern Illinois, as well as portions of southern Canada (Conant and Collins 1998).

In Georgia, the spotted turtle is confined to the Coastal Plain. This secretive turtle seems to prefer shallow-water habitats with standing or slow-moving water, mucky or peaty soils, abundant herbaceous vegetation, and fallen logs and other structures for cover in seepage bogs, swamps, small streams, and cypress-gum ponds. This species also uses upland habitats during certain times of the year (Jensen 1999; Akre and Fahey 2008).

The diet of the spotted turtle includes algae, aquatic grasses and forbs, aquatic insect larvae, crusta-ceans, snails, tadpoles, salamanders, and fishes. Known predators of spotted turtles include raccoons, skunks, common snapping turtles, and bald eagles, but probably also include coyotes, foxes, mink, and river otters (Akre and Fahey 2008).

The spotted turtle is most active in late winter and early spring, when it moves overland from one wetland to another. Mating occurs in early spring, and nests are constructed in early summer (Akre and Fahey 2008). At other times of the year the spotted turtle may lie dormant in moist organic soil or muck, sometimes in groups (Jensen 1999).

Despite a wide distribution in Georgia's Coastal Plain, the spotted turtle is only occasionally seen in the wild. Though population trends in the state are not known, it has probably been adversely affected by loss or degradation of wetland habitats in the Coastal Plain. It is currently protected with a status of Unusual under Georgia law. More research is needed to verify the distribution and habitat requirements of this secretive turtle (Georgia Department of Natural Resources 1999).

Townsend Wildlife Management Area

An easily accessible seepage slope swamp and shrub bog can be observed in the Townsend Wildlife Management Area (McIntosh County). This nearly impenetrable seepage area occurs at the base of a slope that extends upland to where it transitions into xeric sandhill vegetation. The seepage bog is dominated by loblolly bay, saw palmetto, coastal sweet-pepperbush, dahoon, ti-ti, shining fetterbush, sweet bay, and bamboo-vine. Although swamp bay is abundant, most of the plants are currently dead or dying from laurel wilt disease. Emergent trees include swamp tupelo, pond pine, and shortleaf pine. The forest floor of this site is hummocky with numerous downed and decaying trees toppled from prior windstorms. In addition to the adjacent sandhill, communities associated with the seepage slope include bottomland hardwoods dominated by laurel oak and Ogeechee lime toward the Altamaha River floodplain.

Location: From U.S. 84/Ga. Hwy. 38 in Ludowici, take Hwy. 57 south for 4.2 miles. Turn right onto Old Barrington Rd. After crossing the McIntosh County line signpost, continue for 1.9 miles and take a right into the wetland management area. Go approximately 2 miles and a seepage swamp and shrub bog is present along the left of the road. From Darien, at I-95, take Ga. Hwy. 251 west for 3.1 miles. Bear left onto Cox Rd. and do not turn to the right with Ga. 251. Follow Cox Rd. for 9.3 miles to the end of the pavement. Continue straight on dirt road for 2 miles. Turn left on road into the wildlife management area and go approximately 2 miles as above. Google Earth GPS approximate coordinates at the Old Barrington Road entrance: N 31.529751/W 081.602325.

Depression Marshes and Cypress Savannas

Depression marshes and cypress savannas are meadow-like wetlands or open cypress stands that occur in seasonally flooded shallow depressions, such as Carolina bays and limesinks. The substrate is usually sandy and is underlain by a clayey layer that impedes drainage, so that water saturates the soils for at least part of the year. These wetlands have a rich, dense herbaceous vegetation of grasses and sedges. In cypress savannas, an open canopy of pond-cypress and other trees such as black gum or pond pine is present. These geographically isolated wetlands are a superlative habitat for many wading birds and amphibians, as well as for American alligators, and are important in contributing to regional biodiversity because they provide habitat for species that are uniquely adapted to extremes in fluctuating hydrologic conditions as well as periodic fire. Because they rarely support fish, they provide safe breeding habitats for frogs and salamanders.

Depression marshes and cypress savannas are becoming increasingly rare in Georgia due to lack of legal protection from alterations such as dredging or filling or due to fire suppression. The examples of depressional wetlands remaining that are the least disturbed are usually associated with sites in which the surrounding uplands are natural longleaf pine forests that are managed with frequent prescribed fire. In such sites, the transition area between the two communities is often exceptionally floristically diverse.

PHYSICAL SETTING AND ECOLOGY

Depression marshes and cypress savannas occur in shallow basins such as Carolina bays, limesink depressions (see geographically isolated depressional wetlands) or in basins within the rolling terrain of the Fall Line Sandhills. Depressional wetlands are more common in the upper Coastal Plain but may also occur within flatwoods communities. These wetlands have sandy surficial soils (8–20 inches) that are underlain with impervious clay or sandy clay layers. Organic substrates (histosols) typically do not build up because these depressions dry out often enough to enable plant litter to decompose. Fire also may play a role in reducing organic matter accumulation (Sharitz and Gresham 1998). The water is usually nutrient-poor and acidic (Newman and Schalles 1990; Battle and Golladay 1999).

The impervious clay layers create a perched water table (i.e., water that is restricted from vertical movement and thus is held above the regional deep water table) that fluctuates in response to precipitation and some lateral flow of surficial groundwater (E. L. Hendricks and Goodwin 1952; Lide et al. 1995). These wetlands frequently dry down during periods of low precipitation and high evapotranspiration—particularly in summer months, when the vegetation has high water demands and rain events are irregular. The hydroperiod for an individual wetland is dependent on shape, depth, and surrounding landscape. Annual fluctuations in a wetland may range from ponded, with water levels more than 6 feet deep, to completely dry. The length of the hydroperiod varies from year to year as well as spatially, depending on the occurrence of storms. The hydroperiod directly influences vegetation composition by filtering out species based on their tolerance of inundated or dry conditions. Hydroperiod also regulates fire frequency and intensity (i.e., during dry periods, upland and wetland sites will burn, but they are not susceptible to fire when inundated, even under prescribed fire management). Regional fire suppression and landscape fragmentation have significantly altered the degree of influence of fire in plant community succession in many to most of these wetlands (Kirkman et al. 2000).

While all Coastal Plain wetlands in Georgia have suffered historic declines, depression marshes are now particularly rare. Periods of dry-down provide opportunities for timber harvest, construction of ditches to convert these wetlands to agricultural or silvicultural uses, or excavation for small fish ponds. Even in cases in which a depression marsh has not been cultivated or destroyed, land use changes in the surrounding landscape have disconnected many of these wetlands from upland fire regimes, and, consequently, hardwood succession has occurred, eliminating the herbaceous vege-

Depression marsh

tation. Studies of upland-wetland ecotones in high-quality longleaf pine sites managed with frequent fire indicate that this zone harbors exceptionally high plant species richness when a fire corridor is maintained (Kirkman, Drew, and Edwards 1998).

Pond-cypress trees are often harvested during dry periods, primarily for horticultural mulch (Ewel 1998). Consequently, few of these woodlands remain with large, old-growth pond-cypress. Numerous cypress savannas have been drained and planted in pines. Cypress savannas that have been severely fire-suppressed eventually succeed into depression swamps with a mixture of swamp tupelo and other flood-tolerant hardwoods (Monk 1966; Clewell 1971; D. B. Hamilton 1984). Given similarities in physiography, geologic substrate, and hydrologic regimes between depression marshes and cypress savannas, the development of one vegetation type over another is due partly to chance in the periodicity and sequence of inundation and fire events that influence the establishment of cypress. Thus, a range of vegetation types may be suitable as potential restoration goals for a given disturbed wetland depression (Kirkman et al. 2000).

GEOGRAPHICALLY ISOLATED DEPRESSIONAL WETLANDS

Geographically isolated depressional wetlands of the southeastern Coastal Plain are shallow basins that are completely surrounded by uplands (not connected by surface flow to streams or lakes), and their hydrology is driven primarily by rainfall and shallow, subsurface water flow. These wetland depressions range in size from hundreds of acres to less than one acre. In Georgia, they are known by many local names, including Grady ponds, Carolina bays, cypress ponds, Citronelle ponds, flat-bottom ponds, seasonally ponded isolated wetlands, karst ponds, gum ponds, nonalluvial wetlands, nonriverine wetlands, depression marshes, depression meadows, and sinkhole ponds. Water levels range from nearly permanently inundated to frequently dry and fluctuate seasonally and among years, depending on precipitation and evapotranspiration. Consequently, these wetlands support unique communities of plants and animals adapted to cycles of wetting and drying and are especially important habitats for breeding amphibians. Although these wetlands are conspicuous landscape features, their significance and contribution to regional biodiversity have been largely overlooked.

Differences in geomorphic characteristics and origin occur among depressional wetlands in the Southeast, even among those that are similar hydrologically and ecologically. See discussion below of Carolina bays and limesinks. We classify isolated depressional wetlands based primarily on dominant vegetation, which is significantly influenced by hydrology, soil substrate, landscape position, and fire frequency.

In the Coastal Plain of Georgia, depressional wetlands are common but are being rapidly degraded or destroyed because they do not receive the same federal protection as other wetlands that are associated with flowing water drainage systems. The regulatory policy of protection of isolated wetlands has been controversial. Federal legislation enacted in 1972 under the U.S. Clean Water Act prohibited the placement of dredge or fill materials into waters of the United States without a permit. This regulation, as administered by the U.S. Army Corps of Engineers, included protection of larger, isolated wetlands, while small, isolated wetlands lacked the legal protection afforded riparian or lacustrine wetlands. In 2001, even this level of federal protection was challenged and the U.S. Supreme Court limited the kind of wetlands that are within the jurisdiction of the Clean Water Act. As a result, nonnavigable, isolated waters are no longer regulated (SWANCC decision, *Solid Waste Agency of Northern Cook County v. U.S. Army Corps of Engineers*). State-level initiatives for regulating isolated wetlands have emerged in several states, but such legal protection is not present in Georgia. The 2009 Clean Water Restoration Act removed the questionable term "navigable water" from the Clean Water Act, and guidelines for jurisdictional implementation remain to be developed.

LIMESINK WETLANDS

Limesink wetlands are depressional wetlands that are thought to originate from dissolution of underlying limestone and subsidence of surface soils (Beck 1986). These wetlands tend to have a more irregular shape than those of classic Carolina bays and range from deep, steep-sided depressions to large, flat basins. In Georgia, they are most prevalent in the Gulf Coastal Plain, particularly on the karst landscape of the Dougherty Plain.

The solution process begins as rainwater percolates downward through the soil, reaching an underlying layer of limestone. The water is weakly acidic (a solution of carbon dioxide in water, called "carbonic acid") and dissolves the calcium carbonate of the limestone as it moves through interconnected pores or fractures. As the rock dissolves, an underground cavern may be formed. With time, the ceiling of the cavern becomes thinner. When the water table drops due to drought or well withdrawals, the surface soil may become too heavy for the ceiling to support in the absence of hydrostatic pressure, and a depression or collapse of the land surface occurs (Beck 1986; Hicks, Gill, and Longsworth 1987). Depending on the depth of the overburden material above the limestone, the resulting depression may be a deep, steep-sided hole or a more gradual subsidence. A solution sinkhole may occur where the overburden is thin or absent and surficial material is transported downward along solution-enlarged channels in the limestone.

With continued surficial water movement, sand and clay soil particles are transported into the depression. Eventually, layers of clay alternating with layers of sand may form a hardpan that retards vertical movement of water. Thus, the depression will pond water from precipitation (Hendricks and Goodwin 1952;

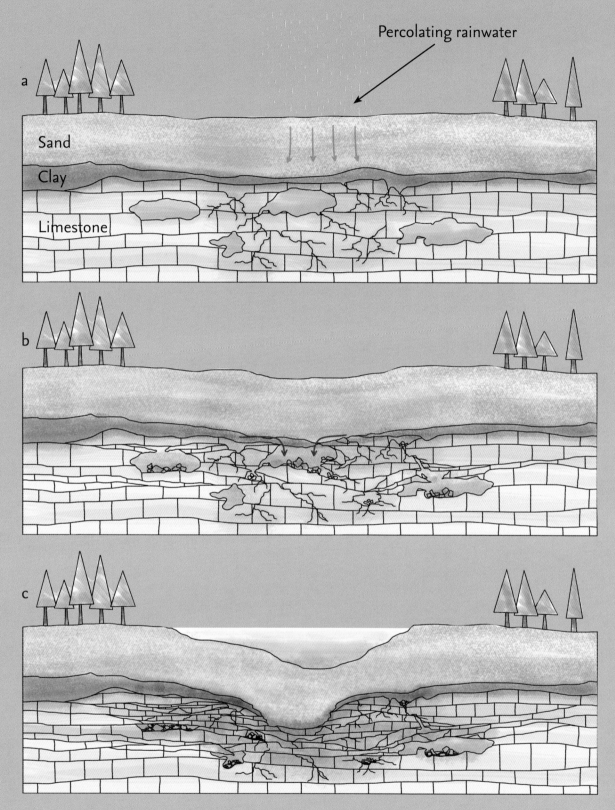

Percolating rainwater

a

Sand

Clay

Limestone

b

c

Sinkhole and limesink depressional wetland development

a. Rainwater percolates through sandy soils until it reaches the limestone.

b. The acidic water dissolves the calcium carbonate in the limestone. Voids, caverns, and surface slumping of the soil occur.

c. Over time, fine soil particles accumulate, forming an impervious clayey layer that ponds water on the ground surface.

Lide et al. 1995). In south-central Georgia, the western edge of the Carolina bay range meets the eastern edge of limesink pond predominance. In this area, depressional wetlands exhibiting characteristics of both types can be found. Grand Bay, near Valdosta, is a particularly large example of a depressional wetland in this region and may be the largest Carolina bay in the state.

CAROLINA BAYS

Carolina bays are shallow geomorphic formations that are unique to the Coastal Plain of the southeastern United States, extending from Maryland to Florida and west to Alabama. They have a unique and characteristic structure that distinguishes them from other depresssional wetlands. These wetlands have an elliptical to ovoid shape and a distinctive northwest-southeast orientation of the long axis. Because of this consistent orientation, Carolina bays appear approximately parallel to one another across a landscape. Some bays have a sandy rim that is most prominent along the southeastern edge. Estimates of the number of these wetlands vary depending on the exact definition of a Carolina bay. Wetlands with these well-defined physical characteristics occur most commonly in North and South Carolina but are also present in abundance in the Atlantic Coastal Plain of Georgia. Similar depressional wetlands that are less distinctive in shape and orientation occur throughout the Coastal Plain (Lide 1997). From an ecological perspective, they are similar to other depressional wetlands that may have formed as subsidence features in karst landscapes (limesink regions, such as the Dougherty Plain, in which limestone bedrock is close to the soil surface).

The geomorphic origin of Carolina bays has been long debated. Various causes have been suggested, including meteor showers, subsurface dissolution processes, as well as wave and prevailing wind action; however, no consensus has emerged on the formation of the depressions (Sharitz and Gresham 1998). There is also dispute over their age. Even though Carolina bays are restricted to sandy soil regions of the Coastal Plain, they are positioned on several different geological formations (Sharitz and Gresham 1998).

VEGETATION

The vegetation in depression marshes and cypress savanna wetlands is a rich herbaceous flora that is often distributed in a distinct zonal pattern of dominant species relative to water depth. Often, floating species such as white waterlily, yellow pondlily, or big floating heart, dominate in the deepest part of the depression. Emergent grasses and sedges, including cutgrass, beakrushes, witchgrasses, panic grasses, and jointgrass, usually occur in more intermediate water depth and hydroperiod conditions. Woody shrubs such as gallberry and myrtle holly may be present along the edges. Droughts or periods of greater than average precipitation may result in shifts in species zones. Based on observations of aerial photographs, many depression marshes appear to be temporally stable if they have escaped direct hydrologic alterations (Kirkman et al. 1996). They can be dominated by herbaceous vegetation for many decades without succeeding to hardwoods or cypress. Because fire and inundation both inhibit establishment of woody species, the absence of one may be offset by the presence of the other; consequently, change in the plant community can be very slow. In depressions with prolonged or semipermanent inundation, hydrology alone may exclude woody establishment. Alternatively, extended dry periods in the absence of fire can result in rapid hardwood shrub and tree encroachment. In some cases, these wetlands can succeed to mesic communities (K. L. Martin and Kirkman 2009). (See depression oak forests.)

Plants inhabiting irregularly inundated freshwater wetlands are subject to a wide range of environmental conditions. These plants must cope with anaerobic soil conditions when soils are saturated or inundated, partial submergence of leaves during inundation, periods of dry soil or even drought conditions, and potentially fire. Adaptations to "amphibious" habitats include physiological (Crawford 1982), morphological (Hook 1984; Brändle and Crawford 1987), life-history (van der Valk and Davis 1980), and growth response traits (Osmond, Winter, and Ziegler 1982; Ridge 1987). Most wetland plants develop internal, gas-filled channels in the stems and roots, called "aerenchyma," that allow oxygen movement from the aerial portions

Pale meadow-beauty

cess in wetland communities include seed dispersal by animals or water, nutritional value to waterfowl, and first-year reproductive maturity of perennials, such as that of many witchgrasses.

The upland-wetland transitional zones of wetlands in fire-managed landscapes, such as the longleaf pine communities that have escaped soil-disturbing activities, have extremely high species richness (Kirkman, Drew, and Edwards 1998). Because many herbaceous marsh species can persist when wetlands are dry, they are also tolerant of conditions existing in transitional zones. They are also usually adapted to fire. In addition, there are numerous species that are characteristic of these transitional areas such as toothache grass, Florida dropseed, erect-leaved witchgrass, licorice goldenrod, and smooth meadow-beauty. In the presence of abrupt firebreaks, roads, or adjacent cultivated fields, the edges of depression marshes may become encroached with oak species such as live oak, laurel oak, and water oak. (See depression oak forests.)

Cypress savannas are similar to marshes floristically but have an open to sparse canopy (25–50% cover) of pond-cypress and an herbaceous ground cover dominated by grasses and sedges. Although often a monospecific woodland, other occasional tree species may include swamp tupelo, loblolly pine, slash pine, and sweet gum. Shrubs, including gallberry, shining fetterbush, and maleberry, may be present, particularly around the edges. Herbaceous ground cover frequently includes maidencane, panic grasses, witchgrasses, beakrushes, nutrush, old-field broomsedge, cutgrass, meadow-beauties, rayless-goldenrod, marsh fleabane, water-primroses, spikerushes, flatsedges, and milkworts.

For cypress to become established, the wetland must be dry long enough for seeds to germinate because they cannot germinate when soils are flooded (Demaree 1932). Cypress seedlings grow slowly and become established only when they reach a height that will not be submerged and a size that can withstand fire. Once established, mature pond-cypress trees are relatively fire-tolerant and are extremely flood-tolerant (Ewel 1995, 1998). With prolonged dry-down and absence of fire, cypress savannas can become invaded by hardwoods, particularly oaks and gum (Ewel 1998).

The trunks of cypress trees are often buttressed or greatly enlarged at their base, and their root systems develop vertical projections known as "knees." The buttressing characteristic and formation of knees are

of the plant down into the roots. Flood-induced petiole elongation has been demonstrated in several herbaceous plant species, such as maidencane and cutgrass, as a mechanism to maintain leaves above the surface of the water and avoid carbon dioxide and oxygen shortages. If inundation occurs during the growing season, these species rapidly elongate and persist as emergent grasses (Kirkman and Sharitz 1993). In depression marshes with irregularly fluctuating water levels, a persistent seedbank is usually present and guilds of species adapted to germination under different hydrologic conditions have been identified (Kirkman and Sharitz 1994; Poiani and Dixon 1995; Collins and Battaglia 2001; Mulhouse, Burbage, and Sharitz 2005). Some species are adapted to drought and germinate in exposed soil conditions; others are stimulated to germinate only under water; and some are generalists and can germinate in both flooded and dry soil conditions (Hook 1984). In addition to seed dormancy characteristics, other life-history traits that contribute to suc-

CHARACTERISTIC PLANTS OF DEPRESSION MARSHES AND CYPRESS SAVANNAS

TREES (PRIMARILY IN CYPRESS SAVANNAS)

Swamp tupelo—Nyssa biflora
Pond-cypress—Taxodium ascendens

SHRUBS AND WOODY VINES

Mayhaw—Crataegus aestivalis
Myrtle holly—Ilex myrtifolia

GROUND COVER

Blue maiden-cane—Amphicarpum
  muhlenbergianum
Old-field broomsedge—Andropogon
  virginicus
Longleaf three-awn grass—Aristida
  palustris

Blue sedge—Carex glaucescens
Wrinkled jointgrass—Coelorachis
  rugosa
Redroot flatsedge—Cyperus
  erythrorhizos
Wright's witchgrass—Dichanthelium
  wrightianum
Spikerush—Eleocharis quadrangulata
Pipewort—Eriocaulon decangulare
Flat-topped goldenrod—Euthamia
  caroliniana
Narrowleaf sunflower—Helianthus
  angustifolius
Redroot—Lachnanthes caroliniana
Southern bogbutton—Lachnocaulon
  beyrichianum
Cutgrass—Leersia hexandra

Alternate-leaf seedbox—Ludwigia
  alternifolia
Maidencane—Panicum hemitomom
Florida paspalum—Paspalum
  floridanum
Waterpepper—Persicaria hydropiperoides
Pale meadow-beauty—Rhexia mariana
Globe beaksedge—Rhynchospora
  globularis
Woolgrass bulrush—Scirpus cyperinus
Netted nutrush—Scleria reticularis
Gaping panic grass—Steinchisma hians
Water dawnflower—Stylisma aquatica
Swollen bladderwort—Utricularia
  inflata
Drummond's yellow-eyed grass—Xyris
  drummondii

---

structural features that probably aid in supporting the tree in saturated soils. Pond-cypress trees are rarely up-rooted, even during storm events with strong winds. Although oxygen transport to the roots has been suggested as a function of the knees, there has been no demonstration of this phenomenon (Mitsch and Gosselink 1993). Cypress trees are also adapted to dry periods. This species may nearly defoliate during drought conditions as a means to prevent water loss. Occasionally, the buttressed base of a cypress tree may be damaged by fire, creating a deep crevice that provides a refuge for alligators or other animals.

ANIMALS

Due to fluctuating water levels, many depressional wetlands do not support fish populations (Snodgrass et al. 1996). The absence of predaceous fish provides habitat that is particularly favorable for breeding amphibians and larval insects. Depressional wetlands are also particularly valuable as foraging sites for wading birds and waterfowl. Even though the landscape connectivity of these wetlands with that of upland habitats, as well as with other wetlands, is critical for biotic support (Ewel 1998), their role in maintaining regional biodiversity has not been adequately recognized or valued by society (Semlitsch and Bodie 1998; Kirkman et al. 1999; Batzer, Cooper, and Wissinger 2006).

Wading birds such as the great blue heron, great egret, little blue heron, snowy egret, and tricolored heron forage for fish, amphibians, reptiles, and invertebrates in grass-sedge marshes when water is low. They usually nest in nearby riverine swamps or in more permanently inundated cypress ponds. The wood stork, an Endangered species, feeds on similar prey in depressional marshes as well as tidally influenced salt marshes (Depkin, Coulter, and Bryan 1992; Bryan 1996; Gaines et al. 1998). Wood stork breeding in Georgia was first documented in 1965. Now, about 1,400 pairs nest annually in the state. Previously found more commonly in Florida and extreme southern Georgia, this species has expanded its range northward and inland, while losing habitat to development in Florida (Coulter et al. 1999; M. J. Harris 1999). Numerous species of birds, including the pied-billed grebe, red-winged blackbird, and purple gallinule, nest in the emergent vegetation of depression marshes (Yasukawa and Searcy 1995; Muller and Storer 1999). In cypress savannas, the open canopy of the cypress also provides perch sites for predatory birds such as hawks and other raptors. Swallow-tailed and Mississippi kites can be seen feeding on dragonflies, beetles, and other invertebrates associated with these wetland sites.

The abundance of isolated wetlands in the Southeast has contributed to the high diversity of amphibians in the region and recognition of it as a hotspot of amphibian species richness. Isolated wetlands provide breeding or primary habitat for 36 amphibian species (Moler and Franz 1987; Petranka 1998; Liner et al. 2008). Within Georgia, the principal breeding habitat for 10 frog and 5 salamander species is restricted to these wetland habitats (Moler and Franz 1987; Petranka 1998). Amphibian-monitoring studies in South Carolina (Gibbons and Semlitsch 1981) and Georgia (Liner et al. 2008) revealed that thousands of individual frogs and salamanders can enter and exit a single depression during the breeding season in wet years. The movement of numerous amphibians from wetlands to uplands as they mature may represent a significant flow of nutrients in a complex food web. The need for upland-wetland habitat connectivity for amphibian species also suggests that optimal habitat management for these species will require maintaining or restoring fire corridors between uplands and wetlands (Dodd and Cade 1998; Semlitsch and Bodie 1998). Thus, hydrologic alterations that maintain water year round, coupled with introductions of fish, can be extremely detrimental to amphibians.

Emergent grasses of depression marshes and cypress savannas provide a substrate for egg deposition when wetlands are inundated. Species that can commonly be heard calling in these wetlands include the bullfrog, southern cricket frog, pig frog, gopher frog (see the Featured Animal), green treefrog, pinewoods treefrog, and barking treefrog. Different species of frogs breed in different seasons. Salamanders that are associated with depression marshes include the tiger salamander and striped newt (L. L. Smith 2008; Stevenson and Cash 2008). One species of concern inhabiting depression marshes and cypress savannas is the flatwoods salamander, which is considered Imperiled in Georgia (Jensen and Stevenson 2008). During autumn rain showers, this salamander moves from longleaf pine forest uplands into small cypress savannas to breed. The chicken turtle prefers isolated herb-dominated depressional wetlands of the Coastal Plain as a primary habitat. The diet of this species consists primarily of crayfish and other aquatic invertebrates (Buhlmann 2008). During winter, most individuals will emerge from the wetlands and bury themselves in the soil of adjacent uplands. Spotted turtles are restricted to the Coastal Plain and usually associated with shallow wetland habitats with emergent vegetation. This small, attractive turtle with its yellow spots has been popular in the pet trade, although the degree to which commercial take has impacted populations in Georgia is unknown. Recent studies have documented the role of isolated wetlands in the ecology of the American alligator, which uses these habitats alternatively with flowing streams and rivers during the breeding season (Subalusky, Fitzgerald, and Smith 2009). The alligator plays a significant role within these wetlands by digging large burrows. As the water level of the wetland recedes, these holes create refugia for many wetland invertebrates and amphibians during the dry period (Mazzotti and Brandt 1994).

As with plant communities, grass-sedge marshes and cypress savannas have greater diversity and density of aquatic invertebrates than other wetland types, probably due to habitat complexity associated with emergent macrophytes (Golladay, Taylor, and Palik 1997; Battle and Golladay 1999). Numerous taxa of tiny crustaceans feed on periphyton. These crustaceans form the basis of the diet of numerous species of carnivorous insect larvae that, in turn, provide the food source of larval amphibians.

Gopher Frog (*Rana capito*)

The gopher frog obtains its name from the gopher tortoise, whose burrow it frequently inhabits. The preferred breeding habitats are cypress savannas or grass-sedge marsh depressional wetlands because these ephemeral ponds usually lack predatory fish. Thus, their habitat includes longleaf pine forests containing gopher tortoise burrows with embedded depressional wetlands within a mile from the burrows (Moler 1992). The gopher frog has a stout body with a large head and mouth. It has prominent warts on the back and a light brown color with brown or black spots that blends in well with sandy soil. After heavy rains in January through March, individuals congregate to breed (Cash, Jensen, and Stevenson 2008). Males call with a very deep snoring sound. The globular egg masses are attached to emergent or submerged plant stems in the

wetland and hatch within four to five days. The tadpole stage lasts from about 85 to 100 days. Upon metamorphosis, adults disperse to uplands. Adults are very secretive and spend most of the day hiding in gopher tortoise burrows. They are active nocturnally and feed on insects and other frogs.

In Georgia, this species occurs primarily in the southeastern and south-central to southwestern parts of the Coastal Plain. Populations are thought to be declining from wetland habitat loss by drainage, filling, or stocking of fish and from upland habitat loss through development, fragmentation, and fire suppression (Bailey 1991). Fire suppression has been linked to population declines because it reduces habitat quality for gopher tortoises. Fire suppression also affects habitat quality of breeding ponds through changes in vegetation (Greenberg 2001). Because of its rarity in Georgia, the gopher frog is protected by state law.

Chickasawhatchee Wildlife Management Area

The Chickasawhatchee Wildlife Management Area is a 20,900-acre state-owned wetland complex located in Dougherty, Calhoun, and Baker Counties. The property is significant in that it is the largest wetland system in the Flint River basin and the second largest wetland system in the state (only the Okefenokee Swamp is larger). It is composed of extensive bottomlands and swamps, as well as numerous depressional wetlands. Although most of the upland forests were converted to industrial pine plantations by the previous owner, many of the wetlands remain as relatively intact communities. Public hiking trails are not developed on this property; however, well-maintained dirt roads occur throughout the property, offering numerous opportunities to access examples of cypress savannas, grass-sedge marshes, and cypress-gum ponds.

Location: From downtown Albany take Ga. Hwy. 91 south 4 miles to junction with Ga. Hwy. 62; turn right (west) and go 8.5 miles; the entrance road will be just across the highway from Mud Creek Rd. Google Earth GPS approximate coordinates at the entrance: N 31.503957/W 084.353907.

Cypress-Gum Ponds

Cypress-gum ponds are geographically isolated wetlands that occur in seasonally flooded depressions, such as Carolina bays and limesinks. These forested wetlands are relatively common throughout the Coastal Plain of Georgia. They are seasonally to semipermanently inundated, and the hydrologic regime fluctuates with precipitation. Surface soils are usually organic and are underlain by impervious clayey soils. These wetlands are dominated by pond-cypress and/or swamp tupelo. The shrub layer is usually sparse and includes species such as buttonbush, ti-ti, myrtle holly, and staggerbush. Herbaceous vegetation primarily includes floating aquatics or species rooted on stumps and floating logs. They are important sites for migratory waterfowl and nesting sites (rookeries) for wading birds, including the federally Endangered wood stork (see the Featured Animal). Several rare plant species are associated with the edge of ecotones that surround the ponds.

PHYSICAL SETTING AND ECOLOGY

Cypress-gum ponds tend to develop in depressions with longer hydroperiods than those of cypress savannas or grass-sedge marshes and may even be semipermanently inundated (Kirkman et al. 2000). These depression swamps occur throughout the Coastal Plain and are generally located in inter-ridge landscape positions in the upper Coastal Plain or surrounded by pine flatwoods or shrub bogs in the lower Coastal Plain. Although the hydrologic regime is usually dominated by precipitation, these wetlands may also receive lateral inputs from surficial groundwater. Some wetlands may even be spring-fed, with direct hydrologic recharge or discharge features connecting them to deeper aquifers. The surface soils are usually organic mucks and peats with a pH of 3.5 to 4.1 and are nutrient-deficient. Peat forms when plant materials are inhibited from decaying fully by acidic, waterlogged conditions. Because of the longer hydroperiod, the probability of fire is less frequent than in cypress savannas or grass-sedge marshes, although they are subject to burn during dry periods, particu-

Cypress-gum pond

larly if the surrounding uplands are fire-maintained pinelands.

Alteration of regional water tables may influence the hydrologic dynamics of isolated wetlands, even in situations where precipitation has been the dominant influence on hydrologic regime. For example, the construction of large reservoirs, such as Lake Seminole in 1957 on the Georgia-Florida state line, has drastically altered the hydroperiod of nearby wetlands from fluctuating water levels to that of nearly permanently inundated conditions (Dalton, Aulenback, and Torak 2004; Torak, Crilley, and Painter 2006). Such alterations in hydrology result in vegetation changes as well as altered animal use of the habitat. Many cypress-gum ponds of the Coastal Plain have been drained, bedded, and site-converted to industrial pine plantations.

VEGETATION

The canopy composition of cypress-gum ponds ranges from monospecific stands of either pond-cypress or swamp black gum to a mixture of both species. The presence of one species over the other may reflect chance historical establishment conditions and fire events or even timber harvest patterns in which cypress was preferentially removed. Species associated with this wetland forest type include slash pine, red maple, American snowbell, shining fetterbush, coastal sweet-pepperbush, red bay, ti-ti, and sweet bay. In some wetlands the trees form a dome-like profile with the taller, older, and more fire-protected trees in the center of the swamp and shorter, younger ones on the edges—these wetlands may be called "cypress domes" or "gum domes" (Ewel 1998). A cypress dome with open water in the center is sometimes called a "cypress doughnut." The presence of a closed canopy and frequent inundation result in sparse herbaceous ground cover, but woody vines such as bamboo-vine and coral greenbrier are very common. Some less flood-tolerant herbs such as false-nettle or St. John's-worts may germinate on old stumps. Cinnamon fern and Virginia chain fern frequently occur along the margins, where water depth is lower.

American snowbell

Swamp tupelo is a very flood-tolerant hardwood, and its fleshy fruits are dispersed by floating on water and by birds.

ANIMALS

Many wading birds, particularly herons, ibis, and great egrets, nest in the trees of cypress-gum ponds, primarily in sites that are permanently inundated. These communities are also used by nesting wood ducks and migratory waterfowl (Hepp and Bellrose 1995). Characteristic passerine birds include the prothonotary warbler, northern parula, and common grackle (Burleigh 1958; Moldenhauer and Regelski 1996; Peer and Bollinger 1997; Petit 1999).

Numerous reptiles and amphibians, including common musk turtle, marbled salamander, mole salamander, two-toed amphiuma, lesser and greater sirens, and southern dusky salamander, can be found in depression swamps. In more permanently inundated sites or during conditions when these depressions are connected to other bodies of water, predatory fish are likely to be present. Consequently, fewer frog species are found in these types of wetlands than in cypress savannas or depression marshes. Bullfrogs, southern cricket frogs, and southern leopard frogs frequently inhabit these wetlands (Liner et al. 2008). Detritivorous crustaceans (invertebrates that consume plant remains) are particularly abundant in the depression swamps in which accumulation of organic material occurs (Golladay, Taylor, and Palik 1997).

In addition to hydrologic regime, fire is an important factor in the development of plant communities in these wetland environments. Because pond-cypress is more fire-tolerant than swamp gum, more frequently burned sites may be maintained as monospecific stands of cypress (Ewel and Mitsch 1978). Protection from fire in addition to commercial harvesting of cypress increases the dominance of hardwoods.

CHARACTERISTIC PLANTS OF CYPRESS-GUM PONDS

TREES

Red maple—Acer rubrum
Swamp tupelo—Nyssa biflora
Laurel oak—Quercus laurifolia
Pond-cypress—Taxodium ascendens

SHRUBS AND WOODY VINES

Peppervine—Ampelopsis arborea
Buttonbush—Cephalanthus occidentalis
Coastal sweet-pepperbush—Clethra
    alnifolia

Coastal fetterbush—Eubotrys racemosa
Virginia-willow—Itea virginica
Shining fetterbush—Lyonia lucida
Whiteleaf greenbrier—Smilax glauca
Coral greenbrier—Smilax walteri
American snowbell—Styrax americanus

GROUND COVER

False-nettle—Boehmeria cylindrica
Blue sedge—Carex glaucescens
Joor's sedge—Carex joori

Southern blue flag—Iris virginica
Cinnamon fern—Osmundastrum
    cinnamomeum
Short-bristle horned beaksedge—
    Rhynchospora corniculata
Lizard's-tail—Saururus cernuus
Virginia chain fern—Woodwardia
    virginica

ROOKERIES

Colonial nesting wading birds are a group of medium to large birds, including great blue heron, great egret, little blue heron, snowy egret, tricolored heron, white ibis, glossy ibis, and wood stork, which nest in large multispecies colonies. The nesting sites, called "rookeries," are often located in the center of cypress-gum ponds with open water and large cypress trees. A rookery may consist of a few nests of a single species to hundreds or thousands of nests of several species. Multiple nests may be present in a single tree. The platform-like nests are built of small sticks. Nest sites are usually in cypress trees in standing water that affords protection from terrestrial nest predators, such as raccoons. If the water dries up, raccoons have easy access to nests and can eliminate an entire colony. The presence of alligators when the swamp is flooded also helps to deter predation by raccoons (M. J. Harris 1999; Winn and Ozier 2010). Colony sites are often used year after year. As a group, colonial nesting wading birds are of conservation concern because their reproductive strategy leaves them especially vulnerable to habitat degradation. Impacts to a colony can affect hundreds of breeding pairs of several species (Winn and Ozier 2010).

When nesting space is limited, larger species such as wood storks and great egrets prefer nesting on stout, lateral branches in the top of the canopy, whereas yellow-crowned night-herons, little blue herons, tricolored herons, and snowy egrets nest lower, often in shrubby habitat (Beaver, Osborn, and Custer 1980). Colonial wading birds feed primarily on fish, crabs, crayfish, and amphibians in shallow water. The glossy and white ibises use their long bills to probe the soil for invertebrates in moist soil and shallow water. With their longer legs, the great blue heron and great egret are able to feed in deeper water. The great blue heron also feeds opportunistically on small birds and mammals (Butler 1992; Melvin 2010a). Numerous wading bird rookeries have been documented throughout the Coastal Plain of Georgia, particularly in the coastal areas of Chatham, McIntosh, Glynn, and Camden Counties. They also occur sporadically in appropriate habitat in other parts of the state. Wading bird conservation has been a focus of the Georgia Department of Natural Resources Nongame Conservation Section, which monitors populations, identifies key population factors, and works to conserve important rookery sites. The success of colonial waterbird conservation will depend on an ecosystem management approach that includes foraging and nesting habitat.

American white ibis rookery

Wood Stork (*Mycteria americana*)

The wood stork, also known as wood ibis, ironhead, flinthead, gourdhead, gannet, preacher, Spanish buzzard, Colorado turkey, and wood-pelican, is a large, long-legged wading bird with a long, down-curved bill. The plumage is mostly white, but the wing-tips, trailing edge of the wings, and tail are black. The neck and head of adults are not feathered, and thus, the gray/black skin has a scaly appearance.

The wood stork's breeding range includes the southeastern United States, Central America, and South America. In the United States, wood storks breed in Florida, Georgia, and the Carolinas. A few wood storks may be seen in the Georgia Piedmont during late summer and fall, but most are found in the coastal marshes.

Beginning in late summer, wood storks from many widely separated breeding colonies gather into communal roosts along the coast. These colonial nesters use a wide variety of freshwater and estuarine wetlands for breeding, feeding, and roosting. Nests may be located in large or small trees, but the trees must be in standing water or on islands surrounded by water. Storks will use the same colonies for many years unless disturbance or changes in water levels make the site unsuitable (M. C. Coulter et al. 1987, 1999).

Wood storks feed on fish, amphibians, and crayfish by tactolocation or grope feeding. The birds wade through shallow water, moving their partially opened beaks back and forth beneath the surface (M. C. Coulter et al. 1999). When the bill touches a fish or other prey, it snaps shut in an exceedingly quick reflex. When a fish is caught, the bird raises its head and swallows the prey.

Loss of habitat is the primary threat to wood storks. An increase in nesting has occurred in South Carolina and Georgia since the early 1980s as the large colonies in southern Florida have steadily declined (M. J. Harris 1999; Winn and Ozier 2010). Protection of foraging and breeding habitat is critical for recovery of this species.

Big Dukes Pond Natural Area

Big Dukes Pond Natural Area (Jenkins County) is owned by the state of Georgia and managed by the Georgia Department of Natural Resources. This 1,220-acre tract includes most of the 1,800-acre Big Dukes Pond Carolina bay. In spite of decades of anthropogenic disturbances of ditching, fire suppression, agriculture, and timber management, there are good examples of remnant or recovering vegetation of cypress-gum swamps and cypress savannas, bay swamps, and mixed hardwoods. The wetland supports two federally listed Endangered species, Canby's dropwort (also known as Canby's cowbane) and the wood stork.

Classic Carolina bay features of an elliptical depression surrounded by a sandy rim along the southeastern edge and a long axis slightly oriented northwest to southeast can best be observed from an aerial perspective. A trail follows the edge of the state/private boundary. A large portion of the interior wetland is dominated by cypress-gum swamp or cypress savanna. The diverse ground cover of the cypress savanna commonly includes umbrella-sedges, meadow-beauties, maidencane, sedges, St. John's-worts, pipeworts, arrowheads, milkworts, yellow-eyed grasses, water-primroses, and bladderworts. A ring of shrubby bay forest and vine thicket occurs along the eastern edge of the bay, dominated by loblolly bay, sweet bay, swamp bay, and red bay. Restoration of the natural hydrologic regime, use of prescribed fire, and canopy conversion of off-site pine plantations are under way.

Location: From Statesboro Rd. (U.S. 25/Ga. Hwy. 121) in Millen, take Ga. Hwy. 17 west approximately 0.9 mile, then turn right onto Old Louisville Rd. (CR 79). Continue north about 7.3 miles and turn left at the entrance sign. The entrance road bears sharply left from CR 79 and continues along the edge of the property boundary to the parking area. Google Earth GPS approximate coordinates at the parking area: N 32.874452/W 082.029912.

Depression Oak Forests

Depression oak forests occur in shallow basins that are infrequently inundated and have been excluded from fire. These depressions are often "islands" or "hammocks" of evergreen hardwoods, particularly live oak, laurel oak, and water oak, within a matrix of fire-maintained longleaf pine uplands. Heavy shade, periodic standing water, and a thick layer of live oak leaf litter lead to a species-poor ground layer. The oak-dominated plant community appears to represent a persistent alternate state to herb-dominated wetlands that would otherwise be present with frequent fire. Even when situated in fire-managed upland sites, the oak-dominated vegetation probably has become more prevalent in recent decades because of the common use of prescribed fire in winter months when the depressions are most likely to have standing water and would exclude fire. These hardwood-dominated de-pressions are particularly abundant in the Dougherty Plain, developing in sinkholes. In urban environments, these depressions are often converted to surface water holding ponds or even municipal parks.

PHYSICAL SETTING AND ECOLOGY

Depression oak forests develop in shallow depressions that occasionally pond water. They usually have mineral soils with a clayey impervious layer beneath. These communities are characterized on the drier end of the wetland hydrologic gradient. Although these wetlands may be completely dry in most years, they are inundated for several months, including the growing season, if precipitation is high (K. L. Martin and Kirkman 2009). During winter, with increased rainfall and decreased evapotranspiration, the wetlands would be most likely to pond water and thus deter fire. As a consequence, the potential for fire entering a wetland may be lessened due to timing of managed burns. During dry periods, mesophytic oaks become established and

Depression oak forest

are then protected from fire when the wetlands are ponded or have saturated soils. Both shading and the accumulation of a thick layer of oakleaf litter beneath the oaks eliminate herbaceous species that would otherwise provide fuel to carry fire. On the soil surface, the evergreen oak leaves retain moisture and become very resistant to ignition (Kane, Varner, and Hiers 2008); thus, the absence of fuels further perpetuates fire suppression within the depression (Myers 1990; K. L. Martin and Kirkman 2009). The frequent dry conditions and rapid decomposition generally prevent accumulation of organic soils.

VEGETATION

Depression oak forests are dominated by a closed canopy of oak species, particularly live oak, laurel oak, and water oak. The largest and oldest trees usually occur in the deepest part of the depression, where these fire-intolerant species are able to establish initially (K. L. Martin and Kirkman 2009). These oaks are tolerant of periodic inundation. Other species commonly present include American persimmon, swamp tu-

pelo, and sweet gum. The litterfall of live oaks is particularly resistant to decomposition and suppresses nearly all herbaceous ground cover. Because the layer of oak leaves also holds moisture, the leaf litter becomes increasingly less prone to carry fire. Thus, over time, as fire is prevented from being carried beneath the oaks, additional oaks become established and the oak-dominated patch encroaches outward. It is possible that increased evapotranspiration of evergreen oaks may exceed that of herbaceous wetland plants, and thus the wetlands may tend to have even shorter hydroperiods once these species become dominant (Sun et al. 2001).

Anthropogenic influences have probably resulted in a greater prevalence of depression oak hammocks today than occurred in prior history. Current land use with altered fire regimes and disturbances that create barriers to the movement of fire (fire shadows) have promoted hardwood encroachment throughout the Coastal Plain of Georgia. Although depression oak hammocks have been a natural component of the longleaf pine landscape and provide habitat diversity for

CHARACTERISTIC PLANTS OF DEPRESSION OAK FORESTS

TREES

American persimmon—*Diospyros virginiana*
Sweet gum—*Liquidambar styraciflua*
Swamp tupelo—*Nyssa biflora*
Laurel oak—*Quercus laurifolia*
Water oak—*Quercus nigra*
Live oak—*Quercus virginiana*

SHRUBS AND WOODY VINES

Peppervine—*Ampelopsis arborea*
Mayhaw—*Crataegus aestivalis*
Cockspur hawthorn—*Crataegus crus-galli*
Mayberry—*Vaccinium elliottii*

FERN

Resurrection fern—*Polypodium polypodioides*

some species, the significant regional loss of species-rich depression marshes and mesic longleaf pine sites has influenced efforts to restore hardwood-encroached depressions to open fire-maintained grassy habitats. In sites where maintaining regional biodiversity is an eco-system management directive, such restoration goals require hardwood removal and reintroduction of frequent fire. In such hardwood-dominated depressions in southwestern Georgia, a persistent soil seedbank of obligate wetland herbs has been documented beneath the closed canopy of live oaks with almost no ground cover vegetation (K. L. Martin and Kirkman 2009). This finding supports the hypothesis that the vegetation of these depressional wetlands has changed drastically from that of a former condition. Five years after hardwood canopy was removed in an associated restoration case study, dense herbaceous ground cover had recovered to the extent that it provided fuels necessary to sustain prescribed fire.

ANIMALS

Because of the relatively short hydroperiod, these wetlands typically are not as important as breeding sites for amphibians as other wetland depressions except in the wetter years. The depression oak forests are not a preferred habitat for many wildlife species due to the absence of cover and food sources. Nonetheless, oak acorns are eaten by squirrels and turkeys, the canopy provides nesting sites for northern parula, and the dense layer of leaf litter provides foraging grounds for towhees. Barred owls use these sites for nesting in cavities of large trees or for foraging (see the Featured Animal). Rat snakes are commonly found in these forested wetlands.

Live oak limb draped with Spansh-moss

Barred Owl (*Strix varia*)

The barred owl, also known as the hoot owl, wood owl, laughing owl, black-eyed owl, round-headed owl, and rain owl, is a large and relatively common bird of upland and lowland forests in the eastern United States and portions of Canada, ranging as far south as Central America and as far north as southeastern Alaska. Adult barred owls are 17 to 24 inches long, with a 40- to 50-inch wingspan, dark barring on the upper breast, and dark vertical streaking on the lower body (Terres 1980).

This species can be distinguished from other owls of the eastern United States by its coloration, lack of ear tufts, and dark eyes (other owls have yellow eyes, except for the barn owl). The barred owl is well known for its loud, hooting call, heard primarily at night but also on cloudy days. This call is often described phonetically as "Who cooks for you? Who cooks for you-all?" Though shy, the barred owl will often respond to imitations of its hooting call by calling and flying closer; it can also be enticed by imitating the squeaks of mice or birds. Of all of the North American owls, the barred owl is the most likely to be active during daylight hours (Dunn and Alderfer 2008).

Barred owls typically build their nests in tree cavities. However, when these favored nesting sites are scarce or absent, they may make use of the abandoned nests of squirrels or hawks (Terres 1980). The diet of the barred owl consists mostly of mice but may also include other mammals ranging in size from shrews to gray foxes, including various ground- and tree-nesting birds, frogs, salamanders, lizards, snakes, insects, and even fiddler crabs. This owl typically hunts by flying through the woods and swooping down on its prey or by perching on a high branch and waiting for prey to pass underneath (Terres 1980).

Depression Oak Forest Sites

Most sites in public ownership in urbanized areas have been converted into storm retention ponds. Numerous examples of forested depressions occur on private properties, particularly in the Dougherty Plain.

Riverine Floodplains

Riverine floodplains of the southeastern Coastal Plain are forested wetlands flanking rivers and streams that are influenced, at least periodically, by flooding. These ecosystems have a linear form as a consequence of their proximity to river or stream channels. As a result, these ecosystems are connected to upstream and downstream ecosystems as habitat corridors and as conduits for the exchange of nutrients and particulates. Riparian ecosystems can be broad alluvial valleys several miles wide or narrow strips of stream bank vegetation. Fluvial processes result in heterogeneous patterns of soil texture and drainage, particularly in larger floodplains. Natural levees that form along stream banks have coarse-textured soils as a result of sediment deposition when streams overflow their banks. Inceptisols occur where rapidly moving water deposits heavier sediments. Within former river channels or sloughs where slower-moving floodwaters are retained, deposition of finer-textured clays and silts occur (Stanturf and Schoenholtz 1998). The vegetation may be a mosaic of plant communities depending on soil and hydrologic characteristics that determine floodplain physical features.

Often, a primary distinction is whether the stream originates in the Piedmont or Coastal Plain. This sepa-ration has resulted in terms such as "alluvial" versus "nonalluvial" and "blackwater" versus "brownwater" rivers. Application of these terms may be useful for describing general characteristics; however, the variation in landforms in Georgia and regions with significant presence of limestone bedrock, groundwater, and spring inputs has rendered these terms somewhat confusing to consistently apply to all river systems in the state.

Rivers that originate in the Piedmont generally transport large amounts of suspended and dissolved materials relative to those originating in the Coastal Plain because of differences in water velocity and steepness of the grade. Thus, Piedmont streams that flow across the Coastal Plain are often called "alluvial" rivers because they result in significant deposits of sediment and the development of well-defined bottomland floodplains and other depositional floodplain features. A classic example of this type of river system is the Altamaha River, which flows from the Georgia Piedmont across the Coastal Plain to the Atlantic Ocean. As this river flows onto the Coastal Plain, the floodplain becomes more sinuous and complex. In contrast, those streams that originate in the Coastal Plain are termed "nonalluvial" due to a rela-

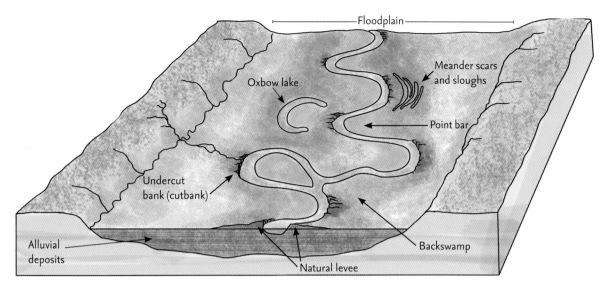

Floodplain characteristics

Floodplain: A level area near a river channel, constructed by the river, which overflows during moderate flow events.

Undercut bank (cutbank): A steep bank in the outer portion of a meander, formed by erosive action of a stream as the main current of the stream (the thalweg) is directed toward the bank.

Point bar: The inner portion of a meander across from the cutbank, where sediment is deposited because the stream is moving slowly in this portion of the channel.

Natural levee: A long, low ridge that forms on stream banks when water overflows the stream channel, slows down, and deposits coarse, sandy sediments. Natural levees slope sharply toward the river and more gently away from the river. Levees in a particular site may be building or eroding, depending upon

stream dynamics. Not all streams or stream stretches have levees.

Backswamp: A low-lying, often hydric area of the floodplain behind the natural levees. It is often characterized by higher, hummocky, mesic areas that are remnants of landforms built when the stream channel was positioned differently.

Slough: A slowly flowing, shallow swamp that forms in meander scars.

Oxbow lake: A body of permanently standing water that results from the cutoff of meanders.

Meander scars: Depressions and ridges on the convex side of bends in the river. Meander scars result in ridge and swale topography.

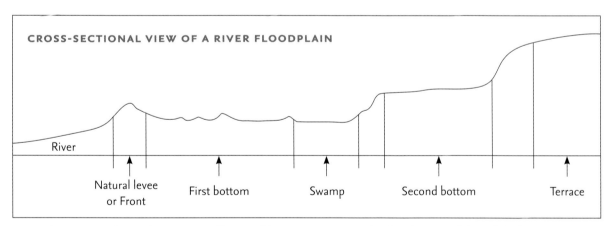

River: A large stream of water that is open at all times of the year.

Natural levee or front: A high, well-drained ridge that forms from repeated floods that overflow the frontlands.

First bottom: Relatively recent or present floodplains that contain newer deposits of alluvium and less mature soils. They consist of a series of ridges and flats and sloughs derived from meander scars.

Swamp: An abandoned section of channel that becomes an oxbow lake and, and as sedimentation continues, a swamp.

Second bottom: Remnants from former floodplains left when a general uplift or tilting of the earth's surface caused the riverbed to erode its way to a lower elevation.

Terrace: An abandoned floodplain, not connected to present floodplain.

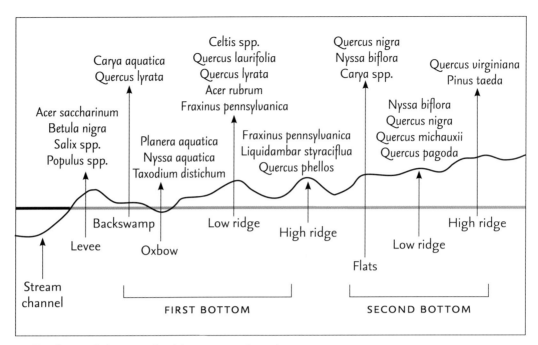

Carya aquatica
Quercus lyrata

Celtis spp.
Quercus laurifolia
Quercus lyrata
Acer rubrum
Fraxinus pennsylvanica

Quercus nigra
Nyssa biflora
Carya spp.

Quercus virginiana
Pinus taeda

Acer saccharinum
Betula nigra
Salix spp.
Populus spp.

Planera aquatica
Nyssa aquatica
Taxodium distichum

Fraxinus pennsylvanica
Liquidambar styraciflua
Quercus phellos

Nyssa biflora
Quercus nigra
Quercus michauxii
Quercus pagoda

Backswamp

Low ridge

High ridge

High ridge

Levee

Oxbow

Low ridge

Flats

Stream
channel

FIRST BOTTOM

SECOND BOTTOM

Profile of Coastal Plain river floodplain topography and vegetation

tively moderate degree of alluvial floodplain processes. This type of river is illustrated by the Ohoopee River, which arises in the lower Coastal Plain, flows sluggishly into the Altamaha River, and has a relatively inconspicuous floodplain associated with it.

The terms "blackwater" and "brownwater" relate to the water chemistry of the river systems, which is also determined by the physiographic characteristics of their sources. Blackwater streams are named for the clear but tea-colored water that seeps out of sandy soil underlying swamps or marshes. The sandy soils of the Coastal Plain headwaters do not retain the dissolved organic matter (DOM—primarily fulvic and humic acid) that is leached from terrestrial vegetation; hence, the DOM is transferred into the water. The high level of DOM stains the water a dark amber or garnet to black. As a result of the organic acids, the pH is low (Wharton and Brinson 1979; J. L. Meyer 1990). The hydrologic regimes of blackwater rivers are strongly driven by local precipitation. Due to the flat terrain, surface runoff is usually restricted to periods in which the water table is at or near the surface, usually in winter and spring. Floodplains on blackwater rivers may be underlain by an impermeable soil layer. During low-water or drought conditions, rainfall reaches blackwater streams primarily through surficial ground water, called "base flow." Because they are usually a low-gradient flow,

these streams carry little suspended material and the water is low in turbidity. The blackwater rivers of Georgia are often quite picturesque, with a striking contrast of white sands with the dark-colored water that may range in color from black (deep water) to garnet or amber (shallow water). In contrast, rivers that originate in the mountains or Piedmont have little DOM relative to the amount of inorganic materials transported. The water is derived primarily from surface runoff within the watershed; thus, they carry large amounts of suspended material that results in turbid conditions, and they are called "alluvial" or "brownwater" rivers.

Deviations from these strongly defined characteristics associated with Piedmont versus Coastal Plain origins are also prevalent in the river systems of Georgia. In southwestern Georgia, the Flint River is an example of a river that originates in the Piedmont and thus would be considered a typical alluvial system as it flows onto the Coastal Plain, where a vast Fall Line swamp is formed as sediments are deposited with decreased flow velocity. As it flows through the lower portion of the river basin, it traverses the Dougherty Plain, a physiographic district of shallow limestone formation. Here the river has cut into the Ocala limestone to reach the water table of the upper Floridan aquifer, and the river corridor is bounded by steep limestone bluffs and limestone shoals are abundant in

Alapaha River

the river (LaForge et al. 1925). Extensive bottomland floodplains are not associated with this section of the river, or they are fairly localized. Often, upland pine stands may be continuous to the river edge, where frequent prescribed fire has been applied to the uplands. Groundwater seeps into the river through the limestone bedrock or bubbles up through springs. During droughts, the base flow from the Floridan aquifer is the primary source of water. Then, the Flint River is very clear, lacking the turbidity normally associated with an alluvial river, when surface flows dominate.

In other cases, large streams such as Ichawaynochaway Creek, Kinchafoonee Creek, and Muckalee Creek originate in headwater swamps and wetland complexes of seeps and springs. Downstream, they flow into the Dougherty Plain limestone region. Thus, in periods of low flow, these streams appear clear and unstained as a result of dominance of groundwater aquifer input. Alternatively, during high flows, when streamflow is dominated by discharge from swamps and wetlands, the water appears stained (LaForge et al. 1925). Water chemistry based on DOM in these streams and rivers varies seasonally, so at times they may be considered blackwater streams and at other periods more closely resemble brownwater streams (Golladay and Battle 2002).

Likewise, differences among water chemistry of rivers can be explained by their different origins, even when they are entirely within the Coastal Plain (Smock and Gilinsky 1992). Peat-draining streams originate in swamps, bogs, and marshes and are more frequently found in the lower Coastal Plain. Streams that drain mineral soils occur most often in the upper Coastal Plain and the sandhills. The waters of the Satilla River, arising in the Tifton Uplands or lower Coastal Plain terraces of southeastern Georgia, are soft, acidic, and highly organic. The Ogeechee River is a low-gradient and stained blackwater river that meanders most of its length through Coastal Plain swamps; however, the water chemistry of this river differs from the low pH and low alkalinity typical of many blackwater rivers. The increased hardness, pH, and nutrients reflect the input from geologic formations of its headwaters at the edge of the Piedmont and from discharge of carbonate-rich waters from Magnolia Springs near Millen and several springs between Midville and Millen (Smock, Wright, and Benke 2005). Another example is the Ochlockonee River. It originates in the Coastal Plain and there has blackwater features; as it flows through the Tallahassee Hills, it picks up sand, silt, and clay, and thereby has alluvial river characteristics downstream (LaForge et al. 1925).

Our classification of vegetation of floodplain forests is determined by the dominant vegetation types that have established as a result of the dynamic and sometimes ancient river flow processes.

Cypress-Tupelo River Swamps

Cypress-tupelo river swamps are forested wetlands that occur in the floodplains of blackwater and brownwater rivers and larger streams in the Coastal Plain. These swamps develop in backswamps, secondary channels, sloughs, and swales of the river floodplain that are most frequently inundated. Long periods of inundation and anaerobic soil conditions restrict vegetation to species such as bald-cypress, Ogeechee lime, and/or water tupelo. These swamps may have standing water nearly all year.

At one time, many river swamps harbored cypress trees of immense size and great age. Cypress trees can live more than 1,000 years and attain a diameter of more than 11 feet. Most of the trees were cut long ago for timber, but occasionally enormous trees remain due to their inaccessibility or because they are hollow and

of little economic value. These ancient giants provide a historical glimpse into the immense cypress-tupelo forest stands that once occurred in Georgia and throughout the Southeast. Outstanding examples of old cypress stands in Georgia occur on Lewis Island in the Altamaha Basin (McIntosh County) and in Ebenezer Creek (Effingham County) (see the Featured Place).

PHYSICAL SETTING AND ECOLOGY

Cypress-tupelo river swamps are usually linear communities that range in size from less than 0.5 mile wide up to several miles wide. These river swamps are found in lower floodplains, secondary channels, oxbows, and sloughs that are seasonally to semipermanently flooded and are often referred to as deep water swamps (Penfound 1952; Sharitz and Mitsch 1993; W. H. Conner and Buford 1998). The flood regime and physiographic characteristics are the primary factors that interact to control the development of the floodplain vegetation through slight changes in elevation. The soils of the flats and sloughs are usually finer-textured sands and silts rather than the coarser, well-drained soils deposited on the levees or ridges. Significant deposits of organic muck occur in deep pools and sloughs, particularly in large alluvial rivers that originate outside the Coastal Plain and carry large sediment loads. These substrates provide nutrient-rich habitats for benthic organisms and are important in supporting fish and other vertebrate consumers in the river system.

The physiological stress caused by flooding and anaerobic conditions may be responsible for extremely slow growth rates of bald-cypress and water tupelo. They are very long-lived, with some reports of trees that are more than 1,000 years old (Stahle, Cleaveland, and Hehr 1998). A dwarf cypress swamp on the Alapaha River in Irwin County contains small, stunted pond-cypress trees approximately 800 years old.

The continuously moist conditions usually prohibit fire. Alternatively, fire may occur during prolonged periods of drought with significant or even catastrophic results. While mature cypress trees are generally tolerant to fire, broad-leaved swamp trees are very susceptible to injury and death (Ewel and Mitsch 1978). Stand-replacing fires may occur in cypress-dominated sites when drought conditions allow organic soils to smolder for long periods of time.

The most common silvicultural method of regenerating cypress-tupelo swamps following clearcutting or high-grading for timber is through stump sprouting and natural seeding coupled with control of competing species. Both species require a period of water drawdown for germination and establishment. Restoration attempts through planting seedlings of bald-cypress have demonstrated some success. Altered hydrologic conditions due to stream channelization or construction of roads, canals, levees, or dams that impact the frequency and timing of flooding can be problematic for long-term restoration and management. Dry-down events may not coincide with seedfall or the period of time needed for germination and seedling establishment (W. H. Conner and Buford 1988).

Cypress seedling establishment during dry period

VEGETATION

Cypress-tupelo swamp vegetation is dominated by bald-cypress, water tupelo, Ogeechee lime, and/or swamp tupelo. These species, particularly bald-cypress and water tupelo, are very tolerant of prolonged inundation. Dominance by water tupelo versus bald-cypress is probably related to a history of selective harvesting of cypress trees coupled with the insignificant degree of stump and root sprouting response of this species, thereby shifting the dominance of some former cypress-dominated swamps to water tupelo stands (Putnam, Furnival, and McKnight 1960). Other tree species may include black willow, cottonwood, water locust, water-elm and green ash. Swamp tupelo is less tolerant of prolonged inundation and occurs on higher, drier sites (Penfound 1952). The understory tree/shrub vegetation is usually patchy, often consisting of species such as swamp-privet, silky dogwood, red maple, and Carolina ash. Frequently present on elevated stumps are shrub species such as Virginia-willow, ti-ti, coastal sweet-pepperbush, coastal fetterbush, shining fetterbush, and bamboo-vine. Few herbaceous species are present, except on logs and stumps. During dry-down some ground cover species, such as lizard's-tail, knotweeds, and false-nettle, may be present.

Water tupelo buttress

ANIMALS

Birds are often more abundant in cypress-tupelo swamps than in adjacent uplands. These wetland forests provide feeding and nesting habitat for red-shouldered hawks, ospreys, and bald eagles and wintering sites for numerous songbirds. Swallow-tailed kites (see the Featured Animal) nest in super-emergent canopy pines interspersed on small sandy "islands" among bottomland forests (Swan 2010). The yellow-crowned night-heron, great blue heron, great egret, and white ibis also commonly occur in this zone. Swainson's warblers and prothonotary warblers are characteristic of

CHARACTERISTIC PLANTS OF CYPRESS-TUPELO RIVER SWAMPS

TREES

Carolina ash—*Fraxinus caroliniana*
Water locust—*Gleditsia aquatica*
Water tupelo—*Nyssa aquatica*
Swamp tupelo—*Nyssa biflora*
Ogeechee lime—*Nyssa ogeche*
Pond-cypress—*Taxodium ascendens*
Bald-cypress—*Taxodium distichum*

SHRUBS AND WOODY VINES

Coastal sweet-pepperbush—*Clethra alnifolia*
Silky dogwood—*Cornus amomum*
Ti-ti—*Cyrilla racemiflora*
Coastal fetterbush—*Eubotrys racemosa*
Swamp-privet—*Forestiera acuminata*
Shining fetterbush—*Lyonia lucida*

GROUND COVER

False-nettle—*Boehmeria cylindrica*
Sensitive fern—*Onoclea sensibilis*
Royal fern—*Osmunda regalis*
Knotweeds—*Polygonum spp.*
Lizard's-tail—*Saururus cernuus*
Netted chain fern—*Woodwardia areolata*
Virginia chain fern—*Woodwardia virginiana*

southern swamps and bottomlands (R. E. Brown and Dickson 1994; Petit 1999). Wood ducks are common in these habitats, especially where hollow trees are prevalent (Hepp and Bellrose 1995).

Sloughs and other semipermanently flooded environments on the floodplain also support several aquatic amphibians, including waterdogs, sirens, and amphiumas. Only a few frogs are restricted to river swamps, such as the bird-voiced treefrog. American alligators frequently use the river floodplain as habitat. They also may have direct travel corridors to upland ponds for nesting sites. Common snakes include the red-bellied, the brown watersnake, and the cottonmouth. Because of their coloration with dark brown splotches and large size, brown watersnakes are often confused with the venomous cottonmouth. Cottonmouths are distinctive, with a dark stripe on the side of the jaw, heat-sensing pits on the face, and vertical pupils. Seldom-seen snakes include the rainbow, mud, black swamp, and striped crayfish snake (Wharton et al. 1982; Jensen, Dorcas, and Gibbons 2008; T. Mills 2008; Winne and Poppy 2008). A river turtle that is particularly associated with swamps is the common musk turtle (Metts 2008).

Species richness of macroinvertebrates in Coastal Plain streams and associated floodplain forests is very high, including numerous species of crayfish (Wharton et al. 1981; Smock, Wright, and Benke 2005). Freshwater mussels are associated with the river channel, where they live on the river bottom or burrow into river sediments. River drainages often have unique assemblages of mussels and even harbor species endemic to the drainage system.

The most characteristic fish in sloughs are mosquito fish, swamp darter, cypress nubbiworm, redfin pickerel, bowfin, and chain pickerel. Fish concentrate in deep holes during periodic dry-downs. River otters and mink feed heavily on crayfish in river swamps. Beaver are frequent along smaller streams and feed on tree bark.

Cypress knees

Swallow-Tailed Kite (*Elanoides forficatus*)

The swallow-tailed kite is a migratory raptor that breeds in the southeastern United States and winters in south-central South America, primarily in Brazil (K. D. Meyer 1995). Also known as the fork-tailed kite, this bird is easily recognized by its black-and-white color pattern and its elongated, deeply forked tail (Swan 2010). Prior to the 1900s, the swallow-tailed kite nested in as many as 21 states, ranging as far north

as Minnesota. Populations declined precipitously during the early 20th century, however, due to shooting, egg-collecting, and habitat destruction. The current breeding range is limited to the South Atlantic and Gulf Coast states from South Carolina to Texas (K. D. Meyer 1995), with a few recent nesting occurrences documented from Arkansas and North Carolina (Swan 2010). Florida accounts for approximately two-thirds of the U.S. population. In Georgia, the swallow-tailed kite is found primarily along the river swamps of the Altamaha, Ogeechee, and Satilla Rivers as well as in the Okefenokee Swamp and other wetlands along the southern border of the state. Recent surveys have also located nests along the Withlacoochee, Alapaha, Ocmulgee, and Oconee Rivers (Swan 2010). Most nests in Georgia are located in the tops of very tall loblolly pines within or adjacent to bottomland forests associated with the river. The majority of these nests are located on private lands managed by industrial forest companies.

The swallow-tailed kite feeds primarily by soaring over forests or fields and capturing flying insects, which form the major part of its diet. During the breeding season, however, this raptor also feeds on small amphibians, reptiles, and nestling birds, usually collecting these directly from trees and shrubs (K. D. Meyer 1995).

Though no longer threatened by shooting or egg collection, this species is still impacted by loss of nesting and foraging habitat. Since 1997, the Georgia Department of Natural Resources has conducted surveys of nesting sites and worked to obtain management agreements with private landowners to protect nest trees. The swallow-tailed kite is listed as Rare in Georgia.

Ebenezer Creek Boat Ramp

Ebenezer Creek Boat Ramp is a small tract (about 1.5 acres) owned by Effingham County where Longbridge Road (County Road 307) crosses Ebenezer Creek. A boat ramp offers an opportunity for canoe trips down the lower portion of the creek. At this site, cypress-water tupelo swamps can also be approached from the uplands. At low water, the floodplain is very accessible from the parking lot. Although there is no designated trail, walk westward (upstream) a short distance along the creek. Near the edge of the parking lot, the uplands are dominated by sand laurel oak, loblolly pine, and saw palmetto. Downslope, this forest transitions into a swamp dominated by bald-cypress and water tupelo with red maple, sweet gum, and Carolina ash. The swamp is infested with the invasive Chinese tallow-tree. The section of Ebenezer Creek from Longbridge Road to the confluence with the Savannah River (about 7 miles downstream) is a designated National Natural Landmark as well as the only State Scenic River in the Coastal Plain of Georgia. The lower portion of this blackwater creek represents a former coastal embayment and is broad with a very low gradient near the mouth of the creek. It is considered a "backwater swamp" because water levels in the creek rise and fall with flow levels in the Savannah River (these are not tidal fluctuations—the limit of tidal influence is downstream near Bear Island). Along this 7-mile stretch, outstanding examples of mature and old-growth cypress-tupelo swamp can be viewed by boat. Some bald-cypress trees are more than 1,000 years old (Wharton 1978). Just below the confluence with the Savannah River is a privately owned boat ramp that can be used as a take-out point.

Location: Go north from Rincon on Ga. Hwy. 21 to Ga. Hwy. 275, turn right, and go east to CR 307, then north to the parking area on the left just before the bridge. Google Earth GPS approximate coordinates at the bridge: N 32.364419/W 081.230885.

Bottomland Hardwoods

Bottomland hardwood forests occur on relict natural levees, terraces, point bar ridges, and other relatively high parts of floodplain flats along blackwater and alluvial streams in the Coastal Plain. They are an important vegetation type in Georgia in terms of areal extent and overall species diversity. The mosaic distribution of microtopography and soil textures results in diverse assemblages of deciduous hardwood species adapted to periods of inundation. These include water oak, willow oak, red maple, sweet gum, Shumard oak, swamp chestnut oak, laurel oak, green ash, overcup oak, and water hickory, and evergreen species such as southern magnolia and live oak. Because of their linear association with streams and rivers, bottomland forests are extremely important wildlife corridors.

PHYSICAL SETTING AND ECOLOGY

Bottomland forests occur on the first bottoms, or flats, adjacent to river levees and are usually flooded in winter and early spring. Inundated conditions may extend well into the growing season, depending on rainfall and topographic position. With the exception of sloughs and backswamps, this zone has the longest hydroperiod of the floodplain. Soils vary from highly organic to well-drained sands, depending on depositional patterns with flooding in the floodplain. Bottomlands may extend for thousands of acres, particularly along the floodplains of large river systems such as the Altamaha River. Flooding regulates the chemical properties of floodplain soils through exogenous input of sediments and nutrients, production of anaerobic soil conditions, the importing of dissolved organic matter, and the exporting of accumulations of organic detritus. Due to periodic nutrient input with inundation, the bottomland soils are often very fertile and tree growth is rapid.

Bottomland hardwood forests of the Coastal Plain represent an important wetland type in Georgia in terms of overall species diversity and areal extent. These forests are a source of commercially valuable timber, particularly bottomland oak species and bald-cypress. Bottomland forests have a long history of human disturbance, with cultivation extending back to Native Americans and early settlement timber harvest along navigable streams. Thousands of acres of Coastal Plain floodplains in Georgia have been cleared for agriculture or timber, resulting in significant alteration or loss of habitat. In many cases, these floodplains have been ditched and converted to pine plantations. Often, forest disturbances such as clearcutting or road construction have created opportunities for invasion of exotic species such as Chinese privet, Nepal grass, and Japanese honeysuckle.

Construction of reservoirs on several major alluvial rivers in Georgia has greatly modified the hydrology of Coastal Plain bottomland hardwood forests. As a result of hydrologic control, the timing, duration, and extent of overbank flooding events have been altered and significantly influence forest successional dynamics.

Today, old-growth bottomland hardwood stands are very rare in the Southeast (Mitchell et al. 2009). In spite of this, mature second-growth stands provide some of the structural characteristics important for biodiversity. For many species of woodpeckers, old and senescing trees supply quality nesting and foraging habitats. Other species, including Rafinesque's big-eared bat and wood ducks, also depend on mature trees for roosting habitat. Fragmentation of expansive forested habitat is detrimental to species with large ranges such as black bear or Florida panther. Disruption of habitat by agricultural use or development may also result in patches too small to support viable populations of some bird species. Estimates of desired bottomland forest patch sizes for some interior bird species range from 40,000 to 100,000 acres (Twedt, Uihlein, and Elliott 2006).

One management opportunity to enlarge and buffer existing mature tracts on public and private land is to "grow" additional forests with mature growth characteristics (R. B. Hamilton, Barrow, and Ouchley 2005). To encourage development of mature bottomland forests, long-rotation timber management, protected set-asides, and conservation easements need to be implemented (Mitchell et al. 2009).

VEGETATION

Zonation of bottomland hardwood forests is strongly driven by the periodicity and duration of inundation and the tolerance of species to the stresses of flood conditions. Inundated conditions alter soil chemical properties by producing low-oxygen conditions and altering nutrient availability. Other environmental factors such as nutrient status, competition, and soil texture are also determinants. Thus, the distribution of vegetation is complex. Typically, dominant canopy species include laurel oak, red maple, green ash, swamp tupelo, American elm, overcup oak, willow oak, and water hickory. Carolina ash occasionally dominates in slightly wetter depressions. Exceptional examples of old-growth bottomland forests are found in the Moody Forest Natural Area (see the Featured Place) and in tributaries of the Ocmulgee River.

On somewhat better-drained sites, with flooding for approximately one to four weeks in the growing season, bitternut hickory, winged elm, swamp chestnut oak, sweet gum, water oak, and cherrybark oak may occur. Shumard oak is also present, particularly in areas associated with basic soil conditions, such as bottomlands in the Flint River and Chattahoochee River drainages. Two pine species, spruce pine and loblolly pine, occur in many bottomlands. Transitional areas to upland forests include black cherry, American beech, southern magnolia, sassafras, white oak, flowering dogwood, basswood, common pawpaw, red hickory, pignut hickory, and wafer-ash (Kellison et al. 1998).

Piedmont azalea

Canebrake

Mature bottomland forests may have trees with large crowns forming a closed canopy with a very sparse understory or herbaceous layer due to frequent flooding or insufficient light. Stands that have been disturbed may have thick shrub layers of Virginia-willow, shining fetterbush, horsesugar, coastal sweet-pepperbush, dwarf palmetto, and coastal fetterbush.

In some upland-wetland transition zones or even on some broad interstream flats, an almost impenetrable understory of river cane becomes established following disturbances such as fire, treefalls, and severe floods. Once established, river cane can persist for long periods in closed-canopy floodplain forests, but without periodic fire it will gradually decrease in abundance. A characteristic understory dominant of bottomland forests in the Chickasawhatchee Wildlife Management Area is needle palm.

Extensive stands of river cane (also called giant cane), are more common and more extensive along large alluvial rivers than those with blackwater characteristics. Early explorers referred to extensive riparian cane bottoms and canebrakes; obviously, this community type has declined significantly since pre-Columbian times (Bartram 1791; Hawkins 1799). Whether canebrakes have declined with regional fire suppression or whether the prevalence of this species was once associated with fires ignited by Native Americans is debated (S. G. Platt and Brantley 1997). Also, extensively practiced woodland cattle grazing may have contributed to decline. A large canebrake occurs in the Ocmulgee River basin, south of Macon. An example of a canebrake in this watershed can be viewed at the Bond Swamp National Wildlife Refuge (Bibb and Twiggs Counties). Cane is a clonal species that rapidly responds to canopy openings. It usually dies after flowering. The role of successful pollination and seed production in maintenance of the population is unknown (Gagnon, Platt, and Moser 2007). Restoration efforts include hardwood canopy removal and control of competing species such as the exotic Chinese privet and reintroduction of fire. Transplantation of culms obtained from donor sites has shown some promise, but survivorship is extremely dependent on precipitation (Klaus and Klaus 2009).

THE LOST GORDONIA (*FRANKLINIA ALATAMAHA*)

Lost gordonia

Franklinia, also known as the Franklin tree or lost gordonia, is a botanical enigma in Georgia. This beautiful shrub was discovered in 1765 by John and William Bartram as they explored the swamplands of the Altamaha River. The exact site is not known but is thought to have been a 2- to 3-acre stand within a sandhill seepage swamp in McIntosh County along the Altamaha River (F. Harper 1998). They named the tree in honor of their friend Benjamin Franklin and the site of discovery, along the Altamaha River. William Bartram returned to this same population again in the 1770s and noted that he knew of no other locations of the plant. The last definitive sighting of the tree in nature occurred in 1803. All Franklin trees today are descendants propagated from seed collections made by the Bartrams and taken to their Philadelphia garden. Whether or not this tree is actually native to Georgia has been debated, but its possible origin remains a mystery (Lewis 2004). The Franklin tree is a deciduous small tree or large shrub in the family Theaceae (somewhat resembling its relative, loblolly bay). The Franklin tree attains a height of 15–20 feet and has deciduous dark green leaves that turn red, orange, or pink in the fall. Its most striking feature is its fragrant and showy 2- to 3-inch snow-white flowers, with clusters of golden yellow stamens in the centers. The tree flowers from late summer until frost. It actually does not grow well or reproduce in the Coastal Plain but seems to grow best in climates with cooler summer temperatures and in well-drained soils.

CHARACTERISTIC PLANTS OF BOTTOMLAND HARDWOODS

TREES

Red maple—Acer rubrum

Common pawpaw—Asimina triloba

Musclewood—Carpinus caroliniana

Water hickory—Carya aquatica

Bitternut hickory—Carya cordiformis

Sugarberry—Celtis laevigata

American persimmon—Diospyros virginiana

Green ash—Fraxinus pennsylvanica

Common two-wing silverbell— Halesia diptera

Sweet gum—Liquidambar styraciflua

Swamp tupelo—Nyssa biflora

Ironwood—Ostrya virginiana

Spruce pine—Pinus glabra

Loblolly pine—Pinus taeda

Laurel oak—Quercus laurifolia

Swamp chestnut oak—Quercus michauxii

Water oak—Quercus nigra

Cherrybark oak—Quercus pagoda

Willow oak—Quercus phellos

Shumard oak—Quercus shumardii

Live oak—Quercus virginiana

American elm—Ulmus americana

SHRUBS AND WOODY VINES

Peppervine—Ampelopsis arborea

American rattan—Berchemia scandens

Trumpet-creeper—Campsis radicans

Sweet bay—Magnolia virginiana

Virginia-creeper—Parthenocissus quinquefolia

Dwarf palmetto—Sabal minor

Whiteleaf greenbrier—Smilax glauca

Poison ivy—Toxicodendron radicans

ANIMALS

The abundance of mast-producing species, as well as bole and branch cavities of the overstory trees, contribute to the value of bottomland hardwoods as wildlife habitat, particularly in contrast to adjacent conifer-dominated uplands. The linear distribution of hardwood forests functions as important corridors for local and regional movements of animals, and water flow fosters larval dispersal of invertebrates (Sharitz and Mitsch 1993).

Many species of birds use the floodplain forests, and turkeys and woodcocks are particularly associated with bottomland hardwoods. Barred owls, red-shouldered hawks, and woodpeckers usually nest in the larger trees. Bottomland sites are important for wintering wood ducks that take advantage of rising and falling water levels for enhanced foraging opportunities. The extensive bottomland forests of the Coastal Plain of Georgia serve as a major migration flyway for sandhill cranes, bald eagles, Mississippi kites, and blue-gray gnatcatchers. The swamp complex of the Altamaha and Ocmulgee Rivers harbors one of the richest avian faunas in the region and provides a critical stopover habitat for millions of migrant birds each spring and fall. Particularly noteworthy specialists are the prothonotary warbler and Swainson's warbler (see the Featured Animal). The prothonotary warbler prefers flooded bottomlands and requires extensive tracts of streamside riparian zones. Other bottomland breeding birds include hooded warblers and Acadian flycatchers. The loss of habitat has had detrimental effects on this species in the Southeast and is of growing conservation concern. The loss of large acreage of the ancient bottom-land forests, with their huge old-growth trees, cane-brakes, and frequent snags, has probably also resulted in the extinction of two bird species, the Bachman's warbler and the ivory-billed woodpecker.

No reptiles are specialists in this habitat, but many are abundant. Eastern box turtles and mud turtles are common, as well as numerous species of non-venomous snakes such as banded watersnakes, common kingsnakes, brown watersnakes, and red-bellied snakes. Timber rattlesnakes (also known as cane-brake rattlesnakes in the Coastal Plain) are associated with bottomland hardwood forests and other stream corridors, avoiding open, frequently burned longleaf pine uplands (W. H. Martin, Stevenson, and Spivey 2008). With widespread fire suppression of upland habitats and increased composition of hardwoods and mixed pine-hardwoods, Coastal Plain populations of timber rattlesnakes have likely increased. Glossy cray-fish snakes are limited to the Coastal Plain and are found primarily in bottomland wetlands, seldom far from water. Relatively few records of this snake have been reported (Dorcas and Gibbons 2008).

Several lepidopteran caterpillars, including Carolina roadside skipper, southern pearly-eye, and creole pearly-eye, are cane specialists (S. G. Platt, Brantly, and Rainwater 2001). Abundant mast from hickories and oaks supports large numbers of deer. Other generalist mammals that frequent bottomlands include the black bear, gray fox, raccoon, and bobcat. Although primarily in the Piedmont of Georgia, swamp rabbits also inhabit canebrakes in the Coastal Plain. These large rabbits forage on cane shoots and have earned the local names "cane cutter" and "cane jake."

Swainson's Warbler
(*Limnothlypis swainsonii*)

Swainson's warbler is small and rather nondescript, being plain olive-brown above and pale yellow-white below. Swainson's warblers have a whitish eyebrow stripe that runs above their eye, and the top of their head is a rusty brown. Males and females are very similar in appearance. This is a migratory species, with part of the population wintering in the Greater Antilles and part wintering in the Yucatán Peninsula region (R. E. Brown and Dickson 1994; Somershoe, Hudman, and Chandler 2003).

Swainson's warbler breeds in southeastern bottomland forests and more rarely occurs in rhododendron thickets in the southern Appalachian Mountains. The nests are fairly large and bulky and are constructed from moss, grass, and small leaves. They are usually situated above ground in a tangle of tall reeds or vines (Somershoe, Hudman, and Chandler 2003). Thickets of small cane and river cane are associated with breed-

ing success (R. E. Brown and Dickson 1994; Klaus 2010b). They will also nest in vine tangles of grapes, cross-vine, poison ivy, greenbriers, trumpet-creeper, peppervine, Virginia-creeper, American rattan, and blackberry.

Populations of Swainson's warblers have declined during recent decades as bottomland forests have come under increasingly intensive management and large areas have been converted to other land uses. In the Coastal Plain and Piedmont, it is most common in mature forests that have a fairly dense upper canopy, a dense mid-story canopy and shrub layer, and little herbaceous cover on the ground. It also occurs at times in early successional forests with a dense layer of shrubs and little herbaceous ground cover (Somershoe, Hudman, and Chandler 2003; Klaus 2010b).

Swainson's warblers can be viewed in bottomland hardwoods along the Altamaha River at Big Hammock Wildlife Management Area (Tattnall County) and Moody Forest Natural Area (Appling County) and at Bond Swamp National Wildlife Refuge (Twiggs and Bibb Counties) along the Ocmulgee River.

Moody Forest Natural Area

The Altamaha River Trail in Moody Forest Natural Area is a 2-mile hike through the floodplain of the Altamaha River and features several plant communities. Beginning at an upland site near the parking area kiosk, the trail traverses an early successional forest dominated by oaks and hickories, including water oak, willow oak, laurel oak, and pignut hickory. The trail continues into a beautiful and extensive old-growth bottomland forest. Here the floodplain forest is dominated by massive swamp chestnut oak, cherrybark oak, overcup oak, American elm, water hickory, spruce pine, and musclewood. Dwarf palmetto is a dominant in the understory. At one point, the trail crosses over a slough, a former river channel where deep water is ponded when the river is high or flooding. Here large bald-cypress and water tupelo dominate. Another ex-ample of the shifting river channel can be viewed along the bank overlooking Alligator Lake. Formerly this lake was the main channel of the Altamaha River, but deposition of soils has altered the course of the river, leaving behind a long, narrow lake cut off from the main flow of the river. As the trail approaches the river, the distinctively higher ground of the river levee can be observed.

Location: From U.S. Hwy. 341 in Baxley, take U.S. 1/Ga. Hwy. 15 (north) for approximately 9 miles. Turn right (east) on Lennox Rd. Turn left onto Spring Branch until a T-intersection with East River Rd. Turn right on East River Rd. Turn left (north) onto Morris Landing Rd. The River Trail trailhead is on the right at the parking area. Google Earth GPS approximate coordinates at the parking area: N 31.906962/W 082.312153.

Riverbanks and Levees

Riverbank and levee forests are hardwood-dominated forests that border river channels. They develop on the active levees and stable banks of medium to large blackwater and alluvial streams, as well as on sand bars that form on the inward sides of river meanders. These are geomorphically active areas that support pioneer species such as American sycamore, red maple, river birch, and southern catalpa.

PHYSICAL SETTING AND ECOLOGY

River levees are generally the highest elevations on the floodplain and are formed from deposition of sediments from overbank flooding. The ridge usually slopes sharply toward the river and more gently away from it. The height, width, soil texture, and drainage characteristics of natural levees vary considerably depending on the velocity and volume of water. These ridges only occupy a small portion of a floodplain, but because of the variations on individual levees forming

microenvironments these sites often harbor the highest tree species richness on the floodplain. Levees of alluvial rivers, particularly near the Fall Line, are generally larger and topographically higher because the sudden reduction in current velocity causes large-sized sediments to settle quickly. Because blackwater rivers carry less sediment, levee formation is usually less striking than that of alluvial rivers. Blackwater river levees are rarely continuous, having frequent openings of sloughs and tributaries that drain adjacent flats into the river. These natural breaks in levees facilitate the spread of riverflow throughout the floodplain. Flooding of levees occurs nearly every year for at least a portion of the growing season.

Levee communities are dominated by forces of the river and are frequently disturbed by shifting alluvium and the energy of floodwaters. For this reason, species tolerant of physical disturbance are usually present. As the river channel is altered, a levee will become inactive, forming a ridge and swale within the more recent floodplain adjacent to a swale. The soil on this ridge is better drained and may support species less tolerant of long periods of inundation than in the adjacent swale or bottomland. Although blackwater and alluvial river systems in Georgia differ in water chemistry, hydrology, and species assemblages, the plant species found on stream banks of these river systems are often very similar.

Unrestricted cattle-grazing along stream banks can have significant negative impacts on water quality, bank stability, and riparian vegetation. Increased nutrient and fecal bacteria concentrations are often detected in flowing water as a result of direct fecal deposition into the stream. Increased sediment load and stream turbidity are associated with use of stream banks by livestock. During flood events, stream bank stability declines with loss of vegetation as a result of soil compaction and trampling (Armour, Duff, and Elmore 1991).

In addition to stabilization of the bank, the vegetation of the stream bank has an important role in contributing coarse woody debris to the stream (Palik et al. 1998). Particularly along stream reaches with higher terraces, tree mortality may be associated with flood events. These dead trees wash into the stream and provide substrate for fish and invertebrates, as well as contribute organic matter to the stream ecosystem (Benke et al. 1984, 1985). Although rehabilitation strategies for streams often include selective placement of coarse woody debris in the channel (Gore and Shields 1995), this may be considered a short-term solution. The preservation and restoration of streamside forests as a source of input of dead trees into the stream is recommended (Palik et al. 1998). In Georgia, riparian zones of Coastal Plain streams and rivers are protected from disturbance that removes vegetation or involves grading within a 25-foot buffer from the edge of the stream.

VEGETATION

On newly formed sand bars or recently exposed river margins, cottonwood, black willow, or ti-ti may become established. As river banks become more stabilized, sweet gum, sycamore, river birch, water-elm, silver maple, and southern catalpa are prevalent in this community. On levees that have become inactive due to changes in stream flows, forests may succeed to more typical bottomland hardwood forests (Sharitz and Mitsch 1993; Hupp 2000). A series of levees and sloughs along the Altamaha River in Big Hammock Wildlife Management Area can be viewed along the

Virginia-willow

main road where it parallels the river. On levees of deep, well-drained soils, white oak, southern sugar maple, northern witch-hazel, tulip-tree, southern magnolia, and live oak often occur. The highest ridges often support eastern red cedar, especially in areas associated with limestone. Tree diversity associated with stream banks is extremely high in some cases. For example, a study on the streamside of natural levees of Ichawaynochaway Creek (Baker County) reported 47 woody species, dominated by Carolina ash, live oak, and eastern red cedar (Palik et al. 1998). Along lower-lying river fronts, bald-cypress, swamp tupelo, water tupelo, or Ogeechee lime are often prevalent. Vines are common along riverbanks because of the availability of sunlight. Conspicuous vines that climb into the tree canopies include peppervine, trumpet-creeper, cross-vine, grape vines, American rattan, and woolly dutchman's-pipe. In addition, poison ivy and greenbriers are common.

CHARACTERISTIC PLANTS OF RIVERBANKS AND LEVEES

TREES

Southern sugar maple—Acer floridanum

Red maple—Acer rubrum

Silver maple—Acer saccharinum

Tag alder—Alnus serrulata

River birch—Betula nigra

Bitternut hickory—Carya cordiformis

Pignut hickory—Carya glabra

Southern catalpa—Catalpa bignonioides

Green ash—Fraxinus pennsylvanica

Eastern red cedar—Juniperus virginiana

Sweet gum—Liquidambar styraciflua

Water-elm—Planera aquatica

American sycamore—Platanus occidentalis

Laurel oak—Quercus laurifolia

Water oak—Quercus nigra

Black willow—Salix nigra

Winged elm—Ulmus alata

SHRUBS AND WOODY VINES

Tall indigo-bush—Amorpha fruticosa

Cross-vine—Bignonia capreolata

Trumpet-creeper—Campsis radicans

Woolly dutchman's-pipe—Isotrema tomentosum

Virginia-willow—Itea virginica

Catbrier—Smilax bona-nox

Whiteleaf greenbrier—Smilax glauca

Common greenbrier—Smilax rotundifolia

Poison ivy—Toxicodendron radicans

Sparkleberry—Vaccinium arboreum

Southern wild raisin—Viburnum nudum

GROUND COVER

River oats—Chasmanthium latifolium

Slender spikegrass—Chasmanthium laxum

Eastern needlegrass—Piptochaetium avenaceum

Riverbank with break in levee

River oats

ANIMALS

The forested stream edge offers unique foraging and nesting habitats. The belted kingfisher occurs throughout the state but is exclusively associated with river and stream courses and other bodies of water such as ponds. In addition to a requirement for waters with fish and other prey (tadpoles, frogs), the kingfisher prefers to nest in cavities dug in stream banks. During the breeding season the mated pair defends a territory against other kingfishers (Hamas 1994). Louisiana waterthrushes strictly require forested streams for food and nesting habitat, preferring forested riparian buffers greater than 350 feet in width. Prothonotary warblers nest along large rivers with forested margins greater than 100 feet (Jensen 2010). They usually build their nests in tree cavities over the water or even in cypress knees. Kentucky warblers and yellow-billed cuckoos nest along stream banks, particularly if dense understory vegetation is present. Other species that are often associated with stream banks are bald eagles, turkey vultures, ospreys, great blue herons, and wood ducks.

River frogs are found on river banks and breed in the river. Other frogs that can often be heard calling from stream banks are the oak toad, bird-voiced treefrog, Cope's gray treefrog, green treefrog, and green frog. Turtles spend much of their lives in the water but sun along the shore. Species such as river cooters, pond sliders, and alligator snapping turtles frequently nest along the riverbank. The state Threatened Barbour's map turtle nests along the edge of rivers and streams of the Flint and Chattahoochee River drainages (L. L. Smith et al. 2006).

Typical snakes include the ringnecked snake, mud snake, scarlet kingsnake, red-bellied snake, banded watersnake, brown watersnake, and rough green snake. In open areas, such as frequently burned longleaf pine uplands, the timber rattlesnake is limited to forested stream corridors (W. H. Martin, Stevenson, and Spivey 2008). A strongly aquatic and secretive snake, the rainbow snake, occurs along spring runs and moving water in the Coastal Plain (T. Mills 2008).

River Otter (*Lontra canadensis*)

River otters are common throughout the state in lakes, ponds, marshes, rivers, and streams. While many states experienced significant declines during the mid-1800s to 1900s due to excessive trapping for the fur trade, populations in Georgia remained fairly healthy. Today, river otters are abundant throughout the state, including in north Georgia where their numbers were once notably diminished (Georgia Wildlife Web 2008).

These charismatic members of the weasel family (Mustelidae) range in size from 3 to 5 feet long and weigh 15 to 30 pounds. River otters are amphibious and can stay submerged for several minutes. The torpedo-shaped body and muscular tail aid them in swimming and diving. The sleek, thick fur is usually dark brown but may range from almost black to reddish on the back and sides. The belly is usually silvery or grayish brown, and the throat and cheeks are silvery to yellowish brown. River otters reach sexual maturity at the age of two years. Breeding takes place in March through April and typically two to four young, called "kits," are born in underground dens the following late winter or early spring (Georgia Wildlife Web 2008).

River otters primarily use waterways as travel paths but also travel overland between rivers, streams, or ponds on terrestrial paths that are regularly used for years. They use scent posts along these paths and waterways to mark territories and communicate with other otters in the area. They also communicate with a series of chirps and whistles. Males may occupy up to 50 miles of a stream throughout the course of a year, whereas females have a much smaller home range. River otters are carnivores, mostly preying on fish, but they also eat crustaceans, amphibians, reptiles, birds, mammals, and insects. In coastal habitats, crabs and young alligators are often consumed.

Altamaha Park

The short gravel trail from the parking lot of Altamaha Park (Glenn County) enters a bottomland forest dominated by spruce pine, pignut hickory, laurel oak, and live oak. Mid-story dominants include musclewood, American holly, and parsley haw. Within a short distance into the forest northward and parallel to the Altamaha River, an impressive bald-cypress-gum swamp associated with a meandering slough will be encountered near its exit to the river. The slough surrounds a small bottomland forested area, forming a swamp island. Just downstream from the mouth of the slough is a distinctively elevated river levee formation. Along the riverbank, the vegetation is dominated by spruce pine, loblolly pine, sweet gum, river birch,

water-elm, musclewood, Sebastian-bush, American holly, and live oak. Trumpet-creeper, grape vines, greenbriers, and poison ivy are tangled into the tree crowns. Several species of grass form a dense ground cover.

Location: From U.S. Hwy. 341 in Everett, take the Altamaha Park Rd. Pavement ends; continue on the dirt road through the private fish camp along river. Go past parking by the general store to the end of the road and the public parking area. The trail from the parking is gravel north along the river. Follow the trail to the river and a slough. The distinctive levee feature occurs along the riverbank just downstream from this point. Google Earth GPS approximate coordinates at the parking area: N 31.429142/W 081.607567.

Small Stream Floodplain Forests

Small stream floodplain forests occur on narrow flood-plains of headwater drainages and low-gradient small creeks and streams throughout the Coastal Plain. Although the drainage gradient is low and little accumulated litter or sediments are transported, the gradient is enough to promote streamflow as opposed to the development of a seepage swamp. These forests often have highly acidic and nutrient-poor soils. Streams that arise from seepage waters of swamps are often darkly stained with tannic acids and are called "blackwater branches" or "blackwater streams." The wetland vegetation of the stream floodplain is dominated by a dense forest of broad-leaved evergreen and deciduous trees, shrubs, and vines.

PHYSICAL SETTING AND ECOLOGY

Small stream floodplains are found along the channels of small creeks and headwater streams that originate in the Coastal Plain. Generally, floodplains are narrow, and features such as levees, ridges, basins, and sloughs are less apparent. The stream banks are seldom well defined, and extensive bottomland forests are not usually associated with these small drainages. Although stream meanders occur, the resulting ridges and sloughs are not well developed and soil texture varies less across the floodplain than on larger drainages (J. D. Hodges 1998). Soils along the stream edge are generally sands or sandy loams with finer-textured sands and silts on the flats and sloughs. Delineating a small stream or branch versus a river is arbitrary and somewhat difficult to quantify in terms of size. Small streams with blackwater characteristics may eventually flow into large alluvial rivers with an abrupt change in physical characteristics. The change is much more gradual when the streams are more equal in size. The hydrologic regime of small blackwater streams is extremely variable, with floods of short duration that are dependent on local weather events. Particularly during summer months, the discharge in streams may dwindle to near zero. Some streams may have temporal characteristics that are more similar to alluvial conditions, carrying suspended sediments due to agricultural inputs following storm events.

In Georgia, small stream floodplain forests occur throughout the Coastal Plain and are particularly well developed in the Tifton Uplands in southwestern Georgia, forming a dense dendritic pattern across the landscape. Here they are important as buffers to non-point-source agricultural chemical, nutrient, and sediment input throughout the regional watershed because the forest vegetation helps retard excessive runoff (Lowrance 1992; Lowrance et al. 1984, 1997). Good examples are the Little River watershed (Tift County) and Warrior Creek watershed (Worth County). Many of the floodplains associated with headwaters and small drainages have been impounded as farm ponds or have been impacted by grazing, planted pines, or fire suppression.

Conservation efforts to retain vegetation of small stream floodplains to serve as buffers for protecting streams from non-point-source pollution are needed and are particularly important in agricultural landscapes for the interception of sediment, nutrients, and pesticides. Poorly engineered dirt roads can add significant amounts of sediment to streams and riparian habitats where they cross or encroach upon these habitats. In some cases where fire is used in adjacent uplands, firebreaks are plowed to exclude these corridors from fire, resulting in loss of ecotonal species between upland and riparian habitats. In some cases, these firebreaks actually function as ditches, altering water flow or contributing to runoff. Implementation of best management practices for agriculture and forestry activities, regulations regarding surface water withdrawals, and enlisting conservation easements and incentive programs are necessary to protect the small stream corridor from disturbance.

VEGETATION

Generally, no well-defined riverbank and levee forest or bottomland hardwood forest is associated with these floodplains because of the small drainage area and low flow. Consequently, species that might be more readily associated with distinct levees or backswamps in larger river systems occur in more mixed stands in this community. Thus, small stream floodplains are distinguished from river swamps or bottomland floodplains based on the absence of alluvial landforms that promote levee forests or bottomland hardwoods; however, this distinction is fairly arbitrary. Small stream floodplains transition rapidly into upland communities, which are distinguished by a prevalence of upland rather than obligate wetland species (J. D. Hodges 1998). With fire suppression, the more fire-intolerant hardwood species become established in upland sites.

The swamp vegetation associated with this narrow floodplain is dominated by bald-cypress, swamp

Cinnamon fern

CHARACTERISTIC PLANTS OF SMALL STREAM FLOODPLAIN FORESTS

TREES

Red maple—Acer rubrum
Sweet gum—Liquidambar styraciflua
Swamp tupelo—Nyssa biflora
Ogeechee lime—Nyssa ogeche
Laurel oak—Quercus laurifolia
Overcup oak—Quercus lyrata
Water oak—Quercus nigra
Cherrybark oak—Quercus pagoda
Bald-cypress—Taxodium distichum

SHRUBS AND WOODY VINES

Peppervine—Ampelopsis arborea
American rattan—Berchemia scandens
Buckwheat-tree—Cliftonia monophylla
Ti-ti—Cyrilla racemiflora
Loblolly bay—Gordonia lasianthus
Dahoon—Ilex cassine
Virginia-willow—Itea virginica
Sweet bay—Magnolia virginiana
Water-elm—Planera aquatica
Swamp rose—Rosa palustris
Whiteleaf greenbrier—Smilax glauca
Bamboo-vine—Smilax laurifolia
Common greenbrier—Smilax rotundifolia
Jackson-brier—Smilax smallii
Coral greenbrier—Smilax walteri
Poison ivy—Toxicodendron radicans

GROUND COVER

Sensitive fern—Onoclea sensibilis
Cinnamon fern—Osmundastrum cinnamomeum
Lizard's-tail—Saururus cernuus

tupelo, or Ogeechee lime. Other tree and shrub species include red maple, laurel oak, overcup oak, cherrybark oak, water oak, sweet gum, common two-wing silverbell, southern sugar maple, northern witch-hazel, swamp bay, loblolly bay, sweet bay, ti-ti, Virginia-willow, buckwheat-tree, water-elm, and dahoon. Numerous species of woody vines occur such as American rattan, coral greenbrier, bamboo-vine, and peppervine. The herbaceous flora is often sparse, and includes cinnamon fern, sensitive fern, and lizard's-tail.

ANIMALS

The fauna is similar to that of other swamp systems. Several attributes of these small stream floodplains are important to wildlife, particularly in regions where most of the surrounding uplands have been cleared for agriculture. The narrow riparian forest provides roosting and foraging sites as well as tree cavities for numerous species of birds. The linear configurations also serve as corridors for dispersal and migration. Breeding bird species include Kentucky warblers and yellow-billed cuckoos, particularly if dense understory vegetation is present. Although a habitat generalist, the red-shouldered hawk is often found nesting along small stream floodplains. Typical snakes include timber rattlesnake, ringnecked snake, red-bellied mud snake, scarlet kingsnake, red-bellied snake, banded watersnake, brown watersnake, smooth earth snake, and rough green snake. The small aquatic black swamp snake occurs in many aquatic habitats, particularly in slow-moving water where aquatic vegetation is prevalent (Winne and Poppy 2008). Turtles are predominantly the Florida cooter. The spotted turtle is often associated with smaller streams with diverse vegetative structure. These turtles are more frequently observed in late winter and early spring rather than in the summer months.

Bluenose Shiner (*Pteronotropis welaka*)

The bluenose shiner is a slender freshwater fish approximately 2 inches long, with a laterally compressed body and a pointed snout. This minnow has a wide, dark stripe, often flecked with silvery scales, that runs the length of the body between the snout and the tail spot in both males and females. A thin, light yellow stripe lies just above the black lateral stripe (Page and Burr 1991; Albanese and Freeman 2009).

The bluenose shiner occurs below the Fall Line in the Apalachicola River drainage and westward to the Pearl River drainage in Mississippi and Louisiana. A disjunct population is also known from the St. Johns River drainage in Florida (Lee et al. 1980; Page and Burr 1991). In Georgia, the bluenose shiner is currently known from nine locations within tributaries to the Flint River. These sites are clustered in the Spring Creek, Ichawaynochaway Creek, and Pennhatchee Creek drainages (Albanese and Freeman 2009). Bluenose shiners inhabit small- to medium-size streams. They are typically found in moderate to deep pools with sluggish current. Preferred sites have soft sediments and are heavily vegetated with aquatic plants such as bur-reed, arrowheads, and bladderworts. In contrast to Mississippi populations, which occur primarily in small headwater streams, bluenose shiners in Georgia tend to be present in larger streams, often at sites that are within or near the largest streams in the watershed (Albanese and Freeman 2009).

During the breeding season, adult males undergo a dramatic transformation in color and body shape. The snout becomes bright blue, and the dorsal, pelvic, and anal fins become greatly enlarged. The dorsal fin becomes black with a pale band near its base, and the anal and pelvic fins turn white to golden yellow with contrasting black pigments. This species is one of a small group of minnows known to lay eggs in the saucer-shaped nests constructed by male sunfishes (Albanese and Freeman 2009).

Due to its restricted range and the isolated nature of individual populations, the bluenose shiner is state-protected as Threatened. Specific threats include sedimentation and nutrient runoff from agricultural areas and excessive water withdrawal.

Little Ocmulgee State Park

Little Ocmulgee State Park (Wheeler County) has several small streams that are tributaries to the Little Ocmulgee River, which is now an impoundment within the park. The Oak Ridge and Short Loop trails traverse sandhills, seepage slopes, and small stream drainages that illustrate the relationship of plant community development and land form. As is the case of many small stream drainages in the Coastal Plain, the present vegetation of the adjacent uplands is reflective of prolonged fire suppression that has permitted hardwoods to encroach into upland habitats from the narrow floodplain. With more frequent fire, the sandy upland soils probably once featured longleaf pine communities. The community changes have likely been exacerbated with a raised water table associated with the impoundment that created more mesic conditions. The Short Loop Trail crosses a small stream that

drains the seepage along the slope of the xeric sandhill. The vegetation associated with the small stream includes loblolly pine, big gallberry, water tupelo, red maple, and shining fetterbush. With fire suppression, the adjacent forest on slightly more upland areas consists of sand hickory, pignut hickory, and laurel oak, intermixed with loblolly and longleaf pines. The Short Loop Trail joins with the Oak Ridge Trail that transitions to the longleaf pine–turkey oak uplands. Ongoing restoration efforts include prescribed burning of the uplands. Reintroduction of frequent fire throughout the site will eventually provide greater definition of the transition zone from the small stream floodplains to the xeric uplands.

Location: From McRae, take U.S. Hwy. 319/441 north for 2 miles to park entrance. Google Earth GPS approximate coordinates at the park entrance: N 32.091692/W 082.884571.

Okefenokee Swamp

The Okefenokee Swamp is one of the most significant wetland systems in the United States, sprawling over 700 square miles, extending into the Pinhook Swamp in Florida, and forming the headwaters of the St. Marys and Suwannee Rivers. Approximately 371,000 acres of the swamp were designated as the Okefenokee National Wildlife Refuge and a large portion of the refuge was designated as a wilderness, making it the third largest national wilderness area east of the Mississippi River. It has been nominated as a World Heritage Site, a place of outstanding global value because of its size as a freshwater wetland, because of its impressive diversity of amphibians, reptiles, birds, and invertebrates, and because it serves as a source of two major rivers.

The swamp is a vast mosaic of communities, including pine uplands; forested wetlands of bay, cypress, and swamp tupelo; scrub/shrub wetlands; and extensive prairies of emergent aquatic vegetation. The name Okefenokee comes from the Native American term "O-ke-fin-o-cau," meaning "land of the trembling earth," referring to the areas of peat in the swamp that shake when walked on (F. Harper and Presley 1981). The presence of peat creates much of the character of the swamp, from the acidic conditions to the tea-colored water, as well as to the fire-maintained habitats.

The human history of the Okefenokee Swamp is rich. Native Americans inhabited the islands and uplands for nearly 4,000 years before they were driven out in the late 19th century. Since that time, several events have greatly shaped the condition of the swamp as it is today. In the 1890s, a canal was built in an attempt to drain the swamp into the St. Marys River for exploitation of the cypress and to convert the land to crops. Although this early attempt was aborted, much of the expansive stands of virgin cypress and pine was then harvested and removed by more than 500 miles of narrow gauge rail lines. At the turn of the century, more than 2,000 people were employed in the swamp in timber harvest or turpentining activities and more than 431 million board feet of timber were extracted. Such extensive timber harvest altered the forested communities, creating large areas of dense shrub growth (D. B. Hamilton 1984; Loftin 1998).

Interest in preservation of the natural community, engendered by prominent biologists including Francis Harper and A. H. Wright, resulted in the federal acquisition and establishment of the Okefenokee National Wildlife Refuge in 1936. Another event that greatly affected the ecosystem was the 1960 construction of a 4.5-mile-long sill (earthen dike) and two water control devices on the southwestern edge to restrict the outflow of water into the Suwanee River during periods of drought. This water retention effort was implemented for the purpose of fire suppression following large-scale fires that occurred during droughts in 1954–1955. The Suwanee River sill reduced the natural fluctuations of water within the vicinity of the dike, but overall, it had minimal impact on the hydrology of the swamp during drought because of the series of natural terrace features that exist within the swamp (Loftin 1998). Although the water control devices are no longer operational, there is considerable interest in breaching the sill and restoring surrounding bottomlands.

PHYSICAL SETTING AND ECOLOGY

The Okefenokee Swamp lies within an enormous peat-filled, saucer-shaped sandy depression. The geologic origin of the basin has been debated (Cohen et al. 1984). One theory suggested by R. M. Harper (1909) and Cooke (1943) is that the swamp formed in an ancient marine lagoon that developed when seawater was trapped between sand bars as ocean levels receded during glaciations. Over time, salt water was presumably replaced with fresh water, vegetation and organic material began to accumulate, and the peat and swamp vegetation developed. An alternative theory (Veatch and Stephenson 1911) hypothesizes that basin development involved a complex series of events, including formation of a series of step-like terraces by fluctuating ocean levels, delta bars formed by ancient rivers, thick deposition of clay, and geologic uplifts. According to this theory, the eastern edge of the swamp basin was formed by an ancient beach ridge, known today as Trail Ridge (Parrish and Rykiel 1979). This broad sand ridge extends approximately 130 miles from southeast-

ern Georgia into north-central Florida (LaForge et al. 1925). In this scenario, peat accumulation occurred in more recent times (within the last 5,000 years) with changes in vegetation, climate, and water levels. With retreat of recent glaciers, vegetation within the basin evolved from upland oak savannas to longleaf pine forests. Subsequently, increased precipitation, coupled with rising water levels, led to ponding of water on the clayey substrate and invasion by cypress and mesic hardwoods. As peat accumulated, water levels began to rise and the swamp grew both laterally and vertically (Parrish and Rykiel 1979). The entire floor of the swamp is covered by a bed of peat varying from a few inches thick at the swamp's edge to 3 to 15 feet thick in the interior (Cohen et al. 1984). Former delta bars and barrier islands constitute the uplands on islands and peninsulas within the swamp today. Seasonally ponded isolated wetlands occur throughout the uplands in association with sandy soils.

The dark-stained, acidic waters of the Okefenokee Swamp flow slowly but continuously toward two outlets: the Suwannee River, the primary outflow on the west side, and the St. Marys River on the southeast. The flow of the St. Marys River southward is directed by the presence of Trail Ridge. The hydrology of the swamp is primarily driven by precipitation (70%) and to a lesser degree by surface runoff (30%) (Rykiel 1977). Thus, water-level fluctuations have been closely associated with climatic regimes. A small degree of groundwater seepage may occur from the Floridan aquifer, but in general the calcareous clay layer of the Hawthorne Formation beneath the swamp is an effective barrier between the swamp and the Floridan aquifer below (Rykiel 1977; Loftin 1998).

The low pH (3.3–4.6) and tea-colored waters of the Okefenokee Swamp are due to the presence of tannins released from decaying vegetation. Peat forms when plant material is prevented from decaying fully by waterlogged conditions, where the absence of oxygen inhibits microbial decomposition activities. Unlike many peatlands in which the dominant vegetation is sphagnum moss, in the Okefenokee Swamp peat is composed mainly of plant remains of water lilies, bald-cypress, and Virginia chain fern. The formation of peat is a very slow process, with accumulations of 0.5 inch occurring over a 10- to 20-year period. Both the rate of accumulation and the types of plant material in peat can provide informative data regarding climate change over thousands of years.

Water levels are a very important factor in determining fire effects within the swamp. The degree of inundation determines whether the fire will burn into the swamp or remain confined to uplands, or whether natural barriers within the swamp effectively isolate fires. Inundation levels, in turn, are determined by precipitation. Extreme droughts foster fire, which plays a large role in shaping the swamp's topography and its characteristic vegetation (Cypert 1972, 1973). Indeed, fire is an integral part of the evolution of the Okefenokee Swamp. Charcoal in peat cores provides evidence of frequent fire since the beginning of peat deposition thousands of years ago (Bond 1970; Cohen 1974). Historical accounts of fires associated with major droughts date back to 1844. Other significant fires occurred in 1911, 1932, 1954 (Cypert 1961, 1972), 2007, and 2011.

In years of average precipitation, most fires are likely to be surficial, where only the aerial portion of vegetation is burned and the vegetation regrows from root sprouts. In contrast, during periods of prolonged drought the peat layer dries out, becomes extremely flammable, and will burn or smolder for months until extinguished by rains or until it burns down to a water table or sand bed (Cypert 1961; D. B. Hamilton 1984). With severe droughts, fire will burn into the root mat, creating permanent openings, or burn deeply into peat, creating new lakes and prairies (Cypert 1973). Many of the lakes found in the swamp have been attributed to the 1844 fire (D. B. Hamilton 1984). This process is cyclical, with regrowth of vegetation, filling by organic matter accumulation, and burning out of peat and root mats. Peat accumulation requires saturated conditions to slow down decomposition of vegetation. In dry conditions, decomposition rates are accelerated; thus, peat formation requires a synchronization of hydroperiod and water levels. Thus, the convergence of 30-year drought cycles and 75- to 100-year fuel accumulations appear to be necessary to produce a large, hot fire that alters the landscape structure and creates the "moving mosaic" of communities within the swamp (Loftin 1998).

Wildfires are a natural part of the swamp ecosystem and are inevitable events given the flammability of peat and vegetation during drought periods and the high incidence of lightning strikes in the region. From 1960 to 1989, there were no large fires mainly due to low fuel levels after the 1954–1955 fires and active suppression when they were discovered. A fire in 1990, called the "Shorts Fire," demonstrated that once a large fire was established in the swamp, it was impossible to extinguish it despite spending millions of dollars attempting to do so. At the same time, an increased recognition was growing among resource managers that fire was the only way to maintain the swamp and to prevent it from changing into a forested bog. Subsequently, fire-suppression activities have focused on confining the fires to within the refuge boundary. Since 2002, 13 fires over 3,000 acres have occurred within the swamp.

Although active prescribed fire management has been conducted on the uplands throughout the refuge for several decades, adjacent privately held properties have become vulnerable, particularly where prescribed fire is not a routine management objective. Fewer and fewer forest landowners are using prescribed fire to reduce fuels because of economics, reduced growth of trees, and liability of smoke. Where large accumulations of fuel occur under fire-suppressed stands, containment of wildfires becomes very difficult. Smoke management is a concern, particularly as the region becomes more urbanized. Recognition of the need to manipulate habitat for fuel reduction through partnerships with adjacent landowners is growing. In addition, conservation easements and incentives on adjacent private lands may be necessary to implement longer rotation timber management to facilitate the growth of older pine trees necessary for red-cockaded woodpeckers and other species of conservation concern.

The wilderness status of the swamp also leads to questions of what management activities are or should be permitted, particularly in regard to use of mechanized equipment and monitoring of rare species populations. Pollution from air, light, and noise with increasing industrial and urban development degrades the wilderness resource and the human experience of wilderness. Monitoring for these intrusions, as well as for contaminants such as mercury, lead, pesticides, and nitrogen inputs, is needed. Under low pH conditions, mercury and lead are available to aquatic biota with the potential for bioaccumulation through the food chain, possibly affecting reproduction, hormone levels, and behavior of the fauna.

Promotion of upland linkages to ephemeral wetlands for flatwoods salamander, striped newt, gopher frog, and other amphibians is an important management consideration for the refuge. Restoration of the hydrology of ephemeral wetlands that have been disrupted by ditches should be promoted.

In addition to the Suwanee River sill, other hydrologic management issues have surfaced. The importance of Trail Ridge in maintaining the surface water and groundwater hydrology of the swamp became regionally recognized with a controversial proposal to mine titanium along Trail Ridge. In 1996, E. I. Dupont De Nemours and Company, Inc., sought permits for a 50-year surface mining project on 22,000 acres along Trail Ridge, just southeast of the refuge boundary. Given the environmental concerns of the public, Dupont abandoned the project and donated 16,000 acres to the Conservation Fund for conservation purposes.

Golden club

WILDFIRE IN 2007

A wildfire known as the Sweat Farm Road Fire started on April 16, 2007, in Ware County, just east of Waycross, Georgia, when a tree limb downed a powerline.

Prolonged drought conditions and record low water levels in the Okefenokee Swamp set the stage for this major wildfire burning into the mix of scrub/shrub, cypress swamp, wetland prairies, peat, and longleaf pine forest. As it moved into the northwestern section of the refuge three days after ignition, it was called the

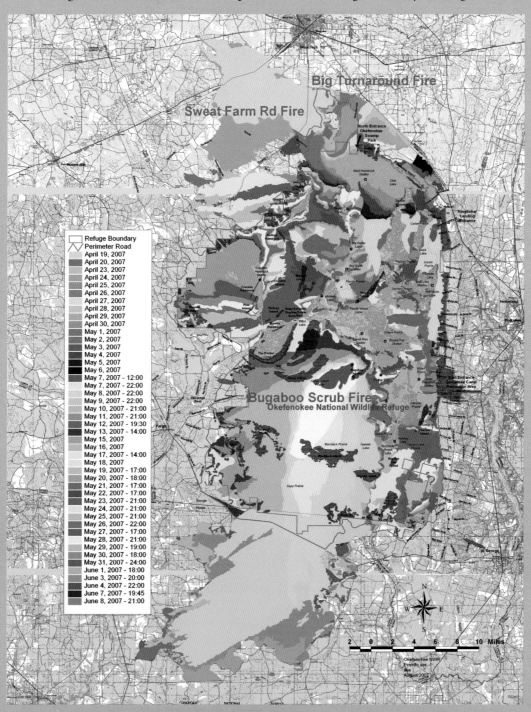

Progression of the 2007 complex of fires in the Okefenokee National Wildlife Refuge

Aerial view of 2007 fire. The Big Turnaround Fire in 2007 consumed fuels that had not burned since the 1932 wildfires.

2009 wildfire at night, Okefenokee Swamp

Intentional burnout operation along the eastern boundary of the refuge to prevent spread of fire into adjacent private properties

Blackjack Island in 2007 immediately following fire

"Big Turnaround Fire Complex." Meanwhile, another fire, the "Bugaboo Scrub Fire," was ignited by lightning on Bugaboo Island within the swamp on May 9. These raging fires quickly became one fire and ultimately the largest fire in the history of both Georgia and Florida, burning nearly 600,000 acres on state and private lands, the Okefenokee National Wildlife Refuge, and the Osceola National Forest. The fires burned very fast and showed some of the most erratic fire behavior ever seen in this part of the country due to frequently shifting winds. At times, flame lengths were estimated at 100 feet. An unusually low-altitude jet stream carried embers up to 2 miles ahead of the fire. Smoke plumes reaching 30,000 feet suddenly collapsed, "blowing out" the fire in all directions. Atmospheric inversions pushed the smoke close to the ground and shut down interstate and state highways. On windy days, the plume traveled hundreds of miles, obscuring city skylines as far away as Mississippi and North Carolina. Firefighting teams corralled the fire until nearly 5 inches of rain fell in early June. It was declared extinguished on December 12, 2007, eight months after it started. The upland pine forests that had been maintained with prescribed fire fared well in stark contrast to the blackened commercial slash pine plantations outside the refuge's boundary, which had not been frequently burned. Some mortality of longleaf pine on the refuge occurred because of accumulations of duff beneath the largest trees that resulted in more deeply penetrating burns.

As a result of this prolonged fire, approximately 81% of the swamp burned, including some areas that had not been exposed to fire for 75 years. Fire moved sporadically through the shrub swamps, bays, prairies, and riverine habitats, depending on fuels and winds. The resulting mosaic of fire included areas where trees and shrubs were burned to the ground, where fire skipped across the prairies burning tree islands, and where fire moved slowly through the duff underneath the trees. In the latter case of smoldering duff, trees toppled over but were not burned, leaving extensive areas looking like a huge pile of toothpicks.

The swamp vegetation began to recover quickly following the fire in some areas with regrowth of shrubs and greenbriers. Hardwoods that were toppled by fire will likely result in complete stand replacement. Cypress trees are typically more resistant to fire than hardwoods, with the result that some stands may become dominated by cypress.

Fire damage to slash pine plantations on adjacent private land that had not been maintained with prescribed fire

Fallen trees following prolonged smoldering of peat

VEGETATION

The vegetation of the Okefenokee Swamp is a complex mosaic of plant communities that reflects successional development and disturbance history. A general successional pathway is considered from prairie to cypress swamp to black gum or bay swamp, though fire can disrupt this trajectory. When surface fires occur, existing vegetation is maintained with rapid regrowth of vegetation. When deep-burning fires occur, most or all vegetation is killed and the process is reset to an earlier successional stage (see Prairies, below). The extensive timber that was removed from the swamp has also altered community dynamics and interactions with fire regimes (Loftin 1998). Most of the cypress trees harvested in the swamp were between 400 and 900 years old (Hopkins 1947). Because resprouting of older cypress is minimal and few seed trees were left behind, reestablishment of cypress was severely constrained. Thus, most areas in which cypress was removed are now dominated by hardwoods (D. B. Hamilton 1984). The following vegetation types are found in the swamp.

Bay Swamp. This is a closed-canopy forest dominated by evergreen species such as loblolly bay, red bay, sweet bay, and dahoon and deciduous species including swamp tupelo and red maple. Pond-cypress is a minor component of the canopy, although many of these sites were formerly dominated by large cypress prior to timber removal in the early 20th century. Some sites that are more strongly dominated by large gums today probably reflect former harvests that were restricted to cypress, particularly in the northwestern part of the swamp (D. B. Hamilton 1984). Understory vegetation is often sparse beneath the dense overstory. Due to the depth of peat, large swamp tupelo and bay trees of the swamp are usually rooted in the upper layer of the peat bed and are not in contact with the underlying mineral soil (Cypert 1972).

Cypress Swamp. Cypress swamps occur as large stands or small patches interspersed with other vegetation. Although 90% of the merchantable cypress was removed by logging operations, small old-growth stands of cypress still exist in the north-central and south-

Bay swamp

eastern parts of the swamp because they occurred in sites where the volume of timber limited the economic incentive for harvest. The subcanopy of these stands may include many of the species of the bay swamp, and the understory supports scrub/shrub species. Cypress swamp communities are maintained by periodic low-intensity fires that prevent transition to bay swamp or mixed swamp (D. B. Hamilton 1984). Based on evidence from several historic and recent fires, severe peat burns can destroy root systems and convert cypress swamps into open prairies (Cypert 1973).

Scrub/Shrub Swamp. The scrub/shrub community develops as a dense thicket of evergreen and deciduous shrubs and trees. Greenbriers often completely overtop the shrub canopy, forming an impenetrable evergreen shroud. Common wetland shrub species include

Cypress swamp

Cypress swamp

Scrub/shrub swamp

ti-ti, shining fetterbush, dahoon, gallberry, button-bush, coastal sweet-pepperbush, maleberry, stagger-bushes, and Virginia-willow. On drier sites, patches of slash pine, cypress, or hardwoods may be present. Scrub/shrub dominance often develops in response to timber removal or periodic fires (Penfound 1952; D. B. Hamilton 1984). Shrubs commonly invade shallower water along edges of upland, where the water level drops below the peat surface as a result of drought, draining, peat buildup, or battery formation (see description below).

Prairies. The shallow marshes of emergent and aquatic species are locally called "prairies" and are a very distinctive community of the swamp. Within the prairie, the depth of peat ranges from 4 to 15 feet. These areas are subject to more continuous flooding and are dominated by aquatic macrophytes, including white water-lily, big floating heart, and broadleaf pondlily. Slightly higher elevations include herbaceous emergents such as heartleaf pickerelweed, golden club, green arrow-arum, pipewort, yellow-eyed grass, southern blue flag, pitcherplants, maidencane, blue maiden-

cane, and showy bur-marigold. The larger marshes near the center of the swamp, such as Chase Prairie, have remained marsh for thousands of years because they overlie an extremely deep trough of peat that was probably the remnants of earlier water courses (Cohen 1973; Parrish and Rykiel 1979; Glasser 1986). Other marshes were created more recently when fire burned into the peat of scrub/shrub or cypress wetlands. Numerous peat islands that support herbaceous and woody communities of varying ages are scattered throughout the marshes. For example, in Chase Prairie, more than 4,000 tree islands are present and vary in size from a few square feet to 20 acres (Glasser 1985).

Island transitional stages are readily apparent, providing an exceptional illustration of primary succession, as well as the ephemeral nature of peat islands. Through microbial action within the peat and the decay of oxygen-filled cells of water lilies, gases are produced that cause the peat to be buoyant. Peat mats that break away from the bottom of the bed of peat and float to the surface are called "batteries." Many of these floating batteries are present for only a few years and are resubmerged. Batteries of peat that per-

The shallow marshes of emergent and aquatic species are called "prairies."

Peat mats that break away from the bottom of the bed of peat and float to the surface are called "batteries."

As trees and surrounding shrubs become a mass of dome-shaped vegetation, they are referred to as "tree houses" or "heads."

Mature tree house

CHARACTERISTIC PLANTS OF THE OKEFENOKEE SWAMP

TREES

Red maple—*Acer rubrum*
Loblolly bay—*Gordonia lasianthus*
Sweet bay—*Magnolia virginiana*
Swamp tupelo—*Nyssa biflora*
Ogeechee lime—*Nyssa ogeche*
Pond-cypress—*Taxodium ascendens*
Bald-cypress—*Taxodium distichum*

SHRUBS AND WOODY VINES

Coastal sweet-pepperbush—*Clethra alnifolia*
Ti-ti—*Cyrilla racemiflora*
Coastal fetterbush—*Eubotrys racemosa*

Dahoon—*Ilex cassine*
Virginia-willow—*Itea virginica*
Crookedwood—*Lyonia ferruginea*
Staggerbush—*Lyonia fruticosa*
Shining fetterbush—*Lyonia lucida*
Swamp bay—*Persea palustris*
Bristly greenbrier—*Smilax hispida*
Bamboo-vine—*Smilax laurifolia*

GROUND COVER

Southern blue flag—*Iris virginica*
Redroot—*Lacnanthes caroliniana*
Cutgrass—*Leersia hexandra*
Broadleaf pondlily—*Nuphar orbiculata*

White waterlily—*Nymphaea odorata*
Big floating heart—*Nymphoides aquatica*
Golden club—*Orontium aquaticum*
Maidencane—*Panicum hemitomon*
Smooth meadow-beauty—*Rhexia alifanus*
Pale meadow-beauty—*Rhexia mariana*
American cupscale—*Sacciolepis striata*
Pitcherplants—*Sarracenia* spp.
Lizard's-tail—*Saururus cernuus*
Woolgrass bulrush—*Scirpus cyperinus*
Bladderworts—*Utricularia* spp.

sist slightly above the surface of the water may provide favorable habitat for colonization by emergents and shrubs. This stage, typified by shrubs and small trees in the center and grasses along the edges, is called a "bonnet." Over time, the battery builds with bulk until it resettles onto the underlying peat and larger trees begin to invade, with the roots stabilizing the substrate. As trees and surrounding shrubs become a mass of dome-shaped vegetation, they are referred to as "tree houses" or "heads" (Wright and Wright 1932; Cypert 1972; Glasser 1985). The dominant species on the islands differs from place to place, primarily because of patterns of seed dispersal, fire, and island age (Glasser 1985).

Uplands. Longleaf pine forests occurred on many of the sand islands within the swamp and surrounding upland sites where frequent fires occurred, extending from the edges of the swamp to well-drained sandy soil ridges. Approximately 30,000 acres of uplands occur within the refuge. The old-growth longleaf pine forest was eliminated with timber harvest or turpentine operations, and many of the uplands were replanted with slash pine. In spite of this, second-growth stands of longleaf pine do occur, and extensive uplands are actively managed to encourage longleaf pine regeneration. Along edges of drains with less frequent fire, longleaf pine is intermixed with slash pine, loblolly pine, and shortleaf pine. On the driest sites, scrub

oaks such as laurel oak, sand live oak, and live oak are also present. With fire exclusion, oaks may dominate, and larger, well-developed stands are called "oak hammocks." Species such as devilwood, horsesugar, red bay, and southern magnolia may also be present, such as that seen along Ridleys Trail in the Chesser Hammock. Often, hardwood hammocks are associated with old homesites. On the well-drained ridges of frequently burned longleaf pine, ground cover is dominated by southern wiregrass. Other species include dwarf pawpaw, prickly-pear, saw palmetto, and dwarf blueberry. On much of the upland habitat of the refuge, the somewhat poorly drained soils support longleaf pine flatwoods vegetation. Here a notable increase in abundance of palmetto and diversity of herbaceous species typically associated with pine flatwoods is present.

ANIMALS

The Okefenokee Swamp is an extremely important habitat for native fauna because of its spatial extent and diversity of habitats. Its significant role in the conservation of migratory birds was a primary motive in its establishment as a national wildlife refuge, but the swamp is also renowned for its species richness of amphibians and reptiles as well as important habitat for several mammal species of conservation concern.

Within the national wildlife refuge, 48 species of mammals have been documented. The Florida black bear (sometimes called a hog bear) is the subspecies of black bear found in the Okefenokee Swamp. The habitat for this subspecies has been greatly reduced as a result of land use conversion to agriculture and pulpwood silviculture. Bears were not legally hunted in southern Georgia between the 1930s and 1981. The population of black bear extending from the Okefenokee Swamp into the Osceola National Forest in Florida is estimated at 400 individuals (Dobey et al. 2005). Bears prefer the gum-bay-cypress habitats and forage on the mast of black gum fruit. They will also forage on saw palmetto and acorns of upland sites. In Georgia, the round-tailed muskrat is restricted primarily to the Okefenokee Swamp and the Grand Bay–Banks Lake wetland complex. The species is listed as Threatened and is protected from hunting and trapping. Round-tailed muskrats inhabit shallow marshes, and their dome-shaped nests of grasses are common in the prairies, frequently located at the base of a cypress tree (see the Featured Animal). Rafinesque's big-eared bat is a species of concern in Georgia, although it ranges throughout the southeastern United States. In the Okefenokee Swamp, the primary roost sites for this species are hollow cavities in large cypress trees. The long ears (more than 1 inch) are conspicuous. No other species of bat in Georgia has such pronounced ears. The Okefenokee Swamp provides habitat for one of the largest populations of bobcat in the state.

Studies of amphibians in the swamp were conducted in the early 1900s (Wright 1932) and the high diversity of frogs (more than 20 species) has long been appreciated. The carpenter frog, an Atlantic Coastal Plain endemic, reaches its southernmost distribution in the Okefenokee Swamp in Georgia and adjacent Pinhook Swamp in Florida (Moler 1992). Its habitat is restricted to acidic, peaty swamps, and in the Okefenokee Swamp it commonly occurs in open prairies and in cypress or black gum stands.

The American alligator is regarded as an icon of the Okefenokee Swamp, with present population estimates of around 10,000–12,000 individuals (U.S. Fish and Wildlife Service 2006c). Alligators are considered "ecosystem engineers" in the swamp because of their trails through the prairies and the holes that they excavate in the peat. They may be responsible for dislodging peat that forms batteries, and many other wildlife species use the trails as travel corridors. Populations of alligators had declined precipitously throughout their range by the mid-1900s. Although legislation was enacted to protect the species, illegal hunting and trade of hide were widespread. Even so, the remoteness of vast areas of the swamp permitted the population of alligators to persist in this part of Georgia.

The diverse and vast habitats of the swamp support many wading bird species. Great egrets, great blue herons, white ibises, and little blue herons are common in the open prairies. The resident population of Florida sandhill cranes at the Okefenokee National Wildlife Refuge is considered to be distinct from other populations of cranes in the Southeast (U.S. Fish and Wildlife Service 2006a). During winter months, more than 1,000 migratory greater sandhill cranes over-winter with the resident cranes. The Okefenokee Swamp is a stopping point for waterfowl migrating along the Atlantic Flyway, including ring-necked ducks, mallards, blue-winged teal, and green-winged teal. Wood ducks are the most common resident species (U.S. Fish and Wildlife Service 2006a). Ospreys can be spotted in open areas, particularly the prairies. Bald eagles are encountered infrequently.

Several rare bird species are present or were once known to occur in the swamp. Wood storks (federally Endangered) move into the swamp in late summer after the nesting season, depending on the fluctuating water conditions. Here they feed on small fish that are concentrated in shallow ponds and sloughs as water levels decline during dry periods. They are often seen in feeding groups in Grand, Chesser, and Chase Prairies. Sightings of the Endangered and probably now extinct ivory-billed woodpecker were made as late as the 1940s (Burleigh 1958). A specimen of the ivory-billed woodpecker was shot in the swamp in 1913 (J. A. Jackson 2002). The demise of this species is attributed to loss of old-growth swamp habitat. Swallow-tailed kites were reported in the swamp by Wright and Harper (1913). This species nests in large pine trees within mature bottomland forests and occasionally in cypress or even oaks. One nest has been reported on the western boundary of the Okefenokee National Wildlife Refuge. Populations of swallow-tailed kites have declined steadily since the early 1900s. The federally Endangered red-cockaded woodpecker occurs on pine islands in the interior of the swamp and in uplands along the perimeter of the swamp. The wildlife refuge has been designated as part of the Osceola National Forest/Okefenokee National Wildlife Refuge recovery population under the U.S. Fish and Wildlife Service Red-cockaded Woodpecker Recovery Plan (U.S. Fish and Wildlife Service 2003).

Round-Tailed Muskrat (*Neofiber alleni*)

The round-tailed muskrat, also known as the Florida water rat, is a medium-sized rodent about 8 to 9 inches in body length, with a tail length of 4 to 7 inches. Its dense fur is rich brown in color and overlain with long, coarse guard hairs. The ears are small, and the front feet are smaller than the slightly webbed rear feet. The sparsely haired tail is round in cross-section, which helps distinguish this species from the common muskrat, which has a tail that is flattened from side to side (Burt and Grossenheider 1980; Ozier 1999b).

Round-tailed muskrats are found throughout much of peninsular Florida and portions of southern Georgia, including the Okefenokee Swamp, Grand Bay, and other large wetland complexes, but do not coexist in the same habitat with common muskrat (Guilday 1971). They live in shallow grass ponds, marshes, and bogs or in open-water ponds with emergent sedges and floating macrophytes. Their diet consists of aquatic grasses, as well as some animal material. Round-tailed muskrats weave dome-shaped houses of grasses, sedges, cattails, and other aquatic vegetation on top of floating mats of sphagnum or peat or attached to the base of woody vegetation. Two escape holes typically lead from the bottom of the house to tunnels in the vegetation mat. Each individual uses several houses, and more than one individual may occupy a house.

Populations of this muskrat are limited by the amount of suitable habitat. Under natural conditions, periodic fires burn off encroaching woody vegetation and reduce the underlying peat, maintaining open-water areas dominated by floating and emergent plants. Winter droughts can also be important in maintaining floating mat habitat by exposing plant roots to freezing temperatures. Fire exclusion or alteration of natural hydrologic conditions can reduce or eliminate habitat for this species. Because of its rarity in Georgia, the round-tailed muskrat is protected by state law (Ozier 1999b).

Okefenokee National Wildlife Refuge

Although the Okefenokee National Wildlife Refuge is vast and most of the property is inaccessible except by helicopter, excellent examples of the dominant swamp and upland communities along trails and boardwalks are available to the public. By entering the east entrance, approximately 11 miles southwest of Folkston, a gradient of upland and wetland communities can be examined. Here visitors can explore the swamp by car, bicycle, canoe, or on foot. (See also pine flatwoods.) A 0.75-mile boardwalk trail to Sea Grove Lake winds through a scrub/shrub community, an impenetrable tangle of evergreen and deciduous shrubs, overtopped by greenbrier. In spring, flowering loblolly bay is extremely showy; in fall, the reddish colored leaves of the deciduous cypress are focal. Vine-wicky, a particularly interesting species that grows under the bark of cypress trees, can be observed along this trail. Along a spur trail, evidence of the May 2007 wildfire can be viewed where large stands of loblolly bay were killed.

A 50-foot observation tower offers spectacular views into Sea Grove Lake and a panorama of Chesser Prairie with the successional sequence of peat batteries, bonnets, and tree houses. Often, sandhill cranes feeding in the marsh can be viewed from this tower location. During dry periods, burned tree stumps are exposed above the water surface. For a closer look, guided boat tours and wilderness canoeing (120 miles of canoe trails) are available in the Suwannee Canal Recreation Area. The canal penetrates 11 miles into the swamp, where boaters can access Chesser, Grand, and Mizell Prairies, some of the swamp's most extensive open areas.

Another entrance into the swamp is through Stephen C. Foster State Park, located about 17 miles from Fargo. In this part of the swamp, a mix of habitats can be viewed, including cypress swamps, bay swamps, blackwater lakes, open water courses, and islands with upland vegetation. A section along the Red Canoe Trail between the state park entrance and Minnie's Lake provides an excellent illustration of this diversity of habitat. Billy's Lake is surrounded by a bay swamp mixed with dramatic stragglers of large, mature cypress. The fire of 2007 burned through the vegetation to the east. Stumps from the 1955 fire are present in the lake. Heading north toward Minnie's Lake into the beginning of the Suwanee River are spectacular views of dense, mature cypress with understory shrubs of the bay swamps. Along the lake edges are dense patches of yellow-eyed grass, maidencane, and American cupscale. These areas are particularly showy in spring when southern blue flag iris is in bloom. The river alternates between sharp, narrow bends and broad, gentle curves. Nearing Minnie's Lake, the vegetation changes to bay swamp and shrub swamp, probably the result of the 1955 fire. Along some stretches, numerous toppled trees are the signature of the 2007 fire, where the shallow-rooted trees and shrubs were burned from below as the peat smoldered. Minnie's Lake is a narrow, mile-long lake surrounded by picturesque cypress. Again, many fire-toppled trees are present. Depending on the severity of the fire, large cypress trees survived the fire, whereas hollow cypress trees were readily consumed by the flames. Billy's Island, a 5 mile by 2 mile sandy upland, with its open slash pine–longleaf pine flatwoods vegetation, contrasts sharply with the surrounding swamp vegetation. This island was inhabited by nearly 600 people at the turn of the 20th century, and vestiges of this occupancy can be seen in the scattered old metal machine parts, cemetery, and introduced plants. Within Foster State Park, the Trembling Earth Nature Trail offers boardwalk access to hammock vegetation, bay swamps, and views of fire-scarred vegetation where fingers of the 2007 fire entered the swamp vegetation. An interesting successional feature along this trail is the common presence of tussock growth, where shrubby vegetation becomes established in the old stumps of cypress.

Location: East entrance: From Main St. in Folkston, take Okefenokee Dr. (Ga. Hwy. 121/23 S/Okefenokee Pkwy.) for 7 miles to the refuge entrance at the Suwannee Canal Recreation Area. Stephen C. Foster State Park entrance: From the intersection of Ga. Hwy. 94 and U.S. Hwy. 441 in Fargo, go south on Ga. 89 S/Ga. 94 E/U.S. 441/Barton St. Turn left onto Ga. 177 N and proceed for 17 miles. The park entrance is on the right. Google Earth approximate coordinates at the park entrance: N 30.8164621/W 082.368042.

Vine-wicky grows beneath the bark of cypress trees.

Chapter 7

MARITIME ECOREGION

Overview

The Maritime ecoregion of Georgia includes the lowest elevations in the state as well as the most dynamic environments. Natural communities in this region are shaped and influenced by ocean tides and currents, prevailing winds and storm events, and outflows from major rivers. Salinity, moisture, and thermal gradients produce complex and visually striking patterns of natural communities across the coastal landscape.

The relatively intact condition of Georgia's coastal environments is due in part to their history of land ownership and use as well as to concerted protection efforts. Remarkably, the coastline of Georgia accounts for approximately one-third of the remaining salt marsh habitat on the East Coast as well as the majority of protected maritime forest in the South Atlantic region. Georgia also has one of the most extensive areas of tidal freshwater wetlands on the East Coast. This part of the state conveys a sense of a world apart, with expansive salt marshes, windswept maritime dunes, wide beaches, and maritime forests of stately pines and contorted oaks draped in Spanish-moss.

The Maritime ecoregion corresponds to the Sea Islands/Coastal Marsh Level IV ecoregion (G. E. Griffith et al. 2001) within the southern Coastal Plain (lower Coastal Plain). This 1,295-square-mile area includes the coastal barrier islands, salt marshes, and estuaries, as well as mainland environments that lie within the zone of tidal influence. The Georgia coastline spans approximately 110 miles from the Savannah River on the north to the St. Marys River on the south.

It is flanked by 13 major islands arranged in 8 clusters and separated from the mainland by an extensive system of salt marshes, tidal estuaries, and sounds. These islands are known as "barrier islands" because they help buffer the mainland from the full force of tidal energy and storm events. The salt marshes also help absorb energy from waves and storms, so they are actually part of the "barrier" system as well.

Coastal marsh is the major land cover type in this region, representing 35.3% of the landscape. Other major land cover types include evergreen forest (20%), forested wetland (13.7%), and open water (9%). Low-intensity and high-intensity urban lands together account for 10% of the total area of this region. Primary conservation land managers in this region include the state of Georgia (101,560 acres), the National Park Service (34,420 acres), the U.S. Fish and Wildlife Service (29,971 acres), and the Department of Defense (14,171 acres). Approximately 21% of the Maritime region is conservation land managed by state or federal agencies.

GEOLOGY, TOPOGRAPHY, AND SOILS

The continental shelf extends approximately 80 miles eastward from the Georgia coast, sloping downward at a very gentle rate of 1 to 2 feet per mile to its eastern edge. From the Pleistocene epoch to the present, climatic changes and corresponding changes in sea level have caused Georgia's coastline to shift between the outer portion of the continental shelf to a point approximately 60 miles inland from the present shoreline. Sedimentation processes during these sea-level shifts produced a series of seven successive barrier island profiles (Hoyt 1968). Georgia's present-day barrier islands are remnants of the "Silver Bluff" dunes, a system of beach dunes extending from the middle of the South Carolina coast to the mouth of the St. Johns River near Jacksonville, Florida (Hoyt 1968). The extremely gradual slope of the continental shelf, low wave energies, and a gradual rise in sea level over thousands of years allowed the Georgia barrier islands to develop gradually as large, discrete islands rather than being destroyed or flattened into narrow spits of sand (Hoyt et al. 1964; Hails and Hoyt 1969).

Georgia's barrier islands are actually composed of two sets of islands that formed at different time periods: from 35,000 to 40,000 years ago during the Pleis-

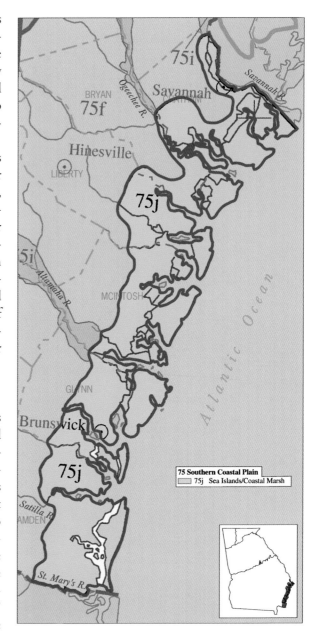

tocene, and from 4,000 to 5,000 years ago during the Holocene. Some of the islands (Tybee, Little Tybee, Wassaw, Blackbeard, Wolf, Little St. Simons, Little Cumberland, and Sea Island) are composed entirely of Holocene sediments. The remaining islands (Ossabaw, St. Catherines, Sapelo, St. Simons, Jekyll, and Cumberland Island) are composed mostly of Pleistocene-age sediments, with strips of Holocene sediments attached along their eastern edges. In general, the Holocene islands are smaller and occur just eastward of the larger islands.

Approximately 5,000 years ago, the rate of sea-level rise slowed to a fairly constant rate of 1 foot per 100 years. These conditions made it possible for the barrier islands to accumulate additional sediments and increase significantly in size. The characteristic "drumstick" shape of the Holocene islands is thought to be due to the large tidal range along the Georgia coast as well as the fact that littoral currents (offshore currents flowing parallel to the coast) move sediments southward from offshore bars to the northern ends of the islands (Hayes 1979). The barrier islands continue to change in size and shape as storms, nearshore currents, sea breezes, and sea-level rise interact to cause a landward migration of sediments. Evidence of this continual landward migration can be seen in peat deposits, tree stumps, and oyster shells that are now exposed on the beaches of these islands (Chalmers 1997).

The fine quartz sands that make up the beaches and dunes of the Georgia coast are easily transported by winds, ocean currents, and tides. During the winter months, large quantities of sand are swept off the beaches by storms and transported to new locations, such as offshore bars. During the summer months, much of this sand is returned to the beach by wave action. This phenomenon is known as the sand-sharing system (Hoyt 1968). Once sand is deposited on the beach, strong ocean breezes transport it landward, rebuilding the upper beach and dunes. Thus, the net movement of sand between the beach and offshore sand bars varies according to a seasonal pattern punctuated by storm events.

The main sources of sediment to Georgia's tidal marshes, swamps, and beaches are major alluvial rivers such as the Altamaha and Savannah Rivers, smaller Coastal Plain rivers that empty to the Atlantic Ocean, and suspended material transported landward from the continental shelf by wave and tide action. Analyses of the composition of minerals on Georgia beaches indicate that the major alluvial rivers that drain the Piedmont are more important contributors to offshore sediments than are blackwater Coastal Plain rivers such as the Satilla, Ogeechee, and St. Marys (A. S. Johnson et al. 1974). Along the coast, interacting currents and differences in water velocities result in a sorting of sediments and lead to the formation of mud and sand bars, levees, and estuarine marsh flats. Most of the soils of the Georgia barrier islands originated from quartz sand that was deposited as primary dunes during island for-

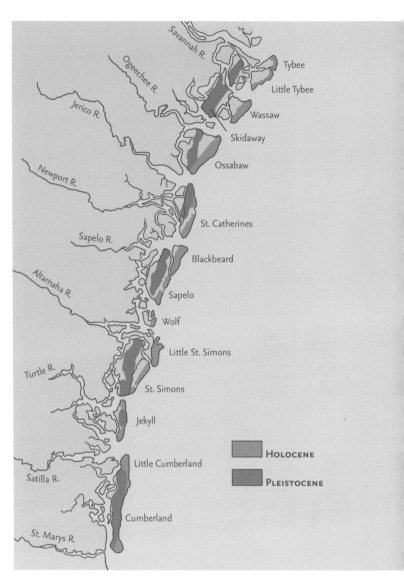

Distribution of Pleistocene and Holocene sediments on Georgia's barrier islands. Adapted from Schoettle 1993 and Lenz 2002, with permission of Taylor Schoettle and Danny Woodward / SherpaGuides.com.

mation. Sands on Georgia beaches are finer grained and contain fewer shell fragments than those of beaches farther north and south along the Atlantic coast, due to lower wave energies (Giles and Pilkey 1965).

The sandy soils of the barrier islands and nearshore upland areas drain quickly, retain few nutrients, and are acidic. Most of the ion exchange capacity in these soils is provided by decay-resistant organic materials produced by the microbial decomposition of plant materials. In general, soils on the Pleistocene islands have

Beach sediments are shifted and rearranged by storms and tides.

greater variety and better soil development (though not as much as Pleistocene soils on the mainland), with some B horizon development, more organic material, and more clays and loams than those of the Holocene islands, which are generally composed of unstratified recent sediments (G. E. Griffith et al. 2001).

In contrast to the sandy soils of upland communities, the soils of tidal saltwater and freshwater marshes are a mixture of sand, silt, and clay and typically include significant amounts of organic material. These submerged mucky soils retain water for long periods of time and are generally anoxic (lacking in oxygen). Because of low light penetration in sediment-laden waters and anoxic conditions in the lower soil levels, most of the productivity of these soils is limited to the uppermost soil layers where photosynthesis can occur (Pomeroy and Wiegert 1981).

RIVER BASINS AND GROUNDWATER

This ecoregion includes the lowermost portions of five major river systems: the Savannah, Ogeechee, Altamaha, Satilla, and St. Marys. By far the largest of these rivers are the Altamaha and Savannah. The Altamaha has an average discharge of 13,520 cubic feet per second, while the Savannah's discharge averages 11,720 cubic feet per second. In addition to these rivers whose headwaters lie well outside the ecoregion, numerous tidal (or "tidewater") rivers originate within or just outside of the ecoregion. Examples include the Bull, Medway, Newport, Sapelo, Mud, Little Satilla, and Crooked Rivers. Many of these tidal rivers are interconnected due to the coastal region's extremely low gradient. At the coast, rivers broaden significantly to form sounds. Hundreds of tidal creeks can be found along the Georgia coast, forming intricate dendritic patterns within coastal marshes.

The Maritime ecoregion's groundwater resources include a surficial aquifer as well as deeper aquifers. The surficial aquifer consists of Pliocene and Miocene sediments interspersed with younger sediments and can be more than 200 feet thick. This aquifer serves as the primary source of groundwater discharge to surface waters, including rivers, tidal creeks, and isolated wetlands. Below the surficial aquifer lie the Brunswick and Floridan aquifers. These deeper aquifers are confined by relatively impermeable layers and have limited connection with the surficial aquifer. They discharge fresh water directly to the ocean at the coastline. The Brunswick aquifer is roughly 20 to 200 feet thick and consists mainly of Miocene sands. The upper and lower Floridan aquifers are composed of limestone and other carbonate rocks and are several hundred to more than 2,000 feet thick. The upper Floridan aquifer is the primary source of fresh water for coastal Georgia (Spechler 2001; Falls et al. 2001; Falls et al. 2005).

On barrier islands, groundwater reserves of fresh water lie near the soil surface and extend to the edges of the island. This "lens" of fresh water is usually deepest in the center of the island and decreases abruptly in depth at the edges of the island (Bellis 1995). Because fresh water is less dense than saline water, it floats on top of salt water within the sediments comprising the island (J. S. Brown 1925; Crandell 1962).

Rain is the only source for recharging the surficial aquifer on barrier islands (Art et al. 1974). As rain collects on the island, it moves downward and laterally through the underlying sediments, ultimately dis-

Tidally influenced stretch of lower Altamaha River

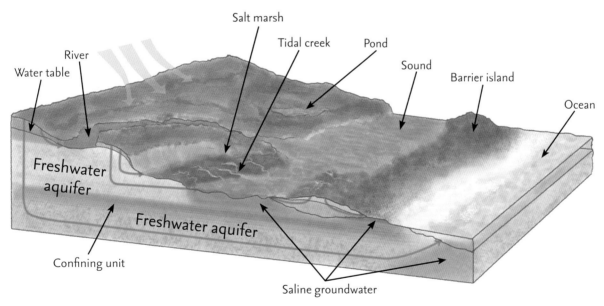

Patterns of surface water and groundwater flows in an idealized coastal watershed. Redrawn from Barlow 2003.

charging to the open ocean below sea level along the margins of the island. The downward and outward flow of fresh water prevents adjacent salt water from penetrating the surface soil layers (Art et al. 1974). Salts entering the surficial aquifer from storm surges and salt spray are diluted by precipitation and flushed from the system (W. H. Collins and Easely 1999).

The water table, or top of the surficial aquifer, drops as groundwater is removed from the system by lateral flow, evaporation, and transpiration by plants, or by direct groundwater withdrawal. The water table rises when significant rain events recharge the supply of groundwater. The ratio of the size of the island to the quantity of water in the freshwater lens determines the magnitude of change in the water table caused by a given precipitation event. Larger islands have a larger surface area on which to receive rainfall, which helps buffer the underlying surficial aquifer and associated wetland habitats against short-term fluctuations in rainfall. On smaller islands, summer droughts may result in rapid dewatering of freshwater wetlands.

Saltwater intrusion is the movement of saline water into freshwater aquifers and may occur naturally due to tides and fluctuations in river discharges. In other instances, saltwater intrusion is a result of human activities such as groundwater pumping from coastal wells, construction of large ditches in the tidal zone, or deepening of navigation channels in tidal rivers. All of these activities can facilitate the incursion of salt water into freshwater habitats and aquifers within a given locality. Groundwater withdrawals from the upper Floridan aquifer have resulted in saltwater contamination in several locations on the Georgia coast, most notably at Savannah and Brunswick (Barlow 2003). Over longer periods of time, sea-level rise due to climatic shifts causes saltwater intrusion along the entire coast.

ENVIRONMENTAL FACTORS

An ocean-moderated climate and intense storm events greatly influence vegetation patterns in the Maritime ecoregion. Temperature fluctuations on the barrier islands and in nearshore mainland areas are generally less extreme than on the interior portions of the Coastal Plain due to the influence of ocean waters and sea breezes. In summer, most precipitation comes in

South Atlantic Bight and Continental Shelf. Data sources: ESRI Online Maps and Data (http://www.arcgis .com) and Georgia GIS Data Clearinghouse (https://data .georgiaspatial.org)

the form of afternoon thundershowers that develop from local convection currents, as warm, moist air from the ocean moves inland, rises, cools, and releases its moisture (M. Teal and J. Teal 1964; Schoettle 1993). In late summer, large continental storm fronts move across the coastal region, bringing extended periods of rain. During the winter months, strong storms with northeasterly winds ("nor'easters") supply most of the precipitation along the Georgia coast (A. S. Johnson et al. 1974). These storms may bring gale-force or even hurricane-force winds and persist from several hours to several days (Stalter and Odum 1993).

TIDES AND WAVES

Twice each day incoming tides deliver nutrients, planktonic organisms, and other materials that contribute to the overall productivity of the coastal marshes and estuaries. Receding tides flush decaying vegetation, sediments, and organisms into the ocean. These tides are produced by the gravitational force of the sun and moon acting on the earth's oceans, which causes a bulge of water on the side of the earth closest to the moon (or sun) as well as a corresponding bulge on the opposite side. There are two tides per day because the earth passes through both bulges during its daily rotation (Bertness 2007).

When the earth, moon, and sun are aligned (during new and full moons), the two bulges of water caused by the moon and sun coincide, leading to higher than average high tides and lower than average low tides; these are known as "spring tides." When the earth, moon, and sun form a right angle, the high tide caused by the moon's gravitational pull coincides with the low tide produced by the sun's force. This results in lower than average high tides and higher than average low tides, which are known as "neap tides" (Bertness 2007; Proudman Oceanographic Laboratory 2009).

As tidal waters approach the Georgia coast, they are funneled together by the concave shape of the South Atlantic Bight and the increasingly shallow continental shelf. This causes a vertical mounding of tidal waters. The result is that the tidal range (difference in sea level between high and low tides) on the Georgia coast is higher than any other location on the Atlantic coast south of Cape Cod. The average tidal range along the Georgia coast is approximately 7.5 feet. During a spring tide with easterly winds, the tidal range may exceed 9 feet (Schelske and Odum 1961). The high tidal range and low elevational gradient of the lower Coastal Plain allow tidal waters to travel inland several miles, creating the most extensive tidal marsh system anywhere along the Atlantic coast.

Georgia has lower wave energy than states farther south and north along the Atlantic coast. This is due in large part to the extent and gradient of the continental shelf. As ocean waves move toward the Georgia coast they must travel across the broad, shallow continental shelf. In the process, these waves lose some of their energy to friction as the wave swells drag across the sea floor and encounter submerged sand bars and shoals. This reduces average wave height and, together with strong tidal flows, contributes to a relatively stable configuration of relatively thick barrier islands separated by broad, stable inlets. In contrast, the coast of North Carolina has much higher wave energies, due in large part to the fact that it lies much closer to the edge of the continental shelf and its nearshore waters are deeper. Here waves have less opportunity to be diminished by bottom friction, and tidal ranges are comparatively low due to the convex shape of the coast. Ocean waves hit the North Carolina coast with much more force and, in combination with relatively weak tidal currents, produce a series of narrow, elongate barrier islands separated by narrow and relatively unstable inlets (Stallins 2000).

One of the most important factors determining the distribution of plants and animals in coastal environments is salinity. Sea salt (a mixture of sodium chloride, magnesium, sulfate ions, and trace minerals) is both a nutrient and a stressor, and organisms that inhabit the coastal region exhibit various adaptations to a salty environment. Plants that are adapted to elevated salt levels in soil or water are known as "halophytes." In most cases, these plants do not actually require salt but are able to outcompete other plants that are more sensitive to elevated levels of salt. Few plants are adapted to high-salinity conditions, so species diversity generally decreases with increasing salinity (Wiegert and Freeman 1990). Only a very few coastal plants, such as glassworts and saltwort, actually require salt.

Salinity generally increases with proximity to the ocean; however, there are a few exceptions. Isolated flats that are infrequently flooded and experience high evaporation rates often have salinities that are well in excess of those in the open ocean. These hyperhaline environments are known as "salt flats" and are usually sparsely vegetated with halophytes. Specific adaptations to increased salinity include physiological mechanisms that allow plant roots to exclude salt when taking in water, glands that secrete salt, salt-concentrating organs (often leaves) that are periodi-

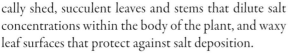
Glasswort, a common halophyte of salt flats

Fire in saw palmetto understory

cally shed, succulent leaves and stems that dilute salt concentrations within the body of the plant, and waxy leaf surfaces that protect against salt deposition.

In the surf zone, tiny droplets of salt water are ejected into the air from breaking waves, and winds carry large amounts of these droplets onto the islands. Most are deposited in close proximity to the intertidal beach, though the effects of salt spray can extend well beyond the beach and dune environments. Injury to plant tissues often occurs when sea salt is deposited and concentrated on the surfaces of leaves and twigs. Salt spray also provides several mineral nutrients that are essential to plants living in upper beach and dune environments, however.

Salinity gradients in the lower reaches of tidal rivers determine the distribution of freshwater and brackish marshes. Tidal freshwater marshes are generally found in a narrow zone along the edges of rivers, while brackish marshes may be found in a variety of settings, including just downstream from freshwater marshes as well as upslope from salt marshes where frequent rainfall dilutes the soil salinity, allowing less salt-tolerant plants to survive.

Lightning-ignited fires occur periodically along the Georgia coast, though generally less frequently than on the mainland. Within this region, the maritime forest represents the primary fire-adapted community. Maritime dunes and interdunal wetlands burn less frequently, and salt and brackish marshes, freshwater tidal marshes, and tidal swamps are thought to

burn only rarely under natural conditions. In general, the incidence of lightning-caused fires increases with decreasing latitude along the South Atlantic coast and is positively correlated with the amount of contiguous upland habitat; natural fires are not uncommon on the larger barrier islands, especially during drought years (S. Turner 1984).

The composition and structure of maritime vegetation influence the ability of a particular natural community to carry lightning-caused fires. In turn, the frequency and intensity of fires play an important role in determining the composition of natural communities in this region. For example, infrequent low-intensity fires in maritime forests may help maintain live oak as a canopy dominant (Laessle and Monk 1961), while more frequent and intense fires may shift the canopy dominance to favor longleaf, slash, or pond pine. Litter in oak-dominated stands is fire-resistant and usually produces a cooler fire than in pine-dominated stands. An abundance of saw palmetto in the understory, however, supports occasional high-intensity fires with long flame lengths.

Other environmental factors interacting with fire to determine the composition and structure of Maritime communities include soil moisture, humidity, prevailing winds, and periodic physical and biological perturbations (Davison 1984; G. R. McPherson 1988). Strong coastal winds can increase the intensity of fires, causing high mortality of trees in the canopy and shifting species composition (Davison 1984). In addition, episodic disturbances such as storm surges or outbreaks of insect pests can kill large numbers of trees, producing excessive amounts of woody fuels and increasing the probability of high-intensity fires.

The land management practices of Native Americans included use of fire, and it is likely that they used this management tool to influence upland barrier island and nearshore coastal habitats. European settlers who followed the Native American inhabitants used fire to improve grazing land for livestock, reduce the abundance of unwanted vegetation, improve habitat for desired game species, repel snakes and other "pests," and maintain open areas (Bellis 1995). More recently, managers of barrier islands and other coastal lands have used prescribed fire in both upland and wetland sites to improve wildlife habitat, reduce unwanted competition in timber stands, and reduce fuels to prevent catastrophic wildfires.

There is little documentation of the natural fire regime in coastal marshes and maritime dunes of the southeastern United States. There is also little information about whether these habitats were intentionally burned by Native Americans. Fires set in upland areas may have occasionally spread into coastal marshes and scrub (M. G. Turner and Bratton 1987). In addition, it is likely that lightning-ignited fires from nearby upland pine forests occasionally spread into adjoining coastal marshes if conditions were favorable (e.g., during low tide).

LAND USE HISTORY AND HUMAN IMPACT

Indigenous Peoples. There is evidence that humans occupied coastal portions of the southeastern United States more than 10,000 years ago (A. S. Johnson et al. 1974). Due to sea-level changes and the constant shifting of landforms along the coast, however, nearly all visible traces of human habitation older than 6,000 years have been obliterated. The primary sites of known settlements were mostly Pleistocene sand ridges 6 to 15 feet above mean sea level. Most were adjacent to marshes and often occurred where tidal creeks met upland habitats (McMichael 1977).

Extensive shell rings or middens are found along the coastal mainland and on the barrier islands. These structures, composed primarily of oyster and other mollusk shells, were created by Native Americans from 3,000 to 4,200 years ago. Though the purpose of these shell rings remains the subject of much debate, they indicate both long-term settlement and a dependence on shellfish as a food source (Simpkins 1975; Thompson 2005). Today, these calcium-rich shell deposits influence the composition of local plant communities.

Archaeological evidence from coastal sites dating from approximately A.D. 500 to 1300 indicates that the native inhabitants lived in established communities and cultivated crops such as corn, beans, melons, squash, and pumpkins (A. S. Johnson et al. 1974). By the time Spanish explorers reached the Georgia coast in 1540, much of the region was occupied by Guale Indians. These Native Americans hunted and fished on the barrier islands and mainland and lived in settlements where they cultivated a variety of crops (National Park Service 2009).

Post-settlement. In the 1560s, Spanish clergy, settlers, and soldiers came to the Georgia coast and established a series of missions that persisted for more than a century. They also introduced non-native species such as swine, goats, oranges, and figs (A. S. Johnson et al. 1974). During the 170 years that followed this initial settlement, Georgia became a British colony with Savannah as its first city; the colony was expanded south as far as St. Simons. Following a series of military skirmishes, Spanish troops were defeated at the famous "Battle of Bloody Marsh" in 1742. After this battle, the Spanish withdrew southward, leaving the Georgia coast under British control until the American Revolution (Green 1989; Schoettle 1993).

Agriculture and Timber Harvest. By the date of America's independence in 1776, cities such as Savannah, Richmond Hill, Midway, Sunbury, Darien, Brunswick, and St. Marys were well established. The economy of the region was based on naval stores, timber, and agriculture (A.S. Johnson et al. 1974). Because of its strength, density, and curved shape, live oak timber was in great demand for use in the construction of wooden ship hulls. To meet this demand, large tracts of maritime forest were cleared along the coast. The first federally protected barrier island on the Georgia coast, Blackbeard Island, was purchased by the federal government in 1800 as a reserve of live oak timber for the U.S. Navy. Only a small portion of the live oak trees on the island was actually harvested, however, because wooden sailing ships became obsolete soon afterward (U.S. Fish and Wildlife Service 2006a).

Rice and cotton were especially important crops for the coastal region of Georgia from the late 1700s

Ruins of Couper Plantation, St. Simons Island

through the mid-1800s. Many of the major tidal river floodplains along the coast were cleared of trees, diked, and placed into rice cultivation using a system of tidal gates. This extensive alteration of the tidal river systems resulted in significant losses of tidal river swamps as well as changes in water flows in coastal streams. Long-staple cotton imported from the Bahamas was grown on cleared fields on many of the barrier islands of Georgia and South Carolina. Because its longer, stronger strands made it easier to process, this "sea island cotton" was much more desirable than the variety of cotton grown on the mainland and served as an important cash crop for the region (A. S. Johnson et al. 1974).

Trade in cotton and rice created enormous wealth in coastal Georgia and spurred the development of extensive plantations as well as the growth of cities such as Savannah. St. Simons Island alone had as many as 14 plantations (Green 1989; Schoettle 1993). Because this plantation-based economy required intensive inputs of human labor and large expanses of cultivated land, it firmly established the institution of slavery as the primary means of agricultural production in the state and led to widespread habitat destruction in the coastal region.

Even before the outbreak of the Civil War, the coastal plantations began to decline due to soil depletion, a decline in cotton prices, and a shortage of slave labor (Green 1989). Following the Civil War and invasion of the boll weevil around 1915, the economy

of coastal Georgia collapsed and the plantations were largely abandoned. Many of the barrier islands were essentially unpopulated until the late 1800s and early 1900s, when these lands became popular with wealthy northern industrialists as private retreats, working plantations, or remote hunting lands. Some of the new landowners introduced exotic game species to the islands (Norris 1956). Others introduced or augmented island populations of domestic livestock, including cattle, horses, donkeys, goats, and swine.

Patterns of Land Ownership and Development. In the latter half of the 20th century, several of the privately owned barrier islands were sold to public agencies or private conservation organizations. Examples include Wassaw, Wolf, and Cumberland Islands (now in federal ownership); Ossabaw, Sapelo, Little Tybee, and Jekyll Islands (now in state ownership); and Little St. Simons and St. Catherines Islands (now in private conservation ownership). Though these islands are protected from development today, they are not pristine; most of the barrier islands have been subjected to intensive agriculture, timber harvest, and the impacts of exotic species. The current condition and configuration of natural communities on the islands vary according to each island's land use history and physical features (Somes and Ashbaugh 1973). Unlike most of the islands of the Atlantic coast, Georgia's barrier islands remain largely undeveloped. Only four of the barrier islands (Tybee, Jekyll, St. Simons, and Sea Island) are accessible by car.

Throughout much of the 20th century, economic growth and development along the Georgia coast was depressed, though areas such as Savannah, St. Simons, Brunswick, and Jekyll Island grew modestly. The coastal economy was based on pulp and timber production, the seafood industry, military base operations, and various manufacturing firms (A. S. Johnson et al. 1974). Beginning in the 1970s and continuing to the present, this region has seen a substantial increase in growth and development (Green 1989; DeScherer et al. 2007; Georgia Office of Planning and Budget 2010).

Industrial Forestry. Another significant development following the Civil War was the growth of the timber industry in south Georgia. Land was inexpensive, and timber supplies were seemingly inexhaustible. Investors from the northern states formed timber companies and built railroads and tram lines to cut and transport trees from the pinelands and swamps of coastal Georgia to mills or ports (Green 1989). From the 1870s to the early 1900s, vast areas of coastal Georgia forest were cut. In swampy areas large ditches were constructed to make the areas more productive for silvicultural uses (Barrows, Phillips, and Brantly 1917). Tram lines with cables were constructed to log ancient cypress and hardwood trees in the river swamps. Savannah, Brunswick, and Darien were leading exporters of naval stores and timber during this period. By the 1930s, nearly all of the old-growth timber in the coastal region had been harvested and replaced with second-growth regeneration or pine plantations.

In the mid-20th century, timber corporations bought up large tracts of land in the coastal counties and invested in intensive silvicultural operations to produce pulp for paper mills. These mills were sited near the coast to take advantage of ample groundwater supplies and large coastal rivers to receive the mill effluent. The operation of these mills and similar industries caused a significant depression of groundwater levels that extended as far as the barrier islands, where some artesian wells stopped flowing and groundwater-fed wetlands were impacted (Hillestad et al. 1975).

In recent years, timber corporations have divested many of their properties in this region, selling them to timber investment management organizations, real estate developers, or individual landowners. While pine plantations are not ecologically equivalent to natural communities, many of these timber lands contain embedded natural communities such as isolated wetlands or sandhills; they provide habitat for native wildlife and help maintain water quality in the region. The long-term impacts of recent shifts in land ownership in this region are difficult to predict. It is likely, however, that intensive development of former timber tracts will result in significant negative environmental impacts in some areas.

Water Quantity and Quality. Human agricultural activities over the past three centuries have contributed to expansion of tidal wetlands along the Atlantic coast by increasing sediment input to the coast (C. J. Anderson and Lockaby 2007). This situation has changed recently due to the construction of dams on major alluvial rivers that drain the Atlantic Coastal Plain (Komar 1998). Upstream dams on the Savannah have greatly altered the flooding and nutrient regimes of this large river. These dams dampen peak flows and

Paper mill, Brunswick, Georgia

raise the level of minimum flows, allowing tides to dominate coastal reaches of the river for longer periods each day (Day, Williams, and Warzewski 2007). Because prolonged periods of low flow are needed to allow regeneration of some tidal swamps, this reduction in flow variability likely alters the process of succession in tidal swamps. The estimated reduction of sediment input to the lower Savannah River by the Lake Thurmond (Clarks Hill) dam is 22%, and the Lake Thurmond and Lake Hartwell dams together trap 90% of the sediment that otherwise would be transported downstream to the lower Savannah system (Duberstein and Kitchens 2007). Though the Altamaha River system also has upstream dams on the Oconee and Ocmulgee Rivers, the relative influence of these dams on flows and sediment transport in the lower reaches of the Altamaha is less significant due to the much greater size of the Altamaha drainage basin.

Dredging of tidal rivers for navigational purposes is another factor influencing the distribution and condition of coastal wetlands. Periodic dredging of the Savannah River began as early as the mid-1700s but was very minor in extent and impact. More significant dredging began in the mid-1800s and has continued to the present (Duberstein and Kitchens 2007). The current depth of the Savannah River channel is 44 feet below mean low water (MLW) at the mouth, 42 feet below MLW at Savannah, and 36 feet below MLW from Savannah up to Port Wentworth, 31 miles up-

Butler Island, Altamaha Wildlife Management Area
(McIntosh County)

Artesian well at St. Andrews Beach Picnic Area, Jekyll Island.
This well was drilled in 1958 and is 396 feet deep, tapping
a Miocene aquifer. Sulfur-reducing bacteria produce the
whitish color at the base of the well.

stream; plans are to deepen the channel to 47 feet to accommodate even larger container ships in the Port of Savannah. The current depth of the dredged channel allows significant saltwater intrusion upstream, increasing salinity levels in the Savannah National Wildlife Refuge and converting freshwater marshes to brackish marsh along the river. Due to dredging, the tidal range actually increases upstream from Savannah to Port Wentworth (Day, Williams, and Warzewski 2007).

The extensive system of drainage ditches constructed in the lower Coastal Plain to benefit agriculture and silviculture also impacts coastal environments. In addition to dewatering adjacent wetlands, these ditches contribute to more rapid movement of surface water runoff into streams and rivers following rain events (G. Rogers, Flint Riverkeeper, pers. comm.). Within the tidal zone, ditches and dikes constructed nearly 300 years ago to benefit rice cultivation are influencing the process of succession; many long-abandoned rice fields are slowly reverting to tidal swamps or marshes, though hydrologic conditions are significantly altered. Examples of former rice fields that are being managed as seasonal impoundments to benefit game and nongame waterfowl can be seen at Butler and Champney Islands in the Altamaha Wildlife Management Area.

Rapid population growth in coastal Georgia, increased tourism, and sustained industrial activity have adversely affected coastal Georgia's water resources and limited the available water supply. The Floridan aquifer water was first tapped in the late 1800s and has been used extensively since that time (Spechler 2001; Falls et al. 2005). Significant withdrawals from the aquifer have resulted in saltwater contamination of drinking water and decreased groundwater input to springs, ponds, marshes, and streams. In an attempt to manage saltwater intrusion, the Georgia Environmental Protection Division limits groundwater withdrawals to 1997 rates in the Savannah and Brunswick areas.

The impact of water withdrawal on the Floridan and Brunswick aquifers was illustrated in 2002, when a large paper company in St. Marys, Georgia, ceased operations. This resulted in decreased groundwater withdrawal in Camden County by 35.6 million gallons per day and a corresponding rise of 140 feet in the level of the local water table (Peck et al. 2005). Many wells in the St. Marys area flowed for the first time since the mill began operations in 1941. Proposed

Red bay succumbing to laurel wilt disease

residential developments in the same area that could require groundwater withdrawals of 2 million gallons per day could result in significant groundwater impacts, potentially affecting interdunal wetlands on Cumberland Island (Priest and Clarke 2005).

Non-native Invasive Species. Non-native invasive species represent significant threats to coastal ecosystems. Feral swine are a significant problem here as elsewhere in the state, impacting a wide variety of habitats. Flathead catfish, native to the Mississippi River basin, have been introduced to Atlantic coast rivers, and significant populations have developed in the Altamaha and Satilla Rivers. These voracious bottom-dwellers have greatly impacted the redbreast sunfish population in the Satilla and may threaten recovery of the robust redhorse, a federal candidate species, in the Altamaha watershed. Other invasive species of concern in aquatic environments include water hyacinth, alligatorweed, and the Asian clam, *Corbicula fluminea*. In freshwater and brackish marshes, common reed, Chinese tallow-tree, marsh dewflower, giant reed, and wild taro represent threats to native biodiversity.

Perhaps the most significant impact to maritime forests in recent years has been the introduction of laurel wilt disease, a lethal fungal infection spread by a non-native ambrosia beetle. This beetle is thought to have been accidentally introduced to the Georgia coast in wooden packing material arriving at the Savannah Harbor around 2002 (Cameron, Bates, and Johnson 2008; J. Johnson et al. 2010). Species susceptible to this disease include red bay, sassafras, pondberry, avocado, pond spicebush, and other members of the Laurel family. In only a few years, this disease has greatly reduced the abundance of red bay trees throughout the coastal zone, nearly eliminating this species as an understory species in maritime forests. All of Georgia's coastal counties now have confirmed laurel wilt, and the disease is moving northward in South Carolina, southward in Florida, and inland at an alarming rate. It remains to be seen whether surviving red bay seedlings can develop resistance to this fungal disease, or whether control measures can be developed to halt the spread of the exotic beetle (J. Johnson et al. 2010).

Other non-native species of concern in upland habitats include Chinese privet, cogongrass, Japanese climbing fern, chinaberry, golden bamboo, and saltcedar (*Tamarix* spp.).

COASTAL CONSERVATION AND RESEARCH PROGRAMS

By some estimates, the population of the coastal region of Georgia is expected to double in the next 20 years. Most of the commercial and residential development pressure is concentrated on barrier islands, marsh hammocks, and mainland sites near the ocean or tidal rivers. These areas contain some of the most sensitive and ecologically significant natural communities in the state, as well as one of the greatest concentrations of globally imperiled species on the entire South Atlantic coast (Georgia Department of Natural Resources 2005a).

As development pressures in this region have grown, there has been a corresponding increase in public awareness of the ecological and economic value of naturally functioning coastal ecosystems and the impacts of human activities on those ecosystems. State laws protecting coastal dunes and salt marshes were passed in the early 1970s. More recently, regu-

lations protecting specific intertidal bars and spits as critically important shorebird nesting areas were established.

In 1972, Congress passed the Coastal Zone Management Act. This federal law established a national goal: "to preserve, protect, develop and where possible, to restore and enhance the resources of the nation's coastal zone for this and succeeding generations." The act created the National Estuarine Research Reserve system, a network of sites that serve as laboratories and classrooms where the effects of natural and human activities can be monitored and studied.

In 1992, the state of Georgia initiated the development of the Georgia Coastal Management Program. Authorized by the state legislature in 1997, the Georgia Coastal Management Program seeks to balance economic development in the coastal zone with preservation of natural, environmental, historic, archaeological, and recreational resources. This objective is pursued through environmental review of proposed development projects, environmental education and outreach programs, technical assistance programs di-

East River industrial area, Brunswick, Georgia

rected at local governments, grant programs for research and habitat conservation, interaction with local stakeholder groups on land-use issues, and enforcement of the Coastal Marshlands Protection Act and Shore Protection Act (Georgia Department of Natural Resources 2007b).

The Coastal Marshlands Protection Act of 1970 limits the amount of direct impact to coastal marshes resulting from physical disturbance or fill but does not address indirect impacts such as creation of impervious surfaces in close proximity to the marshes or hydrologic changes elsewhere in the watershed. While the extent of this law's jurisdiction is being debated, most agree that better land use planning in the coastal region is needed to minimize impacts from development on natural habitats (DeScherer et al. 2007).

Sapelo Island and its surrounding marshes and waters have been the subject of a considerable amount of biological and ecological research since the early 1950s, when the University of Georgia Marine Institute was established on the island. In 1976, the state of Georgia and the National Oceanic and Atmospheric Administration established Sapelo Island National Estuarine Research Reserve. The research conducted here and at other facilities has demonstrated the various ecological services provided by naturally functioning coastal ecosystems and has helped inform efforts to conserve these ecosystems (Georgia Department of Natural Resources 1990).

Global climate change represents a particularly significant threat to natural communities of the Maritime region. Projected increases in sea level due to climate change will undoubtedly impact the distribution of salt and brackish marshes, freshwater tidal marshes, and tidal swamps along the Georgia coast. Rising sea levels will likely drown some salt marsh areas, increase shoreline erosion, and cause salt or brackish marshes to migrate inland into freshwater marsh areas (Craft et al. 2009). Global warming may also result in changes in the frequency and intensity of tropical storms (Michener et al. 1997; Scavia et al. 2002). Conservation plans for coastal areas must consider these potential future impacts in order to protect the remaining natural biodiversity of this region.

Research conducted by the University of Georgia Marine Institute has shown that the productivity of salt marshes is among the highest of all known ecosystems.

Natural Communities of the Georgia Maritime

SPARSELY VEGETATED OR UNVEGETATED INTERTIDAL COMMUNITIES

Intertidal Beaches, Sand Bars, and Mud Flats. Essentially unvegetated intertidal communities with a substrate of unconsolidated sand or mud. They are found along ocean-facing edges of barrier islands, in estuaries, and in nearshore marine environments.

UPLAND AND ISOLATED WETLAND COMMUNITIES

Maritime Dunes. Sparsely vegetated herbaceous and woodland communities occurring on exposed sand dunes, swales, and sand flats on barrier islands and some nearshore mainland areas. Grasses and forbs predominate, with scattered shrubs and trees occupying the landward, more stable portions of these dune systems. Also included in this upland environment are shrub-dominated communities occupying transition zones adjacent to maritime forest, as well as nontidal flats that are occasionally flooded by storm surges.

Maritime Forests. Upland communities that include a variety of mixed pine–evergreen hardwood forests and woodlands found in coastal settings, including barrier islands, back-barrier islands (marsh hammocks), and low ridges and bluffs near the coast. Canopy dominants may include several species of oaks (especially live oak), longleaf pine, pond pine, slash pine, southern red cedar, and cabbage palmetto.

Interdunal Wetlands. Swamps or open-water wetlands typically found in flats and depressions between dune ridges on Georgia's coastal barrier islands. Depending on their location on the barrier island, they may be surrounded by maritime forest or by grass- or shrub-dominated maritime dune communities. They also occur in some near-coastal mainland settings where relict dune structures persist. They are also known as "freshwater sloughs" or "barrier island ponds."

TIDAL MARSHES AND SWAMPS

Salt Marshes and Brackish Tidal Marshes. Marshes that occur along the edges of tidal rivers, estuaries, and sounds, and on the mainland-facing sides of barrier islands. They are dominated by grasses, rushes, sedges, and forbs that are inundated regularly by salty tidal waters. By far the most abundant plant is smooth cordgrass. Other characteristic plants include black needlerush, sea lavender, seaside oxeye, saltgrass, and maritime marsh-elder.

Freshwater and Oligohaline Tidal Marshes. Marshes found along the edges of tidally influenced rivers, upstream of salt marshes and brackish tidal marshes. This natural community includes marshes with salinities ranging from less than 0.5 parts per thousand to 5 parts per thousand. Typical plant communities are dominated by a variety of emergent graminoids and forbs, such as giant cutgrass, sawgrass, southern wildrice, giant cordgrass, pickerelweed, cattails, and green arrow-arum.

Tidal Swamps. Freshwater forested wetlands that exist as narrow to wide bands along the floodplains of tidal rivers and creeks. The canopy is usually dominated by bald-cypress and water tupelo, but may also include sweet gum, swamp tupelo, green ash, swamp red maple, water oak, and swamp bay.

Intertidal Beaches, Sand Bars, and Mud Flats

Intertidal beaches occur as distinctive and easily recognized linear features along the ocean-facing portions of the Atlantic coastline. Beach environments represent high-energy transition zones between terrestrial and marine habitats. Though nearly devoid of vascular plant life, they provide critical foraging habitat for coastal shorebirds, fishes, and invertebrates, including several rare species such as the loggerhead sea turtle, Wilson's plover, and American oystercatcher. This ecologically significant natural community is also recreationally and economically important, as the beach is a primary destination of visitors to the Georgia coast.

Mud flats and sand bars are found at the mouths of tidal rivers and in nearshore marine and estuarine environments. They occur as patches ranging in size from less than an acre to more than 100 acres. These intertidal habitats are generally less accessible and less appreciated by the public but are also of great importance in terms of the ecological services they provide. Beaches, sand bars, and mud flats are treated as a single natural community type in the sections that follow.

PHYSICAL SETTING AND ECOLOGY

Wave action, tidal fluctuations, offshore currents, and prevailing winds greatly influence the configuration of beaches and contribute to their dynamic, high-energy character. The substrate in this environment is constantly shifting, producing a scouring effect on stationary objects. These conditions, together with constant exposure to salt water, result in an intertidal habitat with few or no vascular plants.

Closely related to intertidal beaches in terms of their ecological functions, intertidal bars and flats are regularly or intermittently exposed sandy or muddy areas within the estuarine or nearshore marine zone. Bars are intertidal sediment deposits configured as low islands separated from the adjacent uplands, while flats are more gently sloping and continuous with ter-

St. Catherines Bar, Liberty County. This important shorebird habitat is protected as a state Natural Area.

restrial habitats. The configuration and microtopography of sand bars and mud flats change constantly in response to water currents (Hoyt 1962; Wiegert and Freeman 1990).

The combination of low wave energies and high tidal range along the Georgia coast produces wide, gently sloping beaches. These beaches typically include runnels, shallow linear troughs that lie below and parallel to the high tide line and that are bordered upslope and downslope by small sand ridges or lateral bars. On beaches with higher wave energies, the slope of the beach is more constant, and there is often a scarp or ledge at the upper end of the beach (Stallins 2000).

Beach configuration varies from site to site along a particular barrier island and is determined by the pattern of sediment deposition along the coast. Sediment deposition patterns and rates are in turn greatly affected by the volume of sediment transported by coastal rivers, prevailing winds, and offshore currents

that mix, sort, and move these sediments along the coast. Thus, the shapes of barrier islands are in constant flux (Hoyt and Henry 1967; Hayes 1979). The southern ends of barrier islands tend to be areas of accretion (beach growth), while the northern ends typically experience periods of accretion followed by periods of erosion. Offshore currents carry sediments toward the islands, and these sediments are deposited as sand bars. As these sand bars grow and are pushed landward, they may form spits that are recurved toward the mainland. Examples of recurved spits can be seen at the south ends of Jekyll Island and Sea Island (Schoettle 1987). Tidal mud flats often occur in more sheltered parts of the estuary, landward of the barrier islands, on former river or creek channels filled with recent sediment, and along the edges of existing channels and point bars (Hayes 1994).

The variable patterns of accretion and erosion on the northern ends of barrier islands are caused by

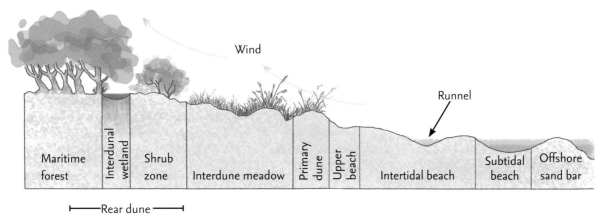

Profile of beach and dune environments on a barrier island. Adapted from Lenz 2002, with permission of Woodward / SherpaGuides.com.

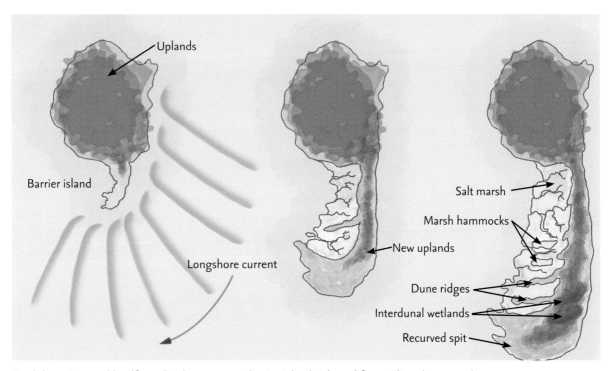

Sand deposition and landform development on a barrier island. Adapted from Schoettle 1993 and Lenz 2002, with permission from Taylor Schoettle and Danny Woodward / SherpaGuides.com.

the interaction of two types of currents—tidal currents moving in and out of the inlets between barrier islands, and longshore currents moving roughly parallel to the coast from north to south. The confluence of these currents causes suspended sediments to settle out near the mouths of the inlets. As these sediments are transported southward by the longshore currents, they tend to move in a clockwise direction around the northern end of the islands, occasionally becoming attached to the island and leading to beach accretion. Intense storms periodically remove these beach sediments, making them available for transport southward along the ocean-facing edge of the island. Georgia's barrier islands are thought to be in dynamic equilibrium, gaining as much sediment from accretion as they lose from erosion (Hoyt and Henry 1967).

Oyster reef at low tide, Little St. Simons Island

Soils of this natural community are unconsolidated Holocene sands, usually mapped as "Beach Association" in published soil surveys. Silts and clays are the most common substrates in areas with relatively low wave energy, such as the landward sides of barrier islands and edges of tidal sounds, while sands are found in areas with higher turbulence and velocity (Wiegert and Freeman 1990).

Type of sediment determines the composition and diversity of the benthic (bottom-dwelling) invertebrate communities that characterize these habitats. Silts and clays support higher populations of bacteria than do sands, perhaps because finer sediments provide much greater surface area for a given volume of sediment (Pomeroy 1959; Pomeroy and Wiegert 1981). Small benthic invertebrates such as burrowing nematodes are also much more abundant in fine sediments than in sand (Wiegert and Freeman 1990). The typical mixture of clays, silts, fine sands, and organic matter that covers the bottom of most estuaries of Georgia supports animal communities dominated by polychaete worms (primitive segmented worms) and mussels (Wiegert and Freeman 1990).

Within the intertidal zone, some organisms create microhabitats used by many other species. In shallow waters near salt marshes, oysters often colonize shell rakes or sites with woody debris and form oyster reefs. In Georgia, the typical oyster reef consists of roughly 82% living oyster and oyster shell and 18% other organisms, silt, and clay (Bahr and Lanier 1981). These intertidal hard-bottom habitats have greater structural diversity than the relatively featureless mud flats and sand bars and support a wide variety of marine organisms (Dardeau et al. 1992). Oyster reefs also help dissipate wave energies and protect the shoreline from erosion resulting from storm events.

Salinity is another important factor influencing the distribution of benthic invertebrates. In general, brackish or oligohaline areas tend to support high densities of relatively few species, while areas of higher and lower salinity support a greater diversity of benthic organisms (Pomeroy and Wiegert 1981; Wiegert and Freeman 1990). Though oysters are capable of growing in a wide range of salinities and actually thrive in high-salinity waters, they are generally limited to areas of lower salinities due to the fact that the oyster drill, a major predator, is unable to live in these less-saline waters (Dardeau et al. 1992).

NUTRIENT EXCHANGE AT THE SHORELINE

Primary productivity in the intertidal zone is supported largely by diatoms (one-celled algae) in the water and upper layers of the sediment. Tidal and wave action contribute to nutrient and energy exchanges within the intertidal zone. One of the primary sources of nutrients on the upper beach is marsh vegetation and other organic material deposited by incoming waves. Plant and animal material, known collectively as beach wrack, is washed up onto the beach by waves and storm surges. Much of the wrack material is composed of smooth cordgrass from nearby salt marshes, as well as marine algae and various other organisms. The wrack line (upper edge of the zone of deposited beach wrack) marks the high tide line and is especially noticeable after strong storms, when it may contain large amounts of shell material as well as dead fish, crustaceans, and coelenterates (starfishes, sea urchins, and sea cucumbers).

While considered unsightly by some beach visitors, beach wrack serves many important ecological functions. It provides food, a moist environment, and a hiding place for small terrestrial invertebrates such as beach hoppers (amphipods) and numerous insects, and foraging habitat for crustaceans such as the ghost crab and many coastal shorebirds. It also helps to trap and stabilize recently deposited sand and add to the development of the primary dunes. As it decomposes, the beach wrack provides nutrients to primary dune vegetation and to soil microorganisms in the upper beach and dune areas. Beach wrack may also transport seeds from plants such as beach morning-glory and southeastern sea rocket from one section of beach to another (Behnke 2009). In recent years, outreach campaigns by conservation groups and educators have increased public awareness of the ecological importance of beach wrack in nutrient exchange and dune formation.

Wrack on Georgia beaches is composed mostly of smooth cordgrass transported from nearby salt marshes.

CHARACTERISTIC PLANTS OF INTERTIDAL BEACHES, SAND BARS, AND MUD FLATS

Southeastern sea rocket—Cakile harperi

Silverleaf croton—Croton punctatus

Dune water-pennywort—Hydrocotyle bonariensis

Beach morning-glory—Ipomoea imperati

Railroad vine—Ipomoea pes-caprae

Bitter seabeach grass—Panicum amarum

Sand knotgrass—Paspalum vaginatum

Small sea-purslane—Sesuvium maritimum

Large sea-purslane—Sesuvium portulacastrum

Large saltmeadow cordgrass—Spartina patens

Seashore dropseed—Sporobolus virginicus

Beaches, sand bars, and mud flats are impacted by alteration of coastal sediment transport processes, including channelization of coastal rivers, development of upstream impoundments, construction of seawalls and jetties (low rock walls extending into the ocean), and artificial beach renourishment. The dredged shipping channel between St. Simons and Jekyll Island has impacted the inlet shoal system at the north end of Jekyll Island, resulting in greater beach erosion (Schoettle 1987).

Construction of seawalls and jetties causes a disruption of the sand-sharing system that moves sediments along the shorelines of barrier islands, resulting in accelerated beach erosion in adjacent "unarmored" areas. The effects of seawall construction are evident along portions of Georgia's more developed barrier islands. These seawalls are both expensive and impermanent, requiring periodic repair and reconstruction in response to the effects of storms and tides. Seawalls and exposed lines of rip-rap also serve as barriers to sea turtle nesting (see p. 534).

Artificial beach renourishment projects involving the application of dredged sediments to eroded beaches can decimate populations of benthic invertebrates by burying them under thick layers of dense, fine-grained sediments. Research has shown that recovery of benthic invertebrate populations following beach renourishment may take up to two years (Reilly and Bellis 1983).

VEGETATION

Intertidal beach, bar, and flat environments are largely unvegetated. Along the upper edge of the spring high tide line on beaches a few herbs may be found. This sparsely vegetated zone is continuous with the seaward edge of the primary dune zone (see maritime dunes), and includes salt-tolerant forbs and grasses. Other indicator plants of the intertidal beach/bar/flat environment are species of marine or estuarine algae.

ANIMALS

Sand beaches are harsh environments, and animals that live in these environments have special adaptations to deal with high salinity, high levels of solar radiation, and high desiccation (drying) rates. Many permanent residents of this environment burrow into the exposed beach sand at low tide, reemerging as water levels rise with the next incoming tide. The distribution of burrowing species in the intertidal zone is determined by the availability of oxygen and moisture, which in turn is influenced by sediment particle size. The sorting of beach sediments by waves results in a zonation of burrowing species along the beach slope (Pearse, Humm, and Wharton 1942; A. S. Johnson et al. 1974).

Typical burrowing animals of intertidal beaches include ghost shrimp, mole crabs, polychaete worms, razor clams, acorn worms, and sea cucumbers (Frey and Howard 1969). The secretive ghost shrimp constructs deep and elaborate burrows that persist even in relict beach deposits; the presence of "fossil" ghost shrimp burrows has been used to determine sea levels and patterns of sedimentation during the Pleistocene (Hoyt 1968; A. S. Johnson et al. 1974). Other aquatic invertebrates of intertidal beaches, including sand dollars, horseshoe crabs, starfish, coquinas (beach clams), and marine gastropods (snails), move up and down the beach surface or burrow shallowly into the sediments. Horseshoe crabs congregate in large numbers along

Keyhole sand dollar

Atlantic ghost crab

Horseshoe crab

Animal) siphon water through their mantle cavities and filter out algae, bacteria, or small bits of suspended organic matter. Sand fiddler crabs, common along the upper edges of beaches, pick up globs of moist sand and place these in their mouths; they remove small food particles from the sediment through a sieving process and place the remaining material back on the surface of the sand in the form of round, moist pellets. Two closely related species, the mud fiddler crab and red-jointed fiddler crab, forage primarily on mud flats and in salt marshes (Teal 1958; Crane 1975).

Predatory aquatic invertebrates of intertidal habitats include aquatic gastropods such as the oyster drill, moon snail, lightning whelk, and knobbed whelk, which feed primarily on bivalves; echinoderms such as the starfish, which feed on bivalves, gastropods, and other invertebrates; cephalopods such as squid; and crustaceans such as blue crabs, which forage over the lower intertidal zone for a wide variety of prey items, venturing into shallower unvegetated areas and adjacent salt marshes during high tides (Dahlberg 1972). Ghost crabs are true opportunists, feeding primarily at night on a wide variety of plant and animal material, living or dead, at the exposed upper beach during low tide. They often search through the beach wrack for prey items.

Fishes of intertidal habitats include a wide variety of marine or estuarine species such as mullet, flounder, silversides, killifish, sheepshead, menhaden, jack,

beaches in the spring or early summer to breed and lay eggs. Each female horseshoe crab can lay up to 4,000 eggs in a single cluster and up to 100,000 per spawning season. Both the eggs and hatchling horseshoe crabs serve as an important food source for migrating shorebirds (U.S. Fish and Wildlife Service 2006b).

Many intertidal invertebrates obtain their nutrients by harvesting plankton or benthic detritus. Beach clams such as the ubiquitous coquina (see Featured

pompano, permit, pigfish, lookdown, Atlantic moon-fish, silver perch, spotted seatrout, sailfin molly, king-fishes, skates, and rays (Dahlberg 1972). Some species, such as oyster toadfish and skilletfish, are closely associated with oyster reefs, but other species are found in multiple intertidal habitats.

Mammals making use of beach habitats are few, and include mice, raccoons, and white-tailed deer. The eastern harvest mouse, cotton mouse, and old field mouse glean seeds from the upper beach, while raccoons feed on a wide variety of animal material. White-tailed deer occasionally graze on vegetation at the upper edge of the beach. Amphibians are generally absent from these harsh environments, and typical reptiles are limited to sea turtles, which traverse intertidal beaches on their way to and from nesting areas located just above the high tide line (A. S. Johnson et al. 1974; Olsen 2006). Georgia beaches represent

critical nesting habitats for the state and federally protected loggerhead sea turtle. Other sea turtles that nest along the Georgia coast infrequently include the leatherback and green.

Intertidal beaches, sand bars, and mud flats are particularly important foraging habitats for coastal shorebirds. American oystercatchers, plovers, dowitchers, willets, red knots, sandpipers, and sanderlings feed at low tide on a variety of invertebrates, while terns and skimmers catch small fishes in the surf zone. Gulls, vultures, eagles, osprey, and fish crows scavenge for food along the upper beach and in the primary dunes (A. S. Johnson et al. 1974). Mud flats are important foraging sites for herons, egrets, and ibises and "loafing" habitat for gulls and terns. In addition, these unvegetated soft-bottom areas support many species of diving ducks, including scaup, scoters, ruddy ducks, and buffleheads (Dardeau et al. 1992).

"Johnson Rocks" at North Beach, Jekyll Island. These boulders, placed here in the 1960s to reduce beach erosion, prevent female loggerhead sea turtles from accessing potential nesting sites on the upper beach and primary dunes.

WATERBIRD CONSERVATION INITIATIVE

Human population growth in the coastal region of Georgia has placed waterbird habitats associated with the barrier island beaches, coastal salt marshes, and freshwater wetlands under increasing threat from development. In 1998, the Waterbird Conservation Initiative was launched by the Wildlife Resources Division of the Georgia Department of Natural Resources to address conservation needs for these species. Conservation efforts include protection and management of five sand island locations specifically for beach-nesting birds. These are Egg Island Bar, at the mouth of the Altamaha River; St. Catherines Bar, at the northern end of St. Catherines Island; Pelican Spit, between St. Simons and Little St. Simons Island; Satilla River Marsh Island, at the mouth of the Satilla River; and Williamson Island, at the southern end of Little Tybee Island. These five islands were dedicated as state natural areas, and regulations limiting access by visitors were developed and adopted by the Board of the Georgia Department of Natural Resources in 1998. This effort has been particularly valuable for seabirds, but both resident and migratory shorebirds also benefit from protection of critical nesting areas on these islands. One of the areas, Egg Island Bar, supports the largest concentration of nesting seabirds on the South Atlantic coast.

Surveys of migrant and wintering shorebirds along the Georgia coast have documented important staging areas for red knots in the late summer and fall, a spring staging of whimbrels that may include 20% of the Atlantic Flyway population, the single largest concentration of wintering semipalmated plovers in the United States, and an important Atlantic coast concentration of wintering piping plovers from all three breeding populations. Recent surveys for American oystercatchers and Wilson's plovers provided the first comprehensive information on breeding populations of these species in the state (Georgia Department of Natural Resources 2007a). These studies demonstrate the critical importance of Georgia beaches and intertidal bars to the conservation of native waterbirds of the Atlantic seaboard.

Shorebirds feeding on horseshoe crab eggs to fuel their migration north. Short-billed dowitchers, dunlins, sanderlings, red knots, willets, and semipalmated sandpipers. St. Catherines Island Bar, Liberty County.

Coquina (*Donax variabilis*)

The coquina is a small, colorful clam found in the intertidal zone of beaches along the Atlantic and Gulf coasts from Virginia to Texas (Ruppert and Fox 1988). The coquina has a wedge-shaped shell less than 1 inch in length, with radiating bands of various colors (hence the name "variabilis"). Because it is so widely distributed and found within the surf zone of sand beaches, this small clam is familiar to many beachgoers. Coquinas are commonly observed burrowing in intertidal sands as waves recede and can easily be collected by digging in the wet sand. Empty coquina shells found at the upper edges of the beach are often collected and made into jewelry. Some people even harvest this small clam for food.

The coquina is well adapted for life in the intertidal zone, where water levels change constantly. Its compact size and relatively large and muscular foot enable it to quickly bury itself in the sand. While submerged, it extends its siphon tube above the surface of the sand and takes in water, extracting small floating food particles (DeLancey 2006). This highly active clam is capable of migrating up and down the beach with the tide, maintaining itself within the zone where food is most abundant. As the tide recedes, the coquina digs deeper into the sand, retracting its siphon and closing its shell tightly. It remains dormant, conserving moisture and avoiding predation, until it is inundated by the next incoming tide.

Surveys of various beaches in the Southeast have demonstrated that the coquina is one of the most abundant macroinvertebrates of intertidal beaches (DeLancey 2006). This species serves as an important source of food for sport fish and shorebirds and is considered an indicator of beach ecosystem health (Finucane 1969; W. G. Nelson 1986; DeLancey 1989; J. G. Wilson 1999).

North and South Beaches, Jekyll Island

The northern and southern ends of Jekyll Island (Glynn County) provide dramatic examples of coastal sedimentation processes and their effects on beach communities. The shoreline at the north end of the island is actively eroding, evidenced by a "boneyard beach" of live oaks extending approximately 90 to 100 feet seaward from the high tide line. Ghost crabs and shorebirds can be seen foraging in the beach wrack at the top of the beach, which consists mainly of smooth cordgrass stems. At the upper end of the beach the vegetation is dominated by cabbage palmetto, live oak, and loblolly pine, with dune water-pennywort, dune greenbrier, and bitter seabeach grass. A wind-pruned low hedge of yaupon, tough buckthorn, catbrier, and dune prickly-pear lies at the upper end of the beach. Just south of the point where an access trail intersects the beach, near beach marker 2, low tide exposes "Johnson rocks"—granite boulders put in place in the 1960s (during the Johnson administration) in an effort to retard beach erosion. These rocks serve as obstacles to nesting loggerhead sea turtles.

In contrast, the south end of Jekyll Island is an area of active accretion. Here sand is being piled up to form a series of parallel dunes. The upper beach area provides critical nesting habitat for loggerhead turtles and numerous shorebirds. Vegetation at the upper end of the beach includes dune water-pennywort, railroad vine, beach morning-glory, dune marsh-elder, sea oats, saltgrass, and bitter seabeach grass. As you walk along the upper beach, watch for markers indicating loggerhead sea turtle nests, and be careful not to walk on the dunes.

Location: North Beach: Approximately 2.7 miles north of the intersection of North Beachview and Captain Wylly Rds. is a small parking area near the Clam Creek bike trail. Park on the left side of road and follow the bike trail for about 85 yards; continue on the foot path another 150 yards to the "Driftwood Beach." South Beach: Park at the South Dunes Picnic Area along South Beachview Dr. The boardwalk starts at the picnic area, traverses maritime dune habitats, and ends at the beach. Google Earth GPS approximate coordinates at North Beach parking area: N 31.104103/W 081.406591; at South Beach parking area: N 31.033103/W 081.417374.

Maritime Dunes

Maritime dune communities are found on sand dunes, swales, and flats on barrier islands and some nearshore mainland areas. Grasses and forbs predominate, with scattered shrubs and trees occupying the landward, more stable portions of these dune systems. The maritime dune community also includes shrub-dominated transition zones adjacent to maritime forests.

This community occurs as a large-patch or local matrix system, with large patches ranging from several hundred to more than a thousand acres along extensive beachfronts such as the Atlantic coast of Florida (NatureServe 2009c). The best and most intact examples are found as discontinuous patches along the protected barrier islands of Georgia. Adjacent natural communities seaward of maritime dunes are intertidal beaches; to the landward (upslope) side of maritime dunes are maritime forests.

Maritime dunes are among the most picturesque environments of the coastal region and are very popular as recreational sites. These dynamic environments provide important habitat for nesting shorebirds, sea turtles, and other species of conservation concern. In addition, they help protect inland habitats from the impacts of storms.

PHYSICAL SETTING AND ECOLOGY

Maritime dune habitats are highly dynamic environments that are subject to shifting substrates, changing salinities, and fluctuations in moisture availability. Indeed, the local topography of dune habitats can literally change overnight. Plants and animals found on maritime dunes are subject to extreme environmental conditions, including high salinity, flooding, shifting substrate, exposure to salt spray, high solar radiation, high summer temperatures, and desiccating winds. In many areas, especially sand flats, occasional inundation by storm surges followed by evaporation of seawater can create temporary hypersaline conditions. Constantly shifting, active dunes also present great challenges for colonization by vascular plants. The combination of these factors prevents the dominance of woody vegetation in this environment.

The composition of maritime dune communities is determined by a combination of physical environmental factors that vary by location along the South Atlantic Bight (Stallins 2000). Overwash, the overland movement of large amounts of sediment and seawater by storms, is an infrequent event on the Georgia coast (Deery and Howard 1977; Hayes 1994; Fenster and Dolan 1996). Georgia's large tidal range limits the impact of storm surges to periods of high tides, and wide tidal inlets help dissipate water and energy from storm surges (P. J. Godfrey 1976; Riggs 1976; Sexton and Hayes 1991). The combination of low wave energy, high tidal range, and wide tidal inlets on the Georgia coast results in a gradual and consistent pattern of sediment deposition, allowing the development of pronounced dune structures with characteristic ridge and swale topography (Oertel and Larson 1976; Psuty 1988).

Tread-softly

DUNE FORMATION

Maritime dune formation represents a complex interaction between sediment deposition, microtopographic gradients, and vegetation composition. Pioneer plants such as sea oats colonize new sand deposits landward of the high tide line, and their fibrous root systems help to stabilize the incipient or "embryo" dune system. These plants trap windblown sand, forming small mounds of sand at their bases that slowly increase the height of the dunes. By producing new leaves and runners in response to accumulating sand, sea oats are able to maintain their position on the dune (Wagner 1964). In fall and early winter, sea oat seeds are dispersed by sea breezes. Those landing on sites where sand is accreting are buried and have a chance of germinating in spring, while many of those remaining exposed on the sand surface are eaten by birds, small mammals, or invertebrates (A. S. Johnson et al. 1974). Beach wrack deposited at the high tide line on the beach may be transported landward by strong breezes. This decaying plant and animal material provides important nutrients and moisture and helps trap the seeds of sea oats and other wind-dispersed species.

Because of its height, aggressive growth pattern, and tolerance of salt, drought, and shifting sands, sea oats is by far the most important species for dune formation on the Georgia coast (Wagner 1964), but bitter seabeach grass, large saltmeadow cordgrass, and seashore dropseed are also important dune colonizers. Other characteristic dune plants tend to be found on lower, temporary dunes because they lack an extensive root system to bind the loose sand, are less tolerant of being buried by shifting sand, or are less tolerant of dry conditions as the dunes grow in height (Kurz 1942). Sprawling plants such as dune water-pennywort, beach morning-glory, creeping frogfruit, railroad vine, and butterfly pea form mats on the surface of the soil and help bind the soil. Being low in stature, they are vulnerable to burial by new sand deposits and tend to persist only in areas where the rate of accretion is relatively low.

Over time, the dune system increases in height to the maximum elevation to which prevailing winds can transport sediments from the beach, typically 10 to 12 feet on the Georgia coast but sometimes much higher (A. S. Johnson et al. 1974). At that point, a second row of dunes often forms seaward of the first ridge, and a swale (linear depression or trough) is maintained between the two ridges. This ridge and swale topography provides resistance to overwash, enhances environmental diversity, and supports greater species richness than does a more uniform slope from beachfront to rear dune (Stallins 2000).

The roots of sea oats bind sand on primary dunes.

Dunes encroaching on maritime forest, South Beach, Jekyll Island

Even established and well-vegetated dunes are subject to blowouts due to storms. Strong storm surges may breach the dunes, especially in areas where erosion has occurred due to natural processes or anthropogenic impacts. Where sediments are not stabilized on the windward side of foredunes they may be transported landward by sea breezes and deposited on top of the existing rear dunes. This phenomenon, known as "marching dunes," is evident at Dungeness Beach on Cumberland Island, where destabilization of the foredunes by horses and other grazers has caused the rear dunes to encroach upon and overtop the adjacent maritime forest (A. S. Johnson et al. 1974). Other examples can be seen on portions of Jekyll Island, where past disturbance of dune vegetation has caused a landward migration of dunes (Schoettle 1987).

Holocene sediments comprise the beaches and active dunes of nearly all of Georgia's barrier islands. These sediments are typically excessively drained on the higher dunes but may alternate between dry and saturated conditions. Because they are primarily quartz sand, the soils of the primary dunes or foredunes are very well drained, very low in nutrient-holding capacity, and acidic. Nitrogen is a primary limiting nutrient for plant growth in maritime dune environments. In general, the wind-sorted sediments on the foredunes are composed of finer sands than those in the interdune swales (Woodhouse 1982; Hayes 1994).

Aerial deposition of sea salt provides a continuous source of inorganic nutrients to the dune environment. Maritime dune soils do not build up high levels of salinity because rainwater leaches the salts through the coarse sediments (Boyce 1954). For this reason, soil salinity is a less important factor than direct salt deposition, desiccation, and interspecific competition in determining the distribution of dune plants (Oosting and Billings 1942; Boyce 1954).

Within interdune swales the soil surface is somewhat protected from high winds, reducing the rate of desiccation and increasing substrate stability. There is less impact from salt spray and the water table is closer to the soil surface. Organic material tends to accumulate and decompose in these swales, leading to higher levels of soil organic matter. Low interdune ridges have

Primary dune, interdune swale, and shrub-dominated rear dune

higher species richness and vegetative cover than the primary dunes because they are moister and have soils with higher organic content. Wax-myrtle, a prominent shrub in the interdune zone, is able to fix nitrogen and thus thrive in this relatively protected but nitrogen-poor environment. By enriching the soil, it makes the interdune habitat more suitable for colonization by other woody species.

Soils of the rear dunes are older and more stable, providing a relatively consistent substrate for growth of woody shrubs and trees. Though these soils contain more organic material than those of the primary dunes, they may be low in available moisture. Because this area receives a significant amount of salt spray, salt-tolerant species such as sea oats may be found among the trees and shrubs on the windward face of the rear dunes. At the crest of the rear dunes the long-term effect of salty sea breezes on exposed woody vegetation is clearly demonstrated. Salt deposited on the ocean-facing surfaces of trees and shrubs causes death of exposed leaves and branches and stimulates the de-

velopment of lateral buds (Boyce 1954). This chemical pruning process, together with mechanical pruning by strong winds that break twigs and branches, results in trees and shrubs with dense, asymmetrical crowns.

Fire is not considered to be a major factor in shaping maritime dune communities. Primary dunes are sparsely vegetated and unlikely to carry fire. Interdune meadows and shrub-dominated rear dunes produce higher levels of combustible fuels and may carry fires that originate in adjacent upland communities. These fires would likely be infrequent under natural conditions, however (NatureServe 2009c). In many coastal states, maritime dune communities have been greatly impacted by motorized vehicle traffic. Fortunately, few maritime dune areas in Georgia are accessible to vehicular traffic. In some popular beach access areas, foot traffic has resulted in degradation of dunes, but today these impacts are relatively minor and localized. Public outreach campaigns have been effective in educating the public about the sensitivity and ecological significance of maritime dune environments.

Salt-pruned shrub thicket at maritime dune–forest ecotone

VEGETATION

Plant communities of maritime dunes exhibit patterns of zonation based on substrate stability, exposure to salt spray, soil organic content, and soil moisture. These communities are typically dominated by salt-tolerant grasses and forbs on the primary dunes and interdune areas but include scattered shrubs and trees on rear dunes. The major vegetation zones within the maritime dune environment have been referred to as primary dune, interdune meadow, and shrub zones (Wharton 1978).

Primary dunes are typically dominated by salt-tolerant species such as sea oats, bitter seabeach grass, beach morning-glory, railroad vine, southeastern sea rocket, tread-softly, large saltmeadow cordgrass, saltwort, large sea-purslane, dune water-pennywort, and northern seaside spurge. Other species often found in this area include dune marsh-elder and Spanish dagger. Low interdune ridges have vegetation that is similar to that of the primary dunes but with higher species richness and vegetative cover.

The greatest diversity of plants within the maritime dune community is found in the relatively protected interdune swales and flats. Herb-dominated "interdune meadows" are characterized by a variety of grasses and forbs, including camphorweed, perennial sand bean, dune water-pennywort, seabeach evening-primrose, dune hairgrass, butterfly pea, silkgrass, and tread-softly (Schoettle 1993). Some woody species are found here, too, including yaupon, wax-myrtle, southern red cedar, and live oak (A. S. Johnson et al. 1974).

Landward of the interdune zone, shrubs such as wax-myrtle, Hercules'-club, yaupon, groundsel tree, tough buckthorn, and saw palmetto can be found on the rear dunes. Scattered trees are also present, including live oak, cabbage palmetto, loblolly pine, slash pine, southern red cedar, and red bay (Wharton 1978). Abundance of woody species is highest on the crest and lee side of the rear dunes, where this natural community abuts the maritime forest. Once established, shrubs such as yaupon, tough buckthorn, and wax-myrtle often form dense thickets that support vines such as dune green-

Spanish dagger

brier, peppervine, and climbing hempweed and provide shelter for a few shade-tolerant herbs.

The relative position and stability of these vegetation zones depend in large part on larger-scale sediment dynamics (M. Taylor and Stone 1996). In stable or moderately accreting beach environments, the primary dune, interdune, and rear dune vegetation zones are typically well developed. In areas of rapidly eroding beaches, these vegetation zones may be extremely compressed and disrupted, with shrubs or even dying trees interspersed with pioneer dune plants at the upper end of the intertidal zone. A study of Nannygoat Beach on Sapelo Island (McIntosh County) indicated that wax-myrtle, creeping frogfruit, and dune hairgrass colonized swales and inhibited growth of other plants through competition and allelopathy. In contrast, large saltmeadow cordgrass was more abundant in areas subjected to periodic overwash (Stallins 2000).

ANIMALS

The faunal communities of maritime dunes are relatively depauperate (Wharton 1978). The ghost crab is a dominant member of the terrestrial invertebrate community, feeding at night on a variety of plant and animal matter. Other predatory or scavenging

CHARACTERISTIC PLANTS OF MARITIME DUNES

TREES

Southern red cedar—Juniperus
  virginiana var. silicicola
Live oak—Quercus virginiana

SHRUBS AND WOODY VINES

Peppervine—Ampelopsis arboreum
Groundsel tree—Baccharis halimifolia
Yaupon—Ilex vomitoria
Dune marsh-elder—Iva imbricata
Wax-myrtle—Morella cerifera
Saw palmetto—Serenoa repens
Tough buckthorn—Sideroxylon tenax
Dune greenbrier—Smilax auriculata
Hercules'-club—Xanthoxylum
  clava-herculis
Spanish dagger—Yucca aloifolia

GROUND COVER

Southeastern sea rocket—Cakile
  harperi
Butterfly pea—Clitoria mariana
Tread-softly—Cnidoscolus stimulosus
Northern seaside spurge—Euphorbia
  polygonifolia
Camphorweed—Heterotheca
  subaxillaris
Dune water-pennywort—Hydrocotyle
  bonariensis
Beach morning-glory—Ipomoea
  imperati
Railroad vine—Ipomoea pes-caprae
Creeping frogfruit—Lippia nodiflora
Dune hairgrass—Muhlenbergia sericea

Seabeach evening-primrose—
  Oenothera humifusa
Dune prickly-pear—Opuntia pusilla
Bitter seabeach grass—Panicum
  amarum
Sand knotgrass—Paspalum vaginatum
Silkgrass—Pityopsis graminifolia
Large sea-purslane—Sesuvium
  portulacustrum
Large saltmeadow cordgrass—
  Spartina patens
Seashore dropseed—Sporobolus
  virginicus

White beach tiger beetle, a predatory insect of beach and dune environments

arthropods include several species of tiger beetles, rove beetles, earwigs, springtails, and spiders (Pearse, Humm, and Wharton 1942). Herbivorous arthropods are also found in this environment, feeding on sea oats and other dune grasses.

The primary dunes provide critical nesting habitat for sea turtles, primarily loggerheads and occasionally leatherbacks. The number of loggerhead turtles successfully nesting along Georgia's beaches has increased gradually over the past two decades, due in large part to reductions in accidental capture in shrimp nets, protection of nests from depredation by raccoons and hogs, and maintenance of naturally functioning beach and dune environments (Georgia Department of Natural Resources 2010). The Georgia Department of Natural Resources, Georgia Sea Turtle Center, University of Georgia Marine Extension Service, and other conservation organizations conduct outreach programs to educate the public about conservation needs of sea turtles and coastal beach and dune habi-

Hatchling loggerhead sea turtles making their way to the sea

Feral horse, Cumberland Island National Seashore. Feral horses can cause significant damage to maritime dune communities by trampling and grazing vegetation.

tats. Other reptiles in this environment are found primarily on the rear dunes, and include six-lined racerunner, black racer, and coachwhip.

The primary dune and interdune zones are also very important nesting habitats for numerous species of coastal shorebirds, including the royal tern, least tern, American oystercatcher, Wilson's plover, black skimmer, gull-billed tern, and willet. Piping plovers and other migratory shorebirds winter along the Georgia coast, foraging in the intertidal zone and primary dunes. More common birds inhabiting maritime dunes include red-winged blackbird, song sparrow, and wild turkey (A. S. Johnson et al. 1974).

Mammals of maritime dune environments include the eastern mole, eastern harvest mouse, old field mouse, cotton mouse, and marsh rabbit. Though widespread on the mainland, the old field mouse has only been recorded from one of the barrier islands, Cumberland Island. Larger mammals found occasionally in maritime dune environments include the raccoon, white-tailed deer, and feral swine. Depending on the barrier island and time period, cattle, horses, goats, fallow deer, red deer, and Sicilian donkeys have also grazed or browsed these dune habitats. Of all barrier island habitats, maritime dunes have been impacted most severely by these non-native herbivores (Stalter and Odum 1993). The impacts of feral horses on dune habitats of Cumberland Island have been documented through exclosure studies; these impacts include destabilization of dunes by trampling, as well as removal of dune grasses through foraging activities (Bratton 1986).

Efforts by state and federal agencies to reduce or eliminate feral livestock on barrier islands have been ongoing for several years. Significant improvements in the condition of dune habitats on Sapelo, Ossabaw, and Cumberland Islands have resulted from reductions in feral grazers and browsers. The greatest remaining management challenge is reduction or elimination of feral swine. These prolific omnivores pose a threat to dune plant communities as well as populations of coastal shorebirds and sea turtles.

Wilson's Plover (*Charadrius wilsoni*)

Wilson's plover is a medium-sized migratory shore-bird that can be distinguished from other plovers by its larger size and heavy black bill. Primary habitats in Georgia include maritime dunes, beaches, overwash fans, intertidal mud flats and sandflats, salt pans, and spits at the mouths of large rivers (Winn 2010). The diet of Wilson's plover includes fiddler crabs, ghost crabs, shrimp, crayfishes, marine worms, mollusks, beetles, flies, and spiders (Terres 1980). It feeds within the intertidal beach slope, along the upper beach edge, and within sandflats and intertidal pools.

This species nests from late April through June, with most nesting occurring in May. Preferred nest sites include sandy flats or terraces above the high tide line, overwash fans, and sparsely vegetated dunes (Winn 2010). The nests are shallow depressions that are scraped out by the male, often near clumps of grass, small shrubs, or other vegetation. Wilson's plovers are territorial during the nesting season but engage in group defense of their nesting areas. During the breeding season they congregate in groups of 30 or more, sometimes with other species of plovers (Corbat and Bergstrom 2000).

Corbat (1990) estimated a total nesting population of 200 to 250 pairs along the Georgia coast in 1986–1987. More recent surveys by the Georgia Department of Natural Resources indicate that the state's nesting population of Wilson's plovers is approximately 100 pairs (Winn 2010). Major threats to this species include loss or degradation of habitat due to beachfront development, disruption of nesting activity by humans, vehicles, and pets, and predation by wild, feral, and domestic animals. Protection of breeding habitat, reduction of disturbance by humans, and reduction of nest predation are needed to ensure the existence of this species along the Georgia coast. Wilson's plover is currently listed as Threatened by the state of Georgia (Winn 2010).

South End Beach, Jekyll Island State Park

Public access to maritime dune habitats in Jekyll Island State Park (Glynn County) is provided from the South Dunes Picnic Area, approximately 2 miles south of the Jekyll Island Conference Center. An elevated boardwalk trail leads from the picnic area across the dunes, providing an overview of the rear dune, interdune, and foredune zones as you approach the beach. The windshear effect on live oaks and other woody species of the rear dunes is dramatically exhibited in this area. Vegetation on the lee slope of the rear dunes is dominated by live oak, saw palmetto, cabbage palmetto, red bay, devilwood, Spanish bayonet, American beautyberry, dune greenbrier, butterfly pea, and muscadine.

Where the boardwalk crosses the top of the rear dune, the understory is dominated by grass-leaved goldenaster, muscadine, butterfly pea, and dune sandbur. Farther toward the beach, the boardwalk over-

looks an interdune meadow, with a variety of herbs and trailing vines, including sea oats, large saltmeadow cordgrass, butterfly pea, and silkgrass, with scattered live oaks and Spanish bayonet. Near the end of the boardwalk one can see young dunes recently colonized by pioneer plants as well as a series of older vegetated dunes forming parallel ridges. The primary dunes are dominated by species such as sea oats, bitter seabeach grass, railroad vine, large saltmeadow cordgrass, dune marsh-elder, and beach morning-glory.

Location: From the end of the Jekyll Island Causeway, turn right on Beachview Dr. and go south approximately 2 miles. The South Dunes Picnic Area will be on your left. The boardwalk trail is located at the east end of the picnic area. Google Earth GPS approximate coordinates at the picnic area: N 31.033103 /W 081.417374.

Maritime Forests

Maritime forest communities include a variety of mixed pine–evergreen hardwood forests and woodlands found in coastal upland settings, including on barrier islands, marsh hammocks, and low ridges and bluffs near the coast. This natural community is found from central South Carolina to the northern portion of Florida's Atlantic coast (NatureServe 2009c). The structure and composition of maritime forests are influenced by salt spray, severe storms, and periodic fire.

Georgia's maritime forests can be distinguished from maritime forests of the central and northern portions of the Atlantic coast by a higher prevalence of fire-adapted species, including longleaf pine, pond pine, and slash pine, as well as the presence of species such as cabbage palmetto. Other dominant or characteristic species of Georgia's maritime forest communities include several species of oaks (live oak, sand

laurel oak, Chapman oak, and myrtle oak) in the canopy and understory, as well as species such as southern magnolia, red bay, southern red cedar, and saw palmetto. Many high-quality examples of this natural environment can be found on public and private lands within the coastal region of Georgia.

PHYSICAL SETTING AND ECOLOGY

Maritime forests are found on stabilized dunes on barrier islands, on low, sandy islands surrounded by salt marsh landward of the barrier islands ("marsh hammocks"), and on low ridges and bluffs on the mainland near the coast. These landforms typically represent former coastal beaches and active dunes of Pleistocene or Holocene age (A. S. Johnson et al. 1974). Sites where maritime forests occur are generally protected from tidal inundation but may be flooded occasionally during storm surges. Aerosol salt deposition, strong and persistent winds, high summer temperatures, and sandy soils contribute to harsh, desiccating conditions,

Marsh hammock or back-barrier island surrounded by salt marsh and brackish marsh, with salt flat in foreground

especially at the edges of the forest. The interior portions of larger patches of maritime forest exhibit more mesic conditions, often supporting an abundance of vines, ferns, and moisture-loving herbs (Stalter and Odum 1993).

The primary area of maritime forest occurrence in Georgia is the chain of barrier islands that flank the coast. Here maritime forests occupy the major portion of each island, bordered by beach and dune habitats on the ocean-facing side and by salt and brackish marsh communities on the landward side and dissected by tidal streams. A significant matrix habitat of barrier islands, maritime forests may surround or encompass wetland communities such as interdunal wetlands and tidal flats, as well as more xeric environments such as maritime dunes. The juxtaposition of these different habitats within a relatively small area supports a diverse group of species. Nevertheless, maritime forests on barrier islands are generally less species-rich than their counterparts on the mainland.

Back-barrier islands, known colloquially as "marsh hammocks," also contain examples of maritime forests.

These islands may form when relict dune ridges on the back edges of barrier islands become fragmented and isolated by salt marsh or tidal creeks, or they may result from overwash and sediment accretion in these sites (Oertel 1979; Howard and Frey 1985). A recent inventory of Georgia's six ocean-facing coastal counties documented approximately 1,200 hammocks ranging in size from less than 1 acre to more than 1,000 acres. Nearly 85% of these are less than 10 acres in area. The total acreage of Georgia's marsh hammocks is more than 17,000 acres; however, 64% of the total acreage can be accounted for in only 41 hammocks (Georgia Department of Natural Resources 2002a). Species diversity on these back-barrier islands is positively correlated with size of the island (Albers and Alber 2003; Fabrizio and Calvi 2003).

The natural fire frequency for maritime forests has been estimated at 20 to 30 years (NatureServe 2009c), though this varies greatly from site to site. Lightning-ignited fires are not infrequent along the Georgia coast. One such fire burned 117 acres of Blackbeard Island in 2006 (U.S. Fish and Wildlife Service 2006a),

Southern red cedar is a common component of maritime forests.

and another burned more than 750 acres on Ossabaw Island in 2007 (B. Winn, Ga. DNR, pers. comm.). A lightning-ignited fire on Sapelo Island burned over 3,700 acres in 2011 (F. Hay, Ga. DNR, pers. comm.). Three lightning-ignited fires occurring within the same portion of Cumberland Island were documented in 1934, 1956, and 1981, and corresponded to years of lower than average rainfall (S. Turner 1984).

Fire behavior and resulting impacts in maritime forest stands are influenced by the relative dominance of oaks and pines, as well as the composition of the understory. In general, oak-dominated stands are more resistant to ignition but under dry conditions may carry fires that originate in adjacent pine-dominated stands or other habitats (Davison 1984). Litter in oak-dominated stands is fire-resistant and usually produces a cooler fire than that in pine-dominated stands. A predominance of saw palmetto or a buildup of woody debris in the understory, however, can support high-intensity fires.

Strong winds along the coast can contribute to intense fires that cause high mortality in canopy trees, including fire-adapted species such as longleaf pine and slash pine; in some cases, these infrequent but intense fires favor oak regeneration over that of pines (Davison 1984). In the absence of fire or other disturbance, these mixed maritime forests eventually transition to hardwood forests dominated by less fire-tolerant species such as sand laurel oak, red bay, American holly, southern magnolia, flowering dogwood, and sassafras, with an abundance of vines such as Virginia-creeper, greenbrier, summer grape, and poison ivy (Hillestad et al. 1975; Georgia Department of Natural Resources 2001c).

Some woody species of maritime forests exhibit specific adaptations to fire. Southern pines and live oaks resist damage from fire due to their thick bark, while cabbage palmetto is protected by its sheathing leaf bases and flame-resistant terminal bud. Other characteristic species such as red bay, wax-myrtle, staggerbush, dwarf palmetto, saw palmetto, sparkleberry, and American holly are not fire-resistant but are able to quickly resprout following fires (Bellis 1995). Southern red cedar is fire-intolerant but can often persist on isolated spits and hammocks that are protected from fire. In addition, its seeds are readily spread by birds,

Cumberland Island, looking north from south end. Maritime forests are the upland matrix communities of the Georgia barrier islands.

so it is often one of the first trees to colonize newly formed islands.

Georgia has the largest amount of intact maritime forest of any state along the South Atlantic coast. This is due to the fact that most of the state's barrier islands are protected through federal (Blackbeard, Wassaw, and Cumberland Islands), state (Little Tybee/Cabbage, Ossabaw, Sapelo, and Jekyll Islands), or private (Little St. Simons, St. Catherines, and Little Cumberland Islands) ownership. Other important conservation areas containing maritime forest include Skidaway Island State Park, Richmond Hill Wildlife Management Area, Hofwyl-Broadfield Plantation State Historic Site, Harris Neck National Wildlife Refuge, and Crooked River State Park (see the Featured Place). In many other portions of the South Atlantic coast, maritime forest habitats have been fragmented severely by development (Bellis 1995). While barrier island examples of this natural community are generally well protected in Georgia, increasing development in the coastal region represents a significant threat to maritime forest communities on the mainland and on many marsh hammocks.

As matrix habitats of coastal uplands, maritime forests encompass and influence many other, more discrete small-patch communities, including interdunal wetlands, coastal scrub habitats, and active dunes. Conservation of maritime forests requires careful management of fire, control of invasive species, and protection against fragmentation and isolation of habitats resulting from development. As these forests become increasingly dissected by roads, utility corridors, and other developments, their ecological functions are compromised. Where residential or commercial developments encroach upon these environments, the ability to apply prescribed fire or to let natural fires run their course is greatly constrained. Hydrologic connections with adjacent wetland and aquatic habitats are impaired by ditches, berms, and other structures constructed to facilitate land development, and invasive species problems are exacerbated by the creation of corridors and edges dominated by non-native species. As development progresses, the remnant fragments of maritime forest cease to exist as fully functioning natural communities due to disruptions in environmental gradients and disturbance regimes and introduction of exotic species.

Impacts of concentrated human recreational use on maritime forest communities are also evident in several areas, especially at campgrounds and picnic areas in publicly accessible sites. These impacts include trampling of herbaceous vegetation, cutting and removal of live woody vegetation and deadfalls, soil compression, and littering. Though these impacts are usually local and relatively minor, they point out the need to manage recreational uses to maintain maritime forest communities.

VEGETATION

Maritime forests vary widely in terms of species composition and structure but generally include a combination of southern pines, live oak and/or other dry-site oaks, a fairly dense and diverse understory/shrub layer, and a relatively depauperate herbaceous community. Canopy and subcanopy dominants of maritime forest communities vary depending on topographic position, soil type, and fire frequency (Bozeman and Fuller 1975; Wharton 1978; Duncan 1982; Davison 1984; Schafale and Weakley 1990).

On old, stabilized dunes protected from salt spray and flooding that do not burn frequently, the canopy of the maritime forest community is often dominated by live oak and/or sand laurel oak, with a mixture of slash or loblolly pine, southern magnolia, pignut hickory, and cabbage palmetto. The understory often includes red bay, cabbage palmetto, American holly, and southern red cedar. The shrub layer may be dominated by saw palmetto or by a more diverse combination of shrubs and vines, including crookedwood, devilwood, horsesugar, wax-myrtle, sparkleberry, catbrier, Spanish dagger, Virginia-creeper, and muscadine. The herbaceous layer is typically very sparse.

On sites that are slightly higher and drier and burn more frequently, the canopy is often dominated by a combination of longleaf, slash, and/or loblolly pine (the latter being more prevalent in sites that were formerly cultivated). Oaks are found in lower numbers,

often in clusters, and generally include species that are more fire-tolerant (e.g., live oak and sand laurel oak). These maritime forest communities often have a more diverse understory ground cover of grasses and forbs, including patches of southern wiregrass. Saw palmetto often occurs in isolated patches in the understory. In previously disturbed sites, loblolly or slash pine may predominate in large patches, often with sand laurel oak as a co-dominant instead of live oak (Bratton and Davison 1985). Pond pine is often prevalent in acidic wet depressions and swales within the maritime forest environment.

Maritime forests also occur in low-lying areas adjacent to or surrounded by salt marsh or brackish marsh, including small back-barrier islands. These maritime forest communities are typically dominated by live oak, southern red cedar, and cabbage palmetto, with a shrub layer of yaupon, wax-myrtle, groundsel tree, Hercules'-club, catbrier, and Florida-privet (Bozeman and Fuller 1975). Florida soapberry and small-flowered buckthorn are often understory components of these forests, especially where calcium-rich shell mounds are present.

Davison (1984) described maritime forest communities on Cumberland Island that were located on sites with well-drained soils. In these forests, live oak and myrtle oak form a low, open canopy and are interspersed with slash and pond pine. Saw palmetto often dominates the understory, along with Chapman oak, devilwood, red bay, wax-myrtle, and crookedwood. The herb layer consists mostly of panic grasses. In slightly lower areas with a higher water table pond pine may dominate the canopy. This subtype is similar to live oak hammock habitats described in northeastern Florida (Laessle and Monk 1961) and subxeric evergreen hardwood forests of inland sandhills in Georgia (Bozeman 1971).

In mainland settings as well as in protected swales and depressions of coastal islands, more mesic site conditions allow the development of maritime forest communities dominated by a mixture of loblolly or slash pine, live oak, sand laurel oak, laurel oak, southern red oak, water oak, sweet gum, pignut hickory, sand hickory, loblolly bay, American elm, and occasionally cabbage palmetto. Understory trees in these forests include ironwood, flowering dogwood, American holly, red maple, sparkleberry, southern red cedar, sassafras, black gum, and witch-hazel. The shrub/vine layer may contain muscadine, summer grape,

Yaupon

Partridge-berry

CHARACTERISTIC PLANTS OF MARITIME FORESTS

TREES

Pignut hickory—*Carya glabra*
American holly—*Ilex opaca*
Southern red cedar—*Juniperus virginiana* var. *silicicola*
Southern magnolia—*Magnolia grandiflora*
Red bay—*Persea borbonia*
Slash pine—*Pinus elliottii*
Longleaf pine—*Pinus palustris*
Loblolly pine—*Pinus taeda*
Sand live oak—*Quercus geminata*
Sand laurel oak—*Quercus hemisphaerica*
Live oak—*Quercus virginiana*
Cabbage palmetto—*Sabal palmetto*

SHRUBS AND WOODY VINES

Peppervine—*Ampelopsis arborea*
American beautyberry—*Callicarpa americana*
Yaupon—*Ilex vomitoria*
Crookedwood—*Lyonia ferruginea*
Wax-myrtle—*Morella cerifera*
Virginia-creeper—*Parthenocissus quinquefolius*
Saw palmetto—*Serenoa repens*
Sparkleberry—*Vaccinium arboreum*
Mayberry—*Vaccinium elliottii*
Muscadine—*Vitis rotundifolia*
Hercules'-club—*Zanthoxylum clava-herculis*

GROUND COVER

Ebony spleenwort—*Asplenium platyneuron*
Longleaf spikegrass—*Chasmanthium sessiliflorum*
Coastal Plain elephant's-foot—*Elephantopus nudatus*
Partridge-berry—*Mitchella repens*
Cinnamon fern—*Osmundastrum cinnamomeum*
Eastern needlegrass—*Piptochaetium avenaceum*
Bracken fern—*Pteridium aquilinum*

American beautyberry, Virginia-creeper, Carolina jessamine, catbrier, winged sumac, poison ivy, and mayberry (Schafale and Weakley 1990).

ANIMALS

Maritime forests are structurally diverse, with overstory and understory trees, shrubs, vines, and epiphytes. This structural diversity supports a wide array of animal species. In many cases, a single plant may provide critical food, foraging habitat, or nesting habitat for a wide variety of animals. For example, Spanish-moss provides nesting habitat for parula warblers, yellow-throated warblers, painted buntings, red bats, and Seminole bats, as well as a haven for chiggers, spiders, rat snakes, and black racers (M. Teal and J. Teal 1964). Live oak acorns are important food items for a wide variety of animals, including white-tailed deer, wild turkey, raccoon, gray squirrel, southern flying squirrel, and many species of waterfowl. Other important wildlife food plants of maritime forests include sand laurel oak, southern magnolia, red bay, sweet bay, saw palmetto, catbrier, American holly, yaupon, dahoon, wax-myrtle, muscadine, Virginia-creeper, and American beautyberry (A. S. Johnson et al. 1974; Miller and Miller 2005).

Gibbons and Coker (1978, cited in Bellis 1995) compared lists of reptiles and amphibians known from barrier islands of the Southeast. They found that the number of species in this group on a particular island was correlated to the amount of forest or woodland habitat present on the island rather than the size of the island itself, indicating that maritime forest communities constitute the primary habitat for most herpetofaunal species found on barrier islands.

Many lizards of the mainland are found on Georgia barrier islands, including the green anole, fence lizard, six-lined racerunner, ground skink, five-lined skink, broadhead skink, southeastern five-lined skink, eastern glass lizard, and island glass lizard (Martof 1963; A. S. Johnson et al. 1974). Snakes are also well represented in maritime forest and woodland communities of barrier islands; typical species include garter snake, black racer, coachwhip, corn snake, scarlet snake, rough green snake, rat snake, eastern diamondback rattlesnake, cottonmouth, and eastern kingsnake. Turtle species known from maritime forest environments are relatively few, but include the eastern box turtle and eastern mud turtle. The gopher tortoise was introduced to St. Catherines Island and Cumberland Island (A. S. Johnson et al. 1974; Hillestad et al. 1975; Bellis 1995).

Salamanders are particularly poor colonizers of island habitats, and representatives of this vertebrate group inhabiting maritime forests on the Georgia barrier islands are limited primarily to the eastern newt

Juvenile black racer in Spanish-moss

and mole salamander. Other amphibians found in maritime forests include the eastern spadefoot, oak toad, southern toad, eastern narrow-mouthed toad, green treefrog, squirrel treefrog, and pine woods treefrog (Hillestad et al. 1975; Stalter and Odum 1993; Chalmers 1997).

Examples of native mammals found in maritime forest communities include raccoon, white-tailed deer, gray squirrel, southern flying squirrel, gray fox, bobcat, opossum, short-tailed shrew, least shrew, eastern mole, cotton mouse, hispid cotton rat, red bat, Seminole bat, eastern pipistrelle, big brown bat, yellow bat, and southeastern myotis. The opossum, common on Cumberland Island in the 1800s, may have been extirpated as a result of subsistence hunting after the Civil War. Other native mammals, including the fox squirrel, bobcat, and white-tailed deer have been introduced (or reintroduced) to one or more of the barrier islands by humans (A. S. Johnson et al. 1974).

Three taxonomically distinct mammals have been described from Georgia barrier islands: Blackbeard's white-tailed deer (*Odocoileus virginianus nigribarbis*), St. Simons Island raccoon (*Procyon lotor litoreus*), and Cumberland Island pocket gopher (*Geomys cumberlandius*), though the latter was found by Laerm (1981) to be taxonomically indistinct from other coastal populations of pocket gopher.

Maritime forests are important environments for birds, including numerous neotropical migrants as well as year-round residents. The variety of foods found in this environment and the relatively dense and complex structure of the understory vegetation provide niches for many species. A. S. Johnson et al. (1974, pp. 171–190) provided a comprehensive list of 246 species of birds documented from forests, clearings, freshwater marshes, and ponds in Georgia's coastal region. This list included more than 93 native and introduced species known to breed on the barrier islands, of which more than 50 species could be considered native birds of maritime forests.

Painted Bunting (*Passerina ciris*)

As its name suggests, the painted bunting is a brightly colored, conspicuous bird. The male painted bunting has a bright blue head, red breast, yellow shoulders, and green back. The female is mostly greenish in color (Terres 1980). This migratory bird is typically found in shrub-scrub and open grassy habitats, open mature pine forests, and maritime forests closely associated with freshwater wetlands. It breeds in two separate areas: the south-central region of the United States and coastal areas of North Carolina, South Carolina, Georgia, and Florida. In Georgia, its breeding distribution is primarily the barrier islands and near-coastal mainland, with scattered occurrences along major river corridors of the Coastal Plain (T. M. Schneider and Sykes 2010).

During the first half of the 20th century this bird was considered a common resident along the Georgia coast and lower Savannah River, but was rarely seen in more inland sites. Recent surveys have documented breeding individuals north of the Fall Line near Augusta and Macon as well as in southwestern Georgia (T.M. Schneider and Sykes 2010). Anecdotal evidence indicates that the painted bunting population on the Atlantic coast is rapidly declining. Much of this population decline can be attributed to loss of breeding habitat due to development, nest parasitism by brown-headed cowbirds, impacts from feral animals, and the illegal pet trade. On barrier islands where hog populations are high, nest destruction and direct predation on painted buntings can be significant. In residential areas along the coast, domestic and feral cats can decimate populations of painted buntings. In Cuba, wintering male buntings are often trapped and sold as caged birds. The U.S. Fish and Wildlife Service and several conservation groups are partnering to curb the illegal wild bird trade in Central America and the Caribbean (T.M. Schneider and Sykes 2010).

Crooked River State Park

The Sempervirens Trail at Crooked River State Park (Camden County) provides access to an exceptional example of maritime forest. Park at the trailhead located just past the park cottages. As you walk along the trailhead, notice that longleaf pine, Chapman's oak, myrtle oak, sparkleberry, and sand live oak predominate in the pine flatwoods habitat. Farther along, the trail decreases slightly in elevation and saw palmetto, laurel oak, and muscadine become more prevalent, while slash pine becomes more common in the canopy. At the start of the Sempervirens loop trail, American basswood, pignut hickory, and American holly are prevalent. At the first boardwalk, where the trail crosses a shell midden, the forest is much more diverse, with basswood, black cherry, sugarberry, southern magnolia, live oak, sweet gum, southern red cedar, and cabbage palmetto dominating the overstory; red buckeye, muscadine, Florida soapberry, saw palmetto, dwarf palmetto, and yaupon occur in the understory. The ground cover vegetation is very sparse, with longleaf spikegrass common.

Farther along the trail is a second boardwalk: Florida soapberry, sugarberry, red buckeye, and southern red cedar are evident in this area. At the end of the boardwalk, a short side trail leads to a view of an adjacent salt marsh. Continue on the main trail to another shell mound exposure, where Godfrey's forestiera occurs in a large patch behind a live oak. Farther along the trail, a gap caused by the death of a large basswood provides space for many smaller trees, including basswood and ash. The return to the start of the loop trail is marked by an increase in cabbage palmetto, southern red cedar, American holly, and sweet gum in the overstory, with American beautyberry and red buckeye in the understory.

Location: The park entrance is near the end of Ga. Spur 40 north of St. Marys at Elliotts Bluff. Enter the park and travel just past the cottages to a small parking area near the trailhead. Google Earth GPS approximate coordinates at the parking area: N 31.846070/ W 081.546616.

Interdunal Wetlands

Interdunal wetlands are typically found in flats and depressions that occur between dune ridges on Georgia's coastal barrier islands. Depending on their location, they may be surrounded by maritime forest or by grass- or shrub-dominated maritime dune communities. They also occur in some near-coastal mainland settings where relict dune structures persist. Also known as "freshwater sloughs" or "barrier island ponds," these small-patch wetland communities are usually less than an acre in size but often occur in complexes of several ponds in close proximity (NatureServe 2009c).

These environments may support nontidal marsh vegetation, shrub- or tree-dominated swamps, or open-water ponds with aquatic macrophytes. Precipitation provides most of the hydrologic input to these wetlands, but periodic overwash from storm events may cause them to become temporarily brackish. Species composition and vegetation structure vary widely in this environment.

Interdunal wetlands represent unique freshwater "oases" within the salty and drought-prone barrier island environment. They provide critical feeding and breeding habitat for a wide variety of animals and serve as refugia for plants adapted to mesic or freshwater environments.

PHYSICAL SETTING AND ECOLOGY

Interdunal wetland vegetation is extremely variable; ponds on the same barrier island often contain very different plant communities, and this variation is dependent on topographic position, hydroperiod, exposure to salt spray, and the composition of surrounding plant communities. These plant communities also vary seasonally with fluctuations in water levels and salinity. In many respects, interdunal wetlands are similar to other depressional wetlands in the lower Coastal Plain, but fluctuating salinity and frequent storm events contribute to ecological and floristic differences.

Interdunal wetlands vary considerably in size and depth. Water levels often fluctuate widely, both within a wetland itself and among different ponds in the same area. Some interdunal wetlands dry up completely in summer, while others contain water throughout the year. The water in these ponds is often stained with tannins; for this reason, light penetrates only a short distance below the surface of the water. Deeper ponds may be dominated by shrubs; emergent aquatics such as cattails, pickerelweed, and arrow-arum; and free-floating plants such as duckweed, mosquito fern, and watermeal. Shallow ponds may have a more uniform coverage of emergent sedges, grasses, and forbs. Some ponds are connected with the surficial aquifer, while others are more or less perched on an underlying layer of clay or organic material. W. E. Odum and Harvey (1988) found that freshwater ponds within maritime forests tended to be circumneutral and poorly buffered; pH levels tended to fluctuate widely in a given pond.

Some interdunal wetlands are periodically inundated by spring or storm tides and thus have fluctuating salinity. These inundations may also include deposition of new sediments, which can reduce the depth of the wetlands. Because of their limited extent, soils of interdunal wetlands are usually not differentiated in soil survey reports from the surrounding upland soils. A pollen analysis of sediment cores taken from a freshwater pond on St. Catherines Island indicated that this pond experienced several distinct periods of sedimentation and shifts in vegetation composition during its formation (Booth et al. 1999).

Interdunal wetlands may form quickly, especially in areas of rapidly accreting beaches. For example, one pond near the southern end of St. Simons Island at East Beach formed over a period of only two years, after new sand deposits isolated a small embayment (Schoettle 1993). Similarly, interdunal ponds near eroding beaches may be breached and destroyed in a single storm event. In contrast, interdunal wetlands in more interior portions of barrier islands are more protected from such rapid geomorphological changes; in addition, they also experience less daily and seasonal variability in temperature, water levels, and salinity due to their more inland location and the ameliorating effects of surrounding woody vegetation.

Succession in barrier island ponds typically involves a shift in dominance from floating macrophytes to deep-water emergents (e.g., cattails and pickerelweed) and finally to shallow-water emergents (saw-grass, sand cordgrass, and water-oleander), shrubs (eastern

rose-mallow and dahoon), and trees (red maple, Carolina willow, and swamp tupelo). As aquatic plants senesce and die, their tissues are incorporated into soil organic matter and contribute to the overall productivity of the wetlands. This process of eutrophication (an increase in chemical nutrients typically resulting in higher primary productivity and lower dissolved oxygen levels in the water) may be accelerated by deposition of sand from shifting dunes and by the addition of nutrients from bird guano and other organic materials (A. S. Johnson et al. 1974).

Fires occurring during periods of extended drought can oxidize organic materials in the bottom of the wetland, reducing the abundance of woody species and creating conditions more typical of earlier successional stages (Hillestad et al. 1975). Severe storms can reduce canopy cover and kill salt-intolerant species by flooding with seawater. In the absence of fire or severe storms, these wetlands typically succeed to hardwood swamps dominated by swamp bay, red maple, swamp tupelo, and water oak (Hillestad et al. 1975; Bellis 1995). With more frequent fire, they may be maintained as herb-dominated communities.

Pumping of groundwater from the underlying aquifers may dewater freshwater ponds that are hydrologically connected to the groundwater or that formerly received water from artesian flows (Spechler 2001). State and federal agencies have considered the construction of wells to supplement freshwater input to interdunal wetlands, but cost considerations may make this approach infeasible. On many barrier islands, networks of shallow ditches constructed many decades ago still impact the hydrology of freshwater sloughs and other wetlands.

On undeveloped barrier islands, management programs intended to maintain interdunal wetlands in a variety of seral stages are generally planned and implemented in concert with management of upland communities. Rather than creating artificial firebreaks around these small wetlands, many land managers allow natural or prescribed fires to spread from upland areas. In designated federal wilderness areas such as portions of Wassaw and Cumberland Islands, the policy is to allow lightning-ignited fires to run their course (U.S. Fish and Wildlife Service 2006d).

Invasive plants, including Chinese tallow-tree, water hyacinth, Brazilian coontail, banana water-lily, giant reed, and alligatorweed are problematic in some interdunal wetlands. Nutria were introduced

Freshwater wetland located in interior of Jekyll Island

on Blackbeard Island in 1949 to control the growth of aquatic plants; after proving ineffectual, these non-native rodents were later eliminated from the island (A. S. Johnson et al. 1974; U.S. Fish and Wildlife Service 2006a). By far the most destructive non-native animals of interdunal wetlands are feral swine.

VEGETATION

As noted above, these wetlands are highly variable in physiognomy and species composition. Deeper, more permanently flooded ponds often have a large expanse of open water, while shallower ponds are usually dominated by a combination of submergent, emergent, and/or floating macrophytes. Trees and shrubs are present mainly along the edges of the wetlands.

Four general plant communities have been described from freshwater wetland environments on Ossabaw Island (Chatham County). These include (1) open-water ponds with scattered herbaceous emer-

gents and buttonbush, found throughout the Pleistocene portion of the island; (2) a mixed emergent community dominated by sedges, yellow-eyed grass, pickerelweed, common rush, sand cordgrass, southern cattail, Carolina willow, wax-myrtle, and buttonbush, often found adjacent to shrub marsh or lowland mixed hardwood forest; (3) communities dominated by sawgrass or sand cordgrass, found primarily in Goose Pond and Rocket Pond in the southern end of the island; and (4) shrub marsh dominated by wax-myrtle and Carolina willow, with scattered buttonbush, found adjacent to Goose Pond, Rocket Pond, Egret Pond, and Rice Pond (Georgia Department of Natural Resources 2001c).

Cumberland Island (Camden County) has the largest and most diverse wetland system of any of Georgia's barrier islands (Hillestad et al. 1975). In addition to more than 16,500 acres of salt marshes, mud flats, and tidal creeks, there are more than 2,500 acres of

Interdunal wetland, Ossabaw Island

freshwater wetlands that range from permanent and semipermanent ponds to seasonal wetland areas including emergent, scrub/shrub, and forested palustrine areas. Many of these wetlands are associated with dune and swale topography (W. E. Odum and Harvey 1988; Frick et al. 2002).

Whitney Lake is distinct from all other freshwater wetlands on Cumberland Island due to its size and its direct surface connection to the ocean. Whitney Lake includes approximately 10 acres of open-water habitat and has a maximum depth of nearly 5 feet near its eastern edge (Lambert 1992). A dense growth of emergent and floating aquatic vegetation surrounds the open-water portion of this lake. A comparison of photos taken in 1991 (Lambert 1992) with those taken by Frick et al. (2002) indicated that the area of floating aquatic vegetation had grown significantly in recent years.

Lake Retta, another Cumberland Island pond, is a shrub-dominated wetland that formed within or adjacent to foredunes that have impeded the natural drainage of surface water and shallow groundwater. Lake Retta is less than 10 feet above sea level and less than

Eastern rose-mallow

CHARACTERISTIC PLANTS OF INTERDUNAL WETLANDS

TREES

Red maple—*Acer rubrum*
Swamp tupelo—*Nyssa biflora*
Swamp bay—*Persea palustris*
Cabbage palmetto—*Sabal palmetto*
Carolina willow—*Salix caroliniana*

SHRUBS

Buttonbush—*Cephalanthus occidentalis*
Water-oleander—*Decodon verticillatus*
Eastern rose-mallow—*Hibiscus moscheutos*
Wax-myrtle—*Morella cerifera*

GROUND COVER

Eastern mosquito fern—*Azolla caroliniana*
Water-shield—*Brasenia schreberi*
Sawgrass—*Cladium jamaicense*
Common rush—*Juncus effusus*
Duckweed—*Lemna spp.*
American frog's-bit—*Limnobium spongia*
American lotus-lily—*Nelumbo lutea*
Broadleaf pondlily—*Nuphar advena*
White waterlily—*Nymphaea odorata*
Big floating heart—*Nymphoides aquatica*
Green arrow-arum—*Peltandra virginica*
Pickerelweed—*Pontederia cordata*
Pondweed—*Potamogeton spp.*
Grassy arrowhead—*Sagittaria graminea*
Broadleaf arrowhead—*Sagittaria latifolia*
Sand cordgrass—*Spartina bakeri*
Narrowleaf cattail—*Typha angustifolia*
Southern cattail—*Typha domingensis*
Common cattail—*Typha latifolia*
Bladderworts—*Utricularia spp.*
Watermeal—*Wolffia columbiana*

1,500 feet west of the mean high tide and may be susceptible to the influence of salt aerosols blown by the wind. Hillestad et al. (1975) indicated that open water in Lake Retta is likely maintained by occasional input of seawater that kills emergent and floating vegetation.

Few detailed studies of interdunal wetlands have been undertaken in Georgia (Frick et al. 2002). Recent surveys by Georgia Department of Natural Resources biologists conducted as part of a detailed habitat mapping effort for Georgia's coastal counties have revealed several exemplary freshwater wetland communities, including a newly described plant association (Southern Atlantic Coastal Plain Carolina willow dune swale) on Jekyll Island that is thought to be globally imperiled (J. Thompson and E. Leonard, Ga. DNR, pers. comm.).

ANIMALS

Interdunal wetlands are very important sources of fresh water for animals of barrier islands. Though limited in size, they contribute greatly to barrier island faunal diversity, providing critical habitats for freshwater fishes, amphibians, watersnakes, and many invertebrates. They also serve as important foraging, roosting, and/or breeding sites for wading birds and waterfowl and provide drinking water for terrestrial mammals.

In the fall, these wetlands serve as important resting and feeding areas for migrating and wintering waterfowl that feed on emergent and floating aquatic plants as well as acorns and other mast from nearby trees (A. S. Johnson et al. 1974). In the spring, large numbers of herons, egrets, and other wading birds nest in rookeries in the canopies of tree-dominated interdunal wetlands. They typically select deeper, semipermanently flooded ponds that provide better protection against nest predation by raccoons. These deeper ponds usually contain alligators and cottonmouths, and these reptiles feed on young birds that fall from the nests. The presence of alligators deters raccoons from entering the wetlands to climb the rookery trees and feed on bird eggs or young. Freshwater sloughs are very important habitats for the American alligator on barrier islands (see Featured Animal). Other reptiles found in this environment include banded watersnake, garter snake, ribbon snake, rat snake, green anole, ground skink, and eastern kingsnake (Hillestad et al. 1975; Stalter and Odum 1993).

Shallow, temporarily flooded sloughs and ponds are more suitable for amphibians because these wetlands generally lack predatory fishes. Amphibians utilizing interdunal wetlands include bullfrog, pig frog, southern leopard frog, eastern narrow-mouthed toad, oak toad, southern toad, eastern spadefoot, pine woods treefrog, green treefrog, grass frog, southern chorus frog, eastern newt, and two-toed amphiuma (A. S. Johnson et al. 1974). The mole salamander is the only

Mixed-species wading bird rookery

ambystomatid salamander known to occur on Georgia's barrier islands (Floyd 2008b).

Fish communities of interdunal wetlands vary greatly based on size and depth of the pond. Large, deep ponds are generally dominated by predatory sunfishes; ponds with fluctuating water and salinity levels tend to have a greater diversity of smaller insectivorous or omnivorous fishes (Wharton 1978). The bluefin killifish, a state-protected species in Georgia, is restricted to freshwater ponds on Sapelo and Blackbeard Islands and a few other locations. It is not known whether these barrier island occurrences represent natural populations or are the result of deliberate introductions. Fishes documented from barrier island ponds on Cumberland Island include mosquitofish, sailfin molly, striped mullet, sheepshead minnow, mottled mojarra, striped killifish, warmouth, and bluegill (Frick et al. 2002).

Invertebrates of freshwater wetlands on the Georgia barrier islands have generally received little atten-

tion from researchers. Aquatic insects representing 54 distinct taxa dominate the invertebrate communities in freshwater wetland habitats on Cumberland Island (Frick et al. 2002). The majority of these were of the orders Hemiptera and Coleoptera. Water boatmen (Corixidae) were the most abundant group.

Seasonal changes in water levels in interdunal wetlands profoundly influence predator-prey relationships. During the spring, prey species such as frogs, small fishes, and macroinvertebrates are able to expand their populations due to ample food supplies. As water levels fall during the summer months, these prey species become concentrated and vulnerable to increased predation by snakes, wading birds, and alligators. At extremely low water levels, many prey species are able to avoid further predation by hiding in inundated holes and burrows on the floor of the wetland or under wet leaf packs. When water levels increase again the prey populations rebound rapidly (Hillestad et al. 1975).

American Alligator
(*Alligator mississipiensis*)

The American alligator is a large, primitive reptile whose geographic range extends from the southern tip of Texas to the northeastern part of North Carolina (Conant and Collins 1998). In Georgia, the alligator's range includes the entire Coastal Plain. Alligators occupy a variety of wetland habitats, including marshes, swamps, interdunal wetlands, and rivers. Alligators are primarily carnivorous and will eat almost anything they can capture in their powerful jaws. During the first few years of life their diet consists mainly of small prey such as snails, crayfish, frogs, insects, and other invertebrates. Larger alligators eat fish, turtles, snakes, waterfowl, raccoons, beavers, and otters, as well as smaller alligators and carrion (Georgia Department of Natural Resources 2001a).

In their natural habitat, alligators help regulate populations of native prey species. In addition, they help to shape and modify habitats. During times of severe drought, alligators often dig holes in the bottom of drying wetlands to concentrate water. These "gator holes" help the alligator survive and provide habitat for other aquatic species as well (Waters 2008). Severe drought conditions may cause alligators to move considerable distances in search of suitable waters (Georgia Department of Natural Resources 2001a).

The alligator was hunted to near extinction in the 1950s and early 1960s, and was listed as Endangered by the U.S. Fish and Wildlife Service in 1967 (Waters 2008). Protective measures taken by state and federal governments halted the precipitous decline of this species and allowed it to recover to levels of relative abundance. As a result, the alligator was "downlisted" in its protected status in 1987. It currently has a status of "Threatened due to Similarity of Appearance" because of its resemblance to rarer crocodilians that are still imperiled. Today, a limited annual harvest of alligators by hunters is allowed by the Georgia Department of Natural Resources.

Jekyll Island State Park

Two easily accessed sites on Jekyll Island provide opportunities to observe two different types of interdunal wetlands. The first is located along a loop trail located across Beachview Drive from the parking lot for the 4H Center. A short walk down the trail leads to a densely vegetated freshwater wetland dominated by Carolina willow, with eastern rose-mallow, wax-myrtle, false-nettle, common rush, royal fern, dotted smartweed, lizard's-tail, common dog-fennel, and several species of sedges. Surrounding trees and shrubs include live oak and cabbage palmetto. This community has recently been described as a unique plant association (Southern Atlantic Coastal Plain Carolina willow dune swale) by Georgia Department of Natural Resources staff.

Farther north on the island, just west of the Jekyll Island Conference Center, is a forested interdunal wetland dominated by red maple, with occasional swamp tupelo, sweet gum, water oak, musclewood, red bay, and willow oak. The understory is very open, with a few woody vines such as American rattan, poison ivy, and muscadine. The herb layer is very sparse. This plant association has been recently described as a red maple–tupelo maritime swamp forest by the Georgia Department of Natural Resources. This wetland floods seasonally to a depth of less than 6 inches.

Location: Site #1: From the end of the Jekyll Island Causeway, turn right on Beachview Dr. and travel south to the parking area for the 4H Center. Cross Beachview Dr. to the trailhead. Google Earth GPS approximate coordinates: N 31.018727/W 081.425362. Site #2: Park at the Jekyll Island Conference Center and enter the woods just west of the building. A short walk downslope will bring you to the forested wetland. Google Earth GPS approximate coordinates: N 31.048625/W 081.412910.

Salt Marshes and Brackish Tidal Marshes

Salt marshes and brackish tidal marshes are found along the edges of tidal rivers, estuaries, and sounds as well as the mainland-facing sides of barrier islands. These wetland communities are dominated by grasses, rushes, sedges, and forbs that are inundated regularly by salty tidal waters. By far the most common plant in Georgia salt marshes is smooth cordgrass. Other characteristic plants include black needlerush, sea lavender, seaside oxeye, saltgrass, sand knotgrass, and annual and perennial saltmarsh asters.

Georgia's coast accounts for a large portion of the total area of tidal marsh along the Atlantic coast, roughly 378,000 acres. Salt and brackish marshes are among the most productive ecosystems in the world. These large-patch or matrix communities serve as nursery grounds for fishes, crustaceans, insects, and shellfish as well as feeding grounds for wading birds, shorebirds, and other animals. They also help buffer upland habitats against the impacts of hurricanes and storm surges by absorbing energy from tidal surges and floods and reducing erosion. Salt and brackish marshes provide critical ecological links between freshwater and marine systems, as well as between aquatic and terrestrial coastal ecosystems.

PHYSICAL SETTING AND ECOLOGY

Salt marsh and brackish tidal marsh environments are influenced by tidal patterns, salinity levels, sedimentation patterns, and topography (Niering and Warren 1977). These marshes are distributed widely throughout the intertidal zone of Georgia's coast where waters range from moderate to high salinity. In contrast to the Gulf Coast, where salt marshes often occur as a narrow fringe along the oceanfront, the primary area for salt marsh development in Georgia is the broad, shallow area of sediment deposition between the barrier islands and the mainland (A. S. Johnson et al. 1974).

Tidal flooding is a primary ecological factor that shapes and nourishes salt and brackish marshes. Incoming tides bring sediments, dissolved nutrients, and

Salt flat near Driftwood Beach, Jekyll Island State Park

organic materials into the marshes from surrounding waters, while outgoing tides remove marsh detritus, planktonic organisms, and other materials. This bidirectional flow of water, nutrients, and other materials is one of the most important influences on the development, species composition, stability, and productivity of salt marsh and brackish marsh environments (Wiegert and Freeman 1990). Georgia's high tidal range results in significant shifts of water between the intertidal marshes and adjacent estuaries. At high tide the emergent marsh grasses may be nearly completely inundated, while at low tide much of the marsh substrate is exposed to the atmosphere.

Storms may push seawater into brackish areas and higher-elevation zones, acting as a disturbance or stressor to vegetation in these areas. In salt marshes, strong storms can deposit thick bands of organic debris (wrack) that can smother vegetation. In marshes located adjacent to barrier islands, periodic overwash caused by storms may deposit sand over the marsh surface. If sufficient amounts of sand are deposited, a portion of the marsh may be converted to intertidal beach habitat (NatureServe 2009c).

Salinity within salt marsh environments generally ranges from hyperhaline (salt concentrations greater than 40 parts per thousand) to mesohaline (between 5 and 18 parts per thousand). The saltiest (hyperhaline) areas are salt pans or flats within the intertidal marshes. These embedded plant communities often form in shallow depressions or flats where seawater collects in pools after flooding, then evaporates, concentrating salts in the soil. Soil salinities in salt pans can exceed 100 parts per thousand, but are usually in the range of 40 to 60 parts per thousand (Antlfinger and Dunn 1979; Wiegert and Freeman 1990).

Along the lower ends of tidal rivers, brackish marsh communities are generally found downstream from, and may be interfingered with, freshwater and oligohaline (salt concentrations between 0.5 and 5 parts per thousand) tidal marsh communities. Other areas suitable for brackish tidal marsh development include borders of open estuaries, sounds, and tidal creeks where salinities are in the 2 to 14 parts per thousand range. Brackish marshes can also develop as a linear transition zone between the upper extent of the salt marsh and upland communities, and in slightly elevated areas within the upper salt marsh zone. In these infrequently flooded environments, precipitation dilutes the soil salinity, providing conditions more favorable to brackish marsh associates.

The primary sources of sediments on which salt and brackish marshes form are the rivers that empty to the Atlantic Ocean at the coast (Neiheisel and Weaver 1967). Coastal rivers continuously transport sediment derived from upstream sites. At the mouths of these rivers the topography flattens, the channel broadens, and waters move more slowly because of the extremely low elevation gradient. This decrease in flow rate causes suspended sediments to be deposited, forming extensive deltas at the mouths of the rivers. These deltas typically include a network of tidal creeks interspersed with bars composed of sand, silt, and clay particles. Superficial deposits are often 6 feet deep in the intertidal zone, while the total depth of recent marsh sediments may range from 30 to 50 feet (A. S. Johnson et al. 1974).

As incoming tidal waters overflow the creek banks, coarser-grained suspended sediments settle out first, followed by finer particles. Over time, this process of sediment deposition results in the development of a pronounced levee along the tidal creek bank, similar to the banks of alluvial streams on the mainland. These creek banks may eventually reach a height at which they are overtopped only by higher tides. In this situation, the tidal flows are pushed up to the heads of the tidal creeks, where they then spread out over the marsh. During the ebb tide some water may be temporarily trapped behind the levee, but usually returns to the creek channel by draining through fiddler crab burrows or by gravity flow (Wiegert, Chalmers, and Randerson 1983). Between the levee and the marsh-upland interface, slight topographic variations result in different levels and frequencies of flooding. In general, marsh sites near the tidal creeks are flooded more frequently and deeply than sites farther from the creeks.

Soils of brackish marshes are very poorly drained organic or mineral soils underlain by sand or clay sediments. Soils of salt marsh habitats are similar but are higher in salt and sulfur content. In Georgia marshes, soils along the tidal creek banks average 50% clay and almost 20% sand; at the high end of the marsh, soils are composed almost entirely of sand (Wiegert and Freeman 1990). This is due to the fact that small clay particles are deposited closer to the creek banks soon

Tidal creek at ebb tide

after inundation. At the high end of the marsh the soil is less influenced by tidal deposition and is similar to soils of adjacent upland environments (J. M. Teal 1962).

Soils of salt and brackish marsh environments are typically very fertile because of the influx of nutrients contained in seawater as well as inputs of nutrient-laden silt, organic materials, and organisms from rivers. These soils are frequently inundated, which creates anaerobic (low-oxygen) conditions near the soil surface. Under these conditions, the breakdown of organic materials by bacteria results in production of hydrogen sulfide, creating the "rotten egg" smell so familiar to coastal residents and visitors. When soils are not flooded, oxygen levels in the upper few inches of the soil are sufficient to allow bacteria to break down material through aerobic respiration.

PRODUCTIVITY AND ENERGY EXCHANGE

Various estimates of above-ground productivity in Georgia salt marshes range from 1,350 to 3,700 $g/m^2/$year (E. P. Odum 1961; Gallagher and Plumley 1979; Gallagher et al. 1980; Schubauer and Hopkinson 1984). This equates to roughly 10 to 20 tons of organic material (dry weight) produced per acre each year. Several studies have shown that salt marsh vegetation is primarily limited by the availability of nitrogen (Mitsch and Gosselink 1993). However, phosphorus, another important nutrient, is available in large quantities (Pomeroy and Wiegert 1981).

Varying successional ages and levels of environmental stress contribute to variability in productivity from site to site (Morris 1988). In addition, grazing by periwinkle snails and other herbivores can have a dramatic local effect on primary productivity. High densities of periwinkle snails can suppress cordgrass production, especially during drought periods (Bertness 2007).

Non-native grazers such as feral horses can also significantly impact primary productivity of salt marshes, though these impacts are usually local and temporary (M. G. Turner and Bratton 1987).

The base of the food web in salt marshes is plant tissue produced from photosynthesis. Some of this plant material is eaten by herbivores, but the majority becomes detritus that feeds algae, bacteria, nematodes, and other benthic organisms, which in turn become food for other animals. Decomposition of detritus concentrates its protein content and enhances its food value to consumers.

In many areas, nearly half of the net production of organic material is washed out with the tide and serves as an energy source for adjacent aquatic communities. The export of organic nutrients to surrounding estuaries varies both geographically and seasonally. However, several studies have demonstrated the critical role that salt marshes provide to the productivity of fish and shellfish populations on the Georgia coast and elsewhere (Mitsch and Gosselink 1993; Wiegert and Freeman 1990).

Little is known of the natural fire regime of salt and brackish marshes, though it is likely that under natural conditions fire would be an infrequent disturbance. Since the incidence of lightning strikes increases southward along the Atlantic coast, Georgia salt marshes are presumably more prone to lightning-induced fires than those in the mid-Atlantic states. Under certain conditions (e.g., neap tides and/or extended drought conditions) fires that originate in adjacent upland areas may spread into intertidal marshes (Hermann 2009).

Davison (1984) documented the effects of two natural fires on Cumberland Island (Camden County). The larger of these two fires primarily impacted pine scrub, oak scrub, maritime forest, and freshwater marsh but also affected a small portion of adjacent salt marsh, brackish marsh, and salt flat habitats. The salt marsh and salt flat habitats did not carry fire to a significant extent, due in large part to the fact that the marsh plants were sparse, heavily grazed by horses, and regularly inundated. In contrast, brackish marshes located upslope from the salt marsh and dominated by large saltmeadow cordgrass burned as

thoroughly as the freshwater marshes, but recovered quickly (Davison 1984).

Salt and brackish marshes have been adversely affected by upstream impoundments, dredging of river channels for navigational purposes, extensive ditching of tidal streams, and residential and commercial development along the coast. Impoundment, dredging, and flow regulations of rivers cause disruptions in the natural patterns of sediment deposition, which in turn affects the distribution and nutrient inputs of salt marshes. Pollution from industrial and residential development along the coast includes chemical effluent from industrial sites as well as sedimentation resulting from soil disturbance and removal of vegetation near tidal streams.

Periodic die-offs of smooth cordgrass along the Atlantic coast have caused alarm among residents and some researchers in recent years, but these events appear to be tied primarily to extended drought conditions (Alber 2008). In addition to direct mortality, drought-induced stress increases the vulnerability of smooth cordgrass to impacts from herbivores such as the common periwinkle snail (Silliman et al. 2005).

Common periwinkle, an abundant herbivore of salt marshes

VEGETATION

Plant communities within this environment are typically demarcated by salinity gradients. Salt marshes dominated by smooth cordgrass can form wherever salinities are greater than 2 parts per thousand but are usually found at higher salinities. Smooth cordgrass actually grows better in very low-salinity conditions but does not compete well against other plants in these environments. Its tolerance of saline conditions allows it to outcompete other emergent marsh plants in salinities of 25 parts per thousand or greater (Wiegert and Freeman 1990).

Salt marsh communities typically exhibit zonal patterns in vegetation structure. Along the tidal creek bank is a sparsely vegetated zone. Adjacent to this zone is the streamside marsh, a relatively narrow band of tall smooth cordgrass. On the natural levee landward of the creek is a zone of smooth cordgrass of intermediate height. At slightly higher elevations, the cordgrass marsh is much shorter and more widely spaced. Near the marsh-upland interface, hyperhaline flats dominated by saltwort often occur (J. M. Teal 1962).

Salt marshes have a remarkably low diversity of vascular plants, being dominated almost entirely by smooth cordgrass. The algal flora, however, while poorly known, is very diverse, comprising several hundred species of diatoms that together form 75% to 93% of the benthic algal biomass (R. B. Williams 1962). As sources of organic material used by other organisms, these phytoplanktonic species are significant contributors to the overall productivity of the salt marsh ecosystem. On hyperhaline salt flats, plants such as saltwort, glassworts, and saltgrass have a competitive advantage over smooth cordgrass and black needlerush because of their ability to tolerate high-salinity conditions. On the other hand, these low-growing plants are not able to compete with black needlerush and smooth cordgrass in less saline areas that are regularly inundated. In addition to a patchy cover of vascular plants, soils of salt flats are often topped by a thin film of blue-green algae (Frey and Basan 1985).

Brackish marshes are typically dominated by a small group of emergent herbs, including black needlerush, giant cordgrass, and threesquare. Other characteristic plants include salt marsh bulrush, softstem bulrush, large saltmeadow cordgrass, southern cattail, narrowleaf cattail, and pickerelweed. Shrubs

The projected impacts of global climate change on Georgia's salt and brackish marshes are a significant long-term concern. Increases in sea level due to climate change will undoubtedly impact the distribution of salt and brackish marshes along the Georgia coast. Under some scenarios of sea-level rise, the overall extent of coastal marshes could remain constant or increase, if vertical accretion of the marsh sediments is equal to the rate of coastal submergence (Knutson 1988; Morris 1988). Rising sea level will likely drown some salt marshes, increase shoreline erosion in some areas, and cause salt or brackish marshes to migrate inland into areas currently occupied by freshwater marsh (Craft et al. 2009).

Transitions between smooth cordgrass marsh and black needlerush marsh are usually abrupt.

are very sparse and trees are generally absent except at the upslope edges of this community. It is sometimes difficult to map a clear and simple boundary between salt marsh and brackish marsh because of the complex interaction of various factors (e.g., topography, tides, and freshwater flows) within the coastal zone (Wharton 1978). For example, black needlerush marsh exists as a zonal community type along tidal creeks that flow through salt marshes as well as circular or irregularly shaped patches on slight rises or mounds in the salt marsh intertidal zone. The boundaries between patches dominated by black needlerush and those dominated by smooth cordgrass are almost always sharp and visually distinct, however.

Within the Altamaha River delta three distinct marsh vegetation zones are distributed along the salinity gradient: the lower estuary, characterized by typical salt marsh vegetation; the middle estuary, with brackish and salt marsh vegetation; and the upper estuary, characterized by typical tidal freshwater marsh vegetation. Within the middle estuary, the three most

prevalent emergent plants are smooth cordgrass, black needlerush, and giant cordgrass (Gallagher and Reismold 1973).

Successional processes in salt marshes are intricately linked with deposition patterns of river-borne sediments (Frey and Basan 1985). In the early stages of salt marsh development, tidal creeks are dynamic, often meandering within the salt marsh zone. These drainage patterns stabilize over time, and the marsh sediments grow both vertically and laterally. In later periods, the rate of accretion slows as the marsh sediments reach an equilibrium based on prevailing topography, stream flows, and sediment supply. Changes in tidal flows and sediment levels are reflected in changes in community composition. Early in successional development, smooth cordgrass marsh is predominant, but over time this community gives way to one dominated by black needlerush. Eventually, terrestrial plants begin to invade the area formerly dominated by smooth cordgrass and black needlerush, and shrubs such as groundsel tree, seaside oxeye, and wax-myrtle become established (Frey and Basan 1985).

Seaside oxeye

Black needlerush, a dominant plant of brackish marshes

CHARACTERISTIC PLANTS OF SALT MARSHES AND BRACKISH TIDAL MARSHES

TREES

Southern red cedar—Juniperus
  virginiana var. silicicola
Cabbage palmetto—Sabal palmetto

SHRUBS

Groundsel tree—Baccharis halimifolia
Seaside oxeye—Borrichia frutescens
Yaupon—Ilex vomitoria
Maritime marsh-elder—Iva frutescens
Southern seashore-mallow—
  Kosteletzkya virginica
Wax-myrtle—Morella cerifera

GROUND COVER

Saltwort—Batis maritima
Salt marsh bulrush—Bolboschoenus
  robustus
Sawgrass—Cladium jamaicense
Saltgrass—Distichlis spicata
Black needlerush—Juncus roemerianus
Pickerelweed—Pontedaria cordata
Glassworts—Salicornia virginica;
  S. bigelovii; Sarcocornia pacifica
Threesquare—Schoenoplectus
  americanus
Softstem bulrush—Schoenoplectus
  tabernaemontani

Smooth cordgrass—Spartina
  alterniflora
Sand cordgrass—Spartina bakeri
Giant cordgrass—Spartina cynosuroides
Large saltmeadow cordgrass—
  Spartina patens
Annual saltmarsh aster—
  Symphiotrichum subulatum
Perennial saltmarsh aster—
  Symphiotricum tenuifolium
Narrowleaf cattail—Typha angustifolia
Southern cattail—Typha domingensis

ANIMALS

The fauna of tidal salt and brackish marshes includes numerous terrestrial and aquatic species. Aquatic animals are by far the most abundant group within the salt marsh, and range in size from tiny zooplankton to large vertebrate species. Common aquatic invertebrates include various crabs (e.g., blue, wharf, mud fiddler, and sand fiddler crabs) and mollusks, including the ubiquitous periwinkle snail found on smooth cordgrass stalks, the marsh snail found on exposed mud flats, the ribbed mussel, and the eastern oyster. Mud fiddler crabs feed on benthic microorganisms within the tidal cordgrass marsh, while sand fiddler crabs are generally found on exposed sand flats and the upper edges of the marsh (J. M. Teal 1958; Crane 1975). Blue crabs move up and down the marsh elevational gradient with the tides to search for prey and to avoid capture by predators (Fitz and Wiegert 1991).

Zooplanktonic animals found in salt and brackish marshes include microscopic copepods (tiny aquatic crustaceans) as well as the larval stages of snails, crabs, starfish, shrimp, and fish. These tiny organisms serve as the food source for a wide variety of larger aquatic consumers in the marshes and adjacent estuaries. Benthic organisms, especially polychaete worms (primitive segmented worms) and nematodes (roundworms), are very abundant in these habitats.

The most abundant terrestrial species of salt marshes are herbivorous arthropods, including a number of grasshoppers and leafhoppers. Smooth cordgrass marshes in Georgia, South Carolina, and North Carolina support 109 species of herbivorous insects (Wiegert and Freeman 1990). The two most abundant insect herbivores are the salt marsh grasshopper and a tiny planthopper. Spiders and mites are the most abundant terrestrial predators in salt marsh communities (Wiegert and Freeman 1990). The rare skipper is a butterfly species of conservation concern that appears to be restricted to brackish and freshwater coastal marsh environments (P. Howard, Georgia Conservancy, pers. comm.)

Tidal salt marshes are very important nursery grounds for fishes, including many desirable sport or food fishes such as sheepshead, snook, pompano, black sea bass, spotted seatrout, red drum, striped mullet, spot, and several species of flounder. More

Mud fiddler crabs forage on salt marsh sediments at low tide.

Snowy egret

than 90 fishes are known to inhabit tidal salt marshes of the southeastern Atlantic coast (Wiegert and Freeman 1990). In general, the diversity of fishes is greater in salt water than in brackish waters (Dahlberg 1972).

Notable reptilian species of salt and brackish tidal marshes include the American alligator, rat snake, banded watersnake, cottonmouth, eastern mud turtle, and diamondback terrapin (see the Featured Animal). Amphibians are rare in these inhospitable salt-rich environments, though southern leopard frogs have been collected in Florida salt marshes (Montague and Wiegert 1990).

Salt and brackish marshes provide foraging and/or nesting habitat for waterfowl and wading birds, including herons, egrets, bitterns, ibises, wood storks, and rails (Wiegert and Freeman 1990). Insectivorous birds such as the marsh wren, seaside sparrow, swallows, and red-winged blackbirds are also common in these habitats. Clapper rails and king rails are common inhabitants but are rarely seen as they typically remain under the canopy of dense grasses. Studies of marsh wrens and seaside sparrows indicate that these two birds avoid competition for food resources by feeding at different levels within the cordgrass; seaside sparrows forage primarily on the surface of the marsh mud, while marsh wrens forage in the cordgrass canopy (Kale 1965).

Salt marshes provide habitat for several medium-sized mammals such as raccoon, mink, otter, and marsh rabbits. River otters and minks are at home in the marshes and tidal creeks, where they feed on fish and clams. Raccoons tend to use these areas only at low tide, feeding on fiddler crabs, fish, diamondback terrapin eggs, bird eggs, and carrion. Other mammals found in salt marshes include the rice rat, cotton mouse, meadow vole, hispid cotton rat, eastern mole, and least shrew. The rice rat has an unusual diet for a rodent in that it is primarily carnivorous, feeding on fiddler crabs, snails, bird eggs, and insect larvae as well as a variety of plant materials. This semiaquatic rodent constructs a nest made of grass within dense cordgrass stands or may occupy the abandoned nest of a marsh wren (A. S. Johnson et al. 1974).

Marine mammals such as the manatee and bottlenose dolphin are found in tidal rivers and creeks adjacent to the marsh. Manatees feed on submerged aquatic vegetation in the estuarine zone, occasionally venturing upstream into fresh or oligohaline waters. Bottlenose dolphins often feed by chasing fish up tidal creeks and trapping them against the muddy creek banks with their bodies; other favored food items include squid and crustaceans.

Diamondback Terrapin
(*Malaclemys terrapin*)

The diamondback terrapin is a resident of brackish and saltwater habitats, including tidal creeks, rivers, sounds, and occasionally nearshore marine waters. It rarely wanders from these habitats, and is uniquely adapted for life in the vast salt marshes and tidal creeks of the coastal region (Conant and Collins 1998).

In late spring and summer, egg-bearing females emerge from the water to find nesting sites. Virtually any area of exposed sandy soil near water or a marsh may be used, including sand bars, spits, dunes, and creek banks as well as the edges of roads and parking lots (Spivey 2008).

The diet of diamondback terrapins includes clams, snails, crustaceans (mainly small crabs), insects, and carrion. The abundant salt marsh periwinkle snail is an important food source. During high tide, diamondback terrapins forage in the upper reaches of salt marshes, but they retreat with the falling tide to avoid predators such as raccoons, river otters, and bald eagles (Spivey 2008).

During the height of popularity of turtle soup in the early 1900s, populations of the diamondback terrapin were significantly impacted by commercial harvest, and some local populations were extirpated. In the decades that followed, reduced demand for turtle meat facilitated the recovery of diamondback terrapin populations. Today, the major threats to diamondback terrapins are automobiles and crab traps. Heavily traveled roads near salt marshes and tidal creeks contribute to mortality during the nesting season. A more important threat may be commercial and recreational crab traps that drown many diamondback terrapins each year. Especially problematic are abandoned or lost "ghost traps," each of which may capture and drown more than 100 diamondback terrapins (Maerz and Grosse 2010). Fortunately, "turtle excluder devices" can be installed on the crab traps to allow diamondback terrapins to escape while retaining the crabs. The diamondback terrapin is a state-protected species, listed as Unusual by the Georgia Department of Natural Resources (Spivey 2008).

Earth Day Nature Trail

This interpretive nature trail is located at the Georgia Department of Natural Resources Coastal Resources Division headquarters in Brunswick (Glynn County). The site is easily accessed from U.S. Highway 17 and is open to the public daily during daylight hours. Earth Day Nature Trail provides views of salt and brackish marsh environments as well as a restored tidal pond habitat. The site on which the nature trail is located includes two small hammocks surrounded by salt marsh. The nature trail consists of two loops on the high ground connected by a footbridge. Typical salt marsh plants seen along the loop trail include smooth cordgrass, seaside oxeye, black needlerush, maritime marshelder, and yaupon. An observation platform located near the southern end of the first loop of the trail provides an overview of a salt flat and opportunities to view saltwort, saltgrass, mud fiddler crabs, and other species typical of this environment. An observation tower on the second loop also provides views of the salt marsh and salt flat, as well St. Simons Sound, the Atlantic Ocean, St. Simons Island, and Jekyll Island. A boardwalk that branches off of the loop trail provides closer access to the salt marsh.

The tidal pond and marsh area in the middle of the trail was excavated and revegetated as part of a wetland mitigation project. This is a good spot to observe wading birds such as snowy egrets and great egrets. Other animals that may occasionally be seen from the observation platforms or from the trail include black-crowned night-heron, osprey, diamondback terrapin, and numerous songbirds.

Location: From Brunswick, head south on U.S. Hwy. 17 toward Jekyll Island. Look for a Georgia DNR sign on the right (west) side of the road just north of the Sidney Lanier Bridge. Turn right, cross under the highway, and continue to the Coastal Resources Division headquarters parking lot. Google Earth GPS approximate coordinates: N 31.124732/W 081.477883.

Freshwater and Oligohaline Tidal Marshes

Freshwater and oligohaline tidal marshes are found along the edges of tidally influenced rivers upstream of salt marsh and brackish marsh environments. These environments typically contain plant communities dominated by emergent herbs such as giant cutgrass, sawgrass, southern wild-rice, giant cordgrass, picker-elweed, cattail, and green arrow-arum. Trees are absent or very sparse, and shrubs are minor components of the community. Freshwater and oligohaline tidal marshes are herb-dominated ecotones between tidal rivers and adjoining uplands, swamps, and bottom-land forests. Though they share some characteristics of salt marshes and inland (nontidal) freshwater marshes, their unique environmental setting (tidal fluctuations, seasonal flooding, and very low salinity levels) supports species assemblages that differ significantly in composi-tion and appearance. Plant diversity in freshwater tidal marshes is typically high, and the vegetation is hetero-geneous and seasonally variable. In addition, freshwater tidal marshes support diverse faunal assemblages (San-difer et al. 1980; W. E. Odum et al. 1984).

Because the differences in species composition between freshwater and oligohaline tidal marshes are very subtle, both types are referred to as "freshwater tidal marshes" in the sections that follow.

PHYSICAL SETTING AND ECOLOGY

Along many of the region's smaller rivers, the fresh-water tidal marsh zone is a relatively narrow and dis-continuous band. The most extensive examples of this natural community are found along the lower reaches of the Savannah and Altamaha Rivers (Seabrook 2006). W. E. Odum et al. (1984) estimated the total area of freshwater tidal marsh on the Atlantic coast to be approximately 405,000 acres. Georgia has the third largest area of freshwater tidal marsh (47,000 acres) on the Atlantic coast, trailing New Jersey (220,000 acres) and South Carolina (64,500 acres). This means that while representing less than 5% of the Atlantic coastline, Georgia accounts for nearly 12% of its freshwater tidal marsh habitat.

Perhaps the most important environmental factor shaping these marsh communities is tidal flow. Tidal fluctuations allow for nutrient import and export and the maintenance of high levels of primary production. Other important influences are the subtle salinity gradients in this tidal regime, river hydrology, soil texture and nutrient levels, sedimentation patterns, and fire frequency. As is the case with salt marshes and brackish marshes, these factors interact to form complex gradients that shape the biotic communities of this environment (W. E. Odum 1988).

Freshwater tidal marshes occur as a result of the interaction of river waters and tidal influences from the ocean. Researchers disagree over the exact mechanism of this interaction, whether a "tidal dam" effect causes overbank flooding or whether river flows simply mix with and dilute saline tidal waters (W. E. Odum et al. 1984). Whatever the mechanism, the net result is twice-daily overbank flow and inundation of areas adjacent to the river with fresh or oligohaline waters.

As the influence of tides decreases upstream, these marshes more closely resemble inland marshes. There is no clear-cut line of distinction between tidal and nontidal riverine marshes based on species composition. Instead, these biotic communities reflect a continuum of environmental influences, including tidal influence, salinity, and sediment deposition.

Soils of freshwater tidal marshes are composed primarily of sediments deposited during the Holocene, when rising sea levels drowned coastal river valleys that had formed during the Pleistocene epoch (Hoyt 1968). The thickness of these sediments varies from 3 feet to more than 30 feet (W. E. Odum et al. 1984). Wharton (1978) reported that former rice fields in the Savannah National Wildlife Refuge contained surface muck 12 to 24 inches thick underlain by 48 to 60 inches of peat subsoil and 72 inches of clay.

Tides and river currents influence the deposition of sediments, creating a gradual increase in elevation from the edge of the tidal river into adjacent freshwater marshes (W. E. Odum et al. 1984). This elevation gradient often includes a low berm or levee along the edge of the tidal river or creek, analogous to the levees on tidal streams within the salt marsh system.

Soils of freshwater tidal marshes are typically circumneutral or only slightly acidic, with pH levels ranging from 6.0 to 6.5 (W. E. Odum et al. 1984). Regularly flooded marshes are thought to be more productive than irregularly flooded marshes because they receive greater amounts of river-borne nutrients. Irregularly flooded marshes tend to accumulate organic materials as layers of peat in the soil. The amount of peat deposition also varies with plant community composition, however; for example, marshes dominated by cattails tend to have higher rates of peat deposition (W. E. Odum et al. 1984).

Where sedimentation rates are very high, deposited clays and silts may result in the development of unvegetated mud flats. Where sedimentation rates are lower, plants have an opportunity to colonize and stabilize newly deposited sediments. Within freshwater tidal marshes, nutrients are retained during the growing season, being bound up in plant tissue, but are lost to floods or tidal flushing or become sequestered in below-ground plant tissues during the winter months.

Only a small portion of the primary productivity from freshwater tidal marshes (approximately 10%) is consumed directly by animals. The remaining 90% becomes available to consumers through detrital (decomposition) food webs (W. E. Odum 1988). The rate of decomposition varies significantly by plant species. Broad-leaved perennials such as pickerelweed and green arrow-arum have high concentrations of nitrogen in their leaves, and their fleshy tissue tends to decompose rapidly. In contrast, high marsh grasses such as southern wild-rice are low in nitrogen and decompose more slowly, allowing the buildup of litter within the freshwater marsh (H. T. Odum and Heywood 1978). In marshes that receive large amounts of sediment, some organic matter may be buried and removed from the detrital food web (Hatton 1981).

Natural fire regimes of freshwater marshes are not well understood (K. McPherson 2009b). In presettlement times, periodic lightning-caused fires may have influenced the species composition of freshwater tidal marshes. The frequency and intensity of naturally occurring fires in this community type probably varied greatly from site to site, influenced by topographic and vegetational gradients. A fire-return interval of three to five years has been cited for freshwater tidal marshes adjacent to fire-prone upland communities, whereas marshes isolated from uplands by river channels or other fire barriers would presumably rarely burn (Schafale and Weakley 1990). Freshwater tidal marshes probably burned most frequently and extensively during low-water conditions, but the seasonality of burns is uncertain. Lightning strikes are more common during the summer, but some marsh vegetation is very difficult to burn when green (Nyman and Chabreck 1995).

Freshwater tidal marshes are now relatively rare natural habitats along the Atlantic and Gulf Coasts because many have been lost to saltwater intrusion, hydrologic changes due to development and agriculture, or other landscape modifications. Remaining freshwater marshes in the Savannah National Wildlife Refuge may be threatened by saltwater intrusion caused by the deepening of the Savannah Harbor as well as by groundwater pumping for commercial and industrial uses.

Extensive areas of freshwater marsh can be found in sites of former rice plantations in the tidewater region of Georgia (particularly in the lower Savannah, Altamaha, and Satilla drainages); these are anthropogenic communities established following the logging of tidal swamps. Many of these former rice fields are now managed with dikes and water control structures to provide habitat for waterfowl (e.g., in Savannah National Wildlife Refuge and Altamaha Wildlife Management Area).

Rising sea levels brought on by global climate change will cause shifts in the distribution of freshwater tidal marshes. Sea-level rise is currently advancing salinity gradients upstream, leading to shifts in vegetation composition and the conversion of some tidal freshwater marshes into brackish marshes (Craft et al. 2009). At the same time, rising water levels in the lower reaches of coastal rivers are drowning tidal swamps in some areas and causing a transition to freshwater tidal marsh.

Invasive species represent a significant threat to freshwater tidal marshes. A non-native form of common reed has been introduced into the lower Altamaha River system and is spreading, displacing native marsh grasses. The Nature Conservancy and the Georgia Department of Natural Resources have identified patches of this plant, and with assistance from the U.S. Fish and Wildlife Service have initiated control efforts using herbicides. Other non-native species that threaten freshwater tidal marshes include water hyacinth, marsh dewflower, giant reed, wild taro, and Chinese tallow-tree.

VEGETATION

Elevational differences across the freshwater tidal marsh are reflected in different assemblages of plants, though in many cases these assemblages are too variable in composition to be considered discrete plant communities (Mitsch and Gosselink 1993; W. E. Odum and Hoover 1988). Submerged vascular plants such as broadleaf pondlily, golden club, pondweed, and water milfoil grow at the edges of tidal streams and in floodplain ponds and oxbow lakes. The creek banks and levees are only sparsely vegetated during the winter but may be covered with annual plants such as dotted smartweed, salt-marsh water-hemp, and showy bur-marigold during the growing season (Mitsch and Gosselink 1993).

Landward of the stream levee the frequently flooded "low marsh" zone often contains broad-leaved emergents such as green arrow-arum, pickerelweed, and bulltongue arrowhead. Toward the upper end of the elevational gradient the "high marsh" vegetation is often dominated by a diverse group of annual and perennial plants, referred to by W. E. Odum et al. (1984) as the "mixed aquatic community type." Characteristic forbs of this zone include showy bur-marigold, halberd-leaf tearthumb, arrowleaf tearthumb, orange jewelweed, and salt-marsh water-hemp; perennial shrubs such eastern rose-mallow, wax-myrtle, groundsel tree, and maritime marsh-elder are often scattered in the high marsh zone. In addition, these shallow areas may have dense stands of southern wild-rice, cattails, giant cutgrass, bulrushes, and giant cordgrass (Wharton 1978).

No plant species endemic to freshwater tidal marshes are known, and in fact most species of this environment are widely distributed along the Atlantic coast (Whigham and Simpson 1975). The tidal marsh obedient-plant, a species of conservation concern in Georgia, is largely restricted to freshwater marshes, with additional occurrences in wetlands of southwest Georgia. Regional differences in plant community composition are generally acknowledged but have not been well researched. W. E. Odum et al. (1984) described eight general plant communities based on data from sites ranging from Massachusetts to northern Florida. They noted that marshes of the mid-Atlantic and South Atlantic regions (including the Georgia coast) typically contain as many as 50–60 species at a single location, often with several co-dominant species.

Freshwater tidal marsh often occurs as a narrow band along the edges of tidal rivers and creeks.

Plant community composition within freshwater tidal swamps is largely determined by the ability of individual plants to germinate and survive in the fluctuating water conditions of the tidal marsh. Some species, such as showy bur-marigold and orange jewelweed, are restricted to the high-marsh zone because their seedlings are not tolerant of extended flooding (Simpson et al. 1983). In addition to vascular plants, diatoms, green algae, and blue-green algae are common components of freshwater tidal marshes.

Tidal marsh obedient-plant

PRODUCTIVITY OF FRESHWATER TIDAL MARSHES

Because of the ample sunlight, water, and nutrients available in this environment, freshwater marshes are extraordinarily productive and can produce tall stands of grasses and sedges within a single growing season. Freshwater tidal marshes in nutrient-rich sites have high levels of biomass and net primary production (1,000 to 3,500 g/m^2/year), equaling or exceeding the productivity of salt marshes (W. E. Odum et al. 1984). The vegetation of freshwater tidal marshes varies spatially within the marsh and temporally over the course of the seasons. The low salinity levels and relatively high nutrient levels in these habitats support a greater diversity of vascular plants than do salt marshes (R. H. Moore 1992).

Freshwater tidal marshes exhibit dramatic seasonal changes in vegetation throughout the year because of the diversity of plants and varying periods of dominance. While primary productivity and overall plant abundance are highest by the end of summer, the diversity of plants in freshwater tidal marshes allows for a predictable transition of dominants during the growing season (W. E. Odum and Hoover 1988). Freezing temperatures in late fall and winter kill back the above-ground vegetation, and the dead plant material is removed from the marsh surface through decomposition and tidal flushing (W. E. Odum et al. 1984). Nutrient cycles in freshwater tidal marshes are more seasonally variable than those in salt marsh systems, with more rapid growth, decay, and decomposition of plant tissues (R. H. Moore 1992). Primary productivity is less variable spatially than in salt and brackish marshes, however, presumably because there is less salinity-induced stress along the elevational gradient (W. E. Odum and Hoover 1988).

CHARACTERISTIC PLANTS OF FRESHWATER AND OLIGOHALINE TIDAL MARSHES

TREES

Water tupelo—*Nyssa aquatica* (occasional)

Bald-cypress—*Taxodium distichum* (occasional)

SHRUBS

Groundsel tree—*Baccharis halimifolia*

Eastern rose-mallow—*Hibiscus moscheutos*

Maritime marsh-elder—*Iva frutescens*

Wax-myrtle—*Morella cerifera*

GROUND COVER

European calamus—*Acorus calamus*

Salt-marsh water-hemp—*Amaranthus cannabinus*

Showy bur-marigold—*Bidens laevis*

Sawgrass—*Cladium jamaicense*

Spikerushes—*Eleocharis spp.*

Orange jewelweed—*Impatiens capensis*

Southern blue flag—*Iris virginica*

Rice cutgrass—*Leersia oryzoides*

Broadleaf pondlily—*Nuphar advena*

Golden club—*Orontium aquaticum*

Green arrow-arum—*Peltandra virginica*

Halberd-leaf tearthumb—*Persicaria arifolia*

Dotted smartweed—*Persicaria punctata*

Arrowleaf tearthumb—*Persicaria sagittata*

Pickerelweed—*Pontedaria cordata*

Sugarcane plume grass—*Saccharum giganteum*

Bulltongue arrowhead—*Sagittaria lancifolia*

Threesquare—*Schoenoplectus americanus*

Softstem bulrush—*Schoenoplectus tabernaemontani*

Giant cordgrass—*Spartina cynosuroides*

Southern cattail—*Typha domingensis*

Common cattail—*Typha latifolia*

Southern wild-rice—*Zizania aquatica*

Giant cutgrass—*Zizaniopsis miliacea*

ANIMALS

Freshwater tidal marshes support diverse faunal communities. Within the Atlantic coast region from southern New England to northern Florida, these environments are utilized by as many as 125 species of fish, 102 species of amphibians and reptiles, 280 species of birds, and 46 species of mammals (W. E. Odum et al. 1984). More birds use freshwater tidal marshes for feeding, nesting, and breeding than any other type of marsh. These marsh communities are important for both freshwater and saltwater organisms. Freshwater fish feed in the marshes, and many estuarine and marine species use them as nursery habitat (R. H. Moore 1992).

As in salt marshes, food webs in freshwater tidal marshes are fueled by the physical and chemical breakdown of detritus (Mitsch and Gosselink 1993). Bacteria and protozoa decompose the dead plant material and in turn are consumed by larger invertebrates, primarily nematodes, which compose the bulk of organisms living in the sediments (Sikora et al. 1977). Slightly larger invertebrates living in the benthic layer include amphipods, oligochaete worms, freshwater snails, freshwater shrimp, and insects. These invertebrates serve as food for young fishes, amphibians, birds, and other animals. Common macroinvertebrates in freshwater tidal marshes include grass shrimp, blue crabs, red-jointed fiddler crabs, wharf crabs, and mud crabs (Rozas and Odum 1987; R. H. Moore 1992). In general, invertebrate communities of freshwater tidal marsh habitats are less diverse than those of nontidal freshwater habitats due to a combination of lower overall habitat diversity and higher stress from fluctuating salinities (W. E. Odum, Rozas, and McIvor 1988). In addition, freshwater tidal marshes generally have fewer species of bivalves, crustaceans, and polychaetes than salt marsh environments (W. E. Odum et al. 1984).

The fish communities of strictly freshwater tidal marshes are typically dominated by resident freshwater species, although estuarine and anadromous fishes (fishes that live as adults in the ocean but spawn in fresh water) also use these habitats; oligohaline tidal marshes usually have a more even distribution of freshwater, estuarine, and marine species (W. E. Odum, Rozas, and McIvor 1988). The most common groups of fishes include cyprinids (minnows, shiners, and carp), centrarchids (sunfish, crappie, and bass), and ictalurids (catfish). Freshwater tidal marshes are used as primary habitat by some fishes and as spawning or nursery grounds by others (W. E. Odum et al. 1984).

Wharf crab

Typical resident freshwater species include redbreast sunfish, banded killifish, spottail shiner, bluegill, and yellow bullhead (Dahlberg 1972; W. E. Odum, Rozas, and McIvor 1988). Rozas and Odum (1987) found that while the composition of fish communities did not vary significantly between tidal headwater streams, tidal creeks, and tidal rivers, fishes were significantly more abundant in headwater and main creek habitats. This may be because these small tidal streams have a greater coverage of submerged aquatic vegetation, providing fishes with a refuge from predators and/or a place to forage for food at low tide. Anadromous fishes pass through these marshes on their way upstream to spawning sites; for many of these species, freshwater tidal marshes serve as very important nursery grounds for juveniles. Examples of these fishes include Atlantic sturgeon, short-nosed sturgeon, American shad, striped bass, and herring. The American eel is a catadromous species (a fish that lives as an adult in fresh water but breeds in salt water) that also uses this environment (Helfman et al. 1984). Some estuarine or marine fishes are also frequently found in freshwater tidal marshes, including striped mullet, mummichog, bay anchovy, inland silverside, tidewater silverside, and spot (W. E. Odum et al. 1984; Rozas and Odum 1987).

Common amphibians of freshwater tidal marshes include bullfrog, pig frog, green frog, southern leopard frog, southern cricket frog, and spring peeper. Salamanders are less well represented, but include the two-toed amphiuma, dwarf waterdog, lesser siren, and greater siren. Reptiles encountered in these environments include aquatic snakes such as the cottonmouth, banded watersnake, glossy crayfish snake, swamp black snake, mud snake, and rainbow snake. Though seldom observed, secretive mud and rainbow snakes appear to be fairly common in tidal freshwater marshes, the former feeding primarily on amphiumas and sirens, the latter preferring eels (T. Mills 2008; Young and Gibbons 2008). Other characteristic reptiles of freshwater tidal marshes include the eastern mud turtle, common musk turtle, common snapping turtle, spotted turtle, pond slider, Florida cooter, and American alligator. Lizards are uncommon in these environments, but include green anoles and broadhead skinks. As might be expected, the herpetofaunal communities of freshwater tidal marshes are more diverse than those in adjacent salt marsh environments (R. H. Moore 1992).

Freshwater tidal wetlands support approximately 215 species of birds in Georgia; of this total, 64 species are restricted to freshwater tidal marshes, and the remaining 151 species also utilize habitats adjacent to these marshes (W. E. Odum et al. 1984). Factors contributing to the high avifaunal diversity in freshwater tidal marshes include the high species diversity of the vegetation as well the spatial and temporal habitat heterogeneity provided by this dynamic environment (Mitsch and Gosselink 1993).

Freshwater tidal marshes provide a variety of foraging opportunities for birds. Shorebirds typically forage on temporarily exposed mud flats, while wading birds such as herons, ibises, egrets, and bitterns feed in areas of shallow water, searching for freshwater invertebrates, small fishes, and amphibians. The interspersion of open-water and herb-dominated communities provides habitat for wintering ducks and geese as well as foraging areas for rails, coots, and gallinules. Shrubs and trees at the edges of freshwater tidal marshes provide perches for a wide variety of birds, including flycatchers, sparrows, swallows, wood warblers, juncos, finches, blackbirds, and wrens. Raptors such as northern harriers, ospreys, swallow-tailed kites, and bald eagles are frequently observed flying or perching over freshwater tidal marshes. The dense marsh vegetation also provides habitat for insectivorous and seed-eating songbirds (Wharton 1978; W. E. Odum et al. 1984).

Mammals typically found in tidal freshwater marshes include large and medium-sized species such as white-tailed deer, raccoon, opossum, beaver, mink, gray squirrel, southern flying squirrel, nine-banded armadillo, and marsh rabbit. Other species such as gray and red foxes, bobcats, striped skunks, and coyotes occasionally forage in this habitat. The red wolf was formerly a top predator in this and other coastal habitats (Stalter and Odum 1993). Muskrats are common in freshwater tidal marshes along the Gulf Coast and northern Atlantic coast but inexplicably absent from coastal areas in South Carolina, Georgia, and portions of Florida (K. McPherson 2009a). Small mammals recorded from freshwater tidal marshes in Georgia include the eastern mole, starnose mole, southeastern shrew, least shrew, short-tailed shrew, eastern harvest mouse, cotton mouse, eastern woodrat, silver-haired bat, Seminole bat, and big brown bat (W. E. Odum et al. 1984).

Marsh Rabbit (*Sylvilagus palustris*)

The marsh rabbit, also known as the "marsh hare" or "pontoon," is the smallest member of the family Leporidae in Georgia. Its range extends from southern Alabama to extreme southeastern Virginia. In Georgia, the marsh rabbit is distributed throughout the Coastal Plain, including the barrier islands (A. S. Johnson et al. 1974; Georgia Museum of Natural History 2008). The marsh rabbit generally resembles its more common relative, the eastern cottontail, but is uniformly darker in color, with shorter ears, feet, and tail (Georgia Department of Natural Resources 2005b).

Marsh rabbits are found primarily in wet habitats, including freshwater and brackish marshes, bottomland hardwood forests, and river swamps. In addition to a variety of settings on the mainland, they can be found on barrier islands, marsh hammocks, and islands within coastal river deltas (Georgia Museum of Natural History 2008). Primarily nocturnal,

marsh rabbits forage at night, feeding on the leaves, stems, and roots of herbaceous plants as well as the leaves and twigs of woody plants. During the day they remain hidden in shallow excavated soil depressions surrounded by dense vegetation, in hollow logs, or in abandoned burrows of other animals.

Marsh rabbits exhibit several unique behavioral adaptations to their environment. Though they can hop like other rabbits, they often walk on all fours with widely spread toes, a mode of locomotion that works well in mucky terrain (Whitaker and Hamilton 1998). They are also capable of walking on their hind legs for short distances. Marsh rabbits are strong swimmers and readily take to the water to avoid predators. Known predators include bobcats, coyotes, foxes, owls, hawks, eagles, rattlesnakes, and cottonmouths (Burt and Grossenheider 1980). The marsh rabbit is an important game animal in Georgia (Georgia Department of Natural Resources 2005b).

Butler Island and Champney Island, Altamaha Wildlife Management Area

Butler Island and Champney Island are located within Altamaha Wildlife Management Area, a 29,300-acre state-owned property managed by the Georgia Department of Natural Resources (McIntosh County). Butler Island was once the home of one of the most successful tidewater rice and sugar plantations in antebellum America, developed in the early 1800s by Major Pierce Butler after vast stands of cypress-dominated tidal swamps had been removed from the island (Lenz 2002). The Butler Island plan-

tation was abandoned following the Civil War, and the property was later purchased by the state of Georgia. Today, the majority of Butler Island is composed of seasonally impounded freshwater wetland habitats managed to provide valuable foraging habitat for migrating and wintering waterfowl. Adjacent to Butler Island, Champney Island was also the site of an antebellum rice plantation and is also currently managed to provide habitat for waterfowl. It is the site of the 34-acre Ansley-Hodges Memorial M.A.R.S.H. (Matching Aid to Restore State Habitats) Project, a waterfowl habitat enhancement project sponsored by Ducks Unlimited and the Georgia Department of Natural Resources. An observation tower a short distance from a parking area located west of U.S. Highway 17 offers views of freshwater marsh within the impoundments. Freshwater emergents such as giant cutgrass, pickerelweed, wild-rice, and cattails are common in the impoundments and in natural freshwater tidal marsh along the edge of the islands. East of U.S. Highway 17, the James Allen Williamson Champney River Park includes a boat ramp and ample parking. A walkway near the boat ramp provides views of freshwater tidal marsh along the river.

Location: Heading south on U.S. Hwy. 17 about 2 miles from Darien, look for the Champney Island parking area and interpretive trail on the right, just south of the Champney River. James Allen Williamson Champney River Park is located east of U.S. 17 just south of the river. Google Earth GPS approximate coordinates for entrance to Champney River Park: N 31.335780/ W 081.448710.

Tidal Swamps

Tidal swamps are freshwater forested wetlands that are found within the floodplains of major tidal rivers emptying to the Atlantic Ocean as well as smaller creeks, sloughs, and flats that receive regular or periodic inundation from freshwater tidal flows. The canopy is usually dominated by bald-cypress and water tupelo but may also include sweet gum, swamp tupelo, green ash, red maple, water oak, and swamp bay.

Tidal river swamps lie downstream from nontidal river swamps and upstream from freshwater or brackish marshes. On the lower floodplains of major alluvial rivers such as the Savannah and Altamaha, they may occur as relatively homogeneous patches several thousands of acres in size (NatureServe 2009c). Tidal swamps also occur along blackwater river systems such as the Ogeechee, Satilla, and St. Marys, but are less extensive (Wharton 1978).

These wetland environments share some characteristics with nontidal river swamps and bottomland hardwood forests, including a freshwater regime and periodic overbank flooding. They are distinguished primarily by their tidal regime, which influences species composition, productivity, and nutrient exchange with other natural communities.

PHYSICAL SETTING AND ECOLOGY

Tidal swamps are flooded and drained regularly or irregularly by freshwater tidal flows. The forest floor is covered twice a day for several hours and may remain inundated for days during flood or storm events (Wharton et al. 1982). Tidal swamps are also affected periodically by elevated tides associated with storm events along the coast. Storm tides are surges in coastal water levels created through a combination of low atmospheric pressure and winds blowing across the surface of ocean waters. Superimposed on the normal tide pattern, these periodic storm surges can quickly elevate water levels, causing extreme flooding in low-lying coastal areas and creating a strong tidal influx that contributes to elevated hydroperiods in tidal swamps and adjacent communities.

Tidal ranges vary by season due to seasonal cycles of heating and cooling that lead to thermal expansion and contraction of ocean water. This seasonal fluctuation in tidal range is inversely correlated with the seasonal pattern of river flows in the lower Coastal Plain. In summer and fall, tides are typically high, while river flows are relatively low; in winter and spring, river flows are high, while tides are lower. The head of the tide (upper end of the tidal zone) moves upriver and downriver seasonally due to fluctuations in river discharge and tide range (Day, Williams, and Warzewski 2007). This seasonal fluctuation creates shifting patterns of salinity and sediment deposition (Doyle et al. 2007). When the head of the tide moves upstream, tidal swamps experience higher salinity levels and more tidal flushing. When the head of the tide moves downstream, salinity levels decrease and the tidal influence is diminished relative to the influence of the river.

The movement of water in and out of the interior areas of extensive tidal swamps may be quite slow; soils in these interior areas may remain saturated even during extreme droughts (Duberstein and Kitchens 2007). While the hydrology of such swamp systems is poorly understood, it may be that tides actually force groundwater flows, maintaining saturated soil conditions for extended periods of time. Under these conditions, the water table within the tidal floodplain rises and falls with the tide, even if there is no overbank flooding (Wharton 1978; Wharton et al. 1982).

Given the very low elevational gradient in tidal swamps, microtopography is a major factor in determining the pattern of species dominance within this community. A common feature of tidal swamps is a pattern of "hummocks" (low mounds or islands) and "hollows" (lower areas representing the base of the swamp). While elevational differences between hummocks and hollows may be only 6–8 inches, this variability is important in determining which species can germinate and survive within the tidally influenced environment (C. J. Anderson and Lockaby 2007).

As noted above, this is considered a freshwater wetland community, which means that the salinity of the water is usually less than 0.5 parts per thousand. However, salinity levels fluctuate seasonally accord-

Tidal swamps typically have sparse or patchy ground cover. The swamp floor is nearly always wet to flooded, and vegetation composition is influenced by microtopography.

ing to flood and tide regimes, and these fluctuations influence community composition. Infrequent influxes of saline water represent an important periodic disturbance factor in this environment, causing injury or death to salt-intolerant species and affecting the growth rate of canopy dominants such as bald-cypress (W. H. Conner, Krauss, and Doyle 2007; NatureServe 2009c).

Periodic saltwater intrusion can occur as a result of storm surges, as salt water is pushed upstream in coastal rivers, affecting both surface water and groundwater (Day, Williams, and Warzewski 2007). Since salt water is denser than fresh water, it flows upstream along the bottom of the river, forming a wedge beneath the fresh water. Mixing occurs along the freshwater-saltwater boundary, adding to the salinity of the upper water layers. If river flows are lowered by prolonged drought or upstream impoundments, the saltwater intrusion can proceed farther up the river and induce salt stress to freshwater species. In general, however, the relationship between river salinity and the salinity of tidal swamp sediments is poorly understood (W. H. Conner, Krauss, and Doyle 2007).

Tidal river swamps are strongly influenced by nutrient and organic material inputs from upstream areas as well as by nutrients and sediments borne by incoming tidal flows. Their soils tend to be highly organic, composed of highly decomposed muck and peat and bound together in the upper soil layers by interwoven root mats (W. H. Conner and Buford 1998). In general, the soils of blackwater tidal swamps have higher levels of organic matter (46%) than those of brownwater (alluvial) tidal swamps (31%). Soils of brownwater tidal swamps are more fertile, however, with a much higher concentration of fine sediments and higher levels of inorganic nitrogen and phosphorus (C. J. Anderson and Lockaby 2007).

Tidal swamps are reportedly more productive than nontidal river swamps due to higher levels of nutrient input. Wharton et al. (1982) reported that tidal freshwater swamps had the highest concentrations of soil organic matter of all swamps studied in the Southeast. They hypothesized that this was a result of suppressed decomposition and higher productivity. Tidal hydrology may suppress methane production relative to other swamp systems (C. J. Anderson and Lockaby 2007).

Naturally occurring fire is very infrequent in these systems but in some cases may be important in deter-mining the boundary between tidal swamps and tidal marshes (NatureServe 2009c). Consistently wet soils, long periods of flooding, and a sparse herbaceous layer make these communities resistant to fire (Schafale and Weakley 1990). It is likely that these environments burn only during very prolonged droughts and in situations where they are located in close proximity to fire-prone upland habitats (W. H. Conner and Buford 1998).

An estimated 494,000 acres of tidal freshwater swamps exist in the Southeast; the largest extent (more than 99,000 acres) is found in South Carolina, followed by Virginia (approximately 69,000 acres) and Georgia (approximately 59,000 acres). The greatest losses of tidal freshwater swamps have occurred in Louisiana, followed by South Carolina, Texas, Virginia, Florida, and Georgia (Doyle et al. 2007). The lower Altamaha, Ogeechee, Savannah, and Satilla Rivers still contain extensive stands of tidal river swamp. The lower Savannah River system includes an estimated 9,600 acres of tidal swamp (Duberstein and Kitchens 2007).

Tidal swamps are among the most sensitive systems to climate change, as they are profoundly impacted by changes in streamflow, salinity, and periodicity of droughts and floods. Current models of sea-level rise predict displacement of much of the tidal freshwater swamp zone by the year 2100, as well as an acceleration of saltwater intrusion (Doyle et al. 2007; Craft et al. 2009). Sea-level rise is likely to replace these and other tidal swamps along the Georgia coast with freshwater or brackish marsh. This transition may occur fairly abruptly following the death of overstory tree species and woody shrubs that are salt-intolerant (Schafale and Weakley 1990). Tidal swamps associated with blackwater rivers are likely more vulnerable to impacts from rising sea level, since these systems accumulate sediments at a much lower rate than tidal swamps along alluvial rivers (W. H. Conner, Krauss, and Doyle 2007).

VEGETATION

Species composition of the tidal swamp canopy and subcanopy is influenced strongly by microtopography and landscape position (e.g., distance from the main river channel), as well as hydrologic regime. Duberstein and Kitchens (2007) described four general types of tidal swamp plant communities in the lower Savannah River basin: shrub hummock, water tupelo,

CHARACTERISTIC PLANTS OF TIDAL SWAMPS

TREES

Red maple—*Acer rubrum*
Musclewood—*Carpinus caroliniana*
Carolina ash—*Fraxinus caroliniana*
Sweet gum—*Liquidambar styraciflua*
Water tupelo—*Nyssa aquatica*
Swamp tupelo—*Nyssa biflora*
Swamp bay—*Persea palustris*
Water oak—*Quercus nigra*
Bald-cypress—*Taxodium distichum*

SHRUBS AND WOODY VINES

Tag alder—*Alnus serrulata*
Buttonbush—*Cephalanthus occidentalis*

Southern leatherflower—*Clematis crispa*
Southern swamp dogwood—*Cornus stricta*
Ti-ti—*Cyrilla racemiflora*
Climbing hydrangea—*Decumaria barbara*
Coastal fetterbush—*Eubotrys racemosa*
Swamp-privet—*Forestiera acuminata*
Dahoon—*Ilex cassine*
Virginia-willow—*Itea virginica*
Wax-myrtle—*Morella cerifera*
Water-elm—*Planera aquatica*
Dwarf palmetto—*Sabal minor*
Southern wild raisin—*Viburnum nudum*

Small-leaf viburnum—*Viburnum obovatum*

GROUND COVER

Green dragon—*Arisaema dracontium*
Coastal Plain water-willow—*Justicia ovata* var. *ovata*
Sensitive fern—*Onoclea sensibilis*
Royal fern—*Osmunda regalis*
Cinnamon fern—*Osmundastrum cinnamomeum*
Green arrow-arum—*Peltandra virginica*
Netted chain fern—*Woodwardia areolata*

swamp tupelo–alder, and water oak–swamp bay swamps. Of these, the swamp tupelo-alder type is the most abundant and "typical" plant community of tidal swamps within the Savannah National Wildlife Refuge. It has a tall canopy dominated by swamp tupelo, with bald-cypress, red maple, swamp bay, and water oak. Dominants in the shrub/understory layer include tag alder, southern swamp dogwood, buttonbush, dahoon, swamp bay, sweet gum, southern wild raisin, and musclewood (Duberstein and Kitchens 2007).

Shrub hummock communities are found mostly in backswamp areas, on low mounds (hummocks) within the floodplain. The canopy consists mostly of water tupelo and bald-cypress, with dahoon, Virginia-willow, coastal fetterbush, and wax-myrtle. Other characteristic species include small-leaf viburnum, shining fetterbush, and southern wild raisin. The water tupelo community is found mainly in tidal creeks and sloughs and consists of a fairly open stand of water tupelo, with a poorly developed shrub layer and well-developed herb layer. Other characteristic species include water oak, Carolina ash, red maple, southern swamp dogwood, and bald-cypress (Duberstein and Kitchens 2007).

The water oak–swamp bay community is found along the main channel of the Savannah River and the largest tidal creeks and drainages in the floodplain. This community has a canopy similar to that of the swamp tupelo–alder community but with no alder.

In addition, the subcanopy of this plant community is dominated by young Carolina ash, red maple, water tupelo, swamp tupelo, bald-cypress, swamp bay, water oak, and musclewood trees (Duberstein and Kitchens 2007).

Tidal swamps of the Altamaha River are similar, with a canopy dominated by bald-cypress, sweet gum, water oak, water tupelo, and swamp tupelo. Typical understory trees and shrubs include swamp bay, swamp-privet, and dwarf palmetto, with black willow, southern swamp dogwood, tag alder, small-leaf viburnum, water-elm, Ogeechee lime, red maple, and buttonbush common along streams and sloughs. Ground cover vegetation is generally sparse in the shaded interior of the swamp. Typical vines and ground cover species include climbing hydrangea, southern leatherflower, green dragon, sensitive fern, royal fern, cinnamon fern, netted chain fern, green arrow-arum, and Coastal Plain water-willow (Wharton 1978).

ANIMALS

Tidal swamps provide habitat for a wide variety of resident and migratory animals. Wharton (1978) suggested that animal communities of tidal swamps are probably more influenced by the tidal regime than are plant communities. Invertebrate communities of tidal floodplains may be similar to those of nontidal river swamps, with high abundance and diversity of cray-

Red bat

fishes, clams, oligochaete worms, snails, freshwater shrimp, amphipods, and insects (W. H. Conner and Buford 1998). Mammals typically found in this environment include medium-sized terrestrial generalists such as the opossum, raccoon, and gray fox. Gray squirrels, red bats, and Rafinesque's big-eared bats make use of canopy trees, and small mammals such as the least shrew, marsh rabbit, eastern woodrat, and rice rat utilize the swamp floor. River otters are commonly observed in sloughs and oxbows, while feral swine and white-tailed deer range widely through the swamp. Black bear and bobcats are less common residents of tidal swamps (Wharton 1978).

Birds associated with tidal swamps include long-legged waders such as the great blue heron, snowy egret, yellow-crowned night-heron, Louisiana heron, green heron, glossy ibis, common egret, white ibis, and wood stork. Characteristic perching birds include the belted kingfisher, pileated woodpecker, hairy woodpecker, prothonotary warbler, northern parula, hooded warbler, Swainson's warbler, Carolina chickadee, tufted titmouse, blue-gray gnatcatcher, red-eyed vireo, white-eyed vireo, northern cardinal, and Carolina wren. Raptors such as the red-shouldered hawk, barred owl, swallow-tailed kite, Mississippi kite, and bald eagle are also frequently observed in this habitat. Characteristic waterbirds include the anhinga, mallard, black duck, hooded merganser, and wood duck, the latter two species being particularly common where mature trees with nesting cavities are present (Wharton 1978; McKenzie and Barclay 1980; Wharton et al. 1982).

Turtles typically found in tidal swamps include the common snapping turtle, pond slider, Florida cooter, eastern mud turtle, loggerhead musk turtle, common musk turtle, and spotted turtle. Snakes associated with this environment include the banded watersnake, brown watersnake, glossy crayfish snake, cottonmouth, timber rattlesnake, eastern kingsnake, black racer, rat snake, black swamp snake, mud snake, and rainbow snake. Lizards are uncommon in this wet habitat but include the green anole and broadhead skink (Wharton 1978; McKenzie and Barclay 1980).

Because they provide many shallow pools, fallen logs, and consistently moist substrates, tidal swamps are particularly favorable environments for amphibians. A wide variety can be found here, including seldom-encountered species such as the greater siren and two-toed amphiuma, as well as more commonly observed species such as the southern dusky salamander, many-lined salamander, dwarf salamander, mud salamander, two-lined salamander, spotted salamander, eastern narrow-mouthed toad, eastern spadefoot, oak toad, southern toad, bullfrog, green frog, southern cricket frog, southern leopard frog, green treefrog, bird-voiced treefrog, and squirrel treefrog (Wharton 1978; McKenzie and Barclay 1980; W. H. Conner and Buford 1998).

Fishes of tidal swamps include sportfish such as bluegill, green sunfish, redbreast sunfish, chain pickerel, yellow bullhead, and largemouth bass. Other fishes typically found in this habitat include the starhead topminnow, mosquitofish, banded pygmy sunfish, longnose gar, bowfin, cypress minnow, silvery minnow, and spotted sucker (McKenzie and Barclay 1980). Tidal river swamps serve an important role as spawning grounds and nurseries for a wide variety of fish species, presumably because of the variety of aquatic habitats found within the floodplain and the abundant inputs of organic materials (Wharton 1978; Wharton et al. 1982).

Prothonotary Warbler
(*Protonotaria citrea*)

The prothonotary warbler, also known as the "swamp canary" or "golden swamp warbler," is a member of the family Parulidae (wood-warblers). Males in breeding plumage have a bright yellow head, neck, breast, and belly and an olive-green back. Females are slightly duller in coloration, with a yellow breast and belly and a greenish yellow head and neck (Dunn and Alderfer 2008). This species was named for its yellow plumage, reminiscent of the bright yellow robes worn by papal clerks (prothonotaries) in the Roman Catholic Church (Petit 1999).

The prothonotary warbler winters in mangrove swamps and coastal tropical forests from southern Mexico and the Yucatan peninsula to northern South America. Its primary breeding grounds are located within the southeastern United States. In Georgia, this species breeds widely throughout the Coastal Plain and locally in the Piedmont and the Cumberland Plateau / Ridge and Valley (Jensen 2010). Within its breeding range, the prothonotary warbler is commonly found along stream banks, near sloughs and oxbow lakes, and in depressional wetlands such as cypress-gum ponds. It often sings from a low perch near the water, making it especially conspicuous to boaters and anglers during the spring and summer.

The only eastern wood-warbler that nests in tree cavities, the prothonotary warbler often chooses a hollow tree or branch near water, but may use abandoned holes of downy woodpeckers or chickadees (Terres 1980; Petit 1999). Its diet includes beetles, spiders, mayflies, caterpillars, aquatic insect larvae, and some seeds. Like other migratory songbirds, the prothonotary warbler depends on nesting and wintering habitats that lie hundreds or even thousands of miles apart. Logging and agricultural conversion of bottomland hardwood forests and river swamps in the southeastern United States have been detrimental to breeding populations. An even greater threat may be the destruction of mangrove habitats in South America (Petit 1999; Jensen 2010).

Lewis Island, Altamaha Wildlife Management Area

Lewis Island (McIntosh County) is located in the lower Altamaha River corridor, bounded on the southwest by the main river channel and on the northeast by Lewis Creek. This 5,633-acre tract, a designated National Natural Landmark, is managed by the Georgia Department of Natural Resources as a part of Altamaha Wildlife Management Area. Lewis Island contains Georgia's largest known virgin stand of tidal swamp dominated by bald-cypress and water tupelo trees. One stand of bald-cypress in the center of the tract has scattered trees 6 to 7 feet in diameter that are estimated to be more than 1,100 years old, with one tree believed to be more than 1,300 years old (Lenz 2002).

The terrain of Lewis Island is low-lying and mucky, with several sloughs of varying depths. In addition to being influenced by seasonal overbank flooding, this site experiences twice-daily inputs of water from incoming tides. During spring tides, these flows can flood the island with several feet of standing water in a period of only a few hours (Wharton 1978). The understory of Lewis Island is fairly open, with widely spaced, old-growth canopy trees. In addition to bald-cypress and water tupelo, characteristic trees include sweet gum, swamp tupelo, and swamp bay. Dwarf palmetto, swamp-privet, water-elm, tag alder, black willow, southern swamp dogwood, and small-leaf viburnum are components of the shrub layer. Characteristic components of the vine-herb layer include climbing hydrangea, southern leatherflower, green dragon, sensitive fern, royal fern, and Coastal Plain water-willow (Wharton 1978).

Location: Lewis Island is located approximately 5 miles upriver from the town of Darien. This site is accessible only by boat, and an experienced guide is recommended. A 0.5-mile trail leading to the stand of virgin bald-cypress trees is flagged with colored plastic tape. The trailhead is located approximately 0.75 mile southeast of the intersection of Studhorse Creek and Pico Creek. Google Earth GPS approximate coordinates for center of Lewis Island: N 31.382420/ W 081.521330.

Ogeechee lime in a slough along the lower Altamaha River

Red maple leaves covered in Spanish-moss

Golden silk orb-weaver

Chapter 8

FUTURE CONSERVATION CHALLENGES

THIS BOOK HAS described the natural communities of Georgia as they exist in the early part of the 21st century. The environment of this state today is different than it was in pre-settlement times, when longleaf pine extended throughout the Coastal Plain, the American chestnut produced mast in profusion every fall in the mountains, and the Piedmont had far thicker, richer soils and was most likely a mosaic of old-growth forests, woodlands, and savannas. In spite of these changes, Georgia remains a state of beauty and native diversity. Conservation of the state's remaining natural communities requires an understanding of current and impending threats, identification of key species and habitats at risk, development of regional and place-specific conservation plans, and advocacy for action by the populace to address these issues in the context of an ever-changing environment. In addition, effective conservation programs require a commitment to monitor and adapt management approaches to achieve successive improvements and to deal with new and emerging challenges (Georgia Department of Natural Resources 2005a).

Four broad goals that are commonly incorporated into biological conservation plans include the following (adapted from Baydack et al. 1999; cited in Nelson 2005): (1) conserve representative examples of all natural communities within their ranges of variability; (2) maintain viable populations of all native species in natural patterns of abundance, interaction, and distribution; (3) maintain ecological and evolutionary processes including natural disturbance regimes, nutrient cycles, and biotic interactions; and (4) manage landscapes and natural communities to be resilient to short-term and long-term climatic and land use changes. These goals, while impossible to achieve

across the entire state, represent essential elements of biodiversity conservation that must be addressed within high priority landscapes where conservation is an option.

Perhaps the greatest challenges facing natural resource managers today are the pace and scale of change in the physical environment of Georgia. Increasing human population growth and urban/suburban sprawl will continue to fragment and isolate natural environments. Human-induced climate change is likely resulting in altered precipitation patterns, drought frequencies, tropical storm intensities and frequencies, average temperatures, temperature variability, and length of the growing season. These changes in turn will likely impact plant phenology, migration patterns of wide-ranging animals, conditions for plant germination, and disturbance regimes, all of which will impact species dispersal and survival. It is expected that natural communities will not move en masse and intact to new locations. Rather, as occurred during the dramatic climate changes of the late Pleistocene and early Holocene, species will most likely move to new locales in an individualistic manner. Some species will be extirpated, and others will form novel assemblages that do not exist today and that may be extant for only short periods of time. These assemblages will most likely contain species now considered non-native invasives.

Under this scenario, and given the significant changes in hydrology, soils, fire regimes, and the distribution of natural habitats that have occurred to Georgia's landscape since the arrival of European settlers, the goal of re-creating historic or prehistoric patterns of plant and animal communities may not be possible or even desirable, although such patterns may serve as useful goals and guideposts in many instances. Conservationists and land managers will face a complex task of evaluating how changes from past conditions can be considered in light of potential changes to come and determining what will best conserve Georgia's impressive storehouse of biodiversity. This task will be made more difficult by the variability in climate model outputs and lack of data on predicted species/ habitat responses to potential changes. Conservation management will require alternative approaches based on maintaining or restoring ecological functionality within broad regions of the state, maximizing habitat diversity, and providing opportunities for species to migrate and community composition to shift. Protection of exemplary sites within a broad range of environmental gradients, restoration of matrix habitats, maintenance of migration corridors, and restoration of ecological drivers of natural environments (e.g., hydrology, sediment transport) will be key components of conservation in the future. Multiscale coordination of these "climate change adaptation" strategies will need to be facilitated by statewide collaborative efforts as well as regional and national consortia of researchers and conservation groups (Association of Fish and Wildlife Agencies 2009).

The ability to manage and protect Georgia's natural environments in the future will also depend upon an informed and engaged public. Many Georgians are unaware of the ecological and biological diversity in the state, the threats to this diversity, and opportunities for involvement in programs or activities that will help protect their natural heritage. Various organizations have developed conservation messages and materials that can contribute to a better public understanding of Georgia's natural diversity. There is a need to make this information available to a wider range of audience and to tailor the messages to make them relevant to local or regional conditions, however. Outreach programs focused on approaches and techniques for restoration and management of natural environments are particularly important.

Another important outreach objective is broader recognition of the significant economic value of various "ecological services" provided by intact natural environments and the importance of maintaining "green infrastructure" in land use planning. Ultimately, maintenance of ecological functions within a given region will require some constraints on development. Effective use of biodiversity data for environmental review, public outreach, permitting, and development of site management plans can help minimize impacts of development on priority species and habitats. Land use plans that incorporate protection of natural environments can help ensure the protection of biotic diversity while allowing sustainable development.

Conservation measures to protect or restore representative examples of natural environments in Georgia will require financial, technical, and other resources well in excess of those currently available to conservation organizations in Georgia. To build on the major state acquisitions of the last decade, additional funding and support for local, state, and national conservation programs to protect natural environments will be necessary to meet the goal of sustaining natural diversity in Georgia. Regional conservation partnerships are important for coordination of conservation efforts and development of greater capacity to address regional conservation needs. Other important approaches include development of in-state partnerships to share resources and expertise, reallocation of existing staff to address areas of greatest conservation need, and development of stable funding sources.

Finally, comprehensive monitoring programs will be needed to assess the success of conservation programs and to make adjustments in these programs to increase their efficacy. Information on the quantity, distribution, and condition of habitats and populations will be needed to gauge the success or failure of conservation efforts. The development and coordination of comprehensive habitat monitoring programs will require participation by a variety of partners, both public and private (Schoonmaker and Lunscombe 2005).

Future challenges to conserve Georgia's natural diversity will be daunting and complex. Continuation of efforts to understand this state's impressive array of natural environments, the threats facing these environments, and the management needs of individual species and habitats will allow for development of more informed conservation strategies. It is our hope that this book will serve as a foundation for future research, education, outreach, and land protection efforts to help conserve the natural communities of this state.

Crosswalk of Community Names with NatureServe (2012) Ecological Systems and Wharton (1978) Natural Environments of Georgia

Natural Community	NatureServe	Wharton
BLUE RIDGE		
Northern hardwood and boulderfield forests	CES202.029 Southern Appalachian Northern Hardwood Forest	52 Broadleaf Deciduous Cove Forest (in part); 53 Boulderfields; 60 Broadleaf Deciduous-Hemlock Forest
Montane oak forests	CES202.596 Central and Southern Appalachian Montane Oak Forest	54 Oak Ridge Forest; 58 Shrub Bald
Cove forests	CES202.373 Southern and Central Appalachian Cove Forest	52 Broadleaf Deciduous Cove Forest (in part)
Low- to mid-elevation oak forests	CES202.886 Southern Appalachian Oak Forest	56 Chestnut Oak Ridge Forest; 57 Oak-Chestnut-Hickory Forest
Pine-oak woodlands and forests	CES202.331 Southern Appalachian Montane Pine Forest and Woodland; CES202.332 Southern Appalachian Low-Elevation Pine Forest	59 Broadleaf Deciduous Ridge Forest; 62 Broadleaf Deciduous–Pine Ridge Forest
Ultramafic barrens and woodlands	CES202.347 Eastern Serpentine Woodland	———
High-elevation rock outcrops	CES202.327 Southern Appalachian Rocky Summit	63 Cliffs and Gorge Walls
Low- to mid-elevation mafic domes, glades, and barrens	CES202.348 Southern and Central Appalachian Mafic Glade and Barrens; CES202.297 Southern Appalachian Granitic Dome	———
Low- to mid-elevation acidic cliffs and outcrops	CES202.330 Southern Appalachian Montane Cliff and Talus	63 Cliffs and Gorge Walls
Mountain bogs	CES202. 300 Southern and Central Appalachian Bog and Fen	34 Mountain and Piedmont Bogs; Spring Seep
Seepage wetlands	CES202.317 Southern Appalachian Seepage Wetland	4 Wet Cliffs and Outcrops (in part)
Spray cliffs	CES202.288 Southern Appalachian Spray Cliff	4 Wet Cliffs and Outcrops (in part)
Floodplains, bottomlands, and riparian zones	CES202.705 South-Central Interior Large Floodplain; CES202.706 South-Central Interior Small Stream and Floodplain	5 Mountain Rivers

Natural Community	NatureServe	Wharton
CUMBERLAND PLATEAU / RIDGE AND VALLEY		
Mesic forests	CES202.887 South-Central Interior Mesophytic Forest	40 Bluff and Ravine Forest; 41 Forests on Colluvial Flats; 45 Ravine, Gorge and Cove Forests
Dry calcareous forests	CES202.457 Southern Ridge and Valley Cumberland Dry Calcareous Forest	43 Forests of the Chickamauga Valley (in part); 44 Deciduous Forests of the Great Valley (in part); 47 Armuchee Ridge Forest (in part)
Acidic oak-pine-hickory forests	CES202.359 Allegheny-Cumberland Dry Oak Forest and Woodland; CES202.309 Cumberland Acidic Cliffs and Rockhouses	42 Submesic Ridge and Slope Forest; 43 Forest of the Chickamauga Valley (in part); 44 Deciduous Forests of the Great Valley (in part); 46 Oak-Pine Forests of the Great Valley; 47 Armuchee Ridge Forest (in part)
Pine-oak woodlands	CES202.332 Southern Appalachian Low-Elevation Pine Forest	50 Rock Outcrops (in part); 47 Armuchee Ridge Forest (in part)
Montane longleaf woodlands and forests (also for Piedmont and Blue Ridge ecoregions)	CES202.319 Southeastern Interior Longleaf Pine Woodland	74 Pine-Broadleaf Deciduous Subcanopy Xeric Forests
Calcareous prairies and barrens (Coosa prairies)	CES202.453 Southern Ridge and Valley Patch Prairie	———
Calcareous glades, barrens, and woodlands (cedar glades)	CES202.024 Southern Ridge and Valley Calcareous Glade and Woodland	48 Cedar Glades
Acidic glades and barrens	CES202.337 Cumberland Sandstone Glade and Barrens	50 Rock Outcrops (in part); 4 Wet Cliffs and Outcrops (in part)
Calcareous cliffs	CES202.356 Southern Interior Calcareous Cliff	50 Rock Outcrops (in part); 4 Wet Cliffs and Outcrops (in part)
Acidic cliffs and rock outcrops	ces202.309 Cumberland Acidic Cliffs and Rockhouses	4 Wet Cliffs and Outcrops (in part); 50 Rock Outcrops (in part)
Flatwoods	CES202.336 Piedmont Upland Depression Swamp	———
Calcareous seepage fens	CES202.458: Southern Ridge and Valley Seepage Fen	Wharton 34 Mountain and Seepage Bog (in part)
Acidic seepage wetlands	CES202.361 Cumberland Seepage Forest	34 Mountain and Seepage Bog (in part)
Sagponds and sinkholes	CES202.018 Central Interior Highlands and Appalachian Sinkhole and Depression Pond	36 Sagpond

Natural Community	NatureServe	Wharton
Floodplains, bottomlands, and riparian zones	CES202.705 South-Central Interior Large Floodplain; CES202.706 South-Central Interior Small Stream and Riparian; CES202.036 Cumberland Riverscour	5 Mountain Rivers (in part); 11 Coosa River and Swamp System
PIEDMONT		
Mesic forests	CES202.342 Southern Piedmont Mesic Forest	64 Bluff and Ravine Forests of Northern Affinities; 65 Bluff, Slope and Ravine Forests; 66 Ravine Forest of Mixed Affinities; 73 Mixed Pine-Hardwood Colluvial Forests
Oak-pine-hickory forests	CES202.339 Southern Piedmont Dry Oak-(Pine) Forest	68 Oak-Hickory Climax Forest; 67 Evergreen Heath Bluffs; 72 Successional Forest Stages
Pine-oak woodlands and forests	CES202.268 Piedmont Hardpan Woodland and Forest	75 Pine-Hardwood Xeric Ridge and Slope Forest
Prairies and savannas	No crosswalk	————
Glades, barrens, and woodlands	CES202.328 Southern Piedmont Glade and Barrens	76 Rock Outcrops (in part)
Granite outcrops	CES292.329 Southern Piedmont Granite Flatrock	71 Pine Climax Forest; Rock Outcrops
Ultramafic barrens and woodlands	CES202.347 Eastern Serpentine Woodland	68 Oak-Hickory Climax Forest (in part); 74 Pine-Broadleaf Deciduous Subcanopy Xeric Forest (in part)
Cliffs, bluffs, and outcrops	CES202.386 Southern Piedmont Cliff	70 Xeric Bluffs
Flatwoods	CES202.336 Piedmont Upland Depression Swamp	69 Piedmont Flatwoods
Seepage wetlands	CES202.298 Piedmont Seepage Wetland	34 Mountain and Piedmont Bog; Spring Seep
Floodplains, bottomlands, and riparian zones	CES202.324 Southern Piedmont Large Floodplain forest (in part); CES202.323 Southern Piedmont Small Floodplain and Riparian Forest	9 Alluvial River and Swamp System—Piedmont
COASTAL PLAIN		
Sandhills and river dunes	CES203.254 Atlantic Coastal Plain Fall-line Sandhills Longleaf Pine Woodland; CES203.497 Atlantic Coastal Plain Xeric River Dune; CES203.281 Atlantic Coastal Plain Upland Longleaf Pine Woodland (in part)	86 Dwarf Oak–Evergreen Shrub Forest

Natural Community	NatureServe	Wharton
Dry upland longleaf pine woodlands	CES203.281 Atlantic Coastal Plain Upland Longleaf Pine Woodland; CES203.496 East Gulf Coastal Plain Interior Upland Longleaf Pine Woodland (in part)	85 Dwarf Oak Forest (Longleaf Pine–Turkey Oak)
Mesic uplands longleaf pine woodlands	CES203.281 Atlantic Coastal Plain Upland Longleaf Pine Woodland (in part); CES203.496 East Gulf Coastal Plain Interior Upland Longleaf Pine Woodland (in part)	95 Longleaf Pine Upland Forest; 96 Loblolly-Shortleaf Pine Upland Forest
Dry evergreen oak woodlands	CES203.494 Southern Coastal Plain Oak Dome and Hammock (in part)	91 Upland Broadleaf Evergreen Forest (in part)
Dry deciduous hardwood forests	CES203.560 Southern Coastal Plain Dry Upland Hardwood Forest; CES203.241 Southern Coastal Plain Dry and Dry-Mesic Oak Forest	83 Upland Broadleaf Deciduous-Needleleaf Evergreen Forest (in part); 84 Clay Ridge Forest; 85 Dwarf Oak Forest (in part)
Mesic slope forests	CES203.476 Southern Coastal Plain Mesic Slope Forest; CES203.242 Southern Atlantic Coastal Plain Mesic Hardwood Forest; CES203.502 Southern Coastal Plain Limestone Forest	77 Mesic Slope Forests (Bluff Forests of Northern Affinities); 78 Bluff and Slope Forests; 79 Chattahoochee Ravines; 80 Torreya Ravines 81; Solution Ravines; 82 Tifton Upland Ravines (in part)
Acidic glades, barrens, and rocky woodlands	CES203.281 Atlantic Coastal Plain Upland Longleaf Pine Woodland (in part)	100 Sandstone outcrops; 82 Tifton Upland Ravines (in part); 84 Clay Ridge Forest (in part)
Blackland prairies and woodlands	CES203.478 Southern Coastal Plain Blackland Prairie and Woodland	———
Pine flatwoods	CES203.536 Southern Atlantic Coastal Plain Wet Pine Savanna and Flatwoods	94 Mesic Pine Lowland Forest (Pine Flatwoods)
Seepage slope herb bogs	CES203.253 Atlantic Coastal Plain Sandhill Seep (in part); CES203.536 Southern Atlantic Coastal Plain Wet Pine Savanna and Flatwoods (in part); CES203.078 Southern Coastal Plain Herbaceous Seep and Bog	32 Herb Bog (Pitcher Plant Bog)
Seepage slope swamps and shrub bogs	CES203.253, Atlantic Coastal Plain Sandhill Seep (in part); CES203.252 Atlantic Coastal Plain Streamhead Seepage Swamp, Pocosin, and Baygall (in part); CES203.505 Southern Coastal Plain Seepage Swamp and Baygall; CES203.385 East Gulf Coastal Plain Interior Shrub Bog	33 Shrub Bog, Bay Swamps

Natural Community	NatureServe	Wharton
Depression marshes and cypress savannas	CES203.245 Atlantic Coastal Plain Clay-Based Carolina Bay Wetland (in part)	28 Carolina Bays (in part); 31 Cypress Savannah; 35 Limesinks (in part)
Cypress-gum ponds	CES203.245 Atlantic Coastal Plain Clay-Based Carolina Bay Wetland (in part); CES203.448 Southern Coastal Plain Nonriverine Cypress Dome	26 Cypress Pond; 27 Gum Pond; 28 Carolina Bays; 35 Limesinks (in part)
Depression oak forests	CES203.494 Southern Coastal Plain Oak Dome and Hammock (in part)	90 Lowland Broadleaf evergreen Forest (in part); 91 Upland Broadleaf Evergreen Forest (in part)
Cypress-tupelo river swamps	CES203.249 Atlantic Coastal Plain Small Blackwater River Floodplain Forest (in part); CES203.493 Southern Coastal Plain Blackwater River Floodplain Forest (in part); CES203.248 Atlantic Coastal Plain Brownwater Stream Floodplain Forest; CES203.066 Southern Atlantic Coastal Plain Large River Floodplain Forest (in part); CES203.489 East Gulf Coastal Plain Large River Floodplain Forest (in part); CES203.559 East Gulf Coastal Plain Small Stream and River Floodplain Forest (in part)	7 Blackwater River and Swamp System; 10 Alluvial River and Floodplain (in part)
Bottomland hardwoods	CES203.248 Atlantic Coastal Plain Brownwater Stream Floodplain Forest (in part); CES203.250 Atlantic Coastal Plain Small Brownwater River Floodplain Forest (in part); CES203.066 Southern Atlantic Coastal Plain Large River Floodplain Forest (in part); CES203.559 East Gulf Coastal Plain Small Stream and River Floodplain Forest (in part); CES203.493 Southern Coastal Plain Blackwater River Floodplain Forest (in part)	10 Alluvial River and Swamp System — Coastal Plain (in part)

Natural Community	NatureServe	Wharton
Riverbanks and levees	CES203.248 Atlantic Coastal Plain Brownwater Stream Floodplain Forest; CES203.250 Atlantic Coastal Plain Small Brownwater River Floodplain Forest (in part); CES203.066 Southern Atlantic Coastal Plain Large River Floodplain Forest (in part); CES203.559 East Gulf Coastal Plain Small Stream and River Floodplain Forest (in part); CES203.493 Atlantic Coastal Plain Blackwater River Floodplain Forest (in part)	7 Blackwater River and Swamp System (in part); 10 Alluvial River and Floodplain (in part)
Small stream floodplain forests	CES203.247 Atlantic Coastal Plain Blackwater Stream Floodplain Forest; CES203.249 Southern Coastal Plain Small Blackwater River Floodplain Forest	8 Blackwater branch or creek swamps
Okefenokee Swamp	CES203.384 Southern Coastal Plain Nonriverine Basin Swamp; CES203.505 Southern Coastal Plain Seepage Swamp and Baygall; CES203.493 Southern Coastal Plain Blackwater River Floodplain Forest (in part); CES203.536 Southern Atlantic Coastal Plain Wet Pine Savanna and Flatwoods; CES203.281 Atlantic Coastal Plain Upland Longleaf Pine Woodland (in part)	30 Bog Swamp (Okefenokee)
MARITIME		
Intertidal beaches, sand bars, and mud flats	CES203.383 Southern Atlantic Coastal Plain Sea Island Beach; CES203.535 Atlantic Coastal Plain Southern Beach	24 Oyster Reefs; 25 Beach
Maritime dunes	CES203.273 Southern Atlantic Coastal Plain Dune and Maritime Grassland	97 Interdune Type; 98 Dune Meadow Type; 99 Dune Oak-Evergreen Shrub Type
Maritime forests	CES203.537 Southern Atlantic Coastal Plain Maritime Forest	87 Lowland Maritime Forest; 88 Maritime Strand Forest; 89 Upland Maritime Forest
Interdunal wetlands	CES203.258 Southeastern Coastal Plain Interdunal Wetland	37 Marsh Ponds (in part)
Salt marshes and brackish tidal marshes	CES203.270 Southern Atlantic Coastal Plain Salt and Brackish Tidal Marsh	15 Smooth Cordgrass Marsh; 16 Salt Grass Marsh; 17 Needlerush Marsh; 18 Edge Zone; 19 Brackish Marsh; 20 Tidal Pools

Natural Community	NatureServe	Wharton
Freshwater and oligohaline tidal marshes	CES203.376 Southern Atlantic Coastal Plain Fresh and Oligohaline Tidal Marsh	14 River Marsh and Fresh Water Marsh; 21 Oligohaline Creek (in part)
Tidal swamps	CES203.240 Southern Atlantic Coastal Plain Tidal Wooded Swamp	12 Tidewater River and Swamp System

Common and Scientific Names of Plants

Most of the common and scientific plant names are derived from *Flora of the Carolinas, Florida, Georgia, and the Surrounding Areas* (Weakley 2010, 2011). In the few instances where common names were not provided in the flora, or would be, in the judgment of the authors, overly confusing to the Georgia audience, common names often used in Georgia were utilized. In most cases, plants are identified to the species, rather than variety, taxonomic level. This is because varieties can be difficult to determine in the field and are often not provided in the source literature that was consulted for this work.

COMMON NAME	SCIENTIFIC NAME	COMMON NAME	SCIENTIFIC NAME
Adder's-tongue fern	*Ophioglossum* spp.	Anise-root	*Osmorhiza longistylis*
Alabama azalea	*Rhododendron speciosum*	Annual salt-marsh aster	*Symphyotrichum subulatum*
Alabama black cherry	*Prunus alabamensis*	Appalachian beardtongue	*Penstemon canescens*
Alabama leatherflower	*Clematis socialis*	Appalachian bunchflower	*Veratrum parviflorum*
Alabama warbonnet	*Jamesianthus alabamensis*	Appalachian milkwort	*Polygala curtissii*
Alders	*Alnus* spp.	Appalachian mock-orange	*Philadelphus inodorus*
Alexander's rock aster	*Eurybia avita*	Appalachian ragwort	*Packera anonyma*
Allegheny blackberry	*Rubus allegheniensis*	Appalachian rockcap fern	*Polypodium appalachianum*
Alligatorweed	*Alternanthera philoxeroides*	Appalachian rock-pink	*Phemeranthus teretifolius*
Alternate-leaf dogwood	*Cornus alternifolia*	Appalachian sandwort	*Minuartia glabra*
Alternate-leaf seedbox	*Ludwigia alternifolia*	Appalachian shoe-string fern	*Vittaria appalachiana*
Alumroots	*Heuchera* spp.	Appalachian sunflower	*Helianthus atrorubens*
American aster	*Symphyotrichum adnatum*	Appalacian cow-wheat	*Melampyrum lineare*
American beautyberry	*Callicarpa americana*	Arrowfeather	*Aristida purpurascens*
American beech	*Fagus grandifolia*	Arrowheads	*Sagittaria* spp.
American bellflower	*Campanula americana*	Arrowleaf tearthumb	*Persicaria sagittata*
American chestnut	*Castanea dentata*	Ashes	*Fraxinus* spp.
American columbo	*Frasera caroliniensis*	Ashy hydrangea	*Hydrangea cinerea*
American cupscale	*Sacciolepis striata*	Ashy sunflower	*Helianthus mollis*
American elm	*Ulmus americana*	Asters	*Symphyotrichum* spp.
American frog's-bit	*Limnobium spongia*	Atamasco-lily	*Zephyranthes atamasca*
American hazelnut	*Corylus americana*	Atlantic white cedar	*Chamaecyparis thyoides*
American holly	*Ilex opaca*	Autumn beakrush	*Rhynchospora solitaria*
American lopseed	*Phryma leptostachya*	Autumn coralroot	*Corallorhiza odontorhiza*
American lotus-lily	*Nelumbo lutea*	Autumn-olive	*Elaeagnus umbellata*
American lovage	*Ligusticum canadense*	Axil-flower	*Mecardonia acuminata*
American persimmon	*Diospyros virginiana*	Azaleas	*Rhododendron* spp.
American rattan	*Berchemia scandens*	Azure sage	*Salvia azurea*
American snowbell	*Styrax americanus*	Bahia grass	*Paspalum notatum*
American trout lily	*Erythronium americanum*	Bald-cypress	*Taxodium distichum*
American wall-rue	*Asplenium ruta-muraria*	Balsam ragwort	*Packera paupercula*
American water-willow	*Justicia americana*	Bamboo-vine	*Smilax laurifolia*
American wisteria	*Wisteria frutescens*	Banana waterlily	*Nymphaea mexicana*
American wood-sorrel	*Oxalis montana*	Barbed rattlesnake-root	*Prenanthes barbata*
Angle-stem beaksedge	*Rhynchospora caduca*		

COMMON NAME	SCIENTIFIC NAME
Barren strawberry	*Geum donianum*
Barrens milkweed	*Asclepias hirtella*
Barrens silky aster	*Symphyotrichum pratense*
Barrens St. John's-wort	*Hypericum sphaerocarpum*
Basswood	*Tilia americana*
Bastard oak	*Quercus sinuata*
Beach morning-glory	*Ipomoea imperati*
Beadle's mountain-mint	*Pycnanthemum beadlei*
Beaked hazelnut	*Corylus cornuta*
Beaked panic grass	*Panicum anceps*
Beaksedges	*Rhynchospora* spp.
Bear huckleberry	*Gaylussacia ursina*
Bee-balm	*Monarda didyma;*
	M. fistulosa
Beechdrops	*Epifagus virginiana*
Bent trillium	*Trillium flexipes*
Bent-awn plume grass	*Saccharum brevibarbe*
Bermuda grass	*Cynodon dactylon*
Bicolor lespedeza	*Lespedeza bicolor*
Big bishopweed	*Ptilimnium costatum*
Big bluestem	*Andropogon gerardii*
Big floating heart	*Nymphoides aquatica*
Big gallberry	*Ilex coriacea*
Bigleaf magnolia	*Magnolia macrophylla*
Bigleaf snowbell	*Styrax grandifolius*
Bird's-foot violet	*Viola pedata*
Bitter seabeach grass	*Panicum amarum*
Bittercresses	*Cardamine* spp.
Bitternut hickory	*Carya cordiformis*
Black birch	*Betula lenta*
Black bulrush	*Scirpus atrovirens*
Black cherry	*Prunus serotina*
Black chokeberry	*Aronia melanocarpa*
Black gum	*Nyssa sylvatica*
Black haw	*Viburnum prunifolium*
Black huckleberry	*Gaylussacia baccata*
Black locust	*Robinia pseudoacacia*
Black needlerush	*Juncus roemerianus*
Black oak	*Quercus velutina*
Black quillwort	*Isoetes melanospora*
Black snakeroot	*Sanicula canadensis*
Black walnut	*Juglans nigra*
Black willow	*Salix nigra*
Blackberries; raspberries;	
dewberries	*Rubus* spp.
Black-eyed Susan	*Rudbeckia hirta*
Blackjack oak	*Quercus marilandica*
Blackroot	*Pterocaulon pycnostachyum*
Bladderpod	*Sesbania vesicarium*
Bladderworts	*Utricularia* spp.

COMMON NAME	SCIENTIFIC NAME
Bland sweet cicely	*Osmorhiza claytonia*
Blazing-star	*Liatris squarrulosa*
Bloodroot	*Sanguinaria canadensis*
Blue ash	*Fraxinus quadrangulata*
Blue butterwort	*Pinguicula caerulea*
Blue maiden-cane	*Amphicarpum*
	muhlenbergianum
Blue marsh violet	*Viola cucullata*
Blue Ridge white	
heart-leaved aster	*Eurybia chlorolepis*
Blue sedge	*Carex glaucescens*
Blue-stars	*Amsonia tabernaemontana*
Blue twinflower	*Dyschoriste oblongifolia*
Blue wild indigo	*Baptisia australis*
Bluebells	*Mertensia virginica*
Blueberries	*Vaccinium* spp.
Blue-eyed grass	*Sisyrinchium* spp.
Bluejack oak	*Quercus incana*
Bluestems	*Andropogon* spp.
Blunt-lobed cliff fern	*Woodsia obtusa*
Bog honeycomb-head	*Balduina atropurpurea*
Boneset	*Eupatorium perfoliatum*
Bosc's witchgrass	*Dichanthelium boscii*
Bottlebrush buckeye	*Aesculus parviflora*
Box elder	*Acer negundo*
Bowmans-root	*Gillenia trifoliata*
Boykin's milkwort	*Polygala boykinii*
Bracken fern	*Pteridium aquilinum*
Bradford pear	*Pyrus calleryana*
Bradley's spleenwort	*Asplenium bradleyi*
Branch lettuce	*Micranthes micranthidifolia*
Brazilian coontail	*Ceratophyllum demersum*
Bristly greenbrier	*Smilax hispida*
Bristly locust	*Robinia hispida*
Broad beech fern	*Phegopteris hexagonoptera*
Broadleaf arrowhead	*Sagittaria latifolia*
Broadleaf pondlily	*Nuphar advena; N. orbiculata*
Brook-saxifrage	*Boykinia aconitifolia*
Brownish beaksedge	*Rhynchospora capitellata*
Buckeyes	*Aesculus* spp.
Buckthorn bumelia	*Sideroxylon lycioides*
Buckwheat-tree	*Cliftonia monophylla*
Buffalo-nut	*Pyrularia pubera*
Bugleweeds	*Lycopus* spp.
Bulbous bittercress	*Cardamine bulbosa*
Bulltongue arrowhead	*Sagittaria lancifolia*
Bulrushes	*Bolboschoenus* spp.
Bur-marigolds	*Bidens* spp.
Bur-reeds	*Sparganium* spp.
Bush clover	*Lespedeza capitata*

COMMON NAME	SCIENTIFIC NAME	COMMON NAME	SCIENTIFIC NAME
Bushy bluestem	*Andropogon glomeratus*	Christmas fern	*Polystichum acrostichoides*
Butterfly pea	*Clitoria mariana*	Cinnamon fern	*Osmundastrum*
Butterweed	*Packera glabella*		*cinnamomeum*
Buttonbush	*Cephalanthus occidentalis*	Cliff saxifrage	*Hydatica petiolaris*
Cabbage palmetto	*Sabal palmetto*	Climbing dogbane	*Trachelospermum difforme*
Camphorweed	*Heterotheca subaxillaris*	Climbing hempweed	*Mikania scandens*
Canada bluet	*Houstonia canadensis*	Climbing hydrangea	*Decumaria barbara*
Canada columbine	*Aquilegia canadensis*	Club mosses	*Lycopodium* spp.
Canada mayflower	*Maianthemum canadense*	Coastal doghobble	*Leucothoe axillaris*
Canada waterleaf	*Hydrophyllum canadense*	Coastal fetterbush	*Eubotrys racemosa*
Candyroot	*Polygala nana*	Coastal Plain	
Canyby's dropwort	*Oxypolis canbyi*	elephant's-foot	*Elephantopus nudatus*
Cardinal flower	*Lobelia cardinalis*	Coastal Plain	
Caribbean miterwort	*Mitreola petiolata*	water-willow	*Justicia ovata* var. *ovata*
Carolina ash	*Fraxinus caroliniana*	Coastal sweet-pepperbush	*Clethra alnifolia*
Carolina bog myrtle	*Kalmia carolina*	Cockspur hawthorn	*Crataegus crus-galli*
Carolina buckthorn	*Frangula caroliniana*	Colic-roots	*Aletris* spp.
Carolina hemlock	*Tsuga caroliniana*	Combs panic grass	*Coleataenia longifolia*
Carolina jessamine	*Gelsemium sempervirens*	Common black-cohosh	*Actaea racemosa*
Carolina laurel cherry	*Prunus caroliniana*	Common blue cohosh	*Caulophyllum thalictroides*
Carolina lily	*Lilium michauxii*	Common bluecurls	*Trichostema dichotomum*
Carolina phlox	*Phlox caroliniana*	Common bogbuttons	*Lachnocaulon anceps*
Carolina rhododendron	*Rhododendron carolinianum*	Common bottlebrush	
Carolina rose	*Rosa carolina*	grass	*Elymus hystrix* var. *hystrix*
Carolina shagbark	*Carya carolinae-*	Common butterfly-weed	*Asclepias tuberosa*
hickory	*septentrionalis*	Common cattail	*Typha latifolia*
Carolina spinypod	*Matelea carolinensis*	Common cinquefoil	*Potentilla canadensis*
Carolina spring-beauty	*Claytonia caroliniana*	Common clasping aster	*Symphyotrichum patens*
Carolina thistle	*Cirsium carolinianum*	Common dog-fennel	*Eupatorium capillifolium*
Carolina wild-petunia	*Ruellia caroliniensis*	Common eastern	
Carolina willow	*Salix caroliniana*	coneflower	*Rudbeckia fulgida*
Catawba rhododendron	*Rhododendron catawbiense*	Common elderberry	*Sambucus canadensis*
Catbrier	*Smilax bona-nox*	Common elegant	
Catesby's trillium	*Trillium catesbaei*	blazing-star	*Liatris elegans*
Cattails	*Typha* spp.	Common elephant's-foot	*Elephantopus tomentosus*
Cave alumroot	*Heuchera parviflora*	Common grass-pink	*Calapogon tuberosus*
Cedar glade daisy	*Erigeron strigosus*	Common greenbrier	*Smilax rotundifolia*
fleabane	var. *calcicola*	Common groundnut	*Apios americana*
Celandine-poppy	*Stylophorum diphyllum*	Common hairsedge	*Bulbostylis capillaris*
Chaffseed	*Schwalbea americana*	Common marsh-pink	*Sabatia angularis*
Chalk maple	*Acer leucoderme*	Common New Jersey tea	*Ceanothus americanus*
Chapman oak	*Quercus chapmanii*	Common pawpaw	*Asimina triloba*
Chattahoochee trillium	*Trillium decipiens*	Common reed	*Phragmites australis*
Cherokee sedge	*Carex cherokeensis*	Common rockcap fern	*Polypodium virginianum*
Cherrybark oak	*Quercus pagoda*	Common rough fleabane	*Erigeron strigosus*
Chinaberry	*Melia azedarach*	Common roundleaf	
Chinese privet	*Ligustrum sinense*	eupatorium	*Eupatorium rotundifolium*
Chinese tallow-tree	*Triadica sebifera*	Common rush	*Juncus effusus*
Chinese wisteria	*Wisteria sinensis*	Common shagbark	
Chinquapin oak	*Quercus muehlenbergii*	hickory	*Carya ovata*
Chokeberries	*Aronia* spp.	Common silverbell	*Halesia tetraptera*

COMMON NAME	SCIENTIFIC NAME
Common smooth rockcress	*Boechera laevigata*
Common sneezeweed	*Helenium autumnale*
Common toadflax	*Nuttallanthus canadensis*
Common white heart-leaved aster	*Eurybia divaricata*
Common wild quinine	*Parthenium integrifolium*
Common wild yam	*Dioscorea villosa*
Common wingstem	*Verbesina alternifolia*
Common yellow thistle	*Cirsium horridulum*
Confederate daisy	*Helianthus porteri*
Coppery St. John's-wort	*Hypericum denticulatum*
Coral beads	*Cocculus carolinus*
Coral greenbrier	*Smilax walteri*
Coral honeysuckle	*Lonicera sempervirens*
Coralberry	*Ardisia crenata*
Cottonwood	*Populus deltoides*
Cowbane	*Oxypolis rigidior*
Cranefly orchid	*Tipularia discolor*
Creamy wild indigo	*Baptisia bracteata*
Creeping aster	*Eurybia surculosa*
Creeping frogfruit	*Phyla nodiflora*
Creeping Jenny	*Lysimachia nummularia*
Creeping phlox	*Phlox stolonifera*
Crested fringed orchid	*Platanthera cristata*
Crested iris	*Iris cristata*
Crookedwood	*Lyonia ferruginea*
Croomia	*Croomia pauciflora*
Cross-vine	*Bignonia capreolata*
Cucumber magnolia	*Magnolia acuminata*
Cumberland oak-leach	*Aureolaria patula*
Cumberland rose-gentian	*Sabatia capitata*
Cumberland spurge	*Euphorbia mercurialina*
Curlyheads	*Clematis ochroleuca*
Curlyleaf yucca	*Yucca filamentosa*
Cutgrass	*Leersia hexandra*
Cuthbert's onion	*Allium cuthbertii*
Cuthbert's turtlehead	*Chelone cuthbertii*
Cutleaf coneflower	*Rudbeckia laciniata*
Cutleaf toothwort	*Cardamine concatenata*
Dahoon	*Ilex cassine*
Daisy fleabanes	*Erigeron* spp.
Dakota vervain	*Glandularia bipinnatifida*
Dallis grass	*Paspalum dilatum*
Dangleberry	*Gaylussacia frondosa*
Decumbent trillium	*Trillium decumbens*
Deerberry	*Vaccinium stamineum*
Deer's-tongue	*Trilisa odoratissima*
Delicate fern moss	*Thuidium delicatulum*
Devil's-bit	*Chamaelirium luteum*
Devilwood	*Osmanthus americanus*

COMMON NAME	SCIENTIFIC NAME
Diamond-flower	*Houstonia nigricans*
Dimpled trout lily	*Erythronium umbilicatum*
Dissected toothwort	*Cardamine dissecta*
Dixie Mountain breadroot	*Pediomelum piedmontanum*
Dollarweed	*Rhynchosia reniformis*
Dolls'-eyes	*Actaea pachypoda*
Dotted smartweed	*Persicaria punctata*
Downy agrimony	*Agrimonia pubescens*
Downy lobelia	*Lobelia puberula*
Downy rattlesnake-orchid	*Goodyera pubescens*
Downy serviceberry	*Amelanchier arborea*
Dropseeds	*Sporobolus* spp.
Drummond's skullcap	*Scutellaria drummondii*
Drummond's yellow-eyed gass	*Xyris drummondii*
Duckweeds	*Lemna* spp.
Dune greenbrier	*Smilax auriculata*
Dune hairgrass	*Muhlenbergia sericea*
Dune marsh-elder	*Iva imbricata*
Dune prickly-pear	*Opuntia pusilla*
Dune water-pennywort	*Hydrocotyle bonariensis*
Dutchman's britches	*Dicentra cucullaria*
Dutchman's-pipe	*Isotrema macrophyllum*
Dwarf filmy fern	*Didymoglossum petersii*
Dwarf ginseng	*Panax trifolius*
Dwarf hackberry	*Celtis tenuifolia*
Dwarf huckleberry	*Gaylussacia dumosa*
Dwarf larkspur	*Delphinium tricorne*
Dwarf live oak	*Quercus minima*
Dwarf palmetto	*Sabal minor*
Dwarf sundew	*Drosera brevifolia*
Dwarf-dandelions	*Krigia* spp.
Early meadowrue	*Thalictrum dioicum*
Early saxifrage	*Micranthes virginiensis*
Eastern beardgrass	*Gymnopogon ambiguus*
Eastern blue monkshood	*Aconitum uncinatum*
Eastern blue phlox	*Phlox divaricata*
Eastern boneset	*Brickellia eupatorioides*
Eastern flowering spurge	*Euphorbia corollata*
Eastern gray goldenrod	*Solidago nemoralis*
Eastern gum bumelia	*Sideroxylon lanuginosum*
Eastern hemlock	*Tsuga canadensis*
Eastern mosquito fern	*Azolla caroliniana*
Eastern needlegrass	*Piptochaetium avenaceum*
Eastern ninebark	*Physocarpus opulifolius*
Eastern prairie anemone	*Anemone berlandieri*
Eastern prickly-pear	*Opuntia humifusa*
Eastern red cedar	*Juniperus virginiana*
Eastern redbud	*Cercis canadensis*

COMMON NAME	SCIENTIFIC NAME	COMMON NAME	SCIENTIFIC NAME
Eastern rose-mallow	*Hibiscus moscheutos*	Fragrant rabbit tobacco	*Pseudognaphalium obtusifolium*
Eastern roughleaf dogwood	*Cornus asperifolia*	Fragrant sumac	*Rhus aromatica*
Eastern sensitive-briar	*Mimosa microphylla*	Franklin tree	*Franklinia alatamaha*
Eastern shooting star	*Primula meadia*	Fraser magnolia	*Magnolia fraseri*
Eastern silvery aster	*Symphyotrichum concolor*	Fremont's clematis	*Clematis fremontii*
Ebony spleenwort	*Asplenium platyneuron*	Fringe tree	*Chionanthus virginicus*
Eggleston's violet	*Viola egglestonii*	Fringed campion	*Silene polypetala*
Elf-orpine	*Diamorpha cymosa*	Fringed loosestrife	*Lysimachia ciliata*
Elliott's bluestem	*Andropogon elliottii*	Galax	*Galax urceolata*
Elms	*Ulmus* spp.	Gallberry	*Ilex glabra*
English ivy	*Hedera helix*	Gaping panic grass	*Steinchisma hians*
Erect milkpea	*Galactia erecta*	Georgia aster	*Symphyotrichum georgianum*
Erect-leaved witchgrass	*Dichanthelium erectifolium*	Georgia beardtongue	*Penstem dissectus*
European calamus	*Acorus calamus*	Georgia beargrass	*Nolina georgiana*
Evergreen bayberry	*Morella caroliniensis*	Georgia calamint	*Clinopodium georgianum*
False garlic	*Nothoscordum bivalve*	Georgia oak	*Quercus georgiana*
False nutsedge	*Cyperus strigosus*	Georgia phacelia	*Phacelia dubia*
False-aloe	*Manfreda virginica*	Georgia rockcress	*Arabis georgiana*
False-pimpernel	*Anagallis minima*	Georgia rush	*Juncus georgianus*
False-nettle	*Boehmeria cylindrica*	Georgia-plume	*Elliottia racemosa*
Fancy fern	*Dryopteris intermedia*	Giant chickweed	*Stellaria pubera*
Fernleaf phacelia	*Phacelia bipinnatifida*	Giant cordgrass	*Spartina cynosuroides*
Few-flowered nutrush	*Scleria oligantha*	Giant cutgrass	*Zizaniopsis miliacea*
Fire cherry	*Prunus pensylvanica*	Giant reed	*Arundo donax*
Fire pink	*Silene virginiana*	Ginseng	*Panax quinquefolius*
Fireweed	*Erechtites hieraciifolius*	Glade blue curls	*Trichostema brachiatum*
Flame azalea	*Rhododendron calendulaceum*	Glade cresses	*Leavenworthia* spp.
		Glade knotweed	*Polygonum tenue*
Flatrock draba	*Draba aprica*	Glade rushfoil	*Croton willldenowii*
Flatrock onion	*Allium speculae*	Glade St. John's-wort	*Hypericum dolabriforme*
Flatrock phacelia	*Phacelia maculata*	Glassworts	*Salicornia* spp.
Flatrock pimpernel	*Lindernia monticola*	Globe beaksedge	*Rhynchospora globularis*
Flat-topped goldenrod	*Euthamia caroliniana*	Goat's-beard	*Aruncus dioicus*
Florida dropseed	*Sporobolus floridanus*	Goat's-rues	*Tephrosia* spp.
Florida flame azalea	*Rhododendron austrinum*	Godfrey's forestiera	*Forestiera godfreyi*
Florida paspalum	*Paspalum floridanum*	Golden bamboo	*Phyllostachys aurea*
Florida sensitive-briar	*Mimosa quadrivalvis*	Golden club	*Orontium aquaticum*
Florida soapberry	*Sapindus marginatus*	Golden colic-root	*Aletris aurea*
Florida tick-trefoil	*Desmodium floridanum*	Golden ragwort	*Packera aurea*
Florida torreya	*Torreya taxifolia*	Goldenrods	*Solidago* spp.
Florida yew	*Taxus floridana*	Golden-seal	*Hydrastis canadensis*
Florida-privet	*Forestiera segregata*	Goldie's wood-fern	*Dryopteris goldiana*
Florist's gayfeather	*Liatris spicata*	Gopher-apple	*Licania michauxii*
Flowering dogwood	*Cornus florida*	Gorge rhododendron	*Rhododendron minus*
Flowering raspberry	*Rubus odoratus*	Granite dome hypericum	*Hypericum buckleyi*
Fly-poison	*Amianthium muscitoxicum*	Granite flatsedge	*Cyperus granitophilus*
Flyr's false-boneset	*Brickellia cordifolia*	Grapes	*Vitis* spp.
Foamflower	*Tiarella cordifolia; T. wherryi*	Grassy arrowhead	*Sagittaria graminea*
Foxglove beardtongue	*Penstemon digitalis*	Greasy grass	*Tridens flavus*
Fragile fern	*Cystopteris fragilis*	Great blue lobelia	*Lobelia siphilitica*

COMMON NAME	SCIENTIFIC NAME	COMMON NAME	SCIENTIFIC NAME
Great laurel	*Rhododendron maximum*	Hooded pitcherplant	*Sarracenia minor*
Great plains		Horned bladderwort	*Utricularia cornuta*
ladies'-tresses	*Spiranthes magnicamporum*	Horsebalms	*Collinsonia* spp.
Great rhododendron	*Rhododendron maximum*	Horse-nettle	*Solanum carolinense*
Great white trillium	*Trillium grandiflorum*	Horsesugar	*Symplocos tinctoria*
Great yellow wood sorrel	*Oxalis grandis*	Huckleberry	*Gaylussacia* spp.
Green arrow-arum	*Peltandra virginica*	Hyssopleaf eupatorium	*Eupatorium hyssopifolium*
Green ash	*Fraxinus pennsylvanica*	Indian cucumber-root	*Medeola virginiana*
Green dragon	*Arisaema dracontium*	Indian pink	*Spigelia marilandica*
Green milkweed	*Asclepias viridiflora*	Indian pipes	*Monotropa uniflora*
Green pitcherplant	*Sarracenia oreophila*	Ironweed	*Veronia glauca*
Green violet	*Hybanthus concolor*	Ironwood	*Ostrya virginiana*
Greenbriers	*Smilax* spp.	Jack-in-the-pulpit	*Arisaema triphyllum*
Green-fly orchid	*Epidendrum magnoliae*	Jackson-brier	*Smilax smallii*
Greenfruit clearweed	*Pilea pumila*	Japanese climbing fern	*Lygodium japonicum*
Grit purslane	*Portulaca biloba*	Japanese honeysuckle	*Lonicera japonica*
Groundsel tree	*Baccharis halimifolia*	Japanese knotweed	*Reynoutria japonica*
Hackberries	*Celtis occidentalis;*	Japanese spirea	*Spirea japonica*
	C. tenuifolia	Kidney-leaved	
Haircap moss	*Polytrichum commune*	grass-of-Parnassus	*Parnassia asarifolia*
Hairgrass	*Muhlenbergia capillaris*	Knotweeds	*Polygonum* spp.
Hairy angelica	*Angelica venenosa*	Kudzu	*Pueraria montana*
Hairy buttercup	*Ranunculus hispidus*	Ladies'-tresses	*Spiranthes praecox*
Hairy coreopsis	*Coreopsis pubescens*	Lady-rue	*Thalictrum clavatum*
Hairy lespedeza	*Lespedeza hirta*	Lanceleaf trillium	*Trillium lancifolium*
Hairy lipfern	*Cheilanthes lanosa*	Large saltmeadow	
Hairy mock-orange	*Philadelphus hirsutus*	cordgrass	*Spartina patens*
Hairy phlox	*Phlox amoena*	Large sea-purslane	*Sesuvium portulacastrum*
Hairy southern		Large spreading pogonia	*Cleistes divaricata*
bush-honeysuckle	*Diervilla rivularis*	Large-flowered coreopsis	*Coreopsis grandiflora*
Hairy spiderwort	*Tradescantia hirsuticaulis*	Large-flowered rock-pink	*Phemeranthus mengesii*
Hairy sunflower	*Helianthus hirsutus*	Large-flowered trillium	*Trillium grandiflorum*
Hairy umbrella-sedge	*Fuirena squarrosa*	Laurel oak	*Quercus laurifolia*
Hairy wicky	*Kalmia hirsuta*	Lax hornpod	*Mitreola petiolata*
Hairy wild-petunia	*Ruellia humilis*	Least glade cress	*Leavenworthia exigua*
Halberd-leaf tearthumb	*Persicaria arifolia*	Least trillium	*Trillium pusillum*
Halberd-leaf violet	*Viola hastata*	Leatherleaf mahonia	*Mahonia bealei*
Hammock spiderlily	*Hymenocallis occidentalis*	Leatherwood	*Dirca palustris*
Hawthorns	*Crataegus* spp.	Leathery rush	*Juncus coriaceus*
Hay-scented fern	*Dennstaedtia punctilobula*	Leechbrush	*Nestronia umbellula*
Heal-all	*Prunella* spp.	Lespedezas	*Lespedeza* spp.
Helmet skullcap	*Scutellaria integrifolia*	Lichen	*Acarospora* sp.
Hemp dogbane	*Apocynum cannabinum*	Lichen	*Buellia* spp.
Hercules'-club	*Zanthoxylum clava-herculis*	Lichen	*Dermatocarpon luridum*
Hickory	*Carya* spp.	Lichen	*Diploschistes* sp.
Hillside blueberry	*Vaccinium pallidum*	Lichen	*Lecanora oreinoides*
Hoary puccoon	*Lithospermum canescens*	Lichen	*Rinodina tephraspis*
Hollow-stem		Licorice goldenrod	*Solidago odora*
Joe-pye-weed	*Eutrochium fistulosum*	Lime stonecrop	*Sedum pulchellum*
Honesty weed	*Baptisia tinctoria*	Lime-barren sandwort	*Minuartia patula*
Honey locust	*Gleditsia triacanthos*	Lipferns	*Cheilanthes* spp.

COMMON NAME	SCIENTIFIC NAME	COMMON NAME	SCIENTIFIC NAME
Little bluestem	*Schizachyrium scoparium*	Milkweeds	*Asclepias* spp.
Little brown jugs	*Hexastylis arifolia*	Milkpeas	*Galactia* spp.
Little gallberry	*Ilex glabra*	Mimosa	*Albizia julibrissin*
Little people	*Lepuropetalon spathulatum*	Minniebush	*Menziesia pilosa*
Littlehip hawthorn	*Crataegus spathulata*	Missouri rockcress	*Boechera missouriensis*
Live oak	*Quercus virginiana*	Mockernut hickory	*Carya alba*
Liverwort	*Dumotiera hirsuta*	Mohr's Barbara's-buttons	*Marshallia mohrii*
Liverwort	*Plagiochila caduciloba*	Monkey-face orchid	*Platanthera integrilabia*
Lizard's-tail	*Saururus cernuus*	Monkey-flowers	*Mimulus* spp.
Lobelias	*Lobelia* spp.	Mottled trillium	*Trillium maculatum*
Loblolly bay	*Gordonia lasianthus*	Mountain angelica	*Angelica triquinata*
Loblolly pine	*Pinus taeda*	Mountain-ash	*Sorbus americana*
Longleaf pine	*Pinus palustris*	Mountain black-cohosh	*Actaea podocarpa*
Longleaf spikegrass	*Chasmanthium sessiliflorum*	Mountain bunchflower	*Veratrum parviflorum*
Longleaf three-awn	*Aristida palustris*	Mountain doghobble	*Leucothoe fontanesiana*
Longspur creeping bladderwort	*Utricularia biflora*	Mountain dwarf-dandelion	*Krigia montana*
Long-spurred violet	*Viola rostrata*	Mountain highbush blueberry	*Vaccinium simulatum*
Long-stalked aster	*Symphyotrichum dumosum*	Mountain holly	*Ilex montana*
Long-stalked holly	*Ilex collina*	Mountain Indian-physic	*Gillenia trifoliata*
Lopsided indiangrass	*Sorghastrum secundum*	Mountain laurel	*Kalmia latifolia*
Lost gordonia	*Franklinia alatamaha*	Mountain maple	*Acer spicatum*
Louisiana blue-star	*Amsonia ludoviciana*	Mountain meadowrue	*Thalictrum clavatum*
Lovegrasses	*Eragrostis* spp.	Mountain-mints	*Pycnanthemum* spp.
Lupine scurfpea	*Orbexilum lupinellum*	Mountain oat-grass	*Danthonia compressa*
Lyreleaf rockcress	*Arabidopsis lyrata*	Mountain spleenwort	*Asplenium montanum*
Lyreleaf sage	*Salvia lyrata*	Mountain stonecrop	*Sedum ternatum*
Maidencane	*Panicum hemitomon*	Mountain sweet-pepperbush	*Clethra acuminata*
Maidenhair spleenwort	*Asplenium trichomanes*	Multiflora rose	*Rosa multiflora*
Maleberry	*Lyonia ligustrina*	Muscadine	*Vitis rotundifolia*
Mapleleaf viburnum	*Viburnum acerifolium*	Musclewood	*Carpinus caroliniana*
Marginal wood-fern	*Dryopteris marginalis*	Myrtle holly	*Ilex myrtifolia*
Maritime marsh-elder	*Iva frutescens*	Myrtle oak	*Quercus myrtifolia*
Marsh bellflower	*Campanula aparinoides*	Naked tick-trefoil	*Hylodesmum nudiflorum*
Marsh dewflower	*Murdannia keisak*	Narrowleaf cattail	*Typha angustifolia*
Marsh fern	*Thelypteris palustris* var. *pubescens*	Narrowleaf sunflower	*Helianthus angustifolius*
Marsh fleabane	*Pluchea baccharis*	Narrowleaf vervain	*Verbena simplex*
Marsh St.John's-wort	*Hypericum fraseri*	Narrowleaf whitetop sedge	*Rhynchospora colorata*
Marsh-elders	*Iva* spp.	Narrow-leaf white-topped aster	*Sericocarpus linifolius*
Maryland golden-aster	*Chrysopsis mariana*	Narrow-leaved lespedeza	*Lespedeza angustifolia*
Mat-forming quillwort	*Isoetes tegetiformans*	Narrow-leaved smooth aster	*Symphyotrichum laeve*
May-apple	*Podophyllum peltatum*	Nashville breadroot	*Pediomelum subacaule*
Mayberry	*Vaccinium elliottii*	Needle palm	*Rhapidophyllum hystrix*
Mayhaw	*Crataegus aestivalis*	Needle witchgrass	*Dichanthelium aciculare*
Maypops	*Passiflora incarnata*	Nepal grass	*Microstegium vimineum*
Meadow spikemoss	*Selaginella apoda*	Netted chain fern	*Woodwardia areolata*
Meadow-beauties	*Rhexia* spp.		
Melic grass	*Melica mutica*		
Mexican plum	*Prunus mexicana*		
Michigan lily	*Lilium michiganense*		

COMMON NAME	SCIENTIFIC NAME	COMMON NAME	SCIENTIFIC NAME
Netted nutrush	*Scleria reticularis*	Pickerelweed	*Pontederia cordata*
Nettleleaf noseburn	*Tragia urticifolia*	Piedmont azalea	*Rhododendron canescens*
Nettle-leaf sage	*Salvia urticifolia*	Piedmont quillwort	*Isoetes piedmontana*
New England aster	*Symphyotrichum novae-angliae*	Pignut hickory	*Carya glabra*
		Pine lily	*Lilium catesbaei*
New York fern	*Thelypteris noveboracensis*	Pineland	
Nodding ladies'-tresses	*Spiranthes cernua*	Barbara's-buttons	*Marshallia ramosa*
Nodding onion	*Allium cernuum*	Pineland three-awn	*Aristida stricta*
Northern hackberry	*Celtis occidentalis*	Pineland tick-trefoil	*Desmodium strictum*
Northern horsebalm	*Collinsonia canadensis*	Pineweed	*Hypericum gentianoides*
Northern leatherflower	*Clematis viorna*	Pineywoods dropseed	*Sporobolus junceus*
Northern maidenhair		Pink lady's-slipper	*Cypripedium acaule*
fern	*Adiantum pedatum*	Pink sandhill lupine	*Lupinus villosus*
Northern red oak	*Quercus rubra*	Pinweed	*Lechea intermedia*
Northern seaside spurge	*Euphorbia polygonifolia*		var. *intermedia*
Northern spicebush	*Lindera benzoin*	Pipewort	*Eriocaulon decangulare*
Northern white		Pipsissewa	*Chimaphila maculata*
colic-root	*Aletris farinosa*	Pitch pine	*Pinus rigida*
Northern wild raisin	*Viburnum cassinoides*	Pitted stripeseed	*Piriqueta caroliniana*
Nuttall's reed-grass	*Calamagrostis coarctata*	Plumleaf azalea	*Rhododendron prunifolium*
Oakleaf hydrangea	*Hydrangea quercifolia*	Poison ivy	*Toxicodendron radicans*
Oat-grasses	*Danthonia* spp.	Poison oak	*Toxicodendron pubescens*
Obedient-plant	*Physostegia virginiana*	Poison sumac	*Toxicodendron vernix*
Oconee azalea	*Rhododendron flammeum*	Pond-cypress	*Taxodium ascendens*
Odorless bayberry	*Morella inodora*	Pond pine	*Pinus serotina*
Ogeechee lime	*Nyssa ogeche*	Pond spicebush	*Lindera melissifolia*
Oglethorpe oak	*Quercus oglethorpensis*	Pondspice	*Litsea aestivalis*
Ohio buckeye	*Aesculus glabra*	Pondweeds	*Potamogeton* spp.
Old-field broomsedge	*Andropogon virginicus*	Poorjoe	*Diodia teres*
One-flower hawthorn	*Crataegus uniflora*	Possum-haw	*Ilex decidua*
Orange dwarf-dandelion	*Krigia biflora*	Post oak	*Quercus stellata*
Orange jewelweed	*Impatiens capensis*	Poverty dropseed	*Sporobolus vaginiflorus*
Orange milkwort	*Polygala lutea*	Poverty oat-grass	*Danthonia spicata*
Oriental bittersweet	*Celastrus orbiculatus*	Prairie bluehearts	*Buchnera americana*
Oval ladies'-tresses	*Spiranthes ovalis*	Prairie coneflower	*Ratibida pinnata*
Overcup oak	*Quercus lyrata*	Prairie dropseed	*Sporobolus heterolepis*
Ozark bedstraw	*Galium virgatum*	Prairie grass-leaved aster	*Eurybia hemispherica*
Painted buckeye	*Aesculus sylvatica*	Prairie larkspur	*Delphinium carolinianum*
Painted trillium	*Trillium undulatum*	Prairie purple coneflower	*Echinacea simulata*
Pale meadow-beauty	*Rhexia mariana*	Prairie-dock	*Silphium terebinthinaceum*
Panic grasses	*Panicum* spp.	Prickly-ash	*Aralia spinosa*
Parrot pitcherplant	*Sarracenia psittacina*	Prickly gooseberry	*Ribes cynosbati*
Parsley haw	*Crataegus marshallii*	Prickly-pear cacti	*Opuntia* spp.
Partridge-berry	*Mitchella repens*	Primrose-leaf violet	*Viola primulifolia*
Peat moss	*Sphagnum cyclophyllum*	Princess tree	*Paulownia tomentosa*
Peat mosses	*Sphagnum* spp.	Puck's orpine	*Sedum pusillum*
Pencil-flower	*Stylosanthes biflora*	Purple cliff-brake	*Pellaea atropurpurea*
Peppervine	*Ampelopsis arborea*	Purple fringeless orchid	*Platanthera peramoena*
Perennial saltmarsh aster	*Symphyotrichum tenuifolium*	Purple lovegrass	*Eragrostis spectabilis*
Perennial sand bean	*Strophostyles umbellata*	Purple milkweed	*Asclepias purpurascens*
Perfoliate bellwort	*Uvularia perfoliata*	Purple pitcherplant	*Sarracenia purpurea*

COMMON NAME	SCIENTIFIC NAME
Purple tassels	*Dalea gattingeri*
Purple-node Joe-pye-weed	*Eutrochium purpureum*
Pursh's rattlebox	*Crotalaria purshii*
Pussytoes	*Antennaria* spp.
Quaker ladies	*Houstonia caerulea*
Quillworts	*Isoetes* spp.
Rabbitbells	*Crotalaria rotundifolia*
Ragweed	*Ambrosia artemisiifolia*
Ragworts	*Packera* spp.
Railroad vine	*Ipomoea pes-caprae*
Ramps	*Allium tricoccum*
Rattlebox	*Sesbania punicea*
Rattlesnake fern	*Botrypus virginianus*
Rattlesnake-master	*Eryngium yuccifolium*
Rattlesnake-roots	*Prenanthes* spp.
Rayless-goldenrod	*Bigelowia nudata*
Red bay	*Persea borbonia*
Red buckeye	*Aesculus pavia*
Red chokeberry	*Aronia arbutifolia*
Red elderberry	*Sambucus racemosa*
Red hickory	*Carya ovalis*
Red maple	*Acer rubrum*
Red mulberry	*Morus rubra*
Red trillium	*Trillium erectum*
Redroot	*Lachnanthes caroliniana*
Redroot flatsedge	*Cyperus erythrorhizos*
Reindeer lichens	*Cladina* spp.; *Cladonia* spp.
Relict trillium	*Trillium reliquum*
Resurrection fern	*Pleopeltis polypodioides*
Rice cutgrass	*Leersia oryzoides*
Riddell's goldenrod	*Solidago riddellii*
River birch	*Betula nigra*
River cane	*Arundinaria gigantea*
River oats	*Chasmanthium latifolium*
Robin's plantain	*Erigeron pulchellus* var. *pulchellus*
Rock alumroot	*Heuchera villosa*
Rock chestnut oak	*Quercus montana*
Rock clubmoss	*Huperzia porophila*
Rock harlequin	*Capnoides sempervirens*
Rock moss	*Grimmia laevigata*
Rock spikemoss	*Selaginella rupestris*
Rockcresses	*Boechera* spp.
Rock-pinks	*Phemeranthus* spp.
Rose pogonia	*Pogonia ophioglossoides*
Rose-gentians	*Sabatia* spp.
Rosinweed	*Silphium* spp.
Rosy twisted stalk	*Streptopus lanceolatus*
Rough blazing-star	*Liatris aspera*
Rough dropseed	*Sporobolus clandestinus*

COMMON NAME	SCIENTIFIC NAME
Roughleaf goldenrod	*Solidago patula*
Roundleaf firepink	*Silene rotundifolia*
Roundleaf ragwort	*Packera obovata*
Roundleaf serviceberry	*Amelanchier sanguinea*
Roundleaf sundew	*Drosera rotundifolia*
Round-leaf violet	*Viola rotundifolia*
Round-lobed hepatica	*Anemone americana*
Royal fern	*Osmunda regalis*
Rue-anenome	*Thalictrum thalictroides*
Rugel's nailwort	*Paronychia rugellii*
Running oak	*Quercus elliottii*
Running strawberry-bush	*Euonymus obovatus*
Rushes	*Juncus* spp.
Sacred-bamboo	*Nandina domestica*
Saltgrass	*Distichlis spicata*
Salt-marsh bulrush	*Bolboschoenus robustus*
Salt-marsh asters	*Symphyotrichum* spp.
Salt-marsh water-hemp	*Amaranthus cannabinus*
Saltmeadow cordgrass	*Spartina patens*
Saltwort	*Batis maritima*
Sand blackberry	*Rubus cuneifolius*
Sand cordgrass	*Spartina bakeri*
Sand hickory	*Carya pallida*
Sand knotgrass	*Paspalum vaginatum*
Sand laurel oak	*Quercus hemisphaerica*
Sand live oak	*Quercus geminata*
Sand myrtle	*Kalmia buxifolia*
Sand post oak	*Quercus margarettae*
Sand spikemoss	*Selaginella arenicola*
Sandhill angelica	*Angelica dentata*
Sandhill beaksedge	*Rhynchospora megalocarpa*
Sandhill goldenaster	*Pityopsis pinifolia*
Sandhill jointweed	*Polygonella polygama*
Sandhill rosemary	*Ceratiola ericoides*
Sandhill skullcap	*Scutellaria arenicola*
Sandhill wild-buckwheat	*Eriogonum tomentosum*
Sandhills blue-star	*Amsonia ciliata*
Sandhills dropseed	*Sporobolus junceus*
Sandwort	*Minuartia uniflora*
Sarsaparilla-vine	*Smilax pumila*
Sassafras	*Sassafras albidum*
Savanna cowbane	*Oxypolis ternata*
Savanna hairsedge	*Bulbostylis ciliatifolia*
Saw palmetto	*Serenoa repens*
Sawgrass	*Cladium jamaicense*
Saxifrages	*Micranthes* spp.
Scarlet oak	*Quercus coccinea*
Scarlet wild basil	*Clinopodium coccineum*
Sea lavender	*Limonium carolinianum*
Sea oats	*Uniola paniculata*

COMMON NAME	SCIENTIFIC NAME
Seabeach evening-primrose	*Oenothera humifusa*
Seashore dropseed	*Sporobolus virginicus*
Seaside oxeye	*Borrichia frutescens*
Sebastian-bush	*Ditrysinia fruticosa*
Sedge	*Carex crinita*
Sedges	*Carex* spp.
Senna seymeria	*Seymeria cassioides*
Sensitive fern	*Onoclea sensibilis*
September elm	*Ulmus serotina*
Sesbania	*Sesbania herbacea*
Sessile-leaf eupatorium	*Eupatorium sessilifolium*
Shale-barren skullcap	*Scutellaria leonardii*
Shallow sedge	*Carex lurida*
Sharp-lobed hepatica	*Anemone acutiloba*
Shining fetterbush	*Lyonia lucida*
Shoestring fern	*Vittaria lineata*
Short-bristle horned beaksedge	*Rhynchospora corniculata*
Shortleaf pine	*Pinus echinata*
Short-spurred corydalis	*Corydalis flavula*
Showy bur-marigold	*Bidens laevis*
Showy orchis	*Galearis spectabilis*
Shrubby St. John's-wort	*Hypericum prolificum*
Shumard oak	*Quercus shumardii*
Side-oats grama	*Bouteloua curtipendula*
Silkgrass	*Pityopsis graminifolia; P. aspera*
Silky dogwood	*Cornus amomum*
Silky dwarf morning-glory	*Evolvulus sericeus*
Silky oat-grass	*Danthonia sericea*
Silver croton	*Croton argyranthemus*
Silver grass	*Miscanthus sinensis*
Silver maple	*Acer saccharinum*
Silver plume grass	*Saccharum alopecuroides*
Silverleaf croton	*Croton punctatus*
Silverling	*Paronychia argyrocoma*
Silvery glade fern	*Diplazium pycnocarpon*
Silvery spleenwort	*Deparia acrostichoides*
Skullcaps	*Scutellaria* spp.
Skunk meadowrue	*Thalictrum revolutum*
Slash pine	*Pinus elliottii*
Slender bluestem	*Schizachyrium tenerum*
Slender marsh-pink	*Sabatia campanulata*
Slender muhly	*Muhlenbergia tenuiflora*
Slender spikegrass	*Chasmanthium laxum*
Slender-stemmed witchgrass	*Dichanthelium acuminatum*
Slimleaf pawpaw	*Asimina angustifolia*
Slippery elm	*Ulmus rubra*
Small cane	*Arundinaria tecta*
Small carpgrass	*Arthraxon hispidus*
Small green wood orchid	*Platanthera clavellata*
Small sea-purslane	*Sesuvium maritimum*
Small white fringed orchid	*Platanthera blephariglottis*
Small-flowered buckthorn	*Sageretia minutiflora*
Small-flowered white meadow-beauty	*Rhexia parviflora*
Small-fruited pawpaw	*Asimina parviflora*
Small-fruited seedbox	*Ludwigia microcarpa*
Smallhead rush	*Juncus brachycephalus*
Small-headed sunflower	*Helianthus microcephalus*
Small-leaf viburnum	*Viburnum obovatum*
Small-leaved white snakeroot	*Ageratina aromatica*
Small's portulaca	*Portulaca smallii*
Smooth blackberry	*Rubus canadensis*
Smooth cordgrass	*Spartina alterniflora*
Smooth highbush blueberry	*Vaccinium corymbosum*
Smooth hydrangea	*Hydrangea arborescens*
Smooth meadow-beauty	*Rhexia alifanus*
Smooth purple coneflower	*Echinacea laevigata*
Smooth rockcress	*Boechera laevigata*
Smooth southern bush-honeysuckle	*Diervilla sessilifolia*
Smooth spiderwort	*Tradescantia ohiensis*
Smooth sumac	*Rhus glabra*
Smooth trailing lespedeza	*Lespedeza repens*
Snorkelwort	*Gratiola amphiantha*
Snoutbeans	*Rhynchosia* spp.
Snowy orchid	*Platanthera nivea*
Soapwort gentian	*Gentiana saponaria*
Softstem bulrush	*Schoenoplectus tabernaemontani*
Solomon's-plume	*Maianthemum racemosum*
Solomon's-seal	*Polygonatum biflorum*
Sourwood	*Oxydendrum arboreum*
Southeastern bold goldenrod	*Solidago rigida*
Southeastern sea rocket	*Cakile harperi*
Southern agrimony	*Agrimonia parviflora*
Southern bentgrass	*Agrostis elliottiana*
Southern black haw	*Viburnum rufidulum*
Southern blue flag	*Iris virginica*

COMMON NAME	SCIENTIFIC NAME	COMMON NAME	SCIENTIFIC NAME
Southern bogbutton	*Lachnocaulon beyrichianum*	St. Andrew's cross	*Hypericum hypericoides;*
Southern catalpa	*Catalpa bignonioides*		*H. stragulum*
Southern cattail	*Typha domingensis*	St. John's-worts	*Hypericum* spp.
Southern evergreen		Staggerbush	*Lyonia fruticosa; L. mariana*
blueberry	*Vaccinium myrsinites*	Starflower	*Trientalis borealis*
Southern harebell	*Campanula divaricata*	Starry rosinweed	*Silphium asteriscus*
Southern lady fern	*Athyrium asplenioides*	Stemless ironweed	*Vernonia acaulis*
Southern leatherflower	*Clematis crispa*	Stiff-leaved aster	*Ionactis linariifolia*
Southern lobelia	*Lobelia amoena*	Stone Mountain-mint	*Pycnanthemum flexuosum*
Southern magnolia	*Magnolia grandiflora*	Strawberry-bush	*Euonymus americanus*
Southern maidenhair	*Adiantum capillus-veneris*	Striped maple	*Acer pensylvanicum*
Southern nodding		Sugar maple	*Acer saccharum*
trillium	*Trillium rugelii*	Sugarberry	*Celtis laevigata*
Southern oak-leach	*Aureolaria pectinata*	Sugarcane plume grass	*Saccharum giganteum*
Southern red cedar	*Juniperus virginiana*	Sumacs	*Rhus* spp.
	var. *silicicola*	Summer bluets	*Houstonia purpurea*
Southern red oak	*Quercus falcata*	Summer farewell	*Dalea pinnata*
Southern red trillium	*Trillium sulcatum*	Summer grape	*Vitis aestivalis*
Southern sandgrass	*Triplasis americana*	Sunbonnets	*Chaptalia tomentosa*
Southern		Sundrops	*Oenothera fruticosa*
seashore-mallow	*Kosteletskya virginica*	Sunflowers	*Helianthus* spp.
Southern sugar maple	*Acer floridanum*	Swamp aster	*Symphyotrichum puniceum*
Southern swamp		Swamp azalea	*Rhododendron viscosum*
dogwood	*Cornus stricta*	Swamp bay	*Persea palustris*
Southern twayblade	*Listera australis*	Swamp chestnut oak	*Quercus michauxii*
Southern water-plantain	*Alisma subcordatum*	Swamp dewberry	*Rubus hispidus*
Southern wild raisin	*Viburnum nudum*	Swamp lousewort	*Pedicularis lanceolata*
Southern wild-rice	*Zizania aquatica*	Swamp pink	*Helonias bullata*
Southern wiregrass	*Aristida beyrichiana*	Swamp rose	*Rosa palustris*
Southern-privet	*Forestiera ligustrina*	Swamp thistle	*Cirsium muticum*
Spanish bayonet	*Yucca gloriosa*	Swamp tupelo	*Nyssa biflora*
Spanish dagger	*Yucca aloifolia*	Swamp-privet	*Forestiera acuminata*
Spanish-moss	*Tillandsia usneoides*	Sweet azalea	*Rhododendron arborescens*
Sparkleberry	*Vaccinium arboreum*	Sweet bay	*Magnolia virginiana*
Speckled wood-lily	*Clintonia umbellulata*	Sweet Betsy	*Trillium cuneatum*
Spider milkweed	*Asclepias viridis*	Sweet cicely	*Osmorhiza* spp.
Spiderworts	*Tradescantia* spp.	Sweet gum	*Liquidambar styraciflua*
Spikemosses	*Selaginella* spp.	Sweet pitcherplant	*Sarracenia rubra*
Spikerush	*Eleocharis atropurpurea*	Sweet white trillium	*Trillium simile*
Spikerush	*Eleocharis quadrangulata*	Sweet white violet	*Viola blanda*
Spikerushes	*Eleocharis* spp.	Sweet-shrub	*Calycanthus floridus*
Splitbeard bluestem	*Andropogon ternarius*	Switchcane	*Arundinaria tecta*
Spotted mandarin	*Prosartes maculata*	Switchgrass	*Panicum virgatum*
Spotted pondweed	*Potamogeton pulcher*	Swollen bladderwort	*Utricularia inflata*
Spreading rockcress	*Arabis patens*	Sycamore	*Platanus occidentalis*
Spreading sunflower	*Helianthus divaricatus*	Table Mountain pine	*Pinus pungens*
Spring-beauty	*Claytonia virginica*	Tag alder	*Alnus serrulata*
Spruce pine	*Pinus glabra*	Tall indigo-bush	*Amorpha fruticosa*
Spurred butterfly pea	*Centrosema virginianum*	Tall ironweed	*Vernonia angustifolia*
Squirrel corn	*Dicentra canadensis*	Tall milkweed	*Asclepias exaltata*

COMMON NAME	SCIENTIFIC NAME	COMMON NAME	SCIENTIFIC NAME
Tall thoroughwort	*Eupatorium altissimum*	Upland willow	*Salix humilis*
Tall white violet	*Viola canadensis*	Vasey's trillium	*Trillium vaseyi*
	var. *canadensis*	Veiny hawkweed	*Hieracium venosum*
Tassel-rue	*Trautvetteria caroliniensis*	Velvety lespedeza	*Lespedeza stuevei*
Teaberry	*Gaultheria procumbens*	Vine-wicky	*Pieris phillyreifolia*
Tennessee yellow-eyed		Violet wood-sorrel	*Oxalis violacea*
grass	*Xyris tennesseensis*	Violets	*Viola* spp.
Texas plains rush	*Juncus filipendulus*	Virginia bluebells	*Mertensia virginica*
Thick-pod wild white		Virginia bugleweed	*Lycopus virginicus*
indigo	*Baptisia alba*	Virginia chain fern	*Woodwardia virginica*
Thimbleweed	*Anemone virginiana*	Virginia goat's-rue	*Tephrosia virginiana*
Tidal marsh		Virginia marbleseed	*Onosmodium virginianum*
obedient-plant	*Physostegia leptophylla*	Virginia meadow-beauty	*Rhexia virginica*
Thorne's beaksedge	*Rhynchospora thornei*	Virginia mountain-mint	*Pycnanthemum virginianum*
Thorny-olive	*Elaeagnus pungens*	Virginia pine	*Pinus virginiana*
Thoroughworts	*Eupatorium* spp.	Virginia snakeroot	*Endodeca serpentaria*
Three-awn grasses	*Aristida* spp.	Virginia spirea	*Spiraea virginiana*
Threeflower hawthorn	*Crataegus triflora*	Virginia-creeper	*Parthenocissus quinquefolia*
Threesquare	*Schoenoplectus americanus*	Virginia-willow	*Itea virginica*
Three-toothed cinquefoil	*Sibbaldia tridentata*	Wafer-ash	*Ptelea trifoliata*
Threeway sedge	*Dulichium arundinaceum*	Walking fern	*Asplenium rhizophyllum*
Thyme-leaf bluet	*Houstonia serpyllifolia*	Walter's aster	*Symphyotrichum walteri*
Ti-ti	*Cyrilla racemiflora*	Walter's violet	*Viola walteri*
Toothache grass	*Ctenium aromaticum*	Wand goldenrod	*Solidago stricta*
Toothed white-topped		Water dawnflower	*Stylisma aquatica*
aster	*Sericocarpus asteroides*	Water hickory	*Carya aquatica*
Toothworts	*Cardamine* spp.	Water hyacinth	*Eichhornia crassipes*
Tough buckthorn	*Sideroxylon tenax*	Water locust	*Gleditsia aquatica*
Tracy's bluestem	*Andropogon tracyi*	Water milfoil	*Myriophyllum* spp.
Tracy's sundew	*Drosera tracyi*	Water oak	*Quercus nigra*
Trailing arbutus	*Epigaea repens*	Water oleander	*Decodon verticillatus*
Trailing meadowrue	*Thalictrum debile*	Water tupelo	*Nyssa aquatica*
Trailing phlox	*Phlox nivalis*	Water-elm	*Planera aquatica*
Tread-softly	*Cnidoscolus stimulosus*	Waterleafs	*Hydrophyllum* spp.
Tree-of-heaven	*Ailanthus altissima*	Watermeal	*Wolffia columbiana*
Trilliums	*Trillium* spp.	Waterpepper	*Persicaria hydropiperoides*
Trumpet pitcherplant	*Sarracenia flava*	Water-shield	*Brasenia schreberi*
Trumpet-creeper	*Campsis radicans*	Wavy hairgrass	*Avenella flexuosa*
Tulip-tree	*Liriodendron tulipifera*	Wax-myrtle	*Morella cerifera*
Tung-oil tree	*Vernicia fordii*	White ash	*Fraxinus americana*
Turkey oak	*Quercus laevis*	White goldenrod	*Solidago bicolor*
Turk's-cap lily	*Lilium superbum*	White oak	*Quercus alba*
Turtleheads	*Chelone* spp.	White pine	*Pinus strobus*
Twinleaf	*Jeffersonia diphylla*	White prairie-goldenrod	*Solidago ptarmicoides*
Twisted-hair spikemoss	*Selaginella tortipila*	White snakeroot	*Ageratina altissima*
Two-leaved miterwort	*Mitella diphylla*	White tassels	*Dalea albida*
Two-wing silverbell	*Halesia diptera*	White turtlehead	*Chelone glabra*
Umbrella magnolia	*Magnolia tripetala*	White waterlily	*Nymphaea odorata*
Umbrella-leaf	*Diphylleia cymosa*	Whiteleaf greenbrier	*Smilax glauca*
Underwood's trillium	*Trillium underwoodii*	Whitetop pitcherplant	*Sarracenia leucophylla*
Upland dwarf iris	*Iris verna*	Whitlow-grass	*Draba cuneifolia*

COMMON NAME	SCIENTIFIC NAME	COMMON NAME	SCIENTIFIC NAME
Whorled aster	*Oclemena acuminata*	Woodland coreopsis	*Coreopsis major*
Whorled loosestrife	*Lysimachia quadrifolia*	Woodland muhly	*Muhlenbergia sylvatica*
Whorled milkweed	*Asclepias verticillata*	Wood-nettle	*Laportea canadensis*
Whorled sunflower	*Helianthus verticillatus*	Woody goldenrod	*Chrysoma pauciflosculosa*
Wide-leaved spiderwort	*Tradescantia subaspera*	Woolgrass bulrush	*Scirpus cyperinus*
Wild bergamot	*Monarda fistulosa*	Woolly dutchman's-pipe	*Isotrema tomentosum*
Wild bleeding heart	*Dicentra eximia*	Woolly lipfern	*Cheilanthes tomentosa*
Wild comfrey	*Cynoglossum virginianum*	Woolly ragwort	*Packera tomentosa*
Wild geranium	*Geranium maculatum*	Wright's witchgrass	*Dichanthelium wrightianum*
Wild ginger	*Asarum canadense*	Wrinkled jointgrass	*Coelorachis rugosa*
Wild hyacinth	*Camassia scilloides*	Yaupon	*Ilex vomitoria*
Wild hydrangea	*Hydrangea arborescens*	Yellow birch	*Betula alleghaniensis*
Wild indigoes	*Baptisia* spp.	Yellow buckeye	*Aesculus flava*
Wild onion	*Allium canadense*	Yellow fringed orchid	*Plantanthera ciliaris*
Wild taro	*Colocasia esculenta*	Yellow hatpins	*Syngonanthus flavidulus*
Willow oak	*Quercus phellos*	Yellow hawthorn	*Crataegus flava*
Winged elm	*Ulmus alata*	Yellow honeysuckle	*Lonicera flava*
Winged monkey-flower	*Mimulus alatus*	Yellow indiangrass	*Sorghastrum nutans*
Winged sumac	*Rhus copallinum*	Yellow jewelweed	*Impatiens pallida*
Wingstems	*Verbesina* spp.	Yellow lady's-slipper	*Cypripedium parviflorum*
Winterberry	*Ilex verticillata*	Yellow mandarin	*Prosartes lanuginosa*
Winter-cresses	*Barbarea* spp.	Yellow nailwort	*Paronychia virginica*
Wintergreen quillwort	*Isoetes hyemalis*	Yellow passionflower	*Passiflora lutea* var. *lutea*
Wireleaf dropseed	*Sporobolus teretifolius*	Yellow pinelily	*Nuphar orbiculata*
Wire-plant	*Stipulicida setacea*	Yellow stargrass	*Hypoxis hirsuta*
Witchgrasses	*Dichanthelium* spp.	Yellow sunnybell	*Schoenolirion croceum*
Witch-hazel	*Hamamelis virginiana*	Yellow-eyed grasses	*Xyris* spp.
Witch's-hobble	*Viburnum lantanoides*	Yellowroot	*Xanthorhiza simplicissima*
Wood anemone	*Anemone quinquefolia*	Yellow-wood	*Cladrastis kentukea*

Common and Scientific Names of Animals

Most of the common and scientific names that appear below were derived from NatureServe, *The Breeding Bird Atlas of Georgia* (Schneider et al. 2010), and *Amphibians and Reptiles of Georgia* (Jensen et al. 2008).

COMMON NAME	SCIENTIFIC NAME	COMMON NAME	SCIENTIFIC NAME
Acadian flycatcher	*Empidonax virescens*	Barred owl	*Strix varia*
Acorn worm	Class Enteropneusta (multiple species)	Bay anchovy	*Anchoa mitchilli*
		Beach hoppers	Family Haustoriidae (multiple species)
Alabama map turtle	*Graptemys pulchra*		
Alligator snapping turtle	*Macrochelys temminckii*	Beaver	*Castor canadensis*
American alligator	*Alligator mississippiensis*	Belted kingfisher	*Megaceryle alcyon*
American black duck	*Anas rubripes*	Big brown bat	*Eptesicus fuscus*
American eel	*Anguilla rostrata*	Bird-voiced treefrog	*Hyla avivoca*
American goldfinch	*Spinus tristis*	Black bear	*Ursus americanus*
American kestrel	*Falco sparverius*	Black racer	*Coluber constrictor*
American oystercatcher	*Haematopus palliatus*	Black rail	*Laterallus jamaicensis*
American redstart	*Setophaga ruticilla*	Black sea bass	*Centropristis striata*
American shad	*Alosa sapidissima*	Black skimmer	*Rynchops niger*
American toad	*Bufo americanus* (= *Anaxyrus americanus*)	Black swallowtail	*Papilio polyxenes*
		Black swamp snake	*Seminatrix pygaea*
American woodcock	*Scolopax minor*	Black vulture	*Coragyps atratus*
Anhinga	*Anhinga anhinga*	Black-and-white warbler	*Mniotilta varia*
Antlion	Family Myrmeleontidae (multiple species)	Black-bellied salamander	*Desmognathus quadramaculatus*
Apalachicola dusky salamander	*Desmognathus apalachicolae*	Black-billed cuckoo	*Coccyzus erythropthalmus*
		Blackburnian warbler	*Dendroica fusca*
Aphrodite fritillary	*Speyeria aphrodite*	Black-crowned night-heron	*Nycticorax nycticorax*
Appalachian eyed brown	*Lethe appalachia*		
Atlantic ghost crab	*Ocypode quadrata*	Black-throated blue warbler	*Dendroica caerulescens*
Atlantic menhaden	*Brevoortia tyrannus*		
Atlantic moonfish	*Selene setapinnus*	Black-throated green warbler	*Dendroica virens*
Atlantic oyster drill	*Urosalpinx cinerea*		
Atlantic silverside	*Menidia menidia*	Blue crab	*Callinectes sapidus*
Atlantic stingray	*Dasyatis sabina*	Blue grosbeak	*Passerina caerulea*
Atlantic sturgeon	*Acipenser oxyrinchus*	Blue jay	*Cyanocitta cristata*
Bachman's sparrow	*Aimophila aestivalis*	Blue Ridge two-lined salamander	*Eurycea wilderae*
Bachman's warbler	*Vermivora bachmanii*		
Bald eagle	*Haliaeetus leucocephalus*	Blueback herring	*Alosa aestivalis*
Banded killifish	*Fundulus diaphanus*	Bluefin killifish	*Lucania goodei*
Banded pygmy sunfish	*Elassoma zonatum*	Bluegill	*Lepomis macrochirus*
Banded watersnake	*Nerodia fasciata*	Blue-gray gnatcatcher	*Polioptila caerulea*
Barbour's map turtle	*Graptemys barbouri*	Blue-headed vireo	*Vireo solitarius*
Barking treefrog	*Hyla gratiosa*	Bluenose shiner	*Pteronotropis welaka*
Barn swallow	*Hirundo rustica*	Blue-winged teal	*Anas discors*

COMMON NAME	SCIENTIFIC NAME	COMMON NAME	SCIENTIFIC NAME
Bobcat	*Lynx rufus*	Common snapping turtle	*Chelydra serpentina*
Bog turtle	*Glyptemys muhlenbergii*	Common wood nymph	*Cercyonis pegala*
Bottlenose dolphin	*Tursiops truncatus*	Common yellowthroat	*Geothlypis trichas*
Bowfin	*Amia calva*	Cooper's hawk	*Accipiter cooperii*
Broadhead skink	*Plestiodon laticeps*	Cope's gray treefrog	*Hyla chrysoscelis*
Broad-winged hawk	*Buteo platypterus*	Copperhead	*Agkistrodon contortrix*
Brown creeper	*Certhia americana*	Coquina	*Donax variabilis*
Brown thrasher	*Toxostoma rufum*	Coral hairstreak	*Satyrium titus*
Brown watersnake	*Nerodia taxispilota*	Corn snake	*Elaphe guttata*
Brown-headed nuthatch	*Sitta pusilla*		(= *Pantherophis guttatus*)
Bufflehead	*Bucephala albeola*	Cotton mouse	*Peromyscus gossypinus*
Bullfrog	*Rana catesbeiana*	Cottonmouth	*Agkistrodon piscivorus*
	(= *Lithobates catesbeiana*)	Coyote	*Canis latrans*
Caddisfly	Order Trichoptera	Creole pearly-eye	*Lethe creola*
	(multiple species)	Crevalle jack	*Caranx hippos*
Canada warbler	*Wilsonia canadensis*	Cypress minnow	*Hybognathus hayi*
Cape May warbler	*Dendroica tigrina*	Dark-eyed junco	*Junco hyemalis*
Carolina chickadee	*Poecile carolinensis*	Deer mouse	*Peromyscus maniculatus*
Carolina roadside		Diamondback terrapin	*Malaclemys terrapin*
skipper	*Amblyscirtes carolina*	Diana fritillary	*Speyeria diana*
Carolina wren	*Thryothorus ludovicianus*	Dowitchers	*Limnodromus griseus;*
Carpenter frog	*Rana virgatipes*		*L. scolopaceus*
	(= *Lithobates virgatipes*)	Downy woodpecker	*Picoides pubescens*
Cave salamander	*Eurycea lucifuga*	Dun skipper	*Euphyes vestris*
Cedar waxwing	*Bombycilla cedrorum*	Dwarf black-bellied	
Cerulean warbler	*Dendroica cerulea*	salamander	*Desmognathus folkertsi*
Chain pickerel	*Esox niger*	Dwarf salamander	*Eurycea quadridigitata*
Chattahoochee slimy		Dwarf waterdog	*Necturus punctatus*
salamander	*Plethodon chattahoochee*	Eastern bluebird	*Sialia sialis*
Chestnut-sided warbler	*Dendroica pensylvanica*	Eastern box turtle	*Terrapene carolina*
Chicken turtle	*Deirochelys reticularia*	Eastern chipmunk	*Tamias striatus*
Chimney swift	*Chaetura pelagica*	Eastern coral snake	*Micrurus fulvius*
Chipping sparrow	*Spizella passerina*	Eastern diamondback	
Chuck-wills-widow	*Caprimulgus carolinensis*	rattlesnake	*Crotalus adamanteus*
Clapper rail	*Rallus longirostris*	Eastern fence lizard	*Sceloporus undulatus*
Clearnose skate	*Raja eglanteria*	Eastern glass lizard	*Ophisaurus ventralis*
Cloudless sulphur	*Phoebis sennae*	Eastern grass shrimp	*Palaemonetes paludosus*
Coachwhip	*Masticophis flagellum*	Eastern harvest mouse	*Reithrodontomys humulis*
Coal skink	*Eumeces anthracinus*	Eastern harvester ant	*Pogonomyrmex badius*
	(= *Plestiodon anthracinus*)	Eastern hognose snake	*Heterodon platirhinos*
Common buckeye	*Junonia coenia*	Eastern indigo snake	*Drymarchon couperi*
Common garter snake	*Thamnophis sirtalis*	Eastern kingsnake	*Lampropeltis getula getula*
Common grackle	*Quiscalus quiscula*	Eastern milk snake	*Lampropeltis triangulum*
Common ground-dove	*Columbina passerina*		*triangulum*
Common kingsnake	*Lampropeltis getula*	Eastern mole	*Scalopus aquaticus*
Common map turtle	*Graptemys geographica*	Eastern mud turtle	*Kinosternon subrubrum*
Common musk turtle	*Sternotherus odoratus*	Eastern narrow-mouthed	
Common nighthawk	*Chordeiles minor*	toad	*Gastrophryne carolinensis*
Common periwinkle	*Littorina littorea*	Eastern newt	*Notophthalmus viridescens*
Common raven	*Corvus corax*	Eastern phoebe	*Sayornis phoebe*

COMMON NAME	SCIENTIFIC NAME	COMMON NAME	SCIENTIFIC NAME
Eastern pipistrelle	*Perimyotis subflavus*	Greater scaup	*Aythya marila*
Eastern ribbon snake	*Thamnophis sauritus*	Greater siren	*Siren lacertina*
Eastern silvery minnow	*Hybognathus regius*	Great-spangled fritillary	*Speyeria cybele*
Eastern small-footed		Green anole	*Anolis carolinensis*
myotis	*Myotis leibii*	Green comma	*Polygonia faunus*
Eastern spadefoot	*Scaphiopus holbrookii*	Green frog	*Rana clamitans*
Eastern tailed-blue	*Cupido comyntas*		(= *Lithobates clamitans*)
Eastern tiger swallowtail	*Papilio glaucus*	Green heron	*Butorides virescens*
Eastern towhee	*Pipilo erythrophthalmus*	Green salamander	*Aneides aeneus*
Eastern wood-pewee	*Contopus virens*	Green sea turtle	*Chelonia mydas*
Eastern woodrat	*Neotoma floridana*	Green sunfish	*Lepomis cyanellus*
Eastern worm snake	*Carphophis amoenus*	Green treefrog	*Hyla cinerea*
Evening bat	*Nycticeius humeralis*	Green-winged teal	*Anas crecca*
Feral hog; feral swine	*Sus scrofa*	Ground dove	*Columbina passerina*
Fiddler crabs	*Uca* spp.	Ground skink	*Scincella lateralis*
Field sparrow	*Spizella pusilla*	Guinea fowl	Family Phasianidae
Five-lined skink	*Eumeces fasciatus*		(multiple species)
	(= *Plestiodon fasciatus*)	Gulf Coast mud	*Pseudotriton montanus*
Flatwoods salamander	*Ambystoma bishopi;*	salamander	*flavissimus*
	A. cingulatum	Gulf fritillary	*Agraulis vanillae*
Florida cooter	*Pseudemys floridana*	Gull-billed tern	*Gelochelidon nilotica*
Florida pine snake	*Pituophis melanoleucus*	Hairy woodpecker	*Picoides villosus*
	mugitus	Hairy-tailed mole	*Parascalops breweri*
Flounder	Family Bothidae	Henslow's sparrow	*Ammodramus henslowii*
	(multiple species)	Hessels' hairstreak	*Callophrys hesseli*
Four-toed salamander	*Hemidactylium scutatum*	Hickory hairstreak	*Satyrium caraevorus*
Fowler's toad	*Bufo fowleri*	Hispid cotton rat	*Sigmodon hispidus*
	(= *Anaxyrus fowleri*)	Hoary bat	*Lasiurus cinereus*
Fox squirrel	*Sciurus niger*	Hooded merganser	*Lophodytes cucullatus*
Georgia satyr	*Neonympha areolatus*	Hooded warbler	*Wilsonia citrina*
Ghost shrimp	*Callichirus major;*	Horseshoe crab	*Limulus polyphemus*
	Callianassa major	House wren	*Troglodytes aedon*
Gizzard shad	*Dorosoma cepedianum*	Indiana bat	*Myotis sodalis*
Glossy crayfish snake	*Regina rigida*	Indigo bunting	*Passerina cyanea*
Glossy ibis	*Plegadis falcinellus*	Inland silverside	*Menidia beryllina*
Golden mouse	*Ochrotomys nuttalli*	Island glass lizard	*Ophisaurus compressus*
Golden silk orb-weaver	*Nephila clavipes*	Ivory-billed woodpecker	*Campephilus principalis*
Golden-crowned kinglet	*Regulus satrapa*	Kentucky warbler	*Oporornis formosus*
Golden-winged warbler	*Vermivora chrysoptera*	King rail	*Rallus elegans*
Gopher frog	*Rana capito*	Kingfish	*Menticirrhus americanus;*
Gopher tortoise	*Gopherus polyphemus*		*M. littoralis; M.saxatilis*
Grasshopper sparrow	*Ammodramus savannarum*	Knobbed whelk	*Busycon carica*
Gray catbird	*Dumetella carolinensis*	Largemouth bass	*Micropterus salmoides*
Gray fox	*Urocyon cinereoargenteus*	Least bittern	*Ixobrychus exilis*
Gray myotis	*Myotis grisescens*	Least shrew	*Cryptotis parva*
Gray squirrel	*Sciurus carolinensis*	Least tern	*Sternula antillarum*
Gray treefrog	*Hyla versicolor*	Least weasel	*Mustela nivalis*
Great blue heron	*Ardea herodias*	Leatherback sea turtle	*Dermochelys coriacea*
Great crested flycatcher	*Myiarchus crinitus*	Lesser scaup	*Aythya affinis*
Great egret	*Ardea alba*	Lesser siren	*Siren intermedia*

COMMON NAME	SCIENTIFIC NAME	COMMON NAME	SCIENTIFIC NAME
Lightning whelk	*Busycon sinistrum*	Northern short-tailed shew	*Blarina brevicauda*
Little blue heron	*Egretta caerulea*	Northern slimy salamander	*Plethodon glutinosus glutinosus*
Little grass frog	*Pseudacris ocularis*		
Loggerhead musk turtle	*Sternotherus minor*	Northern watersnake	*Nerodia sipedon*
Loggerhead sea turtle	*Caretta caretta*	Northern yellow bat	*Lasiurus intermedius*
Longnose gar	*Lepisosteus osseus*	Oak toad	*Bufo quercicus*
Long-tailed shrew	*Sorex dispar*		(= *Anaxyrus quercicus*)
Long-tailed skipper	*Urbanus proteus*	Ocoee salamander	*Desmognathus ocoee*
Long-tailed weasel	*Mustela frenata*	Ohoopee dunes moth	*Narraga georgiana*
Lookdown	*Selene vomer*	Oldfield mouse	*Peromyscus polionotus*
Louisiana waterthrush	*Seiurus motacilla*	Opossum	*Didelphis virginiana*
Mallard	*Anas platyrhynchos*	Osprey	*Pandion haliaetus*
Manatee	*Trichechus manatus*	Ouachita map turtle	*Graptemys ouachitensis*
Many-lined salamander	*Stereochilus marginatus*	Ovenbird	*Seiurus aurocapilla*
Marbled salamander	*Ambystoma opacum*	Oyster toadfish	*Opsanus tau*
Marsh rabbit	*Sylvilagus palustris*	Oyster	*Crassostrea virginica*
Marsh wren	*Cistothorus palustris*	Painted bunting	*Passerina ciris*
Masked shrew	*Sorex cinereus*	Painted turtle	*Chrysemys picta*
Meadow vole	*Microtus pennsylvanicus*	Palamedes swallowtail	*Papilio palamedes*
Mexican free-tailed bat	*Tadarida brasiliensis*	Palmetto tortoise beetle	*Hemisphaerota cyanea*
Mimic glass lizard	*Ophisaurus mimicus*	Peregrine falcon	*Falco peregrinus*
Mink	*Neovison vison*	Permit	*Trachinotus falcatus*
Mississippi kite	*Ictinia mississippiensis*	Pickerel frog	*Lithobates palustris*
Mole crab	*Emerita talpoida*	Pied-billed grebe	*Podilymbus podiceps*
Mole salamander	*Ambystoma talpoideum*	Pig frog	*Rana grylio*
Mole skink	*Plestiodon egregius*		(= *Lithobates grylio*)
Moon snail; shark eye	*Neverita duplicata*	Pigeon Mountain salamander	*Plethodon petraeus*
Mosquitofish	*Gambusia affinis; G. holbrooki*		
		Pigfish	*Orthopristis chrysoptera*
Mottled mojarra	*Eucinostomus lefroyi*	Pileated woodpecker	*Dryocopus pileatus*
Mourning dove	*Zenaida macroura*	Pine barrens treefrog	*Hyla andersonii*
Mud crab	*Eurytium limosum*	Pine siskin	*Spinus pinus*
Mud fiddler crab	*Uca pugnax*	Pine vole	*Microtus pinetorum*
Mud salamander	*Pseudotriton montanus*	Pine warbler	*Dendroica pinus*
Mud snake	*Farancia abacura*	Pine woods snake; yellow-lipped snake	*Rhadinea flavilata*
Mudpuppy	*Necturus maculosus*		
Mummichog	*Fundulus heteroclitus*	Pine woods treefrog	*Hyla femoralis*
Muskrat	*Ondatra zibethica*	Pipevine swallowtail	*Battus philenor*
Nine-banded armadillo	*Dasypus novemcinctus*	Piping plover	*Charadrius melodus*
Northern bobwhite	*Colinus virginianus*	Plain-bellied watersnake	*Nerodia erythrogaster*
Northern cardinal	*Cardinalis cardinalis*	Pompano	*Trachinotus carolinus*
Northern cricket frog	*Acris crepitans*	Pond slider	*Trachemys scripta*
Northern flicker	*Colaptes auratus*	Prairie warbler	*Dendroica discolor*
Northern harrier	*Circus cyaneus*	Prothonotary warbler	*Protonotaria citrea*
Northern parula	*Parula americana*	Purple finch	*Carpodacus purpureus*
Northern pine snake	*Pituophis melanoleucus melanoleucus*	Purple gallinule	*Porphyrio martinica*
		Pygmy rattlesnake	*Sistrurus miliarius*
Northern rough-winged swallow	*Stelgidopteryx serripennis*	Pygmy shrew	*Sorex hoyi*
Northern saw-whet owl	*Aegolius acadicus*	Queen snake	*Regina septemvittata*

COMMON NAME	SCIENTIFIC NAME
Question mark	*Polygonia interrogationis*
Raccoon	*Procyon lotor*
Rafinesque's big-eared bat	*Corynorhinus rafinesquii*
Rainbow snake	*Farancia erytrogamma*
Rare skipper	*Problema bulenta*
Rat snake	*Elaphe obsoleta* (= *Pantherophis obsoletus*)
Razor clam	*Tagelus plebeius; Ensis directus*
Red admiral	*Vanessa atalanta*
Red bat	*Lasiurus borealis*
Red crossbill	*Loxia curvirostra*
Red deer	*Cervus elaphus*
Red drum	*Sciaenops ocellatus*
Red fox	*Vulpes vulpes*
Red imported fire ant	*Solenopsis invicta*
Red knot	*Calidris canutus*
Red salamander	*Pseudotriton ruber*
Red squirrel	*Tamiasciurus hudsonicus*
Red wolf	*Canis rufus*
Red-bellied snake	*Storeria occipitomaculata*
Red-bellied watersnake	*Nerodia erythrogaster*
Red-bellied woodpecker	*Melanerpes carolinus*
Redbreast sunfish	*Lepomis auritus*
Red-cockaded woodpecker	*Picoides borealis*
Red-eyed vireo	*Vireo olivaceus*
Redfin pickerel	*Esox americanus*
Red-headed woodpecker	*Melanerpes erythrocephalus*
Red-jointed fiddler crab	*Uca minax*
Red-legged salamander	*Plethodon shermani*
Red-shouldered hawk	*Buteo lineatus*
Red-spotted purple	*Limenitis arthemis astyanax*
Red-tailed hawk	*Buteo jamaicensis*
Red-winged blackbird	*Agelaius phoeniceus*
Rice rat	*Oryzomys palustris*
Ring-necked duck	*Aythya collaris*
Ringnecked snake	*Diadophis punctatus*
River cooter	*Pseudemys concinna*
River frog	*Rana heckscheri* (= *Lithobates heckscheri*)
River otter	*Luntra canadensis*
Rock or lichen grasshopper	*Trimerotropis saxatilis*
Rose-breasted grosbeak	*Pheucticus ludovicianus*
Rough green snake	*Opheodrys aestivus*
Round-tailed muskrat	*Neofiber alleni*
Rove beetles	Family Staphylinidae (multiple species)

COMMON NAME	SCIENTIFIC NAME
Royal tern	*Thalasseus maximus*
Ruby-throated hummingbird	*Archilochus colubris*
Ruddy duck	*Oxyura jamaicensis*
Ruffed grouse	*Bonasa umbellus*
Sailfin molly	*Poecilia latipinna*
Salt marsh grasshopper	*Orchelimum fidicinum*
Sand dollar	*Mellita isometra; Mellita quinquiesperforata*
Sand fiddler crab	*Uca pugilator*
Sanderling	*Calidris alba*
Sandhill crane	*Grus canadensis*
Say's spiketail	*Cordulegaster sayi*
Scarab beetles	*Aphodius aegrotus; A. haldemani; A. laevigatus; Copris gopheri; Mycotrupes* spp.; *Onthophagus polyphemi; Polyphylla donalsoni*
Scarlet kingsnake	*Lampropeltis triangulum elapsoides*
Scarlet snake	*Cemophora coccinea*
Scarlet tanager	*Piranga olivacea*
Scoter	*Melanitta americana; M. perspicillata*
Sea cucumber	Class Holothuroidea (multiple species)
Seal salamander	*Desmognathus monticola*
Seaside sparrow	*Ammodramus maritimus*
Seepage salamander	*Desmognathus aeneus*
Seminole bat	*Lasiurus seminolus*
Sharp-shinned hawk	*Accipiter striatus*
Sheepshead	*Archosargus probatocephalus*
Sherman's fox squirrel	*Sciurus niger shermani*
Shortnose sturgeon	*Acipenser brevirostrum*
Short-tailed shrew	*Blarina brevicauda; B. carolinensis*
Silver perch	*Bairdiella chrysoura*
Silver-haired bat	*Lasionycteris noctivagans*
Six-lined racerunner	*Aspidoscelis sexlineatus*
Skilletfish	*Gobiesox strumosus*
Sleepy orange	*Abaeis nicippe* (= *Eurema nicippe*)
Slender glass lizard	*Ophisaurus attenuatus*
Slimy salamander	*Plethodon glutinosus*
Smoky shrew	*Sorex fumeus*
Smooth earth snake	*Virginia valeriae*
Snook	*Centropomus undecimalis*
Snowy egret	*Egretta thula*
Song sparrow	*Melospiza melodia*

COMMON NAME	SCIENTIFIC NAME	COMMON NAME	SCIENTIFIC NAME
Southeastern crowned snake	*Tantilla coronata*	Starhead topminnow	*Fundulus dispar*
Southeastern five-lined skink	*Eumeces inexpectatus* (= *Plestiodon inexpectatus*)	Starnose mole	*Condylura cristata*
		Striped bass	*Morone saxatilis*
Southeastern myotis	*Myotis austroriparius*	Striped crayfish snake	*Regina alleni*
Southeastern pocket gopher	*Geomys pinetis*	Striped killifish	*Fundulus majalis*
		Striped mud turtle	*Kinosternon baurii*
Southeastern shrew	*Sorex longirostris*	Striped mullet	*Mugil cephalus*
Southern Appalachian salamander	*Plethodon teyahalee*	Striped newt	*Notophthalmus perstriatus*
		Striped skunk	*Mephitis mephitis*
Southern bog lemming	*Synaptomys cooperi*	Summer tanager	*Piranga rubra*
Southern cricket frog	*Acris gryllus*	Swainson's warbler	*Limnothlypis swainsonii*
Southern dusky salamander	*Desmognathus auriculatus*	Swallow-tailed kite	*Elanoides forficatus*
		Swamp darter	*Etheostoma fusiforme*
Southern flying squirrel	*Glaucomys volans*	Swamp rabbit	*Sylvilagus aquaticus*
Southern gray-cheeked salamander	*Plethodon metcalfi*	Swamp sparrow	*Melospiza georgiana*
		Three-lined salamander	*Eurycea guttolineata*
Southern hognose snake	*Heterodon simus*	Tiger beetles	Subfamily Cicindelinae (multiple species)
Southern leopard frog	*Rana sphenocephala* (= *Lithobates sphenocephalus*)	Tiger salamander	*Ambystoma tigrinum*
		Timber rattlesnake	*Crotalus horridus*
Southern pearly-eye	*Lethe portlandia*	Trapdoor spider	*Myrmekiaphila torreya*
Southern pine beetle	*Dendroctonus frontalis*	Tricolored heron	*Egretta tricolor*
Southern red-backed salamander	*Plethodon serratus*	Tufted titmouse	*Baeolophus bicolor*
		Turkey vulture	*Cathartes aura*
Southern stingray	*Dasyatis americana*	Two-toed amphiuma	*Amphiuma means*
Southern toad	*Bufo terrestris* (= *Anaxyrus terrestris*)	Upland chorus frog	*Pseudacris feriarum*
		Veery	*Catharus fuscescens*
Southern two-lined salamander	*Eurycea cirrigera*	Warmouth	*Lepomis gulosus*
		Water shrew	*Sorex palustris*
Southern zigzag salamander	*Plethodon ventralis*	Waterdogs	*Necturus* spp.
		Webster's salamander	*Plethodon websteri*
Spicebush swallowtail	*Papilio troilus*	Wharf crab	*Sesarma cinereum*
Spiny softshell	*Apalone spinifera*	Whip-poor-will	*Caprimulgus vociferus*
Spot	*Leiostomus xanthurus*	White ibis	*Eudocimus albus*
Spottail shiner	*Notropis hudsonius*	White tiger beetle	*Cicindela dorsalis media*
Spotted dusky salamander	*Desmognathus conanti*	White-eyed vireo	*Vireo griseus*
		White-footed mouse	*Peromyscus leucopus*
Spotted salamander	*Ambystoma maculatum*	White-tailed deer	*Odocoileus virginianus*
Spotted sandpiper	*Actitis macularius*	White-throated sparrow	*Zonotrichia albicollis*
Spotted seatrout	*Cynoscion nebulosus*	Wild turkey	*Meleagris gallopavo*
Spotted skunk	*Spilogale putorius*	Willet	*Tringa semipalmata*
Spotted sucker	*Minytrema melanops*	Willow flycatcher	*Empidonax traillii*
Spotted turtle	*Clemmys guttata*	Wilson's plover	*Charadrius wilsonia*
Spring peeper	*Pseudacris crucifer*	Winter wren	*Troglodytes troglodytes*
Spring salamander	*Gyrinophilus porphyriticus*	Wood duck	*Aix sponsa*
Springtails	Subclass Collembola (multiple species)	Wood frog	*Rana sylvatica* (= *Lithobates sylvaticus*)
		Wood stork	*Mycteria americana*
Squirrel treefrog	*Hyla squirella*	Wood thrush	*Hylocichla mustelina*
Starfish	Class Asteroidea (multiple species)	Woodland jumping mouse	*Napaeozapus insignis*
		Worm-eating warbler	*Helmitheros vermivorum*

County Map of Georgia

Literature Cited

Abrahamson, W. G., and D. C. Hartnett. 1990. Pine flatwoods and dry prairies. Pp. 103–149 *in* R. L. Myers and J. J. Ewel, eds., Ecosystems of Florida. Orlando: University of Central Florida Press.

Abrahamson, W. G., A. F. Johnson, J. N. Layne, and P. A. Peroni. 1984. Vegetation of the Archbold Biological Station, Florida: An example of the southern Lake Wales Ridge. Florida Science 47:209–250.

Abrams, M. D. 2000. Fire and the ecological history of oak forests in the Eastern United States. Pp. 46–55 *in* Proceedings: Workshop on Fire, People, and the Central Hardwoods, General Technical Report NE-274, USDA Forest Service, Northeastern Research Station.

Akre, T. S. B., and K. M. Fahey. 2008. Spotted turtle (*Clemmys guttata*). Pp. 469–471 *in* J. B. Jensen, C. D. Camp, W. Gibbons, and M. J. Elliott, eds., Amphibians and Reptiles of Georgia. Athens: University of Georgia Press.

Albanese, B., and B. J. Freeman. 2009. Bluenose shiner (*Pteronotropis welaka*). Georgia Department of Natural Resources Wildlife Resources Division Website. Last modified February 10, 2009, http://www.georgiawildlife.com/sites/default/files/uploads/wildlife/nongame/pdf/accounts/fishes/pteronotropis_welaka.pdf.

Alber, M. 2008. Update on coastal marsh dieback. Coastal Georgia Research Council. Online report available at http://www.gcrc.uga.edu/FocusAreas/marsh_dieback.htm.

Albers, G., and M. Alber. 2003. A vegetative survey of back-barrier islands near Sapelo Island, Georgia. *In* K. J. Hatcher, ed., Proceedings of the 2003 Georgia Water Resources Conference. University of Georgia, Institute of Ecology, Athens, Ga.

Allen, C. R., D. M. Epperson, and A. S. Garmestani. 2004. Red imported fire ant impacts on wildlife: A decade of research. American Midland Naturalist 152:88–103.

Allison, J. R. 1995. Prairies in Georgia: They are for real. Tipularia 10:2–8.

Allison, J. R., M. W. Morris, and A. N. Egan. 2006. A new species of *Pediomelum* (Fabaceae) from the lower Piedmont Plateau of Georgia and South Carolina. Sida 22:227–241.

Ambrose, J. 1994. Georgia's Natural Communities: A Preliminary List. Georgia Department of Natural Resources. Unpublished report.

Ambrose, J. 1990. Rare wetlands. DNR Outdoor Report. Georgia Department of Natural Resources. 5(1): 6–7.

American Rivers. 2009. America's most endangered rivers: 2009 edition. Available at http://www.americanrivers.org/our-work/protecting-rivers/endangered-rivers/background/past-reports.htm. Accessed June 29, 2009.

American Rivers. 2002. America's most endangered rivers: 2002 edition. Available at http://www.americanrivers.org/our-work/protecting-rivers/endangered-rivers/background/past-reports.html. Accessed June 29, 2009.

America's Longleaf. 2009. Range-wide Conservation Plan for Longleaf Pine. America's Longleaf website, last modified February 17, 2009. Available at http://www.americaslongleaf.net/resources/the-conservation-plan/Conservation Plan.pdf.

Anderson, C. J., and B. G. Lockaby. 2007. Soils and biogeochemistry of tidal freshwater forested wetlands. Pp. 65–88 *in* W. H. Conner, T. W. Doyle, and K. W. Krauss, eds., Ecology of Tidal Freshwater Forested Wetlands of the Southeastern United States. The Netherlands: Springer, Dordrecht.

Anderson, M. D. 2003. *Juniperus virginiana*. *In* Fire Effects Information System. U.S. Department of Agriculture, Forest Service, Rocky Mountain Research Station, Fire Sciences Laboratory. Available at http://www.fs.fed.us/database/fei.

Anderson, R. C., and M. L. Bowles. 1999. Deep-Soil savannas and barrens of the Midwestern United States. Pp. 155–170 *in* R. C. Anderson, J. S. Fralish, and J. M. Baskin, eds., Savannas, Barrens, and Rock Outcrop Plant Communities of North America. Cambridge: Cambridge University Press.

Anderson, R. C., J. S. Fralish, and J. M. Baskin. 1999. Introduction. Pp. 1–6 *in* R. C. Anderson, J. S. Fralish, and J. M. Baskin, eds., Savannas, Barrens, and Rock Outcrop Plant Communities of North America. Cambridge: Cambridge University Press.

Andrews, E. F. 1917. Agency of fire in the propagation of longleaf pine. Botanical Gazette 64:497–508.

Andrews, K. M., and W. Gibbons. 2008a. Black racer (*Coluber constrictor*). Pp. 333–335 *in* J. B. Jensen, C. D. Camp, W. Gibbons, and M. J. Elliott, eds., Amphibians and Reptiles of Georgia. Athens: University of Georgia Press.

Andrews, K. M., and W. Gibbons. 2008b. Ringneck snake (*Diadophis punctatus*). Pp. 336–338 *in* J. B. Jensen, C. D. Camp, W. Gibbons, and M. J. Elliott, eds., Amphibians and Reptiles of Georgia. Athens: University of Georgia Press.

Antlfinger, A. E., and E. L. Dunn. 1979. Seasonal patterns of CO_2 and water vapor exchange of three salt-marsh succulents. Oecologia 43:249–260.

Arabas, K. B. 2000. Spatial and temporal relationships among fire frequency, vegetation and soil in an eastern North American serpentine barren. Journal of the Torrey Botanical Society 127(1):51–65.

Armour, C. L., D. A. Duff, and W. Elmore. 1991. The effects of livestock grazing on riparian and stream ecosystems. Fisheries 16:7–11.

Art, H., F. H. Bormann, G. K. Voight, and G. M. Woodwell. 1974. Barrier island forest ecosystems: Role of meteorological inputs. Science 184:60–62.

Arthur, M. A., R. D. Paratley, and B. A. Blankenship. 1998. Single and repeated fires affect survival and regeneration of woody and herbaceous species in an oak-pine forest. Journal of the Torrey Botanical Society 125(3):225–236.

Association of Fish and Wildlife Agencies. 2009. Voluntary Guidance for States to Incorporate Climate Change into State Wildlife Action Plans and Other Management Plans. Washington, D.C.

Ayers, H. B., and W. W. Ashe. 1905. The Southern Appalachian Forests. Series H, Forestry Professional Paper, no. 37. U.S. Geological Survey, Washington, D.C.

Bahr, L. M., Jr., and W. P. Lanier. 1981. The Ecology of Intertidal Oyster Reefs of the South Atlantic Coast: A Community Profile. FWS/OBS-81-15. U.S. Fish and Wildlife Service, Washington, D.C.

Bailey, M. A. 1991. The dusky gopher frog in Alabama. Journal of the Alabama Academy of Science 62:28–34.

Bakeless, J. E. 1961. The Eyes of Discovery: America as Seen by the First Explorers. New York: Dover.

Baltz, M. E., and S. C. Latta. 1998. Cape May warbler (*Dendroica tigrina*). *In* A. Poole and F. Gill, eds., The Birds of North America, no. 332. Philadelphia: The Birds of North America, Inc.

Bardgett, R. D. 2005. The Biology of Soil: A Community and Ecosystem Approach. Oxford: Oxford University Press.

Barlow, P. M. 2003. Ground water in fresh water/salt water environments of the Atlantic Coast. U.S. Geological Survey Circular 1262.

Barnett, R., I. Barnes, M. J. Phillips, L. D. Mentin, C. R. Harrington, J. C. Leonard, and A. Cooper. 2005.

Evolution of the extinct sabertooths and the American cheetah-like cat. Current Biology 15(15): R589–R590.

Barrows, H. H., J. V. Phillips, and J. E. Brantly. 1917. Agricultural Drainage in Georgia. Geological Survey of Georgia Bulletin, no. 32.

Bartram, W. 1791. Travels of William Bartram. New York: Dover Publications.

Baskin, J. M., and C. C. Baskin. 1999. Cedar glades of the southeastern United States. Pp. 99–118 *in* R. C. Anderson, J. S. Fralish, and J. M. Baskin, eds., Savannas, Barrens, and Rock Outcrop Plant Communities of North America. Cambridge: Cambridge University Press.

Baskin, J. M., and C. C. Baskin. 1978. Plant ecology of cedar glades in the Big Barren Region of Kentucky. Rhodora 80:545–557.

Baskin, J. M., C. C. Baskin, and E. W. Chester. 1999. The Big Barrens Region of Kentucky and Tennessee. Pp. 190–220 *in* R. C. Anderson, J. S. Fralish, and J. M. Baskin, eds., Savannas, Barrens, and Rock Outcrop Plant Communities of North America. Cambridge: Cambridge University Press.

Batista, W. B., and W. J. Platt. 1997. An Old-growth Definition for Southern Mixed Hardwood Forests. U.S. Department of Agriculture, Forest Service, Southern Research Station, General Technical Report SRS-9.

Batista, W. B., W. J. Platt, and R. E. Macchiavelli. 1998. Demography of a shade-tolerant tree (*Fagus grandifolia*) in a hurricane-disturbed forest. Ecology 79:38–53.

Battle, J., and S. W. Golladay. 1999. Water quality and aquatic macroinvertebrates in 3 types of reference limesink wetlands in southwest Georgia. Pp. 439–442 *in* K. J. Hatcher, ed., Proceedings of the 1999 Georgia Water Resources Conference. University of Georgia, Institute of Ecology, Athens, Ga.

Batzer, D. P., R. Cooper, and S. A. Wissinger. 2006. Wetland animal ecology. Pp. 242–284 *in* D. P. Batzer and R. R. Sharitz, eds., Ecology of Freshwater and Estuarine Wetlands. Berkeley: University of California Press.

Baydack, R. K., H. Campa III, and J. G. Haufler. 1999. Practical Approaches to the Conservation of Biological Diversity. Washington, D.C.: Island Press.

Beaton, G. 2010a. Common yellowthroat (*Geothlypis trichas*). Pp. 360–361 *in* T. Schneider, G. Beaton, T. Keyes, and N. Klaus, eds., The Breeding Bird Atlas of Georgia. Athens: University of Georgia Press.

Beaton, G. 2010b. Ovenbird (*Seiurus aurocapilla*). Pp. 354–355 *in* T. Schneider, G. Beaton, T. Keyes, and N. Klaus, eds., The Breeding Bird Atlas of Georgia. Athens: University of Georgia Press.

Beaton, G. 2010c. Worm-eating warbler (*Helmitheras vermivorun*). Pp. 350–351 *in* T. Schneider, G. Beaton,

T. Keyes, and N. Klaus, eds., The Breeding Bird Atlas of Georgia. Athens: University of Georgia Press.

Beaton, G. 2008a. Say's spiketail (*Cordulegaster sayi*). Georgia Department of Natural Resources Wildlife Resources Division website, Accessed August 13, 2011. Available at http://www.georgiawildlife.com/sites /default/files/uploads/wildlife/nongame/pdf/accounts /invertebrates/cordulegaster_sayi.pdf.

Beaton, G. 2008b. Species profile for Cherokee clubtail, *Gomphus consanguis*. Georgia Department of Natural Resources. Available at http://www.georgiawildlife.com /conservation.

Beaton, G. 2007. Dragonflies and Damselflies of Georgia and the Southeast. Athens: University of Georgia Press.

Beaton, G., P. W. Sykes, and J. W. Parrish. 2003. Annotated Checklist of Georgia Birds. 5th ed. Georgia Ornithological Society Occasional Publications 14.

Beaver, D. L., R. G. Osborn, and T. W. Custer. 1980. Nest-site and colony characteristics of wading birds in selected Atlantic coast colonies. Wilson Bulletin 92:200–220.

Beck, B. F. 1986. A generalized genetic framework for the development of sinkholes and karst in Florida, USA. Environmental Geological and Water Sciences 8:5–18.

Beck, B. F., L. Asmussen, and R. Leonard. 1985. Relationship of geology, physiography, agricultural land use, and ground-water quality in southwest Georgia. Ground Water 23:627–634.

Behnke, P. 2009. That bunch of seaweed on the beach. Skimmer 35(6):1–3.

Bell, M., III. 1966. Some notes and reflections upon a letter from Benjamin Franklin to Noble Wimberly Jones October 7, 1772. Darien, Ga.: The Ashantilly Press.

Bellis, V. J. 1995. Ecology of Maritime Forests of the Southern Atlantic Coast: A Community Profile. U.S. Department of the Interior, National Biological Service, Biological Report, no. 30. Washington, D.C.

Bellrose, F. C., and D. J. Holm. 1994. Ecology and Management of the Wood Duck. Mechanicsburg, Pa.: Stackpole Books.

Benke, A., R. L. Henry III, D. M. Gillespie, and R. J. Hunter. 1985. Importance of snag habitat for animal production in southeastern streams. Fisheries 10:8–13.

Benke, A. C., T. C. Van Arsdall Jr., D. M. Gillespie, and F. K. Parrish. 1984. Invertebrate productivity in a subtropical blackwater river: The importance of habitat and life history. Ecological Monographs 54:25–63.

Bentley, M. L., and J. A. Stallins. 2005. Climatology of cloud-to-ground lightning in Georgia, USA, 1992–2003. International Journal of Climatology 25:1979–1996.

Benton, M. W. 2005. When Life Nearly Died: The Greatest Mass Extinction of All Time. London: Thames and Hudson.

Beohm, M. 2010. West-central Georgia butterflies. Yucca giant-skipper. Available at http://www.georgiabutterflies .com/id100.html.

Berg, E. E., and J. L. Hamrick. 1994. Spatial and genetic structure of two sandhills oaks: *Quercus laevis* and *Quercus margaretta* (Fagaceae). American Journal of Botany 81:7–14.

Bertness, M. D. 2007. Atlantic Shorelines: Natural History and Ecology. Princeton, N.J.: Princeton University Press.

Beshear, R. J. 1969. Observations on the life history of *Hemisphaerota cyanea* in Georgia (Coleoptera: Chrysomelidae). Journal of the Georgia Entomological Society 4:168–170.

Bettinger, K. 2010. Yellow-throated warbler (*Dendroica dominica*). Pp. 336–337 *in* T. Schneider, G. Beaton, T. Keyes, and N. Klaus, eds., The Breeding Bird Atlas of Georgia. Athens: University of Georgia Press.

Biggerstaff, M. S., and C. W. Beck. 2007. Effects of method of English ivy removal and seed addition on regeneration of vegetation in a southeastern Piedmont forest. American Midland Naturalist 158(1):206–220.

Blevins, D., and M. P. Schafale. 2011. Wild North Carolina: Discovering the Wonders of our State's Natural Communities. Chapel Hill: University of North Carolina Press.

Boarman, W., and B. Heinrich. 1999. Common raven (*Corvus corax*). *In* A. Poole and F. Gill, eds., The Birds of North America, no. 476. Philadelphia: The Birds of North America, Inc.

Bond, T. A. 1970. Radiocarbon dates of peat from Okefenokee Swamp, Georgia. Southeastern Geology 11:199–201.

Booth, R. K., F. J. Rich, G. A. Bishop, and N. A. Brannen. 1999. Evolution of a freshwater barrier island marsh in coastal Georgia, USA. Wetlands 19:570–577.

Boring, L. R., J. Hendricks, and M. B. Edwards. 1990. Loss, retention, and replacement of nitrogen associated with site preparation burning in southern pine-hardwood forests. Pp. 145–153 *in* S. D. Nodvin, and T. A. Waldrop, eds., Fire and the Environment: Ecological and Cultural Perspectives. General Technical Report SE-69.

Boring, L. R., J. J. Hendricks, C. A. Wilson, and R. J. Mitchell. 2004. Season of burn and nutrient losses in a longleaf pine ecosystem. International Journal of Wildland Fire 13:443–453.

Bowman, R. 2002. Common ground-dove (*Columbina passerina*). *In* A. Poole and F. Gill, eds., The Birds of North America, no. 645. Philadelphia: The Birds of North America, Inc.

Bowring, S. A., D. H. Erwin, Y. G. Jin, M. W. Martin, K. Davidek, and W. Wang. 1998. U/Pb zircon geochronology and tempo of the end-Permian mass extinction. Science 280(5366):1039–1045.

Boyce, S. G. 1954. The salt spray community. Ecological Monographs 24:29–67.

Boyd, R. S., and J. M. Moffett Jr. 2003. Management of *Xyris tennesseensis* (Tennessee yellow-eyed grass), a federally endangered plant species. Unpublished report to the Georgia Department of Transportation, U.S. Department of Transportation and Federal Highway Administration. http://www.dot.state.ga.us/doingbusiness/research /Documents/reports/RP2003.pdf.

Boyer, W. D. 1987. Annual and geographic variation in cone production by longleaf pine. Pp. 73–76 *in* D. R. Phillips, ed., Proceedings of the Fourth Biennial Southern Silvicultural Research Conference. U.S. Department of Agriculture, Forest Service General Technical Report SE-42.

Bozeman, J. R. 1971. A sociologic and geographic study of the sand ridge vegetation in the Coastal Plain of Georgia. Ph.D. dissertation. University of North Carolina, Chapel Hill.

Bozeman, J. R., and R. M. Fuller. 1975. The vegetation of Cumberland Island. Pp. 63–117 *in* H. O. Hillestad, J. R. Bozeman, A. S. Johnson, C. W. Berisford, and J. I. Richardson, eds., The Ecology of Cumberland Island National Seashore, Camden County, Georgia. Georgia Marine Science Center Technical Report Serial 75–5.

Brändle, R., and R. M. M. Crawford. 1987. Rhizome anoxia tolerance and habitat specialization in wetland plants. Pp. 397–410 *in* R. M. M. Crawford, ed., Plant Life in Aquatic and Amphibious Habitats. Oxford: Blackwell Scientific Publications.

Bratton, S. P. 1994. Logging and fragmentation of broadleaved deciduous forests: Are we asking the right ecological question? Conservation Biology 8(1):295–297.

Bratton, S. P. 1986. Feral horses: Grazing impacts, genetics, and birth control. Park Science 7:23–24.

Bratton, S. P. 1975. The effect of the European wild boar, *Sus scrofa*, on gray beech forest in the Great Smoky Mountains. Ecology 56:1356–1366.

Bratton, S. P. and K. L. Davison. 1985. The disturbance history of Buxton Woods, Cape Hatteras, North Carolina. National Park Service, Cooperative Parks Studies Technical Report 16. Institute of Ecology, University of Georgia.

Bratton, S. P., and A. J. Meier. 1998. The recent vegetation disturbance history of the Chattooga River Watershed. Castanea 63(3):372–381.

Braun, E. L. 1950. Deciduous Forests of Eastern North America. Caldwell, N.J.: Blackburn Press, 2001, reprint of the 1st edition.

Brennan, L. A. 1999. Northern bobwhite (*Colinus virginianus*). *In* A. Poole and F. Gill, eds., The Birds of North America, no. 397. Philadelphia: The Birds of North America, Inc.

Brewer, J. S., and W. J. Platt. 1994. Effects of fire season and herbivory on reproductive success in a clonal forb, *Pityopsis graminifolia*. Journal of Ecology 82: 665–675.

Brokaw, N. V. L. 1985. Treefalls, regrowth and community structure in tropical forests. Pp. 53–70 *in* S. T. A. Pickett and P. S. White, eds., The Ecology of Natural Disturbance and Patch Dynamics. San Diego: Academic Press.

Brooks, R. R. 1987. Serpentine and Its Vegetation: A Multidisciplinary Approach. Hong Kong: Dioscorides Press.

Brose, P. A., and T. A. Waldrop. 2006. Fire and the origin of Table Mountain pine-pitch pine communities in the southern Appalachian Mountains, USA. Canadian Journal of Forest Research 36:710–718.

Brown, J. S. 1925. A Study of Coastal Ground Water with Special Reference to Connecticut. USGS Water Supply Paper, no. 537. U.S. Department of the Interior, Washington, D.C.

Brown, L. 1997. A Guide to the Mammals of the Southeastern United States. Knoxville: University of Tennessee Press.

Brown, R. B., E. L. Stone, and V. W. Carlisle. 1990. Soils. Pp. 35–69 *in* R. and J. J. Ewel, eds., Ecosystems of Florida. Orlando: University Central Florida Press.

Brown, R. E., and J. G. Dickson. 1994. Swainson's warbler (*Limnothlypis swainsonii*). *In* A. Poole and F. Gill, eds., The Birds of North America, no. 126. Philadelphia: Academy of Natural Sciences; Washington, D.C.: American Ornithologists' Union.

Brown, R. H. 2002. The Greening of Georgia: The Improvement of the Environment in the Twentieth Century. Macon, Ga.: Mercer University Press.

Brown, R. L. 2003. Paleoenvironment and biogeography of the Mississippi Black Belt: Evidence from insects. Pp. 11–26 *in* E. Peacock and T. Schauwecker, eds., Blackland Prairies of the Gulf Coastal Plain: Nature, Culture, and Sustainability. Tuscaloosa: University of Alabama Press.

Bryan, A. L., Jr. 1996. The Foraging Ecology of Wood Storks Nesting in the Coastal Zone of Georgia and South Carolina in 1995. Annual Report. Brunswick: Georgia Department of Natural Resources, Nongame-Endangered Wildlife Program.

Bryson, C. T., and R. Carter. 1993. Cogongrass, *Imperata cylindrica*, in the United States. Weed Technology 7:1005–1009.

Buckley, N. J. 1999. Black vulture (*Coragyps atratus*). *In* A. Poole and F. Gill, eds., The Birds of North America, no. 411. Philadelphia: The Birds of North America, Inc.

Buell, M. F., and R. L. Cain. 1943. The successional role of southern white cedar, *Chamaecyparis thyoides*, in southeastern North Carolina. Ecology 24:85–93.

Buhlmann, K. A. 2008. Chicken turtle (*Deirochelys reticularia*). Pp. 475–477 *in* J. B. Jensen, C. D. Camp, W. Gibbons, and M. J. Elliott, eds., Amphibians and Reptiles of Georgia. Athens: University of Georgia Press.

Bunn, S. E., and A. H. Arthington. 2002. Basic principles and ecological consequences of altered flow regimes for aquatic biodiversity. Environmental Management 30:492–507.

Buol, S. W. 1973. Soils of the Southern States and Puerto Rico. U.S. Department of Agriculture, Soil Conservation Service, Agricultural Experiment Stations of the Southern States and Puerto Rico. Southern Cooperative Services Bulletin no. 174.

Burbanck, M. P., and D. L. Phillips. 1983. Evidence of plant succession on granite outcrops of the Georgia Piedmont. American Midland Naturalist 109:94–104.

Burbanck, M. P., and R. B. Platt. 1964. Granite outcrop communities of the Piedmont Plateau in Georgia. Ecology 45:292–306.

Burleigh, T. D. 1958. Georgia Birds. Norman: University of Oklahoma Press.

Burns, R. M., and B. H. Honkala, tech. coords. 1990. Silvics of North America: 1. Conifers. Agriculture Handbook 654. U.S. Department of Agriculture, Forest Service, Washington, D.C. vol. 2.

Burt, W. H., and R. P. Grossenheider. 1980. A Field Guide to the Mammals: North America North of Mexico. Boston: Houghton Mifflin.

Bury, R. B. 1979. Review of the Ecology and Conservation of the Bog Turtle, *Clemmys muhlenbergii*. U.S. Fish and Wildlife Service Special Scientific Report, Wildlife, no. 219.

Butler, R. W. 1992. Great blue heron (*Ardea herodius*). *In* A. Poole, P. Stettenheim, and F. Gill, eds., The Birds of North America, no. 25. Philadelphia: Academy of Natural Sciences; Washington, D.C.: American Ornithologists' Union.

Butterflies and Moths of North America. Falcate orangetip (*Anthocharis midea*). Available at http://www.butterfliesandmoths.org/species?l=1416. Accessed June 11, 2009.

Butterflies and Moths of North America. Polyphemus moth (*Antheraea polyphemus*). Available at http://www.butterfliesandmoths.org/species?l=3290. Accessed June 9, 2009.

Butts, C., and B. Gildersbee. 1948. Geology and Mineral Resources of the Paleozoic Area in Northwest Georgia. Geological Department of Mines, Mining, and Geology in cooperation with the Tennessee Valley Authority. Georgia Geological Survey Bulletin, no. 54.

Cameron, R. S., C. Bates, and J. Johnson. 2008. Distribution and spread of laurel wilt disease in Georgia: 2006–08 survey and field observations. Georgia Forestry Commission. Available at http://www.gatrees.org/ForestManagement/documents/GeorgiaLaurelWiltReport2006–08.pdf. Accessed January 6, 2009.

Camp, C. D. 2008a. Dwarf black-bellied salamander, *Desmognathus folkertsi*. Pp. 172–174 *in* J. B. Jensen, C. D. Camp, W. Gibbons, and M. J. Elliott, eds., Amphibians and Reptiles of Georgia. Athens: University of Georgia Press.

Camp, C. D. 2008b. Southern redback salamander, *Plethodon serratus*. Pp. 224–226 *in* J. B. Jensen, C. D. Camp, W. Gibbons, and M. J. Elliott, eds., Amphibians and Reptiles of Georgia. Athens: University of Georgia Press.

Camp, C. D. 2008c. Webster's salamander (*Plethodon websteri*). Pp. 230–232 *in* J. B. Jensen, C. D. Camp, W. Gibbons, and M. J. Elliott, eds., Amphibians and Reptiles of Georgia. Athens: University of Georgia Press.

Camp, C. D. 1999. Intraspecific aggressive behavior in southeastern small species of *Plethodon*: Inferences for the evolution of aggression in terrestrial salamanders. Herpetologica 55:248–254.

Camp, C. D. 1988. Aspects of the life history of the southern red-back salamander *Plethodon serratus* Grobman in the southeastern United States. American Midland Naturalist 119:93–100.

Camp, C. D. 1986. Distribution and habitat of the southern red-back salamander, *Plethodon serratus* Grobman (Amphibia: Plethodontidae). Georgia. Georgia Journal of Science 44:136–146.

Camp, C. D., and J. B. Jensen. 2008. Pigeon Mountain salamander (*Plethodon petraeus*). Pp. 221–223 *in* J. B. Jensen, C. D. Camp, W. Gibbons, and M. J. Elliott, eds., Amphibians and Reptiles of Georgia. Athens: University of Georgia Press.

Camp, C. D., and J. B. Jensen. 2007. Use of twilight zones of caves by plethodontid salamanders. Copeia 2007:594–604.

Camp, C. D., J. L. Marshall, K. R. Landau, R. M. Austin Jr., and S. G. Tilley. 2000. Sympatric occurrence of two species of the two-lined salamander (*Eurycea bislineata*) complex. Copeia 2000:572–578.

Camp, C. D., S. G. Tilley, R. M. Austin Jr., and J. L. Marshall. 2002. A new species of black-bellied salamander (genus *Desmognathus*) from the Appalachian Mountains of northern Georgia. Herpetologica 58:471–484.

Canham, C. D., and P. L. Marks. 1985. The response of woody plants to disturbance: Patterns of establishment and growth. Pp. 197–216 *in* S. T. A. Pickett and P. S. White, eds., The Ecology of Natural Disturbances and Patch Dynamics. San Diego: Academic Press.

Capon, B. 1994. Plant Survival: Adapting to a Hostile World. Portland, Ore.: Timber Press.

Carey, J. H. 1993. *Tsuga canadensis. In* Fire Effects Information System [online]. U.S. Department of Agriculture, Forest Service, Rocky Mountain Research Station, Fire Sciences Laboratory. Available at http://www.fs.fed.us/database/feis/.

Carey, J. H. 1992a. *Pinus echinata. In* Fire Effects Information System [online]. Department of Agriculture, Forest Service, Rocky Mountain Research Station, Fire Sciences Laboratory. Available at http://www.fs.fed.us/database/feis/.

Carey, J. H. 1992b. *Pinus pungens. In* Fire Effects Information System [online]. U.S. Department of Agriculture, Forest Service, Rocky Mountain Research Station, Fire Sciences Laboratory. Available at http://www.fs.fed.us/database/feis/.

Carey, J. H. 1992c. *Pinus rigida. In* Fire Effects Information System [online]. U.S. Department of Agriculture, Forest Service, Rocky Mountain Research Station, Fire Sciences Laboratory. Available at http://www.fs.fed.us/database/feis/.

Carey, M. D., E. Burhans, and D. A. Nelson. 1994. Field sparrow (*Spizella pusilla*). *In* A. Poole and F. Gill, eds., The Birds of North America, no. 103. Philadelphia: Academy of Natural Sciences; Washington, D.C.: American Ornithologists' Union.

Carlson, P. J. 1995. An Assessment of the Old-Growth Forest Resource on National Forest System Lands in the Chattooga River Watershed. Chattooga Ecosystem Demonstration Project, USDA Forest Service Region 8.

Carr, A. 1952. Handbook of Turtles. Ithaca: Cornell University Press.

Carter, K. K., and A. G. Snow. 1990. *Pinus virginiana* Mill. Virginia pine. Pp. 513–519 *in* R. M. Burns and B. H. Honkala, tech. coords., Silvics of North America: vol. 1. Conifers. USDA Forest Service. Agriculture Handbook, no. 654. Washington, D.C.

Carter, R. C., and A. J. Londo. 2003. Remnant fire disturbed montane longleaf pine forest in west central Georgia. Pp. 475–477 *in* K. F. Connor, ed., Proceedings of the 13th Biennial southern Silvicultural Research Conference. Gen Tech. Rep SRS 92. Asheville, N.C.: U.S. Department of Agriculture, Forest Service, Southern Research Station.

Case, G. R., and D. R. Schwimmer. 1988. Late Cretaceous fish from the Blufftown Formation (Campanian) in western Georgia. Journal of Paleontology 62(2): 290–301.

Cash, W. B. 2008. Pine woods treefrog (*Hyla femoralis*). Pp. 62–64 *in* J. B. Jensen, C. D. Camp, W. Gibbons, and M. J. Elliott, eds., Amphibians and Reptiles of Georgia. Athens: University of Georgia Press.

Cash, W. B., and W. Gibbons. 2008. Eastern box turtle (*Terrapene carolina*). Pp. 497–499 *in* J. B. Jensen, C. D. Camp, W. Gibbons, and M. J. Elliott, eds., Amphibians and Reptiles of Georgia. Athens: University of Georgia Press.

Cash, W. B., J. B. Jensen, and D. J. Stevenson. 2008. Gopher frog (*Rana* [*Lithobates*] *capito*). Pp. 102–104 *in* J. B. Jensen, C. D. Camp, W. Gibbons, and M. J. Elliott, eds., Amphibians and Reptiles of Georgia. Athens: University of Georgia Press.

Cavender-Bares, J., K. Kitajima, and F. A. Bazzaz. 2004. Multiple trait associations in relation to habitat differentiation among 17 Floridian oak species. Ecological Monographs 74:635–662.

Cavitt, J. F., and C. A. Haas. 2000. Brown thrasher (*Toxostoma rufum*). *In* A. Poole and F. Gill, eds., The Birds of North America, no. 557. Philadelphia: The Birds of North America, Inc.

Certini, G. 2005. Effects of fire on properties of forest soils: A review. Oecologia 143:1–10.

Chafin, L. G. 2007. Field Guide to the Rare Plants of Georgia. Athens: University of Georgia Press.

Chafin, L. G. 1988. A floristic comparison and community analysis of two southern Appalachian boulderfields. Master's thesis. University of Georgia, Athens.

Chafin, L. G., and S. B. Jones Jr. 1989. Community structure of two southern Appalachian boulderfields. Castanea 54(4):230–237.

Chalmers, A. G. 1997. The Ecology of the Sapelo Island National Estuarine Research Reserve. University of Georgia Marine Institute, Sapelo Island, Georgia.

Christensen, N. L. 2000. Vegetation of the southeastern Coastal Plain. Pp. 449–499 *in* M. G. Barbour and W. D. Billings, eds., North American Terrestrial Vegetation. 2nd ed. Cambridge: Cambridge University Press.

Christopherson, R. W. 2009. Geosystems, 7th ed. Upper Saddle River, N.J.: Prentice Hall.

Cimprich, D. A., and F. R. Moore. 1995. Gray catbird (*Dumetella carolinensis*). *In* A. Poole and F. Gill, eds., The Birds of North America, no. 167. Philadelphia: Academy of Natural Sciences; Washington, D.C.: American Ornithologists' Union.

Cink, C. L. 2002. Whip-poor-will (*Caprimulgus vociferous*). *In* A. Poole and F. Gill, eds., The Birds of North America, no. 620. Philadelphia: The Birds of North America, Inc.

Clark, J. R., and J. Benforado. 1981. Impact workgroup report II: Characteristics of wetlands ecosystems of

Southeastern bottomland hardwood forest ecosystems. Pp. 275–300 *in* J. R. Clark and J. Benforado, eds., Wetlands of Bottomland Hardwood Forests: Proceedings of a Workshop on Bottomland Hardwood Forest Wetlands of the Southeastern United States. New York: Elsevier Scientific Publishing.

Clark, W. Z., Jr., and A. C. Zisa. 1976. Physiographic Map of Georgia. Georgia Department of Natural Resources, Atlanta, Ga.

Clarke, J. S., C. M. Hacke, and M. F. Peck. 1990. Geology and ground-water resources of the coastal area of Georgia: Georgia Geologic Survey Information Circular, no. 113.

Clebsch, E. E. C., and R. T. Busing. 1989. Secondary succession, gap dynamics, and community structure in a southern Appalachian cove forest. Ecology 70(3): 728–735.

Clewell, A. F. 1989. Natural history of wiregrass (*Aristida stricta* Michx., Gramineae). Natural Areas Journal 9: 223–233.

Clewell, A. F. 1986. Natural Setting and Vegetation of the Florida Panhandle. COESAM/PDEI-86/001. U.S. Army Corps of Engineers, Mobile District.

Clewell, A. F. 1971. The Vegetation of the Apalachicola National Forest: An Ecological Perspective. Final Report: Contract no. 38–2249. Atlanta: U.S. Department of Agriculture, U.S. Forest Service, Southern Region.

Clutter, M., B. Mendell, D. Newman, D. Wear, and J. Greis. 2005. Strategic factors driving timberland ownership changes in the U.S. South. Available at http://www.srs.fs.usda.gov/econ/pubs/southernmarkets. Accessed August 2011.

Cocker, M. D. 1991a. Economic geology of altered serpentinites in the Burks Mountain complex, Columbia County, Georgia. Georgia Geological Survey Bulletin, no. 123.

Cocker, M. D. 1991b. Geology and geochemistry of altered serpentinites in the Burks Mountain complex, Columbia County, Georgia. Georgia Geological Survey Bulletin, no. 124.

Cohen, A. D. 1974. Petrography and paleoecology of Holocene peats from the Okefenokee Swamp-marsh complex of Georgia. Journal of Sedimentary Research 44:716–726.

Cohen, A. D. 1973. Petrology of some Holocene peat sediments from the Okefenokee Swamp-marsh complex of southern Georgia. Geological Society of America Bulletin 84:3867–3878.

Cohen, A. D., M. J. Andrejko, W. Spackman, and D. Corvinus. 1984. Peat deposits of the Okefenokee Swamp. Pp. 493–553 *in* A. D. Cohen, D. J. Casagrande,

M. J. Andrejko, and G. R. Best, eds., The Okefenokee Swamp: Its Natural History, Geology, and Geochemistry. Los Alamos, N.M.: Wetland Surveys.

Coladonato, M. 1991. *Fagus grandifolia*. *In* Fire Effects Information System [online]. Available at http://www.fs.fed.us/database/feis/.

Collier, M., R. H. Webb, and J. C. Schmidt. 2000. Dams and Rivers: A Primer on the Downstream Effects of Dams. U.S. Department of the Interior, U.S. Geological Survey Circular 1126.

Collins, B., R. Sharitz, K. Madden, and J. Dilustro. 2006. Comparison of sandhills and mixed pine-hardwood communities at Fort Benning, Georgia. Southeastern Naturalist 5:93–102.

Collins, B. S., and L. L. Battaglia. 2001. Hydrology effects on propagule bank expression and vegetation in six Carolina bays. Community Ecology 2:21–33.

Collins, B. S., K. P. Dunne, and S. T. A. Pickett. 1985. Responses of forest herbs to canopy gaps. Pp. 218–234 *in* S. T. A. Pickett and P. S. White, eds., The Ecology of Natural Disturbance and Patch Dynamics. San Diego: Academic Press.

Collins, W. H., and D. H. Easley. 1999. Freshwater lens formation in an unconfined barrier island aquifer. Journal of the American Water Resources Association 35:1–21.

Comer, P., D. Faber-Langendoen, R. Evans, S. Gawler, C. Josse, G. Kittel, S. Menard, M. Pyne, M. Reid, K. Schulz, K. Snow, and J. Teague. 2003. Ecological Systems of the United States: A Working Classification of U.S. Terrestrial Systems. Arlington, Va.: NatureServe.

Conant, R., and J. T. Collins. 1998. Field Guide to Reptiles and Amphibians of Eastern and Central North America. 3rd ed., exp. Boston: Houghton Mifflin.

Conner, L. M. 2001. Survival and cause-specific mortality of adult fox squirrels in southwestern Georgia. Journal of Wildlife Management 65:200–204.

Conner, L. M., and I. A. Godbois. 2003. Habitat associated with daytime refugia of fox squirrels in a longleaf pine forest. American Midland Naturalist 150:123–129.

Conner, R. N., D. C. Rudolph, D. Saenz, and R. R. Schaefer. 1994. Heartwood, sapwood, and fungal decay associated with red-cockaded woodpecker cavity trees. Journal of Wildlife Management 58:728–734.

Conner, W. H., and M. A. Buford. 1998. Southern deepwater swamps. Pp. 261–290 *in* M. G. Messina and W. H. Conner, eds., Southern Forested Wetlands: Ecology and Management. Boca Raton, Fla.: Lewis Publishers.

Conner, W. H., K. W. Krauss, and T. W. Doyle. 2007. Ecology of tidal freshwater forests in coastal deltaic Louisiana and northeastern South Carolina. Pp.

223–254 *in* W. H. Conner, T. W. Doyle, and K. W. Krauss, eds., Ecology of Tidal Freshwater Forested Wetlands of the Southeastern United States. The Netherlands: Springer, Dordrecht.

Converse, C. K. 1983. The Nature Conservancy Element Stewardship Abstract for *Juniperus virginiana*. Arlington, Va.: The Nature Conservancy.

Cooke, C. W. 1945. Geology of Florida. Florida Geological Survey, Geological Bulletin, no. 29.

Cooke, C. W. 1943. Geology of the Coastal Plain of Georgia. U.S. Geological Survey Bulletin, no. 941.

Corbat, C. A. 1990. Nesting ecology of selected beach-nesting birds in Georgia. Ph.D. dissertation. University of Georgia, Athens.

Corbat, C. A., and P. W. Bergstrom. 2000. Wilson's plover (*Charadrius wilsonia*). *In* A. Poole, ed., The Birds of North America Online. Ithaca: Cornell Lab of Ornithology. Available at http://bna.birds.cornell.edu /bna/species/516.

Couch, C., E. Hopkins, and P. S. Hardy. 1996. Influences of Environmental Settings on Aquatic Ecosystems in the Apalachicola-Chattahoochee-Flint River Basin. Water-Resources Investigations Report 95–4278. U.S. Geological Survey, Atlanta, Ga.

Coulter, E. M. 1956. Auraria: The Story of a Georgia Gold Mining Town. Athens: University of Georgia Press.

Coulter, M. C., W. D. McCort, and A. L. Bryan Jr. 1987. Creation of artificial foraging habitat for wood storks. Colonial Waterbirds 10:203–210.

Coulter, M. C., J. A. Rodgers, J. C. Ogden, and F. C. Depkin. 1999. Wood stork (*Mycteria americana*). *In* A. Poole and F. Gill, eds., The Birds of North America, no. 409. Philadelphia: The Birds of North America, Inc.

Covell, C. V., Jr. 1984. A Field Guide to Moths of Eastern North America. Boston: Houghton Mifflin.

Cowardin, L. M., V. Carer, F. C. Golet, and E. T. LaRoe. 1979. Classification of Wetlands and Deepwater Habitats of the United States. Fish and Wildlife Service FWS/OBS-79/31.

Cowell, C. M. 1998. Historical change in vegetation and disturbance on the Georgia Piedmont. American Midland Naturalist 140(1):78–89.

Cowell, C. M. 1995. Presettlement Piedmont forests— patterns of composition and disturbance in central Georgia. Annals of the Association of American Geographers 85(1):65–83.

Cowell, C. M. 1992. Historical change in Georgia Piedmont forests: Human and environmental influences. Ph.D. dissertation. University of Georgia, Athens.

Cowie, G., ed. 2002. Reservoirs in Georgia: Meeting Water Supply Needs While Minimizing Impacts. River Basin Science and Policy Center, University of Georgia,

Athens. Available at http://www.rivercenter.uga.edu /publications/pdf/reservoir.pdf. Accessed on August 13, 2011.

Craft, C., J. Clough, J. Ehman, S. Joye, R. Park, S. Pennings, H. Guo, and M. Machmuller. 2009. Forecasting the effects of accelerated sea-level rise on tidal marsh ecosystem services. Frontiers in Ecology and the Environment 7(2):73–78.

Crandell, H. C. 1962. Geology and Ground-water Resources of Plum Island, Suffolk County, New York. USGS Water Supply Paper 1539-X.

Crane, J. 1975. Fiddler Crabs of the World. Princeton, N.J.: Princeton University Press.

Crawford, R. M. M. 1982. Physiological responses to flooding. Pp. 453–477 *in* O. L. Lange, P. F. Noble, C. B. Osmond, and H. Ziegler, eds., Encyclopedia of Plant Physiology. Vol. 12B. Physiological Plant Ecology II. Water Relations and Carbon Assimilation. Berlin: Springer-Verlag.

Crawford, R. M. M., L. S. Monk, and Z. M. Zochowski. 1987. Enhancement of anoxia tolerance by removal of volatile products of anaerobiosis. *In* R. M. M. Crawford, ed., Plant Life in Aquatic and Amphibious Habitats. Oxford: Blackwell Scientific Publications.

Cressler, A. M. 1998. Ground-Water Conditions in Georgia, 1997. U.S. Geological Survey Open-File Report 98–172.

Cronk, J. K., and M. S. Fennessy. 2001. Wetland Plants: Biology and Ecology. Boca Raton, Fla.: Lewis Publishers.

Cruse, J. 1997. Vascular flora of Currahee and Soapstone Mountains. Master's thesis. University of Georgia, Athens.

Cullina, W. 2008. Native Ferns, Moss and Grasses. Boston: Houghton Mifflin.

Currie, K., J. M. Varner, J. Kush, and M. Cipollini. 2006. A survey of the herbaceous vegetation found in the Berry Longleaf Pine Management Area. *In* M. L. Cipollini, comp., Proceedings of the Second Montane Longleaf Pine Conference Workshop, November 18–19, 2005, Berry College, Mount Berry, Georgia, Longleaf Alliance Report, no. 9.

Cypert, E. 1973. Plant succession on burned areas in Okefenokee Swamp following the fires of 1954 and 1955. Proceedings of the Tall Timbers Fire Ecology Conference 12:199–217.

Cypert, E. 1972. The origin of houses in the Okefenokee prairies. American Midland Naturalist 87:448–458.

Cypert, E. 1961. The effects of fires in the Okefenokee Swamp in 1954 and 1955. American Midland Naturalist 66:485–503.

Dahl, T. E., and C. E. Johnson. 1991. Status and Trends of Wetlands in the Conterminous United States, mid-1970's to mid-1980's. U.S. Department of the Interior, Fish and Wildlife Service, Washington, D.C.

Dahlberg, M. D. 1972. An ecological study of Georgia coastal fishes. Fisheries Bulletin 70:323–354.

Dale, V. H., S. C. Beyeler, and B. Jackson. 2002. Understory vegetation indicators of anthropogenic disturbance in longleaf pine forests at Fort Benning, Georgia, USA. Ecological Indicators 1:155–170.

Dalton, M. S., B. T. Aulenbach, and L. J. Torak. 2004. Ground-water and Surface-water Flow and Estimated Water Budget for Lake Seminole, Southwestern Georgia and Northwestern Florida. U.S. Geological Survey, Scientific Investigations Report 2004–5073.

Daniels, J. C. 2008. Featured creatures: Yucca giant-skipper butterfly. Available at http://www.entnemdept.ufl.edu /creatures/bfly/yucca_skipper.htm.

Dardeau, M. R., R. F. Modlin, W. W. Schroeder, and J. P. Stout. 1992. Estuaries. Pp. 615–744 in C. T. Hackney, S. M. Adams, and W. H. Martin, eds., Biodiversity of the Southeastern United States: Aquatic Communities. New York: Wiley.

Daubenmire, R. 1990. The Magnolia grandiflora-Quercus virginiana forest of Florida. American Midland Naturalist 123:331–347.

Davis, D. E. 2000. Where There Are Mountains: An Environmental History of the Southern Appalachians. Athens: University of Georgia Press.

Davis, M. M., and D. W. Hicks. 2001. Water resources of the upper Suwannee River watershed. Pp. 70–74 in K. J. Hatcher, ed., Proceedings of the 2001 Georgia Water Resources Conference. University of Georgia, Institute of Ecology, Athens, Ga.

Davis, W. E., Jr., and J. A. Kushlan. 1994. Green heron (Butorides virescens). In A. Poole and F. Gill, eds., The Birds of North America, no. 129. Philadelphia: Academy of Natural Sciences; Washington, D.C.: American Ornithologists' Union.

Davison, K. L. 1984. Vegetation Response and Regrowth after Fire on Cumberland Island National Seashore, Georgia. U.S. Department of the Interior, National Park Service, Research/Resource Management Report SER-69.

Day, R. H., T. M. Williams, and C. M. Warzewski. 2007. Hydrology of tidal freshwater forested wetlands of the southeastern United States. Pp. 29–64 in W. H. Conner, T. W. Doyle, and K. W. Krauss, eds., Ecology of Tidal Freshwater Forested Wetlands of the Southeastern United States. The Netherlands: Springer, Dordrecht.

DeBano, L. F., D. G. Neary, and P. F. Folliott. 1998. Fire's Effects on Ecosystems. New York: Wiley.

Deery, J. R., and J. D. Howard. 1977. Origin and character of washover fans on the Georgia Coast, USA. Transactions of the Gulf Coast Association of Geological Societies 7:259–271.

DeLancey, L. B. 2006. Coquina clam (Donax variabilis). In Comprehensive Wildlife Conservation Strategy, South Carolina Department of Natural Resources, Columbia S.C. Available at http://www.dnr.sc.gov/cwcs/index .html. Accessed July 16, 2009.

DeLancey, L. B. 1989. Trophic relationships in the surf zone at Folly Beach, South Carolina. Journal of Coastal Research 5:477–488.

DeLapp, J. A. 1978. Gradient analysis and classification of the high elevation red oak community of the southern Appalachians. Master's thesis. North Carolina State University, Raleigh.

Delcourt, H. R. 2002. Forests in Peril: Tracking Deciduous Trees from Ice-Age Refuges into the Greenhouse World. Blacksburg, Va.: McDonald and Woodward.

Delcourt, H. R., and P. A. Delcourt. 2000. Eastern deciduous forests. Pp. 358–395 in M. G. Barbour and W. D. Billings, eds., North American Terrestrial Vegetation. 2nd ed. Cambridge: Cambridge University Press.

Delcourt, P. A., and H. R. Delcourt. 2008. Chapter 4: Paleoclimates, paleovegetation, and paleofloras of North America North of Mexico during the late Quaternary. In Flora of North America. Available at http://www.fna .org/Volume/V01/Chapter04.

Delcourt, P. A., and H. R. Delcourt. 1997. The influence of prehistoric human-set fires on oak-chestnut forests in the Southern Appalachians. Castanea 63(3): 337–345.

Delcourt, P. A., H. R. Delcourt, D. F. Morse, and P. A. Morse. 1993. History, evolution, and organization of vegetation and human culture. Pp. 47–79 in W. H. Martin, S. G. Boyce, and A. C. Echternacht, eds., Biodiversity of the Southeastern United States: Lowland Terrestrial Communities. New York: Wiley.

Demaree, D. 1932. Submerging experiments with Taxodium. Ecology 13:258–262.

Depkin, F. C., M. C. Coulter, and A. L. Bryan Jr. 1992. Food of nestling wood storks in east-central Georgia. Colonial Waterbirds 15:219–225.

DeScherer, C. K., L. P. Fabrizio, W. W. Sapp, D. A. Lewis, and A. M. Kron. 2007. At the Tipping Point: A Comprehensive Assessment and Conservation Action Plan for the Georgia Coast. Atlanta: Southern Environmental Law Center.

DeSelm, H. R., and N. Murdock. 1993. Grass-dominated communities. Pp. 87–142 in W. H. Martin, S. G. Boyce, and A. C. Echternacht, eds., Biodiversity of the Southeastern United States: Upland Terrestrial Communities. New York: Wiley.

Diemer, J. E., and D. W. Speake. 1983. The distribution of the eastern indigo snake, Drymarchon corais couperi, in Georgia. Journal of Herpetology 17:256–264.

Dilustro, J., B. Collins, and L. Duncan. 2006. Land use history effects in mixed pine hardwood forests at Fort

Benning. Journal of Torrey Botanical Society 133:460–467.

Dilustro, J., B. Collins, L. Duncan, and R. Sharitz. 2002. Soil texture, land-use intensity, and vegetation of Fort Benning upland forest sites. Journal of the Torrey Botanical Society 129:289–297.

Dobbs, M. 2010. American woodcock (*Scolopax minor*). Pp. 170–171 *in* T. M. Schneider, G. Beaton, T. S. Keyes, and N. A. Klaus, eds., The Breeding Bird Atlas of Georgia. Athens: University of Georgia Press.

Dobey, S., D. V. Masters, B. K. Scheick, J. D. Clark, M. R. Pelton, and M. E. Sunquist. 2005. Ecology of Florida black bears in the Okefenokee-Osceola ecosystem. Wildlife Monographs 158:1–41.

Dodd, C. K., Jr., and B. S. Cade. 1998. Movement patterns and the conservation of amphibians breeding in small, temporary wetlands. Conservation Biology 12:331–339.

Donovan, L. A., J. B. West, and K. W. McLeod. 2000. *Quercus* species differ in water and nutrient characteristics in a resource-limited fall-line sandhill habitat. Tree Physiology 20:929–936.

Dorcas, M. E. 2008. Northern watersnake (*Nerodia sipedon*). Pp. 380–382 *in* J. B. Jensen, C. D. Camp, W. Gibbons, and M. J. Elliott, eds., Amphibians and Reptiles of Georgia. Athens: University of Georgia Press.

Dorcas, M. E., and W. Gibbons. 2008. Glossy crayfish snake (*Regina rigida*). Pp. 393–394 *in* J. B. Jensen, C. D. Camp, W. Gibbons, and M. J. Elliott, eds., Amphibians and Reptiles of Georgia. Athens: University of Georgia Press.

Doyle, T. W., C. P. O'Neil, M. P. V. Melder, A. S. From, and M. M. Palta. 2007. Tidal freshwater swamps of the southeastern United States: Effects of land use, hurricanes, sea-level rise, and climate change. Pp. 1–28 *in* W. H. Conner, T. W. Doyle, and K. W. Krauss, eds., Ecology of Tidal Freshwater Forested Wetlands of the Southeastern United States. The Netherlands: Springer, Dordrecht.

Drew, M. B., L. K. Kirkman, and A. K. Gholson Jr. 1998. The vascular flora of Ichauway, Baker County, Georgia: A remnant longleaf pine/wiregrass ecosystem. Castanea 63:1–24.

Duberstein, J., and W. Kitchens. 2007. Community composition of select areas of tidal freshwater forest along the Savannah River. Pp. 321–349 *in* W. H. Conner, T. W. Doyle, and K. W. Krauss, eds., Ecology of Tidal Freshwater Forested Wetlands of the Southeastern United States. The Netherlands: Springer, Dordrecht.

Duffy, D. C. 1993. Seeing the forest for the trees: Response to Johnson, et al. Conservation Biology 7(2):436–439.

Dugger, B. D., K. M. Dugger, and L. H. Fredrickson. 1994. Hooded merganser (*Lophodytes cucullatus*). *In*

A. Poole and F. Gill, eds., The Birds of North America, no. 98. Philadelphia: Academy of Natural Sciences; Washington, D.C.: American Ornithologists' Union.

Duncan, W. H. 1982. The Vascular Vegetation of Sapelo Island. Botany Department, University of Georgia, and Georgia Department of Natural Resources.

Dunkle, S. W. 2000. Dragonflies Through Binoculars. New York: Oxford University Press.

Dunn, J. L., and J. Alderfer. 2008. National Geographic Field Guide to the Birds of North America. Washington, D.C.: National Geographic.

Dunning, J. B. 1993. Bachman's sparrow (*Aimophila aestivalis*). *In* A. Poole, P. Stettenheim, and F. Gill, eds., The Birds of North America, no. 38. Philadelphia: Academy of Natural Sciences; Washington, D.C.: American Ornithologists' Union.

Earley, L. S. 2004. Looking for Longleaf: The Fall and Rise of an American Forest. Chapel Hill: University of North Carolina Press.

Echols, S. L. 2007. Vascular flora of the remnant blackland prairies and associated vegetation of Georgia. Master's thesis. University of Georgia, Athens.

Edmisten, J. E. 1963. The ecology of the Florida pine flatwoods. Ph.D. dissertation. University of Florida, Gainesville.

Edwards, L. 2010. The land, climate, and vegetation of Georgia. Pp. 148–31 *in* T. M. Schneider, G. Beaton, T. S. Keyes, and N. A. Klaus, eds., The Breeding Bird Atlas of Georgia. Athens: University of Georgia Press.

Edwards, L. 2001. Vegetation dynamics and biogeomorphic influences in a highly eroded landscape. Ph.D. dissertation. University of Georgia, Athens.

Edwards, L., C. Sturm, J. Carles, and C. Stoughton. 1999. The impact of past and present land use on two Georgia Piedmont streams. Pp. 192–195 *in* K. J. Hatcher, ed., Proceedings of the 1999 Georgia Water Resources Conference. University of Georgia, Institute of Ecology, Athens, Ga.

Ehrlich, P. R., D. S. Dubkin, and D. Wheye. 1988. The Birder's Handbook. New York: Simon & Schuster Inc.

Elliott, K. J., and J. M. Vose. 2005. Effects of understory prescribed burning on shortleaf pine (*Pinus echinata* Mill.)/mixed-hardwood forests. Journal of the Torrey Botanical Society 132(2):236–251.

Elliott, K. J., J. M. Vose, B. D. Clinton, and J. K. Knoepp. 2004. Effects of understory burning in a mesic mixed-oak forest of the southern Appalachians. *In* T. Engstrom, K. E. M. Galley, and W. J. de Groot, eds., Proceedings of the 22nd Tall Timbers Fire Ecology Conference: Fire in Temperate, Boreal and Montane Ecosystems. Tallahassee, Fla.: Tall Timbers Research Station.

Elliott, M. J. 2008a. Green salamander (*Aneides aeneus*). Pp. 158–160 *in* J. B. Jensen, C. D. Camp, W. Gibbons, and M. J. Elliott, eds., Amphibians and Reptiles of Georgia. Athens: University of Georgia Press.

Elliott, M. J. 2008b. Four-toed salamander (*Hemidactylium scutatum*). Pp. 211–213 *in* J. B. Jensen, C. D. Camp, W. Gibbons, and M. J. Elliott, eds., Amphibians and Reptiles of Georgia. Athens: University of Georgia Press.

Enge, K. M. 2005. Herpetofaunal drift-fence surveys of steephead ravines in the Florida panhandle. Southeastern Naturalist 4:657–678.

Enge, K. M. 1998. Herpetofaunal survey of an upland hardwood forest in Gadsden County, Florida. Florida Scientist 61:141–159.

Engeman, R. M., A. Stevens, J. Allen, J. Dunlap, M. Dunlap, D. Teague, and B. Constantin. 2007. Feral swine management for conservation of an imperiled wetland habitat: Florida's vanishing seepage slope. Biological Conservation 134:440–446.

Engstrom, R. T. 1993. Characteristic mammals and birds of longleaf pine forests. Pp. 127–138 *in* S. M. Hermann, ed., The Longleaf Pine Ecosystem: Ecology, Restoration and Management. Proceedings of Tall Timbers Fire Ecology Conference 18.

Engstrom, R. T., and F. J. Sanders. 1997. Red-cockaded woodpecker foraging ecology in an old-growth longleaf pine forest. Wilson Bulletin 109:203–217.

Entrekin, S. A., S. W. Golladay, M. Ruhlman, and C. Hedman. 1999. Unique steephead stream segments in southwest Georgia: Invertebrate diversity and biomonitoring. Pp. 295–298 *in* K. J. Hatcher, ed., Proceedings of the 1999 Georgia Water Resources Conference. University of Georgia, Institute of Ecology, Athens, Ga.

Environmental Protection Agency. 2007. Level III Ecoregions of the Continental United States. Available at ftp://ftp.epa.gov/wed/ecoregions/us/Eco_Level_III _US.pdf. last updated October 2, 2007.

Ernst, C. H., and E. M. Ernst. 2003. Snakes of the United States and Canada. Washington, D.C.: Smithsonian Books.

Ernst, C. H., J. E. Lovich, and R. W. Barbour. 1994. Turtles of the United States and Canada. Washington, D.C., and London: Smithsonian Institution Press.

Eschtruth, A. K., and J. J. Battles. 2008. Deer herbivory alters forest response to canopy decline caused by an exotic insect pest. Ecological Applications 18(2): 360–376.

Eubanks, J. O., J. W. Hollister, C. Guyer, and W. K. Michener. 2002. Reserve area requirements for gopher tortoises (*Gopherus polyphemus*). Chelonian Conservation and Biology 4:464–471.

Eubanks, J. O., W. K. Michener, and C. Guyer. 2003. Patterns of movement and burrow use in a population of

gopher tortoises (*Gopherus polyphemus*). Herpetologica 59:311–321.

Evans Ogden, L. J., and B. J. Stutchbury. 1994. Hooded warbler (*Wilsonia citrina*). *In* A. Poole and F. Gill, eds., The Birds of North America, no. 110. Philadelphia: Academy of Natural Sciences; Washington, D.C.: American Ornithologists' Union.

Ewel, K. C. 1998. Pondcypress swamps. Pp. 405–420 *in* M. G. Messina and W. H. Conner, eds., Southern Forested Wetlands: Ecology and Management. Boca Raton, Fla.: Lewis Publishers.

Ewel, K. C. 1995. Fire in cypress swamps in the southeastern United States. Pp. 111–116 *in* S. I. Cerulean and R. T. Engstrom, eds., Fire in Wetlands: A Management Perspective. Proceedings of the Tall Timbers Fire Ecology Conference 19.

Ewel, K. C., and W. J. Mitsch. 1978. The effects of fire on species composition in cypress dome ecosystems. Florida Scientist 41:25–31.

Fabrizio, L., and M. S. Calvi. 2003. Georgia's Marsh Hammocks: A Biological Survey. Southern Environmental Law Center, 200 West Franklin St., Suite 330, Chapel Hill, NC 27516

Fahey, K. M. 2008. Bog turtle (*Clemmys* [*Glyptemys*] *muhlenbergii*). Pp. 472–474 *in* J. B. Jensen, C. D. Camp, W. Gibbons, and M. J. Elliott, eds., Amphibians and Reptiles of Georgia. Athens: University of Georgia Press.

Falls, W. F., L. G. Harrelson, K. J. Conlon, and M. D. Petkewich. 2001. Hydrogeology and water quality of the lower Floridan aquifer, Coastal Georgia, 1999–2000. Pp. 652–655 *in* K. J. Hatcher, ed., Proceedings of the 2001 Georgia Water Resources Conference. University of Georgia, Institute of Ecology, Athens, Ga.

Falls, W. F., C. Ransom, J. E. Landmeyer, E. J. Reuber, and L. E. Edwards. 2005. Hydrogeology, Water Quality, and Saltwater Intrusion in the Upper Floridan Aquifer in the Offshore Area near Hilton Head Island, South Carolina, and Tybee Island, Georgia, 1999–2002. U.S. Geological Survey Scientific Investigations Report 2005–5134.

Faust, W. Z. 1976. A vegetation analysis of the Georgia fall-line sandhills. Rhodora 78:525–531.

Fenster, M., and R. Dolan. 1996. Assessing the impact of tidal inlets on adjacent barrier island shorelines. Journal of Coastal Research 12(1):294–310.

Fergus, C. 2003. Wildlife of Virginia and Maryland. Mechanicsburg, Pa.: Stackpole Books.

Ferguson, B. K. 1997. Flood and sediment interpretation at the historic Scull Shoals mill. Pp. 253–256 *in* K. J. Hatcher, ed., Proceedings of the 1997 Georgia Water Resources Conference. University of Georgia, Institute of Ecology, Athens, Ga.

Ferrari, J. B. 2010. Pine warbler (*Dendroica pinus*). Pp. 338–339 *in* T. M. Schneider, G. Beaton, T. S. Keyes, and

N. A. Klaus, eds., The Breeding Bird Atlas of Georgia. Athens: University of Georgia Press.

Fesenmyer, K. A., and N. L. Christensen, Jr. 2010. Reconstructing Holocene fire history in a southern Appalachian forest using soil charcoal. Ecology 91(3):662–670.

Finucane, J. H. 1969. Ecology of the pompano (*Trachinotus carolinus*) and the permit (*T. falcatus*) in Florida. Transactions of the American Fisheries Society 98: 437–456.

Fisher, H. M., and E. L. Stone. 1990. Air-conducting porosity in slash pine roots from saturated soils. Forest Science 36:18–33.

Fitch, H. S. 1960. Autecology of the copperhead. University of Kansas Publications, Museum of Natural History 13:85–288.

Fitz, H. C., and R. G. Wiegert. 1991. Utilization of the intertidal zone of a salt marsh by the blue crab, *Callinectes sapidus*: Density, return frequency, and feeding habits. Marine Ecology Progress Series 76:249–260.

Floyd, T. M. 2008a. American toad (*Bufo [Anaxyrus] americanus*). Pp. 36–38 *in* J. B. Jensen, C. D. Camp, W. Gibbons, and M. J. Elliott, eds., Amphibians and Reptiles of Georgia. Athens: University of Georgia Press.

Floyd, T. M. 2008b. Mole salamander (*Ambystoma talpoideum*). Pp. 142–144 *in* J. B. Jensen, C. D. Camp, W. Gibbons, and M. J. Elliott, eds., Amphibians and Reptiles of Georgia. Athens: University of Georgia Press.

Floyd, T. M., and C. D. Camp. 2008. Spotted dusky salamander (*Desmognathus conanti*). Pp. 169–171 *in* J. B. Jensen, C. D. Camp, W. Gibbons, and M. J. Elliott, eds., Amphibians and Reptiles of Georgia. Athens: University of Georgia Press.

Folkerts, G. W. 1991. A preliminary classification of pitcher plant habitats in the southeastern United States. Journal of the Alabama Academy of Science 62:199–225.

Folkerts, G. W. 1982. The Gulf Coast pitcher plant bogs. American Scientist 70:260–267.

Folkerts, G. W., M. A. Deyrup, and D. C. Sisson. 1993. Arthropods associated with xcric longleaf pine habitats in the southeastern United States: A brief overview. Pp. 159–192 *in* S. M. Hermann, ed., The Longleaf Pine Ecosystem: Ecology, Restoration and Management. Proceedings of Tall Timbers Fire Ecology Conference 18.

Fonda, R. W. 2001. Burning characteristics of needles from eight pine species. Forest Science 47:390–396.

Ford, W. M., B. R. Chapman, M. A. Menzel, and R. H. Odom. 2002. Stand-age and habitat influences on salamanders in Appalachian cove hardwood forests. Forest Ecology and Management 155:131–141.

Foskett, K. 2006. Plans endanger bears' habitat, developer wants homes on forestland. Atlanta Journal Constitution, November 19 (Main Edition), Section E1. Available at http:www.ajc.com.

Fowler, C., and E. Konopik. 2007. The history of fire in the southeastern United States. Human Ecology Review 14(2):165–176.

Franz, R. 2005. Up close and personal: A glimpse into the life of the Florida pine snake in a north Florida sand hill. Pp. 120–131 *in* W. E. Meshaka Jr. and K. J. Babbitt, eds., Amphibians and Reptiles: Status and Conservation in Florida. Malabar, Fla.: Krieger Press.

Franz, R. 1992. Florida pine snake, *Pituophis melanoleucus mugitus* Barbour. Pp. 254–258 in P. E. Moler, ed., Rare and Endangered Biota of Florida. Vol. III. Amphibians and Reptiles. Gainesville: University Press of Florida.

Freshley, P. D. 2006. Understanding soils and soil fertility. *In* K. Kammermeyer, K. V. Miller, and L. Thomas, eds., Quality Food Plots. Quality Deer Management Association.

Frey, R. W., and P. B. Basan. 1985. Coastal salt marshes. Pp. 225–301 *in* R. A. Davis Jr., ed., Coastal Sedimentary Environments. 2nd ed. New York: Springer-Verlag.

Frey, R. W., and J. D. Howard. 1969. A profile of biogenic sedimentary structures in a Holocene barrier island-salt marsh complex, Georgia. Transactions of the Gulf Coast Association of Geological Societies 19:427–444.

Frick, E. A., M. B. Gregory, D. L. Calhoun, and E. H. Hopkins. 2002. Water Quality and Aquatic Communities of Upland Wetlands, Cumberland Island National Seashore, Georgia, April 1999 to July 2000. U.S. Geological Survey, Water Resources Investigations Report 02-4082.

Frost, C. C. 2006. History and future of the longleaf pine ecosystem. Pp. 9–42 *in* S. Jose, E. J. Jokela, and D. L. Miller, eds., The Longleaf Pine Ecosystem: Ecology, Silviculture, and Restoration. New York: Springer Science Business Media, LLC.

Frost, C. C. 1998. Presettlement fire frequency regimes of the United States: A first approximation. Pp. 70–81 *in* Proceedings of the 20th Tall Timbers Fire Ecology Conference; Fire in Ecosystem Management: Shifting the Paradigm from Suppression to Prescription, May 7–10, 1996, Boise, Idaho. Tallahassee: Tall Timbers Research Station.

Frost, C. C., J. Walker, and R. K. Peet. 1986. Fire-dependent savannahs and prairies of the southeast: Original extent, preservation status, and management problems. Pp. 348–357 *in* D. L. Kulhavy and R. N. Conner, eds., Wilderness and Natural Areas in the Eastern United States: A Management Challenge. Nacogdoches, Tex.: Center for Applied

Sciences, School of Forestry, Stephen F. Austin State University.

Gaddy, L. L. 2000. A Naturalist's Guide to the Southern Blue Ridge Front. Columbia: University of South Carolina Press.

Gaddy, L. L. 1988. Biological Investigations of Tallulah Gorge and Other Georgia Power FERC License Project, no. 2354, Lands in Northeastern Georgia.

Gagnon, P. R., W. J. Platt, and E. B. Moser. 2007. Response of a native bamboo [*Arundinaria gigantea* (Walt.) Muhl] in a wind-disturbed forest. Forest Ecology and Management 241:288–294.

Gaines, K. F., A. L. Bryan Jr., P. M. Dixon, and M. J. Harris. 1998. Foraging habitat use by wood storks nesting in the coastal zone of Georgia, USA. Colonial Waterbirds 21:43–52.

Gallagher, J. L., and F. G. Plumley. 1979. Underground biomass profiles and productivity in Atlantic coastal marshes. American Journal of Botany 66:156–161.

Gallagher, J. L., and R. J. Reimold. 1973. Tidal marsh plant distribution and productivity patterns from the sea to fresh water—a challenge in resolution and discrimination. Pp. 165–181 *in* S. S. Cooper, R. L. Vadas, and S. E. Manzer, eds., Proceedings of the 4th Biennial Workshop on Color Aerial Photography. Falls Church, Va.: American Society of Photogrammetry.

Gallagher, J. L., R. J. Reimold, R. A. Linthurst, and W. J. Pfeiffer. 1980. Aerial production, mortality, and mineral accumulation-export dynamics in *Spartina alterniflora* and *Juncus roemerianus* plant stands. Ecology 61:303–312.

Gammons, D. J., M. T. Mengak, and L. M. Conner. 2009. Armadillo habitat selection in southwestern Georgia. Journal of Mammalogy 90:356–362.

Georgia Department of Natural Resources. 2012. Mink Fact Sheet. Available at http://georgiawildlife.com/node/898. Accessed January 15, 2012.

Georgia Department of Natural Resources. 2010. Conserving Georgia's Nongame Wildlife: 2008–2009 Report. Wildlife Resources Division, Nongame Conservation Section, Social Circle.

Georgia Department of Natural Resources. 2009a. Georgia Invasive Species Strategy. Wildlife Resources Division, Social Circle.

Georgia Department of Natural Resources. 2009b. The State of Georgia's Environment. 2009. Atlanta: Environmental Protection Division.

Georgia Department of Natural Resources. 2009c. Wildlife Resources Division Nongame Conservation Section.. Zahnd Natural Area, Walker County, Georgia: Fifty-Year Site Management Plan 2008–2058. Social Circle, Ga. Unpublished report.

Georgia Department of Natural Resources. 2007a. Conserving Georgia's Nongame Wildlife: 2004–2007 Report. Wildlife Resources Division, Nongame Conservation Section, Social Circle.

Georgia Department of Natural Resources. 2007b. Georgia Coastal Management Program: Legislative Report of Accomplishments, 2003–2007. Coastal Resources Division, Brunswick.

Georgia Department of Natural Resources. 2005a. A Comprehensive Wildlife Conservation Strategy for Georgia. Social Circle, Ga.: Georgia Department of Natural Resources, Georgia Wildlife Resources Division.

Georgia Department of Natural Resources. 2005b. Rabbit Fact Sheet. Available at http://www.georgiawildlife.com.

Georgia Department of Natural Resources. 2005c. Skunk Fact Sheet. Wildlife Resources Division, Social Circle. Available at http://www.georgiawildlife.com.

Georgia Department of Natural Resources. 2004. Fox Fact Sheet. Available at http://www.georgiawildlife.com.

Georgia Department of Natural Resources. 2003. Beaver Fact Sheet. Available at http://www.georgiawildlife.com.

Georgia Department of Natural Resources. 2002a. Report of the Coastal Marsh Hammocks Advisory Council. Atlanta: Georgia Department of Natural Resources.

Georgia Department of Natural Resources. 2002b. Water Quality Assessment. Environmental Protection Division. Atlanta.

Georgia Department of Natural Resources. 2001a. Alligator Fact Sheet. Available at http://www.georgiawildlife.com.

Georgia Department of Natural Resources. 2001b. A Guide to Georgia Wetlands. Wildlife Resources Division, Nongame Wildlife & Natural Heritage Section. Social Circle, Ga. Unpublished report.

Georgia Department of Natural Resources. 2001c. Ossabaw Island Comprehensive Management Plan. Wildlife Resources Division. Social Circle, Ga. Unpublished report.

Georgia Department of Natural Resources. 1999. Protected Animals of Georgia. Forsyth: Georgia Department of Natural Resources.

Georgia Department of Natural Resources. 1990. Sapelo Island National Estuarine Research Reserve Management Plan. National Estuarine Research Reserve Program, Washington, D.C.: U.S. Department of Commerce.

Georgia Museum of Natural History. 2008. Marsh rabbit (*Sylvilagus palustris*). Available at http://dromus.nhm.uga.edu/~GMNH/gawildlife/index.php?page=speciespages/species_page&key=spalustris.

Georgia Office of Planning and Budget. 2010. Georgia 2030: Population Projections. Last updated March 2010.

Available at http://opb.georgia.gov/vgn/images/portal /cit_1210/6/63/162904242georgia%20population%20 projections%20-%20march%202010.pdf.

Georgia Wildlife Web. 2008. University of Georgia Museum of Natural History. Available at http:// naturalhistory.uga.edu/~GMNH/gawildlife/index.php.

Gerber, A. S., and A. R. Templeton. 1996. Population sizes and within-deme movements of *Trimerotropis saxatilis* (Acrididae), a grasshopper with a fragmented distribution. Oecologia 105:343–350.

Gibbons, J. W., and J. W. Coker. 1978. Herpetofaunal colonization patterns of Atlantic Coast barrier islands. American Midland Naturalist 99:219–233.

Gibbons, J. W., and M. E. Dorcas. 2004. North American Watersnakes: A Natural History. Norman: University of Oklahoma Press.

Gibbons, J. W., and R. D. Semlitsch. 1981. Terrestrial drift fences with pitfall traps: An effective technique for quantitative sampling of animal populations. Brimleyana 7:1–16.

Giles, R. T., and O. H. Pilkey. 1965. Atlantic beach and dune sediments of the southern United States. Journal of Sedimentary Petrology 35(4):900–910.

Glasser, J. E. 1986. Pattern, diversity and succession of vegetation in Chase Prairie, Okefenokee Swamp: A hierarchical study. Ph.D. dissertation. University of Georgia, Athens.

Glasser, J. E. 1985. Successional trends on tree islands in the Okefenokee Swamp as determined by interspecific association analysis. American Midland Naturalist 113:287–293.

Glaudas, X. 2008. Pigmy rattlesnake (*Sistrurus miliarius*). Pp. 437–439 *in* J. B. Jensen, C. D. Camp, W. Gibbons, and M. J. Elliott, eds., Amphibians and Reptiles of Georgia. Athens: University of Georgia Press.

Glitzenstein, J. S., D. R. Streng, R. E. Masters, and W. J. Platt. 2008. Clarifying long-term impacts of fire frequency and fire season in southeastern Coastal Plain pine savannas. Pp. 14–24 *in* W. Stringer, J. Andrae, and G. Yarrow, eds., Managing an Ecosystem on the Edge: Proceedings of the 6th Eastern Native Grass Symposium.

Glitzenstein, J. S., D. R. Streng, and D. D. Wade. 2003. Fire frequency effects on longleaf pine (*Pinus palutris* P. Miller) vegetation in South Carolina and northeast Florida, USA. Natural Areas Journal 23:22–37.

Gobris, N. 2010. Bachman's sparrow (*Aimophila aestivalis*). Pp. 374–375 *in* T. M. Schneider, G. Beaton, T. S. Keyes, and N. A. Klaus, eds., The Breeding Bird Atlas of Georgia. Athens: University of Georgia Press.

Godfrey, M. A. 1997. Field Guide to the Piedmont. Chapel Hill: University of North Carolina Press.

Godfrey, P. J. 1976. Comparative ecology of East Coast barrier islands: Hydrology, soil, vegetation. *In* Barrier Island and Beaches: Technical Proceedings of the 1976 Barrier Island Workshop. Annapolis, Md.: The Conservation Foundation.

Godt, M. J. W., and J. L. Hamrick. 1999. Population genetic analysis of *Elliottia racemosa* (Ericaceae), a rare Georgia shrub. Molecular Ecology 8:75–82.

Godwin, J. C. 2008a. Pickerel frog (*Rana* [*Lithobates*] *palustris*). Pp. 118–120 *in* J. B. Jensen, C. D. Camp, W. Gibbons, and M. J. Elliott, eds., Amphibians and Reptiles of Georgia. Athens: University of Georgia Press.

Godwin, J. C. 2008b. Long-tailed salamander (*Eurycea longicauda*). Pp. 192–194 *in* J. B. Jensen, C. D. Camp, W. Gibbons, and M. J. Elliott, eds., Amphibians and Reptiles of Georgia. Athens: University of Georgia Press.

Goebel, P. C., B. J. Palik, L. K. Kirkman, M. B. Drew, L. West, and D. C. Pederson. 2001. Forest ecosystems of a Lower Gulf Coastal Plain landscape: Multifactor classification and analysis. Journal of the Torrey Botanical Society 128:47–75.

Golladay, S. W., and J. M. Battle. 2002. Effects of flooding and drought on water quality in Gulf Coastal Plain streams in Georgia. Journal of Environmental Quality 31:1266–1272.

Golladay, S. W., G. P. Gagon, M. Kearns, J. M. Battle, and D. W. Hicks. 2004. Response of freshwater mussel assemblages (Bivalvia: Unionidae) to record drought in the Gulf Coastal Plain of southwest Georgia. Journal of the North American Benthological Society 23: 494–506.

Golladay, S. W., B. W. Taylor, and B. J. Palik. 1997. Invertebrate communities of forested limesink wetlands in southwest Georgia, USA: Habitat use and influence of extended inundation. Wetlands 17:383–393.

Gomez, C. H. 2003. Flora of New Echota State Historic Site. Tipularia 18:24–35.

Gordon, D. M. 1984. The harvester ant (*Pogonomyrmex badius*) midden: Refuse or boundary? Ecological Entomology 9:403–412.

Gore, J. A., and F. D. Shields Jr. 1995. Can large rivers be restored? BioScience 45:142–152.

Govus, T. E. 2003a. Ecological Reconnaissance of Prairie Related Communities Associated with the Temple-Inland Flatwoods Conservation Easement Site. Unpublished report to Temple-Inland.

Govus, T. E. 2003b. Plant Association Descriptions and Vegetation Mapping of the Chicopee Woods Nature Preserve. Unpublished report to the Elachee Nature Science Center.

Govus, T. E. 2002a. Notes on Shortleaf Pine Ecosystems and Restoration Efforts in the Southern Appalachians. Unpublished NatureServe report prepared for the U.S. Department of Agriculture Forest Service, Cherokee National Forest.

Govus, T. E. 2002b. Summary Report: Protected Plant Survey of High Elevation Rock Outcrop Areas on the Chattahoochee National Forest, Georgia. Unpublished report submitted to the Chattahoochee-Oconee National Forest and The Georgia Natural Heritage Program.

Govus, T. E. 2001. Summary Report Survey on Plant Survey of Ultramafic Outcrop Barren in Chattahoochee National Forest, Georgia. Unpublished report submitted to the Chattahoochee-Oconee Forest.

Gowaty, P. A., and J. H. Plissner. 1998. Eastern bluebird (*Sialia sialis*). *In* A. Poole and F. Gill, eds., The Birds of North America, no. 381. Philadelphia: The Birds of North America, Inc.

Graeter, G. J. 2008. Green anole (*Anolis carolinensis*). Pp. 296–298 *in* J. B. Jensen, C. D. Camp, W. Gibbons, and M. J. Elliott, eds., Amphibians and Reptiles of Georgia. Athens: University of Georgia Press.

Graham, A. 2008. Chapter 3; History of North American Vegetation—Cretaceous (Maastrichtian)—Tertiary *in* Flora of North America. Available at http://www.fna.org/Volume/V01/Chapter03.

Graham, A. 1999. Late Cretaceous and Cenozoic History of North American Vegetation. Oxford: Oxford University Press.

Gray, A. 1875. A pilgrimage to Torreya. American Agriculturist 34:266–267. Reprinted: Scientific papers of Asa Gray. 1:188–195, 1889.

Greear, P. F. 1967. Composition, diversity and structure of some natural ponds in northwest Georgia. Ph.D. dissertation. University of Georgia, Athens.

Green, R. E. 1989. St. Simons Island: A Brief Summary of its History. Rome, N.Y.: Arner Publications.

Greenberg, C. H. 2001. Spatio-temporal dynamics of pond use and recruitment in Florida gopher frogs (*Rana capito aesopus*). Journal of Herpetology 35:74–85.

Greenberg, C. H., and R. W. Simons. 1999. Age, composition, and stand structure of old-growth oak sites in the Florida high pine landscape: Implications for ecosystem management and restoration. Natural Areas Journal 19:39–40.

Greenlaw, J. S. 1996. Eastern towhee (*Pipilo erythrophthalmus*). *In* A. Poole and F. Gill, eds., The Birds of North America, no. 262. Philadelphia: Academy of Natural Sciences; Washington, D.C.: American Ornithologists' Union.

Greer, G. C. 2008. Cope's gray treefrog (*Hyla chrysoscelis*). Pp. 56–58 *in* J. B. Jensen, C. D. Camp, W. Gibbons, and M. J. Elliott, eds., Amphibians and Reptiles of Georgia. Athens: University of Georgia Press.

Griffith, G. E., and J. M. Omernik. 2008. Ecoregions of Alabama and Georgia (EPA). *In* J. Cutler, ed., Encyclopedia of Earth. Washington, D.C.: Environmental Information Coalition, National Council for Science and the Environment). Available at http://www.eoearth.org/article/Ecoregions_of_Alabama_and_Georgia_(EPA).

Griffith, G. E., J. M. Omernik, J. A. Comstock, S. Lawrence, G. Martin, A. Goddard, V. J. Hulcher, and T. Foster. 2001. Ecoregions of Alabama and Georgia (color poster with map, descriptive text, summary tables, and photographs). Reston, Va.: U.S. Geological Survey (map scale 1:1,700,000).

Griffith, R. S. 1991. *Fraxinus americana. In* Fire Effects Information System. Available at http://www.fs.fed.us/database/feis/.

Grime, J. P. 2001. Plant Strategies, Vegetation Processes, and Ecosystem Properties. 2nd ed. Chichester, England: Wiley.

Grossman, D. H., D. Faber-Langendoen, A. S. Weakley, M. Anderson, P. Bourgeron, R. Crawford, K. Goodin, S. Landaal, K. Metzler, K. D. Patterson, M. Pyne, M. Reid, and L. Sneddon. 1998. International Classification of Ecological Communities: Terrestrial Vegetation of the United States. Vol. I. The National Vegetation Classification System: Development, Status, and Applications. Arlington, Va.: The Nature Conservancy.

Guerin, D. N. 1993. Oak dome clonal structure and fire ecology in a Florida longleaf pine dominated community. Bulletin of the Torrey Botanical Club 120:107–114.

Guilday, J. E. 1971. The Pleistocene history of the Appalachian mammal fauna. Pp. 233–262 *in* P. C. Holt, R. A. Patterson, and J. P. Hubbard, eds., The Distributional History of the Biota of the Southern Appalachians. Part III: Vertebrates. Blacksburg: Virginia Polytechnic Institute and State University.

Gunter, H. 1921. Florida Geological Survey Report 13: 207–209.

Guzy, M. J., and G. Ritchison. 1999. Common yellowthroat (*Geothlypis trichas*). *In* A. Poole and F. Gill, eds., The Birds of North America, no. 448. Philadelphia: The Birds of North America, Inc.

Hails, J. R., and J. H. Hoyt. 1969. An appraisal of the evolution of the lower Atlantic coastal plain of Georgia, USA. Transactions of the Institute of British Geographers 46:53–68.

Hainds, M. J., R. J. Mitchell, B. J. Palik, L. R. Boring, and D. H. Gjerstad. 1999. Distribution of native legumes (Leguminoseae) in frequently burned longleaf pine

(Pinaceae)-wiregrass (Poaceae) ecosystems. American Journal of Botany 86:1606–1614.

Hamas, M. J. 1994. Belted kingfisher (*Ceryle alcyon*). *In* A. Poole and F. Gill, eds., The Birds of North America, no. 84. Philadelphia: Academy of Natural Sciences; Washington, D.C.: American Ornithologists' Union.

Hamel, P. B. 2000. Cerulean warbler (*Dendroica cerulea*). *In* A. Poole and F. Gill, eds., The Birds of North America, no. 84. Philadelphia: Academy of Natural Sciences; Washington, D.C.: American Ornithologists' Union.

Hamilton, D. B. 1984. Plant succession and the influence of disturbance in the Okefenokee Swamp. Pp. 86–111 *in* A. D. Cohen, D. J. Casagrande, M. J. Andrejko, and G. R. Best, eds., The Okefenokee Swamp: Its Natural History, Geology, and Geochemistry. Los Alamos, N.M.: Wetland Surveys.

Hamilton, R. B., W. C. Barrow Jr., and K. Ouchley. 2005. Old-growth bottomland hardwood forests as bird habitat: Implications for contemporary forest management. Pp. 373–388 *in* L. H. Frederickson, S. L. King, and R. M. Kaminski, eds., Ecology and Management of Bottomland Hardwood Systems: The State of Our Understanding. Gaylord Memorial Laboratory Special Publication no. 10. Puxico: University of Missouri-Columbia.

Hanners, L. A., and S. R. Patton. 1998. Worm-eating warbler (*Helimitheros vermivorus*). *In* A. Poole and F. Gill, eds., The Birds of North America, no. 367. Philadelphia: The Birds of North America, Inc.

Hanski, I., and D. Y. Zhang. 1993. Migration, meta-population dynamics, and fugitive co-existence. Journal of Theoretical Biology 163:491–504.

Hanula, J. L., S. Horn, and J. W. Taylor. 2009. Chinese privet (*Ligustrum sinense*) removal and its effect on native plant communities of riparian forests. Invasive Plant Science and Management 2:292–300.

Hardin, E. D., and D. L. White. 1989. Rare vascular plant taxa associated with wiregrass (*Aristida stricta*) in the southeastern forest lands. Natural Areas Journal 9: 234–245.

Harmon, M. E., S. P. Bratton, and P. S. White. 1983. Disturbance and vegetation response in relation to environmental gradients in the Great Smoky Mountains. Vegetatio 55:129–139.

Harms, W. R., W. M. Aust, and J. A. Burger. 1998. Wet flatwoods. Pp. 421–444 *in* M. G. Messina and W. H. Conner, eds., Southern Forested Wetlands: Ecology and Management. Boca Raton, Fla.: Lewis Publishers.

Harper, F. 1998. The Travels of William Bartram: Naturalist edition. Athens: University of Georgia Press.

Harper, F., and D. E. Presley. 1981. Okefenokee Album. Athens: University of Georgia Press.

Harper, R. M. 1943. Forests of Alabama. Geological Survey of Alabama, Monograph 10.

Harper, R. M. 1909. Okefinokee Swamp. Popular Science Monthly 74:596–614.

Harper, R. M. 1906. A phytogeographic sketch of the Altamaha Grit region of the coastal plain of Georgia. Annals of the New York Academy of Science 17:241–25.

Harper, R. M. 1905a. "Hammock," "hommock" or "hummock"? Science 22:400–402.

Harper, R. M. 1905b. Phytogeographical explorations in the Coastal Plain of Georgia in 1903. Bulletin of the Torrey Botanical Club 32:141–171.

Harris, L. C., Jr. 1972. Butterflies of Georgia. Norman: University of Oklahoma Press.

Harris, M. J. 1999. Wood stork (*Mycteria americana*). Pp. 52–53 *in* T. W. Johnson, J. C. Ozier, J. L. Bohannon, J. B. Jensen, and C. Skelton, eds., Protected Animals of Georgia. Georgia Department of Natural Resources, Wildlife Resources Division, Nongame Wildlife–Natural Heritage Section.

Harrison, J. R. 2005. *Desmognathus aeneus*. Pp. 696–698 *in* M. Lannoo, ed., Declining Amphibians: The Conservation Status of United States Species. Berkeley: University of California Press.

Harrison, K. A., and A. Tyson. 2001. Agricultural irrigation trends in Georgia. Pp. 114–117 *in* K. J. Hatcher, ed., Proceedings of the Georgia 2001 Water Resources Conference. University of Georgia, Institute of Ecology, Athens, Ga.

Harrod, J., P. S. White, and M. E. Harmon. 1998. Changes in xeric forests in western Great Smoky Mountains National Park, 1936–1995. Castanea 63(3):346–360.

Harrod, J. C., M. E. Harmon, and P. S. White. 2000. Post-fire succession and 20th century reduction in fire frequency on xeric southern Appalachian sites. Journal of Vegetation Science 11:465–472.

Hartley, M. E., and H. M. Penley. 1974. The Lake Chatuge Sill Outlining the Brasstown Antiform. Georgia Geological Society Guidebook 13. Georgia Department of Natural Resources.

Harvey, M. J., J. S. Altenbach, and T. L. Best. 1999. Bats of the United States. Little Rock: Arkansas Game and Fish Commission.

Hatton, R. S. 1981. Aspects of marsh accretion and geochemistry: Barrataria Basin, Louisiana. Master's thesis. Louisiana State University, Baton Rouge.

Hawkins, B. 1799. A Sketch of the Creek Country in the Years 1798–1799. Reprint of Vol. III, Part I, Georgia Historical Society. Americus, Ga.: American Book Company, 1938.

Hayes, M. O. 1994. The Georgia Bight barrier system. Pp. 223–304 *in* R. A. Davis, ed., Geology of Holocene Barrier Island Systems. Berlin: Springer-Verlag.

Hayes, M. O. 1979. Barrier island morphology as a function of tidal and wave regime. Pp. 1–28 *in* S. P. Leatherman, ed., Barrier Islands. New York: Academic Press.

Hedman, C. W., S. L. Grace, and S. E. King. 2000. Vegetation composition and structure of southern Coastal Plain pine forests: An ecological comparison. Forest Ecology and Management 134:233–247.

Heikens, A. L. 1999. Savannas, barrens, and glade communities of the Ozark Plateaus Province. Pp. 220–230 *in* R. C. Anderson, J. S. Fralish, and J. M. Baskin, eds., Savannas, Barrens, and Rock Outcrop Plant Communities of North America. Cambridge: Cambridge University Press.

Heimlich, R. E., K. D. Wiebe, R. Claassen, D. Gadsby, and R. M. House. 1998. Wetlands and Agriculture: Private Interests and Public Benefits. Resource Economics Division, Economic Research Service, U.S. Department of Agriculture. Agricultural Economic Report No. 765.

Hein, C. D., S. B. Castleberry, and K. V. Miller. 2008. Male Seminole bat winter roost-site selection in a managed forest. Journal of Wildlife Management 72:1756–1764.

Hein, C. D., S. B. Castleberry, and K. V. Miller. 2005. Winter roost-site selection by Seminole bats in the Lower Coastal Plain of South Carolina. Southeastern Naturalist 4:473–478.

Helfman, G. S., E. L. Bozeman, and E. B. Brothers. 1984. Size, sex, and age of American eels in a Georgia river. Transactions of the American Fisheries Society 113: 132–141.

Helton, R. C., L. K. Kirkman, and L. J. Musselman. 2000. Host preference of the federally endangered hemiparasite *Schwalbea americana* L. (Scrophulariaceae). Journal of the Torrey Botanical Society 127:300–306.

Hendricks, E. L., and M. H. Goodwin Jr. 1952. Water-level Fluctuations in Limestone Sinks in Southwestern Georgia. U.S. Geological Survey, Geologic Survey Water-Supply Paper 1110–E.

Hendricks, J. J., and L. R. Boring. 1999. N_2-fixation by native herbaceous legumes in burned pine ecosystems of the southeastern United States. Forest Ecology and Management 113:167–177.

Hepp, G. R., and F. C. Bellrose. 1995. Wood duck (*Aix sponsa*). *In* A. Poole and F. Gill, eds., The Birds of North America, no. 169. Philadelphia: Academy of Natural Sciences,; Washington, D.C.: American Ornithologists' Union.

Herkert, J. R., C. M. Nixon, and L. P. Hansen. 1992. Dynamics of exploited and unexploited fox squirrel (*Sciurus niger*) populations in the midwestern United States. Pp. 864–874 *in* D. R. McCullough and R. H. Barrett, eds., Wildlife 2001: Populations. New York: Elsevier Applied Science.

Hermann, S. 2009. Fire regime of coastal marshes. *In* Forest Encyclopedia Network. Available at http://www.forestencyclopedia.net/p/p4/p142/p154/p213. Accessed July 12, 2009.

Hermann, S. M., J. S. Kush, and J. P. Stowe Jr. 2008. Fire in montane/piedmont longleaf forests: An overview. Pp. 2–8 *in* J. S. Kush and S. M. Hermann, comps., Proceedings of the Third Montane Longleaf Conference, March 11–12, 2008, Auburn University, Alabama. Longleaf Alliance Report no. 13.

Herrington, B. 2008. Barking treefrog (*Hyla gratiosa*). Pp. 65–67 *in* J. B. Jensen, C. D. Camp, W. Gibbons, and M. J. Elliott, eds., Amphibians and Reptiles of Georgia. Athens: University of Georgia Press.

Hess, C. A., and F. C. James. 1998. Diet of the red-cockaded woodpecker in the Apalachicola National Forest. Journal of Wildlife Management 62:509–517.

Hester, J. J. 1970. Ecology of the North American paleo-Indian. BioScience 20(4):213–217.

Heyward, F. 1939. The relation of fire to stand composition of longleaf pine forests. Ecology 20:287–304.

Hicks, D. W. 1995. The Independence Day Flood of 1994 and effects on water levels in the Upper Floridan Aquifer, Albany area, Georgia. Proceedings of the 1995 Georgia Water Resources Conference, University of Georgia, Institute of Ecology, Athens, Ga.

Hicks, D. W., H. E. Gill, and S. A. Longsworth. 1987. Hydrogeology, chemical quality, and availability of groundwater in the upper Floridan aquifer, Albany area, Georgia. U.S. Geological Survey, Water-Resource Investigations Report 87–4145.

Hiers, J. K., R. Wyatt, and R. J. Mitchell. 2000. The effects of fire regime on legume reproduction in longleaf pine savannas: Is a season selective? Oecologia 125:521–530.

Highton, R. 1962. Geographic variation in the life history of the slimy salamander. Copeia 1962:597–613.

Highton, R., and R. B. Peabody. 2000. Geographic protein variation and speciation in salamanders of the *Plethodon jordani* and *Plethodon glutinosus* complexes in the southern Appalachian Mountains with the description of four new species. Pp. 31–93 *in* R. C. Bruce, R. G. Jaeger, and L. D. Houck, eds., The Biology of *Plethodontid* Salamanders. New York: Klewer Academic /Plenum Publishers.

Hill, J. G. 2009. The grasshopper (Orthoptera: Acrididae) fauna of sand dunes along the Little Ohoopee River, Emanuel County, Georgia, USA. Journal of Orthoptera Research 18:29–35.

Hillestad, H. O., J. R. Bozeman, A. S. Johnson, C. W. Berisford, and J. I. Richardson. 1975. The Ecology of Cumberland Island National Seashore, Camden County, Georgia. Georgia Marine Science Center Technical Report Serial 75–5.

Hinkle, C. R., W. C. McComb, J. M. Safley Jr., and P. A. Schmalzer. 1993. Mixed mesophytic forests. Pp. 1–34 *in* W. H. Martin, S. G. Boyce, and A. C. Echternacht, eds., Biodiversity of the Southeastern United States: Upland Terrestrial Communities. New York: Wiley.

Hobbs, H. H., Jr. 1981. The crayfishes of Georgia. Smithsonian Contributions to Zoology, no. 318.

Hodges, A. W. 2006. The naval stores industry. Pp. 43–48 *in* S. Jose, E. J. Jokela, and D. L. Miller, eds., The Longleaf Pine Ecosystem: Ecology, Silviculture, and Restoration. New York: Springer Science Business Media, LLC.

Hodges, J. D. 1998. Minor alluvial floodplains. Pp. 325–341 *in* M. G. Messina and W. H. Conner, eds., Southern Forested Wetlands: Ecology and Management. Boca Raton, Fla.: Lewis Publishers.

Hodges, J. D, W. W. Elam, W. F. Watson, and T. E. Nebeker. 1979. Oleoresin characteristics and susceptibility of four southern pines to southern pine beetle (Coleoptera: Scolytidae) attacks. Canadian Entomologist 111:889–896.

Hodges, M. F., Jr. 2010. Common ground-dove (*Columbina passerina*). Pp. 190–191 *in* T. M. Schneider, G. Beaton, T. S. Keyes, and N. A. Klaus, eds., The Breeding Bird Atlas of Georgia. Athens: University of Georgia Press.

Hodler, T., and H. A. Schretter. 1986. The Atlas of Georgia. Athens: Institute of Community and Area Development, University of Georgia, p. 14.

Hofslund, P. B. 1959. A life history of the yellowthroat *Geothlypis trichas*. Proceedings of the Minnesota Academy of Science 27:144–174.

Holland, W. J. 1968. The Moth Book: A Popular Guide to Knowledge of the Moths of North America. New York: Dover Publications.

Hölldobler, B. 1971. *Steatoda fulva* (Theridiidae), a spider that feeds on harvester ants. Psyche 77:202–208.

Holman, J. A. 1967. A Pleistocene herpetofauna from Ladds, Georgia. Bulletin of the Georgia Academy of Sciences 25(3):154–166.

Hook, D. D. 1984. Adaptations to flooding with fresh water. Pp. 265–294 *in* T. T. Kozlowski, ed., Flooding and Plant Growth. New York: Academic Press.

Hooper, R. G., M. R. Lennartz, and H. D. Muse. 1991. Heart rot and cavity tree selection by red-cockaded woodpeckers. Journal of Wildlife Management 55:323–327.

Hopkins, J. M. 1947. Forty-five years with the Okefenokee Swamp. Bulletin of the Georgia Society of Naturalists 4:1–69.

Hopp, S. L., A. Kirby, and C. A. Boone. 1995. White-eyed vireo (*Vireo griseus*). *In* A. Poole and F. Gill, eds., The Birds of North America, no. 168. Philadelphia: Academy of Natural Sciences; Washington, D.C.: American Ornithologists' Union.

Hotchkin, P. E., C. D. Camp, and J. L. Marshall. 2001. Aspects of the life history and ecology of the coal skink, *Eumeces anthracinus*. Georgia. Journal of Herpetology 35:145–148.

Howard, J. D., and R. W. Frey. 1985. Physical and biogenic aspects of backbarrier sedimentary sequences, Georgia coast, USA. Marine Geology 63:77–127.

Hoyt, J. H. 1968. Geology of the Golden Isles and lower Georgia Cosastal Plain. Pp. 18–32 *in* D. S. Maney, F. C. Marland, and C. B. West, eds., The Future of the Marshlands and Sea Islands of Georgia. Georgia Natural Areas Council and Coastal Area Planning and Development Commission. Athens: University of Georgia Marine Institute.

Hoyt, J. H. 1962. High angle beach stratification, Sapelo Island, Georgia. Journal of Sedimentary Petrology 32:309–311.

Hoyt, J. H., and J. R. Hails. 1967. Pleistocene shoreline sediments in coastal Georgia: Deposition and modification. Science 155:15411–15543.

Hoyt, J. H., and V. J. Henry Jr. 1967. Influence of island migration on barrier-island sedimentation. Bulletin of the Geological Society of America 78:77–86.

Hoyt, J. H., R. J. Weimer, and V. J. Henry Jr. 1964. Late Pleistocene and recent sedimentation, central Georgia coast, USA. Pp. 170–176 *in* L. M. J. U. van Straaten, ed., Developments in Sedimentology, Vol. 1: Deltaic and Shallow Marine Sediments. Amsterdam: Elsevier Publishing.

Hubbard, R. K., C. R. Berdanier, H. F. Perkins, and R. A. Leonard. 1985. Characteristics of selected upland soils of the Georgia Coastal Plain. Agricultural Research Service ARS–37.

Hubble, T. H., A. M. Laessle, and J. C. Dickinson. 1956. The Flint-Chattahoochee-Apalachicola region and its environments. Bulletin of the Florida State Museum 1:1–73.

Huddlestun, P. F. 1988. A revision of the lithostratigraphic units of the Coastal Plain of Georgia: The Miocene through Holocene. Georgia Department of Natural Resources, Environmental Protection Division. Georgia Geologic Survey Bulletin 104.

Hudson, C. 1976. The Southeastern Indians. Knoxville: University of Tennessee Press.

Hughes, J. M. 1999. Yellow-billed cuckoo (*Coccyzus americanus*). *In* A. Poole and F. Gill, eds., The Birds of North America, no. 418. Philadelphia: The Birds of North America, Inc.

Hunt, C. B. 1967. Physiography of the United States. San Francisco: W. H. Freeman.

Hunt, P. D., and D. J. Flaspohler. 1998. Yellow-rumped warbler (*Dendroica coronata*). *In* A. Poole and F. Gill, eds., The Birds of North America, no. 376. Philadelphia: The Birds of North America, Inc.

Hupp, C. R. 2000. Hydrology, geomorphology and vegetation of Coastal Plain rivers in the south-eastern USA. Hydrologic Processes 14:2991–3010.

Hutchens, J. J., and J. B. Wallace. 2002. Ecosystem linkages between southern Appalachian headwater streams and their banks: Leaf litter breakdown and invertebrate assemblages. Ecosystems 5:80–91.

Iacona, G. D., L. K. Kirkman, and E. M. Bruna. 2010. Effects of resource availability on seedling recruitment in a fire-maintained savanna. Oecologia 163:171–180.

Ingold, J. L. 1993. Blue grosbeak (*Guiraca caerulea*). *In* A. Poole and F. Gill, eds., The Birds of North America, no. 79. Philadelphia: Academy of Natural Sciences; Washington, D.C.: American Ornithologists' Union.

Ivester, A. H., and D. S. Leigh. 2003. Riverine dunes on the Coastal Plain of Georgia, USA. Geomorphology 51:289–311.

Jack, S. B., W. L. Neel, and R. J. Mitchell. 2006. The Stoddard-Neel approach. Pp. 242–245 *in* S. Jose, E. J. Jokela, and D. L. Miller, eds., The Longleaf Pine Ecosystem: Ecology, Silviculture, and Restoration. New York: Springer Science Business Media, LLC.

Jackson, J. A. 2002. Ivory-billed woodpecker (*Campephilus principalis*). *In* A. Poole and F. Gill, eds., The Birds of North America, no. 711. Philadelphia: The Birds of North America, Inc.

Jackson, J. A. 1994. Red-cockaded woodpecker (*Picoides borealis*). *In* A. Poole and F. Gill, eds., The Birds of North America, no. 85. Philadelphia: Academy of Natural Sciences; Washington, D.C.: American Ornithologists' Union.

Jackson, S. T., and R. J. Hobbs. 2009. Ecological restoration in the light of ecological history. Science 325. Available at www.sciencemag.org.

Jacobs, D. F. 2007. Toward development of silvical strategies for forest restoration of American chestnut (*Castanea dentata*) using blight-resistant hybrids. Biological Conservation 137:497–450.

Jacqmain, E. I., R. H. Jones, and R. J. Mitchell. 1999. Influences of frequent cool-season burning across a soil moisture gradient on oak community structure in longleaf pine ecosystems. American Midland Naturalist 141:85–100.

Jaeger, R. G. 1978. Plant climbing by salamanders: Periodic availability of plant-dwelling prey. Copeia 1978: 686–691.

Jenny, H. 1941. Factors of Soil Formation. New York: McGraw-Hill.

Jensen, J. B. 2010. Prothonotary warbler (*Protonaria citrea*). Pp. 348–349 *in* T. M. Schneider, G. Beaton, T. S. Keyes, and N. A. Klaus, eds., The Breeding Bird Atlas of Georgia. Athens: University of Georgia Press.

Jensen, J. B. 2008a. Eastern milksnake (*Lampropeltis triangulum triangulum*). Pp. 366–368 *in* J. B. Jensen, C. D. Camp, J. W. Gibbons, and M. J. Elliott, eds., Amphibians and Reptiles of Georgia. Athens: University of Georgia Press.

Jensen, J. B. 2008b. Mimic glass lizard (*Ophisaurus mimicus*). Pp. 285–286 *in* J. B. Jensen, C. D. Camp, W. Gibbons, and M. J. Elliott, eds., Amphibians and Reptiles of Georgia. Athens: University of Georgia Press.

Jensen, J. B. 2008c. Southern cricket frog (*Acris gryllus*). Pp. 50–52 *in* J. B. Jensen, C. D. Camp, W. Gibbons, and M. J. Elliott, eds., Amphibians and Reptiles of Georgia. Athens: University of Georgia Press.

Jensen, J. B. 1999. Spotted turtle (*Clemmys guttata*). Pp. 69–70 *in* T. W. Johnson, T. W., J. C. Ozier, J. L. Bohannon, J. B. Jensen, and C. Skelton, eds., Protected Animals of Georgia. Georgia Department of Natural Resources, Wildlife Resources Division, Nongame Wildlife-Natural Heritage Section.

Jensen, J. B., C. D. Camp, and J. L. Marshall. 2002. Ecology and life history of the Pigeon Mountain salamander. Southeastern Naturalist 1:3–16.

Jensen, J. B., C. D. Camp, W. Gibbons, and M. J. Elliott, eds. 2008. Amphibians and Reptiles of Georgia. Athens: University of Georgia Press.

Jensen, J. B., M. E. Dorcas, and W. Gibbons. 2008. Striped crayfish snake (*Regina alleni*). Pp. 391–392 *in* J. B. Jensen, C. D. Camp, W. Gibbons, and M. J. Elliott, eds., Amphibians and Reptiles of Georgia. Athens: University of Georgia Press.

Jensen, J. B., and D. J. Stevenson. 2008. Flatwoods salamander (*Ambystoma cingulatum*). Pp. 133–135 *in* J. B. Jensen, C. D. Camp, W. Gibbons, and M. J. Elliott, eds., Amphibians and Reptiles of Georgia. Athens: University of Georgia Press.

Johnson, A. S., H. O. Hillestad, S. F. Shanholtzer, and G. F. Shanholtzer. 1974. An ecological survey of the coastal region of Georgia. U.S. National Park Service Scientific Monograph Series no. 3. Washington, D.C.

Johnson, F. L., and P. G. Risser. 1974. Biomass, annual net primary production, and dynamics of six mineral elements in a post oak-blackjack oak forest. Ecology 55(6):1246–1258.

Johnson, J., L. Reid, B. Mayfield, D. Duerr, and S. Fraedrich. 2010. Laurel wilt disease associated with redbay ambrosia beetle. Available at http://www.gfc.state.ga.us/ForestManagement/LaurelWilt.cfm.

Johnson, K. 2000. Unpublished Soil Surveys and Site Descriptions for Selected *Xyris tennesseensis* Sites in the Ridge and Valley Ecoregion of Alabama. U.S. Department of Agriculture, Grovehill, Ala.: Natural Resources Conservation Service.

Johnson, K. R., and L. J. Hickey. 1991. Megafloral change across the Cretaceous Tertiary boundary in the Northern Great Plains and Rocky Mountains. *In* V. I. Sharpton and P. D. Ward, eds., Global Catastrophes in Earth History: An Interdisciplinary Conference on Impacts, Volcanism, and Mass Mortality, Geological Society of America.

Johnson, T. W. 2010a. Ruby-throated hummingbird (*Archilochus colubris*). Pp. 214–215 *in* T. M. Schneider, G. Beaton, T. S. Keyes, and N. A. Klaus, eds., The Breeding Bird Atlas of Georgia. Athens: University of Georgia Press.

Johnson, T. W. 2010b. Common raven (*Corvus corax*). Pp. 266–267 *in* T. M. Schneider, G. Beaton, T. S. Keyes, and N. A. Klaus, eds. The Breeding Bird Atlas of Georgia. Athens: University of Georgia Press.

Jolley, D. B. 2007. Reproduction and herpetofauna depredation of feral hogs at Fort Benning, Georgia. Master's thesis. Auburn University, Auburn, Ala.

Jones, L. E. 2001. Saltwater contamination in the upper Floridan aquifer at Brunswick, Georgia. Pp. 644–647 *in* K.J. Hatcher, ed., Proceedings of the 2001 Georgia Water Resources Conference. University of Georgia, Institute of Ecology, Athens, Ga.

Jones, S. B., Jr. 1974. The flora and phytogeography of the Pine Mountain region of Georgia. Castanea 39(2): 113–149.

Jones, S. B., Jr., and N. C. Coile. 1988. The Distribution of the Vascular Flora of Georgia. Athens: privately printed.

Juras, P. 1997. The presettlement Piedmont savanna: A model for landscape design and architecture. Master's thesis. University of Georgia, Athens.

Kale, H. W., III. 1965. Ecology and bioenergetics of the long-billed marsh wren, *Telmatodytes palustris griseus* (Brewster) in Georgia salt marshes. Pp. 589–591 *in* Nuttall Ornithological Club Publication 5. Cambridge, Mass.

Kane, J. M., J. M. Varner, and J. K. Hiers. 2008. The burning characteristics of southeastern oaks: Discriminating fire facilitators from fire impeders. Forest Ecology and Management 256:2039–2045.

Kellison, R. C., M. J. Young, R. R. Braham, and E. J. Jones. 1998. Major alluvial floodplains. Pp. 291–323 *in* M. G. Messina and W. H. Conner, eds., Southern Forested Wetlands: Ecology and Management. Boca Raton, Fla.: Lewis Publishers.

Kellog, F. E., G. L. Doster, E. V. Komarek Sr., and R. Komarek. 1972. The one quail per acre myth. Pp. 15–20 *in* J. Morrison and J. Lewis, eds., Proceedings of the First National Bobwhite Quail Symposium.

Kelly, C., and J. Cumming. 2005. *Pinus virginiana* succession influences soils and arbuscular mycorrhizae of a serpentine grassland. Poster abstract for Ecological Society of America Meeting.

Keppie, D. M., and R. M. Whiting Jr. 1994. American woodcock (*Scolopax minor*). *In* A. Poole and F. Gill, eds., The Birds of North America, no. 100. Philadelphia: Academy of Natural Sciences; Washington, D.C.: American Ornithologists' Union.

Kesler, T. R., L. C. Anderson, and S. M. Hermann. 2003. A taxonomic reevaluation of *Aristida stricta* (Poaceae) using anatomy and morphology. Southeastern Naturalist 2:1–10.

Keyes, T. S. 2010. Loggerhead shrike (*Lanius ludovicianus*). Pp. 250–251 *in* T. M. Schneider, G. Beaton, T. S. Keyes, and N. A. Klaus, eds., The Breeding Bird Atlas of Georgia. Athens: University of Georgia Press.

Keyes, T. S. 2010. White-eyed vireo (*Vireo griseus*). Pp. 252–253 *in* T. Schneider, G. Beaton, T. Keyes, and N. Klaus, eds., The Breeding Bird Atlas of Georgia. Athens: University of Georgia Press.

Kilgo, J. C., H. S. Ray, C. Ruth, and K. V. Miller. 2010. Can coyotes affect deer populations in southeastern North America? Journal of Wildlife Management 74(5): 929–933.

King, J. R., W. R. Tschinkel, and K. G. Ross. 2009. A case study of human exacerbation of the invasive species problem: Transport and establishment of polygyne fire ants in Tallahassee, Florida, USA. Biological Invasions 11: 373–377.

Kinlaw, A. 1995. *Spilogale putorius*. Mammalian species no. 511. American Society of Mammalogists.

Kirk, D. A., and M. J. Mossman. 1998. Turkey vulture (*Cathartes aura*). *In* A. Poole and F. Gill, eds., The Birds of North America, no. 339. Philadelphia: The Birds of North America, Inc.

Kirkman, L. K., K. L. Coffey, R. J. Mitchell, and E. B. Moser. 2004a. Ground cover recovery patterns and life history traits: Implications for restoration obstacles and opportunities in a species-rich savanna. Journal of Ecology 92:409–421.

Kirkman, L. K., M. B. Drew, and D. Edwards. 1998. Effects of experimental fire regimes on the population dynamics of *Schwalbea americana* L. Plant Ecology 137:115–137.

Kirkman, L. K., M. B. Drew, L. T. West, and E. R. Blood. 1998. Ecotone characterization between upland longleaf pine/wiregrass stands and seasonally-ponded isolated wetlands. Wetlands 18:346–364.

Kirkman, L. K., S. W. Golladay, L. LaClaire, and R. Sutter. 1999. Biodiversity in southeastern seasonally ponded, isolated wetlands: Management and policy perspectives for research and conservation. Journal of the North American Benthological Society 18:553–562.

Kirkman, L. K., P. C. Goebel, B. J. Palik, and L. T. West. 2004b. Predicting plant species diversity in a longleaf pine landscape. Ecoscience 11:80–93.

Kirkman, L. K., P. C. Goebel, L. West, M. B. Drew, and B. J. Palik. 2000. Depressional wetland vegetation types: A question of plant community development. Wetlands 20:373–385.

Kirkman, L. K., R. F. Lide, G. Wein, and R. R. Sharitz. 1996. Vegetation changes and land-use legacies of depression wetlands of the western coastal plain of South Carolina: 1951–1992. Wetlands 16:564–576.

Kirkman, L. K., and R. J. Mitchell. 2006. Conservation management of *Pinus palustris* ecosystems from a landscape perspective. Applied Vegetation Science 9:67–74.

Kirkman, L. K., R. J. Mitchell, R. C. Helton, and M. B. Drew. 2001. Productivity and species richness across an environmental gradient in a fire-dependent ecosystem. American Journal of Botany 88:2119–2128.

Kirkman, L. K., R. J. Mitchell, M. J. Kaeser, S. D. Pecot, and K. L. Coffey. 2007. The perpetual forest: Using undesirable species to bridge restoration. Journal of Applied Ecology 44:604–614.

Kirkman, L. K., and R. R. Sharitz. 1994. Vegetation disturbance and maintenance of diversity in intermittently flooded Carolina bays in South Carolina. Ecological Applications 4:177–188.

Kirkman, L. K., and R. R. Sharitz. 1993. Growth in controlled water regimes of three grasses common in freshwater wetlands of the southeastern USA. Aquatic Botany 44:345–359.

Klaus, N. 2006. Historic fire regimes and species composition of two Georgia mountain longleaf communities. *In* M. L. Cipollini, comp., Proceedings of the Second Montane Longleaf Pine Conference Workshop, November 18–19, 2005, Berry College, Mount Berry, Georgia, Longleaf Alliance Report, no. 9, p. 13.

Klaus, N. A. 2010a. Cerulean warbler (*Dendroica cerulean*). Pp. 342–343 *in* T. M. Schneider, G. Beaton, T. S. Keyes, and N. A. Klaus, eds., The Breeding Bird Atlas of Georgia. Athens: University of Georgia Press.

Klaus, N. A. 2010b. Swainson's warbler (*Limnothlypis swainsonii*). Pp. 352–353 *in* T. M. Schneider, G. Beaton, T. S. Keyes, and N. A. Klaus, eds., The Breeding Bird Atlas of Georgia. Athens: University of Georgia Press.

Klaus, N. A., and J. M. Klaus. 2009. Evaluating tolerance of herbicide and transplantation by cane (a native bamboo) for canebrake restoration. Restoration Ecology 19:344–350.

Knight, T. 2006. Dendrochronological investigations of longleaf pine on Lavender Mountain. Pp. 18–24 *in* M. L. Cipollini, comp., Proceedings of the Second Montane Longleaf Pine Conference Workshop, November 18–19, 2005, Berry College, Mount Berry, Georgia, Longleaf Alliance Report, no. 9.

Knutson, P. L. 1988. Role of coastal marshes in energy dissipation and shore protection. Pp. 161–175 *in* D. D. Hook, W. H. McKee Jr., H. K. Smith, J. Gregory, V. G. Burrell Jr., M. R. DeVoe, R. E. Sojka, S. Gilbert, R. Banks, L. H. Stolzy, C. Brooks, T. D. Matthews, and T. H. Shear, eds., The Ecology and Management of Wetlands. Vol. 1: Ecology of Wetlands. Portland, Ore.: Timber Press.

Komar, P. D. 1998. Beach Processes and Sedimentation. Upper Saddle River, N.J.: Simon and Schuster.

Komarek, E. V. 1974. Effects of fire on temperate forests and related ecosystems: Southeastern United States. Pp. 251–277 *in* T. T. Kozlowski and C. E. Ahlgren, eds., Fire and Ecosystems. New York: Academic Press.

Kral, R. 1990. A Status Report on *Xyris tennesseensis*. Unpublished report submitted to the U.S. Fish and Wildlife Service, Jackson, Mississippi.

Kral, R. 1983. *Xyris tennesseensis*. Pp. 166–169 *in* A Report on Some Rare, Threatened, or Endangered Forest-related Vascular Plants of the South, Vol. 1, U.S. Department of Agriculture Forest Service, Technical Publication R8-TP 2.

Krause, R. E., and R. B. Randolph. 1989. Hydrology of the Floridan aquifer system in southeast Georgia and adjacent parts of Florida and South Carolina. U.S. Geological Survey Professional Paper 1403D.

Krebs, C. J. 2001. Ecology. 5th ed. San Francisco: Addison Wesley Longman.

Kreech, S., III. 1999. The Ecological Indian: Myth and History. New York: W. W. Norton.

Kricher, J. C. 1995. Black-and-white warbler (*Mniotilta varia*). *In* A. Poole and F. Gill, eds., The Birds of North America, no. 158. Philadelphia: Academy of Natural Sciences; Washington, D.C.: American Ornithologists' Union.

Kruse, L. M. 2003. Vascular flora of the Upper Etowah River Watershed, Georgia. Master's thesis. University of Georgia, Athens.

Krysko, K. L. 2008. Common kingsnake (*Lampropeltis getula*). Pp. 361–363 *in* J. B. Jensen, C. D. Camp, W. Gibbons, and M. J. Elliott, eds., Amphibians and Reptiles of Georgia. Athens: University of Georgia Press.

Krysko, K. L., and D. B. Means. 2008. Mole kingsnake (*Lampropeltis calligaster*). Pp. 359–360 *in* J. B. Jensen,

C. D. Camp, W. Gibbons, and M. J. Elliott, eds., Amphibians and Reptiles of Georgia. Athens: University of Georgia Press.

Kundell, J. E., and M. Myszewski. 2007. Urban sprawl. *In* The New Georgia Encyclopedia. Available at http://www.georgiaencyclopedia.org/nge/Article.jsp?id=h-763 updated 12/05/2002.

Kurtin, B. 1972. The Age of Mammals. New York: Columbia University Press.

Kurz, H. 1942. Florida dunes and scrub, vegetation and geology. Florida State Board Conservation Geological Bulletin no. 23, pp. 1–154.

Kush, J. S., and J. M. Varner. 2006. Burn slowly and carry a water bag: Lessons learned from 10 years of restoration burning. *In* M. L. Cipollini, comp., Proceedings of the Second Montane Longleaf Pine Conference Workshop, November 18–19, 2005, Berry College, Mount Berry, Georgia, Longleaf Alliance Report, no. 9.

Kwit, C., M. W. Schwartz, W. J. Platt, and J. P. Geaghan. 1998. The distribution of tree species in steepheads of the Apalachicola River Bluffs, Florida. Journal of the Torrey Botanical Society 125:309–318.

Laderman, A. D. 1989. The ecology of the Atlantic white cedar wetlands: A community profile. U.S. Fish and Wildlife Service Biological Report 85(7.21).

Laerm, J. 1981. Systematic status of the Cumberland Island pocket gopher, *Geomys cumberlandius*. Brimleyana 6:141–151.

Laessle, A. M. 1958. The origin and successional relationship of sandhill vegetation and sand-pine scrub. Ecological Monographs 28:361–387.

Laessle, A. M. 1942. The Plant Communities of the Welaka Area. Biological Science Series, Vol. IV. Gainesville: University of Florida Press.

Laessle, A. M., and C. D. Monk. 1961. Some live oak forests of northeastern Florida. Quarterly Journal of Florida Academy of Science 24:39–55.

Lafon, C. W., D. Y. Graybeal, and K. H. Orvis. Patterns of ice accumulation and forest disturbance during two ice storms in southwestern Virginia. Physical Geography 20(2):97–115.

LaForge, L., W. Cook, A. Keith, and M. R. Campbell. 1925. Physical Geography of Georgia. Geological Survey of Georgia Bulletin no. 42.

Lamb, T., and W. Gibbons. 2008. Pine woods snake (*Rhadinaea flavilata*). Pp. 397–398 *in* J. B. Jensen, C. D. Camp, W. Gibbons, and M. J. Elliott, eds., Amphibians and Reptiles of Georgia. Athens: University of Georgia Press.

Lambert, C. L. 1992. Spatial vegetation dynamics of Lake Whitney—a freshwater wetland on Cumberland Island, Georgia. Master's thesis. University of Georgia, Athens.

Lancaster, J. 1996. Scaling the effects of predation and disturbance in a patchy environment. Oecologia 107(3):321–331.

Landers, J. 1991. Disturbance influences on pine traits in the Southeastern United States. Pp. 61–95 *in* High Intensity Fire in Wildlands: Management Challenges and Options, Proceedings of the Tall Timbers Fire Ecology Conference 17.

Lanyon, W. E. 1997. Great crested flycatcher (*Myiarchus crinitus*). *In* A. Poole and F. Gill, eds., The Birds of North America, no. 300. Philadelphia: Academy of Natural Sciences; Washington, D.C.: American Ornithologists' Union.

Larson, D. W., U. Matthes, and P. E. Kelly. 2000. Cliff Ecology: Pattern and Process in Cliff Ecosystems. Cambridge: Cambridge University Press.

Lawless, P. J. 2005. Xeric limestone prairies of the eastern United States. Ph.D. dissertation. University of Kentucky, Lexington.

Lee, D. S., C. R. Gilbert, C. H. Hocutt, R. E. Jenkins, D. E. McAllister, and J. R. Stauffer Jr. 1980. Atlas of North American Freshwater Fishes. Raleigh: North Carolina State Museum of Natural History.

Lemon, P. C. 1949. Successional responses of herbs in the longleaf-slash pine forest after fire. Ecology 30:135–145.

Lenz, R. J. 2002. Longstreet Highroad Guide to the Georgia Coast & Okefenokee. Longstreet Press. Available at http://www.sherpaguides.com/georgia/coast/central_coast/altamaha_river_bioreserve.html.

Lewis, A. J., III. 2004. Historic, Heritage and Heirloom Plants of Georgia and the American South. Athens: The State Botanical Garden of Georgia.

Lide, R. F. 1997. When is a depression wetland a Carolina bay? Southeastern Geographer 37:90–98.

Lide, R. F., V. G. Meentemeyer, J. E. Pinder III, and L. M. Beatty. 1995. Hydrology of a Carolina bay located on the upper Coastal Plain of western South Carolina. Wetlands 15:47–57.

Liner, A. E., L. L. Smith, S. W. Golladay, S. B. Castleberry, and J. W. Gibbons. 2008. Amphibian distributions within three types of isolated wetlands in southwest Georgia. American Midland Naturalist 160:69–81.

Linzey, D. W. 1995. Mammals of Great Smoky Mountains National Park. Blacksburg, Va.: The McDonald & Woodward Publishing Company, Inc.

Lippincott, C. L. 1997. Ecological consequences of *Imperata cylindrica* (Cogongrass) invasion in Florida Sandhill. Ph.D. dissertation. University of Florida, Gainesville.

Lipps, E. L., and H. R. DeSelm. 1969. The vascular flora of the Marshall Forest, Rome, Georgia. Castanea 34:414–432.

Lipps, L., and C. E. Ray. 1967. The Pleistocene fossiliferous deposit at Ladds, Bartow County, Georgia. Bulletin of the Georgia Academy of Sciences 25(3):113–118.

Lipps, W. L. 1966. Plant communities of a portion of Floyd County, Georgia—especially the Marshall Forest. Ph.D. dissertation. University of Tennessee, Knoxville.

Lockaby, B. G., J. Stanturf, and M. Messina. 1997. Effects of silvicultural activity on ecological processes in floodplain forests of the southern United States: A review of existing report. Forest Ecology and Management 90:93–100.

Lockaby, B. G., F. C. Thornton, R. H. Jones, and R. G. Clawson. 1994. Ecological responses of an oligotrophic floodplain forest to harvesting. Journal of Environmental Quality 23:901–906.

Loehle, C. 2007. Predicting Pleistocene climate from vegetation in North America. Climate of the Past 3: 109–118.

Loftin, C. S. 1998. Assessing patterns and processes of landscape change in Okefenokee Swamp, Georgia. Ph.D. dissertation. University of Florida, Gainesville.

Lohoefener, R., and L. Lohmeier. 1981. Comparison of gopher tortoise (*Gopherus polyphemus*) habitats in young slash pine and old longleaf pine areas of southern Mississippi. Journal of Herpetology 15:239–242.

Lorimer, C. G. 1993. Causes of the oak regeneration problem. *In* Proceedings, Oak Regeneration: Serious Problems, Practical Recommendations, September 8–10, 1992, Knoxville, Tenn.: Gen. Tech. Rep. SE-84. St. Paul, Minn.: U.S. Department of Agriculture, Forest Service, North Central Forest Experiment: 14–39.

Lowrance, R. R. 1992. Groundwater nitrate and denitrification in a Coastal Plain riparian forest. Journal of Environmental Quality 21:401–405.

Lowrance, R. R., R. Todd, J. Fail Jr., O. C. Hendrickson Jr., R. Leonard, and L. Asmussen. 1984. Riparian forests as nutrient filters in agricultural watersheds. Bioscience 34:374–377.

Lowrance, R. R., G. Vellidis, R. D. Wauchope, P. Gay, and D. D. Bosch. 1997. Herbicide transport in a managed riparian forest buffer system. Transactions of the ASAE 40:1047–1057.

Mack, R N., D. Simberloff, W. M. Lonsdale, H. Evans, M. Clout, and F. A. Bazzaz. 2000. Biotic invasions: Causes, epidemiology, global consequences, and control. Ecological Applications 10:689–710.

MacNeil, F. S. 1950. Pleistocene Shore Lines in Florida and Georgia. U.S. Geological Survey Professional Paper 221-F:95–107.

Maerz, J. C., and A. M. Grosse. 2010. Relationship between Diamondback Terrapin Abundance and Road and Crabbing Pressures along Coastal Georgia. Unpublished report to the Georgia Department of Natural Resources.

Magilligan, F. J., and M. L. Stamp. 1997. Historical land-cover changes and hydrogeomorphic adjustment in a small Georgia watershed. Annals of the Association of American Geographers 87:614–635.

Malanson, G. P. 1993. Riparian Landscapes. Cambridge: Cambridge University Press.

Mansberg, L., and T. R. Wentworth. 1984. Vegetation and soils of a serpentine barren in western North Carolina. Bulletin of the Torrey Botanical Club 111(3):273–286.

Marshall, L. G. 1988. Land mammals and the Great American Interchange. American Scientist 76(4):380–389.

Martin, G. 2010. Evaluating the location, extent, and condition of isolated wetlands in the Dougherty Plain, Georgia, USA. Master's thesis. University of Georgia, Athens.

Martin, K. L., and L. K. Kirkman. 2009. Management of ecological thresholds to re-establish disturbance-maintained herbaceous wetlands of the south-eastern USA. Journal of Applied Ecology 46:906–914.

Martin, W. H., D. J. Stevenson, and P. B. Spivey. 2008. Timber rattlesnake (*Crotalus horridus*). Pp. 433–436 *in* J. B. Jensen, C. D. Camp, W. Gibbons, and M. J. Elliott, eds., Amphibians and Reptiles of Georgia. Athens: University of Georgia Press.

Martof, B. S. 1963. Some observations on the herpetofauna of Sapelo Island, Georgia. Herpetologica 19:70–72.

Mattoon, W. R. 1922. Longleaf Pine. U.S. Department of Agriculture Forest Service Bulletin no. 1061.

Mattsson, B. J., and R. J. Cooper. 2007. Which life-history components determine breeding productivity for individual songbirds? A case study of the Louisiana waterthrush (*Seirus montacilla*). Auk 124:1186–2000.

Mazzotti, F. J., and L. A. Brandt. 1994. Ecology of the American alligator in a seasonally fluctuating environment. Pp. 485–506 *in* S. M. Davis and J. C. Ogden, eds., Everglades: The Ecosystem and its Restoration. Boca Raton, Fla.: St. Lucie Press.

McCallie, S. W. 1908. A preliminary report on the underground water of Georgia. Geological Survey of Georgia Bulletin no. 15.

McCarty, J. P. 1996. Eastern wood-pewee (*Contopus virens*). *In* A. Poole and F. Gill, eds., The Birds of North America, no. 245. Philadelphia: Academy of Natural Sciences; Washington, D.C.: American Ornithologists' Union.

McDaniel, S. T. 1971. The genus *Sarracenia*. Bulletin of the Tall Timbers Research Station 9:36.

McGuire, J. P., R. J. Mitchell, E. B. Moser, S. D. Pecot, D. H. Gjerstad, and C. W. Hedman. 2001. Gaps in a gappy forest: Plant resources, longleaf pine regeneration, and understory response to tree removal in longleaf pine savannas. Canadian Journal of Forest Research 31:765–778.

McIntyre, R. K., S. B. Jack, R. J. Mitchell, J. K. Hiers, and W. L. Neel. 2008. Multiple Value Management: The Stoddard-Neel Approach to Ecological Forestry in Longleaf Pine Grasslands. Newton, Ga.: Joseph W. Jones Ecological Research Center.

McKenzie, M. D., and L. A. Barclay. 1980. Ecological Characterization of the Sea Island Coastal Region of South Carolina and Georgia: Executive Summary. FWS/OBS-79/45. U.S. Fish and Wildlife Service, Washington, D.C.

McMichael, A. E. 1977. A model for barrier island settlement pattern. Florida Anthropologist 30:179–195.

McPherson, G. R. 1988. Boundary Dynamics on Cumberland Island National Seashore. Institute of Ecology, University of Georgia. Cooperative Park Studies Unit Technical Report 49.

McPherson, K. 2009a. Freshwater marshes: Community description. Forest Network. Available at http://www.forestencyclopedia.net/p/p4/p142/p146/p253. Accessed July 12, 2009.

McPherson, K. 2009b. Fire regime of freshwater marshes. Forest Encyclopedia Network. Available at http://www.forestencyclopedia.net/p/p4/p142/p146/p254. Accessed July 12, 2009.

Means, D. B. 2008a. Apalachicola dusky salamander (*Desmognathus apalachicolae*). Pp. 163–165 *in* J. B. Jensen, C. D. Camp, W. Gibbons, and M. J. Elliott, eds., Amphibians and Reptiles of Georgia. Athens: University of Georgia Press.

Means, D. B. 2008b. Southern dusky salamander (*Desmognathus auriculatus*). Pp. 166–168 *in* J. B. Jensen, C. D. Camp, W. Gibbons, and M. J. Elliott, eds., Amphibians and Reptiles of Georgia. Athens: University of Georgia Press.

Means, D. B. 2006. Vertebrate faunal diversity of longleaf pine ecosystems. Pp. 157–213 *in* S. Jose, E. J. Jokela, and D. L. Miller, eds., The Longleaf Pine Ecosystem: Ecology, Silviculture, and Restoration. New York: Springer Science Business Media, LLC.

Means, D. B. 2000. Southeastern U.S. Coastal Plain habitats of the Plethodontidae: The importance of relief, ravines, and seepage. Pp. 287–302 *in* R. C. Bruce, R. G. Jaeger, and L. D. Houck, eds., The Biology of Plethodontid Salamanders. New York: Plenum Publishers.

Melvin, S. L. 2010a. Great blue heron (*Ardea herodias*). Pp. 92–93 *in* T. M. Schneider, G. Beaton, T. S. Keyes, and N. A. Klaus, eds., The Breeding Bird Atlas of Georgia. Athens: University of Georgia Press.

Melvin, S. L. 2010b. Green heron (*Butorides virescens*). Pp. 104–105 *in* T. M. Schneider, G. Beaton, T. S. Keyes, and N. A. Klaus, eds., The Breeding Bird Atlas of Georgia. Athens: University of Georgia Press.

Merrill, M. D., M. C. Freeman, B. J. Freeman, E. A. Kramer, and L. M. Hartle. 2001. Stream loss and fragmentation due to impoundments in the Upper Oconee Watershed. Pp. 66–69 *in* K. J. Hatcher, ed., Proceedings of the 2001 Georgia Water Resource Conference, Institute of Ecology, University of Georgia, Athens, Ga.

Metts, B. S. 2008. Common musk turtle (*Sternotherus odoratus*). Pp. 511–513 *in* J. B. Jensen, C. D. Camp, W. Gibbons, and M. J. Elliott, eds., Amphibians and Reptiles of Georgia. Athens: University of Georgia Press.

Meyer, A. M. 1937. An ecological study of cedar glade invertebrates near Nashville, Tennessee. Ecological Monographs 7:404–443.

Meyer, J. L. 1990. A blackwater perspective on riverine ecosystems. BioScience 40:643–651.

Meyer, J. L., K. L. Jones, G. C. Poole, C. R. Jackson, J. E. Kundell, B. L. Rivenbark, E. L. Kramer, and W. Bumback. 2005. Implications of Changes in Riparian Buffer Protection for Georgia's Trout Streams. Institute of Ecology, University of Georgia, Athens. Available at http://www.rivercenter.uga.edu/publications/pdf/buffer_science.pdf. Accessed June 12, 2011.

Meyer, J. L., D. L. Strayer, J. B. Wallace, S. L. Eggert, G. S. Helfman, and N. E. Leonard. 2007. The contribution of headwater streams to biodiversity in river networks. Journal of the American Water Resources Association 43(1):86–103.

Meyer, K. D. 1995. Swallow-tailed kite (*Elanoides forficatus*). *In* A. Poole and F. Gill, eds., The Birds of North America, no. 138. Philadelphia: Academy of Natural Sciences; Washington, D.C.: American Ornithologists' Union.

Michener, W. K., E. R. Blood, K. L. Bildstein, M. M. Brinson, and L. R. Gardner. 1997. Climate change, hurricanes and tropical storms, and rising sea level in coastal wetlands. Ecological Applications 7(3):770–801.

Middleton, A. L. A. 1998. Chipping sparrow (*Spizella passerina*). *In* A. Poole and F. Gill, eds., The Birds of North America, no. 334. Philadelphia: The Birds of North America, Inc.

Middleton, A. L. A. 1993. American goldfinch (*Carduelis tristis*). *In* A. Poole and F. Gill, eds., The Birds of North America, no. 80. Philadelphia: Academy of Natural Sciences; Washington, D.C.: American Ornithologists' Union.

Mikan, C. J., D. A. Orwig, and M. D. Abrams. 1994. Age structure and successional dynamics of a presettlement-origin chestnut oak forest in the Pennsylvania Piedmont. Bulletin of the Torrey Botanical Club 121(1):13–23.

Milius, S. 1998. "How bright is a butterfly?" Science News Online. Available at http://www.sciencenews.org/sn_arc98/4_11_98/bob1.htm. Accessed November 24, 2008.

Miller, J. H. 2003. Nonnative invasive plants of the southern forests: A field guide for identification and control. U.S. Department of Agriculture Forest Service Southern Research Station General Technical Report SRS-62.

Miller, J. H., and K. V. Miller. 2005. Forest Plants of the Southeast and their Wildlife Uses. Athens: University of Georgia Press.

Mills, T. 2008. Rainbow snake (*Farancia erytrogramma*). Pp. 351–352 *in* J. B. Jensen, C. D. Camp, W. Gibbons, and M. J. Elliott, eds., Amphibians and Reptiles of Georgia. Athens: University of Georgia Press.

Mirarchi, R. E., and T. S. Baskett. 1994. Mourning dove (*Zenaida macroura*). *In* A. Poole and F. Gill, eds., The Birds of North America, no. 117. Philadelphia: Academy of Natural Sciences; Washington, D.C.: American Ornithologists' Union.

Mitchell, R., T. Engstrom, R. R. Sharitz, D. De Steven, K. Hiers, R Cooper, and L. K. Kirkman. 2009. Old forests and endangered woodpeckers: Old-growth in the southern Coastal Plain. Natural Areas Journal 29:301–310.

Mitsch, W. J., and J. G. Gosselink. 1993. Wetlands. 2nd ed. New York: Van Nostrand Reinhold.

Moffett, J. M., Jr. 2008. *Xyris tennesseensis*: Status survey, habitat restoration/management concerns, and relation to a new xyrid, *Xyris spathifolia*. Ph.D. dissertation. Auburn University, Auburn. Available at Auburn University's electronic archive of Master's theses and Ph.D. dissertations repository. URL: http://etd.auburn.edu/etd/handle/10415/1534.

Moldenhauer, R. R., and D. J. Regelski. 1996. Northern parula (*Parula americana*) in A. Poole and F. Gill, eds., The Birds of North America, no. 215. Philadelphia: Academy of Natural Sciences; Washington, D.C.: American Ornithologists' Union.

Moler, P. 1985. Distribution of the eastern indigo snake, *Drymarchon corais couperi*, in Florida. Herpetological Review 16:37–38.

Moler, P. E. 1992. Rare and Endangered Biota of Florida. Vol. III. Amphibians and Reptiles. Gainesville: University Press of Florida.

Moler, P. E., and R. Franz. 1987. Wildlife values of small isolated wetlands in the Southeastern Coastal Plain. Pp. 234–241 *in* R. R. Odom, K. A. Riddleberger, and J. C. Ozier, eds., Proceedings of the Third Southeastern Nongame and Endangered Wildlife Symposium.

Monk, C. D. 1968. Successional and environmental relationships of the forest vegetation of north central Florida. American Midland Naturalist 79:441–457.

Monk, C. D. 1967. Tree species diversity in the eastern deciduous forest with particular reference to north-central Florida. American Naturalist 101:173–187.

Monk, C. D. 1966. An ecological significance of evergreenness. Ecology 47:649–654.

Monk, C. D. 1965. Southern mixed hardwood forests of north central Florida. Ecological Monographs 35:335–354.

Montague, C. L., and R. G. Wiegert. 1990. Salt marshes. Pp. 481–516 *in* R. L. Myers and J. J. Ewel, eds., Ecosystems of Florida. Orlando: University of Central Florida Press.

Mooney, H. A., and R. J. Hobbs. 2000. Invasive Species in a Changing World. Washington, D.C.: Island Press.

Moore, J., and L. Fogo. 2008. Montane longleaf = Piedmont longleaf? Does it matter what we call it? *In* J. S. Kush and S. M. Hermann, comps., Proceedings of the Third Montane Longleaf Conference, March 11–12, 2008, Auburn University, Alabama, Longleaf Alliance.

Moore, R. H. 1992. Low-salinity backbays and lagoons. Pp. 541–614 *in* C. T. Hackney, S. M. Adams, and W. H. Martin, eds., Biodiversity of the Southeastern United States: Aquatic Communities. New York: Wiley.

Moore, W. S. 1995. Northern flicker (*Colaptes auratus*). *In* A. Poole and F. Gill, eds., The Birds of North America, no. 166. Philadelphia: Academy of Natural Sciences; Washington, D.C.: American Ornithologists' Union.

Morehead, K. K., and I. M. Rossell. 1998. Southern Mountain Fens. Pp. 379–403 *in* M. G. Messina and W. H. Conner, eds., Southern Forested Wetlands. Boca Raton, Fla.: Lewis Publishers.

Morgan, D. R., and D. E. Soltis, 1993. Phylogenetic relationships among members of *Saxifragaceae sensulato* based on rbcL sequence data. Annals of the Missouri Botanical Garden 80:631–660.

Moriarty Lemmon, E. C. 2008. Upland chorus frog (*Pseudacris feriarum*). Pp. 80–82 *in* J. B. Jensen, C. D. Camp, W. Gibbons, and M. J. Elliott, eds., Amphibians and Reptiles of Georgia. Athens: University of Georgia Press.

Morris, J. T. 1988. Pathways and controls of the carbon cycle in salt marshes. Pp. 497–510 *in* D. D. Hook, W. H. McKee Jr., H. K. Smith, J. Gregory, V. G. Burrell Jr., M. R. DeVoe, R. E. Sojka, S. Gilbert, R. Banks, L. H. Stolzy, C. Brooks, T. D. Matthews, and T. H. Shear, eds., The Ecology and Management of Wetlands. Vol. 1: Ecology of Wetlands. Portland, Ore.: Timber Press.

Morris, M. W., J. Williams, M. Pschandl, and R. Van Cleave. 2008. A floristic study of Burks Mountain Ultramafic Woodland, Columbia County, Georgia. Southeastern Biology 55:352–353.

Morse, D. H. 1994. Blackburnian warbler (*Dendroica fusca*). *In* A. Poole and F. Gill, eds., The Birds of North America, no. 102. Philadelphia: Academy of Natural Sciences; Washington, D.C.: American Ornithologists' Union.

Morse, D. H. 1993. Black-throated green warbler (*Dendroica virens*). *In* A. Poole and F. Gill, eds., The Birds of North America, no. 55. Philadelphia: Academy of Natural Sciences; Washington, D.C.: American Ornithologists' Union.

Moulis, R. A. 2008. Alabama map turtle (*Graptemys pulchra*). Pp. 483–484 *in* J. B. Jensen, C. D. Camp, J. W. Gibbons, and M. J. Elliott, eds., Amphibians and Reptiles of Georgia. Athens: University of Georgia Press.

Mou, P., and M. P. Warillow. Ice storm damage to a mixed hardwood forest and its impacts on forest regeneration in the ridge and valley region of southwestern Virginia. Journal of the Torrey Botanical Society 127(1):66–82.

Mount, R. H. 1975. The Reptiles and Amphibians of Alabama. Auburn: Auburn University.

Mowbray, T. B. 1997. Swamp sparrow (*Melospiza georgiana*). *In* A. Poole and F. Gill, eds., The Birds of North America, no. 279. Philadelphia: Academy of Natural Sciences; Washington, D.C.: American Ornithologists' Union.

Mulhouse, J. M., L. E. Burbage, and R. R. Sharitz. 2005. Seed bank-vegetation relationships in herbaceous Carolina bays: Responses to climatic variability. Wetlands 25:738–747.

Muller, M. J., and R. W. Storer. 1999. Pied-billed grebe (*Podilymbus podiceps*). *In* A. Poole and F. Gill, eds., The Birds of North America, no. 410. Philadelphia: The Birds of North America, Inc.

Mulligan, M. K., and S. M. Hermann. 2004. Fort Benning Longleaf Pine Reference Communities. A report to the Department of Defense under cooperative agreement DAMD17-00-2-0017. Fort Benning, Ga.: The Nature Conservancy of Georgia.

Mulligan, M. K., L. K. Kirkman, and R. J. Mitchell. 2002. *Aristida beyrichiana* (wiregrass) establishment and recruitment: Implications for restoration. Ecological Restoration 10:68–72.

Murdy, W. H. 1968. Plant speciation associated with granite outcrop communities of the southeastern Piedmont. Rhodora 70:394–407.

Murdy, W. H., and M. E. Brown Carter. 2000. Guide to the Plants of Granite Outcrops. Athens: University of Georgia Press.

Mutch, R. 1970. Wildland fires and ecosystems—a hypothesis. Ecology 51:1046–1051.

Myers, R. L. 1990. Scrub and high pine. Pp. 150–193 *in* R. L. Myers and J. J. Ewel, eds., Ecosystems of Florida. Orlando: University of Central Florida Press.

National Oceanic and Atmospheric Administration. 2012. Weather Forecast Office. Available at http://www.srh.moaa.gov/ffc/?n+clisumls. Accessed January 3, 2012.

National Park Service. 2009. Echoes from the past: The archaeology of Fort Pulaski. Available at http://www.nps.gov/seac/pulaski/index.htm. Accessed August 11, 2009.

The Nature Conservancy. 2009. Banks Lake Preserve. Available at http://www.nature.org/ourinitiatives/regions/northamerica/unitedstates/georgia/placesweprotect/banks-lake.xml. Accessed December 2011.

The Nature Conservancy. 1999. TNC Ecoregions and Divisions of the Lower 48 United States. Available at http://gis.tnc.org/data/MapbookWebsite/map_page.php?map_id=9. Accessed August, 2011.

NatureServe. 2009a. About Us. Available at http://www.natureserve.org/aboutUs/. Accessed October 6, 2009.

NatureServe. 2009b. *Dendroica pinus*. Available at http://www.natureserve.org/explorer/servlet/NatureServe?searchName=Dendroica+pinus. Accessed June 11, 2009.

NatureServe. 2009c. NatureServe Explorer: An Online Encyclopedia of Life. Version 7.1. Arlington, Va.: NatureServe. Available at http://www.natureserve.org/explorer. Accessed June 11, 2009.

NatureServe. 2006. NatureServe Explorer: An online encyclopedia of life. Version 6.1. NatureServe, Arlington, Virginia. Available at http://www.natureserve.org/explorer.

NatureServe Ecology South. 2008. Chickamauga and Chattanooga National Military Park calcareous glade monitoring: A resampling of baseline transects established in 1993.

Neel, L., P. S. Sutter, and A. G. Way. 2010. The Art of Managing Longleaf: A Personal History of the Stoddard-Neel Approach. Athens: University of Georgia Press.

Neiheisel, J., and C. E. Weaver. 1967. Transportation and deposition of clay minerals, southeastern United States. Journal of Sedimentology and Petrology 37(4): 1084–1116.

Nelson, P. 2004. Classification and characterization of savannas and woodlands in Missouri. *In* G. Hartman, S. Holst, and B. Palmer, eds., Proceedings of SRM 2002 Savanna/Woodland Symposium, Conservation Commission of the State of Missouri.

Nelson, P. W. 2005. The Terrestrial Natural Communities of Missouri. Missouri Department of Natural Resources.

Nelson, W. G. 1986. Predation and prey population variation in a high energy sand beach macrofaunal community. Ophelia 26:305–316.

Newell, C. L., and R. K. Peet. 1998. Vegetation of Linville Gorge Wilderness, North Carolina. Castanea 63(3): 275–322.

Newman, M. C., and J. F. Schalles. 1990. The water chemistry of Carolina bays: A regional study. Archive für Hydrobiologie 118:147–168.

Niering, W. A., and R. S. Warren. 1977. Salt marshes. Pp. 697–702 *in* J. R. Clark, ed., Coastal Ecosystem Management. New York: Wiley.

Nixon, C. M., R. W. Donohoe, and T. Nash. 1974. Overharvest of fox squirrels from two woodlots in western Ohio. Journal of Wildlife Management 38:67–80.

Norden, A. H., and L. K. Kirkman. 2004. Persistence and prolonged winter dormancy of the federally endangered *Schwalbea americana* L. (Scrophulariaceae) following experimental management techniques. Natural Areas Journal 24:129–134.

Norris, R. A. 1956. Introduction of exotic game birds in Georgia. Oriole 21:1–6.

Noss, R. F., E. T. Laroe III, and J. M. Scott. 1985. Endangered Ecosystems of the United States: A Preliminary Assessment of Loss and Degradation. U.S. Department of Interior, National Biological Service, Biological Report 28.

Nourse, H., and C. Nourse. 2007. Favorite Wildflower Walks in Georgia. Athens: University of Georgia Press.

Nyman, J. A., and R. H. Chabreck. 1995. Fire in coastal marshes: History and recent concerns. Pp. 134–141 *in* S. I. Cerulean and R. T. Engstrom, eds., Fire in Wetlands: A Management Perspective. Tallahassee, Fla.: Tall Timbers Research, Inc.

Odum, E. P. 1961. The role of tidal marshes in estuarine productivity. New York Conservationist 15(6):12–15, 35.

Odum, E. P., and M. G. Turner. 1987. The Georgia Landscape: A Changing Resource. Final Report of the Kellogg Physical Resources Task Force. Athens: University of Georgia Institute of Ecology.

Odum, H. T., and M. A. Heywood. 1978. Decomposition of intertidal freshwater marsh plants. Pp. 89–97 *in* R. E. Good, D. G. Whigham, and R. L. Simpson, eds., Freshwater Wetlands: Ecological Processes and Management Potential. New York: Academic Press.

Odum, W. E. 1988. Comparative ecology of tidal freshwater and salt marshes. Annual Review of Ecology and Systematics 19:147–176.

Odum, W. E., and J. W. Harvey. 1988. Barrier island interdunal freshwater wetlands. Association of Southeastern Biologists Bulletin 35:149–155.

Odum, W. E., and J. K. Hoover. 1988. A comparison of vascular plant communities in tidal freshwater and saltwater marshes. Pp. 526–534 *in* D. D. Hook, W. H. McKee Jr., H. K. Smith, J. Gregory, V. G. Burrell Jr., M. R. DeVoe, R. E. Sojka, S. Gilbert, R. Banks, L. H. Stolzy, C. Brooks, T. D. Matthews, and T. H. Shear, eds., The Ecology and Management of Wetlands. Vol. 1: Ecology of Wetlands. Portland, Ore.: Timber Press.

Odum, W. E., L. P. Rozas, and C. C. McIvor. 1988. A comparison of fish and invertebrate community composition in tidal freshwater and oligohaline marsh systems. Pp. 561–569 *in* D. D. Hook, W. H. McKee Jr., H. K. Smith, J. Gregory, V. G. Burrell Jr., M. R. DeVoe, R. E. Sojka, S. Gilbert, R. Banks, L. H. Stolzy, C. Brooks, T. D. Matthews, and T. H. Shear, eds., The Ecology and Management of Wetlands. Vol. 1: Ecology of Wetlands. Portland, Ore.: Timber Press.

Odum, W. E., T. J. Smith III, J. K. Hoover, and C. C. McIvor. 1984. Ecology of Tidal Freshwater Marshes of the United States East Coast: A Community Profile. FWS/OBS-83/17. Washington, D.C.: U.S. Fish and Wildlife Service.

Oertel, G. F. 1979. Barrier island development during the Holocene Recession, southeastern United States. Pp. 273–290 *in* S. P. Leatherman, ed., Barrier Islands from the Gulf of St. Lawrence to the Gulf of Mexico. New York: Academic Press.

Oertel, G. F., and M. Larsen. 1976. Developmental sequences in Georgia coastal dunes and distributions of dune plants. Bulletin of the Georgia Academy of Science 34:35–48.

Olsen, M. 2006. Know the Connection: The Beach. Georgia Department of Natural Resources, Coastal Resources Division. Available at ehttp://www.knowtheconnection.com/int_beach.htm.

Olson, A. L., T. H. Hubbell, and H. F. Howden. 1954. The burrowing beetles of the genus *Mycotrupes* (Coleoptera: Scarabaeidae: Geotrupinae). Miscellaneous Publications of the Museum of Zoology, University of Michigan 84:1–59.

Omernik, J. M. 1987. Ecoregions of the conterminous United States. Annals of the Association of American Geographers 77:118–125.

Oosting, H. J., and W. D. Billings. 1942. Factors affecting vegetation zonation on coastal dunes. Ecology 23:131–142.

Osmond, C. B., K. Winter, and H. Ziegler. 1982. Functional significance of different pathways of CO_2 fixation in photosynthesis. Pp. 479–547 *in* O. L. Lange, P. S. Nobel, C. B. Osmond, and H. Ziegler, eds., Encyclopedia of Plant Physiology, Vol. 12B, Physiological Plant Ecology II. Water Relations and Carbon Assimilation. Berlin: Springer-Verlag.

Outcalt, K. W. 2008. Lightning, fire and longleaf pine: using natural disturbance to guide management. Forest Ecology and Management 255:3351–3359.

Outcalt, K. W. 1994. Seed production of wiregrass in central Florida following growing-season prescribed burns. International Journal of Wildland Fire 4:123–125.

Outcalt, K. W. 1992. Factors affecting wiregrass (*Aristida stricta* Michx.) cover on uncut and site prepared sandhills areas in central Florida. Ecological Engineering 1:245–251.

Outcalt, K. W., and C. E. Lewis. 1990. Response of wiregrass (*Aristida stricta*) to mechanical site preparation. Pp. 60–71 *in* L. C. Duever and R. F. Noss, eds., Proceedings of the Symposium on Wiregrass Biology and Management.

Ozier, J. 2008. Species profile for Rafinesque's big-eared bat, *Corynorhinus rafinesquii*. Georgia Department of Natural Resources. Available at http://www.georgiawildlife.com/conservation.

Ozier, J. C. 1999a. Red-cockaded woodpecker, *Picoides borealis*. Pp. 54–55 *in* T. W. Johnson, J. C. Ozier, J. L. Bohannon, J. B. Jensen, and C. Skelton, eds., Protected Animals of Georgia. Georgia Department of Natural Resources, Wildlife Resources Division, Nongame Wildlife–Natural Heritage Section.

Ozier, J. C. 1999b. Round-tailed muskrat (*Neofiber alleni*). Pp. 25–26 *in* T. W. Johnson, J. C. Ozier, J. L. Bohannon, J. B. Jensen, and C. Skelton, eds., Protected Animals of Georgia. Georgia Department of Natural Resources, Wildlife Resources Division, Nongame Wildlife–Natural Heritage Section.

Page, L. M., and B. M. Burr. 1991. A Field Guide to Freshwater Fishes of North America North of Mexico. Boston: Houghton Mifflin.

Paine, J., S. Newton, and D. Baugman. 2009. Chattahoochee River dam removal and aquatic ecosystem restoration: Design considerations. Proceedings of the 2009 Georgia Water Resources Conference, University of Georgia, Institute of Ecology, Athens, Ga.

Palik, B. J., S. W. Golladay, P. C. Goebel, and B. W. Taylor. 1998. Geomorphic variation in riparian tree mortality and stream coarse woody debris recruitment from record flooding in a coastal plain stream. Ecoscience 5:551–560.

Palik, B. J., and N. Pederson. 1996. Overstory mortality and canopy disturbances in longleaf pine ecosystems. Canadian Journal of Forest Research 26:2035–2047.

Pallardy, S. G., and T. T. Kozlowski. 2008. Physiology of Woody Plants. San Diego: Academic Press.

Parrish, F. K., and E. J. Rykiel. 1979. Okefenokee Swamp origin: Review and reconsideration. Journal of the Elisha Mitchell Scientific Society 95:17–31.

Parrish, J. W., Jr. 2010a. American kestrel (*Falco sparverius*). Pp. 140–141 *in* T. M. Schneider, G. Beaton, T. S. Keyes, and N. A. Klaus, eds., The Breeding Bird Atlas of Georgia. Athens: University of Georgia Press.

Parrott, R. T. 1967. A study of wiregrass (*Aristida stricta* Michx.) with particular reference to fire. Master's thesis. Duke University, Durham.

Patrick, T. S., J. R. Allison, and G. A. Krakow. 1995. Protected Plants of Georgia: An Information Manual on Plants Designated by the State of Georgia as Endangered, Threatened, Rare, or Unusual. Georgia Department of Natural Resources.

Payne, R. B. 1992. Indigo bunting (*Passerina cyanea*). *In* A. Poole and F. Gill, eds., The Birds of North America, no. 4. Philadelphia: Academy of Natural Sciences; Washington, D.C.: American Ornithologists' Union.

Peacock, E., and T. Schauwecker. 2003. Blackland Prairies of the Gulf Coastal Plain: Nature, Culture, and Sustainability. Tuscaloosa: University of Alabama Press.

Pearse, A. S., H. J. Humm, and G. W. Wharton. 1942. Ecology of sand beaches at Beaufort, N.C. Ecological Monographs 12(2):136–190.

Peck, M. F., C. N. Joiner, J. S. Clarke, and A. M. Cressler. 1990. Ground-Water Conditions in Georgia, 1989. U.S. Geological Survey Open-File Report 90–706.

Peck, M. F., K. W. McFadden, and D. C. Leeth. 2005. Impact of a major industrial shutdown on groundwater flow and quality in the St. Marys area, southeastern Georgia and northeastern Florida. Pp. 2001–2003 *in* K. J. Hatcher, ed., Proceedings of the 2005 Georgia Water Resources Conference, University of Georgia, Institute of Ecology, Athens, Ga.

Peer, B. D., and E. K. Bollinger. 1997. Common grackle (*Quiscalus quiscula*). *In* A. Poole and F. Gill, eds., The Birds of North America, no. 271. Philadelphia: Academy of Natural Sciences; Washington, D.C.: American Ornithologists' Union.

Peet, R. K. 2006. Ecological classification of longleaf pine woodlands. Pp. 51–93 *in* S. Jose, E. J. Jokela, and D. L. Miller, eds., The Longleaf Pine Ecosystem: Ecology, Silviculture, and Restoration. New York: Springer Science Business Media, LLC.

Peet, R. K. 1993. A taxonomic study of *Aristida stricta* and *A. beyrichiana*. Rhodora 95:25–37.

Penfound, W. T. 1952. Southern swamps and marshes. The Botanical Review 18:413–446.

Perkins, M. W., and L. M. Conner. 2004. Habitat use of fox squirrels in southwestern Georgia. Journal of Wildlife Management 68:509–513.

Perkins, M. W., L. M. Conner, and M. B. Howze. 2008. The importance of hardwood trees in the longleaf pine forest ecosystem for Sherman's fox squirrels. Forest Ecology and Management 255:1618–1625.

Pessin, L. J. 1933. Forest associations in the uplands of the lower Gulf Coastal Plain (longleaf pine belt). Ecology 14:1–14.

Petit, L. J. 1999. Prothonotary warbler (*Protonotaria citrea*). *In* A. Poole and F. Gill, eds., The Birds of North America, no. 408. Philadelphia: The Birds of North America, Inc.

Petranka, J. W. 1998. Salamanders of the United States and Canada. Washington, D.C.: Smithsonian Institution Press.

Petranka, J. W., M. E. Eldridge, and K. E. Haley. 1993. Effects of timber harvesting on southern Appalachian salamanders. Conservation Biology 7:363–370.

Pickett, S. T. A., and P. S. White. 1985. The ecology of natural disturbance and patch dynamics. Pp. 3–13 in S. T. A. Pickett and P. S. White, eds., The Ecology of Natural Disturbance and Patch Dynamics. New York: Academic Press.

Pinter, N., S. Fiedel, and J. E. Keeley. 2011. Fire and vegetation shifts in the Americas at the vanguard of paleoindian migration. Quaternary Science Reviews 30(3–4):269–272.

Pittillo, J. D., R. D. Hatcher Jr., and S. W. Buol. 1998. Introduction to the Environment and Vegetation of the Southern Blue Ridge Province. Castanea 63(3):202–216.

Platt, S. G., and C. G. Brantley. 1997. Canebrakes: An ecological and historical perspective. Castanea 62:8–21.

Platt, S. G., C. G. Brantley, and T. R. Rainwater. 2001. Canebrake fauna: Wildlife diversity in a critically endangered ecosystem. Journal of the Elisha Mitchell Scientific Society 117:119.

Platt, W. J., G. W. Evans, and M. M. Davis. 1988. Effects of fire season on flowering of forbs and shrubs in longleaf pine forests. Oecologia 76:353–363.

Platt, W. J., G. W. Evans, and S. L. Rathbun. 1988. The population dynamics of a long-lived conifer (Pinus palustris). American Naturalist 131:491–525.

Platt, W. J., and M. W. Schwartz. 1990. Temperate hardwood forests. Pp. 194–229 in R. L. Myers and J. J. Ewel, eds., Ecosystems of Florida. Orlando: University of Central Florida Press.

Plummer, G. L. 1963. Soils of the pitcher plant habitats in the Georgia Coastal Plain. Ecology 44:727–734.

Poiani, K. A., and P. M. Dixon. 1995. Seed banks of Carolina bays: Potential contributions from surrounding landscape vegetation. American Midland Naturalist 134:140–154.

Pomeroy, L. R. 1959. Algal productivity in salt marshes of Georgia. Limnology and Oceanography 4:386–397.

Pomeroy, L. R., and R. G. Wiegert. 1981. Ecology of a Salt Marsh. Ecological Studies Series, Vol. 38. New York: Springer-Verlag.

Ponnamperuma, F. N. 1984. Effects of flooding on soils. Pp. 9–45 in T. T. Kozlowski, ed., Flooding and Plant Growth. New York: Academic Press.

Porcher, R. D., and D. A. Rayner. 2001. A Guide to the Wildflowers of South Carolina. Columbia: University of South Carolina Press.

Poulin, R. G., S. D. Grindal, and R. M. Brigham. 1996. Common nighthawk (Chordeiles minor). In A. Poole and F. Gill, eds., The Birds of North America, no. 213. Philadelphia: Academy of Natural Sciences; Washington, D.C.: American Ornithologists' Union.

Priest, S., and J. S. Clarke. 2005. Potential effects of groundwater development in eastern Camden County, Georgia on groundwater resources of Cumberland Island National Seashore. In K. J. Hatcher, ed., Proceedings of the 2005 Georgia Water Resources Conference, University of Georgia, Institute of Ecology, Athens, Ga.

Pringle, C. M., and F. J. Triska. 2000. Emergent biological patterns and surface-subsurface interactions at landscape scales. Pp. 167–193 in J. B. Jones and P. J. Mulholland, eds., Streams and Ground Waters. San Diego: Academic Press.

Prothero, D. R. 2006. After the Dinosaurs: The Age of Mammals. Bloomington: Indiana University Press.

Proudman Oceanographic Laboratory. 2009. Questions and Answers About Tides. Available at http://www.pol.ac.uk/home/insight/tidefaq.html Accessed August 6, 2009.

Provencher, L., B. J. Herring, D. R. Gordon, H. L. Rodgers, K. E. M. Galley, G. W. Tanner, J. L. Hardesty, and L. A. Brennan. 2001. Effects of hardwood reduction techniques on longleaf pine sandhill vegetation in northwest Florida. Restoration Ecology 9:13–27.

Psuty, N. B. 1988. Sediment budget and dune/beach interaction. Journal of Coastal Research 3:1–4

Putnam, J. A., G. M. Furnival, and J. S. McKnight. 1960. Management and inventory of southern hardwoods. U.S. Department of Agriculture, Forest Service, Agriculture Handbook no. 181.

Pyne, S. J. 1982. Fire in America: A Cultural History of Wildland and Rural Fire. Seattle: University of Washington Press.

Quarterman, E., M. P. Burbanck, and D. J. Shure. 1993. Rock outcrop communities: Limestone, sandstone, and granite. Pp. 35–86 in W. H. Martin, S. G. Boyce, and A. C. Echternacht, eds., Biodiversity of the Southeastern United States: Upland Terrestrial Communities. New York: Wiley.

Radford, A. E., and D. L. Martin. 1975. Potential Ecological Natural Landmarks: Piedmont Region, Eastern United States. Unpublished report for the Department of Botany, University of North Carolina at Chapel Hill.

Raison, R. J. 1979. Modification of the soil environment by vegetation fires, with particular reference to nitrogen transformations: A review. Plant and Soil 51:73–108.

Ramos, I. 2001. Battus philenor. Animal Diversity Web. Available at http://animaldiversity.ummz.umich.edu/site/accounts/information/Battus_philenor.html. Accessed November 24, 2008,

Ranger, L. S. 2007. The Vascular Flora of Kennesaw Mountain. Unpublished report.

Ray, C. E. 1967. Pleistocene mammals from Ladds, Bartow County, Georgia. Bulletin of the Georgia Academy of Sciences 25(3):120–150.

Rebertus, A. J., G. B. Williamson, and E. B. Moser. 1989. Longleaf pine pyrogenicity and turkey oak mortality in Florida xeric sandhills. Ecology 70:60–70.

Reed, F. W. 1905. A Working Plan for Forest Lands in Central Alabama. USDA Forest Service Bulletin 71.

Reed, R. N., and W. Gibbons. 2008. Common garter snake (*Thamnophis sirtalis*). Pp. 413–415 *in* J. B. Jensen, C. D. Camp, W. Gibbons, and M. J. Elliott, eds., Amphibians and Reptiles of Georgia. Athens: University of Georgia Press.

Reeder, T. W., C. J. Cole, and H. C. Dessauer. 2002. Phylogenetic relationships of whiptail lizards of the genus *Cnemidophorus* (Squamata: Teiidae): A test of monophyly, reevaluation of karyotypic evolution, and review of hybrid origins. American Museum Novitiates 3365:1–61.

Reilly, F. J., and V. J. Bellis. 1983. The Ecological Impact of Beach Nourishment with Dredged Materials on the Intertidal Zone at Bogue Banks, North Carolina, U.S. Army Corps of Engineers. Coastal Engineering Research Center, Miscellaneous Report no. 83.

Reinert, H. K., D. Cundall, and L. M. Bushar. 1984. Foraging behavior of the timber rattlesnake, *Crotalus horridus*. Copeia 1984:976–981.

Richardson, C. J., and J. W. Gibbons. 1993. Pocosins, Carolina bays, and mountain bogs. Pp. 258–310 *in* W. H. Martin, S. G. Boyce, and A. C. Echternacht, eds., Biodiversity of the Southeastern United States: Lowland Terrestrial Communities. New York: Wiley.

Riddle, J. 2005. Selected Statistics on Old-Growth Stands in the Chattahoochee National Forest: A Site by Site Summary of the Findings of the Georgia ForestWatch Old Growth Project. Unpublished report to Georgia ForestWatch.

Ridge, I. 1987. Ethylene and growth control in amphibious plants. Pp. 53–76 *in* R. M. M. Crawford, ed., Plant Life in Aquatic and Amphibious Habitats. Oxford: Blackwell Scientific Publications.

Riggs, S. R. 1976. Barrier islands as storm dependent systems. *In* Technical Proceedings of the 1976 Barrier Island Workshop. Annapolis, Md.: The Conservation Foundation.

Robbins, L. E., and R. L. Myers. 1992. Seasonal Effects of Prescribed Burning in Florida: A Review. Miscellaneous Publication no. 8. Tallahassee, Fla.: Tall Timbers Research, Inc.

Roberts, D. C. 1996. Peterson Field Guide to Geology of Eastern North America. Boston: Houghton Mifflin.

Robertson, E. B. 1996. The palynology of early Eocene samples from Burke County, Georgia and Aiken and Barnwell Counties, South Carolina. Georgia Journal of Science 54(3):155–163.

Robinson, T. R., R. Sargent, and M. B. Sargent. 1996. Ruby-throated hummingbird (*Archilochus colubris*). *In* A. Poole and F. Gill, eds., The Birds of North America, no. 151. Philadelphia: Academy of Natural Sciences; Washington, D.C.: American Ornithologists' Union.

Robinson, W. D. 1995. Louisiana waterthrush (*Seiurus motacilla*). *In* A. Poole and F. Gill, eds., The Birds of North America, no. 151. Philadelphia: Academy of Natural Sciences; Washington, D.C.: American Ornithologists' Union.

Rodewald, P. G., J. H. Withgott, and K. G. Smith. 1999. Pine warbler (*Dendroica pinus*). *In* A. Poole and F. Gill, eds., The Birds of North America, no. 438. Philadelphia: The Birds of North America, Inc.

Rosser, G. K., and R. K. Moore. 1982. A study of Alabama Black-Belt soils. Pp. 210–225 *in* K. R. Demars and R. C. Chaney, eds., Geotechnical Properties, Behavior, and Performance of Calcareous Soils, ASTM STP 777. American Society for Testing and Materials.

Rostlund, E. 1957. The myth of a natural prairie belt in Alabama: An interpretation of historical records. Annals of the Association of American Geographers 47:392–411.

Roth, D. R., and A. Ambrose. 1996. Metropolitan Frontiers: A Short History of Atlanta. Atlanta: Longstreet Press.

Rothermel, B. 2008. Green treefrog (*Hyla cinerea*). Pp. 59–61 *in* J. B. Jensen, C. D. Camp, J. W. Gibbons, and M. J. Elliott, eds., Amphibians and Reptiles of Georgia. Athens: University of Georgia Press.

Rothermel, B. B., J. B. Jensen, C. D. Camp, and T. D. Schwaner. 2007. Geographic distribution. *Desmognathus folkertsi*. Herpetological Review 38:213.

Rozas, L. P., and W. E. Odum. 1987. Use of tidal freshwater marshes by fishes and macrofaunal crustaceans along a marsh stream-order gradient. Estuaries 10:36–43.

Rugel, K. C. R. Jackson, J. J. Romeis, S. W. Golladay, D. W. Hicks, and J. F. Dowd. 2011. Effects of irrigation withdrawals on streamflows in a karst environment: Lower Flint River Basin, Georgia, USA. Hydrological Processes. DOI: 10.1002/hyp.8149

Runkle, J. R. 1985. Disturbance regimes in temperate forests. Pp. 17–33 *in* S. T. A. Pickett and P. S. White, eds., The Ecology of Natural Disturbance and Patch Dynamics. New York: Academic Press.

Ruppert, H. H., and R. S. Fox. 1988. Seashore Animals of the Southeast. Columbia: University of South Carolina Press.

Rykiel, E. J., Jr. 1977. The Okefenokee Swamp watershed: Water balance and nutrient budgets. Ph.D. dissertation. University of Georgia, Athens.

Rymal, D. E., and G. W. Folkerts. 1982. Insects associated with pitcher plants (*Sarracenia*: Sarraceniaceae) and their relationship to pitcher plant conservation: A review. Journal of the Alabama Academy of Science 53:131–151.

Sanders, Albert E. 2002. Additions to the Pleistocene mammal faunas of South Carolina, North Carolina, and Georgia. Transactions of the American Philosophical Society, vol. 92, p. 5.

Sandifer, P. A., J. V. Miglarese, D. R. Calder, J. J. Manzie, and L. A. Barclay, eds. 1980. Ecological Characterization of the Sea Island Coastal Region of South Carolina and Georgia, vol. 3. Biological Features of the Characterization area. Marine Resources Division, South Carolina Wildlife and Marine Resources Department, Charleston.

Scavia, D., J. C. Field, D. F. Boesch, R. W. Buddemeier, V. Burkett, D. R. Cayan, M. Fogarty, M. A. Harwell, R. W. Howarth, C. Mason, D. J. Reed, T. C. Royer, A. H. Sallenger, and J. G. Titus. 2002. Climate change impacts on U.S. coastal and marine ecosystems. Estuaries 25(2):149–164.

Schafale, M. P., and A. S. Weakley. 1990. Classification of the Natural Communities of North Carolina. North Carolina Natural Heritage Program, Division of Parks and Recreation, North Carolina Department of Environmental, Health, and Natural Resources.

Schelske, C. L., and E. P. Odum. 1961. Mechanisms maintaining high productivity in Georgia estuaries. Gulf and Caribbean Fisheries Institute Proceedings 14:75–80.

Schmalz, G. 2010. Turkey vulture (Cathartes aura). Pp. 118–119 in T. M. Schneider, G. Beaton, T. S. Keyes, and N. A. Klaus, eds., The Breeding Bird Atlas of Georgia. Athens: University of Georgia Press.

Schneck, W. M., and W. J. Fritz. 1985. An amphibian trackway (Cincosaurus cobbi) from the Lower Pennsylvanian ("Pottsville") of Lookout Mountain, Georgia: A first occurrence. Journal of Paleontology 59(5):1243–1250.

Schneider, R. 2002. History of the Chattahoochee-Oconee National Forests. Available at http://www.fs.fed.us/conf/chatto_history.htm.

Schneider, T., and T. Keyes. 2010. Species profile for Bachman's sparrow, Aimophila aestivalis. Georgia Department of Natural Resources. Available at http://www.georgiawildlife.com/conservation.

Schneider, T. M., G. Beaton, T. S. Keyes, and N. A. Klaus. 2010. The Breeding Bird Atlas of Georgia. Athens: University of Georgia Press.

Schneider, T. M., and P. W. Sykes Jr. 2010. Painted bunting (Passerina ciris). Pp. 396–397 in T. M. Schneider, G. Beaton, T. S. Keyes, and N. A. Klaus, eds., The Breeding Bird Atlas of Georgia. Athens: University of Georgia Press.

Schnell, D. E. 2002. Carnivorous Plants of the United States and Canada. Portland, Ore.: Timber Press.

Schnurr, J. L., R. S. Ostedl, and C. D. Canham. 2002. Direct and indirect effects of masting on rodent populations and tree seed survival. Oikos 96(3):402–410.

Schoettle, H. E. T. 1993. A Naturalist's Guide to St. Simons Island. St. Simons Island, Ga.: Watermarks Printing.

Schoettle, H. E. T. 1987. A Field Guide to Jekyll Island. Georgia Sea Grant College Program, Athens, University of Georgia.

Scholtens, B. 2005. Diana fritillary (Speyeria diana). In South Carolina Department of Natural Resources. Comprehensive Wildlife Conservation Strategy. Columbia.

Schoonmaker, P., and W. Lunscombe. 2005. Habitat Monitoring: An Approach for Reporting Status and Trends for State Comprehensive Wildlife Conservation Strategies. Portland, Ore.: Illahee.

Schotz, A. R., and M. S. Barbour. 2009. Ecological Assessment and Terrestrial Vertebrate Surveys for Black Belt Prairies in Alabama. Alabama Natural Heritage Program report submitted to Alabama Department of Conservation and Natural Resources, Montgomery, Ala.

Schowalter, T. D. 1985. Adaptations of insects to disturbance. Pp. 235–252 in S. T. A. Pickett and P. S. White, eds., The Ecology of Natural Disturbance and Patch Dynamics. San Diego: Academic Press.

Schubauer, J. P., and C. S. Hopkinson. 1984. Above- and below-ground emergent macrophyte production and turnover in a coastal marsh ecosystem, Georgia Limnology and Oceanography 29:1056–1065.

Schuler, T. M., and W. R. McClain. 2003. Fire History of a Ridge and Valley Oak Forest. U.S. Department of Agriculture Forest Service Northeastern Research Station Research Paper NE-724.

Schwimmer, D. R., K. Padian, and A. B. Woodhead. 1985. First pterosaur records from Georgia; open marine facies, Eutaw Formation (Santonian). Journal of Paleontology 59(3):674–676.

Scott, D. E. 2005. Ambystoma opacum. Pp. 627–632 in M. Lannoo, ed., Amphibian Declines: The Conservation Status of United States Species. Berkeley: University of California Press.

Seabrook, C. 2006. Tidal marshes. In New Georgia Encyclopedia. Available at http://www.georgiaencyclopedia.org/nge/Article.jsp?id=h-1183.

Seamon, P. A., R. L. Myers, L. E. Robbins, and G. S. Seamon. 1989. Wiregrass reproduction and community restoration. Natural Areas Journal 9:264–265.

Semlitsch, R. 2000. Principles for management of aquatic-breeding amphibians. Journal of Wildlife Management 64:615–631.

Semlitsch, R. D., and J. R. Bodie. 2003. Biological criteria for buffer zones around wetlands and riparian habitats for amphibians and reptiles. Conservation Biology 17:1219–1228.

Semlitsch, R. D., and J. R. Bodie. 1998. Are small, isolated wetlands expendable? Conservation Biology 12: 1129–1133.

Semlitsch, R. D., and C. A. West. 1983. Aspects of the life history and ecology of Webster's salamander, *Plethodon websteri*. Copeia 1983:339–346.

Sexton, W. J., and M. O. Hayes. 1991. The geologic impact of Hurricane Hugo and post-storm recovery along the underdeveloped coastline of South Carolina, Dewees Island to the Santee Delta. Journal of Coastal Research 8:275–290.

Sharitz, R. R., and C. A. Gresham. 1998. Pocosins and Carolina bays. Pp. 343–377 *in* M. G. Messina and W. H. Conner, eds., Southern Forested Wetlands: Ecology and Management. Boca Raton, Fla.: Lewis Publishers.

Sharitz, R. R., and W. J. Mitsch. 1993. Southern floodplain forests. Pp. 311–372 *in* W. H. Martin, S. G. Boyce, and A. C. Echternacht, eds., Biodiversity of the Southeastern United States: Lowland Terrestrial Communities. New York: Wiley.

Shepard, J. P., S. J. Brady, N. D. Cost, and C. G. Storrs. 1998. Pp. 1–28 *in* M. G. Messina and W. H. Conner, eds., Southern Forested Wetlands: Ecology and Management. Boca Raton, Fla.: Lewis Publishers.

Shure, D. J. 1999. Granite outcrops of the southeastern United States. Pp. 99–118 *in* R. C. Anderson, J. S. Fralish, and J. M. Baskin, eds., Savannas, Barrens, and Rock Outcrop Plant Communities of North America. Cambridge: Cambridge University Press.

Sikora, J. P., W. B. Sikora, C. W. Erkenbrecher, and B. C. Coull. 1977. Significance of ATP, carbon and caloric content of meiobenthic nematodes in partitioning benthic biomass. Marine Bulletin 44:7–14.

Silliman, B. R., J. Van de Koppel, M. D. Bertness, L. E. Staton, and I. A. Mendelssohn. 2005. Drought, snails, and large-scale dieoff of southern U.S. marshes. Science 310:1803–1806.

Silver, T. 1990. A New Face on the Countryside: Indians, Colonists, and Slaves in South Atlantic Forests, 1500–1800. Cambridge: Cambridge University Press.

Simberloff, D. 2000. Introduced species: The threat to biodiversity & what can be done. American Institute of Biological Sciences. Available at http://www.actionbioscience.org/biodiversity/simberloff.html. Accessed July 2010.

Simpkins, D. L. 1975. A preliminary report on test excavations at the Sapelo Island Shell Ring, 1975. Early Georgia 3:15–37.

Simpson, R. L., R. E. Good, M. A. Leck, and D. F. Whigham. 1983. The ecology of freshwater tidal wetlands. Bioscience 33:255–259.

Singer, F. J., W. T. Swank, and E. E. C. Clebsch. 1984. Effects of wild pig rooting in a deciduous forest. Journal of Wildlife Management 48:464–473.

Sisk, L. 1975. The Changed Look of the Countryside. Franklin Springs, Ga.: Advocate Press.

Skeate, S. T. 1987. Interactions between birds and fruits in a northern Florida hammock community. Ecology 68:297–309.

Skeen, J. N., P. D. Doerr, and D. H. Van Lear. 1993. Oak-hickory-pine forests. Pp. 1–34 *in* W. H. Martin, S. G. Boyce, and A. C. Echternacht, eds., Biodiversity of the Southeastern United States: Upland Terrestrial Communities. New York: Wiley.

Skelley, P. E. 2003. Review of the tribe Melolonthini in the southeastern United States (Coleoptera: Scarabaeidae: Melolonthinae). Insecta Mundi 17:129–156.

Skelley, P. E., and R. D. Gordon. 2001. Scarab beetles from pocket gopher burrows in the southeastern United States (Coleoptera: Scarabaeidae). *Insecta Mundi* 15: 77–93.

Skelton, C. E. 2008. Conasauga blue burrower (*Cambarus cymatilis*). Georgia Department of Natural Resources, Wildlife Resources Division website. Available at http://georgiawildlife.dnr.state.ga.us/assets/documents/gnhp/cambarus_cymatilis.pdf.

Skelton, C. E., S. Cammack, and E. VanDeGenachte. 2000. Surveys of Rare Burrowing Crayfish Species. Unpublished report to the Georgia Department of Natural Resources.

Small, C. J., and T. R. Wentworth. 1998. Characterization of montane cedar-hardwood woodlands in the Piedmont and Blue Ridge Provinces of North Carolina. Castanea 63(3):241–261.

Smith, J. E., R. Molina, and D. A. Perry. 1995. Occurrence of ectomycorrhizas on ericaceous and coniferous seedlings grown in soils from the Oregon Coast Range. New Phytologist 129(1):73–81.

Smith, K. G., J. H. Withgott, and P. G. Rodewald. 2000. Red-headed woodpecker (*Melanerpes erythrocephalus*). *In* A. Poole and F. Gill, eds., The Birds of North America, no. 518. Philadelphia: The Birds of North America, Inc.

Smith, L. L. 2008. Tiger salamander (*Ambystoma tigrinum*). Pp. 145–147 *in* J. B. Jensen, C. D. Camp, W. Gibbons, and M. J. Elliott, eds., Amphibians and Reptiles of Georgia. Athens: University of Georgia Press.

Smith, L. L., D. A. Steen, J. M. Stober, M. C. Freeman, S. W. Golladay, L. M. Conner, and J. C. Cochrane.

2006. The vertebrate fauna of Ichauway, Baker County, Ga. Southeastern Naturalist 5:599–620.

Smith, R. N. 1991. Species composition, stand structure, and woody detrital dynamics associated with pine mortality in the southern Appalachians. Master's thesis. University of Georgia, Athens.

Smith, S. N. 2008. Two-lined salamanders (*Eurycea bislineata* complex). Pp. 186–189 *in* J. B. Jensen, C. D. Camp, W. Gibbons, and M. J. Elliott, eds., Amphibians and Reptiles of Georgia. Athens: University of Georgia Press.

Smock, L. A., and E. Gilinsky. 1992. Coastal Plain blackwater streams. Pp. 272–311 *in* C. T. Hackney, S. M. Adams, and W. H. Martin, eds., Biodiversity of the Southeastern United States: Aquatic Communities. New York: John Wiley and Sons.

Smock, L. A., A. B. Wright, and A. C. Benke. 2005. Atlantic coast rivers of the southeastern United States. Pp. 73–122 *in* A. C. Benke and C. E. Cusing, eds., Rivers of North America. Burlington, Mass.: Elsevier Academic Press.

Snedaker, S. C., and A. E. Lugo. 1972. Ecology of the Ocala National Forest. Atlanta, Ga.: U.S. Forest Service, Southern Region.

Snodgrass, J. W., A. L. Bryon Jr., R. F. Lide, and G. M. Smith. 1996. Factors affecting the occurrence and structure of fish assemblages in isolated wetlands of the upper coastal plain, USA. Canadian Journal of Fisheries and Aquatic Sciences 53:443–454.

Somers, A. B., K. A. Bridle, D. W. Herman, and A. B. Nelson. 2000. The Restoration & Management of Small Wetlands of the Mountains & Piedmont in the Southeast: A Manual Emphasizing Endangered & Threatened Species Habitat with a Focus on Bog Turtles. Joint Publication of the Watershed Science & Wetland Science Institutes of the Natural Resources Conservation Service, University of North Carolina at Greensboro, and Pilot View Resource Conservation & Development, Inc.

Somershoe, S. G., S. P. Hudman, and C. R. Chandler. 2003. Habitat use by Swainson's warblers in a managed bottomland forest. Wilson Bulletin 115:148–154.

Somes, H. A., Jr., and J. R. Ashbaugh. 1973. Vegetation of St. Catherines Island, Georgia. Unpublished report. Devon, Pa.: Jack McCormick and Associates.

Sorenson, K. 2008. Two-toed amphiuma (*Amphiuma means*). Pp. 148–150 *in* J. B. Jensen, C. D. Camp, W. Gibbons, and M. J. Elliott, eds., Amphibians and Reptiles of Georgia. Athens: University of Georgia Press.

Sorenson, K., and P. E. Moler. 2008. Greater siren (*Siren lacertina*). Pp. 263–265 *in* J. B. Jensen, C. D. Camp, W. Gibbons, and M. J. Elliott, eds., Amphibians and Reptiles of Georgia. Athens: University of Georgia Press.

Southeast Regional Climate Center. 2009. Historical climate summaries for Georgia. University of North Carolina, Chapel Hill. Available at http://www.sercc.com/climateinfo/historical/historical_ga.html

Southern Appalachian Man and the Biosphere (SAMAB). 1996a. The Southern Appalachian Assessment Atmospheric Technical Report. Report 2 of 5. Atlanta: U.S. Department of Agriculture, Forest Service, Southern Region.

Southern Appalachian Man and the Biosphere (SAMAB). 1996b. The Southern Appalachian Assessment Social /Cultural/Economic Technical Report. Report 4 of 5. Atlanta: U.S. Department of Agriculture, Forest Service, Southern Region.

Southern Appalachian Man and the Biosphere (SAMAB). 1996c. The Southern Appalachian Assessment Terrestrial Technical Report. Report 5 of 5. Atlanta: U.S. Department of Agriculture, Forest Service, Southern Region.

Spalding, P. 1991. Part 1: Colonial Period. Pp. 9–70 *in* K. Coleman, ed., A History of Georgia. Athens: University of Georgia Press.

Spechler, R. M. 2001. The relationship between structure and saltwater intrusion in the Floridan Aquifer system, northeastern Florida. Pp. 25–29 *in* E. L. Kuniansky, ed., USGS Karst Interest Group Proceedings, Water-Resources Investigations Report 01–4011, Washington, D.C.

Spira, T. P. 2011. Wildflowers and Plant Communities of the Southern Appalachian Mountains and Piedmont. Chapel Hill: University of North Carolina Press.

Spivey, P. 2008. Diamondback terrapin (*Malaclemys terrapin*). Pp. 485–487 *in* J. B. Jensen, C. D. Camp, W. Gibbons, and M. J. Elliott, eds., Amphibians and Reptiles of Georgia. Athens: University of Georgia Press.

Spivey, P. B. 2010. Red-bellied woodpecker (*Melanerpus carolinus*). Pp. 220–221 *in* T. Schneider, G. Beaton, T. Keyes, and N. Klaus, eds., The Breeding Bird Atlas of Georgia. Athens: University of Georgia Press.

Stahle, D. W., M. K. Cleaveland, and J. G. Hehr. 1988. North Carolina climate changes reconstructed from tree rings: A. D. 372 to 1985. *Science* 240:1517–1519.

Stallings, D. T. 1997. *Reithrodontomys humilis*. Mammalian species 565:1–6. American Society of Mammalogists.

Stallins, J. A. 2000. Barrier Island morphology and dune vegetation pattern and process in the Georgia Bight. Ph.D. dissertation. University of Georgia, Athens.

Stalter, R., and W. E. Odum. 1993. Maritime communities. Pp. 117–163 *in* W. H. Martin, S. G. Boyce, and A. C. Echternacht, eds., Biodiversity of the Southeastern United States: Lowland Terrestrial Communities. New York: Wiley.

Stamp, N. E., and J. R. Lucas. 1990. Spatial patterns and dispersal distances of explosively dispersing plants in

Florida sandhill vegetation. Journal of Ecology 78: 589–600.

Stanturf, J. A., and S. H. Schoenholtz. 1998. Soils and landforms. Pp. 123–147 *in* M. G. Messina and W. H. Conner, eds., Southern Forested Wetlands: Ecology and Management. Boca Raton, Fla.: Lewis Publishers.

Stephenson, S. L., A. N. Ash, and D. F. Stauffer. 1993. Appalachian oak forests. Pp. 255–304 *in* W. H. Martin, S. G. Boyce, and A. C. Echternacht, eds., Biodiversity of the Southeastern United States: Upland Terrestrial Communities. New York: Wiley.

Stevenson, D. J., and C. D. Camp. 2008. Eastern newt (*Notophthalmus viridescens*). Pp. 254–256 *in* J. B. Jensen, C. D. Camp, W. Gibbons, and M. J. Elliott, eds., Amphibians and Reptiles of Georgia. Athens: University of Georgia Press.

Stevenson, D. J., and W. B. Cash. 2008. Striped newt (*Notophthalmus perstriatus*). Pp. 251–253 *in* J. B. Jensen, C. D. Camp, W. Gibbons, and M. J. Elliott, eds., Amphibians and Reptiles of Georgia. Athens: University of Georgia Press.

Stevenson, D. J., and R. A. Moulis. 2008. Eastern coral snake (*Micrurus fulvius*). Pp. 421–423 *in* J. B. Jensen, C. D. Camp, W. Gibbons, and M. J. Elliott, eds., Amphibians and Reptiles of Georgia. Athens: University of Georgia Press.

Stevenson, D. J., R. A. Moulis, and N. L. Hyslop. 2008. Eastern indigo snake (*Drymarchon couperi*). Pp. 339–341 *in* J. B. Jensen, C. D. Camp, W. Gibbons, and M. J. Elliott, eds., Amphibians and Reptiles of Georgia. Athens: University of Georgia Press.

Stevenson, H. M., and B. H. Anderson. 1994. The Bird Life of Florida. Gainesville: University of Florida Press.

Stewart, M. A. 1996. "What Nature Suffers to Groe": Life, Labor, and Landscape on the Georgia Coast. 1680–1920. Athens: University of Georgia Press.

Stoddard, H. L. 1935. Use of controlled fire in southeastern upland game management. Journal of Forestry 333: 346–351.

Stoddard, H. L. 1931. The Bobwhite Quail: Its Habits, Preservation and Increase. New York: Charles Scribner's Sons.

Stoddard, H. L., and E. V. Komarek. 1941. The carrying capacity of southeastern quail lands. Transactions of the North American Wildlife Conference 6:149–155.

Stooksberry, D. E. 2003. Historical droughts in Georgia and drought assessment and management. In Kathryn J. Hatcher, ed., Proceedings of the 2003 Georgia Water Resources Conference. University of Georgia, Institute of Ecology, Athens, Ga.

Stout, I. J., and W. R. Marion. 1993. Pine flatwoods and xeric pine forests of the southern (Lower) Coastal Plain.

Pp. 373–446 *in* W. H. Martin, S. G. Boyce, and A. C. Echternacht, eds., Biodiversity of the Southeastern United States: Lowland Terrestrial Communities. New York: John Wiley and Sons, Inc.

Straight, C. A. 2010a. Common nighthawk (*Chordeiles minor*). Pp. 206–207 *in* T. M. Schneider, G. Beaton, T. S. Keyes, and N. A. Klaus, eds., The Breeding Bird Atlas of Georgia. Athens: University of Georgia Press.

Straight, C. A. 2010b. Whip-poor-will (*Caprimulgus vociferus*). Pp. 210–211 *in* T. Schneider, G. Beaton, T. Keyes, and N. Klaus, eds., The Breeding Bird Atlas of Georgia. Athens: University of Georgia Press.

Straight, C. A., and R. J. Cooper. 2000. Chuck-will's-widow (*Caprimulgus carolinensis*). *In* A. Poole and F. Gill, eds., The Birds of North America, no. 499. Philadelphia: The Birds of North America, Inc.

Stuble, K. L., L. K. Kirkman, and C.R. Carroll. 2009. Patterns of abundance of fire ants and native ants in a native ecosystem. Ecological Entomology 34:520–526.

Subalusky, A. L., L. A. Fitzgerald, and L. L. Smith. 2009. Ontogenetic niche shifts in the American alligator establish functional connectivity between aquatic systems. Biological Conservation 142:1507–1514.

Sullivan, J. 1994. *Tilia americana. In* Fire Effects Information System . U.S. Department of Agriculture, Forest Service, Rock Mountain Research station, Fire Sciences Laboratory (Producer). Available at http://www .fs.fed.us/database/feis/.Sullivan, J. 1993. *Pinus virginiana. In* Fire Effects Information System . U.S. Department of Agriculture, Forest Service, Rock Mountain Research station, Fire Sciences Laboratory (Producer). Available at http://www.fs.fed.us/database/feis/.

Sun, G., S. G. McNulty, J. P. Shepard, D. M. Amatya, H. Riekerk, N. B. Comerford, R. W. Skaggs, and L. Swift Jr., 2001. Effects of timber management on the hydrology of wetland forests in the Southern United States. Forest Ecology and Management 143:227–236.

Sutter, R. D. Undated. The Effects of Restoration and Human Impacts at Sunset Rock, a Climbing and Hiking Site on Lookout Mountain, Chickamauga-Chattanooga National Military Park, Tennessee, U.S. Unpublished Report for the National Park Service.

Sutter, R. D., T. E. Govus, R. L. Smyth, C. Nordman, M. Pyne, and T. Hogan. 2011. Monitoring change in a central U.S. calcareous glade: Resampling transects established in 1993. Natural Areas Journal 31(2):163–172.

Swan, D. 2010. Swallow-tailed kite (*Elanoides forficatus*). Pp. 122–123 *in* T. M. Schneider, G. Beaton, T. S. Keyes, and N. A. Klaus. The Breeding Bird Atlas of Georgia. Athens: University of Georgia Press.

Taylor, M., and G. W. Stone. 1996. Beach ridges: A review. Journal of Coastal Research 12(3):612–621.

Teal, J. M. 1962. Energy flow in the salt marsh ecosystem of Georgia. Ecology 43(4):614–624.

Teal, J. M. 1958. Distribution of fiddler crabs in Georgia salt marshes. Ecology 39(2):185–193.

Teal, M., and J. Teal. 1964. Portrait of an Island. New York: Atheneum Press.

Terres, J. K. 1980. The Audubon Society Encyclopedia of North American Birds. New York: Knopf.

Thackston, R. E. 2010. Northern bobwhite (*Colinus virginianus*). Pp. 80–81 *in* T. Schneider, G. Beaton, T. Keyes, and N. Klaus, eds., The Breeding Bird Atlas of Georgia. Athens: University of Georgia Press.

Thieme, D. M. 2006. Talbot shoreline at Mount Pleasant. *In* T. Chowns, ed., Quaternary Stratigraphy and Depositional Environments—Jekyll Island and the Golden Isles Parkway. Georgia Geological Society Guidebook 26:80–83.

Thomas, P. 2000. Trees: Their Natural History. Cambridge: Cambridge University Press.

Thompson, V. 2005. Coastal shell rings. The New Georgia Encyclopedia. http://www.georgiaencyclopedia.org/nge /Article.jsp?id+h-2530. Accessed January 15, 2012.

Thorne, R. F. 1949a. Inland plants on the Gulf Coastal Plain of Georgia. Castanea 14:88–97.

Thorne, R. F. 1949b. The flora of southwestern Georgia. Ph.D. dissertation. Cornell University, Ithaca, N.Y.

Tiner, R. W. 1999. Wetland Indicators: A Guide to Wetland Identification, Delineation, Classification, and Mapping. Boca Raton, Fla.: Lewis Publishers.

Tomer, M. 2003. Mine reclamation may bury history. The Atlanta Journal-Constitution. September 9, pp. A-1, A-7.

Topa, M. A., and K. W. McLeod. 1986. Responses of *Pinus clausa*, *Pinus serotina* and *Pinus taeda* seedlings to anaerobic solution culture. II. Changes in tissue nutrient concentration and net acquisition. Physiologia Plantarum 68:532–539.

Torak, L. J., D. M. Crilley, and J. A. Painter. 2006. Physical and Hydrochemical Evidence of Lake Leakage Near Jim Woodruff Lock and Dam and of Ground-water Inflow to Lake Seminole, and an Assessment of Karst Features in and near the Lake, Southwestern Georgia and Northwestern Florida. U.S. Geological Survey, Scientific Investigations Report 2005–5084.

Torak, L. J., G. S. Davis, G. A. Strain, and J. G. Herndon. 1991. Geohydrology and evaluation of water-resource potential of the Upper Floridan aquifer in the Albany area, southwestern Georgia: U.S. Geological Survey Open-File Report 91–52.

Torak, L. J., and J. A. Painter. 2006. Geohydrology of the Lower Apalachicola-Chattahoochee-Flint River Basin, Southwestern Georgia, Northwestern Florida, and Southeastern Alabama. U.S Geological Survey, Scientific Investigations Report 2006-5070.

Trimble, S. W. 1985. Perspectives on the history of soil erosion control in the eastern United States. Agricultural History 59:162–180.

Trimble, S. W. 1974. Man-induced Soil Erosion on the Southern Piedmont, 1700–1970. Ankeny, Iowa: Soil Conservation Society of America.

Tuberville, T. D., and K. A. Buhlmann. 2008. Eastern hognose snake (*Heterodon platirhinos*). Pp. 353–355 *in* J. B. Jensen, C. D. Camp, W. Gibbons, and M. J. Elliott, eds., Amphibians and Reptiles of Georgia. Athens: University of Georgia Press.

Tuberville, T. D., and W. Gibbons. 2008. Coachwhip (*Masticophis flagellum*). Pp. 369–371 *in* J. B. Jensen, C. D. Camp, W. Gibbons, and M. J. Elliott, eds., Amphibians and Reptiles of Georgia. Athens: University of Georgia Press.

Tuberville, T. D., and P. A. Mason. 2008. Pine snake (*Pituophis melanoleucus*). Pp. 388–390 *in* J. B. Jensen, C. D. Camp, W. Gibbons, and M. J. Elliott, eds., Amphibians and Reptiles of Georgia. Athens: University of Georgia Press.

Turner, M. G., and S. P. Bratton. 1987. Fire, grazing, and the landscape heterogeneity of a Georgia barrier island. Pp. 85–101 *in* M. G. Turner, ed., Landscape Heterogeneity and Disturbance. Ecological Series 64. New York: Springer-Verlag.

Turner, S. 1984. The Fire History of Cumberland Island National Seashore 1900–1983. Institute of Ecology, University of Georgia. Cooperative Park Studies Unit Technical Report, no. 7.

Tuttle, J. P., and E. A. Kramer. 2005. Georgia Historic Vegetation Reconstruction Pilot Project. Natural Resources Spatial Analysis Laboratory, Institute of Ecology, University of Georgia, Athens. Unpublished report.

Twedt, D. J., W. B. Uihlein III, and A. B. Elliott. 2006. A spatially explicit decision support model for restoration of forest bird habitat. Conservation Biology 20:100–110.

Tyndall, R. W., and J. C. Hull. 1999. Vegetation, flora and plant physiological ecology of serpentine barrens of eastern North America. Pp. 67–82 *in* R. C. Anderson, J. S. Fralish, and J. M. Baskin, eds., Savannas, Barrens, and Rock Outcrop Plant Communities of North America. Cambridge: Cambridge University Press.

University of Georgia. 2011. Georgia Automated Environmental Monitoring Network. Available at http://www.griffin.uga.edu/aemn/. Last modified September 9, 2010.

University of Georgia. Warnell School of Forestry. 2011. "Research Projects in the Merkle Lab." Available at http://www.warnell.uga.edu/research/merkle/. Accessed July 29, 2011.

U.S. Department of Agriculture. 2009. Natural Resources Conservation Division (NRCD) Plants database. Available at http://plants.usda.gov/wetinfo.html accessed October 30, 2009.

U.S. Department of Agriculture. 1975. Soil Taxonomy. U.S. Department of Agriculture Handbook no. 436. Washington, D.C.: U.S. Government Printing Office.

U.S. Department of Agriculture. 1956. Agricultural Research Service. Land use and development: southern coastal plain. U.S. Department of Agriculture Information Bulletin 154.

U.S. Fish and Wildlife Service. 2010. White nose syndrome: Questions and answers for the U.S. Fish and Wildlife Service Cave Advisory. Available at http://www.fws.gov/WhiteNoseSyndrome/caveadvisoryfaqs.html.

U.S. Fish and Wildlife Service. 2006a. Blackbeard Island National Wildlife Refuge annual narrative. Townsend, Ga.

U.S. Fish and Wildlife Service. 2006b. The Horseshoe Crab, *Limulus polyphemus*: A living fossil. Available at http://www.fws.gov/northeast/pdf/horseshoe.fs.pdf. Accessed August 11, 2009.

U.S. Fish and Wildlife Service. 2006c. Okefenokee National Wildlife Refuge Comprehensive Conservation Plan. U.S. Fish and Wildlife Service, Southeast Region.

U.S. Fish and Wildlife Service. 2006d. Wassaw Island National Wildlife Refuge annual narrative. Savannah, Georgia.

U.S. Fish and Wildlife Service. 2003. Recovery Plan for the Red-cockaded Woodpecker (*Picoides borealis*). 2nd rev. U.S. Fish and Wildlife Service, Southeast Region.

U.S. Fish and Wildlife Service. 1990. Gopher Tortoise Recovery Plan. U.S. Fish and Wildlife Service, Southeast Region.

U.S. Soil Conservation Service. 1987. Hydric Soils of the United States in cooperation with the National Technical Committee for Hydric Soils, Washington, D.C.

van der Valk, A. G., and C. B. Davis. 1980. The impact of a natural drawdown on the growth of four emergent species in a prairie glacial marsh. Aquatic Botany 9: 301–322.

Van Horn, G. S. 1991. Cedar glades of northwest Georgia. Tipularia 6(1):22–27.

Van Horn, M. A., and T. M. Donovan. 1994. Ovenbird (*Seiurus aurocapillus*). *In* A. Poole and F. Gill, eds., The Birds of North America, no. 88. Philadelphia: Academy of Natural Sciences; Washington, D.C.: American Ornithologists' Union.

VandeGenachte, E., and S. Cammack. 2002. Carolina Bays of Georgia: Their Distribution, Condition and Conservation. Social Circle: Georgia Department of Natural Resources, Wildlife Resources Division. Available at http://www.georgiawildlife.com/node/819.

Varner, M. J., III, D. R. Gordon, F. E. Putz, and J. K. Hiers. 2005. Restoring fire to long-unburned *Pinus palustris* ecosystems: Novel fire effects and consequences for long-unburned ecosystems. Restoration Ecology 13: 536–544.

Vaughan, D. M., and M. D. Shepherd. 2005a. Species profile: *Mitoura hesseli*. *In* M. D. Shepherd, D. M. Vaughan, and S. H. Black, eds., Red List of Pollinator Insects of North America. CD-ROM Version 1 (May 2005). Portland, Ore.: The Xerces Society for Invertebrate Conservation.

Vaughan, D. M., and M. D. Shepherd. 2005b. Species profile: *Speyeria diana*. *In* M. D. Shepherd, D. M. Vaughan, and S. H. Black (Eds.) Red list of pollinator insects of North America. CD-ROM version 1 (May 2005). Portland, Ore.: The Xerces Society for Invertebrate Conservation.

Veatch, O., and L. W. Stephenson. 1911. Preliminary Report on the Geology of the Coastal Plain of Georgia. Geological Survey of Georgia Bulletin no. 26.

Vickery, P. D. 1996. Grasshopper sparrow (*Ammodramus savannarum*). *In* A. Poole and F. Gill, eds., The Birds of North America, no. 239. Philadelphia: Academy of Natural Sciences; Washington, D.C.: American Ornithologists' Union.

Voorhies, M. R. 1974. Pleistocene vertebrates with boreal affinities in the Georgia Piedmont. Quaternary Research 4:85–93.

Voorhies, M. R. 1971. The Watkins Quarry, a new Late Pleistocene mammal locality in Glynn County, Georgia. Bulletin of the Georgia Academy of Science 29(2):128.

Wade, D. D., and J. D. Lunsford. 1989. A Guide for Prescribed Fire in Southern Forests. U.S. Department of Agriculture, Forest Service, Southern Region, Technical Publication R8-TP 11.

Wade, D. D., and D. E. Ward. 1973. An Analysis of the Air Force Bomb Range Fire. U.S. Department of Agriculture, Forest Service, Southeastern Forest and Range Experiment Station, Research Paper SE-105.

Wagner, R. H. 1964. The ecology of *Uniola paniculata* in the Dunes Strand habitat of North Carolina. Ecological Monographs 34:79–125.

Wahlenberg, W. G. 1946. Longleaf Pine: Its Uses, Ecology, Regeneration, Protection, Growth, and Management. Washington, D.C.: Charles Lathrop Pack Forestry Foundation.

Wakeley, P. C. 1954. Planting the southern pines. U.S. Department of Agriculture Agricultural Monograph 18.

Wakeley, P. C. 1935. Artificial reforestation in the southern pine region. U.S. Department of Agriculture Technical Bulletin No 492. Washington, D.C.

Walbridge, M. R., and B. G. Lockaby. 1994. Effects of forest management on biogeochemical functions in southern forested wetlands. Wetlands 14:10–17.

Waldrop, T. A., H. H. Mohr, and P. H. Brose. 2006. Early dynamics of Table Mountain pine stands following stand-replacement prescribed fires of varying intensity. Pp. 471–474 in General Technical Report SRS-92, Asheville, N.C.: U.S. Department of Agriculture. Forest Service, Southern Research Station.

Walker, L. 1991. The Southern Forest: A Chronicle. Austin: University of Texas Press.

Ware, R. T., Sr. 1999. Summary Report: Survey for Clematis Socialis and Other Rare Plants of the Significant Calcareous or Coosa Flatwoods in the Ridge and Valley Province of Northwest Georgia. Report to the Georgia Natural Heritage Program. Social Circle, unpub. rep.

Ware, S., C. Frost, and P. D. Doerr. 1993. Southern mixed hardwood forest: The former longleaf pine forest. Pp. 447–493 in W. H. Martin, S. G. Boyce, and A. C. Echternacht, eds., Biodiversity of the Southeastern United States: Lowland Terrestrial Communities. New York: John Wiley and Sons, Inc.

Waters, G. 2008. American alligator (Alligator mississippiensis). Pp. 272–274 in J. B. Jensen, C. D. Camp, W. Gibbons, and M. J. Elliott, eds., Amphibians and Reptiles of Georgia. Athens: University of Georgia Press.

Weakley, A. S. 2011. Flora of the Southern and Mid-Atlantic States. University of North Carolina Herbarium (NCU). North Carolina Botanical Garden, University of North Carolina at Chapel Hill.

Weakley, A. S. 2010. Flora of the Carolinas, Florida, Georgia, and the Surrounding Areas. University of North Carolina Herbarium (NCU). North Carolina Botanical Garden, University of North Carolina at Chapel Hill.

Wear, D. N., and D. H. Newman. 2004. The speculative shadow over timberland values in the US South. Journal of Forestry 102:25–31.

Weaver, T. W., III. 1969. Gradients in the Carolina fall-line sandhills: Environment, vegetation, and comparative ecology of the oaks. Ph.D. dissertation. Duke University, Durham.

Weeks, H. P., Jr. 1994. Eastern phoebe (Sayornis phoebe). In A. Poole and F. Gill, eds., The Birds of North America, no. 94. Philadelphia: Academy of Natural Sciences; Washington, D.C.: American Ornithologists' Union.

Weigl, P. D., M. A. Steele, L. J. Sherman, J. C. Ha, and T. S. Sharpe. 1989. The ecology of the fox squirrel (Sciurus niger) in North Carolina: Implications for survival in the Southeast. Bulletin of Tall Timbers Research Station Bulletin 24:1–93.

Wells, B., and I. V. Shunk. 1931. The vegetation and habitat factors of coarser sands of the North Carolina Coastal Plain: An ecological study. Ecological Monographs 1:465–520.

Wetherington, M. V. 1994. The New South Comes to Wiregrass Georgia, 1860–1910. Knoxville: University of Tennessee Press.

Wharton, C. H. 1998. Natural Environments of the State Botanical Garden of Georgia. Athens, Georgia, The State Botanical Garden of Georgia, University of Georgia, Athens. Unpublished report to The State Botanical Garden.

Wharton, C. H. 1994. A Natural Resource Study of the Chicopee Woods Nature Preserve. Unpublished report to the Elachee Nature Science Center.

Wharton, C. H. 1978. The Natural Environments of Georgia. Atlanta, Ga.: Department of Natural Resources.

Wharton, C. H. 1968. Distribution of the red squirrel in Georgia. Journal of Mammalogy 49(1):153–155.

Wharton, C. H., and M. M. Brinson. 1979. Characteristics of southeastern river systems. Pp. 32–40 in R. R. Johnson and J. F. McCormick, eds., Strategies for Protection and Management of Floodplain Wetlands and Other Riparian Ecosystems: Proceedings of the Symposium. U.S. Department of Agriculture, Forest Service Publication GTR-WO-12.

Wharton, C. H., W. H. Kitchens, E. C. Pendlenton, and T. W. Snipe. 1982. The Ecology of Bottomland Hardwood Swamps of the Southeast: A Community Profile. U.S. Fish and Wildlife Service FWS/OBS-81/37.

Wharton, C. H., V. W. Lambou, J. Newson, P. V. Winger, L. L. Gaddy, and R. Mancke. 1981. The fauna of bottomland hardwoods in the southeastern United States. Pp. 87–100 in J. R. Clark and J. Benforado, eds., Wetlands of Bottomland Hardwood Forests. Amsterdam: Elsevier Scientific Publishing.

Whigham, D. F., and R. L. Simpson. 1975. Ecological Studies of the Hamilton Marshes. Progress report for the period June 1974–January 1975. Rider College, Biology Department, Lawrenceville, N.J.

Whitaker, J. O., Jr. 1999. Woodland jumping mouse. Pp. 665–666 in D. E. Wilson and S. Ruff, eds., The Smithsonian Book of North American Mammals. Washington, D.C.: Smithsonian Institution Press.

Whitaker, J. O., Jr., and W. J. Hamilton Jr. 1998. Mammals of the Eastern United States, 3rd ed. Ithaca, N.Y.: Cornell University Press.

White, P. S., E. Buckner, J. D. Pittillo, and C. V. Cogbill. 1993. High-elevation forests: Spruce-fir forests, northern hardwoods forest, and associated communities. Pp. 305–338 in W. H. Martin, S. G. Boyce, and A. C. Echternacht, eds., Biodiversity of the Southeastern United States: Upland Terrestrial Communities. New York: Wiley.

Whitehead, D. R., and T. Taylor. 2002. Acadian flycatcher (*Empidonax virescens*). *In* A. Poole and F. Gill, eds., The Birds of North America, no. 614. Philadelphia: The Birds of North America, Inc.

Whittaker, R. 1956. Vegetation of the Great Smoky Mountains. Ecological Monographs 26(1):1–80.

Wiegert, R. G., A. G. Chalmers, and P. F. Randerson. 1983. Productivity patterns in salt marshes: The response of *Spartina alterniflora* to experimentally manipulated soil water movement. Oikos 41:1–6.

Wiegert, R. G., and B. J. Freeman. 1990. Tidal salt marshes of the Southeast Atlantic coast: A community profile. Biological Report 85(7.29). Washington, D.C.: U.S. Department of the Interior, Fish and Wildlife Service.

Williams, R. B. 1962. The ecology of diatom populations in a Georgia salt marsh. Ph.D. dissertation. Harvard University, Cambridge.

Wilson, J. D., and M. E. Dorcas. 2004. Aspects of the ecology of small fossorial snakes in the western Piedmont of North Carolina. Southeastern Naturalist 3:1–12.

Wilson, J. G. 1999. Population dynamics and energy budget for a population of *Donax variabilis* (Say) on an exposed South Carolina beach. Journal of Experimental Marine Biology and Ecology 239:61–83.

Winn, B. 2010. Wilson's plover (*Charadrius wilsonia*). Pp. 160–161 *in* T. M. Schneider, G. Beaton, T. S. Keyes, and N. A. Klaus, eds., The Breeding Bird Atlas of Georgia. Athens: University of Georgia Press.

Winn, B., and J. C. Ozier. 2010. Wood stork (*Mycteria americana*). Pp. 114–115 *in* T. M. Schneider, G. Beaton, T. S. Keyes, and N. A. Klaus, eds., The Breeding Bird Atlas of Georgia. Athens: University of Georgia Press.

Winne, C. T. 2008. Six-lined racerunner (*Cnemidophorus sexlineatus* [*Aspidoscelis sexlineata*]). Pp. 320–321 *in* J. B. Jensen, C. D. Camp, W. Gibbons, and M. J. Elliott, eds., Amphibians and Reptiles of Georgia. Athens: University of Georgia Press.

Winne, C. T., and S. M. Poppy. 2008. Black swamp snake (*Seminatrix pygaea*). Pp. 399–400 *in* J. B. Jensen, C. D. Camp, W. Gibbons, and M. J. Elliott, eds., Amphibians and Reptiles of Georgia. Athens: University of Georgia Press.

Wiser, S. K. 1998. Comparison of Southern Appalachian high-elevation outcrop plant communities with their Northern Appalachian counterparts. Journal of Biogeography 25:501–513.

Wiser, S. K. 1994. High-elevation cliffs and outcrops of the Southern Appalachians: Vascular plants and biogeography. Castanea 59(2):85–116.

Wiser, S. K., R. K. Peet, and P. S. White. 1996. High-elevation rock outcrop vegetation of the Southern Appalachian Mountains. Journal of Vegetation History 7:703–722.

Withgott, J. H., and K. G. Smith. 1998. Brown-headed nuthatch (*Sitta pusilla*). *In* A. Poole and F. Gill, eds., The Birds of North America, no. 349. Philadelphia: The Birds of North America, Inc.

Witmer, M. C. 1996. Annual diet of cedar waxwings based on U.S. Biological Survey records (1885–1950) compared to diet of American robins: Contrasts in dietary patterns and natural history. Auk 113:414–430.

Witmer, M. C., D. J. Mountjoy, and L. Elliot. 1997. Cedar waxwing (*Bombycilla cedrorum*). In A. Poole and F. Gill, eds., The Birds of North America, no. 309. Philadelphia: Academy of Natural Sciences; Washington, D.C.: American Ornithologists' Union.

Witz, B. W., D. S. Wilson, and M. D. Palmer. 1991. Distribution of *Gopherus polyphemus* and its vertebrate symbionts in three burrow categories. American Midland Naturalist 126:152–158.

Woo, S. M., and H. Y. Wetzstein. 2008. Morphological and histological evaluations of in vitro regeneration in *Elliottia racemosa* leaf explants induced on media with thidiazuron. Journal of American Society of Horticultural Science 133:167–172.

Woodhouse, W. W., Jr. 1982. Coastal sand dunes of the United States. Pp. 1–44 *in* R. R. Lewis, ed., Creation and Restoration of Coastal Plant Communities. Boca Raton, Fla.: CRC Press.

Woods, J. C. 1967. Soil Survey of Houston and Peach Counties, Georgia. Washington, D.C.: U.S. Department of Agriculture, Soil Conservation Service.

Wright, A. H. 1932. Life-histories of the Frogs of Okefinokee Swamp, Georgia. New York: Macmillan Company.

Wright, A. H., and F. Harper. 1913. A biological reconnaissance of Okefenokee Swamp: The birds. The Auk 30:477–505.

Wright, A. H., and A. A. Wright. 1932. The habitats and composition of the vegetation of Okefinokee Swamp. Ecological Monographs 2:109–232.

Wunderlin, R. P, and B. F. Hansen. 2003. Guide to the Vascular Plants of Florida. 2nd ed. Gainesville: University Press of Florida.

Wyatt, R. 1981. Ant-pollination of the granite outcrop endemic *Diamorpha smallii* (Crassulaceae). American Journal of Botany 68:1212–1217.

Wyatt, R., and J. R. Allison. 2000. Flora and vegetation of granite outcrops in the Southeastern United States. Pp. 409–434 *in* S. Porembski and W. Barthlott, eds., Inselbergs: Biotic Diversity of Isolated Rock Outcrops in Tropical and Temperate Regions. Heidelberg: Springer-Verlag.

Yarnell S. L. 1995. The Southern Appalachians: A History of the Landscape [September 1995 draft]. Southeast Center for Forest Economics Research. Research Triangle Park, N.C.

Yasukawa, K., and W. A. Searcy. 1995. Red-winged blackbird (*Agelaius phoeniceus*). *In* A. Poole and F. Gill, eds., The Birds of North America, no. 184. Philadelphia: Academy of Natural Sciences; Washington, D.C. American Ornithologists' Union.

Yosef, R. 1996. Loggerhead shrike (*Lanius ludovicianus*). *In* A. Poole, ed., The Birds of North America Online. Ithaca, Cornell Lab of Ornithology; Retrieved from the Birds of North America Available at http://bna.birds .cornell.edu/bna/species/231.

Young, C. A., and W. Gibbons. 2008. Mud snake (*Farancia abacura*). Pp. 348–350 *in* J. B. Jensen, C. D. Camp, W. Gibbons, and M. J. Elliott, eds., Amphibians and Reptiles of Georgia. Athens: University of Georgia Press.

Zartman, C. E., and J. D. Pittillo. 1998. Spray cliff communities of the Chattooga Basin. Castanea 63(3):217–240.

Photo Credits

Except as noted below, all photographs were provided by Hugh and Carol Nourse:

James R. Allison: 5, 112, 119, 581 (bottom)

Jonathan Ambrose: vi–vii, 475, 520, 523, 531, 534, 548, 562 (bottom), 568, 586

Jerry Amerson: 392 (left), 474

Simon Pierre Barrette (Cephas): 102

Giff Beaton (www .giffbeaton.com): 236

Claud L. Brown: 458, 479

Richard T. Bryant: 16 (bottom), 346–347, 357 (top), 387, 483

Melissa Caspary: 305

Ed Corey, NCDENR: 87

Alan Cressler: 93, 129, 130, 131, 224, 514, 521, 522 (right), 524, 533 (top left), 541, 544, 545 (top), 561, 571, 583, 593, 594 (all)

Julie W. Duncan, Georgia DNR, Wildlife Resources Division: 556

Leslie Edwards: 288

Wilson Faircloth, USDA Agricultural Research Service, Bugwood.org: 363

James F. Flynn Jr.: 384

Kenneth D. Foote: 277

Christopher M. Funk: 487

Georgia DNR, Wildlife Resources Division: 15, 422, 518 (right), 545 (bottom)

S. P. Graham: 187, 213

© Bob Gress: 176

© Bill Harbin: 139, 208

Phillip Hardy: 481

Ichauway Collection: 357 (bottom)

Ichauway Collection; photo by Kim Coffey: 382

Ichauway Collection; photo by Melanie Kaeser: 370

Ichauway Collection; photo by Nathalie Smith: 359

N. Tyrus Ivey : 116, 195, 241, 557, 592

Howard L. Jelks, U.S. Geological Survey: 492

John B. Jensen, Georgia DNR, Wildlife Resources Division: 109, 127, 182, 218, 243, 254, 428

Timothy Keyes, Georgia DNR, Wildlife Resources Division: 459, 564, 566

Barry Mansell: 290, 507, 591

Linda May, Georgia DNR, Wildlife Resources Division: 170, 329, 536

Howard McCullough, USFWS, Okefenokee NWR: 499 (top right)

Darlene J. Moore: 78

Michael Wayne Morris: 315, 316 (left)

NASA (http://visibleearth .nasa.gov): 12

Jay W. Pakchar: 23 (right), 31, 269

Todd W. Pierson: 133, 247, 283 (top)

L. Bruce Railsback, Department of Geology, University of Georgia: 264 (left)

William Reeves (The Hawk): 323, 565

Naomi Rice: 312

Todd Schneider, Georgia DNR, Wildlife Resources Division: 201, 585

Jason Scott: 377

Ann and Rob Simpson: 69

Tom Simpson, GNPA, SPS, PSA: 460

Chris Skelton: 343 (both)

Lora Smith: 355

South Carolina DNR: 295

State Archives of Florida: 360

D. Stevenson, The Orianne Society: 122, 398, 403, 444, 454

Kevin M. Stohlgren: 144, 410, 576

Randy Tate, Georgia DNR, Parks, Recreation, and Historic Sites Division: 20 (bottom)

Roger F. Thoma: 229

Trees Atlanta: 16 (top), 270 (both)

USDA, FSA Aerial Photography Field Office, National Agricultural Imagery Program: 461 (right)

USDA, Natural Resources Conservation Service: 361

USFWS, Okefenokee NWR: 499 (top left, bottom left and right)

Daniel F. Vickers: 149, 301, 318, 335, 385, 416, 437, 465, 547

Robert Weller, Georgia DNR, Wildlife Resources Division: 364

Brad Winn, Georgia DNR, Wildlife Resources Division: 528, 535, 552, 562 (top)

Index

fire (*continued*)
505, 507; Okefenokee
wildfire, 425, 498–500;
in Piedmont ecoregion,
261–263, 266, 274, 298;
in pine flatwoods, 425;
and pines of Blue Ridge
ecoregion, 99–100; in
prairies and savannas,
293; prescribed, 17–18,
56, 162, 193, 266, 360,
367–368; Prescribed
Fire Council, 18; season
of, 367–368; in upland
longleaf pine woodlands,
366–368; and wiregrass
biology, 370–371
Flat Tub Landing Wildlife
Management Area
(featured place), 417
flatwoods: Berry Flatwoods
(featured place),
230; in Coastal Plain
ecoregion, 351, 365, 424–
427; in Cumberland
Plateau / Ridge and
Valley ecoregion, 161,
166, 226–229; defined,
4, 166, 271; in Piedmont
ecoregion, 271, 325–328
flint kaolin, 414
Flint River, 363, 373, 468–
469; basin, 10, 33; in
Coastal Plain ecoregion,
351; corridor, and
land acquisition, 7; in
Dougherty Plain, 349–
350, 352; floodplain, in
Piedmont ecoregion,
260; and Floridan
aquifer, 352, 354–
355, 363–364; gorges,
259, 260; levees, 338;
Riverside Trail, at
Camp Thunder, 324;
and steepheads, 406;
tributaries, 350
floodplain characteristics,
466–468
floodplains, bottomlands,
and riparian zones: in
Blue Ridge ecoregion,
61, 146–148, 150–151;

in Coastal Plain, 466–
468; in Cumberland
Plateau / Ridge and
Valley ecoregion,
166, 249–254, 255; in
Piedmont ecoregion,
272, 337–342, 344
Florida torreya, 408–409
Floridan aquifer. *See under*
aquifer
Floyd County prairies. *See*
calcareous prairies and
barrens
Forestry: ecological, 371;
and timber production,
55–56, 360, 520–521. *See
also* industrial forestry
Fort Benning, 374, 401,
414, 415; gopher tortoise
habitat at, 384; and lack
of wiregrass, 389; Malone
Canebrake at, 442; red-
cockaded woodpecker
populations at, 376
Fort Mountain State Park,
49, 81, 90, 98
Fort Payne chert, 156, 157,
171
Fort Stewart, 361, 376, 384,
397
Fort Yargo State Park, 280
Franklin Delano Roosevelt
(FDR) State Park, 190,
191, 192, 275
Franklinia, 479
freshwater and oligohaline
tidal marshes, 526, 568,
578–584, 586

gabbro rock: defined, 22; in
lower Piedmont, 259; in
Monticello Glades, 325,
326, 330
gap phase disturbance. *See
under* disturbance agent
geology, 21, 24; of Blue
Ridge ecoregion, 49–
51; of Coastal Plain
ecoregion, 348–
351; and common
rocks of Georgia,
22; of Cumberland
Plateau / Ridge and

Valley ecoregion, 153,
154–155, 156–157, 160;
of Maritime ecoregion,
512–514; of Paleozoic to
Cenozoic eras, 43–44;
of Piedmont ecoregion,
258–261, 280
George L. Smith State Park,
372
Georgia Invasive Species
Task Force, 16
Georgia Prescribed Fire
Council, 18
Georgia-plume, 319, 395,
397, 399, 417
Gizzard formation, 155, 156,
157, 184, 220
glades, barrens, and
woodlands, 271, 297–
300, 302, 412–417
glades, calcareous. *See*
calcareous glades,
barrens, and woodlands
glades, defined, 5
gneiss, defined, 22
golden-winged warbler,
77, 92
gopher frog, 376, 453, 496;
featured animal, 454
gopher tortoise, 375, 382,
383, 384; burrows, 372,
376, 391, 397, 417; and
fragmented landscape,
362; and longleaf pine
forests, 391, 397, 417
Gordonia-Alatamaha State
Park, 431
grady ponds (isolated
depressional wetlands),
18, 448–450
granite, 10, 258;
composition and
weathering of, 22. *See
also* granite outcrops
granite outcrops, 7, 204,
313; lichens of, 310; of
Piedmont ecoregion,
259, 261, 271, 303–312,
313; recreational impacts
on, 267; vegetation
communities and
succession in, 304–306,
308–309

gray fox (featured animal),
290
Great Valley, 51, 154, 157,
162, 249
green salamander, 217, 222,
323; featured animal, 127
groundwater withdrawal:
and altered hydrology,
18–19, 20; in Coastal
Plain ecoregion,
363–364, 448, 490;
in Cumberland
Plateau / Ridge and
Valley ecoregion, 164; in
Maritime ecoregion, 516,
522–523
gum domes (isolated
depressional wetlands),
18, 448–450, 457
gypsy moth, 15, 59, 92, 139

habitat fragmentation
and loss, 7–10, 14; in
Blue Ridge ecoregion,
59, 78; in Coastal Plain
ecoregion, 362, 366, 447,
477; in Cumberland
Plateau / Ridge and
Valley ecoregion, 231;
in Maritime ecoregion,
552–553; in Piedmont
ecoregion, 266, 268, 277,
279
hammock (depression oak
forests), 462
Hard Labor Creek State
Park, 280
heath bluffs, 275, 280–281
Helton Creek Falls
(featured place), 145
hemlock, eastern, 57, 66, 81;
old-growth, 82, 83; and
warblers, 148. *See also*
acidic cove forests
hemlock woolly adelgid, 15,
43, 59, 80, 84–85
high-elevation rock
outcrops, 53, 60, 111–
115, 117
hydrology: altered, 18–
20; in Blue Ridge
ecoregion, 53, 112, 124,
130, 141; channelization,

Wagon Train Trail (featured place), 70
water quantity and quality: in Blue Ridge ecoregion, 59; in Coastal Plain ecoregion, 363–364; in Cumberland Plateau / Ridge and Valley ecoregion, 163–164; in Maritime ecoregion, 521–523; in Piedmont ecoregion, 268–270
Waterbird Conservation Initiative, 535
waterfowl impoundments, 522, 580, 586
watersheds. *See* river basins
waves, 512, 517, 531, 532, 536
Weeks Act, 57
wet prairies, 198
wetlands, 55, 149, 388, 565; and altered hydrology, 18–20, 59, 358, 522–523; defined and characteristics of, 29–30; depressional, 161, 394, 448, 450, 454, 461; hydric soils, 30, 226; plant adaptations to, 30–31; protection of, 13, 20, 521; types, 31–32; wet prairies, 198. *See also* calcareous seepage fens; Chickasawhatchee Wildlife Management Area; cypress-gum ponds; cypress-tupelo river swamps; depression marshes and cypress savannas; depression oak forests; flatwoods; freshwater and oligohaline tidal marshes; interdunal wetlands; mountain bogs; Okefenokee Swamp complex; pine flatwoods; sagponds and sinkholes; salt marshes and brackish tidal marshes; seepage slope herb bogs; seepage slope swamps and shrub bogs; seepage wetlands; tidal swamps

Wetlands Reserve Program, 13
white nose syndrome, 15, 16, 163
white-tailed deer: herbivory, 42–43, 274; in maritime forests, 555, 556; in montane oak forests, 77; in prairies and savannas, 294; and wildlife openings, 56
Whitley Gap Trail (featured place), 79
Wildcat Mountain, 74, 124
wildlife management areas, 56, 58, 379, 380; Altamaha Wildlife Management Area, 522, 580; Beaverdam Wildlife Management Area, 349; Big Hammock Wildlife Management Area, 399, 481, 484; Big Lazer Creek Wildlife Management Area, 275; Chickasawhatchee Wildlife Management Area (featured place), 361–362, 455, 478; Crockford-Pigeon Mountain Wildlife Management Area (featured place), 156, 173, 219; Dawson Forest Wildlife Management Area, 285, 336; Flat Tub Landing Wildlife Management Area (featured place), 417; Johns Mountain Wildlife Management Area, 173; Lake Seminole Wildlife Management Area, 362; Oaky Woods Wildlife Management Area (featured place), 407, 408, 418, 419, 423; Ocmulgee Wildlife Management Area, 418; Richmond Hill Wildlife Management Area, 552; River Creek Wildlife Management Area, 425; Silver Lake Wildlife Management Area (featured place), 394; Townsend Wildlife Management Area (featured place), 445
Wilson's plover, 527, 535, 546; featured animal, 547
wiregrass, southern, 365, 379, 380; biology of, 370–371; and fire, 38, 363, 368, 388–389, 427
wood stork, 452, 456, 506; featured animal, 460
woodland jumping mouse (featured animal), 87
woodlands, defined, 4. *See also* pine-oak woodlands; pine-oak woodlands and forests
woolly adelgid. *See* hemlock woolly adelgid

yellow birch, 62, 63, 67, 70
yucca giant-skipper (featured animal), 416

Zahnd Natural Area, 155, 210, 221, 253; featured place, 188
Zahnd Natural Area Sagpond (featured place), 248